Explore Australia

Viking
A division of Penguin Books Australia Ltd
487 Maroondah Highway, PO Box 257
Ringwood, Victoria 3134, Australia
Penguin Books Ltd
Harmondsworth, Middlesex, England
Viking Penguin, A division of Penguin Books USA Inc.
375 Hudson Street, New York, New York 10014, USA
Penguin Books Canada Limited
10 Alcorn Avenue, Toronto, Ontario, Canada M4V 3B2
Penguin Books (N.Z.) Ltd
182–190 Wairau Road, Auckland 10, New Zealand

This fifteenth edition published by Penguin Books Australia Ltd, 1996
First published by George Philip & O'Neil Pty Ltd, 1980
Second edition 1981   Fourth edition 1985
Third edition 1983   Fifth edition 1986
Reprinted 1984
Sixth edition published by Penguin Books Australia, 1987
Seventh edition 1988 Eleventh edition 1992
Eighth edition 1989   Twelfth edition 1993
Ninth edition 1990   Thirteenth edition 1994
Tenth edition 1991   Fourteenth edition 1995

Copyright © Penguin Books Australia Ltd, 1996

ISBN 0 670 86691 1

All rights reserved. Without limiting the rights under copyright reserved above, no part of this publication may be reproduced, stored in or introduced into a retrieval system, or transmitted in any form or by any means (electronic, mechanical, photocopying, recording or otherwise) without the prior written permission of both the copyright owner and the above publisher of this book.

Printed and bound in Australia by Southbank Book

Publisher's Note: Every effort has been made to ensure that the information in this book is accurate at the time of going to press. The publisher welcomes information and suggestions for corrections or improvement. A Suggestion Form is provided on page 583.

Disclaimers: The publisher cannot accept responsibility for any errors or omissions. The representation on the maps of any road or track is not necessarily evidence of public right of way.
The population figures given in *Explore Australia* have been taken from the most recent Census result available. They are intended to provide only an approximate idea of the size of the various cities and towns. Accommodation listed is a guide to accommodation available in each town.

HALF-TITLE PAGE: Lawn Hill National Park, Queensland (Bill Bachman)
TITLE PAGE: Channel Country, Queensland (Lincoln Fowler/Horizon International Photo Library)

Explore Australia

The COMPLETE TOURING COMPANION

VIKING

Acknowledgements

State Cartographic Consultants
Australian Capital Territory:
Paul Sjoberg
New South Wales: Bruce Whitehouse (Ass. Dip. Cart.)
Northern Territory: Len Carter, AMAIC
Queensland: David Gooding (Ass. Dip. Cart.), Brenda Gooding (Cert. Cart.)
South Australia: George Ricketts, MAIC
Tasmania: Phil Broughton, FAIC
Victoria: Christopher Crook ARMIT (Cartog.)
Western Australia: Peter Tarwin, AMAIC

General editor
Fran Church, EdInk Pty Ltd

Photographers
George Bareth; Ross Barnett; Andrew Chapman; Diana Calder; Rick de Carteret; Stuart Grant; Richard l'Anson; Alex Julius; Gary Lewis; Lochman Transparencies: Brian Downs, David Hancock, Jiri Lochman, Dennis Sarson, Len Stewart; Ern Mainka; PD Munchenberg; Pajinka Wilderness Lodge; Nick Rains; Don Skirrow; Robin Smith; Ken Stepnell; Warren Steptoe; Bruce Stewart; Stock Photos: Bill Bachman, Benaji, Diana Calder, John Carr, Roger Du Buisson, Peter Elliston, Excitations, Trevern Dawes, Robert Fox, Ron Gale, Phillip Hayson, Owen Hughes, Noeline Kelly, Russell Kord, Mark Laricchia, Lance Nelson, Otto Rogge, Don Skirrow, Paul Steel, Ken Stepnell, Stocktake, Michael Wennrich; South Australian Tourism Commission.

Text
For the preparation of this edition, each tourist information centre for the towns described was contacted and the information for each town checked. The revision of this edition could not have occurred without their assistance. As well, assistance was received from the following organisations:

New South Wales
Sydney Visitors and Convention Bureau
National Parks and Wildlife Service
Geographical Names Board
Australian Capital Territory
Canberra Tourism
ACT Parks and Conservation Service
Nomenclature Committee
Victoria
Tourism Victoria
Melbourne Convention and Marketing Bureau
Department of Conservation and Natural Resources
Place Names Committee
South Australia
South Australian Tourism Commission
Adelaide Convention and Tourism Authority
Department of Environment and Natural Resources
Geographical Names Advisory Committee
Western Australia
Western Australia Tourism Commission
Department of Conservation and Land Management
Geographic Names Committee

Northern Territory
Central Australian Tourism Industry Association
Darwin Region Tourism Association
Australian Nature Conservation Agency
Parks and Wildlife Commission of the Northern Territory
Northern and Central land councils
Place Names Committee
Queensland
Queensland Tourist and Travel Corporation
Brisbane Visitors and Convention Bureau
Department of Environment and Heritage
Department of Natural Resources (place names)
Tasmania
Department of Tourism, Sport and Recreation
Tasmanian Parks and Wildlife Service
Nomenclature Board of Tasmania

Maps
The publisher acknowledges the assistance to revise and check the maps from the various regional tourism authorities, place name committees, local government offices, Aboriginal communities and land councils, and state cartographic consultants.

The publisher also wishes to acknowledge Geoff Rasmussen of Edutech Productions for preparation of the indexing software; Lloyd Junor of Aussie Outback Escorted Tours for assistance with the Spare Parts listing; the Bureau of Meteorology for the Climate Guides; Royal Automobile Club of Victoria for motoring information; The Quill Consultancy for assistance with Gourmet Island (Tas.); and St John Ambulance Australia for accident action information.

Contents

Inside front cover:
Major inter-capital city routes

Fold-out page:
Symbols used on the maps
How to use this book

Inside back cover:
Accident action

INTRODUCTION 1
Planning Ahead 2
Advance Information 2
How Far Ahead to Start 2
Useful Information 3
Motoring Organisations 3
Tourist Bureaus 3
Accommodation 3
Emergency 3
When to Go 4
Which Way to Go 4
Other Touring Possibilities 5
Where to Stay 5
Other Information 6
Pets 6
Before Departure 6
Carrying a Camera 6
Time Zones 6
Quarantine Regulations 6
Dividing Up the Dollars 7
Car Maintenance Courses 7
Insurance 8
Itineraries 8
Clothing 8
First-aid Kit 8
Useful Extras 8

Inter-city Route Maps 9
Sydney–Melbourne *via* Hume Hwy/Fwy 10
Sydney–Melbourne *via* Princes Hwy 10
Sydney–Brisbane *via* Pacific Hwy 10
Melbourne–Adelaide *via* Western & Dukes Hwys 10
Melbourne–Adelaide *via* Princes Hwy 10
Melbourne–Brisbane *via* Newell Hwy 11
Adelaide–Darwin *via* Stuart Hwy 11
Adelaide–Perth *via* Eyre & Great Eastern Hwys 11
Adelaide–Sydney *via* Hume & Sturt Hwys 11
Perth–Darwin *via* Brand, Northwest Coastal, Great Northern, Victoria & Stuart Hwys 11
Sydney–Brisbane *via* New England Hwy 12
Brisbane–Darwin *via* Warrego, Landsborough, Barkly & Stuart Hwys 12
Brisbane–Cairns *via* Bruce Hwy 12
Hobart–Launceston *via* Midland Hwy 12
Hobart–Devonport *via* Midland & Bass Hwys 12

Have A Good Trip 13
Checking the Car 13
Hazards 14
Flood 14
Bushfire 14
Animals 14
Packing the Car 15
When to Set Off 15
Leaving Home 15
Better Driving 16
Driving Emergencies 16
Safe Driving 17
Basic Traffic Laws 17
Positioning 17
In Case of Accident 17
Towing 18
Checklist 18
Outback Motoring 19
Driving Conditions 19
Surviving in the Outback 20
Direction Finding 20
How to Obtain Water 20
Outback Advice 21
Critical Rules for Outback Motoring 21
Outback Advice Service 21
Sharing the Outback 21
Breakdowns 22
Modern Vehicles 22
Earlier-model Vehicles 22
When the Engine Stops 22
Tools and Spare Parts 23
Tools 23
Spare Parts 23
Fuel 23
Trouble Shooting 24
Child's Play 26
Dos and Don'ts 26
Handy Hints 26
Child Restraints 26
Games 27

Mountain Ash, Yarra Ranges National Park, Victoria

Contents

Scenic mountain road, Victoria

Safety 27
Safe Swimming, Surfing 27
Safe Skiing 27
Safe Boating 27

NEW SOUTH WALES
Introduction 29
   Not to be Missed in New South Wales 29
   Calendar of Events 30
   Climate Guide 31
   Calendar of Events (contd) 32
Sydney 33
   Not to be Missed in Sydney 34
   City on the Water 35
   Sydney on Foot 36
   Accommodation 37
   A Colonial Past 38
Tours from Sydney 41
   The Blue Mountains 42
New South Wales from A to Z 44
The Hawkesbury 46
Southern Highlands 49
Port Stephens 51
The Illawarra Coast 53
The South Coast 55
National Parks 58
The Snowy Mountains 65
New England 69
The Newell 75
Vineyards and Wineries 81
Caves and Caverns 85

Maps
Location Map 91
Central Sydney 92
Sydney Approach & Bypass Routes 93
Sydney & Western Suburbs 94
Northern Suburbs, Sydney 96
Southern Suburbs, Sydney 98
Sydney Region 100
The Blue Mountains 102
Hawkesbury & Central Coast 104
Port Macquarie Region 105
Newcastle 106
Newcastle Approach & Bypass Routes 107
Newcastle Region 108
Lower Hunter Vineyards 109
Wollongong 110
Wollongong Approach & Bypass Routes 111
Southern Highlands 112
South Coast 113
Snowy Mountains Region 114
South Eastern New South Wales 115
Central Eastern New South Wales 116
North Eastern New South Wales 118
North Western New South Wales 120
South Western New South Wales 122

AUSTRALIAN CAPITAL TERRITORY
Introduction 125
   Not to be Missed in the Australian Capital Territory 125
   Calendar of Events 126
   Climate Guide 126
Canberra 127
   Canberra on Foot 128
   Accommodation 129
   Wining and Dining 131
Tours from Canberra 132

Maps
Location Map 133
Central Canberra 134
Australian Capital Territory 135
Canberra & Northern Suburbs 136
Canberra & Southern Suburbs 137
Canberra Region 138

VICTORIA
Introduction 141
   Not to be Missed in Victoria 141
   Calendar of Events 142
   Climate Guide 143
Melbourne 144
   Not to be Missed in Melbourne 144
   Accommodation 145
   Parks and Gardens 146
   Melbourne on Foot 148
Tours from Melbourne 152
   The Mornington Peninsula 154
   The Dandenongs 156
Victoria from A to Z 157
The Golden Age 161
Phillip Island 169
National Parks 174
Alpine Country 182
The Great Ocean Road 187
The Prom 188
Gippsland Lakes 193
Wine Regions 197
The Grampians 198
The Mighty Murray 201
The Wimmera 203
The Western District 204

Maps
Location Map 205
Central Melbourne 206
Melbourne Approach & Bypass Routes 207
Melbourne & Western Suburbs 208
Eastern Suburbs, Melbourne 210
Southern Suburbs, Melbourne 211
Melbourne Region 212
Mornington Peninsula 214
Yarra Valley Region 216
Otway Region 217
Geelong 218
Geelong Region 219
Bendigo 220
Ballarat 221
Goldfields Region 222
Alpine Region 224
Southern Central Victoria 226
South Western Victoria 228
Central Western Victoria 230
North Western Victoria 232
North Central Victoria 234
North Eastern Victoria 236

Blue Lake, Mount Gambier, South Australia

Contents vii

Glen Helen Gorge, Northern Territory

SOUTH AUSTRALIA
Introduction 239
   Not to be Missed in South Australia 239
   Calendar of Events 240
   Climate Guide 241
Adelaide 242
   Not to be Missed in Adelaide 242
   Accommodation 239
   Adelaide on Foot 245
Tours from Adelaide 246
   The Adelaide Hills 247
   Festival Fun 248
South Australia from A to Z 250
The Yorke Peninsula 255
The Eyre Peninsula 256
Vineyards and Wineries 259
National Parks 262
Kangaroo Island 269
The Flinders Ranges 273
The Coorong 274
The Fleurieu Peninsula 276
The Outback 279

Maps
Location Map 281
Central Adelaide 282
Adelaide Approach & Bypass Routes 283
Adelaide & Southern Suburbs 284
Northern Suburbs, Adelaide 286
Adelaide Region, North 288
Adelaide Region, South 289
McLaren Region 290
Flinders Ranges 291
Barossa Valley 292
South Eastern South Australia 293
South Central South Australia 294
Central South Australia 296
North Eastern South Australia 298
North Western South Australia 300
South Western South Australia 302

WESTERN AUSTRALIA
Introduction 305
   Not to be Missed in Western Australia 305
   Calendar of Events 306
   Climate Guide 307
Perth 308
   Not to be Missed in Perth 308
   Accommodation 309
   Perth on Foot 310
Tours from Perth 311
   Rottnest Island 312
Western Australia from A to Z 313
Western Wildflowers 317
The South-west 319
National Parks 322
The Great Southern 329
Crossing the Nullarbor 333
The Goldfields 336
The Pilbara 339
The Hamersley Range 343
The Kimberley 344
The Ord River 347

Maps
Location Map 349
Central Perth 350
Perth Approach & Bypass Routes 351
Perth & Southern Suburbs 352
Northern Suburbs, Perth 354
Perth & Northern Region 356
Southern Region, Perth 357
Fremantle 358
Margaret River Region 359
Albany Region 360
Kimberley Region 362
South Western Western Australia 364
Central Western Western Australia 365
Southern Western Australia 366
Central Western Australia 368
North Western Australia 370

NORTHERN TERRITORY
Introduction 373
   Not to be Missed in the Northern Territory 373
   Calendar of Events 374
   Climate Guide 375
Darwin 376
   Not to be Missed in Darwin 376
   Accommodation 377
   Darwin on Foot 378
Tours from Darwin 379
Northern Territory from A to Z 381
The Red Centre 382
   The Mereenie Loop Road 383
The Top End 385
Aboriginal Art 386
Aboriginal Lands 389
Aboriginal-operated Tours 391
National Parks 392
Fishing in the Territory 395
The Gove Peninsula 396

Maps
Location Map 397
Central Darwin 398
Darwin & Northern Suburbs 399
North Eastern Suburbs, Darwin 400
Kakadu National Park 401
Darwin Region 402
The Red Centre 404
Northern Northern Territory 406
Central Northern Territory 408
Southern Northern Territory 410

QUEENSLAND
Introduction 413
   Not to be Missed in Queensland 413
   Calendar of Events 414
   Climate Guide 415

Contents

Aboriginal art, Northern Territory

Brisbane 416
   Not to be Missed in Brisbane 416
   Accommodation 417
   Brisbane on Foot 418
   Mount Coot-tha 419
Tours from Brisbane 420
   The Gold Coast 422
Queensland from A to Z 424
The Sunshine Coast 429
Fraser and Moreton Bay Islands 433
Great Barrier Reef 437
Gladstone Region 445
The Far North 448
   Atherton Tableland 449
Cape York 453
Thursday Island 455
National Parks 456
Fishing in Queensland 463
Darling Downs 465
Capricorn Region 469
Channel Country 472
Gulf Savannah 474

Maps
Location Map 475
Central Brisbane 476
Brisbane Approach & Bypass Routes 477
Brisbane & Northern Suburbs 478
Southern Suburbs, Brisbane 480
Brisbane Region 482
Gold Coast Approach & Bypass Routes 484
The Gold Coast 485
The Sunshine Coast 486
Townsville 487
Cairns 488
Cairns Region 489
South Eastern Queensland 490
North Eastern Queensland 492
Far North Eastern Queensland 494
Cape York Peninsula 496
Far North Western Queensland 497
North Western Queensland 498
South Western Queensland 500

TASMANIA
Introduction 503
   Not to be Missed in Tasmania 503
   Calendar of Events 504
   Climate Guide 505
Hobart 506
   Not to be Missed in Hobart 506
   Accommodation 507
   Hobart on Foot 508
   Battery Point 508
Tours from Hobart 509
Tasmania from A to Z 511
Scenic Island State 514
A Convict Past 517
National Parks 520
Rural Landscapes 522
The Gourmet Island 525

Brisbane cityscape, Queensland

Stately Homes 527
The West Coast 528
The Bass Strait Islands 531
Angler's Paradise 533
Maps
Location Map 534
Central Hobart 535
Hobart & Suburbs 536
Hobart Region 538
Launceston Region 540
Southern Tasmania 542
Northern Tasmania 544

Index of Place Names 546
Suggestion Form 583

INTRODUCTION

Australia's deserts are as vast as the Sahara; its snowfields are huge and dramatically picturesque; its surfing beaches are among the best in the world. The entire continent is criss-crossed by a combination of bitumen highways, sealed roads and rough bush tracks, almost all navigable in the modern motor car, although some require 4WD vehicles.

Australia comprises an area of some 8.5 million square kilometres; it covers a distance of 3700 kilometres from north to south, and 4000 kilometres east to west. Within these boundaries there is an extraordinary range of flora and fauna, a variety of climatic extremes and a vast array of geological wonders.

Australia's temperatures vary from an average 36°C in the midsummer of the Red Centre to an average of 6°C in the highlands in winter.

It is a land of extremes. The parched deserts of central Australia may be totally dry for years until flooding rains produce a short-term sea. Sydney has a population of approximately 4 million, whereas Innamincka in South Australia, near the Queensland border, has only 14 permanent residents.

Australia has been the home of Aborigines for over 40 000 years and evidence of their early occupation abounds, particularly in cave paintings and rock carvings made thousands of years ago and found at numerous locations across the continent.

The predominant colours of the Australian landscape are red, blue and green. Inland, the stark red of the Simpson Desert sand dunes contrasts dramatically with the deep azure blue of the noonday sky. Dotted here and there are clumps of velvet-green scrub and, after rain, Sturt's desert pea blooms scarlet.

Uluru (Ayers Rock), that superb monolith sited almost in the centre of this island continent, is in the Red Centre where the moonscapes of sand and rocky tors, and hardy bush scrub have a forbidding beauty all their own, even in times of drought. After rain, gardens of brilliant wildflowers are added to the landscape. Across the Far North, from Cape York Peninsula in the east to the Kimberleys in the west, tropical rainforests are in parts impenetrable, and of a green so luxuriant as to rival the colour from an artist's paintbrush.

Almost all Australia is accessible to the exploring traveller. It is possible to drive from Melbourne in the south of the mainland to Cooktown in the Far North. The intrepid can plan a trip from the Pacific to the Indian Ocean; from the rainforests in the north to the temperate beaches of the southern coast. And for the traveller seeking peace and tranquillity, there are the green pasturelands and rugged, splendidly scenic mountain areas of Tasmania, the Island State.

Simply put, Australia is a wonderland. And in order to discover what it has to offer, either for a one-day tour or as a full-year, once-in-a-lifetime adventure, *Explore Australia* is an invaluable travelling companion. It is designed to be of assistance with every facet of your travel itinerary. It is an encouragement and an almanac; a manual and a tour guide. It is recommended that you read it as part of your travel planning, particularly for long-distance journeys. For experienced road travellers, it will reinforce knowledge acquired in the past; for less experienced road travellers, it can ensure the utmost pleasure from the holiday you have planned, and help to make it trouble-free.

Have a good trip – and remember to drive carefully!

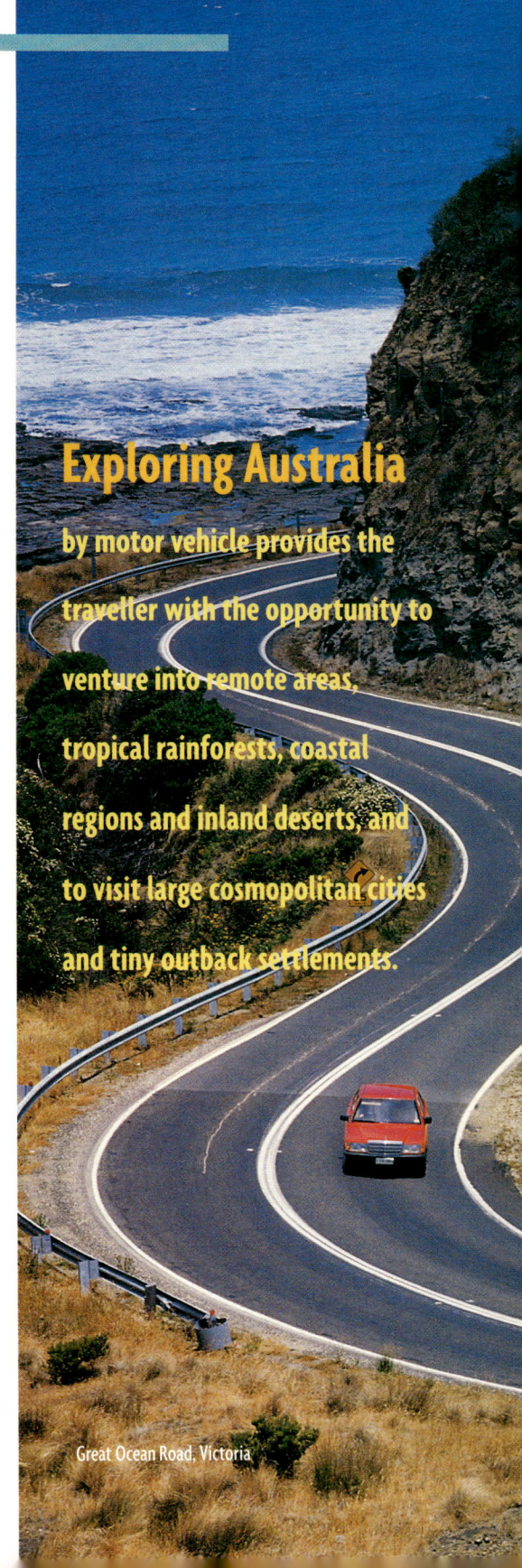

Exploring Australia by motor vehicle provides the traveller with the opportunity to venture into remote areas, tropical rainforests, coastal regions and inland deserts, and to visit large cosmopolitan cities and tiny outback settlements.

Great Ocean Road, Victoria

PLANNING Ahead

A network of sealed roads ensures pleasant touring

INTRODUCTION

There is so much of Australia to see and so many ways to see it. Today, even the most remote sections of this vast continent are accessible, particularly to 4WD vehicles designed for use on bush tracks and unmade roads.

For some, exploring Australia will mean touring the made highways and staying in motels and hotels. Others will tow their accommodation behind them in the form of a caravan or camper, and probably, as a result, stay mainly on made roads. Still others will fit out a commercial van with sleeping and cooking facilities and produce a mobile home, and yet another group, perhaps the true adventurers, will load a tent, a mobile fridge and a barbecue into the back of a 4WD station wagon and go bush. In all cases, careful planning will enhance the journey immeasurably.

Obviously a one-, two- or three-day tour will not require the time and effort necessary for a round-Australia jaunt, but in any case, advance planning of the route and of overnight stopping-points, and a careful estimate of travel time – make for safety, comfort and enjoyment. So, indeed, will the roadworthiness of the vehicle. While as a matter of course your travel vehicle will be properly maintained and in reliable condition, some extra attention will not go astray, especially for long journeys. More of that later.

Advance Information

Any journey will benefit from careful advance planning. The idea of throwing a bag in the back and taking off is attractive in theory but creates complications in practice. Try to gather as much information as possible as far ahead of your planned departure as you can. Remember, the planning is half the fun. Research will confirm, or perhaps deny, your original choice of destination; it also will reveal ways and means, and problems where they exist. And bear in mind that although information sources are extensive, there is nothing like local 'on-the-spot' knowledge.

The first places to obtain information are: **State tourist bureaus** and **motoring organisations** (**see:** Useful Information). They are excellent sources for travel brochures, regional maps and accommodation guides, and they usually have up-to-date knowledge of local conditions. For details of specific areas, they can put you in touch with the appropriate tourist authority.

Travel agencies, **airline travel centres** and the **main railway booking offices** in each State can help if you are planning a fly/drive holiday, or intend to combine rail and motor travel.

This book. The introductions to each State provide information on main tourist areas. Once you have decided on your destination, check it out by consulting the A–Z entries for specific towns and the feature articles for the major tourist regions. Do note that while the capital cities and towns have been covered quite comprehensively in this book, the fine detail will be available at local information centres.

How Far Ahead to Start

It can be a major disappointment to decide on a certain destination and then discover that motels, caravan parks and camping grounds in the area are booked out. In some regions at certain times of the year – Christmas, Easter, school holiday periods – accommodation can be booked out a year in advance. Explore all possibilities and, on long journeys, remember the travel-time factor. When booking accommodation in advance, always remember to allow enough time to travel comfortably to your destination. Your trip will lose a great deal of its charm if you have to rush from one point to the next (see: Itineraries).

While all popular destinations are likely to be busy at holiday peak times, some will be booked out around the time of special events: Melbourne at Melbourne Cup time; Adelaide at the time of the Adelaide Festival of Arts, for

Useful Information

MOTORING ORGANISATIONS

There are motoring organisations in all Australian States and territories. All are affiliated under the Australian Automobile Association and reciprocal rights are available to their members. Membership can consist of service and social membership or service membership only.

- **Service membership**. When planning a trip it would be advisable for you to take out service membership of the motoring organisation in your home State. Not only will this ensure that you receive service in that State, but by producing your membership card you can request assistance from the equivalent organisation in other States.

The advantages of service membership of a motoring organisation are wide-ranging. They include emergency breakdown and towing services, vehicle inspection and 'approved repairer' services; tuition in safe and defensive driving for licensed drivers; legal advice on matters like the procedure to be followed after motor vehicle accidents or traffic charges, and the possible penalties; and motor vehicle insurance cover.

Service membership also provides touring information and advice for motoring holidays, including guides, maps and reports on road conditions, accommodation and travel bookings; and package holidays, accommodation at concessional rates, and a variety of car accessories.

- **Social membership**. Social or 'club' membership entitles members to the use of club facilities and accommodation, including reciprocal use in some 50 clubs throughout Australia.

The following lists the main office for each State's motoring organisation:

New South Wales
National Roads & Motorists' Association (NRMA)
151 Clarence St, Sydney 2000
132 132; Fax: (02) 9292 8548

Australian Capital Territory
National Roads & Motorists' Association (NRMA)
92 Northbourne Ave, Braddon 2601
132 132; Fax: (06) 240 4229

Victoria
Royal Automobile Club of Victoria Ltd (RACV)
360 Bourke St, Melbourne 3000
(03) 9790 3333; Fax: (03) 9670 8605

South Australia
Royal Automobile Association of S.A. Inc. (RAA)
41 Hindmarsh Sq., Adelaide 5000
(08) 8202 4600; Fax: (08) 8202 4520

Western Australia
Royal Automobile Club of W.A. Inc. (RAC)
228 Adelaide Tce, Perth 6000
(09) 421 4444; Fax: (09) 221 1887

Northern Territory
Automobile Association of the N.T. Inc. (AANT)
79–81 Smith St, Darwin 0800
(08) 8981 3837; Fax: (08) 8941 2965

Queensland
Royal Automobile Club of Queensland (RACQ)
300 St Pauls Tce, Brisbane 4000
(07) 3361 2444; Fax: (07) 3257 1863

Tasmania
Royal Automobile Club of Tasmania (RACT)
cnr Patrick and Murray Sts, Hobart 7000
(03) 6232 6300; Fax: (03) 6234 8784

TOURIST BUREAUS

New South Wales
NSW Travel Centre
19 Castlereagh St, Sydney 2000
(02) 9231 4444; Fax: (02) 9232 6080

Australian Capital Territory
Canberra Tourism
Visitor Information Centre
Northbourne Ave, Dickson 2602
(06) 205 0044; Fax: (06) 205 0776

Victoria
Victorian Visitor Information Centre
cnr Little Collins and Swanston Sts,
Melbourne 3000
(03) 9650 1522; Fax: (03) 9650 1212

South Australia
South Australian Travel Centre
1 King William St, Adelaide 5000
(08) 8212 1505, 1800 88 2092; Fax: (08) 8303 2249

Western Australia
WA Tourist Centre, Albert Facey House
cnr Forrest Pl. and Wellington St, Perth 6000
(09) 483 1111; Fax: (09) 481 0190

Northern Territory
Darwin Region Tourism Association
33 Smith St Mall, Darwin 0800
(08) 8981 4300; Fax: (08) 8981 7346

Central Australian Tourism Industry Association
Centrepoint Building
cnr Gregory Tce and Hartley St, Alice Springs 0871
(08) 8952 5199; Fax: (08) 8953 0295

Queensland
Queensland Government Travel Centre
cnr Adelaide and Edward Sts, Brisbane 4000
(07) 3221 6111; Fax: (07) 3221 5320

Tasmania
Tasmanian Travel and Information Centre
20 Davey St, Hobart 7001
(03) 6230 8233; Fax: (03) 6224 0289

ACCOMMODATION

Backpackers Resorts of Australia (head office)
PO Box 600, Cannon Hill, Brisbane 4170
(07) 3890 2767; Fax: (07) 3348 8566

Bed and Breakfast Australia (head office)
PO Box 408, Gordon NSW 2072
(02) 9498 5344; Fax: (02) 9498 6438

Farm holidays
The following is a list of contact addresses in each State if you wish to arrange a farm holiday.

- **New South Wales**
  Australian Farm Host Holidays Pty Ltd
  PO Box 65, Culcairn 2660
  (060) 29 8621; Fax: (060) 29 8770
  (Properties available Australia-wide)

- **Victoria**
  Host Farms Association Inc.
  6th Floor, 230 Collins St, Melbourne
  (03) 9650 2922; Fax: (03) 9650 9434

- **South Australia**
  SA Host Farms Association Inc.
  PO Box 74, Burra North 5417
  (08) 8892 2755; Fax: (08) 8892 2383

- **Western Australia**
  WA Farm and Country Holidays Association
  Evedon Park, Burekup 6227
  (097) 26 3012; Fax: (097) 26 3397

- **Northern Territory**
  Northern Territory Holiday Centre
  PO Box 2532, Alice Springs 0871
  1800 62 1336; Fax: (08) 8951 8581

- **Queensland**
  Queensland Host Farm Association
  RACQ Travel Service
  PO Box 537, Fortitude Valley 4006
  (07) 3361 2390, 1800 77 7888;
  Fax: (07) 3257 1504

- **Tasmania**
  Homehost Tasmania Pty Ltd
  PO Box 780, Sandy Bay 7005
  (03) 6224 1612; Fax: (03) 6224 0472

YHA Australia (head office)
10 Mallett St, Camperdown NSW 2050
(02) 9565 1699; Fax (02) 9565 1325

Emergency (for all States)
For police, ambulance and fire-brigade services, dial 000.

Planning Ahead

The Ghan journeys between Adelaide and Alice Springs

example. Always check ahead for the timing of local special events (**see**: Calendar of Events in the introduction to each State).

If you wish to go to a favourite hotel or try a special type of accommodation – a farm homestead, a houseboat or charter boat – book well ahead. Other holiday-makers will have the same interests. And remember, most national parks require advance notice to give permission for camping within their boundaries.

When to Go

With a few exceptions you can travel Australia at any time of the year. The exceptions include parts of the Far North between October and May, that is, in the 'wet' or tropical monsoon season (this applies particularly if you plan to use bush tracks and unmade roads, many of which are impassable for months). Tropical cyclones are random summer hazards between November and March. In the New South Wales and Victorian high country, from about May to August many roads will be snow-bound. The Red Centre is not especially inviting in midsummer, when daytime temperatures can reach 45°C, while it can be bitterly cold at night.

Otherwise, remember the holiday peaks. If you can avoid travelling in the dense traffic during these major vacation periods, do so.

Which Way to Go

If you flinch at the thought of driving seemingly endless kilometres, you should consider an alternative: both fly/drive packages and MotoRail facilities eliminate time-consuming travel and allow for concentration on areas of interest. Given fuel costs, neither of these is necessarily an extravagance. Cost them out against the expenses involved in using your own car for the entire trip.

Fly/drive. Contact a travel agent or airline travel centre for advice and information on fly/drive packages.

MotoRail. For information on this easy way of covering long distances, contact the State tourist bureaus (**see**: Useful Information) or the main State railway offices (see below). Enquire about CAPER fares; a reduction in rail fare is available on some interstate services if travel is booked and paid for in advance. For all Rail-travel reservations and inquiries phone 13 2232. For the price of a local call you will reach your nearest capital city, where operators will give you Australia-wide information. The following lists MotoRail services:

• **Perth–Sydney–Perth**
Indian–Pacific
Crosses the continent, ocean to ocean; over the Blue Mountains and across the Nullarbor Plain. Two services a week each way: leaves Sydney Mon. and Thurs., leaves Perth Fri. and Mon.; 66 hours.

• **Perth–Adelaide–Perth**
Indian–Pacific
Two services a week each way: leaves Adelaide Tues. and Fri., leaves Perth Mon. and Fri.; 38 hours. This service connects with *The Overland* to Melbourne.

• **Melbourne–Adelaide–Melbourne**
The Overland
Daily, each way (overnight); 12 hours.

• **Adelaide–Alice Springs–Adelaide**
The Ghan
A classic and historic journey. Travel in luxury across the desert May–October, 2 services a week each way; November–April, 1 service a week each way; 22 hours.

• **Brisbane–Townsville–Cairns–Townsville–Brisbane**
The Queenslander
One service a week each way: leaves Brisbane Sun., leaves Cairns Tues.; 33 hours. An additional service once a week each way, includes Proserpine stop; check frequency.

• **Brisbane–Longreach**
Spirit of the Outback
Two services a week each way: leaves Brisbane Tues. and Fri., leaves Longreach Thurs. and Sun.

Note: There are no MotoRail services between Melbourne–Sydney and Sydney–Brisbane.

For further information contact the following main State railway offices:

New South Wales
Country Link Travel Centre
Wynyard Station
11–31 York St, Sydney 2000
(02) 9224 4744 (for timetables only; reservations have to be made in person)

Victoria
V/Line Reservations and Information
Level 2, Transport House
589 Collins St, Melbourne 3000
(03) 9619 5000

South Australia
Australian National Passenger
Reservations and Enquiries
1 Richmond Rd, Keswick 5035
(08) 8217 4111

Western Australia
Westrail Centre
West Pde, East Perth 6000
(09) 326 2222

Queensland
Queensland Rail
305 Edward St, Brisbane 4000
(07) 3235 2222

Other Touring Possibilities

▌ **Spirit of Tasmania.** This passenger and car ferry makes three return voyages weekly between Melbourne and Devonport, northern Tasmania. Bookings can be made through the TT Line Tasmania at Port Melbourne and at Dockside, Devonport, or through your local Tasmanian Travel Centre.

▌ **Campervan rental.** Available in all States and most cities and major towns, the campervans are fully equipped and vary in size and level of luxury. Costs vary accordingly and also with the season. There are often restrictions on where you can take a campervan; so check first.

▌ **Escorted group trips.** If you are interested in a full-on adventure tour, but are intimidated by the thought of doing it alone, motoring organisations and many private tour operators provide escorted group trips into more remote areas, Cape York for example. These tag-along tours save you the worry of navigation and planning (except for your vehicle) and also provide expert help and backup in case of a mechanical breakdown.

Spirit of Tasmania, a car and passenger ferry between Melbourne and Devonport

▌ **Other ideas.** You also could leave your vehicle behind and tour in a 4WD coach, or take a camel trek or try a canoe adventure – or travel almost any way you choose. Check with your travel agent or tourist bureau (**see:** Useful Information).

Where to Stay

State motoring organisations, tourist bureaus and booksellers – all have accommodation guides; some include information on camping and caravan parks. Travel agents and airline travel centres can also provide information.

▌ **Resorts, hotels and motels.** Contact State tourist bureaus, motoring organisations (**see:** Useful Information), your travel agent or airline travel centres for details and bookings. Major motel chains, such as Best Western and Flag, cover most of the country and have head offices in each capital city. Brochures detailing accommodation are available from these head offices.

▌ **Serviced or self-service holiday flats.** If you are planning a stay in a city or at any holiday destination for a length of time, this provides a sensible family alternative to motel or hotel accommodation. The relevant tourist bureau (**see:** Useful Information) will provide you with the details.

▌ **House swapping.** This is yet another possibility for a lengthy stay. This can be arranged through organisations such as Latitudes Home Exchange, PO Box 436, South Perth WA 6151; (09) 367 9412. In addition, advertisements for those seeking a house-swapping holiday often appear in the classified sections of the newspapers. Make sure you are totally satisfied with the arrangements made concerning your commitments and that you are happy with the people with whom you are dealing. Also check that your householder's insurance covers you in such circumstances (**see:** Insurance).

Campervans are available for rental in all States

Other Information

Houseboats at Lake Eildon, Victoria

Pets
Do not forget: whether you are leaving your pets behind or taking them with you, you will need to make arrangements for them also.

Leaving them behind
- Pet care services (see *Yellow Pages* telephone book): provide care of pets in their own environment. They also will care for plants and property, etc.
- Dog boarding kennels and catteries (see *Yellow Pages*): provide care and accommodation. Some have pickup and delivery services.
- Animal welfare organisations/veterinary surgeons (see *Yellow Pages*): for advice and information.

Taking them with you
- Make sure, in advance, that the accommodation or mode of travel booked permits animals. Many caravan parks and most national parks do not admit animals.
- During the trip, carry additional water and stop at regular intervals for toileting and exercise.
- Do not leave an animal unattended in a vehicle for any length of time; always provide fresh air.
- Allow sufficient room in the vehicle to comfortably accommodate the animal.
- Do not transport an animal in a moving caravan.

Before Departure
- Cancel newspapers, mail deliveries.
- Make arrangements for the garden to be watered and lawns mowed. Board out your indoor plants or place them in the sink, surround with damp peat and water thoroughly. Encasing each in a sealed polythene bag also helps retain moisture.
- If you have a pet, arrange for its safekeeping well in advance (**see:** Pets).
- Arrange for a neighbour to keep an eye on the house. Contact your local police and inform them of your absence. Alternatively, consult a professional home security service (see *Yellow Pages*).
- Valuable items, such as jewellery, are best left for safekeeping at your bank.
- Turn the electricity off at the mains and leave the fridge door open. If you have equipment that must operate in your absence, for example a stocked freezer, leave power on and remove plugs from all other power points. Make sure that everything else that should be turned off is off.
- Check that all windows and doors are locked; then check again.
- Always leave a contact address with a friend or neighbour.

Carrying a Camera
You probably will want to preserve the highlights of your trip on film. Check the following points:
- If you have recently bought or hired a camera, take at least one test film before departure so that you know how the equipment reacts to different light conditions.
- As weather conditions may vary, it is a good idea to carry film with a range of speeds. If you are not an expert, talk to your local dealer about the varieties of film available.
- Before you leave, have a good supply of film, batteries and a lens brush. Other useful accessories are a close-up lens, exposure meter, lens hood, filters and a tripod.
- Keep your equipment in a plastic bag inside a camera bag to protect it from water, heat, sand and dust. It can get very hot in a closed car, so always keep the camera in the shade. The best place is on the floor, on the side opposite the exhaust pipe. Make sure, however, that the bag can not rattle around.
- High temperatures and humidity can damage colour film. Store your film in the coolest spot available and do not break the watertight vapour seal until just before use. Once the film is used, remove it from the camera, mark it with an E for 'exposed' and send it for processing as soon as possible.
- When using the camera in hot conditions, even with automatic exposure, it may be necessary to allow one stop or half of a stop down to compensate for the brilliance of the light. If in doubt, consult the instruction sheet included with the film.
- Check that your personal property insurance covers the loss of cameras and photographic equipment while travelling (**see:** Insurance).

Time Zones
Australia has 4 time zones:
- **Eastern Standard Time** (EST), in Queensland, Australian Capital Territory, New South Wales, Victoria and Tasmania. (Note: Broken Hill, in central western New South Wales, operates on CST, half an hour behind the rest of New South Wales.)
- **Central Standard Time** (CST is half an hour behind EST), in South Australia and Northern Territory.
- **Western Standard Time** (WST is 2 hours behind EST), in Western Australia.
- **Central Western Time** (CWT is 45 minutes ahead of WST), a local time zone operating from 3 km east of Caiguna in Western Australia to the South Australian border.

Daylight saving is adopted by some States in summer. In New South Wales, Victoria, Tasmania, Australian Capital Territory and South Australia, clocks are put forward 1 hour at the beginning of summer. Northern Territory, Western Australia and Queensland do not have daylight saving.

Quarantine Regulations
Throughout Australia, State quarantine regulations prohibit the transport by travellers of certain plants and foods, and even soil, across State borders. Further information is available from offices of agricultural departments in all States.

Planning Ahead

Backpacker accommodation in Kings Cross, Sydney

■ **Host farms.** Such accommodation varies from spartan to luxurious and, in some cases, guests are invited to take part in farm life. Associations in each State (**see:** Useful Information) or tourist authorities will provide details.

■ **Bed and breakfast accommodation.** Contact Bed & Breakfast Australia (**see:** Useful Information) for information on bed and breakfast accommodation in homestay or farmstay environments throughout Australia.

■ **Backpacker accommodation.** This type of accommodation is provided at budget rates in a communal environment and is becoming very popular. Note, however, that the accommodation offered is not always suitable for children. During the holiday season, some hostels may not accept telephone reservations without payment and it is advisable to book well in advance. To obtain information on the range of accommodation available, contact Backpackers Resorts of Australia (**see:** Useful Information). A Backpackers VIP Discount Kit costing $20 (add $5 for postage and handling, if purchasing by mail), valid in 21 countries with an accommodation guide (free) to 127 hostels Australia-wide, is available from this organisation.

■ **Youth hostels.** For the young at heart, there are over 100 youth hostels throughout Australia. For information, contact the main headquarters of YHA Australia (**see:** Useful Information).

■ **Floating accommodation.** If you are into staying afloat, consider hiring a paddle-wheeler on the Murray or a houseboat on the Hawkesbury River or Eildon Weir, or even chartering a yacht to cruise in the Whitsundays. Obtain details from your travel agent or State tourist bureau (**see:** Useful Information).

Dividing Up the Dollars

Very few people can afford the 'money-no-object' approach to holidays, no matter what the length of stay. Your planning should include budgeting. You will need principally to consider accommodation, food, fuel and entertainment, although emergency funds should not be forgotten. Travel insurance is a wise precaution (**see:** Insurance).

■ **Accommodation.** Accommodation costs can be estimated when you book, but you might simply average the figure. If you do, estimate high rather than low.

■ **Food.** This is a matter of personal choice: you may eat out every night or prepare all or some of your meals yourself. Be realistic when budgeting the cost of eating out or preparing meals: allow for the unexpected, and for the higher cost of food and meals in popular holiday destinations or in remote areas. Budget for snacks and recreational treats, if you are travelling with children.

■ **Fuel.** Once you know your vehicle's fuel consumption you can work out your fuel costs in advance. The usual method is based on litres per 100 kilometres. If your vehicle uses 16 litres per 100 kilometres and your journey distance works out at 5000 kilometres, you will use 50 times 16 litres of fuel, or 800 litres. Allow for rises in the cost of petrol and other vehicle expenses, and also for the fact that fuel is more expensive in remote areas.

■ **Entertainment and other costs.** When budgeting, allow for such 'budget biters' as admission charges, postcards, camera film, chemist's items, tips, bridge tolls and car repairs. Remember also that accommodation, travel and rental charges rise during peak periods.

Carrying large amounts of cash with you is not a good idea, hence travellers cheques were invented. Use them, or credit cards, but also make arrangements with your bank to enable you to draw from the bank's branches on your route.

Car Maintenance Courses

If you plan to tour in the remoter areas, you should acquire basic mechanical knowledge and skills. In general you should have a broad understanding of the technology of your vehicle and know how much roadside repair is possible in the event of a breakdown (**see also:** Breakdowns). You should also have some specific knowledge; for example how to change a tyre on the vehicle you will be using; and whether you can use jumper leads to start your car and if so, how it is done. Car care and basic car-maintenance courses are run by Adult Education centres, TAFE Colleges and motoring organisations in all States. The courses vary widely in content and

8 Planning Ahead

Shark Bay, near Monkey Mia in Western Australia

length. A call to these organisations will ascertain what course is available and appropriate. Test your knowledge by reading through the Trouble Shooting flow-charts and the Tools and Spare Parts list (**see:** Breakdowns).

Insurance

The benefits of a comprehensive insurance policy on your vehicle, caravan or trailer are obvious. As well as cover against loss or damage due to accident, theft and vandalism, your personal effects are covered against loss or damage when they are in the insured vehicle. Additional policies will cover such eventualities as, for example, the cost of temporary accommodation should your caravan become uninhabitable. Some companies provide short-term (maximum 6 weeks) travel insurance, for example, to cover loss of luggage or the cancellation of accommodation bookings, etc. Information and advice can be obtained from the various motoring organisations (**see:** Useful Information) and insurance companies.

Itineraries

Some people make itineraries and stick to them; others do not. At the very least, a rough schedule to ensure a mixture of travel and sightseeing time is essential. Allow some flexibility. You never know what might detain you: the weather (frequent rest breaks are necessary in extreme heat), or children, who have a low tolerance for long periods without a break (**see:** Child's Play).

Clothing

Be strict with yourself and the family when you are packing and travel as lightly as you can. It is better to spend an hour at a laundromat than overburden your vehicle with clothing you probably will not wear.

Essentials are a jumper or jacket, even in summer; sensible comfortable shoes; and a wide-brimmed hat to protect yourself from the sun at all times. Non-irons are practical. Carry items like swimwear, towels, spare socks and jumpers in a bag that can be kept within easy reach. Gumboots are a handy item also.

First-aid Kit

A first-aid kit is essential. Include band-aids, antiseptic, bandages, headache tablets, extra blockout, sunburn cream, insect repellent and a soothing lotion for bites. Eye drops are a good idea, as is a thermometer and a tourniquet. Kits are available from various suppliers including St John Ambulance Australia, which also conducts basic courses in first aid. As car sickness is often a problem on long journeys, particularly with young children, include medication to counter this. Your chemist or a doctor will advise you.

Useful Extras

Depending on the length and nature of your tour, some items are valuable, some essential (**see:** Tools and Spare Parts). Carry picnic and barbecue equipment, tissues, toilet paper and a container or plastic bag for rubbish – and take it with you rather than leaving it behind, at least until you can find a legitimate rubbish tip. Rugs or blankets are a necessary extra, as is a large sheet of plastic, which can be used as an emergency windscreen. Having a mobile phone may be useful if you are travelling within signal range; check the coverage before departure. If you are going to the outback, a necessary item is some type of shade cover, such as a tarpaulin, as sun protection in case of an emergency stop (**see:** Outback Motoring).

Accidents do happen; the right insurance prevents financial disaster

Inter-city Route Maps

The following inter-city route maps will help you plan your route between major cities. As well, you can use the maps during your journey, since they provide information on distances between towns along the route, roadside rest areas, road conditions and which towns are described in the A–Z listings. The map below provides an overview of the routes mapped.

Sydney - Melbourne via Highway/Freeway [31] 10
Sydney - Melbourne via Highway [1] 10
Sydney - Brisbane via Highway [1] 10
Melbourne - Adelaide via Highways [8] [1] 10
Melbourne - Adelaide via Highway [1] 10
Melbourne - Brisbane via Highways [31] [39] [42] [15] 11
Adelaide - Darwin via Highways [87] [1] 11
Adelaide - Perth via Highways [1] [94] 11
Adelaide - Sydney via Highways [31] [20] 11
Perth - Darwin via Highway [1] 11
Sydney - Brisbane via Highways [1] [92] [15] 12
Brisbane - Darwin via Highways [15] [54] [71] [66] [87] [1] 12
Brisbane - Cairns via Highway [1] 12
Hobart - Launceston via Highway [1] 12
Hobart - Devonport via Highway [1] 12

10 Inter-city Route Maps

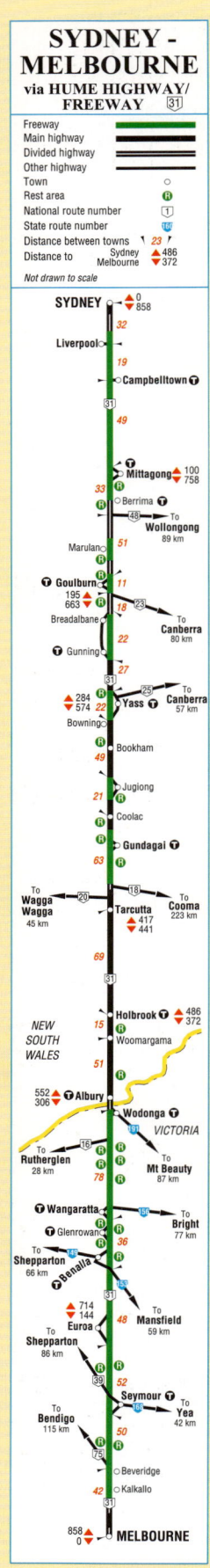
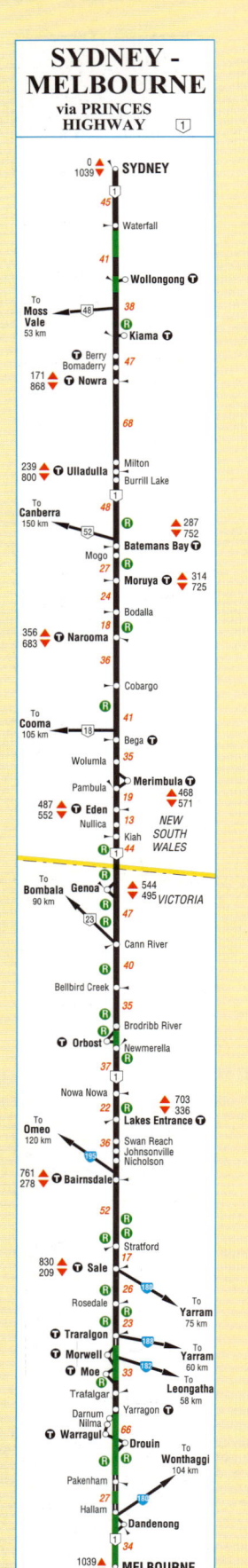
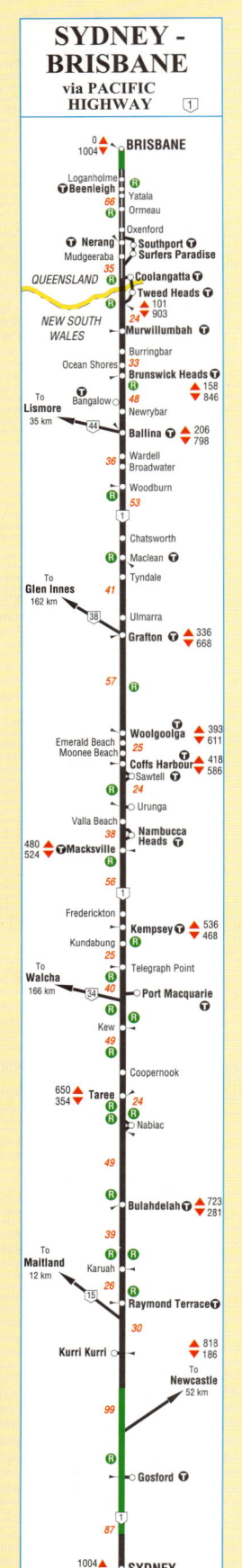
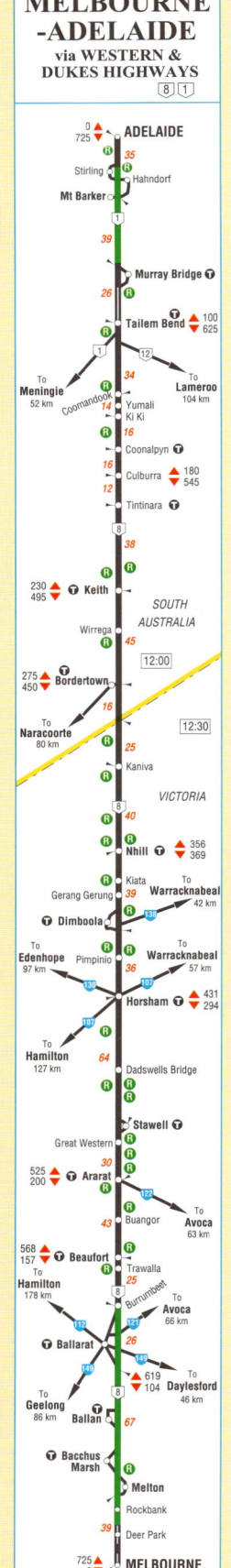
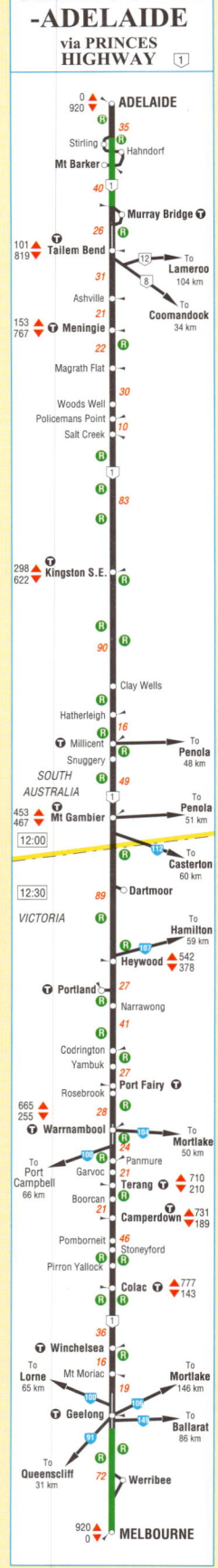

Inter-city Route Maps

MELBOURNE-BRISBANE
via NEWELL HIGHWAY

ADELAIDE-DARWIN
via STUART HIGHWAY

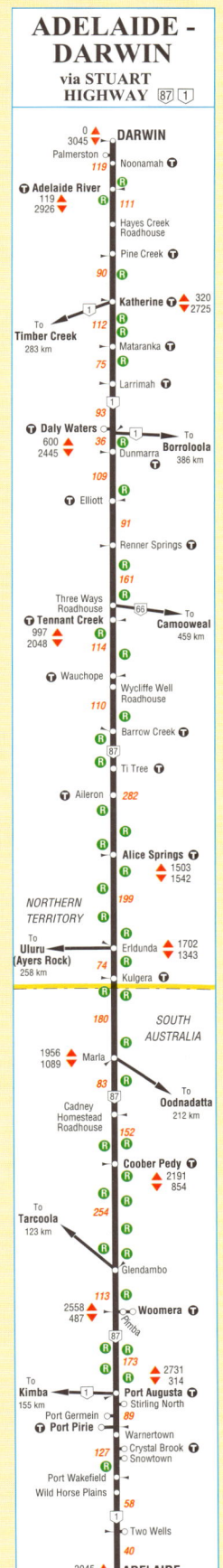

ADELAIDE-PERTH
via EYRE & GREAT EASTERN HIGHWAYS

ADELAIDE-SYDNEY
via STURT & HUME HIGHWAYS

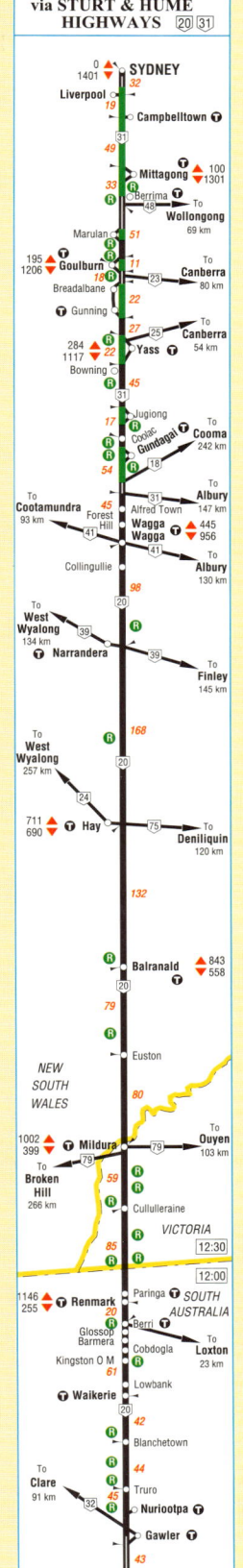

PERTH-DARWIN
via BRAND, NORTH-WEST COASTAL, GREAT NORTHERN, VICTORIA & STUART HIGHWAYS

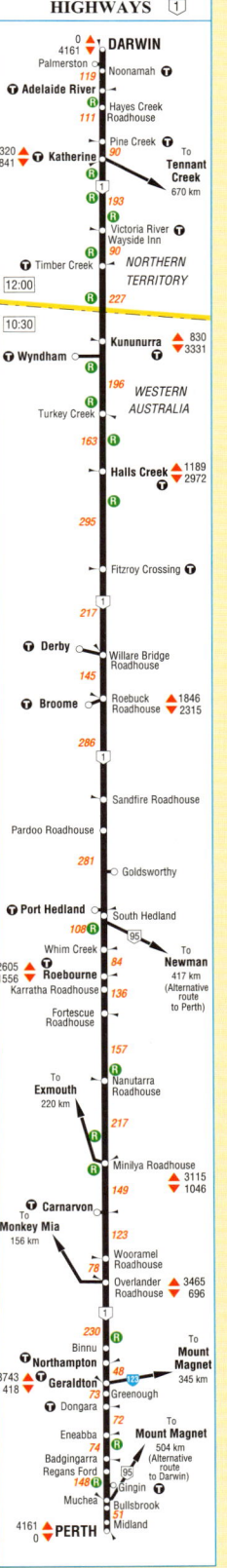

12 Inter-city Route Maps

SYDNEY - BRISBANE
via NEW ENGLAND HIGHWAY

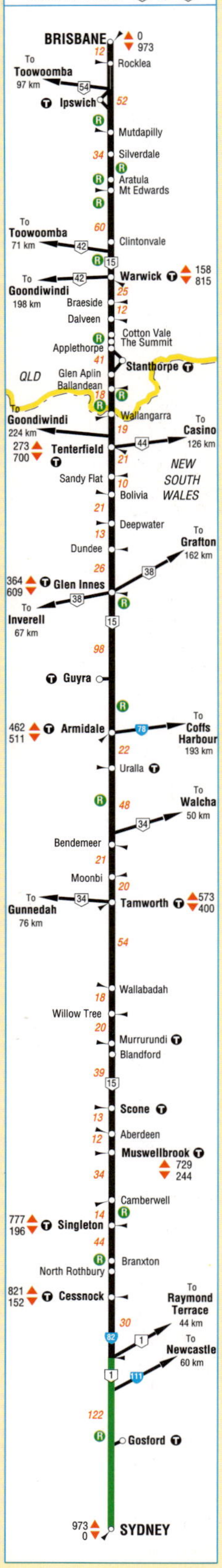

BRISBANE - DARWIN
via WARREGO, LANDSBOROUGH, BARKLY & STUART HIGHWAYS

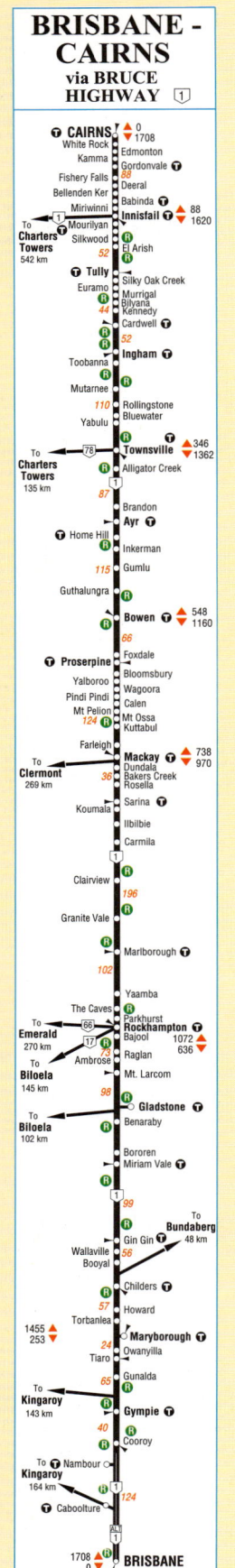

BRISBANE - CAIRNS
via BRUCE HIGHWAY

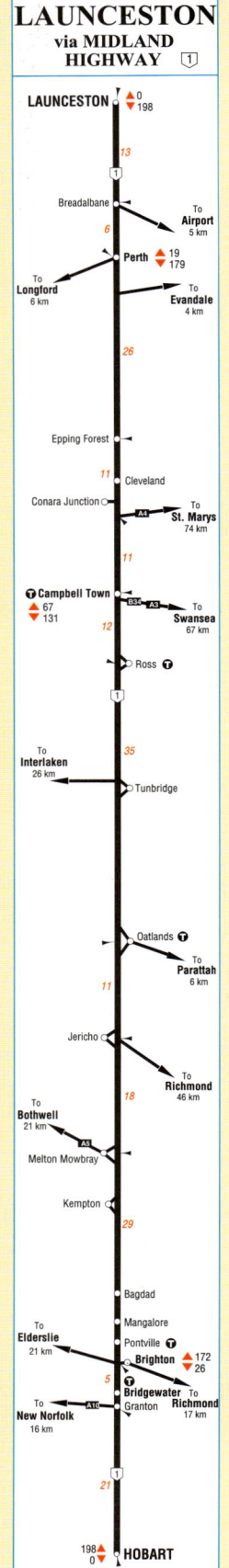

HOBART - LAUNCESTON
via MIDLAND HIGHWAY

HOBART - DEVONPORT
via MIDLAND & BASS HIGHWAYS

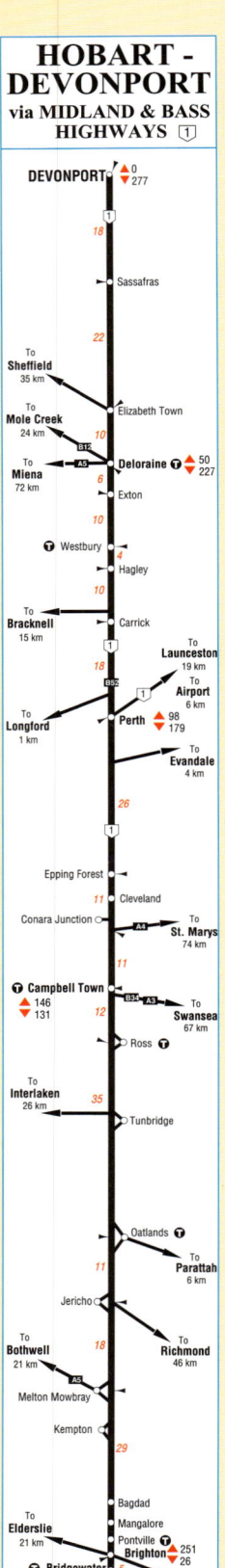

Have a GOOD TRIP

Checking the Car

All the care that you devote to your own comfort can be for nothing if you do not make sure that the car checks out too.

For a one-, two- or three-day tour, you could simply fuel up, check the tyre pressures, clean all the windows and head off; if you maintain your vehicle at all times in reasonable condition – as indeed you should – probably little further preparation is required. However, a vacation of a week or more, or any time involving long-distance driving, will need more thorough preparation. If you intend travelling through remote areas, for example, you should first check that your vehicle is able to handle off-road conditions. The service department of your State motoring organisations (**see:** Useful Information) will give advice and will make a preliminary inspection of your vehicle.

Regardless of the length of your tour, you should check the wheelbrace, jack and under-vehicle jacking points, in case you have to change a tyre.

Unless you are able to service your vehicle yourself, this preparation should be left to your mechanic. To avoid breakdowns and to confirm the reliability of safety-related items, ask the mechanic to include a check of the fuel supply, electrics, brakes, tyres and certain ancillary equipment, as follows.

■ **Fuel supply.** Check fuel pump for flow. Check carburettor for wear and potential blockages or check condition of electronic or mechanical fuel injection. When the tank is almost empty, remove the drain plug and drain the tank, to check that the remaining fuel is perfectly clean. Check fuel-supply lines for cracks and poor connections, and make sure no fuel line is exposed to damage by rocks or low-clearance projections.

■ **Electrics.** Check battery output and condition (including terminals), alternator/generator output and condition, spark plugs, condenser, coil, distributor and all terminals and cables. If the vehicle is fitted with electronic ignition it should be checked in the prescribed manner.

■ **Lights.** Check all lights, not just to see that they work, but to make sure that

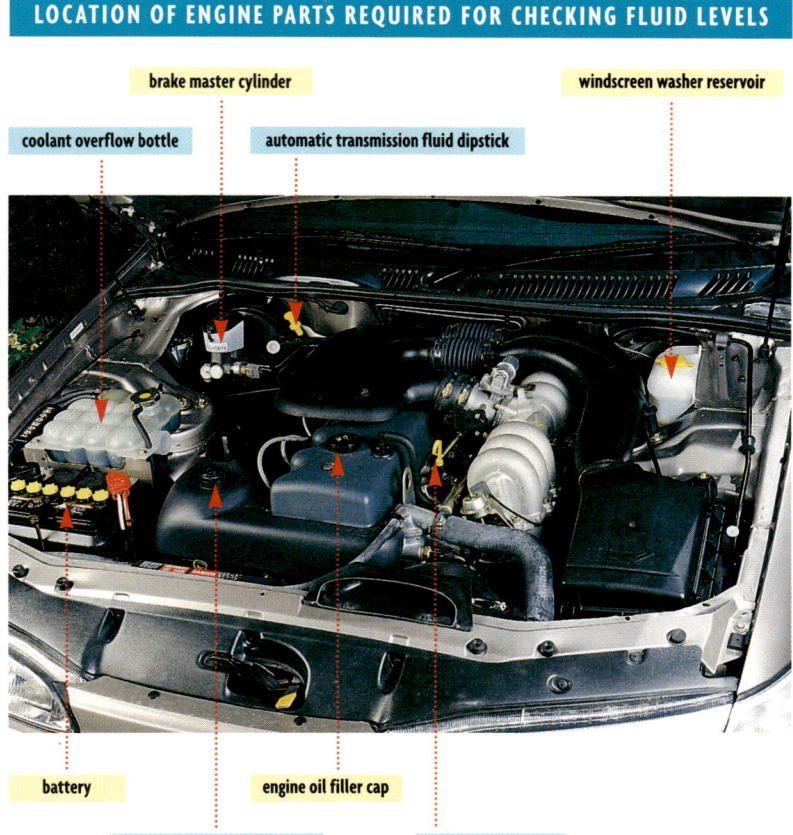

LOCATION OF ENGINE PARTS REQUIRED FOR CHECKING FLUID LEVELS

brake master cylinder • windscreen washer reservoir • coolant overflow bottle • automatic transmission fluid dipstick • battery • engine oil filler cap • power-steering fluid dipstick • engine oil dipstick

they are aligned correctly and are likely to continue to work. It can be very, very dark at night in outback Australia.

■ **Brakes**. Check wear of pads and/or linings, check discs for runout and drums for scoring. Brake dust should be cleaned off. Check brake lines and hoses for cracks and wear. Make sure brake lines are not liable to be damaged by rocks or low projections. Check parking brake for adjustment and cable stretch.

■ **Tyres.** Check for uneven or excessive wear. Check walls for cracks and stone or kerb fractures. Check pressures. Include spare (or spares) in all checks. Make sure that the spare wheel matches those on the car, and uses the same kind of wheel nuts.

■ **Windscreen-wiper blades.** Check for wear and proper contact, and washers for direction and effectiveness. Include rear wiper and washer, where fitted.

■ **Windscreen glass.** Check for cracks and replace if necessary.

■ **Seat mountings and adjustments.** Check.

■ **Lubricant levels.** Check (including brake and clutch fluid) and either top up or drain and refill.

■ **Wheel bearings.** Check for play and adjust or replace.

■ **Universal and constant velocity joints.** Check, where appropriate, and replace if necessary.

■ **Dust and water sealing.** A pre-run test in appropriate conditions will reveal any problems. What you do not need is dust, exhaust fumes or water inside the vehicle.

■ **Roof rack.** Check mounts and welds for weaknesses and cracks.

■ **Seat belts**. Check for tears or sun-hardening. Replace if necessary. Also check inertia reels.

■ **Radiator water level and condition.** Check; drain and flush if necessary.

Hazards

Flood

In some remote areas, floods can occur without warning. Do not camp in dry river beds or close to the edges of creeks or streams. Always exercise extreme caution when approaching flooded roads or bridges. Floodwaters are deceptive; always check the depth before attempting to cross. If you do find yourself stranded in deep water:
- Do not panic.
- Wind up all the windows, to slow down or prevent water entering. (You should have closed all the windows before you tried to cross.)
- When the car has stabilised, undo the seatbelts.
- Turn the headlights on to help rescuers locate the car.
- If the car does not sink, but drifts (which is often the case with a well-sealed car), wait until it reaches shallow water or is close to the bank, then open the door or windows and climb out.
- Form a human chain and help children to keep their heads above water.
- If the car is sinking, it will be necessary to wait for the water pressure to equalise before you can open the doors or windows. As a last resort, kick out the windscreen or rear window.

Exercise extreme caution when crossing flooded areas

Bushfire

If you have to travel on days of critical fire danger (that is, total fire ban days), make sure you carry some woollen blankets and a filled water container. If you are trapped as a bushfire approaches:
- Do not panic.
- Stop the car in the nearest cleared area.
- Wind up all the windows.
- Turn on the hazard lights to warn any other traffic.
- DO NOT GET OUT OF YOUR CAR. The temperature may become unbearably hot, but it is still safer to stay in the car.
- Lie on the car floor, below window level, to avoid radiant heat.
- Cover yourself and your passengers with blankets.

The car will not explode or catch fire, and a fast-moving wildfire will pass quickly overhead.

Animals

Although some species of Australia's unique wildlife are immensely appealing, some species are extremely dangerous.

Marine life

- **Box jellyfish** (or **marine stingers**). These are found in the coastal waters of Queensland and northern Australia in the summer months (from October–May). A sting from their many long tentacles can be lethal, and for that reason swimming on coastal beaches north of Rockhampton is prohibited at this time. Also, walking barefoot at the water's edge in this region in summer is not advisable.
- **Stonefish.** Among Australia's several species of poisonous stinging fish, the stonefish, found all around the northern coastline, is best avoided.
- **Blue-ringed octopus.** Common in Australian coastal waters, its bite can paralyse in 15 minutes resulting in death. Do not handle in any circumstances.
- **Sharks.** Sharks are common in Australian waters. Avoid swimming in deep water and do not swim where sharks have been seen.
- **Freshwater and saltwater crocodiles.** These are found in north and north-western Australia. The saltwater crocodile is particularly dangerous and may be found in both salt water and fresh water. The freshwater crocodile will also bite, thus caution is necessary for both species. Neither species is easy to see in the water. Heed local warning signs and do not swim or paddle in natural waterways or allow children or animals near the water's edge. People standing in water feeding or cleaning fish are particularly vulnerable.

Snakes

As a rule, snakes are timid and generally do not attack unless threatened. However, several species are highly venomous.

Spiders

Funnel-web spider and **red-back spider.** The bite from both species can be deadly. The funnel-web is found in and around Sydney. The red-back is found in most Australian States.

Insects

Wasps, **bees**, **ticks**, **ants** (particularly the **bull-ant**), **scorpions** and **centipedes.** These insects are found throughout Australia. Their sting or bite normally is not harmful, except to those people who are allergy-prone, but it may cause pain and discomfort. Ticks should be removed promptly.

Study Australia's wildlife and learn to identify dangerous species. Remember also that some plant species are poisonous. When visiting a new area, check with local authorities to ascertain which dangerous species, if any, are found there.

Marine stinger warning sign

Check radiator for leaks and radiator pressure cap for pressure release accuracy. Check water-pump operation. Check radiator and heater hoses for cracks and general condition, and replace if necessary. Check hose clamps.
▌ **Fan belt.** Check for tension and fraying.
▌ Check anything else you might think is worthwhile.

All this should be done as near as practicable to your departure date. Allow time for unexpected work or part replacement, and for a return to the garage if a particular problem persists. Note: *Nothing should be overlooked* – lives may be at stake.

Packing the Car

First and most important, you should carry only those items that are absolutely necessary with you in the passenger compartment. In a sedan this is not difficult. You have a boot, and that is where most items should be carried; but in a station wagon it is much more difficult. Loose items in the passenger compartment get under your feet (especially hazardous for the driver), interfere with your comfort and will become dangerous projectiles if you have a collision. So for your station wagon, buy or rig up a safety net, which can be fitted behind the rear seat to separate you from the objects that could otherwise harm you.

This rule applies also to food and drink. Empty bottles and cartons should be stowed out of the way in a rubbish bag, until you are able to dispose of them properly.

And if you are short of space, cull some non-essential items.

In order to provide extra space, many drivers fix a roof rack to their vehicle. This is not recommended. Laden roof racks upset the balance of the vehicle by changing its centre of gravity, making it top-heavy. They disturb the air flow, which can destabilise the vehicle, and they certainly increase fuel consumption by interfering with the aerodynamics. In some circumstances they can snag on overhanging limbs of trees.

If you must use a roof rack, carry as little on it as possible and keep the maximum loading height as low as you can. Protect the load by wrapping it in a tarpaulin or groundsheet and, if possible, create a sharp (aerofoil) leading edge on the load to improve air flow.

A better alternative to a roof rack is a small, strong, lightweight trailer, but

An early start, Mt Rowland in Tasmania

there are times when this will be a disadvantage also.

If you are towing a caravan, some items can be carried inside the van on the floor, preferably strapped down (anything loose will be flung about) and located over the axle (or axles). In some States, caravans must be fitted with a fire extinguisher. (And remember, no people or animals are to be transported in a towed caravan.)

Once your vehicle is loaded, and preferably with the passengers aboard, check the tyre pressures (yes, even as you leave home on day one). The additional load will mean higher pressures are needed. The tyre placard or owner's handbook can be used as a guideline, but modern steel radials, fully laden, are best inflated to around 250 kilopascals (36 psi). This is not too high. For a country trip with a heavy load on a hot day 280 kPa (40 psi) is about right. Light vans and 4WD vehicles should have higher pressure: at least 315 kPa (45 psi) for the highway, and as high as 350 kPa (50 psi) for highway travel on a hot day with a heavy load. The tyre will bag if it is under-inflated and destabilise the car. It also will offer a baggy sidewall to rocks and stones, encouraging wall fractures and potential blowouts. Laden-tyre pressure requirements vary with tyre size and design, but the pressure is important. If you are in any doubt contact the tyre manufacturer.

When to Set Off

There is evidence to suggest that people drive best during the hours in which they are accustomed to being awake, and probably at work. As drowsiness is deadly in drivers, this is worth noting. Leaving home, for example at 1 a.m., might avoid the heat of the day and beat the traffic to a large extent, but somewhere between 3 and 5 a.m. you may find yourself wanting to doze off again.

Plan to share long-distance driving as much as possible. Depart around or just before sunrise and stop no later than sundown. Allow regular stops, not just to stretch your legs but to take nourishment as well. Food helps keep the energy levels up. You might care to leave later if you are travelling east, to avoid the rising sun shining in your eyes, and finish earlier if you are travelling west, for the converse reason.

Leaving Home

Everyone knows the feeling that usually comes when you are a good distance from home: did I lock all the windows, turn off the electricity at the meter, cancel the newspaper and mail delivery? Usually all is well, but it is reassuring to double-check everything before you leave (**see**: Before Departure).

Better DRIVING

Take extra care on icy roads

In skilful driving, the two most important ingredients are concentration and smoothness.

Concentration. Find a position that is comfortable position and stay comfortable; discomfort destroys concentration. Lack of concentration is the biggest single cause of road accidents.

Wear the right clothes: loose-fitting, cool or warm as appropriate, but capable of being changed (not while you are driving!) as temperatures change. Lightweight shoes are better than boots. (There are such things as driving shoes, which are excellent.) Wear good quality antiglare sunglasses. Sit comfortably: neither too close to the steering wheel and cramped, nor too far back and stretching; and be sure you can reach the foot controls through the entire length of their movement. Drive with both hands all the time. No one can control a car properly with one hand. Driving gloves are recommended. Make all seat, belt and rear-view mirror adjustments before you drive off. (Particularly if you share the driving with someone not your size.)

Concentration means *no distractions*. It is probably unrealistic to suggest that no conversation takes place while you are driving, but do not allow conversations to interfere with your concentration. Aim to keep the children quiet and amused (**see:** Child's Play). If an important issue needs to be resolved, first stop the car and then sort it out.

Smoothness. Smoothness is vital for the vehicle's safe, effective operation, but unfortunately many people are not smooth drivers. A vehicle in motion is a tonne or so of iron, steel and plastic sitting atop a set of springs. It is inherently unstable and prone to influences such as pitch and roll. This is difficult enough to control in normal motion, but worse when the driver exaggerates these instabilities by stabbing at the brakes, jerking the steering wheel and crashing the gears. Two things derive from being a smooth driver. The first is passenger comfort; on a long trip, everyone will arrive much fresher and more relaxed if the driver has provided a smooth and therefore pleasant journey. The second is increased safety; the vehicle will react better to smooth driving than it will to hamfisted driving. Smooth driving brings even further benefits: less wear and tear and lower fuel consumption.

However, to define better driving as a combination of concentration and smoothness only would not be wholly accurate. There are other factors:

Know your vehicle. Understand its breaking capacities, especially in emergencies – some cars move around a lot, or become directionally unstable under harsh braking. Be aware of its usable power and its limitations. And drive well within the cornering and road-holding limits of the vehicle's suspension and tyre combination.

Drive defensively. Assume all other drivers are asleep, inattentive or devoid of skill. It is remarkable how your driving awareness is increased by such an attitude.

Do not be impatient. Advance planning should have provided you with ample time for the day's journey.

Do not drive with an incapacitating illness or injury. Something as simple as a bruised elbow might restrict rapid arm movement when you most need it.

Driving Emergencies

Of course, the best way to handle emergencies is to avoid them. However, to suggest one problem or another will never occur is unrealistic. A course in defensive driving is an advantage; contact your local motoring organisation to obtain more information (**see:** Useful Information).

Skidding. The possibility of skidding worries most drivers, as well it should. There are a number of causes of a skid, some of them composite. Essentially skidding occurs when the tyres lose their grip on the road.

The most common form is a front-wheel (or sometimes all-wheel) skid caused by over-braking. When the wheels stop rolling, the vehicle will no longer react to steering input. If you avoid jumping on the brake pedal, (that is, drive smoothly), you will avoid this type of skid. However if you do skid, quickly ease just sufficient pressure off the brake pedal to allow the wheels to roll again. The steering will come back, which at least will allow you to take avoiding action as well as to slow down.

A rear-wheel skid also may occur as a result of harsh braking, usually while turning at the same time (for example corner entry speed too high, braking too harsh). In slippery conditions the tail of the car may also fishtail because you have entered a corner too fast or, in rear-wheel drive vehicles, because too much power has been applied too soon, causing the rear tyres to break traction. A rear-wheel skid of any kind requires some reverse steering, often only briefly. It is not enough to advise turning the steering in the direction of the skid: the question is, by how much? Turn the steering wheels to point them in the direction you wish to travel and, at the same time, try to recognise what you did to cause the skid in the first place. If it was because of excessive acceleration, back off a little and re-apply the accelerator more gently. If it was because you entered the corner too fast or because of your braking (or both at the same time), ease the brakes and let your corrective steering realign the car and then, smoothly, increase the power again by gently applying the accelerator.

Skids can be complex and difficult to control. Over-correction is common, with the result that the vehicle swings into another skid in the opposite direction. It is important not to panic, and to be smooth in your reaction. Easy to say – not so easy to do!

■ **Aquaplaning.** This is a form of skidding where the tyres roll a layer of water up in front of the vehicle and then ride on to it, breaking contact with the road surface. What you sense is a sudden loss of driving 'feel'. Slow down, very smoothly, until the tyres come off the layer of water and then proceed more carefully. Watch out for deep puddles: they are the danger.

Driving in snow, ice and mud also produces adhesion problems. Once again, smooth, steady progress, while 'feeling' the vehicle and staying on top of its movements, is the only answer.

■ **Icy roads.** For a visit to the snow, your vehicle should be fitted with chains. If it is not and the car's back wheels begin to spin wildly on packed and rutted snow or ice:
- Stop the car.
- Look for and remove any obstructions under the car.
- Pack loose gravel, sticks or vegetation under the driving wheels.
- Remember that on a level surface a gentle push sometimes will get the car moving again.

Because it cannot be seen, ice can be more dangerous than snow.

■ **Foggy conditions.** When driving in fog:
- Switch on dipped headlights, or foglights if your car is fitted with them.
- Use front and back demisters.
- If visibility is reduced to such an extent that driving becomes an ordeal, pull as far off the road as you can, switch on your emergency lights and wait until the fog lifts and you feel able to continue.

The advice in this section applies equally to driving in the cities and in the outback. The techniques are the same; only the conditions vary (**see**: Outback Motoring for more detail on driving in the outback).

Safe Driving

Basic Traffic Laws

There are variations in road traffic laws from State to State throughout Australia. Some affect the traveller, some do not. Drivers are expected to know and observe those rules that apply to a vehicle's operation; however, specific State laws that affect the registration of vehicles, trailers or caravans, for example, are not enforced between States.

The city of Melbourne, which is the last stronghold of the tram, has its unique hook turn, where at some inner-city intersections a vehicle making a righthand turn must move to the far left of the intersection and wait until the traffic clears and the traffic lights change before completing the turn. Overtaking on the right of a tram is forbidden and no vehicle may pass a stationary tram at a recognised tram stop.

Drink-driving laws are extremely strict in all States and drivers can be pulled up at random and be required to take a blood alcohol test.

Speed regulations vary in each State. In some States, the use of cameras to catch speeding drivers, both in the city and country, is widespread; as well, cameras are positioned at traffic lights on many intersections to record drivers who do not stop at the red light.

In most other respects, the road traffic laws are essentially the same from State to State. However, legislation is subject to change and the cautious driver will check first with the relevant State motoring organisation (**see**: Useful Information) for answers to any questions raised on specific regulations.

Positioning

Positioning is vital on any road.
- Try to stagger the position of your car in the line of traffic so that you can see well ahead.

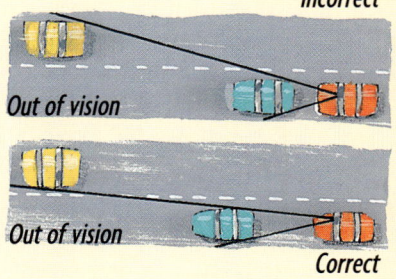

- When turning right on a two-lane highway, do not angle the car; keep it square to the other traffic so that cars can pass on the left.

In Case of Accident

In all States of Australia, any accident in which someone is injured or killed *must* be reported to police at once, or within 24 hours. In Western Australia, all car accidents must be reported.

It is highly advisable to report to police any accident that involves substantial property damage. Police may or may not decide to attend the scene, but they at least will have your report on record, which may well be useful should there be legal proceedings or insurance claims.

When involved in an accident and if required by police, you *must* give your name and address and produce your driver's licence. If you do not have it with you, you may be liable for an on-the-spot fine. It is advisable to obtain the insurance details of the other parties involved.

All parties involved in the accident should exchange names and addresses, and insurance details. *Do not volunteer any other information.* In particular, do not discuss the accident. Should court action result, you may find something said in the stress of the aftermath of the accident used against you. Above all, *do not admit you are at fault in any way.*

You are not obliged to make a statement to police. If you are disturbed and upset, wait until you can think clearly.

An accident that involves damage to persons or property should be reported to your insurance company as soon as possible.

TOWING

Touring near the Hamersley Range, Western Australia

INTRODUCTION

Towing your accommodation behind you will provide the advantage of low-budget touring and flexibility with stopovers. It can be a disadvantage also, in that it may restrict access to some areas. You can, however, use the caravan for most sections of your journey and park it somewhere while you go off in the car and explore the more difficult tracks.

■ **Obtain advice.** If you are new to towing, the first thing you must do is to get expert advice from your local motoring organisation (**see**: Useful Information) on your towing hitch. It is very important that the rig (that is, car and caravan, boat or trailer) is balanced and the weight over the tow ball is not excessive. An adjustable height hitch with spring bars is best.

■ **Learn to reverse.** Once you have decided on the hitch and you have learned how to hook up and unhook, you must learn to reverse the rig. Find a wide open area, an empty car park for example, and practise. Get the feel of the rig and aim to be proficient at reversing before you depart.

■ **Allow for added length.** On the road, remember to make allowances for the added overall length and give yourself extra space for turning and extra distance for overtaking. The added weight will obviously affect the towing vehicle's performance with regard to acceleration and braking.

■ **Know the speed limit.** In most States there are speed limits on articulated vehicles and you should know what they are before departure and abide by them (**see**: Basic Traffic Laws). High-speed towing of vans and trailers can cause major difficulties, magnifying driving problems substantially.

■ **Avoid trailer sway.** Cross-winds can be a problem when towing a caravan, the van's slab sides acting like sails. The combination of high speed and cross-winds can cause trailer sway, a dangerous characteristic that dramatically destabilises both towing vehicle and caravan. You probably will feel it happening before you see it, but checking in the rear-view mirrors will confirm it. Should the trailer begin to move about, ease back on your speed, braking if necessary, but very gently. Harsh or sudden braking will compound the problem. When the caravan stabilises, resume speed, perhaps very gradually if you are continuing in a cross-wind area.

■ **Fit good-quality towing mirrors on your vehicle.** It is very important that your rear view down both sides of the trailer or caravan is not obscured.

■ **Be courteous.** If, because of the relative slowness of your progress, you observe in the rear-view mirror a line of vehicles banking up behind you, be courteous and pull over when and where you can, to allow vehicles to overtake.

■ **Locate load correctly.** The carrying of goods and equipment in a caravan has been mentioned, but it is worth repeating that such items should be located as much as possible over and just to the front of the caravan axle (or axles), never behind, which will lift the front of the caravan and the tow ball.

■ **Check the rig.** Before setting off and every day of the trip, whatever the vehicle, always check and double-check that the hitch is secure, that the safety chains are correctly fitted, and that the electrical connections are working so that indicator lights function at the rear of the towed vehicle.

■ **Allow extra time.** Remember to allow extra time for each day's travel, and remain alert.

Checklist

When towing anything:
- Check the hitch for security. The law in most States demands that tow bars are fitted with safety chains.
- Check that the tail and stop lights, marker lights and signal lights are working.
- Remember to check the air pressure in the caravan or trailer tyres.
- If towing a boat, check the lashings.
- Check that caravan doors, windows and roof vents are closed before departure.
- If the caravan or trailer is fitted with separate brakes, check these as soon as you start to move.

OUTBACK Motoring

A 4WD vehicle negotiating bulldust

Australia's size and remoteness deter many people from exploring it. However, properly set up and equipped, and armed with common sense and a little background knowledge, every intending traveller can explore the country's huge open spaces.

If you intend travelling in the outback, planning ahead is vital, for it is possible to travel in some sections of the Australian outback and not see another vehicle or person for several days. (The Canning Stock Route is a good example.)

It is possible to travel in some areas of the outback in a 2WD vehicle, but it is safer and much more practical to do so in a 4WD vehicle suited to off-road conditions. Remember that if you rent a vehicle, there may be restrictions on insurance if you drive on unclassified roads; seek advice before you make any plans.

Your vehicle should be fitted with air conditioning to counteract high inland daytime temperatures and to allow you to drive with all the windows closed through dusty areas. You should be able to carry out small running repairs and must carry an owner's manual for the vehicle, tools and spare parts (**see:** Tools and Spare Parts).

Driving Conditions

Outback driving conditions vary greatly. The deserts are usually dry; conditions change after rain. Many parts of the tropics are accessible only in the 'dry' season, and even then there are streams to ford and washaways to contend with.

Pre-reading road conditions is vital. Recognising that a patch of different colour may represent a change in surface is an example. Sand can give way to rock; rock may lead to mud; hard surfaces become bulldust with little warning.

■ **Soft sand, bulldust and mud.** These are best negotiated at the highest reasonable speed and in the highest possible gear *and* in 4WD. However, examine the road surface first. Never enter deep mud or mud covered with water without first establishing the depth of either or both.

■ **Deep sand.** Requires low tyre pressures. Carry a tyre pressure gauge and drop pressures to about 10 psi. Reinflate when on gravel or bitumen roads again, because the soft tyres will perform very badly and may blow out as a result of stone fractures on hard surfaces.

■ **Crossing a creek or stream.** Stop to check the track across for clear passage and water depth. If the water is deep but fordable, cover the front of the vehicle with a tarpaulin and remove the fan belt to stop water being sprayed over the engine electrics. Drive through in low range second gear or high range first gear, and clear the opposite embankment before stopping again. If it has rained, beware of flash flooding.

■ **Dips.** Dips are common on outback roads and can break suspension components if you enter too fast. To cross a dip, brake on entry to drop the vehicle's nose, and hold the brake on until just before the bottom of the depression. Then accelerate again to lift the nose and therefore the suspension, as you exit. This will prevent the springs from bottoming out and will also give maximum clearance.

■ **Cattle grids.** Also a potential hazard, as they are often neglected, with broken approaches and exits. If a grid appears to be in disrepair, stop and check first, before attempting to cross.

■ **Road trains.** These multi-trailered, long trucks are difficult and often dangerous to overtake, particularly on dusty roads. Wait for a chance to get the front of your vehicle out to a position where the road-train driver can see you in the rear-view mirror, but even then do not try to overtake until the driver has signalled acknowledgement that you are there. Sometimes it is prudent to stop and take a break, rather than try to overtake a road train. If you meet an oncoming road train, pull over and stop until it has passed.

■ **Animals.** There are vast areas of unfenced property in the outback where stock roam free. A bullock or a large kangaroo can seriously damage your vehicle. Be especially wary around sunrise and sunset when animals are more active. A bull-bar or roo-bar provides limited protection at low speeds only, especially against larger animals. Driver concentration should be at as high a level as in city peak hours.

Surviving in the Outback

You might be stranded in a remote area with a major mechanical breakdown, or if your vehicle becomes bogged. For this eventuality you should be equipped to wait at that spot until you are found. Always carry a week's supply of spare water, minimum 20 litres per head. Keep it for an emergency. Emergency supplies of dry biscuits and canned food will keep hunger at bay, but body evaporation and thirst is the vital factor. Do not drink radiator coolant. Often it is not water but a chemical compound, and even if it is water, usually it has been treated with chemicals. (See: How to Obtain Water.)

Do not try to walk out of a remote area. You are going to survive only if you wait by the car. Before entering a remote area, check with police or a local authority, and tell them where and when you are going, and when you expect to arrive. When you reach your destination, telephone and advise of your arrival. This is important as failure to do so causes unneccessary and expensive searches.

If stranded, set up some type of shelter and, in the heat of the day, remain in its shade as motionless as possible. Movement accelerates fluid loss. (See: How to obtain Water.)

Direction Finding

Clever electronic hand-held navigation devices, using the Global Positioning System (GPS), are now available from bushwalking shops and outdoor centres. These can be used with or without a map and are much more sophisticated and accurate than a magnetic compass.

If you cannot read a map or use a compass – or if you have no navigational device with you – it is vital to have some means of orientating yourself if you are lost.

A simple method of finding north is to use a conventional wristwatch.

Place the 12 on the watch in line with the sun and bisect the angle between it and the hour hand. This will give a fairly accurate indication of north.

At night, the Southern Cross can be used to determine south.

When exploring a side track off the main road, make a rough sketch of the route you are following, noting all turnoffs and distances between them (using the speedometer), together with any prominent landmarks. When you return, reconcile your return route with the sketch, point by point.

How to Obtain Water

Less than 24 hours without water can be fatal in outback heat.
- It is essential to conserve body moisture. Take advantage of any shade that can be found.
- **Do not LEAVE your vehicle.** It may be the only effective shade available.
- Ration your drinking water. Do not drink your car's radiator coolant.

Although a river or creek bed may be dry, there is often an underground water source. A hole dug about a metre deep may produce a useful soak.

Making an Arizona Still

Where there is vegetation, it is possible to extract water from it using an Arizona still.
- Dig a hole about one metre across and a little more than half a metre deep.
- Put a vessel of some kind in the hole's centre to collect the water.
- Surround the vessel with cut vegetation. (Fleshy plants hold more moisture than drier saltbush.)
- Cover the hole with a plastic sheet held down by closely packed rocks, so that the hole is sealed off.
- Put a small stone in the centre of the sheet, directly above the collection vessel.

The sun's heat will evaporate moisture from the plants. This moisture will condense on the inside of the plastic, run down the cone formed by the weight of the stone and drip off into the vessel. In uninterrupted sunlight, with suitable plants, about one litre of water should be collected about every six hours. The Arizona still takes about three hours to start producing and it will become less efficient as the ground moisture dries out. A new hole will need to be dug at intervals.

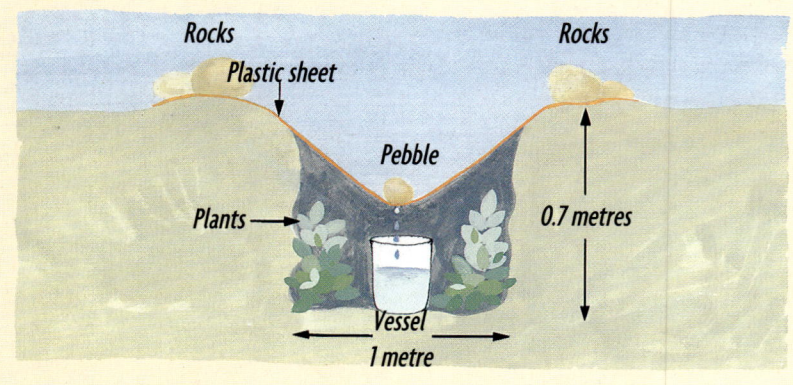

Outback Advice

Critical Rules for Outback Motoring
- Check intended routes carefully.
- Check the best time of year to travel.
- Check that your vehicle is suited to outback conditions.
- Check your load; keep it to a minimum.
- Check ahead for local road conditions, weather forecasts and fuel availability.
- Check that you have advised someone of your route, destination and arrival time.
- Check that you have essential supplies: water, food, fuel, spare parts.
- Carry detailed maps.
- Carry one week's extra supply of food and water in case of emergency.
- Always remain with your vehicle if it breaks down.

Warning. When driving on desert roads remember:
- There is no water, except after rains.
- Unmade roads can be extremely hazardous, especially when wet.
- Traffic is almost non-existent, except on main roads.

Sign beside the Eyre Highway in South Australia

Outback Advice Service
The Royal Flying Doctor Service of Australia offers a service to tourists who plan to tour the outback. Royal Flying Doctor Service bases and Visitors Centres provide advice on outback touring and on proper emergency procedures. Bases at Broken Hill (NSW), Charleville (Qld) and Jandakot (WA) also hire out transceiver sets with a fixed emergency call button in case of accident or sickness, at a very reasonable cost. Those bases that do not hire out sets, can suggest local outlets for them.

New South Wales
Broken Hill: Broken Hill Airport, 2880; (080) 88 0777. Open: Mon.–Fri. 10.30 a.m.–12 noon, 3.30–5 p.m.; Sat.–Sun. 10.30 a.m.–12 noon.

South Australia
Port Augusta: 4 Vincent St, 5700; (086) 42 2044. Open: Mon.–Fri. 10 a.m.–3 p.m.

Western Australia
Derby: Clarendon St, 6728; (091) 91 1211. Open: Mon.–Fri. 8 a.m.–12 noon, 2.30–3.30 p.m.
Jandakot: 3 Eagle Dr., Jandakot Airport 6164; (09) 414 1200. Open Mon. and Thurs. 10 a.m.–4 p.m.; bookings essential for tours of base.

Kalgoorlie: St Albans Rd, 6430; (090) 21 2899. Open Mon.–Fri. 8.30 a.m.–5 p.m.; tours of base Mon. and Thurs. 10.30 a.m.

Northern Territory
Alice Springs: Stuart Tce, 0870; (08) 8952 1033. Open Mon.–Sat. 9 a.m.–4 p.m., Sun. 1–4 p.m.

Queensland
Cairns: 1 Junction St, 4870; (070) 53 1952. Open Mon.–Fri. 8.30 a.m.–5 p.m., Sat.–Sun. 9.30 a.m.–4 p.m.
Charleville: Old Cunnamulla Rd, 4470; (076) 54 3057. Telephone for details of service.
Mount Isa: Barkly Highway, 4825; (077) 43 2800. Open Mon.–Fri. 9 a.m.–5 p.m., Sat. 9 a.m.–1 p.m.; subject to change during off-season.

For general information relating to the services offered by the Royal Flying Doctor Service, contact: The Australian Council of the Royal Flying Doctor Service of Australia, Level 5, 15–17 Young St, Sydney 2000; (02) 9241 2411, fax (02) 9247 3351.

Sharing the Outback
As you travel through the outback, remember you are sharing the land with its traditional Aboriginal owners, pastoralists, other tourists – and even nature itself. In order to protect and preserve the outback for future visitors:

- Respect Aboriginal sacred and cultural sites, and heritage buildings and pioneer relics.
- Protect native flora and fauna; take photographs not specimens.
- Follow restrictions on the use of firearms and shooting. These restrictions protect wildlife and stock.
- Carry your own fuel source (for example a portable gas stove), to avoid lighting fires in fire-sensitive areas.
- When lighting a campfire (if you must), keep it small and use any fallen wood sparingly. Never leave a fire unattended; extinguish completely before you move on.
- Do not drive off-road.
- Do not camp immediately adjacent to water sources (for example on riverbanks or by dams). Allow access for stock and native animals.
- Do not bury your rubbish; carry out everything you take in.
- Dispose of faecal waste by burial.
- Leave gates as you find them: open or shut.
- Do not ignore signs warning of dangers or entry restrictions. These are there for your protection.

BREAKDOWNS

Roadside repairs in northern Queensland

INTRODUCTION

There are many causes of motor vehicle breakdown, but fortunately modern vehicle technology has vastly reduced the possibility of being stuck by the roadside. Breakdowns that do occur can sometimes be cured with a roadside 'fix'; but this is often less possible with today's computer-driven vehicles. Inexpert or makeshift repairs may lead to further complications and a bigger repair bill.

Proper vehicle preparation and maintenance should at least reduce the possibility of roadside breakdowns and, on long journeys, the regular vehicle-service schedule should be maintained.

In areas where you have access to service through a motoring organisation, it is better to leave even slightly complicated repairs to the specialist. (Remember to carry your membership card, which entitles you to assistance in other States; **see**: Useful Information.) If you are driving a rental car, most rental companies list their recognised repair organisations in the manual supplied. (Before you drive the car, you should check that these details are provided.) If your rental vehicle cannot be repaired immediately, you should request an exchange vehicle.

If you plan to journey into remote areas, it is a good idea to first take a basic course in vehicle maintenance (**see**: Car Maintenance Courses). As well, you should carry a range of tools and spare parts (**see**: Tools and Spare Parts).

Modern Vehicles

Most modern vehicles are fitted with electronic engine-management systems, or with electronic ignition and fuel injection. Generally these are more reliable than older systems and usually, in case of partial failure of the system, they have a 'limp home' mode, which enables travelling a limited distance at limited speed. However, total failure of such a system is difficult or impossible to remedy at the roadside without expert knowledge and equipment. This means that travel into remote areas is rendered much safer by travelling with at least one other vehicle, and by installing or hiring an appropriate long-range radio transmitter, receiver and aerial (**see**: Outback Advice).

Earlier-model Vehicles

For those who drive earlier-model vehicles with less complex electrics and fuel systems, the trouble-shooting flow-charts are designed to be of assistance (**see**: Trouble Shooting). But first, always remember to:

▎**Watch warning gauges.** These have been installed to warn that things *may* be going wrong. A flickering battery warning light will suggest all is not well with the generator/alternator charge rate and should be attended to. A fluctuating temperature gauge *may* suggest the onset of a problem with the cooling system. Act on the warning at the earliest opportunity.

▎**Make a daily check** of fluid levels. Check fuel, water and oil (including spare supplies); also tyre pressures, and fan-belt tension and condition.

▎**Make a regular check** of brake-fluid and battery-acid levels, and pressure of spare tyre.

If the vehicle develops an unexplained sound, move to the side of the road as soon as possible. Park on flat ground if you can. You may have to spend some time under the bonnet, so look for shade or shelter. A loud, 'serious' sound usually indicates a major problem. Try to locate the source of the sound. If it is coming from the engine, do nothing and seek help.

When the Engine Stops

When the engine either splutters to a stop, constantly misfires or stops suddenly but was otherwise running smoothly, the problem is probably in one of two areas: fuel supply or electrics. Use the Trouble Shooting flow-charts to establish where the problem lies. If the problem is within the drive-train – the gearbox, drive-shaft or differential – once again, seek help.

Tools and Spare Parts

Be prepared when travelling in remote areas

Remote-area travelling requires that someone in the vehicle knows, at least, the basics of breakdown repairs (**see**: Breakdowns). This means carrying emergency tools, spare parts and spare fuel, and the *vehicle owner's manual*. The following is a guide to what may be appropriate for your vehicle:

Tools

- Set of screwdrivers (blade and Phillips head)
- Small set of socket spanners
- Set of open-end/ring combination spanners
- Small and medium adjustable wrenches
- Small ball pein (engineer's) hammer
- Pliers and wire-cutters
- Hand drill and bits
- Workshop scissors
- Aerosol puncture repair can
- Tyre pump
- Puncture repair kit
- Tyre-pressure gauge
- Wheel brace
- Jack with supplementary wide base for sand or mud (block of wood, approximately the size of an A4 sheet of paper and 3 cm thick)
- Jumper leads (capacitor-type if for EFL engine)
- Hydrometer
- Small spade
- Vice grips
- Good quality tow-rope
- Heavy duty torch, spare batteries and globe
- Pocket knife
- Fire extinguisher(s)

Spare Parts

- Epoxy resin bonding 'goo' (for repair of punctured fuel tank)
- Plastic insulating tape
- Spare radiator and heater hoses
- Engine accessory belts (fan, alternator, power steering, etc.)
- Roll of cloth adhesive tape
- 1 metre fuel line (reinforced plastic)
- Insulated electric wire
- Spare electrical connections (range)
- Spare hose-clips (range)
- Distributor cap
- Set of high tension leads
- Condenser (where appropriate)
- Rotor
- Set of spark plugs
- Can of dewatering spray
- Set of points
- Spare fuel, air and oil filters
- Fuel pump kit, water pump kit
- Small-diameter plastic tubing
- Range of spare light globes and fuses
- Nuts, bolts, washers, split pins
- Lubricants: automatic transmission and power steering fluid
- Radiator sealant
- Tube of hand cleaner, clean rags

Fuel

- Spare fuel (40 litres minimum) in steel jerry cans. (Do *not* use non-approved plastic containers; some plastics react with fuel.) Also check fuel range, and the distance between refuelling points.
- At least one spare wheel (slightly over-inflated to allow for some air loss). If travelling in remote areas, consider additional tyres/tubes.

Trouble Shooting (for earlier-model vehicles)

King Leopold Range in the Kimberley, Western Australia

Engine will not turn over

Check battery for charge.

If flat...
recharge or replace, or tow-start (if manual transmission vehicle) until next service opportunity. (If automatic, check handbook. Most autos cannot be tow- or clutch-started.)

▼

If battery OK...
check if battery terminals and straps are loose, broken or dirty. If so, clean, repair or replace.

▼

If terminals OK...
check for jammed starter motor. For manual vehicle, put in top gear and rock back and forth to try to free pinion. An indication that starter may be jammed is an audible click when you try to start the engine and it will not turn over. With an automatic vehicle, try to turn engine back and forth with a spanner on crankshaft pulley to free pinion. Put gearbox into 'N' first.

▼

If the starter motor is free...
it is possible a solenoid has failed. Unless you are an auto electrician and carry a spare, seek help.

Starter motor whirrs but will not turn engine

Very likely, you have stripped a starter ring-gear, which means major repair work. But check to see that the starter motor is fully bolted to its mounting bracket, and tighten if not.

Engine turns over but will not fire, or fires but will not run cleanly, or misfires regularly, or runs and stops

Problem may be electrics or fuel supply. If unsure, begin with electrics.

Electrics

1 Check that spark is getting to spark plugs. Remove high tension (HT) lead from No. 1 plug and remove No. 1 plug. Reattach HT lead to plug and hold plug body with pliers 1 mm from cylinder-head bolt or similar and turn engine over. Plug should produce strong blue spark at regular intervals.

▼

2 If not...
the simplest and fastest way to deal with an electrical problem is to replace parts, either at once or progressively, with spares (**see**: Tools and Spare Parts). Replace coil and all HT leads and try engine. If problem persists, remove distributor cap and replace condenser and points. Re-set points and fit new rotor and distributor cap. Engine should start and run cleanly.

▼

3 If you carry no spare parts, you can still confirm electrics as the problem by a process of elimination. If there is no spark at the spark plugs, the problem has to be between battery and plug. Check that low tension lead at side of distributor is connected properly and tightly mounted. If so, remove distributor cap and check for cracks. If there is a crack, repair with an epoxy glue/filler until it can be replaced. Check that condenser is tightly mounted and its LT wire is connected. Check that points open and close properly by turning engine over by hand slowly and watching for a spark between points. Points may be burned or deeply pitted. If so, remove points and use nail-file to clean up faces, then replace and re-set. If, however, you have established an electrical problem and you have no spares, seek assistance.

▼

4 If you have a spark at the plugs, most likely you have a fuel-supply problem.

Fuel supply

Check fuel tank for fuel, despite gauge reading. (It may be faulty.)

1 If fuel OK...
Check accelerator cable connection and for free operation, and check choke cable and operation. For vehicle with automatic choke, remove air-cleaner carrier and element, and look down choke tube. If

choke butterfly is not fully open, open it and check to see if it stays open. If it closes again, engine is flooding, and may not run for that reason. A faulty auto choke cannot be repaired at the roadside.

▼

2 If accelerator and choke cables are operating correctly...
do not replace air cleaner; remove fuel line to carburettor and turn engine over. Fuel should flow freely. If so, check it is not contaminated by pumping small amount into clear glass or plastic container and examine for water and/or dirt.

▼

3 If water or dirt are apparent...
check and replace fuel filter and remove and check fuel pump. Examine glass for contamination. If none or very little, replace fuel line to carburettor and try engine again.

▼

Touring in northern Queensland

4 If there is substantial contamination...
it may be coming from fuel tank. Tank will need to be drained and perhaps flushed. Drained fuel should be saved and strained back. If you are travelling a long way before next fuel stop, be careful not to waste fuel.

▼

5 If no fuel at fuel line and no apparent blockage...
fuel pump has failed for some reason. If you are carrying a spare, replace pump. If not, seek assistance.

▼

6 If fuel is clean and running freely...
blockage may be inside carburettor. Carefully remove top and then main jet and float. Clear main jet and clean out float bowl. Be careful not to interfere with float level. Replace parts and try engine again.

Overheating in a water-cooled engine

(Occurs when coolant level falls or circulation is interrupted. Dash gauge gives warning, but vehicle also will lose power.)

1 Stop vehicle. Do not remove radiator cap. Check hoses and hose connections for signs of leakage—steam if system is boiling. Any identified leak can be cured temporarily with spare hoses or binding with cloth tape.

▼

2 If no sign of leakage...
After about 10 minutes and holding radiator cap with a thick cloth, slowly remove cap, letting out steam under pressure at same time. Top up radiator and fill with engine running and car's heater on hot setting. Do not add cold water until engine is running and then mix cold with hot water.

▼

3 Check again for leaks.

▼

4 If there is a slow drip from radiator core itself...
fix with an internal chemical sealant or externally with an epoxy filler or adhesive.

▼

5 If no leak is apparent...
check fanbelt for tension. It may be slipping and not driving water pump. If so, tighten by releasing bolts on generator/ alternator and increasing tension and re-tightening.

▼

**6 If you cannot account for overheating by any of the preceding, you may have a failed waterpump, a blocked system, a failed pressure cap or a combination of all three. Seek help as soon as possible, but you may drive on if you can continue topping up.

Child's **PLAY**

Everyone in the family looks forward to a holiday, but most parents dread a long car trip when children travelling in the back seat can become bored and irritable passengers.

Most children are good travellers, but there are some car journeys that are inappropriate for small children (say, under the age of 10). Usually, however, children will consider every trip an adventure and start looking forward to it for weeks ahead. A little thought and planning by parents will avoid the boredom of a long drive and ease the strain on all concerned, particularly the driver, who needs to be able to apply total concentration.

Dos and Don'ts

Several days before setting out, make a list of 'dos' and 'don'ts' for the children and explain, seriously, why their cooperation is necessary. Make it quite clear that you expect them to observe the rules because they are safety measures, and reinforce this message at the time of departure. For example:

- DO NOT fight or yell while the car is in motion. This distracts the driver and can cause a collision or a serious mishap, which might bring the holiday to an abrupt end.
- DO NOT play with door handles or locks. (Set the child-proof locks on rear doors before departure.)
- DO keep head, arms and hands inside the car. DO NOT lean out of the windows, ever.
- DO NOT unbuckle seat belts or restraints while the car is in motion.

Handy Hints

- Any long car trip, even with frequent stops, can be tiring. Make sure the children are as cool and comfortable as possible. Curtains (or substitutes, for example a towel) or sun screens on rear windows are advisable. Babies and pre-school children may need their security blankets or favourite soft toy. These items can save the day if the children are upset or sleepy.
- Pack a small bag – a cosmetic bag is ideal – with packets of moist towelettes or a damp face cloth.
- Make sure your first-aid kit contains some junior aspirin and supplies of any other medication taken by the children. It is important to carry some insect repellent and sunblock, since children tend to get bitten easily, and their skin must be protected from the sun. Also bring a mosquito net to cover your baby's bassinette when you are outdoors.
- Make up a 'busy box' for the children to take on the trip. Use a small box – a shoe box is best – and keep it on the back seat where the children can reach it easily. Fill the box with small note-pads, crayons or felt-tipped pens (pencils break and need to be sharpened) and activity books. Choose activity books for each child's age group. Do not forget to include your children's favourite storybooks.
- If your car has a radio and cassette player, include some tapes of stories for entertainment, and children's songs for 'quiet times'. Music soothes and lulls children to sleep.
- Although your primary concern will be to keep the children happy and occupied during the car trip, it is also important to take along some games, such as Snakes and Ladders, pocket-sized video games or a pack of cards, to keep them amused in the evenings and on rainy days. Also encourage older children to keep a diary. A rubber ball and skipping rope will be welcomed by young children who enjoy playing outdoors.
- If you have room, breakfast trays can be used as book supports for drawing or colouring-in. If not, a clipboard will serve as well.
- When travelling with young children, make sure that you stop the car every hour or so, so that they can stretch their legs and let off steam. Try to stop at a park or an area with some play equipment. If it is raining, stop at a newsagent or bookshop where the children can browse and perhaps buy something to read.
- If children complain of feeling sick, stop the car as soon as possible and let them out for some fresh air. Sit with them for a while and persuade them to take a sip of water before returning to the car and continuing the trip.
- When approaching a rest area, a garage or a small town, offer the children a toilet stop. Do not delay until they get desperate and cannot wait.
- Even though you plan to stop for meals and snacks on your journey, you should still pack some food and drink. Children become very hungry and thirsty when travelling and it is important that they eat little but often. Pack small snacks in their own lunch boxes. Avoid chocolate, which is messy and can make children feel sick, and potato chips which are almost as messy and encourage thirst. Avoid greasy foods. Sultanas, nuts (for older children only), bananas, grapes, cheese cubes, celery and carrot sticks, and boiled sweets are good for snacks. For lunches, pack easy-to-eat meals like chicken drumsticks or bite-size rolled-up pieces of cold meat with ready-spread bread on the side. Children can find large sandwiches difficult to handle, so remember to cut their sandwiches small. Sandwich fillings require some thought, avoid anything moist or runny.
- Avoid spills and breakages by buying milk or fruit juice in small cartons and making sure you have a good supply of drinking straws. If you carry drinks in a flask, take training cups for younger children. For older children use paper or styrofoam cups with tight-fitting lids and with straws, and recycle as much as possible.
- Have plastic bags for waste paper and empty drink cartons in the cars.
- When eating out, choose places that have fast service – or have meals sent to your room.

Child Restraints

Note that the law in each State and Territory is very specific when it comes to child restraints in cars. As the law differs from State to State, it is important to check with the State motoring organisation (**see:** Useful Information) when travelling with children. Under certain ages and weights, children in passenger cars are required to be seated in the rear seat, and in an approved child restraint.

Child's Play

Games

To while away the long hours you will spend in the car with your children, here are some games for them to play.

For younger children

- **Colour contest:** Each child selects one colour, then tries to spot cars of that colour. The first with ten cars wins.
- **Spot the mistake in the story:** Either you or an older child tells a story with obvious mistakes. For example, 'Once upon a time, there was a little boy called Goldilocks, and he visited the house of the seven dwarfs.'
- **Scavenger:** Make a list of 10 things you are likely to come across during your trip, for example farmhouse, bus stop, cow, lamb, chemist shop, woman with a hat. Ask the children to spot them, one at a time. Older children cross the objects off the list as they are seen.
- **Alphabet game:** Select a letter and ask the children to spot as many things as possible beginning with that particular letter of the alphabet.

For older children

- **Rhyme stories:** One child starts a story, and the next has to take up the story with a line that rhymes. The second child also continues the story with a line of new rhyme. For example:

1st child: 'I know a man called Sam.'
2nd child: 'He loves to eat ham.
 The more he eats the more he wants.'

- **Cliff-hangers:** One child begins a story and stops at the most exciting part, leaving the next child to continue.
- **I packed my bag...** (a good memory game): Each player has to name one object she or he puts into a bag. As each child takes a turn, she or he lists all the objects in order and adds a new item to the list. For example:

1st child: 'I packed my bag and put an apple in it.'
2nd child: 'I packed my bag and put an apple and a comb in it.'
3rd child: 'I packed my bag and put an apple, a comb and a key in it.'
4th child: 'I packed my bag and put an apple, a comb, a key and a ball in it.'

- **What am I?** This is an old favourite. One player thinks of an object or an animal and keeps it secret. The others take turns to ask questions, which must be answered only by 'Yes' or 'No', for clues to the identity of the object or animal.
- **Number-plate messages:** Note the letters of the number plate on a nearby car and ask the children to make up a message or conversation from them. For example: WFL: 'What's for lunch?'
- **Navigation:** All you need is a spare road-map covering the route you are taking. The children can follow your progress with a coloured marker.
- **Word scramble:** Prepare a list of words with jumbled letters and get the children to unscramble them.
- **Crossword:** Draw crossword squares on several note-pads. During the trip, play the crossword game by calling out letters at random. The children write the letters in any square they wish and try to make up words.

Safety

Note the following safety hints:

Safe Swimming, Surfing

- Swim or surf only at those beaches patrolled by lifesavers.
- Swim or surf within the area indicated by the red and yellow flags. (An amber flag indicates that the surf is dangerous. A red flag and sign 'Danger – closed to bathing' indicates the beach is unsafe; do not swim or surf in this area.)
- Do not enter the water directly after a meal or under the influence of alcohol.
- If you are caught in a rip or strong current, swim diagonally across it. If you tire or cannot avoid the current, do not panic. Straighten, raise one arm as a distress signal and float until help arrives.
- If seized with a cramp, keep the affected part perfectly still, raise one arm as before and float until help arrives.

Safe Skiing

Skiing is fun, but like any sport, there is the risk of injury. It is also strenuous. If possible, train beforehand, and avoid overdoing it on the slopes. All ski resorts have instructors if you need to take lessons.

- Choose slopes that suit your ability.
- Wear clothing suited to the conditions.
- Check equipment before setting out.
- Avoid skiing alone; if you must, then tell someone where you are going.
- If lost, stay where you are; only retrace your tracks if they are very clear.

Cross-country skiing requires careful planning.

- Tell someone in authority the route you intend to take.
- Travel in a group.
- Take plenty of food and adequate equipment for your survival.
- Protect yourself against sunburn.
- Watch the weather.
- Be alert for signs of exposure (hypothermia): tiredness, reluctance to carry on, clumsiness, loss of judgement and collapse.

Safe Boating

- Tell someone where you are going.
- Carry adequate equipment.
- Carry effective life jackets.
- Carry enough fuel and water.
- Ensure engine reliability.
- Guard against fire.
- Do not overload the craft.
- Know the boating rules and local regulations; also distress signals.
- Watch the weather.
- Do not drink alcohol while boating.

New South Wales

NEW SOUTH WALES

Founding State

New South Wales is a State of contrasts, covering an area of 801 428 square kilometres, with extremes of country ranging from subtropical to alpine. The State's capital, Sydney, is Australia's largest city.

In 1770 Captain Cook took possession for the British of all Australian territories east of the 135th meridian of east longitude and named them New South Wales. Today the founding State has shrunk somewhat and occupies just 10 per cent of the continent. The settlement at Sydney Cove, established as the site of a penal colony in 1788, was developed under the guiding hand of Governor Arthur Phillip. Following his departure in 1792, however, much of Phillip's initial planning was negated, owing to the influence of the infamous New South Wales Corps, until 1810 heralded the arrival of the redoubtable Governor Macquarie.

In 1813 Blaxland, Lawson and Wentworth discovered the lands to the west of the Blue Mountains. Further exploration quickly followed and settlement fanned out from Sydney. Sydney itself thrived and its citizens agitated against the stigma of the penal presence, with the result that transportation of convicts ended in 1840. The goldrushes of the 1850s swelled the population and led to much development throughout the State. In 1856, with the granting of responsible government, the founding State was well on its way.

Today New South Wales is the most populous State and its central region, around Sydney, Newcastle and Wollongong-Port Kembla, has been described as 'the heart of industrial Australia'. New South Wales produces two-thirds of the nation's black coal, and the silver-lead-zinc mines of Broken Hill are a major source of mineral wealth. Primary production is diversified and thriving – New South Wales is the nation's main wheat producer and has more than one-third of the nation's sheep population.

The State is divided naturally into four regions: the sparsely populated western plains, which take up two-thirds of the state; the high tablelands and peaks of the Great Dividing Range; the pastoral and farming country of the Range's western slopes; and the fertile coastal region. The climate varies with the landscape: subtropical along the north coast, temperate on the south coast. The north-west has dry summers, and the high country has brisk winters with extremes of cold in the highest alpine areas. Sydney has a midsummer average of 25.7°C, a midwinter average of 15.8°C and boasts sunshine for an average of 342 days a year.

Lively and sophisticated, Sydney offers the shopping, restaurants and nightlife expected of a great cosmopolitan city, yet within a 200-kilometre radius is much of the best country in New South Wales: superb beaches, the myriad of intricate bays and inlets of Pittwater, the Hawkesbury River, Tuggerah Lakes and the breathtaking Illawarra coastline. The scenic Blue Mountains and the Jenolan Caves can be reached in a day trip. Most of the State's highways

NOT TO BE MISSED
in New South Wales

- **Berrima** – historic town in the beautiful Southern Highlands
- **Fossicker's Way** – a scenic drive through the mineral-rich villages of New England
- **Hill End** – once a boom town, now a fascinating ghost town
- **Hunter Valley** – for good food and good wine in delightful country surroundings
- **Jenolan Caves** – magnificent limestone caves surrounded by a flora and fauna reserve
- **Mailboat run** – an unusual way to cruise the Hawkesbury River
- **Scenic Railway** – a hair-raising ride down a cliff face into the Jamison Valley
- **Skitube** – for an exciting train ride through Thredbo Valley in the Snowy Mountains
- **Western Plains Zoo** – where landscaped parklands provide natural habitats for the animals and walking trails for visitors
- **Warrumbungle National Park** – spectacular scenery with gorges, rocky outcrops and freshwater springs

Flynn's Beach at Port Macquarie, a major holiday destination

Mudgee, an attractive town west of the Hunter Valley

lead out from the capital. The Pacific Highway runs north via the industrial city of Newcastle and the popular resort town of Port Macquarie. Diverting inland, you can sample the products of the rich Hunter Valley vineyards, considered to be one of the most important wine-growing areas in the country. Further north, the highway passes through country that is hilly and subtropical, with irresistible golden beaches to the east and

CALENDAR OF EVENTS

Note: The information given here was accurate at the time of printing. However, as the timing of events held annually is subject to change and some events may extend into the following month, it is best to check with the local tourism authority or event organisers to confirm the details. The calendar is not exhaustive. Most towns and regions hold sporting competitions, arts and craft exhibitions, agricultural and flower shows, music festivals and other such events annually. Details of these events are available from local tourism outlets.

JANUARY
Public holidays: New Year's Day; Australia Day. **Sydney:** Sydney festival and carnivalé (includes Opera in the park; Ferry boat race). **Bermagui:** Blue water fishing classic. **Brunswick Heads:** Fish and chips (wood chop) festival. **Byron Bay:** Arts and music festival. **Cooma:** Rodeo. **Corowa:** Federation festival. **Culburra:** Open fishing carnival. **Deniliquin:** Sun festival. **Gunnedah:** National tomato competition. **Guyra:** Lamb and potato festival (includes Hydrangea festival). **Hay:** Australia Day 'Surf' carnival. **Kundabung:** Australasian bull-riding titles. **Lake Cargelligo:** Hovercraft meeting; Bowling festival. **Nelligen:** Country music festival. **Quirindi:** Wallabadah New Year's Day Cup meeting. **Tamworth:** Australasian country music festival. **The Entrance:** Australia Day family concert and fireworks. **Tumbarumba:** New Year's Day rodeo. **Walcha:** Australia Day breakfast in the park. **Wentworth Falls:** Australia Day regatta. **Wingham:** National rodeo titles.

FEBRUARY
Sydney: Gay and Lesbian mardi gras. **Blue Mountains:** Blue Mountains Summer Classic held at Blackheath, Leura and Katoomba golf courses. **Adaminaby:** Race meeting. **Albury:** Festival of sport. **Bega:** Far South Coast national show. **Berry:** Agricultural show. **Camden:** Heritage wine and food fair. **Cessnock:** Vintage festival. **Gunning:** Agricultural show. **Kiama:** Jazz festival. **Nelson Bay:** Game-fishing tournament. **Orange:** Banjo Paterson festival. **Rylstone-Kandos:** Show. **Temora:** Golden Gift (foot race). **Tweed Heads:** Tweed Valley triathlon. **Walcha:** Agricultural show.

MARCH
Albury: Festival of sport (contd). **Alstonville:** Tibouchina festival. **Bega:** Cheese Pro-Am. **Blayney:** Agricultural show. **Bulahdelah:** Prawn festival. **Eden:** Amateur fish club competition. **Inverell:** Art exhibition. **Jamberoo:** Illawarra folk festival. **Jindabyne:** Strzelecki Polish festival. **Moruya:** Music festival. **Moss Vale:** Agricultural show. **Narrandera:** John O'Brien folk festival. **Newcastle:** Surfest. **Orange:** Banjo Paterson festival (contd). **Raymond Terrace:** Oz ski. **Robertson:** Agricultural show. **Thirlmere:** Festival of steam. **Wagga Wagga:** Australian veterans games. **Wauchope:** Lasiandra festival. **Wellington:** The Wellington Boot (horseraces); Vintage fair. **Wingham:** Agricultural show. **Wyong:** Festival of arts. **Yass:** Agricultural show.

EASTER
Public holidays: Good Friday; Easter Monday. **Sydney:** Royal Easter show. **Balranald:** Homebush gymkhana. **Bermagui:** Four Winds Easter concerts. **Berridale:** Fair. **Bingara:** Gold rush festival; Easterfish. **Brunswick Heads:** Blessing of the fleet; Fishing competition. **Byron Bay:** East Coast Blues festival. **Canowindra:** Model aircraft championships. **Coonabarabran:** Carnival. **Deniliquin:** Jazz festival. **Gilgandra:** Goat races; Rodeo. **Grenfell:** Guinea pig races. **Griffith:** Wine and food festival. **Holbrook:** Ultra Fly-In (biennial, even-numbered years). **Huskisson:** White Sands carnival. **Leeton:** Sunrice Country festival (biennial, even-numbered years). **Maclean:** Highland gathering. **Moree:** Carnival of sport. **Moulamein:** Yabby races. **Narooma:** Tilba festival. **Taree:** Aquatic festival; National power-boat titles. **Tocumwal:** Festival of Family Fun. **Ulladulla:** Blessing of the fleet.

APRIL
Public holiday: Anzac Day. **Sydney:** AJC autumn racing carnival, includes Sydney Cup Week; Australian international dragon

New South Wales

to the west the New England tablelands – high mountain and grazing country, at its best in autumn.

The State's extreme north-west is still frontier territory and has limited tourist facilities. If you enjoy getting off the beaten track, and if you and your car are well prepared, the region can be very rewarding. Highlights include the spectacular Nandewar and Warrumbungle Ranges, Lightning Ridge and the green oasis of Broken Hill, the State's storehouse of mineral wealth. The best time for touring is between March and November when the temperature is relatively cool and the winter days are clear and dry, but remember, if you break down in the 'outback' areas, stay with your vehicle.

Many relics of the early goldmining and agricultural history of the State can be seen in and around such inland towns as Bathurst, Dubbo, Wellington, Griffith and Wagga Wagga. Towards the Victorian border, where the Murray River forms a natural State boundary, irrigation greens the countryside and supports many vineyards and citrus groves.

CLIMATE GUIDE

SYDNEY

	J	F	M	A	M	J	J	A	S	O	N	D
Maximum °C	26	26	25	22	19	17	16	18	20	22	24	25
Minimum °C	19	19	17	15	11	9	8	9	11	13	16	17
Rainfall mm	104	113	134	126	121	131	101	80	69	79	83	78
Raindays	12	12	13	12	12	12	10	10	11	12	11	12

COFFS HARBOUR REGION

	J	F	M	A	M	J	J	A	S	O	N	D
Maximum °C	27	27	26	24	21	19	19	20	22	23	25	26
Minimum °C	19	19	18	15	11	9	7	8	11	14	16	18
Rainfall mm	197	221	241	180	161	119	73	90	67	97	125	150
Raindays	16	15	17	13	11	10	8	8	9	12	11	14

ALPINE REGION

	J	F	M	A	M	J	J	A	S	O	N	D
Maximum °C	21	21	18	14	10	6	5	6	9	13	16	19
Minimum °C	7	7	6	2	0	-3	-4	-2	-1	2	3	5
Rainfall mm	110	90	122	131	183	146	144	184	200	220	161	113
Raindays	11	10	11	13	15	16	16	17	17	17	15	12

MERIMBULA REGION

	J	F	M	A	M	J	J	A	S	O	N	D
Maximum °C	24	25	23	21	19	16	16	17	18	20	21	23
Minimum °C	15	15	14	11	8	6	4	5	7	9	12	14
Rainfall mm	80	71	95	71	70	64	37	45	52	77	85	65
Raindays	10	9	10	9	10	9	7	9	10	11	12	11

---

boat festival. **Albury:** Finish of the Big NSW bike ride. **Bathurst:** Start of the Big NSW bike ride. **Batlow:** Festival. **Bourke:** Fred Hollows foot race (to Sydney). **Brewarrina:** Agricultural show. **Bundanoon:** Bundanoon is Brigadoon annual highland gathering. **Campbelltown:** Show. **Gulgong:** Foundation Day. **Kempsey:** Agricultural show. **Macksville:** Nambucca River show. **Maitland:** Hunter Valley Steamfest; Indoor equestrian dressage championships. **Molong:** Cabonne country day. **Murrurundi:** Sheepdog trials. **Muswellbrook:** Agricultural show. **Narrabri:** Agricultural show. **Nyngan:** Anzac Day race meeting. **Shellharbour:** Sunshine festival. **Taree:** Taree and district eisteddfod. **Tumut:** Festival of the falling leaf. **Wee Waa:** Agricultural show. **Wingham:** Manning Valley beef week.

MAY

Casino: Beef week festival. **Cobar:** Agricultural show. **Dubbo:** Agricultural show. **Gilgandra:** Agricultural show. **Glen Innes:** Celtic festival. **Lismore:** Trinity arts festival. **Merriwa:** Polocrosse carnival. **Nyngan:** Agricultural show. **Scone:** Horse week festival. **Sussex Inlet:** Fishing carnival. **Tamworth:** Gold Cup race meeting. **Taree:** Taree and district eisteddfod. **Tathra:** Game-fishing competition. **Tumut:** Festival of the falling leaf (contd). **Warialda:** Agricultural show. **Warren:** Golden Fleece Day. **White Cliffs:** Gymkhana and rodeo. **Windsor:** Bridge to bridge power boat classic. **Yanco:** Murrumbidgee farm fair.

JUNE

Public holiday: Queen's Birthday. **Sydney:** Film festival; Food and wine festival (at Manly). **Blue Mountains:** Yulefest. **Bourke:** Bourke to B–Bash (charity car rally). **Casino:** Agricultural show. **Coonamble:** Rodeo. **Dubbo:** Eisteddfod. **Grenfell:** Henry Lawson festival of arts. **Gulgong:** Henry Lawson festival. **Jerilderie:** League of silent flight (model planes). **Manilla:** Lake Keepit kool sailing regatta. **Merimbula:** Jazz festival. **Merriwa:** Festival of fleeces. **Nambucca Heads:** Ken Howard memorial bowls competition. **Parkes:** Central West jazz triduum. **Snowy Mountains Region:** Opening of ski season (long weekend). **Southern Highlands Region:** Christmas in June. **Tibooburra:** Festival (sometimes held in July).

JULY

Boggabri: Wean picnic races. **Blue Mountains:** Yulefest (contd). **Iluka:** Amateur fishing classic. **Kyogle:** Rodeo. **Stroud:** International brick and rolling-pin throwing. **Urunga:** Bowling club carnival. **White Cliffs:** Royal flying doctor ball.

AUGUST

Sydney: Sun city to surf (fun run to Bondi Beach). **Bellingen:** Jazz festival. **Blue Mountains:** Yulefest (contd). **Condobolin:** Agricultural show. **Cootamundra:** Wattle time festival and garden fair. **Dungog:** Canoe Classic. **Evans Head:** Bowling carnival. **Forster:** Australian veteran cycling championships. **Gunnedah:** Ag Quip, agricultural field day. **Murwillumbah:** Banana festival. **Nambucca Heads:** VW Spectacular (biennial, odd-numbered years). **Narrandera:** Camellia show. **Newcastle:** Jazz festival. **Nundle:** Camp drafting and dog trials. **Pitt Town:** Fun run. **Quirindi:** Polo carnival. **Shellharbour:** Shelkove aquatic and outdoor expo. **Snowy Mountains Region:** FIS Australian championships; Continental Cup (both snow skiing). **Tweed Heads:** Bowls tournament. **Wellington:** Eisteddfod. **Wollongong:** South Coast youth arts and skills festival.

SEPTEMBER

Sydney: Rugby league grand final; Festival of the winds (kite flying), held at Bondi. **Armidale:** Springfest. **Barham:** Pro-Am golf tournament. **Batlow:** Daffodil show. **Bega:** Festival. **Bellingen:** Springtime in the valley. **Bourke:** Mateship festival (includes paddleboat regatta). **Bowral:** Tulip time festival; District art society exhibition. **Broke:** Village fair. **Broken Hill:** Silver city show. **Brunswick Heads:** River festival. **Canowindra:** Agricultural show. **Coffs Harbour:** Garden competition. **Cowra:** World peace day. **Dungog:** Spring festival. **Finley:** Agricultural show. **Forbes:** Show Day. **Glen Innes:** Minerama gem festival. **Gloucester:** Mountain man triathlon. **Henty:**

NEW SOUTH WALES

Shoalhaven River at Nowra on the Illawarra Coast

The Murray River towns retain much of the history of the riverboat era when the Murray was a major transport route.

The Princes Highway leads south from Sydney down the Illawarra Coast, famous for its panoramic views, excellent beaches and numerous national parks. Good fishing of all kinds can be enjoyed and there is splendid bushwalking and climbing in the nearby foothills of the Southern Highlands. Nearby, the Snowy Mountains area includes the natural grandeur of the Kosciusko National Park and the wonder of the Snowy Mountains hydro-electric scheme.

Linked by a network of freeways, highways and roads, New South Wales offers a wide variety of regions to explore.

CALENDAR OF EVENTS

Machinery field days. **Kempsey:** Country music festival. **Lake Cargelligo:** Lake show. **Lismore:** Cup Day. **Maclean:** Cane harvest festival. **Merimbula:** Food and wine frolic. **Mudgee:** Wine festival. **Mullumbimby:** Chincogan fiesta. **Murrumburrah:** Agricultural show. **Muswellbrook:** Art prize. **Nambucca Heads:** Septemberfest carnival. **Nimbin:** Show. **Nundle:** Camp drafting and dog trials (contd). **Richmond:** Hawkesbury District orchid spring show. **Stroud:** Rodeo. **Toukley:** Azalea festival. **Wagga Wagga:** National festival of the voice. **West Wyalong:** Agricultural show. **Yamba:** Family fishing festival.

OCTOBER
Public Holiday: Labour Day. **Armidale:** Springfest (contd). **Bathurst:** 1000 car races. **Bega:** Bega Valley art awards. **Berrigan:** Agricultural show. **Bingara:** Country music talent quest. **Bourke:** Back o'Bourke stampede (rodeo). **Bowral:** Tulip Time festival (contd). **Broken Hill:** Country music festival. **Bundanoon:** Gullies Gallop fun run. **Camden:** Camden to Goulburn cycle classic. **Cessnock:** Jazz concerts. **Cobar:** Back to Cobar. **Condobolin:** Art exhibition. **Coonabarabran:** Sky and space astrofest. **Coonamble:** Cup race meeting. **Cowra:** Sakura Matsuri; Japanese cultural exhibition. **Gilgandra:** Coo-ee festival. **Glen Innes:** Australian music festival. **Gosford:** Mangrove Mountain District country fair; Agricultural show. **Grafton:** Jacaranda festival; Bridge to bridge ski race. **Griffith:** Festival of gardens. **Gundagai:** Spring flower show. **Gunnedah:** Dorothea MacKellar children's festival. **Inverell:** Sapphire City floral festival. **Kiama:** Seaside festival. **Kyogle:** Show. **Leura:** Gardens festival. **Lismore:** Folk festival; North Coast national show. **Lithgow:** National Go-Kart championships. **Macksville:** Pro-Ag field day. **Manilla:** Festival of spring flowers. **Merimbula:** Veterans tennis. **Milton:** Settlers fair. **Murrurundi:** Bushman's carnival. **Muswellbrook:** Spring wine festival. **Nambucca Heads:** Show'n'Shine hot rod exhibition. **Narrabri:** Spring festival. **Narrandera:** Tree-mendous festival. **Narromine:** Festival of sport. **Nowra:** Spring festival. **Parkes:** Country music jamboree. **Raymond Terrace:** Twin Rivers festival. **Singleton:** Festival of wine and roses. **Stroud:** Rodeo (contd). **Tenterfield:** Federation festival; Spring wine festival; Highland gathering. **Tibooburra:** Gymkhana and rodeo. **Toukley:** Cycle Classic. **Walgett:** Weekend extravaganza. **Wauchope:** Colonial carnival. **West Wyalong:** Highways festival (biennial, odd-numbered years). **Wyong:** Cycle classic. **Yamba:** Family fishing festival (contd).

NOVEMBER
Armidale: Springfest (contd). **Barraba:** Fine music festival. **Batemans Bay:** Neptune festival. **Bulahdelah:** Show and rodeo. **Campbelltown:** Festival of Fisher's ghost. **Coonamble:** Western Sandfly supercross motorbike race. **Glen Innes:** Land of the Beardies bush festival. **Grafton:** Jacaranda festival (contd). **Gundagai:** Dog on the Tuckerbox festival. **Holbrook:** Agricultural show. **Kyogle:** Festival; Golf tournament. **Lithgow:** Festival of the valley (biennial, even-numbered years). **Moree:** Golden grain festival. **Queanbeyan:** Festival, Agricultural show. **Scone:** Rodeo. **Tenterfield:** Gem festival. **The Entrance:** Celtic festival. **Tumbarumba:** Heritage week. **Uralla:** Thunderbolt picnic race meeting. **Wagga Wagga:** Festival. **Warren:** Cotton Cup carnival. **Wellington:** Festival of dance. **Wentworth:** Wentworth Cup (horserace). **Windsor:** Bridge to bridge water ski classic. **Young:** National cherry festival.

DECEMBER
Public holidays: Christmas Day; Boxing Day. **Sydney:** World series cricket; Carols by candlelight (in the Domain); Sydney–Hobart yacht race. **Abercrombie Caves:** Carols in the caves. **Adelong:** Boat regatta. **Corowa:** National skydiving championships. **Jindabyne:** Lake Jindabyne Sailing Club hobie cat races. **Moulamein:** Horseracing Cup. **Nundle:** Camp drafting and dog trials. **Queanbeyan:** Country music festival. **The Entrance:** Tuggerah Lakes mardi gras festival. **Wollongong:** Junior surf lifesaving championships. **Young:** National cherry festival (contd).

SYDNEY

Australia's First City

Luna Park, Harbour Bridge and city skyline

Sydney, a thriving harbourside metropolis populated by almost 4 million people, is Australia's largest and best-known city. It was the first site of European settlement on the Australian continent – one vastly different from today's cosmopolitan showcase.

Command of the first colonial expedition was entrusted to Captain Arthur Phillip. On his arrival at Botany Bay in 1788, Phillip was not impressed with this proposed settlement site and decided to look further afield. On 26 January he sailed into a beautiful natural harbour, where he dropped anchor, named the area Sydney Cove, hoisted the flag and proclaimed the colony of New South Wales.

Sydney Cove, now Circular Quay, saw those First Fleet convicts toiling to clear a site for the settlement that was to become the city of Sydney. Testament to their endeavours is **The Rocks**, an area of winding lanes and sandstone buildings situated near the Harbour Bridge. An integral part of Sydney's history, providing rich memories of how the city was forged, today The Rocks features outdoor cafes, art and craft centres, weekend markets, museums, curio shops and rollicking pubs. Nearby the **Sydney Observatory**, a group of colonial buildings, houses a museum of astronomy with some hands-on displays.

In the sandstone building alongside Circular Quay is the **Museum of Contemporary Art**, which houses splendid collections of Australian and Aboriginal art. It is Australia's first major museum dedicated to the contemporary visual arts.

Sydney Cove has remained the gateway to Australia, situated in calm waters some 11 kilometres from the towering bluffs that flank the harbour mouth: **North Head** and **South Head**. Both headlands command a breathtaking view back along the harbour to the shimmering city skyline and its highlights the **Harbour Bridge**, the **Opera House** and **Sydney Tower**.

While these three structures may be the city's best known landmarks, it is **Sydney Harbour** itself that is the city's pride and joy. Its innumerable waterways extend in all directions, the product of a drowned valley system that finds bottom in the depths of the Pacific Ocean. Its surface is a glistening blue aquatic playground for Sydneysiders.

With the harbour as its heart, the city proper is bounded by water to the north and west and fringed to the east by the extensive green parklands of the Botanic Gardens and the Domain. Hyde Park, in the middle of the city, provides areas of tranquil, verdant delight in a bustling central business district. Within these boundaries, Sydney is an exciting and rewarding city to explore.

In line with Sydney's boundaries, the city's bus services terminate at three main points: **Circular Quay** in the north, **Wynyard Square** in the west and, in the south, **Central Railway Station**, the grand, domed building that is the outlet for all country and interstate train services. An underground train service travels on the ground outside the central business area and connects the city with outlying suburbs. The **Sydney Explorer** tourist bus loops around 28 kilometres of the city daily, stopping at 27 leading attractions and allowing passengers to alight and rejoin following buses at will.

Where Phillip's First Fleet dropped anchor, the shoreline has become a neat U-shaped area, with major wharves on either arm and harbour-ferry terminals at its base. **Circular Quay** was built in the nineteenth century to handle overseas shipping and, in the final great era of sail, the days of the superb clipper ships, Sydney Cove was a forest of majestic masts. Today it boasts a huge international shipping terminal with anchorage for ships of 40 000 tonnes and is the hub of Sydney's water traffic: its ferries, jetcats, cruise boats and water taxis. Circular Quay is a bright, colourful part of town where buskers play for the entertainment of strolling lunchtime shoppers, and where there are various restaurants offering superb harbour views while you dine.

Across the water from the Quay, the Harbour Bridge disgorges its congested traffic into Sydney's mini-twin **North Sydney**, a high-rise, high-density satellite of the 1960s. The **Harbour Tunnel**, which runs beneath the harbour, also links both business districts. **Mary MacKillop Place** museum, commemorating the life of Australia's first saint, is in Mount Street, North Sydney. Nearby on the harbour foreshore is **Luna Park** fun park which offers a variety of rides with spectacular views of Sydney.

Under the shadow of the Bridge on the city side of the harbour is **Pier One**, a complex of shops, restaurants (specialising in seafood) and a tavern decorated in Old Sydney style. It was once a disembarkation point for immigrants. Further along is **Pier Four**, which has been converted into a permanent home for the Sydney Theatre Company. The Wharf Theatre is the venue for the Sydney Theatre Company's year-round calendar, while the Wharf Restaurant, with award-winning cuisine, commands one of Sydney's best views.

Standing sentinel at the eastern end of Sydney Cove is the **Sydney Opera House**, a building whose aspect is breathtaking against the blue of the harbour. Its white arches seem to rise out of the water like sails scudding up from the waves. At weekends, the Opera House promenade is the venue for a variety of free outdoor concerts.

The Quay is typically waterfront. **Circular Quay Plaza** and the Rocks area are the home of some of the city's oldest pubs, many of which are early openers, catering for night-shift workers from 6 a.m. Detached from these, and from its high-rise neighbours, the old **Customs House,** in the centre of the Plaza, continues to preside over the scene, a monument in sandstone to nineteenth-century Sydney. Its time-honoured clock is surrounded by tridents and dolphins, and the coat of arms above the entrance is one of the best stone carvings in Australia.

Immediately behind Circular Quay Plaza, a series of maritime-flavoured laneways and narrow streets culminates in **Macquarie Place** and its sheltering canopies of giant Moreton Bay fig trees. An anchor and a cannon from Phillip's flagship HMS *Sirius* are preserved in the park, which they share with gas lamps, an 1857 drinking fountain, an ornate Victorian 'gents' (classified by the National Trust) and a weathered obelisk from which distances to all points in the colony used to be measured. In the surrounding laneways look for one of the world's smallest churches, the tiny **Marist Chapel** at 5 Young Street, run by the Marist Fathers. Further east on the corner of Bridge and Phillip Streets is the new **Museum of Sydney**, on the site of the first Government House.

The present **Government House** is an imposing neo-Gothic sandstone mansion of the 1840s, not open to the public but easily admired from the adjacent Botanic Gardens. Between the entrances to both, the fortress-like lines of the **NSW Conservatorium of Music** successfully conceal the building's origin as stables, designed in 1816 by the renowned convict architect Francis Greenway, and completed in 1821 as part of an earlier Government House on the site.

The **Royal Botanic Gardens**, more than 24 hectares of formal landscaping, were originally dedicated in 1816. Today they are a perennial landscape of colour where more than 17 000 native and exotic plants bloom throughout the year. In one small corner there is a stone wall, over 200 years old, marking the original plot of the colony's first vegetable garden, planted at the direction of Governor Phillip. The Pyramid greenhouse contains Australian tropical plants. Nearby, the elegant glass Ark, a major tropical-plant centre, houses some of the world's rarest plants.

An imposing sandstone building on the western side of Macquarie Street, the **State Library of New South Wales**, overlooks the Botanic Gardens. In the library's Mitchell and Dixson wings is one of the world's great repositories of national archives and memorabilia, a priceless collection of Australiana and historical records. The new wing of the State Library is sited between the old building and Parliament House. This high-tech building features the latest technology, including study aids for the disabled. A brochure for a self-guide tour of the library is available.

Adjacent to the Library are two of Sydney's oldest buildings, the **New South Wales Parliament** and the **Colonial Mint** which houses the fascinating **Sydney Mint Museum**. The museum tells the story of gold in Australia and there is a shop selling a range of gold items and coins.

Parliament House and the former Mint were once a part of the original

NOT TO BE MISSED
in Sydney

- **Art Gallery of New South Wales** – one of the most comprehensive collections in the country
- **Circular Quay** – watch the action on the harbour from the waterfront walkway
- **Darling Harbour** – an impressive complex with its National Maritime Museum, Sydney Aquarium and Powerhouse Museum
- **Ferry trip on the harbour** – the best way to appreciate the magnificent harbour
- **Opera House** – wander around the forecourt of this distinctive landmark
- **Royal Botanic Gardens** – beautiful gardens in harbourside setting
- **Strand Arcade** – the city's most elegant arcade
- **Sydney Explorer** – a convenient way to see the city's major attractions
- **View from the top of the Sydney Tower** – for a bird's-eye view of the city
- **Weekend markets at the Rocks** – an innovative street market in this historic area

City on the Water

In the arid continent of Australia, Sydney is a cosmopolitan, subtropical oasis, set around the bays and inlets of Port Jackson, and extending north and south along the coast. The foreshore stretching over 250 kilometres is scalloped with white sandy beaches, while the South Pacific Ocean caresses the shores of sheltered coves and thunders in on some of the best surf beaches in the country. The climate is mild, the water warm enough for swimming most of the year.

Australia's best-known city sits majestically on the shores of its beautiful natural **harbour** – a harbour bustling with commuter ferries and jetcats, small tugs and massive container ships, and visiting luxury liners. Sydneysiders are rightly proud of their city. It is the cradle of Australian history and, industrially and commercially, the focal point of the South Pacific. The people are relaxed yet sophisticated. The water that surrounds them has a major impact on their lifestyle; many office workers commute by ferry and spend their lunch hours by the foreshore, enjoying the cool sea breeze in hot summer months. At weekends Sydneysiders collectively stretch out on the beaches or set sail.

Sydney owes a lot to its harbour, first discovered in 1770 by Captain James Cook, who named it Port Jackson. In 1788 Captain Arthur Phillip declared it 'the finest harbour in the world'. Today, due to its vast size, its protection from storms, its uniform depth, small tides, freedom from silting, and lack of navigational hazards, together with its wharves conveniently situated close to the city's business centre – it is arguably the world's best natural harbour. It embraces more than 55 square kilometres of water and caters for more than 6000 vessels each year.

At weekends sailing boats, speedboats, yachts and launches join the busy harbour traffic. Sydney Harbour is also the venue for many boating classics, including the Sydney to Hobart Yacht Race which starts on Boxing Day, and the Festival of Sydney's Ferry Boat Race in January.

Between Sydney's two most famous landmarks, the Opera House and the Harbour Bridge, is Sydney Cove – the birthplace of the city, State and nation. In 1788, Captain Arthur Phillip chose this inlet for the first colony because of its deep bay and running stream of fresh water. Its foreshore, now **Circular Quay**, in the heart of the city, is dwarfed by skyscrapers, with the City Circle Railway passing immediately overhead and the Cahill Expressway forming a canopy over the railway.

Ferry passing the Opera House on Sydney's beautiful harbour

Circular Quay is the nucleus of a network of ferry services that links the city to its waterfront suburbs (Manly, Mosman, Neutral Bay, Balmain and Parramatta), beaches, Darling Harbour and Taronga Zoo. Most ferry routes pass close to Fort Denison, also known as Pinchgut, where convicts were once imprisoned on a diet of bread and water. Today this fortress island can be hired for special functions. It is possible also to hire an aqua cab (water taxi) to take you to any point around the harbour, while special cruises go to Middle Harbour, the Lane Cove and Parramatta Rivers, and up the coast to Broken Bay and the Hawkesbury River.

The ferry service to **Manly** dates back to 1854. This resort suburb took as its slogan around the turn of the century: 'seven miles from Sydney and a thousand miles from care', and it stands as true today. Named by Captain Phillip after the 'manly' behaviour of the Aborigines, this suburb can be reached by a 35-minute ferry ride, a 15-minute journey in a jetcat or an even quicker trip in a UTA catamaran. Each summer, Manly's population doubles, thanks to the mild climate and the popularity of the harbour and ocean beaches nearby.

Between Grotto Point and Middle Head is the fishing and boating haven of **Middle Harbour**. Here the Spit Bridge opens for vessels visiting the area's many bays, small coves and beaches.

Along the **northern shore** of Port Jackson are several well-known beaches: Chowder Bay, where American whalers concocted their famous dish using Sydney rock oysters; Neutral Bay, where ships from foreign countries once anchored; and the picturesque Mosman Bay and Chinamans Beach.

On the **southern foreshore**, there are almost 100 hectares of parkland in the Domain and Royal Botanic Gardens. City workers flock to the gardens for a quiet lunch break, a stroll or jog along the foreshore, or a quick game of cricket.

Sydney is also renowned for its fine **surf beaches**. The scenic northern beaches stretch from Manly to Palm Beach. To the south, Bondi, just 7 kilometres from the General Post Office, is the most popular and most famous metropolitan beach. Coogee and Cronulla are also popular. The smaller beaches at Clovelly, Tamarama and Bronte offer quiet seclusion. Sydney's thirty-four surfing beaches are patrolled by volunteer lifesavers, who stage colourful large-scale carnivals throughout the summer. Lady Jane and Reef beaches on the harbour cater for nude sunbathers. Surfers should take heed of warning flags placed on the sand, which mark the areas safe for surfing on that day. Rock pools are abundant and are ideal for children. It is not advisable to swim in the harbour.

The 'city on the water' has a pronounced maritime character, its appearance dominated by the many bays and inlets of its harbour, and its white sandy beaches.

The Strand arcade

buildings, the **Domain** – location for such annual events as Opera in the park (part of the Sydney festival held in Jan.) and Carols by candlelight – separates the rear of Macquarie Street from the **Art Gallery of New South Wales**. During January, when the annual **Sydney Festival and Carnivalé** is in full swing, the Domain becomes a giant outdoor concert hall where hundreds of thousands of Sydneysiders flock to hear jazz, opera and symphonies in the park.

Macquarie Street leads to **Queens Square**, arguably one of Sydney's most elegant precincts. The square is encircled by Hyde Park, the towering **Law Courts** building and Francis Greenway's pre-1820 masterpieces, **St James's Church** and **Hyde Park Barracks** (now a social history museum with unique relics from Sydney's convict origins). Flowing harmoniously on from the old barracks are two great neo-Gothic triumphs of the nineteenth century: the **Registrar-General's Building** and **St Mary's Roman Catholic Cathedral**.

Hyde Park is divided in two by Park Street. One half is dominated by the **Archibald Fountain** – a legacy to the city from the first publisher of the *Bulletin* – and the other by a **Pool of Remembrance** and the **Anzac War Memorial**. At night, Hyde Park's avenues of trees are lit with thousands of fairy lights. On the park's eastern boundary, in College Street, stand the **Australian Museum**; one of Sydney's oldest colleges, **Sydney Grammar School**; and two high-rise neighbours, the **Returned Servicemen's League** headquarters and the **NSW Police Department** administration building.

On the city side of Hyde Park runs **Elizabeth Street.** No longer the major city artery it once was, it now serves as a vital, almost continuous, bus feeder route, particularly where two underground railway stations, **St James** and **Museum**, disgorge. It is still, however, noteworthy for one of Sydney's historic buildings, the **Great Synagogue**, and for the headquarters of one of Australia's great retailing empires, **David Jones**. David Jones, with its liveried doormen, marble floors and title of 'the most beautiful store in the world', stands on the corner of Elizabeth Street and Market Street and is a Sydney landmark. 'I'll see you on DJ's corner' was, and still is, a regular Sydney rendezvous. From here, Elizabeth Street continues north to the spacious semicircle of **Chifley Square**, named in honour of former Prime Minister J.B. Chifley.

In a wedge-shaped sector of blocks made by Bent, Bridge, Young, Phillip and Loftus Streets stand the office buildings of colonial New South Wales, elaborately constructed from Sydney's superb Hawkesbury sandstone, on which the city is built. Mostly late Victorian, the buildings still serve their original purpose as housing for State government departments.

The disordered pattern of the surrounding streets is a product of the complete lack of planning in the period after Governor Phillip's recall from Sydney. Bullock tracks and cow paths determined the town plan until Governor Macquarie attempted to impose order some 20 years later. Today the result contributes to Sydney's charm.

Castlereagh Street, parallel to Elizabeth Street, also loses itself in the tangle of colonial office blocks above the Quay. In **Martin Place**, a traffic-free plaza running from Elizabeth Street through Castlereagh and Pitt Streets and finishing at George Street, lunchtime office workers attend outdoor concerts in the amphitheatre, flower sellers hawk their wares from colourful barrows, and cut-price theatre and concert tickets are on sale at a Halftix booth. The **GPO** sits in Martin Place, between Pitt and George Streets. South of Martin Place the character of the area

colonial hospital, which was known as the Rum Hospital. When there was a shortage of coinage in the colony and rum was the currency, the builders were paid in casks of the spirit. Between them, in all its dour Victorian splendour, is **Sydney Hospital**, a city institution, which opened in 1879. Behind the

SYDNEY ON FOOT

There are numerous walking tours around Sydney and the following list is a small selection. All are guided tours organised by private companies; bookings are essential and a charge applies.

- **Aboriginal Australia:** Aboriginal exhibits at the Art Gallery and the Australian Museum.
- **Art galleries:** tour of Sydney's contemporary art scene.
- **Behind the scenes:** of the Australian Broadcasting Commission, the Law Courts, NSW Parliament House and other institutions.
- **Chinatown:** discover this colourful area of Sydney.
- **Coffee houses of Darlinghurst:** guided tour with plenty of caffeine!
- **Fish Markets:** see fish auctions and eat fish and chips.
- **Kings Cross:** discover the historical side of this somewhat raffish area.
- **Sydney city and Opera House:** includes the city's major attractions.
- **Sydney Harbour Bush Walk:** follows shoreline around Middle Harbour.
- **The Rocks:** numerous guided tours available.

For further information contact NSW Travel Centre, 19 Castlereagh St, Sydney; (02) 9231 4444.

changes from a merchant belt to a shopping mecca. The **MLC Centre** dominates almost a whole block and contains suites of luxurious offices, and at ground level, some exclusive shops, mostly jewellers and fashionable boutiques. The complex also houses a convenient fast-food area, the Australia Tavern, a cinema (the Dendy) and, for the theatre-goer, Sydney's prestigious **Theatre Royal**. The King and Castlereagh Streets crossroads, with its collection of elite retail traders such as Chanel and Gucci, has been compared to New York's Fifth Avenue and London's Bond Street.

Only two of Sydney's north-south arteries actually make a complete journey from Circular Quay to Central Railway Station: Pitt Street and George Street. As Pitt Street between King and Market Streets is a pedestrian mall, traffic must make this journey using George Street only. Sydney has several shopping arcades that run off Pitt and George Streets. One of these, **The Strand**, is particularly noteworthy, having been restored to its 1892 splendour and housing some of Australia's leading fashion designers, jewellers and craftspeople.

In both Pitt and George Streets there is little trace of colonial Sydney, although handsome turn-of-the-century commercial buildings are carefully watched over by devoted citizens and the National Trust, lest developers' ambitions exceed their sense of history and good taste. Of the two streets, **Pitt Street** is probably the more exciting in terms of shops, cafes and street hawkers. The monorail beside Pitt Street winds through the city above street level, linking it to the Darling Harbour Complex.

Between King and Park Streets is **Pitt Street Mall** with department stores, including **Grace Bros** and **Centrepoint**; another popular sporting club, **City Tattersalls**; the Pitt Street side of the Methodist Church's Wesley headquarters; cinemas; and, dominating the two blocks, the soaring **Sydney Tower**, the tallest building in Sydney. This 270-metre golden tower has two revolving restaurants and from the observation decks at its summit, high-powered binoculars and a video television camera enhance the spectacular views of the city particularly at night.

Pitt Street becomes rather nondescript as it heads south, with its secondhand stores, places that offer cheap accommodation, and a laneway that leads to a nineteenth-century police headquarters building, now more a city watchhouse and serving as cells for the grim **Central Criminal Court** building on one of the cross-streets, Liverpool Street.

On carnival-thronged evenings along the entertainment section of **George Street**, cinema complexes, fast-food houses, pin-ball alleys, all-night bookshops and erotic movie houses – all compete for the jostling crowd's attention. Apart from its entertainment area that makes its nights so boisterous, George Street boasts a number of Sydney's most important and interesting buildings, both old and new. Twenty years ago, Sydney's and Australia's tallest building was the **Australia Square Tower**. Tall and circular in shape, it has an observation platform on the forty-eighth floor and a revolving restaurant. These days the tower is dwarfed by more recent buildings on Sydney's ever-changing skyline.

South from here are Wynyard underground railway station and the remarkable **Queen Victoria Building** (QVB), which monopolises an entire block. The restoration of the QVB included the refurbishing of its enormous copper dome, which once loomed over the older city skyline. The building now houses many restaurants and over 160 shops. A landmark of the city's earlier days is to be found opposite the Queen Victoria building, through the George Street entrance to the Hilton Hotel. In the hotel's basement, restored to its original ornate detail, is the superb **Marble Bar** of the old Adams Hotel, which once stood on the site of the Hilton. On the next corner stands the spiralling blue **Coopers and Lybrand tower**. With its art deco design, it has been dubbed the Superman Building because of its similarity to the fictitious Daily Planet building depicted in film and comic strip.

The **Town Hall**, now dwarfed but not overshadowed by a modern council administration block, is Italian Renaissance in style. Built of mellow brown sandstone, it was completed in 1874. A graceful, shaded pedestrian plaza, **Sydney Square** borders the Town Hall and separates it from Sydney's Anglican Cathedral, **St Andrew's**.

Further west is the impressive complex **Darling Harbour**, which includes: the **Chinese Garden of Friendship**, the **Sydney Convention and Exhibition Centre**, waterside walks, a variety of eating places, 7-day-a-week shopping, and splendid parklands around a busy harbour inlet that was once a dull industrial port. Sydney's temporary **Casino** is on the northern arm of Darling Harbour. At the western end of the National Trust-classified Pyrmont Bridge is the **National Maritime Museum** and near the eastern end of this one-time traffic carrier, now used as a walkway, is the fascinating **Sydney Aquarium** – with giant sharks, large saltwater crocodiles and fur seals.

The **Powerhouse Museum** on the southern edge of the Darling Harbour Complex is also well worth a visit. Its size is such that it can exhibit aeroplanes, trams, boats and steam engines, plus many equally fascinating smaller

ACCOMMODATION

HOTELS

Hotel Nikko Darling Harbour
161 Sussex St, Sydney
(02) 9299 1231

Quay West Apartments
98 Gloucester St, The Rocks
(02) 9240 6000

Regent, Sydney
199 George St, Sydney
(02) 9238 0000

Ritz Carlton
93 Macquarie St, Sydney
(02) 9252 4600

Sebel of Sydney
23 Elizabeth Bay Rd, Elizabeth Bay
(02) 9358 3244

Sheraton on the Park
161 Elizabeth St, Sydney
(02) 9286 6000

Sydney Hilton
259 Pitt St, Sydney
(02) 9266 0610

Sydney Renaissance
30 Pitt St, Sydney
(02) 9259 7000

The Observatory
89–113 Kent St, The Rocks
(02) 9256 2222

FAMILY AND BUDGET

Russell
143a George St, The Rocks
(02) 9241 3543

The York
5 York St, Sydney
(02) 9210 5000

YWCA
5–11 Wentworth Ave, Darlinghurst
(02) 9264 2451

MOTEL GROUPS: BOOKINGS

Best Western 131 779
Flag 13 2400
Travelodge 1800 22 2446

This list is for information only; inclusion is not necessarily a recommendation.

A Colonial Past

At the first settlement at Sydney Cove, Captain Watkin Tench of the Marines wrote: 'to proceed on a narrow, confined scale in a country of the extensive limits we possess, would be unpardonable... (the) extent of Empire demands grandeur of design'.

Such grand design began in 1810, when the vision of the new Governor, Lachlan Macquarie, was put into practice by the convict architect Francis Greenway, resulting in a heritage of splendid buildings, many of which are landmarks today. It continued through nearly a century of growth and lofty ideals to create a prosperous and busy metropolis – a great symbol of colonial aspirations.

As Sydney developed, it was both 'mean and princely', a mixture of broad, tree-lined avenues and narrow streets and alleys, grand buildings and crowded cottages and terraces. Its switchback, craggy hills around the indented harbour made orderly Georgian-style planning impossible, and the grand outlines of earlier days soon became blurred by the city's growth from first settlement to colonial seat, to State capital to modern city.

In modern Sydney with its gleaming towers, its crowds and its traffic, substantial remnants of old Sydney can still be seen. Some parts of the city, like **the Rocks** area adjacent to Circular Quay, are almost pure history. Here the old hotels and bandstands, sandstone cottages and terrace houses, the Argyle Cut and Agar Steps, the Garrison Church and the village green form an oasis separated from the bustling city by Flagstaff Hill, where the old Observatory stands, and the approaches to the Harbour Bridge are seen.

There are many other inner suburban areas that are reminiscent of the feeling of old Sydney. **Paddington** is the showplace historic suburb, with its picturesque terraces and cottages, most superbly restored. The narrow streets of this once working-class suburb provide an intimate, neighbourly feeling. Balmain, Leichhardt and Redfern are becoming popular as the advantages of inner-suburban living attract owners who are conscious of the aesthetic quality of the old sandstone cottages.

In the city itself, the street that best reflects the past is probably **Macquarie Street**, which overlooks both the Botanic Gardens and the Domain, where Government House, the Conservatorium of Music, and the State Library and Art Gallery of NSW are situated. Governor Macquarie planned for the east

Modern city skyscrapers contrast with historic buildings at the Rocks

side of the street to be occupied by official buildings and for the west to contain the town houses of wealthy citizens; the west side is now occupied mainly by medical practitioners.

Other interesting buildings in Macquarie Street are: Parliament House (1816), a verandahed sandstone building, originally one wing of the Rum Hospital; the adjoining Mint Building, restored from the other wing of the original Rum Hospital; Sydney Hospital, whose buildings replaced the central block of the Rum Hospital; the Royal College of Physicians; and the Hyde Park Barracks (1819), now a museum. In nearby Queens Square is the classical St James's Church.

At the harbour end of Mrs Macquarie's Road is a reminder of the Macquarie era – a sandstone shell known as Mrs Macquarie's Chair. The Governor's wife is said to have sat here and gazed upon the great harbour, now one of the world's busiest and most picturesque waterways.

There are a number of other **major buildings** in or near the city, including Elizabeth Bay House, in Regency style, now restored and a showplace for the rich furnishings of the time when it looked over a harbour backed by cliff and woodland; the General Post Office in Martin Place, completed in 1887 in classic Renaissance style; the Great Hall at Sydney University, and St Andrew's Cathedral, both designed by Edmund Blacket; St Mary's Cathedral, designed by William Wardell; the Greek Revival court house in Taylor Square, designed by Mortimer Lewis; and Vaucluse House, the former home of William Charles Wentworth, father of the NSW Constitution. Perhaps the most striking example of colonial architecture in Sydney is Victoria Barracks in Darlinghurst. This two-storeyed building of severe Georgian style, 74 metres long, with white-painted upper and lower verandahs, is a model of elegance. (Visit on Thursday at 10 a.m., watch the changing of the guard and be entertained by the Australian Army Band, Sydney, and follow with a guided tour of this historic group of buildings.)

As settlement extended from the harbourside colony, villages were established, first in the upper **Hawkesbury region** to the north-west, then to the south and finally, as the Blue Mountains were breached, out to the western plains and throughout New South Wales.

In the upper Hawkesbury valley are the sister towns of Windsor and Richmond, two of the Macquarie Towns both beautifully sited on the river and retaining the peaceful charm, as well as many of the buildings, of earlier days. Windsor has a number of fine buildings: Claremont Cottage, St Matthew's Anglican Church, the Macquarie Arms, Tebbutt's Observatory, the Doctor's House and the Toll House, to name a few. At Richmond are Belmont, Hobartville, Toxana House, the School of Arts and St Peter's Anglican Church.

In the **Southern Highlands**, the settlements of Mittagong, Moss Vale, Berrima and Bowral are full of historic interest. The Berrima Village Trust is responsible for the preservation of the village as it was in the 19th century. Sited in a valley, Berrima contains a number of fine sandstone buildings grouped around a central common, among them the gaol and court house, the Surveyor-General Inn, the Church of the Holy Trinity, Harper's Mansion and Allington. New South Wales has many other historic towns and properties bearing the hallmarks of the nation's foundation.

For further information on colonial towns and buildings, contact the National Trust of Australia office in your State.

Picturesque terraces at Paddington, an inner-city suburb

Bungan Beach, north of the city

exhibits. Opposite is the **Sydney Entertainment Centre,** a major venue for concerts and conventions. Nearby lies **Dixon Street**, the pedestrianised heart of Sydney's **China Town,** a traditional area of restaurants, warehouses, specialty stores and Chinese grocers, where even banks and service stations are labelled in Chinese script. At its southern end the visitor will find **Paddy's Markets,** which reopened in 1994.

Not far from Darling Harbour is Australia's largest fish market, the **Sydney Fish Market** at Pyrmont; it has retail stores, coffee shops, restaurant, souvenir outlets and Australia's first seafood school. Walking tours are available.

Of the city's cross-streets, two handsome boulevards are noteworthy: **Park Street** and **Martin Place**. The authentic heart of the city, Martin Place, with its memorial **Cenotaph** to Australia's war dead, is the annual stage for the city's Anzac Day March on April 25. It is also a stage for a variety of free lunchtime entertainment.

Park Street ambles east splitting Hyde Park in two before turning into William Street which leads to **Kings Cross,** Sydney's version of Soho and Greenwich Village. Yet the Cross has its unique flavour: the breath of a Sydney Harbour breeze and a glimpse of blue water are a delight. Whatever the Cross has borrowed from other cities in its strip joints, gaudy nightspots and colourful characters, it has its own bohemian traditions. In its backyard are **Garden Island** dockyard, where the Fleet is nearly always in, and the encircling apartment houses of select **Elizabeth Bay**. On its boundaries are the lively suburbs of Darlinghurst and Woolloomooloo.

The once notorious **Darlinghurst,** a long-time haunt of pimps, prostitutes and gangsters, boasts the historic Darlinghurst Gaol (where bushrangers were hanged) as one of its attractions. Today, however, the face of Darlinghurst has changed dramatically and it is now the home of artists, musicians and poets. Its main artery, **Oxford Street**, with its adult bookshops, pubs, clothing stores and restaurants, is the gay capital of Australia. Nearby in Surry Hills, **Brett Whiteley's studio** displays a range of the late artist's work.

Woolloomooloo has seen its cramped houses and narrow streets skyrocket in price as the desire for trendy inner-city living escalates. Individual restaurants and bars are many and various. Trendy brasseries compete amid the leftovers of 'sleaze' on Bayswater Road and Kellett Street, where the gentrification of the Cross is most apparent. But, even so, there are a great number of erotic movie houses and specialty bookshops still left in the Cross. A less controversial landmark is the dandelion-shaped **El Alamein Fountain** commemorating the World War II battle.

In the other direction, Darlinghurst Road and Bayswater Road lead to Sydney's trendiest area, **Paddington,** a suburb of steep hills, unplanned streets and picturesque terrace houses, hardly one without ornate Victorian wrought-iron railings and fences and lots of trees. The old-fashioned pubs are now terribly chic; well-spoken children and large dogs exercise on streets once the domain of street urchins, before Paddington underwent its fashionable revival back in the late fifties. Next door to 'Paddo' is **Centennial Park,** Sydney's equivalent to New York's Central and London's Regent Park, where horseriding, cycling and picnicking are weekend activities.

Paddington's counterpart on the other side of Sydney, **Glebe** (bordering historic **Sydney University**) is not quite so leafy or picturesque, and certainly not as expensive. Nearby **Balmain** with its harbour frontage has also undergone a fashionable revival.

At every turn these inner suburbs reveal something old and handsome in weathered sandstone: a church, a cottage, a school from Sydney's past. They have also given rise to a Sydney phenomenon: village markets, usually held on Saturdays and featuring colourful identities plying their wares at open-air stalls in the grounds of schools or churches, or in local parks. The colourful **Paddington Markets** are Sydney's trendiest.

So is the rest of Australia's first city: from Paddington's neighbours, **Woollahra** and **Rushcutters Bay**, through the harbourside suburbs of exclusive **Double Bay**, **Rose Bay** and **Vaucluse**, to **The Gap** and **South Head**; or across the harbour by ferry, jetcat, Harbour Bridge or Harbour Tunnel to **Manly** and the long line of ocean beaches stretching north to beautiful **Palm Beach**, competing in terms of wealth and privilege with the precipitous bush gorges and superior heights of the elegant **North Shore** suburbs. A floatplane service at Rose Bay has flights between Sydney and Palm Beach, Gosford and Newcastle; and there are cruises from Circular Quay up the coast into Broken Bay and the Hawkesbury River.

The **Olympic Games site**, west of the city at Homebush Bay, is a hive of activity in preparation for the games due to be held here in the year 2000. Here and beyond lies the metropolitan heartland of Sydney's great urban sprawl – 75 kilometres from the harbour across the vast, flat western suburbs to the foothills of the **Blue Mountains**.

In Sydney one can dine out on the cuisines of virtually every nation in the world. (However, it should be mentioned that Sydney is famous for its rock oyster and the Balmain Bug – an odd-looking but tasty crustacean.) The choice of cinema, live theatre and live-theatre restaurants, and jazz and blues clubs, is just as comprehensive.

For further information on Sydney, contact the Sydney Visitor and Convention Bureau, Level 5, 80 Williams St, Sydney or the NSW Travel Centre, 19 Castlereagh St, Sydney; (02) 9231 4444. For information regarding public transport, contact the Transport Infoline 131500. A SydneyPass provides unlimited travel for 3 days on all public buses, harbour ferries and Jetcats, Sydney Explorer buses, the Rocks Shuttle (a continuous service linking the Opera House, The Rocks and Darling Harbour) and the Airport Express.

TOURS from Sydney

Monument at Captain Cook's Landing Place, Kurnell

Sydney's range of available day tours out and about is almost unrivalled for the variety of scenic and recreational attractions on offer. In the frantic rush to get out of the city, however, it is easy to overlook two of Sydney's greatest assets: **Royal National Park**, little more than an hour's drive south from the GPO, and **Ku-Ring-Gai Chase National Park**, 40 km north; both offer good bushwalking.

Harbour Cruises

An ideal way to view Sydney and its harbour is by boat. Sydney ferries criss-cross the harbour as a means of public transport; as well several cruises are available. State Transit run three cruises: a two-and-a-half hour Morning River Cruise (daily from Wharf 4 at Circular Quay) through the main reach of the harbour then west along the Parramatta River; a two-and-a-half hour Afternoon Harbour Cruise (weekdays) down the main harbour and Middle Harbour; and an Evening Harbour Lights Cruise (Mon.–Sat. from Wharf 5), a one-and-a-half hour cruise of the main harbour at night offering splendid views of the city's lights. Bookings are not necessary.

Captain Cook Cruises offer a wide variety of cruises (which leave from Wharf 6) including the *Sydney Harbour Explorer* which stops at six harbourside attractions enabling passengers to disembark, explore then catch the next *Explorer*; coffee cruises, which run twice daily through Main and Middle Harbours; luncheon cruises travel to Cockatoo Island; and the *John Cadman* makes a dinner cruise nightly. Captain Cook Cruises also conduct tours daily to Fort Denison, one of the most historic relics in Australia. Matilda Cruises offer a range of harbour discovery cruises of one-and-a-half or two-hour duration, departing from the Aquarium Wharf at Darling Harbour and Circular Quay. As well they offer cruises aboard the *Solway Lass*, a restored sailing-ship. Another Tall Ship, the *Bounty* departs from the Rocks daily for lunch cruises, and at weekends for brunch and dinner cruises. Sail Venture Cruises use large sailing catamarans for their sightseeing, lunch, cocktail or dinner cruises. Departure is from the Aquarium Wharf at Darling Harbour or the East Pontoon at Circular Quay.

Taronga Zoo

12 minutes by ferry from Circular Quay, Wharf 2

Taronga is set in 30 ha of harbourside bushland, giving it a magnificent and unique setting: the views back to the city are splendid. Of particular interest are the displays of Australian native animals and the nocturnal house. Children will enjoy meeting the tame animals at the Friendship Farm (open daily).

Manly

Manly ferry or Jetcat from Circular Quay

Manly on the north side of the harbour has traditionally been a popular day trip for both locals and visitors. The historic Manly Wharf and modern Harbourside Centre offer specialty shops, restaurants, a ferris wheel and a merry-go-round. The Corso, a pedestrian walkway, links the harbour side of Manly to the famous ocean beach with its Norfolk Pines.

Palm Beach

48 km from Sydney via Pittwater Road

This beautiful beach in bush surroundings offers swimming and boating facilities, and a choice of ocean or Pittwater beaches. The drive from Sydney reveals many of Sydney's lovely northern beaches and it is tempting to stop at every one. The Mona Vale Road provides a shorter route if you are based in the northern suburbs; allow time to visit Waratah Park, a fauna reserve at Terrey Hills.

Captain Cook's Landing Place, Kurnell

35 km from Sydney via Princes Highway and Captain Cook Bridge

The site of the first recorded landing by Europeans on the east coast of Australia in 1770 is set aside as a historic site on a pleasant reserve. An excellent museum displays items related to Captain James Cook's life and discoveries. A short

The Blue Mountains

The famous rock formation the Three Sisters is a major attraction near Katoomba

For more than a century, the Blue Mountains have been a favourite holiday resort for Sydneysiders. Rising from the coastal plain 65 kilometres west of Sydney, they combine a unique blend of superb mountain scenery, outstanding geographical features, beautiful gardens and highly developed tourist attractions.

The towering cliffs of the Blue Mountains presented a seemingly impassable barrier to the early European settlers until Blaxland, Lawson and Wentworth made their historic crossing in 1813 – thus opening up much-needed pasture-land beyond. In the late 1870s the well-to-do of Sydney discovered the area's charms as a resort, and started to build elaborate holiday houses to escape the summer heat of the coast. At first they travelled by Cobb & Co. coach, later by train. Now the mountains are less than two hours from Sydney by road or rail. One-day round-trip coach tours run daily between Sydney and Katoomba.

The Blue Mountains are justly famous for their spectacular scenery of high precipices rising from densely wooded valleys. Their highest point is about 1100 metres above sea level. Bushwalking is a very popular pastime in the mountains and several self-guide brochures are available from Tourist information with details of routes, highlights and grades of walks. Deep gorges and high rocks in this area make some of the terrain inaccessible except to skilled bushwalkers and mountaineers. Climbing schools offer rock-climbing weekends for beginners, and there are day courses in beginners' abseiling.

The panoramic **Blue Mountains National Park**, which covers an area of 218 100 hectares, is the fourth largest national park in the state. The park protects some of the best-known scenery in New South Wales.

The City of Blue Mountains incorporates 26 towns and villages, the main towns being **Katoomba**, Blackheath, Wentworth Falls, Springwood and Glenbrook. All these towns depend on tourism and are geared for the holiday trade. They offer a wide range of accommodation, from bed and breakfast at old-style guest houses to luxury living at modern resorts.

The Blue Mountains' reputation for natural wonders is rapidly being rivalled by its popularity as a gastronomic centre. Wining and dining to suit all tastes and budgets is available.

For further information, contact the Blue Mountains Tourism Authority, PO Box 8, Glenbrook 2773; (047) 39 6266, or visit the Information Centres at Echo Point, Katoomba or Glenbrook on the Great Western Hwy. *The Blue Mountains Holiday Book*, produced by the BMTA, also details accommodation and activities in the area. **See also:** National Parks; and entry for Katoomba in A–Z listing. **Map references:** 100 I6, 102, 103, 112 A1, 115 H1, 116 I8.

Why are the Blue Mountains so blue? The whole area is heavily timbered with eucalypts, which constantly disperse fine droplets of oil into the atmosphere. These droplets cause the blue light-rays of the sun to be scattered more effectively, thus intensifying the usual light refraction phenomenon (Rayleigh Scattering), which causes distant objects to appear blue.

Winery in the Hunter Valley region

historical walk takes visitors past several points of interest. There are picnic/barbecue facilities in the grounds.

Parramatta

22 km from Sydney via Great Western Highway

Although it is now a city within Sydney, Parramatta retains its individuality and has some interesting buildings. Pick up a *Historic Houses* self-guide leaflet from Tourist information, cnr Church and Market Sts; (02) 9630 3703. Elizabeth Farm (1793), at 70 Alice St, contains part of the oldest surviving European building in Australia and, as the home of Elizabeth and John Macarthur, was for the first 40 years of the colony the social, political and agricultural centre – do not miss the audiovisual presentation and the period gardens (1830s). Hambledon Cottage (1824) in Hassall St was part of the original Elizabeth Farm property. Experiment Farm Cottage in Ruse St was the site of James Ruse's 'experiment' to support himself from the land in the early years of the colony. Closer to the centre of the city are two historic sites: Old Government House and St John's Church. Old Government House in attractive Parramatta Park, has been beautifully restored from its 1799 beginnings (enlarged 1815) and is maintained by the National Trust. A guided tour is available Tues.–Sun. St John's Cathedral (1850s), in the heart of the shopping district, is open Tues.–Fri.; guides are on duty Fri. St John's cemetery is a block away from the church itself and contains the oldest headstone in the colony, dated January 1791. A short trip north along Pennant Hills Rd leads to the Koala Park Sanctuary (Castle Hill Rd, West Pennant Hills) where koalas are on show all day.

Historic Camden and Campbelltown

60 km from Sydney via Liverpool, on Hume Highway

Liverpool, situated 32 km from Sydney and a major retail and commercial centre, has many buildings of historic interest: St Luke's Church (1818); Liverpool Hospital (1825-30), designed by Francis Greenway and now the Liverpool College of TAFE; and Glenfield Farm (1817). The ultra-modern Liverpool Museum, built as a bicentennial project, fronts Collingwood Cottage, built in 1810 for a whaling captain. A good stopping-point is Chipping Norton Lakes, a reclaimed area with picnic and barbecue facilities, and walking tracks. Further down the highway, lovers of history can enjoy a relaxed stroll around the streets of two early towns of New South Wales, Camden and Campbelltown. **See:** Entries for Camden and Campbelltown in A–Z listing.

Windsor and Richmond

60 km from Sydney via Great Western Highway and Windsor Road

These two towns near the Hawkesbury River are reminders of the earliest days of settlement in New South Wales, and are a must for lovers of history and early architecture **See:** Entries for Windsor and Richmond in A–Z listing.

Katoomba and the Blue Mountains via Penrith

104 km from Sydney via Western Motorway

The historic town of Penrith, 57 km from Sydney, dates back to the opening of the Blue Mountains road in 1815, when a court house and a small gaol were built there. Today it makes a pleasant stopover en route to the Blue Mountains. Penrith's attractions include the Museum of Fire in Castlereagh St, the Nepean Belle paddle-boat, which cruises the Nepean Gorge, Vicary's Winery, south of the town, and the Lewers Bequest and Penrith Regional Art Gallery at Emu Plains.

It is worth diverting from the motorway to Featherdale Wildlife Park in Kildare Rd, Doonside to see the extensive fauna collection and to visit their souvenir shop. Another diversion off the motorway near Eastern Creek is the popular Australia's Wonderland wildlife park. **See:** The Blue Mountains; and Katoomba entry in A–Z listing.

The Hunter Valley Vineyards

160 km from Sydney via Pacific Highway

Although it is possible to do this trip in a day, this certainly would not do the area justice – and it is definitely not a good idea if you plan to do any wine-tasting! The best time to visit the Hunter Valley is at vintage time, when you can see the grapes being fermented in great open vats. Picking starts any time from the end of January, but this can vary considerably, and sometimes does not start until well into February. Tyrrell's and Drayton's wineries were established within a few years of each other in the 1850s. At Tyrrell's you can still see the classic hand-presses being used during vintage and fermentation. Most of the wineries are open daily and welcome visitors. Visits can be arranged with the wineries direct or at Tourist information, Turner Park, Aberdare Rd, Cessnock; (049) 90 4477. **See also:** Vineyards and Wineries; and Cessnock entry in A–Z listing.

NEW SOUTH WALES from A to Z

Lake Eucumbene, near Adaminaby, renowned for its excellent fishing

Adaminaby   Pop. 375

MAP REF. 114 H5, 115 D8, 138 E9, 237 L1

This small town was moved in the 1950s to its present site; the old town site was flooded to form Lake Eucumbene as part of the Snowy Mountains Scheme. Located on the Snowy Mountains Hwy it is a good base for cross-country skiers and anglers. The ski area of Mt Selwyn is nearby. Adaminaby is the stepping-off point for Lake Eucumbene, where there are a range of lakeside holiday resorts and excellent fishing. **Of interest:** World's largest trout, Baker St. Boats available for hire. Feb.: Race meeting. **In the area:** Fishing-boat hire at Buckenderra, 44 km S. Yarrangobilly Caves and thermal pool, off Snowy Mountains Hwy, 53 km NW. Horse-riding and alpine horseback safaris. **Tourist information:** Post Office, 3 Denison St; (064) 54 2303. **Accommodation:** 1 hotel/motel, 2 motels, 1 cara./camp. park.

Adelong   Pop. 795

MAP REF. 115 B5, 116 A13

Both fossickers and goldfields historians are attracted to this picturesque table-lands town on the Snowy Mountains Hwy. In the mid-1850s it produced 200 tonnes of gold and drew many thousands of hopeful miners. **Of interest:** National Trust-classified Tumut St, from Campbell to Neil Sts; some buildings, such as old Bank of NSW, of great historical interest. Also in Tumut St: Gold Fields Galleries, for art and craft; restored Old Pharmacy with Old Prison Clock (over 125 years old) originally from Kiandra court house. Dec.: Boat regatta. **In the area:** Adelong Falls, a scenic picnic area, also gold fossicking; 2 km N on Tumblong–Gundagai Rd. **Tourist information:** York's News-agency, Tumut St; (069) 46 2051. **Accommodation:** 3 hotels, 1 B&B, 1 cara./camp. park.

Albury   Pop. 39 975

MAP REF. 123 Q13, 235 P4, 236 C1

Albury-Wodonga is situated beside the Murray River, 572 km SW from Sydney. Once the meeting-place for local Aboriginal tribes, today the Albury region makes a convenient stopover for motorists driving via the Hume Hwy between Sydney and Melbourne. The building of the Hume Weir in 1936 created Lake Hume, one of the most extensive and beautiful artificial lakes in Australia. **Of interest:** Albury Regional Museum, in former Turk's Head Hotel, Wodonga Pl. Botanical Gardens (1871), cnr Wodonga Pl. and Dean St. The Parklands, comprising Hovell Tree Reserve, Noreuil and Australia Parks, for riverside walks, river swimming, kiosk and picnic areas; on western side of Wodonga Pl. at town entrance. PS *Cumberoona* offers Murray River cruises; embarkation points within parks. Albury Regional Art Centre, features extensive Sir Russell Drysdale collection; Dean St. Performing Arts Centre, Civic Centre, Swift St. 360° views from Albury Monument Hill at end of Dean St. Frog Hollow Leisure Park, Olive St, offers maze, theatre and mini-golf. Sales of local dairy products at Haberfield's Milk Dairy Shop, Hovell St; tours during business hours. Feb.–Mar.: Festival of sport. **In the area:** Ettamogah Wildlife Sanctuary, 12 km NE on Hume Hwy. Cartoonist Ken Maynard's Ettamogah Pub, worth photographing. Cooper's Ettamogah Winery, 3 km further along hwy. Australian Newsprint Mill, 15 km N; tours by appt. Jindera Pioneer Museum, 14 km NW, in former general store. Hume and Hovell Walking Track from Albury to Gunning, 370 km NE; the track offers a 20-day trek for long distance walkers but design caters for half-day, one-day and weekend walks along the way; contact the Department of Lands, 22–23 Bridge St, Sydney; (02) 9228 6111. Day trips to wineries of Rutherglen, 47 km W, and into Mad Dan Morgan (the infamous bushranger) country, 200 km round trip N. Bogong Mountains, gateway to Victorian snow-fields and high country, 130 km S. Hume Weir, a paradise for anglers, canoeists, swimmers, sailors, water-skiers, speedboat enthusiasts and wind-surfers, 14 km E. Hume Weir Trout Farm, nearby, offers trout feeding and fishing. Upstream of weir, Wymah Ferry, still in operation, carries two cars at a time 800 m across river. **Tourist information:** Choices Information Centre, Hume Hwy, Ettamogah (12 km NE near Table Top); (060) 40 2114; accommodation booking line 1800 80 6939. **Accommodation** (in Albury-Wodonga): 2 hotels, 55 motels, 13 cara./camp. parks.

Alstonville
Pop. 3678

MAP REF. 119 Q3, 491 Q12

The village of Alstonville nestles in lush surroundings at the top of the Ballina Cutting between Ballina and Lismore. Famous for the beautiful purple Tibouchina tree, the town holds a Tibouchina festival during blossom time in Mar. Surrounding properties produce potatoes, sugarcane, tropical fruits, macadamia nuts and avocados. **Of interest:** Prize-winning town in 'Tidy Towns' competition since 1986. Lumley Park, Bruxner Hwy, features open-air pioneer transport museum. In Budgen Ave: Kolinda Gallery and Ward's Antiques for local art and craft. Elizabeth Ann Brown Park, a rainforest park with picnic facilities; Main St. Mar.: Tibouchina festival. **In the area:** House With No Steps, 10 km S, a unique enterprise with nursery, crafts, fruit sales and tearooms run by disabled. Nearby, Victoria Park features boardwalks and picnic area. Art and craft at John Cook Studio Gallery, Forest Rd (off Uralba Rd), 6 km E. **Tourist information:** Ballina Tourist Information Centre, Las Balsas Plaza, Ballina; (066) 86 3484. **Accommodation:** 1 hotel, 1 motel.

Armidale
Pop. 21 605

MAP REF. 119 L9

Situated midway between Sydney and Brisbane in the New England Ranges (altitude 980 m), this university city is the centre of the New England district and an attractive tourist centre, with more than 30 National Trust-classified buildings. **Of interest:** New England Regional Art Museum, Kentucky St, contains Hinton Collection, Australia's most valuable provincial art collection. Also in Kentucky St, Aboriginal Centre and Keeping Place, a museum and education centre. Folk Museum with display of pioneer relics, in National Trust-classified building, cnr Faulkner and Rusden Sts. In Dangar St: St Mary's Roman Catholic Cathedral (1912), magnificent Gothic revival structure; St Peter's Anglican Cathedral (1875), built of 'Armidale blues' bricks. The Stables (1872), Moore St, now craft shop. Court house (1860) and Imperial Hotel (1889) in Beardy St. Central Park, pleasant city park with useful relief map of area; Dangar St. Self-guide heritage walk and heritage drive of city, and numerous self-drive scenic drives of area; pamphlets available at Tourist information. Markets in Mall, last Sun. each month. Sept.-Nov.: Springfest. **In the area:** Excellent trout fishing. University of New England, 5 km NW, features historic Booloominbah homestead now administration building, Antiquities Museum, Zoology Museum, and kangaroo and deer park. Dumaresq Dam, 15 km NE, features walking tracks, non-power boating, swimming and fishing for trout (Oct.–June). Mt Yarrowyck Aboriginal rock-art site and cultural walk, 23 km NW off Bundarra Rd. National Trust-owned Saumarez Homestead (1888), 6 km S; check opening times. Rural Life and Industry Museum with exhibits of goldmining equipment at ghost town of Hillgrove, 27 km E. Oxley Wild Rivers National Park, 39 km E, includes Wollomombi Falls, one of the highest falls in the State, plunging 220 m, Dangars Falls and Mihi Falls. Fine views of Bellinger Valley from Point Lookout (1500 m) and excellent walking trails in World Heritage-listed New England National Park, 80 km E; on road into park, L.P. Dutton Trout Hatchery. Cathedral Rock National Park boasts magnificent granite tors; entrance from road to Ebor. **Tourist information:** Visitors Centre & Coach Station, 82 Marsh St; (067) 73 8527, Freecall (1800) 62 7736. **Accommodation:** 5 hotels, 21 motels, 3 B&B, 2 cara./camp. parks. **See also:** New England.

Ashford
Pop. 567

MAP REF. 119 K4, 491 L13

This small New England town is the centre of a tobacco-growing district. **In the area:** Network of limestone caves and spectacular Macintyre Falls, 36 km NW. Pindari Dam, 20 km S, offers swimming and fishing, and camping, bushwalking, picnic/barbecue facilities in surrounds. **Tourist information:** Shire Tourism Committee, Water Towers Complex, Campbell St, Inverell; (067) 22 1693. **Accommodation:** 1 hotel, 1 cara./camp. park. **See also:** New England.

Ballina
Pop. 14 554

MAP REF. 119 Q3, 491 R12

Ballina is a fishing town at the mouth of the Richmond River in northern NSW. Ideal year-round temperatures, golden beaches, picturesque farmlands and friendly rural atmosphere make the area a popular family holiday destination. Cedar cutters were among the first European settlers, attracted by the red cedar trees along the shores of the river. Farmers followed and by 1900 the dairy-farming industry was established alongside sugarcane plantations. **Of interest:** Naval Museum, adjacent to Tourist information, features restored Las Balsas Expedition rafts that sailed from South America in 1973. B Framed Gallery, River St. Quilts and Collectables, Martin St. Ballina Outdoor Entertainment Reserve, Canal Rd. The Big Prawn Complex, Pacific Hwy, features fresh seafood, antiques, opal and gem museum, and art and craft. *Richmond Princess* river cruises. **In the area:** MacKay Harrison Galleries, 2 km N on Lennox Head Rd. Freshwater Lake Ainsworth, 12 km N, at Lennox Head. Thursday Plantation Tea Tree Oil, 3 km W; guided tours available. **Tourist information:** Las Balsas Plaza, cnr River and Norton Sts; (066) 86 3484. **Accommodation:** 18 motels, 3 B&B, 1 hostel, 8 cara./camp. parks.

Balranald
Pop. 1327

MAP REF. 122 H2, 233 N6

On the Murrumbidgee River, Balranald is 438 km NW of Melbourne, in a wool, cattle, wheat, fruit and timber area. **Of interest:** Historical Museum and Heritage Park, Market St, includes gaol, Murray pine school house and Tourist information centre. Lions Park has picnic/barbecue facilities and playground. Easter: Homebush gymkhana. **In the area:** Balranald (low-level) Weir for picnics, barbecues and fishing. Yanga Lake, 7 km SE, offers good fishing and water sports. Historic Homebush Hotel (1878), 25 km N. Mungo National Park, 150 km NW within Willandra Lakes World Heritage Region, features the Walls of China; the lakes preserve record of 40 000 years of Aboriginal life. **Tourist information:** Market St; (050) 20 1599. **Accommodation:** 1 hotel/motel, 5 motels, 1 cara./camp. park.

Bangalow
Pop. 819

MAP REF. 119 Q2, 491 Q12

Bangalow is a delightful village, with rustic charm and set amid magnificent scenery, 10 km SW of Byron Bay. **Of interest:** Art, craft and antique shops. Market, every 4th Sun. **In the area:**

Byron Creek walking track, through splendid rainforest to picnic area. Beaches at Byron Bay, 12 km E. **Tourist information:** Byron Tourist Information Office, 80 Jonson St, Byron Bay; (066) 85 8050. **Accommodation:** 1 hotel, 1 motel.

Barham Pop. 1217

MAP REF. 122 I12, 231 Q2, 233 Q13, 234 B1

Barham and its twin town Koondrook, on the other side of the Murray River, are centres for the timber, cattle, fat-lamb, dairying and tourism industries. **Of interest:** Barham Lakes Complex, Murray St, includes artificial lakes, walking track, picnic/barbecue facilities, swimming, paddle-boats and canoe hire. Bonum Red Gum Saw Mill, Moulamein Rd. Sept.: Pro-Am golf tournament. **In the area:** Around Koondrook: Shannkirst Park Zoological Reserve; Gannawarra Wetlander Cruises, 15 km S; Kerang Ibis Rookery, 28 km SW on Murray Valley Hwy; State Forest, East Barham Rd; Red-gum woodcraft at Brady's Burls, 2½ km NW on Murrabit Rd. At Murrabit, 20 km NW: Karaweena Alpacas, open Sun. and public holidays; market, 1st Sat. each month. **Tourist information:** 25 Murray St; (054) 53 3100. **Accommodation:** 3 hotels, 6 motels, 3 cara./camp. parks.

Barooga Pop. 843

MAP REF. 123 M13, 235 J3

A small but rapidly growing town near the Victorian town of Cobram, Barooga's beautiful setting and abundant wildlife make it a popular holiday resort. **Of interest:** Sandy beaches along Murray River. Binghi Boomerang Factory, Tocumwal Rd. Jan., Easter, June, Aug.: major golf events. **In the area:** Citrus- and grape-growing. Brentwood Fruit Juices, 6 km E. **Tourist information:** The Old Grain Shed, cnr Station St and Punt Rd, Cobram; (058) 72 2132. **Accommodation:** 1 hotel, 4 motels, 1 B&B, 3 cara./camp. parks.

Barraba Pop. 1427

MAP REF. 118 I8

Surrounded by magnificent mountain scenery on the Manilla River in the Nandewar Ranges, Barraba is an agricultural and pastoral centre, and an ideal base for exploring the eastern part of the Nandewar Mountains. **Of interest:** Nandewar Historical Museum, Queen St; open by appt. Clay Pan Fuller Gallery, Queen St. Beautiful old organ in St Laurence's Anglican Church, Fitzroy St. Nov.: Fine music festival. **In the area:** Adam's Lookout, 4 km N. Elembee Fine Fibre Farm, a goat stud in 500 ha of bushland offering walks, fossicking and wildlife; Houghton Falls Rd, 32 km W. Horton River Falls and Horton Valley, 38 km W towards Mt Kaputar National Park. Split Rock Dam Recreation Area, 5 km SE. **Tourist information:** 116 Queen St; (067) 82 1255. **Accommodation:** 3 hotels, 1 motel, 2 cara./camp. parks. **See also:** New England.

The Hawkesbury

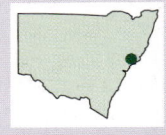

The Hawkesbury River, north of Sydney, is one of the most attractive rivers in Australia and also played an important role in Sydney's early colonial history. The first European settlers arrived in 1794 to establish farming settlements to help feed the starving colony. In 1810 Governor Macquarie founded the towns of **Windsor**, **Richmond**, Castlereagh, Wilberforce and **Pitt Town** in the upper Hawkesbury valley. Today much of this land is still used for agriculture and there are many oyster leases on the lower river.

Although farming has been pursued since the late 18th century, the charm of the Hawkesbury lies mainly in the fact that the river is still surrounded by large areas of untouched bushland. Four national parks front the river: upstream the **Dharug National Park**, noted for its Aboriginal rock carvings; Marramarra National Park, noted for its flora; downstream the **Ku-Ring-Gai Chase National Park**, a bushland haven; and **Brisbane Water National Park**, with its Aboriginal rock engravings and colourful displays of waratahs and Christmas bush.

Car ferry crossing the river at Berowra Waters

The Hawkesbury River is a popular recreational waterway, particularly at its lower and wider reaches between Brooklyn and Pittwater. One of the best ways of exploring the Hawkesbury is by boat. Craft of all types, from small rowing dinghies to cruisers and houseboats, are available for hire at Brooklyn, Bobbin Head, Berowra Waters and Wisemans Ferry. A delightful way to see the river is to join the mailboat run, which leaves Brooklyn on weekdays and takes 3 hours. Cruises on the river are also available, from 2 hours to a full day, on the *Deerubbun* and other craft, departing from the wharf at Brooklyn.

If you are travelling north from Sydney by road, the Newcastle–Sydney Freeway crosses the Hawkesbury and its tributary, Mooney Mooney Creek. Here, the freeway cuts through magnificent sandstone cliffs and offers spectacular views.

For further information, contact the Hawkesbury Visitors Centre, Ham Common Bicentenary Park, Richmond Rd, Clarendon; (045) 88 5895. **See also:** National Parks; and individual entries in A–Z listing for those parks and towns indicated by bold type. **Map references:** 101 M4, 104 C10, 117 K6.

Batemans Bay–Bellingen

Batemans Bay
Pop. 8320

MAP REF. 115 H7, 139 N7

Crayfish and oysters are the specialty of this attractive resort town on the Princes Hwy 285 km S of Sydney. Located at the estuary of the Clyde River, Batemans Bay provides convenient access to both the Pacific Ocean and the safe waters of the Clyde. **Of interest:** *Clyde Princess*, for river cruises; departs Ferry Wharf. On Beach Rd: 27-hole golf course; Birdland Animal Park, features a rainforest trail. Houseboats available for hire. Fishing charters available. Markets, each 2nd and 4th Sun. Nov.: Neptune festival. **In the area:** Excellent fishing. Murramarang National Park, 10 km NE, a coastal park noted for its mostly undisturbed coastline. Durras Lake, 8 km NE, for fishing and swimming. Historic Nelligen, 10 km NW, on Clyde River; has Country music festival each Jan. Araluen, old goldmining town, 82 km W. At Mogo, 8 km S: art and craft outlets; Mogo Goldfields Park features working goldmine; Old Mogo Town, 19th-century recreated goldmining town; Mogo Zoo. Calligraphy Gallery, for local art; 12 km SE. Surfing at Malua Bay, 14 km SE. **Tourist information:** Eurobodalla Coast Visitors Centre, cnr Princes Hwy and Beach Rd; (044) 72 6900. **Accommodation:** 18 motels, 3 B&B, 8 cara./camp. parks. **See also:** The South Coast.

Bathurst
Pop. 24 682

MAP REF. 100 B4, 116 H6

Bathurst, 210 km W of Sydney on the Macquarie River, and the centre of a pastoral and fruit- and grain-growing district, has many historic connections. The birthplace of former Prime Minister, J.B. Chifley, it is better known today for its famous motor-racing circuit, Mount Panorama. **Of interest:** Self-guide historic walking tour and Fossicker's self-drive tour; leaflets at Tourist information. Ben Chifley's Cottage, Busby St. Historical Society Museum in East Wing of court house, Russell St. Miss Traill's house (c. 1845), 321 Russell St, contains items collected by one family over 100 years, which record history of town and reflect family's passion for horse-breeding and racing. Bathurst Regional Art Gallery, Keppel St. Oct.: Bathurst 1000 car races. **In the area:** South-west of city centre at Mt Panorama on Panorama Ave: Bathurst Gold Diggings, a reconstruction of goldmining era; Bathurst Motor Racing Museum, at Mt Panorama Circuit; magnificent views from summit of Mt Panorama; nearby, McPhillamy Park features Sir Joseph Banks Nature Reserve. Abercrombie Caves, limestone cave system containing Arch Cave, considered one of finest natural arches in world and larger than Grand Arch at Jenolan Caves (Carols in the caves held in Dec.); 72 km S, on Bathurst–Goulburn Rd. Abercrombie House (1870s), baronial-style Gothic mansion; 6 km W on Ophir Rd. Hill End Historic Site, 86 km NW: former goldfield with many original buildings; Visitor centre in old Hill End Hospital, and equipment for panning and fossicking available for hire. Other old gold towns nearby include Rockley, O'Connell, Trunkey Creek and Sofala. Bathurst Sheep and Cattle Drome at Rossmore Park, 6 km NE on Limekilns Rd features performing sheep and cattle, and milking, shearing and sheepdog demonstrations. **Tourist information:** 28 William St; (063) 32 1444. **Accommodation:** 4 hotels, 12 motels, 20 B&B, 1 cara./camp. park.

Batlow
Pop. 1143

MAP REF. 115 B6, 116 D13, 138 A4

This timber-milling and former goldmining town, situated in the Great Dividing Range 33 km S of Tumut, is located in a district renowned for its apples, pears and berry fruits. **Of interest:** Historical Society Museum, Mayday Rd. Mountain Maid Cannery, off Kurrajong Ave. Batlow Fruit Packing Complex, Forest Rd. Superb views of town and peaks of Snowy Mountains from Weemala Lookout Flora and Fauna Reserve, H.V. Smith Dr. Apr.: Festival. Sept.: Daffodil show. **In the area:** Hume and Hovell Lookout, 6 km E, for views over Lake Blowering; picnic area at site where explorers paused in 1824. Lake Blowering, 20 km E. Springfield Orchard, Tumut Rd, 6 km N, grows 16 apple varieties; picnic/barbecue facilities available. Pick-your-own berry fruits and cherries at farms on Tumut Rd. Access points for shorter section walks on 370-km Hume and Hovell Walking Track, which runs from Gunning to Albury. Bushwalks and drives through scenic areas on south-west slopes of Bago State Forest, 11 km SW. Spectacular Buddong Falls, 25 km S; accessible during fine weather only. **Tourist information:** Springfield Orchard, Tumut Rd; (069) 49 1021. **Accommodation:** 1 hotel, 1 motel, 1 B&B, 1 cara./camp. park.

Bega
Pop. 4202

MAP REF. 113 F7, 115 G10, 237 Q6

It is possible to surf and ski on the same day from Bega, set as it is between the beach and the Kosciusko snow resorts. The town is near the junction of the Princes and Snowy Mountains Hwys, which link Sydney, Melbourne and Canberra. **Of interest:** Bega Family Historical Museum, cnr Bega and Auckland Sts. Feb.: Far South Coast national show. Mar.: Cheese Pro-Am. Sept.: Festival. Oct.: Bega Valley art awards. **In the area:** Fine views from Dr George Lookout (8 km NE) and Bega Valley Lookout (2 km N). Bega Cheese Heritage Centre, restored original cheese factory with displays of old cheese-making techniques, also has art gallery; 3 km N. See cows being milked at Brogo Valley Rotolactor, 18 km N. Mumbulla Falls picnic area with beautiful rock pools and natural waterslide, 15 km NE. Grevillea Estate Winery, 5 km W on Buckajo Rd. Historic village of Candelo, 23 km SW, with its old-world charm untouched by time, art gallery and market held 1st Sun. each month. Tathra, 18 km SE, has beautiful beaches, historic wharf, Mimosa Rocks National Park to the north and Wallagoot Lake and Bournda National Park to the south. **Tourist information:** Gipps St; (064) 92 2045. **Accommodation:** 5 hotels, 5 motels, 1 hostel, 1 cara./camp. park. **See also:** The South Coast.

Bellingen
Pop. 2298

MAP REF. 119 P8

Bellingen is an attractive tree-lined town on the banks of the Bellinger River in the rich dairylands of the Bellinger Valley. In pioneer days it was a timber-getting and ship-building centre. **Of interest:** Much of town classified by Heritage Commission. Restored Hammond and Wheatley Emporium, Hyde St, now houses Sweetwater Gallery. Local art and craft at Yellow Shed, cnr Hyde and Prince Sts, and Butter Factory Complex, Dopel Lane. Canoe hire available. Markets, 3rd Sat. each month. Aug.: Jazz festival. Sept.: Springtime in the valley. **In the area:**

River-side walks and canoeing on Bellinger River. Scenic island in river, with flying fox colony. Picnicking at Thora, 14 km NW, at foot of Mt Dorrigo. State forests for bushwalking and horseriding. Trout fishing in streams on Dorrigo Plateau. Scenic drive north-east through farmlands and wooded valleys, across Never Never Creek to the Promised Land; several swimming holes and picnic areas along the way; road continues to Dorrigo National Park. Gambaarri Aboriginal Cultural Tours offer a tour to same area with Aboriginal guide. **Tourist information:** Bellingen Travel, 42 Hyde St; (066) 55 2055. **Accommodation:** 1 hotel, 1 motel, 8 B&B, 1 hostel, 1 cara./camp. park.

Bermagui Pop. 1166

MAP REF. 113 H4, 115 H9, 139 M13, 237 R4

Fishing in all forms – lake, estuary, deep-sea and big-game – is excellent in this delightful small port, 13 km from the Princes Hwy. It was much publicised for its fishing by American novelist-sportsman Zane Grey in the 1930s. Craft market, last Sun. each month. Jan.: Blue water fishing classic. Easter: Four Winds Easter concerts. **In the area:** Beautiful rock pools, particularly Blue Pool, rugged coastline and unspoiled countryside. Charter boats offer diving, deep sea and game-fishing trips; depart from harbour. Fresh fish and prawns for sale at Fish Co-op at harbourside. Safe swimming at Horseshoe Bay Beach. Good surfing at Beares, Mooreheads, Cuttagee and Haywards beaches. Coastal walk (8 km) to Wallaga Lake passing through wetland flora and fauna reserves, and remnants of Montreal Goldfields. At Wallaga Lake, 8 km N: Camel Rock, unusual rock formation on shoreline; Umbarra Cultural Centre, offers Aboriginal cultural tours; Wallaga Lake National Park, for boating, fishing, swimming, bushwalking and picnicking, and walking trail to summit of Mt Dromedary. Central Tilba historic village, a National Trust-classified town, 14 km N. Montague Island, 23 km NE, has seal colony and fairy penguins; surrounding waters a mecca for anglers. Cobargo, on Princes Hwy 19 km W, an unspoiled old working village with several art galleries, wood and leather crafts, iron forge, pottery and tearooms; country market held 3rd Sun. each month in grounds of Co-op. Mimosa Rocks National Park, 20 km S. **Tourist information:** BP Bermagui, 8 Coluga St; (064) 93 4174. **Accommodation:** 1 hotel, 4 motels, 5 cara./camp. parks. **See also:** The South Coast.

Berridale Pop. 949

MAP REF. 114 I10, 115 D9, 138 E12, 237 L4

Located near Lake Eucumbene, Lake Jindabyne and the southern ski fields. **Of interest:** St Marys Church (1860), off Kosciusko Rd. Berridale School (1883), Oliver St. Berridale Inn (1863), in Exchange Sq. Easter: Fair. **In the area:** On Old Dalgety Rd: Snowy River Winery, 12 km S; Snowy River Ag Barn and Fibre Centre, 15 km S. Eucumbene Trout Farm, 30 km N, offers sales, horseriding and tours. **Tourist information:** Berridale Store, 64 Jindabyne Rd; (064) 56 3206. **Accommodation:** 1 hotel, 5 motels, 1 cara./camp. park.

Berrigan Pop. 949

MAP REF. 123 N12, 235 J1

A traditional country town with many old buildings reflecting a bygone era, Berrigan is best known for its connections with horseracing. **Of interest:** Historic buildings. Berrigan Racecourse and Kilfenora Racing Stables. Sojourn Station Art Studio. Oct.: Agricultural show. **Tourist information:** River Foreshore, Tocumwal; (058) 74 2131. **Accommodation:** 3 hotels, 1 hotel/motel, 1 motel, 1 cara./camp. park.

Berrima Pop. 723

MAP REF. 112 B6, 115 H3, 117 J10

A superbly preserved 1830s Australian town, Berrima is on the Old Hume Hwy in the Southern Highlands. **Of interest:** Self-guide historic walking tour, contact Tourist information. Many old buildings restored as craft and antique shops, restaurants and galleries. In Market Pl.: White Horse Inn (1832), now a restaurant; historical museum; Australian Alpaca Centre, sells knitwear. Australia's oldest continually licensed hotel the Surveyor General (1835), Old Hume Highway. Gaol (1839), still in use; Argyle St. Court house (1838), finest building in the town, first trial by jury in Australia held here in 1841, now a museum with displays and an excellent video of early Berrima; Wilshire St. Harper's Mansion (1830s) cnr Wilkinson St and Old Hume Hwy. **In the area:** Joadja Winery, 8 km NW, open for tastings; weekends and school holidays. Amber Park Emu and Ostrich Farm, 11 km NW. **Tourist information:** Southern Highlands Visitor Information Centre, Winifred West Park, Old Hume Hwy, Mittagong; (048) 71 2888. **Accommodation:** 1 hotel, 2 motels, 6 B&B. **See also:** Southern Highlands.

Berry Pop. 1570

MAP REF. 112 F11, 115 I4, 117 K11

Old English trees add to the charm of this town on the Princes Hwy, 18 km NE of Nowra. In rich dairying country, it was founded by David Berry, whose brother Alexander was the first European settler in the Shoalhaven area. **Of interest:** Many National Trust-classified buildings including Historical Museum, Queen St. Impressive concentration of antique shops and galleries. Market at Showgrounds, 1st Sun. each month. Feb.: Agricultural show. **In the area:** Cambewarra Lookout, 14 km SW. Coolangatta, a group of convict-built cottages, restored to historic village, winery and resort; 11 km SE, on site of first European settlement in area in 1822. Wineries open for tastings and sales: Jasper Valley Wines, 4 km S; The Silos Winery; 6 km S; Coolangatta Estate, 11 km SE; Cambewarra Estate (open weekends and public holidays), 14 km SW. **Tourist information:** Princes Hwy, Bomaderry; (044) 21 0778. **Accommodation:** 1 hotel, 1 hotel/motel, 1 motel, 3 B&B.

Bingara Pop. 1231

MAP REF. 118 I6

Sapphires, tourmalines and gold may be found in the creeks and rivers around this fascinating town. **Of interest:** Stamper battery at site of former All Nations Gold Mine, top of Hill St. National Trust-classified Museum (1860), in slab building thought to be town's first hotel, displays furniture and photographs from last-century settlement, gems and minerals, and has a working smithy. Murray Cod Hatchery, Bandalong St; open by appt. Gwydir River Rides (train rides), Maitland St. Easter: Gold rush festival; Easterfish. Oct.: Country music talent quest. **In the area:** Excellent fishing. Rocky Creek glacial area, 37 km SW. Sawn Rocks, pipe-shaped volcanic rock formations;

70 km SW. At Upper Bingara 24 km S: remains of old gold and copper mines; Three Creeks Tourist Goldmine, a working mine where visitors can pan and fossick for gold. Copeton Dam, 42 km E, for fishing and boating; excellent camping and accommodation nearby. **Tourist information:** Museum, Maitland St; (067) 24 1726. **Accommodation:** 2 hotels, 1 motel, 1 cara./camp. park. **See also:** New England.

Blayney Pop. 2652

MAP REF. 116 G6

A progressive country town with a growing goldmining industry on the Mid Western Hwy between Cowra and Bathurst, and close to the historic villages of Carcoar and Millthrope. **Of interest:** Buildings classified by National Trust. Avenues of deciduous trees, particularly beautiful in autumn. Forever Country, Adelaide St, for local crafts. Heritage Park, Adelaide St. Carrington Park, Church St. Mar.: Agricultural show. **In the area:** Carcoar Dam, 12 km SW, for water sports; camping and picnic/barbecue facilities nearby. National Trust-classified village of Carcoar, 14 km SW, scene of NSW's first bank hold-up in 1863. At Newbridge, 20 km E, historic buildings and craft outlets. Local art and craft at Taroona Wool Pack (5 km) and Cottesbrook Gallery (15 km) both NE on Mid Western Hwy. Millthorpe, 11 km NW, a National Trust-classified village featuring Golden Memories Museum and craft shops. **Tourist information:** Mid West Mini Market, 20 Adelaide St; (063) 68 2570. **Accommodation:** 4 hotels, 2 motels, 1 B&B, 1 cara./camp. park.

Boggabri Pop. 751

MAP REF. 118 H9

Situated 115 km NW of Tamworth, this town is the centre of a wool, wheat and cotton area. **Of interest:** Historical Museum, Brent St. Honey factory, Lynn St; open by appt. July: Wean picnic races. **In the area:** Fishing. Dripping Rock waterfall, Manilla Rd, 35 km E. Gin's Leap, a rock formation; 4 km N. **Tourist information:** Narrabri Information Centre, Newell Hwy, Narrabri; (067) 92 3583. **Accommodation:** 3 hotels, 1 motel, 1 cara./camp. park.

Bombala Pop. 1404

MAP REF. 113 A9, 115 E11, 237 N7

This small town on the Monaro Hwy, 89 km S of Cooma, is the centre for the surrounding wool, beef cattle, sheep, vegetable and timber-producing area. The area is also renowned for its rich trout fishing. **Of interest:** Self-guide historical walk (1 hr) includes court house, cnr High and Dickinson Sts; School of Art, Caveat St; leaflet from Tourist information. Toorallie Knitting Mill, Maybe St; inquire at Tourist

Southern Highlands

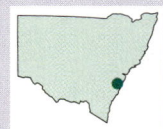

When Governor Lachlan Macquarie visited the area to the south of Sydney that came to be known as the Southern Highlands, he recorded in his diary for that year, 1820: 'the situation of the New Settlers, four miles southwest of Throsby Park, is particularly beautiful and rich, resembling a fine extensive pleasure ground in England'.

Located within the Sydney-Canberra-Melbourne transport corridor formed by the Hume Highway and the main railway between Sydney and Melbourne, the Southern Highlands is easily accessible, with Canberra to the south (170 kilometres from Bowral), Wollongong and the coast to the east (50 kilometres from Bowral) and Sydney to the north (130 kilometres from Bowral).

The thriving towns of **Mittagong**, **Bowral**, **Berrima**, **Moss Vale**, **Robertson** and **Bundanoon** are surrounded by the gentle softness of a rural landscape varied by the changing colours of the seasons.

The crisp mountain air has long attracted visitors. The area offers colourful gardens, and in the towns and villages the visitor will find galleries, antiques, and arts and crafts. There are also rugged mountain ranges, rolling green hillsides, plunging waterfalls and marvellous bushwalks.

The landscape ranges from gently undulating to rugged, at 650–860 metres above sea level. The eastern side of the region is bounded by the cliffs and ravines of the Illawarra escarpment and **Morton National Park**. There are small sections of remnant rainforest in the vicinity of Robertson.

The major natural attraction in the region are the picturesque Fitzroy Falls, part of Morton National Park. Wombeyan Caves, 67 kilometres north-west of Mittagong, are remarkable for their limestone formations. Budderoo National Park is small, but noted for its views and excellent walking tracks. Other popular attractions include the Alpaca Centre at Berrima, the Butterfly House at Mittagong, the Equestrian Centre at Sutton Forest (14 kilometres south-west of Moss Vale), the Tulip Time festival, held in late September, early October at Bowral and 'Christmas in June' held in towns and villages throughout the region.

For further information, contact the Southern Highlands Visitor Information Centre, Winifred West Park, Old Hume Hwy, Mittagong; (048) 71 2888. **See also:** National Parks; and individual town entries in A–Z listing for those parks and towns indicated by bold type. **Map reference:** 112.

Moss Vale, one of the major centres in the Southern Highlands

NEW SOUTH WALES

information. In Caveat St: White House Gallery (c.1835); Endeavour Reserve, features 2-km return walking track. In Mahratta St: Folk Museum, displays local artifacts and farm implements; Bicentennial Park, with river walk. **In the area:** Burnima historic homestead, 6 km N on Monaro Hwy; open by appt. Goldmines at Craigie, 33 km SW. Early Settlers Hut at Delegate, 36 km SW. Scenic drive (gold fossicking along route, with landowners' permission) to Bendoc Mines in Vic., 57 km SW. Coolumbooka Nature Reserve, 15 km NE. **Tourist information:** Mobil Service Station, 125 Maybe St; (064) 58 3047. **Accommodation:** 3 hotels, 1 motel, 1 B&B, 1 cara./camp. park.

Bourke Pop. 2976

MAP REF. 121 N5

Anything 'Back o' Bourke' is the real outback. Bourke itself is the service centre of a vast area of sheep country that produces up to 55 000 bales of wool a year. It is claimed to be the largest centre for wool shipment in the world. Crops in the area including cotton have been successful due to the weir on the Darling River providing irrigation. **Of interest:** Many colonial buildings; self-guide historical tour available, contact Tourist information. Tourist information in Old Railway Station, Anson St, has displays of Aboriginal artifacts, products of local industries and local history. In Cobar Rd: Fred Hollows' grave and Memorial in cemetery; Cotton Gin, open for tours. Fishing for cod, Darling River. Bridge (1883) over Darling River, first lift-up bridge in NSW. Lock, only lock on Darling. Replica of historic wharf, Sturt St, a reminder of days when Bourke was a busy paddlesteamer port. Apr.: Fred Hollows footrace (to Sydney). June: Bourke to B-Bash (charity car rally, different destination each year, always starting with 'B'). Sept.: Mateship festival (includes paddleboat regatta). Oct.: Back o' Bourke stampede (rodeo). **In the area:** Replica of Fort Bourke Stockade, 20 km SW, testament to early explorer Major Thomas Mitchell. Mt Gunderbooka, 74 km S, wildlife sanctuary featuring caves with Aboriginal art. Mt Oxley, 40 km E, views of plains from summit. **Tourist information:** Old Railway Station, 45 Anson Street; (068) 72 2280. **Accommodation:** 6 hotels, 5 motels, 1 hostel, 3 cara./camp. parks.

Bowral Pop. 7929

MAP REF. 112 C6, 115 I3, 117 J10

The friendly township of Bowral nestles below Mount Gibraltar, 114 km S of Sydney. Originally a popular summer retreat for wealthy Sydney residents, who left a legacy of stately mansions and beautiful gardens, Bowral today is the commercial centre of the Southern Highlands region. **Of interest:** Corbett Gardens, Merrigang St, showpiece of Tulip Time festival (Sept.-Oct.). Bradman Oval, near house where cricketer Sir Donald Bradman spent his youth, and Bradman Museum, St Jude St. Historic buildings, mostly in Wingecarribee and Bendooley Sts. Specialty shopping in antiques, especially Bong Bong St. Sept.-Oct.: Tulip Time festival; District Art Society exhibition. **In the area:** Lookout on Mt Gibraltar, 2 km N; also bushwalking trails. **Tourist information:** Southern Highlands Visitor Information Centre, Winifred West Park, Old Hume Hwy, Mittagong; (048) 71 2888. **Accommodation:** 3 hotels, 7 motels, 4 B&B.

Braidwood Pop. 976

MAP REF. 115 G6, 116 H13, 139 L4

This old town, 84 km S of Goulburn, has been declared an historic village by the National Trust. Gold was discovered in the area in 1851 and Braidwood developed as the principal town of the southern goldfields. Much of the architecture from this period has survived. *Ned Kelly* (1969) and *The Year My Voice Broke* (1986) and *On Our Selection* (1994) – all filmed here. **Of interest:** Museum, Wallace St, displays of local Aboriginal history, Chinese settlement and gold-mining artifacts. Historic buildings include: St Andrews Church, Elrington St; St Bedes, Wallace St; Royal Mail Hotel with its beautiful iron lacework, Wallace St. Self-guide tour of historic buildings, also scenic drive; leaflets from Tourist information. Galleries; craft and antique shops. **In the area:** The Big Hole, a large sink hole, and the Marble Arch rock formation, 45 km S. **Tourist information:** Museum, Wallace St; (048) 42 2310. **Accommodation:** 1 hotel, 3 motels, 3 B&B, 1 hostel.

Brewarrina Pop. 1168

MAP REF. 121 Q5

Located 95 km E of Bourke, this town takes its name from an Aboriginal word meaning 'good fishing'; it is still an ideal base for the keen angler. The main industries include wool and wheat production. **Of interest:** Ancient Aboriginal stonefish traps in Darling River, once a major food source for local Aborigines. Aboriginal Cultural Museum, Bathurst St, displays aspects of Aboriginal life from Dreamtime to present; open Mon.–Fri. Many 19th-century buildings built when town was a thriving river port. Self-guide drive, contact Tourist information. Wildlife park, Doyle St. Apr.: Agricultural show. **In the area:** Narran Lake, 40 km NE, features native birdlife and other fauna. **Tourist information:** Shire Offices, Bathurst St; (068) 39 2106. **Accommodation:** 2 hotels, 1 motel, 1 cara./camp. park.

Broken Hill Pop. 23 263

MAP REF. 120 B12

This artificial oasis in the vast arid lands of far western NSW was created to serve the miners working in the rich silver-lead-zinc mines of the Barrier Range. The mines produce 2 million tonnes of ore annually. The green parks and colourful gardens, 1170 km NW of Sydney, seem unreal in the semi-desert setting. The city's water supply comes from local storage schemes and the Menindee Lakes on the Darling River. Note that Broken Hill operates on Central Standard Time, half an hour behind the rest of NSW. **Of interest:** Self-guide heritage trails, contact Tourist information for pamphlets. National Trust-classified historic streetscape, Argent St. Railway, Mineral and Train Museum, cnr Blende and Bromide Sts. Geo Centre Museum, cnr Crystal and Bromide Sts. White's Mineral Art and Mining Museum, Allendale St. Joe Keenan's Lookout, Marks St, for view of town and mine dumps, and information boards displaying town history. Many art galleries, including City Art Gallery, cnr Blende and Chloride Sts, featuring Silver Tree, commissioned by Charles Rasp, discoverer of Broken Hill orebody in 1883. Broken Hill is home of Brushmen of the Bush, a group of artists that includes Pro Hart and Jack Absalom. Inspection of School of the Air, cnr McCulloch and Lane Sts; book at Tourist information. Mine tours to Delprat's Mine, off Crystal St. Moslem Mosque (1891), Buck St, built by

Afghan community then living in town. Zinc Twin Lakes, off Wentworth Rd, South Broken Hill. Sept.: Silver city show. Oct.: Country music festival. **In the area:** Inspection of Royal Flying Doctor Service, 10 km S; book at Tourist information. Water sports, fishing and camping at Menindee Lakes, 110 km SE. Mootwingee National Park, 130 km NE, features magnificent scenery and Aboriginal historic site, rich in rock art and stencils (access to site limited, contact Tourist information); visitors are advised to be fully self-sufficient in food, water and fuel. Fred Hollows Sculpture Symposium and The Living Desert, 6 km N on Nine Mile Rd; leaflet from Tourist information. Excellent viewing of wildlife on Sundown Nature Trail (2.8 km return), begins 9 km N on Tibooburra Rd; contact Tourist information for leaflet (take water). Silverton, 23 km NW, silver chlorides were discovered here in 1883 and town has been location for films *Wake in Fright*, *Mad Max 2* and *A Town Like Alice*; tours of Day Dream Mine; heritage walking trail; several galleries featuring work of resident artists; Silverton Hotel (c. 1880); Old Gaol Museum displaying historic items; camel rides available. Mundi Mundi Plains Lookout, 4 km further N, and a further 9 km N, Umberumberka Reservoir Lookout. **Tourist information:** Cnr Blende and Bromide Sts; (080) 87 6077. **Accommodation:** 12 hotels, 13 motels, 2 hostels, 3 cara./camp. parks.

Brunswick Heads
Pop. 1662

MAP REF. 119 Q2, 491 Q12

This town at the mouth of the Brunswick River is well known for its outstanding fishing, and is the base for a large commercial fishing fleet. **Of interest:** Canoe and paddleboat hire at the *Pirate Ship* on the river off

Port Stephens

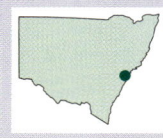

The white volcanic sand and aquamarine waters of the beaches of Port Stephens have a distinctly tropical look, and the annual average temperature is within about 2°C of that of the Gold Coast. This large deep-water port, less than an hour's drive from Newcastle, is one of the most unspoiled and attractive seaside holiday areas on the New South Wales coast. Two-and-a-half times the size of Sydney Harbour, and almost enclosed by two volcanic headlands, the harbour is fringed by sheltered white sandy beaches backed by stretches of natural bushland. In spring, wildflowers grow in profusion.

The deep, calm waters of the harbour are ideal for boating and offer excellent fishing. You can hire a wide range of boats, from aquascooters and catamarans to sailing and power boats. Various cruises are available, including the popular Dolphin Watch and the Myall River cruise. Game-fishing waters are within reach outside the harbour, but local fishing clubs warn against going outside the heads unless you are an experienced sailor with a two-motor boat. The best way to reach these waters is aboard one of the many charter boats licensed to take anglers and sightseers outside the heads. Early in the afternoon you can watch the local fishing fleet coming into **Nelson Bay**, the main anchorage of the port.

Restaurants in the area – not surprisingly – offer fresh seafood as a specialty. Sample a superb lobster supreme, washed down by a fine Hunter Valley or Port Stephens wine. For dedicated oyster lovers, a trip to Moffat's Oyster Barn, Swan Bay, is a must. As well as seeing oysters under cultivation

One of the many sheltered inlets at Port Stephens

and learning about their 4-year life cycle, you can also enjoy a delicious meal of oysters. If you go by boat, make sure you do not run aground on an oyster lease!

You can hire almost anything in the area including bicycles (try a tandem), beach umbrellas and fishing tackle. There are also golf courses, bowling greens and all the other usual sporting facilities.

For surfing, you can visit the spectacular ocean beaches that stretch in both directions outside the harbour. Within about 6 kilometres of Nelson Bay are Zenith, Wreck and Box beaches, Fingal Bay and One Mile Beach. Always popular is the Coastal Explorer 4WD tour along Newcastle Bight, the largest sand-dune expanse on the east coast. An experienced guide will take you along the beach to view Aboriginal shell middens, the *Sygna* wreck and World War II lines of defence.

Other local attractions include: art galleries; craft markets; Aussie Ewe and Lamb Centre, Anna Bay; the toboggan run at Toboggan Hill Park, Salamander Bay; Oakvale Farm and Fauna World; and Fighter World, RAAF Base Williamtown. There is a wide variety of accommodation available in the area, including caravan and camping parks. The main towns, apart from Nelson Bay, are Shoal Bay, Fingal Bay, Anna Bay, Tanilba Bay, Lemon Tree Passage and Soldiers Point on the south shore, and Tea Gardens and Hawks Nest on the north shore.

For further information about the area, including such nearby attractions as the Myall Lakes National Park, contact the Port Stephens Visitors Centre, Victoria Pde, Nelson Bay; (049) 81 1579. **See also:** Town entry for Nelson Bay in A–Z listing. **Map references:** 108 G2, 117 O4.

Mullumbimby St. Surfing and swimming. Market 1st Sat. each month. Jan.: Fish and chips (wood chop) festival. Easter: Blessing of the fleet; Fishing competition. Sept.: Brunswick river festival. **In the area:** New Brighton Hotel, an old pub with character at Billinudgel 7 km NW. Mullumbimby, 10 km W. Cape Byron lighthouse at Byron Bay, 19 km S. **Tourist information:** 80 Jonson St, Byron Bay; (066) 85 8050. **Accommodation:** 1 hotel, 4 motels, 4 cara./camp. parks.

Bulahdelah Pop. 1097

MAP REF. 117 O3

Situated on the Pacific Hwy at the foot of Alum Mountain, Bulahdelah is a good base for a bushwalking or houseboating holiday. The town is surrounded by State forests and the beautiful Myall Lakes. Mar.: Prawn festival. Nov.: Show and rodeo. **In the area:** Bulahdelah Mountain Park, a lovely park with picnic/barbecue facilities, remains of machinery used for alunite mining, rare orchids and walking track. In Bulahdelah State Forest, 14 km N off the Lakes Way, is State's tallest known tree, a flooded gum *Eucalyptus grandis*. Bulahdelah Logging Railway, 19 km N, full-size steam train offers rides Fri., Sat. and school holidays. Myall Lakes National Park, 12 km E, contains one of State's largest networks (10 000 ha) of coastal lakes, ideal for water sports, bushwalking and camping in rainforest; houseboats available for hire. Beaches and camping at Seal Rocks, 40 km E. **Tourist information:** Little St, Forster; (065) 54 8799. **Accommodation:** 4 motels, 2 cara./camp. parks.

Bundanoon Pop. 1513

MAP REF. 112 A9, 115 H3, 117 J10

This town is 32 km SW of Mittagong. The area is famous for its deep gullies and views over the rugged mountains and gorges of Morton National Park. Walk or drive to lookouts. Bundanoon was once a honeymoon resort; today it boasts an English-style pub, delightful guest houses and a health resort. The train stops in the heart of town. Apr.: Bundanoon is Brigadoon annual highland gathering. Oct.: Gullies Gallop fun run. **In the area:** Exeter, a small village 6 km N; the surrounding area boasts some of the finest horse studs in the country. Bundanoon section of Moreton National Park, 4 km S, particularly scenic with spectacular lookouts, walking tracks and the famous glow worms visible at night in Glow Worm Glen (access is via the end of William St, a 25-minute walk, or Riverview Rd, a 40-minute walk). **Tourist information:** Southern Highlands Visitor Information Centre, Winifred West Park, Old Hume Hwy, Mittagong; (048) 71 2888. **Accommodation:** 1 hotel, 2 motels, 1 cara./camp. park, 1 camping ground.

Byron Bay Pop. 5001

MAP REF. 119 R2, 491 R12

Surfers from near and far gravitate to Wategos Beach, on Cape Byron. Its northerly aspect makes it one of the best beaches for surfboard riding on the east coast. Visitors can go bushwalking, horseriding, fishing, swimming, scuba diving, trikeflying or skydiving, or just enjoy the delightful climate and relaxing lifestyle of this idyllic spot. Dairy products, bacon, beef and tropical fruits are produced locally. Market, 1st Sun. each month. Jan.: Arts and music festival. Easter: East Coast Blues festival. **In the area:** On Cape Byron, most easterly point on Australian mainland, 3 km SE: Cape Byron Lighthouse, Australia's most powerful lighthouse; Byron Bay Whale Centre, in Lighthouse, celebrates majesty of whales with educational displays and spectacular audio/visual 'Journey with the Whales'; walking trail, leaflet available at Tourist information; lookouts (humpback whales pass the Cape May–Dec., dolphins can be seen all year). Ocean Shores Golf Course, 1½ km N, considered to be best in State. **Tourist information:** 80 Jonson St; (066) 85 8050. **Accommodation:** 2 hotels, 23 motels, 6 hostels, 7 cara./camp. parks.

Camden Pop. 8440

MAP REF. 101 K10, 112 F1, 115 I1, 117 K8

In 1805 John Macarthur was granted 5000 acres (2023 ha) at what was known as the Cowpastures which he called Camden Park. It was here he conducted his famous sheep-breeding experiments. The town of Camden dates from 1840, and is 60 km SW of Sydney on Camden Valley Way. **Of interest:** Many historic buildings, including Belgenny Farm (1819) and Camden Park House (1834), both part of Macarthur's Camden Estate, Elizabeth Macarthur Dr.; Church of St John the Evangelist (1840–49), John St; Camelot, designed by J. Horbury Hunt, and Kirkham Stables (1816), both in Kirkham Lane. Camden History Museum, John St. Self-guide walk and scenic drive available, contact Tourist information. Cobbitty Markets, 1st Sun. each month. Feb.: Heritage wine and food fair. Oct.: Camden to Goulburn cycle classic. **In the area:** Museum of Aviation, Narellan, 3 km NE. Mt Annan Botanic Garden, Narellan Rd. Struggletown Fine Arts Complex, 3 km N. Historic Gledswood Homestead and winery, 10 km N on Camden Valley Way, presents a unique opportunity for visitors to experience a working colonial farm; craft market held last Sun. each month. Vicarys Winery, 25 km N; open weekends. Camden Aerodrome, 3 km NW, ballooning, gliding, vintage aircraft. Oran Park Raceway, 4 km W, venue for bike, car and truck racing. Wollondilly Heritage Centre and slab-built St Matthew's Church (1838) at The Oaks, 16 km W. Burragorang Lookout for views over Lake Burragorang; 24 km W. Further west, Yerranderie, fascinating, but remote, old silver-mining town; reached by 6-hour 4WD journey from Camden or 30-min. plane flight. **Tourist information:** Oxley Cottage, Camden Valley Way, Elderslie; (046) 58 1370. **Accommodation:** 1 hotel, 4 motels, 1 cara./camp. park. **See also:** Vineyards and Wineries.

Campbelltown Pop. 10 004

MAP REF. 101 L10, 112 G1, 117 K8

Named by Governor Macquarie in 1820 after his wife's maiden name, Campbelltown is now a rapidly growing city. It is also the location for the legend of Fisher's ghost. In 1826 an ex-convict Frederick Fisher disappeared. The ghost of Fisher is alleged to have pointed to the place where his body was subsequently found and as a result the murderer was brought to justice. **Of interest:** Campbelltown City Bicentennial Art Gallery and Japanese Gardens, Art Gallery Rd, cnr Camden and Appin Rds. Historic buildings: Glenalvon (1840) and Richmond Villa (1830–40), Lithgow St; Colonial Houses, 284–298 Queen St; St Peter's Church (1823), Cordeaux St; Old St John's Church, cnr Broughton and George Sts, with grave of James Ruse; Emily Cottage (1840), cnr Menangle and Camden Rds; and

Campbelltown Art and Craft Society (licensed as Farrier's Arms Inn in 1843) and Fisher's Ghost Restaurant, formerly Kendall's Millhouse (1844), both in Queen St. Self-guide heritage walk, leaflet available at Tourist information. Apr.: Show. Nov.: Festival of Fisher's ghost. **In the area:** Eschol Park House (1820), 15 km N. Mount Annan Botanic Garden, 10 km W on Narellan Rd. Menangle House (1839) and St James's Church at Menangle, 9 km SW. Steam and Machinery Museum, 5 km S on Menangle Rd. **Tourist information:** Council Offices, 91 Queen St; (046) 20 1510. **Accommodation:** 4 motels.

Canowindra   Pop. 1721

MAP REF. 116 E7

Bushranger Ben Hall and his gang commandeered this township in 1863. Canowindra today is known as the 'Balloon Capital of Australia' as more balloon flights take place here annually than anywhere else in Australia. Fish fossils of world significance, 360 million years old were discovered in 1956, 9 km SW, and another major dig took place in 1993. Situated on the Belubula River, Canowindra is noted for its curving main street and notable buildings; the entire commercial section in Gaskill St has been classified by the National Trust as a Heritage Conservation Area. Easter: Model aircraft championship. Sept.: Agricultural show. **Of interest:** In Gaskill St: Educational Centre, displays of fish fossils (open by appt, contact Tourist information); museum exhibits local memorabilia (Sun. p.m.); antique shops. Gondwana Dreaming Fossil Tours, 2nd weekend each month. Hot-air balloon rides, Mar.–Nov., weather permitting. **Tourist information:** Canowindra Bakery, Gaskill St; (063) 44 1399. **Accommodation:** 3 hotels, 1 motel, 1 cara./camp. park.

Casino   Pop. 10 850

MAP REF. 119 P3, 491 P12

This important commercial centre beside the Richmond River is a typical country town with its wide streets and verandahed hotels. It is the centre for the surrounding beef-cattle region. **Of interest:** Casino Folk Museum, Walker St; open Wed. p.m. and Sun. p.m. Many fine buildings including public school and court house, both in Walker St; St Mark's Church of England, West St; and Cecil Hotel, post office and Tattersall's Hotel, all in Barker St. Eight parks in town and attractive picnic spots beside Richmond River. Tours of meat works by appt only. May: Beef week festival. June: Agricultural show. **In the area:** Freshwater fishing on Cooke's Weir and Richmond River. Aboriginal rock carvings, 20 km W on Tenterfield Rd. **Tourist information:** Memorial Baths Centre, Centre St; (066) 62 3566. **Accommodation:** 4 hotels, 5 motels, 2 cara./camp. parks.

Cessnock   Pop. 17 506

MAP REF. 108 B10, 109 E12, 117 M4

Many excellent Hunter River table wines are produced in the Cessnock district. The economy of the city, formerly based on coal mining, is now centred on wine and tourism. **Of interest:** Galleries, antique and craft shops. Feb.: Vintage festival. Oct.: Jazz concerts. **In the area:** More than 55 quality wineries in Pokolbin area, most open for tastings and cellar-door sales (see Lower Hunter Vineyards map). Hot-air ballooning at Rothbury, 11 km N. Rusa Park Zoo, an exotic wildlife park at Nulkaba, 7 km NW. Picturesque village of Wollombi, 29 km SW, has wealth of historic buildings, including beautiful St John's Anglican Church; court house, now Endeavour Museum (open weekends); old-style combined general store and post office; Aboriginal cave paintings; tours. Watagan Mountains and State Forest, 33 km SE; splendid views and picnic/barbecue facilities at Heaton, Hunter's and McLean's Lookouts. At Pelaw Main, 17 km E, Richmond Main Mining Museum offers steam-train

The Illawarra Coast

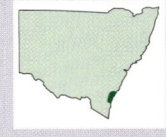

Magnificent panoramic views along the rugged Illawarra coast more than compensate for the often winding route of the Princes Highway, which runs the length of it. 'Illawarra' is a corruption of an Aboriginal word appropriately meaning 'high and pleasant place by the sea'. Stretching from Sydney south to Batemans Bay, the Illawarra coast is bounded on the west by the Southern Highlands.

Fine surf beaches stretch along Illawarra's craggy coast, which is liberally dotted with mountain streams, waterfalls, inlets and lakes – ideal for prawning and water sports. Wildflowers and fauna abound in the many reserves along the coast, and the distinctive vegetation includes cabbage palms, tree ferns and giant fig trees. This is the setting for the State's third largest city, **Wollongong**, which

View from Stanwell Park near Wollongong

has many tourist attractions, scenic lookouts and beautiful beaches.

The other main towns on the coast are **Shellharbour**, a popular holiday resort and residential town south of Lake Illawarra; **Kiama**, the centre of a prosperous dairying and mixed-farming district; **Nowra**, the main town of the fascinating Shoalhaven River district; and **Ulladulla**, a picturesque little fishing town and popular summer holiday resort.

For further information, contact Tourism Wollongong, 93 Crown St, Wollongong; (042) 28 0300. **See also:** individual entries in A–Z listing for those towns indicated by bold type. **Map references:** 112 G13, 117 K12.

rides. Richmond Vale Mining Museum, 13 km NE; open 1st, 2nd and 3rd Sun. each month. **Tourist information:** Turner Park, Aberdare Rd; (049) 90 4477. **Accommodation:** 7 hotels, 68 motels, 3 cara./camp. parks.

Cobar Pop. 4138

MAP REF. 121 N10, 123 Q3

A progressive copper, gold, silver, lead and zinc mining town with wide tree-lined streets, Cobar is 723 km NW of Sydney. The town is on the Barrier Hwy, used by travellers to visit outback areas of NSW, Qld and NT. Since the opening of the CSA Copper Mine in the mid-1960s, and the introduction of a channel water supply, the town has been transformed from an arid landscape to a green oasis. There is an abundance of native flora and fauna in the area. The CSA Mine has an annual output of 600 000 tonnes of copper and copper-zinc ores. The Elura silver-lead-zinc mine opened in 1983 and the Peak goldmine in 1992. Wool is the main local primary industry. **Of interest:** Great Cobar Outback Heritage Centre, Barrier Hwy, features pastoral, mining and technological displays; open daily. Fine early architecture, including court house and police station, Barton St; St Laurence O'Toole Catholic Church, Prince St; Great Western Hotel, Marshall St, with longest iron-lace verandah in State. Commonwealth Meteorological Station, Louth Rd; open by appt. May: Agricultural show: Oct.: Back to Cobar. **In the area:** Mt Grenfell Aboriginal cave paintings, turn-off 40 km W on Barrier Hwy, near Mt Grenfell homestead; picnic area nearby. **Tourist information:** Great Cobar Outback Heritage Centre, Barrier Hwy; (068) 36 1452. **Accommodation:** 2 hotels, 1 hotel/motel, 6 motels, 1 cara./camp. park.

Coffs Harbour Pop. 20 326

MAP REF. 119 P8

One of the larger centres on the Holiday Coast, this subtropical resort town is 580 km N of Sydney on the Pacific Hwy. The surrounding districts produce timber, bananas, vegetables, dairy products and fish. Coffs Harbour is really two towns – one on the highway and the other near the harbour and railway station. **Of interest:** In High St: Historic Pier Hotel (rebuilt 1920s) and jetty (1892); Coffs Harbour Museum. The Marina, departure point for fishing charters and scuba-diving trips to the Solitary Islands. A walk along northern sea wall of harbour leads to Muttonbird Island National Park, a great vantage point to view annual migration of humpback whales May–Dec. North of jetty, Pet Porpoise Pool, Orlando St, features performing porpoises and seals; also research and nursery facilities. Aquajet Waterslide, Park Beach Rd. North Coast Regional Botanical Gardens complex, with its splendid rainforest and prolific birdlife; Hardacre St. Sept.: Garden competition. **In the area:** Hot-air ballooning, white-water rafting, canoeing, game-fishing, scuba diving, horseriding and 4WD tours; Gambaari Aboriginal Cultural Tour of coastal area; self-guide tours through Wedding Bells State Forest and the Dorrigo Region (4WD only) – for further information, contact Tourist information. Coastline views from surrounding area. Clog-making and Dutch village at Clog Barn on Pacific Hwy, 2 km N. The Big Banana, 4 km N along Pacific Hwy; unusual concrete landmark in form of huge banana with displays illustrating banana industry; alongside, Big Banana Theme Park features Aboriginal Dreamtime Cave experience and 'realistic' bunyip; World of Horticulture, with monorail, is nearby. Coffs Harbour Zoo, 14 km N. Bruxner Park Flora Reserve, Korora, 9 km NW, a dense tropical jungle area of vines, ferns and orchids; bushwalking tracks and picnic area at Park Creek. Georges Gold Mine tours, 38 km W. **Tourist information:** Visitors and Convention Bureau, Pacific Hwy; (066) 52 8824. **Accommodation:** 8 resorts, 9 hotels, 37 motels, 6 cara./camp. parks.

Coleambally Pop. 580

MAP REF. 123 N9

This recently established town, officially opened in June 1968 and the centre of the Coleambally Irrigation Area, is south of the Murrumbidgee River. Rice is the main crop of the 87 600 ha under irrigation; vegetables, grain, sorghum, safflower and soya beans also are grown. The town has a modern shopping centre and a rice mill. **Of interest:** Wineglass Water Tower, Brolga Pl. **Tourist information:** Coleambally Motel, Kingfisher Ave; (069) 54 4233. **Accommodation:** 1 hotel, 1 motel, 1 cara./camp. park.

Condobolin Pop. 3163

MAP REF. 116 A5

On the Lachlan River, 475 km W of Sydney, Condobolin is the centre of a red-soil plains district producing wool, beef cattle, fat lambs, fruit and mixed farm products. The town is the southernmost point to which road trains operate from NT and Qld. Aug.: Agricultural show. Oct.: Art exhibition. **In the area:** Aboriginal relics, 40 km W, including monument marking burial place of one of last Lachlan tribal elders. Gum Bend Lake, 5 km W. Agricultural research station, 10 km E; open by appt. Mt Tilga, 8 km N, said to be geographic centre of NSW; stiff climb to summit but view is worth it. **Tourist information:** Shire Offices, 62–64 Molong St; (068) 95 2377. **Accommodation:** 3 hotels, 1 hotel/motel, 2 motels, 1 cara./camp. park.

Cooma Pop. 7385

MAP REF. 113 A9, 115 E9, 138 G11, 237 M3

This lively, modern tourist centre at the junction of the Monaro and Snowy Mountains Hwys, on the Southern Tablelands of NSW, was once dubbed Australia's most cosmopolitan town. Thousands of migrants from many different countries worked in the region on the Snowy Mountains Scheme. It is a busy tourist centre year-round, and the jumping-off point for the Snowies. Motorists are advised to check their tyres and stock up on petrol and provisions before setting off for the snow country. **Of interest:** Self-guide Lambie St walk highlighting National Trust-classified buildings, brochure available from Tourist information. Old Gaol Museum, Vale St. In Centennial Park, Sharp St: International Avenue of Flags, with flags of 27 countries unfurled in 1959 to commemorate 10th anniversary of Snowy Mountains Hydro-electric Authority and in recognition of nationalities of people who worked on project; The Time Walk, a Bicentennial project presenting district history in 40 ceramic mosaics. Also in Sharp St, Southern Cloud Park, features display (with audiotape) of remains of *Southern Cloud* aircraft, which crashed here in 1931 and found 1958. Snowy Mountains Authority Information Centre, Monaro Hwy, has displays and films on Snowy Mountains Scheme. Nannygoat Lookout, Massie St. Local art and craft at

The South Coast

Coast near Merimbula

The southern coast of New South Wales, from Batemans Bay to the Victorian border, is an angler's paradise. Hemmed by the Great Dividing Range, it is one of the finest areas for fishing in southern Australia. It is also a haven for anyone who enjoys swimming, surfing or bushwalking in an unspoiled setting.

One of the attractions of this stretch of coast is the variety of country: superb white surf beaches and crystal-clear blue sea against a backdrop of craggy mountains, gentle hills, lakes, inlets and forests. The coast is dotted with quaint little fishing and holiday towns, offering a wide range of accommodation, including caravan parks. These towns are not highly commercialised, although many of them triple their population in the peak summer months. Boats of all kinds can be hired at the major towns.

Peaceful **Batemans Bay**, at the estuary of the Clyde River, is very popular with the landlocked residents of Canberra, the national capital. **Narooma**, Montague Island and **Bermagui** are well known for their game-fishing. Black marlin, blue fin and hammerhead sharks are the main catch. Narooma also boasts an 18-hole cliff-side golf course where you tee off from the third hole across a narrow canyon.

Bega, to the south, is the unofficial capital of the area and is an important dairying and cheese-making centre. As Bega is about 10 minutes inland from the coast and 2 hours from the snow fields, the town's proud boast is that you can ski in the Snowies and surf in the Pacific on the same day. Further south is the popular holiday resort of **Merimbula** and its sister village of Pambula.

The southernmost town of the region is the quaint old fishing village of **Eden**, and its former rival settlement, Boydtown, both reminders of the colourful whaling days of the last century. Whale-watching is popular in Eden in the months of October and November.

Fishing is excellent all along the coast. You can catch a variety of fish, including rock cod, bream and jewfish, from the beach or net crayfish off the rockier parts of the coast. Prawning is good in the scattered inlets; and trout and perch can be caught in the many rivers draining from the mountains.

The region's all-year-round mild climate has made it a favourite with visitors, but you must book well ahead in the peak holiday period.

For further information, contact the Sapphire Coast Tourism Association, 2/163 Auckland St, Bega; (064) 92 3313. **See also:** individual entries in A–Z listing for those towns indicated by bold type. **Map references:** 113, 115, 139.

Japanese Garden, just north of Cowra

NEW SOUTH WALES

Loegoss Gallery and The Little Gallery, both in Sharp St; and Raglan Gallery, Lambie St. Market, 3rd Sun. each month in Centennial Park. Jan.: Rodeo. **In the area:** Cloyne Nursery, specialising in roses and geraniums; 8 km N. Clog Maker, 2.5 km W on Snowy Mountains Hwy, clog-making demonstration by Dutch artisans. Mt Gladstone Lookout, 3 km W. Llama World, 13 km W on Snowy Mountains Hwy; open Fri., Sat. and Sun. **Tourist information:** 119 Sharp St; (064) 50 1742. **Accommodation:** 6 hotels, 21 motels, 2 hostels, 3 cara./camp. parks.

Coonabarabran   Pop. 2959

MAP REF. 118 F11

A tourist-conscious town in the Warrumbungle Mountains on the Castlereagh River, 465 km NW of Sydney, near Warrumbungle National Park. **Of interest:** Woollen Yarn and Exhibition, Dalgarno St, displays of local wool industry and range of woollen products. Crystal Kingdom, Oxley Hwy, exhibits unique collection of minerals from Warrumbungle Range. Easter: Carnival (includes market on Easter Sat.). Oct.: Sky and space astrofest. **In the area:** Skywatch Night'n'Day Observatory, 2 km NW on National Park road, has interactive display and planetarium. Pilliga Pottery, 34 km NW, off Newell Hwy, mudbrick workshop and showrooms in bushland setting, also German-style tearooms. Pilliga Scrub 'A million wild acres' near Baradine, 44 km NW, a 450 000-ha forest (biggest in NSW) mainly white cypress pine and ironbark plains of dense heath and scrub; location of picnic areas, forest drives and walking tracks from Baradine Forestry Office or Tourist information. Miniland, 8 km W, life-size models of prehistoric animals displayed in bushland setting, as well as an historical museum, children's fun park and waterslide, kiosk and picnic/barbecue facilities. Siding Spring Observatory set atop an extinct volcano, 24 km W, has largest optical telescope (3.9 m) in Australia (open day annually in Oct.), and permanent hands-on exhibition 'Exploring the Universe'. Warrumbungle National Park, 35 km W, features 'The Breadknife' a volcanic plug and offers bushwalking, rock climbing, colourful wildflowers, nature study, photography and camping facilities. **Tourist information:** Bicentennial Centre, Newell Hwy; (068) 42 1441. **Accommodation:** 3 hotels, 12 motels, 2 B&B, 2 hostels, 2 cara./camp. parks. **See also:** The Newell.

Coonamble   Pop. 2886

MAP REF. 118 C10

This town on the Castlereagh Hwy is situated on the Western Plains, 518 km NW of Sydney. It serves a district that produces wheat, wool, lamb, beef, cypress pine and hardwood timber. **Of interest:** Historical Museum, in former police station and stables, Aberford St. Warrana Creek Weir, for boating and swimming, on southern outskirts of town. June: Rodeo. Oct.: Cup race meeting. Nov.: Western Sandfly super-cross motorbike race. **In the area:** Macquarie Marshes, 80 km NW, a breeding-ground for waterbirds. Swimming at Hollywood Bore, 45 km NE. Warrumbungle National Park and Siding Spring Observatory, 80 km SE. **Tourist information:** Historical Museum, Aberford St; (068) 22 3040. **Accommodation:** 5 hotels, 3 motels, 1 cara./camp. park.

Cootamundra   Pop. 6386

MAP REF. 115 B3, 116 D10

This town on the Olympic Way, 427 km SW of Sydney, is less than 2 hours' drive from Canberra, and is well known for the Cootamundra wattle (*Acacia baileyana*). It has a strong retail sector and is a large stock-selling centre for the surrounding pastoral and agricultural rural holdings. **Of interest:** Self-guide 'Two Foot Tour' around town; contact Tourist information for brochure. Birthplace of Sir Donald Bradman, town's most famous son, at 89 Adams St; open weekends. Cootamundra Public School Museum, Cooper St; check opening times. Aug.: Wattle time festival and garden fair. **In the area:** Wineries in the Harden area, 78 km E. Inglenook Deer Farm at Wallendbeen, 19 km NE. Yandilla Mustard Seed Oil, 26 km N; tours by appt. **Tourist information:** Railway station, Hovell St; (069) 42 4212. **Accommodation:** 7 hotels, 4 motels, 1 cara./camp. park.

Corowa   Pop. 5064

MAP REF. 123 O13, 235 M3

Birthplace of Australia's Federation, Corowa took its name from *Currawa*, an Aboriginal word describing the pine trees that once grew there in profusion. A typical Australian country town, Corowa's wide main street, Sanger St, lined with turn-of-the-century verandahed buildings, runs down to the banks of the Murray River. Tom Roberts' painting *Shearing of the Rams* displayed in the National Gallery of Victoria, was completed at Brocklesby Station, just out of town, in 1889. **Of interest:** Federation Museum, Queen St. Self-guide historic walk (guide available on request for groups), lake and river cruises available; contact Tourist information. Market, 1st Sun. each month. Jan.: Federation festival. Dec.: National skydiving championships. **In the area:** Rutherglen wineries, begin 4 km S, only a short drive or bicycle ride away. **Tourist information:** Railway station building, John St; (060) 33 3221. **Accommodation:** 6 hotels, 17 motels, 4 cara./camp. parks.

Cowra   Pop. 8422

MAP REF. 116 F8

The peaceful air of this busy country town on the Lachlan River belies its dramatic recent history. On 5 August 1944, over 1000 Japanese prisoners attempted to escape from a nearby POW camp. Four Australian soldiers and 231 Japanese prisoners were killed in the ensuing struggle. **Of interest:** Australia's World Peace Bell, Darling St. Cowra Rose Garden, adjacent to Tourist information centre. Lachlan Valley Railway and Steam Museum, Campbell St, displays and train rides; check times. Sept.: World peace day (ceremony at Peace Bell). Oct.: Sakura Matsuri (Cherry blossom festival); Japanese cultural exhibition. **In the area:** Australian and Japanese War Cemeteries, 5 km N, beside Cowra-Canowindra Rd (Australian soldiers who died are buried in Australian War Cemetery; Japanese soldiers who died during escape, and Japanese internees who died elsewhere in Australia, are buried in Japanese War Cemetery). Sakura Ave, 5 km of flowering cherry trees, links site with POW camp, Breakout Walking Track and Japanese Garden and Cultural Centre; Cultural Centre includes traditional teahouse, bonsai house, pottery and display of Japanese artifacts. Historic Croote Cottage, Gooloogong, 25 km NW, built by convicts and raided by bushrangers; open by appt. Conimbla National Park, 27 km W. Quarry Cellars winery, 4 km S, on Boorowa Rd. Wyangala Waters State Recreation Area, 40 km SE, a mecca for water sports and fishing enthusiasts. Mid State Pioneer Rail Museum, 5 km E on Sydney Rd. **Tourist information:** Olympic Park, junction Boorowa, Grenfell and Young Rds; (063) 42 4333. **Accommodation:** 4 hotels, 2 hotel/ motels, 8 motels, 12 B&B, 3 cara./camp. parks.

Crookwell   Pop. 1966

MAP REF. 115 F2, 116 H10

Located 45 km NW of Goulburn, Crookwell is the centre of a rich agricultural and pastoral district, producing wool, beef, fat lambs, apples, pears and cherries, and is the State's major supplier of certified seed potatoes. **Of interest:** Stevensons Mill, Roberts St, a flour mill restored by local historians; open Wed. or by appt. Weaving Mill and Gallery, Denison Lane; open Wed.–Sun. Self-drive bushranger trails, contact Tourist information. Market, 1st Sat. each month. **In the area:** Many quaint historic villages associated with gold and copper mining, and bushranging including Tuena, Peelwood, Laggan, Bigga, Binda (all north of town) and Roslyn (south, and birthplace of poet Dame Mary Gilmore). Redground Lookout, 8 km NE. Willow Vale Mill at Laggan, 9 km NE, restored flour mill with restaurant and accommodation. Wombeyan Caves, 60 km NE, has five caves open to public. Abercrombie Caves, 64 km N along Bathurst Rd; set in a 220-hectare reserve featuring the largest natural bridge in the southern hemisphere; tours available. Snowy Mountain Lookout, 42 km NE. Upper reaches of Lake Wyangala and Grabine State Recreation Area, 65 km NW, for waterskiing, picnicking, fishing, bushwalking and camping. **Tourist information:** Crookwell Promotion Centre, 44 Goulburn St; (048) 32 1988. **Accommodation:** 4 hotels, 2 motels, 1 cara./ camp. park.

Culburra   Pop. 3145

MAP REF. 112 G13, 117 K11

Famous for its prawning and fishing, this town is situated 23 km SE of Nowra near Wollumboola Lake. **Of interest:** Surfing, swimming, and lake, shore and rock fishing. The beach is patrolled in summer holidays. Jan.: Open fishing carnival. **Tourist information:** Shoalhaven Tourist Centre, 254 Princes Hwy, Bomaderry; (044) 21 0778. **Accommodation:** 1 motel, 2 cara./camp. parks.

Culcairn   Pop. 1175

MAP REF. 123 Q12, 235 Q1

Dating back to 1880 and planned to service the railway between Sydney and Melbourne, Culcairn today reflects the district's rural prosperity. Bushranger Dan Morgan began his life of crime at Round Hill Station, with a hold-up on 19 June 1864. The town owes its picturesque tree-lined streets and parks to its unlimited underground water supply (discovered in 1926). **Of interest:** Historic Culcairn Hotel (1891), Railway Pde. Many National Trust-classified buildings in Railway Pde and on Olympic Way. Also in Railway Pde, French's Furniture, rustic Australian-style furniture. Local crafts at N & H Crafts, Balfour St. Centenary Mural, Main St. Artesian pumping station, Gordon St. **In the area:** John McLean's Grave, 3 km E; a price was put on Morgan's head after he shot McLean. Round Hill Station, Holbrook Rd. At Walla Walla, 18 km W: Old Schoolhouse (1875), museum and largest Lutheran church (1924) in NSW; Morgan's Lookout, 4 km N. Premier Yabbies, 7 km S. Pioneer Museum at Jindera, 42 km S. **Tourist information:** Post office, 33a Balfour St; (060) 29 8521. **Accommodation:** 1 hotel, 1 motel, 1 cara./camp. park.

Deniliquin   Pop. 7895

MAP REF. 123 L11

At the centre of the largest irrigation complex in Australia, beside the Edward River, 750 km SW of Sydney, Deniliquin has the largest rice mill in the southern hemisphere. The northern part of the district is famed for merino sheep studs, including Wanganella and Boonoke. **Of interest:** Sunrice Visitors Centre, at rice mill; Ricemill Rd. Peppin Heritage Centre (1879), a museum dedicated to the development of merino sheep industry by the Peppin family last century; George St. Waring Gardens, Cressy St. Island Sanctuary, off Cressy St footbridge, free-ranging emus and kangaroos, and prolific birdlife. River beaches, including McLean and Willoughby's beaches. Market, 4th Sat. each month. Jan.: Sun festival. Easter: Jazz festival. **In the area:** Pioneer Tourist Resort and Garden Centre, 6 km N, features antique steam and pump display. Bird Observatory Tower at Mathoura, 34 km S. Irrigation works

National Parks

The national parks of New South Wales encompass areas ranging from World Heritage-listed rainforests to unspoiled beaches. Tourists return time and time again to these popular scenic retreats, which offer a wide range of activities for holidaymakers. Many of the State's parks are found along the coast, their rugged headlands, quiet inlets and sweeping beaches pounded by the crashing surf. The easy accessibility of these coastal parks accounts for their popularity.

Around Sydney

Sydney Harbour National Park is made up of pockets of bushland encircling Sydney Harbour and is the closest national park to the city. Daily visits to Fort Denison and Goat Island leave from Circular Quay.

Just south of Sydney is **Botany Bay National Park** which is divided into two sections: the northern section contains the sandy beaches of La Perouse and a maritime museum (guided tours available), while the southern section at Kurnell protects the site of Captain Cook's first Australian landing in 1770. Here the Discovery Centre features exhibitions of the history of the area.

The **Royal National Park**, just 32 kilometres south of Sydney, was the first national park to be proclaimed in Australia. It was established in 1879, and has over 16 000 hectares of sandstone plateau country, broken here and there by fine surf beaches, including Wattamolla and Garie. The Hacking River runs almost the entire length of the park. Boats may be hired at Audley and visitors can row in leisurely fashion up the river, following its twisting course.

Lane Cove National Park, located within the northern urban area of Sydney, offers good walks and is extremely popular with families. There are many picnic areas next to the river, some of which can be reserved. The river is good for boating (non-powered only) and fishing, and visitors can enjoy a ride on the paddlewheeler *Turrumburra*. A wildlife shelter and wildlife shop are popular features of the park.

Further inland, to the west of Sydney, are splendid parks nestling in the mountains that overawed the early explorers. Year after year, innumerable visitors return to the **Blue Mountains National Park**, where mysterious blue mists shroud the immense valleys of the Grose and Coxs rivers, creating ever-changing patterns of green, blue and purple. At Katoomba, pillars of weathered sandstone rise abruptly like isolated church spires: these are the Three Sisters, the most popular tourist attraction in the Blue Mountains. The Grose and Jamison Valleys offer many walks with spectacular views.

Just north of Sydney are two prominent national parks, on the southern and northern shores of the Hawkesbury River: **Ku-Ring-Gai**

Patonga and headlands in Brisbane Water National Park

National Parks

Chase and Brisbane Water National Parks, which offer sheltered creeks and inlets, ideal for boating, and bushland walking tracks adorned with wildflowers.

Ku-Ring-Gai Chase, established in 1894 and only 24 kilometres from Sydney, hugs the shores of Cowan Creek, Broken Bay and Pitt Water. Comprising 15 000 hectares of open rainforest, eucalypt forest, scrub and heath, it is the home of a wide range of animal life, including the shy swamp wallaby, the elusive lyrebird, honeyeaters, waterbirds, colourful parrots and lorikeets. A small colony of koalas live in the eucalypt forest. A network of walking tracks leads to Aboriginal hand stencils and rock engravings.

Brisbane Water also has sandstone landscapes rich in Aboriginal art. There are scenic views from Warrah Trig and Staples Lookout, while Somersby Falls and Girakool picnic areas mark the beginning of rainforest walks.

Nearby on the coast is Bouddi National Park which protects the coast and bush at the eastern entrance to Broken Bay and on the coastal foreshore from Killcare Heights to McMasters Beach; it also covers a large offshore area near the beautiful Maitland Bay. An extensive network of walking tracks leads to secluded, unspoiled beaches and pockets of rainforest.

Upsteam along the Hawkesbury River is Dharug National Park, its sandstone cliffs rising high above the meandering river. A network of walking tracks includes a section of the convict-built Old Great North Road.

In the north-east of the State

The largest coastal lake system in New South Wales is protected by the Myall Lakes National Park, an important waterbird habitat. Water is the focus of tourist activities: you can enjoy sailing and canoeing on the quiet lake waters, or surfing and beach fishing off the shores of the Pacific Ocean.

Barrington Tops, one of the State's most popular national parks, is a World Heritage Area with wilderness values. It has a mountainous plateau (1600 metres), providing spectacular views of the surrounding Hunter Valley and, in the distance, the Pacific Ocean, but visitors must be prepared for sudden bad weather. The stands of snow gums here give way, at about 1000 metres, to forests of Antarctic beech, with lichens, mosses and tree ferns. The lowest areas of the park feature subtropical rainforests, rivers, waterfalls and rapids. Many of the walking tracks in the park are suitable for families. Longer walks, ranging from 4–5 hours to overnight, are suitable for more experienced bushwalkers.

The World Heritage New England National Park, which preserves one of the largest remaining areas of rainforest in New South Wales, is 576 kilometres north-east of Sydney. Its 29 985 hectares cover three distinct zones: subalpine with tall snow gums; temperate forests of ancient moss-covered Antarctic beeches; and true subtropical rainforests, rich in ferns, vines and orchids. The park has a diverse range of flora and fauna, including the rare rufous scrub-bird. Some 20 kilometres of walking tracks reveal to visitors the charm of the rainforest, while the trackless wilderness attracts more experienced bushwalkers. Nearby, the World Heritage Dorrigo National Park protects the rainforests of northern New South Wales. At the Rainforest Centre, visitors can experience the sights, sounds and smells of rainforests. The Skywalk provides magnificent views over the rainforest canopy to the Bellinger Valley and Pacific Ocean beyond.

Yuraygir and Bundjalung National Parks, to the north and south respectively of the Clarence River on the far north coast, are a water wonderland with isolated beaches, quiet lakes and striking scenery. The parks deserve their reputation as prime areas for fishing. Surfing is also popular; waterways invite exploration by canoe; and the estuaries offer safe swimming. Heathwalking offers opportunities for birdwatching and nature photography, particularly in spring when both parks explode in a spectacle of colour.

In the far north of the State, Border Ranges, Mount Warning and Nightcap National Parks offer the visitor vistas of World Heritage-listed rainforest. The 31 508-hectare Border Ranges National Park includes the rim of the ancient volcano once centred on Mt Warning to the east. The best access is via the spectacular Tweed Scenic Drive. Stunning escarpments, waterfalls, and walking tracks from picnic areas abound in the eastern part.

Known to the Aborigines as 'Wollumbin', the cloud-catcher, Mt Warning (1157 metres) dominates the landscape and catches the first rays of the rising sun on the continent. A walk through Breakfast Creek rainforest leads to a steep climb and the summit viewing platform. Nightcap National Park is part of the volcanic remnants of Mt Warning and includes the popular summit viewing platform and Protector Falls.

Further inland are two well-known national parks: Warrumbungle and Mount Kaputar.

NEW SOUTH WALES

Warrumbungle National Park, on the western slopes of the Great Divide, is 491 kilometres north-west of Sydney. Here is some of the most spectacular scenery in the nation: sheltered gorges, rocky spires, permanent freshwater springs. At Warrumbungle, east meets west: the dry western plains and moist eastern coast combine to give high peaks covered with gums and lower forests filled with fragrant native trees and shrubs. Walking trails lead to lookout points where hikers are rewarded with magnificent views. In the spring and summer months the colourful displays of wildflowers and the calls of brightly plumaged birds lure many visitors. There are also easy access tracks for families and the disabled.

Mount Kaputar National Park, near Narrabri, is one of Australia's most accessible wilderness areas. Several lookouts can be reached by car or are only a short walk from your car. Its vegetation ranges from rainforest to subalpine, and the park is rich in flora and fauna. One of the highlights of the park is Sawn Rocks, a 40-metre-high rock formation resembling a series of organ pipes. This is some of the finest columnar jointing in the country and represents one of the various volcanic formations found in the park. Limited cabin accommodation is available within the park.

The remarkable Walls of China in Mungo National Park

In the south-east of the State

There are a number of national parks in the southern part of the State, including **Morton National Park**, particularly known for the Fitzroy, Belmore and Carrington Falls, and **Budderoo National Park**, which includes the award-winning Minnamurra Rainforest Centre, where an elevated boardwalk takes you into the rainforest canopy.

Over 9000 hectares of rocky but beautiful coastline flanking Twofold Bay make up **Ben Boyd National Park**. Flowering heaths and colourful banksias add to the area's attraction. Boyd's Tower, constructed in the 1840s, is a prominent feature of the park.

The largest national park in New South Wales is **Kosciusko**. Its 647 097 hectares include mainland Australia's only glacial lakes, as well as limestone caves, grasslands, heaths and woodlands. Situated 450 kilometres south-west of Sydney, this park is of particular significance because it embraces a large area of the continent's largest alpine region and contains Australia's highest mountains as well as the sources of the important Murray, Snowy and Murrumbidgee Rivers. The most extensive snowfields of the nation are located here, centred around Thredbo, Perisher, Smiggin Holes, Mt Blue Cow, Mt Selwyn and Charlotte Pass. There are easy grades for beginners and slopes for expert skiers. Although Kosciusko is associated with winter sports, it is also a superb summer retreat with its crisp, clean air, crystal-clear lakes and a wonderful display of alpine wildflowers. It is a popular venue for those who enjoy camping, fishing, boating and bushwalking. Yarrangobilly Caves, perhaps the first site within the park to be developed for tourism, is open all-year round, subject to winter road conditions. Yarrangobilly boasts five tourist caves – one with wheelchair access – a naturally heated thermal pool, nature trails and facilities for BYO picnics.

In the west of the State

In the far west of New South Wales are four outstanding national parks. **Kinchega**, 110 kilometres south-east of Broken Hill, contains the beautiful saucer-shaped overflow lakes of the Darling River. The lakes provide a most important breeding ground for a wide variety of waterbirds, including herons, ibises, spoonbills and black swans. Walking tracks pass through forests of river red gums, and scenic drives follow the course of the river and the lake shores.

North-east of Wentworth is the World Heritage-listed **Mungo National Park**, part of the Willandra Lakes World Heritage Area. The shores of the now dry lake hold a continuous record of Aboriginal life dating back more than 40 000 years. The remarkable Walls of China, a great crescent-shaped dune, stretches along the eastern shore of the lake bed. Visitors can enjoy the park on a day trip or take advantage of the shearers' quarters accommodation or camping facilities. Self-guide walking tracks and a 60-kilometre self-guide drive tour provide visitors with the opportunity to see and learn about the many attractions of the park.

Mootwingee National Park, covering an area of 68 912 hectares and 130 kilometres north-east of Broken Hill, offers breathtaking scenery and a rich heritage of Aboriginal art.

The most remote national park in the State is **Sturt**, 1400 kilometres from Sydney and 330 kilometres north of Broken Hill. This is an ideal place for those who want to get away from it all and experience the real Australian outback. The park's 310 634 hectares comprise scenic red sand dunes, rocky ridges, ephemeral lakes and billabongs, and Mitchell grass plains. Visitors must come well prepared but may camp in the park and enjoy bushwalking over the sandplains. Wildflowers, which include the scarlet and black Sturt's desert pea, are abundant in good seasons. Fort Grey, where Sturt and his party built a stockade to protect their supplies, is worth a visit, even though there is little evidence of his occupation today.

For further information about the national parks of New South Wales, contact the National Parks and Wildlife Service, 43 Bridge St (PO Box 1967), Hurstville, NSW 2220; (02) 9585 6333. National Parks and Wildlife Service has produced an excellent brochure *Visitor Guide to National Parks in NSW* which can be obtained from their centres or by mail.

at Lawsons Syphon, 6 km E and Stevens Weir, 26 km W. **Tourist information:** Peppin Heritage Centre, George St; (058) 81 2878. **Accommodation:** 6 hotels, 3 hotel/motels, 8 motels, 1 hostel, 5 cara./camp. parks.

Dorrigo   Pop. 1135

MAP REF. 119 O8

This important timber town is surrounded by magnificent river, mountain and forest scenery. **Of interest:** Old railway station, Tallowood St, has large collection of locomotive and rolling stock. Calico Cottage, Hickory St, for local crafts. **In the area:** Excellent trout fishing in district. Dangar Falls, 2 km N. On Tyringham Rd: Dorrigo Pottery, 8 km W. At Bostobrick, 14 km W, Golden Bowl Pottery. Dutton Trout Hatchery near Ebor, 63 km W. Nearby, Ebor Falls, favourite with photographers. Point Lookout, 60 km W, in New England National Park, for stunning views over head of Bellinger Valley across to ocean; claimed to be one of the best views on the east coast. Dorrigo National Park, 5 km E, has a Skywalk (begins at Rainforest Centre) offering birds' eye views over canopy of World Heritage-listed rainforest. **Tourist information:** Hickory St; (066) 57 2486. **Accommodation:** 2 hotel/motels, 1 cara./camp. park.

Dubbo   Pop. 28 064

MAP REF. 116 E2

This pleasant city on the banks of the Macquarie River, 420 km NW of Sydney, is recognised as the regional capital of western NSW, and supports many agricultural and secondary industries. **Of interest:** In Macquarie St: Old Dubbo Gaol, featuring original gallows and solitary confinement cells, and animatronic robots telling story of convicts; Dubbo Museum. Dubbo Regional Art Gallery, Darling St. Indoor Kart Centre, Mountbatten Dr. May: Agricultural show. June: Eisteddfod. **In the area:** Western Plains Zoo, 5 km S, Australia's first open-range zoo with over 300 ha of landscaped park and animals from six continents, some roaming in natural surroundings. Military Museum, 8 km S, with open-air exhibits; 4 km further S, Yarrabar Pottery. Restored Dundullimal Homestead (1840s), 7 km SE on Obley Rd. Golfworld has driving range and mini-golf course; Fitzroy St, 3 km N. Jinchilla Gardens and Gallery, 12 km N, off Gilgandra Rd. **Tourist information:** cnr Erskine and Macquarie Sts; (068) 84 1422. **Accommodation:** 6 hotels, 33 motels, 1 B&B, 1 hostel, 5 cara./camp. parks. **See also:** The Newell.

Dungog   Pop. 2187

MAP REF. 108 A1, 117 N3

These days an ideal base for bushwalking enthusiasts, Dungog was established in 1838 as a military post to prevent bushranging in the area. Situated on the upper reaches of the Williams River, it is on one of the main access routes to Barrington Tops National Park. Aug.: Canoe Classic. Sept.: Spring festival. **In the area:** Lake Chichester, 23 km N, in picturesque mountain setting; nearby Duncan Park is ideal for picnicking. Telegherry Forest Park, 30 km N, with walking trails to waterfalls along Telegherry River and picnic, swimming and camping spots. Barrington Tops National Park, 40 km N, noted for its unusual native flora and rich variety of wildlife; good bushwalking and forest drives. Superb views from Mt Allyn (1100 m), 40 km NW. Clarence Town historic village, 25 km S. **Tourist information:** Shire Offices, cnr Brown and Dowling Sts; (049) 92 1224. **Accommodation:** 3 hotels, 1 motel.

Eden   Pop. 3277

MAP REF. 113 F11, 115 G11, 237 Q8

Eden is a quiet former whaling town on Twofold Bay, 512 km S of Sydney, with an outstanding natural harbour. Fishing and timber-getting are the main industries. **Of interest:** Eden Killer Whale Museum, Imlay St, features skeleton of notorious 'Tom the killer whale'. Bay cruises available. Mar.: Amateur fish club competition. **In the area:** Whale-watching Oct.–Nov. Ben Boyd National Park, extending 8 km N and 19 km S of Eden, has outstanding scenery and is ideal for fishing, swimming, camping and bushwalking; prominent park features include Boyd's Tower (1840s) at Red Point and the red and white earth formations, the Pinnacles, located 8 km N. On perimeter of park, 9 km S, at Nullica Bay, former rival settlement of Boydtown has convict-built Sea Horse Inn, still licensed, safe beach and excellent fishing. Davidson Whaling Station Historic Site on Kiah Inlet, 14 km S. Harris Daishowa Chipmill Visitors Centre, Jews Head, 26 km S (other side of Twofold Bay), has video and static displays on logging and milling operations; tours, Thurs. 10.30 a.m. Good fishing at Wonboyn Lake, 40 km S; scenic area in between Ben Boyd National Park and Nadgee Nature Reserve. **Tourist information:** Princes Hwy; (064) 96 1953. **Accommodation:** 2 hotels, 10 motels, 6 B&B, 1 hostel, 6 cara./camp. parks. **See also:** The South Coast.

Eugowra   Pop. 572

MAP REF. 116 E6

It was near this small town on the Orange–Forbes road that 'the great gold-escort robbery' occurred in 1862. **Of interest:** Eugowra Museum, displaying Aboriginal artifacts, gemstones, early farm equipment and wagons. Nangar Gems, Norton St, for sapphires, opals, emeralds and garnets. **In the area:** Escort Rock, 3 km E, where bushranger Frank Gardiner and gang hid before ambush of Forbes gold escort; rock is on private property, but plaque on road gives details, unlocked gate allows entry. **Tourist information:** Visitors Centre, Civic Gardens, Byng St, Orange; (063) 61 5226. **Accommodation:** 2 hotels.

Evans Head   Pop. 2375

MAP REF. 119 Q4, 491 Q13

This holiday and fishing town, and centre of the NSW prawning industry, is situated off the Pacific Hwy via Woodburn. It has safe surf beaches and sandy river flats. Rock, beach and ocean fishing, boating and windsurfing are popular activities. Aug.: Bowling carnival. **In the area:** Bundjalung National Park, just south, renowned for its fishing; also Aboriginal relics. Broadwater National Park, 5 km N, for bushwalking, birdwatching, fishing and swimming. At Woodburn, 10 km NW, Riverside Park beside Richmond River; further 14 km S at New Italy, monument and remains of settlement, result of ill-fated Marquis de Rays' expedition in 1880. **Tourist information:** The Professionals Real Estate, 9 Oak St; (066) 82 4611. **Accommodation:** 1 hotel, 1 motel, 1 cara./camp. park.

Finley   Pop. 2220

MAP REF. 123 M12, 234 I1

This town on the Newell Hwy, 20 km

Gerringong, a delightful seaside town on the Illawarra Coast

from the Victorian border, is the centre of the Berriquin irrigation scheme. **Of interest:** Log Cabin (replica) and Museum, with display of rural heritage, Mary Lawson Wayside Rest, Newell Hwy; open daily. Finley Lake, Newell Hwy, for boating and sailing, picnic areas on lake banks. Sept.: Agricultural show. **Tourist information:** River Foreshore, Tocumwal; (058) 74 2131. **Accommodation:** 3 hotels, 5 motels, 1 cara./camp. park.

Forbes   Pop. 7552

MAP REF. 116 D6

Noted bushranger Ben Hall is buried in this former goldmining town, 386 km W of Sydney beside the Lachlan River. He was shot by police just outside the town in 1865. Today the town's industries include an abattoir, feed lots, and export of beef and hay. **Of interest:** Many historic buildings, especially in Camp and Lachlan Sts. Historic museum, Cross St, featuring relics associated with Ben Hall. Forbes Cemetery, Bogan Gate Rd, has graves of Ben Hall, Ned Kelly's sister, Kate Foster, and Captain Cook's niece, Rebecca Shields. Memorial in King George V Park, Lawler St, where 'German Harry' discovered gold in 1861. In small park in Dowling St, memorial marks spot where explorer John Oxley first passed through Forbes. Sept.: Show Day. **In the area:** Sandhills Vineyard, 6 km E on Eugowra Rd.

Lachlan Valley Wines, 5 km SE. Lachlan Vintage Village, 1 km S, a re-creation of gold-rush era with emphasis on lifestyles. Gum Swamp Sanctuary for native fauna, 4 km W. **Tourist information:** Old Railway Station, Union St; (068) 52 4155. **Accommodation:** 9 hotels, 6 motels, 4 cara./camp. parks. **See also:** The Newell.

Forster   Pop. 14 578

MAP REF. 117 P2

Forster is connected by a bridge to its twin town Tuncurry on the opposite side of Wallis Lake, a holiday area in the Great Lakes district. Launches and boats may be hired for lake and deep-sea fishing, and tours are available. The area is well known for its fishing. **Of interest:** Forster Art and Craft Centre, Breese Pde. Aug.: Australian veteran cycling championships. **In the area:** Curtis Collection of vintage cars, 3 km S. The Green Cathedral, an unusual 'open-air cathedral' at Tiona on shores of Wallis Lake, 13 km S. Booti Booti National Park, 17 km S. Sugar Creek Toymakers at Bungwahl, 22 km S. Wallingat State Forest, 25 km S. Myall Lakes National Park, 35 km S; houseboat hire available. Camping and beaches at Seal Rocks, 40 km S. **Tourist information:** Great Lakes Tourism, Little St; (065) 54 8799. **Accommodation:** 2 hotels, 19 motels, 1 hostel, 12 cara./camp. parks.

Gerringong   Pop. 2478

MAP REF. 112 G10, 117 K11

Spectacular views of white sand and rolling breakers can be seen from this town, 11 km S of Kiama on the Illawarra Coast. Market, 2nd Sun. each month. **In the area:** Surfing, fishing and swimming at local beaches. Gerroa and Seven Mile beaches, 3 km S, world-famous as windsurfing locations. Memorial to pioneer aviator Sir Charles Kingsford Smith and lookout at northern end of Seven Mile Beach, site of his takeoff to New Zealand in the *Southern Cross* in 1933. Bushwalks through Seven Mile Beach National Park, 13 km S; camping and picnic areas. Wild Country Park in natural rainforest setting at Foxground, 8 km W. **Tourist information:** Visitors Centre, Blowhole Pt, Kiama; (042) 32 3322. **Accommodation:** 1 hotel, 3 motels, 3 cara./camp. parks.

Gilgandra   Pop. 2890

MAP REF. 118 D13

An historic town at the junction of three highways, Gilgandra is the centre for the surrounding wool and farming country. It was the home of the famous 'Coo-ee March', which left from Gilgandra for Sydney in 1915 in a drive to recruit more soldiers for World War I. The area is also known for its windmills, which once provided sub-artesian water. **Of interest:** Australian Collection, Miller St, features Aboriginal artifacts, display of minerals, fossils and marine specimens, and Gwen Collison watercolours. The Observatory and Display Centre, cnr Wamboin and Willie Sts. Museum, Newell Hwy, displays memorabilia from 'Coo-ee March'. Film *The Chant of Jimmy Blacksmith* was based on Breelong Massacre, which took place near Gilgandra; related items in museum. Orana Cactus World, Newell Hwy. Coo-ee Tourist Walk, historic walk based on 1915 march; tourist drive around town and to Flora Reserve; brochures available at Tourist information. Easter: Goat races; Rodeo. May: Agricultural show. Oct.: Coo-ee festival. **In the area:** Gilgandra Flora Reserve, 14 km NE, has wildflowers in spring. Warrumbungle National Park, 82 km NE. **Tourist information:** Coo-ee March Memorial Park, Newell Hwy; (068) 47 2045. **Accommodation:** 3 hotels, 8 motels, 4 cara./camp. parks.

Glen Innes
Pop. 6140

MAP REF. 119 L6

Gazetted in 1852, this mountain town was the scene of many bushranging exploits. In a beautiful setting, at an elevation of 1073 m, it is now the centre of a lush farming district where sapphire mining is an important industry. **Of interest:** Many original public buildings, particularly in Grey St; self-guide walks, contact Tourist information for brochures. Centennial Parklands with Martin's Lookout, Meade St, now site of Celtic monument 'Australian Standing Stones'. Land of the Beardies History House, cnr Ferguson St and West Ave, a folk museum housed in town's first hospital and set in extensive grounds, with reconstructed slab hut, period room settings and pioneer relics. May: Celtic festival. Sept.: Minerama gem festival. Oct.: Australian music festival. Nov.: Land of the Beardies bush festival. **In the area:** Scenic mountain and riverside country. Good fishing for trout, perch and cod. Fossicking for sapphire, topaz and quartz, within 45-km radius of town. Horse treks, with accommodation at historic bush pubs. Convict-carved tunnel, halfway between Glen Innes and Grafton, on Old Grafton Rd. Gibraltar Range National Park, 70 km NE, has impressive falls, and The Needles and Anvil Rock granite formations. World Heritage-listed Washpool National Park, 75 km NE, a rainforest wilderness area. Fishing safaris at Deepwater, 25 km N. Fossicking at old mining town, Emmaville, 38 km NW. Fossicking and unique rock formations at Torrington, 66 km NW. Gem fossicking and unusual balancing rock formation, 18 km S. Guy Fawkes River National Park, 77 km SE, wild river area ideal for bushwalking, canoeing and fishing. **Tourist information:** Church St; (067) 32 2397. **Accommodation:** 4 hotels, 10 motels, 6 cara./camp. parks. See also: New England.

Gloucester
Pop. 2465

MAP REF. 117 N1

This town lies at the foot of a range of monolithic hills, The Bucketts. It is at the junction of three tributaries of the Manning River, which has excellent trout and perch fishing. **Of interest:** The Bucketts Walk (1½ hrs return) up Bucketts Mountain Range offers good views; immediately west of town. Gloucester District Park, outstanding sporting complex. Sept.: Mountain man triathlon (mountain-biking, kayaking and running). **In the area:** Scenic flights, aerodrome; 4 km S. Views from Mograni Lookout (5 km E), Kia-ora Lookout (4 km N) and Berrico Trig Station (14 km W). Mountain Maid Gold Mine at Copeland, 16 km W. Excellent bushwalking and forest drives in Barrington Tops National Park, 60 km W. **Tourist information:** cnr Church and Denison Sts; (065) 58 1408. **Accommodation:** 1 hotel, 1 hotel/motel, 2 motels, 2 B&B, 1 cara./camp. park.

Gosford
Pop. 38 205

MAP REF. 101 P4, 104 F6, 117 M6

Gosford is 85 km N of Sydney on the beautiful Brisbane Water. Oct.: Mangrove Mountain District country fair; Agricultural show. **In the area:** Henry Kendall Cottage (1838), 3 km SW in Henry Kendall St, where poet lived 1874–5; picnic/barbecue facilities in pleasant grounds. Australian Reptile Park and Wildlife Sanctuary, 9 km SW, features taipans, pythons, goannas, and a platypus. Opposite, Old Sydney Town, a reconstruction of early pioneer settlement. Somersby Falls, near Old Sydney Town, ideal picnic spot. Aboriginal engraving site Bulgandry in Brisbane Water National Park, 10 km SW; also spectacular waratahs in spring. Bouddi National Park, 17 km SE, for bushwalking, camping, fishing and swimming. Central Park Family Fun Centre, Forresters Beach, 31 km E. The Ferneries, a rainforest area with children's playground, picnic/barbecue facilities, paddle-boats and Devonshire teas; Oak Rd, Matcham, 11 km NE. Elizabeth's Berry Farm, a blueberry farm with tearooms; 12 km NE. Award-winning Forest of Tranquillity at Ourimbah, 14 km NW. **Tourist information:** 200 Mann St; (043) 25 2835. **Accommodation:** 3 hotels, 10 motels, 1 cara./camp. park.

Goulburn
Pop. 21 451

MAP REF. 115 G3, 116 H11

This provincial city, steeped in history (proclaimed a city in 1833), can be accessed from the Hume Hwy bypass some 209 km SW of Sydney. It is the centre of a wealthy farming district at the junction of the Wollondilly and Mulwarry Rivers beyond the Southern Highlands. **Of interest:** National Trust-classified coaching-house Riversdale (1840), Maud St. St Clair History House (c.1843), Sloane St, a 20-room mansion restored by local historical society. Garroorigang, Braidwood Rd, South Goulburn (1857), private home in almost original condition; open by appt. Old Goulburn Brewery Hotel, Bungonia Rd. Goulburn Court House, Montague St. In Bourke St: Regional Art Gallery; Cathedral of St Saviour. Cathedral of St Peter and St Paul, cnr Bourke and Verner Sts. Goulburn Yurt Works, Copford Rd, tours (by appt) of factory making prefabricated round houses. Make-your-own fabrics at Fibre Designs gallery, Montague St. Wood-turning Gallery, Grafton St. Lindner Sock Factory, Cathcart St, open for inspection and sock sales. The Big Merino, a 15-m sculptured relief, Hume Hwy, has displays of wool products and Australiana items for sale. Goulburn Steam Museum, Fitzroy St, includes rides on Leisureland Express; check times. South Hill, Garoorigang Rd, features woollen art. Excellent picnic/barbecue facilities on Wollondilly River at Marsden Weir. Rocky Hill War Memorial, Memorial Dr., city's best-known landmark, built in memory of local World War I soldiers. **In the area:** Shearing and sheepdog demonstrations (by appt) at Pelican Sheep Station, 10 km S. Geologically interesting Bungonia State Recreation Area, 35 km E; range of walks available, including one through the spectacular Bungonia Gorge; information about walks available from visitors' centre. **Tourist information:** 6 Montague St; (048) 21 5343. **Accommodation:** 7 hotels, 1 hotel/motel, 13 motels, 3 cara./camp. parks.

Grafton
Pop. 16 642

MAP REF. 119 P6

A garden city, famous for its riverbank parks and the jacaranda, wheel and flame trees lining its wide streets, Grafton is situated at the junction of the Pacific and Gwydir Hwys, 665 km N of Sydney. **Of interest:** Numerous National Trust buildings. Schaeffer House (1900), Fitzroy St, now district historical museum. Stately Prentice House, Fitzroy St, one of Australia's finest regional art galleries. Susan Island in Clarence River, a recreation reserve covered with rainforest and home to large fruit-bat colony. **Oct.:** Bridge to bridge ski race. **Oct.-Nov.:** Jacaranda festival. **In the area:** Four major national parks within hour's drive: Yuraygir (50 km E), Bundjalung (70 km N), Washpool (88 km NW) and Gibraltar Range (92 km NW). National Trust-classified Ulmarra village, 12 km NE, a fine example of turn-of-the-century river port. Houseboat hire at Brushgrove, 20 km NE. Weekend gliding at Eatonsville, 18 km NW. Canoeing and rafting on wild-river systems in surrounding area; also many scenic drives. **Tourist information:** cnr Spring St and Pacific Hwy, South Grafton; (066) 42 4677. **Accommodation:** 17 hotels, 14 motels, 3 cara./camp. parks.

Grenfell   Pop. 2037

MAP REF. 115 B1, 116 D8

The birthplace of poet and short-story writer Henry Lawson, this small town is 377 km W of Sydney, on the Mid Western Hwy. **Of interest:** Museum, Camp St; open weekends. Off Camp St, O'Brien's Lookout, where gold was discovered, has walkway and picnic facilities. Henry Lawson Obelisk, next to Lawson Park on road south to Young, on site of house where poet is believed to have been born in 1867. **Easter:** Guinea pig races. **June:** Henry Lawson festival of arts. **In the area:** Weddin Mountains National Park, 18 km SW, for bushwalking, camping and picnicking; area used as hideout by bushrangers Ben Hall, Frank Gardiner, Johnnie Gilbert and others; easy walk to Ben Hall's Cave. **Tourist information:** CWA Craft Centre, 68 Main St; (063) 43 1612. **Accommodation:** 5 hotels, 1 motel, 1 hostel, 1 cara./camp. park.

Griffith   Pop. 13 296

MAP REF. 123 N7

A thriving city developed as a result of the introduction of irrigation, Griffith was designed by Walter Burley Griffin, architect of Canberra, and named after Sir Arthur Griffith, the first Minister for Public Works in the NSW government. Of a diversity of industries, rice is the most profitable, followed by citrus fruits, grapes, vegetables, eggs and poultry. Griffith is well known as a wine-producing area; there are over a dozen wineries in the district. The Murrumbidgee Irrigation Area produces 80 per cent of the State's wines. **Of interest:** Two Foot Tour walk around town, brochure available at Tourist information. Koala Gourmet Foods, Whybrow St; tours available. In Banna Ave: Regional Theatre has stage curtain designed and created by efforts of 300 residents to reflect city, surrounding villages and industries; Regional Art Gallery, has monthly exhibitions. Griffith Cottage Gallery, Bridge Rd. Crafty Spot, Benerembah St. Market, each Sun. in Wakaden St. **Easter:** Wine and food festival. **Oct.:** Festival of gardens. **In the area:** Pioneer Park Museum, set in 18 ha of bushland 2 km N, features drop-log buildings, memorabilia from early 20th century and Bagtown village, recreated to give insight into development of area. Lake Wyangan, 10 km NW, for water sports. Bagtown Cemetery, 5 km S, a reminder of pioneering days. Catania Fruit Salad Farm, a horticultural farm offering demonstrations of processes; Cox Rd, Hanwood, 6 km S, open weekdays p.m., weekends by appt. Cocoparra National Park, 25 km NE. Many wineries in area, most open for tastings and sales; contact Tourist information. **Tourist information:** cnr Banna and Jondaryan Aves; (069) 62 4145. **Accommodation:** 2 hotels, 1 hotel/motel, 8 motels, 1 hostel, 2 cara./camp. parks. **See also:** Vineyards and Wineries.

Gulgong   Pop. 2042

MAP REF. 116 H2

This old goldmining town, 29 km NW of Mudgee, is known as 'the town on the (original) $10 note'. In its heyday in the 1870s it was packed with fortune hunters from all over the world. Some of its glory remains in the many restored buildings; the town's narrow streets are lined with clapboard and iron buildings decorated in their original iron lace. **Of interest:** Henry Lawson Centre, Mayne St, boasts largest collection of Lawson memorabilia outside Sydney's Mitchell Library. Historic buildings on self-guide Town Trail (brochures available from Tourist information) include Prince of Wales Opera House, Mayne St; Ten Dollar Town Motel (formerly Royal Hotel), cnr Mayne and Medley Sts; American Tobacco Warehouse and Fancy Goods Emporium, Mayne St; Pioneers Museum, cnr Herbert and Bayly Sts. **Apr.:** Foundation Day. **June:** Henry Lawson festival. **In the area:** Ulan Coal Mine, viewing areas overlook this large open-cut mine; Hands on the Rock, rock paintings; The Drips, curtains of water dripping through rocks alongside Goulburn River – all 25 km N. **Tourist information:** 109 Herbert St; (063) 74 1202. **Accommodation:** 4 hotels, 3 motels, 1 cara./camp. park.

Gundagai   Pop. 2069

MAP REF. 115 B5, 116 D12

Much celebrated in song and verse, this town on the Murrumbidgee River at the foot of Mt Parnassus, 398 km SW of Sydney, has become part of Australian folklore. Its history includes Australia's worst flood disaster in 1852 when 89 people drowned, nearby gold rushes, and many bushranging attacks. Today it is the centre of a rich pastoral and agricultural district that produces wool, wheat, fruit and vegetables. **Of interest:** Marble carving of cathedral, comprising over 20 000 pieces, by Frank Rusconi (sculptor of tuckerbox dog) on display in Tourist Information Centre, Sheridan St. Also in Sheridan St: Gabriel Gallery, with its outstanding collection of early photographs, letters and possessions of poet Henry Lawson; National Trust-classified court house (1859), scene of many historic trials, including that of notorious bushranger Captain Moonlite; Prince Alfred Bridge (1866), longest timber viaduct in Australia, also National Trust-classified. Historical museum, Homer St. National Trust-classified St John's Anglican Church (1861), cnr Otway and Punch Sts. Excellent views from Mt Parnassus Lookout, Hanley St, and Rotary Lookout, Luke St, South Gundagai. **Oct.:** Spring flower show. **Nov.:** Dog on the Tuckerbox festival. **In the area:** Dog on the Tuckerbox, 'five miles from' or 8 km N, monument to pioneer teamsters and their dogs, celebrated in song by Jack O'Hagan; nearby larger-than-life copper statues of Dad and Dave characters from radio serial; kiosk; fern-house; and ruins of Five Mile Pub. Asparagus plantation at Jugiong, 21 km NE. **Tourist information:** Sheridan St; (069) 44 1341. **Accommodation:** 4 hotels, 6 motels, 1 B&B, 2 cara./camp. parks.

Gunnedah   Pop. 8874

MAP REF. 118 H10

A prosperous town on the banks of the Namoi River, Gunnedah is the centre of rich pastoral and agricultural country,

The Snowy Mountains

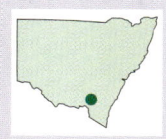

The Snowy Mountains are a magnet to tourists all year round. The combination of easily accessible mountains, alpine heathlands, forests, lakes, streams and dams is hard to beat. In winter, skiers flock to the snug, well-equipped snow resorts in the area. When the snow melts it is time for fishing, bushwalking, cycling, horse-riding, water-skiing and boating.

The creation of the Snowy Mountains Hydro-electric Scheme was indirectly responsible for boosting tourism. The roads built for the scheme through the previously difficult and sometimes inaccessible mountain country helped to open up the area, which is now used for a range of recreational activities year-round.

All the ski resorts of the Snowy Mountains are within Kosciusko National Park, which is the largest national park in the State and includes the highest plateau in the Australian continent. Mt Kosciusko (2228 m) is its highest peak. The major ski areas are: Thredbo, Perisher, Smiggin Holes, Mt Blue Cow and Charlotte Pass in the southern part of Kosciusko National Park; and Mt Selwyn in the northern part of the park.

The resorts are easily accessible and the major centres have first-class amenities such as motels, hotels, restaurants, lodges, apres-ski entertainment, chairlifts, ski-tows and expert instruction. The snow sports season officially begins on the long weekend in June and continues until the October long weekend.

Thredbo Village, 98 kilometres from Cooma at the foot of the Crackenback Range. Thredbo hosted the World Cup ski race in 1989, and has facilities for skiers at all levels, including ski hire and instruction. The chairlift to the summit of Mt Crackenback operates year-round. The village has a wide range of amenities, restaurants, cultural entertainment and outdoor recreation for every season.

Charlotte Pass, 104 kilometres from Cooma and 8 kilometres from the summit of Mt Kosciusko. A convenient base for ski tours to some of Australia's highest peaks and most spectacular ski runs.

Perisher, 94 kilometres from Cooma. One of the highest and most popular ski resorts in the area; all the facilities of a small town. Caters for both downhill and cross-country skiers. The new Nordic Centre caters especially for cross-country skiers. Ski hire and instruction available.

Smiggin Holes, 92 kilometres from Cooma. Linked to Perisher by ski-lifts and a free shuttle bus service. Essentially for beginners and intermediate skiers. Ski hire and instruction available.

Mt Blue Cow can be reached by skitube underground railway which runs from Bullocks Flat Terminal near Jindabyne up to Perisher and on to Mt Blue Cow, by road to Guthega, or from Perisher by the 'Interceptor' quad chairlift. Limited overnight accommodation at Guthega. No overnight accommodation at Mt Blue Cow. Ski hire and instruction available at Mt Blue Cow and Guthega.

A wide variety of accommodation is available at Perisher and Smiggin Holes. However, overnight parking is limited; overnight visitors are advised to use Skitube from Bullocks Flat on the Alpine Way. Perisher, Mt Blue Cow and Guthega resorts have merged to become Perisher Blue Ski Resort.

Mt Selwyn, at the northern end of Kosciusko National Park, has been designed for beginners, families and school groups. Mt Selwyn is one of the main centres for cross-country skiing. No overnight accommodation. Accommodation is available in nearby towns like Adaminaby. Ski hire and instruction available.

For further information on the Snowy Mountains, contact the National Parks and Wildlife Service Visitors Centre at Sawpit Creek; (064) 56 1700 or the Snowy Region Information Centre in Jindabyne; (064) 56 2444. **See also:** Safe Skiing. **Map reference:** 114.

Snow scene at Three Mile Dam on the Kiandra–Cabramurra road

Witcombe Memorial Fountain, Lachlan St, Hay

and is one of the largest stock-marketing and killing centres in NSW. Other industries include a brickworks, a tannery, flour mills and open-cut and underground coal mining. **Of interest:** In Anzac Park, South St: Water Tower Museum; Dorothea MacKellar Memorial statue. Rural Museum, Mullaley Rd. Red Chief Memorial to an Aboriginal warrior of Gunn-e-dar group, State Office building, Abbott St. Old Bank Gallery, Conadilly St. Creative Arts Centre, Chandos St. Eighth Division Memorial Avenue of flowering gums. Self-drive town tour; self-guide Bindea Town Walk; brochures available from Tourist information. Market, 3rd Sat. each month in Wolsely Park, Conadilly St. Jan.: National tomato competition. Aug.: Ag Quip, agricultural field day. Oct.: Dorothea MacKellar children's festival. **In the area:** Porcupine Lookout, 3 km SE, offers views over town and surrounding agricultural area. Lake Keepit Dam and State Recreation Centre, 34 km NE, water sports, bushwalking, gliding club, picnicking, camping, caravan park. 150° East Time Meridian, 28 km W. **Tourist information:** Anzac Park, South St; (067) 42 4300. **Accommodation:** 6 hotels, 7 motels, 1 cara./camp. park.

Gunning   Pop. 497

MAP REF. 115 E4, 116 G11

This town, on the Old Hume Hwy between Goulburn and Yass, is in the centre of pastoral country. **Of interest:** In Yass St: Pye Cottage, a slab-style pioneer cottage; historic post office; Telegraph Hotel; old court house; Do Duck Inn. Feb.: Agricultural show. **In the area:** Greendale Pioneer Cemetery, Gunning–Boorowa Rd. Hume and Hovell Walking Track extends from Gunning to Albury, a distance of 370 km and a 20-day trek for long distance walkers, but half-day, one-day and weekend walks at various points along the route; for information on this walking track contact the Department of Lands, 22–23 Bridge St, Sydney; (02) 9228 6111. **Tourist information:** Gunning Motel, Yass St; (048) 45 1191. **Accommodation:** 1 hotel, 1 motel, 2 B&B.

Guyra   Pop. 1942

MAP REF. 119 L8

Guyra is Aboriginal for 'fish may be caught', and the local streams are excellent for fishing. At 1300 m, this small town in the Great Dividing Range is one of the highest in NSW. Guyra is the centre of a highly productive area known for fat lambs, beef, wool and potatoes. **Of interest:** Historical Society Museum, Bradley St; open Sun. or by appt. Railway station, Bradley St, has large display of antique machinery. Waterbirds at Mother of Ducks Lagoon, McKie Pde. Jan.: Lamb and potato festival (includes Hydrangea festival). **In the area:** Chandler's Peak, for spectacular views; 20 km E. Llangothlin Handcraft Hall on Hwy, 13 km N. Thunderbolt's Cave, 10 km S. Ebor Falls and picnic reserve, 75 km SE. **Tourist information:** Penns Art Gallery, New England Hwy; (067) 79 1206. **Accommodation:** 2 hotels, 2 motels, 1 cara. park. **See also:** New England.

Hartley   Pop. 5

MAP REF. 100 G5, 116 I7

This historic village just off the Great Western Hwy, 134 km NW of Sydney, was an important stopover for travellers in the early colonial days. Situated in the Hartley Valley, it is now administered by the National Parks and Wildlife Service. **Of interest:** Self-guide leaflet (from Tourist information) introduces several historic buildings, including convict-built court house (1837), designed by colonial architect Mortimer Lewis; Royal Hotel (early 1840s); Old Trahlee Cottage; post office (1846); St Bernard's Church and Presbytery (1842); Farmer's Inn; Ivy Cottage; and Shamrock Inn. **Tourist information:** 285 Main St, Lithgow; (063) 51 2307. **Accommodation:** 1 cara./camp. park.

Hay   Pop. 2817

MAP REF. 123 K8

Hay, the commercial centre for a huge area of semi-arid grazing country, is located on the banks of the Murrumbidgee River at the junction of the Cobb, Mid Western and Sturt Hwys. Increasing irrigation from the Murrumbidgee has led to an expansion in vegetable- and fruit-growing. Many world-famous sheep studs, including Mungadal, Uardry and Cedar Grove, are in the area. **Of interest:** In Lachlan St: historic buildings; Witcombe Memorial Fountain (1883) and plaque, commemorating journey of explorer Charles Sturt along Murrumbidgee and Murray Rivers in 1829-30; coach house in main shopping area, featuring original Cobb & Co. coach that plied Deniliquin–Hay–Wilcannia run until 1901. Hay Gaol Museum, Church St, has pioneer relics. Restored court house, Moppett St. Hay Park, cnr of Moppett and Pine Sts. Signposted scenic drive around town. Sandy river beaches along Murrumbidgee for swimming, boating and fishing; Sandy Point Beach is venue for Australia Day 'Surf' Carnival. Birdwatching area close to town; breeding ground for many inland species. Bishop's Lodge, South Hay (1888), restored as museum, exhibition gallery and conference centre. Jan.: Australia Day 'Surf' carnival. **In the area:** Ruberto's Winery, Sturt Hwy, South Hay. Sunset viewing area, 16 km N on Booligal Rd. Weir on Murrumbidgee River, 12 km W. Villages of Maude (53 km W), with its attractive picnic areas near weir; and Oxley (87 km NW) with its river red gums along river and prolific wildlife (best seen at dusk). **Tourist information:** 407 Moppett St; (069) 93 4045. **Accommodation:** 7 hotels, 6 motels, 2 cara./camp. parks.

Henty   Pop. 840

MAP REF. 116 A13, 123 Q11

The historic pastoral township of Henty, the 'home of the header', is in the heart of Morgan Country, so called because of the infamous but ill-fated bushranger Dan Morgan. Almost midway between Albury-Wodonga and Wagga Wagga, Henty can be reached by the Olympic Way or by the Hume Hwy and Boomerang Way. **Of interest:** Headlie Taylor Header Memorial, Henty Park, off Allen St, a tribute to machine (invented 1914) that revolutionised the grain industry. Sept.: Machinery field days. **In the area:** Sergeant Smith Memorial Stone, 2 km W on Pleasant Hills Rd, marks site where Dan Morgan fatally wounded a policeman. Doodle Cooma Swamp (2000 ha), breeding area for waterbirds, is visible from memorial stone. Buckarginga Woolshed, built of chocks and logs (no nails), located on Cookardinia Rd, 11 km E. Squatters Arms Inn (1848), Cookardinia, 24 km E. **Tourist information:** Doodle Cooma Arms Hotel, Sladen St; (069) 29 3013. **Accommodation:** 2 hotels.

Holbrook Pop. 1369

MAP REF. 123 R12, 235 R1

This small town is a well known stock-breeding centre, 521 km SW of Sydney, on the Hume Hwy. **Of interest:** Commander Holbrook submarine in Holbrook Park, Hume Hwy, scaled model of submarine in which Commander N. D. Holbrook won VC in World War I; town (formerly Germonton) was renamed in his honour. Woolpack Inn Museum, in former hotel (1860), features the complete plant of old cordial factory, bakery, horse-drawn vehicles and farm equipment. Ten Mile Creek, behind museum, attractive area for picnics and walks. Easter: Ultra Fly-in (biennial, even-numbered years). Nov.: Agricultural show. **In the area:** Ultralight Centre, Holbrook airport; 3 km N. **Tourist information:** Woolpack Inn Museum, 83 Albury St (Hume Hwy); (060) 36 2131. **Accommodation:** 2 hotels, 7 motels, 1 cara./camp. park.

Huskisson Pop. 900

MAP REF. 115 I5, 117 K12, 139 R1

A thriving town, Huskisson is 24 km SE of Nowra, on the shores of Jervis Bay. **Of interest:** Lady Denman Heritage Complex, Dent St, provides history of wooden shipbuilding at Huskisson (check opening times); also in Complex, Laddie Timbery's Aboriginal Art and Craft Centre, artifacts made on site by Aboriginal artisans; and Museum of Jervis Bay Science and the Sea, with its fine maritime and surveying collections. Antique and craft shops. Diving and dolphin watch cruises available. Market, 2nd Sun. each month at White Sands Park. Easter: White Sands carnival. **In the area:** At Jervis Bay: water sports, particularly scuba diving, also excellent fishing; Bay renowned for its clean water and is frequently used to film underwater sequences; Barry's Bushtucker Tours; Wreck Bay Walkabout Tours; contact Tourist information for details. **Tourist information:** Shoalhaven Tourist Centre, 254 Princes Hwy, Bomaderry; (044) 21 0778. **Accommodation:** 4 motels, 2 cara./camp. parks.

Iluka Pop. 1795

MAP REF. 119 Q5

A coastal resort alongside the mouth of the Clarence River, Iluka is well known for its fishing. A deep-sea fishing fleet operates from the harbour. **Of interest:** Daily passenger ferry services to Yamba. River cruises available from Boatshed, Wed. & Fri. 11.45 a.m. July: Amateur fishing classic. **In the area:** World Heritage-listed Iluka Rainforest, at northern edge of town, for excellent walks. Further north, Bundjalung National Park, a beautiful coastal park offering excellent fishing, swimming, surfing, canoeing, walking and camping. Woombah Coffee Plantation, 14 km W, world's southernmost coffee plantation; tours by appt. **Tourist information:** Lower Clarence Visitors Centre, Ferry Park, Pacific Hwy, Maclean; (066) 45 4121. **Accommodation:** 1 motel, 3 cara./camp. parks.

Inverell Pop. 9736

MAP REF. 119 K6

Known as 'Sapphire City', this town, 67 km W of Glen Innes, is in fertile farming land also rich in minerals. Industrial diamonds, zircons, tin and sapphires are mined in the area. **Of interest:** National Trust-classified court house, Otho St. Pioneer Village, Tingha Rd, has buildings dating from 1840, moved from their original sites, including Grove Homestead, Paddy's Pub and Mt Drummond Woolshed. Tour Centre and Mining Museum in Water Towers Complex, Campbell St. Art Society Gallery, Evans St. Gem Centre, Byron St. Town Stroll, a self-guide walk; contact Tourist information. Sapphire City market, 3rd Sun. each month. Mar.: Art exhibition. Oct.: Sapphire City floral festival. **In the area:** Fossicking. Lake Inverell Reserve, 3 km E. Draught Horse Centre, Fishers Rd, 4 km E, with six breeds, has display of harness and memorabilia. See working sapphire mine at DeJon Sapphire Centre, 19 km E on Glen Innis Rd. Goonoowigall Bushland Reserve, 5 km S. Gilgai Winery, 12 km S. Green Valley Farm and museum, 35 km S. Copeton Dam State Recreation Area, 40 km SW, for boating, water-skiing, swimming, fishing, bushwalking, rock climbing, adventure playgrounds, waterslides and picnic/barbecue facilities. Honey Farm and Bottle Museum, 8 km W. Gwydir Ranch 4WD Park, 28 km W. **Tourist information:** Water Towers Complex, Campbell St; (067) 22 1693. **Accommodation:** 4 hotels, 6 motels, 3 B&B, 3 cara./camp. parks. **See also:** New England.

Jamberoo Pop. 704

MAP REF. 112 G9, 117 K10

Jamberoo, 10 km W of Kiama, is in one of the most picturesque areas of the NSW coast, with lush pastures surrounded by towering escarpments. The district has been well-known for the quality of its dairy products since early European settlement days. **Of interest:** Jamberoo Hotel, Allowrie St, features bush bands Sun. p.m. Mar.: Illawarra folk festival. **In the area:** Jamberoo Recreation Park, 3 km N. Saddleback Lookout, 7 km S, for 180° views of coast and starting point for Hoddles Trail, a one-hour walk to Barren Grounds escarpment. Jamberoo Pass, 8 km SW, for excellent views. Walking trails in Barren Grounds Bird Observatory, 10 km SW. Breathtaking State-award-winning Minnamurra Rainforest, 4 km W, features elevated timber boardwalk through rainforest area; enables visitors to view the flora and fauna. **Tourist information:** Kiama Visitors Centre, Blowhole Point, Kiama; (042) 32 3322. **Accommodation:** 1 hotel, 1 motel/lodge, 1 B&B.

Jerilderie Pop. 898

MAP REF. 123 M11

This town on the Newell Hwy was held by the Kelly gang for two days in 1879 when they captured the police station, cut the telegraph wires and robbed the bank. Today it is the centre of the largest merino stud area in NSW and also supports an expanding vegetable industry. **Of interest:** Telegraph Office Museum, Powell St; next door, The Willows historic home, for crafts, Devonshire teas and light lunches. Court house, near library on Newell Hwy. Doll World, displays large collection from around the World, Bolton St. Lake Jerilderie for water sports; adjacent Luke Park features Steel Wings, one of largest windmills in southern hemisphere, and shady picnic areas. June: League of silent flight (model, radio-controlled planes). **In the area:** Tomato and onion factory, 2 km E; tours by appt. **Tourist information:** The Willows, Powell St; (058) 86 1666. **Accommodation:** 1 hotel/motel, 3 motels, 1 cara./camp. park. See also: The Newell.

Jindabyne — Pop. 4601

MAP REF. 114 G11, 115 D9, 138 C12, 237 K4

Now on the shores of Lake Jindabyne at the foothills of the Snowy Mountains, the original township was on the banks of the Snowy River. From 1962, residents of the old town moved to the new site chosen by the Snowy Mountains Hydro-electric Authority. This made way for the damming of the Snowy River to form a water storage as part of the Snowy Mountains Scheme. At an altitude of 930 m and situated in the heart of the Snowy Mountains, Jindabyne attracts skiers in winter and anglers, water-sports enthusiasts and bushwalkers in summer. Mar.: Strzelecki Polish festival. Dec.: Lake Jindabyne Sailing Club hobie cat races. **In the area:** Lake Jindabyne, well stocked with trout, also ideal for boating, water-skiing and other water sports. Kosciusko National Park Headquarters and Information Centre, Sawpit Creek, 20 km NW, on Kosciusko Rd. Winter shuttle-bus service to Bullocks Flat, Smiggin Holes and Thredbo. Crackenback Cottage, 12 km SW, has craft shop, timber maze and restaurant. At Bullocks Flat, 20 km SW, terminal for Skitube, a fascinating train ride to Perisher and Mt Blue Cow; operates daily, winter, Easter and Christmas holidays. After snow has melted, 50-min. drive south-west from Jindabyne leads to Charlotte Pass and 300-m boardwalk to view main range; 16-km round trip to summit of Mt Kosciusko. At Thredbo, 37 km W, chairlift operates all year; in summer provides easy access over steel-mesh track to summit of Mt Kosciusko, 13-km round trip. Kunama Galleries, 7 km NE. **Tourist information:** Snowy Region Information Centre, Snowy Mountains Plaza, Kosciusko Rd; (064) 56 2444. **Accommodation:** 2 hotel/motels, 5 motels, 1 hostel, 2 cara./camp. parks.

Junee — Pop. 3673

MAP REF. 115 A4, 116 C11, 123 R9

Junee is an important railhead town and commercial centre 482 km SW of Sydney on the Olympic Way. **Of interest:** Monte Cristo Homestead, overlooking town, a restored colonial mansion with carriage collection. Roundhouse Museum, Harold St, features 32-m turntable for swivelling train engines to attach to carriages, 42 repair bays, original workshop, locomotives and memorabilia. Endeavour Park, Olympic Way. Memorial Park, Main St. Hobbin Pond, Peel St. **In the area:** Historic Hotel Shirley, Bethungra, 30 km NE. Turnoff at Bethungra for Bethungra Dam, ideal for canoeing and sailing. Bethungra Rail Spiral 33 km NE, a unique engineering feat. **Tourist information:** Shire Offices; (069) 24 1277. **Accommodation:** 4 hotels, 1 motel, 1 cara./camp. park.

Katoomba — Pop. 16 927

MAP REF. 100 H7, 102 E9, 117 J7

Katoomba is the highly developed tourism centre of the Blue Mountains area which attracts 3 million people each year. Nearby, the smaller towns of Leura and Wentworth Falls have many interesting features as well as superb mountain scenery. Originally developed as a coal mine last century, it was not long before Katoomba was attracting wealthy Sydney holidaymakers. The coal mine foundered, but Katoomba continued to develop as a tourist resort. Natural and created attractions abound in the Blue Mountains region. **In the area:** Excellent bushwalking, 4-wheel driving and cycling; also scenic flights, contact Tourist information for details. *Around Katoomba:* Scenic Skyway and Railway Complex, Violet St/Cliff Dr: Skyway, first horizontal passenger-carrying ropeway in Australia, travels 350 m across mountain gorge above Cooks Crossing giving magnificent views of Katoomba Falls, Orphan Rock, Jamison Valley; the Scenic Railway, built in late 1800s by founder of Katoomba coal mine to bring out coal and transport miners, is reputed to be world's steepest railway descending into Jamison Valley at an average incline of 45°, through a sunlit, tree-clad gorge approximately 445 m in length. Famous rock formations (The Three Sisters, Orphan Rock) and Katoomba Falls, floodlit at night. *At Leura, 3 km E:* Leura Mall, tree-lined main street and gardens (beautiful in spring and autumn) with many specialty shops, galleries and restaurants. Everglades Garden, Everglades Ave, one of Australia's great gardens built in 1930s, includes a gallery devoted to its creator, Danish master gardener Paul Sorenson. Leuralla, Olympian Pde, a historic art deco mansion with major collection of 19th-century Australian art and one of Australia's largest collections of toys, dolls, trains and railway memorabilia as well as memorial museum to Dr H. V. Evatt. Dramatic views from Sublime Point; Cliff Drive follows cliff tops around Katoomba-Leura offering spectacular views at many lookouts and picnic spots. Walking tracks along cliff tops and descending into Jamison Valley; Gardens festival in Oct. *At Wentworth Falls, 7 km E:* Yester Grange (1870s), a colonial homestead-museum on 4.7-ha site, has been restored and furnished to late-Victorian splendour. Norman Lindsay Gallery and Museum near Faulconbridge, 32 km E; open Tues.–Sun. Hydro Majestic Hotel at Medlow Bath, 5 km NW; once a health resort. Conservation Hut Cafe, an eco-designed cafe with splendid views; Australia Day regatta on lake in Jan. *Around Blackheath, 8 km NW:* Jemby-Rinjah Lodge on edge of Blue Mountains National Park, includes environmental studies centre; Evans Lookout; on Govetts Leap Rd, National Parks and Wildlife Heritage Centre, centre is starting point for Fairfax Heritage Track walk, and Govetts Leap Lookout; rhododendrons and azaleas at Bacchante Gardens; Pulpit Rock Reserve and Lookout. Horseriding in Megalong and Kanimbla Valleys. Mount Victoria, 16 km NW of Katoomba, a National Trust-classified village with craft shops and museum. Jenolan Caves, some of the most splendid underground caves and above-ground arches in Australia, in flora and fauna reserve 76 km SW of Katoomba. Yerranderie, silver-mining ghost town surrounded by 2430-ha wildlife reserve, 200 km S of Katoomba via Oberon (4WD), features several historic buildings including museum and quaint hostel-style accommodation. **Tourist information:** Great Western Hwy, Glenbrook; (047) 39 6266. **Accommodation:** 2 hotels, 7 motels, several lodges and guesthouses, 1 cara./camp. park. **See also:** The Blue Mountains.

Kempsey   Pop. 9049

MAP REF. 105 G3, 119 O11

Kempsey, situated in the Macleay River Valley, 428 km N of Sydney, is the commercial centre of a growing district of dairying, horticulture, tourism and light industry, including the Akubra hat factory. The town celebrated its sesquicentenary in 1986. **Of interest:** Macleay River Historical Society Museum and Settlers Cottage, Pacific Hwy, South Kempsey. Number of 19th-century buildings in Kemp, Elbow, Sea and Belgrave Sts, West Kempsey. Apr.: Agricultural show. Sept.: Country music festival. **In the area:** At South West Rocks, 35 km NE: good beach; hand-feeding of fish at Everglades Aquarium; nearby, Trial Bay Gaol, 40 km NE, built by prisoners in 1880s; Smoky Cape Lighthouse and restored Boatmans Cottage (1902). Hat Head National Park, 32 km E, a coastal park with magnificent sand dunes and unspoiled beaches. Crescent Head, 20 km SE, popular seaside holiday town. Limeburners Creek Nature Reserve, 34 km SE. Fish Rock Cave, noted for scuba diving, just off Smoky Cape. At Kundabung, 12 km S, Australasian bull riding titles held each Jan. Mindubella Animal Park and Farm Nursery, 30 km NW, a miniature horse and pony stud; rides available. Ronbara Equestrian Park, 36 km NW, offers horseriding, gig rides, canoeing; also tearooms and overnight accommodation. Bellbrook, 47 km NW, a National Trust-classified village. **Tourist information:** Pacific Hwy, South Kempsey; (065) 63 1555. **Accommodation:** 5 hotels, 12 motels, 5 cara./camp. parks.

Khancoban   Pop. 416

MAP REF. 114 A9, 115 B9, 236 I3

Set in the lush green Murray Valley at the western end of the Alpine Way, 109 km NW of Jindabyne, this small modern town was built by the Snowy Mountains Authority. **Of interest:** Lady Hudson Rose Garden, Mitchell Ave. National Parks and Wildlife Service, Scott St, have videos of the Snowy Mountains Scheme and Kosciusko National Park. **In the area:** Trout fishing, water sports and whitewater rafting. Permit required for vehicles entering National Park; contact Tourist information. Murray 1 Power Station 10 km SE on Alpine Way; guided tours daily. Excellent picnic and rest areas along Alpine Way; brilliant roadside displays of wildflowers in spring and autumn. Spectacular mountain views from Scammel's Spur Lookout, 20 km SE. Fishing tours.

New England

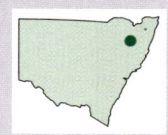

Despite the scenery, it is worth keeping your eyes on the ground if you pull over for a rest in the New England area. Some of the best fossicking specimens in the district have been found by the roadside. All kinds of quartz, jaspers, serpentine, crystal and chalcedony are found right throughout this area – not to mention sapphires, diamonds and gold, though these require a little more effort to find.

The round trip from Nundle, through **Tamworth**, **Manilla**, **Barraba**, **Bingara**, **Warialda**, then on to the New England towns of **Inverell** and **Glen Innes** and back, is known as 'The Fossickers' Way' and tourist signs have been placed at intervals to guide the motorist. Nearby is the Copeton Dam, which holds two-and-a-half times as much water as Sydney Harbour, with part of its foreshores forming Copeton State Recreational Area.

Glen Innes and Inverell have nearby sapphire reserves where fossickers may hire tools and try their luck; anything you find is yours. The largest find to date in the Nullamanna Fossicking Reserve, near Inverell, is a 70-carat blue, valued at $3000.

The New England district is the largest area of highlands in Australia, and has plenty to offer

Lookout in Boonoo Boonoo National Park, north-east of Tenterfield

besides gemstones. The countryside is varied and lovely, with magnificent mountains, and streams cascading into spectacular gorges, contrasting with the rich blacksoil plains of wheat and cotton to the west. Some of the State's most outstanding national parks and World Heritage features are found in New England, and the southern hemisphere's largest granite monolith, Bald Rock, is located near **Tenterfield**.

Fishing is excellent, with trout in the streams of the tablelands, and cod and yellow-belly in the lower New England rivers to the west. You can also fish, picnic, swim, sail or water-ski at Pindari and Copeton dams.

Other towns in New England, **Ashford**, Delungra, **Guyra**, **Tingha**, **Walcha**, **Uralla** and Deepwater, and the city of **Armidale**, have much to offer.

For further information, contact the Visitors Centre and Coach Station, 82 Marsh St, Armidale; (067) 73 8527, Freecall 1800 62 7736. **See also:** individual entries in A–Z listing for those towns indicated by bold type. **Map reference:** 119 M7.

View from Mt Pleasant, south of Kiama

Tourist information: National Parks and Wildlife Service, Scott St; (060) 76 9373. **Accommodation:** 1 hotel/motel, 4 B&B, 1 hostel, 1 cara./camp. park.

Kiama   Pop. 10 631

MAP REF. 112 H9, 117 K10

The spectacular Blowhole is the best known attraction of this resort town. Discovered by explorer George Bass in 1797, it sprays water up to heights of 60 m and is floodlit each evening. Kiama is the centre of a prosperous dairying and mixed farming district. **Of interest:** Terrace houses, specialty and craft shops in Collins St. Family History Centre, Railway Pde, contains world-wide collection of records for tracing family history. Heritage Walk, contact Tourist information. At Blowhole Point: Blowhole; Pilots Cottage Historical Museum. Kiama Beach for surfing, swimming and fishing. Market, 3rd Sun. each month. Feb.: Jazz festival. Oct.: Seaside festival. **In the area:** Little Blowhole, 2 km S, off Tingira Cres. Cathedral Rocks, a scenic rocky outcrop, best at dawn; 3 km N at Jones Beach. **Tourist information:** Blowhole Point Rd; (042) 32 3322. **Accommodation:** 2 hotels, 6 motels, 1 B&B, 1 hostel, 4 cara./camp. parks. **See also:** The Illawarra Coast.

Kyogle   Pop. 2912

MAP REF. 119 P2, 491 P12

Kyogle makes a good base for exploring the mountains nearby. It is also the centre of a lush dairy and mixed-farming area on the upper reaches of the Richmond River near the Qld border. July: Rodeo. Oct.: Show. Nov.: Festival; Golf tournament. **In the area:** World Heritage-listed Border Ranges National Park, 27 km N: forestry road access; walking tracks; camping facilities; views of Mt Warning and Tweed Valley; in eastern section, Tweed Range Scenic Drive (64 km) through pristine rainforest with deep gorges and waterfalls plunging into crystal-clear creeks. Scenic forest drive via Mt Lindesay, 45 km NW on NSW-Qld border, magnificent views; and Toonumbar Dam, 31 km W, with bushwalking and picnic/barbecue facilities; at Bell's Bay, 2 km from dam, excellent bass fishing and camping. Picnic spots include Roseberry Nursery, 23 km N; Sheepstation Creek, in Border Ranges National Park. **Tourist information:** Old 66 Caltex Garage, Summerland Way; (066) 32 1042. **Accommodation:** 2 hotels, 1 motel, 3 cara./camp. parks.

Lake Cargelligo   Pop. 1256

MAP REF. 123 O4

A small township, 586 km W of Sydney, with the same name as the lake alongside, Lake Cargelligo serves the surrounding agricultural and pastoral district. **Of interest:** The lake, 8 km long and 3.5 km wide, ideal for fishing, boating, sailing, water-skiing and swimming. The lake is also home to many species of bird, including at times, the rare black cockatoo. Tourist information centre, Foster St, has a large gem collection. Jan.: Hovercraft meeting; Bowling festival. Sept.: Lake show. **Tourist information:** Foster St; (068) 98 1501. **Accommodation:** 3 hotels, 2 motels, 1 cara./camp. park.

Laurieton   Pop. 4385

MAP REF. 105 F10, 119 O12

The villages of Laurieton, North Haven and Dunbogan are scattered around the foreshore of a large inlet formed by the Camden Haven River at its mouth, 44 km S of Port Macquarie. This tidal inlet is ideal for estuary fishing. **Of interest:** Historical Museum, in old post office, Laurie St; open by appt. **In the area:** Oysters, lobsters, crabs, bream and flathead in local rivers and lakes. Seafront well-known fishing spot. Delightful bushwalks along seafront and around lakes. River cruises available. Crowdy Bay National Park, 5 km S, renowned for its prolific birdlife and magnificent ocean beach; walking tracks provide spectacular ocean view. Panoramic views from North Brother Mountain, 6 km SW. Big Fella Gum Tree, 18 km SW, one of three exceptionally large trees in Middle Brother State Forest. At Kendall, 10 km W: several art and craft galleries including Craft Co-op in railway station; markets on 1st and 3rd Sun. each month. Rainforest with waterfalls, 60 km W at Comboyne Plateau. **Tourist information:** Pacific Hwy, Kew; (065) 59 4400. **Accommodation:** 1 hotel, 3 motels, 2 cara./camp. parks.

Leeton   Pop. 6245

MAP REF. 123 O8

Located 560 km SW of Sydney, Leeton is the first of the planned towns in the Murrumbidgee Irrigation Area and was designed by American architect Walter Burley Griffin. The town is an important administrative and processing centre for this intensive fruit-, rice- and wine-grape-growing area. **Of interest:** Historic Hydro Hotel (1919), Chelmsford Pl. Tours weekdays at Sunrice Country Visitors Centre at rice mill, Calrose St and Quelch Juice Factory, Brady Way. Riverina Cheese Factory, Massey Ave; open Sun.–Thurs. (9.30 a.m.–2.30 p.m.). Easter: Sunrice country festival, 10-day festival culminates Easter Mon. (biennial; even-numbered years). **In the area:** Wine tastings at Toorak and Lillypilly Estate wineries, both near town. Fivebough Swamp, 2 km N, a waterbird sanctuary. Gliding, hot-air ballooning at Brobenah airfield, 9 km N. Whitton Court House Museum, 23 km W. Gogeldrie Weir, 23 km SW. Yanco, 7 km S. Murrumbidgee State Forest, 12 km S. **Tourist information:** Chelmsford Pl.; (069) 53 2832. **Accommodation:** 2 hotels, 3 motels, 2 cara./parks. **See also:** Vineyards and Wineries.

Lennox Head   Pop. 3036

MAP REF. 119 R3, 491 R12

Just north of Ballina, Lennox Head has a charming seaside village atmosphere. The area is famous for its surfing beaches. **Of interest:** Freshwater Lake Ainsworth, 50 m from surfing beach and popular with windsurfers. Market, 2nd Sun. each month. **In the area:** Swimming, surfing and snorkelling. Many scenic walks and rainforests a short drive away. Pat Morton Lookout, 1 km S, whale-watching Aug.–Dec. **Tourist information:** Ballina Tourist Information Centre, Las Balsas Plaza, cnr River and Norton Sts, Ballina; (066) 86 3484. **Accommodation:** 3 motels, 1 hostel, 1 cara./camp. park.

Lightning Ridge   Pop. 1522

MAP REF. 118 B5

Lightning Ridge is a small opal-mining town in the famous opal fields, 74 km N of Walgett, via the Castlereagh Hwy. The valuable black opal found in the area attracts gem enthusiasts worldwide. **Of interest:** Many displays of art and craft, including opal jewellery and gem opals. Underground mine tours available, contact Tourist information. In Opal St: Bottle House Museum, has collection of bottles, minerals and mining relics; paintings and photographs at John Murray Art. Gemopal, Pandora St, for local pottery. Bush Moozeum at Simms Hill opal field, eastern outskirts of town off Pandora St. Opal-cutting demonstrations at the Three Mile Field, southern outskirts of town. **In the area:** Cactus Nursery, 2 km N, off Bald Hill Rd. Fauna Orphanage, Opal St, 3 km S. Hot Artesian Bore Baths (free), 2 km NE. Nature reserves, fossicking. **Tourist information:** Morilla St; (068) 29 1466. **Accommodation:** 4 motels, 5 cara./camp. parks.

Lismore   Pop. 27 246

MAP REF. 119 Q3, 491 Q12

Regional centre of the Northern Rivers district of NSW, a closely settled and intensively cultivated rural area, Lismore is situated beside the Wilsons River (formerly the north arm of the Richmond River), 821 km N of Sydney. It is best known for its rainforest heritage, including the Rotary Rainforest Reserve in the residential area of the city. **Of interest:** Lismore Visitor and Heritage Centre, Foleys Rd, has indoor rainforest walk, and displays of local arts and crafts. Picnic areas and mini steam train rides in surrounding Heritage Park, cnr Ballina and Molesworth Sts. Also in Foleys Rd, the Chocolate Factory, an art and craft gallery. Cedar Log Memorial, Ballina St. Richmond River Historical Museum and Lismore Regional Art Gallery, both in Molesworth St. Robinson's Lookout, Robinson Ave. Claude Riley Memorial Lookout, New Ballina Rd. Wilsons Park, Wyrallah St, East Lismore. River cruises on MV *Bennelong*, The Wharf, Magellan St. Car boot market, 1st and 3rd Sun. each month at Lismore Shopping Square. Heritage Park market, 5th Sun. each month. May: Trinity arts festival. Sept.: Cup Day. Oct.: Folk festival; North Coast national show. **In the area:** At Alphadale, 11 km E: Macadamia Magic, a macadamia processing plant and tourist complex; Stephen Morris Glassware. Boatharbour Reserve, 5 km N on Bangalow Rd. Rocky Creek Dam, 25 km N. Minyon Falls and Peates Mountain Lookout in Whian Whian State Forest, 25 km N. Among six World Heritage-listed areas in vicinity: Border Ranges National Park, 40 km N of Kyogle, and Nightcap National Park, 25 km N of Nimbin with its spectacular Protestor Falls. Lismore Lake, 3 km S, pleasant lagoon for swimming with picnic/barbecue facilities and adventure park on foreshore. Tucki Tucki Koala Reserve, 15 km S, adjacent to Lismore–Woodburn Rd; Aboriginal ceremonial ground nearby. **Tourist information:** cnr Ballina and Molesworth Sts; (066) 22 0122. **Accommodation:** 9 hotels, 12 motels, 8 B&B, 3 hostels, 6 cara./camp. parks.

Lithgow   Pop. 11 968

MAP REF. 100 G5, 116 I6

This important coal-mining city on the north-west fringes of the Blue Mountains is a must for railway enthusiasts. The city itself is highly industrialised with two power stations and several large factories; the surrounding countryside is beautiful. **Of interest:** Eskbank House, Bennett St, built 1841 by Thomas Brown, who discovered Lithgow coal seam, now museum with fine collection of 19th-century furniture and vehicles, and displays depicting industrial history of area; open Sat.–Sun. Blast Furnace Park, a wetland restoration area off Inch St, with ruins of Australia's first blast furnace complex. Oct.: National Go-Kart championships. Nov.: Festival of the valley (biennial; even-numbered years). **In the area:** Zig Zag Steam Railway, 10 km E via Bells Line of Road, a breathtaking stretch of railway built in 1869 and later restored, offers train trips. Mt Tomah Botanic Gardens at Berambing, 35 km E. Lake Wallace, Wallerawang, 11 km NW; sailing, trout fishing. Mt Piper Power Station, 21 km NW; open daily 9 a.m.– 4 p.m., guided tours, admission free. Lake Lyell, 9 km W, for power boating, water-skiing and trout fishing. Hassans Walls Lookout, 5 km S via Hassans Walls Rd. Hartley historic village, outstanding architecturally and historically, 12 km SE, off Great Western Hwy, features convict-built court house (1837). Jenolan Caves, 60 km SE. **Tourist information:** 285 Main St; (063) 51 2307. **Accommodation:** 7 hotels, 5 motels, 1 hostel, 1 cara./camp. park.

Lockhart   Pop. 887

MAP REF. 123 P10

This pleasant historic town, situated 65 km SW of Wagga, was originally known as Green's Gunyah and was renamed Lockhart in 1897. **Of interest:** National Trust-classified Green St, fine example of turn-of-the-century streetscape, with wide, shady shop front verandahs. **In the area:** Galore Hill, 3 km S, features caves where bushranger Mad Dog Morgan hid; also walking tracks, lookouts and picnic/barbecue facilities. **Tourist information:** Tarcutta St, Wagga Wagga; (069) 23 5402. **Accommodation:** 1 hotel, 1 motel, 1 cara. park.

Macksville   Pop. 2869

MAP REF. 119 P9

Macksville is an attractive town near the Nambucca River, south of Nambucca

Hunter Valley Steamfest held at Maitland in April

Heads. **Of interest:** In River St: Mary Boulton Pioneer Cottage, replica of pioneer home with furniture, costumes and museum of horse-drawn vehicles; Star Hotel (1885). Craft markets on riverbank, 4th Sat. each month. Apr.: Nambucca River show. Oct.: Pro-Ag field day. **In the area:** Nambucca Valley Crafters Cottage co-op, 4 km N. More than 4000 dolls at Flo's House of Dolls; 4 km N. Joseph and Eliza Newman Folk Museum; Sat. markets (a.m.) at Bowraville (the 'verandah-post town'), 16 km NW. Bakers Creek Station, 30 km W, for horseriding, fishing, rainforest walking, canoeing and picnicking; accommodation available. Cosmopolitan Hotel (1903), the 'pub with no beer', made famous by song, at Taylors Arm, 26 km SW. Yarahappini Mt Lookout, 10 km S, for 360° views. Scotts Head, 18 km SE, has excellent surfing, swimming and fishing; dolphins often seen offshore. **Tourist information:** 4 Pacific Hwy, Nambucca Heads; (065) 68 6954. **Accommodation:** 2 hotels, 3 motels, 2 cara./parks.

Maclean   Pop. 2890

MAP REF. 119 P5

Fishing and river prawning fleets are based at Maclean, on the Clarence River, about 740 km N of Sydney. Professional anglers from this pretty town and from the nearby towns of Yamba and Iluka catch about 20 per cent of the State's seafood. Sugarcane, maize and mixed farm crops are grown in the area. **Of interest:** In River St: Scottish Corner; Civic Hall (1903). Free Presbyterian Church (1864), cnr Wharf and River Sts. Self-guide historic buildings walk, contact Tourist information. Bicentennial Museum and adjacent Stone Cottage (1879), Wharf St, top of Maclean Lookout and Pinnacle Rocks. Arts and crafts, Ferry Park. Rainforest walking track from High School. Market, 2nd Sun. each month. Easter: Highland gathering. Sept.: Cane harvest festival. **In the area:** Houseboat hire at Brushgrove, 21 km SW. Yuraygir National Park, 24 km SE. **Tourist information:** Lower Clarence Visitors Centre, Ferry Park, Pacific Hwy; (066) 45 4121. **Accommodation:** 3 hotels, 2 motels, 1 B&B, 2 cara./camp. parks.

Maitland   Pop. 45 209

MAP REF. 108 C7, 117 M4

On the Hunter River, 28 km NW of Newcastle, Maitland dates back to early colonial days. The flourishing city's winding High St has been recorded by the National Trust as a Conservation Area and most of the buildings date back to the 1800s. First settled in 1818, when convicts were put to work as cedar-cutters, it was a flourishing township by the 1840s. **Of interest:** National Trust properties Grossmann House (1862), Georgian-style folk museum, and Brough House (1870), containing city's art collection, are mirror images; both in Church St. Cintra, a Victorian mansion offering weekend B&B; Regent St. Self-guide heritage walks: East Maitland, Maitland Central Precinct and one designed for children; brochures available at Tourist information. Poetry in the Pub, Queens Arms, High St, last Mon. in month. Market, 1st Sun. each month at Showground. Apr.: Hunter Valley Steamfest; Indoor equestrian dressage championships. **In the area:** At Morpeth, 5 km NE: historic buildings with superb iron lace; craft shops open Thurs.–Sun.; Heritage walk, contact Tourist information. Scenic drive (inquire at Tourist information) to Walka Waterworks, 3 km N, former pumping station, now excellent recreation area. Scenic drive north-west to historic settlements of Tocal and Paterson. At Lochinvar, 13 km W, Windermere Colonial Homestead, a private residence built of sandstone brick by convict labour in 1820s, was favourite residence of William Charles Wentworth and has museum in dungeons where convicts were housed; open by appt (contact Tourist information for details). Also at Lochinvar, NSW Equestrian Centre; open to bus tours only. **Tourist information:** Maitland Visitor Centre, cnr Banks St and New England Hwy; (049) 33 2611. **Accommodation:** 4 hotels, 6 motels, 2 B&B, 1 cara./camp. park.

Manilla   Pop. 2110

MAP REF. 122 J9

This small town, located 42 km NW of Tamworth, is renowned for its meadery, one of only two meaderys in the State. **Of interest:** Dutton's Meadery, Barraba St, has tastings and sales of fresh honey and mead. Picturesque Manilla St: antique and coffee shops; Royce Cottage Historical Museum. June: Lake Keepit kool sailing regatta. Oct.: Festival of spring flowers. **In the area:** Manilla Ski Gardens on Lake Keepit, 20 km SW. Warrabah National Park, 40 km NE, a peaceful riverside retreat. Swimming, fishing and canoeing on Namoi and Manilla Rivers. **Tourist information:** Cnr Murray and Peel Sts, Tamworth; (067) 66 9422. **Accommodation:** 4 hotels, 1 motel, 1 cara./camp. park. **See also:** New England.

Menindee
Pop. 467

MAP REF. 120 E13, 122 E1

It was at this small town, 110 km SE of Broken Hill, that the ill-fated Burke and Wills stayed in 1860 on their journey north. **Of interest:** Maiden's Hotel (where they lodged). Ah Chung's Bakehouse Gallery, Menindee St. Menindee Lakes Lookout. **In the area:** Menindee Lake, 1 km NW, part of water-storage scheme that guarantees an unfailing water supply to Broken Hill. Yachting, fishing and swimming on lakes in area. Copi Hollow, 12 km E, attracts water-skiers and power boat enthusiasts. Kinchega National Park, 1 km W, has prolific wildlife and restored shearers' quarters. **Tourist information:** Broken Hill Tourist Information Centre, cnr Blende and Bromide Sts, Broken Hill; (080) 87 6077. **Accommodation:** 2 hotels, 1 motel, 3 cara./camp. parks.

Merimbula
Pop. 4259

MAP REF. 113 F9, 115 G11, 237 Q7

Excellent surfing, fishing and prawning at this small sea and lake town. Its sister village of Pambula also offers fine fishing and surfing. **Of interest:** Aquarium at Merimbula Wharf, Lake St. Old School Museum, Main St. June: Jazz festival. Sept.: Food and wine frolic. Oct.: Veterans tennis. **In the area:** Lake cruises; boat hire available. Magic Mountain Family Recreation Park, 5 km N on Sapphire Coast Dr. Tura Beach, 5 km NE. Pambula, 7 km SW, historic village; market held 2nd Sun. each month. Walking track and lookout at nearby Pambula Beach, 10 km S. **Tourist information:** Beach St; (064) 95 1129. **Accommodation:** 16 motels, 1 hostel, 4 cara./camp. parks. **See also:** The South Coast.

Merriwa
Pop. 962

MAP REF. 117 J2

This small town in the western Hunter region is noted for its many historic buildings. **Of interest:** Self-guide historic walks, brochures from Tourist information. Historical Museum in stone cottage (1857), Bettington St. Bottle Museum, Vennacher St. May: Polocrosse carnival. June: Festival of fleeces (includes fireworks). **In the area:** The Drips (curtains of water dripping through rocks) picnic area, at Goulburn River National Park, 35 km S. Convict-built Flags Rd, runs from town to Gungal, 25 km SE. Old gold-boom town of Cassilis, 45 km NW, historic sandstone buildings. Official gem-fossicking area 27 km SW. **Tourist information:** Historical Museum, Bettington St; (065) 48 2607. **Accommodation:** 2 hotels, 1 motel, 1 B&B, 1 cara./camp. park.

Mittagong
Pop. 5666

MAP REF. 112 C6, 115 I2, 117 J10

The gateway to the Southern Highlands, Mittagong is 110 km S of Sydney. **Of interest:** Historic cemeteries and many gracious old buildings. Butterfly House, Bessemer St. Natural wonders of Lake Alexandra, Queen St. **In the area:** Well-planned walk through nearby hills at Box Vale, turnoff 4 km SW. Loopline Scenic Drive north-east includes Thirlmere Lakes National Park, Thirlmere Railway Museum, potteries and orchards. Wombeyan Caves, 60 km NW; reached by scenic but narrow road (not suitable for caravans) **Tourist information:** Southern Highlands Visitor Information Centre, Winifred West Park, Main St; (048) 71 2888. **Accommodation:** 2 hotels, 6 motels, 1 B&B, 1 cara./camp. park. **See also:** Southern Highlands.

Molong
Pop. 1563

MAP REF. 116 F5

Molong is a small rural town on the Mitchell Hwy, 35 km NW of Orange. **Of interest:** Yarn Market, Craft Cottage and Coach House Gallery, Bank St. Molong Country Markets, Railway Station, 2nd Sun. each month (not winter). Apr.: Cabonne country day. **In the area:** Grave of Yuranigh, Aboriginal guide of explorer Sir Thomas Mitchell, 2 km E; grave marked by a headstone that pays tribute to his courage and fidelity. Mitchell's Monument, 21 km S, marks site of explorer's base camp. **Tourist information:** Visitors Centre, Civic Gardens, Byng St, Orange; (063) 61 5226 or Railway Station Complex, Mitchell Hwy, Molong. **Accommodation:** 2 hotels, 1 motel, 2 B&B, 1 cara./camp. park.

Moree
Pop. 10 062

MAP REF. 118 G5

Situated on the Mehi River, 640 km NW of Sydney, this town is the nucleus of a large cotton and wheat region. It is best known for its artesian spa baths, said to relieve arthritis and rheumatism. **Of interest:** Spa complex, Anne St. Mary Brand Park, Gwydir St. National Trust-classified Moree Lands Office (1894), cnr Frome and Heber Sts. Moree Plains Regional Gallery, Heber St. Historic walk, contact Tourist information. Yurundiali Aboriginal Corporation, Endeavour Lane, a screen-print clothing factory. Plains Pottery and Craft Centre, 36 Auburn St. The Big Plane, a DC3 transport plane at Amaroo Tavern; Amaroo Dr. Market, 1st Sun. each month at Jellicoe Park, Balo St. Easter: Carnival of sport. Nov.: Golden grain festival. **In the area:** Pecan Nut Farm, 35 km E; tours available. Inspection of cotton gins during harvesting season (Apr.–July); contact Tourist information. **Tourist information:** Lyle Houlihan Park, Newell Hwy; (067) 52 7479. **Accommodation:** 4 hotels, 1 hotel/motel, 17 motels, 3 cara./camp. parks. **See also:** The Newell.

Moruya
Pop. 2520

MAP REF. 115 H7, 139 M8

Many well known old dairying estates were founded near this town, which was once a gateway to the Araluen and Braidwood goldfields. Situated on the Moruya River, 322 km S of Sydney, it is now a dairying, timber and oyster-farming centre. Granite used in the pylons of the Sydney Harbour Bridge was quarried in the district. **Of interest:** Eurobodalla Historic Museum, in town centre, depicts discovery of gold at Mogo and general history of district. Court house (1880), on Princes Hwy. Catholic Church (1889), Queen St. Mar.: Music festival. **In the area:** Good fishing, surfing and water sports. Black swan and sea eagle colonies located up-river at Yarragee. Deua National Park, 20 km W, variety of flora and fauna; Hanging Mountain and Mt Wanderer Lookouts located in park. Nerrigundah, 44 km SW, former gold-mining town. At Bodalla, 24 km S: Coomerang House, home of 19th-century industrialist and dairy farmer Thomas Sutcliffe Mort; Mort Memorial Church and historic cemetery. **Tourist information:** cnr Princes Hwy and Beach Rd, Batemans Bay; (044) 72 6900, and Narooma; (044) 76 2881. **Accommodation:** 1 hotel, 1 hotel/motel, 2 motels, 2 B&B, 2 cara./camp. parks.

Moss Vale — Pop. 5690

MAP REF. 112 B7, 115 I3, 117 J10

The industrial and agricultural centre of the Southern Highlands, this town stands on part of the 1000-acre parcel of land granted to Charles Throsby in 1819. **Of interest:** Leighton Gardens. Historic walk, contact Tourist information. Mar.: Agricultural show. **In the area:** Cecil Hoskins Nature Reserve with abundance of birdlife; 3 km NE. At Sutton Forest, 6 km SW: A Little Piece of Scotland, for all things Scottish; Everything Shop, for recycled timber furniture and antiques. Exeter, 4 km further S. Fitzroy Falls, Morton National Park, 20 km SE. **Tourist information:** Southern Highlands Visitor Information Centre, Winifred West Park, Main St, Mittagong; (048) 71 2888. **Accommodation:** 3 hotels, 2 motels, 4 B&B, 2 cara./camp. parks. **See also:** Southern Highlands.

Moulamein — Pop. 459

MAP REF. 122 I10, 233 P9

This is the oldest town in the Riverina, already well established in the 1870s as a prosperous inland port on the Edward River. Today the town is noted for its fishing. **Of interest:** Old wharf, Morago St. Restored court house, Nyang St (obtain key from Tourist information). Riverside picnic areas. Lake Moulamein, Brougham St. Easter: Yabby races. Dec.: Horseracing Cup. **Tourist information:** Moulamein Business Centre, Morago St; (058) 87 5354. **Accommodation:** 1 hotel, 1 cara./camp. park.

Mudgee — Pop. 7447

MAP REF. 116 H3

This attractively designed town is the centre of a productive agricultural area on the Cudgegong River, 264 km NW of Sydney. Wine grapes, fine wool, sheep, cattle and honey are among the local produce. There are horse studs in the area. **Of interest:** Many fine buildings. In Market St: St John's Church of England (1860); St Mary's Roman Catholic Church; railway station; town hall; Colonial Inn Museum (open Sun. and public holidays); Mudgee Gallery for local art. Judy's Doll Museum, Gladstone St. Mt Vincent Meadery, Common Rd. Honey Haven, cnr Hill End and Gulgong Rds, and Mudgee Honey, Robertson St. Mudgee Creative Yarns, Sydney Rd, offers tours of working mill and sales. Market, 1st Sat. each month. Sept.: Wine festival. **In the area:** Henry Lawson's boyhood home memorial, plaque on remains of demolished cottage, 6 km N. Cudgegong River Park, 39 km W, on eastern foreshores of Burrendong Dam, for water sports and excellent fishing. Pick-Your-Own Farm, 12 km S, variety of fruit and vegetables Oct.–May. Water sports and trout fishing at Windamere Dam, 24 km SE; camping facilities on shore. Twenty local wineries, including Craigmoor, Montrose, Huntington Estate, Botobolar; contact Tourist information for details. **Tourist information:** 84 Market St; (063) 72 5875. **Accommodation:** 5 hotels, 9 motels, 22 B&B, 3 cara./camp. parks. **See also:** Vineyards and Wineries.

Mullumbimby — Pop. 2612

MAP REF. 119 Q2, 491 Q12

Situated in lush subtropical country, Mullumbimby is some 850 km NE of Sydney. **Of interest:** Art Gallery, cnr Burringbar and Stuart Sts. Restored Cedar House, Dalley St, National Trust-classified, with antiques gallery. Brunswick Valley Historical Museum, in old post office (1907), Stuart St. Brunswick Valley Heritage Park, preservation of rainforest plants; Tyagarah St. Market, 3rd Sat. each month. Sept.: Chincogan fiesta. **In the area:** Sakura Farm run by Buddhist monk, offers unique retreat-style holidays; 15 km W. Wanganui Gorge and rainforest walking track, 20 km W. Crystal Castle, 7 km SW, large display of natural quartz. Skydiving and paragliding at airstrip at Tyagarah, on Pacific Hwy, 13 km SE. **Tourist information:** 80 Jonson St, Byron Bay; (066) 85 8050. **Accommodation:** 2 hotels, 2 motels, 1 camp. park.

Mulwala — Pop. 1330

MAP REF. 123 N13, 235 L3

On the foreshores of Lake Mulwala, the town is a major aquatic centre. Lake Mulwala is an artificial lake of over 6000 ha, formed by the damming of the Murray River at Yarrawonga Weir in 1939 to provide water for irrigation. **Of interest:** Yachting, water-skiing, sailboarding, swimming, canoeing and fishing. Linley Animal Park, Corowa Rd, has native and exotic animals, and horse and pony rides. Tunzafun Amusement Park, Melbourne St, for mini-golf, mini-train and dodgem cars. Cruises available on Lake Mulwala. **Tourist information:** Irvine Pde, Yarrawonga; (057) 44 1989. **Accommodation:** 2 hotels, 10 motels, 3 B&B, 6 cara./camp. parks.

Murrumburrah — Pop. 2016

MAP REF. 115 C3, 116 E10

Murrumburrah, 357 km SW of Sydney, with its twin town Harden were settled in 1830. The surrounding area is rich grain and stock country. **Of interest:** In Albury St: Harden-Murrumburrah Historical Museum, open weekends; Which Craft and Coffee Cottage for local crafts; Coddington Park for picnics. Sept.: Agricultural show. **In the area:** Newson Park, in Albury St Harden, has picnic/barbecue facilities. Barwang Vineyard, 20 km N. Asparagus plantation at Jugiong, 30 km S. **Tourist information:** Which Craft and Coffee Cottage, Albury St; (063) 86 2343. **Accommodation:** 4 hotels, 1 motel, 1 B&B, 1 cara./camp. park.

Murrurundi — Pop. 983

MAP REF. 119 J13

This picturesque town on the New England Hwy, set in a lush valley on the Pages River, is overshadowed by the Liverpool Ranges. **Of interest:** St Joseph's Catholic Church, Polding St, contains 1000 pieces of Italian marble. Murrurundi Museum, Main St. Paradise Park, Paradise Rd, is horseshoe-shaped and surrounded by mountains; visits by wildlife in evening. Apr.: Sheepdog trials. Oct.: Bushman's carnival. **In the area:** Chilcott's Creek, 15 km N, where huge diprotodon remains, now in Sydney Museum, were found. Burning Mountain, a deep coal seam that has been smouldering at least 1000 years, at Wingen, 20 km S. Timor Limestone Caves, 43 km E. **Tourist information:** Council Offices, 47 Mayne St; (065) 46 6205. **Accommodation:** 3 hotels, 2 motels, 1 cara./camp. park.

Murwillumbah — Pop. 8003

MAP REF. 119 Q1, 491 Q11

Situated on the banks of the Tweed River, 31 km S of the Qld border in the beautiful Tweed Valley, Murwillumbah's local industries include cattle-raising and the growing of sugarcane, tropical fruits, tea and coffee. **Of interest:** Tweed River Regional Art Gallery, Tumbulgum Rd. Aug.: Banana festival. **In the area:** Tweed River houseboat hire, on Pacific Hwy, 1 km N of Tourist information. Condong sugar mill, 5 km N; open July–Dec. Tropical Fruitworld, 15 km N. Treetops Environment Centre, 8 km NE. Madura Tea Estates, 12 km NE. Hare Krishna Community Farm, Eungella, 10 km W; visitors welcome. Pioneer Plantation, 25 km SE, a banana plantation with farm animals and native gardens; tours available. World Heritage-listed areas within radius of 50 km include Mt Warning, Nightcap and Border Ranges National Parks. **Tourist information:** cnr Pacific Hwy and Alma St; (066) 72 1340. **Accommodation:** 6 hotels, 4 motels, 2 cara./camp. parks.

Muswellbrook Pop. 10 140

MAP REF. 117 K2

In the Upper Hunter Valley, Muswellbrook is the centre for the surrounding agricultural area. There is also a large open-cut coal-mining industry. **Of interest:** Art Gallery in old town hall, Bridge St. Historical town walk, contact Tourist information for brochure. Apr.: Agricultural show. Sept.: Art prize. Oct.: Spring wine festival. **In the area:** Seven local wineries. Wollemi National Park, 30 km SW, features Aboriginal carvings and paintings. Bayswater Power Station, 16 km S; tours available. Scenic Goulburn River National Park, 50 km W. **Tourist information:** Old Teahouse and Gift Shoppe, 208 Bridge St; (065) 43 3599. **Accommodation:** 3 hotel/motels, 8 motels, 2 cara./camp. parks.

Nambucca Heads Pop. 5683

MAP REF. 119 P9

At the mouth of the Nambucca River, 552 km N of Sydney, this beautifully sited town is ideal for boating, fishing and swimming. **Of interest:** Nambucca Historical Museum, Headland Reserve. Model Train Museum, Pelican Cres. Several rainforest walks, contact Tourist information. Market, 2nd Sun. each month at Nambucca Plaza. June: Ken Howard memorial bowls competition. Aug.: VW spectacular (odd-numbered years). Sept.: Septemberfest carnival. Oct.: Show 'n' Shine hot rod exhibition. **In the area:** Breathtaking views from several local lookouts. Wooden toys at Swiss Toymaker, 5 km N on Pacific Hwy (closed Sun.). Worm Farm Valley has educational worm displays; 7 km N. **Tourist information:** 4 Pacific Hwy; (065) 68 6954. **Accommodation:** 1 hotel, 12 motels, 1 B&B, 1 hostel, 6 cara./camp. parks.

Narooma Pop. 3443

MAP REF. 113 I2, 115 H9, 139 N11, 237 R2

This popular fishing resort situated at the mouth of the Wagonga River on the Princes Hwy, 360 km S of Sydney, is well known for its rock oysters. **Of interest:** Cruises on *Wagonga Princess* (Wed., Fri.–Sun.), depart Riverside Dr. adjacent to Taylors Boat Shed; whale-watching tours (mid Sept.–early Dec.); contact Tourist information. Easter: Tilba Festival. Excellent golf course on scenic cliff top, Ballingalla St. Mystery Bay near Lake Corunna, south of town, haunt of lapidary collectors with its coloured sands and strange rock formations. Other inlets and lakes north and south of town. **In the area:** Central Tilba, a heritage area (founded 1895),

The Newell

With its excellent bitumen surface and long, straight stretches, the Newell provides fast and easy driving right across New South Wales. Driving time between Melbourne and Brisbane is up to 6 hours quicker by this route. The time you save could be put to good use enjoying the many interesting attractions along the way.

From the Murray River town of **Tocumwal** to the Queensland border town of **Goondiwindi**, the highway runs through a wide range of scenery and is well served with motels, roadside cafes and service stations.

Tocumwal, with sandy beaches on the Murray, offers swimming and fishing as well as boating. At **Jerilderie**, 57 kilometres further north, visit the tiny restored post office held up by the Kelly gang in 1879. At **Narrandera** there is an excellent caravan park on the shore of Lake Talbot, a popular water sports centre. Beyond **West Wyalong** to the north is Lake Cowal, the largest natural lake in New South Wales and an important bird sanctuary; further north out of **Forbes** is a major tourist attraction – the Lachlan Vintage Village, a re-creation of a 19th-century goldmining town.

There is plenty to see in **Parkes**, including a vintage car museum and the Henry Parkes Museum. The famous radio telescope is on the highway, 23 kilometres north of the town. **Dubbo** boasts what is probably the most popular tourist attraction on the Newell – the Western Plains Zoo, claimed to be the best open-range wildlife park in Australia.

From Dubbo, the highway passes through the spectacular volcanic **Warrumbungle National Park**, which is ideal for bushwalking. If you have children aboard, do not miss the award-winning fantasy park, Miniland, with its life-size prehistoric animals, just west of **Coonabarabran**. Once you get beyond the Warrumbungle Ranges, the scenery changes dramatically to the vast Pilliga scrub country. **Narrabri**, in the heart of 'cotton country', offers a diversity of attractions, including the CSIRO Telescope Complex, and areas for gemstone fossicking, and is near **Mt Kaputar National Park** which

Western Plains Zoo, Dubbo

features the extraordinary rock formation Sawn Rocks. The northern town of **Moree**, not far from the Queensland border, is well known for its artesian spa baths and pecan nut farm.

For further information, contact the Tourist Information Office, Kelly Reserve, Newell Highway, Parkes 2870; (068) 62 4365. An excellent booklet on the Newell is available at tourist information centres. **See also:** National Parks; and individual entries in A–Z listing for those towns indicated by bold type. **Map references:** 116 C7, 116 D5, 118 F10, 118 H4.

17 km SW just off Princes Hwy, classified as 'unusual mountain village' by National Trust, has old buildings in original 19th-century condition and new buildings to National Trust specifications. Nearby, Deer Park. Montague Island, a wildlife sanctuary 5.7 nautical miles offshore, has large colony of little (fairy) penguins and Australian fur seals; year-round tours, contact Tourist information. **Tourist information:** Narooma Visitor Centre, Princes Hwy; (044) 76 2881. **Accommodation:** 1 hotel, 13 motels, 4 cara./camp. parks. See also: The South Coast.

Narrabri Pop. 6694

MAP REF. 118 G8

Situated between the Nandewar Range, including Mt Kaputar National Park and the extensive Pilliga scrub country, Narrabri is a phenomenally successful cotton-producing centre. **Of interest:** Historic buildings including court house (1886), Maitland St. Self-guide town tour; contact Tourist information. Riverside picnic area, Tibbereena St. Apr.: Agricultural show. Oct.: Spring festival. **In the area:** Tours of cotton fields and gin processing plants, Apr.–June; inquire at Tourist information. Plant Breeding Institute, 9 km N, on Newell Hwy. CSIRO Observatory, 25 km W, six giant radio telescopes; Visitors Centre, open Mon.–Fri. Yarrie Lake, 32 km W. Pilliga State Forest, 23 km SW. Salt Caves, 90 km SW. Mt Kaputar National Park, 53 km E in dramatic, volcanic mountain country; 360° views from peak take in one-tenth of NSW; Sawn Rocks, wilderness area in northern section (via Bingara Rd), with spectacular basaltic formation. **Tourist information:** Newell Hwy; (067) 92 3583. **Accommodation:** 6 hotels, 2 hotel/motels, 8 motels, 4 cara./camp. parks. See also: The Newell.

Narrandera Pop. 4649

MAP REF. 123 P9

This historic town on the Murrumbidgee River, at the junction of the Newell and Sturt Hwys, has been declared an urban conservation area with buildings classified or listed by the National Trust. Located 580 km SW of Sydney, it is the gateway to the Murrumbidgee Irrigation Area. **Of interest:** Lake Talbot Aquatic Playground, Lake Dr. Antique Shops, Larmer St. NSW Forestry Tree Nursery, Broad St. On Newell Hwy: Tiger Moth Memorial; Parkside Cottage Museum, Miniature Zoo and Tourist information centre with 5.8 m-long, playable guitar at Narrandera Park. My Dolls, doll and teddy-bear collection, Dangar Dr. Two Foot town heritage tour, Bundidgerry Walking Track through Nature Reserve, Blue arrow scenic drive; pamphlets available at Tourist information. Market, 2nd Sun. in months Oct.–Apr. Mar.: John O'Brien folk festival. Aug.: Camellia show. Oct.: Tree-mendous festival. **In the area:** Inland Fisheries Research Station has visitors centre (open Mon.–Fri.), 6 km SE. Berembed Weir, 40 km SE. Alabama Ostrich Farm, 30 km N; group tours by appt. Citrus Orchard, 6 km NW; group bookings. Craig Top Deer Farm, 8 km NW; tours daily. Robertson Gladioli Farm, 8 km W; group tours by appt. **Tourist information:** Big Guitar Tourist Information Centre, Narrandera Park, Newell Hwy; (069) 59 1766. **Accommodation:** 5 hotels, 10 motels, 2 B&B, 2 cara./camp. parks. See also: The Newell; Vineyards and Wineries.

Narromine Pop. 3378

MAP REF. 116 D2

On the Macquarie River, 457 km NW of Sydney, the area surrounding Narromine is well-known for quality agricultural products, including citrus fruit, tomatoes, corn, lamb, beef and cotton. It is also regarded as a good gliding area. **Of interest:** On Mitchell Hwy: Waterslide at eastern edge of town. Gliding and ultralight flying at airport, western outskirts of town. Oct.: Festival of Sport. **In the area:** Seedlings grown at Yates Research Station and Narromine Transplants, 2 km N. Swane's Rose Production Nursery, 5 km W, open to public. **Tourist information:** Council Offices, 124 Dandaloo St; (068) 89 1322. **Accommodation:** 4 hotels, 1 hotel/motel, 2 motels, 3 cara./camp. parks.

Nelson Bay Pop. 6766

MAP REF. 108 H2, 117 O4

The beautiful bay on which this town is sited is the main anchorage of Port Stephens, about 60 km N of Newcastle. **Of interest:** Restored Inner Lighthouse, Nelson Head. Contact Tourist information for details of: self-guide heritage walk, from Dutchmans Bay to Little Beach; Dolphin Watch cruises; cruises on harbour, on Myall River and to Broughton Island (Sun. only); dive charters; and boat hire. Feb.: Game-fishing tournament. **In the area:** Fort Tomaree Lookout, 4 km NE, for 360° views (signposted walkway to top). Across bay (70 km by road) Yacaaba Lookout also offers 360° views. Native Flora Reserve at Little Beach, 1 km E. Gan Gan Lookout, 2 km SW on Nelson Bay Rd. Toboggan Hill Park at Salamander Bay, 5 km SW, has toboggan runs, mini-golf course and fun shed. On Nelson Bay Rd: Port Stephens Wines, 10 km SW; Oakvale Farm and Fauna World, 16 km SW at Salt Ash. Convict-built Tanilba House (1831), 37 km W; open Wed., Sat. and Sun. Tomaree National Park, along coastline from Shoal Bay, 3 km NE, to Anna Bay, 10 km SW. **Tourist information:** Port Stephens Visitors Centre, Victoria Pde, Nelson Bay; (049) 81 1579. **Accommodation:** 12 motels, 1 cara./camp. park. See also: Port Stephens.

Newcastle Pop. 262 331

MAP REF. 106, 108 G7, 117 N4

Australia's largest industrial city, located 158 km N of Sydney is encircled by some of the finest surfing beaches in the world and overlooks a huge, spectacular harbour. Rebuilding in some areas has followed the 1989 earthquake. Newcastle is experiencing a boom in tourism as visitors are attracted to the wineries and vineyards, and picturesque villages of the surrounding Hunter Valley region. **Of interest:** Queens Wharf, on Wharf Rd, centrepoint of foreshore redevelopment, has indoor and outdoor restaurants, 'boutique' brewery, observation tower linked by walkway to the City Mall, a part of Hunter St. Sydney-style terrace houses along nearby city streets. City parks and gardens. Regional art gallery, Laman St. City Hall, King St. In King Edward Park, Wolfe St: Obelisk (1850) marks site of Newcastle's first windmill; Soldiers Baths (1880s) off Shortland Espl., now a public pool; Bogey Hole, hole cut in rocks by convict labour, now a public pool; band rotunda (1898). Heritage walk, contact Tourist information. Maritime and Military Museum at Fort Scratchley, Nobbys Rd. Scenic walks along foreshore. Many fine surf beaches. River and harbour cruises. Mar.: Surfest. Aug.: Jazz festival. **In the area:** Lake Macquarie, 20 km S: huge aquatic playground with well-maintained parks lining foreshore. Lake cruises on *Macquarie Lady* and *Macquarie Enterprise*, both leave from Toronto Wharf and Belmont Public Wharf; Dobell House, home of artist Sir William Dobell, has collection of his work and memorabilia; 47 Dobell Dr., Wangi Wangi; tours of power station available at Eraring; Aboriginal art and craft at Bahtabah Land Council Visitors Centre, Lakeview Pde. Frazer Park, a coastal recreation area south of Swansea. Shortland Wetlands, 15 km W, a bird habitat, with a canoe trail. About 50 km NW is Australia's famous wine region, the Hunter Valley. Fighter World, museum and high-tech exhibition at Williamtown RAAF base, 20 km N. Yuelarbah Track, part of Great North Walk from Sydney to Newcastle, covers 25 km from Lake Macquarie to Newcastle harbour; contact Tourist information. **Tourist information:** 92 Scott St; (049) 29 9299. **Accommodation:** 27 hotels, 30 motels, 13 cara./camp. parks.

Nimbin   Pop. 274

MAP REF. 119 Q2, 491 Q12

The Aquarius Softlicks festival in 1973 established Nimbin as the alternative culture capital of Australia. Today Nimbin's peaceful, friendly atmosphere, and the buildings designed and decorated to reflect the community's ideas and beliefs, attract visitors wishing to experience an alternative lifestyle. **Of interest:** In Cullen St: shops, painted in psychedelic colours, feature home-made products, local art and craft; Triple Blah Theaterette, showing variety of short films; Dancing Dervish Restaurant, 'food from the fourth dimension'; original Rainbow Cafe, fresh local organic produce; Nimbin Museum, dedicated to hippy culture and history of St Aquarius; town hall has mural featuring Aboriginal art; Rainbow Power Company, Alternative Way, alternative power supplier, now exporting; tours available. Country Market, 4th Sun. each month at Showgrounds; outlet for local craftspeople. Sept.: Show. **In the area:** Spectacular volcanic Nimbin Rocks, 3 km S, on Lismore Rd. Nearby, Nimbin Rocks Gallery has high-quality art in all mediums. The Channon Craft Market, 15 km SE, 2nd Sun. each month at Coronation Park. World Heritage-listed Nightcap National Park, 10 km NE. Calurla Tea Gardens, 10 km N on Lillian Rock Rd, offers spectacular views, farmhouse cooking and live music. **Tourist information:** Lismore Visitor Information Centre, cnr Ballina and Molesworth Sts; (066) 22 0122. **Accommodation:** 1 hostel, 1 cara./camp. park.

Nowra   Pop. 21 942

MAP REF. 112 E12, 115 H4, 117 K11

A popular tourist centre, Nowra is the principal town of the Shoalhaven district on the south coast. Bomaderry is on the northern side of the river. **Of interest:** Historic Houses Trust-property Meroogal (1885), cnr Worrigee and West Sts; open weekends. Shoalhaven Historical Museum, cnr Plunkett and Kinghorn Sts, in old police station. Fishing, water-skiing, canoeing and sailing on Shoalhaven River. Hanging Rock, via Junction St, has fine views. Nowra Animal Park, Rockhill Rd. Bens Walk, alongside river; Bomaderry Creek Walk from Bomaderry; contact Tourist information for pamphlets. Market, 3rd Sun. each month at Showground. Oct.: Spring festival. **In the area:** Many beautiful beaches within 30 km radius of town. Australian Naval Aviation Museum, at HMAS *Albatross*; 7 km SW. Cambewarra Lookout, 12 km NW. Kangaroo Valley, 23 km NW, historic buildings: Friendly Inn (National Trust-classified); Pioneer Settlement Reserve, reconstruction of dairy farm of 1880s; Hampden Bridge (1898), oldest suspension bridge in Australia. Fitzroy Falls in Morton National Park, 38 km NW; also in park (turn off at Kangaroo Valley), Tallowa Dam water catchment area, 42 km NW, ideal for picnicking; just before park, Sharpley Vale Fruit World, a working fruit farm. Historic Bundanon, 21 km W, gifted to the nation by Arthur and Yvonne Boyd, guided tours only of National Estate-listed homestead including Bundanon collection and Arthur Boyd's studio; tickets need to be obtained from Tourist information (advance bookings recommended). Fresh fish and oyster sales at Greenwell Point, 14 km E. **Tourist information:** Shoalhaven Tourist Centre, 254 Princes Hwy, Bomaderry; (044) 21 0778. **Accommodation:** Nowra: 1 hotel, 10 motels, 5 cara./camp. parks. Bomaderry: 1 hotel, 4 motels, 1 cara./camp. park. **See also:** The Illawarra Coast.

Nundle   Pop. 261

MAP REF. 119 K12

The history of this small town began in the early gold-rush era during the 1850s. Well known for its fishing, Nundle is situated 60 km SE of Tamworth, at the foot of the Great Dividing Range, in a district that supports sheep, cattle, wheat and timber. **Of interest:** In Jenkins St: Court house,

Historic Hampden Bridge, Kangaroo Valley, near Nowra

NEW SOUTH WALES

Town Hall building, Nyngan

antique shop and historic Peel Inn (1860s). Goldmining display in restored coffin factory, Gill St. Aug.-Sept., Dec.: Camp drafting and dog trials. **In the area:** Hanging Rock and Sheba Dams Reserve, 11 km E, for picnicking, bushwalking and camping. Fossicking at Hanging Rock, gold panning on Peel River. Chaffey Dam, 11 km N. **Tourist information:** cnr Peel and Murray Sts, Tamworth; (067) 66 9422. **Accommodation:** 1 hotel, 1 motel, 1 cara./camp. park.

Nyngan Pop. 2311

MAP REF. 121 R10

The centre of a wool-growing district beside the Bogan River, 603 km NW of Sydney. **Of interest:** Historic buildings, especially in Cobar and Bogan Sts. Historical Museum at railway station, Pangee St, has local memorabilia. Apr.: Anzac Day race meeting. May: Agricultural show. **In the area:** Cairn on private property, marking geographic centre of NSW; 65 km S. Grave of Richard Cunningham, botanist with explorer Major Mitchell's party, speared by Aborigines in 1835; 70 km S. Bird sanctuary in Macquarie Marshes, 64 km N. **Tourist information:** Burns Video, Pangee St; (068) 32 1155. **Accommodation:** 2 hotels, 1 hotel/motel, 3 motels, 2 cara./camp. parks.

Orange Pop. 29 635

MAP REF. 116 G6

A prosperous city set in rich red volcanic soil and famous for its apples, parks and gardens, Orange is 264 km NW of Sydney on the slopes of Mt Canobolas. An obelisk marks the birthplace of the city's most famous citizen, poet A.B. (Banjo) Paterson; his birthday is celebrated with the Banjo Paterson festival. **Of interest:** Historic Cook Park, Summer St, has begonia conservatory (flowers Feb.–May), duck ponds, fernery and picnic area. Museum, McNamara St. Civic Centre, Byng St, comprises a theatre, Regional Art Gallery, City Library, Visitors Centre and exhibition rooms. Feb.-Mar.: Banjo Paterson festival. **In the area:** Campbell's Corner, 8 km S on Pinnacle Rd, a roadside picnic/barbecue spot. Lucknow Village, 10 km SE. Golden Memories Museum, Millthorpe, 22 km SE, has over 5000 exhibits, including grandma's kitchen and blacksmith's shop; also art and craft centre. Gallery of Minerals, 1 km E, mineral and fossil collection. Agriculture Research Centre, 5 km N, field days held Nov. Ophir goldfields, 27 km N, site of first discovery of payable gold in Australia in 1851, features fossicking centre, picnic area, walking trails to historic gold tunnels, tours of working goldmine and Ophir Reserve. Borenore Caves, 17 km W, has picnic/barbecue facilities. Lake Canobolas Park, 8 km SW via Cargo Rd, has recreation and camping area, deer park, children's playground, picnic/barbecue facilities; trout-fishing in lake. Mt Canobolas Park, a 1500-ha bird and animal sanctuary, 14 km SW. Wineries: Bloodwood Estate, 3 km NW on Molong Rd; Canobolas Wines, 15 km W on Cargo Rd; Highland Heritage Wines, 3 km E on Bathurst Rd. **Tourist information:** Civic Gardens, Byng St; (063) 61 5226. **Accommodation:** 9 hotels, 9 motels, 15 B&B, 2 cara./camp. parks.

Parkes Pop. 8784

MAP REF. 116 D5

Situated 364 km NW of Sydney on the Newell Hwy, Parkes is the commercial and industrial centre of an important agricultural area. **Of interest:** Motor Museum, cnr Bogan and Dalton Sts, displays vintage and veteran vehicles, local art and craft. Henry Parkes Historical Museum, Clarinda St, has memorabilia, library of 1000 volumes. Imposing views from Shrine of Remembrance at eastern end of Bushman St. In north Parkes: Pioneer Park Museum (Pioneer St), in historic school and church, has displays of early farm machinery and transport; Kelly Reserve (Newell Hwy), picnics and barbecues in bush setting; Bushmans Hill Reserve (Newell Hwy), at site of old goldmine. June: Central West jazz triduum. Oct.: Country music jamboree. **In the area:** CSIRO Radio Telescope Visitors Centre, 23 km N, has excellent educational aids explaining use of giant saucer-shaped telescope. At Peak Hill, 48 km N: open-cut goldmine; lookout offering views of goldmine; camel park. **Tourist information:** Kelly Reserve, Newell Hwy; (068) 62 4365. **Accommodation:** 5 hotels, 11 motels, 4 cara./camp. parks. **See also:** The Newell.

Picton Pop. 2116

MAP REF. 101 J11, 112 E2, 115 I2, 117 K9

Picton, named after Sir Thomas Picton, hero of Waterloo, is 80 km SW of Sydney on Remembrance Dr. (former Hume Hwy). The old buildings and quiet hills of this small town seem to echo the past. **Of interest:** Historic buildings: old railway viaduct (1862) over Stone Quarry Creek, seen from Showgrounds off Menangle St; St Mark's Church (1848), Menangle St; George IV Inn, which incorporates Scharer's Little Brewery, Argyle St. **In the area:** Sydney Skydiving Centre, 5 km E. On Remembrance Dr.: Jarvisfield (1865), 2 km N, family home of pioneer landholders, now clubhouse of Antill Park Golf Club; Wool Away! Woolshed, 3 km N, bush dances Fri. and Sat. nights. At Thirlmere, 5 km SW: Railway Transport Museum; Festival of steam held in Mar. Further 3 km, Thirlmere Lakes National Park protects five linked freshwater lakes; scenic drive around lakes. Wirrimbirra Sanctuary, 13 km S, native flora and fauna; overnight cabins. **Tourist information:** Shire Offices: Menangle St; (046) 77 1161. **Accommodation:** 1 hotel, 1 motel, 1 B&B, 1 cara. park.

Pitt Town Pop. 632

MAP REF. 101 L6

One of the five Macquarie Towns, Pitt Town was named after William Pitt the elder, and was marked out on a site to the east of the present village in January 1811. The rich alluvial river flats provided early Sydney with almost 50 per cent of its food supply, which was transported by boat down the Hawkesbury River and south along the coast to Sydney Town. Aug.: Fun run. **In the area:** Old Manse, belonging to oldest Presbyterian (now Uniting) Church in Australia, 8 km N at Ebenezer. **Tourist information:** Ham Common Bicentenary Park, Richmond Rd, Clarendon; (045) 88 5895. **Accommodation:** None. **See also**: The Hawkesbury.

Port Macquarie   Pop. 26 798

MAP REF. 105 G7, 119 P12

Founded as a convict settlement in 1821, and one of the oldest towns in the State, Port Macquarie is now a major holiday resort, situated at the mouth of the Hastings River, 423 km N of Sydney. **Of interest:** Award-winning Hastings Historical Museum, Clarence St, in 15 rooms of commercial building (built 1835–40); displays of convict and pioneer relics. St Thomas's (1824), Church St, a convict-built church designed by convict architect Thomas Owen. In Horton St: historic cemetery dating from 1842; Kooloonbung Creek Nature Reserve, 50 ha of natural bushland with walking trails. Roto House and Macquarie Nature Reserve, Lord St, a koala hospital and study centre. Port Macquarie Observatory, William St. Fantasy Glades, Pacific Dr., with rainforest gardens and picnic/barbecue facilities. Billabong Koala and Aussie Wildlife Park (Billabong Dr.) and Kingfisher Park (Kingfisher Rd), for close-up look at Australian animals. World of Models, Bay St. Town Beach, has surf at one end, sheltered coves at other. Peppermint Park, has slides, roller-skating. Orchid World, Ocean Dr., features Australian and exotic plants, camel rides and safaris. River cruises daily. Market, 2nd and 4th Sun. each month. **In the area:** Scenic drives to Ellenborough Falls, 85 km SW; to Wauchope and Timbertown, 20 km W; brochures available at Tourist information. Exceptionally good fishing and all water sports. Charter fishing available. Harley Davidson motor-bike tours, horseriding, abseiling. Thrumster Village Pottery, 10 km W. Cassegrain Winery, 13 km W. Sea Acres Rainforest Centre, 4 km S, includes elevated boardwalk and guided tours of rainforest. The Old Butter Factory, an Australiana-theme function centre, holds regular bush dances; 21 km NW. **Tourist information:** cnr Clarence and Hay Sts; (065) 83 1293. **Accommodation:** 1 hotel/motel, 38 motels, 3 B&B, 15 cara./camp. parks.

Queanbeyan   Pop. 19 383

MAP REF. 115 E5, 116 G13, 135 G4, 138 H3

Adjoining Canberra, Queanbeyan has a special relationship with the Australian capital. The town, proclaimed in 1838, is named from a squattage held by an ex-convict innkeeper, Timothy Beard, on the Molonglo River and called 'Quinbean' ('clear waters'). **Of interest:** History Museum, Farrer Pl. Byrne's Mill (1883) now a restaurant, Collett St. Mill House Gallery, cnr Collett and Morisset Sts. Design Plus Gallery, Monaro St, for pottery, silk, leatherwork. Art Centre, Trinculo Pl. Michelago Steam Train rides, depart station in Henderson St; first Sun. in month and special trips. Cottage market, 2nd Sun. each month. Nov.: Festival; Agricultural show. Dec.: Country music festival. **In the area:** At Bungendore, 26 km NE: historic village square contains colonial-style shops; Woodworks sells local art and crafts. Bywong Mining Town, 31 km NE. Googong Dam, 10 km S, fishing; bushwalking and wildlife refuge on shore. London Bridge Woolshed and Shearers' Quarters, 24 km S; walk 1 km to limestone formation. **Tourist information:** cnr Farrer Place and Lowe St; (06) 298 0241. **Accommodation:** 3 hotels, 18 motels, 2 cara./camp. parks.

Quirindi   Pop. 2830

MAP REF. 119 J12

Appropriately named after an Aboriginal word meaning 'nest in the hills', this town in the Liverpool Ranges was proclaimed in 1856. It was one of the first towns in Australia to organise the game of polo. **Of interest:** Historical Cottage and Museum, Station St; open Fri. p.m. and Sat. a.m. Jan.: Wallabadah Cup meeting (New Year's Day). Aug.: Polo carnival. **In the area:** Who'd-A-Thought-It Lookout, 2 km NE, for views over ranges and plains. **Tourist information:** Sports Centre, 248 George St; (067) 46 2128. **Accommodation:** 5 hotels, 2 motels, 1 cara./camp. park.

Raymond Terrace   Pop. 11 159

MAP REF. 108 E6, 117 N4

An important wool-shipping centre in the 1840s, several historic buildings remain in this town, set on the banks of the Hunter and William Rivers. **Of interest:** Significant buildings: court house (1838) (cnr William St and Pacific Hwy), still in use; Church of England and rectory (Glenelg St), built of hand-hewn sandstone in 1830s; and numerous buildings in historic King St, along waterfront. Sketchley Cottage, museum of memorabilia, on Pacific Hwy. Mar.: Oz ski (waterskiing races and events). Oct.: Twin Rivers festival. **In the area:** Hunter Region Botanic Gardens, on Pacific Hwy at Motto Farm, 2 km S. Fighter World, RAAF Base Williamtown, 16 km E. **Tourist information:** Council Offices, 116 Pacific Hwy; (049) 83 1333. **Accommodation:** 5 motels, 2 cara./camp. parks.

Richmond   Pop. 18 766

MAP REF. 101 K6, 117 K7

One of the five Macquarie towns and sister town to Windsor, 5 km E, Richmond was proclaimed a town in 1810. **Of interest:** Historic buildings: Hobartville (privately owned), Castlereagh Rd; Toxana (1841) (art gallery in building, open Sun.), Windsor St; St Peter's Church (1841), also in Windsor St; adjacent graveyard where several notable pioneers, including William Cox and Australia's convict chronicler Margaret Catchpole, are buried. Sept.: Hawkesbury District orchid spring show. **In the area:** RAAF base, 3 km E on Windsor–Richmond Rd, oldest Air Force establishment in Australia; used for civilian flying from 1915. University of Western Sydney, 3 km S; foundation stone laid in 1895. Vale Lookout, for stunning views over Grose Valley; 20 km W. Panorama Point Lookout at Kurrajong Heights, 13 km NW, for views across to Sydney skyline. **Tourist information:** Ham Common Bicentenary Park, Richmond Rd, Clarendon; (045) 88 5895. **Accommodation:** 1 hotel, 1 hotel/motel, 2 motels. **See also:** The Hawkesbury.

Robertson   Pop. 252

MAP REF. 112 E8, 115 I3, 117 K10

The link between the Southern Highlands and the coast, Robertson sits at the top of the Macquarie Pass. Vantage points in the area offer spectacular views of the coast. It is the centre of the largest potato-growing district in NSW. Mar.: Agricultural show. **In the area:** Fitzroy and Belmore Falls in Morton National Park, 10 km SW. Mannings Lookout over Kangaroo Valley, 16 km SW. Robertson Rainforest, 2 km S. Carrington Falls and State-award-winning Minnamurra Rainforest, with elevated boardwalk, in Budderoo National Park; 10 km SE. View from top of Macquarie Pass in national park, over rainforest to coast; 10 km NE. **Tourist information:** Southern Highlands Visitor Information Centre, Winifred West Park, Old Hume Hwy, Mittagong; (048) 71 2888. **Accommodation:** 1 hotel, 1 motel, 1 B&B.

Rylstone   Pop. 721

MAP REF. 116 I4

Aboriginal hand-paintings on a sandstone rock overhang are a feature of the region, which is west of the Great Dividing Range on the Cudgegong River, north-east of Bathurst. **Of interest:** Historic buildings, especially in Louee St, including The Half Pie Gallery (formerly bank), and post office. Feb.: Rylstone-Kandos show. **In the area:** Many camping spots and fishing areas on Capertee, Cudgegong and Turon Rivers. Industrial Museum (open weekends) at Kandos, 3 km S. Fern Tree Gully, 16 km N, tree ferns in subtropical forest. Lake Windemere, 19 km W, for water sports and trout fishing; camping and picnic/barbecue facilities on shore. Glen Davis, 56 km SE on Capertee River, surrounded by sheer cliff faces. Wollemi National Park, 60 km SE, for wilderness bushwalking and canoeing. **Tourist information:** Shire Offices, Louee St, Rylstone; (063) 79 1205. **Accommodation:** 4 hotels, 1 motel, 1 B&B, 1 cara./camp. park.

Sawtell   Pop. 10 809

MAP REF. 119 P8

This peaceful family holiday town, 8 km S of Coffs Harbour, has safe beaches and tidal creeks for fishing, swimming and surfing. **Of interest:** Playground and picnic/barbecue facilities at Boambee Creek Reserve, Sawtell Rd. Enchanting walks and drives in surrounding bush and mountains, including Sawtell Reserve. **In the area:** White-water rafting on Nymboida, Gwydir and Murray Rivers. **Tourist information:** Coffs Harbour Visitors and Convention Centre, cnr Ross Ave and Marcia St, Coffs Harbour; (066) 52 8824. **Accommodation:** 2 hotels, 2 motels, 1 cara./camp. park.

Scone   Pop. 3329

MAP REF. 117 K1

This pleasant town set in beautiful country on the New England Hwy, 280 km N of Sydney, is the world's second largest thoroughbred and horse-breeding centre. **Of interest:** Historical Society Museum, Kingdon St; open Wed. and Sun. Hungry Horse Gallery and Restaurant, part of tourist information centre opposite Elizabeth Park, Kelly St. Market, last Sun. each month. May: Horse week festival. Nov.: Rodeo. **In the area:** Lake Glenbawn, 15 km E, for water sports, picnic/barbecue facilities and camping on shore. Hunter Valley Museum of Rural Life, 2 km W of dam. Barrington Tops National Park, 80 km E, for scenic drives and walks. Jazz festival in Oct. at Moonan Flat, 50 km NE. Burning Mountain at Wingen, 20 km N, a deep coal seam that has been smouldering for at least 1000 years. **Tourist information:** cnr Susan and Kelly Sts; (065) 45 1526. **Accommodation:** 3 hotels, 5 motels, 7 B&B, 1 hostel, 2 cara./camp. parks.

Shellharbour   Pop. 1754

MAP REF. 112 H8, 117 K10

This attractive holiday resort 7 km S of Lake Illawarra is one of the oldest settlements on the south coast. A thriving port in the 1830s, its importance declined once the south coast railway opened. Apr.: Sunshine festival. Aug.: Shelkove aquatic and outdoor expo. **In the area:** Bike paths; bike hire available. Blackbutt Forest Reserve and Killalea Recreation Park, 2 km W. BMX circuit at Croom Regional Sporting Complex, 8 km W. Bass Point Headland and Marine Reserve, 5 km SE, picnic area with views; scuba diving, snorkelling, fishing and surfing. Fine beach at Warilla, 3 km N. Lake Illawarra, 7 km N; boat hire available. **Tourist information:** Lamberton House, Shellharbour Square, Blackbutt; (042) 21 6169. **Accommodation:** 1 hotel, 2 motels, 3 cara./camp. parks. **See also:** The Illawarra Coast.

Singleton   Pop. 11 861

MAP REF. 117 L3

Set beside the Hunter River in rich grazing land, Singleton is the geographical heart of the Hunter Valley. New wealth in the form of huge open-cut coal mines has joined the traditional rural industry and transformed Singleton into one of the most progressive country centres in the State. **Of interest:** Monolithic sundial, largest in southern hemisphere; built as Bicentennial project on riverbank in James Cook Park, Ryan Ave. Sales of herbs at Dullwide Herbs, Falbrook Rd. Oct.: Festival of wine and roses. **In the area:** Royal Australian Infantry Corps Museum of Small Arms, 5 km S, traces development of firearms from 15th century. Village fair held in Sept. at Broke, 26 km S. Broke-Fordwich winery area of Hunter Valley; contact Tourist information for details. Yengo National Park, 15 km S, features extensive Aboriginal carvings and paintings; tours available, contact Tourist information. Wollemi National Park, 15 km SW, a large wilderness park. Bayswater Power Station, biggest thermal power station in southern hemisphere; New England Hwy, 26 km NW. Lake St Clair, 30 km N, extensive recreational and waterway facilities; camping on shore; nearby, magnificent views of Mt Royal Range. **Tourist information:** Shire Offices, Queen St; (065) 72 1866. **Accommodation:** 6 hotels, 2 hotel/motels, 5 motels, 2 B&B, 2 cara./camp. parks.

Stroud   Pop. 556

MAP REF. 117 N3

There are many historic buildings in this delightful, small country town, 75 km N of Newcastle. The convict-built Anglican Church of St John, built in 1833 of local clay bricks, with its beautiful stained glass windows and cedar furnishings, is one of the finest. **Of interest:** Rectory of St John's (1836), Stroud House (1832), Parish House (1837), court house, post office and Quambi House – all in Cowper St. Self-guide heritage tour, leaflet available at Tourist information. Underground silo (one of 8 built in 1841) at Silo Hill Reserve, off Broadway St. July: International brick and rolling-pin throwing. Sept.-Oct.: Rodeo. **Tourist information:** Great Lakes Tourist Board, Little St, Forster; (065) 54 8799.

Lindeman's Winery, Pokolbin, is one of the major wineries in the Hunter Valley

Vineyards and Wineries

A vineyard holiday takes you through peaceful, ordered countryside and gives you the chance to learn more about wine and its making at first hand. It also gives you a perfect excuse for wine-tasting and, later, sampling the local wines with a meal in a first-class restaurant in the area. The obvious place to head for in New South Wales is the famous Hunter Valley. It is not far from Sydney (2 hours' drive each way) and, with some 70 wineries, must rate as one of the most important wine-growing districts in Australia. Although it can be a pleasant day trip from Sydney to the Hunter, it is well worth booking into a motel in the area for at least one night, to do it justice. Mid-week with lower tariffs and fewer crowds, is the best time to visit.

The Hunter is Australia's oldest commercial wine-producing area, wine having first been made there in the 1830s. The Hunter's table wines, both red and white, still rank among the best in Australia.

Most of the early colonial vineyards in the region have vanished. Some family concerns have been taken over by the larger companies such as Lindemans and McWilliams.

The high reputation of the district is maintained by such well-known properties as Mount Pleasant, Oakvale, Drayton's, Tyrrell's, Tulloch's Glen Elgin, Wyndham and Rothbury.

Most wineries welcome visitors and are open for inspection and wine-tastings daily. Several have picnic grounds, barbecue facilities and excellent restaurants which make for a pleasant day's outing.

Pokolbin Cellars at McGuigan Hunter Village, Blaxland's at Pokolbin and the Casuarina at North Pokolbin are among the restaurants in the area.

The McGuigan Hunter Village at Pokolbin has wine tastings, wine sales, a gallery, accommodation at the Vineyard Resort, specialty shops, a cheese factory, a restaurant, kiosk, picnic facilities, an adventure playground for children and an aquagolf driving range.

It is best to go at vintage time – usually around February in the Hunter – if you want to see a vineyard in full swing. However, this is the most hectic time of year for vignerons, so do not expect their undivided attention. For an idea of the range of wineries in the district, try Tyrrell's and Drayton's wineries for a glimpse of the more traditional family approach, and Lindeman or Hunter Estate for the modern 'big company' style.

South of Sydney at **Camden** is Gledswood, birthplace of Australia's wine industry. The first vines were planted here in 1827; the winery was re-established as Gledswood Cellars in 1970. The winery also offers an art gallery, shearing demonstrations and picnic facilities. Hayrides and candle-lit dinners for parties can be arranged.

You could also have an enjoyable wine-tasting holiday in the Riverina towns of **Griffith** and **Leeton**, in the other main winegrowing area of the State. Griffith, Leeton and **Narrandera** are the main towns in the Murrumbidgee Irrigation Area, which grows 80 per cent of the State's wine-producing grapes. Well known wineries such as McWilliam's, de Bortoli and Rosetto & Sons are open to visitors who wish to taste the wines of the Riverina. In Leeton, visitors are welcome to sample the vintages at Toorak Winery and Lillypilly Estate.

Mudgee, 261 kilometres north-west of Sydney, is also in an area where fine wines are produced from some dozen wineries. Other smaller vineyards are scattered throughout the State – some of them quite close to Sydney.

For further information on the Lower Hunter area, contact the Lower Hunter Visitor Information Centre, Turner Park, Aberdare Rd, Cessnock; (049) 90 4477. For information on the other wine areas, contact the local tourist information centres in the area. **See also:** individual entries in A–Z listing for those towns indicated by bold type. **Map reference** for Lower Hunter: 109.

NEW SOUTH WALES

Bridge over Manning River, Taree

Accommodation: 1 hotel, 1 hostel, 1 camp. park.

Tamworth Pop. 31 716

MAP REF. 119 J11

This prosperous city at the junction of the New England and Oxley Hwys is the country music capital of Australia, as well as being the heart of many other cultural and musical activities. Thousands of fans flock here for the 10-day Australasian country music festival, held each Jan. since 1973. Tamworth, with its attractive public buildings and parks and gardens, is also the commercial capital of northern NSW. **Of interest:** Country Music Hands of Fame cornerstone at Hands of Fame Park, Kable Ave, has hand imprints of country music stars, including Tex Morton, Slim Dusty and Smoky Dawson. Country Music Roll of Renown at Radio Centre, on New England Hwy at Calala, dedicated to country-music artists who have contributed to Australia's heritage. National Trust-classified Calala Cottage, Denison St, home of Tamworth's first mayor. City Gallery, Marius St, exhibits works by Turner, Hans Heysen and Will Ashton; also home of National Fibre Collection. Weswal Gallery, Brisbane St. Tininburra Gallery, Moore Creek Rd. Gallery of Stars Wax Museum, Great Australian Ice-creamery and famous Longyard Hotel – all on New England Hwy. Oxley Park Wildlife Sanctuary, north off Brisbane St. Oxley Lookout for views of city and rich Peel Valley, at top of White St; lookout is starting point for Kamilaroi walking track (6.2 km), brochure available at Tourist information. Powerstation Museum, cnr Peel and Darling Sts, traces Tamworth's history as first city in southern hemisphere to have electric street lighting. Market, 2nd Sun. each month at Showground Pavilion. Jan.: Australasian country music festival. May: Gold Cup race meeting. **In the area:** Country Collection, 6 km S on New England Hwy, fascinating gemstone collection and location of 12-metre Golden Guitar. Lake Keepit State Recreation Area, 57 km NW, water sports, visitor facilities. Historic gold-mining township of Nundle nestled in 'Hills of Gold', a 63-km scenic drive SE. Chaffey Dam, 45 km SE, for sailing; Dulegal Arboretum on foreshore. Warrabah National Park, 75 km N. **Tourist information:** cnr Murray and Peel Sts; (067) 66 9422. **Accommodation:** 7 hotels, 2 hotel/motels, 31 motels, 2 B&B, 4 cara./camp. parks.

Taree Pop. 16 303

MAP REF. 105 C13, 117 P1, 119 N13

Taree on the Pacific Hwy, 320 km N of Sydney, serves as the manufacturing and commercial centre of the Manning River district. **Of interest:** Manning River cruises depart from wharf at end of Pulteney St. Houseboats available for hire. The Big Oyster, Pacific Hwy at northern entrance to town. Easter: Aquatic festival; National power-boat titles. Apr.-May: Taree and district eisteddfod. **In the area:** Good surfing beaches on coast 16 km E. Forest drives and walking trails in Manning Valley. Manning River, a 150-km navigable waterway, with beaches, good fishing and holiday spots. Easy car access to top of Ellenborough Falls (160-m drop) on Bulga Plateau, 50 km NW. The Big Buzz Funpark, Lakes Way, Rainbow Flat, 17.5 km S. Crowdy Bay National Park, 40 km NE, offers wildflowers in spring, fishing, swimming and bushwalking. Scenic Coopernook Forest Dr., starts at Forest Headquarters north of Coopernook, 20 km NE; one highlight is Big Nellie (a large volcanic plug), rising 560 m above sea level. Railway Crossing Family Fun Park at Harrington, 30 km N. High Adventure Fun Park, 38 km N on Pacific Hwy, a light airsports (including both paragliding and hang-gliding) training and recreational centre. Middle Brother State Forest, 50 km N. **Tourist information:** Manning Valley Tourist Information Centre, Pacific Hwy, Taree North; (065) 52 1900 or 1800 80 1522. **Accommodation:** 6 hotels, 21 motels, 3 cara./camp. parks.

Tathra Pop. 1571

MAP REF. 113 G8, 115 G10, 237 R6

Tathra is a relaxed seaside town, centrally located on the south coast of NSW, 18 km SE of Bega and midway between Merimbula and Bermagui. Tathra is an ideal place for a family holiday, with its patrolled 3-km long surf beach, safe swimming for small children at Mogareka Inlet (the sandy mouth of the Bega River), and good fishing spots. Diving and deep-sea fishing charters at Kianniny Bay. **Of interest:** National Trust-classified historic wharf (1860s), Wharf Rd. Above wharf, Maritime Museum displays variety of memorabilia of visiting ships. May: Game-fishing competition. **In the area:** Fishing and water sports on Lake Wallagoot, 9.5 km S. Bournda National Park, 11 km S of town, for camping, swimming and bushwalking. Mimosa Rocks National Park, a picturesque coastal park 17 km N. **Tourist information:** Tathra Wharf, Wharf Rd; (064) 94 4062. **Accommodation:** 1 motel, 1 hotel/motel, 1 B&B, 4 cara./ camp. parks.

Temora Pop. 4279

MAP REF. 115 A2, 116 C10, 123 R8

Temora is the commercial centre for the

rich wheat district of the northern and western Riverina, which also supports oats, barley, fat lambs, pigs and cattle. **Of interest:** Temora Rural Museum (open p.m.), has working displays, and rock and mineral collection; Wagga Rd. Feb.: Golden Gift (foot race). **In the area:** Lake Centenary, 3 km N. Paragon Gold Mine at Gidginbung, 15 km N; open by appt. **Tourist information:** Temora Community Centre, Hoskins St; (069) 78 0500. **Accommodation:** 2 hotels, 3 motels, 1 cara./camp. park.

Tenterfield   Pop. 3310

MAP REF. 119 M4, 491 N13

The countryside around Tenterfield, at the northern end of the New England highlands in northern NSW, offers a contrast of rugged mountains and serene rural landscapes. Primarily a sheep- and cattle-grazing area, other industries include logging and saw-milling, and tourism. Autumn in Tenterfield is spectacular. **Of interest:** Centenary Cottage (1871), Logan St, has local history collection. Early residential buildings in Logan St; self-guide Logan St Historic Walk; leaflet available from Tourist information. Sir Henry Parkes Library and Museum in School of Arts (1876), Rouse St, features relics relating to Sir Henry Parkes, who made his famous Federation speech there in 1889. Hand-made saddles at Tenterfield Saddler (1860s), High St. Oct.: Federation festival; Spring wine festival; Highland gathering. Nov.: Gem festival. **In the area:** Mt McKenzie Granite Drive, 30-km circular route beginning and ending at Molesworth St (in town) and including Ghost Gully. Silica mine at Torrington, 70 km SW. Bluff Rock, 10 km S on New England Hwy, unusual granite outcrop. Thunderbolt's Hideout, 11 km NE. Gold mine at Drake, 31 km NE. Boonoo Boonoo Falls (210-m drop), within Boonoo Boonoo National Park, 32 km NE. Good views from summit of Bald Rock, largest granite monolith in Australia, in Bald Rock National Park, 35 km N. Girraween National Park (in Qld) renowned for its wildflowers and granite outcrops. Aboriginal cultural tours to Boonoo Boonoo and Bald Rock National Parks; contact Tourist information. **Tourist information:** 157 Rouse St; (067) 36 1082. **Accommodation:** 4 hotels, 2 hotel/motels, 6 motels, 3 B&B, 3 cara. parks. **See also:** New England.

Terrigal   Pop. 7453

MAP REF. 101 Q4, 104 H5, 117 M6

Excellent surfing is one of the main attractions of this popular holiday town on the Central Coast. **In the area:** The Skillion, a headland offering coastal views; 3 km SE. Good surfing beaches: Wamberal Beach (2.8 km N); Shelly Beach (13 km N); Avoca Beach (7.5 km S). Secluded beaches and pockets of rainforest at Bouddi National Park, 17 km S. **Tourist information:** Rotary Park, Terrigal Dr.; (043) 85 4430. **Accommodation:** 1 hotel, 5 motels, 1 hostel, 1 cara./camp. park.

The Entrance   Pop. 37 831

MAP REF. 101 Q3, 104 H2, 117 M6

Blessed with clear, clean beaches, this beautiful lakeside and ocean town between Sydney and Newcastle is the family holiday playground of these two cities. **Of interest:** Daily pelican feeding at 3.30 p.m. in the Amphitheatre, Memorial Park. Lake cruises depart from public wharf. Art and craft market, each Sun. Concerts by the Sea on Jan. weekends. Jan.: Australia Day family concert and fireworks. Nov.: Celtic festival. Dec.: Tuggerah Lakes mardi gras festival. **In the area:** Fishing on lakes – Tuggerah, Budgewoi and Munmorah – and ocean beach. During summer months, prawning on lakes. Water sports on Lake Tuggerah. Extensive collection of shells at Shell Museum, 1 km N at Dunleith Caravan Park. Bushwalking trails in Wyrrabalong National Park, 6 km N. Crackneck Point Lookout, for coastal views; 6 km S. **Tourist information:** Tuggerah Lakes Tourist Assocn, in Memorial Park, Marine Pde; (043) 32 9282. **Accommodation:** 3 hotels, 10 motels, 12 cara. parks.

The Rock   Pop. 809

MAP REF. 116 B13, 123 Q11

This small town, 32 km SW of Wagga Wagga, is noted for its unusual scenery. Walking trails through a flora and fauna reserve lead to the summit of The Rock (about 365 m). One species, the groundsel plant, is believed to be unique to the area. **Of interest:** Fantasia Dolls, Olympic Way, hand-made porcelain dolls. **Tourist information:** Tourism Wagga Wagga, Tarcutta St, Wagga Wagga; (069)23 5402. **Accommodation:** 1 hotel/motel.

Tibooburra   Pop. 150

MAP REF. 120 D3

The name of this former gold town, 337 km N of Broken Hill, comes from an Aboriginal word meaning 'heaps of rocks'. The town is surrounded by granite outcrops and was previously known as The Granites. **Of interest:** In Briscoe St: buildings of local stone, including court house (1888), Family Hotel (1888) and Tibooburra Hotel (1890); School of the Air; tours during term time. June (or July): Tibooburra festival. Oct.: Gymkhana and rodeo (long weekend). **In the area:** Nearby goldfields. Self-guide historic Gold-mining walk and Granite scenic walk, contact Tourist information for brochures. Sturt National Park, 20 km N, a semi-desert area noted for its wildlife and geological features; Explorers Tree, at western end of park, tree faintly blazed by explorer Charles Sturt; pastoralists display at Mt Wood (27 km E). Check road conditions before travelling in this area; read section on Outback Motoring. Depot Glen billabong, 14 km NW, where Sturt stayed marooned for 6 months in 1845; 1 km further east, grave of James Poole, a member of Sturt's 1845 expedition. Cameron Corner, 140 km NW, where three States meet. At former gold township of Milparinka, 42 km S: restored court house, remains of old police station, bank, general store and post office, but Albert Hotel is town's only active concern. Further 11 km NW of Milparinka is Mt Poole, where cairn commemorates Charles Sturt's expedition (marooned there 1845). **Tourist information:** National Parks and Wildlife Service, Briscoe St; (080) 91 3308. **Accommodation:** 2 hotels, 1 motel/cara./camp. park.

Tingha   Pop. 831

MAP REF. 119 K7

This small tin-mining town is 28 km SE of Inverell. **Of interest:** Campbells Honey Farm, Swimming Pool Rd. Nucoorilma Aboriginal Arts and Crafts, Diamond St. **In the area:** Fossicking for gems. Smith's Mining and Natural History Museum at Green Valley Farm, 10 km S, displays several artifacts, antiques, minerals and gemstones; cabin accommodation available. Good water-skiing, boating and excellent fishing on Copeton Dam, 15 km W. **Tourist information:** Tingha Games Caravan

Park, Swimming Pool Rd; (067) 23 3234. **Accommodation:** 1 hotel, 1 cara. park. **See also:** New England.

Tocumwal Pop. 1587

MAP REF. 123 M12, 234 I2

This peaceful Murray River town on the Newell Hwy is ideal for boating, fishing, swimming and water-skiing. **Of interest:** Huge fibreglass codfish in town square represents Aboriginal legend about giant Murray cod that lived in nearby blowhole. Old Railway Store, Deniliquin St, has scale models of Australian trains. Picnic area with lawns and sandy river beach, 200 m from town square. A 36-hole golf course, Barooga–Corowa Rd on eastern outskirts of town. Easter: Festival of Family Fun. **In the area:** River Murray Heritage Centre, 3 km N. Nallama, 15 km W on Tuppal Rd, a historic farm settlement with grave site and giant gum; check opening times. Ulupna Island flora and fauna reserve, Murray River. Binghi Boomerang Factory at Barooga, 19 km SE. Aerodrome, 5 km NE, largest RAAF base in Australia during World War II, now houses world-renowned Sportavia Soaring Centre; gliding joy flights and tuition packages available. The Rocks and Blowhole, 11 km NE on Rocks Rd, once a stone quarry, now a good picnic spot. **Tourist information:** Tocumwal River Foreshore; (058) 74 2131. **Accommodation:** 3 hotels, 1 hotel/ motel, 10 motels, 6 cara./camp. parks. **See also:** The Newell.

Tooleybuc Pop. 300

MAP REF. 122 G10, 233 M9

A quiet, tranquil, riverside town with a village atmosphere, Tooleybuc is 65 km S of Balranald. **Of interest:** Fishing, picnicking and riverside walks. River Retreat craft shop, Lea St. **Tourist information:** 25 Murray St, Barham; (054) 53 3100. **Accommodation:** 1 hotel, 3 motels, 1 cara./camp. park.

Toukley Pop. 6520

MAP REF. 101 Q2, 117 M6

Situated on the peninsula between Tuggerah and Budgewoi Lakes, this coastal hamlet offers pollution-free beaches and breathtaking scenery. Open-air markets, each Sun. at Shopping Centre carpark. Sept.: Azalea festival. Oct.: Cycle Classic. **In the area:** Lakes, venue for all water sports. During summer months, prawning from lake foreshores. Rock pool at Cabbage Tree Bay, 5 km E. Norah Head Lighthouse, 5 km E. Many bushwalking trails in magnificent Munmorah State Recreation Area, 10 km N, or Red Gum Forest in Wyrrabalong National Park, 4 km S. **Tourist information:** Toukley and District Visitors Centre, Wallarah Point Park, Gorokan; (043) 92 4666. **Accommodation:** 1 hotel, 6 motels, 4 cara./camp. parks.

Tumbarumba Pop. 1548

MAP REF. 115 B7

A former goldmining town in the western foothills of the Snowy Mountains, 504 km SW of Sydney, Tumbarumba has much to offer the visitor who prefers to get off the beaten track. It is an ideal base for day trips to the Snowy Mountains. **Of interest:** Bicentennial Botanic Gardens, Prince St. Historical Society Museum, Bridge St, features working model of water-powered timber mill; open Mon.–Sat. Jan.: New Year's Day rodeo. Nov.: Heritage week. **In the area:** White-water rafting, fly fishing, paragliding, trail rides. Site of old Union Jack Mine, 3 km N. Pioneer Women's Hut, 8 km NW on Wagga Rd, a domestic, rural history museum; open Wed., Sat. and Sun. Paddy's River Falls, 16 km S, cascades drop 60 m; nearby, walking track and picnic area. Henry Angel Trackhead, 7 km SE on Tooma Rd, starting point for a section of Hume and Hovell Walking Track, and has facilities for campers and picnickers. At Tooma, 34 km SE: historic hotel, tearooms and store. Mt Selwyn Ski Resort, 70 km SE. Murray 1 Power Station, 10 km SE of Khancoban on Alpine Way; guided tours daily. **Tourist information:** Tumbarumba Wool and Craft Centre, 10 Bridge St; (069) 48 2805. **Accommodation:** 2 hotels, 1 motel, 2 B&B, 2 cara./camp. parks.

Tumut Pop. 5955

MAP REF. 115 C5, 116 D12, 138 A2

Situated on the Snowy Mountains Hwy, 424 km SW of Sydney, Tumut attracts visitors all year. Close to ski resorts and the great dams of the Snowy Mountains Hydro-electric Scheme, it is also well known for spectacular mountain scenery. **Of interest:** CSR Woodpanels and Softwood, Adelong Rd; open by appt, contact Tourist information. Millet broom factory, Snowy Mountains Hwy. Tours to power stations: Tumut 3 (45 km S) and Tumut 2 (115 km S); contact Tourist information. Apr.–May: Festival of the falling leaf. **In the area:** Excellent fishing in Tumut and Goobraganda Rivers. White-water rafting, canoeing, horseriding, abseiling, powered hang-gliding, scenic flights. Two access points for Hume and Hovell Walking Track (track extends from Gunning to Albury but various access points allow for shorter walks). Largest African violet farm in Australia, 7 km S on Tumut Plains Rd. Blowering Reservoir, 10 km S, major centre for water sports, fishing for rainbow trout, brown trout and perch; lookout over dam wall. Talbingo Dam and Reservoir, 40 km S, set in steep wooded country is second tallest rock-filled dam in Australia and renowned for large trout. Kiandra, 95 km S, an old gold-mining town. **Tourist information:** Fitzroy St (Snowy Mountains Hwy); (069) 47 1849. **Accommodation:** 4 hotels, 2 hotel/motels, 8 motels, 4 B&B, 2 cara./camp. parks.

Tweed Heads Pop. 5360

MAP REF. 119 Q1, 485 I11, 491 Q11

Tweed Heads, the State's most northern town, and its twin town Coolangatta, across the border, are popular holiday destinations at the southern end of the Gold Coast. **Of interest:** World's first laser-beam lighthouse sits atop Point Danger, one half in NSW and the other in Qld; nearby, cliff-edge walk (dolphins may be seen offshore) and picnic spots. Tweed Endeavour cruise boats, operating from River Tce, visit locations along Tweed River. Fishing and diving charters. Houseboats available for hire. Feb.: Tweed Valley triathlon. Aug.: Bowls tournament. **In the area:** Idyllic beaches, reserves and coastal towns on Tweed Coast, particularly Kingscliff, 14 km S, and other villages south including Bogangar and Pottsville. Minjungbal Aboriginal Cultural Centre, just over Boyds Bay Bridge, features Aboriginal ceremonial bora ring, museum and nature walk through sections of mangroves and rainforest. Melaleuca Station, 9 km S on Pacific Hwy at Chinderah, a re-created 1930s railway station set in tea-tree plantation, has train rides, tea-tree oil distillation plant and animal nursery. Tropical

Caves and Caverns

Magical underground limestone caves are one of the wonders of New South Wales. Glittering limestone stalactites and stalagmites, caused by the ceaseless dripping of limestone-impregnated water over tens of thousands of years, glow eerily in cathedral-like caves. These delicate formations of ribbed columns, frozen cascades, 'tapestries' and 'shawls' look like part of a subterranean fairyland.

The most famous are the **Jenolan Caves**. Since being first explored in 1838, several million people have visited them. Situated on a spur of the Great Dividing Range, on the south-west edge of the Blue Mountains, they are open daily for guided tours. The caves are surrounded by a 2416-hectare flora and fauna reserve with walking trails, kiosk, cafe and picnic/barbecue facilities. Accommodation includes the charming Tudor-style guest house, Jenolan Caves House; and Binda Bush Cabins, 8 kilometres from the caves precinct, on the road into the reserve.

The Wombeyan Caves are set in a pleasant valley in the Southern Highlands, 193 kilometres south-west of Sydney. They can be reached from the Wombeyan turn-off, 60 kilometres north-west of Mittagong. From here a well-surfaced but narrow road winds through spectacular mountain scenery. The alternative route (recommended for caravanners) is via Goulburn, Taralga and Richlands. Five of the caves are easily accessible by graded paths. They are fully developed for visitors, with steps and handrails, and are open daily or on demand for self-guide, historical and adventure caving tours. There is a Visitors Centre and facilities exist for camping and family or group accommodation. Three walking tracks lead from the reserve to attractions in the area.

The **Abercrombie Caves** are on the edge of the Great Dividing Range, 72 kilometres south of Cowra; they can also be accessed from Oberon or Goulburn. Regular guided and self-guide tours of the caves area available. The caves are set in a 2200-hectare reserve which features the largest natural bridge in the southern hemisphere; swimming, fishing and fossicking in Grove Creek; scenic bushwalks; rich variety of flora and fauna; a kiosk; and camping facilities.

The **Yarrangobilly Caves**, 6.5 kilometres off the Snowy Mountains Highway, 109 kilometres north-west of Cooma, are open daily, except Christmas Day (but subject to winter road conditions) for self-guide or guided tours. On weekends, school and public holidays, additional tours are available, subject to demand. Among some 250 caves in the area only four have been developed and are open for inspection (one with wheelchair access). During summer and Easter school holidays, tours include a torchlit Adventure Cave Walk. An added attraction in the area is a thermal pool with naturally heated water at 27°C all year round. The caves are a feature of Kosciusko National Park and are surrounded by spectacular limestone gorges and densely forested mountains. But bring your own food and drink; there is no kiosk in the area.

The **Wellington Caves** form part of the Wellington Caves complex which consists of two show caves (the Cathedral Cave with its huge stalagmite and the beautiful Gaden Cave), an animal enclosure, a clock museum, a bottle house, a golf course and a caravan park with self-contained lodges. Guided cave tours are available daily (except Christmas Day). Wellington Caves are located 8 kilometres south of Wellington, 1 kilometre from the Mitchell Highway.

For further information: on Jenolan Caves, contact Jenolan Caves Reserve Trust, (063) 59 3311; on Wombeyan Caves, (048) 43 5976; on Abercrombie Caves, (063) 68 8603; on Yarrangobilly Caves, (064) 54 9597; on Wellington Caves, contact Wellington Shire Offices, (068) 45 1733. **Map references:** for Jenolan Caves, 100 F8, 116 I7; for Wombeyan Caves, 116 I9; for Abercrombie Caves, 115 F1, 116 G8; for Yarrangobilly Caves, 114 D1, 115 C7; and for Wellington Caves, 116 F3.

Jenolan Caves House provides accommodation for visitors to the Jenolan Caves

NEW SOUTH WALES

Bawley Beach, near Ulladulla

Fruitworld, 15 km S on Pacific Hwy. Pioneer Plantation, a working banana plantation featuring a six-wheel-drive trip to top of Banana Mountain; on Pottsville Rd, Mooball. **Tourist information:** cnr Pacific Hwy and Alma St, Murwillumbah; (07) 5536 4244 or (066) 72 1340. **Accommodation:** 2 hotels, 22 motels, 9 cara./camp. parks.

Ulladulla Pop. 7381

MAP REF. 115 I6, 117 J13, 139 P4

Ulladulla, a fishing town, is the main centre along this section of the south coast, a stretch of beautiful coast, coastal lakes and lagoons with white sandy beaches. **Of interest:** Town's oldest building (c. 1868) houses Millard's Cottage Restaurant, Princes Hwy. Funland, Princes Hwy, large indoor family fun park. At Warden Head, lighthouse, views and walking tracks. Native plants, birdlife and walks at South Pacific Heathland Reserve, Dowling St. Ulladulla Wildflower Reserve, cnr Green and Warden Sts. Easter: Blessing of the fleet. **In the area:** Historic Milton, 7 km NW on Princes Hwy; Settlers Fair held in Oct. Pointer Gap Lookout, for coastal views; 20 km NW. Mollymook, 2 km N, for surfing and excellent fishing. Narrawallee Beach, 4 km N. Nearby Narrawallee Inlet has calm, shallow water ideal for children. Bendalong, 36 km N. Sussex Inlet, 47 km N, holds fishing carnival in May. Lakes Conjola (23 km NW) and Burrill (5 km SW), ideal for swimming, fishing and water-skiing. Views from summit of Pigeon House Mountain in Morton National Park, 25 km NW. **Tourist information:** Princes Hwy; (044) 55 1269. **Accommodation:** 3 hotels, 20 motels, 1 B&B, 1 hostel, 4 cara./camp. parks. **See also:** The Illawarra Coast.

Uralla Pop. 2324

MAP REF. 119 L9

'Gentleman' bushranger Thunderbolt was shot dead by a local policeman in 1870, at Kentucky Creek, south-east of this charming New England town. Rich gold discoveries were made in the vicinity in the 1850s. **Of interest:** Self-guide Heritage Walking Tour, contact Tourist information for brochure. In Bridge St: Hassett's Military Museum, displays local and national military history and memorabilia; Statue of Thunderbolt; his grave is in old Uralla Cemetery, John St. McCrossin's Mill (1870), Salisbury St, now a museum with goldfields history displays, a re-created joss house honouring the many Chinese who came to the diggings and Thunderbolt exhibits. Old Uralla court house, Hill St, now houses collection of Thunderbolt paintings. Brass and Iron Lake Foundry, operating since 1872; open Mon.–Fri. Market, 2nd Sun. each month (Sept.–May). Nov.: Thunderbolt picnic race meeting. **In the area:** Mt Yarrowyck Aboriginal rock-art site, 23 km NW off Bundarra Rd. Fossicking at Old Rocky River diggings, 5 km W; nearby, pleasant picnic spot. Gostwyck, 11 km SE, one of oldest properties in area, not open to public, except private chapel open to groups, by appt only. **Tourist information:** Bridge St; (067) 78 4496. **Accommodation:** 1 hotel, 1 hotel/motel, 3 motels, 1 B&B, 2 cara./camp. parks. **See also:** New England.

Urunga Pop. 2666

MAP REF. 119 P9

Located at the junction of the Bellinger and Kalang Rivers, and alongside a broad lagoon, Urunga is one of the best fishing spots on the north coast. The town is 32 km S of Coffs Harbour. **Of interest:** Water sports and fishing. Safe river swimming pool for children, with picnic reserve nearby. July: Bowling club carnival. **In the area:** At Raleigh, 4 km north: winery, horseriding and go-kart complex. **Tourist information:** The Honey Place, Pacific Hwy; (066) 55 6160. **Accommodation:** 1 hotel, 5 motels, 1 B&B, 4 cara./camp. parks.

Wagga Wagga Pop. 40 875

MAP REF. 116 B12, 123 R10

This prosperous city – the largest inland city in NSW – is 478 km SW of Sydney just off the Hume Hwy. Wagga is a major centre for industry, commerce, education, agriculture and the home of two important military bases. The town is renowned for its cultural pursuits and performing arts. **Of interest:** Botanic Gardens (excellent) and Zoo on Willans Hill; a miniature railway runs through gardens. Historical Museum, adjacent to gardens, has indoor and outdoor exhibits. City Art Gallery, Gurwood St, features National Art Glass collection. Riverina Galleries, The Esplanade. Mar.: Australian veterans games. Sept.: National festival of the voice. Nov.: Festival. **In the area:** Lake Albert, 7 km S, for water sports. RAAF Museum, 10 km E. Wagga Wagga Winery, 15 km NE; tasting area and restaurant have early Australiana theme; on road to winery Eunonyhareenyha Cottage, offers teas in delightful riverside setting; usually open weekends. Charles Sturt Winery at Charles Sturt University (Riverina Campus), 6 km NW. Aurora Clydesdale Stud and Pioneer Farm, 9 km W of Collingullie on Sturt Hwy. Tours of military base at Kapooka, 9 km SW. **Tourist information:** Tourism Wagga Wagga,

Tarcutta St; (069) 23 5402. **Accommodation:** 12 hotels, 24 motels, 3 B&B, 6 cara./camp. parks.

Walcha　　　　Pop. 1782

MAP REF. 119 L10

This town on the eastern slopes of the Great Dividing Range was first settled in 1832. **Of interest:** Pioneer Cottage and Museum, Derby St, features first Tiger Moth plane to be used for crop-dusting in Australia, and a replica of blacksmith's shop. Fenwicke House, 19th-century terrace in Fitzroy St, now art gallery. Jan.: Australia Day breakfast in the park. Feb.: Agricultural show. **In the area:** Trout fishing. Ohio Homestead (1842), 4 km E; open by appt. Oxley Wild Rivers National Park, 20 km E, encompasses a high plateau, deep gorges and numerous waterfalls including Wollomombi (220 m) considered the highest in Australia, Apsley and Tia; sections of park developed for visitors centre around the major waterfalls, other areas left as wilderness. **Tourist information:** 106E Fitzroy St; (067) 77 1075. **Accommodation:** 4 hotels, 2 motels, 1 cara./camp. park. **See also:** New England.

Walgett　　　　Pop. 2091

MAP REF. 118 C7

Walgett is situated at the junction of the Barwon and Namoi Rivers, 300 km NW of Dubbo. With its airport and railhead, it is also the gateway to the opal fields around Lightning Ridge. **Of interest:** First European settler's grave on banks of Namoi River, northern end of town. Oct.: Weekend extravaganza with raft races and go-karts. **In the area:** Good fishing all year. Grawin, Glengarry and Sheepyard opal fields, 70 km W. (Motorists are warned water is scarce; adequate supply should be carried.) One of largest inland lakes in Australia, Narran Lake, 96 km W via Cumborah Rd, is a wildlife sanctuary; no facilities for private visits, but light aircraft tours can be arranged through Walgett Aero Club; (068) 28 1344. **Tourist information:** Shire Offices, 77 Fox St; (068) 28 1399. **Accommodation:** 2 hotel/motels, 3 motels, 1 cara./camp. park.

Warialda　　　　Pop. 1285

MAP REF. 118 I5

The first administrative centre in the north-west of the State, this town on Gwydir Hwy, 63 km NW of Inverell, is in a stud farm and wheat-growing district. **Of interest:** Historical buildings, especially on Stephen and Hope Sts. Self-guide historic walk around town and Koorilgur Nature Walks; contact Tourist information. Historic Carinda House, Stephen St, now outlet for crafts. Historic graves (from 1850s) in bushland setting at Pioneer Cemetery, Queen and Stephen Sts. Well's Family Gem and Mineral Collection in Heritage Centre, Hope St; also has Aboriginal artifacts and bottle display. May: Agricultural show. **In the area:** Picnic spots, fossicking, wildflowers (in spring) and prolific wildlife at Cranky Rock Nature Reserve, 8 km E. **Tourist information:** Shire Offices, Hope St; (067) 29 1016. **Accommodation:** 1 hotel, 1 motel, 1 cara./camp. park.

Warren　　　　Pop. 2036

MAP REF. 118 B13

The centre for the surrounding wool, cattle and cotton district, Warren is on the Oxley Hwy, 126 km NW of Dubbo. Located beside the Macquarie River, it is a popular spot for anglers. **Of interest:** Macquarie Park, Burton St, on banks of river. Tiger Bay Wildlife Park, northern outskirts of town on Oxley Hwy. May: Golden Fleece Day. Nov.: Cotton Cup carnival. **In the area:** Excellent racecourse, 3 km W, location for Cotton Cup carnival. Warren Weir, 5 km SE. **Tourist information:** Shire Offices, Dubbo St; (068) 47 4606. **Accommodation:** 2 hotels, 2 motels, 2 cara./camp. parks.

Wauchope　　　　Pop. 4297

MAP REF. 105 E8, 119 O12

A major re-creation of a typical timber town of the 1880s at nearby Timbertown has put Wauchope on the tourist map. The town is the centre of a timber-getting, dairying, beef-cattle and mixed-farming area on the Oxley Hwy, 19 km W of Port Macquarie. **Of interest:** Train Meadows, King Creek Rd, has model-train display. Mar.: Lasiandra festival. Oct.: Colonial carnival. **In the area:** Timbertown, re-created village with shops and school, 3 km W on edge of Broken Bago State Forest, features working bullock team, horse-drawn wagons, smithy, steam-powered train and sleeper-cutting demonstrations. Adjacent small weatherboard church houses Historical Society Museum. Old Bottlebutt, largest known bloodwood tree in State; 5½ km S. The Big Bull, 2 km E off Oxley Hwy, has dairy farming display, hay rides and animal nursery. **Tourist information:** cnr Hay and Clarence Sts, Port Macquarie; (065) 83 1293. **Accommodation:** 2 hotels, 2 motels, 1 cara./camp. park.

Wee Waa　　　　Pop. 2030

MAP REF. 118 F8

This small town near the Namoi River is the centre of a cotton-growing district producing the highest cotton yield in Australia. **Of interest:** Guided tours (Apr.–Aug.) from Namoi Cotton Co-op, Short St, to Merah North Cotton Gin (9 km). Apr.: Agricultural show. **In the area:** Cubbaroo Winery, 45 km W. Cuttabri Wine Shanty, 25 km SW, an original Cobb & Co. coaching-stop between Wee Waa and Pilliga. Yarrie Lake, 24 km S, for boating and birdwatching. **Tourist information:** Newell Hwy, Narrabri; (067) 92 3583. **Accommodation:** 1 hotel, 2 motels, 2 cara. parks.

Wellington　　　　Pop. 5433

MAP REF. 116 F3

Limestone caves are one of the interesting features of this town at the junction of the Macquarie and Bell Rivers, 362 km NW of Sydney. **Of interest:** Town walking tour; contact Tourist information. Historical Museum in old bank (1883), cnr Percy and Warne Sts. Cameron Park, attractive area on western side of main street (Mitchell Hwy). Mar.: The Wellington Boot (horseraces); Vintage fair. Aug.: Eisteddfod. Nov.: Festival of dance. **In the area:** Wellington Caves, 9 km S: Cathedral Cave and smaller Gaden Cave with its rare cave coral; tours available. Nearby, aviary, opal shop, craft shop, bottle house, clock museum, picnic/barbecue facilities and kiosk. Markeita Cellars, 16 km S in village of Neurea. Rabbit Farm, 20 km S, has shearing demonstrations of angora rabbits; also alpacas. Burrendong State Recreation Area, 32 km E: Lake Burrendong, for water-sports and fishing; panoramic views of lake from spillway; Arboretum, a native flora reserve; walking tracks; camping facilities and cabin accommodation. Glenfinlass Wines, 8 km SW on Parkes

Opal fields, White Cliffs

Rd. Nangara Gallery, 26 km SW, Australia-wide collection of Aboriginal artifacts. From Mt Arthur Reserve, 3 km W of town, walking trails to lookout at summit of Mt Binjang; maps from Tourist information. **Tourist information:** Cameron Park, Nanima Cr.; (068) 45 1733. **Accommodation:** 7 hotels, 4 motels, 1 B&B, 4 cara./camp. parks.

Wentworth Pop. 1447

MAP REF. 122 C6, 232 F2

This historic town at the junction of the Murray and Darling Rivers was once a busy riverboat and customs port; today it is a quiet holiday town. **Of interest:** In Beverly St: Rotary Folk Museum; Old Wentworth Gaol (1881). Court house (1870s), Darling St. Historic convent, Cadell St. Apphara Art Gallery, Adams St. Historic PS *Ruby*, in Fotherby Park, Wentworth St. River cruises on MV *Loyalty*; depart from end Darling St. Lock 10, weir and park for picnics. Nov.: Wentworth Cup (held on Melbourne Cup Day). **In the area:** Houseboat hire available. Perry's sand hills, 5 km NW. Model aircraft display at Yelta, 12 km E. At Buronga, 26 km E: Oasis Botanical Gardens, River Road; Orange World and Stanley Wine Co. both on Silver City Hwy. Mungo National Park, 157 km NE, a World Heritage Area. **Tourist information:** Shop 4, Wentworth Pl., Adams St; (050) 27 3624. **Accommodation:** 1 hotel, 6 motels, 2 cara. parks.

West Wyalong Pop. 3458

MAP REF. 116 B8, 123 Q6

This former goldmining town, at the junction of the Mid Western and Newell Hwys, celebrated its centenary in 1994. It is the business centre of a prosperous wheat, wool and mixed-farming area. **Of interest:** On Newell Hwy: Aboriginal Artifacts Gallery (open Mon.–Fri.). Bland District Historical Museum, has historical displays and scale model of a goldmine. Sept.: Agricultural show. Oct.: Highways festival (biennial, odd-numbered years). **In the area:** Bird sanctuary and fishing at Lake Cowal, 48 km NE via Clear Ridge, largest natural lake in NSW. Weethalle Whistlestop, 65 km W on Hay Rd, for Devonshire teas, art and craft. At Barmedman, 32 km SE, Mineral Water Pool, believed to provide relief from arthritis and rheumatism. **Tourist information:** McCann Park, Newell Hwy; (069) 72 3645. **Accommodation:** 6 hotels, 11 motels, 2 cara./camp. parks. **See also:** The Newell.

White Cliffs Pop. 219

MAP REF. 120 F8

White Cliffs 97 km NW of Wilcannia, is a town where pioneering is a way of life. The opal fields were the first commercial fields in NSW; the first lease was granted in 1890, and in the boom years at the turn-of-the-century, the fields were supporting 4500 people. Precious opal is still mined today. Jewelled opal 'pineapples' are found only in this area. Road access to the town is via a graded gravel road, suitable for conventional cars and caravans when driven with care in dry weather. **Of interest:** In town centre: historic buildings including old police station (1897), public school (1900) and post office (1900); camping, barbecue facilities and swimming-pool in Reserve; pioneer children's cemetery; Joe's Stubby Opal Shop, built with glass stubbies; General Store and tourist information. Just south: solar power station; rugged outback golf course. On the southern outskirts around Smith's Hill: Top Level Opals; Outback Treasures; Underground Dugout Motel. On the eastern outskirts around Turley's Hill: Eagles Gallery; Jock's Place, dugout home and museum; P.J.'s Underground B&B. On the northern outskirts: Wellington's Underground Art Gallery; Brian Moore's Opal Showroom; opal fields. Opal cutting and polishing can be seen in many of the opal showrooms. May: Gymkhana and rodeo. July: Royal flying doctor ball. **In the area:** Mootwingee National Park, 90 km SW, guided tours of Aboriginal rock-art sites in cooler months (extremely hot in summer). **Tourist information:** General Store; (080) 91 6611. **Accommodation:** 1 hotel, 1 motel, 1 B&B, 1 cara./camp. park.

Whitton Pop. 340

MAP REF. 123 O8

Whitton, 24 km W of Leeton, is the oldest town in the Murrumbidgee Irrigation Area and has rice and grain storage facilities. **Of interest:** Whitton Court house and Gaol Museum, Gogeldrie St. **In the area:** Gogeldrie Weir, 14 km SE. **Tourist information:** Chelmsford Pl., Leeton; (069) 53 2832. **Accommodation:** 1 hotel.

Wilcannia Pop. 942

MAP REF. 120 G10

Once the 'queen city of the west', this quaint township, 196 km NE of Broken Hill, still has many impressive sandstone buildings. It was proclaimed a town in 1864 and was a key inland port in the days of paddlesteamers. Declining in the early 1920s with the advent of the car, today it is the service centre for a far-flung rural population. **Of interest:** Self-guide Historic Town Tour (brochure available from Tourist information) introduces several fine stone buildings, including in Reid St: post office (1877), prison and court house (1880), and Athenaeum Chambers (1890), now a historical museum. Opening bridge (1895) across Darling River; paddlesteamer wharf upstream. **In the area:** Opal fields at White Cliffs, 97 km NW. **Tourist information:** Shire Offices, Reid St; (080) 91 5909. **Accommodation:** 2 hotels, 2 motels, 1 cara./camp. park.

Windsor Pop. 1869

MAP REF. 101 K6, 117 K7

A town for lovers of history and early architecture, Windsor is one of the oldest towns in Australia, situated 56 km NW of Sydney. **Of interest:** St Matthew's Church, Moses St, oldest Anglican Church in Australia, designed by Francis Greenway and convict-built in 1817. Nearby graveyard is even older. Court house, Court St, is another Greenway building. The Doctor's House (1844), Thompson Sq., privately owned. Many other fine buildings in historic George St and Thompson Sq. Hawkesbury Museum, Thompson Sq., formerly Daniel O'Connell Inn, built in 1843. Craft market, each Sun. May: Bridge to bridge power boat classic. Nov.: Bridge to bridge water ski classic. **In the area:** Cattai National Park, 14 km NE, has historic homestead, friendship farm, horse and pony rides for children, canoe hire, picnic/barbecue facilities and camping area. Australian Pioneer Village, 6 km N, features Rose Cottage, considered oldest timber dwelling in Australia; wagon and buggy collection; good picnic/barbecue facilities and lake with paddle-boats. At Ebenezer, 14 km N: Tizzana Winery; Uniting Church (1809), claimed to be oldest church in Australia still holding regular services; nearby, old cemetery and schoolhouse (1817). **Tourist information:** Ham Common Bicentenary Park, Clarendon; (045) 88 5895. **Accommodation:** 2 hotels, 3 motels, 1 B&B. **See also:** The Hawkesbury.

Wingham Pop. 4407

MAP REF. 105 B13, 117 O1, 119 N13

The oldest town along the Manning River, 13 km NW of Taree, Wingham was established in 1836. The area was important as a source of timber and remains so today together with beef cattle and dairy farming. **Of interest:** Manning Valley Historical Society Museum, part of attractive village square with several prominent historic buildings, bounded by Isabella, Bent, Farquhar and Wynter Sts. Jan.: National rodeo titles. Mar.: Agricultural show. Apr.: Manning Valley beef week. **In the area:** The Wingham Brush, Isabella St, close to town centre, is one of the few remaining subtropical flood-plain rainforests in NSW; with orchids, ferns, Moreton Bay fig trees, grey-headed flying foxes and 100 species of birds. Fine bush scenery. Bulga Forest Dr. through timbered country north-west of town, past Ellenborough Falls, 40 km N, one of the highest single drop falls in State; contact Tourist information for brochure. **Tourist information:** Pacific Hwy, Taree North; (065) 52 1900 or 1800 80 1522. **Accommodation:** 2 hotels, 1 motel.

Wisemans Ferry Pop. 400

MAP REF. 101 M3, 117 K6

Situated beside the Hawkesbury River, 66 km NW of Sydney, Wisemans Ferry is an important recreational area for those interested in water sports. Two vehicular ferries provide transport across the river. **Of interest:** Wisemans Ferry Inn, Old Northern Rd, was named after founder of original ferry service and innkeeper, and is said to be haunted by his wife, whom he allegedly pushed down the front steps of the inn to her death. Dharug National Park, on northern side of river, features wealth of Aboriginal rock engravings; convict-built Great Old North Rd, one of great engineering feats of early colony (walk or cycle along lower section – closed to vehicles – from ferry). **Tourist information:** Ham Common Bicentenary Park, Richmond Rd, Clarendon; (045) 88 5895. **Accommodation:** 1 hotel, 1 motel, 4 cara./camp. parks. **See also:** The Hawkesbury.

Wollongong Pop. 211 417

MAP REF. 110, 112 H6, 117 K10

The area surrounding Wollongong, the third largest city in NSW, contains some of the South Coast's most spectacular scenery. **Of interest:** Illawarra Historical Society Museum, Market St, including a handicraft room and a Victorian parlour. Wollongong City Gallery, cnr Burelli and Kembla Sts. Spectacular mall in Crown St with soaring steel arches and water displays. Botanic Gardens in Northfields Ave. Rhododendron Park, Parish Ave, Mt Pleasant. Surfing beaches and rock pools, to north and south. Foreshore parks for picnicking. Wollongong Harbour, home to fishing fleet. On Endeavour Dr.: fish market; historic lighthouse (1872). On the foreshore of Port Kembla Harbour, at the southern end of the city, is the highly automated steel mill operated by BHP, an export coal loader and the largest grain-handling facility in NSW. Market, each Thurs. and Sat. at Showground. Aug.: South Coast youth arts and skills festival. Dec.: Junior surf lifesaving championships. **In the area:** Lake Illawarra, 5 km S, stretches from South Pacific Ocean to foothills of Illawarra Range: good prawning, fishing and sailing; boat hire available. Seaside village of Shellharbour, 22 km S; walking trails in nearby Blackbutt Reserve. Illawarra Escarpment, forming western backdrop to city, provides vantage points for lookouts at Stanwell Tops, Sublime Point, Mount Keira and Mount Kembla. Bulli Lookout, at top of escarpment near Bulli Pass, a steep, scenic drive down the escarpment (or up) with stunning coastal views. Lawrence Hargraves Memorial and Lookout at Bald Hill, 36 km N, site of aviator Lawrence Hargrave's first attempt at flight in early 1900s; now favourite spot for hang-gliding. Symbio Koala Gardens, 44 km N at Helensburgh. Mt Kembla Village, 15 km W, scene of tragic mining disaster in 1902, features monument in church; original miners' huts; several historic buildings, including former post office now Historical Museum, pioneer kitchen and blacksmith's shop; and reconstruction of Mt Kembla disaster. **Tourist information:** 93 Crown St; (042) 28 0300. **Accommodation:** 4 hotels, 8 motels, 1 B&B, 1 hostel. **See also:** The Illawarra Coast.

Woolgoolga Pop. 3660

MAP REF. 119 P7

This charming seaside town on the Pacific Hwy, 25 km N of Coffs Harbour, is popular with anglers as there is excellent crabbing, prawning and whiting fishing in the area. The banana industry became established in the district in the 1930s attracting a sizeable population of Indian migrants to the town. **Of interest:** Guru Nanak Sikh Temple, River St, place of worship for town's Indian population. Art Gallery, Turon Pde, exhibits paintings and pottery. **In the area:** Clean, sandy beaches, a feature of this coast. Yuraygir National Park, 10 km N, for bushwalking, canoeing, fishing, surfing, swimming, picnicking and camping on this beautiful stretch of unspoiled coastline. Wedding Bells State Forest, 14 km NW. **Tourist information:** Mobil Service Station, Pacific Hwy; (066) 54 1603. **Accommodation:** 7 motels, 3 cara./camp. parks.

Woy Woy Pop. 12 206

MAP REF. 101 P4, 104 F8, 117 L6

Woy Woy, situated 90 km N of Sydney and 6 km S of Gosford, is the commercial centre for the surrounding holiday villages and national parks abutting the magnificent Brisbane Water and Broken Bay. **In the area:** Boating, fishing and swimming on Brisbane Water, Broken Bay and Hawkesbury River. Mt Ettalong Lookout, 6 km SE, for spectacular coastal views. Brisbane Water National Park, 3 km SW, noted for spring wildflowers, bushwalks and birdlife; within the park, features include Staples Lookout (7 km W), for magnificent coastal views; Bulgandry Aboriginal engravings (9 km W); and Warrah Lookout, for both views and spring wildflowers. Bouddi National Park, 12 km E, has good fishing, bushwalks and swimming areas; wreck of PS *Maitland* at Maitland Bay, a beautiful unspoiled coastal environment. Near entrance to park, Marie Byles Lookout offers views of Sydney. Wreck of WW1 ship *Parramatta*, Hawkesbury River near Milson Island; accessible only by boat. **Tourist information:** 200 Mann St, Gosford; (043) 25 2835. **Accommodation:** On peninsula: 3 hotels, 2 motels, 3 cara./camp. parks.

Wyong Pop. 3902

MAP REF. 101 P2, 104 F1, 117 M6

Wyong is situated on the Pacific Hwy between Tuggerah Lakes and the State Forests of Watagan, Olney and Ourimbah. The town developed as a result of the construction of the Sydney to Newcastle railway, completed in 1889. **Of interest:** District Museum, Cape Rd, has historical displays relating to early ferry services across lakes, and forest logging. Mar.: Festival of arts. Oct.: Cycle classic. **In the area:** Hinterland popular for bushwalking and camping. Burbank Nursery, at Tuggerah, 3 km S, features 20 ha of azaleas; flowering time Sept. Fowlers Lookout over forest, 10 km SW. Macadamia Nut Plantation, 18 km W in beautiful Yarramalong Valley. The Durren Pottery, 20 km NW, uses local clay; open by appt, contact Tourist information. Frazer Park, 28 km NE, a recreational park in a natural bush setting. Within the State forests to the north: Mandalong Lookout, Muirs Lookout and picnic area (Onley State Forest); Wishing Well, destination for Watagan Mountains Walking Trail (Watagan State Forest); Flat Rock Lookout and picnic area (Corrabare State Forest). **Tourist information:** Tuggerah Central Coast Tourism, Caltex Twin Service Centre, F3 Freeway; (043) 52 1955. **Accommodation:** 2 hotels, 1 motel, 2 cara./camp. parks.

Yamba Pop. 3707

MAP REF. 119 Q5

This prawning and fishing town at the mouth of the Clarence River offers sea, lake and river fishing. It is the largest coastal resort in the Clarence Valley. **Of interest:** Story House Museum, River St, displays historical records of early Yamba. Views from base of lighthouse, reached via steep Pilot St. Off Yamba Rd, departure point for daily passenger ferry services to Iluka, and river cruises (Wed. and Fri.). Nearby, boat hire available. Sept.-Oct.: Family fishing festival. **In the area:** Houseboat hire at Brushgrove, 35 km SW. Lake Wooloweyah, 4 km S, for fishing and prawning. Yuraygir National Park, 5 km S for swimming, fishing and bushwalking in area dominated by sand ridges and banksia heath. The Blue Pool, 5 km S, at Angourie, a freshwater pool, only 50 m from ocean, of unknown depth and origin; popular swimming and picnic spot. **Tourist information:** Lower Clarence Visitors Centre, Ferry Park, Pacific Hwy, Maclean; (066) 45 4121. **Accommodation:** 1 hotel, 9 motels, 3 cara. parks.

Yanco Pop. 651

MAP REF. 123 O8

Located 8 km S of Leeton, this town is where Sir Samuel McCaughey developed his own irrigation scheme, which led to the establishment of the Murrumbidgee Irrigation Area. **Of interest:** In Binya St: Powerhouse Museum, open by appt; Aquatic Park. May: Murrumbidgee farm fair. **In the area:** McCaughey's mansion, 3 km S, now an agricultural high school; with nearby Yanco Agricultural Institute, open to public. Extensive red gum forests along the Murrumbidgee River. Well-marked forest drives lead to sandy beaches and many pleasant fishing spots. **Tourist information:** Chelmsford Pl., Leeton; (069) 53 2832. **Accommodation:** 1 hotel.

Yass Pop. 4828

MAP REF. 115 D4, 116 F11

Close to the junction of two major highways (the Hume and the Barton), this interesting old town is on the Yass River, surrounded by beautiful, rich, rolling country, 280 km SW of Sydney and 55 km from Canberra. **Of interest:** Grave of Hamilton Hume who discovered Yass Plains in 1824, in Yass Cemetery; signposted from Ross St. National Trust-classified Cooma Cottage (1830), where Hume lived for 40 years; 3 km E, open 10–4 (closed Tues.). Hamilton Hume Museum, Comur St. Self-guide heritage walk, contact Tourist information. Marked walk (2 km) along Yass River, begins Riverbank Park, Comur St. Market, 2nd Sat. each month. Mar.: Agricultural show. **In the area:** Crisp Art Glass and Crisp-Grow Lavender Nursery, 19 km NW on Hume Hwy. At Wee Jasper, 53 km SW: Goodradigbee River for trout fishing; Micalong Creek; Carey's Cave, with superb limestone formations (guided tours, contact Tourist information); access point for Hume and Hovell Walking Track. Burrinjuck State Recreation Area (surrounds Burrinjuck Dam), 54 km SW off Hume Hwy, for bushwalking, water sports and fishing. Numerous wineries in Murrumbateman area, 19 km S, on Barton Hwy. Quamba Emu Farm 10 km NE on Wargeila Rd. **Tourist information:** Coronation Park, Comur St; (06) 226 2557. **Accommodation:** 4 hotels, 8 motels, 1 B&B, 1 cara./camp. park.

Young Pop. 6666

MAP REF. 115 C2, 116 D9

Attractive former goldmining town in the western foothills of the Great Dividing Range, 395 km SW of Sydney. Today, cherries and prunes are the area's best-known exports, as well as flour and fabricated steel. **Of interest:** Lambing Flat Folk Museum, Campbell St, fascinating reminders of town's colourful history, including 'roll-up' flag carried by miners during infamous anti-Chinese Lambing Flat riots of 1861. Burrangon Art Gallery, Olympic Way. Blackguard Gully with historic pug-mill, on Boorowa Rd, a reconstruction showing early goldmining methods. Nov.–Dec.: National cherry festival. **In the area:** Chinaman's Dam recreation area, 4 km SE, with picnic/barbecue facilities, children's playground and scenic walks. At Murringo Village, 24 km E: several historic buildings, home of glass blower and engraver Helmut Hiebel. Wineries open for tastings and sales: Woodonga Hill Winery (12 km N); Nioka Ridge Winery (15 km E). **Tourist information:** Olympic Way; (063) 82 5433. **Accommodation:** 6 hotels, 6 motels, 1 hotel/motel, 2 B&B, 1 cara./camp. park.

New South Wales

Location Map

Other Map Coverage
Central Sydney 92
Sydney Approach & Bypass Routes 93
Sydney & Western Suburbs 94
Northern Suburbs, Sydney 96
Southern Suburbs, Sydney 98
Sydney Region 100

The Blue Mountains 102
Hawkesbury & Central Coast 104
Port Macquarie Region 105
Newcastle 106
Newcastle Approach & Bypass 107
Newcastle Region 108
Lower Hunter Vineyards 109

Wollongong 110
Wollongong Approach & Bypass 111
Southern Highlands 112
South Coast 113
Snowy Mountains Region 114

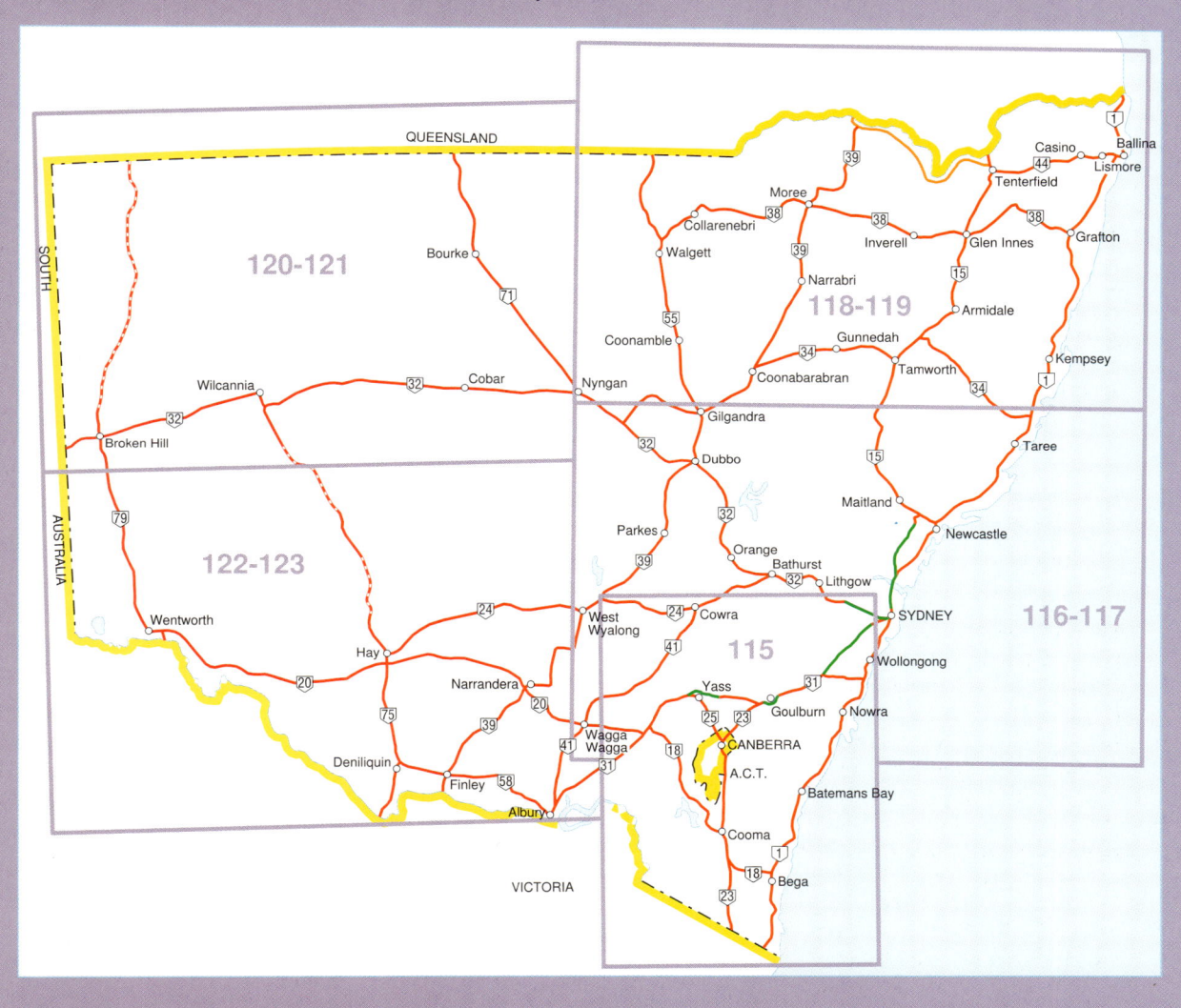

92 Central Sydney

Accommodation
- ANA Hotel 1 D4
- Hilton Hotel 2 E8
- Hotel Intercontinental 3 F5
- Park Hyatt 4 D2
- Quay West Apartments 5 D4
- Ramada Renaissance 6 E5
- Regent 7 D4
- Ritz Carlton 8 F4
- Russell Hotel 9 D4
- York Apartments 10 C6
- YWCA 11 F10

General Information
- AAT Kings/Australian Pacific Coach 12 E3
- Ansett Australia 13 G11
- Captain Cook Cruise 14 E4
- Central Railway Station 15 E13
- General Post Office 16 D7
- Motoring Organisation (NRMA) 17 C7
- Police Headquarters 18 G10
- Pioneer Coach Terminal 19 G11
- Qantas Travel Centre 20 E9, 21 E6
- Rocks Visitors Centre 22 D3
- Tourist Information 23 E6

Places of Interest
- Aquarium 24 B8
- Art Gallery of NSW 25 H7
- Australian Museum 26 G9
- Cadman's Cottage 27 D3
- Cenotaph 28 D7
- Centrepoint/Sydney Tower 29 E8
- Chinese Garden 30 C11
- Dixon Street (Chinatown) 31 D11
- Holy Trinity (Garrison) Church 32 C3
- Government House 33 F3
- Hyde Park Barracks 34 F7
- Mrs Macquaries Chair 35 I3
- Museum of Sydney 36 E5
- The Mint Museum 37 F7
- Museum of Contemporary Art 38 D4
- National Maritime Museum 39 A8
- Opera House 40 F2
- Parliament House 41 F6
- Powerhouse Museum 42 B12
- Queen Victoria Building 43 D8
- State Library of NSW 44 F6
- Sydney Harbour Bridge Pylon Lookout 45 D1
- Sydney Harbour Casino 46 A6
- Sydney Tower/Centrepoint 29 E8
- Town Hall 47 D9

Accommodation Only a sample range is listed; inclusion is not necessarily a recommendation.

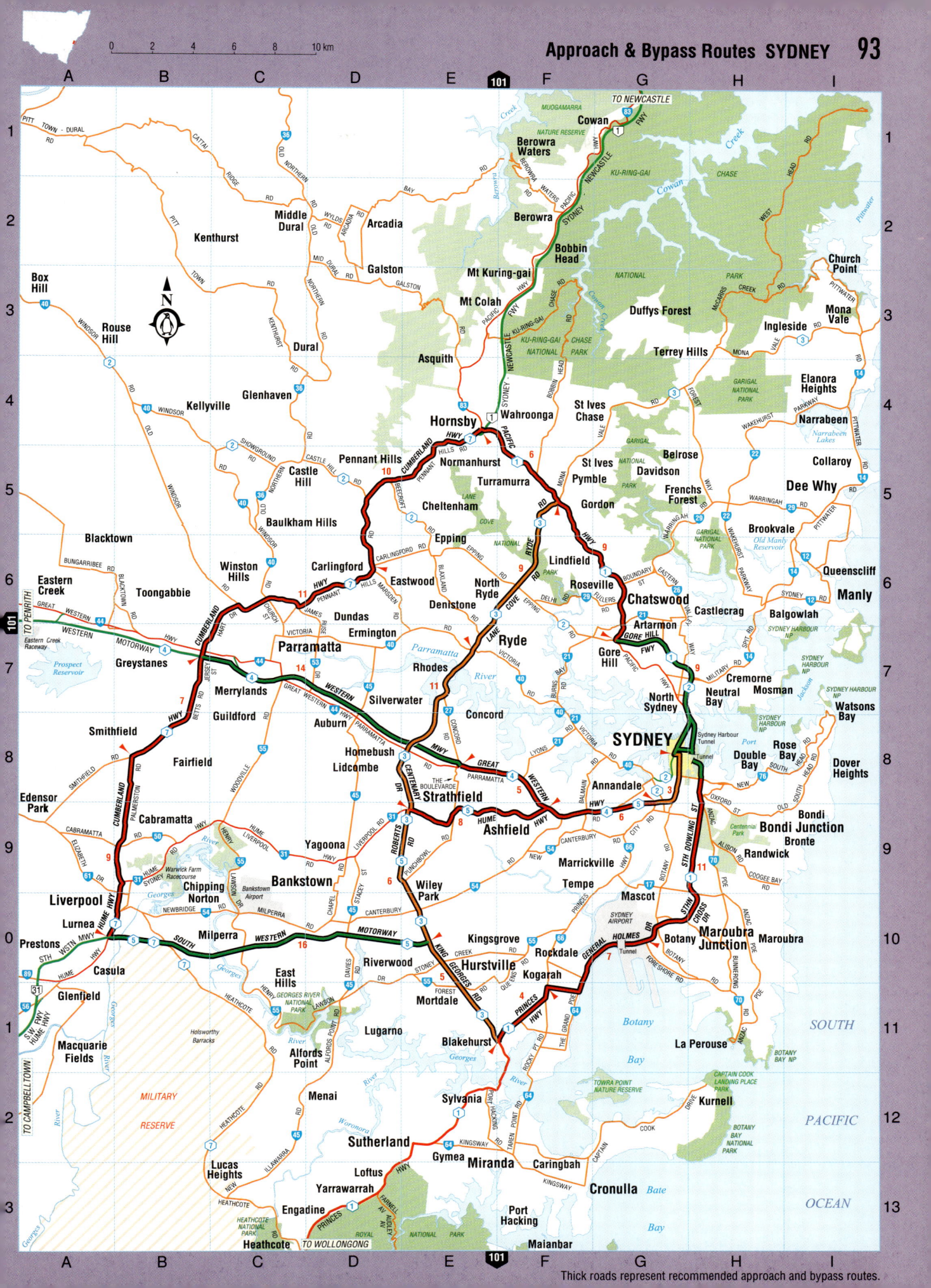

Approach & Bypass Routes SYDNEY 93

Thick roads represent recommended approach and bypass routes.

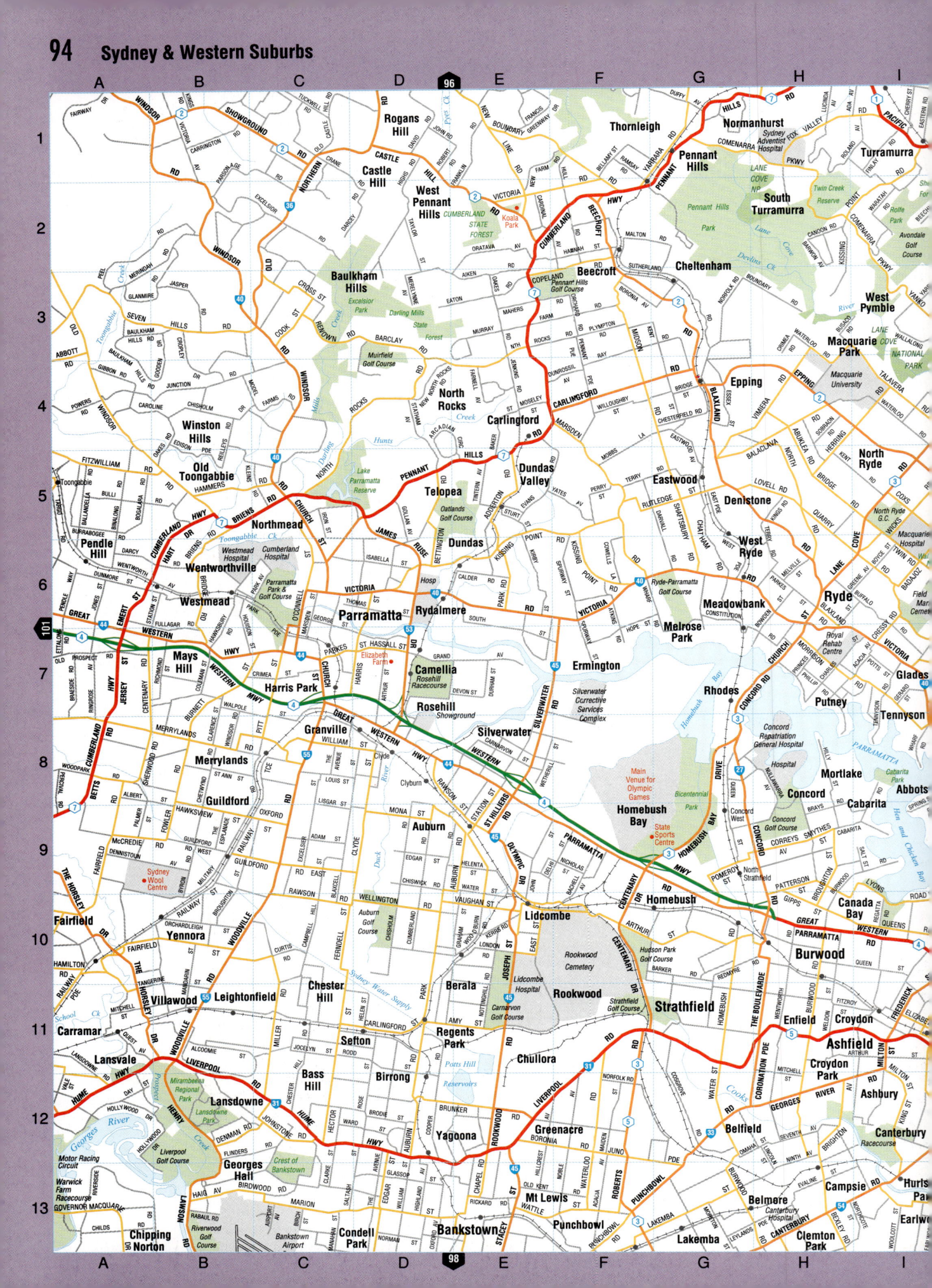

94 Sydney & Western Suburbs

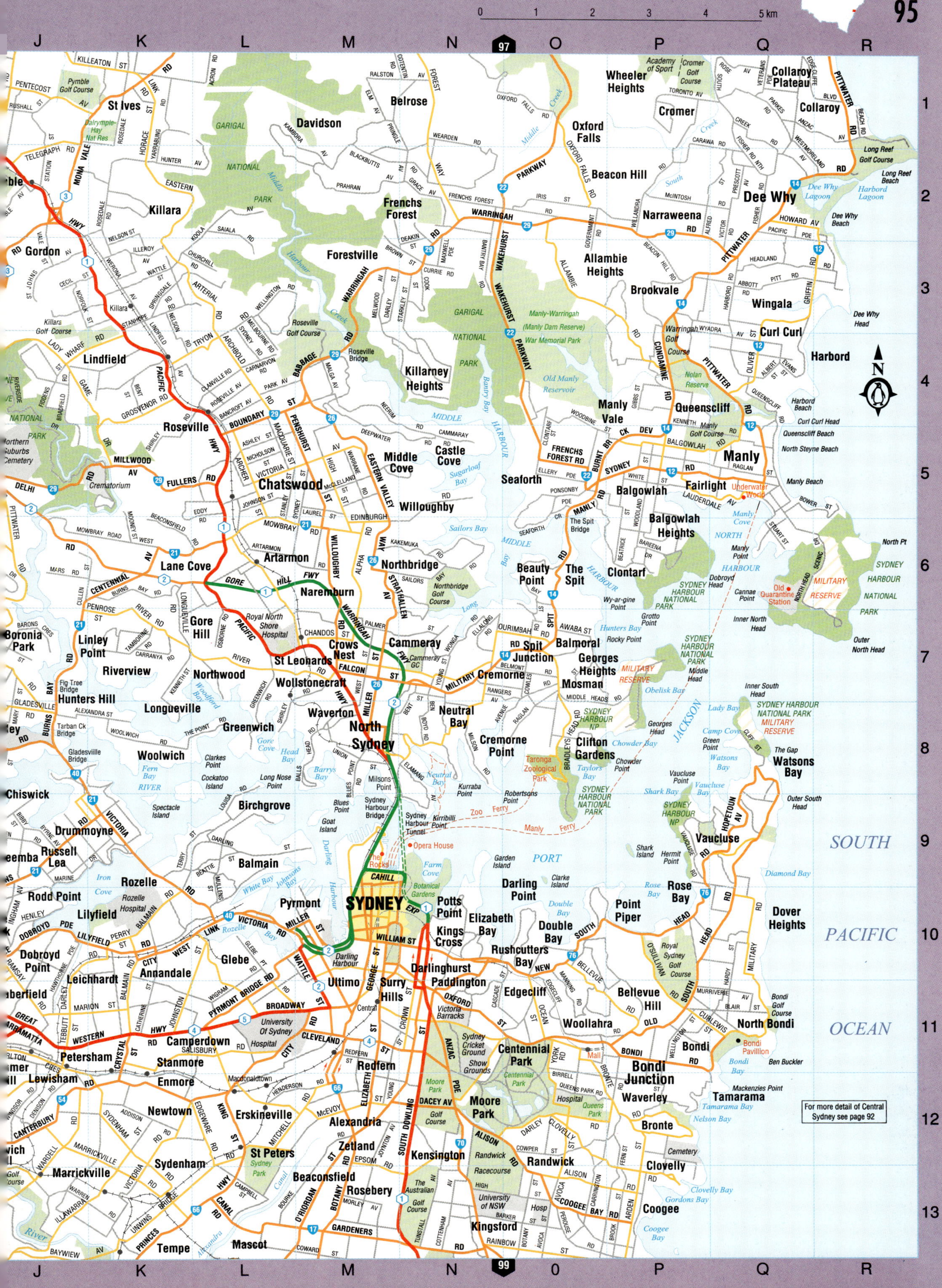
0 1 2 3 4 5 km
97
99
J K L M N O P Q R
1 2 3 4 5 6 7 8 9 10 11 12 13
St Ives
Pymble Golf Course
Davidson
Belrose
Wheeler Heights
Academy of Sport
Cromer Golf Course
Collaroy Plateau
Collaroy
Cromer
Oxford Falls
Beacon Hill
Long Reef Beach
Long Reef Golf Course
Dee Why
Dee Why Lagoon
Harbord Lagoon
Dee Why Beach
Narraweena
Frenchs Forest
Killara
Gordon
Forestville
Allambie Heights
Brookvale
Wingala
Dee Why Head
Curl Curl
Harbord
Killara Golf Course
Roseville Golf Course
Garigal National Park
Manly-Warringah (Manly Dam Reserve) War Memorial Park
Old Manly Reservoir
Lindfield
Killarney Heights
Manly Vale
Queenscliff
Nolan Reserve
Harbord Beach
Curl Curl Head
Queenscliff Beach
North Steyne Beach
Roseville
Manly Golf Course
Manly
Manly Beach
Middle Cove
Castle Cove
Sugarloaf Bay
Chatswood
Seaforth
Balgowlah
Fairlight
Underwater World
Crematorium
Willoughby
Sailors Bay
Middle Harbour
Balgowlah Heights
Manly Cove
North Harbour
Artarmon
Northbridge
Northbridge Golf Course
The Spit Bridge
Beauty Point
The Spit
Clontarf
Dobroyd Head
Cannae Point
Old Quarantine Station
Military Reserve
Sydney Harbour National Park
North Pt
Lane Cove
Naremburn
Grotto Point
Wy-ar-gine Point
Hunters Bay
Rocky Point
Inner North Head
Outer North Head
Gore Hill
Royal North Shore Hospital
Crows Nest
Cammeray
Spit Junction
Balmoral
Linley Point
Riverview
St Leonards
Georges Heights
Mosman
Middle Head
Obelisk Bay
Northwood
Wollstonecraft
Cremorne
Inner South Head
Hunters Hill
Longueville
Waverton
Neutral Bay
North Sydney
Lady Bay
Camp Cove
Green Point
Watsons Bay
The Gap
Greenwich
Cremorne Point
Clifton Gardens
Chowder Bay
Georges Head
Jackson
Woolwich
Taronga Zoological Park
Taylors Bay
Chowder Point
Vaucluse Point
Vaucluse Bay
Shark Bay
Outer South Head
Chiswick
Birchgrove
Milsons Point
Kurraba Point
Robertsons Point
Sydney Harbour Bridge
Sydney Harbour Tunnel
Kirribilli Point
Zoo Ferry
Manly Ferry
Opera House
Vaucluse
South Pacific Ocean
Drummoyne
Russell Lea
Balmain
The Rocks
Farm Cove
Garden Island
Port Jackson
Clarke Island
Shark Island
Hermit Point
Diamond Bay
Rozelle
Rozelle Hospital
Royal Botanical Gardens
Sydney
Potts Point
Darling Point
Double Bay
Point Piper
Rose Bay
Dover Heights
Rodd Point
Lilyfield
Pyrmont
Elizabeth Bay
Kings Cross
Rushcutters Bay
Royal Sydney Golf Course
Dobroyd Point
Leichhardt
Annandale
Glebe
Darling Harbour
Darlinghurst
Paddington
Edgecliff
Bellevue Hill
Ultimo
Surry Hills
Victoria Barracks
Woollahra
North Bondi
Bondi Golf Course
Camperdown
University of Sydney
Petersham
Stanmore
Redfern
Sydney Cricket Ground
Show Grounds
Centennial Park
Bondi Junction
Bondi
Bondi Pavillion
Ben Buckler
Bondi Bay
Lewisham
Enmore
Moore Park
Waverley
Tamarama
Mackenzies Point
Tamarama Bay
Newtown
Erskineville
Alexandria
Queens Park
Bronte
Nelson Bay
For more detail of Central Sydney see page 92
Marrickville
Sydenham
St Peters
Sydney Park
Zetland
Kensington
Randwick Racecourse
Randwick
Clovelly
Clovelly Bay
Gordons Bay
Beaconsfield
Rosebery
The Australian Golf Course
University of NSW
Coogee
Coogee Bay
Kingsford
Tempe
Mascot

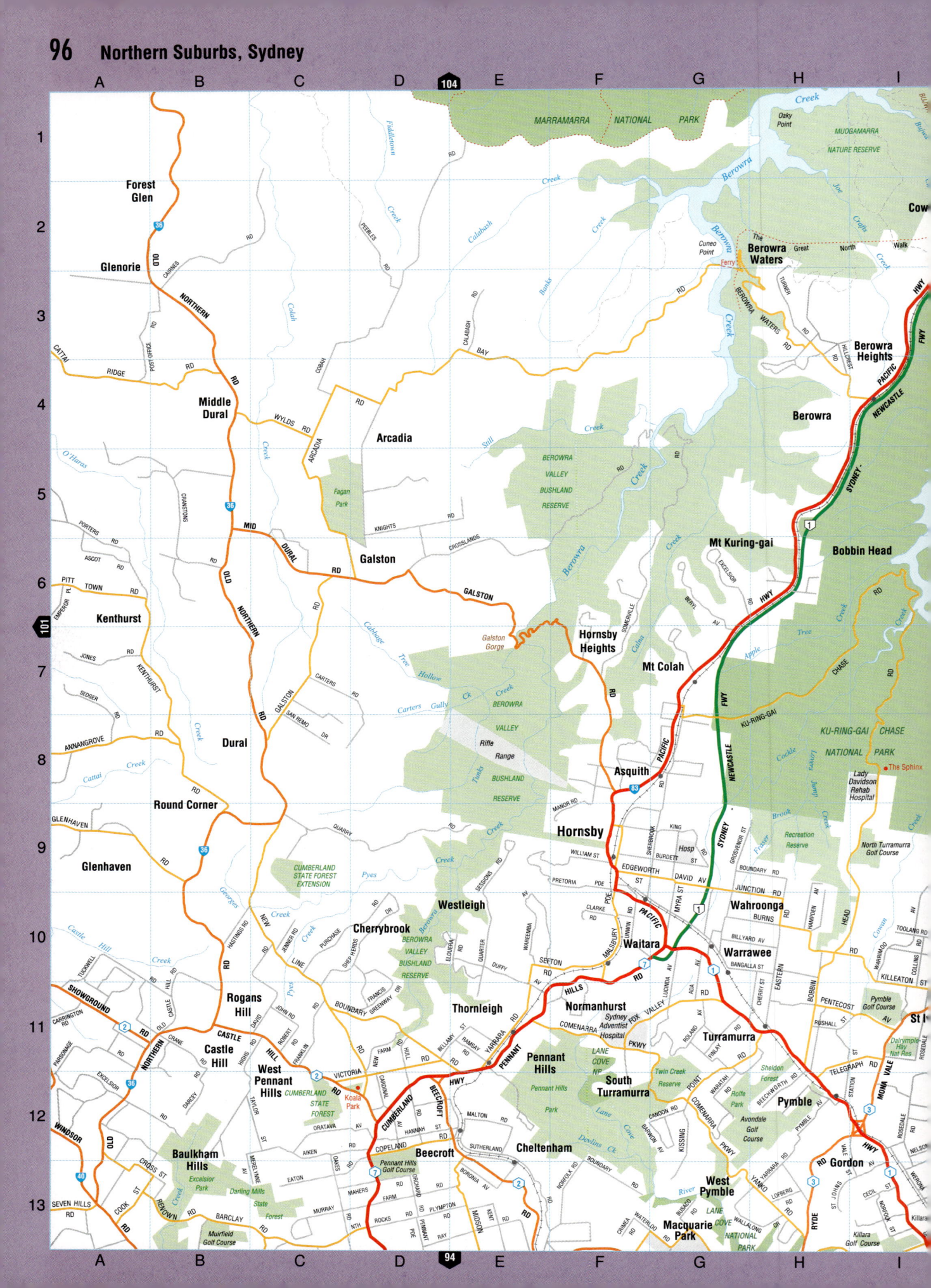

96 Northern Suburbs, Sydney

Palm Beach
Whale Beach
Careel Bay
Avalon
Clareville
Bilgola
Newport
Scotland Island
Church Point
Bayview
Mona Vale
Ingleside
Warriewood
Terrey Hills
Duffys Forest
Elanora Heights
Narrabeen
Wheeler Heights
Collaroy Plateau
Collaroy
Cromer
Oxford Falls
Beacon Hill
Belrose
Davidson
Frenchs Forest
Forestville
Narraweena
Dee Why
Allambie Heights
Brookvale
Wingala
Curl Curl
KU-RING-GAI CHASE NATIONAL PARK
GARIGAL NATIONAL PARK
Barrenjoey Lighthouse
Bangalley Head
St Michaels Cave
Hole in the Wall
Bilgola Head
Bungan Head
Turimetta Head
Narrabeen Head
Long Reef Point
Dee Why Head
Baha'i Temple
Waratah Park
Ku-Ring-Gai Wildflower Garden
St Ives Showground
SOUTH PACIFIC OCEAN
PITTWATER
0 1 2 3 4 5 km

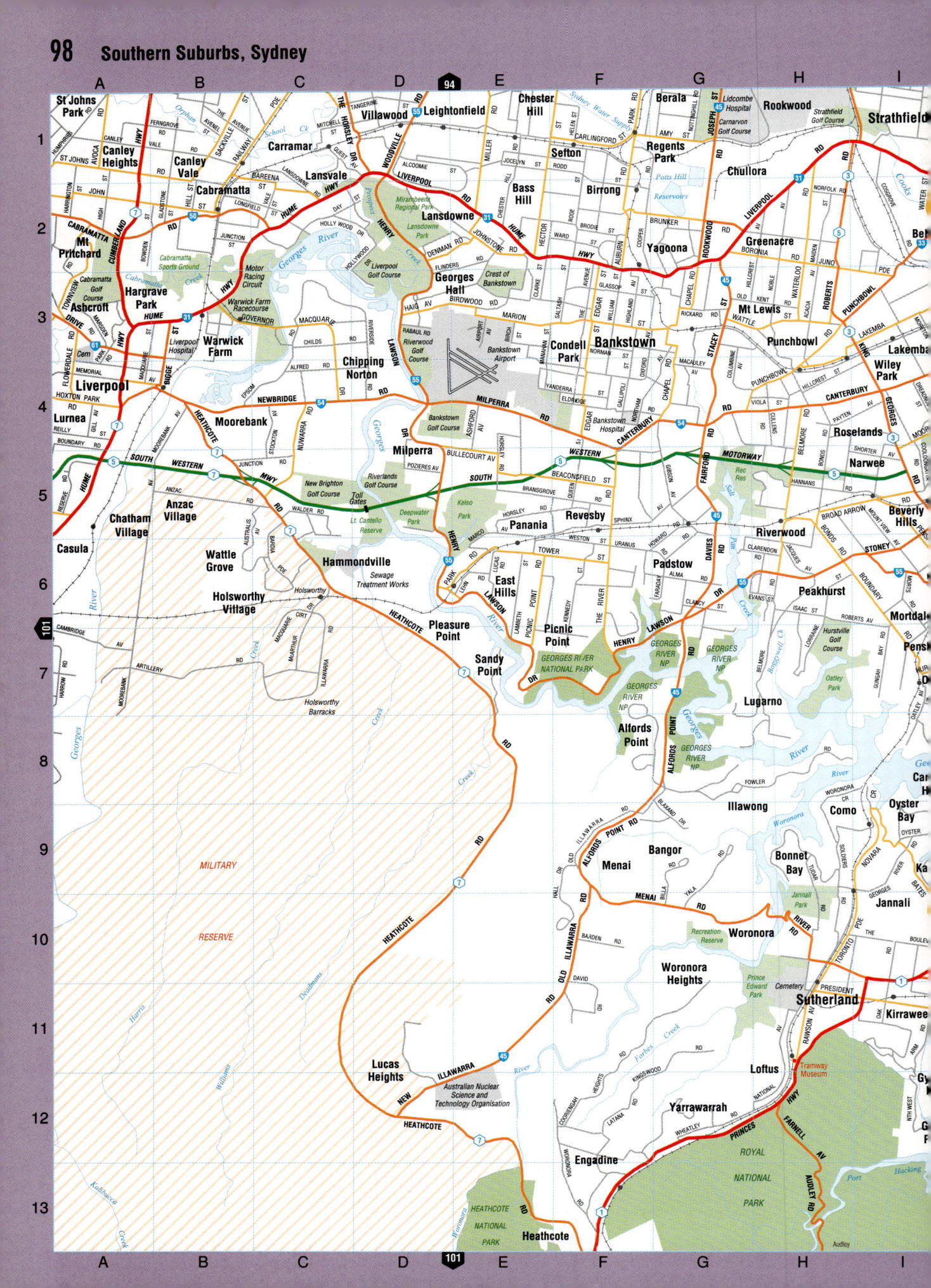

Southern Suburbs, Sydney

0 1 2 3 4 5 km
Enfield
Croydon
Ashfield
Croydon Park
Ashbury
Haberfield
Leichhardt
Annandale
Glebe
Ultimo
Surry Hills
Paddington
Edgecliff
Bellevue Hill
Woollahra
Summer Hill
Petersham
Lewisham
Camperdown
Stanmore
Enmore
University Of Sydney
Redfern
Centennial Park
Bondi
Bondi Junction
Waverley
Canterbury
Dulwich Hill
Newtown
Erskineville
Alexandria
Moore Park
Bronte
Marrickville
Hurlstone Park
Campsie
St Peters
Sydenham
Beaconsfield
Zetland
Kensington
Randwick
Clovelly
Rosebery
Coogee
Earlwood
Clemton Park
Tempe
Mascot
Kingsford
Undercliffe
Turrella
Arncliffe
Bardwell Park
Bexley North
Eastlakes
Daceyville
Sydney Airport
Pagewood
Maroubra Junction
Maroubra
Kingsgrove
Bexley
Banksia
Rockdale
Botany
Kyeemagh
Banksmeadow
Hillsdale
Matraville
Hurstville
Kogarah
Brighton-le-Sands
Malabar
Chifley
Carlton
Allawah
Monterey
Beverley Park
Ramsgate
Connells Point
Carss Park
Blakehurst
Phillip Bay
Little Bay
La Perouse
Dolls Point
Sans Souci
Sandringham
BOTANY BAY
Kurnell
Sylvania
Sylvania Waters
Sylvania Heights
Taren Point
Towra Point Nature Reserve
Quibray Bay
Weeney Bay
Woolooware Bay
Botany Bay National Park
Miranda
Caringbah
Woolooware
Cronulla
Yowie Bay
Dolans Bay
Burraneer
Port Hacking
Lilli Pilli
Maianbar
Port Hacking Point
BATE BAY
SOUTH PACIFIC OCEAN
Cape Banks

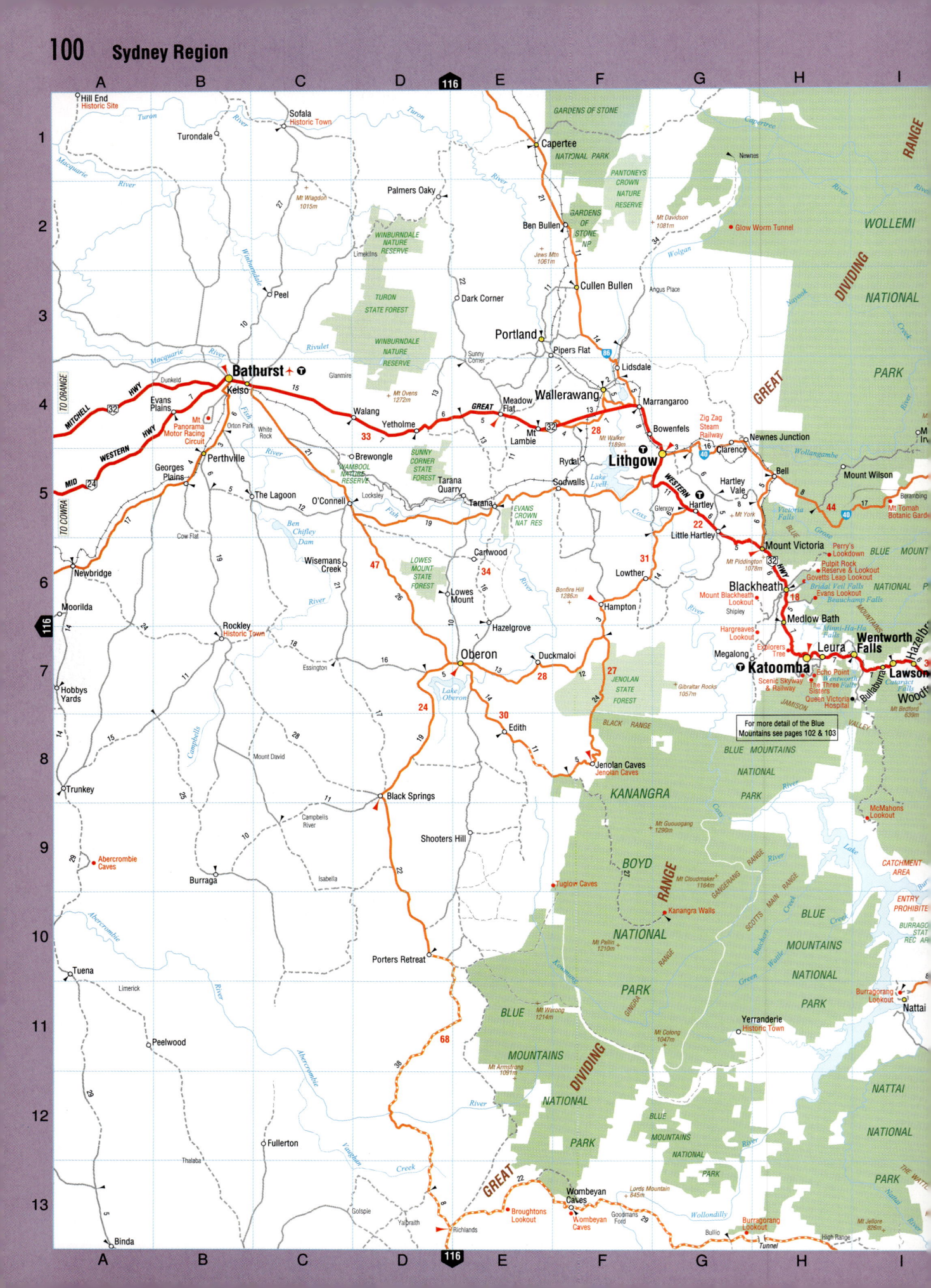

Sydney Region

0 5 10 15 20 km

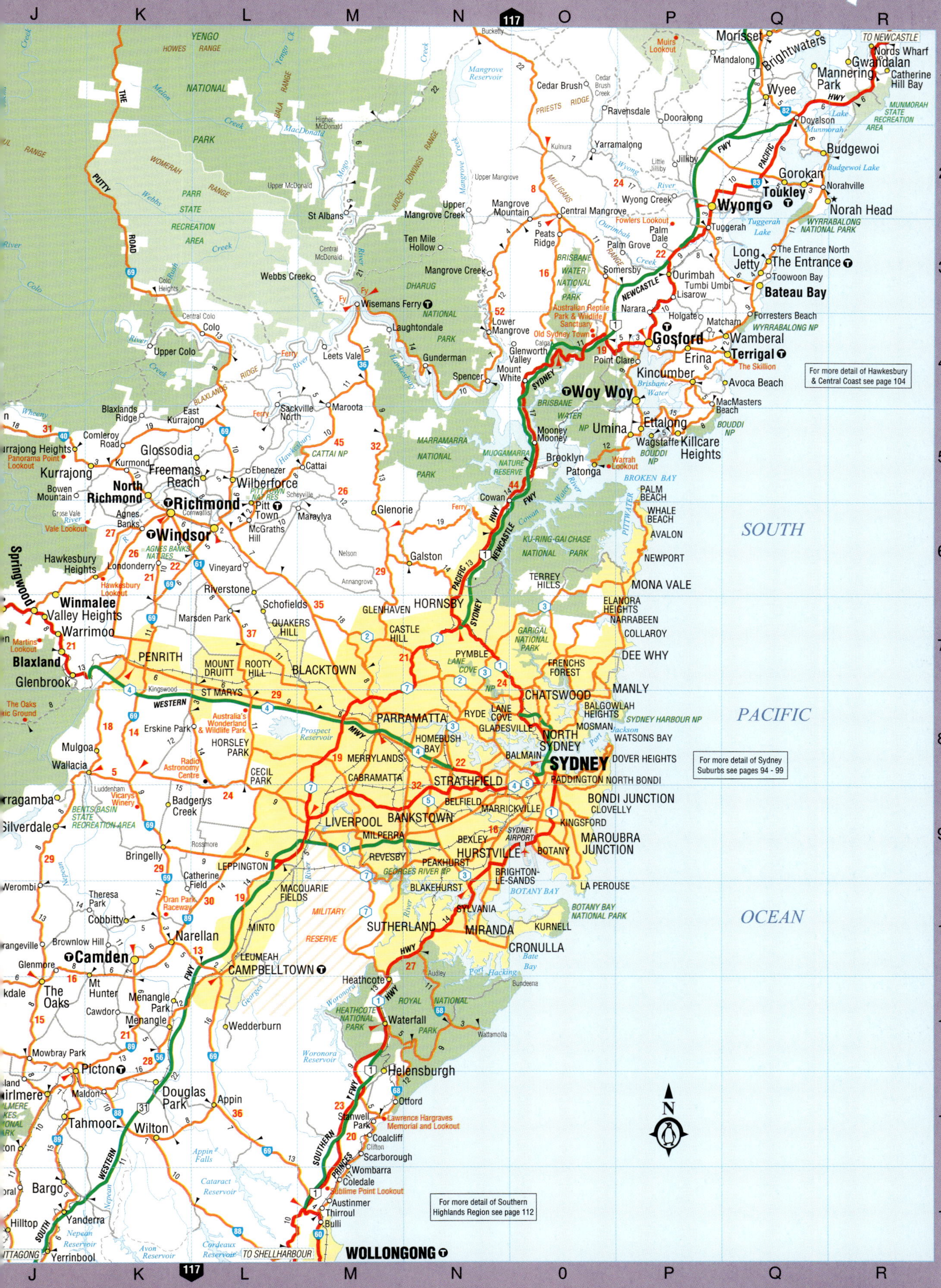

J K L M N O P Q R
117
1 2 3 4 5 6 7 8 9 10 11 12 13
YENGO NATIONAL PARK
PUTTY ROAD
WOMERAH RANGE
PARR STATE RECREATION AREA
DHARUG NATIONAL PARK
BRISBANE WATER NATIONAL PARK
MARRAMARRA NATIONAL PARK
KU-RING-GAI CHASE NATIONAL PARK
GARIGAL NATIONAL PARK
SYDNEY HARBOUR NP
BOTANY BAY NATIONAL PARK
ROYAL NATIONAL PARK
HEATHCOTE NATIONAL PARK
BLUE MOUNTAINS
BENTS BASIN STATE RECREATION AREA
MUNMORAH STATE RECREATION AREA
WYRRABALONG NATIONAL PARK
BOUDDI NATIONAL PARK
MILITARY RESERVE
SOUTH PACIFIC OCEAN
TO NEWCASTLE
Morisset
Mandalong
Brightwaters
Wyee
Mannering Park
Nords Wharf
Gwandalan
Catherine Hill Bay
Doyalson
Budgewoi
Gorokan
Toukley
Norahville
Norah Head
Wyong
Tuggerah
Long Jetty
The Entrance North
The Entrance
Toowoon Bay
Bateau Bay
Forresters Beach
Wamberal
Terrigal
Erina
Gosford
Kincumber
Avoca Beach
MacMasters Beach
Woy Woy
Umina
Ettalong
Killcare Heights
Patonga
Brooklyn
Mooney Mooney
Cowan
Central Mangrove
Mangrove Mountain
Peats Ridge
Somersby
Ourimbah
Lisarow
Narara
Wisemans Ferry
Laughtondale
Gunderman
Spencer
St Albans
Webbs Creek
Colo
Upper Colo
Leets Vale
Maroota
Sackville North
Glenorie
Galston
Kurrajong
North Richmond
Richmond
Windsor
Wilberforce
Pitt Town
Maraylya
McGraths Hill
Vineyard
Riverstone
Schofields
Marsden Park
Quakers Hill
Winmalee
Valley Heights
Warrimoo
Blaxland
Glenbrook
Springwood
Penrith
Mount Druitt
Rooty Hill
Blacktown
St Marys
Kingswood
Erskine Park
Horsley Park
Cecil Park
Mulgoa
Wallacia
Badgerys Creek
Bringelly
Leppington
Catherine Field
Macquarie Fields
Minto
Leumeah
Campbelltown
Narellan
Camden
Cobbitty
The Oaks
Menangle Park
Menangle
Picton
Douglas Park
Wilton
Appin
Tahmoor
Bargo
Yanderra
Hornsby
Glenhaven
Castle Hill
Pymble
Lane Cove
Chatswood
Ryde
Parramatta
Homebush Bay
Merrylands
Cabramatta
Strathfield
Liverpool
Bankstown
Milperra
Revesby
Hurstville
Peakhurst
Blakehurst
Sylvania
Sutherland
Miranda
Cronulla
Kurnell
Brighton-Le-Sands
Marrickville
Balmain
North Sydney
SYDNEY
Mosman
Manly
Dee Why
Collaroy
Narrabeen
Mona Vale
Newport
Avalon
Whale Beach
Palm Beach
Terrey Hills
Frenchs Forest
Balgowlah Heights
Watsons Bay
Dover Heights
North Bondi
Paddington
Bondi Junction
Clovelly
Kingsford
Maroubra Junction
Botany
La Perouse
Botany Bay
Port Hacking
Bundeena
Heathcote
Waterfall
Helensburgh
Otford
Stanwell Park
Coalcliff
Scarborough
Wombarra
Coledale
Austinmer
Thirroul
Bulli
WOLLONGONG
TO SHELLHARBOUR
For more detail of Hawkesbury & Central Coast see page 104
For more detail of Sydney Suburbs see pages 94 - 99
For more detail of Southern Highlands Region see page 112

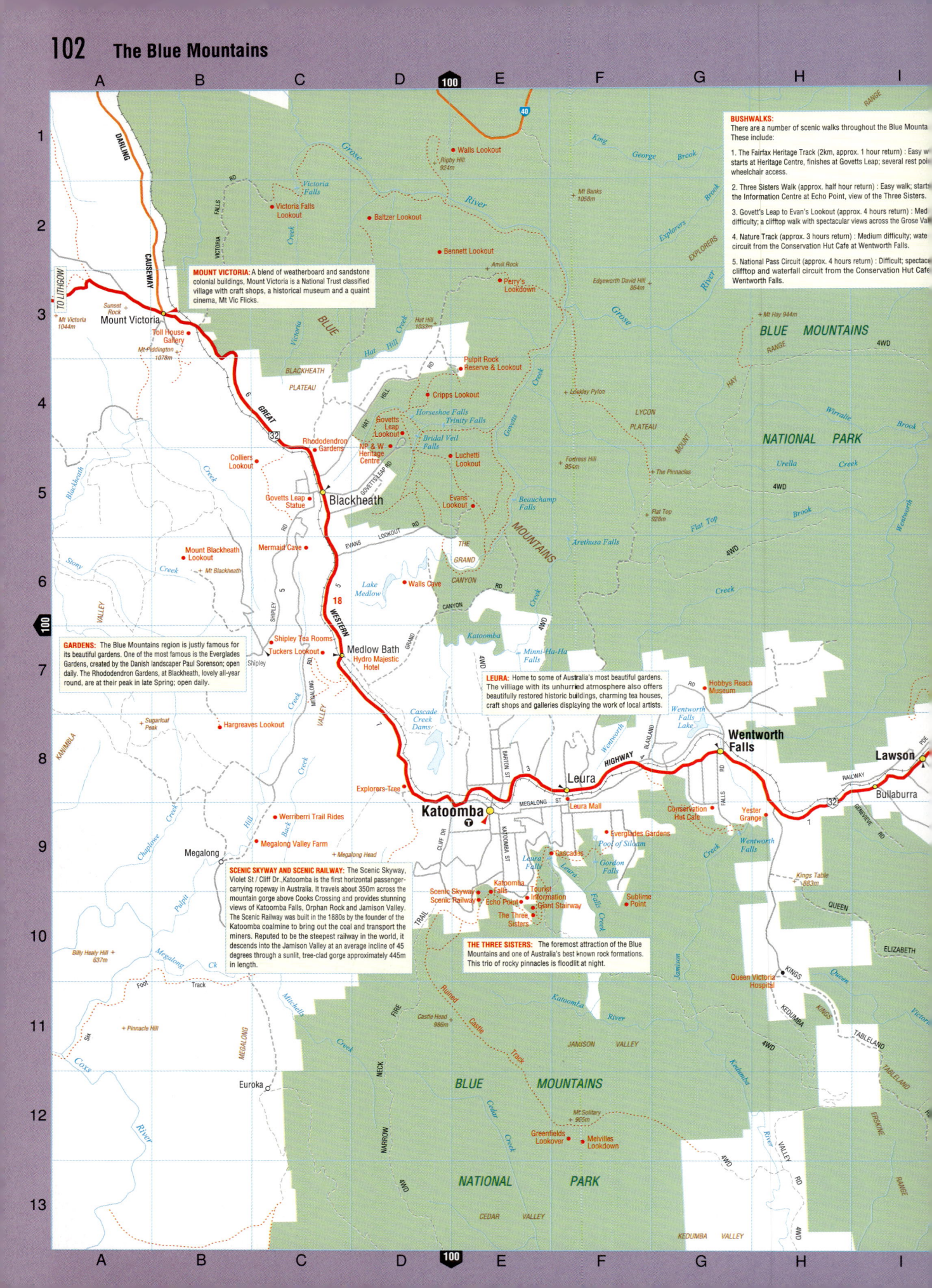

102 The Blue Mountains

BUSHWALKS:
There are a number of scenic walks throughout the Blue Mounta[ins]
These include:

1. The Fairfax Heritage Track (2km, approx. 1 hour return): Easy w[alk]
   starts at Heritage Centre, finishes at Govetts Leap; several rest poi[nts]
   wheelchair access.

2. Three Sisters Walk (approx. half hour return): Easy walk; start[s at]
   the Information Centre at Echo Point, view of the Three Sisters.

3. Govett's Leap to Evan's Lookout (approx. 4 hours return): Med[ium]
   difficulty; a clifftop walk with spectacular views across the Grose Val[ley]

4. Nature Track (approx. 3 hours return): Medium difficulty; wate[rfall]
   circuit from the Conservation Hut Cafe at Wentworth Falls.

5. National Pass Circuit (approx. 4 hours return): Difficult; spectac[ular]
   clifftop and waterfall circuit from the Conservation Hut Cafe [at]
   Wentworth Falls.

MOUNT VICTORIA: A blend of weatherboard and sandstone colonial buildings, Mount Victoria is a National Trust classified village with craft shops, a historical museum and a quaint cinema, Mt Vic Flicks.

GARDENS: The Blue Mountains region is justly famous for its beautiful gardens. One of the most famous is the Everglades Gardens, created by the Danish landscaper Paul Sorenson; open daily. The Rhododendron Gardens, at Blackheath, lovely all-year round, are at their peak in late Spring; open daily.

LEURA: Home to some of Australia's most beautiful gardens. The village with its unhurried atmosphere also offers beautifully restored historic buildings, charming tea houses, craft shops and galleries displaying the work of local artists.

SCENIC SKYWAY AND SCENIC RAILWAY: The Scenic Skyway, Violet St / Cliff Dr., Katoomba is the first horizontal passenger-carrying ropeway in Australia. It travels about 350m across the mountain gorge above Cooks Crossing and provides stunning views of Katoomba Falls, Orphan Rock and Jamison Valley. The Scenic Railway was built in the 1880s by the founder of the Katoomba coalmine to bring out the coal and transport the miners. Reputed to be the steepest railway in the world, it descends into the Jamison Valley at an average incline of 45 degrees through a sunlit, tree-clad gorge approximately 445m in length.

THE THREE SISTERS: The foremost attraction of the Blue Mountains and one of Australia's best known rock formations. This trio of rocky pinnacles is floodlit at night.

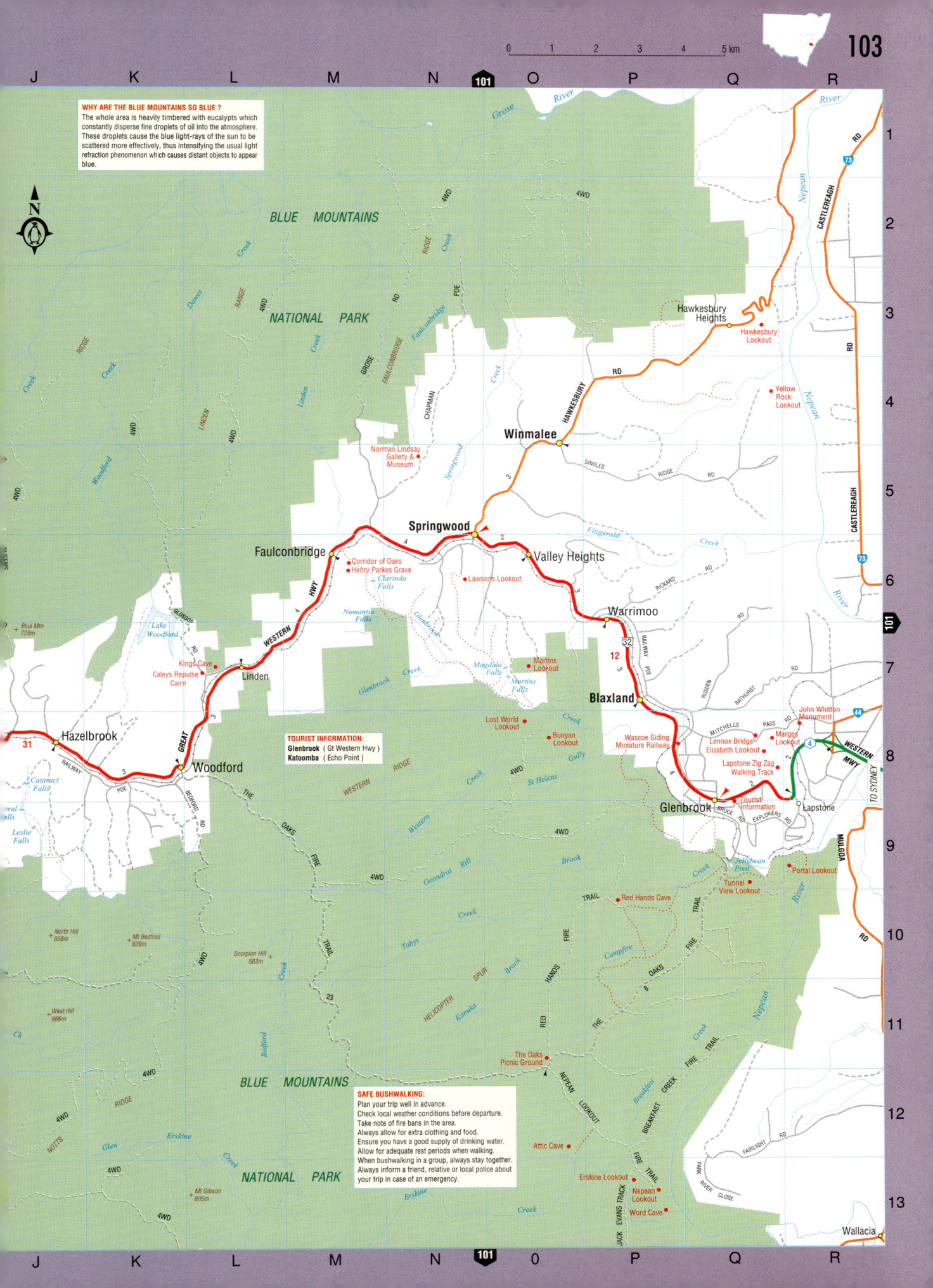

WHY ARE THE BLUE MOUNTAINS SO BLUE?
The whole area is heavily timbered with eucalypts which constantly disperse fine droplets of oil into the atmosphere. These droplets cause the blue light-rays of the sun to be scattered more effectively, thus intensifying the usual light refraction phenomenon which causes distant objects to appear blue.

TOURIST INFORMATION:
Glenbrook (Gt Western Hwy)
Katoomba (Echo Point)

SAFE BUSHWALKING:
Plan your trip well in advance.
Check local weather conditions before departure.
Take note of fire bans in the area.
Always allow for extra clothing and food.
Ensure you have a good supply of drinking water.
Allow for adequate rest periods when walking.
When bushwalking in a group, always stay together.
Always inform a friend, relative or local police about your trip in case of an emergency.

104 Hawkesbury & Central Coast

TOURIST INFORMATION:
The Entrance (Marine Pde)
Gosford &
Woy Woy (200 Main St)
Terrigal (Terrigal Dr)
Wyong (Caltex, Twin Service Centre Sydney - Newcastle Fwy)

PELICAN FEEDING: This unique attraction occurs each afternoon around 3-30 near the children's playground in the Memorial Park at The Entrance.

NATIONAL PARKS: At **Wyrrabalong** swimming is possible at either Bateau Bay or Tuggerah Beach; waterbirds are a feature. **Bouddi** is renowned for its established walking trails and at Maitland Bay, there is a shipwreck half submerged on the beach. **Brisbane Water** offers spectacular water views and has many fine Aboriginal art sites. Further west, **Dharug** lines the river and has a popular family walking trail.

GREAT NORTH WALK: A section of this 250 km walking track, which runs between Sydney and Newcastle, passes through the region. There are numerous access points, facilities and connections to public transport enabling families, campers and day trippers to enjoy day and weekend walks.

HAWKESBURY RIVER: A magnificent waterway navigable as far as Windsor and further for small craft. There are few settlements along the widest section of the river as most of the shore is protected as part of Brisbane Water and Ku-Ring-Gai Chase National Parks.

RIVER MAIL-BOAT: Visitors can join the river mail-boat run which leaves the ferry wharf at Dangar Road Brooklyn on weekdays. It takes three hours, ferrying mail, groceries & other necessities to residents with no road access.

SAFE BOATING:
Tell someone where you are going.
Carry adequate equipment.
Carry effective life jackets.
Carry enough fuel and water.
Ensure engine reliability.
Guard against fire.
Do not overload the craft.
Know the boating rules and local regulations; also distress signals.
Watch the weather.
Do not drink alcohol while boating.

Port Macquarie Region

TOURIST INFORMATION:
- Kempsey (Pacific Hwy, South Kempsey)
- Port Macquarie (Cnr Clarence & Hay Sts)
- Taree (Pacific Hwy, Taree North)

FOREST DRIVES: There are abundant scenic drives through spectacular stands of eucalyptus, and lush rainforest in this timber growing district. Follow parts of the trail of Surveyor General John Oxley where in 1818 he made his way across the Great Dividing Range to the mouth of the Hastings River at Port Macquarie.

TIMBERTOWN: Only 3 km west of Wauchope, this re-created sawmillers village is a tribute to the hardy timber pioneers of 1880. Ride the restored steam-train or Clydesdale-drawn dray to bush camps for demonstrations of sleeper-cutting, shingle-splitting and bullock-yoking. The authentic late 1800s hotel serves damper and roast meats with Australian bushsongs for entertainment.

ELLENBOROUGH FALLS: One of the highest single-drop falls in the state, with a 160-metre sheer descent. A relaxing drive through picturesque dairy country and the Bulga State Forest leads to the falls. The spectacular Ellenborough Falls is on the edge of the New England Tableland.

HASTINGS RIVER: Starting from the slope of eastern streams of the Great Divide and fed by the Ellenborough and Forbes Rivers, this beautiful waterway of deep pools and sandy banks stretches over 100 km. In the wet season the Hastings River swells with rapid torrents excellent for white water rafting and exhilarating canoe adventures.

CAMDEN HAVEN RIVER: This river runs through a cluster of picturesque towns surrounded by forests, national parks, unspoilt coast and cool, clean waterways. Magnificent views from North Border mountain. Sailing, fishing and hang-gliding are popular in the area.

CROWDY BAY NATIONAL PARK: Numerous walking tracks are found within the park linking sand dunes and plains rich in wildflowers to swamp wonderlands - home to the spoonbill, ibis and gracious jabiru. Diamond Head is named for the quartz crystals found in the region's rocks. Crowdy Bay is well-known for the 101 bird species that inhabit the area.

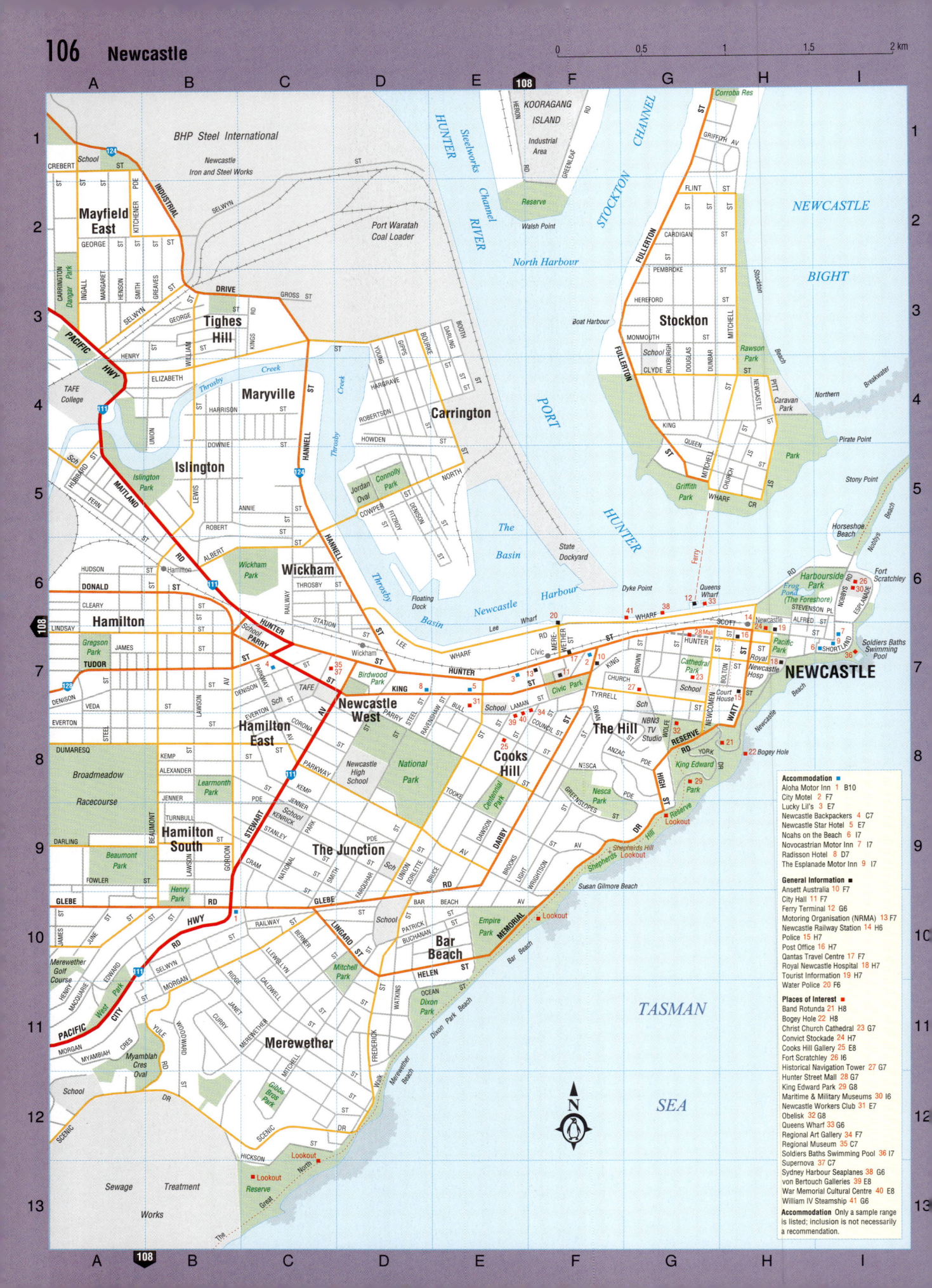

106 Newcastle

Accommodation
- Aloha Motor Inn 1 B10
- City Motel 2 F7
- Lucky Lil's 3 E7
- Newcastle Backpackers 4 C7
- Newcastle Star Hotel 5 E7
- Noahs on the Beach 6 I7
- Novocastrian Motor Inn 7 I7
- Radisson Hotel 8 D7
- The Esplanade Motor Inn 9 I7

General Information
- Ansett Australia 10 F7
- City Hall 11 F7
- Ferry Terminal 12 G6
- Motoring Organisation (NRMA) 13 F7
- Newcastle Railway Station 14 H6
- Police 15 H7
- Post Office 16 H7
- Qantas Travel Centre 17 F7
- Royal Newcastle Hospital 18 H7
- Tourist Information 19 H7
- Water Police 20 F6

Places of Interest
- Band Rotunda 21 H8
- Bogey Hole 22 H8
- Christ Church Cathedral 23 G7
- Convict Stockade 24 H7
- Cooks Hill Gallery 25 E8
- Fort Scratchley 26 I6
- Historical Navigation Tower 27 G7
- Hunter Street Mall 28 G7
- King Edward Park 29 G8
- Maritime & Military Museums 30 I6
- Newcastle Workers Club 31 E7
- Obelisk 32 G8
- Queens Wharf 33 G6
- Regional Art Gallery 34 F7
- Regional Museum 35 C7
- Soldiers Baths Swimming Pool 36 I7
- Supernova 37 C7
- Sydney Harbour Seaplanes 38 G6
- von Bertouch Galleries 39 E8
- War Memorial Cultural Centre 40 E8
- William IV Steamship 41 G6

Accommodation: Only a sample range is listed; inclusion is not necessarily a recommendation.

Approach & Bypass Routes NEWCASTLE 107

Thick roads represent recommended approach and bypass routes.

108 Newcastle Region

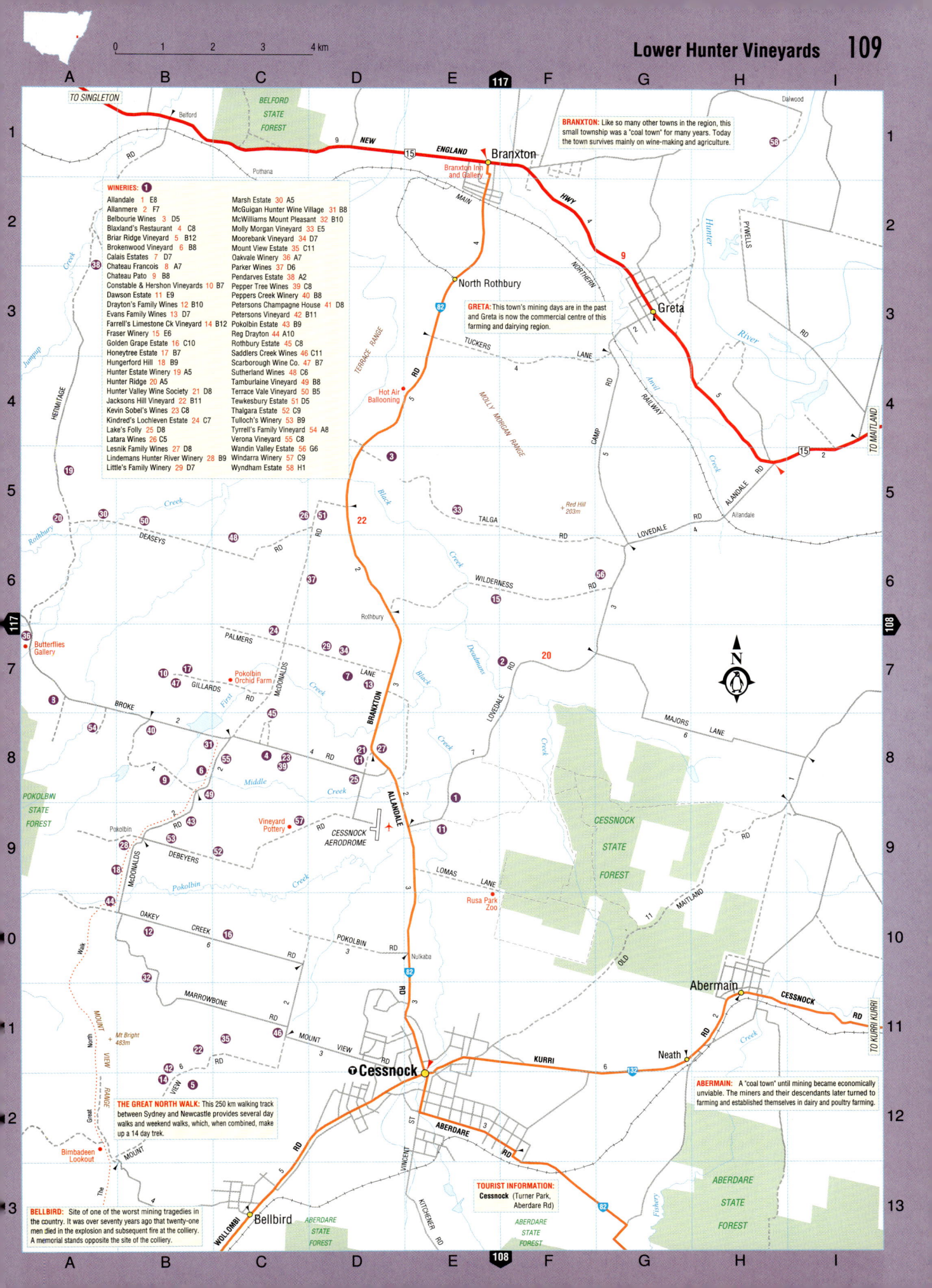

Lower Hunter Vineyards

BRANXTON: Like so many other towns in the region, this small township was a "coal town" for many years. Today the town survives mainly on wine-making and agriculture.

GRETA: This town's mining days are in the past and Greta is now the commercial centre of this farming and dairying region.

ABERMAIN: A "coal town" until mining became economically unviable. The miners and their descendants later turned to farming and established themselves in dairy and poultry farming.

BELLBIRD: Site of one of the worst mining tragedies in the country. It was over seventy years ago that twenty-one men died in the explosion and subsequent fire at the colliery. A memorial stands opposite the site of the colliery.

THE GREAT NORTH WALK: This 250 km walking track between Sydney and Newcastle provides several day walks and weekend walks, which, when combined, make up a 14 day trek.

TOURIST INFORMATION: Cessnock (Turner Park, Aberdare Rd)

WINERIES:

Name	No.	Ref
Allandale	1	E8
Allanmere	2	F7
Belbourie Wines	3	D5
Blaxland's Restaurant	4	C8
Briar Ridge Vineyard	5	B12
Brokenwood Vineyard	6	B8
Calais Estates	7	D7
Chateau Francois	8	A7
Chateau Pato	9	B8
Constable & Hershon Vineyards	10	B7
Dawson Estate	11	E9
Drayton's Family Wines	12	B10
Evans Family Wines	13	D7
Farrell's Limestone Ck Vineyard	14	B12
Fraser Winery	15	E6
Golden Grape Estate	16	C10
Honeytree Estate	17	B7
Hungerford Hill	18	B9
Hunter Estate Winery	19	A5
Hunter Ridge	20	A5
Hunter Valley Wine Society	21	D8
Jacksons Hill Vineyard	22	B11
Kevin Sobel's Wines	23	C8
Kindred's Lochleven Estate	24	C7
Lake's Folly	25	D8
Latara Wines	26	C5
Lesnik Family Wines	27	D8
Lindemans Hunter River Winery	28	B9
Little's Family Winery	29	D7
Marsh Estate	30	A5
McGuigan Hunter Wine Village	31	B8
McWilliams Mount Pleasant	32	B10
Molly Morgan Vineyard	33	E5
Moorebank Vineyard	34	D7
Mount View Estate	35	C11
Oakvale Winery	36	A7
Parker Wines	37	D6
Pendarves Estate	38	A2
Pepper Tree Wines	39	C8
Peppers Creek Winery	40	B8
Petersons Champagne House	41	D8
Petersons Vineyard	42	B11
Pokolbin Estate	43	B9
Reg Drayton	44	A10
Rothbury Estate	45	C8
Saddlers Creek Wines	46	C11
Scarborough Wine Co.	47	B7
Sutherland Wines	48	C6
Tamburlaine Vineyard	49	B8
Terrace Vale Vineyard	50	B5
Tewkesbury Estate	51	D5
Thalgara Estate	52	C9
Tulloch's Winery	53	B9
Tyrrell's Family Vineyard	54	A8
Verona Vineyard	55	C8
Wandin Valley Estate	56	G6
Windarra Winery	57	C9
Wyndham Estate	58	H1

110 Wollongong

Accommodation ■
- Belmore Deluxe Apartments 1 F10
- Boat Harbour Motel 2 F10
- City Pacific Hotel 3 E10
- Downtown Motel 4 F10
- Novotel Northbeach 5 F9
- Park Street Apartments 6 E9
- Surfside 22 Motel 7 F10

General Information ■
- Coach Terminal 8 E10
- General Post Office 9 F10
- Motoring Organisation (NRMA) 10 E11
- Police Headquarters 11 E10
- Tourist Information 12 E10
- Wollongong Railway Station 13 D11

Places of Interest ■
- Art Gallery 14 E10
- Botanic Gardens 15 C8
- Historical Museum 16 F10
- Illawarra Performing Arts Centre 17 F10
- International Centre 18 E11
- McCabe Park 19 E11

Accommodation: Only a sample range is listed; inclusion is not necessarily a recommendation.

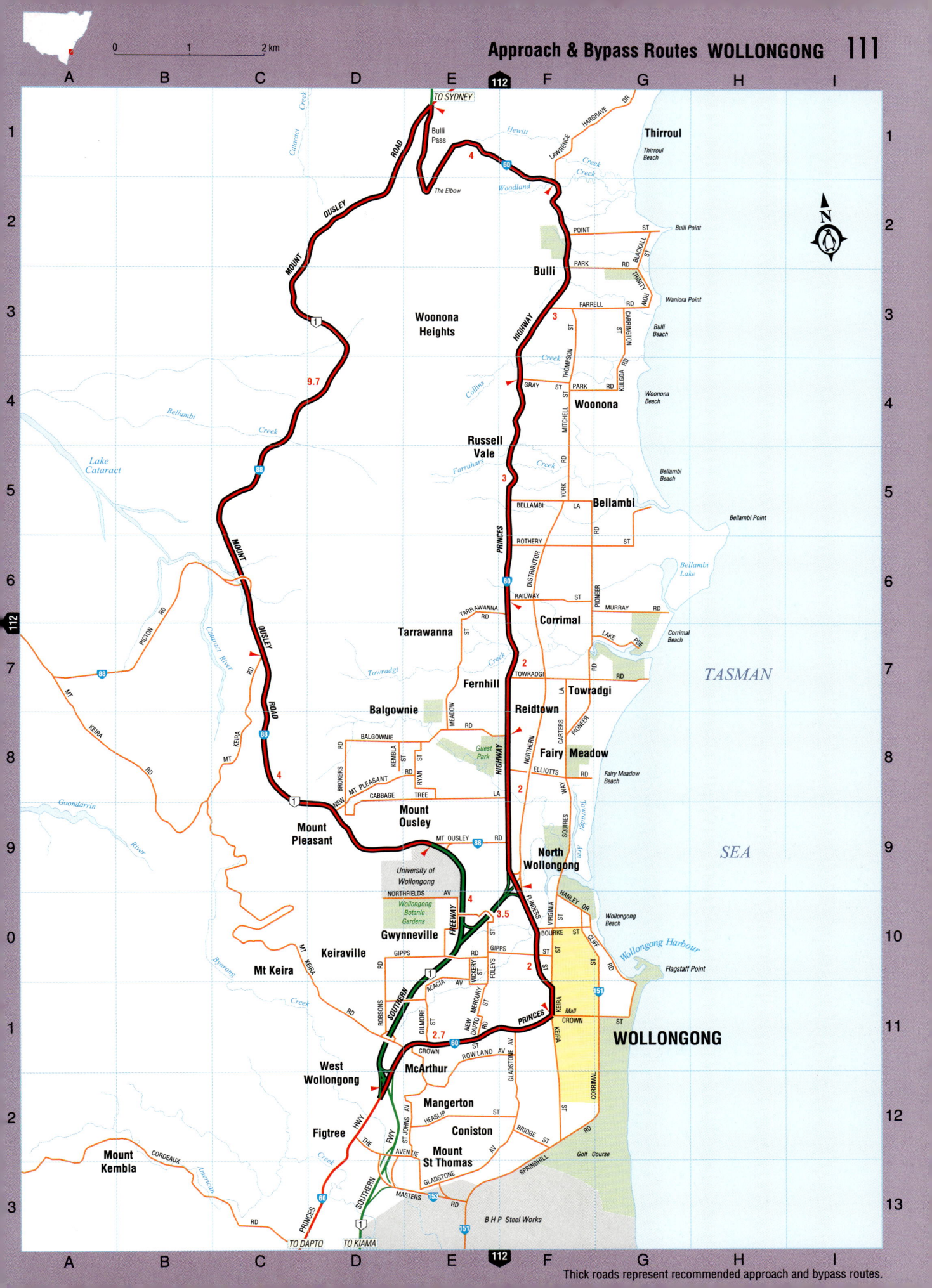

Approach & Bypass Routes WOLLONGONG 111

Thick roads represent recommended approach and bypass routes.

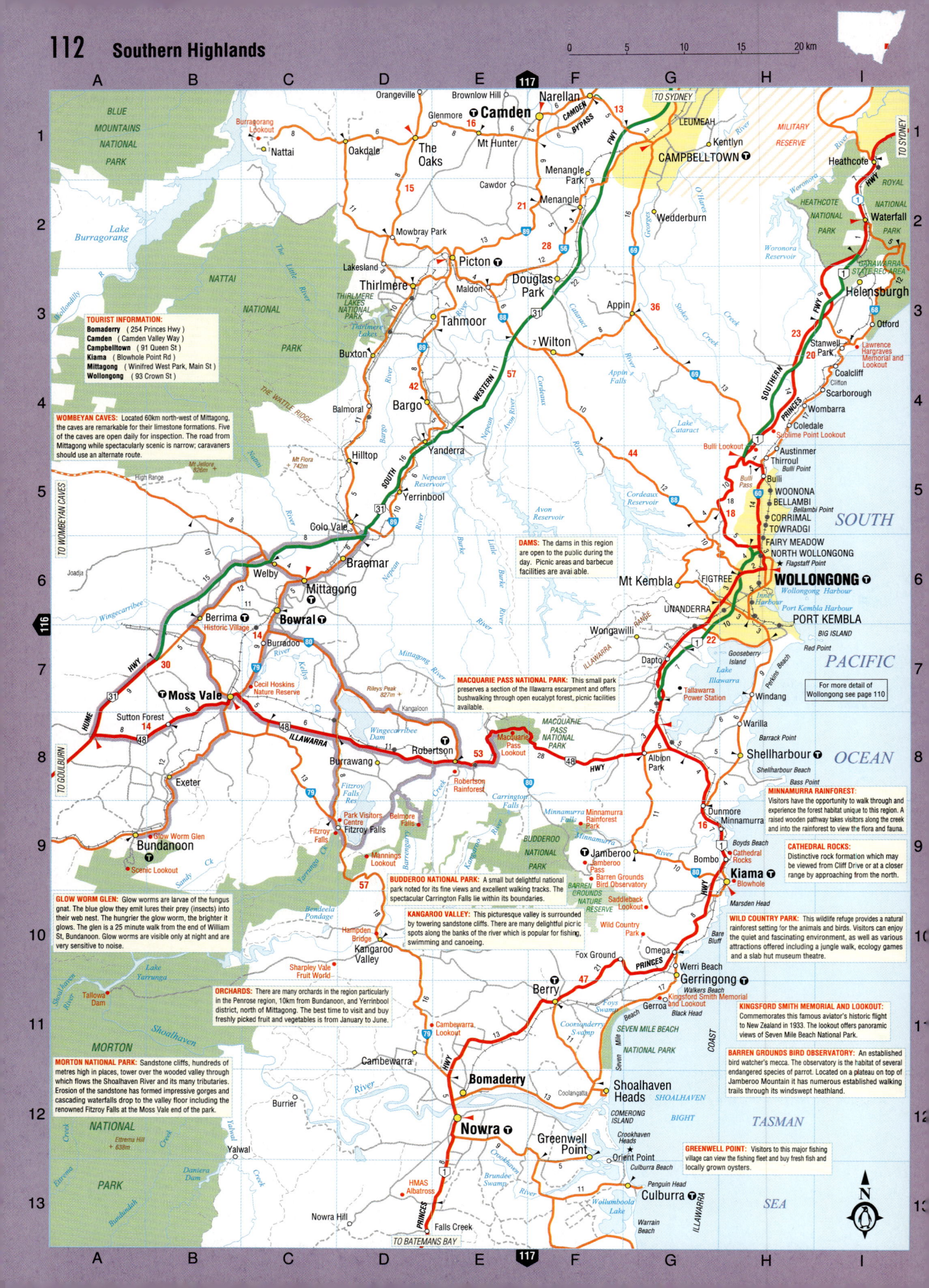

112 Southern Highlands

South Coast 113

Tourist Information:
- **Bega** (Gipps St)
- **Bermagui** (5 Caluga St)
- **Bombala** (125 Maybe St)
- **Cooma** (119 Sharp St)
- **Eden** (Princes Hwy)
- **Merimbula** (Beach St)
- **Narooma** (Princes Hwy)
- **Tathra** (Wharf Rd)

NAROOMA: A popular fishing resort well-known for its rock oysters.

CENTRAL TILBA: Founded in 1895, this town was classified by the National Trust in 1974 to preserve it for posterity. Visitors can enjoy the craft shops, a deer farm, winery and tea rooms.

THE TRIANGLE: So called because on a map the road pattern linking the three towns, Central Tilba, Bermagui, and Cobargo, is distinctly triangular. The surrounding area offers the visitor scenic places, superb fishing facilities and an insight into the country's heritage.

CANDELO: Little has changed in this village since the Nineteenth Century giving it an old-world charm.

PAMBULA: Historic village renowned for its quaint buildings now housing craft shops and restaurants. Sunday markets held second Sunday of each month. Nearby Pambula beach, a patrolled surfing beach, has excellent picnic spots on its foreshore where kangaroos and wallabies may be seen feeding in the early mornings and late afternoons.

FISHING: Every year thousands of anglers come to this section of the Coast to enjoy their favourite sport. Fisheries, however, are limited, and restrictions have been placed in order that they be protected. Contact the NSW Fisheries for information regarding protected species, quantities of fish taken in any one day, minimum sizes and method of capture.

BEN BOYD NATIONAL PARK: Over 9000 hectares of rocky but beautiful coastline flanking Twofold Bay. Flowering heaths and colourful banksias add to the area's attraction. Prominent features in the park include Boyds Tower, constructed in the 1840s, and The Pinnacles, a formation that dates back about 65 million years. The Pinnacles walking track is popular with visitors.

WONBOYN LAKE: Reputed to be the finest fishing spot on this section of the coast, note that the road leading to the lake is unsealed.

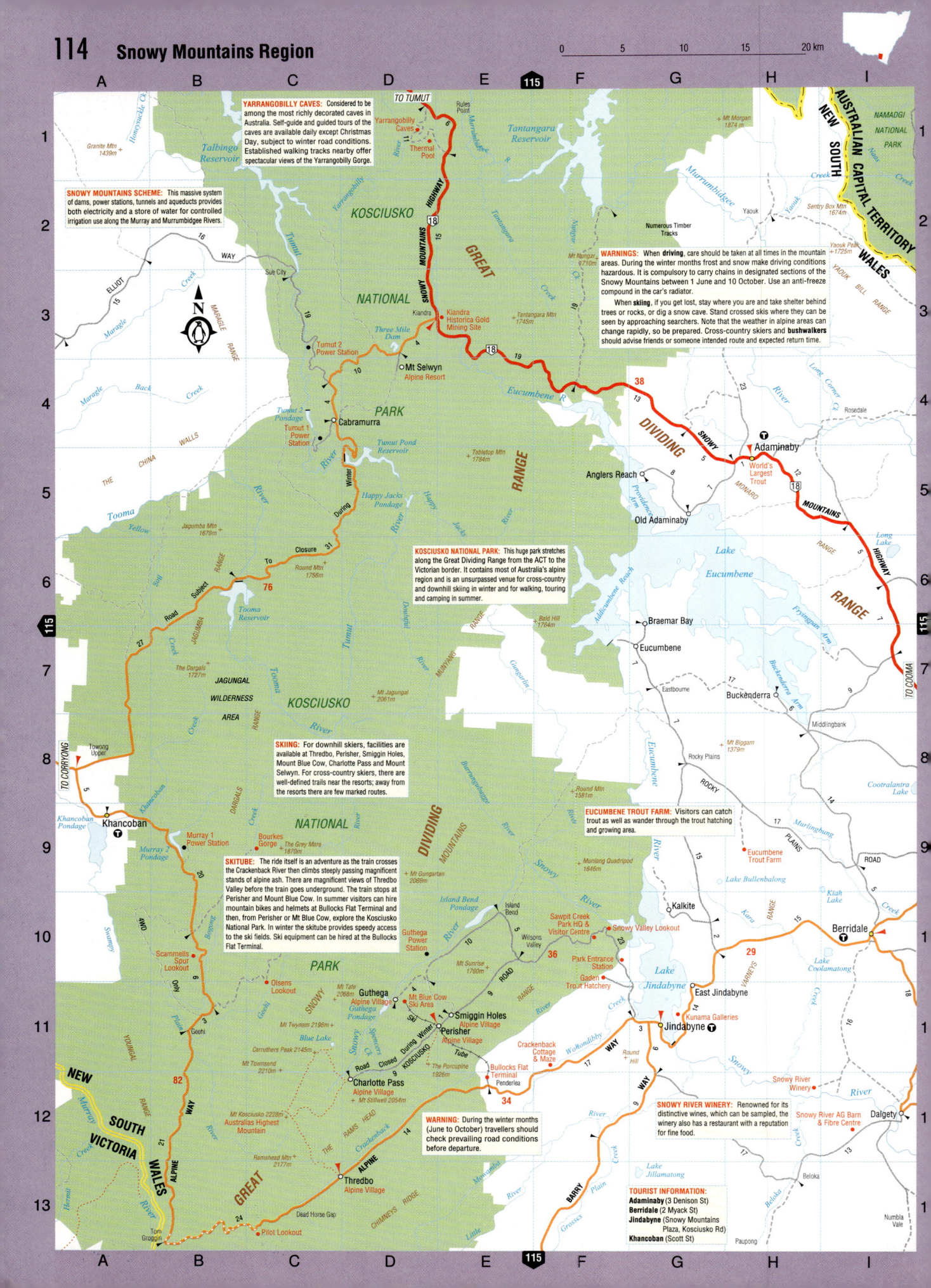

114 Snowy Mountains Region

YARRANGOBILLY CAVES: Considered to be among the most richly decorated caves in Australia. Self-guide and guided tours of the caves are available daily except Christmas Day, subject to winter road conditions. Established walking tracks nearby offer spectacular views of the Yarrangobilly Gorge.

SNOWY MOUNTAINS SCHEME: This massive system of dams, power stations, tunnels and aqueducts provides both electricity and a store of water for controlled irrigation use along the Murray and Murrumbidgee Rivers.

WARNINGS: When **driving**, care should be taken at all times in the mountain areas. During the winter months frost and snow make driving conditions hazardous. It is compulsory to carry chains in designated sections of the Snowy Mountains between 1 June and 10 October. Use an anti-freeze compound in the car's radiator.

When **skiing**, if you get lost, stay where you are and take shelter behind trees or rocks, or dig a snow cave. Stand crossed skis where they can be seen by approaching searchers. Note that the weather in alpine areas can change rapidly, so be prepared. Cross-country skiers and **bushwalkers** should advise friends or someone intended route and expected return time.

KOSCIUSKO NATIONAL PARK: This huge park stretches along the Great Dividing Range from the ACT to the Victorian border. It contains most of Australia's alpine region and is an unsurpassed venue for cross-country and downhill skiing in winter and for walking, touring and camping in summer.

SKIING: For downhill skiers, facilities are available at Thredbo, Perisher, Smiggin Holes, Mount Blue Cow, Charlotte Pass and Mount Selwyn. For cross-country skiers, there are well-defined trails near the resorts; away from the resorts there are few marked routes.

EUCUMBENE TROUT FARM: Visitors can catch trout as well as wander through the trout hatching and growing area.

SKITUBE: The ride itself is an adventure as the train crosses the Crackenback River then climbs steeply passing magnificent stands of alpine ash. There are magnificent views of Thredbo Valley before the train goes underground. The train stops at Perisher and Mount Blue Cow. In summer visitors can hire mountain bikes and helmets at Bullocks Flat Terminal and then, from Perisher or Mt Blue Cow, explore the Kosciusko National Park. In winter the skitube provides speedy access to the ski fields. Ski equipment can be hired at the Bullocks Flat Terminal.

WARNING: During the winter months (June to October) travellers should check prevailing road conditions before departure.

SNOWY RIVER WINERY: Renowned for its distinctive wines, which can be sampled, the winery also has a restaurant with a reputation for fine food.

TOURIST INFORMATION:
Adaminaby (3 Denison St)
Berridale (2 Myack St)
Jindabyne (Snowy Mountains Plaza, Kosciusko Rd)
Khancoban (Scott St)

South Eastern New South Wales

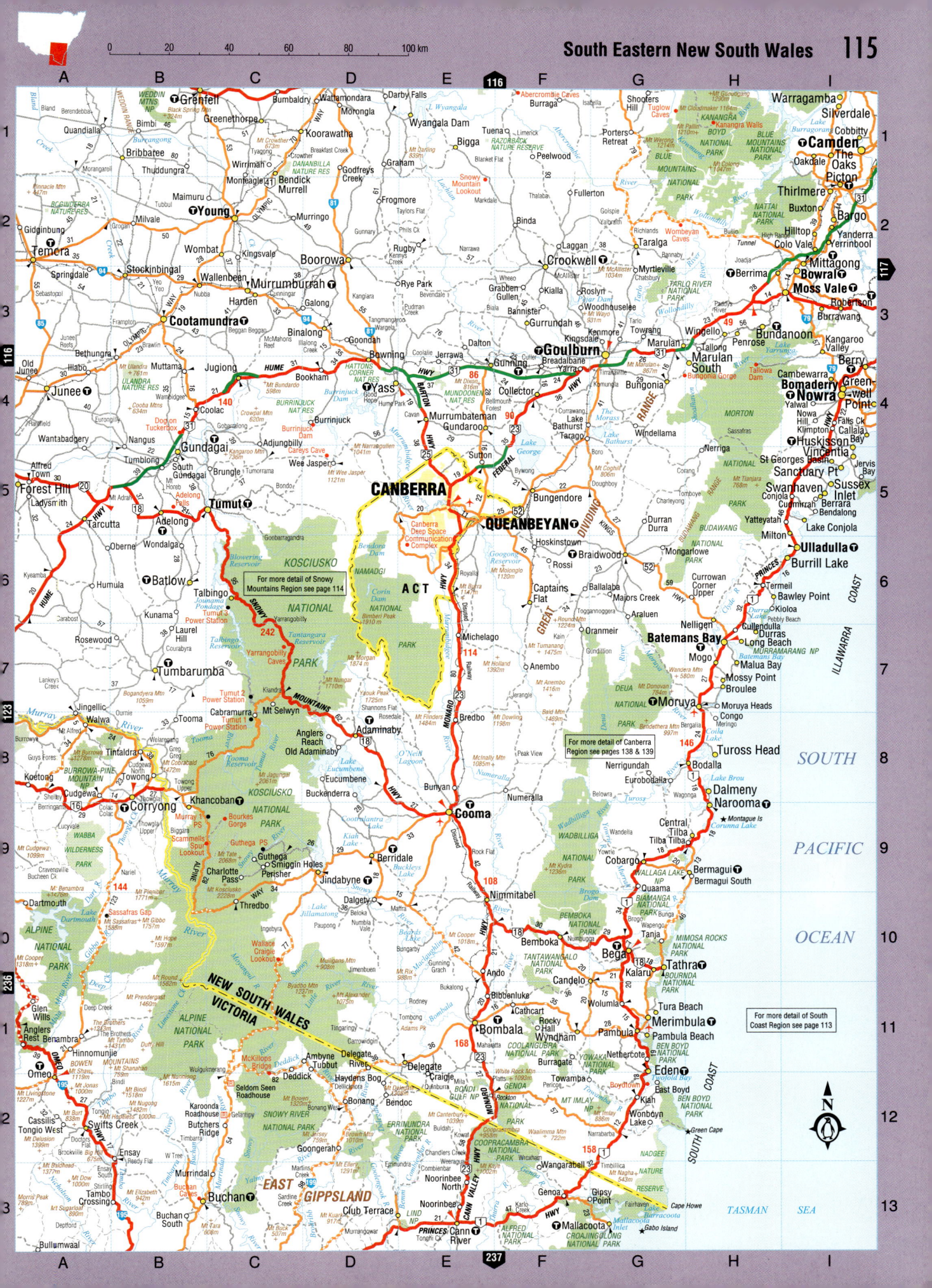

116 Central Eastern New South Wales

0 20 40 60 80 100 km
J K L M N 119 O P Q R
1 2 3 4 5 6 7 8 9 10 11 12 13
Wingen
Scone
Bunnan
Merriwa
Aberdeen
Muswellbrook
Denman
Sandy Hollow
Wybong
Hollydeen
Jerrys Plains
Ravensworth
Camberwell
Mt Olive
Singleton
Warkworth
Bulga
Broke
Moonan Flat
Gundy
Ellerston
GREAT DIVIDING RANGE
BARRINGTON TOPS NATIONAL PARK
Barrington
Copeland
Gloucester
Mount George
Wingham
Marlee
Lansdowne
Coopernook
Moorland
Harrington
CROWDY BAY NATIONAL PARK
Taree
Tinonee
Purfleet
Old Bar
Rainbow Flat
Diamond Beach
Hallidays Point
Burrell Creek
Krambach
Nabiac
Forster Tuncurry
Bunyah
Willina
Coolongolook
Wootton
Pacific Palms
Elizabeth Beach
BOOTI BOOTI NATIONAL PARK
Blueys Beach
Bungwahl
Seal Rocks
Bulahdelah
MYALL LAKES NATIONAL PARK
Broughton Island
Stratford
Craven
Wards River
Stroud Road
Stroud
Markwell
Booral
Dungog
Salisbury
Eccleston
Halton
Bendolba
Bandon Grove
Gresford
Vacy
Paterson
Clarence Town
Branxton
Lochinvar
Woodville
Limeburners Creek
Seaham
Karuah
Tea Gardens
Hawks Nest
Shoal Bay
Nelson Bay
TOMAREE NATIONAL PARK
Anna Bay
Lemon Tree Passage
Williamtown
Raymond Terrace
Morpeth
Maitland
Beresfield
West
Weston
Abermain
Kurri Kurri
Cessnock
Millfield
Paxton
Abernethy
Ellalong
Wollombi
NEWCASTLE
CHARLESTOWN
BELMONT
Rathmines
Wangi Wangi
Cooranbong
Avondale
Morisset
Mannering Park
Catherine Hill Bay
Wyee
Budgewoi
Toukley
Wyong
The Entrance
St Albans
Peats Ridge
Gosford
Terrigal
Kincumber
Woy Woy
Killcare Heights
Mount White
Wisemans Ferry
WOLLEMI NATIONAL PARK
YENGO NATIONAL PARK
Bilpin
Kurrajong Heights
Freemans Reach
Richmond
Windsor
Wilberforce
Galston
Blackheath
Katoomba
Springwood
Lawson
PENRITH
PARRAMATTA
MANLY
Port Jackson
SYDNEY
MAROUBRA
Botany Bay
LIVERPOOL
Mulgoa
Wallacia
Warragamba
Silverdale
Cobbitty
Camden
The Oaks
Oakdale
Picton
Thirlmere
CAMPBELLTOWN
Appin
Heathcote
Waterfall
ROYAL NATIONAL PARK
Helensburgh
Stanwell Park
Coalcliff
Scarborough
Thirroul
Bulli
Buxton
Bargo
Hilltop
Colo Vale
Yanderra
Yerrinbool
Mittagong
Bowral
Moss Vale
WOLLONGONG
PORT KEMBLA
Shellharbour
Bass Point
Burrawang
Robertson
Bundanoon
Jamberoo
Kiama
Kangaroo Valley
Fox Ground
Gerringong
Berry
Cambewarra
Bomaderry
Nowra
Shoalhaven Heads
Greenwell Point
Culburra
Falls Creek
Callala Bay
Currarong
Huskisson
St Georges Basin
Vincentia
Sanctuary Point
Jervis Bay
Sussex Inlet
Swanhaven
Berrara
Cudmirrah
Bendalong
Conjola
Lake Conjola
Milton
Ulladulla
Burrill Lake
Termeil
Bawley Point
Kioloa
For more detail of Newcastle Region see page 108
For more detail of Sydney Region see pages 100 & 101
For more detail of Southern Highlands see page 112
SOUTH PACIFIC OCEAN
TASMAN SEA
N

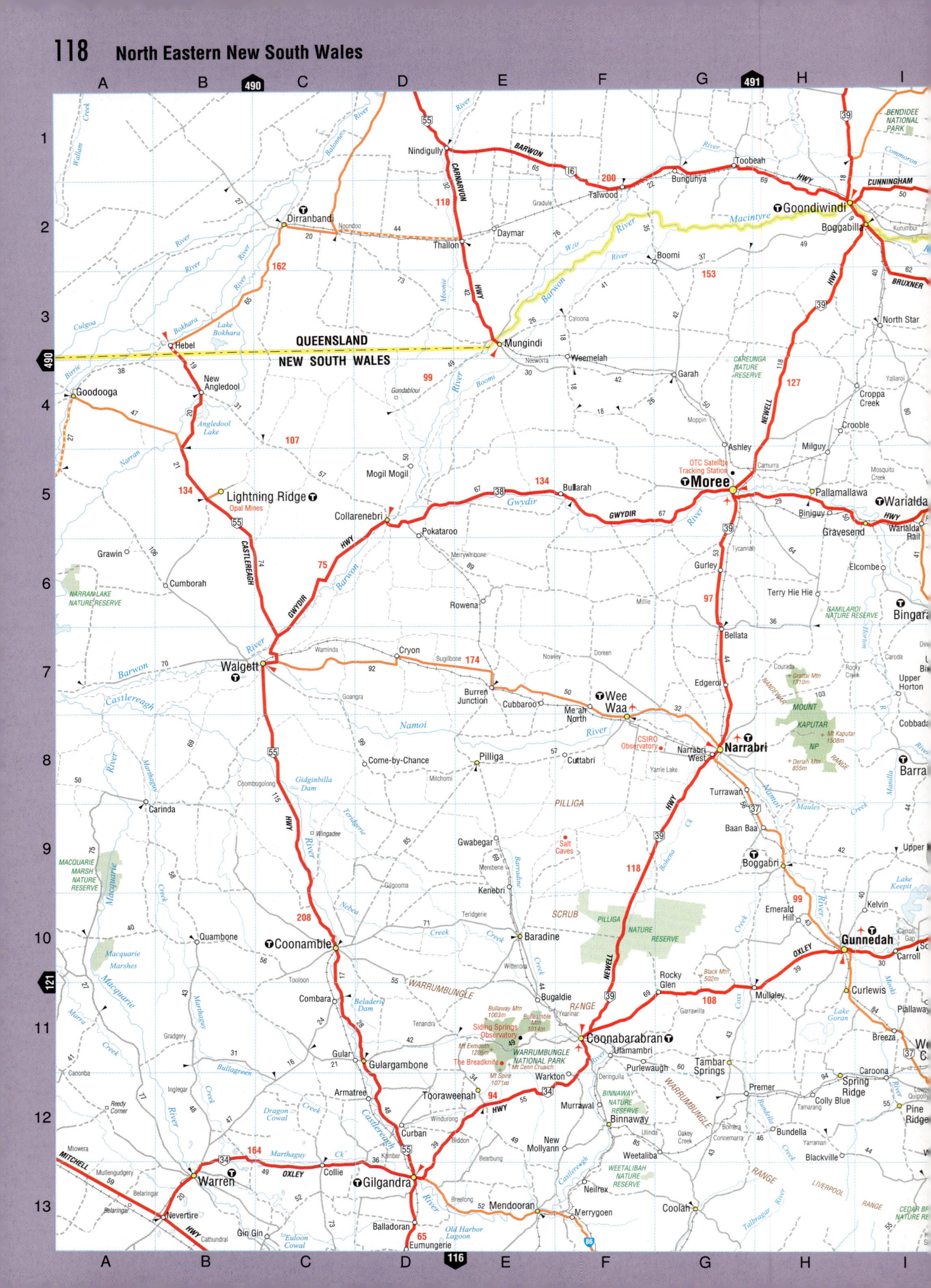

118 North Eastern New South Wales

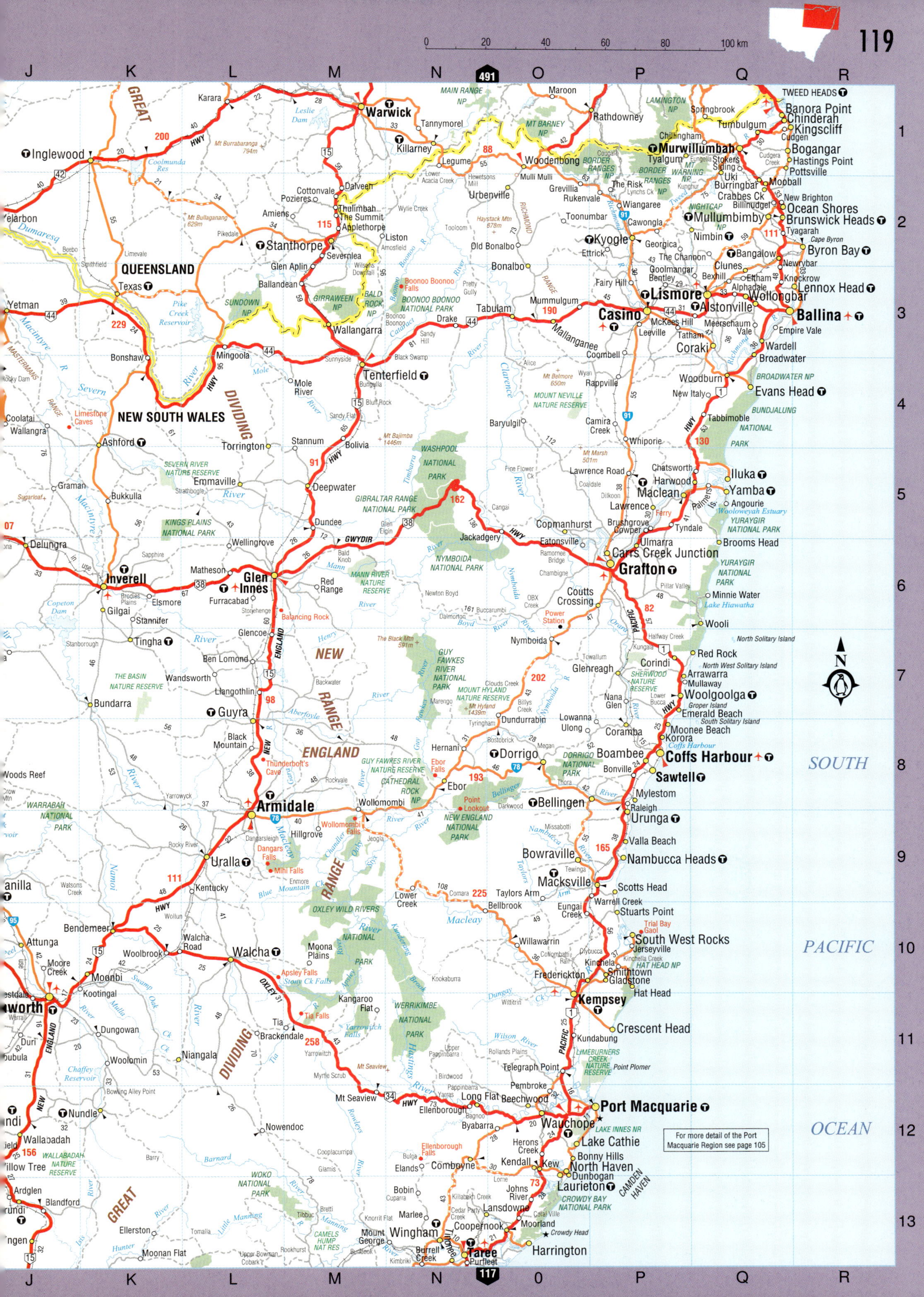

North Western New South Wales

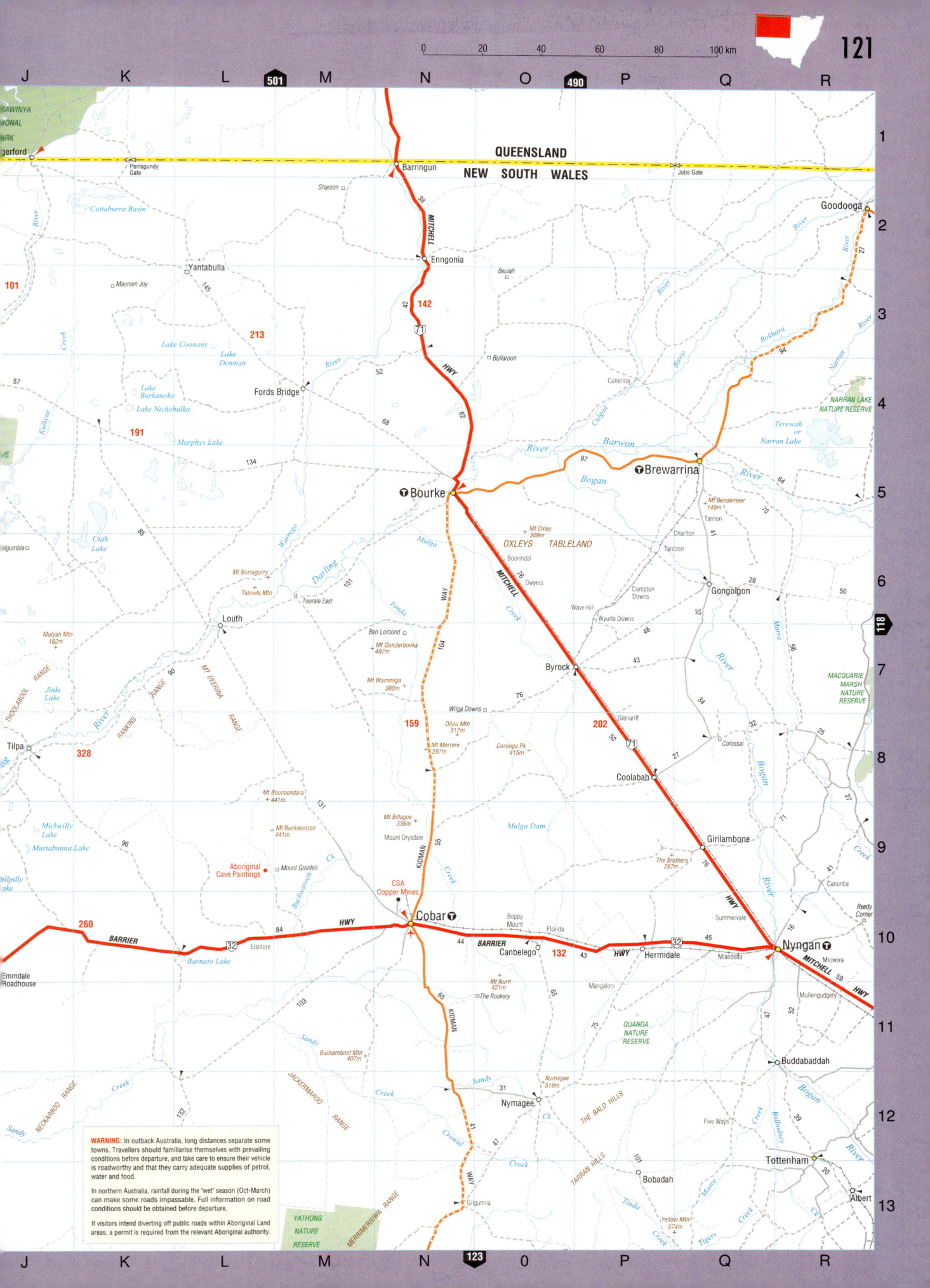

122 South Western New South Wales

0 20 40 60 80 100 km

J K L M N O P Q R

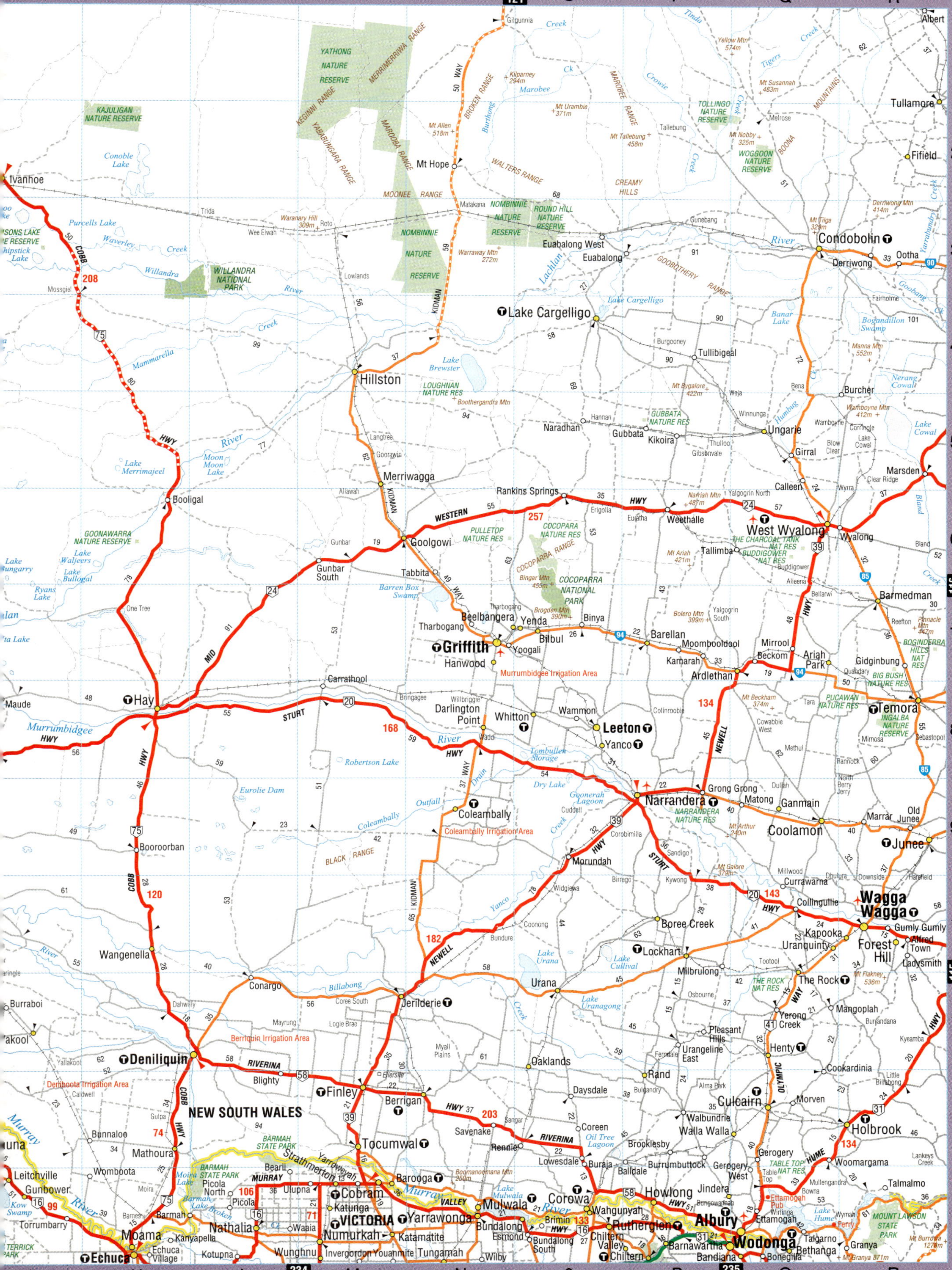

1 2 3 4 5 6 7 8 9 10 11 12 13

Australian Capital Territory

A.C.T.

The Capital State

Australian Capital Territory

The capital State is a 2400 square-kilometre area with an air of spaciousness and grace, typical of eastern rural Australia and enhanced by the beautiful valley of the Molonglo River and the surrounding hills, mountains and pastureland.

The Australian Capital Territory is surrounded by New South Wales and lies roughly halfway between Sydney and Melbourne. It was created by the Commonwealth Constitution Act of 1901 when the Commonwealth of Australia was inaugurated: a nation was formed from the six colonies.

One of the provisions of the Act was that the seat of government should be on land vested in the Commonwealth. Nine years of prolonged wrangling followed, as two Royal Commissions and parliamentary committees considered the various claims of established towns and cities to be the federal capital, before the location of the new territory and the site for the new city was decided. In addition, the area of Jervis Bay on the south coast of New South Wales was ceded to the Commonwealth to provide a seaport for the nation's capital.

Melbourne was the provisional seat of government until 1927 when a temporary building was erected in Canberra. This building was used until 1988 when the new House of Parliament was completed.

Canberra, Australia's modern capital city, was built on an undulating plain in an amphitheatre of the Australian Alps. The Molonglo River, a tributary of the Murrumbidgee River, runs through the city and was dammed in 1964 to create Lake Burley Griffin, around which Canberra has been developed.

It is one of the world's best-known fully-planned cities and has become an increasing source of pride and interest for Australians and for overseas visitors. Its public buildings, its areas of parkland and bush reserves, its leafy suburbs and broad tree-lined streets have resulted from brilliant planning by its architect, Walter Burley Griffin, and from care taken in its development over the years. Its architecture and its atmosphere are unique and stimulating considering there is little over 50 years old. Although the city has an air of being contrived, it contains so much that educates, absorbs and stimulates the visitor, this somewhat sterile quality is soon forgotten.

The land on which the city is sited was discovered in 1820 by Charles Throsby Smith and his party of explorers. The area became known as Limestone Plains and was destined for settlement as grazing property. The first European settler, Joshua Moore, took up a thousand acres (2500 hectares) of land on the Murrumbidgee River in 1824 and named his property Canberry, which is an Aboriginal word meaning 'meeting place'. A year later Robert Campbell, a wealthy Sydney merchant, took up 4000 acres (10 000 hectares) of land, which formed the first part of the Duntroon estate.

When the land on which the city is now built was acquired by the Commonwealth Government in 1911

NOT TO BE MISSED
in the Australian Capital Territory

- **Australian National Botanic Gardens** – splendid collection of Australian native plants
- **Australian War Museum** – one of the world's outstanding war museums
- **Cockington Green** – feel like a giant in a miniature English village
- **Lanyon** – an historic homestead housing a collection of Sidney Nolan's paintings
- **Namadgi National Park** – famous for its rugged beauty and majestic mountain scenery
- **National Film and Sound Archive** – for radio, film, television and sound recording memorabilia
- **National Gallery of Australia** – has an excellent collection of Aboriginal art
- **Parliament House** – impressive architecture: designed to preserve the contour of Capital Hill
- **Questacon** – for hands-on interactive displays from microbes to earthquakes
- **Telstra Tower** – for superb views of Canberra
- **Tidbinbilla Nature Reserve** – home to koalas, kangaroos and other native fauna

Parliament House on Capital Hill

Australian Capital Territory

CLIMATE GUIDE

AUSTRALIAN CAPITAL TERRITORY

	J	F	M	A	M	J	J	A	S	O	N	D
Maximum °C	28	27	24	20	15	12	11	13	16	19	23	26
Minimum °C	13	13	11	7	3	1	0	1	3	6	9	11
Rainfall mm	58	56	53	49	49	37	40	48	52	68	62	53
Raindays	8	7	7	8	9	9	10	11	10	11	10	8

Telstra Tower on Black Mountain has public viewing galleries

Spring in Canberra

it contained only two small villages. Construction of the first public buildings started in 1913, and in 1914 a rail service was opened between Sydney and the new capital. The Depression and World War II slowed building construction, but the rate of development has been spectacular since the mid-1950s and the population is now over 285 000.

There are four distinct seasons: a warm spring, a hot dry summer, a brilliant cool autumn, and a cold winter with occasional snow. Perhaps the best time to visit the ACT is in the autumn, when there is a magnificent display of golden foliage. Over two million Australian and overseas visitors come to the ACT each year.

CALENDAR OF EVENTS

Note: The information given here was accurate at the time of printing. However, as the timing of events held annually is subject to change and some events may extend into the following month, it is best to check with the local tourism authority or event organisers to confirm the details.

JANUARY
Public holidays: New Year's Day; Australia Day.
Canberra: Australia Day in the National Capital; Multicultural festival; Canberra World Cup showjumping and international teams event.

FEBRUARY
Canberra: Royal Canberra Show; Sri Chinmoy triathlon and mini triathlon.

MARCH
Public holiday: Canberra Day.
Canberra: Black opal stakes; Canberra festival.

EASTER
Public holidays: Good Friday; Easter Monday.

APRIL
Public holiday: Anzac Day.
Canberra: Anzac Day Service at Australian War Memorial; National folk festival; Australian science festival.

JUNE
Public holiday: Queen's Birthday.

SEPTEMBER
Canberra: Floriade spring festival.

OCTOBER
Public holiday: Labour Day. **Canberra:** Canberra Cup; Floriade spring festival (contd); Oktoberfest.

NOVEMBER
Canberra: Canberra international car rally.

DECEMBER
Public holidays: Christmas Day; Boxing Day. **Canberra:** Street machine summernats (national hot-rod exhibition and races).

CANBERRA

The Nation's Capital

As well as being Australia's capital, Canberra is a model city. Its unique concentric circular streets, planted with more than 10 million trees and shrubs, are set graciously on the shores of the constructed Lake Burley Griffin. Driving in Canberra can be challenging; it is wise to study a map before beginning to tour.

The old Parliament House, completed in 1927, and a number of government department buildings and hostels for public servants were among the first buildings in the national capital. They are now dwarfed by the grand buildings of later development, which have turned Canberra into a showpiece.

A number of lookouts on the surrounding hills give superb views of the city. The 195-metre **Telstra Tower** on Black Mountain is the highest. **Mount Ainslie** offers fine views of central Canberra and Lake Burley Griffin. **Red Hill** overlooks Parliament House, South Canberra and the Woden Valley. **Mount Pleasant** has memorials to the Royal Regiment of Australian Artillery and the Royal Australian Armoured Corps at its summit.

The city took on a new character in 1964 when Lake Burley Griffin was created. The shoreline totals 35 kilometres and the lake has become popular for swimming, sailboarding, rowing, sailing and fishing, while ferries operating from Acton Jetty offer day and dinner cruises.

In recent years Canberra has spread outwards across the plains, with satellite towns at Belconnen, Woden, Tuggeranong, Weston Creek and Gungahlin, but the focus is still the city centre and the modern architectural development around Lake Burley Griffin.

Black Mountain, close to the city centre and the lakeshore, is topped by a telecommunications tower with public viewing galleries and a revolving restaurant. On the lower slopes of Black Mountain are Canberra's **Botanic Gardens**. They follow Walter Burley Griffin's original plan for an Australian

The impressive Anzac Parade stretches from the War Memorial to Lake Burley Griffin

native garden. The superb gardens have arrowed walks, which allow for varying degrees of stamina, and take visitors through areas of foliage indigenous to various Australian regions. In the rainforest area a misting system simulates rainforest conditions. The **Australian Institute of Sport** is on the edge of Black Mountain Reserve in Bruce. Tours of training facilities and stadiums are conducted daily by resident athletes.

Most of Canberra's major buildings lie within a triangle that is formed by Kings, Commonwealth and Constitution Avenues, with **Capital Hill** at the apex and the central business district on the northern corner. On Capital Hill is the **new Parliament House**, topped by its massive flagpole. A grassed walkway forms the roof of Parliament House and provides visitors with splendid views of Canberra. In front is the **old Parliament House**, open to the public.

On the southern foreshore of Lake Burley Griffin is the **National Gallery of Australia**, which houses an outstanding collection of modern and post-modern art, including a wide representation of Australian painters. In the grounds, works by Australian and international sculptors are placed in a landscape setting. In this Sculpture

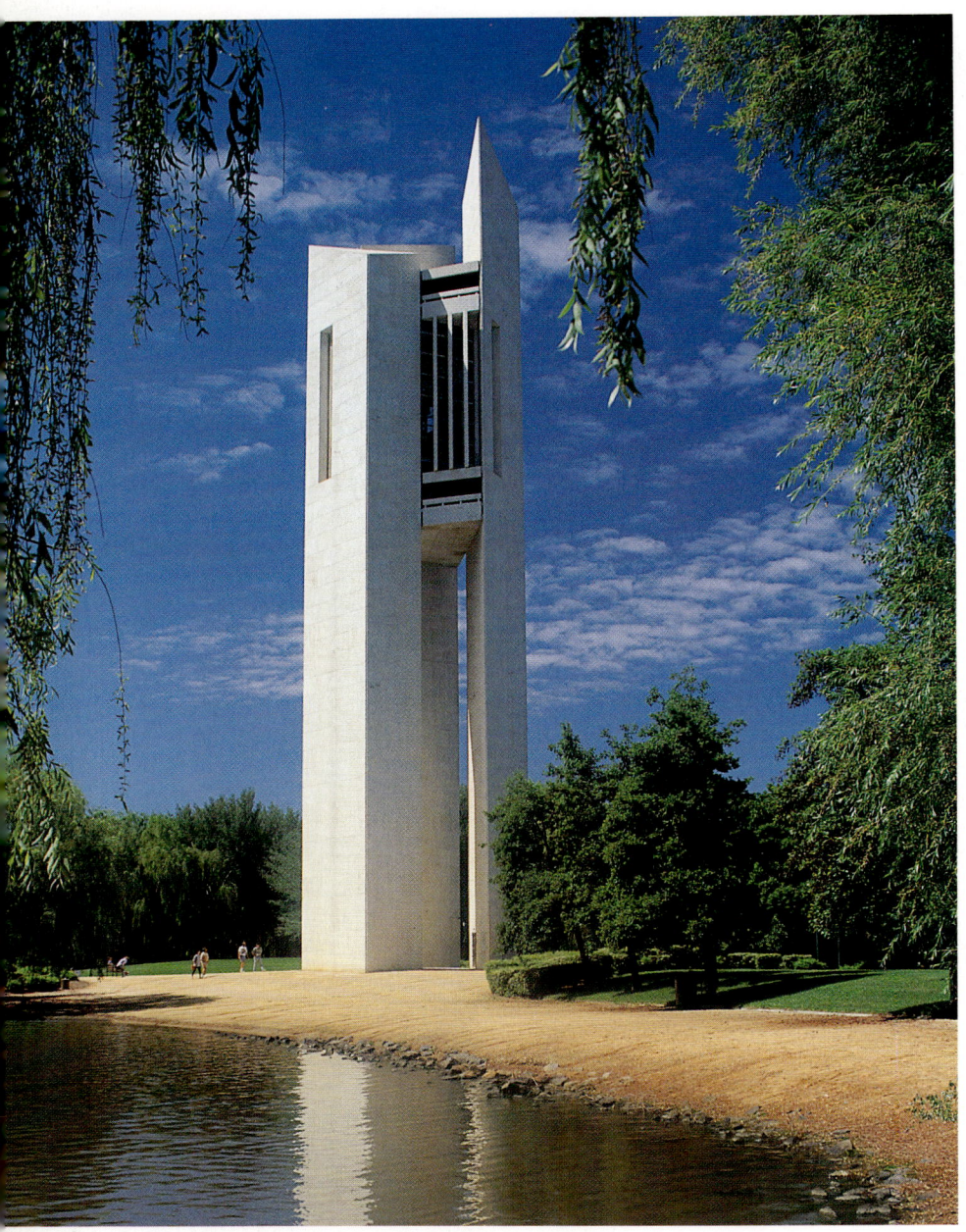

The Carillon, a three-column belltower with 53 bells

CANBERRA ON FOOT

The following are some of the walks around Canberra.

- **National Trust self-guide walks:** 1. A 3-kilometre circuit through the heritage suburb of Reid. 2. Around Lake Burley Griffin.

- **Umbrella Walking Tours:** depart three times daily from the Foundation Stone, Parliament House, for a guided 90-minute walking tour around the heart of Canberra; bookings essential.

Brochures are available for the self-guide walks; for these and for further information, contact Canberra Tourism, Visitors Information Centre, Northbourne Ave, Dickson; (06) 205 0044.

Garden the gallery's restaurant is in a 'misty oasis', an artificial fog sculpture created by the Japanese artist Fujiko Nakaya. A footbridge connects the National Gallery and the **High Court of Australia**, the nation's final court of appeal. The court's lofty public gallery is encircled by open ramps that lead off to the courts, and it features Jan Senbergs' murals reflecting the history, functions and operations of the High Court.

Further along the foreshore is the **National Library**, which contains over 5 million books, as well as newspapers, periodicals, films, historical documents and photographs. The foyer features three magnificent tapestries woven from Australian wool in Aubusson, France, and superb stained-glass windows, the work of the Australian artist Leonard French.

Also on the foreshore of the lake between the National Library and the High Court is **Questacon – The National Science and Technology Centre** in King Edward Terrace. The Centre features hands-on science displays where simple do-it-yourself experiments and explanations make the understanding of everyday scientific principles easy. Adults and children alike are enthralled for hours by the hundreds of exhibits in the five galleries (Waves, Microcosm, Forces, Visions, and 0011-OTC). Further south of the lake is the **Canberra Railway Museum**, which has Australia's oldest working steam locomotive (built in 1878), as well as four other engines and 40 carriages.

Lake Burley Griffin is the centre piece of Canberra. On the lake are three places of interest: the **Carillon** on Aspen Island, a three-column belltower that was a gift from the British Government to mark Canberra's Jubilee; the **Captain Cook Memorial**, a 150-metre water jet and terrestrial globe on the foreshore; and the **National Capital Exhibition** at Regatta Point, which has a pavilion with exhibits showing Canberra's development. Overlooking the lake is the Australian-American Memorial, which celebrates America's contribution to Australia's defence during World War II.

The lake is surrounded by parklands, most with picnic facilities. One of the largest is **Commonwealth Park** on the northern foreshore, with its wading pools and cherry-tree grove. Another lakeside park is **Weston Park**, which features superb conifer trees, a maze, a miniature train and a playground for

Australian Institute of Sport, first-class facilities for the nation's elite athletes

able and disabled children. Cycling is popular in Canberra; there are more than 280 kilometres of cycle paths. It is possible to cycle right round the lake. Bikes can be hired near the ferry terminal. Sightseeing cruises of the lake are available. Paddle-boats, windsurfers and sailing boats also can be hired. Hot-air ballooning is popular throughout the year, and during the **Canberra Festival** in March a fleet of balloons takes off each morning.

Although the **National Museum of Australia** (which will include the Gallery of Aboriginal Australia) is still in the planning stage, its Yarramundi Visitor Centre off Lady Denman Drive on the shores of the lake features objects from the museum's extensive collections, a viewing platform and a theatrette. The **National Aquarium and Australian Wildlife Sanctuary**, further along Lady Denman Drive near Scrivener Dam, has over 60 display tanks containing marine and freshwater fish. It also has koalas, kangaroos, dingos, little (fairy) penguins and a Tasmanian devil.

Anzac Parade stretches from the northern side of the lake to the **Australian War Memorial** and is one of Australia's most frequently visited attractions. The War Memorial houses a huge collection of relics, models and paintings from all theatres of war. Its cloisters, pool of reflection, hall of memory and many galleries of war relics provide an unforgettable experience. It is also the site of the Tomb of the Unknown Soldier.

An interesting walk to the summit of **Mount Ainslie** starts from the picnic grounds behind the War Memorial.

Another distinctive landmark in Canberra is the **Academy of Science**, situated in Gordon Street, Acton. Its copper-covered dome rests on arches set in a circular pool. Nearby, the **National Film and Sound Archive** in McCoy Circuit displays movie memorabilia and has public screenings from its collection of historic films, radio and television programs. Also at Acton is the **Australian National University**, set in 145 hectares of landscaped gardens.

Diplomatic missions bring an international flavour to the city's architecture. It is well worth driving around the suburb of Yarralumla to see the many high commission and embassy buildings. The official residence of

ACCOMMODATION

HOTELS
Capital Parkroyal
1 Binara St, Canberra City
(06) 247 8999

Hyatt Hotel Canberra
Commonwealth Ave, Yarralumla
(06) 270 1234

Hotel Kurrajong
Cnr National Circuit and Bligh St, Barton
(06) 234 4444

Rydges Canberra
London Circuit, Canberra
(06) 247 6244

Rydges Capital Hill
Cnr Canberra Ave and National Circuit, Forrest
(06) 295 3144

FAMILY AND BUDGET
Canberra Motor Village
Kunzea Street, O'Connor
(06) 247 5466

Hotel Heritage
203 Goyder St, Narrabundah
(06) 295 2944

Motel Monaro
27 Dawes St, Kingston
(06) 295 2111

Rydges Resort Eagle Hawk Hill
Federal Hwy, Sutton
(06) 241 6033

MOTEL GROUPS: BOOKINGS
Best Western 13 1779
Flag 13 2400

This list is for information only; inclusion is not necessarily a recommendation.

Canberra

Cockington Green, a popular attraction just out of Canberra

Australia's Governor-General is on Dunrossil Drive at Yarralumla. In Deakin, on the corner of Adelaide Avenue and National Circuit, is the **Prime Minister's Lodge**, the official residence of the Australian Prime Minister. The **Royal Australian Mint** in Denison Street, Deakin, has plate-glass windows in its visitors' gallery, allowing excellent views of the process of making coins.

Despite the gleaming modern style of the city of Canberra, there are still interesting vestiges of the old Limestone Plains settlement. In Campbell the sandstone homestead of the **Duntroon estate**, now the Officer's Mess at Duntroon Royal Military College, is the finest old house in the ACT. The single-storey part of the house was built in 1833 and the two-storey extension was completed in 1856. Guided tours of the **Australian Defence Force Academy** and the **Royal Military College** are available.

The **Church of St John the Baptist** off Anzac Park dates back to 1841 and its tombstones and other memorials provide a record of much of the area's early history. The adjacent schoolhouse containing relics of this history is regularly open to visitors. Many of the stained glass windows of St John's Church commemorate members of the pioneer families, including Robert Campbell, the founder of Duntroon estate. **Blundell's farmhouse** on the northern shore of the lake was built in 1858 by Campbell for his ploughman, and has been furnished by the Canberra and District Historical Society with pieces contemporary to the district's early history. **Calthorpes House**, in Mugga Way, Red Hill, is a 1920s family home that has survived almost unchanged providing a fascinating glimpse of the life-style of those times.

The **central business district** for Canberra surrounds London Circuit at the end of Commonwealth Avenue. **Civic Centre** is the major retail area. At the head of the **Civic Square** is the **Canberra Theatre Centre** and nearby in Petrie Plaza is the old St Kilda merry-go-round, a favourite with children. The **Canberra Casino** is in its permanent home off Binara Street in Glebe Park. For touring the city's attractions, the **Canberra Explorer** bus service runs every hour, 7 days a week, around a 25-kilometre route with 19 stops. Leave the bus any time and reboard, or take the full-hour tour.

Each Saturday and Sunday at the Gorman House Arts Centre, just 5 minutes walk from the city centre in Ainslie Avenue, Braddon, talented young artists and actors present exhibitions and performances, and craftspeople display their wares. The showground at Hall, a small village on the outskirts of Canberra, is covered with over 300 stalls on the first Sunday of the month, selling home produce and folk art. An old bus depot at Kingston provides an undercover market selling quality hand-crafted items each Sunday.

Around Canberra too there are many attractions. **Cockington Green** on the Barton Highway, 9 kilometres north of the city, is a miniature English village (named after Cockington in Devon, UK). Adjacent is the historic village of **Ginninderra**, featuring craft studios, an art gallery, shops and a restaurant. **Federation Square**, a new shopping area nearby, features a number of craft and specialty shops, and children's play areas. Directly opposite Ginninderra on the Barton Highway is the 300-exhibit **National Dinosaur Museum**, between Gold Creek Road and Northbourne Avenue.

The **Australian Heritage Village**, on the corner of Federal Highway and Antill Street, features shops, eating-houses and amusements in a parkland setting, and is open daily, admission free. The **Bywong Mining Town** at Geary's Gap NSW (off the Gundaroo Road), is a re-creation of the mining settlement that prospered in the late 1800s. Tourists can see working machinery and enjoy panning for gold. Bywong is open daily. Special programs as well as guided tours are available.

At the **Tidbinbilla Nature Reserve**, a 40-minute drive south-west of the city, an area of more than 5500 hectares has been developed to enable visitors to see Australian flora and fauna in a bushland

Blundell's farmhouse, an historic building in the heart of Canberra

setting. Nearby is the **Corin Forest Recreation Area**, with a 1-kilometre alpine slide, bushwalking and skiing in winter. Another favourite spot is the **Cotter Dam** and Reserve, 22 km west of the city, where there are pleasant picnic and camping areas, a restaurant, river swimming and a children's playground. Nearby is the **Mount Stromlo Observatory**, its large silver domes and buildings housing the huge telescope of the Department of Astronomy of the Australian National University. Located further south at Tidbinbilla, is the **Canberra Deep Space Communications Complex**, a deep-space tracking station, featuring spacecraft models and audiovisual presentations. It is operated by the Department of Science for the US National Aeronautics and Space Administration.

The historic homestead **Lanyon**, 30 kilometres south of the city, enjoys the National Trust's highest classification. Set in landscaped gardens and picturesque parklands on the banks of the Murrumbidgee River, Lanyon serves as a reminder of nineteenth-century rural living and houses a collection of Sidney Nolan paintings. Further south and also on the Murrumbidgee River is the historic **Cuppacumbalong** homestead with its cottages, outbuildings, private cemetery, craft centre, restaurant, picnic areas and river swimming.

For further information on Canberra and the ACT, contact Canberra Tourism, Visitors Information Centre, Northbourne Ave, Dickson; (06) 205 0044, or 1800 02 6166.

Wining and Dining

Canberra is the Australian base for diplomatic missions from all over the world, and this has resulted in a wide variety of restaurants. Eating out can be a cosmopolitan 'feast' in the national capital. The city has approximately 300 restaurants specialising in modern Australian cuisine and a host of traditional ethnic styles.

Good wine is the natural accompaniment to a good meal and the Canberra district has 16 wineries producing a range of fine cool climate wines.

Wines were first produced in the area in the 1860s, but the burgeoning of boutique wineries in the region has only occurred in recent decades. The wineries are clustered around the townships of Hall and Murrumbateman to the north of Canberra, and Bungendore to the east. The wineries are almost exclusively small, family-owned enterprises, where you can chat to the winemaker when you make your purchase at the cellar door; check first for opening times.

Fine, cool climate wines are produced at local wineries

For further information contact Canberra Tourism, Northbourne Ave, Dickson; (06) 205 0044

TOURS from Canberra

More than 50 per cent of the city of Canberra is national park and nature reserve. Canberra is unique in that bushland is an easy drive from the city centre. A longer leisurely drive takes the visitor to the heart of the Snowy Mountains in the south or to the picturesque coastal resorts in the east.

Bungendore and Braidwood

35 km and 90 km from Canberra via the Kings Highway

This popular route passes Lake George, which mysteriously empties periodically. At Bungendore, the Village Square features an historic re-creation from the 1850s telling the story of a local bushranger. The entire township of Braidwood has been classified by the National Trust. Antique and art and craft shops, museums and restaurants are found in many of the town's lovely old sandstone buildings.

Batemans Bay

150 km from Canberra via the Kings Highway

This popular resort is at the mouth of the Clyde River. Of particular interest are the penguins and other birds at Tollgate Island Wildlife Reserve. In the area are many picturesque coastal resorts and the old gold mining towns of Mogo and Araluen.

The Snowy Mountains

228 km from Canberra via the Monaro and Snowy Mountains Highways

The Snowy Mountains, centre of the world-famous hydro-electric scheme, is an all-year-round resort and tourist area. Thredbo is the centre of activity during the ski season. Lake Eucumbene is very popular for water sports and trout fishing.

Jervis Bay

285 km from Canberra via the Kings and Princes Highways

This fine natural port was the site of the Royal Australian Navy Training College, established in 1915. In that year its jurisdiction was transferred from New South Wales to the ACT, to give the federal capital sea access. Popular Aboriginal-owned Jervis Bay National Park is jointly managed by the Wreck Bay Aboriginal Community Council and the Australian Nature Conservation Agency. The area has several holiday towns ideal for swimming, fishing, boating and bushwalking.

Namadgi National Park

30 km from central Canberra via the Tuggeranong Parkway and Tharwa Drive to Tharwa

Namadgi National Park, the most northerly alpine environment in Australia, covers some 40 per cent of the ACT. The special qualities of remoteness and rugged beauty that make up a wilderness are evident in the area surrounding the park's highest point, Bimberi Peak (1911 m). The Visitor Centre on the Naas Rd provides excellent information on the park and has hands-on displays and audiovisuals. Public access roads in the park pass through majestic mountain scenery. Picnic areas, some with barbecues and toilets, are sited along most roads. The pleasant bushland settings at Mt Clear and Orroral are ideal for low-key camping. Much of Namadgi's attractions lie beyond its main roads and picnic areas. There are over 150 kilometres of marked walking tracks. Bushwalkers who venture into Namadgi's more remote parts reap some of the park's greatest rewards. Namadgi's streams attract trout anglers. Horseriding is permitted in certain areas and cross-country skiing is possible when snow conditions permit.

Batemans Bay, popular with the land-locked residents of Canberra

Australian Capital Territory

Location Map

Other Map Coverage
Central Canberra 134
Canberra Region 138

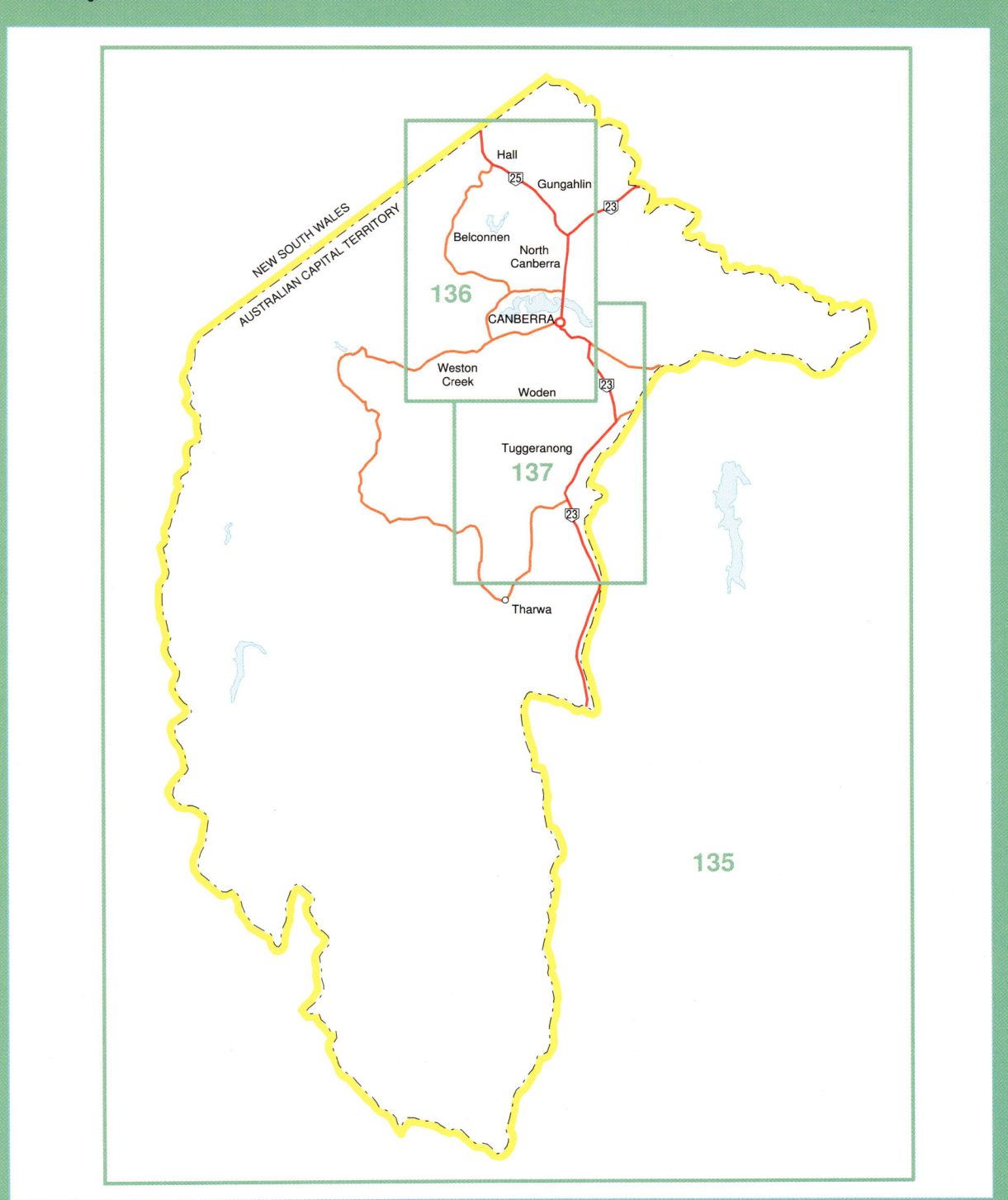

134 Central Canberra

Accommodation
- Capital Parkroyal 1 E4
- Hotel Kurrajong 2 E10
- Hyatt Hotel 3 C8
- James Court Apartment Hotel 4 D2
- Macquarie Hotel 5 E12
- Motel Monaro 6 G13
- Rydges Canberra 7 C5
- Rydges Capital Hill 8 D12

General Information
- Ansett Australia 9 D3
- Canberra Railway Station 10 H13
- Coach/Bus Terminal 11 D3
- General Post Office 12 D3
- Motoring Organisation (NRMA) 13 D2
- Qantas Travel Centre 14 D3

Accommodation: Only a sample is listed; inclusion is not necessarily a recommendation.

Places of Interest
- Australian National Gallery 15 F9
- Australian National University 16 A4
- Australian War Memorial 17 H4
- Blundell's Farmhouse 18 F7
- Canberra Theatre Centre 19 D4
- Captain Cook Memorial Water Jet 20 D7
- Carillon 21 F8
- Casino Canberra 22 E4
- High Court of Australia 23 E8
- Jewish Memorial Centre 24 D12
- National Capital Exhibition, Regatta Point 25 D6
- National Film and Sound Archive 26 B4
- National Library 27 D8
- Questacon 28 D8
- Old Parliament House 29 D9
- Parliament House 30 C11
- Royal Canberra Yacht Club 31 B8
- The Lodge 32 A11

Australian Capital Territory 135

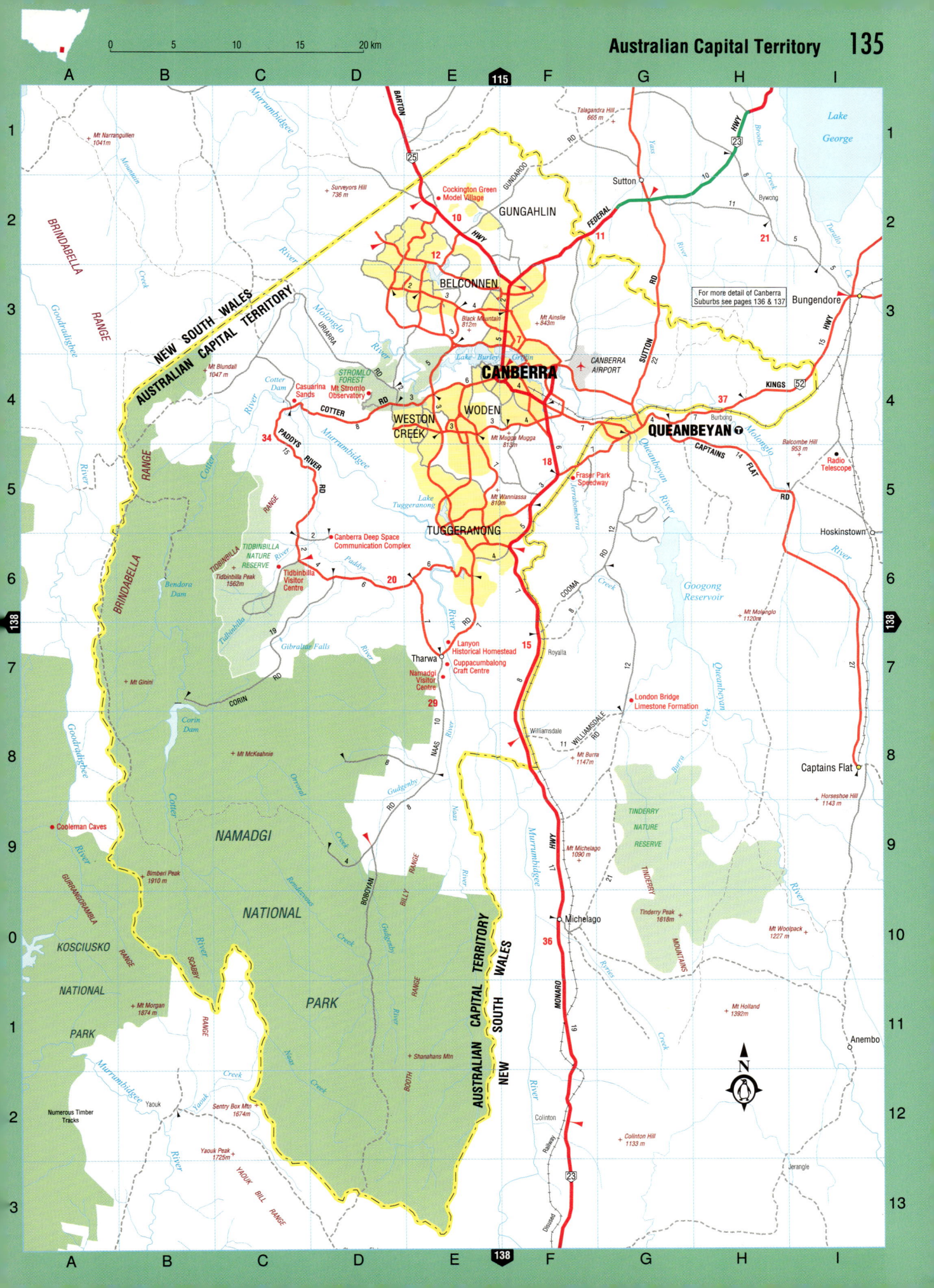

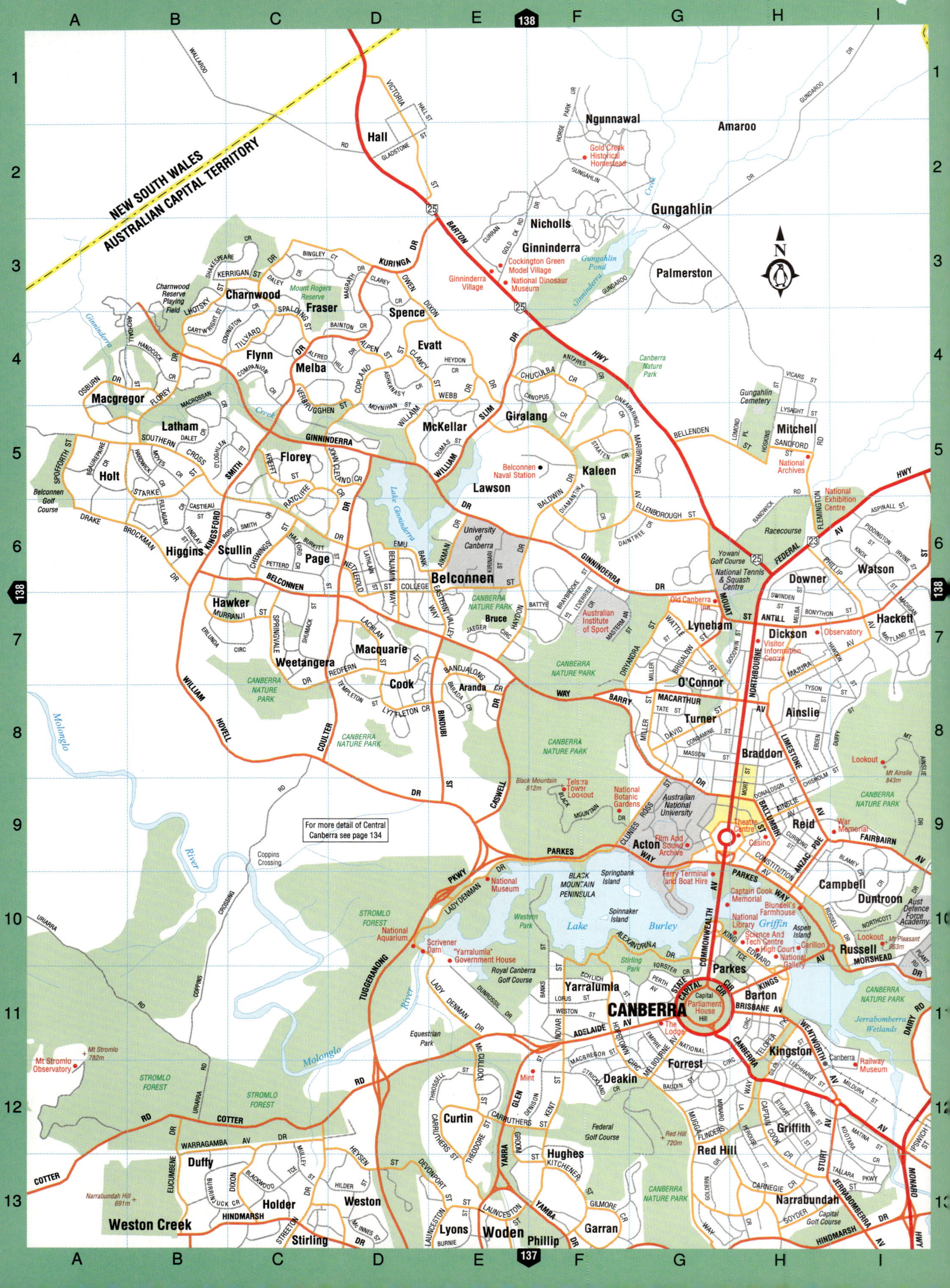

0 1 2 3 km
A B C D E F G H I
1 2 3 4 5 6 7 8 9 10 11 12 13
138
137
NEW SOUTH WALES
AUSTRALIAN CAPITAL TERRITORY
Hall
Ngunnawal
Amaroo
Gold Creek Historical Homestead
Gungahlin
Nicholls
Ginninderra
Palmerston
Cockington Green Model Village
National Dinosaur Museum
Ginninderra Village
Gungahlin Pond
Charnwood
Charnwood Reserve Playing Field
Fraser
Mount Rogers Reserve
Spence
Evatt
Flynn
Melba
Macgregor
Latham
Holt
Belconnen Golf Course
Florey
McKellar
Giralang
Canberra Nature Park
Gungahlin Cemetery
Mitchell
National Archives
Belconnen Naval Station
Kaleen
Lawson
Lake Ginninderra
National Exhibition Centre
Racecourse
Higgins
Scullin
Page
University of Canberra
Belconnen
Hawker
Bruce
Yowani Golf Course
National Tennis & Squash Centre
Downer
Watson
Hackett
Old Canberra Inn
Australian Institute of Sport
Lyneham
Dickson
Observatory
Visitor Information Centre
Macquarie
Weetangera
Cook
Aranda
O'Connor
Turner
Ainslie
Braddon
Lookout
Mt Ainslie 843m
Black Mountain 812m
Telstra Tower Lookout
National Botanic Gardens
Australian National University
Reid
War Memorial
Theatre Centre
Casino
Acton
Film And Sound Archive
For more detail of Central Canberra see page 134
Coppins Crossing
Molonglo River
National Museum
Black Mountain Peninsula
Springbank Island
Ferry Terminal and Boat Hire
Captain Cook Memorial
Blundell's Farmhouse
Campbell
Duntroon
Aust Defence Force Academy
Lake Burley Griffin
Spinnaker Island
Western Park
Aspen Island
National Library
Science And Tech Centre
High Court
Carillon
National Gallery
Russell
Mt Pleasant 663m
Stromlo Forest
National Aquarium
Scrivener Dam
"Yarralumla" Government House
Royal Canberra Golf Course
Stirling Park
Yarralumla
Parkes
Barton
Capital Parliament House Hill
CANBERRA
The Lodge
Kingston
Canberra Railway Museum
Jerrabomberra Wetlands
Mt Stromlo Observatory
Mt Stromlo 782m
Equestrian Park
Forrest
Deakin
Mint
Curtin
Federal Golf Course
Red Hill 720m
Red Hill
Griffith
Hughes
Duffy
Holder
Weston
Weston Creek
Narrabundah Hill 691m
Stirling
Lyons
Woden
Phillip
Garran
Narrabundah
Capital Golf Course
BARTON HWY
FEDERAL HWY
NORTHBOURNE AV
COMMONWEALTH AV
GINNINDERRA DR
BELCONNEN WAY
WILLIAM HOVELL DR
PARKES WAY
TUGGERANONG PKWY
COTTER RD
ADELAIDE AV
CANBERRA AV
MONARO HWY

Canberra & Southern Suburbs 137

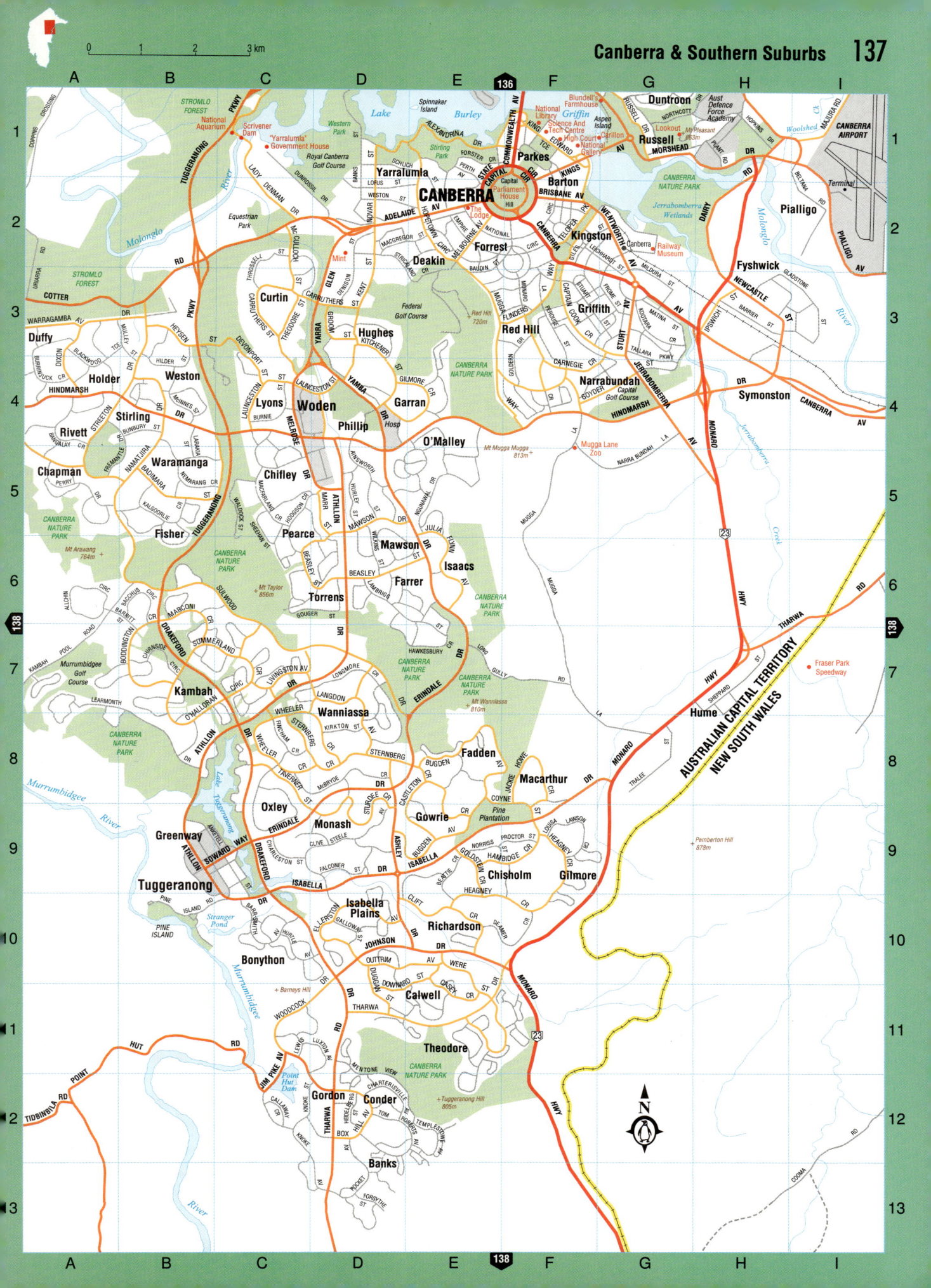

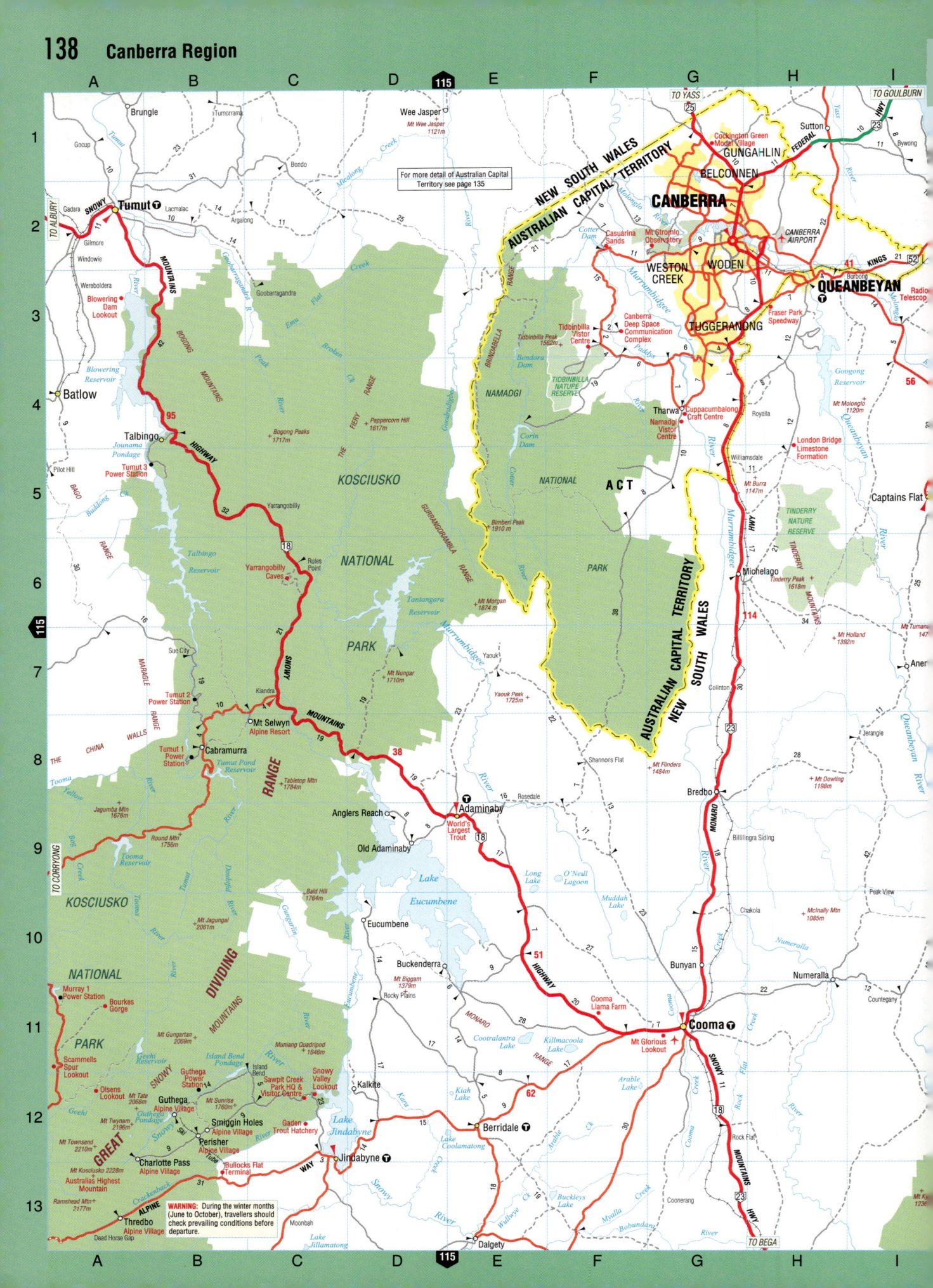

Canberra Region

0 5 10 15 20 km
J K L M N O P Q R
1 2 3 4 5 6 7 8 9 10 11 12 13
115
TO NOWRA
Klimpton
Callala Bay
Huskisson
Vincentia
Tomerong
Wandandian
St Georges Basin
Jervis Bay
Hyams Beach
Sanctuary Point
Jervis Bay
JERVIS BAY TERRITORY
Sussex Inlet
Swan Lake
Green Patch
Cudmirrah
Swanhaven
Berrara
JERVIS BAY NATIONAL PARK
Conjola
Bendalong
Manyana
Cunjurong Point
Lake Conjola
Pointer Gap Lookout
Yatteyatah
Narrawallee
Milton
Mollymook
Ulladulla
Burrill Lake
Tabourie Lake
COAST
Termeil
Bawley Point
MURRAMARANG ABORIGINAL RESERVE
Kioloa
ILLAWARRA
East Lynne
Durras Lake
Pebbly Beach
Depot Beach
Cullendulla
Durras
Long Beach
Batemans Bay
Shell Museum
Batehaven
Batemans Bay
MURRAMARANG NATIONAL PARK
Surf Beach
Malua Bay
Mogo
Rosedale
Bimbimbie
Tomakin
Mossy Point
Broulee
Mullenderee
Moruya
Moruya Heads
Kiora
The Anchorage
Congo
Bergalia
Meringo
Coila Lake
Turlinjah
Tuross Lake
Tuross Head
Bodalla
Potato Point
Lake Brou
Nerrigundah
Eurobodalla
Mummuga Lake
Dalmeny
Wagonga
Kianga
Narooma
Billa Billa Ck
Corunna Lake
Corunna
MONTAGUE IS NATURE RESERVE
Tilba Village Vineyard
Deer Farm
Mt Dromedary
Central Tilba Historic Village
Tilba Tilba
Tilba Tilba Lake
GOURA NAT RES
WALLAGA LAKE NP
Wallaga Lake
Cobargo
Narira
Creek
Bermagui
Bermagui South
BERMAGUEE NATURE RES
TO BEGA
PRINCES HWY
BODALLA STATE FOREST
Wandella
Yowrie
Peak Alone 954m
Belowra
Tuross
WADBILLIGA NATIONAL PARK
Wadbilliga River
Badja Mill
DEUA NATIONAL PARK
Running Creek
Deua
Burra Ck
Donalds Ck
Bendethera Mtn 997m
Mt Donovan 784m
Wandera Mtn 580m
Mogendoura
Yarragee
Gundary
Mt Anembo 1416m
Jinden Ck
Jerrabattgulla
Tinmanmang 1419m
Gundillion
The Big Hole and Marble Arch
Kain
Oranmeir
Round Mtn 1224m
Toggannoggera
Araluen North
Araluen
Bettowynd Ck
Araluen Ck
Runnyford
Buckenbowra
Nelligen
Benandarah
Clyde
Monga
Currowan Corner Upper
Shallow Crossing
Ballalaba
Majors Creek
Reidsdale
Mongarlowe
Braidwood Historic Town
Rossi
DIVIDING RANGE
Eskinstown
Durran Durra
KINGS HWY
Shoalhaven River
Doughboy
Bungendore
Butmaroo
Mt Fairy
Boro
Mt Coghill 806m
Lower Boro
Nerriga
Corang
Charleyong
Tomboye
BUDAWANG RANGE
BUDAWANG NATIONAL PARK
Currockbilly Mtn 823m
Mt Corang 863m
Yadboro
Sassafras
Bulea Brook
Mt Sassafras 823m
Main Ck
MORTON NATIONAL PARK
Mt Tianjara 768m
Pigeon House Mtn 719m
Burrill Lake
Mt Mogood 391m
Carters Ck
Bimberamala River
SOUTH PACIFIC OCEAN
N

Victoria

Garden State

VICTORIA

Victoria is an ideal State for the motoring tourist. In one day's drive, you can explore mountain country, pastoral landscape and spectacular coastline, yet still arrive at your destination in time to watch the sunset.

Victoria's earliest explorers, of course, were from a pre-motor age. What they saw did little to arouse their enthusiasm. After an unsuccessful attempt at settlement in the Port Phillip area in 1803, it was not until 1834 that expeditions from Van Diemen's Land, searching for more arable land, settled along the south-west coast of Victoria. Their glowing reports prompted John Batman and John Fawkner to investigate the Port Phillip area and then purchase land on opposite sides of the Yarra from the local Aborigines. The Colonial Office in London expressed disapproval of these transactions, but in those times possession was nine tenths of the law.

A squatting colony grew rapidly in the district and the new town was named Melbourne after the British Prime Minister of the day. Nervous of inheriting the penal system of settlement, Victoria sought separation from New South Wales; it was granted in 1851. At about that time, gold was discovered near Ballarat and the State's population more than doubled within a year. Apart from a serious but short-lived setback caused by land speculation in the early 1890s, Victoria has gone from strength to strength ever since.

Today Victoria is the most closely settled and industrialised part of the nation, and is responsible for about one-third of the gross national product. Melbourne has been traditionally regarded as the financial capital of the country.

Melbourne's inner areas are graced by spacious parks and street upon street of elegant and well-preserved Victorian and Edwardian architecture, contrasting strongly with modern tower blocks. It is renowned also for its retail shopping, theatres, restaurants, cultural festivals and Australian Rules Football.

Beyond the city, the Dandenong Ranges, fifty kilometres to the east, are noted for their forests of eucalyptus and graceful tree ferns, their many established gardens and an increasing number of restaurants, wineries and galleries that are popular with visitors. Phillip Island, less than two hours' drive from Melbourne, is famed for its unique little (fairy) penguin parade as well as for its good surfing. To the south and south-west, the Mornington and Bellarine peninsulas provide Melbourne with its seaside playgrounds, which are extremely popular during the summer months.

The weather can be unpredictable in Victoria, particularly along the coastal regions. Despite its rather volatile weather, the State enjoys a generally temperate climate. Spring, late summer and autumn provide the most settled and pleasant touring weather. The road system is good and penetrates most areas; as a result much of the State can be reached easily in a day's driving.

Each of Victoria's five main geographical regions has its own special attraction. The central and western districts, due north and west of

NOT TO BE MISSED
in Victoria

- **Gippsland Lakes** – one of the State's most outstanding holiday areas
- **Great Ocean Road** – 320 kilometres of breathtaking coastal scenery
- **Lake Eildon** – sheltered waters ideal for all water sports – and houseboats
- **Paddlesteamer ride on the Murray River** – to appreciate this magnificent waterway
- **Penguin Parade at Phillip Island** – a delightful spectacle each evening at sunset
- **Sovereign Hill** – fascinating re-creation of a goldmining township
- **Spa towns of Daylesford and Hepburn Springs** – mineral springs in scenic surroundings
- **The Grampians** – beautiful scenery and wildflowers, particularly in spring
- **Wilsons Promontory** – an impressive coastal national park
- **Yarra Valley** – good scenery and excellent wineries

The beautiful Fitzroy Gardens in central Melbourne

Victoria

The Twelve Apostles, rock formations in Port Campbell National Park

Melbourne, offer highlights including the historic gold-rush areas, with well-preserved, attractive towns such as Bendigo, Castlemaine and Ballarat, the popular spa towns of Daylesford and Hepburn Springs, and the Grampians, a beautiful national park, particularly noted for its spring wildflowers. Travelling south from these impressive ranges brings you into the western district, where rich grazing land is dotted with many splendid old properties. No exploration of this region would be complete without a drive along the aptly named Great Ocean Road, which runs for 320 kilometres along the dramatic south-west coast. The spectacular rock formations in the Port Campbell National Park are without doubt its most imposing sight, but along its length there are excellent beaches and pleasant small holiday towns.

The north-east high-country region has equally magnificent scenery and is dotted with winter ski resorts. While also popular in spring and summer, this region would hardly ever be described as crowded, and the wildflowers, sweeping views and clear air can be enjoyed with a fair degree of solitude. Fishing, bushwalking and climbing are well provided for. Down in the foothills, the Eildon Reservoir and Fraser National Park area are good for water sports.

Gippsland stretches to the southeast; it contains some of the State's most beautiful and varied country. Rolling pastures lead to densely

CALENDAR OF EVENTS

Note: The information given here was accurate at the time of printing. However, as the timing of events held annually is subject to change and some events may extend into the following month, it is best to check with the local tourism authority or event organisers to confirm the details. The calendar is not exhaustive. Most towns and regions hold sporting competitions, arts and craft exhibitions, agricultural and flower shows, music festivals and other such events annually. Details of these events are available from tourism outlets.

JANUARY
Public holidays: New Year's Day; Australia Day. **Melbourne:** Australian Open (grand slam tennis championships); Summer Live (at the Arts Centre); Montsalvat jazz festival (at Eltham). **Cobram:** Peaches and Cream festival (biennial, odd-numbered years). **Daylesford:** Daylesford Gift (horse race). **Geelong:** Summer festival. **Hanging Rock:** Picnic race meeting. **Heyfield:** Timber festival. **Hoddles Creek:** Upper Yarra draught horse festival. **Jeparit:** Beach carnival. **Lakes Entrance:** Australian wood design exhibition. **Lorne:** Pier to Pub swim; Surf to Mountain foot race. **Maryborough:** Highland gathering. **Murtoa:** Race meeting. **Orbost:** Australian wood display. **Portland:** Foreshore carnival; Fishing competition. **Terang:** Horse carnival. **Yarrawonga:** Sailing regatta.

FEBRUARY
Melbourne: Australian Masters (golf tournament); Formula 500 (motor racing); Autumn racing carnival; Chinese New Year festival. **Beechworth:** Drive Back in Time (car rally). **Camperdown:** Leura festival. **Cohuna:** Aquatic festival. **Donald:** Dead Centre motorbike rally. **Drouin:** Ficifolia festival. **Edenhope:** Henley-on-Lake Wallace. **Halls Gap:** Grampians jazz festival. **Geelong:** Pako multicultural festival. **Hamilton:** Beef expo. **Healesville:** Coldstream country and western festival. **Korumburra:** Coal Creek twilight music and theatre festival. **Leongatha:** Cycling carnival. **Maldon:** Camp draft. **Seymour:** Alternative farming expo. **Traralgon:** Music in the park. **Warrnambool:** Wunta fiesta.

MARCH
Public holiday: Labour Day. **Melbourne:** Australian Formula One Grand Prix; Moomba festival including International Dragon Boat festival; Grape Grazing (Yarra Glen). **Apollo Bay:** Music festival. **Bairnsdale:** Riviera festival. **Ballan:** Arcadian festival. **Ballarat:** Begonia festival; Opera festival. **Bendigo:** Madison 10 000 cycling race. **Casterton:** Vintage car rally. **Cohuna:** Show. **Colac:** Kana festival. **Corryong:** High Country festival. **Eaglehawk:** Dahlia and Arts festival. **Echuca:** Water-ski race. **Erica:** King of the Mountain woodchop. **Geelong:** Highland gathering. **Harrietville:** Bushman's Classic (mountain cattlemen's race). **Healesville:** Australian car rally championship. **Horsham:** Wimmera machinery field days. **Inverloch:** Jazz festival. **Koo-wee-rup:** Potato festival. **Korumburra:** Karmai (Giant Worm) festival. **Kyabram:** Rodeo. **Maffra:** Harvest festival. **Mansfield:** Harvest festival. **Marlay Point (near Sale):** Yacht race to Paynesville. **Metung:** Regatta. **Mildura:** Great Mildura paddleboat race (biennial, odd numbered years). **Moe:** Jazz festival; Blue Rock Classic (cross-country horse race). **Mount Beauty:** Conquestathon fun walk. **Myrtleford:** Tobacco, hops and timber festival. **Nagambie:** Goulburn Valley vintage festival. **Numurkah:** Art show. **Albert:** Fishing competition. **Port Fairy:** Folk festival. **Portland:** Dahlia festival. **Rutherglen:** Tastes of Rutherglen. **Sale:** Sale Cup. **Seymour:** Rafting festival. **Thorpdale:** Potato festival. **Warragul:** Gippsland field days. **Wodonga:** Show.

EASTER
Public holidays: Good Friday; Easter Monday; **State-wide:** Easterbike (various locations). **Alexandra:** Art show. **Beechworth:** Golden Horseshoes festival. **Benalla:** Felix arts festival. **Bendigo:** Fair (features Chinese dragon). **Buchan:** Rodeo. **Echuca:** Working horse fair. **Kyabram:** Antique aeroplane fly-in. **Kyneton:** Antique fair. **Lake Bolac:** Yachting regatta. **Maldon:** Fair. **Mallacoota:** Festival. **Omeo:** Rodeo and market. **Paynesville:** Gold Cup (speedboat races). **Patchewollock:** Easter sports and camel race. **Quambatook:** Australian tractor pull championship. **Stawell:** Easter Gift (professional foot race). **Torquay:** Bells Beach surfing classic. **Warracknabeal:** Vintage machinery and vehicle rally; Wheatlands carnival. **Wunghnu:** Tractor pull festival. **Yarram:** Tarra festival.

APRIL
Public holiday: Anzac Day. **State-wide:** Heritage Week. **Melbourne:** Comedy festival. **Bendigo:** Chrysanthemum show. **Bright:** Autumn festival.

wooded hill country, still relatively unpopulated and peaceful. National parks such as Tarra-Bulga and Wilsons Promontory are all well worth visiting. The coastal region includes the Ninety Mile Beach which borders the Gippsland Lakes system – Australia's largest inland waterway – and the beautiful Croajingolong National Park, a wilderness area.

Following the course of the Murray can be an interesting way of exploring Victoria's north. The river begins as a narrow, rapidly flowing alpine stream near Mt Kosciusko, and changes to a broad expanse near the aquatic playgrounds of Lakes Hume and Mulwala; there are many waterbird and wildlife reserves, national parks, flourishing citrus and wine-growing areas, sandy river beaches, and fascinating glimpses of life in the riverboat era at cities such as Echuca, Swan Hill and Mildura.

A good network of sealed roads means Victoria's unique diversity of attractions, both natural and constructed, are easily accessible to the motoring tourist.

CLIMATE GUIDE

MELBOURNE

	J	F	M	A	M	J	J	A	S	O	N	D
Maximum °C	26	26	24	20	17	14	13	15	17	20	22	24
Minimum °C	14	14	13	11	8	7	6	7	8	9	11	13
Rainfall mm	48	47	52	57	58	49	49	50	59	67	60	59
Raindays	8	7	9	12	14	14	15	16	15	14	12	11

LAKES ENTRANCE REGION

	J	F	M	A	M	J	J	A	S	O	N	D
Maximum °C	24	24	22	20	17	15	15	16	17	19	20	22
Minimum °C	14	15	13	11	8	6	5	6	7	9	11	13
Rainfall mm	57	35	55	61	79	65	55	57	57	61	73	74
Raindays	8	7	10	10	12	13	12	14	13	13	13	11

BENDIGO REGION

	J	F	M	A	M	J	J	A	S	O	N	D
Maximum °C	29	29	25	21	16	13	12	14	16	20	24	26
Minimum °C	14	15	13	9	7	4	3	5	6	8	11	13
Rainfall mm	34	32	36	41	55	60	56	58	54	53	38	33
Raindays	5	4	5	7	10	12	13	13	11	10	7	6

ALPINE REGION

	J	F	M	A	M	J	J	A	S	O	N	D
Maximum °C	18	19	15	10	6	3	1	3	5	9	13	15
Minimum °C	8	9	7	4	1	-2	-4	-2	-1	1	4	5
Rainfall mm	88	59	121	154	195	175	266	256	210	179	168	172
Raindays	10	7	12	12	15	16	19	19	17	15	15	14

Echuca: Barmah muster. **Geelong:** Heritage and vintage rally; Alternative Farmvision. **Inglewood:** Blue Eucalyptus festival (biennial, even-numbered years). **Tallangatta:** Dairy festival. **Wonthaggi:** Turville Shield fishing competition.

MAY
Melbourne: Next Wave festival (biennial, even-numbered years). **Chiltern:** Antique fair. **Daylesford:** Hepburn Swiss-Italian festival. **Halls Gap:** Grampians gourmet weekend. **Kalorama:** Chestnut festival. **Kerang:** Salt and Water festival. **Lake Goldsmith** (near Beaufort): Steam Rally. **Warrnambool:** Southern right whales due at Logans Beach; Racing carnival.

JUNE
Public holiday: Queen's birthday. **Melbourne:** Melbourne international film festival.

Buchan: Woodchop. **Cobram:** Antique fair. **Echuca:** Steam, horse and vintage car rally. **Geelong:** Wool week; Celtic festival. **Rutherglen:** Winery walkabout weekend.

JULY
Melbourne: A Cappella festival (choral singing). **Daylesford:** Mid-winter festival. **Hamilton:** Eisteddfod. **Swan Hill:** Italian fiesta. **Warburton:** Winterfest.

AUGUST
Melbourne: Rhododendron festival (at Olinda). **Ballarat:** Royal South Street Eisteddfod. **Falls Creek:** International Ski Marathon Kangaroo Hoppet. **Hamilton:** Wool heritage week. **Mount Beauty:** Hoppet festival. **Speed:** Mallee machinery field days.

SEPTEMBER
State-wide: Opening of Australia's open garden scheme. **Melbourne:**

Australian football league and association finals; Royal Melbourne show; Tesselaar's tulip festival (at Silvan). **Anglesea:** Angair festival. **Bacchus Marsh:** Pioneer Day festival. **Chiltern:** Art show. **Cowes:** Motor racing. **Halls Gap:** Wildflower exhibition. **Kyneton:** Daffodil and arts festival. **Leongatha:** Daffodil and floral festival. **Maryborough:** Golden wattle festival. **Nhill:** Wildflower exhibition (at Little Desert Lodge). **Wedderburn:** Wool expo. **Yarrawonga:** Ice breaker yacht regatta.

OCTOBER
Melbourne: Oktoberfest; Spring racing carnival, including Caulfield Cup; International festival of the arts; Fringe arts festival; Lygon Street festival. **Ararat:** Golden gateway festival. **Avoca:** Wool and wine festival, includes Avoca Cup (horse race). **Bendigo:**

Orchid Club spring show. **Bright:** Alpine spring festival. **Broadford:** Scottish festival. **Buchan:** Art and craft festival. **Charlton:** Art show. **Cowes:** Superbike championships. **Creswick:** Brackenbury Classic fun run. **Echuca:** Rich river festival. **Euroa:** Wool week; Agricultural show. **Geelong:** Show; Racing carnival. **Heathcote:** Golden grape festival. **Horsham:** Spring garden festival. **Maldon:** Vintage car hill climb. **Moe:** Moe Cup. **Myrtleford:** International festival (biennial, even-numbered years). **Phillip Island:** Grand Prix motorcycle race. **Port Fairy:** Spring music festival. **Pyramid Hill:** Pioneer machinery display; Iron man contest. **Rainbow:** Iris festival. **Tallangatta:** Arts festival. **Warrnambool:** Melbourne –Warrnambool Cycling Classic. **Yarrawonga:** Antique fair.

NOVEMBER
Public holiday: Melbourne Cup Day (Vic metro. only). **Melbourne:** Spring racing carnival, including Melbourne Cup and Oaks Day. **Benalla:** Rose festival. **Bendigo:** National swap meet; Racing carnival. **Casterton:** Street-car drag racing. **Castlemaine:** Spring garden festival (biennial, odd-numbered years). State festival (biennial, even-numbered years); **Dimboola:** Rowing regatta. **Dunkeld:** Dunkeld Cup. **Heathcote:** Show. **Kyneton:** Kyneton Cup. **Lake Goldsmith:** Steam rally; Art show. **Lakes Entrance:** World Cup sport kiting championships. **Macedon:** Mount Macedon festival. **Maldon:** Folk festival. **Mansfield:** Mountain country festival. **Mount Beauty:** Festival of the Bogong Moth. **Natimuk:** Harrow national bush billycart championship. **Omeo:** Agricultural and

pastoral show. **Ouyen:** Farmers festival. **Port Albert:** Regatta. **Portland:** Jazz festival; Antique fair; Pioneer week. **Sale:** Wetlands festival. **Shepparton:** Strawberry festival. **Walhalla:** Goldfields fun day. **Wandin:** Cherry festival. **Wangaratta:** Festival of jazz and blues. **Yarragon:** Dairy fest. **Yarram:** Seabank fishing contest.

DECEMBER
Public holidays: Christmas Day; Boxing Day. **Melbourne:** Finish of Great Victorian bike ride. **Broadford:** Hells Angels concert. **Corryong:** Folk music festival (in Nariel Valley). **Daylesford:** Highland gathering. **Dunkeld:** Festival. **Gisborne:** Festival. **Horsham:** Kannamaroo festival. **Lancefield:** Horse festival. **Nagambie:** Rowing regatta. **Port Fairy:** Moyneyana festival. **Portland:** Surfboat marathon. **Woodend:** Five Mile Creek festival.

MELBOURNE
Most Livable City

The banks of the Yarra River, a peaceful retreat for city dwellers

At first glance, Melbourne may look like any other modern city with its skyline crammed with concrete and glass. However, if you look a little closer you'll find the real Melbourne: clanging trams, swanky boutiques, friendly taxi drivers, Australian Rules football, fickle weather and BYOs (restaurants to which you bring your own liquor) by the hundred. Add to this Melbourne's traditional virtues of tree-lined boulevards, magnificent public gardens, elegant buildings and imposing Victorian churches and banks – and the Melbourne Cricket Ground – and you'll have some idea of the city.

In recent years, Melbourne has become a polyglot society with a huge influx of migrants from many countries, particularly from Asia and Greece; it has one of the largest Greek-speaking populations in the world. This cosmopolitan influence is reflected in Melbourne's bustling markets, delicatessens and restaurants. Eating out has become one of the great Melbourne pastimes, and the numerous city and suburban restaurants provide an opportunity to sample a tempting variety of food cultures.

Situated at the head of Port Phillip and centred on the north bank of the Yarra River, Melbourne has a population of over three million. Suburbs stretch in all directions, particularly round the east coast of the bay and out to the Dandenongs, a picturesque mountain range east of Melbourne.

Both John Batman and John Pascoe Fawkner were associated in the founding of Melbourne in 1835, and Melbourne soon entered a boom period with the discovery of gold in the State in 1851. The goldfields of Bendigo, Ballarat and Castlemaine attracted fortune-hunters from all over the world, and by 1861 Melbourne had become Australia's largest city. By the end of the century it was firmly established as the business and cultural centre of the colony.

Today Melbourne's position as a financial and cultural centre of the nation is shared with Sydney, but it has an elegance and style all its own. Melbourne has been the only Australian capital to retain its network of pollution-free electric trams. The once familiar clang of the old green thunderers is heard less often, although some of these have been given a new lease of life; most have been replaced by new trams and the light rail. The World Health Organisation has rated Melbourne as one of the least polluted cities of its size in the world; Melbourne has also been acclaimed the world's most livable city by the internationally renowned Population Crises Centre, based in Washington D.C., USA.

Melbourne has a huge range of retail stores, and one of its highlights is the shopping in the city area, at **Southgate** across the Yarra, and in such suburbs as fashionable **South Yarra**. Several other

NOT TO BE MISSED
in Melbourne

- **Arthurs Seat** – for panoramic views over both Port Phillip and Western Port
- **Colonial Tramcar restaurant** – dine and see the sights at the same time
- **Healesville Sanctuary** – excellent collection of native fauna
- **National Gallery** – known for its excellent Australian collection
- **Puffing Billy** – see the beautiful Dandenongs by taking a steam-train ride
- **Royal Botanic Gardens** – considered among the best in the world
- **Royal Queen Victoria Market** – always bustling and noisy – and fun
- **Scienceworks** – award-winning science and technology museum
- **Southgate** – wine, dine or shop beside the Yarra River
- **Williamstown** – take a ferry to this fascinating former maritime village

suburbs such as **Carlton**, **Camberwell**, **Prahran**, **Armadale** and **Toorak** rival the city centre with their up-market retail stores and restaurants.

Melburnians are also great sports lovers and this is reflected in the huge crowds that attend cricket and Australian Rules football matches. A peculiarly Melbourne phenomenon is the football fever that grips the city each year, with enthusiasm building up to mass hysteria on Grand Final day in late September.

The **Melbourne Cricket Ground** is the venue for many sporting and entertainment fixtures. Located just outside the Members' entrance, the **Australian Gallery of Sport** celebrates Australian sporting history. The **Olympic Museum**, located in the Gallery of Sport, houses memorabilia dating back to the first modern Olympics, held in Olympia in 1896. The **Melbourne Cricket Club Museum**, featuring members' exhibits, is located in the Members Pavilion.

Horseracing is another popular Melbourne spectator sport and the **Melbourne Cup** at **Flemington Racecourse** brings Australia to a halt for three minutes on the first Tuesday of each November. Melbourne's other main racecourses are at Caulfield, Moonee Valley and Sandown Park; the **Victorian Racing Museum** is at Caulfield Racecourse. The city's 3½ week **Spring Racing Carnival** runs from early October to early November. **Moomba** in March, the **Comedy Festival** in April and the **Melbourne International Festival of the Arts** in October are other outstanding events on the Melbourne calendar.

The **Melbourne Park Tennis Centre** hosts the **Australian Open**, one of the world's four grand slam events, in January each year. The Centre Court with its unique retractable roof can accommodate 16 000 people, and is used also as a venue for a variety of entertainment extravaganzas.

The **Crown Hotel and Casino** are being constructed alongside the Yarra River near the Spencer Street Bridge. Nearby, the *Polly Woodside*, a square-rigged commercial sailing ship built in 1885, is moored (off South Wharf Road) and is the focal point of the **Melbourne Maritime Museum**. Across the river, the **World Congress Centre**, on the corner of Flinders and Spencer Streets, houses the temporary **Crown Casino**. Next door are the **Centra on the Yarra** hotel and the **World Trade Centre** which hosts international trade displays.

Further along Flinders Street past the Banana Alley Vaults is the **Flinders Street Station** complex, the main terminus for the suburban rail system. The **Underground Rail Loop** located on the edge of the central business district has three stations. Above ground, the distinctive burgundy-and-cream **City Circle tram**, which is free, offers a daily 10-minute service (between 10 a.m. and 6 p.m.) around the central city area. The circuit, along Flinders, Spring and Nicholson Streets, Victoria Parade and La Trobe and Spencer Streets, takes 30 minutes. The **City Explorer** tourist bus departs Flinders Street Station hourly between 10 a.m. and 4 p.m., and stops at the major attractions.

To get a different view of Melbourne, take a river cruise on the Yarra; cruise boats depart from the **Princes Walk Terminal**, near Princes Bridge. The Yarra Yarra Water Taxi service is available from Southgate, on the opposite bank of the river. The exciting Southgate development includes several restaurants, wine bars, a licensed food court, outdoor eating areas, shops and the **Sheraton Towers Southgate** hotel. As well, the development includes **Experience Australia**, a sensor vision theatre, providing a thrilling way to experience the historical, natural and cultural aspects of the country.

The Southgate riverside development

ACCOMMODATION

HOTELS

Grand Hyatt Melbourne
123 Collins St, Melbourne
(03) 9657 1234

Le Meridien at Rialto
495 Collins St, Melbourne
(03) 9620 9111

Novotel Melbourne
270 Collins St, Melbourne
(03) 9650 5800

Rockman's Regency
Cnr Exhibition and Lonsdale Sts, Melbourne
(03) 9662 3900

Sheraton Towers Southgate
1 Brown St, South Melbourne
(03) 9696 3100

The Hotel Como
630 Chapel St, South Yarra
(03) 9824 0400

The Regent Melbourne
25 Collins St, Melbourne
(03) 9653 0000

The Windsor
103 Spring St, Melbourne
(03) 9653 0653

FAMILY AND BUDGET

City Limits Motel
20 Little Bourke St, Melbourne
(03) 9662 2544

Lygon Lodge
220 Lygon St, Carlton
(03) 9663 6633

The Hotel Y
489 Elizabeth St, Melbourne
(03) 9329 5188

The Victoria Hotel
215 Little Collins St, Melbourne
(03) 9653 0441

MOTEL GROUPS: BOOKINGS

Best Western 1800 22 2166
Flag 13 2400
Travelodge 1800 22 2446

This list is for information only; inclusion is not necessarily a recommendation.

Parks and Gardens

Sherbrooke Forest, part of the Dandenong Ranges National Park

Melbourne is a city that has grown to become a place of dignity and beauty, designed as it was with wide, tree-shaded streets and magnificent public gardens. The feeling for greenery and open space has been maintained by individual residents, many of whom take great pride in their gardens, whether they be planted with exotic species or with Australian native trees and shrubs.

The jewel of Victoria is the **Royal Botanic Gardens**, situated beside the Yarra River. There there are 36 hectares of plantations, flower-beds, lawns and ornamental lakes, so superbly laid out and cared for that they are considered to be among the best in the world.

The site was selected in 1845 but the main work on their development was carried out by Baron Ferdinand von Mueller, who was appointed Government Botanist in 1852. He was succeeded by W. R. Guilfoyle, a landscape artist, who further remodelled and expanded the gardens. The gardens and the riverside are now a favourite place for people on Sundays. Families flock to picnic, feed the swans and waterbirds on the lakes, or simply take a pleasant stroll.

Adjoining the gardens and flanking St Kilda Road is another large area of parkland, the **Kings Domain**, comprising 43 hectares of tree-shaded lawns and containing the Shrine of Remembrance, La Trobe's Cottage, which was the first Government House, and the Sidney Myer Music Bowl, an unconventional aluminium and steel structure that creates a perfect amphitheatre for outdoor concerts in the summer months, and is converted into an ice-skating rink during winter. This vast garden area is completed by the adjoining **Alexandra** and **Queen Victoria Gardens**, a further 52 hectares of parkland.

The city's first public gardens were the **Flagstaff Gardens** at William Street, West Melbourne. A monument in the gardens bears a plaque describing how the site was used as a signalling station to inform settlers of the arrival and departure of ships at Williamstown. On the other side of the city in East Melbourne are the **Treasury** and **Fitzroy Gardens** close by the State government offices. In the Fitzroy Gardens is the explorer Captain Cook's cottage, which was transported in 1934 from the village of Great

Ayton, Yorkshire, where Cook was born, and which was re-erected to commemorate Melbourne's centenary. Also in these gardens is a model Tudor village, laid out near an ancient tree trunk carved with tiny figures by the late Ola Cohn and known as the fairy tree. Another garden close to the city is the **Carlton Gardens**, in which the domed Exhibition Buildings are situated. They were erected for the Great Exhibition of 1880, and were for 27 years the meeting-place of the Victorian Parliament; Federal Parliament met in the State Parliament buildings while awaiting the building of the nation's capital at Canberra.

Melbourne also has large recreational areas around the city and throughout the urban region, and these meet the demands of a sport-loving populace. The most notable is **Albert Park**, the venue for the annual Australian Formula One Grand Prix car race. The lake is ideal for sailing and rowing, and the surrounding parkland and buildings cater for both outdoor and indoor sports.

In East Melbourne, another large sporting area contains the famous **Melbourne Cricket Ground**, which has been established for more than 100 years as a venue for test cricket and football, and which now has stands that can accommodate 100 000 people. Nearby is the award-winning **Melbourne Park Tennis Centre**, the venue for international tennis tournaments, including the Australian Open each January. Courts are available for public hire. The Melbourne metropolitan area has eighty golf courses, many of which are accessible to the public. The **Royal Melbourne Golf Club** ranks sixth in world ratings, and hosts many world-class tournaments.

The created beauty of Melbourne is surpassed by nature in places such as the **Dandenongs**, heavily forested ranges near Melbourne with magnificent trees and spectacular fern gullies; the **Wilsons Promontory National Park** in Gippsland with its secluded beaches and superb coastal scenery; the **Tarra-Bulga National Park** in the Strzelecki Ranges, with its mountain ash trees and rainforest vegetation; the **Wyperfeld National Park** in the north-west, with its wildflowers and dry-country birdlife; and the **Alpine National Park**, which stretches across 642 000 hectares of the State's high country.

The quality of Victoria's public and private gardens is exceptional wherever you go. Each year, Australia's Open Garden Scheme publishes a guidebook to numerous private gardens open throughout spring, summer and autumn, right across Victoria as well as in four other States. Most major towns have large, meticulously maintained garden areas, each with its own special quality. The Botanical Gardens at **Ararat** are noted for orchid glasshouse displays. The gardens at **Ballarat** are the centre of the notable annual Begonia festival held in March. **Benalla** has a Rose festival every November. In autumn, visitors are attracted to the colours of autumn foliage on the trees in and around the small town of **Bright**.

For more detailed information on various garden festivals and displays, contact the Victorian Visitor Information Centre, cnr Little Collins and Swanston Sts, Melbourne; (03) 9650 1522. **See also:** National Parks.

The beautiful National Rhododendron Gardens at Olinda

The city centre is compact, its wide streets laid out in a grid system. Take a tram to the top of **Collins Street** and wander back down – the street somehow epitomises Melbourne.

Looking down on Collins Street, in Spring Street, is the elegant **Old Treasury Building**, built in 1853, now refurbished and open as a museum featuring the **Melbourne Exhibition** which explores Melbourne's fine architecture and colourful social history. Just down from Spring Street is the august **Melbourne Club**, mecca to Melbourne's Establishment. On the opposite side of the street on the Exhibition Street corner is **Collins Place**, an impressive multi-storey complex that houses **The Regent Melbourne** hotel in one of its high towers. Described as 'the city within the city', this complex has many shops and boutiques open all weekend. Another tall building, **Nauru House**, is diagonally opposite.

Continuing down the hill you will see fashionable boutiques and two old churches, the **Uniting Church** and **Scots Church**. Across the road the **Grand Hyatt** hotel complex has an interesting food hall and shopping plaza at street level. Just down the hill is the graceful porticoed **Baptist Church**, built in 1845, and further down are Melbourne's imposing **Town Hall**, used for receptions and concerts and Melbourne's grandest Gothic Cathedral, **St Paul's** Cathedral in Swanston Walk. The **City Square** located on the corner of Collins Street and Swanston Walk, and the historic but long disused **Regent Theatre** nearby in Collins Street, are both in the process of being refurbished.

Further down Collins Street is the elegant old **Block Arcade** with its mosaic floor, glass and iron-lace roof and stylish shops. The small lane at the back of this arcade (Block Place) leads through to Little Collins Street and to another gracious old arcade. This is the **Royal Arcade** where, every hour, the huge statues of mythical figures, Gog and Magog, strike the hour. This arcade leads through to the **Bourke Street Mall**, between Elizabeth and Swanston Streets. Several department stores and fashion chains, including **Myer**, Australia's largest department store, and **David Jones**, front on to the mall. David Jones has another store on the opposite side and its food hall is worth a visit to see the beautifully presented displays. Nearby, the shopping complex **Centre Point** is a handy place to browse under shelter or to stop for a snack in one of its many coffee bars. You can sit and watch city buskers from the seats provided in the mall, but when crossing the Mall be aware of the trams – the only traffic, apart from delivery and emergency vehicles, allowed in this block. The **Half-Tix** booth in the mall offers the opportunity to purchase theatre tickets for the day's performances at reduced prices. There is also a **tourist information booth** in the mall; half-day, guided, shopping and sightseeing tram tours, which utilise the regular tram service, depart from here; bookings are essential.

Swanston Street Walk, a pedestrian mall, encourages a stroll between Flinders and La Trobe Streets. Window-shop at your leisure or take time for coffee at one of the many sidewalk cafes.

A combination of bookshops and bistros occupies the uppermost block of **Bourke Street**. The front coffee bar at Pellegrini's, a bustling Italian restaurant, is a great favourite. On the Spring Street corner is one of the last of Melbourne's grand old hotels, the elegant **Windsor** (1883), which looks over the peaceful **Treasury Gardens**. Proudly surveying the city from its location on Spring Street is the classical-style **State Parliament House**. The Corinthian style of the Legislative Council Chamber is a legacy of Melbourne's golden era. **St Patrick's Cathedral** with its massive blocks of bluestone can be seen from the elegant gardens that surround Parliament House. Melbourne's gracious and beautifully restored **Princess Theatre**, is also in Spring Street.

Gordon Place, at the top of Little Bourke Street, is a unique building designed by the colonial architect William Pitt in 1883. The building is now an attractive tourist apartment complex.

If you like Chinese food, do not miss Melbourne's **Chinatown** in Little Bourke Street, between Exhibition and Swanston Streets. Dozens of fascinating restaurants, grocery shops and mixed stores date back to Melbourne's post-gold-rush days, when it became the city's Chinese quarter. The standard of the restaurants is good and prices vary from fairly cheap to very expensive. Among the outstanding eating-houses are the Bamboo House, the Flower Drum and the Mask of China. Located in the heart of Chinatown at Cohen Place, the **Museum of Chinese Australian History** is worth a visit.

Further down Little Bourke Street is the **Information Victoria Centre**, which provides the public with access to Victorian Government information resources, including research facilities for public-records.

Just half a block away in Lonsdale Street is the huge retail complex **Melbourne Central** which features a 20-storey, glass cone enclosing a historic shot tower. Melbourne Central and the department store **Daimaru** together occupy most of the block bounded by Lonsdale, Swanston, La Trobe and Elizabeth Streets and are well serviced by Museum station on the underground rail loop. There is a direct walk-through access between Melbourne Central and

---

MELBOURNE ON FOOT

The following is a selection of walking tours available.

- **Art & About:** Guided walks highlighting cultural side of city; bookings essential, charge applies.

- **Booklovers Walk:** Guided walk includes the State Library and various bookshops; bookings essential; charge applies.

- **Chocaholics Walk:** Guided walk around major chocolate outlets; bookings essential; charge applies.

- **Melbourne Heritage Walks:** Various guided walks providing an insight into the city's history and architecture; bookings essential; charge applies.

- **Royal Botanic Gardens:** Guided walk, free of charge.

- **Walking Melbourne:** Various self-guide walks prepared by the National Trust; booklet available.

For further information, contact the Victorian Visitor Information Centre, cnr Little Collins and Swanston Sts, Melbourne; (03) 9650 1522.

the Myer department store. Further east along Lonsdale Street, Greek music cafes and flaky pastry shops make Melbourne a mini-Athens.

The **Museum of Victoria** located in Swanston Street has many interesting exhibits, including a large collection of Australiana, natural history, the legendary racehorse Phar Lap and the **Children's Museum**, a first in Australia. This imposing old building also houses the **Planetarium** (where slides are projected on the ceiling); the magnificent domed **State Library** and the **La Trobe Library**. Further east along La Trobe Street is the **National Philatelic Centre**.

A block away, in Russell Street, is the grim **Old Melbourne Gaol** and **Penal Museum** with its chillingly macabre exhibits, including the gallows where folk-hero and bushranger Ned Kelly swung. The gaol's atmosphere becomes even more dramatic and enthralling during the after-dark tours which incorporate live theatre.

More cheerful sights such as clothing, souvenirs, plants, cheeses, sausages and decoratively arranged vegetables can be seen at Melbourne's bustling **Queen Victoria Market**, bounded by Peel, Victoria and Elizabeth Streets, and open Tuesdays, Thursdays, Fridays, Saturdays and Sundays. Alongside in Victoria Street are cafes and covered outdoor-eating areas. Near the market on the corner of Queen and Franklin Streets is the fascinating **Queen Victoria Arts and Craft Centre**, open daily. From here it is only a short stroll to the beautiful **Flagstaff Gardens**, once used as a pioneer graveyard and later as a signalling station. Today this is a pleasant place for the whole family to relax, with shady old trees, a children's playground, tennis courts and barbecues. Facing the park in King Street you can see **St James' Old Cathedral**, built in 1839.

The lower part of the city is the sedate legal and financial sector. Back towards the city centre along William Street are the former **Royal Mint** and the **Supreme Court** and **Law Courts**, which were built between 1877 and 1884. At the bottom end of Collins Street is the luxury hotel **Le Meridien at Rialto**. The elaborate Rialto building and its neighbours, erected between 1889 and 1893, have been retained as a facade to this towering hotel and office complex, the tallest building in the southern hemisphere. An **observation**

The dome at Melbourne Central, built to protect the shot tower

deck on level 55 provides 360-degree views of Melbourne from large internal and external viewing areas.

In contrast, two of Melbourne's finest city parks, the quiet old **Treasury Gardens** and the beautiful **Fitzroy Gardens**, lie on the eastern boundary of the central city grid. The John F. Kennedy Memorial is located beside the lake in the Treasury Gardens. The Fitzroy Gardens have superb avenues of huge English elms planted along gently contoured lawns, giving them a serene beauty all year round. Attractions within the gardens include **Captain Cook's Cottage**, the intricately carved **Fairy Tree**, a model Tudor village, a restaurant and kiosk, and a children's playground.

The **Carlton Gardens**, located north-east of the city, flank the **Exhibition Buildings** – a grandiose domed hall originally built for the Great Exhibition in 1880 and still used for trade fairs. The southern side of the gardens has an ornamental pond and ornate fountain while the northern section has an adventure playground and a mini-traffic circuit that is popular with junior cyclists. This area is currently being redeveloped for the new Museum of Victoria, due for completion in the year 2000.

The **Victorian Arts Centre** is just over Princes Bridge on St Kilda Road, south of the central business area, and comprises the **National Gallery of Victoria**, the **Melbourne Concert Hall**, three theatres, other performance spaces, several gallery areas, and a variety of restaurants and bars. The National Gallery features a fine collection of Australian and overseas masterpieces. The intricate stained-glass ceiling of the Great Hall was designed by Australian artist Leonard French. The Concert Hall is used for classical music and large concerts. It also contains the **Performing Arts Museum**, which offers a programme of regularly changing exhibitions covering the whole spectrum of the performing arts. The theatres include the **State Theatre** for opera, ballet and large musicals, the **Playhouse** for drama and the **George Fairfax Studio** for experimental theatre. Not far away at the **Malthouse**, 117 Sturt Street, South Melbourne, the Playbox Theatre Company has two theatres.

The **Kings Domain**, across St Kilda Road, is a huge stretch of shady parkland where you will see: the **Myer Music Bowl**, used in the summer months as the venue for outdoor concerts and in the winter months as an ice-skating rink; the tower of **Government House** (open to the public on the third Sunday in October); the majestic, pyramid-style **Shrine of Remembrance,** which dominates St Kilda Road; the **Old Observatory** in Birdwood Avenue and, just past this, **La Trobe's Cottage**, Victoria's first Government House. This quaint cottage with many original furnishings – a reminder of Melbourne's humble beginnings – was brought out from England

Rippon Lea, a National Trust property at Elsternwick

by the first Governor (La Trobe) in prefabricated sections. It is now a National Trust property, furnished in the original style with many of La Trobe's personal belongings. The main entrance to the **Royal Botanic Gardens** is nearby. With lush, beautifully landscaped gardens and gently sloping lawns, attractively grouped trees and shrubs, shady ferneries and ornamental lakes, the gardens are a peaceful retreat for city dwellers. Many of the majestic old oaks in the western end of the garden are over 100 years old. The tearooms, open daily, offer morning and afternoon teas, and lunch. Guided walks operate at 10 a.m. and 11 a.m. daily (not Mondays, Saturdays and public holidays) departing from the Visitor Centre; there is no charge.

If you walk through the gardens you will come to shady **Alexandra Avenue**, which runs beside the Yarra River. Barbecues are dotted along the Yarra's grassy banks and are good for a family picnic. At weekends, you can hire bicycles and ride the scenic **Yarra River Cycle Path**.

Nearby **Albert Park**, just south of St Kilda Road, is another good place for families – and sports enthusiasts. There are barbecues on the edge of the huge Albert Park Lake and boats are available for hire. You can jog or cycle around the lake, or play golf on the adjoining public golf course. This park is the venue for the annual Australian Formula One Grand Prix car race.

Albert Park and its neighbouring suburbs, **South Melbourne** and **Port Melbourne**, are popular places with their trendy restaurants, bookshops, pubs and markets leading down to Melbourne's bayside beaches. The beachfront is ideal for a bayside stroll; the more energetic can hire a bike, a sailboard or a pair of rollerblades and join the local crowd. In Coventry Street, South Melbourne are three portable houses, assembled in the 1850s, of the kind popular in Victoria during the gold-rush era.

Cosmopolitan **St Kilda** is a mixture of London's Soho and an old-fashioned fun resort. **Luna Park** and the enormous **Palais Theatre** are relics of the days when St Kilda was Melbourne's leading seaside playground. **Fitzroy Street**, recently a neon-lit, 24-hour strip of takeaway food shops and nightspots, is undergoing a change as the grand old hotels in the street are restored and their ground floors opened as stylish cafes, bistros, art cinemas and restaurants. St Kilda is worth a visit, particularly on Sundays, when a collection of art and craft stalls appears on the **Esplanade**, and **Acland Street** offers bookshops, restaurants and luscious continental cakes. For a delightful fish meal, visit The Pavilion restaurant or take-away on Jacka Boulevard. The Stokehouse restaurant on the foreshore and the kiosk at the end of St Kilda Pier, are also popular eating places. The **Jewish Museum** is in nearby Alma Road.

Located just outside St Kilda at 192 Hotham Street, Elsternwick, is **Rippon Lea**, a National Trust property, that is open daily. This huge Romanesque mansion is well-known for its beautiful English-style landscaped gardens and strutting peacocks.

Two of Melbourne's wealthiest suburbs are **South Yarra** and **Toorak**. **Como**, another magnificent National Trust mansion, is in Como Avenue, off Toorak Road. Set in pleasant gardens, which once spread down to the river, Como, with its charming balconies, is a perfect example of nineteenth-century colonial grandeur.

Although many of Toorak's and South Yarra's grand old estates have been subdivided, there is no shortage of imposing gates and high walls screening huge mansions. You could easily spend the best part of a day strolling down **Toorak Road**. With its boutiques, expensive restaurants and gourmet food shops – this is a place to see and be seen.

Another of Melbourne's great shopping streets, **Chapel Street**, crosses Toorak Road in South Yarra. Here yet more fashion boutiques, and antique and jewellery shops abound, but the air is not quite so rarefied, nor are the price tags quite as high. The **Jam Factory**, a huge refurbished redbrick factory has shops, an attractive glass-topped courtyard and restaurants. Further on towards Malvern Road, Chapel Street becomes more cosmopolitan and the emphasis shifts from fashion to food. The **Prahran Market** is around the corner in Commercial Road. This market springs to life on Tuesdays, Thursdays, Fridays and Saturdays. Catch a tram down nearby **High Street** to Armadale and you will come to Melbourne's antique area. As well as antique shops, art and craft galleries, and designer-clothes shops stretch along High Street for several blocks.

Melbourne's city centre has been revitalised by Sunday trading and the popularity of the various shopping complexes. Once-depressed inner suburbs north of the Yarra have also been recharged with life. Theatres, theatre restaurants, antique shops, trendy fashion boutiques and dozens of BYOs have bloomed in the suburbs of **Carlton**, **North Fitzroy** and **Richmond**. Most of the elegant iron-lace terrace houses in the more fashionable inner suburbs have been lovingly restored, but these areas still have a lively mixture of migrants and Australian old-timers. Carlton has one of the largest concentrations of beautiful Victorian houses in Melbourne. Its shady wide streets and squares of restored terraces can make you forget you are within walking distance of a modern city.

Lygon Street, known locally as 'little Italy', is lined with Italian restaurants, delicatessens, bookshops, boutiques and 'arty' shops. Have lunch and take in the Carlton scene at Jimmy Watson's, Melbourne's oldest wine bar, at 333 Lygon Street. The wine is good but cheap, the food self-service and the atmosphere frenetic.

Carlton is also the site of **Melbourne University**; located in the University grounds – a mixture of original ivy-clad buildings and modern blocks – are the **Grainger Museum** and the **University Gallery**. Nearby is **Parkville**, another little pocket of gracious Victorian terraces and shady streets. And at the **Melbourne Zoo**, just across nearby **Royal Park**, you can see a magnificent collection of butterflies in the walk-through Butterfly House, families of lions at play from the safety of a 'people cage', an enclosed bridge that takes you right through the lions' large, natural-looking enclosure and other interesting animal enclosures. These innovations are typical of the zoo's policy of making enclosures for animals as large and as natural as possible, with a minimum of bars. There is also an amusement park, bistro and kiosk.

Melbourne's old metropolitan meat market at 42 Courtney Street, North Melbourne has been converted to a large craft gallery and workshop complex. The **Meat Market Craft Centre** features changing exhibitions, as well as demonstrations and sales of high-quality crafts including woodwork.

For more information on craft shops and galleries, contact Craft Victoria on (03) 9417 3111.

Another old inner suburb worth exploring is **Fitzroy**, which is similar in character to Carlton. Raffish **Brunswick Street**, Fitzroy, has an interesting mixture of antique shops, bookshops, clothes boutiques, nurseries, pubs and first-class BYOs. The **Mary MacKillop Centre** is at 11 Brunswick Street, the site of her birth, and features various exhibits relating to her life. In the suburb of **Fairfield**, a few kilometres east of Fitzroy, are the **Fairfield Park Boathouse and Tea Gardens**, with rowing skiffs and canoes for hire.

East Melbourne, another notable area with beautiful terrace houses, has such 'grand old ladies' as **Clarendon Terrace** (in Clarendon Street) with its graceful, colonnaded central portico, and **Tasma Terrace** in Parliament Place, which now houses the National Trust Preservation Bookshop. The **Fire Services Museum of Victoria** is at 48 Gisborne Street, East Melbourne.

Swan Street, **Richmond** has one of the best selections of Greek restaurants in Melbourne. Most are quite cheap and unpretentious with excellent food enhanced by a lively atmosphere. **Victoria Street**, the Vietnamese heartland of the city, is crammed with restaurants, grocery shops and mixed stores. Restored Victorian shops in **Bridge Road** house both boutiques and bargain 'seconds' outlets. As well as Bridge Road, factory outlets and seconds shops can be found in Swan Street and Church Street, making Richmond the bargain shopping district of Melbourne.

It is possible in Melbourne to dine and see the sights at the same time. The **Colonial Tramcar restaurant** is a restaurant aboard a 1927 tram, thus allowing patrons to enjoy a meal in elegant style while travelling through Melbourne and some of its suburbs. This has proved so popular that three old-style trams are now in use. Another novel way to wine and dine is aboard **The Showboat**, a cruising restaurant, which leaves from North Wharf, West Melbourne or hire a Bar-B-Boat, a novel way to enjoy a barbecue while cruising on the Yarra River.

South-west of the city is Melbourne's oldest suburb **Williamstown**, founded in the 1830s. This fascinating former maritime village has many quaint old seafront pubs, churches, cottages and relics of its days as an important seaport. Because it was shielded from modern development until the completion of the **West Gate Bridge** to the city centre, Williamstown retains a strong seafaring character. At weekends you can see over HMAS *Castlemaine* – a World War II minesweeper restored by the Maritime Trust – and picnic along the grassy foreshore. You can also see model ships, early costumes and relics at the Williamstown **Historical Museum** in Electra Street and look over a superb exhibition of old steam locomotives at the **Railway Museum** in Champion Road, North Williamstown. Williamstown bay and river cruises are available.

The award-winning science and technology museum, **Scienceworks**, is located in a former pumping station in the suburb of **Spotswood**, close to Williamstown and only a ten-minute drive from the city. Australia's first plane and car are exhibited here along with a variety of other exhibits. The historic steamship *Wattle* departs from the Scienceworks jetty for cruises around the bay and river, except in January, when it conducts seal-colony viewing cruises from Rye pier to the Mornington Peninsula.

Closer to the city is the **Living Museum of the West**, Australia's first eco-museum, at Pipemakers Park, Van Ness Avenue, in the suburb of **Maribyrnong**. It presents the environment and heritage of the total community, the focus being on the people of the region. Cruises on the Maribyrnong River visit some of the attractions to the west and north-west of Melbourne. At the **Craigieburn** note-printing branch of the Reserve Bank of Australia, visitors can observe the printing of Australian currency notes; ring (03) 9303 0444 for an appointment.

For more information on Melbourne there are a number of guidebooks available. The Victorian Visitor Information Centre, cnr Little Collins and Swanston Sts (03) 9650 1522, provides maps, brochures and other information. As well as the Zone 1 Daily Ticket, **The Met**, Melbourne's public transport system, offers an Explorers Pack consisting of three adult Met passes, a map, and a booklet of tourist attractions in and around Melbourne, and suggested day trips on public transport. Contact (03) 9617 0900 or visit the Met shop at 103 Elizabeth Street.

TOURS from Melbourne

The bridge at San Remo links the mainland and Phillip Island

Some of Australia's most beautiful and interesting tours start from Melbourne and include historic towns and stunning scenery. Many require an overnight stop to do them justice and in such cases booking ahead is strongly recommended.

Ballarat and Sovereign Hill

110 km from Melbourne via the Western Freeway

A must for the tourist if only to visit Sovereign Hill, arguably the most authentic reconstruction of a nineteenth-century goldmining township in the world. **See:** Ballarat entry in A–Z listing; and the Golden Age.

Werribee Park

35 km from Melbourne via the Princes Highway

Just outside the township of Werribee, now almost a suburb of Melbourne, Werribee Park is a large estate with a magnificent Italianate mansion of some sixty rooms, built in the 1870s for the Chirnside brothers, who had established a pastoral empire in the western district. Now owned by the Victorian Government, Werribee Park is open daily. There are extensive formal gardens, including the Victorian State Rose Garden, an open-range zoo, an equestrian centre, restaurant, kiosk, picnic and barbecue facilities, a golf course and tennis courts. Nearby Point Cook RAAF Museum (open Sun.–Fri.) has adjacent picnic and barbecue facilities; the new National Air and Space Museum is being constructed here. There is nude bathing at Campbell's Cove.

Geelong, Queenscliff and Point Lonsdale

107 km from Melbourne via the Princes Highway and Bellarine Highway

Allow two days for this tour. Spend some time in Geelong, especially around the historic waterfront and at the National Wool Museum, before continuing to Queenscliff and Point Lonsdale. Stay overnight at a classic nineteenth-century hotel; try the Vue Grand, Ozone or the Queenscliff, each located in Queenscliff. **See:** Individual town entries for Geelong and Queenscliff in A–Z listing.

The Great Ocean Road and the Otway Range

140 km from Melbourne along the south-west coast
See: The Great Ocean Road.

Yarra Valley wineries

40–60 km from Melbourne via the Maroondah and Melba Highways, or via Heidelberg, Greensborough and the Diamond Valley

Throughout the Yarra Valley, 37 wineries and 82 vineyards, from Cottlesbridge in the north to Warburton in the south (centred on Coldstream/Yarra Glen),

VICTORIA

produce premium reds and whites that are acclaimed world-wide. Of these, 28 have cellar-door facilities and many are open daily. Some offer picnic facilities and several – such as Fergusson's, De Bortoli, Kellybrook and Yarra Burn – have restaurants on the premises. For further information on opening times and a listing of cellar-door details, contact the Yarra Valley Wine Growers' Association; (03) 9735 3929.

Healesville Sanctuary

60 km from Melbourne via the Maroondah Highway

To see all of Australia's distinctive fauna in one huge natural enclosure, take a one-day tour to Healesville Sanctuary. Many of the animals roam freely; there are 'walk-through' aviaries, excellent nocturnal displays and viewing of the extraordinary platypus. The highlight, however, is the 'Where Eagles Fly' exhibit, for which rangers and birds of prey combine in an awe-inspiring display. The sanctuary is open daily and has a kiosk, self-service restaurant, and picnic and barbecue facilities. **See also:** Healesville entry in A–Z listing.

Warburton and the Upper Yarra Reservoir

96 km via the Maroondah and Warburton Highways

This tour through some of Victoria's high country offers excellent scenic driving. Some of the Warburton-Upper Yarra Dam area may be snow-covered in mid-winter. Visit wineries in the Yarra Valley region on the way. If you visit in the warmer months, go trout fishing at Tommy Finn's Trout Farm near Warburton and picnic by the Upper Yarra Reservoir; the road on to Lake Mountain offers superb views. For a longer tour, you can return via the Acheron Way to Warburton, Yarra Junction, cross the range to Noojee, and return via Warragul and the Princes Highway. Further extend your trip and explore the Gourmet Deli region; Gippsland produces some of the world's great cheeses. **See also:** Warburton and Warragul entries in A–Z listing; and Yarra Valley wineries tour, above.

Healesville Sanctuary displays native fauna in a bushland setting

The Dandenong Ranges

50 km from Melbourne via the Burwood Highway
See: The Dandenongs.

Phillip Island

140 km from Melbourne via the South Eastern Freeway and the South Gippsland and Bass Highways
See: Phillip Island; and Cowes entry in A–Z listing.

South Gippsland and Wilsons Promontory

230 km from Melbourne via the South Gippsland Highway

Leaving Melbourne behind, you drive through Cranbourne, Korumburra and Leongatha, and the lush, rolling hills and the spectacular countryside of South Gippsland to Foster, where you turn right towards the southernmost point on the Australian mainland at Wilsons Promontory National Park. See kangaroos and koalas, and take some short (or long) bushwalks to tiny coves and sandy beaches. This tour deserves at least two days. Return along the coast road through Inverloch, a popular seaside town and Wonthaggi, South Gippsland's largest town. **See also:** Individual town entries in A–Z listing; and entry for Wilsons Promontory National Park in National Parks.

Mornington Peninsula

100 km from Melbourne via the Nepean Highway
See: The Mornington Peninsula.

The Mornington Peninsula

Cliff-top walking track at Cape Schanck, the most southerly point on the peninsula

This boot-shaped promontory separating Port Phillip and Western Port, is a mixture of holiday towns, varying in size and tourist development, and inland rural countryside. As well as safe bayside beaches, there are excellent surf beaches, particularly along the stretch of rugged coast between Portsea and Cape Schanck at the end of the Peninsula. The Mornington Peninsula National Park includes the key beaches in this area – Portsea, Sorrento, Diamond Bay, Koonya and Gunnamatta. A number of cliff-top walking tracks have been established linking Cape Schanck to Port Nepean. Swimming is considered safe only in those areas controlled by the Surf Lifesaving Association.

The Western Port side of the Peninsula is less developed, much of its foreshore having remained relatively unspoiled and being still devoted to farming and grazing land. **French Island**, which is set in the centre of this bay, was a Victorian penal settlement for forty years and is now administered by the Victorian government as a State park. The island is notable for its fauna.

The Mornington and Bellarine Peninsulas are linked for vehicle access by the Peninsula Searoad car and passenger ferry, which operates daily between Sorrento and Queenscliff. A passenger ferry links Sorrento, Portsea and Queenscliff in the summer season as well.

Frankston, now mainly a residential area for Melbourne commuters, could also be considered the gateway to the Peninsula. It is a thriving town within easy reach of good beaches on Port Phillip Bay at Daveys Bay, Canadian Bay and Mount Eliza. The National Trust-classified homestead Ballam Park (1855) in Cranbourne Road, Frankston, is open for tours and afternoon teas on Sunday afternoons. McClelland Art Gallery at Langwarrin is open Tuesday to Sunday, and public holidays except Christmas Day and Good Friday.

The Peninsula itself is well developed for tourists, with good sporting facilities and many art galleries, craft shops and restaurants. It is a burgeoning wine-producing area and many vineyards are open for tastings and cellar-door sales. On the long weekend in June, the wine producers on the Peninsula organise 'all wineries under one roof' at the Regional Gallery, Dunns Road, Mornington. Because of the area's popularity it is advisable to book accommodation, well ahead during the summer and Easter seasons. The Port Phillip Bay foreshore from **Dromana** to **Blairgowrie** is almost entirely devoted to campers and caravans during these peak seasons.

Mornington was established in 1864. The deep safe harbour at Schnapper Point first attracted settlers to this area and it has been a popular holiday town ever since. A self-guide walk introduces the town's historic buildings, including the gaol and court house on the Esplanade, and the old post office on the Esplanade corner, which is now a historic museum. The Studio City Pop and Media Museum, on Nepean Highway, has film, television, radio and pop music memorabilia. The Mornington Peninsula Art Gallery is in the Civic Reserve, Dunns Road. Railway workers' motorised trolley rides operate from Bungower Road level crossing near

Tanti Park on Sunday afternoons. A street market operates in Main Street on Wednesday mornings and on the second Sunday of each month. The Mornington Racecourse craft market operates on the second Sunday of each month at the racecourse. The coastline between the town and nearby Mount Martha features sheltered sandy bays separated by rocky bluffs and backed by steep, wooded slopes. Fossil Beach, between Mount Martha and Mornington, is one of only two exposed fossil plains in the world. Located at Mount Martha, The Briars, an old homestead (1866) and property, incorporates established gardens, buildings which house a significant collection of Napoleonic artifacts and furniture, wetland areas, bird hides and woodland walks. The property also produces its own wines.

Dromana rests at the foot of Arthurs Seat, the 305-metre mountain that provides the Peninsula with panoramic views over both bays. Safety Beach has boat-launching ramps and trailer facilities. A good road leads to the summit and a chairlift operates at weekends and school and public holidays from May to mid-September, and daily from then until to the end of April. A lookout tower, picnic reserve and licensed restaurant are at the summit. Nearby, Seawinds has beautiful gardens complete with sculptures, picnic facilities and splendid views.

Main Ridge and **Red Hill** are in the hinterland behind Arthurs Seat. At Main Ridge attractions include Kings Waterfall, in Arthurs Seat State Park; the Drum Drum wildflower farm; Seaview Nursery and tearooms; Sunny Ridge Strawberry Farm; Arthurs Seat Maze; the Pig and Whistle, an English-style pub; Arthurs Seat Riding School; and the Pine Ridge Car Museum. Red Hill is particularly well known for its Community Market, held on the first Saturday of the months September to May.

McCrae, a small resort centre, is noted for the McCrae Homestead, built in 1844 and now a National Trust property, open to the public. It was the first homestead on the Peninsula.

Rosebud is a busy commercial centre with wide foreshore camping areas.

Rye has extensive camping, picnicking and recreational foreshore areas, and boat-launching and parasailing facilities. The steamship **Wattle** runs daily cruises from the pier to the seal colonies during January.

Sorrento was the site of Victoria's first settlement in 1803, when Colonel Collins landed in this area. The early settlers' graves and a memorial to Collins can be found in the cliff-top cemetery overlooking Sullivans Bay. Sorrento was energetically developed as a watering place by George Coppin in the 1870s; the Sorrento, Koonya and Continental Hotels are fine examples of early Victorian architecture. At nearby Point King, the Union Jack was raised for the first time in Australia.

Portsea, situated at the end of the Nepean Highway, is an attractive town with excellent deepwater bayside beaches and first-class surfing at its Back Beach. Victoria's first Quarantine Station (now an Army training camp) was built here in 1856 after 82 deaths from smallpox on the vessel *Ticonderoga* anchored in Weroona Bay. Off-limits to the public until recently, this area is now incorporated into the **Mornington Peninsula National Park** which also includes Fort Nepean, the historic military fortifications that guarded the entrance to Port Phillip; self-guide walks are available. Panoramic views of the impressive rocky coastline can be enjoyed from here. Situated near Back Beach is London Bridge, a spectacular rock formation created by sea erosion.

Flinders, on the Western Port side, is the most southerly Peninsula township. It is a fishing and holiday town with good surfing, swimming and fishing. Cape Schanck lighthouse (1859), the Blowhole and Elephant Rock are all worth visiting.

Hastings, also fronting Western Port, is an attractive fishing port and holiday centre with a seawater swimming pool, yacht club, marina and boat-launching ramps south of the pier. There is a fauna park next to the high school in High Street, and a 52 000-hectare coastal area of designated wetlands north of town. South of town, there is a 2-kilometre coastal wetland walk.

Other towns on the Western Port side include **Shoreham**, a sprawling holiday settlement on Stony Creek, close to the sea. On Red Hill Road is Ashcombe Maze, which features hedge mazes surrounded by gardens. Five kilometres from Shoreham is **Point Leo**, which has one of the safest surf beaches on the Peninsula. Between Point Leo and **Balnarring**, a short access road from the main Flinders-Frankston road leads to a very pleasant beach at Merricks. Emu Plains Craft Market operates on the third Saturday of the months between November and May.

Somers, a quiet village with many holiday homes, has good beaches, excellent fishing, tennis and yacht clubs. Coolart Wetlands and Homestead features a National Trust-classified homestead dating from the 1890s, developed wetlands, bird hides and walking trails, as well as landscaped gardens. Between Somers and Crib Point is HMAS *Cerberus*, the Royal Australian Navy's largest training establishment.

The Mornington Peninsula is a rapidly growing wine-producing area. From the hinterland of Mount Martha to the shores of Western Port, many vineyards open regularly for cellar-door tastings and sales; others open by appointment only. For further detailed information, contact the Mornington Peninsula Vignerons Association.

For further information on the area contact Peninsula Tourism, Nepean Hwy, Dromana; (059) 87 3078, or the Mornington Information Centre, cnr Main and Foam Sts, Mornington; (059) 77 0186.
Map references: 214-15.

Ashcombe Maze, near Shoreham on the Western Port side of the peninsula

The Dandenongs

These ranges, 50 kilometres from the centre of Melbourne, are a tourist attraction renowned for their beauty. Heavy rainfall and rich volcanic soil have created a lush vegetation with spectacular hills and gullies crowded with creepers, tree ferns and soaring mountain ash. The area is fairly closely settled and there are a number of pretty townships dotted about the hills.

It has long been a traditional summer retreat for people from Melbourne and many of the gracious old homes have now been converted into guest houses and restaurants.

The entire area is famous for its beautiful gardens and for its great variety of European trees, particularly attractive in spring and autumn. Many excellent restaurants, art and craft galleries, antique shops and well-stocked plant nurseries add to the charm of these hills, ideally placed for a relaxed day's outing from Melbourne. At 633 metres, Mount Dandenong is the highest point of the ranges, and at its summit there are excellent views, picnic facilities and a restaurant from which a magnificent night-time view of Melbourne can be seen.

Ferntree Gully National Park, Doongalla and Sherbrooke Forest are part of the 1920-hectare **Dandenong Ranges National Park,** where you can see lush trees and ferns, and a wide variety of flora and fauna. The lyrebird and eastern whipbird can be heard here. Sherbrooke Forest, on the road from Belgrave to Kallista, is unspoiled bushland with a large population of lyrebirds. A tourist road runs through the park area from Ferntree Gully to Montrose. William Ricketts Sanctuary, on Mount Dandenong Tourist Road, is a natural forest area in which Ricketts, a musician and naturalist who died in 1993, sculpted a number of Aboriginal figures and symbolic scenes in clay. Near Sherbrooke the Alfred Nicholas Memorial Gardens, 13 hectares of a formerly private garden, are open to the public.

The Puffing Billy narrow-gauge steam train, one of the Dandenongs' most famous attractions, leaves from Belgrave and travels 14 kilometres to Emerald Lake. The Puffing Billy Steam Museum at Menzies Creek, open Saturday, Sunday and public holidays, displays some restored locomotives and rolling-stock. This small train runs daily except on Christmas Day and fire-ban days. A timetable is available from the RACV, 230 Collins St, Melbourne, (03) 9650 1522; or telephone (03) 9870 8411 for recorded information. Each April, the Great Train Race is held: runners attempt to race Puffing Billy from Belgrave to Emerald Lake Park.

Emerald was the first settlement in the area and is situated on a high ridge. It has a number of interesting galleries and in the surrounding countryside there are lavender farms and attractive picnic spots. Olinda, a pretty township, is the location of the National Rhododendron Gardens which is even more beautiful in spring, when the annual show is held. Another spring flower festival is Tesselaar's tulip festival held at Tesselaar's Farm near Silvan.

For further information on the Dandenongs, contact the Tourism hotline on (03) 9751 2344 or the Victorian Visitor Information Centre, cnr Little Collins and Swanston Sts, Melbourne; (03) 9650 1522. **See also:** National Parks; and town entry for Emerald in A–Z listing. **Map references:** 210, 213 M7, 216 A11, 226 E4.

Alfred Nicholas Memorial Gardens, near Sherbrooke

VICTORIA from A to Z

The Great Ocean Road, near Anglesea

Alexandra Pop. 1965

MAP REF. 213 O1, 235 J11

Alexandra is a farming and holiday centre, 24 km W of Lake Eildon. The nearby Goulburn River is one of the most important freshwater fisheries, particularly for fly-fishers, close to Melbourne. **Of interest:** Timber and Tramway Museum in former railway station, Station St. Historic buildings: National Trust-classified post office and adjacent law courts, Downey St. Also in Downey St: Alexandra Potters (closed Sun.); Myrtle House Gallery for local crafts (open weekends). Community Market, last Sat. each month. Easter: Art show. Oct.: Open gardens weekend. **In the area:** Fraser National Park, excellent walks; 12 km E. Bonnie Doon, on Lake Eildon: good base for trail-riding, bushwalking, water sports and scenic drives; 37 km NE. McKenzie Nature Reserve, virgin bushland with abundance of winter and spring orchids; at southern edge of town. Taggerty, 18 km S in the Acheron Valley: good trout fishing in nearby rivers; Pioneer Education Centre. Cathedral Range State Park, 3 km S from Taggerty, for camping, bushwalking, rock climbing and trout fishing. **Tourist information:** Redgate Nursery and Craft Cottage, 73 Downey St; (057) 72 2169; 1800 652 298. **Accommodation:** 4 hotels, 2 motels, 8 B&B, 2 cara./camp. parks.

Anglesea Pop. 1965

MAP REF. 212 E12, 219 C11, 229 Q9

This attractive seaside town on the Great Ocean Rd offers excellent swimming and surfing. The golf course is renowned for its tame kangaroos that graze there. **Of interest:** Melaleuca Gallery, Great Ocean Rd. Coogoorah Park, on Anglesea River: bushland reserve, waterways, islands, boardwalks, bridges and picnic areas. Viewing platform overlooking open-cut, brown-coal mine and power station; behind town in Coalmine Rd. Sept.: Angair wildflower festival. **In the area:** J.E. Loveridge Lookout, 1 km W. Point Roadknight beach, 2 km SW. Angahook-Lorne State Park, attractive reserve with many walking tracks; access from Anglesea or Aireys Inlet (10 km SW on Great Ocean Rd). At Aireys Inlet: Lighthouse; Eagle Rock Pde. Further south, Memorial Arch, commemorating construction of Great Ocean Rd in 1920s. Spectacular 35-km Surf Coast Walk, from Jan Juc (south of Torquay) to Moggs Creek (south of Aireys Inlet); brochure available. Ironbark Basin for walks, birdlife and cliff-top views of coastline; north off Point Addis Rd. **Tourist information:** From caravan, Anglesea Riverbank (Christmas–Easter, daily; winter, Fri.–Mon.). **Accommodation:** 3 motels, 4 cara./ camp. parks. **See also:** The Great Ocean Road; The Western District.

Apollo Bay Pop. 894

MAP REF. 217 G12, 229 N12

The Great Ocean Rd leads to this attractive coastal town, the centre of a rich dairying and fishing area, and the base for a huge fish-freezing plant. The wooded mountainous hinterland offers memorable scenery and there is excellent sea and river fishing in the area. The rugged and beautiful coastline has been the scene of many shipwrecks in the past. **Of interest:** Bass Strait Shell Museum, Noel St. Old Cable Station Museum, Great Ocean Rd. Self-guide walks; leaflet from Tourist information. Mar.: Music festival. **In the area:** Carisbrook Falls, 14 km NE on Great Ocean Rd; nearby walking tracks to spectacular views. Grey River Scenic Reserve, 24 km NE. Marriners Lookout for views across Skenes Creek and Apollo Bay; 1.6 km NW. Crows Nest Lookout; 5 km NW, on Tuxion Rd. Paradise Scenic Reserve in beautiful Barham River Valley; 10 km NW. Beauchamp Falls, 20 km NW; scenic walk from picnic area to falls. Otway National Park, 13 km SW: excellent bushwalking through park to sea; Elliot River and adjacent Shelly Beach; popular Maits Rest rainforest boardwalk, 17 km W; 300-yr-old National Trust-registered native beech tree. Lavers Hill, once a booming timber centre; 53 km W. Melba Gully State Park, 3 km W of Lavers Hill: fern gullies, myrtle beech trees, also glow-worm habitat; self-guide rainforest walk available. Scenic touring roads: Turton's Track, 25 km N; and Wild Dog Road, 3 km E. **Tourist information:** 155 Great Ocean Rd; (052) 37 6529. **Accommodation:** 2 hotels, 20 motels, 6 cara./camp. parks. **See also:** The Great Ocean Road.

Ararat Pop. 7633

MAP REF. 222 D8, 229 K2, 231 K13

The Ararat area gold boom came in 1857. It was short-lived and sheep farming became the basis of the town's economy. Today the town is the commercial centre of a prosperous farming and winegrowing region. The area also produces fine merino wool. The first vines in the district were planted by French settlers in 1863 and the town of

Great Western, 16 km NW of Ararat, gave its name to some of Australia's most famous wines. **Of interest:** Beautiful bluestone buildings in Barkly St: post office, splendid town hall, civic square and war memorial. Also in Barkly St: Ararat Art Gallery, regional gallery specialising in wool and fibre pieces by leading artists. Chinese Gold Discovery Memorial, Lambert St. Langi Morgala Folk Museum, Queen St, displays Aboriginal weapons and artifacts. Alexandra Park and Botanical Gardens, Vincent St: orchid glasshouse display, walk-in fernery and herb garden. J-Ward, Old Ararat Gaol, off Lowe St; open Sun., guided tours, groups by appt. Oct.: Golden gateway festival. **In the area:** Green Hill Lake, a constructed lake, ideal for fishing and water sports; 4 km E off Western Hwy. Langi Ghiran State Park, 14 km E off Western Hwy, has scenic walks and children's playground. At Buangor, 23 km SE: century-old Buangor Hotel and old Cobb & Co. changing station (c. 1860); 18 km further on, Mt Buangor State Park includes Fern Tree Waterfalls. Wineries, most open for tastings and cellar-door sales, north-west of town: Garden Gully Vineyard (15 km), Seppelt's Great Western Vineyards (17 km) established in 1865 and specialising in dry red and sparkling wines (its underground cellars classified by National Trust) and Best's wines (19 km); east of town: Mt Langi Ghiran Wines (20 km); south of town: Montara Winery (3 km); west of town: Cathcart Ridge Winery (6 km). Cathcart 6 km W, and, further 20 km W, Mafeking, once a bustling settlement with 10 000 people. Care must be taken when walking in these areas; watch for deep mine shafts. **Tourist information:** Barkly St; (053) 52 2096. **Accommodation:** 5 hotels, 6 motels, 4 B&B, 2 cara./camp. parks. **See also:** Wine Regions.

Avoca   Pop. 1004

MAP REF. 222 I5, 231 M12

In the Central Highlands region, Avoca was established with the discovery of gold in the area in 1852. Located at the junction of the Sunraysia and Pyrenees Hwys, the surrounding Pyrenees Range foothills offer attractive bushwalking and possible sighting of kangaroos, wallabies and koalas. **Of interest:** Early National Trust-classified bluestone buildings: old gaol and powder magazine, Camp St; court house and one of State's earliest pharmacies, Lalor's, in High St. Rock and Gem Museum, High St. Market, 2nd Sat. each month. Oct.: Wool and wine festival, includes Avoca Cup (horse race). **In the area:** Fishing: Avoca River, near town; Wimmera River 42 km W; Bet Bet Creek, 11 km E. Several wineries including Mt Avoca vineyard, 7 km W; Chateau Remy Vineyards, 8 km W; Redbank Winery, Redbank, 20 km NW; Summerfield Winery, Moonambel Village, 20 km NW; Mountain Creek Vineyard and Warrenmang Vineyard, NE of Moonambel; Taltarni Wines and Dalwhinnie Wines, 5 km W of Moonambel. **Tourist information:** High St; (054) 65 3767. **Accommodation:** 2 hotels, 2 motels, 1 cara./camp. park. **See also:** Wine Regions.

Bacchus Marsh   Pop. 13 000

MAP REF. 212 G5, 223 R13, 226 A3, 229 R4

The trees of the Avenue of Honour provide an impressive entrance from the east to Bacchus Marsh, which is 49 km from Melbourne. This long-established town is in a fertile valley, once marshland, between the Werribee and Lerderderg Rivers. **Of interest:** Manor House, Manor St, home of town's founder, Captain Bacchus; privately owned. In Main St: original blacksmith's shop and cottage; court house, lockup and National Bank (all National Trust-classified); Border Inn (1850), thought to have been first coaching service stop in Victoria when Bacchus Marsh was a staging post for Cobb & Co. coaches travelling to goldfields. In Gisborne Rd: Holy Trinity Anglican Church (1877); Express Building Art Gallery. Ra Ceramics and Crafts, Station St. Big Apple Tourist Orchard, Avenue of Honour. Sept.: Pioneer Day festival. **In the area:** Lerderderg Gorge, for picnics, bushwalking and swimming; 10 km N. At Blackwood, 26 km NW: Mineral Springs Reserve; and Garden of St Erth. Long Forest Flora Reserve features bull mallee, some specimens centuries old; 2 km NE. Merrimu Reservoir and Wombat State Forest; both about 10 km NE. Willows Historic Homestead, Melton, 14 km E. Maddingley open-cut coal mine, 3 km S. Brisbane Ranges National Park, 16 km SW: steep-sided Anakie Gorge, walking tracks and wildflowers in spring. Werribee Gorge, 10 km W. Wineries and vineyards: St Anne's Vineyard on the Western Fwy, 6 km W, has old bluestone cellar built from remains of old Ballarat gaol; Craiglee Winery and Goonawarra Vineyard, Sunbury, 47 km NE; Wildwood Vineyard, Bulla, 9 km SE. **Tourist information:** Shire Offices, Main Street; (053) 67 2111. **Accommodation:** 4 hotels, 1 motel, 1 cara./camp. park. **See also:** The Golden Age.

Bairnsdale   Pop. 10 770

MAP REF. 227 P4, 236 F13

Located on the river flats of the Mitchell River, this East Gippsland trade centre and holiday town is at the junction of the Princes Hwy, the Omeo Hwy and the road east to Lakes Entrance. Its position makes Bairnsdale an excellent base for touring the region. **Of interest:** Historical Museum (1891), contains items of local historical interest; Macarthur St. St Mary's Church, features wall and ceiling murals by Italian artist Francesco Floreani; Main St. Adjacent to post office, Port of Bairnsdale site and river walk. Mar.: Riviera festival. **In the area:** Lindenow, 19 km W. Nearby, Mitchell River National Park: good bushwalking tracks; Den of Nargun, Aboriginal cultural site in gorge. Mitchell River empties into Lake King at Eagle Point Bluff, world's second longest silt jetty. Boardwalk (closed during duck season) across part of McLeod's Morass, a bird wetland habitat; main access about 10 km S. Jolly Jumbuk Country Craft Centre, woollen products for sale; 5 km E on Princes Hwy. Metung, 30 km E: picturesque fishing village on shores of Lake King, some solid pioneer holiday homes still standing. Scenic drive north along Omeo Hwy through Tambo River valley; stunning in spring when wattles bloom. Nicholson River Winery, 10 km E, and Golvinda winery, 5 km N. **Tourist information:** 240 Main Street; (051) 52 3444. **Accommodation:** 3 hotels, 10 motels, 1 B&B, 1 hostel, 3 cara./camp. parks. **See also:** Gippsland Lakes.

Ballan   Pop. 1053

MAP REF. 212 F4, 223 Q12, 229 Q4, 234 C13

A small town on the Werribee River, noted for its mineral springs. **Of interest:** Caledonian Park, eastern edge of town, offers picnic areas and swimming. Mar.: Arcadian festival. **In the area:** Good trout fishing in Pikes Creek Reservoir, 12 km E. **Tourist information:** Shire Offices, cnr Stead and Steiglitz Sts; (053) 68 1001. **Accommodation:** 2 hotels, 2 cara. parks.

The elegant statuary pavilion in the Botanic Gardens, Ballarat

Ballarat
Pop. 64 980

MAP REF. 212 C4, 221, 223 M11, 229 O3, 234 A13

Ballarat is Victoria's largest inland city, situated in the Central Highlands. Its inner areas retain much of the charm of its gold-boom era, with many splendid original buildings still standing. Ballarat was just a small rural township in 1851, when its enormously rich alluvial goldfields were discovered. Within two years it had a population of nearly 40 000. Australia's only civil battle occurred here in 1854, when miners refused to pay Government licence fees and fought with police and troops at the Eureka Stockade. Today Ballarat is a bustling city featuring many galleries, museums, and antique and craft shops. It has excellent recreational facilities and beautiful garden areas and parks, making it most attractive to visitors. The begonia is the city's floral emblem. **Of interest:** In Lydiard St: Fine Art Gallery, Australia's largest and oldest regional gallery, has comprehensive collection of Australian art, including works by Lindsay family, and the original Eureka Flag; Her Majesty's Theatre (1875), oldest, intact, purpose-built theatre in Australia; Craig's Royal Hotel, George Hotel and Ballarat Terrace (1889) for dining and accommodation in old-world surroundings. Constructed Lake Wendouree, used for water sports; paddle-steamer tours with commentary on history of city. Botanic Gardens adjoining the lake area: Robert Clarke Horticultural Centre, showcase for famous begonias; Adam Lindsay Gordon Cottage; Tramway Museum, vintage trams; Prime Ministers' Avenue, displaying busts of Australian prime ministers; elegant statuary pavilion nearby. Vintage Tramway, via Wendouree Pde; rides weekends, public and school holidays. The award-winning Montrose Cottage (1856), first masonry cottage built on the goldfields, and Eureka Museum; Eureka St. Eureka Exhibition, historical information on Eureka Rebellion; cnr Stawell and Eureka Sts. The Old Curiosity Shop, pioneer relics; Queen St. In Stawell St South: Eureka Stockade Park, with life-size replica of the famous battle; self-guide Eureka Trail. Ballarat Wildlife and Reptile Park, cnr of York and Fussell Sts. Sovereign Hill, in Main St, is a major tourist attraction; it is a world-class reconstruction of a goldmining settlement with orientation centre and working displays and features Blood on the Southern Cross, a night sight-and-sound exhibition; panning for gold; re-created shops and businesses; during Begonia festival in Mar., guided lamplight tours of Sovereign Hill; excellent barbecue facilities; kiosk, restaurant and licensed hotel; and Government Camp, comfortable family-type accommodation. Adjoining Sovereign Hill, Gold Museum features exhibits of gold history, large collection of gold coins and display of the uses of gold 'today and tomorrow'. Mar.: Begonia festival; Opera festival. **In the area:** Great Southern Woolshed, an authentic working woolshed with demonstrations by shearers, classers and working sheep dogs; 8 km E. Nearby, Kryal Castle, reconstruction of a medieval castle; family entertainment. White Swan Reservoir, attractive picnic spot with water views; 8 km NE off Daylesford Rd. Lake Burrumbeet: good water sports, scenic picnic spots and excellent trout fishing; 22 km NW. On western edge of city, Avenue of Honour (22 km) and Arch of Victory, honouring those who fought in World War I. Well-known Yellowglen Winery, Smythesdale; 24 km SW. Berringa Mines Historic Reserve, 8 km SE of Smythesdale. Enfield State Park, near Enfield, 16 km S of Ballarat. Mt Buninyong Lookout, 360° views; 13 km SE. Lal Lal Falls (30 m) on Moorabool River, 18 km SE of city. Nearby, Lal Lal Blast Furnace, beautiful archaeological remains from 19th century. **Tourist information:** Cnr Sturt and Albert Sts; (053) 32 2694. **Accommodation:** 11 hotels, 27 motels, 29 B&B, 1 hostel, 8 cara./camp. parks. **See also:** The Golden Age; Wine Regions.

Beaufort
Pop. 1171

MAP REF. 222 H9, 229 M3

This small town on the Western Hwy, midway between Ballarat and Ararat, has a gold-rush history, like so many of the other towns in this area. The discovery of gold at Fiery Creek swelled its population in the late 1850s to nearly 100 000. Today Beaufort is primarily a centre for the surrounding pastoral and agricultural district. **Of interest:** Historic court house (key available from Tourist information), Livingstone St. Turn-of-century band rotunda, Neill St. **In the area:** Mt Cole State Forest, part of Great Dividing Range: peaceful natural area, bushwalks, native flora and fauna, picnic and camping facilities; 16 km NW, via Raglan. Lake Goldsmith, 14 km S; steam rally held in May. **Tourist information:** Shire Offices, 5 Lawrence St; (053) 49 2000, or The Cooperative Crafts, Lawrence St. **Accommodation:** 1 hotel, 1 motel, 1 cara./camp. park.

Beechworth
Pop. 3136

MAP REF. 235 O6, 236 A3

Once the centre of the great Ovens goldmining region, Beechworth lies 24 km off the Ovens Hwy, between Wangaratta and Wodonga on 'The Kelly Way' (Old Sydney Rd). This is one of Victoria's best-preserved and most beautiful gold towns, magnificently sited in the foothills of the Alps. Its public buildings are of architectural merit and the whole

Shamrock Hotel, Bendigo

town has been classified as historically important by the National Trust. The rich alluvial goldfield at Woolshed Creek was discovered by a local shepherd during the 1850s. A total of 4 121 918 ounces of gold was mined in 14 years. A story is told of Daniel Cameron, campaigning to represent the Ovens Valley community: he rode through the town at the head of a procession of miners from Woolshed, on a horse shod with golden shoes. Sceptics claim they were merely gilded, but the tale is an indication of what Beechworth was like during the boom, when its population was 42 000 and it boasted 61 hotels and a theatre at which international celebrities performed. **Of interest:** Fine 1850s government buildings built of local honey-coloured granite, all still in use; especially in Camp and Ford Sts. Daily historic town tour from Tourist information; bookings essential. In Albert Rd: Harness and Carriage Museum, run by National Trust; Tanswell's Hotel, privately restored lacework building; Ned Kelly's cell, under Shire Offices; Beechworth Gaol (1859), still used as a prison. Former Bank of Victoria building, now Rock Cavern with gemstone collection; cnr Camp and Ford Sts. In Ford St: historic former Bank of Australasia, now offering fine dining in elegant surroundings; Country Rustica and Buckland Gallery. In Camp St: Beechworth Galleries; Beechworth Bakery. In Loch St: Robert O'Hara Burke Memorial Museum, displays relics of gold rush and features 16 mini-shops depicting town's main street as it was more than 100 years ago. Feb.: Drive Back in Time (rally of vintage, veteran and classic vehicles). Easter: Golden Horseshoes festival. **In the area:** Beechworth Historic Park, surrounds Beechworth area: Woolshed Falls historic walk through former alluvial goldmining sites; Gorge Scenic Drive (5 km) starts north of town; gold fossicking in limited areas. Golden Hills Trout Farm, 2 km S. Stanley, historic village 4 km S, in hills set above Beechworth, among apple orchards, berry farms, nut plantations and tall forests. Fletcher Dam, Beechworth Forest Drive, 3 km SE towards Stanley. Kelly's lookout, Woolshed Creek, about 4 km N. On road north to Chiltern: Beechworth Cemetery; Chinese burning towers; Chinese cemetery. **Tourist information:** Rock Cavern, cnr Ford and Camp Sts; (057) 28 1374. **Accommodation:** 2 hotels, 5 motels, 11 B&B, 2 cara./camp. parks.

Benalla   Pop. 8334

MAP REF. 224 A2, 235 K7

This small city, just off the Hume Fwy, is 40 km SW of Wangaratta. Lake Benalla, created in the Broken River which runs through the city, has recreation and picnic facilities, and a bird sanctuary. During the late 1870s Benalla experienced the activities of the notorious Kelly Gang, who were eventually captured at nearby Glenrowan in 1880. It is also the birthplace of Sir Edward ('Weary') Dunlop, and Michael J. Savage, NZ Prime Minister in the 1940s. **Of interest:** In Bridge St: Botanical Gardens, with splendid rose gardens; Benalla Art Gallery, on shores of lake, features important Ledger Collection of Australian paintings; open daily. In Mair St: a 3-dimensional ceramic mural; Pots 'n' More, for paintings, pottery and craft; Costume and Pioneer Museum, has Ned Kelly's cummerbund on display. At aerodrome on northern outskirts of town: centre for Gliding Club of Victoria; hot-air ballooning and glider flights available. Easter: Felix arts festival. Nov.: Rose festival. **In the area:** Reef Hills State Park, 4 km S on Midland Hwy: 2 040 ha of forest with wide variety of native flora and fauna. Pleasant day trip south-east to King Valley and spectacular Paradise Falls. Winton Motor Raceway, 10 km NE. **Tourist information:** Pots 'n' More, 14 Mair St; (057) 62 1749. **Accommodation:** 5 hotels, 8 motels, 1 B&B, 1 cara./camp. park.

Bendigo   Pop. 57 427

MAP REF. 220, 223 Q2, 231 Q9, 234 C8

This is one of Victoria's most famous goldmining towns. Sited at the junction of five highways, it is central for trips to many other gold towns nearby. The gold rush began here in 1851 and gold production continued for 100 years. The affluence of the period can still be seen today in many splendid public and commercial buildings. **Of interest:** Shamrock Hotel (1897), Bendigo's famous landmark; cnr Pall Mall and Williamson St. Sacred Heart Cathedral, largest outside Melbourne; Wattle St. Alexandra Fountain at Charing Cross. Renaissance-style post office (1887) and law courts (1896), Pall Mall. Self-guide heritage walk; brochure available from Tourist information. Bendigo Art Gallery (1890), View St; open daily. Central Deborah Gold Mine, in working order, a vivid reminder of Bendigo's history; Violet St, open daily. Vintage Talking Trams (taped commentary), run daily from mine on 8-km city trip; includes stop at Tram Depot Museum displaying 30 vintage trams. Golden Dragon Museum, Bridge St: Chinese history of goldfields and largest display of Chinese processional regalia in the world, including world's oldest imperial dragon 'Loong' and longest imperial dragon 'Sun Loong' (more than 100 m long). National Trust-classified Dudley House (1859), historical display; View St. Lookout tower in Rosalind Park. Discovery Science and Technology Centre, hands-on displays; Railway Pl. Bendigo Woollen Mills, factory tours; Lansell St West. Sun. market, Showgrounds, Holmes Rd. Mar.: Madison 10 000 cycling race. Easter: Fair (first held 1871, features Chinese dragon). Apr.: Chrysanthemum show. Oct.: Orchid club spring show. Nov.: National swap meet (Australia's largest meet for vintage car and bike enthusiasts); Racing carnival. **In the area:** Excellent art and

The Golden Age

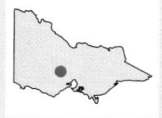

The cities and towns of the goldfields region of Victoria came to a peak of style and affluence in the 1880s, an affluence built on the first gold discoveries in the 1850s. The towns display all the frivolity and grandeur of Victorian architecture, having grown up during a period when it was believed that gold and wealth would be a permanent benefit in Victoria.

The two major cities of the region are Ballarat and Bendigo, but there are many other towns, large and small, in the area. They all have beautiful historic houses and public buildings, and many have other trappings of the past — statues, public gardens (some with lakes), ornamental bandstands and grand avenues of English trees. Spring and autumn are the best seasons to visit this region, because then there are not the extremes of summer and winter temperatures, and the flowers and foliage are at their best.

It is a quiet region now. The remaining small towns serve the surrounding rich pastoral district, and secondary industries and services centre on the two cities.

It was once, however, an area of frantic activity. Gold was found at Clunes in 1851 and within three months 8000 people were on the diggings in the area between Buninyong and Ballarat. Nine months later 30 000 people were on the goldfields and four years later 100 000. The population of the city of Melbourne dwindled alarmingly and immigrants rushed to the diggings from Great Britain, America and many other countries. Ships' crews, and sometimes even their captains, abandoned their vessels and trekked to the diggings to try their luck. Tent cities sprang up on the plains as men dug and panned for gold. There were remarkable finds of huge nuggets in the early days, but finally the amount of gold obtained by panning in the rivers and by digging grew less and less. The communities were remarkable: there were shanty towns, the streets crowded day and night with hawkers and traders; there were pubs and dancing-rooms, and continuous sounds of music and revelry.

As time went on, the surface gold was worked out and expensive company-backed operations followed: mining in deep shafts, then the ore was stamped and crushed in steam-powered plants on the surface. The success of these methods heralded a new era, that of the company mines, outside investors and stock-exchange speculation. It led to a much more stable workforce and to the well-established communities that slowly evolved into the towns of the region today. As the pastoral and industrial potential began to be realised and fully exploited, it was the perfect scene for expansion and optimism.

The years between 1870 and 1890 saw the towns embellished with fine civic buildings, mansions, solid town houses, churches, hotels and all the trappings of affluence. Thus Ballarat, Bendigo, Castlemaine and to a lesser extent Clunes, Creswick, Daylesford and Maldon became extraordinary *nouveau riche* visions of the current British taste.

The Western Highway between Melbourne and Ballarat is at its most scenic as it rises into the Pentland Hills. Rounded volcanic hills encircle **Bacchus Marsh**, which is approached by a magnificent avenue of North American elms commemorating soldiers who died in the Great War. Bacchus Marsh is adjacent to the Lerderderg and Werribee Rivers, which enter dramatic gorges close to the town. Just off the highway are the small rural towns of Myrniong and Ballan, Gordon and Bungaree. South of the highway near Bungaree is Dunnstown, dominated by its bluestone distillery and the bulk of Mount Warrenheip, where an excellent view of the district can be had from the summit.

A turnoff to the south near Ballarat leads to Buninyong, the scene of one of the first gold strikes in Victoria. Gold was discovered here at Hiscock's Gully in 1851. The impressive township of Buninyong with its grand tree-lined main street has a number of striking buildings: the Crown Hotel and white-walled Uniting Church are of the 1860s, while the combined council chambers and court house of 1886 are in rich Italianate design, unified by a central clock tower.

The city of **Ballarat** was laid out to the west of the diggings within twelve months of the first discovery of gold. The design included a magnificent chief thoroughfare, Sturt Street, wide enough for future plantations and monuments. The primitive buildings of early settlement were gradually replaced by boom-style architecture in the 1880s. Italianate, Romanesque, Gothic and French Renaissance styles are mingled; porticoes, colonnades and ornamental stone facades vie with verandahs of lavish cast-iron decoration. There are many superb buildings, the most notable being the post office, the railway station, the town hall, the stock exchange, the former Ballarat gaol, the Wesley Church, the George Hotel, Reids Coffee Palace, the Bailey Mansion, the Roman Catholic bishop's residence, Loreto Abbey and the art gallery. It is a city of many beautiful gardens, particularly the Botanic Gardens adjacent to Lake Wendouree, famous for the annual begonia display in March.

Without doubt the major attraction in Ballarat is Sovereign Hill. This re-created goldmining township is a fascinating place for a day's outing to interest all the family. Begin your outing by visiting the excellent 'Voyage to Discovery' orientation centre, near the main entrance, and end it at 'Blood of the Southern Cross', a sound-and-light spectacular re-creating the Eureka uprising in 1854.

Gold was discovered in Ballarat in 1851, and a visit to the Red Hill Gully Diggings at Sovereign Hill will show you something of the life of those early days. Your visit will not be complete without the chance to pan for 'colour'. A friendly digger will give you a lesson, but you must be sure to purchase your licence first or you may find yourself being arrested by the watchful trooper!

Main Street at Sovereign Hill is lined with faithfully re-created shops and businesses of the 1851–1861 period. These are based on actual shops and businesses that were operating in Ballarat at that time – the services that supported the influx of people to the goldfields. Perhaps you will be tempted by the aroma of freshly-baked bread from the wood-fire brick oven of the Hope Bakery. Next door you may dress in topcoat or crinoline and be photographed in true Victorian pose. Across the road, mid-nineteenth-century printing-presses in the Ballarat *Times* office can be used to print your name on a WANTED poster, similar to that issued for Lalor and Black after the uprising at the Eureka Stockade in 1854.

Few can even pass the well-stocked grocery in Main Street without a surge of nostalgia for days gone by. The tiny sweet shop nearby sells all manner of sweets made to Victorian recipes at Brown's confectionery factory, further up the street. Those with larger appetites may wine and dine at the United States Hotel or enjoy a digger's lunch of soup, roast meat and apple pie at the New York Bakery. For some energetic relaxation, try your hand at ninepin bowling on the 40-metre-long alley in the Empire Bowling Saloon. The accommodation

Main Street at Sovereign Hill, Ballarat's famous tourist attraction

complex, Government Camp, provides comfortable and inexpensive lodging ranging from tents to self-contained units, while Sovereign Hill Lodge, a recent addition, offers quality accommodation.

During school terms you will be enchanted to watch a 'class of 1856' at the Red Hill National School. Here children dress in period costume, learn from actual 1850s texts, and are totally involved in living the lives of mid-nineteenth-century goldfields children.

The towering poppet-head, the hiss of steam and the thunder of the stamper battery will draw you to the Sovereign Quartz Mine. Take a guided tour of the underground area; here you will see examples of early mining techniques and even some original workings of the 1880s.

As you wander through the streets you will meet costumed diggers and businessfolk, and ladies in bell-shaped crinolines and bonnets. Stop and talk to them and you will learn more about life in the days of the 'rush'.

Sovereign Hill is open daily, except on Christmas Day. There are admission charges, and there is ample parking available near the entrance.

The Gold Museum, opposite Sovereign Hill, has a collection of nuggets, alluvial gold and coins, as well as a Eureka Exhibition outlining the Eureka rebellion. While in Ballarat it is also worth visiting historic Montrose Cottage, the Ballarat Wildlife Park, the Fine Art Gallery and the Eureka precinct.

Beyond Ballarat, on the Midland Highway is **Creswick**, a picturesque valley town with a wonderfully ornate town hall. The bluestone tower of St John's Church dominates the town's western hill and on the hilltop across the valley is a Tudor-style hospital building which is now a school of forestry.

Turn off the highway to **Clunes** where gold was discovered in July 1851. It proved difficult to get supplies to this remote township, so the rush was limited and the later discoveries at Buninyong and Ballarat quickly diverted attention from the area. Of particular interest in Clunes are the rich verandahed facades in the shopping area of Fraser Street and the elegant architectural style of the banks, hotels, post office and town hall.

On the Western Highway, 133 kilometres north-west of Ballarat, past **Ararat** (where a gold rush began in 1857), is **Stawell**. Gold was discovered at the present site of Stawell in 1853; by 1857 there was a population of 30 000, and the township was proclaimed in 1858. Goldmining continued in the area until 1920. Today visitors can recapture some of the atmosphere of the gold-rush era at the Mount Pleasant Diggings and Alluvial Gold Memorial.

North-east of Ballarat up the Midland Highway is **Daylesford**, another former goldmining town set in picturesque wooded hills around Wombat Hill

Gardens and Lake Daylesford. The town has many churches in the Gothic Revival style and an imposing town hall, post office and school. On the hill are groves of rhododendrons, exotic trees and a lookout tower that provides a view of Mount Franklin (a perfectly preserved volcanic crater) and Mount Tarrengower. Several kilometres north of Daylesford are natural springs containing lime, iron, magnesia and other minerals. This is the famed Hepburn Spa, which attracted visitors in the nineteenth century for its medicinal properties and is still popular with tourists. Bottling mineral water is the town's main industry.

Further north on the road to Bendigo is **Castlemaine**, a larger town and one of the most picturesque in the region. The streetscape in the centre of the town has remained virtually unaltered since the early days, for the prosperity of the 1860s diminished and the town settled down to a quieter rural life. One of the most notable buildings is the town market, an unusual Palladian-inspired building which was restored in 1974 and which now contains a museum portraying the history of the town and the Mount Alexander goldfields. The town boasts some other fine buildings, including the post office in Italianate style with a central clock tower, the former telegraph office, the mechanics' institute, the Imperial Hotel and the Commercial Banking Company building. The stone and redbrick gaol, and the obelisk built in 1862 to commemorate the ill-fated Burke and Wills expedition, are high on the hill above the town.

Nearby **Maldon** was declared a notable town by the National Trust in 1962. The winding streets are flanked by low buildings, with deep verandahs shading the bluestone pavements laid in 1866.

The city of **Bendigo** is the jewel of the region and is Victoria's most outstanding example of a boom town. Gothic- and classical-style buildings have been designed in vast proportions, richly ornamented and combined with the materials of the age, cast iron and cast cement.

The post office and law courts are among the most impressive high-Victorian public buildings in Australia. Opposite the post office is the Shamrock Hotel — a massive, verandahed structure that once boasted an electric bell to ring for service in each of its 100 rooms. Many of Bendigo's important buildings were designed by the German architect William Charles Vahland. His work included the Benevolent asylum and hospital, the school of mines, the mechanics' institute, the town hall, the Masonic hall, the Capital theatre, four banks and the handsome Alexandra fountain at Charing Cross, the centre of Bendigo.

Bendigo Art Gallery houses a large collection of 19th-century British and European artworks and decorative arts, and an outstanding collection of Australian paintings; including works by the goldfields artist, S.T. Gill.

Central Deborah Goldmine was the last deep-reef goldmine in Bendigo. Sunk in 1909 and closed in 1954, it has been restored and is open for inspection. The underground mine tour is claimed to be the best in Australia. The mine is 411 metres deep with seventeen levels, and the visitor level at 61 metres has a 350-metre circuit illustrating the geological features of the Bendigo region and the machinery used in the gold-retrieval process. At ground level are the 21-metre poppet head, the engine room, installations and other exhibits, all of which can be inspected. The mine is also the point of departure for the 8-kilometre (1-hour) tour

Flora statue in the Botanic Gardens, Ballarat

through Bendigo by the city's famous Vintage Talking Trams, with their taped commentary on attractions and historic points of interest.

The goldfields region can be enjoyed in three days or three weeks, according to time and taste. Bendigo Goldseeker Tours organise gold-fossicking excursions and include instruction in the use of metal detectors. A great way to see the region is via the 'Goldfields Tourist Route', a 450-kilometre triangle road route linking Ballarat, Ararat, Stawell, **Avoca, Maryborough,** Bendigo, Castlemaine and Daylesford. Free maps marking the route are available at the Victorian Visitor Information Centre, cnr Little Collins and Swanston Sts, Melbourne, all RACV offices and various tourist information centres throughout the goldfields.

More detailed information can be obtained from the Bendigo Tourist Information Centre, 51–67 Pall Mall; (054) 47 7788. **See also:** individual entries in A–Z listing for those towns indicated by bold type. **Map references:** 220–23.

antiques. Fortuna Villa mansion (1871), Chum St, 2 km S; open Sun. One Tree Hill observation tower, panoramic views; 4 km S. At Mandurang, 8 km SE, historic Chateau Dore winery, open daily; Orchid Nursery; Tannery Lane Pottery. Camel Farm, rides and treks (check opening times); Sedgwick, 20 km SE. Arakoon Resort, aquatic fun park (check opening times); 18 km SE. Lake Eppalock, 26 km SE: camping, fishing and water sports; nearby (9 km N of Redesdale), Eppalock Ridge winery; open by appt. Bendigo Cactus Gardens, (established 1937) classified by National Trust; White Hills, 3 km NE. At Epsom, 6 km NE: Bendigo Pottery, Australia's oldest working pottery (tours and sales, open daily); Central Victorian Motor Museum, part of Pottery complex; Sun. market. National Trust-classified Chinese Joss House, built by Chinese miners; Emu Point, 1 km N, open daily. At Whipstick State Park, 21 km N: wildlife, old goldmining areas, bushwalking, cycling; goldpanning in gullies after rains; nearby, Hartland's Eucalyptus Factory and Historic Farm (open daily), built 1890 to process eucalyptus oil obtained from surrounding scrub. Eaglehawk, site of goldrush in 1852, 6.5 km NW: reminders of mining days; fine examples of 19th century architecture, many classified by National Trust; self-guide heritage tour, see Tourist information; Dahlia and Arts festival held each Mar. Balgownie Estate winery, open Mon.–Sat.; 10 km NW. Chateau Leaman winery, open Wed.–Mon.; 10 km SW. Bendigo Mohair Farm, Lockwood, 11 km SW; open daily, guided tours Mon.–Fri., admission free. **Tourist information:** 51–67 Pall Mall; (054) 47 7788. **Accommodation:** 5 hotels, 28 motels, 20 B&B, 13 cara./camp. parks. **See also:** The Golden Age; Wine Regions.

Birchip Pop. 827

MAP REF. 122 F13, 231 K4

On the main rail link between Melbourne and Mildura, Birchip gets its water supply from the Wimmera-Mallee stock and domestic channel system. **Of interest:** In Cumming Ave: Big Red (Mallee bull); Historical Society Museum, in old court house (open by appt). **In the area:** Sites within Shire of historic interest are indicated by markers; leaflet from Tourist information. Junction of two major irrigation channels constructed in early 1900s, 1 km N. Sections of original Dog Fence, a vermin-proof barrier constructed in 1883 between Murray River near Swan Hill and South Australian border; 20 km N. Tchum Lake, 8 km E, facilities for motor boats, caravans and camping. **Tourist information:** Council Offices, 22 Cumming Ave; (054) 92 2200. **Accommodation:** 2 hotels, 1 motel, 1 cara./camp. park.

Boort Pop. 801

MAP REF. 122 H13, 231 O5

A pleasant rural and holiday town on the shores of Lake Boort. The lake is popular for water sports, has good picnic facilities and beaches, and offers redfin fishing. There is prolific native birdlife in the area. **Tourist information:** Boort Lake Caravan Park, Durham Ox Rd; (054) 55 2064. **Accommodation:** 1 motel, 1 cara./camp. park.

Uniting Church at Bright, in the beautiful Ovens Valley

Bright Pop. 1881

MAP REF. 225 L5, 235 P8, 236 C6

In the heart of the beautiful Ovens Valley and at the foothills of the Victorian Alps, Bright is an attractive tourist centre. The town offers easy access to the ski resorts of Mt Hotham, Mt Buffalo and Falls Creek, and a number of ski-hire shops in the town stay open late during the winter season. The discovery of gold was responsible for the town's beginnings; remains of alluvial goldfields can still be seen. The area is excellent for bushwalking, horseriding, mountain-bike riding and trout fishing, and is very photogenic, particularly in autumn. **Of interest:** Avenues of deciduous trees, planted in 1930s, particularly beautiful in spring and autumn. In Gavan St: Gallery 90; Country Collectables; Centennial Park with its deep weir, ideal for swimming in summer, children's playground and picnic facilities. Bright Art Gallery and Cultural Centre, Mountbatten Ave. Historical Museum, old railway station, Station Ave. Lotsafun Amusement Park, entrance Mill Rd. Ovens River flows through town; picnic and camping spots alongside. Variety of safe, well-marked walking tracks in Bright area, in particular, Canyon Walk along Ovens River retraces 1850s gold-seekers path; leaflets available at Tourist information. Hanggliding, paragliding and 4WD tours available; inquire at Tourist information. Apr.: Autumn festival. Oct.: Alpine spring festival. **In the area:** Wandiligong, National Trust-classified hamlet in scenic valley, 6 km SE; linked to Bright by road, and walking and cycle track. Scenic drives to: Tower Hill Lookout, 4 km NW; Huggins Lookout, 2 km S; Clearspot (stunning views), 13 km S; from Alpine Road south-east to Mt Hotham, superb views of Mt Feathertop, the Razor Back and Mt Bogong. Porepunkah, 6 km NW of Bright at junction of Ovens and Buckland Rivers, convenient access to Mt Buffalo; Boyntons of Bright Winery, open daily. Further 10 km, Snowline Deer and Emu Farm in Hughes Lane, Eurobin. Mount Buffalo Chalet, 33 km W. **Tourist information:** Gavan St; (057) 55 2275. **Accommodation:** 2 hotel/motels, 11 motels, 6 B&B, 2 hostels, 7 cara./camp. parks.

Broadford Pop. 2215

MAP REF. 213 K1, 234 G11

A small town off the Hume Fwy near Mt Piper. **Of interest:** Display of old printing equipment in *Broadford Courier* building, High St; check opening times. Picnic/barbecue facilities in park in town centre; also replica of drop-slab pioneer cottage. Oct.: Scottish festival. Dec.: Hells Angels concert. **In the area:** Turnoff 20 km E to Strath Creek for beautiful scenic drive through Valley of a Thousand Hills. At Kilmore, 14 km SW: fine old buildings, including Whitburgh Cottage (1857); cable tram rides in Hudson Park. **Tourist information:** Newsagency, 67 High St; (057) 84 1487. **Accommodation:** 2 hotels, 1 motel, 1 B&B.

Buchan Pop. 220

MAP REF. 115 B13, 236 I11

This small town, set in the heart of Gippsland mountain country north-east of Bairnsdale, is famous for its remarkable series of limestone caves. **Of interest:** Tours of Royal and Fairy Caves; conducted daily (adventure tours also available). Park and spring-fed swimming pool located at Caves Reserve. Conorville Heritage Model Village, display of Australian building to 1900; Main St. Easter: Rodeo. June: Woodchop. Oct.: Art and craft festival. **In the area:** Schoolhouse (1865), at Suggan Buggan; 64 km N. Eagle Loft Gallery, for local art and craft; south of Suggan Buggan. Snowy River National Park, for spectacular mountain scenery; 10 km NW of Suggan Buggan. Outstanding views from lookout over Little River Gorge, 70 km N on road to McKillops Bridge; Litte River Falls near Gorge. Stonehenge Rockhounds Museum, Buchan South; 7 km SW. **Tourist information:** General Store, Main St; (051) 55 9202. **Accommodation:** 1 hotel, 1 motel, 1 hostel, 2 cara./camp. parks.

Camperdown Pop. 3315

MAP REF. 217 C5, 229 L8

This south-western town on the Princes Hwy has the English-style charm of gracious buildings and avenues of elms. More than 50 buildings are of historical significance and can be seen by following the Heritage Trail; brochure from Tourist information. The centre for a rich pastoral district, Camperdown is also noted for fishing – in the volcanic crater lakes in the area. **Of interest:** Clock tower (1896), cnr Manifold and Pike Sts. Also in Manifold St: Historical Society Museum; court house; post office. Old Mill, Curdie St: gallery, plant nursery, restored buggies and tearooms in 120-yr-old restored building. Craft Market, Finlay Ave or Theatre Royal, 1st Sun. each month. Feb.: Leura festival (parades and festivities). **In the area:** At Mt Noorat, near Noorat, 21 km NW: Alan Marshall Memorial Walking Track, off Glenormiston Rd, 3-km summit and return (1 hr) or crater-rim 1.5-km circuit (30 min.); excellent views over Western District. Lookout at Mt Leura, 1 km W, extinct volcano next to the perfect cone shape of Mt Sugarloaf; views over numerous crater lakes and volcanoes, north across plains to the Grampians. Cobden, peaceful dairying town; 13 km S. Further 27 km S, at Timboon: Timboon Farmhouse, cheese tastings and sales; Old Timboon Railway Line Walk (10 km). Picturesque road leads from Timboon to tiny seaside village of Port Campbell, 18 km S. Lake Corangamite, Victoria's largest salt lake; 13 km E. Excellent fishing lakes including Bullen Merri, 3 km W; and Purrumbete, 4 km SE, well stocked with Quinnat salmon, also excellent water-sports facilities, picnic spots and caravan park. **Tourist information:** Fragrant Cottage, Old court house building, Manifold St; (055) 93 2288. **Accommodation:** 3 hotels, 3 motels, 3 B&B, 1 cara./camp. park. **See also:** The Western District.

Cann River Pop. 336

MAP REF. 115 E13, 237 N11

A popular stop for Sydney-Melbourne motorists using the Princes Hwy. Excellent fishing and bushwalking in the rugged hinterland. **In the area:** Nulluakgundji, Aboriginal art and craft centre; 1 km N (check at Tourist information for opening times). Croajingolong National Park, main access 27 km S, stretches from Sydenham Inlet to NSW border; incorporates Captain James Cook Lighthouse Reserve at Point Hicks, and Tamboon, Wingan and Mallacoota Inlets. **Tourist information:** Conservation and Natural Resources Information Centre, Princes Hwy; (051) 58 6351. **Accommodation:** 1 hotel, 3 motels, 1 cara./camp. park.

Casterton Pop. 1808

MAP REF. 228 C4

Given the Roman name meaning 'walled city' because of lush hills surrounding the valley, Casterton is on the Glenelg Hwy, 42 km E of the South Australian border. The Glenelg River flows through the town and provides mineral and gem fossicking along its banks near the town, as well as water-skiing at Nelson, some 70 km SW. Launch trips go from Nelson to the river's mouth, on the coast at Discovery Bay. **Of interest:** Casterton Historical Museum, Old Railway Buildings, cnr Jackson and Clarke Sts; open by appt. David Geschke Fine Porcelain Gallery, Casterton Racecourse Rd. In Henty St: Bryan Park; Alma and Judith Zaadstra Fine Art Gallery. Tourist information centre displays local art and craft. Mar.: Vintage car rally. Nov.: Street-car drag racing. **In the area:** Mainly grazing land with rolling hills and areas of natural forest; excellent bushwalks, variety of fauna and flora. Bilston's Tree, arguably world's largest red gum tree in terms of timber mass,

Historic colonial home 'Lake View', Chiltern

and 50 m high; on Glenmia Rd, 30 km N. Baileys Rocks, giant granite boulders, unique green colour; 50 km N, in Dergholm State Park. Other interesting geological formations at the Hummocks, 12 km NE, and Bahgalah Bluff, 20 km SW. Long Lead Swamp has waterbirds, kangaroos and emus; Penola Rd, 11 km W. Angling Club Reserve, Roseneath; 24 km NW. National Trust-classified Warrock Homestead (1843), unique collection of 33 buildings erected by the Station's founder, George Robertson; 26 km NE, open daily. **Tourist information:** Shiels Tce; (055) 81 2070. **Accommodation:** 2 hotel/motels, 1 motel, 1 B&B, 1 cara./camp. park. **See also:** The Western District.

Castlemaine   Pop. 6812

MAP REF. 223 P5, 231 Q11, 234 C10

Along with Kyneton and Maldon, Castlemaine epitomises the goldmining towns of north-western Victoria. An attractive and interesting town, it is built on low hills at the foot of Mt Alexander, on the Calder Hwy, 119 km from Melbourne. In the 1850s and 1860s enormous quantities of gold were found in its surface fields. This gold boom saw Castlemaine grow rapidly and many of its fine old buildings were built during this period. **Of interest:** Market Museum (1862): Palladian style building, National Trust-operated with audiovisual displays, photographic collection and relics of district; Mostyn St, open weekends. Midland and Imperial Hotels, in Templeton and Lyttleton Sts, splendid iron lacework verandahs. Also in Lyttleton St: court house; town hall and library; regional art gallery and museum. Theatre Royal, Hargraves St. Buda Historic Home and Garden, Urquhart St: home from late 1850s of silversmith and jeweller Ernest Leviny and his family, with beautifully preserved home and gardens of the era. Botanic Gardens, Parker St. Old gaol, now restaurant and hostel; Farnsworth St, guided tours daily. Nov.: Spring garden festival (odd-numbered years); State festival (even-numbered years). **In the area:** Excellent restaurants and antique shops. Burnett Gallery and Garden, Burnett Road, North Castlemaine; open weekends. At Harcourt, 10 km NE: Skydances, a walk-through orchid and butterfly nursery; good fishing; scenic picnic spots; Harcourt Valley Vineyard; Blackjack Vineyards; Mt Alexander wineries. On Mt Alexander, koala reserve; 19 km NE. At Malmsbury, 24 km SE: Botanic Gardens, one of oldest in State; nearby, historic reserve. Duke of Cornwall mine buildings, Fryerstown, 10 km SE. Chinese cemetery and mineral springs at Vaughan, 12 km S. At Chewton, 4 km SE: Wattle Gully goldmine; Dingo Farm, puppy time July–Aug. Big Tree, a giant red gum over 500 years old. At Guildford, 11 km SW: At Newstead, 16 km SW: winery; pottery. **Tourist information:** Duke St; (054) 72 3222. **Accommodation:** 5 hotels, 3 motels, 11 B&B, 2 cara./camp. parks. **See also:** The Golden Age.

Charlton   Pop. 1182

MAP REF. 231 M6

A supply centre for a rich wheat district, Charlton is set on the banks of the Avoca River, at the intersection of the Calder and Borung Hwys in north-central Victoria. **Of interest:** Fishing in Avoca River. Walking track along river, from town to weir; about 2 km one way. Oct.: Art show. **In the area:** Wooroonook Lake, for swimming and boating; 12 km W. Bish Deer Farm, further 18 km W. Wychitella State Forest, 27 km E: interesting native flora and fauna, including the lowan (mallee fowl). **Tourist information:** Shire Offices, 1 High St; (054) 91 1755. **Accommodation:** 2 hotels, 2 motels, 1 cara./camp. park.

Chiltern   Pop. 1157

MAP REF. 123 P13, 235 N4, 236 A2

Halfway between Wangaratta and Wodonga, Chiltern is 1 km off the Hume Fwy. It was once a goldmining boom town with 14 suburbs. Many of its attractive buildings have been classified by the National Trust. **Of interest:** In Conness St: Athenaeum Museum (1866), features Goldfields Library collection; The Pharmacy (1868), National Trust-owned chemist shop with its original features; Stephen's Motor Museum, for motoring memorabilia. Self-guide historic walk, leaflet available from Tourist information. Famous Grapevine Attraction, formerly Grape Vine Hotel, boasts the largest grapevine in Australia (in Guinness Book of Records, planted 1867); cnr Conness and Main Sts. National Trust-classified Federal Standard newspaper office, dates from goldmining era (1860–61); Main St, open by appt for groups. Picnic spots with barbecues at Lake Anderson, via Main St. Walking track from lake-shore over bridge to National Trust-classified 'Lake View', Victoria St, home of author Henry Handel Richardson; open weekends, public and school holidays. May: Antique fair. Sept.: Annual art show. **In the area:** Chiltern Regional Park, surrounds the town: bushwalking, nature observation, picnicking, tourist drives and guided walking tours available (contact Tourist information). Magenta open-cut mine, 2 km E. Pioneer Cemetery, 2 km N. Black Dog Creek Pottery, 3 km NW on Chiltern Valley Rd. **Tourist information:** Famous Grapevine Attraction, Main St; (057) 26 1395. **Accommodation:** 1 hotel, 1 motel, 2 B&B, 1 cara./camp. park. **See also:** Wine Regions.

Clunes   Pop. 846

MAP REF. 212 C2, 223 L7, 229 O2, 231 O13, 234 A11

The first reported gold find in the State was made at Clunes on 7 July 1851 when James Esmond announced his discovery of 'pay dirt'. The town, some 35 km N of Ballarat, has several bluestone buildings classified by the National Trust, and the verandahed elegance of Fraser St is worth noting. Surrounding the town are a number of rounded hills (extinct volcanoes) and a good view of them can be obtained about 3 km S, on the road to Ballarat. **Of interest:** Old post office (1873), now second-hand bookshop; cnr Bailey and Service Sts, open weekends. In Bailey St: town hall and court house (1870); Bottle Museum, in former South Clunes State School; Queens Park, established over 100 years ago on banks of Creswick Creek; Butter Factory Gallery, sculpture and art gallery; Cameron St. In Fraser St: the Weavery, handwoven fabrics; Museum, open weekends, public and school holidays. Nov.: Agricultural show. **In the area:** Clunes Homestead Furniture, 1 km NW on Talbot Rd. At Talbot, historic town 18 km NW: many 1860–1870 buildings, particularly in Camp St and Scandinavian Cres.; Arts and Historical Museum, Camp St, in former Primitive Methodist Church (1870); Bull and Mouth restaurant, old bluestone building (1860s) formerly hotel. Mt Beckworth, 8 km W: scenic reserve along with variety of native flora and fauna. **Tourist information:** Clunes Museum, Fraser St; (053) 45 3592. **Accommodation:** 1 hotel, 1 motel, 1 cara./camp. park. **See also:** The Golden Age.

Cobram   Pop. 3797

MAP REF. 123 M13, 235 J3

Magnificent wide sandy beaches are a feature of the stretch of the Murray River at Cobram, so picnicking and water sports are popular. This is also fruit-growing country; the clingstone variety of peach was developed here. **Of interest:** Rotary dairy, 200 cows, on outskirts of town; open at milking time, 4–5 p.m. daily. Jan.: Peaches and Cream festival (odd-numbered years). June: Antique fair. **In the area:** Matata Deer Farm on Tocumwal road, 5 km NW. Sportavia Soaring Centre at Tocumwal airport, 20 km NW. Heritage Farm Wines, with 116-m woodcarving depicting scenes of early River Murray life; on Murray Valley Hwy, 5 km W. At Strathmerton, 16 km W, Spikes and Blooms cactus farm; Coonanga Homestead. Monichino winery, 15 km S towards Numurkah. Strathkellar Wines, 8 km E on Murray Valley Hwy. Binghi Boomerang Factory at Barooga, 4 km NE. **Tourist information:** The Old Grain Shed, cnr Station St and Punt Rd; (058) 72 2132. **Accommodation:** 3 hotels, 4 motels, 3 cara./camp. parks. **See also:** The Mighty Murray.

Cohuna   Pop. 2071

MAP REF. 123 J12, 231 Q3, 234 C2

Between Kerang and Echuca on the Murray Valley Hwy, Cohuna is surrounded by dairy farms. The town is located beside Gunbower Island, formed by the Murray River on the far side and Gunbower Creek just across the highway from the town. This island is covered in red gum and box forest, which provides a home for abundant waterfowl and other birdlife as well as kangaroos and emus. The forest is subject to flooding and a large part of the island has breeding rookeries during the flood periods. Feb.: Aquatic festival. Mar.: Show. **In the area:** Two-hour cruises in the *Wetlander* along Gunbower Creek; inquire at Tourist information. Gunbower Island: birdlife, picnic/barbecue facilities and forest tracks for walking, (map available at local shops). Major Mitchell Trail, 1700-km signposted trail that retraces this famous explorer's footsteps from Mildura to Wodonga via Portland; at Cohuna, signposted trail along Gunbower Creek, down to Mt Hope. National Barefoot Ski Titles held on Gunbower Creek in Apr. Kow Swamp, 23 km S: bird sanctuary; picnic spots and good fishing at Box Bridge. Mount Hope (110 m), about 28 km S: easy rock climbing, good views from summit and beautiful wildflowers in spring. Cohuna Grove Cottage, local art and craft; 4 km SE on Murray Valley Hwy. Kraft factory, shop open a.m. Mon.–Fri., 16 km SE at Leitchville. Torrumbarry Weir, 40 km SE: during winter, entire weir structure is removed from the river; in summer, water-skiing above the weir. Mathers Waterwheel Museum, memorabilia; Brays Rd, 9 km W. **Tourist information:** Golden River Tourism, 25 Murray St, Barham; (054) 53 3100. **Accommodation:** 1 hotel/motel, 1 cara./camp. park.

Colac   Pop. 10 241

MAP REF. 212 B11, 217 G7, 229 N9

Colac is situated on the eastern edge of the volcanic plain that covers much of the Western District of Victoria. It is the centre of a prosperous, closely settled agricultural area and is sited on the shores of Lake Colac, which has good fishing and a variety of water sports. **Of interest:** Historical Centre, Gellibrand St; open Thurs., Fri., Sun. p.m. Botanic Gardens, Queen St. Barongarook Creek, has prolific birdlife and walking track alongside to Sculpture Park. Sculpture Park on Princes Hwy, has permanent and special exhibitions. Self-guide town walk leaflet and information on full-day mountain scenic drive available, contact Tourist information for details. Mar.: Kana festival. **In the area:** Irrewarra Homestead, 15 km N. Red Rock Lookouts, 22 km N near Alvie: 30 volcanic lakes can be seen from here, including Lake Corangamite, Victoria's largest saltwater lake. Floating Island Reserve, 17 km W, a lagoon with islands that change position. Gellibrand Pottery, 10 km S. Burtons Lookout, views of Otway hinterland; 13 km S. Red Rock Winery, 15 km S; check opening times. Otway Ranges, about 30 km S: beautiful winding roads and lush mountain scenery, en route to the coast. Tarndwarncoort Homestead, 15 km E. At Birregurra, 20 km E, interesting old buildings. **Tourist information:** Cnr Murray and Queen Sts; (052) 31 3730. **Accommodation:** 1 hotel/motel, 4 motels, 3 cara./camp. parks.

Coleraine　　Pop. 1089

MAP REF. 228 E4

Situated 35 km NW of Hamilton, the Coleraine area was first settled by the Henty and Whyte brothers in 1838 for pastoral grazing. Today the primary products are fine-wool sheep and beef cattle. **In the area:** Point's Arboretum: unique planting of over 700 native tree and shrub species, and lookout; western edge of town. Historic homesteads: National Trust-classified Warrock Homestead (1843), 20 km W towards Casterton; Glendinning Homestead with wildlife sanctuary, near Balmoral, 50 km N. Rocklands Reservoir, 12 km E of Balmoral: fishing and boating; caravan/camping park nearby. Black Range State Park, on northern shores of reservoir, has walking tracks. Wannon Falls, 14 km SE, and Nigretta Falls, 24 km SE. Gardens of Nareen, property of ex-Prime Minister Malcolm Fraser and his wife, located 31 km NW; open weekdays by appt and through Australia's Open Garden Scheme (closed Christmas, Easter and May–Aug.). **Tourist information:** Old Railway Station, Pilleau St; (055) 75 2733. **Accommodation:** 2 hotels, 1 cara./ camp. park. **See also:** The Western District.

Corryong　　Pop. 1226

MAP REF. 115 B8, 236 G2

Situated in alpine country, Corryong is at the gateway to the Snowy Mountains. The district offers superb mountain scenery and excellent trout fishing. The Murray River near Corryong is a brisk and gurgling stream running through forested hills. **Of interest:** Jack Riley, reputedly 'The Man from Snowy River', came from these parts and his grave is in Corryong cemetery. The Man from Snowy River Folk Museum, features replica of Riley's original shack; Hanson St. Mar.: High country festival. **In the area:** Scenic drive west from Corryong. Scenic views: Players Hill Lookout, 1 km SE; Mt Mittamatite and Emberys Lookout, 10 km N; lookout with views over Kosciusko National Park at Towong, 12 km NE; Sassafras Gap, 66 km S. Trout fishing at Tintaldra; 23 km N. Canoeing and mountain-bike excursions from Walwa, 47 km NW. Burrowa-Pine Mountain National Park, 27 km W: Cudgewa Bluff Falls, excellent scenery and bushwalking tracks. In Nariel Valley, 12 km SW, folk music festival in Dec. Upper Murray Fish Farm, 38 km S. **Tourist information:** Corryong Newsagency, 43–49 Hanson St; (060) 76 1381; or Mt Mittamatite Caravan Park, Tallangatta Rd; (060) 76 1152. **Accommodation:** 2 hotel/motels, 2 motels, 2 cara./camp. parks.

Cowes　　Pop. 2658

MAP REF. 213 L12, 215 O11, 226 E9

This is the main town on Phillip Island, a popular resort area in Western Port linked to the mainland by a bridge at San Remo. Cowes is on the northern side of the island and is the centre for hotel and motel accommodation. It has pleasant beaches, safe for children, and the jetty is popular for fishing and swimming. The town has a number of art and craft shops, and a variety of restaurants. Sept.: Motor racing. Oct.: Grand Prix motorcycle race; Superbike championships. **In the area:** Summerland Beach, on southern shore, about 13 km SW, is famous for its nightly penguin parade. Colonies of fur seals can be seen year-round on Seal Rocks, and off southern shores, also short-tailed shearwaters Oct.–Apr. On Phillip Island Rd: Wildlife Park has native fauna in natural environment, 3 km S; A Maze 'N Things, 7 km SW. Racing circuit, venue for Grand Prix motorbike race; 6 km S. Australian Dairy Centre at Newhaven, 16 km SE: museum and cheese factory. Churchill Island, 2 km from Newhaven: historic homestead and walking tracks. Feed pelicans, 11a.m. on foreshore opposite San Remo Fishing Co-op. Wildlife Wonderland, including the Giant Worm and Wombat World; 9 km W of San Remo. **Tourist information:** Phillip Island Rd, Newhaven; (059) 56 7447 (incl. tickets for Phillip Island attractions). **Accommodation:** 17 hotel/motels, 9 B&B, 1 hostel, 13 cara./ camp. parks. **See also:** Phillip Island.

Creswick　　Pop. 2387

MAP REF. 212 C3, 223 M9, 229 O2, 231 O13, 234 A12

This picturesque town, situated 18 km N of Ballarat on the Midland Hwy, nestles at the foot of the Creswick State Forest. One of the richest alluvial goldfields in the world was discovered here. **Of interest:** Mullock heaps on Lawrence Rd. Creswick Historical Museum, Albert St. Gold Battery, Battery Cres. Cemetery, with early miners' graves and Chinese section; Clunes Rd. In Melbourne Rd: Koala Park; St Georges Lake. Oct.: Brackenbury Classic fun run. **In the area:** Surrounding volcanic bushland and forest areas attract field naturalists and bushwalking enthusiasts. Creswick Forest Nursery, 1 km E. World of Dinosaurs, life-size models in bushland setting; 1.5 km E off Midland Hwy. Gold panning, in Creswick Creek; 4 km E. Tangled Maze Nursery, a maze formed by climbing plants; 5 km E. At Smeaton, 16 km N: Smeaton House (1850s); Anderson's Mill (1860s); Tuki Trout Farm. Tumblers Green Nursery, 1 km W. **Tourist information:** Shire Offices, 68 Albert St; (053) 45 2000. **Accommodation:** 1 motel, 2 B&B, 1 cara./camp. park. **See also:** The Golden Age.

Daylesford　　Pop. 3347

MAP REF. 212 E2, 223 P8, 229 Q2, 231 Q13, 234 B12

Daylesford and Hepburn Springs, 4 km N, together constitute a spa town, with 65 documented mineral springs, many with hand pumps. Daylesford rambles up the side of Wombat Hill, at the top of which are the Botanical Gardens in Central Springs Rd, with a lookout tower from which there are views in all directions. **Of interest:** Hepburn Springs Spa Complex, in the Mineral Springs Reserve, Forest Ave, offers public and private baths, flotation tanks, massage and a sauna; open daily. Convent Gallery, in former girls' school; Daly St. Nearby, Wombat Hill Botanical Gardens and lookout tower. In Vincent St: Alpha Hall Galleria, in former silent movie house (closed Tues.-Wed.); historical museum in former School of Mines (open weekends). Central Springs Spa Reserve and Lake Daylesford, Central Springs Rd; Tipperary Walking Track runs from here to Mineral Springs Reserve (leaflet available). Lyonville spring, 15 km SE. Loddon Falls, 10 km NE. Glenlyon reserve, 11km NE. Market near railway station, Sun. a.m. During market, Central Highlands Tourist Railway runs hourly rail-motor services between Daylesford and Musk, 1st and 3rd Sun. each month, and ganger's trolleys operate to Wombat Forest alternate Sun. Jan.: Daylesford Gift (horse race). May: Hepburn Swiss-Italian festival. July: Mid-winter festival. Nov.: Agricultural show. Dec.: Highland gathering. **In the area:** Breakneck Gorge, 5 km N. Mt Franklin, an extinct volcano,

Phillip Island

Penguin parade at Summerland Beach, one of the State's most popular tourist attractions

Phillip Island (10 300 hectares) is situated at the entrance to Western Port, 120 kilometres south-east of Melbourne. Once over the bridge between San Remo and Newhaven, the greatest attraction for visitors is the fascinating little (fairy) penguin parade on Summerland Beach. The penguins spend the day out at sea catching whitebait for their young. Each evening at sunset they return in small groups and waddle up the beach to their sand-dune burrows. Visitors watch the parade under subdued floodlights from elevated stands and walkways. No flashlight photography is permitted. The Phillip Island Penguin Reserve is open daily. (Inquiries (059) 56 8300; bookings for parade (059) 56 8691.)

Seal Rocks at the south-west tip of the island is home to colonies of fur seals. At the peak of the breeding season, about 5000 seals can be seen there. A ferry service from Cowes allows close-up views of the seals sunbathing on the rocks. Coin-operated telescopes give landlubbers a view of the seals from The Nobbies kiosk. Nearby, The Nobbies, a big rock outcrop can only be reached at low tide. The Blow Hole here is best seen at high tide.

Take the road down to the surf beach at Cape Woolamai, a rugged granite headland. A two-hour walk leads to the highest point on the island, from where there are breathtaking views of the coastline. The sand dunes all along the Cape are the home of many short-tailed shearwaters. Arriving from Siberia on their annual migration, the birds nest in the rookeries here in spring and summer. Koalas can be seen at the Koala Conservation Centre, which features an elevated boardwalk in the treetops.

Visit nearby historic Churchill Island, reached by bridge near Newhaven. A pamphlet available at Tourist information outlines the Homestead Walk (the homestead was built in 1872). There are several walking trails on the island.

Everyone will enjoy hand-feeding the tame emus, kangaroos and wallabies at the Phillip Island Wildlife Park, which is set in 32 hectares of bushland. Other fauna to be seen there include wombats, venomous and non-venomous snakes, eagles and pelicans. Nearly 7 hectares is wetlands, consisting of ponds and waterways that are breeding grounds for rare and endangered birds.

Some unusual bird species make their homes in The Nits at Rhyll, a fishing resort on the northern side of the island. Pelicans, ibis, royal spoonbills, swans and gulls inhabit the swamplands there.

Also on the north coast is **Cowes**, the most popular summer resort on Phillip Island. Its unspoilt beaches are sheltered for safe swimming, yachting and other water sports.

For further information on attractions, ticket sales for the penguin parade, and information and maps for self-guide walks and nature tours, contact the Phillip Island Information Centre, Phillip Island Rd, Newhaven; (059) 56 7447. **See also:** individual town entry for Cowes in A–Z listing. **Map references:** 215 N12, 226 E9.

13 km N. At Trentham, 23 km SE: interesting buildings; waterfalls to the north. Yandoit, a settlement of Swiss-Italian heritage, 18 km NW. Sailors Falls, 10 km S. **Tourist information:** Information Centre, Vincent St; (053) 48 1339. **Accommodation:** 4 hotels, 7 motels, 23 B&B, 1 cara./camp. park. **See also:** The Golden Age.

Derrinallum   Pop. 280

MAP REF. 217 C2, 229 L6

A small rural town servicing the local pastoral farming community and surrounded by volcanic plains. **In the area:** Significant dry-stone walls, immediately west of town. Mt Elephant, a scoria cone of volcanic origin rising high above surrounding plains; 2 km SW. At Darlington, 15 km SW: Elephant Bridge Hotel, a 2-storey bluestone building, classified by National Trust. Lake Tooliorook, 6 km SE, and Deep Lake, 5 km NW; both for fishing and water sports. **Tourist information:** Fragrant Cottage, Old Court house building, Manifold St, Camperdown; (055) 93 2288. **Accommodation:** 1 hotel/motel.

Dimboola   Pop. 1581

MAP REF. 230 F7

This is a peaceful town on the tree-lined Wimmera River, 35 km NW of Horsham. **Of interest:** Walking track along Wimmera River. Oct.: Agricultural show. Nov.: Rowing regatta. **In the area:** Little Desert National Park, 6 km SW, self-guide walks, including Pomponderoo Hill Nature Walk (1 km) from Horseshoe Bend picnic and camping area at river's edge. At Wail, 11 km S, well-stocked Natural Resource League forest nursery. Ebenezer Mission Station (founded 1859), near Antwerp on Jeparit Rd, 15 km N. Pink Lake, coloured salt lake, 9 km NW. At Kiata, 26 km W, mallee fowl can be seen in Lowan Sanctuary all year. **Tourist information:** Mag's Menagerie, 119 Lloyd St; (053) 89 1290. **Accommodation:** 2 hotels, 1 motel, 1 B&B, 1 cara./camp. park. **See also:** The Wimmera.

Donald   Pop. 1505

MAP REF. 231 K7

At the junction of the Sunraysia and Borung Hwys, Donald is situated on the Richardson River in a Wimmera district. **Of interest:** Historic police station (1874), Wood St. Railway steam engine, Steam Loco Park, cnr Hammill and Walker Sts. Agricultural museum, Hammill St. Historic water pump by lake in caravan park. Bullocks Head Lookout, Byrne St. Large, unusual growth on box tree beside Richardson River. Kooka's Country Cookies, has tours and sales; Sunraysia Hwy. Feb.: Dead Centre motorbike rally. **In the area:** Angora Goat Farm, 1 km E on Racecourse Rd. Deer farm, 10 km E on Charlton Rd. Mt Jeffcott, 20 km NE: flora, fauna and views of Lake Buloke. Fishing in Richardson River. Lake Buloke, 10 km N, a wetlands area. Watchem Lake, 30 km N: good fishing and water sports. **Tourist information:** Shire Offices, McCulloch St; (054) 97 1300, or Caravan Park, Hammill St; (054) 97 1764. **Accommodation:** 3 hotels, 2 motels, 2 B&B, 1 cara./camp. park.

Drouin   Pop. 4455

MAP REF. 213 P9, 226 H6

Located on the Princes Hwy not far from Warragul and the La Trobe Valley. Feb.: Ficifolia festival. **In the area:** Camping and picnic spots: beside Tarago River at Glen Cromie Park, 8 km N; Picnic Point on Princes Hwy, 10 km W. At Neerim South, 31 km NE: Tarago River Cheese Company; picnic/barbecue area at Tarago Reservoir; Woodlyn Park, horseriding into adjacent State Forest. At Nayook, 38 km N: Nayook Fruit and Berry Farm; Country Farm Perennials Nursery and Gardens. At Noojee, 40 km NE: Alpine Trout Farm; Noojee Trestle Bridge. At Drouin West, 3 km W: Oakbank Angoras and Alpacas; Fruit and Berry Farm. Victoria's Farm Shed, farm animal and agricultural displays, including shearing, sheepdog workouts and milking; Princes Hwy, Tynong, 22 km W. Gumbaya Park, family fun park; 25 km W on Princes Hwy. Many of the food attractions in the area are featured on the Gourmet Deli Trail; brochure from Tourist information. **Tourist information:** Shop 1, Southside Central, Princess Hwy, Traralgon; (051) 74 3199. **Accommodation:** 2 motels, 3 B&B, 3 cara./camp. parks.

Drysdale   Pop. 1166

MAP REF. 212 H9, 219 H7, 226 B6

This is primarily a service centre for the local farming community on the Bellarine Peninsula. **Of interest:** In High St: Old Court House Museum, home of the Bellarine Historical Society; Drysdale Community Crafts. Community Market, every 3rd Sun. (Sept.–Apr.) at Recreation Reserve, Duke St. **In the area:** Lake Lorne picnic area, 1 km SW. Nearby Bellarine Peninsula Railway offers steam-train rides between Drysdale and Queenscliff, weekends and summer holidays; locomotives and carriages dating back to 1870s on display. Soho Nursery and Fine Arts Gallery, 6 km E. Adjoining township of Clifton Springs had a brief burst of fame in the 1870s when the therapeutic value of its mineral-spring water was discovered. Local wineries include: Scotchmans Hill Winery, Scotchmans Road. Historic Spray Farm, Portarlington Rd; open weekends and public holidays. **Tourist information:** A Maze'N Things, 1570 Bellarine Hwy, cnr Grubb Rd, Wallington; (052) 50 2669. **Accommodation:** 1 hotel.

Dunkeld   Pop. 440

MAP REF. 228 H4

On the Glenelg Hwy, 32 km NE of Hamilton, Dunkeld is the southern gateway to the Grampians and is convenient for trips to the Chimney Pots, a landmark in the Grampians National Park, 25 km N. **Of interest:** Historical museum, in old church, features history of area's Aborigines, and explorer Major Mitchell's journeys; Templeton St. Self-guide walk or drive of historic places of interest; leaflet available from Tourist information. Skin Inn, has sheepskin products and crafts; Parker St. Nov.: Dunkeld Cup (horseracing) Dec.: Festival. **In the area:** Walking tracks to top of Mt Sturgeon (3 km N) and Mt Abrupt (8 km N); both climbs steep, but good views. Easier walk to Mt Piccaninny, 4½ km S. Freshwater Lake Reserve, 8 km N. **Tourist information:** Visitors Centre, Glenelg Hwy; (055) 77 2558. **Accommodation:** 1 hotel/motel, 5 B&B, 1 cara. park, 1 cara./camp. park. **See also:** The Western District.

Dunolly   Pop. 686

MAP REF. 223 L3, 231 O10

A small town in north-central Victoria, in the heart of the gold country and on the Goldfields Tourist Route. 'Welcome Stranger', considered to be the largest nugget ever discovered, was found 15 km NW at Moliagul. The district has

Paddlesteamers on the Murray River at Echuca

produced more nuggets than any other goldfield in Australia; 126 were unearthed in the town itself. Ninety per cent of alluvial gold mined world-wide comes from this area. **Of interest:** Restored Dunolly Court house has display relating to historic gold discoveries in area; open Fri.–Mon., Market St. Next door: original lockup (1859) and stables. In Broadway: handsome original buildings; Bonsai Shop; Goldfields Historical and Arts Society collection, replicas of some of town's most spectacular nuggets, open weekends or by appt. Self-guide bike rides of region; leaflet available at Tourist information. **In the area:** Countryside abounds with spring wildflowers and native fauna. Gold panning in local creeks. Laanecoorie Reservoir, 16 km E. Tarnagulla, 13 km NE, a small mining town; remains of mine and flora reserve nearby. At Moliagul, 15 km NW: monuments mark spot where 'Welcome Stranger' nugget was found 1869, and birthplace of Rev. John Flynn, founder of Royal Flying Doctor Service; Welcome Stranger Discovery Walk, leaflet available at Tourist information. **Tourist information:** Court house, Market St; (054) 68 1205. **Accommodation:** 2 hotels, 1 motel, 6 B&B, 1 cara./camp. park.

Echuca   Pop. 9438

MAP REF. 123 K13, 234 E4

Echuca and its twin town Moama, across the river in NSW, are at the junction of the Murray, Campaspe and Goulburn Rivers. Echuca, now a city and once Australia's largest inland port, took its name from an Aboriginal word meaning 'meeting of the waters', while Moama means 'place of the dead'. An iron bridge joins the two. **Of interest:** Port of Echuca, restored to the period of its heyday with its massive red gum wharf; paddlesteamer *Pevensey* (renamed *Philadelphia* for TV mini-series *All the Rivers Run*); D26 logging barge, PS *Alexander Arbuthnot*; PS *Adelaide*; (all available for cruises, cruise times displayed at wharf entrance). Also part of the Port's attractions, all in Murray Esplanade: Star Hotel, underground bar and escape tunnel; Bridge Hotel, built by Henry Hopwood, founder of Echuca, who ran original punt service; Red Gum Works, woodturning demonstrations; award-winning Sharp's Magic Movie House and Penny Arcade; Echuca Wharf Pottery; Tisdall Wines, tastings and cellar-door sales; Coach House and Carriage collection; Port tour available. In High St: Echuca Historical Society Museum (1867) in former police station; Gumnutland, model village; World in Wax museum. National Holden Museum, Warren St. Cruises available on paddlewheelers *Canberra* and *Pride of the Murray*; accommodation and cruises on paddlesteamer *Emmylou*; MV *Mary Ann* cruising restaurant. Houseboat hire available; inquire at Tourist information. Feb.: Southern 80 ski race from Torrumbarry Weir to Echuca. Easter: Working horse fair. Apr.: Barmah muster. **In the area:** Camping, fishing, water sports and bushwalking. In Moama: Silverstone Go Kart Track; Horseshoe Lagoon reserve; Aqua Farms Yabbie Farm; Market, 2nd Sun. p.m. each month. At Barmah Red Gum Forest 39 km NE: Dharnya Aboriginal Interpretative Centre, has excellent historical display of culture of local Yorta Yorta people; wetlands cruises, fishing, swimming at Barmah Lake. Near Mathoura, 40 km NE: Moira Forest Walkway and Bird Observatory; Picnic Point recreational area. **Tourist information:** Old Pumphouse, cnr Hagarth and Cobb Hwy, Echuca; (054) 80 7555. **Accommodation:** 42 motels, hotels, holiday units and homesteads, 5 B&B, 11 cara. parks. **See also:** The Mighty Murray; Wine Regions.

Edenhope   Pop. 821

MAP REF. 230 C11

On the Wimmera Hwy, just 30 km from the border with South Australia, Edenhope is situated on the shores of Lake Wallace, a haven for waterbirds. When full, the lake is popular for a variety of water sports. **Of interest:** Cairn, beside the lake in Lake St, commemorating visit of first all-Aboriginal cricket team to England; team was coached by T.W. Willis, who was also the founder of Australian Rules football. Feb.: Henley-on-Lake Wallace (carnival with street procession). **In the area:** Harrow, 32 km SE: one of Victoria's oldest inland towns; historic buildings including Hermitage Hotel (1851) and log gaol (1862). Rocklands Reservoir, part of Wimmera-Mallee irrigation system, for fishing and boating; 65 km E. About 50 km W, over SA border, Naracoorte Caves Conservation Park. **Tourist information:** Shire Offices, 49 Elizabeth St; (055) 85 1011. **Accommodation:** 1 hotel, 1 motel, 1 B&B, 1 cara./camp. park.

Eildon   Pop. 740

MAP REF. 213 P2, 224 A12, 235 K11

Built to irrigate a vast stretch of northern Victoria and to provide hydro-electric power, Lake Eildon is the State's largest constructed lake and is a popular resort area, surrounded by the beautiful foothills of the Alps within Eildon State Park. There are excellent recreational facilities around the foreshores, two major boat harbours, launching ramps, picnic grounds and many lookout points. Power boat and houseboat hire available at boat harbours. **In the area:** Signposted Lake Eildon Wall lookout,

Puffing Billy runs between Belgrave and Emerald

1 km N. Lake cruises from Eildon Boat Harbour. Eildon Pondage and Goulburn River, for excellent fishing. There is no closed season for trout in Lake Eildon, which is also stocked with Murray cod; redfin abound naturally. Inland fishing licence required for anglers over 16 years old. Eildon State Park, surrounds town: walking tracks, and camping and picnicking at Jerusalem Inlet. Mt Pinninger (503 m), for panoramic views of Mt Buller, the Alps and lake; 3 km E. Snobs Creek Fish Hatchery, where millions of trout bred and used to stock lakes and rivers; 6 km S, visitors welcome. Eildon Deer Park nearby, on Goulburn Valley Hwy; open weekends and public holidays. Just past the hatchery, Snobs Creek Falls. Rubicon Falls, 18 km SW, via Thornton. Jamieson, 57 km SE, old mining town at junction of Goulburn and Jamieson Rivers, surrounded by dense, bush-clad mountain countryside. Mt Skene, 48 km SE of Jamieson; colourful wildflowers Dec.–Feb. (road closed in winter). Scenic drive to Fraser National Park, 13 km NW: popular Candlebark Gully Nature Walk; other scenic walks in area; camping. **Tourist information:** Redgate Nursery and Craft Cottage, 73 Downey St, Alexandra; (057) 72 2169. **Accommodation:** 4 motels, 12 B&B, 6 cara./camp. parks.

Emerald
Pop. 4693

MAP REF. 213 M7, 216 C13, 226 F5

The Puffing Billy steam railway runs between Belgrave and this pretty town, the first European settlement in the Dandenong Ranges. **Of interest:** Many Galleries and craft shops. Restored Victorian 'red rattler' train, now restaurant with gallery and model railway; Monbulk Rd. Emerald Lake Park, once part of famous Nobelius Nursery; Emerald Lake Rd. Environmental Centre, with walking tracks and barbecues. Emerald Lake, one of the area's most attractive and best-equipped picnic and swimming sites; includes water-slides, paddleboats, model railway, kiosk and tearooms. Lake sited on Dandenongs Walk Track, 40-km trail from Cockatoo and Gembrook to Sassafras. **In the area:** At Menzies Creek, 5 km NW: Cotswold House, fine food and views; Lake Aura Vale, for sailing and picnics. Sherbrooke Art Gallery, Monbulk Rd, Belgrave; 11 km NW. Monbulk Animal Kingdom, Swales Rd, Monbulk; 11 km NW. Tulip farms at Silvan, 14 km NW. At picturesque town of Olinda, 18 km NW: antique galleries; National Rhododendron Garden and nursery; home of settler Edward Henty on Ridge Rd. Australian Rainbow Trout Farm, Macclesfield, 8 km N. Bimbimbie Wildlife Park, Paternoster Rd, Mount Burnett; 12 km SE. Trail rides available at Sherbrooke Equestrian Park, 3 km W on Wellington Rd. Further 2 km along, Cardinia Reservoir Park, for good views, picnic spots and native fauna. **Tourist information:** Possum's Cottage, 348 Main Rd; (059) 68 6110. **Accommodation:** 3 B&B, 1 hostel. **See also:** The Dandenongs.

Euroa
Pop. 2772

MAP REF. 234 I8

A small town 151 km NE of Melbourne, just off the Hume Fwy, Euroa is a good base for exploring the Strathbogie Ranges and tablelands. The town name originated from the Aboriginal *yerao*, meaning 'joyful'. The district was traversed by the explorers Hume and Hovell in 1824 and Major Mitchell in 1836, and in 1879 was proclaimed a municipality. The Kelly gang staged a daring robbery here, rounding up some 50 hostages at the nearby Faithfull Creek station and then making off with £2200. **Of interest:** Seven Creeks Park, Tarcombe St. Farmers Arms historical museum, Kirkland Ave; open Sun. p.m. Miniature steam-train rides, Turnbull St; last Sun. each month. Parachuting School, Drysdale Rd; open weekends. Wildflower walks in spring; leaflet available at Tourist information. Oct.: Agricultural show; Wool week. **In the area:** Seven Creeks Run Woolshed complex, 1 km N: wool memorabilia, bush market and crafts. Forlonge Memorial, commemorating Eliza Forlonge, who with her sister imported first merino sheep into Victoria; off Euroa–Strathbogie road, 10 km SE. Scenic drive to Gooram Falls (20 km SE) and around Strathbogie Ranges. Mt Wombat lookout, spectacular views of surrounding country and Alps; 25 km SE. Balloon Flights Victoria, 10 km SW. At Longwood, 14 km SW: historic buildings, especially White Heart Hotel. Faithfull Creek Waterfall, 9 km NE. **Tourist information:** Mon.–Fri., Community Centre, Binney St; (057) 95 2777. Weekends and public holidays: Tourist Information Centre, Kirkland Ave; (057) 95 1263. **Accommodation:** 3 motels, 1 cara./camp. park.

Foster

Pop. 1078

MAP REF. 227 J10

A picturesque small town within easy reach of Corner Inlet, Waratah Bay and Wilsons Promontory on the south-east coast of Victoria, and about 170 km from Melbourne. **Of interest:** In Main St: Historical Museum, in old post office; Stockyard Gallery. Feb.: Agricultural show. **In the area:** Scenic drive to Fish Creek, 11 km SW; in town, Fish Creek Potters. Pleasant beach resorts: Waratah Bay, 34 km SW; Walkerville, 36 km SW; Port Franklin, 12 km SE. Cape Liptrap, excellent views of rugged coastline and Bass Strait; 46 km SW. Good surf beach at Sandy Point, 22 km S; surrounding protected waters of Shallow Inlet popular for fishing, windsurfing and swimming. Toora, 12 km E: proposed SECV windfarm, in experimental stage; Bonlac milk products. Turtons Creek, 18 km N, old gold-rich area; lyrebirds sometimes seen in tree-fern gullies nearby. Near Turtons Creek, horse-drawn wagons and trail riding. Foster North Lookout, 6 km NW. **Tourist information:** Stockyard Gallery, Main St; (056) 82 1125. **Accommodation:** 2 motels, 10 B&B, 1 cara./camp. park.

Geelong

Pop. 126 306

MAP REF. 212 F9, 218, 219 E7, 226 A6, 229 R7

Geelong, on Corio Bay, is the largest provincial city in Victoria. It is a major manufacturing and processing centre, and has a strong tradition in wool selling and storage. The Corio Bay area was first settled in the 1830s and, apart from a rush to the diggings during the gold boom, Geelong has grown and prospered steadily. It is a pleasant and well-laid-out city with lovely views across the bay. **Of interest:** National Wool Museum in historic bluestone woolstore features sound and audio-visual displays, re-created shearers quarters and millworker's cottage; cnr Moorabool and Brougham Sts (Geelong Otway Tourism Information Centre in foyer). Interesting buildings (more than 100 with National Trust classifications) include: Merchiston Hall (1856), Garden St, East Geelong; Osborne House (1858), bluestone mansion housing Maritime Museum, Swinburne St, North Geelong; beautiful Corio Villa (1856), prefabricated cast-iron house, at Eastern Beach. The following are open to the public: The Heights (1855), 14-roomed prefabricated timber mansion surrounded by delightful gardens, Aphrasia St, Newtown; Barwon Grange (1855), Fernleigh St, Newtown. Christ Church, Moorabool St, oldest Anglican church in Victoria still in continuous use. Customs House, Brougham St. Geelong Art Gallery, State's largest regional gallery; Performing Arts Centre; both in Little Malop St. Wintergarden historic building housing gallery, nursery, antiques and gift shop; 51 McKillop St. Pottage Crafts, 189 Moorabool St. Eastern Beach and Park, swimming in fully restored 1930s seabathing complex. Beachfront Scenic Drive. Botanic Gardens in Eastern Park, overlooking Corio Bay; Garden St. Johnstone Park, cnr Mercer and Gheringhap Sts. Queens Park, Queens Park Rd, Newtown, walks to Buckley's Falls. Balyang Bird Sanctuary, Shannon Ave, Newtown. Extensive walking tracks and bike paths alongside Barwon River. Boat ramps on Corio Bay beaches. Good river and bay fishing. Jan.: Summer festival. Feb.: Pako multicultural festa. Mar.: Highland gathering. Apr.: Heritage and vintage rally; Alternative Farmvision. June: Wool week; Celtic festival. Oct.: Show; Racing carnival. **In the area:** In Greater Geelong: 14 wineries (details from Tourist information); Norlane Water World, 7 km N. Lara, 19 km N, swept by bushfires in 1969 but some historic buildings remain. Nearby, You Yangs, a range of distinctive granite hills in You Yangs Regional Park; walking tracks, picnic grounds and information centre. Between Lara and You Yangs, Serendip Sanctuary, once purely a wildlife research station, now open to public, has nature trails, bird hides and visitors' centre. Anakie, a township at foot of Brisbane Ranges; 31 km N. Brisbane Ranges National Park, 34 km N: many species of ferns and flowering plants; native fauna; Discovery Walk leads to Anakie Gorge (leaflet available). Nearby Fairy Park, with miniature houses and scenes from fairytales. Mt Anakie Winery; Staughton Vale winery; both north of Anakie on Staughton Vale Rd. Steiglitz, 10 km NW of Anakie: once a gold town, now almost deserted; restored court house (1875), open Sun. Batesford, 10 km NW of Geelong, a picturesque market garden township with a history of winemaking; Sandstone Travellers Rest Inn (1849) across Moorabool River from present hotel. Meredith, 46 km NW, one of the oldest towns in Victoria, once a stopping-place for diggers on their way to the goldfields. Fyansford, 5 km W on outskirts of city, one of oldest settlements in region: historic buildings including Swan Inn, Balmoral Hotel (1854) (now an art gallery) and Fyansford Hotel; Information Centre at Common Reserve has interpretative material on history, flora and fauna of region; Monash Bridge across Moorabool River thought to be one of first reinforced-concrete bridges in Victoria. Brownhill Observation Tower, Ceres, 10 km SW, excellent view of surrounding areas; nearby Eastcott Nursery, Violet Farm and tearooms. Deakin University's Institute of the Arts, Waurn Ponds, 13 km SW. At Moriac, 20 km SW, horse-drawn caravan hire. The Bellarine Peninsula begins about 16 km E (see text entries for Drysdale, Portarlington, St Leonards, Queenscliff and Ocean Grove). Great Ocean Rd from Torquay provides spectacular coastal scenery. **Tourist information:** National Wool Museum, 26–32 Moorabool St; (052) 22 2900. **Accommodation:** 7 hotels, 27 motels, 17 B&B, 14 cara./camp. parks. **See also:** The Great Ocean Road; Wine Regions.

Gisborne

Pop. 2819

MAP REF. 212 H3, 226 B2, 234 E13

Once a stopping-place for coaches and foot travellers on their way to the Castlemaine and Bendigo goldfields, Gisborne is an attractive township (now bypassed by the Calder Hwy) on the way to Woodend and Kyneton. Market, cnr Aitken and Hamilton Sts, 1st. Sun. each month (Oct.–May). Dec.: Festival. **In the area:** Mount Macedon, 15 km N, memorial cross at summit. Mt Aitken Estates Winery, 6 km S of Gisborne. **Tourist information:** Ampol Road Pantry; (054) 282 541. **Accommodation:** 2 motels, 1 cara./camp. park (at Macedon). **See also:** Wine Regions.

Glenrowan

Pop. 345

MAP REF. 224 D1, 235 M6

Glenrowan, 220 km NE of Melbourne, is the famous site of the defeat of Ned Kelly and his gang by the police in 1880. **Of interest:** Old Hume Hwy: Ned Kelly Memorial Museum and Homestead; Kate's Cottage, gifts and souvenirs behind huge 6-m high statue of Ned Kelly; engrossing computer-animated show of the capture of Ned Kelly. **In the area:** Nearby wineries: Baileys of

National Parks

Although it is Australia's smallest mainland State, Victoria houses over 100 national, state, wilderness and regional parks. Victoria's parks protect representative samples of a wide range of the State's land and vegetation types: from alps, open grasslands and desert mallee to rainforests, tall forests, coasts, volcanic plains and heathlands. Spring and summer are the best seasons to visit those parks noted for their wildflowers. In summer, sun lovers can head for parks along the coast to swim, surf, canoe, boat or fish. Autumn, with its mild weather, beckons the bushwalker, and winter means skiing at alpine parks.

Around Melbourne

At **Organ Pipes National Park,** only 20 kilometres north-west of Melbourne, there are interesting rock formations: a series of hexagonal basalt columns rising more than 20 metres above Jacksons Creek. These 'organ pipes' were formed when lava cooled in an ancient river bed. While this is the best known feature of the small 85-hectare park, it is also excellent for picnics, walks and bird-observing. Another favourite haunt of bushwalkers, 50 kilometres north-east of Melbourne, is **Kinglake National Park,** where wooded valleys, fern gullies and timbered ridges provide a perfect setting for two beautiful waterfalls, Masons and Wombelano Falls. From a lookout, visitors can enjoy a panoramic view of the Yarra Valley, Port Phillip Bay and the You Yangs Range.

Just 35 kilometres east of Melbourne is the green wonderland of the 1920-hectare **Dandenong Ranges National Park.** This park includes tree-fern gullies in which huge fronds of ferns form a canopy overhead, screening the sun and creating a cool, moist environment in which mosses, delicate ferns and flowers, including over 30 orchid species, all thrive. There are more than 20 species of native animals in the park, including echidnas, platypuses, ringtail possums and sugar gliders; kookaburras, rosellas and cockatoos often visit picnic areas. The spectacular rufous fantail can be seen in the summer months. There are over 100 bird species, but make sure you identify them by sight and not by sound only, because the lyrebird can mimic their calls.

Mornington Peninsula National Park is probably the most interesting park close to Melbourne, mainly because for more than 100 years the Point Nepean area has been out of bounds to most people. It has associations with early settlement, quarantine, shipping and defence.

Unusual basalt columns, Organ Pipes National Park

National Parks

Tidal River in Wilsons Promontory National Park, one of the State's most popular national parks

As one of Victoria's major Bicentennial projects, an information centre, walking tracks, displays and other facilities were provided during 1988-9. Today the total area of the park, including former Cape Schanck Coastal Park, is 2680 hectares. To prevent overcrowding and damage to the environment, no more than 600 people are permitted in the Point Nepean area at any one time; so bookings for day visits (with a park-use fee) are required, especially during summer. Vehicles are not permitted beyond the orientation centre, so walking or taking the transporter are the ways to get around. Highlights of the park are Fort Nepean, the cemetery with burials dating from the 1850s and the fascinating Cheviot Hill walk.

Yarra Ranges National Park, the most recent national park proclaimed in Victoria, is located just north-east of Melbourne. The majestic eucalypts and lush tree-fern glades of the Black Spur on the Maroondah Highway form a dramatic gateway to Marysville, Lake Mountain, Alexandra and Lake Eildon. Further south, along the Yarra Valley via Warburton, is Mt Donna Buang. The park includes one of Melbourne's water catchment areas which had previously been closed to public access. The moist forests of the Yarra Ranges are considered to be of national botanical significance, and they provide vital habitats for many unique animals. In particular, the forests of mountain ash — the world's tallest flowering plant — provide the habitat for Leadbeater's possum, a hollow-dependent endangered species. Thought to be extinct for many years, Leadbeater's possum was rediscovered in these forests in 1961.

Coastal Parks

Wilsons Promontory National Park in Gippsland is the best known coastal park and one of the most popular in Victoria. The Prom, as it is known, really does have something for everyone. There is a concentration of amenities and accommodation, including camping and caravan sites, at Tidal River, as well as the visitor information centre and park office. Leaflets for 80 kilometres of walking tracks are available here, and visitors should also inquire about the long but rewarding lighthouse walk. Other natural attractions include secluded bays and magnificent stretches of beaches, granite outcrops, and spectacular wildflowers that begin blooming in late winter and continue through spring. Wilsons Promontory is very popular in summer, with campsites available only by ballot for the Christmas-holiday period.

The unusual rock structures found at **Port Campbell National Park** — The Twelve Apostles, The Arch and Loch Ard Gorge — are majestic formations sculpted out of soft limestone cliffs by the relentless sea. While it is the spectacular coastal scenery that makes this park so popular, it is also an interesting linear park for birds, with around 100 species being recorded. The park was a popular place with Aboriginal people too, if the number of shell middens along the coast is an indication. And it is especially notorious for being part of the 'Shipwreck Coast'.

Closer to Melbourne are the beautiful lush tree-fern gullies and towering mountain ash forests of the **Otway National Park** and the special **Melba Gully State Park** to the north-west of the national park near Lavers Hill. Because of the treacherous nature of the waters, a lighthouse was the first piece of 'civilisation' at Cape Otway; it was opened in 1848 after two years in the building. Activities to be enjoyed include sightseeing all year (even in winter storms), while camping, surfing, fishing and walking are most enjoyable in spring and summer. There are guided walks in summer to see the glow-worms at Melba Gully.

Eastern Victoria, with its mild and fairly wet climate, has vast areas of dense forest. These are attractive to bushwalkers and campers, who will find here a wide range of trees — mainly eucalypts, but also native pines, banksias and paperbarks.

Some of the most attractive coastal scenery close to any major regional centre can be found in and around **The Lakes National Park.** The park is surrounded by the waters of the extensive Gippsland Lakes system, ideal for sailing, boating and fishing. The 2390-hectare park harbours a large population of kangaroos and more than 140 bird species. Camping, picnicking and an excellent network of walking tracks provide distractions for those who are land-based.

Croajingolong National Park has 87 500 hectares of coastline and hinterland stretching from Sydenham Inlet to the New South Wales border. The area contains remote rainforest, woodland, ocean beaches, rocky promontories, inlets and coves. Several rare species of wildlife can be found here, such as the smoky mouse and the ground parrot, and in spring the visitor will see an array of wildflowers. There is a wide range of activities for visitors at Croajingolong, with a holiday centre at Mallacoota and other towns along the Princes Highway offering accommodation and fine food.

In the north-east of the State

The **Alpine National Park,** created in December 1989 and currently covering approximately 642 000 hectares, is the State's largest national park. Stretching along the Great Dividing Range, the park links with the Kosciusko National Park in New South Wales and its neighbour Namadgi National Park in the Australian Capital Territory in a grouping of national parks that encompasses almost all of south-east Australia's alpine areas. The park protects the habitats of a variety of flora and fauna,

VICTORIA

Snow gums, Baw Baw National Park

including the rare mountain pygmy possum (the world's only exclusively sub-alpine marsupial). The Alps are renowned for their sublime landscapes, features characterised by Mount Bogong and Mount Feathertop (Victoria's highest mountains) and the unique Bogong High Plains. During spring and summer the high plains are carpeted with wildflowers; more than 1100 native plant species are found in the park, including 12 found nowhere else in the world. The park is ideal for bushwalking, horseriding and cross-country skiing. Both Falls Creek and Mount Hotham ski resorts are surrounded by the Alpine National Park. In the summer months most roads provide easy access for vehicles, allowing a range of scenic drives with short walks to lookouts and other points of interest. Some huts in the park, popular places for walkers to visit, are being restored for their historic value.

Mount Buffalo National Park, north-west of Bright, encompasses the Mount Buffalo plateau with its granite tors and rounded boulders. In milder weather, the park, with its bubbling streams and cascading waterfalls, offers visitors over 80 kilometres of marked walking tracks. The wildflowers on the high plains are at their best between November and March. Wombats, wallabies, lyrebirds, rosellas and gang-gang cockatoos may be seen. In winter, skiers can enjoy excellent cross-country skiing.

Canoeists will find excitement shooting the rapids or exploring the gorges of **Snowy River National Park** or **Mitchell River National Park,** both in East Gippsland, while bushwalkers can hike through beautiful forest scenery.

Baw Baw National Park covers the granite Baw Baw plateau at the southern end of Victoria's high country, and sections of the Thomson and Aberfeldy river valleys. It offers good cross-country skiing in winter, Baw Baw Alpine Village abutts the park, and numerous walking tracks in summer, including a 20-kilometre section of the Australian Alps Walking Track, which extends from Walhalla to Cowombat Flat on the New South Wales border. Summer visitors can take short walks to the Track and to the plateau, or follow cross-country ski trails. Colourful wildflowers bloom on the plateau in summer. The park is home to Leadbeater's possum and the Baw Baw frog (both endangered species), wombats, wallabies, echidnas, platypuses, gliders, and several types of snake and lizard. Crimson rosellas, yellow-tailed black cockatoos, gang-gangs and lyrebirds are common.

Fraser National Park centres on Lake Eildon, and offers boating, sailing, water skiing, fishing and swimming, and a number of walking tracks, including a nature trail near Devil Cove. The park's western boundary, along the Puzzle Range, provides scenic views over nearby peaks and Coller Bay. There are many kangaroos and wallabies in the park. Crimson rosellas, cockatoos, galahs and kookaburras visit the camping grounds, and around the lake there are cormorants, pelicans, ducks, swans, herons and ibis.

In the west of the State

The 167 000-hectare **Grampians National Park** offers marvellous scenery, wildlife and tourist facilities. The park is famous for its rugged sandstone ranges, waterfalls, wildflowers, wide variety of birds and mammals, as well as its Aboriginal rock-art sites. The peaks rise to heights of over 1000 metres and form the western edge of the Great Dividing Range. The Grampians is no doubt best seen on foot and there are many walking tracks, such as the easy-graded, well-marked Wonderland Track, through to the more challenging walks across the Major Mitchell Plateau.

Mount Eccles in south-west Victoria, is one of several parks that contain rock formations of great geological interest. An extinct volcano, a lava canal, lava cave and the formation called the Stony Rises are exceptional features, while the crater contains the tranquil Lake Surprise.

The surprise for most visitors to the **Little Desert National Park** is to discover that it is neither little nor a desert. It is best known for its amazing displays of wildflowers in spring; more than 600 flowering-plant species are found here, including more than 40 ground orchids. Another special feature of the Little Desert is that mallee fowl is found here. These birds build mounds for eggs that can be as much as 5 metres in diameter and 1.5 metres high.

Wyperfeld National Park in the north-west, also contains hundreds of species of plants and birdlife, and is also a great park to visit in the spring, autumn and winter. In good rainfall years there are colourful spring wildflower displays, and in the autumn the visitor will enjoy crisp, clear days — perfect for bushwalking and birdwatching.

Murray-Sunset National Park contains a diversity of semi-arid environments from riverine floodplains to heathlands, salt lakes and woodlands, which support a tremendous variety of wildlife, particularly birdlife. It is the second largest national park in the State. This park is best visited in the cooler months of the year.

Another park in the north-west of the State is the smaller **Hattah-Kulkyne National Park**. Typically, summers here are long, hot and dry; rainfall is usually less than 300 millimetres per year. The animals of this area have evolved strategies for avoiding or tolerating heat and dryness: some burrow, others just rest during the heat of the day; some birds catch thermals to cooler air. After rainfall and flooding from the Murray River, the serenely beautiful Hattah Lakes system transforms the park into a bird haven and a wonderful wildflower landscape.

For more information on Victoria's national parks, contact the Department of Conservation and Natural Resources at 240 Victoria Pde, East Melbourne; (03) 9412 4795.

Glenrowan, Taminick Gap Rd; Auldstone Cellars, Booths Rd, Taminick; Booths Taminick Cellars, Booths Rd, Taminick; HJT Vineyards, Keenan Rd. **Tourist information:** Kate's Cottage, Old Hume Hwy; (057) 66 2448. **Accommodation:** 1 motel, 1 cara. park. **See also:** Wine Regions.

Halls Gap Pop. 334

MAP REF. 228 I1, 230 I12

Beautifully sited in the heart of the Grampians, this little village is adjacent to Lake Bellfield and surrounded by the Grampians National Park and a network of scenic roads. Feb.: Grampians jazz festival. May: Grampians gourmet weekend. Sept.–Oct.: Wildflower exhibition. **In the area:** The area is noted for its wildflowers. Bushwalking, camping, rock climbing and abseiling in national park, one of largest in State; Visitors Centre, 2 km from town, open daily. Brambuk Aboriginal Living Cultural Centre, 2 km S. Wallaroo Wildlife Park, 5 km SE. Boroka Vineyards, 2 km E. Lake Fyans, 17 km E: swimming, fishing, yachting and water-skiing. Roses Gap Recreation Park, base for scenic walks, has a fitness track, accommodation and camping; Roses Gap Rd, 21 km N, in Northern Grampians section of park. Reids Lookout and The Balconies, 12 km NW. McKenzie Falls, 17 km NW. Wartook Pottery and Restaurant, 20 km NW. **Tourist information:** Grampians Rd; (053) 56 4247. **Accommodation:** 8 motels, 4 cara./camp. parks. **See also:** The Grampians; National Parks.

Hamilton Pop. 10 200

MAP REF. 228 F5

Known as the 'Wool Capital of the World', Hamilton is a prosperous and pleasant city less than an hour's drive from the coastal centres of Portland, Port Fairy and Warrnambool to the south and the Grampian Ranges to the north. **Of interest:** Big Woolbales Complex, Henty Hwy: focuses on wool industry with shearing demonstrations, woolshed memorabilia and craft centre. Hamilton Country Spun Woollen Mill and Factory, sales and tours (Mon.–Fri.); Peck St. HIRL (Hamilton Institute of Rural Learning), North Boundary Rd: has a nature trail and a breeding area for eastern barred bandicoots. HEAL (Hamilton Environmental Awareness and Learning) conducts land-care tours; bookings essential. Hamilton Art Gallery, Brown St. Lake Hamilton, Ballarat Rd: sandy beach, water sports, trout fishing and picnic facilities. On banks of lake, Sir Reginald Ansett Transport Museum has historical collection and memorabilia of transport industry which began in Hamilton in 1931. Small zoo with free-flight aviary, at Botanical Gardens (established 1870), French St. Hamilton Pastoral Museum, in former St Luke's Lutheran Church; Glenelg Hwy, open by appt. Hamilton History Centre and Aboriginal Keeping Place, Gray St, highlights aspects of local Aboriginal culture. Hamilton is the starting point for Mary MacKillop Pilgrims Drive; grave of Mary's father in cemetery. July: Eisteddfod. Aug.: Wool heritage week. **In the area:** Summit Park, Nigretta Rd, 15 km NW, specialises in the raising of Saxon-Merino sheep for superfine wool production; open daily. Wannon and Nigretta Falls, 15 km NW. At Coleraine, 35 km NW: Points Arboretum, official State collection of eucalypts. Mt Eccles National Park, near Macarthur, 35 km S, features Mt Eccles and crater Lake Surprise, one of 3 extinct volcanoes. Grampians Tour (good day trip from Hamilton) to Dunkeld, Grampians National Park, Halls Gap, Ararat and back via Glenthompson. **Tourist information:** Lonsdale St; (055) 72 3746 and 1800 80 7056. **Accommodation:** 6 hotels, 7 motels, 1 hostel, 2 cara./camp. parks. **See also:** The Western District.

Harrietville Pop. 250

MAP REF. 225 M8, 235 Q9, 236 C7

Tucked into the foothills of Mt Hotham and Mt Feathertop, Harrietville is a convenient accommodation centre for skiers at Mt Hotham or holidaymakers in north-east Victoria. Gold was discovered here in 1862, and the gold-rush village was proclaimed a township in 1879. **Of interest:** Bicycles, horses, fishing rods and gold-panning dishes for hire. Pioneer Park, open-air museum and picnic area; Alpine Rd. Audrey's Dolls and Crafts, hand-made porcelain dolls; Cobungra Court. Aug.: International Ski Marathon Kangaroo Hoppet (Falls Creek). Bushmarket, 3rd Sun. in Jan. and Easter Sun. Mar.: Bushman's Classic (mountain cattlemen's race). **In the area:** Bushwalking in high mountain country of Alpine National Park, which surrounds town (weather conditions can be harsh and change suddenly); walking tracks: Mt Feathertop (1922 m), 20 km return; Mt Hotham (1859 m), about 32 km one way. Mt Hotham Alpine Village, 32 km SE: during summer, bushwalking (Australian Alps Walking Track passes through village) in Bogong High Plains and Dargo High Plains; during winter, excellent downhill and cross-country skiing. Dinner Plain Alpine Village, 44 km SE: during summer, bushwalking and horseriding; during winter, good cross-country skiing. Crystal Waters Trout Farm and, nearby, Mountain Fresh Trout Farm, 5 km N: fishing and educational displays. **Tourist information:** Old General Store, Alpine Rd; (057) 59 2553. **Accommodation:** 1 hotel/motel, 1 cara./camp. park.

Healesville Pop. 6264

MAP REF. 213 N5, 216 E6, 226 F3

Surrounded by mountain forest country, Healesville is about a one and a half hour's drive from Melbourne along the Maroondah Hwy. It has been a popular resort town since the turn of the century, as the climate is cool and pleasant in summer and the area offers excellent bushwalks and beautiful scenic drives. **Of interest:** Trolley rides, Healesville railway station to Yarra Glen; Sun. only. Yarra Valley Winery Tours, inquire at Tourist information. Feb.: Coldstream country and western festival. Mar.: Australian car rally championship. **In the area:** Hedgend Maze, 2 km S. Pottery, lapidary and art gallery at Nigel Court, off Badger Creek Rd, 2 km S. Corranderrk Aboriginal Cemetery, 3 km S. World-famous Healesville Sanctuary, 4 km S, on Badger Creek Rd: 32-ha reserve houses a variety of native birds and animals in largely natural bushland setting; key attractions include displays enabling animals to be seen in close proximity; picnic/barbecue facilities, kiosk and self-service restaurant. Mallesons Lookout, views of Yarra Valley through to Melbourne; 8 km S. Badger Weir Park, majestic park in natural setting; 7 km SE. Tuscany Gallery, 5 km E. Maroondah Reservoir Park, 3 km NE: magnificent park in sylvan setting, walking tracks and lookout nearby. At Donnelly's Weir Park, 4 km N: start of 5000-km Bicentennial National Trail to Cooktown (Qld) for horseriders and walkers. Mt St Leonard, 14 km N, fine views from summit. At Toolangi, 17 km NW: Forest Discovery Centre, displays of timber industry and its history; Singing Garden of C.J. Dennis, a beautiful, formal garden; Toolangi Pottery. At Yarra Glen, 14 km W: historic Grand Hotel; Yarra Valley Racing Centre, 5 km E; Gulf Station (1854), historic homestead, 2 km N. Sugarloaf Reservoir Park, 10 km W of Yarra Glen, for fishing, sailing and walking. **Tourist information:** Yarra Valley Healesville Visitor Information Centre, 127 Maroondah Hwy; (059) 62 2600. **Accommodation:** 5 motels, 20 B&B, 1 hostel, 3 cara./camp. parks. **See also:** Wine Regions.

Heathcote   Pop. 1507

MAP REF. 234 E9

In attractive countryside on the McIvor Hwy, Heathcote is set along the McIvor Creek, 47 km SE of Bendigo. **Of interest:** McIvor Cottage Crafts, in old court house, High St: historical display, art and craft market and tourist information. Pink Cliffs, brilliant mineral staining created by eroded spoil from gold sluices; Pink Cliffs Rd, off Hospital Rd. Old Heathcote Hospital (1859), listed for preservation by National Trust; Hospital Rd. McIvor Range Reserve, off Barrack St. Wineries in town: Heathcote Winery (High St) and Zuber Estate (Northern Hwy). Oct.: Golden grape festival. Nov.: Show. **In the area:** Lake Eppalock, 10 km W, one of the State's largest lakes. Central Victorian Yabbie Farm, on Northern Hwy at South Heathcote. Mount Ida Lookout, 4 km N, excellent views. Wineries nearby: Wild Duck Creek Estate (10 km S); Jasper Hill and Huntleigh Vineyards (6 km N); McIvor Creek Wines (10 km SW) and Eppalock Ridge Vineyards (22 km SW). **Tourist information:** McIvor Cottage, High St; (054) 33 3677. **Accommodation:** 1 hotel, 1 hotel/motel, 1 motel, 1 B&B, 1 cara./camp. park.

Hopetoun   Pop. 704

MAP REF. 122 E12, 230 H3, 232 H13

This small Mallee town, south-east of Wyperfeld National Park, was named after the seventh Earl of Hopetoun, first Governor-General of Australia. Hopetoun was a frequent visitor to the home of Edward Lascelles, who was largely responsible for opening up the Mallee area. **Of interest:** In Evelyn St, two National Trust-classified homes: Hopetoun House (1891) built for Lascelles; Corrong Homestead (1846), home of first European settler in area, Peter McGinnis. Mallee Mural and leadlight window in Shire Office, Lascelles St, depict history of the Mallee. Lake Lascelles, end Austin St, for boating, swimming and picnics. Oct.: Agricultural show. **In the area:** Wyperfeld National Park, 50 km W; information centre in park. Swamp Tank Museum at Turriff, 45 km NE. Nearby at Speed, Mallee machinery field days held in Aug. **Tourist information:** Yarriambiack Shire Council, 75 Lascelles St; (050) 83 3001. **Accommodation:** 1 hotel, 1 hotel/motel, 1 cara./camp. park.

Horsham   Pop. 12 552

MAP REF. 230 G9

At the junction of the Western, Wimmera and Henty Hwys, Horsham is generally regarded as the capital of the Wimmera region. It is a popular base for tours of the region, particularly to the Little Desert National Park, 40 km NW, to the Grampians, some 50 km SE and to Mt Arapiles, 32 km W. **Of interest:** Botanic Gardens, cnr Baker and Firebrace Sts. Horsham Art Gallery, features Mack Jost collection of Australian art; Wilson St. Cottage Delights, Dooen Rd, for plants and crafts. May Park, Dimboola Rd. Apex Adventure Island, children's playground; Barnes Rd. Golf Course Rd: Horsham Rocks and Gems and Country Crafts; Wool Factory, producing top quality, extra-fine wool from Saxon-Merino sheep; tours daily. Olde Horsham Village, Western Hwy at edge of town: historic buildings, art, craft, antiques. Wimmera River flows through town; attractive picnic spots, fishing and good viewing place for spectacular sunsets. Mar.: Wimmera machinery field days. Sept.: Agricultural show. Oct.: Spring garden festival. Dec.: Kannamaroo festival. **In the area:** Good fishing for redfin, trout, Murray cod in lakes in area. Wimmera lakes for fishing and water sports include: Green Lake (13 km SE), Pine Lake (16 km SE), Taylors Lake (18 km SE), Toolondo Reservoir (44 km S), home of the fighting brown trout and Rocklands Reservoir (90 km S) on Glenelg River, built to supplement Wimmera-Mallee irrigation scheme. Redfin and Trout Championship at lakes in Wimmera district, each Oct. Mt Arapiles, 32 km W, popular climbing rock, 360-degree views from lookout. Black Range Cashmere and Thryptomene Farm, 40 km S; 4WD tours available, bookings essential, through Tourist information. Grampians National Park, 50 km SE, famous for its rugged sandstone ranges, wildflowers, waterfalls, birds and mammals and Aboriginal rock-art sites. At Jung, 10 km NE, market last Sat. each month. **Tourist information:** 20 O'Callaghan's Pde; (053) 82 1832. **Accommodation:** 6 hotels, 15 motels, 1 B&B, 2 cara./camp. parks. **See also:** The Wimmera.

Inglewood   Pop. 740

MAP REF. 231 O8, 234 A7

North along the Calder Hwy from Bendigo are the 'Golden Triangle' towns of Inglewood and Bridgewater on Loddon. Sizeable gold nuggets have been found in this area: the largest 'Welcome Stranger' found at Moliagul, weighed 65 kg; two were found at Kingower in the last decade. **Of interest:** Old eucalyptus oil distillery, Calder Hwy (northern end of town). Old court house, now displays historical memorabilia of region (open by appt); Southey St. Inglewood Gipsy Tours, wagons drawn by Clydesdales; Grant St. Apr.: Blue Eucalyptus festival (even-numbered years). **In the area:** Passing Clouds winery at Kingover; 11 km W. Kooyoora State Park, 16 km W: features Melville Caves, once haunt of notorious bushranger Captain Melville; Kangderaar Vineyard (in park). At Bridgewater on Loddon, 8 km SE: fishing, water-skiing, parachute jumping (at weekends) and Water Wheel Vineyards. **Tourist information:** Old Railway Centre, 1 Thompson St; (054) 38 3175. **Accommodation:** 1 hotel, 1 motel, 1 cara./camp. park. **See also:** Wine Regions.

Inverleigh   Pop. 282

MAP REF. 212 E9, 219 B6, 229 P7

On the Leigh River, this little town 29 km W of Geelong has a number of historic buildings. **Of interest:** On Hamilton Hwy: former Horseshoe Inn; two-storey hotel; Church of England; Presbyterian Church; State School. **In the area:** Fishing in Leigh and Barwon Rivers. Inverleigh Common, bushland and fauna reserve; 2 km N. Barunah Plains Homestead (open by appt), 17 km W. **Tourist information:** Geelong Otway Tourist Information Centre, National Wool Museum, 26–32 Moorabool St, Geelong; (052) 22 2900. **Accommodation:** Limited.

Inverloch
Pop. 2195

MAP REF. 226 G10

This is a small seaside resort on Anderson Inlet, east of Wonthaggi. It has long stretches of excellent beach with good surf, and is very popular in summer. **Of interest:** Environment Centre and Shell Museum, in Tourist information building, The Esplanade. Mar.: Jazz festival. **In the area:** Adjacent to town, Anderson's Inlet, most southerly habitat of mangroves. Townsend Bluff and Maher's Landing for birdwatching. Inverloch–Cape Paterson Scenic Rd through Bunurong Cliff Coastal Reserve, 15 km SW; views equal those on Great Ocean Rd. Spear fishing and surfing at Cape Paterson; 13 km SW. Tarwin River, 20 km SE, offers good fishing. Beaches, natural bushland and wildlife at Venus Bay nearby. **Tourist information:** Cnr Ramsay Blvd and The Esplanade; (056) 74 2706. **Accommodation:** 2 motels, 4 B&B, 4 cara./camp. parks.

Jeparit
Pop. 440

MAP REF. 230 F6

This little town in the Wimmera, 37 km N of Dimboola, is 5 km SE of Lake Hindmarsh, the largest natural freshwater lake in Victoria. The late Sir Robert Menzies was born here in 1894. **Of interest:** Sir Robert Menzies Spire, illuminated at night, Sands Ave. Menzies Square, site of dwelling where Menzies was born; cnr Charles and Roy Sts. Wimmera-Mallee Pioneer Museum, Charles St at southern entrance to town: 4-ha complex of colonial buildings furnished in period; also displays of restored farm machinery. Jan.: Beach carnival. Oct.: Agricultural show. **In the area:** Safe beaches, fishing and camping at Lake Hindmarsh, 5 km NW. Wyperfeld National Park, 44 km N and Little Desert National Park, 40 km SW; both feature wildflowers, native fauna and walking tracks. **Tourist information:** Horsham Rural City Visitor Centre, 20 O'Callaghan's Pde, Horsham; (053) 82 1832. **Accommodation:** 2 hotels, 1 cara. park.

Kaniva
Pop. 762

MAP REF. 230 C7

Kaniva in the west Wimmera, 43 km from Bordertown, SA, is just north of the Little Desert, which is noted for its wildflowers in spring. **Of interest:** Historical museum has large collection of items of local history; Commercial St, open by appt. In Progress St: Mayfare Cement Works; Iris farm. Eastwoods herb farm, Western Hwy. **In the area:** Billy-Ho Bush Walk, a 3-km self-guide walk in Little Desert National Park, begins some 10 km S; numbered pegs allow identification of various species of desert flora (brochure available at Tourist information). Mooree Reserve, 20 km SW of town. National Trust-classified railway station (1889) at Serviceton, 23 km W (key available from Serviceton General Store). Waterbird farm, 20 km NW, breeds black swans and other species; open by appt. **Tourist information:** 41 Commercial St; (053) 92 2418. **Accommodation:** 1 hotel, 2 motels, 1 cara./camp. park.

Kerang
Pop. 4024

MAP REF. 122 I12, 231 P3, 233 P13, 234 A2

Some 30 km from the Murray River and 60 km from Swan Hill, Kerang is the centre of a productive rural area and lies at the southern end of a chain of lakes and marshes. Some of the world's largest breeding-grounds for ibis and other waterfowl are found in these marshes. The ibis is closely protected because of its value in controlling locusts and other pests. **Of interest:** Old water tower, cnr Murray Valley Hwy and Shadforth St. Museum, Riverwood Drive, features cars and farm machinery. May: Salt and Water festival. **In the area:** Apex Park recreation area near the first of the three Reedy Lakes (8 km NW); the second has a large ibis rookery. Lakes Meran, Reedy, Kangaroo and Charm are suitable for water sports. Excellent fishing. Gunbower State Forest, significant red-gum habitat, flora and fauna; 25 km N. Murrabit, 29 km N, on the Murray and surrounded by picturesque river forests; country market, 1st Sat. each month. At Koondrook, 20 km NE, historic building and sawmill. Lake Boga, 44 km NW, has good sandy beaches. At Easter, Australian tractor pull championship at Quambatook, 42 km SW. **Tourist information:** Golden Rivers Tourism, 25 Murray St, Barham (NSW); (054) 53 3100. **Accommodation:** 4 hotels, 1 hotel/motel, 3 motels, 2 cara./camp. parks. **See also:** The Mighty Murray.

Picturesque Lake Boga, north-west of Kerang

Koo-wee-rup
Pop. 1106

MAP REF. 213 M10, 226 F7

Well known for its Potato festival held each March, this town is in the middle of a rich market-garden area near Western Port. **Of interest:** Historical Society Museum, Rossiter Rd; open Sun. **In the area:** Bayles Flora and Fauna Park, 8 km NE. At Tynong, 20 km NE: Victoria's Farm Shed, displays; Gumbaya Park, in landscaped native bushland. At Pakenham, 21 km N: Berwick-Pakenham Historical Society Museum, John St; Military Vehicle Museum, Army Rd. Royal Botanic Gardens, Cranbourne, 28 km NW, all native species. At Cardinia, 6 km W, Australian Pioneer Farm offers opportunities to shear sheep and milk cows. Fishing and boating at Tooradin, 10 km W, on Sawtell's Inlet. Between Tooradin and Koo-wee-rup, on the South Gippsland Hwy: Harewood House (1850s), original furnishings (open weekends); Swamp Observation Tower, views of surrounding swamp and Western Port. **Tourist information:** Newsagency, 277 Rossiter Rd; (059) 97 1456. **Accommodation:** 1 motel.

Koroit   Pop. 968

MAP REF. 228 H9

Koroit is 18 km NW of the coastal resort of Warrnambool in the south-west of Victoria. It is an agricultural town with historic botanic gardens. The commercial and church precincts of the town, both with historic buildings, have been classified by the National Trust. **In the area:** Tower Hill State Game Reserve, 3 km S: volcanic area with Natural History Centre, walking tracks and bird hides. Coast between Port Fairy and Warrnambool offers delightful scenery. Mahogany Walking Track, 22-km walking track between Port Fairy and Warrnambool. **Tourist information:** Warrnambool Tourist Information Centre, 600 Raglan St, Warrnambool; (055) 64 7837. **Accommodation:** 1 hotel, 2 B&B, 1 cara./camp. park.

Korumburra   Pop. 2906

MAP REF. 213 O12, 226 H8

The giant Gippsland earthworm, sought by fishermen and geologists alike, is found near this town, situated on the South Gippsland Hwy, 116 km SE of Melbourne. The area surrounding the town is given to dairying and agriculture, and the countryside is hilly. **Of interest:** Coal Creek Historical Village, cnr South Gippsland Hwy and Silkstone Rd: recreation of 19th-century coal-mining village on original site of Coal Creek mine (commenced in 1890s), orientation centre in Mechanics' Institute near entrance. Feb.: Coal Creek twilight music and theatre festival. Mar.: Karmai (giant worm) festival. **In the area:** South Gippsland Railway offers train rides through 40 km of countryside linking Leongatha, Korumburra, Loch and Nyora; Sun. and public holidays. Gooseneck Pottery, Ruby, 4 km SE. Old School Tea Room in 1916 primary-school building; 6 km SE, off South Gippsland Hwy. Leongatha, 14 km SE. Top Paddock Cheeses, tastings and sales of traditional, curd and soft cheeses; Bena, 4 km NW. At Loch, 16 km NW: antiques, art and craft. At Poowong, 18 km NW: Poowong Pioneer Chapel, fine example of German architecture; Mudlark Pottery. **Tourist information:** South Gippsland Tourism, Coal Creek Historical Village, cnr South Gippsland Hwy and Silkstone Rd; (056) 55 2233. **Accommodation:** 2 hotels, 1 motel, 2 B&B, 1 cara./camp. park.

Kyabram   Pop. 5540

MAP REF. 234 G5

A prosperous town in the Murray-Goulburn area, just 40 km NW of Shepparton, Kyabram is in a rich dairying and fruit-growing district. **Of interest:** Community-owned waterfowl and fauna park on Lake Rd: five ponds with waterbirds and 15-ha of open-range parklands with native fauna. The Stables, adjacent to fauna park, pottery and crafts. Mr Ilzyn's Cottages, Breen Ave: mansions, hotels and farmhouses from around the world, all in miniature. Mar.: Rodeo. Easter: Antique aeroplane fly-in. **Tourist information:** Fauna park, 75 Lake Rd; (058) 52 2883. **Accommodation:** 3 hotels, 2 motels, 2 cara./camp. parks. **See also:** The Mighty Murray.

Kyneton   Pop. 3940

MAP REF. 212 G1, 229 R1, 231 R12, 234 D11

Little more than an hour's drive from Melbourne, along the Calder Hwy, Kyneton is a well-preserved, attractive town with several interesting bluestone buildings. Farms around the town prospered during the gold rushes, supplying large quantities of fresh food to the Ballarat and Bendigo diggings. **Of interest:** Kyneton Museum (open Wed.–Sun.), Piper St, in former bank (c.1865); drop-log cottage in grounds. Botanic Gardens, Clowes St, 8-ha area above river with 500 specimen trees. Historic buildings: town's churches; mechanics institute, Mollison St; old police depot, Jenning St. In Piper St: Steam Mill, restored to operational condition, open weekends; Meskills Woolstore, has wool spinning mill, and yarn and garments for sale; Alpaca Shop, tours and demonstrations, sales. Self-guide walks, see Tourist information. Market, 2nd Sun. each month. Easter: Antique fair. Sept.: Daffodil and arts festival. Nov.: Kyneton Cup. **In the area:** Two-storey bluestone mills on either side of town; both on Calder Hwy. Upper Coliban, Lauriston and Malmsbury Reservoirs, all nearby. At Malmsbury, 10 km NW: historic bluestone railway viaduct; Bleak House (1850s) with rose garden; The Mill (1861), National Trust-classified, has gallery, restaurant and accommodation. Cottage Maze Gardens, Drummond, 12 km N. At Trentham, 22 km SW: historic foundry; Jargon Crafts; Minifie's Berry Farm, pick-your-own in season. At Blackwood, further 14 km S, Garden of St Erth. Carlsruhe Gallery and Campaspe Art Gallery at Carlsruhe, 5 km SE. Trentham Falls, 20 km SE. Burke and Wills Camel farm, Woodend; 15 km SE on Calder Hwy. Turpins Falls, Metcalfe, 22 km N. **Tourist information:** Jean Haynes Playground, High St; (054) 22 6110 (closed Tues. and Thurs.). **Accommodation:** 1 hotel, 2 motels, 4 B&B, 1 cara./camp. park.

Lake Bolac   Pop. 266

MAP REF. 222 C13, 229 J5

In the Western District plains area, this small town on the Glenelg Hwy is by a 1460-ha freshwater lake that has sandy beaches around a 20-km shoreline and is good for fishing (eels, trout, perch and yellow-belly), boating and swimming. There are several boat-launching ramps. Easter: Yachting regatta. **Tourist information:** Lake Bolac Motel, Glenelg Hwy; (053) 50 2218. **Accommodation:** 1 motel, 1 B&B, 1 cara./camp. park.

Lakes Entrance   Pop. 4622

MAP REF. 227 R5, 236 H13

This extremely popular holiday town is at the eastern end of the Gippsland Lakes, which form the largest inland network of waterways in Australia. They cover an area of more than 400 sq. km. and are separated from the ocean by a thin sliver of sand dunes forming a large part of the Ninety Mile Beach, which

Royal Cave at Buchan Caves, north of Lakes Entrance

stretches south to Seaspray. A bridge across the Cunningham Arm gives access to the surf beach from Lakes Entrance. The town is well suited for the holiday maker, catering for both seaside recreation and exploration of the mountain country to the north. It is the home port for a large fishing fleet and many pleasure craft. Large cruise vessels conduct regular sightseeing tours of the lakes throughout the year. Boats can also be hired. Fishing, both ocean and beach, is popular, as are swimming and surfing on a variety of good beaches. **Of interest:** Fisherman's Co-operative, Bullock Island, has viewing platform and fish for sale. Shell Museum, the Esplanade. Potteries and galleries. Jan.: Australian wood design exhibition. Nov.: World Cup sport kiting championship. **In the area:** Carriage tours available from East Gippsland Carriage Co., just east of town. Lake Bunga, 3 km E, nature trail on foreshore. Kinkuna Country fauna park and family entertainment centre, Princes Hwy; 3.5 km E. Lake Tyers (6–23 km NE, depending on access point): sheltered waters ideal for fishing, swimming and boating; cruises depart from Fishermans Landing. Braeburne Park Orchards, 6 km N. Woodsedge, 8 km N on Baades Rd: gallery, furniture workshop and glass-blowing demonstrations. Wyanga Park Vineyard and Winery, 10 km N; also reached by boat trip from town. Buchan Caves, 55 km N, well worth a visit. Blue Gum Ostriches, 6 km NW on Hoggs Lane: tours, display of painted eggs; closed Tues. Day trips to old mining areas around Omeo, 126 km NW. Good views: Jemmy's Point, 1 km W, and Nyerimilang Park, 10 km NW; original homestead (north wing 1892). At Metung, 15 km W: boat hire; regatta in Mar. each year. Nicholson River (24 km W), and Golvinda wineries (50 km NW), via Bairnsdale. **Tourist information:** Visitors Information Centre, cnr Esplanade and Marine Pde; (051) 55 1966. **Accommodation:** 2 hotel/motels, 20 motels, 15 cara./camp. parks. **See also:** Gippsland Lakes; Wine Regions.

Lancefield Pop. 1063

MAP REF. 212 I2, 234 E11

This historic township with its wide streets and Victorian buildings is located 67 km NW of Melbourne. **Of interest:** Old Macedonia House (1889), now Antique Centre of Victoria including Crafts cottage (local crafts); Main Rd. Cleveland, an historic home and winery, 2 km E on Shannons Rd. Mechanics Hall (1868), High St. Dec.: Horse festival. **In the area:** A number of wineries and nurseries; horseriding in area; inquire at Tourist information. Monument Creek Herb Farm, Monument Rd, 5 km W. **Tourist information:** Centre Vic Motor Inn, Main Rd; (054) 29 1777. **Accommodation:** 1 motel.

Leongatha Pop. 3968

MAP REF. 213 P13, 226 H9

Located near the foothills of the Strzelecki Ranges, Leongatha is a large dairying area and a good base for trips to Wilsons Promontory and the seaside and fishing resorts on the coast. **Of interest:** Historic Society Museum (check opening times) and Art and Craft Gallery, McCartin St. Mushroom Crafts and Pottery, Bair St. Cash's Weaving Factory, open to public; Holt St. Feb.: Cycling carnival. Sept.: Daffodil and floral festival. **In the area:** South Gippsland Railway tourist train, from Leongatha to Korumburra, Loch and Nyora; Sun. and public holidays. Firelight Museum, 9 km N, features antique lamps and firearms. About 21 km N, excellent scenic driving along Grand Ridge Rd to Tarra-Bulga National Park (120 km E). At Meeniyan, 17 km SE, excellent craft shop. Mossvale Park, 16 km NE: impressive plantation of exotic trees, picnic/barbecue facilities; venue for Victorian State Orchestra performance each Feb. At Mirboo North, 23 km NE: Grand Ridge Brewing Company, viewing of beer-brewing process and sales; Erimae Lavender Farm; Colonial Bank Antiques. Brackenhurst Rotary Dairy, Christoffersens Rd, Nerrena, 5 km E: 350 cows, also museum; open from 3.30 p.m. daily. Gooseneck Pottery, Ruby, 9 km NW. Korumburra, 14 km NW along South Gippsland Hwy. **Tourist information:** CAB, Michael Place Complex; (056) 62 2111. **Accommodation:** 2 motels, 1 B&B, 1 cara./camp. park.

Lorne Pop. 1143

MAP REF. 212 D13, 219 A13, 229 P10

The approaches to Lorne along the Great Ocean Rd, whether from east or west, are quite spectacular. The town is one of Victoria's most attractive coastal resorts. It has a year-round mild climate and the superb mountain scenery of the Otways nearby. Captain Loutit gave the district the name of Loutitt Bay. The village of Lorne was established in 1871, became popular with pastoralists from inland areas, and developed rather in the style of an English seaside resort. When the Great Ocean Rd opened in 1932 Lorne grew more popular; however, the town itself has remained relatively unspoiled, with good beaches, surfing, and excellent bushwalking in the hills. **Of interest:** Teddy's Lookout at edge of George St behind town, for excellent bay views. Foreshore reserve. Shipwreck Walk along beach. Paddle boats available for hire. Qdos Contemporary Art Gallery, Mountjoy Pde. Lorne Fisheries on pier; daily supplies from local fleet. Shell Shop and Museum, William St. Jan.: Pier to Pub swim; Surf to Mountain foot race. **In the area:** Angahook-Lorne

Alpine Country

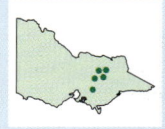

To the east and north-east of Melbourne, the gently rounded peaks of the Victorian Alps stretch, seemingly endlessly, under clear skies. They are much lower than alpine ranges in other parts of the world, lacking sheer escarpments and jagged peaks, but they still stand majestic, especially when covered in snow. These blue ranges are not high enough to have a permanent cover of snow, but the expanses of the rolling mountains are ideal for cross-country and downhill skiing.

The skiing season officially opens on the Queen's Birthday long weekend each June and closes in October, but it often actually extends beyond these dates. Each year, thousands of people flock to the snow for the enjoyment of skiing, for snowboarding or just to enjoy the beauty of nature.

There is bountiful fishing in the lakes and trout streams. Tennis, rock climbing, sailing, swimming, canoeing and water-skiing are popular sports in the summer. Many riding schools in the valleys provide for those who want to explore the countryside on horseback. For the more energetic, bushwalking in this beautiful rugged country is a must. Despite their summer beauty, however, the Alps can still claim the life of an ill-prepared bushwalker. Make sure you have the necessary equipment and knowledge and always tell someone where you are going and when you expect to be back.

Victoria's ski resorts are all located within easy reach of Melbourne.

Mount Donna Buang, 95 km from Melbourne, via Warburton. Sightseeing and novice skiing.

Lake Mountain, 120 km from Melbourne, via Healesville. Sightseeing and cross-country skiing.

Mount Baw Baw, 177 km from Melbourne, via Drouin. Beginners, novices and cross-country skiing. **Mount St Gwinear** nearby, is popular for cross-country skiing.

Mount Buller, 221 km from Melbourne, via Mansfield. For beginners to advanced skiers. Ski hire and instruction.

Mount Stirling, 250 km from Melbourne, near Mount Buller. Cross-country skiing. Most trails start at Telephone Box Junction. Visitor centre with public shelter, ski hire and trail maps.

Mount Buffalo, 331 km from Melbourne, via Myrtleford. Includes Dingo Dell (6 km) and Cresta (10 km). Beginners, families and cross-country skiing. Ski hire and instruction.

Falls Creek, 356 km from Melbourne, via the Snow Road through Oxley. Protected ski runs for novices, intermediate and advanced skiers; good cross-country skiing. Ski hire and instruction.

Mount Hotham, 367 km from Melbourne, via the Snow Road through Oxley. Known as the 'powder snow capital' of Australia. For experienced downhill skiers. Also cross-country skiing. Ski hire and instruction.

Dinner Plain, a 10-minute ski-shuttle ride from Mount Hotham. Offers ski hire, cross-country skiing and horseriding.

For further information on all resorts, contact the Alpine Resorts Commission, Amev House, Whitehorse Road, Box Hill; (03) 9895 6900, or the Falls Creek Information Centre, Bogong High Plains Tourist Rd, Falls Creek; (057) 58 3224. **See also:** Safe Skiing. **Map references:** 222-23; for Lake Mountain, 226 H2; for Mount Donna Buang, 226 G3; and for Mount Baw Baw, 227 J4.

On the slopes at Mount Buller, one of the State's most popular ski resorts

Railway station at Maldon, a National Trust-classified town

State Park, surrounding town: Erskine Falls (5 km NW of town); many walking tracks, including one to Kalimna and Phantom waterfalls from Sheoak Picnic area, about 4 km from town. Scenic drives: west in the Otway Ranges; south-west or north-east along Great Ocean Rd. Allenvale, 2 km W. Cumberland River Valley, 4 km SW: walking tracks and camping ground. Mt Defiance, 10 km SW. Wye River, 17 km SW: fishing and surfing. Gentle Annie Berry Gardens, 26 km NW, via Deans Marsh. **Tourist information:** 144 Mountjoy Pde; (052) 89 1036. **Accommodation:** 2 hotel/motels, 5 motels, 2 B&B, 1 hostel, 5 cara./camp. parks. **See also:** The Great Ocean Road.

Maffra Pop. 3879

MAP REF. 227 M5

The Shire of Maffra extends from the farming lands of the Macalister Irrigation Area north to the mountain scenery of the Great Dividing Range. **Of interest:** Maffra Sugar Beet Museum, River St. Mineral and gemstone display in court house, Johnson St. All Seasons Herb Gardens, Foster St. Mar.: Harvest festival. **In the area:** At Heyfield 10 km W, Timber festival in Jan. Lake Glenmaggie, 11 km N of Heyfield, popular water sports venue. Spectacular scenic drives along forest road north (closed in winter), which follows Macalister Valley to Licola (49 km from Heyfield), and to Mt Tamboritha (20 km NE of Licola) and Mt Howitt (50 km), both in Alpine National Park; or to Jamieson (147 km) and access to snowfields or Lake Eildon. Road north from Maffra, via Briagalong (14 km), leads to historic town of Dargo (86 km N) and over Dargo High Plains. Lake Tarli Karng, located in Alpine National Park, 60 km NE of Licola, is a major focus for bushwalking in season. Trail-riding and horseback tours from Valencia Creek, 17 km N of Maffra, and from Licola. At Briagalong, 22 km NE: historic hotel, art and craft shops and Avonlea Gardens. Australian Wildlife Art Gallery and Sculpture, 25 km E. **Tourist information:** The Court House, 8 Johnson St; (051) 41 1811. **Accommodation:** 3 hotels, 1 motel, 1 B&B, 1 cara./camp. park.

Maldon Pop. 1174

MAP REF. 223 O4, 231 P11, 234 B10

The National Trust has declared Maldon the 'First Notable Town' in Australia, on the basis that no other town has such an interesting collection of 19th-century buildings, nor such a collection of European trees. Situated 20 km NW of Castlemaine in central Victoria, Maldon is very popular with tourists, especially during the Maldon Easter Fair, and in spring when the wildflowers are in bloom. The deep reef goldmines in the area were among Victoria's richest, and at one stage 20 000 men worked on the nearby Tarrangower diggings. Enthusiasts still search for gold in the area. **Of interest:** Anzac Hill, southern end of High St, for good view of town. Many notable buildings, mostly constructed of local stone: Maldon Hospital (1860), cnr Adair and Chapel Sts; post office (1870), High St; old council offices, High St (now folk museum); Dabb's General Store, Main St, has faithfully restored old storefront. National Trust properties: former Denominational (Penny) School; Welsh Congregational Church, cnr Camp and Church Sts; Cumquat Tea Rooms, High St. The Beehive Chimney (1862), south end of Church St. Castlemaine and Maldon Preservation Society runs steam trains from railway station, Hornsby St (Sun. and public holidays). Town walking tour, leaflet available. Feb.: Camp draft. Easter: Fair. Oct.: Vintage car hill climb. Nov.: Folk festival. **In the area:** Delightful bushwalks and intriguing rock formations. Panoramic views from Mt Tarrangower Lookout Tower, 2 km W. Carmen's Tunnel, 2 km SW, a vivid reminder of hardships of goldmining days. Cairn Curran Reservoir, 10 km SW: water sports, fishing, picnics and sailing club near spillway. North-east, goldmining dredge beside road to Bendigo. 'Porcupine Township', 3 km NE, a reconstructed goldmining town. Nuggetty Ranges and Mt Moorol, 2 km N. **Tourist information:** High St; (054) 75 2569. **Accommodation:** 3 motels, 10 B&B, 1 cara./camp. park. **See also:** The Golden Age.

Mallacoota Pop. 961

MAP REF. 115 G13, 237 Q11

On the Gippsland coast, at the mouth of a deep inlet of the same name, Mallacoota is a seaside and fishing township, and a popular holiday centre. The Croajingolong National Park surrounds the town. Bushwalking and birdwatching are popular activities in the area. Easter: Festival. **In the area:** Lake and river cruises; scenic drives, contact Tourist information. Gipsy Point, 16 km NW, set in attractive countryside. Genoa, 24 km NW, on Princes Hwy, last town before entering NSW. Nearby Genoa Peak, for magnificent views. Bastion Point (2 km SE) and Betka (5 km S) are good surfing beaches. **Tourist information:** 57 Maurice Ave; (051) 58 0788. **Accommodation:** 3 motels, 4 cara./camp. parks. **See also:** National Parks.

Mansfield Pop. 2178

MAP REF. 224 C10, 235 L10

A popular inland resort at the junction of the Midland and Maroondah Hwys, Mansfield is 3 km E of the northern arm of Lake Eildon. It is the nearest sizeable town to Mt Buller Alpine Village and Mt

Craig's Hut, near Mansfield, used for filming The Man from Snowy River

Stirling Alpine Resort. **Of interest:** At junction of High St and Midland Hwy, monument to three police officers shot by Ned Kelly at Stringybark Creek, near Tolmie, 1878; graves in Mansfield cemetery. Highton Manor (1896), Highton Lane. Bush market, 4 times a year, check times. Mar.: Harvest festival. Nov.: Mountain country festival. **In the area:** Horse trail-riding. Road north-east over mountains to Whitfield in the King River Valley (62 km) passes through spectacular scenery. Powers Lookout, views over King River Valley (former vantage point for bushranger Harry Power); 44 km NE. Lake William Hovell, 85 km NE, for boating, canoeing and fishing. Scenic drives, picnics, camping and bushwalking at Mt Samaria State Park, 14 km N. At Lake Nillahcootie, 20 km NW: boating, fishing, canoeing and sailing. Houseboat hire at Lake Eildon, 15 km S. South, Howqua, Jamieson and Goulburn rivers offer trout fishing and gold fossicking. Historic buildings at old goldmining town of Jamieson, 37 km S, on Jamieson River. Delatite Winery, on Stoneys Rd, 7 km SE. At Merrijig, 18 km SE, rodeo in Mar. each year. Craig's Hut, 50 km E, used for filming *The Man from Snowy River*; no vehicle access to Craig's Hut in winter. Hot-air balloon flights. Alpine National Park, 60 km E, offers bushwalks. **Tourist information:** In railway station, 167 High St; (057) 75 1464. **Accommodation:** 3 hotels, 4 motels, 5 B&B, 1 hostel, 1 cara./camp. park. **See also:** Wine Regions.

Maryborough
Pop. 7623

MAP REF. 223 L5, 231 O11

First sheep farming, then the gold rush, and now secondary industry have contributed to the development of this small city on the northern slopes of the Great Dividing Range, 70 km N of Ballarat. Maryborough is in the centre of an agricultural and forest area. **Of interest:** Pioneer Memorial Tower, Bristol Hill. Worsley Cottage (1894), a historical museum; Palmerston St. Impressive railway station complex, Railway St. Imposing Civic Square buildings, Clarendon St. Princes Park, Park Rd. Jan.: Highland gathering on New Year's Day. Sept.: Golden wattle festival. Nov.: Energy Breakthrough (energy expo, machine races). **In the area:** Aboriginal wells, 4 km S. Once-thriving gold towns of Bowenvale and Timor; both 6 km NE from town. **Tourist information:** Railway station complex, Railway St; (054) 60 4511. **Accommodation:** 1 hotel/motel, 6 motels, 8 B&B, 1 cara./camp. park.

Marysville
Pop. 662

MAP REF. 213 O4, 216 I3, 226 G2, 235 J13

The peaceful sub-alpine town of Marysville owes its existence first to gold, as it was on the route to the Woods Point goldfields, and later to timber milling. It is 37 km NE of Healesville, off the Maroondah Hwy. The town is surrounded by attractive forest-clad mountain country and is a popular resort all year round. **Of interest:** Hidden Talents, local art and crafts; Murchison St. Goulds Sawmill, Racecourse Rd; open Mon.–Fri. Nicholl's Lookout, Cumberland Rd, for excellent views of surrounding area. Gallipoli Park, Murchison St, has historic display within park. Market, 2nd Sun. each month. **In the area:** Numerous bushwalking tracks lead to a variety of beauty spots: 3 min. walk to Steavenson Falls from Falls Rd (walk and falls illuminated at night); 4-km loop walk in Cumberland Memorial Scenic Reserve, 16 km E; 2-hr walk to Keppel's Lookout; 30-min. walk to Mt Gordon (begins 2 km W of town). Lake Mountain, 19 km E: accessible walking and cross-country skiing trails and tobogganing. Big River State Forest, 30 km E: camping, good fishing and gold fossicking. Lake Eildon, 46 km NE, and Fraser National Park, 59 km NE, within easy driving distance. Fraser National Park offers boating, sailing, water skiing, fishing and swimming, and a number of walking tracks. At Buxton, 10 km NW: Kaz Pottery; zoo; trout farm; Australian Bush Pioneer's Farm, at foot of Mt Cathedral in Cathedral Range State Park. **Tourist information:** The Old Yarra Track Shoppe, 18 Murchison St; (059) 63 3453. **Accommodation:** 1 hotel, 1 hotel/motel, 3 motels, 7 B&B, 1 cara./camp. park.

Milawa
Pop. 120

MAP REF. 224 G1, 235 N6

Milawa is 16 km SE of Wangaratta on what is known as the Snow Road, which links Oxley, Milawa and Markwood with Wangaratta to the west and the Ovens Hwy to the east. Brown Brothers Vineyard has operated here since 1889, producing quality wines. **Of interest:** Milawa Mustards, off Snow Rd: wide range of mustards and attractive cottage garden. Milawa Cheese Company, Factory Rd: for specialist cheeses. At Oxley, 4 km W: Bicycle tours available from Bogong Jack Adventures; John Gehrig Wines; Reads Winery. Other wineries in area: Markwood Estate Winery, 6 km E; Avalon Vineyard, 4 km N of Whitfield; Darling Estate Wines, near Cheshunt. **Tourist information:** Wangaratta and Region Visitors Information Centre, cnr Handley St and Tone Rd, Wangaratta; (057) 21 5711. **Accommodation:** 1 motel, 1 cara./camp. park. **See also:** Wine Regions.

Mildura
Pop. 23 176

MAP REF. 122 D7, 232 G3

Sunny mild winters and picturesque locations on the banks of the Murray River make Mildura and neighbouring towns popular tourist areas. Mildura, on the Sunraysia Hwy, 557 km N of Melbourne, is a small and pleasant city that developed along with the irrigation of the area. Alfred Deakin, statesman and advocate of irrigation, persuaded the Chaffey brothers, Canadian-born irrigation experts, to visit this region. They recognised its potential and selected Mildura as the first site for development. The early days of the project were fraught with setbacks, but by 1900 the citrus-growing industry was well established and, with the locking of the Murray completed in 1928, Mildura soon became a city. **Of interest:** Statue of W.B. Chaffey, Mildura's first mayor; Deakin Ave. Mildura Arts Centre complex, Cureton Ave, includes Rio Vista, original Chaffey home, now museum displaying colonial household items. Paddlesteamers leave from Mildura Wharf, end of Madden Ave, for trips on Murray and Darling Rivers: PS *Melbourne*, 2-hr round trips; PS *Avoca*, luncheon and dinner cruises; PS *Coonawarra*, 5- and 6-day cruises; PV *Rothbury*, day cruise to Trentham Winery each Thurs. Humpty Dumpty Tourist Farm, Cureton Ave. Snakes and Ladders, 17th St, popular with children. Mildura Lock Island and Weir. Aquacoaster waterslide, cnr Seventh St and Orange Ave. Dolls on the Avenue, Benetook Ave. Pioneer Cottage, Hunter St. The Citrus Shop, Deakin Ave. Mar.: Great Mildura Paddleboat Race (odd-numbered years). **In the area:** Many vineyards, including Lindemans Karadoc Winery (20 km S), largest winery in southern hemisphere; Allambie Wine Co. (south off Murray Valley Hwy); Trentham Estate (south off Sturt Hwy); Mildara Wines (9 km W). River Road Pottery, 10 km W. Woodsie's Gem Shop, 6 km SW. Sunbeam Dried Fruits, tours available; at Irymple, 6 km S. Red Cliffs, 15 km S, important area for citrus and dried fruit industries; 'Big Lizzie' steam traction engine in town. Bushwalking in Hattah-Kulkyne National Park, 70 km S. In NSW: Yabbies at Gol Gol Fisheries, 2 km N; Orange World, 6 km N, offers tours of citrus-growing areas. Golden River Zoo, 3 km NW, has both native and exotic species located in natural surroundings. **Tourist information:** 101 Deakin Ave; (050) 21 4424. **Accommodation:** 3 hotels, 44 motels, 25 cara./camp. parks. **See also:** The Mighty Murray; Wine Regions.

Moe
Pop. 17 000

MAP REF. 213 R10, 227 J7

Situated on the Princes Hwy, 134 km SE of Melbourne, Moe is a rapidly growing residential city in the La Trobe Valley and a gateway to the alpine region. **Of interest:** Old Gippstown Pioneer Township, re-creation of 19th-century community with over 30 restored buildings brought from surrounding areas and fine collection of fully restored horse-drawn vehicles; Lloyd St. Cinderella Dolls, display centre; Andrew St. Trout fishing, Narracan Creek. Picturesque race track, Waterloo Rd. Mar.: Jazz festival; Blue Rock Classic (cross-country horse race). Oct.: Moe Cup (horse race). **In the area:** Mair's Coalville Vineyard, Moe South Rd; by appt. Edward Hunter Heritage Bush reserve, 3 km S via Coalville St: bushland and walking tracks. Blue Rock Dam, 20 km NW; fishing, swimming and sailing. Scenic road leads north-east, 46 km to picturesque old mining township of Walhalla, Thomson Reservoir nearby, and through mountains to Jamieson, 147 km further north (check road conditions in winter). North of Willow Grove: Baw Baw plateau, excellent for bushwalking and abundant wildflowers in summer; Mt Baw Baw and Mt Saint Gwinear, for cross-country and downhill skiing. **Tourist information:** Shop 1, Southside Central, Princes Hwy, Traralgon; (051) 74 3199. **Accommodation:** 3 motels, 1 B&B, 1 hostel, 2 cara./camp. parks.

Morwell
Pop. 15 423

MAP REF. 227 J7

Morwell, 150 km SE of Melbourne, is situated in the heart of the La Trobe Valley. This valley contains one of the world's largest deposits of brown coal. Morwell is an industrial town with a number of secondary industries. **Of interest:** PowerWorks, dynamic displays on electrical industry; off Princes Hwy. La Trobe Regional Gallery, Commercial Rd. **In the area:** Scenic day tours can be made from the three main cities in the La Trobe Valley: Morwell, Moe (20 km NW) and Traralgon (12 km NE); brochure available from Tourist information. Lake Narracan and the Hazelwood pondage, 5 km S: warm water and year-round water sports. Tarra-Bulga National Park, 47 km SE: renowned for fern glades, waterfalls, rosellas, lyrebirds and koalas. Morwell National Park, good walking tracks; 12 km S. At Yinnar, 12 km SW, Arts Resource Collective in old butter factory. Views of Moe, Yallourn North and valley between Strzelecki Ranges and Baw Baw mountains at Narracan Falls, about 27 km W. To the north, 66 km through dense mountain country, old mining township of Walhalla. Further on, Thomson Reservoir and the beautiful Tanjil and Thomson River valleys. **Tourist information:** PowerWorks Visitors Centre, Commercial Rd; (051) 35 3415. **Accommodation:** 2 hotels, 9 motels, 2 cara./camp. parks.

Mount Beauty
Pop. 1837

MAP REF. 225 N5, 235 Q8, 236 D6

Situated in the Upper Kiewa Valley, 344 km NE of Melbourne, Mount Beauty was originally an accommodation town for workers on the Kiewa Hydro-electric Scheme in the 1940s. An ideal holiday centre, the town lies at the foot of Mount Bogong, Victoria's highest mountain (1986 m). A multitude of ski hire outlets services skiers on their way to Falls Creek in winter. In summer, the town services bushwalkers heading for the high plains. **Of interest:** At Tourist information: Heritage Museum with local craft and woodworker in action. Leaflets outlining walks, excursions and other activities, from various tourist information centres and National Parks Office. McKay Creek power station, 80 m underground, tours (bookings preferred); access from Bogong Plains Rd, 26 km SE. Mar.: Conquestathon fun walk. Aug.: Hoppet festival (foot race). Nov.: Festival of the Bogong Moth. **In the area:** Mountain-bike hire, horseriding and 4WD tours. Excellent hang-gliding. Scenic road to Falls Creek (30 km SE) and the Bogong High Plains (not accessible in winter); skiing at Falls Creek. Bogong Village, 16 km SE and walks around nearby Lake Guy. Good water sports and fishing at Mount Beauty Pondage, Falls Creek Rd, 26 km SE. Tawonga Gap, 13 km NW, features scenic lookout over two valleys. **Tourist information:** Australian High Country Visitors Centre, Kiewa Valley Hwy; (057) 54 3172. **Accommodation:** 6 motels, 2 cara./camp. parks.

Murtoa
Pop. 878

MAP REF. 230 I9

Murtoa is situated around picturesque Lake Marma, 30 km E of Horsham on the Wimmera Hwy. It is in the centre of Victoria's wheat belt. **Of interest:** Huge wheat-storage silos and facilities. Many buildings c. 1880. Original shopping centre c. 1900, McDonald St. Four-storey railway water-tower (1886), now a museum with James Hill's taxidermy collection of some 500 birds and animals, prepared between 1885 and 1930; Soldiers Pde, open Sun. p.m. Lake Marma, around which is a walking track, offers birdwatching and spectacular sunsets. Stick Shed (1941) built from 640 unmilled tree trunks; Wimmera Hwy, eastern side of town. Jan.: Race meeting on New Years Day. June: Murtoa Cup **In the area:** Town of Rupanyup, 14 km E. Barrabool Forest Reserve, 7 km S, spring wildflowers (difficult access in winter). **Tourist information:** Marma Gully Antiques, 50 Marma St; (053) 85 2422. **Accommodation:** 2 hotels, 1 cara./camp. park.

Myrtleford
Pop. 2862

MAP REF. 225 J2, 235 O7, 236 B5

On the Ovens Hwy, 45 km SE of Wangaratta, the town of Myrtleford is surrounded by an area that produces hops, timber, tobacco, vegetables, chestnuts and wine. It also has some of the largest walnut groves in the southern hemisphere. The Ovens Valley was opened up by graziers. Later gold was discovered, and creeks there are still popular for gold panning and gem fossicking. **Of interest:** The Phoenix Tree, sculptured butt of a red gum, crafted by Hans Knorr, on highway at town entrance. Reform Hill Lookout, end of Halls Rd. Rotary Park, Myrtle St. Many other delightful picnic spots and rest areas. Mar.: Tobacco, hops and timber festival. Oct.: International festival (even-numbered years). **In the area:** On road to Bright: Swinburne Reserve (5 km SE), starting point for self-guide forest walks and fitness track; Rosewhite Vineyards (8 km SE, 4 km off Hwy), open Wed., Fri.–Mon.); Red Deer and Emu Farm at Eurobin (20 km SE). Nug Nug Quarter Horse Stud and Dingo Breeding, 16 km S; open school holidays. Good fishing at Lake Buffalo (25 km S), Ovens River and Buffalo River (31 km S). Mt Buffalo National Park and historic towns of Beechworth, Yackandandah and Bright, within easy driving distance. **Tourist information:** Ponderosa Cabin, 29–31 Clyde St; (057) 52 1727. **Accommodation:** 1 hotel, 1 hotel/motel, 2 motels, 1 hostel, 2 cara./camp. parks.

Nagambie
Pop. 1215

MAP REF. 234 G8

Between Seymour and Shepparton on the Goulburn Valley Hwy, Nagambie is on the shores of Lake Nagambie, which was created by the construction of the Goulburn Weir in 1891. Rowing and yachting regattas, speedboat and water-ski tournaments are held here throughout the year. There is a 65-m water-slide at one of the swimming areas. **Of interest:** Several National Trust-classified buildings. Historical Society display of colonial Victoriana and early horsedrawn vehicles, in old Shire Offices, High St. Pottery, art and craft shops. The Nut House, for Australian nuts and Australian-made products; High St. Mar.: Goulburn Valley vintage festival. Dec.: Rowing regatta on Boxing Day. **In the area:** National Trust-classified buildings at Chateau Tahbilk Winery, 6 km SW. Mitchelton Winery, 10 km SW off Goulburn Valley Hwy, also has 60-m observation tower and scenic river cruises on the Goulburn River; check times. Osicka's Vineyard, Graytown, 24 km W. David Traeger Wines, on Goulburn Valley Hwy, northern end of town. Longleat Winery, 23 km N, near Murchison. At Murchison: Italian War Memorial and chapel; Meteorite Park, site of 1969 meteorite fall. Days Mill, flour mill with buildings dating from 1865, 5 km S of Murchison. **Tourist information:** 145 High St; (057) 94 2647. **Accommodation:** 5 motels, 1 B&B, 3 cara./camp. parks. **See also:** Wine Regions.

Natimuk
Pop. 464

MAP REF. 230 F9

This Wimmera town, 27 km W of Horsham, is close to the striking Mt Arapiles, a 356-m sandstone monolith that has been described as 'Victoria's Ayers Rock' and is located in the Mount Arapiles-Tooan State Park. A drive to the summit reveals a scenic lookout and a telecommunications relay station. The mountain was first climbed by Major Mitchell in 1836 and today is popular with rock-climbing enthusiasts. **Of interest:** In Main St: Arapiles Historical Society Museum in old court house; Arapiles Craft Shop for local craft. Nov.: Harrow national bush billycart championship. **In the area:** Lake Natimuk, 2 km N, for water sports. Duffholme Cabins and Museum, 21 km W. Mount Arapiles-Tooan State Park, 12 km SW. **Tourist information:** Natimuk Hotel, Main St; (053) 87 1300. **Accommodation:** 1 hotel/motel, 1 hostel, 1 cara./camp. park.

Nhill
Pop. 1891

MAP REF. 230 D7

The name of this town is possibly derived from the Aboriginal word *nyell*, meaning 'white mist on water'. A small wheat town on the Western Hwy, exactly half-way between Melbourne and Adelaide, it claims to have the largest single-bin silo in the southern hemisphere. **Of interest:** Historical Society Museum, McPherson St, open weekends or by appt. Cottage of John Shaw Neilson, lyric poet, Shaw Neilson Park, Western Hwy. Draught Horse Memorial to famous Clydesdales, indispensable in opening up Wimmera region; Goldsworthy Park. Post office (1888), National Trust-classified. The Wagan Inn, information display and farming relics. Lowana Craft Shop, local craft. **In the area:** Little Desert National Park and Little Desert Lodge, via Kiata, 23 km S. Little Desert Wildflower Exhibition in Oct. Lake Hindmarsh, 45 km NE, largest freshwater lake in Victoria. Hermans Hill Tourist Walk through mallee and heathland to hill overlooking Big Desert Wilderness Park; inquire at Tourist information. Big Desert Wilderness Park, via Yanac 32 km NW, on track north to Murrayville; exploration of this remote area by walking tracks only. **Tourist information:** Victoria St; (053) 91 3086. **Accommodation:** 3 hotels, 5 motels, 1 cara./camp. park.

Numurkah
Pop. 3128

MAP REF. 123 M13, 234 I4

Numurkah, 35 km N of Shepparton on the Goulburn Valley Hwy, is only half an hour from some sandy beaches and excellent fishing spots on the Murray River. The town is in an irrigation area concentrating on dairying, and was originally developed through the Murray Valley Soldier Settlement Scheme. **Of interest:** In Melville St: Steam and Vintage Machinery Display; historical museum, open Sun. p.m.; Court House Crafts; Street market. Marie's House of Dolls, Neiklejohn St. Mar.: Art show. **In the area:** Potts Herbs, nursery; 5 km N. The Palmyard, specialist palm tree nursery, 6 km N. Glenarron, 8 km N, a tourist dairy farm. Monichino's Winery, Katunga, 11 km N. Ulupna Island flora and fauna reserve, has large koala population; near Strathmerton, 21 km N. Red Gum Wildlife Tours of Ulupna Island. At Strathmerton: Kraft cheese factory; Spikes and Blooms cactus garden (2 ha); Coonanga Historic Homestead, features blacksmith shop. Barmah Forest, largest red gum forest in southern hemisphere; 40 km NW, safari tours available. Morgan's Beach Caravan Park, 27 km N at edge of forest on bank of Murray River: bushwalking and horseriding (horses for hire and facilities for visitors' horses). Waaia Wildlife Park, 10 km NW. Historic buildings set on banks of Broken Creek at Nathalia, 20 km W. At Wunghnu 5 km S: Institute Tavern in restored Mechanics Institute (c. 1880); Tractor pull festival at Easter. Brookfield Historic Holiday Farm and Museum, 6 km SE. **Tourist information:** Spikes and Blooms, Murray Valley Hwy; (058) 74 5271. **Accommodation:** 2 hotels, 2 motels, 1 cara./camp. park.

Ocean Grove   Pop. 10 069

MAP REF. 212 G10, 219 G9, 226 A7, 229 R8

At the mouth of the Barwon River, Ocean Grove offers fishing and surfing, while nearby Barwon Heads offers safe family relaxation along the shores of its protected river. Both holiday towns are linked by a bridge over the Barwon River estuary, and are popular in the summer months as they are the closest ocean beaches to Geelong, 22 km to the NW. **Of interest:** Ocean Grove Nature Reserve, Grubb Rd. **In the area:** Jirrahlinga Koala and Wildlife Sanctuary, Taits Rd, Barwon Heads. Mangrove swamps in Lake Connewarre State Game Reserve, 7 km N. At Wallington, 8 km N: A Maze'N Things; Koombahla Park Equestrian Centre; Country Connection Adventure Park. **Tourist information:** A Maze'N Things, 1570 Bellarine Hwy (at Grubb Rd), Wallington; (052) 50 2669. **Accommodation:** Ocean Grove: 3 motels, 1 hotel/motel, 5 cara./camp. parks. Barwon Heads: 1 hotel, 1 motel, 2 cara./camp. parks.

The Great Ocean Road

Very few roads can offer a continuous stretch of more than 300 kilometres of breathtaking scenery, but the Great Ocean Road, along Victoria's south-west coast, does exactly that. Built to honour the servicemen of World War I and completed in 1932, the road has dramatic stretches of precipitous cliffs, idyllic coves and wide beaches.

The Great Ocean Road begins at **Torquay**, not far from Geelong. This is a popular surfing spot and the road leads past a collection of famous surfing and safe swimming beaches and resorts. **Lorne** is one of the most charming of these. Despite offering modern holiday amenities and plenty of seaside entertainment for families, its gracious old hotels and guest houses remain as a reminder of days gone by. Behind the town, the Otway Ranges, which stretch from **Anglesea** to Cape Otway, offer beautiful hills, waterfalls, and excellent walking tracks.

At **Apollo Bay**, the road leaves the coast and winds through the ferny slopes of Cape Otway. This is rainforest country, silent and untouched, and well worth exploring. Many of the roads are unsealed but quite adequate for standard cars. Try to visit the Melba Gully State Park to the west of the tiny town of Lavers Hill. Shipwreck Trail signs begin on the eastern side of Lavers Hill. This point marks the beginning of the 'Shipwreck Coast', which stretches through **Port Campbell** and **Warrnambool** to **Port Fairy**. Photographers can be seen risking life and limb to take advantage of the dramatic coastal scenery; it is advisable, however, for drivers to keep their eyes firmly on the road. The coastline takes on tortured, twisted shapes, with amazing rock formations like The Twelve Apostles — huge stone pillars looming out of the surf, carved over time by the incessant sea.

At Princetown, the Great Ocean Road returns to hug the coastline along the entire length of **Port Campbell National Park** and follows the coast to the Bay of Islands, 8 kilometres east of the small seaside town of Peterborough, where four shipwrecks are located along the coast. Here the Curdies River enters the sea in a wide, sandy inlet beloved of fishermen.

A section of the Great Ocean Road near Lorne

For further information, contact the Great Ocean Road Visitor Information Centre, Great Ocean Rd, Apollo Bay; (052) 37 6529. **See also:** National Parks, and individual town entries in A–Z listing for those parks and towns indicated by bold type. **Map references:** 217 A10, 217 F12.

Omeo

Pop. 274

MAP REF. 115 A12, 236 F8

The high plains around Omeo were opened up in 1835 when overlanders from the Monaro region moved their stock south to these lush summer pastures. Its name is an Aboriginal word meaning 'mountains', and the township is set in the heart of the Victorian Alps at an altitude of 643 m. It is used as a base for winter traffic approaching Mt Hotham from Bairnsdale, 120 km S, and for bushwalking expeditions to the Bogong High Plains during summer and autumn. Omeo has suffered several natural disasters. It was damaged by earthquakes in 1885 and 1892, and was half destroyed by the Black Friday bushfires of 1939. Nevertheless, several old buildings remain. **Of interest:** In the A.M. Pearson Historical Park, Day Ave, old court house (1861) now museum; present court house (1892); log gaol (1858); stables; blacksmiths. Also in Day Ave: post office (1891); Commercial Bank (1890); Colonial Bank (1889) now bookshop; school (1866); 19th century timber buildings including D.C.N.R. office, C.W.A. Hall and Petersens Gallery. Gold panning popular along Livingstone Creek, which flows through town. Easter: Rodeo and market. Nov.: Agricultural and pastoral show. **In the area:** High-country horseback and 4WD tours, bushwalking, trout fishing, skiing and white-water rafting (in spring). Omeo has a gold-rush history; high cliffs left after sluicing for gold, stone walls and tunnel openings can be seen at the Oriental Claims, 1.5 km W on Alpine Rd. Remains of State's first hydro-electric plant (power for Cassilis goldfield), 25 km W off Victoria Falls Rd. Mt Markey Winery, Cassilis Rd, Cassilis, 15 km S. Blue Duck Inn (1890s) is a base for fishing at Anglers Rest, 29 km NW. Benarubra, 20 km N. Taylors Crossing

The Prom

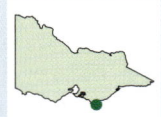

Wilsons Promontory, at the southernmost tip of the mainland, is one of Victoria's largest and most spectacular national parks. 'The Prom', as it is affectionately known to Victorians, has an impressive range of landscapes, including tall forested ranges, luxuriant tree fern valleys, open heaths, salt marshes and long drifts of sand dunes. Its wide, white sandy beaches are truly magnificent, some dominated by spectacular granite tors and washed by a rolling surf. There are also safe swimming beaches, particularly at Norman Bay near the main camping area at Tidal River. At the aptly named Squeaky Beach, the sands squeak underfoot.

Two lookouts in particular offer magnificent views across Bass Strait and offshore islands: Sparkes Lookout, off the main road to Tidal River and the lookout at the Mt Oberon carpark.

Birds and other wildlife abound on the Prom: lorikeets, rosellas and flame robins; kookaburras and blue wrens are in evidence, even in the main general store area at Tidal River village; and for the more dedicated and patient birdwatcher, sightings of treecreepers and herons can be the reward.

Emus feed unperturbed on the open grassland by the side of the main road at the park entry area at Yanakie Isthmus, and kangaroos and wallabies seem unimpressed by their human observers. At night, wombat-spotting by torchlight is a favourite pastime with children staying in the Tidal River area.

There are more than 100 kilometres of walking tracks in the Wilsons Promontory National Park. Some cover short walks, such as the nature trail in Lilly Pilly Gully, where the vegetation varies from bushland inhabited by koalas, to rainforest with ancient tree ferns and trickling streams. Other longer walks can be taken to such places as Sealers Cove or to the tip of the Prom, where there is a lighthouse dating from 1859. Hikers should consider tide times to make creek crossing easier.

At the visitor information centre and park office at Tidal River, leaflets are available detailing walking tracks and the flora and fauna of the park.

Refuge Cove, a beautiful cove on the eastern side of the Prom

During summer and Easter, park rangers give talks and spotlight tours as well as leading children's nature activities. Permits are required for all overnight hikes.

For further information contact the Wilsons Promontory National Park, Park Office, Tidal River; (056) 80 9555, or for bookings (056) 80 9500. **Map reference:** 227 K12.

suspension bridge, part of Australian Alps Walking Track, 44 km NE, off Tablelands Rd. Scenic drives: Tambo River valley between Swifts Creek and Bruthen (97 km S), especially beautiful in autumn; to Benambra then Corryong, 148 km NE; Omeo Hwy through Mitta Mitta to Tallangatta (172 km NW); from Omeo through Dinner Plain to Mt Hotham. Note: all scenic drives listed cross state forests (be alert for timber trucks) or alpine areas (check road conditions in winter). **Tourist information:** Octagon Bookshop, Day Ave; (051) 59 1411. **Accommodation:** 1 hotel, 1 hotel/motel, 1 motel, 4 B&B, 1 cara./camp. park.

Orbost   Pop. 2515

MAP REF. 237 J12

Situated on the banks of the Snowy River, this Gippsland timber town is on the Princes Hwy, surrounded by spectacular coastal and mountain territory. **Of interest:** Historical Museum, Nicholson St. Old Pump House, behind Slab Hut at Information centre, hut (1872) relocated from its original site 40 km away. Rainforest Interpretation Centre, audiovisual display explaining complex nature of rainforest ecology; Lockiel St. Moogji Cultural Display Centre, also offers tours to Aboriginal sites. In Nicholson St: Croajingolong Mohair Farm, has garments, yarns, fleeces, fabrics and leathergoods; Snowy River Country Craft. Netherbyre Gemstone and Art Gallery, cnr Browning and Carlyle Sts. Jan.: Australian wood display. **In the area:** Beautiful Bonang Hwy, unsealed in parts, leads north through mountains to Delegate in NSW. At Bonang, 97 km NE: Aurora Mine, working goldmine, bookings essential. Walking in Snowy River National Park (25 km NW) and Errinundra National Park (54 km NE); also rainforest boardwalk at Errinundra National Park. Tranquil Valley Tavern, on banks of Delegate River near NSW border, about 18 km N of Bonang. Spectacular drive to Buchan, 58 km NW, leads to Little River Falls and McKillop's Bridge on the Snowy River. Scenic coastal drive to Marlo and Cape Conran (30 km E) starts just west of Orbost, returns to Princes Hwy at Cabbage Tree Creek. Cabbage Tree Palms Flora Reserve, 27 km E. Coopracambra National Park, 136 km NE, near NSW border. Bemm River, on Sydenham Inlet, 57 km E, popular centre for bream anglers. Baldwin Spencer Trail, 262-km scenic driving circuit following route of explorer. Croajingolong National Park, stretching east along the coast from Sydenham Inlet to border. **Tourist information:** The Slab Hut, cnr Nicholson and Clarke Sts; (051) 54 2424. **Accommodation:** 2 hotels, 3 motels, 4 B&B, 1 cara./camp. park.

Ouyen   Pop. 1337

MAP REF. 122 E10, 232 H9

At the junction of the Calder and Mallee Hwys, Ouyen is about 100 km S of Mildura, north-east of the Big Desert area. **Of interest:** Nov.: Farmers festival. **In the area:** Hattah-Kulkyne National Park, 34 km N, features abundant wildlife, birdwatching, bushwalking, canoeing and wildflowers in spring. Pink lakes are outstanding subjects for photography in Murray-Sunset National Park, 60 km W. At Patchewollock, 41 km SW, Easter sports (with camel-racing). Tag-along (own vehicle tagging along behind 4WD tour) and 4WD tours are available. **Tourist information:** Resource Centre, Oke St; (050) 92 1763. **Accommodation:** 1 hotel, 2 motels, 1 cara./camp. park. **See also:** The Mallee.

Paynesville   Pop. 2444

MAP REF. 227 Q5

A popular tourist resort 18 km from Bairnsdale on the McMillan Straits, Paynesville is a mecca for fishing and boating enthusiasts, and is noted for yachting and speedboat racing as well as water-skiing. **Of interest:** In the Esplanade: St Peter-by-the-Lake (1961) church, incorporating seafaring symbols; Community Craft Centre. Market at Gilsenan Reserve, 2nd Sun. each month. Easter: Gold Cup speedboat championships. **In the area:** Rotomah Island Bird Observatory, 8 km S by boat. Ninety Mile Beach, 10 km S by boat; free ferry crosses Straits to Raymond Island. Koala Reserve on Raymond Island. The Lakes National Park, to the east, 5 km by boat to Sperm Whale Head; otherwise via Loch Sport. Cruises on MV *Lakes Odyssey*. Organised scenic tours of lakes. Boat charter and hire. Dolphins in bay. **Tourist information:** Paynesville Marine Service, Esplanade; (051) 56 6554. **Accommodation:** 1 motel, 2 B&B, 5 cara./camp. parks. **See also:** Gippsland Lakes.

Port Albert   Pop. 307

MAP REF. 227 L10

This tiny historic town on the south-east coast, 120 km SE from Morwell, was the first established port in Victoria. Sailing boats from Europe and America once docked at the large timber jetty here. Boats from China brought thousands of Chinese to the Gippsland goldfields. Originally established for trade with Tasmania, Port Albert was the supply port for Gippsland pioneers until the railway from Melbourne to Sale was completed (1878). The timber jetty is still crowded today, as Port Albert is a commercial fishing port and its sheltered waters are popular with anglers and boat owners. Some of the original stone buildings are still in use and have been classified by the National Trust. **Of interest:** Historic buildings in Tarraville Rd: original government offices and stores; Bank of Victoria (1861), now Maritime Museum with photographs and relics of the area. Warren Curry Art Gallery, also in Tarraville Rd, features Australian country-town streetscapes. Port Albert Hotel, Wharf St, first licensed in 1842 and possibly the oldest hotel still operating in State. **In the area:** At Tarraville, 5 km NE, Christ Church (1856), first church in Gippsland. Swimming at Mann's Beach, 10 km NE. Surfing at Woodside on Ninety Mile Beach, 34 km NE. Wildlife sanctuary on St Margaret Island, 12 km E. Alberton, 8 km N, once the administrative centre of Central Gippsland. Tarra-Bulga National Park, 41 km NW. **Tourist information:** South Gippsland Tourism, Coal Creek Historical Village, cnr South Gippsland Hwy and Silkstone Rd, Korumburra; (056) 55 2233. **Accommodation:** 1 hotel/motel, 2 cara./camp. parks.

Port Campbell   Pop. 234

MAP REF. 217 A10, 229 K11

This small crayfishing village and seaside resort is situated in the centre of Port Campbell National Park and on a spectacular stretch of the Great Ocean Rd. **Of interest:** Historical Museum, Lord St; open school holidays. Loch Ard Shipwreck Museum, Lord St. Self-guide Discovery Walk (2.5 km); leaflet from Tourist information. Good fishing from rocks and pier. **In the area:** Port Campbell National Park surrounds town, its coastal features include world-famous Twelve Apostles (12 km E), Loch Ard

Port Fairy, a charming coastal fishing village

Gorge (10 km SE), London Bridge (now fallen down), 5 km W and The Arch (6 km W). Glenample, first homestead in area; survivors of *Loch Ard* recuperated there, 12 km E on Great Ocean Rd, (check opening times). Walking tracks, scenic drives and historic shipwreck sites; Historic Shipwreck Trail links sites along 'Shipwreck Coast', from Moonlight Head to Port Fairy. Otway Deer and Wildlife Park, 20 km E. Picturesque road leads north to pretty timbered township of Timboon also centre of dairy area. Just south of Timboon, Timboon Farmhouse has cheese tastings and sales. **Tourist information:** National Parks Office, Morris St; (055) 98 6382. **Accommodation:** 1 hotel, 4 motels, 1 hostel, 1 cara./camp. park. **See also:** The Great Ocean Road.

Port Fairy   Pop. 2467

MAP REF. 228 G9

The home port for a large fishing fleet and an attractive, rambling holiday resort, Port Fairy is 29 km W of Warrnambool with both ocean and river as its borders. The town's history goes back to whaling days. At one time it was one of the largest ports in Australia. Over 50 of its small cottages and bluestone buildings have been classified by the National Trust. This charming old-world fishing village is popular with heritage lovers and holidaymakers. **Of interest:** History Centre, Gipps St, in old court house. Battery Hill, old fort and signal station at mouth of river; end Griffith St. National Trust-classified buildings: splendid timber home of Captain Mills, Gipps St; Mott's Cottage, 5 Sackville St. Other attractive buildings: Old Caledonian Inn, Bank St; Seacombe House and ANZ Bank building, Cox St; St John's Church of England (1856), Regent St; *Gazette* Office (1849), Sackville St. Ornamental Shoe and Boot (displays), Princes Hwy. Hot Glass Studio, Regent St. Self-guide historic walks of town; Historic Shipwreck Trail, linking sites along 'Shipwreck Coast' between Port Fairy and Moonlight Head; Mahogany Walk to Warrnambool, taking 6–7 hr one-way (return by bus); brochures available at Tourist information. Mar.: Award-winning Folk festival. Oct.: Spring music festival. Dec.: Moyneyana festival. **In the area:** Griffiths Island, connected to east of town by causeway, has lighthouse and muttonbird rookeries; spectacular nightly return of the muttonbirds to island during Sept.–Apr. Australia's only mainland colony of muttonbirds at Pea Soup Beach and South Beach, on southern edge of town. Lady Julia Percy Island, 10 km off coast, home for fur seals; only accessible by experienced boat operators in calm weather. Yambuk and Lake Yambuk, 17 km W. Mt Eccles National Park, 56 km NW. Tower Hill, 14 km E, fascinating area with an extinct volcano and crater lake with islands. **Tourist information:** 22 Bank St; (055) 68 2682. **Accommodation:** 7 motels, 11 B&B, 8 cara./camp. parks. **See also:** The Great Ocean Road.

Portarlington   Pop. 2553

MAP REF. 212 H9, 219 I7, 226 B6

Named after an Irish village and with a history of Irish settlement in the area, Portarlington is a popular seaside resort on the Bellarine Peninsula, 31 km E of Geelong. It has a safe bay for children to swim, good fishing and a variety of water sports. **Of interest:** Historic flour mill (1857), restored by National Trust, now venue for historical displays; Turner Crt. Lavender Cottage Gallery, Fenwick St. Public Reserve, Sprout St. **Tourist information:** A Maze'N Things, 1570 Bellarine Hwy; Wallington; (052) 50 2669. **Accommodation:** 1 motel, 3 cara./camp. parks.

Portland   Pop. 10 115

MAP REF. 228 D9

Portland, situated about 75 km E of the South Australian border, is the most western of Victoria's major coastal towns and is the only deep-water port between Melbourne and Adelaide. It was the first permanent settlement in Victoria, founded by the Henty family in 1834. Today it is an important industrial and commercial centre, and a popular summer resort with beaches, surfing, fishing and outstanding coastal and forest scenery. **Of interest:** Number of self-guide and guided walks in and around Portland including the Walk in the Footsteps of Mary MacKillop around sites significant during Mary's time in Portland (guided tours also available); for the more energetic, the 250-km Great South West Walk, a scenic circular track from Tourist information centre through a number of national parks and State forests to Discovery Bay and Cape Nelson (can be covered in easy stages); for all walks, inquire at Tourist information.

Botanical Gardens (1857), Cliff St. More than 200 early buildings, some National Trust-classified: customs house and court house in Cliff St; Steam Packet Inn (1842) and Mac's Hotel in Bentinck St. History House, a historical museum and family research centre in old town hall (1863); Charles St. Fawthrop Lagoon, Glenelg St, has prolific birdlife. Powerhouse Car Museum, Percy St. Good views from Portland Battery, Battery Hill. Portland Aluminium Smelter; guided tours available, check times. Kingsley Winery (tastings and sales outlet), Bancroft St. Jan.: Foreshore carnival. Feb.: Fishing competition. Mar.: Dahlia festival. Nov.: Jazz festival; Antique fair; Pioneer week. Dec.: Surfboat marathon. **In the area:** Alcoa reclamation and revegetation projects. Edward Henty's homestead Burswood, Cape Nelson Rd. Cape Nelson State Park, 11 km SW, offers spectacular coastal scenery and lighthouse, National Trust-classified (check opening times). Safe swimming and surfing at Cape Bridgewater, 21 km SW; also nearby, petrified forest, blowholes, freshwater springs, seal caves and the Watering Place; walks to Cape Duquesne and Discovery Bay, both further west. Barrett's Gorae West Wines, 20 km W. Mt Richmond National Park, 25 km NW, spring wildflowers. Lower Glenelg National Park, 44 km NW via Kentbruck: spectacular gorges, colourful wildflowers, native birds and excellent fishing. Along coastal road is charming hamlet of Nelson, 70 km NW. Nearby Princess Margaret Rose Caves, tours available. Tours up Glenelg River. Narrawong State Forest, 18 km NE. Caledonian Inn, historical displays; Henty Hwy, 8 km N. At Heywood, 22 km N: Cave Hill Gardens; Bower Birds Nest Museum. **Tourist information:** Cliff St; (055) 23 2671 or 1800 03 5567. **Accommodation:** 10 motels, 4 B&B, 4 hostels, 7 cara./camp. parks.

Pyramid Hill Pop. 546

MAP REF. 122 I13, 231 Q5, 234 B4

A small country town some 40 km SW of Cohuna and 100 km N of Bendigo, Pyramid Hill was named for its unusually shaped hill, 187 m high. **Of interest:** Historical museum, McKay St. A climb to the top of Pyramid Hill provides scenic views of the surrounding irrigation and wheat district (there is also a Braille walking trail for visually impaired people). Oct.: Pioneer machinery display; Iron man contest. **In the area:** Terrick Terrick State Park, 11 km SE, large Murray Pine forest reserve with numerous granite outcrops (southernmost outcrop called Mitiamo Rock), walks, variety of birdlife and other fauna. Mt Hope, 10 km NE, named by explorer Major Mitchell. **Tourist information:** Newsagency, 12–14 Kelly St; (054) 55 7036. **Accommodation:** 1 hotel, 1 cara./camp. park.

Queenscliff Pop. 3681

MAP REF. 212 H10, 214 B5, 219 I9, 226 B7

Queenscliff, 31 km E of Geelong on the Bellarine Peninsula, was established as a commercial fishing centre in the 1850s and still has a large fishing fleet based in its harbour. The town looks out across the famous and treacherous Rip at the entrance to Port Phillip. **Of interest:** Queenscliff Maritime Centre, explores town's long association with sea and days of sailing ships; Weeroona Pde. Adjacent Marine Studies Centre, offers summer holiday programme for visitors. Fort Queenscliff (1882), built during the Crimean War, includes Black Lighthouse (1861), White Lighthouse (1862); King St. Other historic buildings include: Vue Grand Hotel, Hesse St; Ozone and Queenscliff Hotels, Gellibrand St. Historical tours leave from pier. Queenscliff Arcade, for local art and craft; Hesse St. Hobson's Choice Gallery, Hobson St. Seaview Gallery in Seaview House, Hesse St. Steam train operates between Queenscliff (station in Symonds St) and Drysdale (8 km NW), weekends and summer holidays; also display of historic locomotives and carriages at station. Regular passenger ferry service operates between Queenscliff and Portsea across bay; summer and school holidays. Vehicle and passenger ferry service between Queenscliff and Sorrento (about 45 min.); daily. 'Snorkelling with the seals', inquire at Tourist information. Point Lonsdale (6 km SW) extensively developed as holiday and tourist resort. Queenscliff market at Symonds St, last Sun. of month, Aug.–Apr. Pt Lonsdale market at Bowen Rd, 2nd Sun. each month. **In the area:** Marine life viewing at Harold Holt Marine Reserve, which includes Mud Island and coastal reserves. Lake Victoria, 1 km W of Point Lonsdale. At Wallington, 13 km NW: A Maze'N Things; horseriding at Australian Equestrian Academy; Country Connection Adventure Park; pick-your-own fruit and vegetable farms. **Tourist information:** A Maze'N Things, 1570 Bellarine Hwy, Wallington; (052) 50 2669. **Accommodation:** Queenscliff: 3 hotels, 4 cara./camp. parks. Point Lonsdale: 2 motels, 2 cara./camp. parks.

Rainbow Pop. 587

MAP REF. 122 D13, 230 F4

This Wimmera township, 70 km N of Dimboola, is near Lake Hindmarsh, popular for fishing, boating and waterskiing. **Of interest:** Pascos Cash Store (1928), Federal St, an original country general store. National Trust-classified Yurunga Homestead (1910) has large selection of antiques and original fittings; in Gray St, on northern edge of town. Oct.: Iris festival. **In the area:** Lutheran church (1901), with old pipe organ, only one other of its kind in State; at Pella, 10 km W. Lake Albacutya Park, 12 km N. Wyperfeld National Park, 30 km N via sealed road north from Yaapeet. **Tourist information:** Shire of Dimboola, 10 Roy St, Jeparit; (053) 97 2070. **Accommodation:** 2 hotels, 1 motel, 1 cara./camp. park.

Robinvale Pop. 1795

MAP REF. 122 F8, 233 J6

This small, well-laid-out town on the NSW border, 80 km SE of Mildura, is almost entirely surrounded by bends in the Murray River. The surrounding area is ideal for the production of citrus, dried fruit and wine grapes. It is a picturesque town, and water sports and fishing are popular along the river. **Of interest:** In Moore St: McWilliams Wines; Lexia Room features historical exhibits. Rural Life Museum, Bromley Rd. **In the area:** Euston weir and lock on Murray, 3 km downstream. Robinvale Wines, Greek-style winery, 5 km S on Sea Lake Rd. Kyndalyn Park almond farm, 23 km SE. Hattah-Kulkyne National Park, 66 km SW. **Tourist information:** Bromley Rd; (050) 26 1388. **Accommodation:** 1 hotel, 3 motels, 2 cara./camp. parks. **See also:** Wine Regions.

Rochester Pop. 2527

MAP REF. 234 E6

On the Campaspe River, 28 km S of Echuca, Rochester is the centre for a rich dairying and tomato-growing area. A small, busy town, it has some attractive older buildings and boasts the largest dairy factory in Australia. **Of interest:** In Moore St: 'The Oppy Museum', open Sun., public holidays; opposite, statue of Sir Hubert Opperman, champion cyclist; Pinpandoor Gallery, for local crafts. Historical Plaque Trail; brochure available at Tourist information. **In the area:** Random House Homestead, amid 4 ha of gardens beside river in Bridge Rd, on eastern edge of town. Campaspe Siphon, 3 km N: an engineering achievement, where the Waranga-Mallee irrigation channel runs under the Campaspe River. District channels are popular with anglers; plentiful cod and bream. Pleasant lakes in district, popular for fishing and water sports, including Greens Lake and Lake Cooper (14 km SE). **Tourist information**: Railway Station, Moore St; (054) 84 1860. **Accommodation:** 3 hotels, 1 motel, 1 cara./camp. park.

Romsey   Pop. 2033

MAP REF. 212 I2, 226 B1, 234 E12

The township of Romsey, 7 km S of Lancefield, was settled in the mid-1850s and possesses some excellent Victorian architecture. **Of interest:** Sydney Seymour Cottage, Palmer St. **In the area:** Cope-Williams Romsey Vineyard, Glenfern Rd. Monegeetta (8 km S), Mintaro Homestead (1882), smaller replica of Melbourne's Government House and built by Captain Gardiner (not open to the public). **Tourist information:** Centre Vic Motor Inn, Main Rd, Lancefield; (054) 29 1777. **Accommodation:** 1 hotel.

Rushworth   Pop. 1012

MAP REF. 234 G7

Rushworth, 20 km W of Murchison, off the Goulburn Valley Hwy, still shows traces of its gold-rush days. **Of interest:** Many of the town's attractive original buildings still stand, witnesses to the days when Rushworth was the commercial centre for the surrounding mining district. Nearly all the buildings in High St are National Trust-classified: St Pauls Church of England, band rotunda, former Imperial Hotel (now a private residence), Glasgow Buildings and the Whistle Stop. History Museum in Mechanics Institute (1913), High St; open by appt. **In the area:** Rushworth State Forest, largest natural ironbark forest in world; 3 km S. Whroo Historic Area, 7 km S: Balaclava Hill open-cut goldmine, Whroo cemetery and Aboriginal waterhole; all with visitor access. Further south, remnants of deserted goldmining towns Angustown, Bailieston and Graytown. Longleat Winery and Campbell's Bend picnic reserve, 20 km E. At Murchison, 21 km E, Meteorite Park, site of meteorite fall 1969. At Waranga Basin, 6 km NE: water sports, fishing, camping and excellent picnic facilities. **Tourist information:** Guided Tours of Victoria, 31 High St; (058) 56 1612. **Accommodation:** 1 hotel, 1 hotel/motel, 2 cara./camp. parks.

Rutherglen   Pop. 1876

MAP REF. 123 O13, 235 N4

Rutherglen is the centre of one of the most important winegrowing areas in Victoria. There is a cluster of vineyards surrounding the town, with winegrowing country stretching south to the Milawa area. Most wineries reflect their history; of particular interest is the National Trust-classified winery building at All Saints, 10 km NW. Other wineries include Anderson's, Bullers, Campbells, Chambers, Cofield, Fairfield, Gehrig Brothers, Jones, Morris's, Mount Prior, Pfeiffers, Stanton and Killeen, and St Leonards. Mar.: Tastes of Rutherglen. June: Winery walkabout weekend. **Of interest:** Walkabout Cellars, Main St. **In the area:** Old Customs House at Wahgunyah, 10 km NW, relic of days when duty was payable on goods coming from NSW. Scenic day trips to Albury-Wodonga, Yarrawonga, Lake Mulwala, Corowa, Beechworth, Bright or Mt Buffalo. Lake Moodemere, 8 km W, water sports; fauna reserve nearby. **Tourist information:** Walkabout Cellars, 84 Main St; (060) 32 9784. **Accommodation:** 2 hotels, 4 motels, 3 B&B, 1 cara./camp. park. **See also:** The Mighty Murray; Wine Regions.

St Arnaud   Pop. 2741

MAP REF. 231 L9

This old goldmining town is on the Sunraysia Hwy between Donald and Avoca, and is surrounded by forest and hill country. Many of the town's historic iron-lacework decorated buildings are National Trust-classified and together form a nationally recognised historic streetscape. **Of interest:** Queen Mary Gardens, Kings Ave. Worm Farm, Millet St. Oct.: Agricultural show. **In the area:** Good fishing in Avoca River and at Teddington Reservoir, 28 km S. St Peter's Church (1869), made of pebbles, at Carapooee, 11 km SE. Melville Caves, famous as haunt of bushranger Captain Melville; 38 km E, between St Arnaud and Inglewood. At Lake Batyo Catyo, 35 km NW: fishing, water sports and camping. **Tourist information:** Josephine Coppens Gallery, 2 Napier St; (054) 95 2313. **Accommodation:** 4 hotels, 3 motels, 2 B&B, 1 cara./camp. park.

St Leonards   Pop. 1206

MAP REF. 212 I9, 214 C2, 219 I8, 226 B6

A small beach resort, 11 km SE of Portarlington on the Bellarine Peninsula, St Leonards has excellent coastal fishing, calm waters for boating and yachting, and is popular for family summer holidays. **Of interest:** Edwards Point Wildlife Reserve, Beach Rd. Memorial on The Esplanade commemorates landing by Matthew Flinders in 1802, and John Batman and his party in 1835. **Tourist information:** A Maze'N Things, 1570 Bellarine Hwy, Wallington; (052) 50 2669. **Accommodation:** 1 hotel, 2 cara./camp. parks.

Sale   Pop. 13 858

MAP REF. 227 N6

Sale is the main administrative city in Gippsland. In nearby Bass Strait, there is a concentration of offshore oil development. Just over 200 km E of Melbourne on the Princes Hwy, Sale is convenient for exploration of the whole Gippsland Lakes area, which extends from Wilsons Promontory to Lakes Entrance, and is bordered to the north by the foothills and mountains of the Great Divide and, most of the way along the coast, by the famous Ninety Mile Beach. **Of interest:** Unique art of Annemieke Mein, wildlife-in-textiles artist, at Central Gippsland Tourism office, on Princes Hwy at western approach to city. Port of Sale, thriving during the days of the paddle-steamers. In Foster St, Lake Guthridge, for picnics, fauna park and adventure playground; Historical museum; Regional Arts Centre; bronze of Mary MacKillop in St Mary's Church. Attractive buildings: Our Lady of Sion Convent; clock tower; Victoria Hall; Criterion Hotel, beautiful lacework verandahs. RAAF base, Raglan St, home of the famous Roulettes aerobatic team. Pedestrian Mall, cnr Cunningham and

Gippsland Lakes

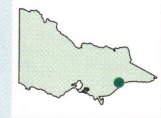

Many people regard the Gippsland Lakes as the most outstanding holiday area in Victoria. Dominated as it is by Australia's largest system of inland waterways, it certainly does live up to all the superlatives accorded it. With the foothills of the high country just to the north and the amazing stretch of the Ninety Mile Beach separating the lakes from the ocean, the region offers a variety of natural beauty and recreation activities. Here the choice really is yours — lake, river or ocean fishing, boating, cruising, surfing, swimming, birdwatching or just sitting by the water.

Within easy reach of the Lakes area the high country begins, so it is possible to vary a waterside trip with days exploring the alpine reaches (roads may be closed in winter) and some of the fascinating little old townships such as **Omeo**, Briagolong and Dargo. The road across the Dargo High Plains and the Omeo Highway leading to Hotham Heights passes through some stunning country. Check your car thoroughly before you set off — service stations are scarce along the way.

Wellington, King, Victoria, Tyers, Reeve and Coleman — these six lakes cover more than 400 square kilometres and stretch parallel to the Ninety Mile Beach for almost its entire length. **Sale**, at the western edge of the region, is the local base for the development of the Bass Strait oil and gas fields. Both Sale and **Bairnsdale**, further east on the banks of the Mitchell River, make excellent bases for holidays on the Lakes or for alpine trips. The main resort towns are **Lakes Entrance**, at the mouth of the Lakes; **Paynesville**, a mecca for boating and fishing enthusiasts; Metung, a departure point for cruising holidays on the Lakes; and Loch Sport, nestled between Ninety Mile Beach, Lake Victoria and the national park.

The Lakes National Park, the **Mitchell River National Park,** and the hills and valleys of the alpine foothills to the north, all provide plenty of opportunities for bushwalking, for enjoying nature or for simply enjoying the peace.

For further information on the Gippsland Lakes area, contact the local tourist information centre in each area: Cnr Esplanade and Marine Pde, Lakes Entrance; (051) 55 1966, or 240 Main St, Bairnsdale; (051) 52 3444, or Princes Hwy, Sale; (051) 44 1108. **See also:** National Parks, and individual town entries in A–Z listing for those parks and towns indicated by bold type. **Map reference:** 227 P6.

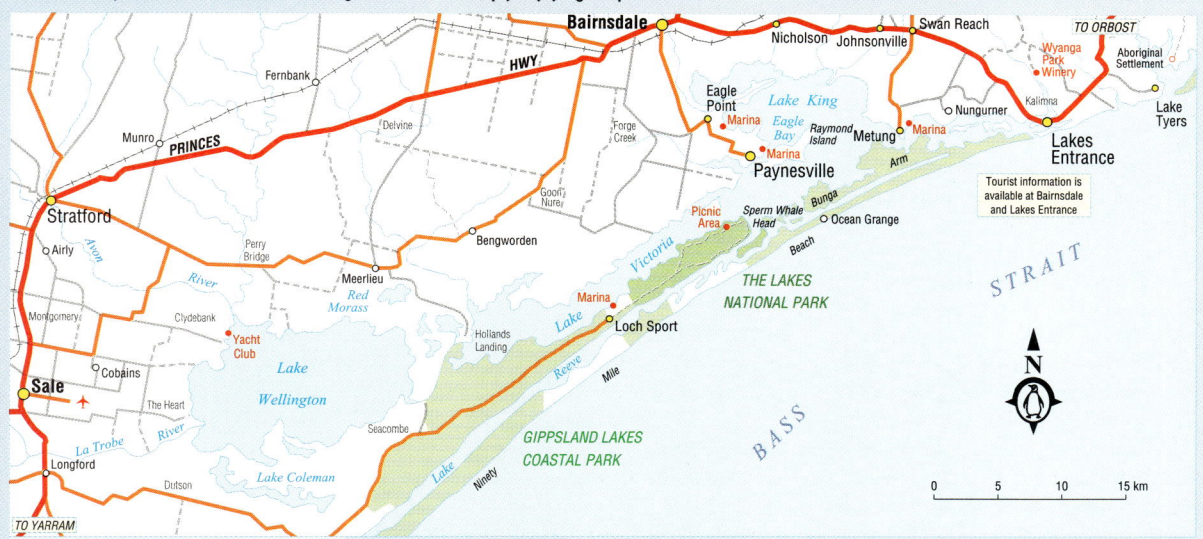

The township of Lakes Entrance at the mouth of the Gippsland Lakes

Museum in the Historical Precinct, Shepparton

Raymond Sts has local art including Annemieke Mein bronzes. Sale Common and State Game Refuge, protected wetlands area with boardwalk; on southern edge of town. Mar.: Sale Cup (horse race). Nov.: Wetlands festival; Agricultural show. **In the area:** To north west: Maffra and Heyfield (18 km), in intensively cultivated country; Lake Glenmaggie, 6 km N of Heyfield. Road to Stratford (18 km N), leads across Dargo High Plains to Mt Hotham; scenic drive through high country (check weather conditions). Holey Plains State Park, 14 km SW. Seaspray, on Ninety Mile Beach, 32 km S: excellent surfing and fishing; also at Golden and Paradise Beaches, 35 km from Sale, and Loch Sport, a further 30 km. Nearby, The Lakes National Park and Rotamah Island Bird Observatory, 15 km from Loch Sport. Marlay Point, 25 km E on shores of Lake Wellington, has extensive boat launching facilities; yacht club here sponsors overnight yacht race to Paynesville each Mar. Popular rivers for fishing include the Avon, close to Marlay Point, and the Macalister, Thomson and La Trobe, especially at Swing Bridge (1883), 5 km S of Sale. **Tourist information:** Central Gippsland Tourism, Princes Hwy; (051) 44 1108. **Accommodation:** 9 motels, 2 B&B, 2 cara./camp. parks. **See also:** Gippsland Lakes.

Seymour   Pop. 6558

MAP REF. 234 G10

Seymour is a commercial, industrial and agricultural town on the Goulburn River, 98 km N of Melbourne. The area was recommended by Lord Kitchener during his visit in 1909 as being suitable for a military base. Nearby Puckapunyal was an important training place for troops during World War II and is still a major army base. **Of interest:** In Emily St: Royal Hotel, featured in Russell Drysdale's famous 1941 painting 'Moody's Pub'; Studio Roest Gallery; Somerset Crossing Vineyard. Goulburn Park, cnr Progress and Guild Sts, has picnic and swimming areas. Old Goulburn Bridge (1891), preserved as historic relic; at end of Emily St. Steam Train Preservation Society; rides Sun. by appt. Feb.: Alternative farming expo. Mar.: Rafting festival. **In the area:** Mitchelton and Chateau Tahbilk Vineyards, near Nagambie, 23 km N. Other wineries: Somerset Crossing Vineyards, 2 km S; Hankin's Wines, 5 km NW on Northwood Rd; Hayward's Winery, 12 km SE near Trawool. Army Tank and Transport Museums at Puckapunyal army base, 10 km W. Trawool Valley Angora Stud, 11 km SE. Spotted Jumbuk, features spotted sheep; Highland Rd, 5 km E. Capalba Park Alpacas, on Kobyboyne Rd 11 km E. **Tourist information:** Somerset Winery, Emily St; (057) 92 2445, or Nagambie Tourist Centre, 320 High St, Nagambie; (057) 94 2647. **Accommodation:** 5 motels, 3 cara./camp. parks. **See also:** Wine Regions.

Shepparton   Pop. 30 511

MAP REF. 234 I6

The 'capital' of the rich Goulburn Valley, this thriving, well-developed city, now known as the Solar City, 175 km N of Melbourne, has 4000 ha of orchards within a 10-km radius and 4000 ha of market gardens along the river valley nearby. The area is irrigated by the Goulburn Irrigation Scheme. The central shopping area is surrounded by parkland. **Of interest:** Solar display at Visitors Centre, Wyndham St. Art gallery in Civic Centre, Welsford St, features Australian paintings and ceramics. On Parkside Dr., International Village and Aboriginal Keeping Place, a tourist, educational and cultural centre. Historical Museum, in Historical Precinct, High St; open Sun. p.m. Redbyrne Pottery, Old Dookie Rd, has variety of local pottery. Victoria Park Lake, Tom Collins Dr. for yachting and water sports. In Andrew Fairley Ave, SPC, a huge cannery; guided tours during fruit season (Jan.–Apr.). Lemnos-Campbells soup cannery and Ardmona fruit cannery at Mooroopna, 5 km W. All three have direct sales. Reedy Swamp Walk, at end of Wanganui Rd: prolific birdlife in wetland area. Fruit Connection, at rest stop on causeway. Feb.: Bush market day. Nov.: Strawberry festival. **In the area:** Mud Factory Pottery, 6 km S on Goulburn Valley Hwy. Several vineyards, including Chateau Tahbilk (1860), 36 km S on Goulburn Valley Hwy, near Nagambie. At Kialla, 5 km SE: Boxwood Pottery; Elm Vale Nursery. Historic Brookfield Homestead, 20 km N on Goulburn Valley Hwy features old farm machinery and shearing sheds; open by appt. Victoria's Irrigation Research Institute, east of Tatura, 16 km W of Shepparton. **Tourist information:** 534 Wyndham St; (058) 31 4400 or 1800 80 8839. **Accommodation:** 4 hotels, 18 motels, 2 B&B, 6 cara./camp. parks. **See also:** Wine Regions.

Skipton   Pop. 462

MAP REF. 222 H13, 229 M4

This township on the Glenelg Hwy, south-west of Ballarat, is situated in an important pastoral and agricultural district. The town was a major centre for merino sheep sales in the 1850s. **Of interest:** Eel factory, Cleveland St: eels netted in region, snap-frozen and exported, mainly to Germany. Adjacent to eel factory, Gibson's Doll Display. Bluestone Presbyterian Church, National Trust-classified, Montgomery St. Nov.: Art show. **In the area:** Mooromong, notable historic homestead; open by appt, 11 km NW. Mt Widderin Cave, 6 km S, volcanic cave with large underground chamber; tours by appt. Kaolin Mine, 10 km E. **Tourist information:** Skipton Hotel, Glenelg Hwy; (053) 40 2111, or Roadhouse, Glenelg Hwy; (053) 40 2131. **Accommodation:** 1 hotel.

Stawell Pop. 6339

MAP REF. 222 C5, 231 J12

North-east of Halls Gap and 123 km NW of Ballarat on the Western Hwy, Stawell is well sited for tours to the northern Grampians. It is the home of the Stawell Easter Gift, Australia's most famous professional foot race. **Of interest:** Stawell Gift Hall of Fame Museum, in Athletic Club, Central Park, cnr Seaby and Napier Sts. Big Hill, local landmark and goldmining site; Pioneers Lookout at summit indicates positions of famous mines. Casper's World in Miniature Tourist Park, London Rd: re-creation of scenes in Australia and Pacific countries using scale working models, dioramas and commentaries. Doll and Toy Museum, Main St, private collection; open Wed.–Sun. p.m. Pleasant Creek Court House Museum, Western Hwy. Easter: Easter Gift (professional foot race); Grampians highland and national dancing club championships. **In the area:** Joyflights and balloon flights. Bunjil's Shelter, Aboriginal rock paintings in ochre; off Pomonal Rd, 11 km S. The Sisters Rocks, 3 km SE, huge granite tors beside Western Hwy. Wineries at Great Western, Ararat and Halls Gap. The Diggings pottery at Great Western, picturesque wine village, 14 km SE. Goldmining at Stawell Gold Mine, 2.5 km E; viewing areas off Reefs Rd. Overdale Station, Landsborough Rd, 10 km E, offers guided tours during school holidays. National Trust property, Tottington Woolshed, rare example of 19th-century woolshed, 55 km NE on road to St Arnaud. Deep Lead Flora and Fauna Reserve, 6 km W, off Western Hwy. Excellent lakes for all water sports: Lake Fyans, 17 km SW; Lake Wartook, in Grampians National Park, 60 km W; Lake Lonsdale, 12 km NW. **Tourist information:** 54 Western Hwy; (053) 58 2314, (053) 58 2823. **Accommodation:** 1 hotel, 8 motels, 3 B&B, 2 cara./camp. parks. **See also:** The Grampians; The Golden Age; Wine Regions.

Swan Hill Pop. 9357

MAP REF. 122 H11, 233 N11

In 1836 when the explorer Thomas Mitchell camped on the banks of the Murray, he named the spot Swan Hill because the black swans had kept him awake all night. The township became a busy 19th-century river port and today it is a pleasant city and major holiday centre on the Murray Valley Hwy, 350 km NW of Melbourne. The climate is mild and sunny, and the river offers good fishing, boating and water sports. **Of interest:** Australia's first heritage museum the Pioneer Settlement, at end of Gray St on Little Murray River, features local Aboriginal culture and life in the last century, staff in period costume, old-fashioned transport and Sound and Light tour (bookings essential); riverboats: PS *Pyap* (daily Murray cruises); stationary PS *Gem* (has restaurant). In Gray St: Regional Gallery of Contemporary Art; Dowling House Art and Craft Centre. Military Museum, Campbell St, has fine collection of militaria dating from 1800. Burke and Wills Fig Tree, considered largest in Australia, commemorates explorers' visit; Curlewis St. July: Italian fiesta. **In the area:** Buller's winery, Beverford, 11 km N. Horseriding at Mulberry Farm, Vinifera, 20 km N. Historic Tyntyndyer Homestead (c. 1846), National Trust-classified, 20 km N on Murray Valley Hwy. Lakeside Nursery and Gardens, with over 300 roses on view; 10 km NW. Tooleybuc, 45 km NW, pleasant spot for fishing and birdwatching. Piambie State Forest, 70 km N. Murray Downs Homestead, historic sheep, cattle and irrigation property, also animal park and children's playground; 2 km NW over bridge into NSW on Moulamein Rd. Daily river cruises from Murray Downs River Cruises wharf on MV *Kookaburra*. Pheasant farm and aviaries at Nowie North, 20 km NW. Amboc Mohair Farm, Mystic Park, 29 km S. Lake Boga, 15 km SE, ideal for water sports. Best's St Andrew's Vineyard near Lake Boga. **Tourist information:** 306 Campbell St; (050) 32 3033. **Accommodation:** 3 hotels, 16 motels, 3 B&B, 4 cara./camp. parks. **See also:** The Mighty Murray; Wine Regions.

Tallangatta Pop. 1021

MAP REF. 235 Q5, 236 D2

When the old town of Tallangatta was submerged for the construction of the Hume Weir, many of its buildings were moved to a location above the shoreline. Today, situated 42 km SE from Wodonga on the Murray Valley Hwy, the town has the benefit of this large lake and boasts an attractive inland beach. It is the easternmost main Murray River town and is directly north of the beautiful alpine region of Victoria. **Of interest:** The Hub, for art and craft; Tallangatta's Community Centre, Towong St. Self-guide walks and drives; leaflets from Tourist information. Apr.: Dairy festival. Oct.: Arts festival. **In the area:** Laurel Hill Trout Farm at Eskdale, 33 km S: buy or catch-your-own; picnic/barbecue facilities. Forest drives recommended extend from Mitta Mitta along Omeo Hwy; including trips to Cravensville, Mt Benambra, Tawonga and Omeo via Snowy Creek Rd. Australian Alps Walking Track passes over Mt Wills, 48 km S of Mitta Mitta. Lake Dartmouth, 58 km SE, has good trout fishing and boating. Traron Alpacas at Bullioh, 15 km E: alpacas, other animals, yarns, garments and Paulownia trees (Chinese trees grown for shade or fodder). **Tourist information:** The Hub, 35–37 Towong St; (060) 71 2695. **Accommodation:** 2 hotels, 1 motel, 1 cara./camp. park. **See also:** The Mighty Murray.

Terang Pop. 1937

MAP REF. 217 A6, 229 K8

Terang, located on the Princes Hwy in a predominantly dairy-farming area, is a well-laid-out town with grand avenues of deciduous trees, recognised by the National Trust. The town has sporting facilities, with a particular emphasis on horse sports. **Of interest:** Early 20th-century commercial architecture. In High St: Gothic-style sandstone Presbyterian church; cottage crafts shop in century-old cottage, originally police station. Historical museum, features replica of early dairy; Princes Hwy. Self-guide historic town walk; leaflet available at Tourist information. Walking track

Airworld Aviation Museum, Wangaratta

(3 km) beside lake beds and National Trust-classified trees; entrance behind Civic Centre, High St. Jan.: Horse carnival and stockhorse weekend. **In the area:** Noorat, 6 km N, birthplace of Alan Marshall, author of *I Can Jump Puddles*; Alan Marshall Walking Track, a gentle climb to summit of extinct volcano with excellent views of crater, surrounding district and across to Grampians. Glenormiston Agricultural College, 4 km further N, tastefully developed around a historic mansion. **Tourist information:** Clarke Saddlery, 105 High St; (055) 92 1164. **Accommodation:** 4 hotels, 2 motels, 1 cara./camp. park.

Torquay Pop. 4887

MAP REF. 212 F11, 219 E10, 229 Q9

The popularity of this resort, 22 km S of Geelong, is well known. Close to the town are the excellent surfing beaches, Bells and Jan Juc, which attract surfers from all over the world. The Torquay Surf Lifesaving Club is the largest in the State. Torquay also marks the eastern end of the Great Ocean Rd, a spectacular drive south-west to Anglesea and beyond. **Of interest:** In Geelong Rd: Mary Elliott Pottery; The Gallery. Surfworld Plaza, cnr Geelong and Beach Rds; surfing products and national surfing museum. Craft Cottage, Anderson St. Barbara Peake's Studio, Sarabande Cr. Torqair Vintage Aeroplane Flights, offers joyflights; Blackgate Rd. Easter: Bells Beach surfing classic. **In the area:** Bicycle track along Surfcoast Hwy, Grovedale to Anglesea; various walks and scenic drives; contact Tourist information. Southern Rose, rose gardens; 1 km S on Great Ocean Rd. Experimental wind-power generator at Breamlea, 10 km NE. Rebenberg Winery (open weekends) and Downunda Weaving Studio at Mt Duneed, 11 km N. Sea Mist, horserides; Wensleydale Station Rd, Moriac, 22 km NW. Museum of early Australian horse-drawn carriages near Bellbrae, 6 km W. At Bellbrae: Pottery Studios, Moores Rd; Atelier Design Centre, Bone Rd; Spring Creek Trail Rides, Poryreath Rd. **Tourist information:** Surfworld Museum, cnr Geelong and Beach Rds; (052) 61 4606. **Accommodation:** 3 motels, 4 cara./ camp. parks. **See also:** The Great Ocean Road.

Traralgon Pop. 19 699

MAP REF. 227 K7

Situated on the Princes Hwy, 164 km SE of Melbourne, Traralgon is one of the La Trobe Valley's main cities, the others being Moe and Morwell. **Of interest:** Walking tours, heritage drive; contact Tourist information. Old post office and court house, cnr Franklin and Kay Sts. Band rotunda and miniature railway at Victory Park. Gippsland Shop, exhibition and sales of local crafts; Princes Hwy. Feb.-Mar.: Music in the park. **In the area:** Loy Yang power station, 5 km S; tours available Sun. p.m., bookings essential. PowerWorks, dynamic displays on electrical industry, off Princes Hwy near Morwell. Giant mountain ash trees and ferns, walks and scenic drives at Tarra-Bulga National Park, about 40 km S. Tarra-Bulga Visitor Centre at Balook, Grand Ridge Road, has interpretive displays. Tambo Cheese Factory, 3 km E of town, for cheese and local craft sales. **Tourist information:** Shop 1, Southside Central, Princes Hwy; (051) 74 3199. **Accommodation:** 9 motels, 5 cara./ camp. parks.

Walhalla Pop. 15

MAP REF. 227 K5

The tiny goldmining town of Walhalla is tucked away in dense mountain country in south-east Gippsland. The drive, 46 km N from Moe, passes through some spectacular scenery. Walhalla is set in a narrow, steep valley, with sides so sheer that its cemetery has graves that have been dug lengthways into the hillside. **Of interest:** Historic buildings and relics of gold-boom days. Excellent local walks. Long Tunnel Extended Goldmine, named after the most successful in the State; guided tours, check times. Rotunda (1896). Spett's Cottage (1871), furnished in the period. Old Fire Station, hand-operated fire engine and fire memorabilia. Post office (1886). Old bakery (1865), oldest surviving building in town, near rebuilt hotel. Museum, gold-era memorabilia. Windsor House (1890). Cricket ground, perched on top of 200-m hill. Walhalla Goldfield Railway, runs Sun. and public holidays. Walhalla Coach Company, drives along main road. Nov.: Goldfields fun day. **In the area:** Australian Alps Walking Track (655 km) commences at Walhalla. Cross-country skiing and walking in Baw Baw National Park, which edges western side of town. Rawson, 8 km SW, built for construction of nearby Thomson Dam. At Erica, 12 km SW: timber industry display at Erica Hotel; Elderberry Cottage, gardens and nursery; Erica Craftworks features resident wood turner; Mountain Saddle Safaris; King of the mountain woodchop, held each Mar. Thomson River, 4 km S: fishing, picnicking, canoe trail and white-water rafting. Moondarra State Park, 30 km S. Traralgon, major city in the La Trobe Valley, 35 km S. Scenic road between Walhalla and Jamieson (140 km N); check weather conditions. **Tourist information:** Museum and General Store, Main St; (051) 65 6250. **Accommodation:** 1 B&B. **See also:** Gippsland Lakes.

Wangaratta Pop. 15 984

MAP REF. 235 M6

The Ovens Hwy to Bright and the Victorian Alps, through the Ovens Valley, branches off the Hume Fwy near Wangaratta, north-east of Melbourne. The surrounding fertile area produces wool, wheat, tobacco, kiwifruit, walnuts, chestnuts, hops and table-wine grapes. **Of interest:** In cemetery, Tone Rd, grave of Daniel 'Mad Dog' Morgan, the bushranger; his headless body was buried here, the head having been sent to Melbourne for examination. Kooringa Native Plants, Warby Range Rd. At Tourist information centre, cnr Tone Rd and Handley St: Mrs Stell's House in Miniature; history of Kelly Gang. Paddys market each Sun. a.m. at Co-Store car park. Oct.: Agricultural show. Nov.: Festival of jazz and blues. **In the area:** Airworld Aviation Museum, 7 km S, has world's largest collection of flying antique civil aircraft. Road 27 km S to Moyhu leads to beautiful King Valley

Wine Regions

Viticulture developed in Victoria following the 1850s gold rush. Unsuccessful diggers began planting vines as a source of income. Later, Edward Henty and William Rye brought cuttings to the new colony and by 1868 more than 1200 hectares of vines had been established. The light, dry wines produced in these vineyards won wide acclaim, but the event of phylloxera saw a promising industry decline until the early 1960s, when it started to re-emerge and develop into what it is today.

One of the oldest regions is in the north-east of the State, 270 kilometres from Melbourne. **Rutherglen** and the other nearby wine-making towns of Wahgunyah, **Glenrowan** and **Milawa** produce wine unique to each of the region's environmental sub-cultures. Many of the wineries are still managed by the descendants of the founders. The region is famed for its rich flavoursome reds, and for the exotic range of fortified wines such as Rutherglen Muscat, Rutherglen Tokay and its famous Port-style wine. On the June long weekend, a winery walkabout is organised so that wine-lovers can visit the vineyards and sample some of the fine wines of the north-east. It is advisable to book accommodation in advance if planning a visit at this time.

West along the Murray, the towns of **Echuca**, **Swan Hill** and **Mildura** are part of the Murray Valley and north-west region known for the production of wines for everyday drinking.

About 200 kilometres west of Melbourne, between Stawell and Ararat, is the little town of Great Western, where the Seppelt and Best wineries developed in the 1860s. Since then they have consistently produced fine wines, including the renowned champagne-style Great Western Special Reserve from the Seppelt winery. The vineyards of Great Western are also noted for their rich red and full-flavoured white table wines.

At **Ararat**, Trevor Mast's Mt Langi Ghiran Wines and the Montara Winery, both produce excellent wine with their own individual character.

To the north-east of Great Western is the region of the Pyrenees with the towns of **Avoca**, Redbank and Moonambel. Here are the Taltarni, Mt Avoca, Redbank, Chateau Remy, Summerfield, Dalwhinnie and Warrenmang wineries.

Stretching from **Shepparton** along to **Nagambie**, **Seymour** and **Mansfield** is the picturesque region of the Goulburn Valley with a contrast in wineries from the historic, classified buildings of Chateau Tahbilk to the modern wineries of Delatite and Mitchelton. One grape variety from the region to win acclaim is the Marsanne, a distinct and rather unusual white wine.

One of the two oldest regions near Melbourne is the Yarra Valley region, which is centred round Cottles Bridge and St Andrews (at the northern end), Yarra Glen, Lilydale, Coldstream and **Healesville** (in the central part of the region), and Seville and **Warburton** (to the south). This region's premium wine has had a rebirth after starting in the early 1850s and petering out as late as the 1920s. There is a wide range of wines produced in the area, from sparkling wine to quality reds and white table wines. Wineries of particular interest include Domaine Chandon for its sparkling wines and splendid tasting room, and Fergusson's, Kellybrook, Yarra Burn and De Bortoli for an enjoyable restaurant lunch in the Valley. There are many other wineries worth visiting, including Bianchet for the merlot and verduzzo wines, and St Huberts, one of the first wineries in the re-birth of the district. Grape Grazing, a food and wine festival, is held in March every year.

Another wine-producing area close to Melbourne is the Mornington Peninsula area. A cool-climate winegrowing district, its vineyards nestle between farming and coastal hamlets. The main spread covers the area from Dromana, through Red Hill and across the Peninsula to Merricks and Balnarring, with Mornington, Main Ridge and Mt Martha offering isolated vineyards. Most vineyards are open, usually on weekends and public holidays, for cellar-door tastings and sales; some open for sales and visits by appointment only.

The wine producers in this area organise 'all wineries under one roof' at the Regional Gallery in Mornington, during the long weekend in June.

North of Melbourne's Tullamarine Airport, wineries dot the landscape with pockets of vines stretching into the Macedon Ranges; some were established in the 1860s, others more recently. They include Knight's Granite Hills, Wildwood, Hanging Rock, Virgin Hills, Craiglee, Goonawarra, Cleveland, Cope-Williams, Flynn and Williams — each with its own distinct quality and character.

The Heathcote-Bendigo region is, like so many of Victoria's wine regions, goldmining country that gave up much hidden wealth in the period 1850–1900. Today there are many wineries scattered throughout the region, around the townships of **Heathcote**, Kingower, **Bendigo** and Bridgewater on Loddon. Wineries include Passing Clouds, Jasper Hill, Osicka's, Zuber Estate, Water Wheel, Le Amon and Mildara's Balgownie.

In the last 30 years Victoria's wine industry has changed from an industry in decline, with about 25 commercial vineyards, to a flourishing concern with about 300 commercial vineyards and 100 smaller ones. Most larger wineries are open daily for tastings and sales; some of the small wineries have restricted opening times, so check with the winery before visiting.

For more information contact: Mornington Peninsula Vignerons Association; (059) 87 3822; or Yarra Valley Wine Growers Association; (03) 9735 3929. Tourism Victoria publish an excellent guide, *Wine Regions of Victoria* describing more than 200 wineries; a copy can be obtained from the Victorian Visitor Information Centre, cnr Little Collins and Swanston Sts, Melbourne, (03) 9650 1522. **See also:** individual entries in A–Z listing for those towns indicated by bold type. **Map reference:** 216, for Yarra Valley region.

Vineyard in the Yarra Valley region

and Paradise Falls. Network of minor roads allows exploration of unspoiled area and tiny townships of Whitfield (54 km S), Cheshunt and Carboor. King Valley scenic drive runs beside King River to Whitfield and Powers Lookout (74 km S). Newton's Prickle Berry Farm at Whitfield. Many vineyards around towns of Glenrowan (SW), Milawa (SE) and Rutherglen (NE). Glenrowan, 16 km SW, famed for its Ned Kelly history. Warby Range State Park, 12 km W: good vantage points, picnic spots and variety of bird and plant life. Interesting old gold township Eldorado (20 km NE): largest gold dredge in the southern hemisphere, built in 1936; historical museum; general store; potteries. Nearby, Reedy Creek, popular with anglers, gold-panners and gem-fossickers. 'Carinya' Ladson Store (1860), Tarrawingee, 11 km SE: historic homestead and old goldfields store, property owned by same family for 110 years (all furnishings original); check times. Wombi Toys, Whorouly, 25 km SE. **Tourist information:** Cnr Tone Rd and Handley St; (057) 21 5711. **Accommodation:** 2 hotels, 1 hotel/motel, 13 motels, 3 B&B, 3 cara./camp. parks. **See also:** Wine Regions.

Warburton Pop. 2504

MAP REF. 213 O6, 216 H9, 226 G3

Warburton was established with the gold finds of the 1880s; however, by the turn of the century it had found its niche as a popular tourist town with fine guest houses. It is surrounded by the foothills of the Great Dividing Range and is only about 90 minutes' drive from Melbourne. **Of interest:** Several art and craft, and old wares shops. July: Winterfest. **In the area:** Bushwalking, riding and birdwatching. Tommy Finn's Trout Farm, 2 km W. Yarra Junction Historical Museum, 10 km W. Upper Yarra draught horse festival in Jan. at Hoddles Creek, 15 km W. Cherry festival in Nov. at Wandin, 27 km W. Mt Donna Buang, 7 km NW, popular day-trip destination from Melbourne, often snow-covered in winter. The Acheron Way begins 2 km E of Warburton, giving access to views of Mt Donna Buang, Mt Victoria and Ben Cairn, on the scenic 37-km drive to St Fillans. Upper Yarra Dam, 23 km NE. South of town along Warburton Hwy, an attractive area of vineyards: Yarra Burn, Lillydale and Oak Ridge Estate. Walk from Powelltown, 27 km SE, to East Warburton (leaflet from Tourist information); this is one branch of the Centenary Trail (the other branch leads from Warburton to Baw Baw National Park). Between Powelltown and Noojee,

The Grampians

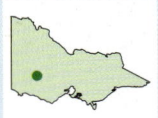

The massive sandstone ranges of the Grampians in western Victoria provide some of the State's most spectacular scenery. Rising in peaks to heights of over 1000 metres, they form the western extremity of the Great Dividing Range. The explorer Major Mitchell climbed and named the highest peak, Mt William, in July 1836 and gave the name 'The Grampians' to the ranges because they reminded him of the Grampians in his native Scotland.

On 1 July, 1984 these rugged mountain ranges became a national park. It is a superb area for scenic drives on good roads; bushwalking and rock climbing are also popular. The western and northern Grampians have Aboriginal rock-art sites. Lake Bellfield provides for sailing and rowing, and there is trout fishing in the lake and in Fyans Creek.

There is plenty of wildlife to be seen: koalas and kangaroos are numerous, and echidnas, possums and platypuses can be found, while more than 100 bird species have been identified.

Apart from their scenic grandeur, the Grampians are best known for the beauty and variety of their wildflowers. There are more than 1000 species of ferns and flowering plants native to the region and they are at their most colourful from August to November. The Halls Gap wildflower exhibition is held annually in September.

The Grampians, rugged sandstone ranges in western Victoria

Halls Gap, which takes its name from a pioneer pastoralist who settled in the eastern Grampians in the early 1840s, is the focal point of the area and offers a wide variety of accommodation.

For further information, contact the Stawell and Grampians Tourism Information Centre, 54 Western Hwy, West Stawell; (053) 58 2314, or the Halls Gap Tourist Information Centre, Grampians Rd, Halls Gap; (053) 56 4247, or the Grampians National Park Visitors Centre, Grampians Rd, Halls Gap; (053) 56 4381. **See also:** Grampians National Park entry in National Parks; entry for Halls Gap in A–Z listing. **Map references:** 222 A7, 228 H1, 230 H12.

rainforest gully walk to Ada Tree, a giant mountain ash. Yellingbo State Fauna Reserve, 25 km SW. **Tourist information:** Yarra Valley-Healesville Visitor Information Centre, 127 Maroondah Hwy, Healesville; (059) 62 2600. **Accommodation:** 1 hotel, 2 motels, 1 cara./camp. park.

Warracknabeal Pop. 2687

MAP REF. 230 H6

Situated on the Henty Hwy, 350 km NW of Melbourne, Warracknabeal is in the centre of a rich grain-growing area. The Aboriginal name means 'the place of the big red gums shading the watercourse'. **Of interest:** Historical Centre, 81 Scott St. Black Arrow Tour of historic buildings (self-guide drive or walk) and other walks; leaflets available from Tourist information. National Trust-classified buildings: Warracknabeal Hotel (1872), Scott St, beautiful iron lacework; original log lockup (1872), Devereaux St, built when town acquired its first permanent policeman. Wheatlands Agricultural Machinery Museum, displays of farm machinery from last 100 yrs; Henty Hwy. Lions Park, on Yarriambiack Creek, has picnic spots, and flora and fauna park. Easter: Vintage machinery and vehicle rally; Wheatlands carnival. **In the area:** Argip Lane Antiques, in old church, 18 km NW on road to Jeparit. At Jeparit, 45 km W, Wimmera-Mallee Pioneer Museum. Nearby, Lake Hindmarsh, largest freshwater lake in Victoria. Lake Buloke, 56 km E. **Tourist information:** 119 Scott St; (053) 98 1632. **Accommodation:** 4 hotels, 3 motels, 1 B&B, 1 cara./camp. park. **See also:** The Wimmera.

Warragul Pop. 8910

MAP REF. 213 P10, 226 H6

Most of Melbourne's milk comes from this prosperous dairy-farming area 103 km SE of Melbourne. It is also an important commercial centre. **Of interest:** West Gippsland Arts Centre, Civic Place. Lillico Garden Railway, Copelands Rd. Mar.: Gippsland field days. **In the area:** Wild Dog Winery, 5 km S on Warragul–Jirynbyrra Rd; open daily by appt. Scenic drives through mountain country near Neerim South, 19 km N. Gourmet Deli Trail, brochure available, guides visitors on a food trip around this scenic region via various farms, cheese producers, wineries, nurseries, restaurants and food outlets. Wildflower sanctuary at Labertouche, 16 km W. Darnum Musical Village, 8 km E. Nature reserves and picnic spots: Glen Cromie (Drouin West), Glen Nayook (south of Nayook) and Toorongo Falls (just north of Noojee). Alpine Trout Farm, west of Noojee. **Tourist information:** Shop 1, Southside Central, Princes Hwy, Traralgon; (051) 74 3199. **Accommodation:** 3 motels, 1 B&B, 1 cara./camp. park.

Flagstaff Hill Maritime Museum, Warrnambool

Warrnambool Pop. 25 500

MAP REF. 228 I9

A beautiful seaside city, Warrnambool is located 263 km SW of Melbourne on Lady Bay, where the Princes Hwy meets the Great Ocean Rd. First-class sporting, cultural and entertainment facilities and beautifully developed and maintained parks and gardens have resulted in Warrnambool being awarded Victoria's Premier Town title a record 3 times. **Of interest:** Flagstaff Hill Maritime Museum, Merri St: reconstructed 19th-century Maritime Village with Entrance Gallery Orientation Centre introducing visitors to Maritime Village experience, featuring Flagstaff Hill tapestry, with themes of Aboriginal history, sealing, whaling, exploration, immigration and settlement. Over 100 ships were wrecked on the coast near Warrnambool; famous earthenware Loch Ard Peacock, recovered from *Loch Ard* wreck in 1878, is on permanent display at Flagstaff Hill Maritime Museum. Annual visit of rare southern right whales, usually May–Oct. (viewing platform east of town at Logans Beach). The Kid's Country Treasure Map (available at Tourist information) provides informative way for the whole family to enjoy Warrnambool. In Timor St: Performing Arts Centre; Art Gallery. In Gilles St: Customs House Gallery; History House, local memorabilia (open by appt). Botanic Gardens (designed by Guilfoyle in 1879), Botanic Rd. Fletcher Jones Gardens, Raglan Pde. Lake Pertobe Adventure Playground, Pertobe Rd. Portugese Padrao, monument to Portugese explorers; Cannon Hill. The Potter's Wheel, Liebig St. Thunder Point Reserve, end Macdonald St. Middle Island, off Pickering Point, colony of little (fairy) penguins. Wollaston Bridge (over 100 years old) unusual design, on northern outskirts of town. Heritage trail walk and arrow tour of city start at Tourist information centre (self-guide leaflets available). Feb.: Wunta fiesta. May: Racing carnival. Oct.: Melbourne–Warrnambool cycling classic. **In the area:** Tower Hill State Game Reserve, 14 km W, features one of Victoria's largest and most recently active volcanoes; nature walk starts at the Natural History Centre within reserve. Port Campbell National Park, 54 km SE, 32-km spectacular stretch of scenic and historic coastline. Robert Ulmann Studio, 4 km E, paintings of Australian flora and fauna. Allansford Cheese World, 10 km E: cheese tasting, sales and viewing of cheese production. Ralph Illidge Sanctuary, 32 km E: wildlife and nature walks. Historic Shipwreck Trail links sites of wrecks along the 'Shipwreck Coast' from Port Fairy (29 km W) to Moonlight Head (112 km E). Mahogany Walk from Warrnambool–Port Fairy (22 km), along beach dunes. Helicopter and joy flights along coast. **Tourist information:** 600 Raglan Pde; (055) 64 7837. **Accommodation:** 10 hotels, 23 motels, 6 B&B, 8 cara./camp. parks. **See also:** The Great Ocean Road.

Wedderburn   Pop. 764

MAP REF. 231 N7

Once one of Victoria's richest goldmining towns in the 'Golden Triangle', Wedderburn is on the Calder Hwy, 74 km NW of Bendigo. Gold is still found around the town. **Of interest:** Hard Hill area, former gold diggings and Government Battery, Wilson St at northern edge of town. In High St: Museum and General Store (1910), restored building furnished and stocked as it was at turn of century; coach-building factory; old bakery, converted into a pottery. Sept.: Wool expo. **In the area:** Christmas Reef Mine, 2 km E. Mount Korong, 16 km SE: rock scrambling and bushwalking. Wychitella Forest Reserve, wildlife sanctuary in mallee forest; 16 km N. **Tourist information:** Shire Offices, High St; (054) 94 3200. **Accommodation:** 1 hotel, 1 motel, 1 cara./camp. park.

Welshpool   Pop. 241

MAP REF. 227 K10

Welshpool is a small dairying town and nearby Port Welshpool is a deep-sea port servicing fishing and oil industries. Barry Beach Marine Terminal, 8 km S of the South Gippsland Hwy, services the offshore oil rigs in Bass Strait. **In the area:** Excellent fishing and boating. At Port Welshpool, Maritime Museum. Tarra-Bulga National Park, 56 km NE. Agnes Falls, 19 km NW, State's highest. Scenic drive west with panoramic views from Mt Fatigue, off South Gippsland Hwy. Near Toora, 11 km W, Franklin River Reserve has nature walk. **Tourist information:** South Gippsland Tourism, Silkstone Rd, Korumburra; (056) 552233. **Accommodation:** 1 motel, 2 cara./camp. parks.

Winchelsea   Pop. 969

MAP REF. 212 D10, 219 A8, 229 P8

This town, in the centre of a farming area, is on the Barwon River, 37 km W of Geelong. It originated as a watering-place and shelter for travellers on the road to Colac from Geelong. **Of interest:** Barwon Bridge, with its graceful stone arches, opened 1867 to handle increasing westward traffic. Alexandra's Antiques and Art Gallery, Main St. Barwon Hotel (1842), houses museum of Australiana. **In the area:** National Trust property, Barwon Park Homestead, 3 km N on Inverleigh Rd; open Sun. and Wed. Country Dahlias, gardens open Feb.–Apr.; 5 km S on Mathieson Rd. **Tourist information:** Shire Offices, Hesse St; (052) 67 2104. **Accommodation:** 1 motel, 1 cara./camp. park.

Wodonga   Pop. 39 975

MAP REF. 123 Q13, 235 P4, 236 B2

Wodonga is the Victorian city – Albury, the NSW city – in a twin-city complex astride the Murray in north-east Victoria. Albury-Wodonga, with the attractions of the Murray and nearby Lake Hume, makes a good base for a holiday. **Of interest:** Gateway complex on Lincoln Causeway: working craft shops, tourist information and restaurant. Miniature steam railway, Diamond Park, off Lincoln Causeway; runs on 3rd Sun. of month. Sumsion Gardens, beautiful lakeside park; Church St. In Melrose Dr., largest outdoor tennis centre in Australia. Border country fair, 2nd Sun. each month. Feb.: Sports festival. Apr.: Wodonga show. Aug.: Wine and food festival. Nov.: World Cup show jumping. **In the area:** Military Museum, Bandiana; 4 km SE. Hume Weir, 15 km E; Hume Weir Trout Farm. Nearby touring areas include: Upper Murray, mountain valleys of north-east Victoria; Murray Valley; Riverina district. Short drive 36 km S leads to picturesque township of Yackandandah. Nearby towns worth visiting: Beechworth (47 km), Wangaratta (68 km), both south-west; and Rutherglen, 42 km NW. **Tourist information:** Gateway Tourist Information Centre, Lincoln Causeway; (060) 41 3875. **Accommodation:** 4 hotels, 11 motels, 2 cara./camp. parks. **See also:** The Mighty Murray.

Wonthaggi   Pop. 5751

MAP REF. 226 G10

Once the main supplier of coal to the Victorian Railways, Wonthaggi, situated 8 km from Cape Paterson in Gippsland, is South Gippsland's largest town. It began as a tent town in 1909 when the coal mines were opened up by the State Government following industrial unrest in the coalfields in NSW. The mines operated until 1968. Apr.: Turville Shield fishing competition. **In the area:** State Coal Mine, 1.5 km S on Cape Paterson Rd: tours of re-opened Eastern Area Mine, with experienced former coalminer as guide, and museum of mining activities. Cape Paterson, 8 km S in Bunurong Marine Park; surfing, swimming, snorkelling, scuba diving and fishing. Scenic drives: beaches at Inverloch, 13 km SE; Tarwin Lower, 35 km SE. Self-guide 25-km tour links places of interest in area. George Bass Coastal Walk from Kilcunda, 11 km NW. Brochures available at Tourist information. Market, 4th Sun. each month at Grantville, north on Bass Hwy. **Tourist information:** Watts St; (056) 72 2484. **Accommodation:** 1 hotel, 2 motels, 1 hostel, 1 cara./camp. park, 1 cara. park.

Woodend   Pop. 2743

MAP REF. 212 G2, 226 A1, 229 R2, 234 D12

The township of Woodend is situated on the Calder Hwy, an hour's drive north of Melbourne. It acquired its name from its position at the end of the Black Forest. During the gold rushes (1850s), travellers sought refuge from mud, bogs and bushrangers at the 'wood's end' around Five Mile Creek. Later the town developed, as shops and services were established for the passing trade. The main danger for today's travellers is 'black ice' in winter; hazard warning lights are installed throughout the area. **Of interest:** Five Mile Creek and bluestone bridge (1862). St Mary's Anglican

The Mighty Murray

P S Cumberoona cruises the river near Albury

As a present-day explorer, a trip following the course of the Murray River is an opportunity to discover a rich cross-section of Australian country and its history, as well as the infinite variety of natural beauty and wildlife the river itself supports.

The source
The Murray has its source on the slopes of Mount Pilot, high in the Alps. Here it is just a gurgling mountain stream, rushing through some breathtaking mountain scenery. This is the area of the Snowy Mountains Hydro-Electric Scheme and the great Australian snowfields.

The upper Murray
The upper reaches of the river flows through the scenic area around Jingellic and Walwa, and on to the beautiful Lake Hume near **Albury** and **Wodonga** before continuing past **Corowa**, the birthplace of Federation, and into Lake Mulwala.

Lakes, beaches and red gums
As it flows from the aquatic playgrounds of Lakes Hume and Mulwala, the Murray becomes a wide and splendid river. Lined with magnificent red gums in the region around **Cobram**, the riverbanks are transformed into wide sandy beaches. This is ideal holiday country with pleasant resort towns: **Yarrawonga**, Mulwala, **Barooga** and **Tocumwal**.

Wine country
Victoria's main winegrowing area is centred around **Rutherglen** and extends to the wineries of Cobram and the Ovens and Goulburn valleys. The wineries welcome visitors and many offer conducted tours.

The heyday of the riverboats
Famous river towns like **Echuca**, **Swan Hill** and **Wentworth** have carefully preserved much of the history of the colourful riverboat era. The Port of Echuca, the Swan Hill Pioneer Settlement and the historic Murray Downs Homestead are a must if you are in the area. Children especially will delight in the 'living museum' aspect of these river towns, with their original buildings, paddlesteamers and old wharves faithfully restored.

Wildlife
The Murray's abundant bird and animal life is protected by national parks and in a number of sanctuaries and reserves stretching from the banks of the river. Spoonbills, herons, eagles, harriers and kites abound. The **Hattah-Kulkyne** and Murray-Kulkyne national parks include a section of the river frontage and the Hattah Lakes system. More than 220 species of birds have been recorded here and red kangaroos can be regularly seen, a rare experience in Victoria. The other major park near the river **Murray-Sunset National Park**, includes a section of the riverine plains of the Murray and supports a varied array of native fauna including the mallee fowl. Near Picnic Point in the Moira State Forest, near Mathoura, waterbirds and wildlife abound and can be seen from the observatory in this beautiful red gum forest. At **Kerang**, which lies at the beginning of a chain of lakes and marshes, you can see huge breeding grounds for the splendid ibis. **Kyabram** has a famous community-owned fauna and waterfowl park which is open daily, and almost all of Gunbower Island is a protected sanctuary for wildlife.

Sunraysia
The beautiful climate of **Mildura** supports flourishing citrus and winegrowing industries as well as attracting countless holidaymakers to the Sunraysia area. Upstream is Red Cliffs, a town founded after World War I by returned soldiers, who turned it into a model irrigation town, and the surrounding areas into prosperous winelands. At the junction of the Murray and the Darling lies **Wentworth**, one of the oldest of the river towns, with an historic gaol and the beautifully preserved paddlesteamer *Ruby*. From Wentworth, holidaymakers can cruise along the Darling River in MV *Loyalty*.

Riverland
The Murray crosses into South Australia and at **Renmark** begins its splendid flow down to its mouth at Lake Alexandrina. The banks are lined with such historic river towns as **Renmark, Morgan** and **Murray Bridge. Goolwa** at its mouth has a strong tradition of shipbuilding, originating from the busy riverboat days. Renmark, like Mildura, is famous for its year-round sunshine. This South Australian stretch of the Murray offers splendid river scenery and birdlife, excellent fishing and water sports, and the chance to enjoy the many wineries in the area.

Further information is available from the tourist information centres in the various towns along the river, including Swan Hill; (050) 32 3033, Mildura; (050) 21 4424, Cobram; (058) 72 2132, Echuca; (054) 80 7555, or Yarrawonga-Mulwala; (057) 44 1989. **See also:** National Parks, and individual entries in A–Z listing for those parks and towns indicated by bold type.

Yackandandah, an historic town classified by the National Trust

Church (1864), Calder Hwy. Court house (1870), Forest St; open by appt. Clock tower, Calder Hwy, built as WWI memorial. Walks, cycling and horse-riding nearby; inquire at Tourist information. Craft market, 3rd Sun. of month (Oct.–May). Dec.: Five Mile Creek festival. **In the area:** Black gum trees *(E. aggregata)*, unique to Woodend. Hanging Rock, 8 km NE: massive rock formation made famous by Joan Lindsay's story and subsequent film *Picnic at Hanging Rock*; picnic races held nearby in Jan. (New Year's Day) and Australia Day; vintage car rally held in Feb. Mt Macedon (1013 m), 10 km E: WWI memorial cross at summit; area around renowned for its beautiful gardens, many open autumn and spring. Nearby, Church of the Resurrection has stained-glass windows designed by Leonard French. Scenic drives and bushwalks in Macedon Regional Park. The town of Macedon, 8 km SE. Over 15 wineries in region; maps available at Tourist information. Wineries close to town: Hanging Rock Winery, Newham (8 km NE); Cope-Williams Winery, Romsey (21 km E); Macedon Ranges 'Budburst' wine festival held last weekend Oct. Camel Farm, safaris and trail rides; 2 km SE. At Gisborne, 18 km SE: Gisborne Steam Park; craft outlets. Barringo Wildlife Reserve at New Gisborne, 21 km SE. Potato-growing area and old goldmining town of Trentham, 25 km SW; nearby, Trentham Falls. Firth Park in Wombat Forest, East Trentham. Art and craft gallery at Tylden, 13 km W. At Lancefield, 28 km NE: Antique Centre, crafts. At Carlsruhe, 18 km NW: galleries, crafts and antiques. **Tourist information:** High St, beside Five Mile Creek; (054) 27 2033. **Accommodation:** 5 B&B, 1 hostel.

Wycheproof Pop. 777

MAP REF. 122 G13, 231 L5

A railway line runs down the middle of the main street of this town on the edge of the Mallee, 140 km from Bendigo. **Of interest:** On Broadway: Centenary Park; Willandra Historical Museum. 'Mt Wycheproof', a mere 43 m high and the smallest mountain in the world; Mount St. Craft shops. **In the area:** Peppercorn Drive Homestead, 5 km NW, country crafts and antique kitchenware for sale. **Tourist information:** Shire Offices, 367 Broadway; (054) 93 7400. **Accommodation:** 2 hotels, 1 motel, 1 cara./camp. park.

Yackandandah Pop. 601

MAP REF. 235 P5, 236 B3

Located about 27 km S of Wodonga, this exceptionally attractive town, with avenues of English trees and traditional verandahed buildings, has been classified by the National Trust. Yackandandah is in the heart of the north-east goldfields (gold was discovered here in 1852), but today it is better known for its historic buildings. **Of interest:** Number of original buildings in High St: post office; several banks and general stores; Bank of Victoria (1865), now historical museum. Self-guide walking tour; brochure from Tourist information. Ray Riddington's Premier Store and Gallery, High St. Art and craft from: Yackandandah Workshop, cnr Kars and Hammond Sts; Haldane Artist Studio, High St; Wildon Thyme, High St. Vintage Sounds Restorations, Wyndham St: old and antique gramophones, telephones and radios. Yackandandah Trail and Coach Rides. Yack Track Tours offer tours of Karrs Reef Goldmine; 4WD tours for wine tasting, goldpanning and bushwalking; bookings essential. Market, 2nd Sat. each month in Memorial Gardens, High St. **In the area:** Creeks and old diggings in Yackandandah area still yield specimens of alluvial gold to amateur prospectors. Lavender Patch Plant Farm, 4 km W on Beechworth Rd. Picturesque Indigo Valley, 6 km NW; scenic drive leads through rolling hills along valley floor to Barnawatha. Near Barnawatha: Koendidda Historic Homestead and gardens, Pooleys Rd. At Allans Flat, 10 km NE: Mr Red's Farm (nursery and native fauna park); Schmidt's Strawberry Winery. At Leneva, 16 km NE, Wombat Valley Tramways, small-gauge railway operates at Easter or by appt for groups. At Dederang, 25 km SE: art, craft and plants. **Tourist information:** Finders Bric-a-Brac and Old Wares, 28 High St; (060) 27 1222. **Accommodation:** 2 hotels, 3 B&B, 1 cara./camp. park.

Yarragon Pop. 708

MAP REF. 213 Q10, 226 I7

This small town in the La Trobe Valley is situated 116 km E of Melbourne in an agricultural and dairying district. It is an ideal base for exploring the Upper La Trobe and Tanjil River valleys in the mountainous area to the north and for scenic drives along the Grand Ridge Rd to the south. **Of interest:** Antiques, crafts, gallery, specialty shops, gourmet food and boutique wines. Nov.: Dairy fest. **In the area:** Mt Worth State

Park, 10 km SW. At Childers, 16 km SE: Sunny Creek Fruit and Berry Farm; Windrush Cottage. At Thorpdale (known for its potatoes), 22 km SE: potato bread from bakery; Potato Festival in Mar. Grand Ridge Rd, spectacular 140-km drive starting at Mirboo North and traversing top of Strzelecki Ranges. Trafalgar Lookout, Narracan Falls and Henderson's Gully near Trafalgar, 8 km E. At Darnum, 7 km NW, musical village housing hundreds of musical instruments. **Tourist information:** Gippsland Food and Wine, Princes Hwy; (056) 34 2451. **Accommodation:** 1 motel.

Yarram   Pop. 2006

MAP REF. 227 L9

This old-established South Gippsland town, 225 km by road from Melbourne, has some interesting original buildings and a pleasant golf course inhabited by relatively tame kangaroos. It is situated between the Strzelecki Ranges and Bass Strait. **Of interest:** Tarra Spinning Wheels, Alberton Rd: spinning wheels, boat wheels and beds; general wood turning. Easter: Tarra festival. Nov.: Seabank fishing contest. **In the area:** Historic towns: Alberton (6 km S), early settlers' graves in cemetery; Tarraville (11 km SE), Christ Church (1856) and maritime museum in old bank building; Port Albert (14 km S), site of first European settlement in Gippsland. Ninety Mile Beach, popular with surfers and anglers, begins just north of Port Albert. Beaches patrolled in summer: Woodside Beach, 29 km E; Seaspray, 68 km NE. Fishing beaches: Manns, 16 km SE; McLoughlins, 29 km E. To the north, Australian Omega Navigation Facility with 432-m-high steel tower; open daily. In the Strzelecki Ranges, 27 km NW: Tarra-Bulga National Park, hilly and densely forested with mountain ash, myrtle and sassafras, spectacular fern glades, splendid river and mountain views, the occasional koala as well as rosellas and lyrebirds. At Tarra Valley: Eilean Donan Gardens and Riverbank Nursery; splendid gardens; two caravan parks; horseriding nearby. At Hiawatha, 46-km circuit drive from Yarram: Minnie Ha Ha Falls, on Albert River, nearby picnic facilities; horses for hire. Won Wron Forest, 16 km N on Hyland Hwy, wildflowers in spring. **Tourist information:** The Court House, Rodger St; (051) 82 6553. **Accommodation:** 2 hotels, 3 motels, 2 cara./camp. parks.

Yarrawonga   Pop. 3603

MAP REF. 123 N13, 235 K3

A pleasant stretch of the Murray and the attractive Lake Mulwala have made this border town and Mulwala (in NSW) extremely popular holiday resorts. The 6000-ha lake was created in 1939 during the building of the Yarrawonga Weir, which controls the irrigation waters in the Murray Valley. **Of interest:** Around

The Wimmera

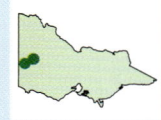

Travelling through the Wimmera on a hot summer day is an unforgettable experience. The Wimmera is the granary of the State; the wheat fields stretch as far as the eye can see, an endless golden plain broken only occasionally by a gentle ripple in the terrain. In the south-east corner, however, are the Grampians, surrounded by a network of lakes, understandably popular with anglers and water-sports lovers.

The region takes its name from an Aboriginal word meaning 'throwing stick'. Evidence of occupation by the original inhabitants, the Wotjobaluk and Jardwa, can still be seen: canoe trees are common and there are many rock-art sites in the Grampians area. The Ebenezer Mission Station at Antwerp, near **Dimboola**, founded by missionaries in 1859 to christianise the Aboriginal population, has been restored by the National Trust and local inhabitants.

Horsham, with its delightful private, public and Botanic gardens, intriguing Olde Horsham Village and the excellent Regional Art Gallery, makes a good base from which to explore the whole region. If you are visiting the region in March, do not miss the annual Wimmera machinery field days, held at the Victorian College of Agriculture and Horticulture at Longerenong. **Natimuk,** 27 km west of Horsham, is the centre for visitors drawn to climb Mt Arapiles, a 356-metre sandstone monolith.

The agricultural life of the last century has been remembered at **Warracknabeal,** the largest wheat-receiving centre in the State, where an agricultural machinery museum houses huge steam-powered chaff-cutters, headers and tractors, and depicts the history of the wheat industry. Near Dimboola, set along the banks of the Wimmera River, is one entrance to the Little Desert National Park. 'Little Desert' is something of a misnomer because the park is not little, and it does not look like a desert. There is a proliferation of plant and animal life, particularly in spring when the scrub and heathlands come into bloom.

For further information, contact the Horsham Rural City Visitor Centre, 20 O'Callaghan's Pde, Horsham; (053) 82 1832. **See also:** individual entries in A–Z listing for those towns indicated by bold type. **Map reference:** 230 D4.

Lake Bellfield, at the south-eastern end of the region

the lake and along the river: sandy beaches and still waters, ideal for water sports; abundant birdlife. The Yarrawonga and Mulwala foreshore areas: shady willows, giant water-slides, barbecues and boat ramps. At Tourist information: Old Yarra Mine Shaft houses a large collection of gems, minerals and fossils. Canning A.R.T.S. Gallery, Belmore St. Tudor House Clock Museum, Lynch St. Daily cruises on *Paradise Queen*, *Lady Murray*; Bank St. Tunzafun Amusement Park, Melbourne St. Robb & Co., horse-drawn coach rides. Canoe and boat hire, horseriding. Bush market, 2nd and 4th Sun. each month at railway station, Sharp St. Jan.: Sailing regatta. Sept.: Ice Breaker yacht regatta. Oct.: Antique fair. **In the area:** At Mulwala: Pioneer Museum, Melbourne St (open Wed.–Sun.). Linley Park Animal Farm and Fauna Park, Corowa Rd. Fishing in Murray River (no licence required). Fyffe Field Winery, 19 km W on Murray Valley Hwy. Matata Deer Farm, Cobram, 42 km W. Historical Museum, Katamatite; 35 km SW. **Tourist information:** Irvine Pde, Yarrawonga; (057) 44 1989. **Accommodation:** 4 hotels, 2 hotel/motels, 16 motels, 10 cara./camp. parks. **See also:** The Mighty Murray.

Yea   Pop. 995

MAP REF. 213 M1, 234 I11

This town, 58 km N of Yarra Glen, stands beside the Yea River, a tributary of the Goulburn. Set in pastoral and dairy-farming land, it is well situated for touring around Mansfield, Eildon and the mountains, and to the gorge country between Yea and Tallarook, as well as south-east to Marysville. There are some beautiful gorges and fern gullies close to the Yea–Tallarook road. **Of interest:** Beaufort Manor (1870s), High St. General Store (1887), High St. **In the area:** Pick-your-own fruit at Berry King Farm, Two Hills Rd, Glenburn; 28 km S. Kinglake National Park, 30 km S: beautiful waterfalls, tall eucalypts, fern gullies and impressive views. Spectacular Wilhelmina Falls, 32 km S via Melba Hwy. In Murrindindi Reserve, 11 km SE: Murrindindi Cascades and wildlife including wombats, platypuses, lyrebirds. Flowerdale Winery, 23 km SW on Whittlesea–Yea Rd. Ibis rookery at Kerrisdale, 17 km W. Grotto at Caveat, 27 km N. Mineral springs at Dropmore, 47 km N off back road to Euroa. Several good campsites along Goulburn River. Many scenic drives in area; contact Tourist information. **Tourist information:** Shire Offices; (057) 97 2209; Legendary Country Tourism, 11 High St, Mansfield; (057) 75 1464. **Accommodation:** 2 motels, 1 cara./camp. park.

The Western District

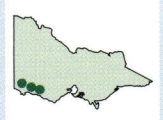

Some famous Australians have been born and bred in this south-western part of Victoria. Many have been members of the land-owning families whose gracious homesteads are dotted about this beautiful pastoral area. The western district supports one-third of Victoria's best sheep and cattle, and the region's merino wool is acknowledged to be the finest in the land.

Many of the western district towns boast splendid pioneer buildings. Of special interest are **Hamilton** – recognised as the 'Wool Capital of the World' – and the attractive towns of **Coleraine** and **Casterton**. Several of the district's historic homesteads are open for inspection, including Warrock (near Casterton), which has 33 original farm buildings still in operation. Of particular interest to nature lovers are the remaining colonies of the eastern barred bandicoot.

Warrnambool, situated on the south coast, is the commercial capital of the western district and a gateway to the spectacular Great Ocean Road. The winter visits of southern right whales along the coast here are a popular attraction.

The heart of the western district is fairly flat grazing land. To the east, the volcanic lake area

Mouth of the Hopkins River, near Warrnambool

around **Camperdown** offers great fishing and water sports. To the south, a rugged coastline stretches from **Anglesea** to the tiny hamlet of Nelson, at the mouth of the Glenelg River. To the north, the high rocky ranges of the Grampians break through the gently rolling countryside. An excellent scenic route to Halls Gap is along the Mt Abrupt Road from **Dunkeld**.

Further information can be obtained from local tourist information centres, especially the Hamilton and District Tourist Information Centre, Lonsdale St, Hamilton; (055) 72 3746, and the Warrnambool Tourist Information Centre, 600 Raglan Pde, Warrnambool; (055) 64 7837. **See also:** individual entries in A–Z listing for those towns indicated by bold type. **Map reference:** 228 C5.

Victoria

Location Map

Other Map Coverage
Central Melbourne 206
Melbourne Approach & Bypass Routes 207
Melbourne & Western Suburbs 208
Eastern Suburbs, Melbourne 210
Southern Suburbs, Melbourne 211
Melbourne Region 212

Mornington Peninsula 214
Yarra Valley Region 216
Otway Region 217
Geelong 218
Geelong Region 219
Bendigo 220
Ballarat 221

Goldfields Region 222
Alpine Region 224

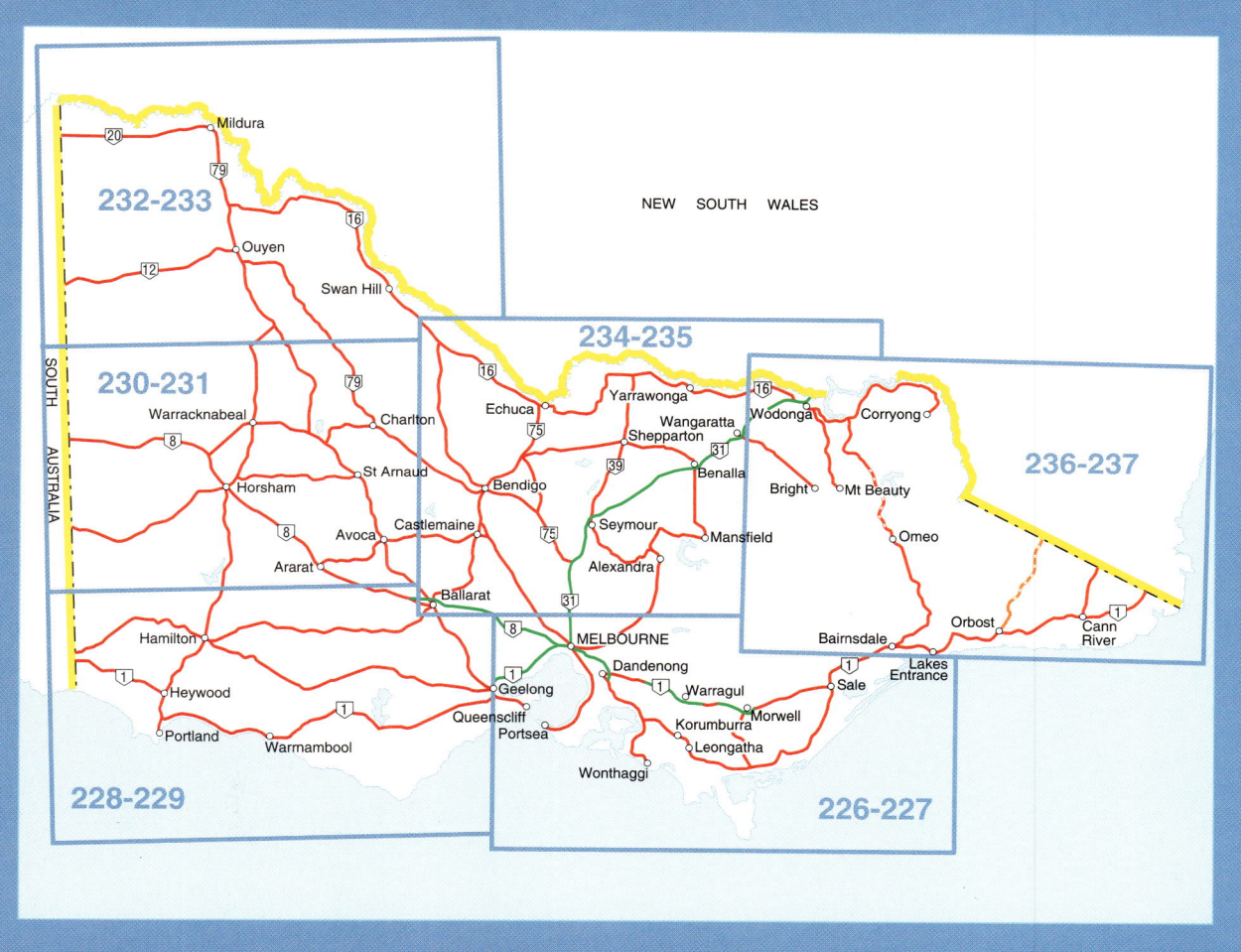

206 Central Melbourne

Accommodation
- Centra Melbourne on the Yarra 1 B10
- Grand Hyatt Melbourne 2 F7
- Hotel Y (YWCA) 3 C5
- Le Meridien at Rialto 4 B9
- Lygon Carlton 5 E2
- Novotel Melbourne on Collins 6 D7
- Oakford Gordon Place 7 F6
- Old Melbourne Hotel 8 B2
- Regent Melbourne 9 G7
- Rockman's Regency 10 F6
- Sheraton Towers Southgate 11 E10
- Windsor Hotel 12 G6

General Information
- Ansett Australia 13 D4
- Australian Coachlines Coach Terminal 14 C5
- Bus Day Tour Departure Point 15 E7
- Flinders Street Station 16 E8
- General Post Office 17 D7
- Melbourne City Police Station 18 A10
- Melbourne River Cruises 19 E9
- Qantas Travel Centres 20 C5, C8, E8
- Spencer Street Coach Terminal 21 A8
- Spencer Street Station 22 A9
- Tourist Information 23 E7

Accommodation
Only a sample range is listed; inclusion is not necessarily a recommendation.

Places of Interest
- Captain Cook's Cottage 24 I7
- Chinatown 25 E6/F6
- Chinese Museum 26 F6
- Crown Casino 27 A10
- Exhibition Buildings 28 F3
- Fire Brigade Museum 29 G5
- Floral Clock 30 F10
- La Trobe's Cottage 31 H13
- Meat Market Craft Centre 32 A2
- Melbourne Cricket Ground 33 I9
- Melbourne Maritime Museum (Polly Woodside) 34 A11
- Museum of Victoria 35 D6
- National Gallery of Victoria 36 F10
- National Tennis Centre 37 H10
- Old Melbourne Gaol 38 E5
- Queen Victoria Market 39 B4
- Rialto Towers Observation Deck 40 B9
- Shrine of Remembrance 41 G13
- Sidney Myer Music Bowl 42 G11
- Southgate 43 E9
- State Library of Victoria 44 D5
- The Australian Gallery of Sport and Olympic Museum 45 I9
- Victorian Arts Centre 46 E10
- World Congress Centre 47 B10
- World Trade Centre 48 A10

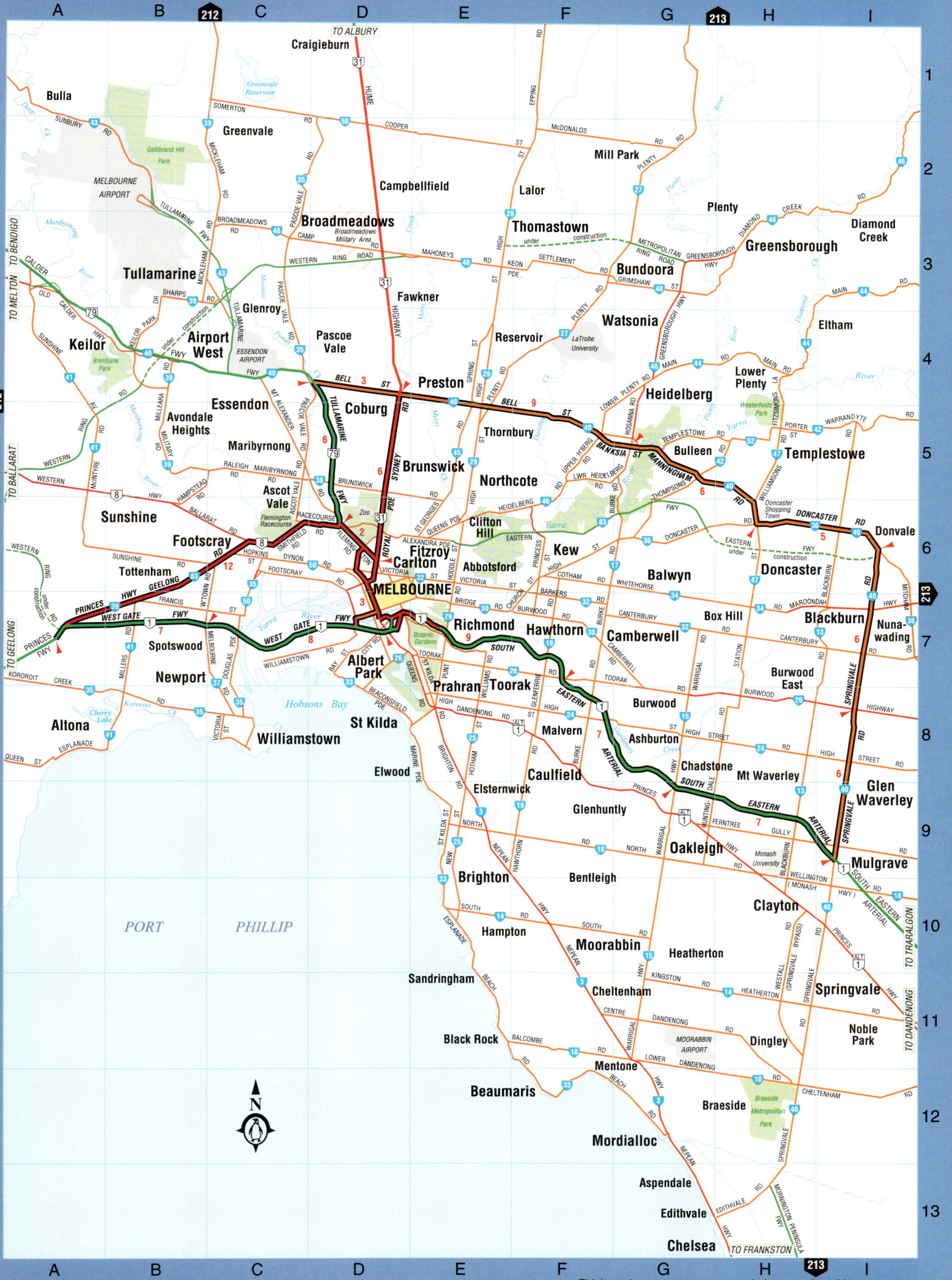

0 2 4 6 8 km
TO ALBURY
Craigieburn
Bulla
Greenvale
Gellibrand Hill Park
MELBOURNE AIRPORT
Campbellfield
Lalor
Mill Park
Broadmeadows
Broadmeadows Military Area
Thomastown
Plenty
Greensborough
Diamond Creek
Tullamarine
Bundoora
Fawkner
Glenroy
Watsonia
Eltham
Keilor
Airport West
Pascoe Vale
Reservoir
LaTrobe University
ESSENDON AIRPORT
Brimbank Park
Preston
Heidelberg
Lower Plenty
Essendon
Coburg
Avondale Heights
Thornbury
Westerfolds Park
Maribyrnong
Bulleen
Templestowe
Brunswick
Northcote
Ascot Vale
Flemington Racecourse
Zoo
Sunshine
Clifton Hill
Doncaster Shopping Town
Donvale
Footscray
Fitzroy
Kew
Carlton
Abbotsford
Tottenham
Doncaster
MELBOURNE
Balwyn
Box Hill
Blackburn
Nunawading
Richmond
Hawthorn
Camberwell
Spotswood
Botanic Gardens
Albert Park
Burwood East
Newport
Prahran
Toorak
Burwood
Hobsons Bay
Altona
Cherry Lake
St Kilda
Malvern
Ashburton
Williamstown
Chadstone
Mt Waverley
Elwood
Caulfield
Glen Waverley
Elsternwick
Glenhuntly
Oakleigh
Monash University
Mulgrave
Brighton
Bentleigh
Clayton
PORT PHILLIP
Hampton
Moorabbin
Heatherton
TO TRARALGON
Sandringham
Cheltenham
Springvale
TO DANDENONG
MOORABBIN AIRPORT
Black Rock
Dingley
Noble Park
Mentone
Beaumaris
Braeside Metropolitan Park
Braeside
Mordialloc
Aspendale
Edithvale
Chelsea
TO FRANKSTON
TO BENDIGO
TO MELTON
TO BALLARAT
TO GEELONG

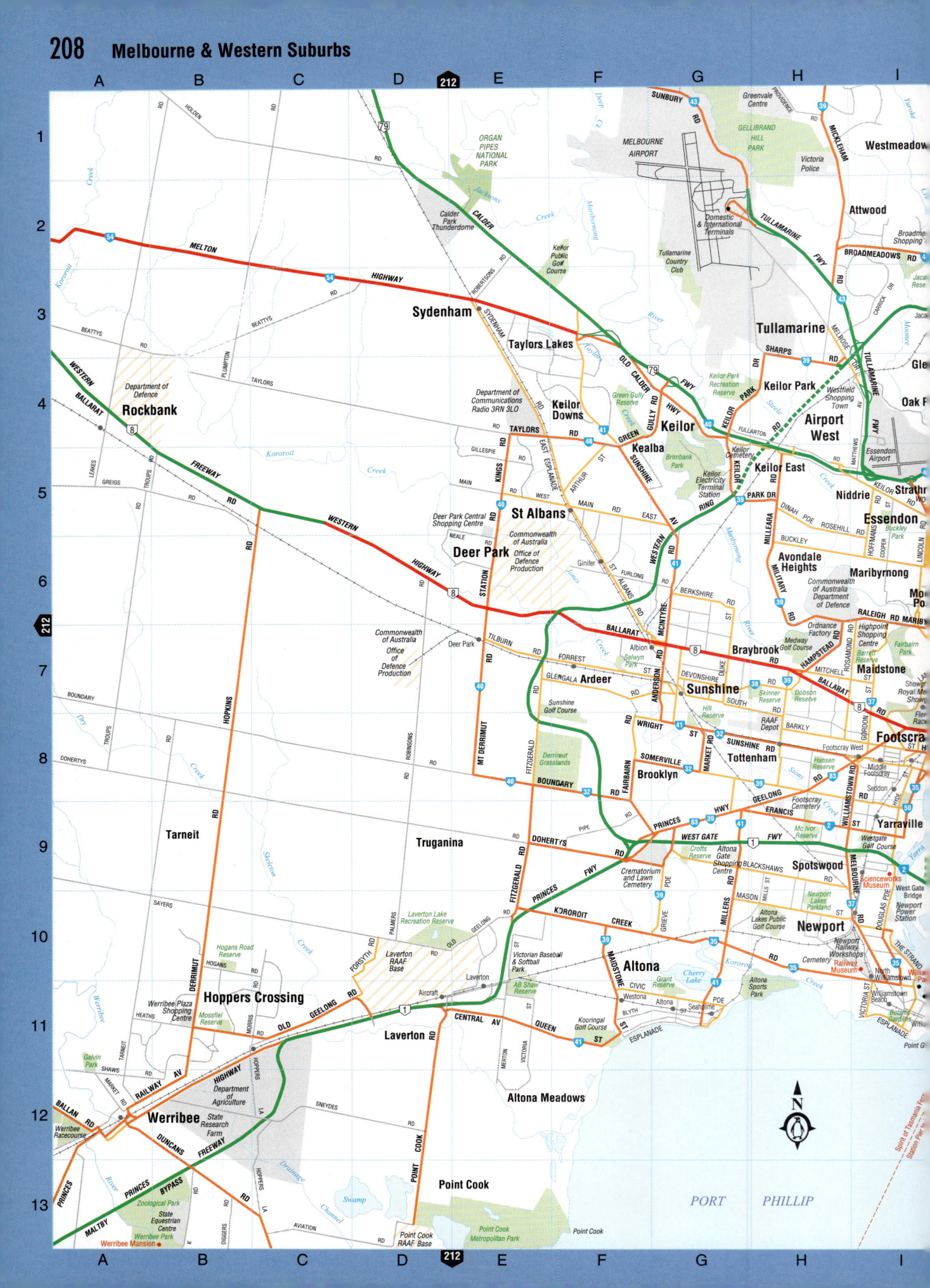

208 Melbourne & Western Suburbs

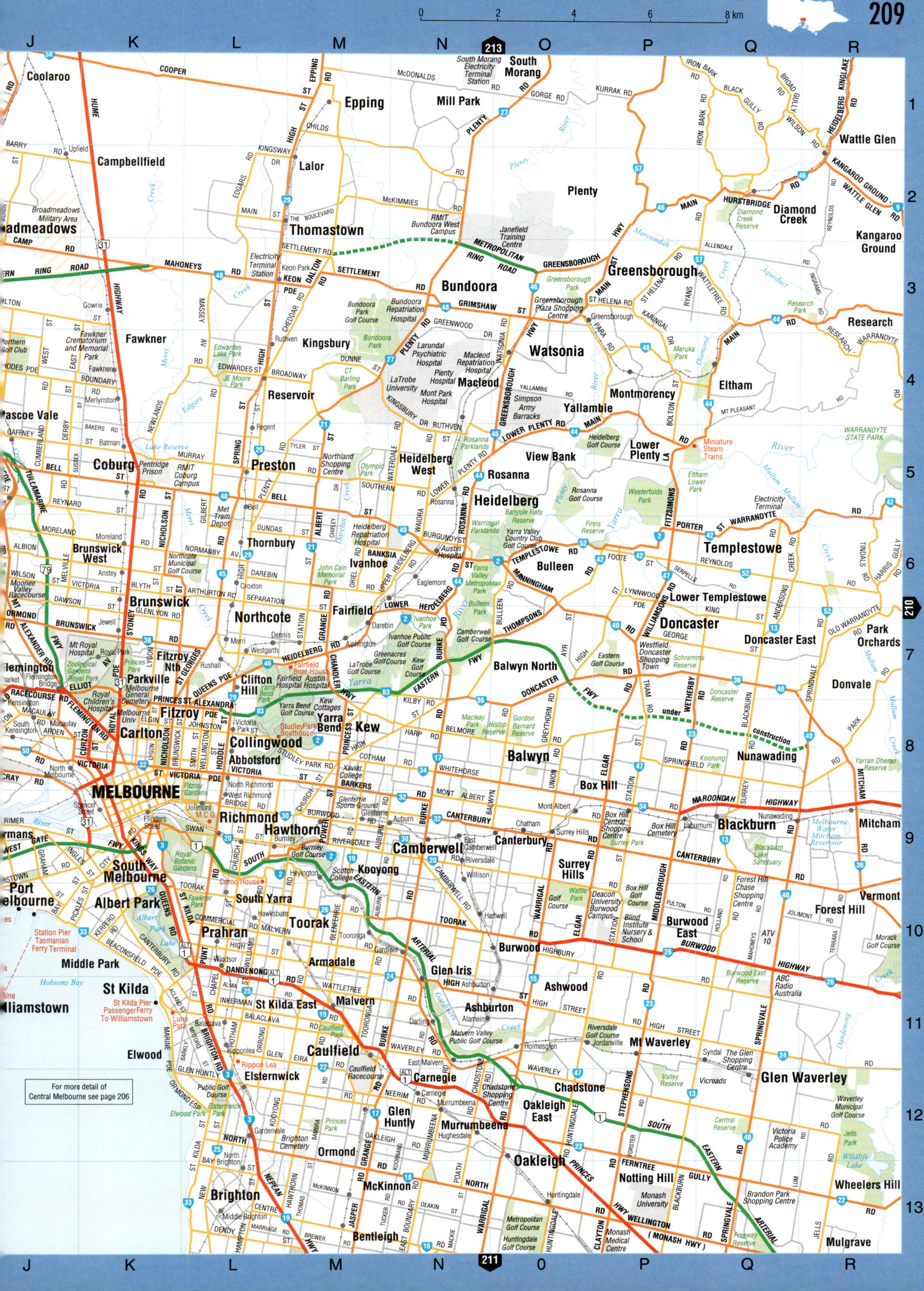
0 2 4 6 8 km
Coolaroo
Campbellfield
Epping
Mill Park
South Morang
Lalor
Thomastown
Plenty
Wattle Glen
Diamond Creek
Kangaroo Ground
Greensborough
Bundoora
Research
Fawkner
Kingsbury
Watsonia
Macleod
Reservoir
Montmorency
Eltham
Yallambie
Pascoe Vale
Coburg
Preston
Heidelberg West
Rosanna
View Bank
Lower Plenty
Heidelberg
Templestowe
Brunswick West
Thornbury
Ivanhoe
Bulleen
Brunswick
Northcote
Fairfield
Lower Templestowe
Doncaster
Doncaster East
Park Orchards
Flemington
Parkville
Fitzroy Nth
Clifton Hill
Balwyn North
Donvale
Fitzroy
Carlton
Collingwood
Abbotsford
Yarra Bend
Kew
Balwyn
Nunawading
Box Hill
MELBOURNE
Richmond
Hawthorn
Camberwell
Canterbury
Blackburn
Mitcham
Port Melbourne
South Melbourne
Albert Park
South Yarra
Kooyong
Surrey Hills
Vermont
Forest Hill
Prahran
Toorak
Burwood
Burwood East
Middle Park
Armadale
Glen Iris
Ashwood
St Kilda
St Kilda East
Malvern
Ashburton
Williamstown
Caulfield
Mt Waverley
Elwood
Elsternwick
Carnegie
Chadstone
Glen Waverley
Glen Huntly
Oakleigh East
Murrumbeena
Ormond
Oakleigh
Notting Hill
Brighton
McKinnon
Wheelers Hill
Bentleigh
Mulgrave
For more detail of Central Melbourne see page 206
213
210
211
J K L M N O P Q R
1 2 3 4 5 6 7 8 9 10 11 12 13

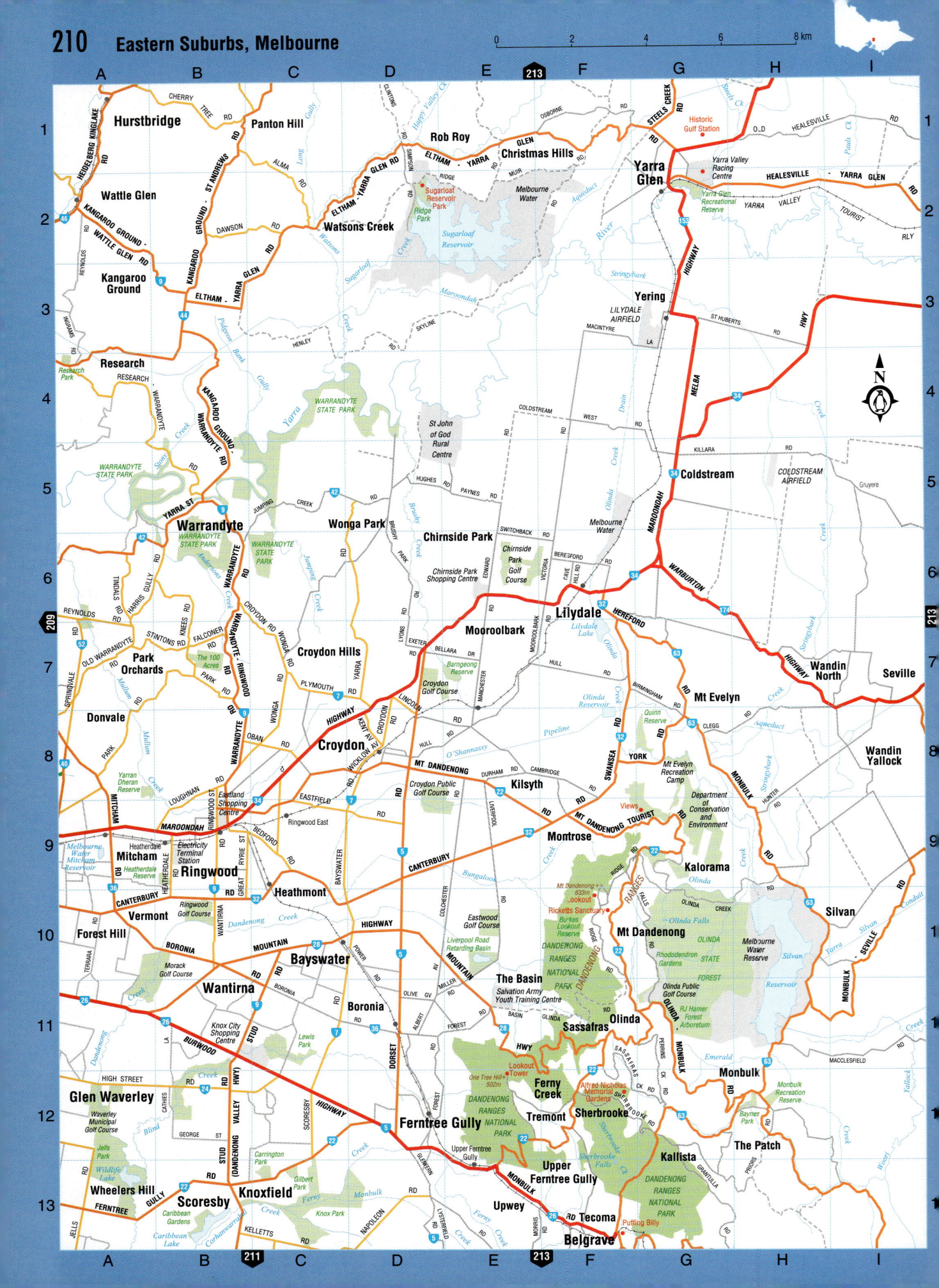

210 Eastern Suburbs, Melbourne

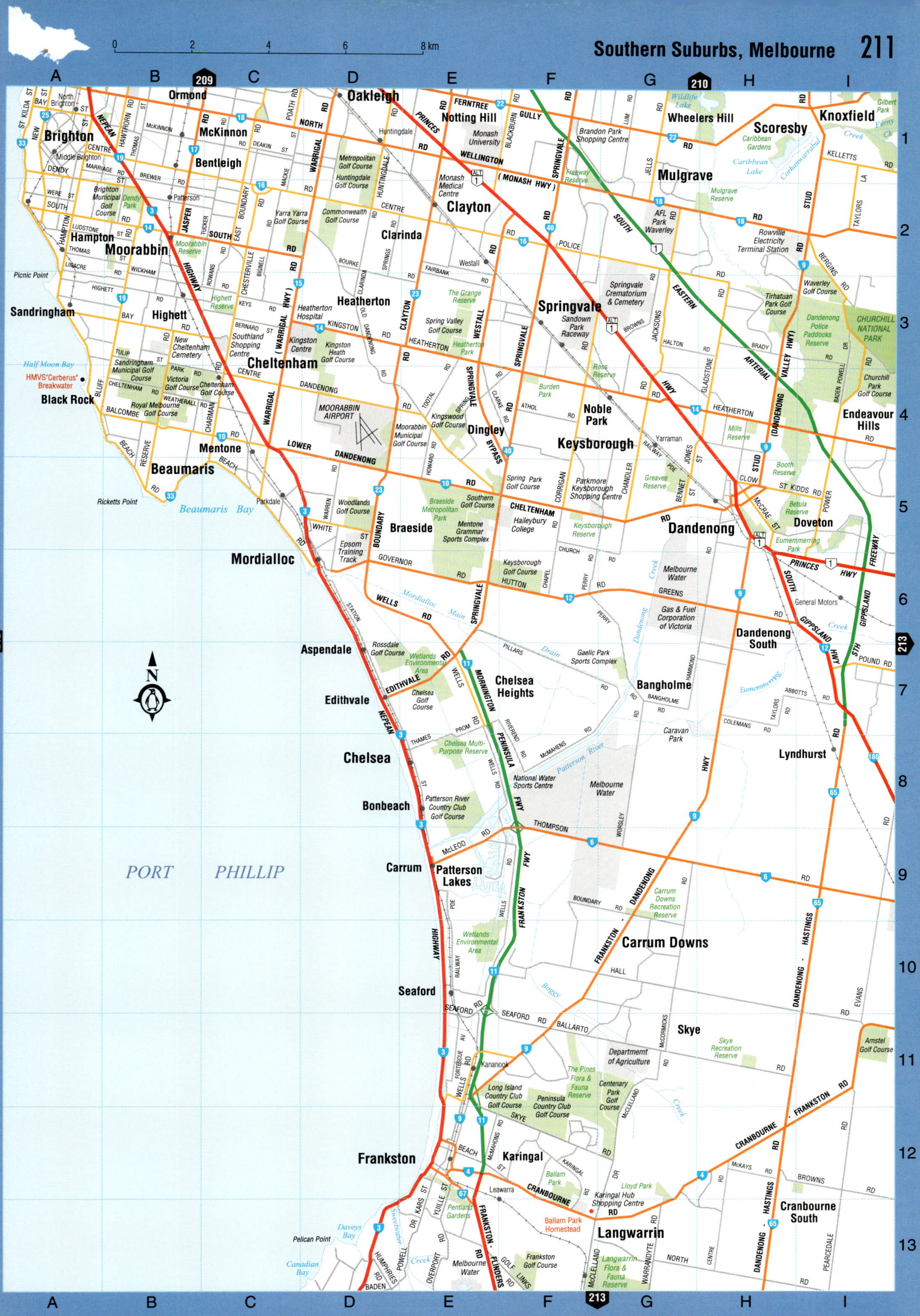
Brighton
Ormond
McKinnon
Bentleigh
Oakleigh
Notting Hill
Wheelers Hill
Scoresby
Knoxfield
Mulgrave
Clayton
Clarinda
Hampton
Moorabbin
Sandringham
Highett
Heatherton
Springvale
Cheltenham
Black Rock
Noble Park
Keysborough
Dingley
Mentone
Beaumaris
Endeavour Hills
Braeside
Dandenong
Doveton
Mordialloc
Dandenong South
Aspendale
Edithvale
Chelsea Heights
Bangholme
Chelsea
Bonbeach
Lyndhurst
Carrum
Patterson Lakes
Carrum Downs
Seaford
Skye
Frankston
Karingal
Langwarrin
Cranbourne South
PORT PHILLIP
Beaumaris Bay
Half Moon Bay
Ricketts Point
Picnic Point
Pelican Point
Daveys Bay
Canadian Bay
Moorabbin Airport
Churchill National Park
HMVS Cerberus Breakwater
Ballam Park Homestead
0 2 4 6 8 km
209
210
213
212

212 Melbourne Region

213

214 Mornington Peninsula

HISTORICAL HOMES: The Mornington Peninsula has an array of magnificently preserved historical homesteads. Visit Coolart at Somers, a century-old mansion nestled in landscaped gardens, or the simple 1844 drop slab cottage McCrae Homestead. The Briars, an 1860's homestead at Mount Martha, houses a significant collection of Napoleonic artefacts and furniture.

DOLPHIN SWIMS: Join professional divers and swim with the friendly bottlenose dolphins that inhabit the bay. Tours depart Sorrento Pier on weekends from November to May.

ARTHURS SEAT STATE PARK: Originally named after a similar mountain near Edinburgh, Scotland during the first exploration of Port Phillip Bay. Take a ride on the 72-seat chairlift for spectacular views of the Peninsula and Bay. Enjoy a short walk to scenic Flinders Lookout and to Seawinds Gardens.

MORNINGTON PENINSULA NATIONAL PARK: This magnificent park extends from the tip of Point Nepean to Cape Schanck. An unusual transporter service operates, taking visitors to Cheviot Beach, Observatory Point and the historical Fort Nepean. Numerous walking tracks provide easy access to London Bridge, Cape Schanck Lighthouse and endless spectacular coastal scenery.

TOURIST INFORMATION:
- Phillip Island (Phillip Island Rd, Newhaven)
- Mornington (cnr Main & Elizabeth Sts)
- Queenscliff (cnr Bellarine Hwy & Grubb Rd)

Please refer to Mornington Peninsula feature on page 155 for more information on this region.

WINERIES:

Balnarring Vineyard	1	L7
Boonooke Estate	2	L8
Craig Avon Vineyard	3	K7
Darling Park Vineyards	4	K8
Dromana Estate Vineyards	5	J7
Dunstan's Poplar Bend	6	I9
Elan Vineyard	7	L6
Ermes Estate	8	L5
Hanns Creek Estate	9	K8
Karina Vineyard	10	J7
Kings Creek Vineyard	11	L7
Main Ridge Estate	12	I8
Merricks Estate	13	K9
Miceli Vineyard	14	I8
Moorooduc Estate	15	L5
Paringa Estate	16	J9
Peninsula Estate	17	J8
Port Phillip Estate	18	K8
Red Hill Estate	19	J9
Ryland River	20	I9
Stonier's Winery	21	K9
Stumpy Gully Vineyard	22	L4
Tanglewood Downs Estate	23	K6
T'Gallant	24	J8
The Briars Vineyard	25	J5
Tucks Ridge	26	J9
Tuerong Estate	27	I9
Vintina Estate	28	K3
Willow Creek Vineyard	29	L7

215

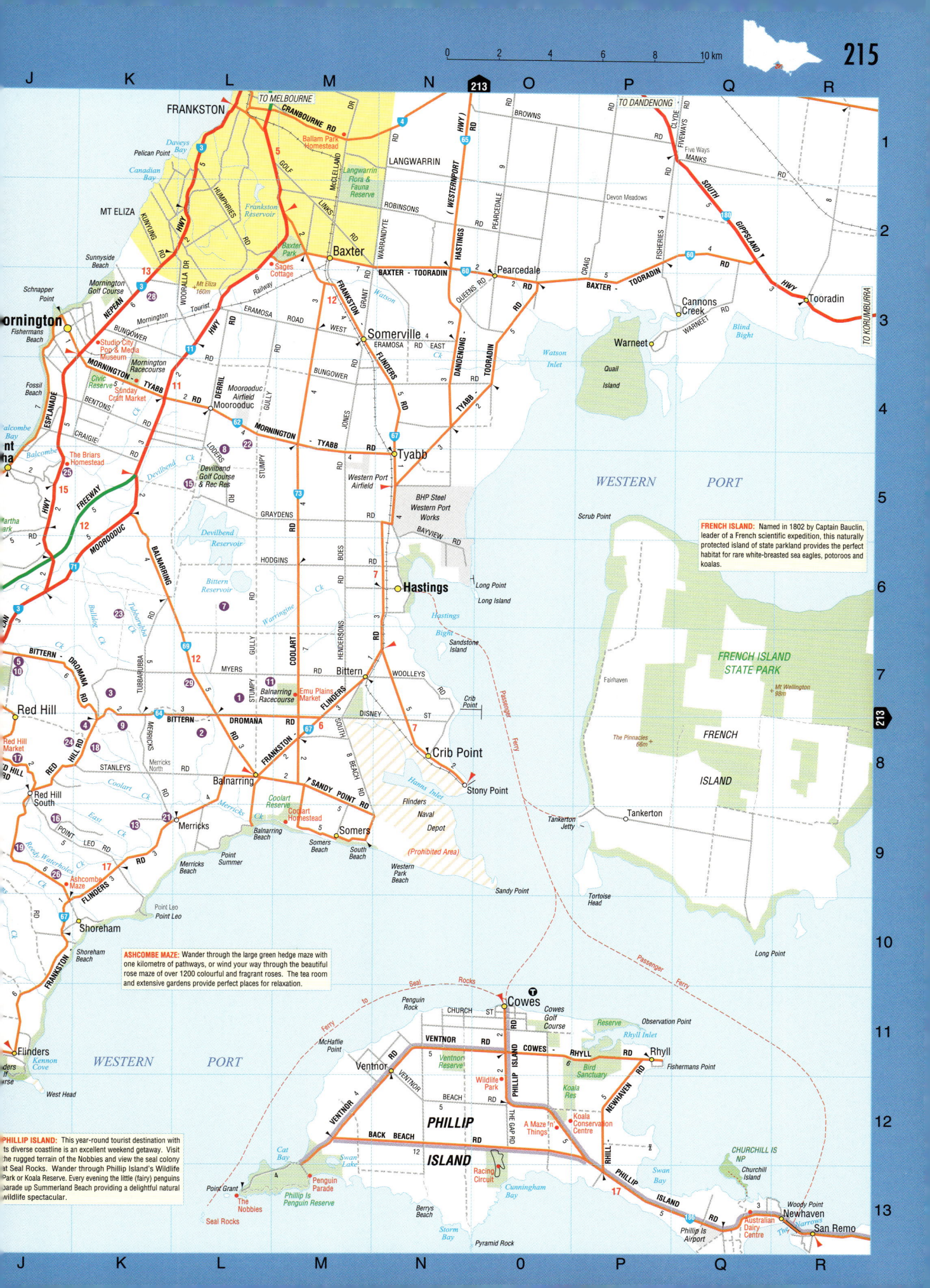

FRENCH ISLAND: Named in 1802 by Captain Bauclin, leader of a French scientific expedition, this naturally protected island of state parkland provides the perfect habitat for rare white-breasted sea eagles, potoroos and koalas.

ASHCOMBE MAZE: Wander through the large green hedge maze with one kilometre of pathways, or wind your way through the beautiful rose maze of over 1200 colourful and fragrant roses. The tea room and extensive gardens provide perfect places for relaxation.

PHILLIP ISLAND: This year-round tourist destination with its diverse coastline is an excellent weekend getaway. Visit the rugged terrain of the Nobbies and view the seal colony at Seal Rocks. Wander through Phillip Island's Wildlife Park or Koala Reserve. Every evening the little (fairy) penguins parade up Summerland Beach providing a delightful natural wildlife spectacular.

216 Yarra Valley Region

WINERIES
- Bianchet Winery 1 A7
- Brahams Creek Winery 2 H8
- Broussard's Chum Creek Winery 3 D5
- Coldstream Hills 4 D8
- De Bortoli Winery and Restaurant 5 C4
- Domaine Chandon Australia 6 C6
- Eyton on Yarra 7 D7
- Fergusson Winery and Restaurant 8 C5
- Kellybrook Winery and Restaurant 9 A7
- Lillydale Vineyards 10 D9
- Lirralirra Estate 11 A8
- Long Gully Estate 12 D5
- Lovey's Estate - Mount Hope Wines 13 C5
- Monbulk Winery 14 C11
- Mt Delancy 15 C9
- Oakridge Estate 16 C10
- Paternoster 17 D13
- St Huberts Vineyard 18 C7
- Shantell Vineyard 19 C4
- Tarrawarra Vineyard 20 D6
- Warramate Vineyard 21 D7
- Yarra Burn Winery and Restaurant 22 F9
- Yarra Edge Vineyard 23 A7
- Yarra Ridge Vineyard 24 B6
- Yarra Yering Vineyard 25 D7
- Yering Station Vineyard 26 B6

KINGLAKE NATIONAL PARK: Home to numerous lyrebirds and wombats, the Kinglake National Park areas were established to protect the remaining wet eucalypt forests on the Great Dividing Range. Tranquil walks through fern gullies and forested spurs take you to the Wombelano and Mason's Falls.

TOOLANGI-BLACK RANGES: Toolangi (once) home of C.J. Dennis, author of "The Sentimental Bloke" is a mountainous berry producing area nestled in the Black Ranges State Forest. Picturesque roadways provide easy access to the spectacular Wilhelmina Falls and Murrindindi Cascades. There are excellent riding tours available in the area, taking you along rugged mountain tracks and tranquil river paths. Trout and Blackfish can be caught in the Murrindindi River.

GULF STATION: Now owned by the National Trust, Gulf Station at Yarra Glen is one of Victoria's oldest pastoral properties dating back to the 1850s. Visitors can step back in time, explore the original timber buildings, cottage gardens and participate in farm activities.

HEALESVILLE SANCTUARY: Home to over 200 of Australia's unique birds, animals and reptiles, including some endangered species. Healesville Sanctuary, open every day of the year, is recognised as Australia's top wildlife park. Spend the day venturing among friendly kangaroos, emus and wombats in naturally designed enclosures.

SILVAN RESERVOIR: Located on the edge of beautiful Olinda State Forest, Stonyford picnic ground at the magnificent Silvan Reservoir provides excellent BBQ facilities. Stop along the Monbulk Road for breathtaking views of the region.

PUFFING BILLY: This superbly restored vintage steam train ambles its way from the ferny stands of Belgrave through the cool rainforest to Emerald Lake.

TOURIST INFORMATION:
Yarra Valley & Healesville (127 Maroondah Hwy, Healesville)
Marysville (18 Murchison St)

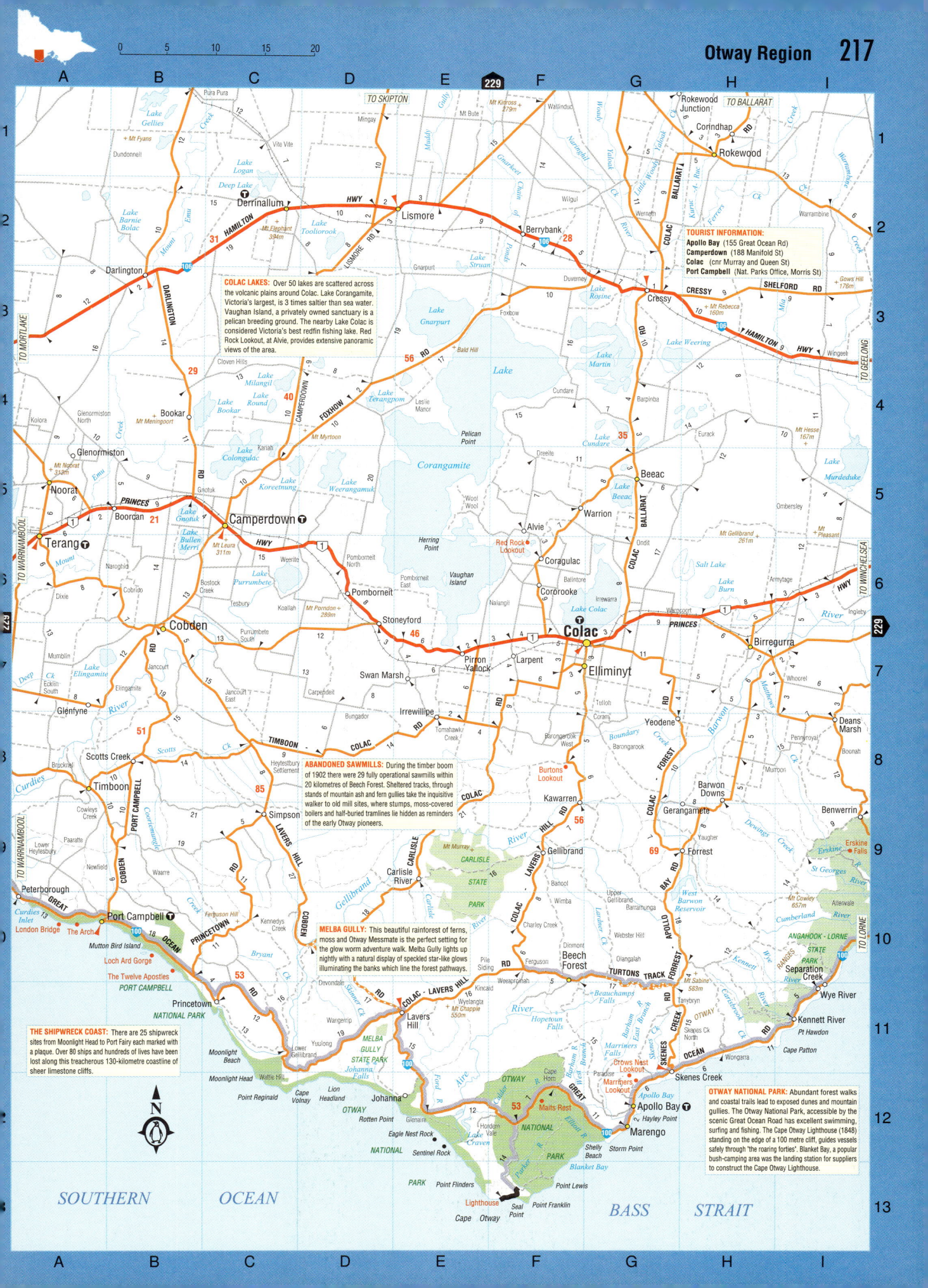

Otway Region 217

TOURIST INFORMATION:
- Apollo Bay (155 Great Ocean Rd)
- Camperdown (188 Manifold St)
- Colac (cnr Murray and Queen St)
- Port Campbell (Nat. Parks Office, Morris St)

COLAC LAKES: Over 50 lakes are scattered across the volcanic plains around Colac. Lake Corangamite, Victoria's largest, is 3 times saltier than sea water. Vaughan Island, a privately owned sanctuary is a pelican breeding ground. The nearby Lake Colac is considered Victoria's best redfin fishing lake. Red Rock Lookout, at Alvie, provides extensive panoramic views of the area.

ABANDONED SAWMILLS: During the timber boom of 1902 there were 29 fully operational sawmills within 20 kilometres of Beech Forest. Sheltered tracks, through stands of mountain ash and fern gullies take the inquisitive walker to old mill sites, where stumps, moss-covered boilers and half-buried tramlines lie hidden as reminders of the early Otway pioneers.

MELBA GULLY: This beautiful rainforest of ferns, moss and Otway Messmate is the perfect setting for the glow worm adventure walk. Melba Gully lights up nightly with a natural display of speckled star-like glows illuminating the banks which line the forest pathways.

THE SHIPWRECK COAST: There are 25 shipwreck sites from Moonlight Head to Port Fairy each marked with a plaque. Over 80 ships and hundreds of lives have been lost along this treacherous 130-kilometre coastline of sheer limestone cliffs.

OTWAY NATIONAL PARK: Abundant forest walks and coastal trails lead to exposed dunes and mountain gullies. The Otway National Park, accessible by the scenic Great Ocean Road has excellent swimming, surfing and fishing. The Cape Otway Lighthouse (1848) standing on the edge of a 100 metre cliff, guides vessels safely through 'the roaring forties'. Blanket Bay, a popular bush-camping area was the landing station for suppliers to construct the Cape Otway Lighthouse.

218 Geelong

Accommodation
- Ambassador Hotel / Motel 1 E7
- Bay City Motel 2 G6
- Colonial Lodge Motel 3 E9
- Geelong Motor Inn 4 D4
- Innkeepers Motor Inn 5 D6
- Shannon Motor Inn 6 B6
- Southside Caravan Park 7 C10
- Youth Hostel (YHA) 8 E8

General Information
- Geelong Hospital 9 F7
- Geelong Railway Station 10 E5
- Geelong Transport Interchange 11 E5
- Motoring Organisation (RACV) 12 E7
- Police 13 E5
- Post Office 14 E7
- Qantas Travel Centre 15 E6
- Tourist Information 16 F6
- Town Hall 17 E6

Places of Interest
- Balyang Bird Sanctuary 18 A9
- Barwon Grange 19 D9
- Barwon Valley Fun Park 20 C9
- Botanic Gardens 21 H6
- Eastern Beach 22 G6
- Geelong Art Gallery 23 E6
- Performing Arts Centre 24 E6
- Geelong Racecourse 25 H11
- National Wool Museum 26 F6
- The Heights 27 A6

Accommodation: Only a sample range is listed; Inclusion is not necessarily a recommendation.

Geelong Region 219

220 Bendigo

Accommodation
- ANA Motor Inn 1 C8
- Bendigo Central Motor Lodge 2 C8
- Central Deborah Motor Inn 3 A11
- Julie Anna Inn 4 I5
- McIvor Motor Inn 5 I8
- Oval Motel 6 C7
- Shamrock Hotel 7 E9

General Information
- All Saints Old Cathedral 8 C9
- Base Hospital 9 F4
- Bendigo Railway Station 10 F12
- Motoring Organisation (RACV) 11 E11
- Municipal Offices 12 F9
- Police 13 E8
- Post Office 14 E9
- R.S.L. 15 D9
- Sacred Heart Cathedral 16 C10
- Town Hall 17 F9

Places of Interest
- Art Gallery 18 D8
- Bendigo Woollen Mills 19 H7
- Capital Theatre 20 C8
- Central Deborah Mine 21 A12
- Chinese Joss House 22 I1
- Conservatory 23 E8
- Golden Dragon Museum 24 F7
- Talking Tram 25 A12
- Tram Museum 26 H7

Accommodation Only a sample range is listed; inclusion is not necessarily a recommendation.

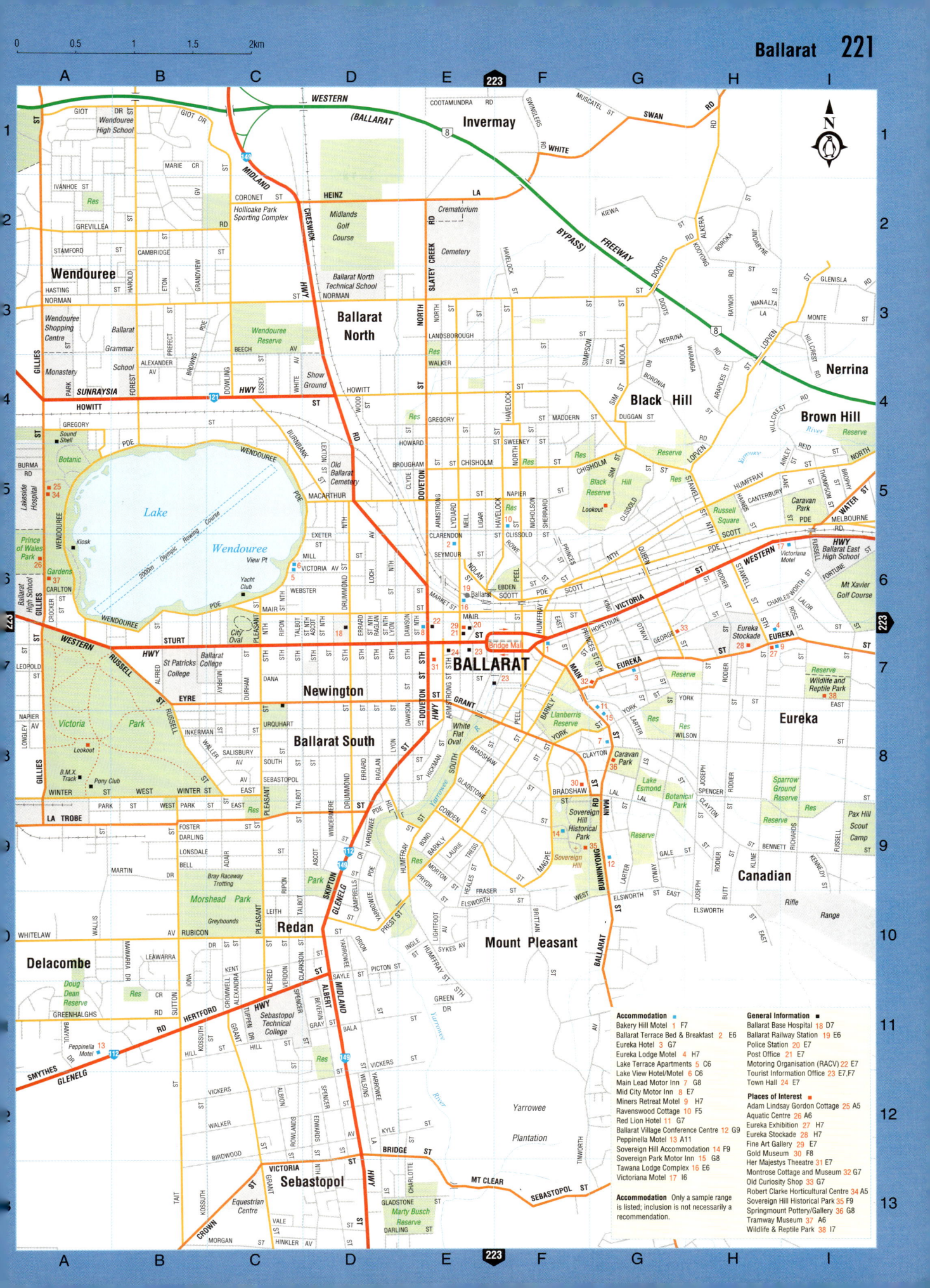

Ballarat 221

Accommodation ■
Bakery Hill Motel	1 F7
Ballarat Terrace Bed & Breakfast	2 E6
Eureka Hotel	3 G7
Eureka Lodge Motel	4 H7
Lake Terrace Apartments	5 C6
Lake View Hotel/Motel	6 C6
Main Lead Motor Inn	7 G8
Mid City Motor Inn	8 E7
Miners Retreat Motel	9 H7
Ravenswood Cottage	10 F5
Red Lion Hotel	11 G7
Ballarat Village Conference Centre	12 G9
Peppinella Motel	13 A11
Sovereign Hill Accommodation	14 F9
Sovereign Park Motor Inn	15 G8
Tawana Lodge Complex	16 E6
Victoriana Motel	17 I6

Accommodation Only a sample range is listed; inclusion is not necessarily a recommendation.

General Information ■
Ballarat Base Hospital	18 D7
Ballarat Railway Station	19 E6
Police Station	20 E7
Post Office	21 E7
Motoring Organisation (RACV)	22 E7
Tourist Information Office	23 E7, F7
Town Hall	24 E7

Places of Interest ■
Adam Lindsay Gordon Cottage	25 A5
Aquatic Centre	26 A6
Eureka Exhibition	27 H7
Eureka Stockade	28 H7
Fine Art Gallery	29 E7
Gold Museum	30 F8
Her Majestys Theeatre	31 E7
Montrose Cottage and Museum	32 G7
Old Curiosity Shop	33 G7
Robert Clarke Horticultural Centre	34 A5
Sovereign Hill Historical Park	35 F9
Springmount Pottery/Gallery	36 G8
Tramway Museum	37 A6
Wildlife & Reptile Park	38 I7

Goldfields Region

GREAT WESTERN: The vineyards of this area are famous for producing high quality champagne-style wine, as well as red and dry white table wines. Wineries where tastings and sales are available include: Best's Concongella Winery, Seppelt Great Western Champagne Cellars and Garden Gully Vineyard.

GRAMPIANS NATIONAL PARK: The park is famous for its waterfalls, wildflowers, wide variety of birds and mammals, as well as its aboriginal rock art sites. The massive sandstone ranges of the Grampians provide some of the state's most spectacular scenery. Popular activities in the park include rock-climbing, bushwalking, and scenic drives; Lake Bellfield is good for sailing and rowing, and there is excellent trout-fishing in the lake and in Fyans Creek.

TOURIST INFORMATION:
- **Ararat** (Barkly St)
- **Avoca** (High St)
- **Ballan** (Cnr Stead & Steiglitz Sts)
- **Ballarat** (Cnr Sturt & Albert Sts)
- **Beaufort** (Lawrence St)
- **Bendigo** (High St, Kangaroo Flat)
- **Castlemaine** (Duke St)
- **Clunes** (Fraser St)
- **Creswick** (Albert St)
- **Dunolly** (Market St)
- **Lake Bolac** (Glenelg Hwy)
- **Maldon** (High St)
- **Maryborough** (Railway St)
- **Stawell** (54 Western Hwy)

223

Map of central Victoria goldfields region, showing cities and towns including Bendigo, Castlemaine, Maryborough, Daylesford, Ballarat, and Bacchus Marsh. Grid references J–R (columns) and 1–13 (rows).

BENDIGO'S TALKING TRAM: Visitors can take a tram ride through the historic centre of Bendigo and enjoy a potted history provided by a recorded commentary.

GOLDFIELDS REGION: The cities and towns of this region came to a peak of style and affluence in the 1880s, a wealth built on the first gold discoveries in the 1850s. The towns display all the frivolity and grandeur of Victorian architecture.

MALDON: The National Trust has declared Maldon the "first notable town" in Victoria; interesting collections of 19th-century buildings, and collection of European trees.

GARDENS: There are many fine historic and public gardens scattered throughout the region. Public gardens of particular note include the Botanic Gardens of Castlemaine, Daylesford and Malmsbury, and the Queen Mary Gardens at St Arnaud. One of the most famous private gardens, open to the public, is Buda Historic Home and garden at Castlemaine.

SPA TOWNS: Daylesford and nearby Hepburn Springs are popular holiday centres, set in attractive hill country. They are both "spa" towns, with 65 documented mineral springs, many with hand pumps.

MT BUNINYONG: An extinct volcanic crater that rises 750 metres above sea level. A sealed road leads up to the lookout which offers stunning 360° views.

SOVEREIGN HILL: This re-created gold-mining township is one of Victoria's major tourist attractions and should not be missed.

224 Alpine Region

225

ALPINE NATIONAL PARK: Stretching along the Great Dividing Range, the park joins the Kosciusko National Park in New South Wales and its neighbour Namadgi National Park in the Australian Capital Territory. The park protects the habitats of a variety of flora and fauna, including the rare mountain pygmy possum. During spring and summer the high plains are carpeted with wildflowers; more than 1100 native plant species are found in the park, including twelve found nowhere else in the world.

WANDILIGONG VALLEY: Classified by the National Trust this beautiful valley can be enjoyed by travelling along the road from Bright which winds between the hills. Wandiligong was once a thriving gold-mining town. A number of historic buildings are preserved in the township. Beyond the town is a huge apple orchard and the much-photographed Wandiligong poplars, at their most beautiful in autumn.

For downhill skiers, facilities are available at Hotham, Dinner Plain, Falls Creek, Mt Buller, and Mt Buffalo. For cross-country skiers, there is a variety of touring country ranging from well defined near the resorts to winter wilderness areas. From the resorts there are few marked routes.

AUSTRALIAN ALPS WALKING TRACK: One of the finest long-distance bushwalking tracks in the country, this 655-km track stretches between Walhalla in Victoria and Canberra in the Australian Capital Territory. To walk the Victorian section of the track takes about thirty days. As the track passes through remote areas for most of its length, it is advisable to only attempt certain sections if you are not a seasoned bushwalker. During summer, water is in short supply in some areas along the track; taking a compass and map is essential.

BOGONG HIGH PLAINS: Considered to contain some of the most awe-inspiring mountain scenery in Victoria, this area is particularly splendid in spring and early summer when the wildflowers cover the plains. Scattered across the plains are historic old huts used by the cattlemen of the lower valley during the summer months. At the end of summer, the cattle were mustered and then taken down to the valley for winter.

WARNING: Road closed during snow season.

WARNING: Road closed during snow season.

BICENTENNIAL NATIONAL TRAIL: Extends from Healesville in Victoria to Cooktown in Queensland and passes through the Alpine National Park. For details of permit requirements, contact a regional office of the Department of Conservation and Natural Resources.

226 Southern Central Victoria

0 10 20 30 40 50 km
J K L M N O P Q R
235
236
1 2 3 4 5 6 7 8 9 10 11 12 13
ALPINE NATIONAL PARK
RANGE
Mt McDonald 1625m
Jamieson
Mt Skene 1571m
Mt Tamboritha 1640m
Mt Kent 1563m
Mt Wellington 1635m
Castle Hill 1448m
Lake Tarli Karng
Wellington River
Wonnangatta River
Crooked River
Dargo
Waterford
Mt Djoandah 610m
Mt Birregun 1463m
Mt Delusion 1399m
Mt Baldhead 1377m
Mt Dow 1000m
Nicholson
Morris Peak 789m
Mt Sugarloaf 890m
Swifts Creek
Doctors Flat
Brookville
Big Hill 675m
Ensay
Reedy Flat
Ensay South
Stirling
Tambo Crossing
Mt Elizabeth 942m
Woods Point
Matlock
Mt Selma 1457m
Gable End 1570m
AVON WILDERNESS PARK
Licola
Jericho
Red Jacket
Aberfeldy
Mt Useful 1432m
Thomson Reservoir
Tabberabbera
Cobbannah
MITCHELL RIVER NATIONAL PARK
EAST GIPPSLAND
Deptford
Bullumwaal
Mt Alfred 503m
Mt Taylor 475m
Mount Taylor
Clifton Creek
Little Dick 320m
OMEO HWY
Bruthen
Wiseleigh
Sarsfield
Culloden
Iguana Ck
Wuk Wuk
Calulu
Lindenow
Glenaladale
Woodglen
Walpa
Coongulmerang
Hillside
Wy Yung
Lucknow
Tambo Upper
Colquhoun
Johnsonville
Swan Reach
Nicholson
PRINCES HWY
Bairnsdale
Lake King
Kalimna West
Metung
Nungurner
Lakes Entrance
Eagle Point
Forge Creek
Paynesville
GIPPSLAND LAKES COASTAL PARK
THE LAKES NATIONAL PARK
GIPPSLAND LAKES
Bren
Mt Baw Baw 1563m
Mt St Gwinear Ski Area
Baw Baw Village
Beardmore
Talbot Peak 1519m
BAW BAW NATIONAL PARK
Ben Cruachan 839m
Stockdale
Valencia Creek
Lake Glenmaggie
Coongulla
Maffra West Upper
Boisdale
Briagolong
Bushy Park
Fernbank
Glenmaggie
Seaton
Newry
Llowalong
Munro
Delvine
Goon Nure
Bengworden
Parkers Corner
Walhalla
Rawson
Erica
Tyers Junction
Coopers Creek
Heyfield
Dawson
Tinamba
Maffra
Stratford
Airly
Perry Bridge
Meerlieu
Cowwarr
Winnindoo
Nambrok
Bandalaguah
Montgomery
Clydebank
Lake Victoria
Loch Sport
Moondarra
MOONDARRA STATE PARK
Moondarra Res
Toongabbie
Tanjil South
TYERS PARK
Glengarry
Kilmany
Fulham
Cobains
Sale
Lake Wellington
Seacombe
Wurruck
The Heart
Kilmany South
GIPPSLAND LAKES COASTAL PARK
Lake Narracan
Yallourn North
Tyers
La Trobe River
Moe
Newborough
Open Cut Mine
PRINCES HWY
Flynn
Rosedale
Longford
Lake Coleman
Reeve
Paradise Beach
Golden Beach
Morwell
Traralgon
Flynns Creek
HOLEY PLAINS STATE PARK
Dutson
Narracan
Loy Yang
Loy Yang Power Station
HYLAND HWY
Willung
Hazelwood
Hazelwood Cooling Pond
Churchill
Yinnar
Traralgon South
Callignee North
Callignee
Gormandale
Hiamdale
Stradbroke West
Stradbroke
Flamingo Beach
Delburn
Jerralang North
MORWELL NATIONAL PARK
Carrajung
Willung South
Carrajung South
Ninety Mile Beach
Seaspray
Boolarra
Budgeree
Jumbuck
Budgeree East
Le Roy
Balook
Blackwarry
Giffard
TARRA-BULGA NATIONAL PARK
Macks Creek
Won Wron
GIPPSLAND HWY
Darriman
Madalya
Ryton
GIPPSLAND
Devon
Jack River
Greenmount
Woodside
Woodside Beach
Gunyah
Wonyip
Binginwarri
Yarram
Hunterston
Mt Best
Woorarra
Alberton
McLoughlins Beach
Gelliondale
Hazel Park
SOUTH
Tarraville
Manns Beach
Agnes
Hedley
Langsborough
Port Albert
Toora
Welshpool
Port Franklin
Port Welshpool
NOORAMUNGA MARINE AND WILDLIFE RESERVE
TASMAN SEA
Corner Inlet
Entrance Point
Mt Hunter 348m
WILSONS PROMONTORY MARINE PARK
Mt Roundback 314m
WILSONS PROMONTORY NATIONAL PARK
Mt Vereker 637m
WILSONS PROMONTORY
Mt La Trobe 759m
Tidal River
Mt Oberon Lookout
Mt Wilson 709m
South East Point
WILSONS PROMONTORY MARINE RESERVE
N

228 South Western Victoria

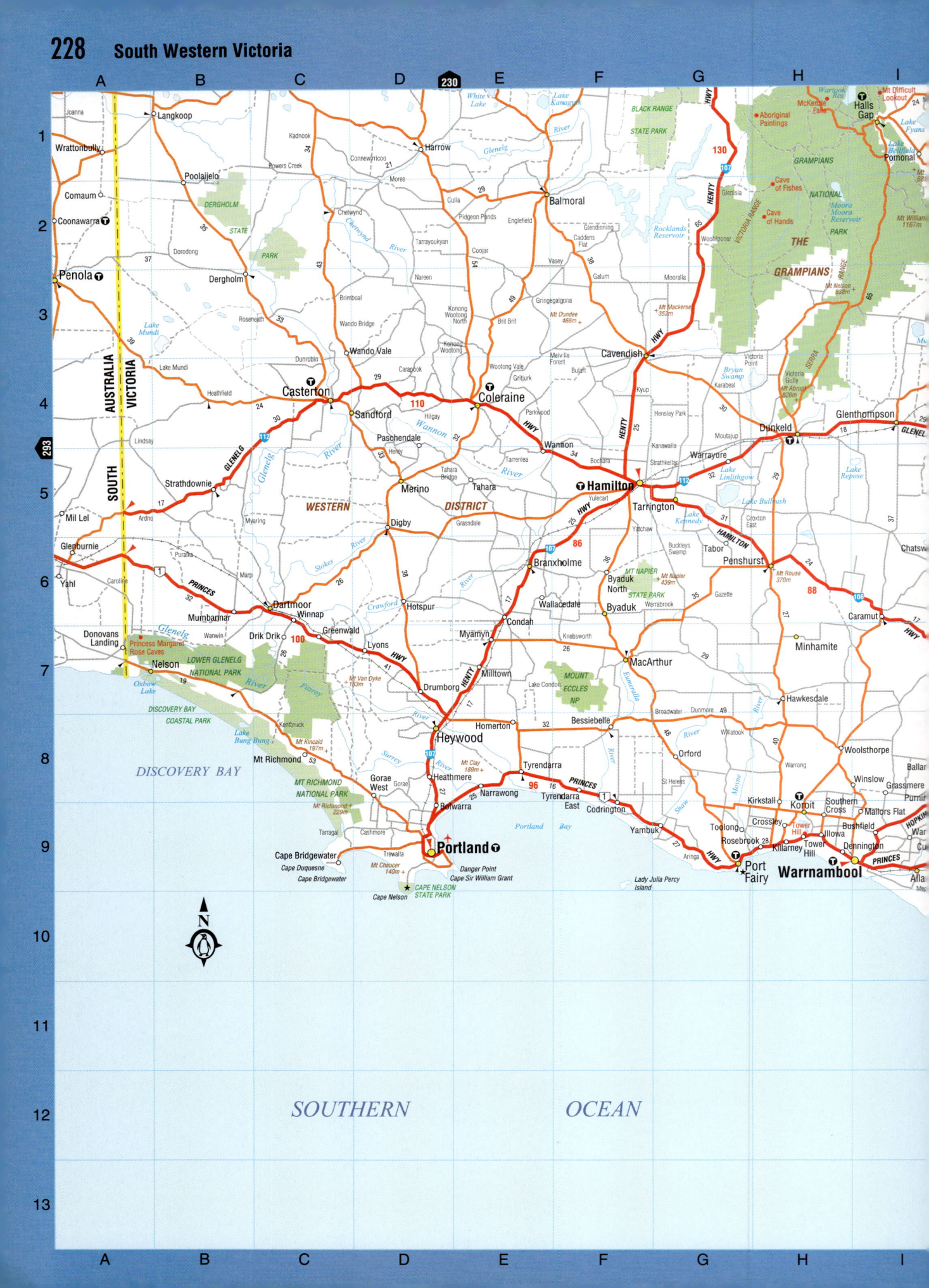

0 10 20 30 40 50 km
J K L M N O P Q R
231
226
For more detail of Goldfields Region see page 222 & 223
For more detail of Ballarat see page 221
For more detail of Geelong Region see page 219
For more detail of Otway Region see page 217
Great Western
Crowlands
Elmhurst
Amphitheatre
Lamplough
Amherst
Paddys Ranges SP
Daisy Hill
Majorca
Talbot
Campbelltown
Yandoit
Vaughan
Taradale
Barfold
Langley
Malmsbury
Lauriston
Kyneton
Carlsruhe
Tylden
Woodend
Trentham
Hepburn Springs
Daylesford
Smeaton
Kingston
Clunes
Lexton
Waubra
Ararat
Moyston
Mt Ararat 616m
Langi-Ghiran State Park
Mt Buangor State Park
Warrak
Raglan
Chute
Beaufort
Trawalla
Burrumbeet
Lake Burrumbeet
Learmonth
Creswick
Broomfield
Newlyn
Dean
Miners Rest
Cardigan Village
Ballarat
Sovereign Hill
Nerrina
Bullarook
Bolwarrah
Bungaree
Wallace
Gordon
Dunnstown
Navigators
Ballan
Greendale
Blackwood
Lerderderg State Park
Myrniong
Lerderderg Gorge
Bacchus Marsh
Parwan
Glenmore
Rowsley
Fiskville
Werribee Gorge State Park
Yendon
Lal Lal
Mount Helen
Buninyong
Napoleons
Haddon
Snake Valley
Smythesdale
Scarsdale
Newtown
Linton
Piggoreet
Happy Valley
Durham Lead
Clarendon
Mt Doran
Mount Wallace
Brisbane Ranges National Park
Enfield
Grenville
Elaine
Cargerie
Mount Mercer
Dereel
Meredith
Anakie Gorge
Balliang
Illabarook
Cape Clear
Rokewood Junction
Corindhap
Rokewood
Steiglitz
Steiglitz Park
Sheoaks
Anakie
Maude
Lethbridge
Little River
Lara
Teesdale
Shelford
Bannockburn
Batesford
Geelong
Fyansford
Gnarwarre
Inverleigh
Mount Moriac
Moriac
Ceres
Marshall
Leopold
Waurn Ponds
Ocean Grove
Barwon Heads
Breamlea
Freshwater Creek
Bellbrae
Torquay
Winchelsea
Anglesea
Aireys Inlet
Fairhaven
Eastern View
Angahook-Lorne State Park
Benwerrin
Deans Marsh
Bambra
Birregurra
Lorne
Separation Creek
Wye River
Kennett River
Cape Patton
Skenes Creek
Apollo Bay
Marengo
Blanket Bay
Otway National Park
Cape Otway
Johanna
Lavers Hill
Melba Gully State Park
Beech Forest
Forrest
Gerangamete
Barwon Downs
Kawarren
Gellibrand
Carlisle River
Carlisle State Park
Yeodene
Elliminyt
Colac
Larpent
Pirron Yallock
Irrewillipe
Swan Marsh
Stoneyford
Pomborneit
Cororooke
Coragulac
Alvie
Warrion
Beeac
Lake Corangamite
Cressy
Berrybank
Lismore
Derrinallum
Darlington
Camperdown
Terang
Boorcan
Noorat
Glenormiston
Bookar
Cobden
Garvoc
Panmure
Laang
Glenfyne
Ayrford
Nullawarre
Scotts Creek
Timboon
Curdie Vale
Simpson
Peterborough
London Bridge
The Arch
Port Campbell
Loch Ard Gorge
The Twelve Apostles
Port Campbell National Park
Princetown
Moonlight Head
Point Reginald
Skipton
Streatham
Westmere
Lake Bolac
Nerrin Nerrin
Mininera
Willaura
Tatyoon
Rossbridge
Maroona
Woorndoo
Mortlake
Framlingham
Ellerslie
Mannibadar
Lake Goldsmith
Lake Wongan
Slater Lake
Lake Bookar
Lake Colongulac
Lake Gnarpurt
Lake Martin
Lake Murdeduke
Lake Connewarre
BASS STRAIT
WESTERN HWY
PYRENEES HWY
SUNRAYSIA HWY
MIDLAND HWY
GLENELG HWY
HAMILTON HWY
PRINCES HWY
PRINCES FWY
WESTERN FWY
GREAT OCEAN RD
CALDER HWY

230 Central Western Victoria

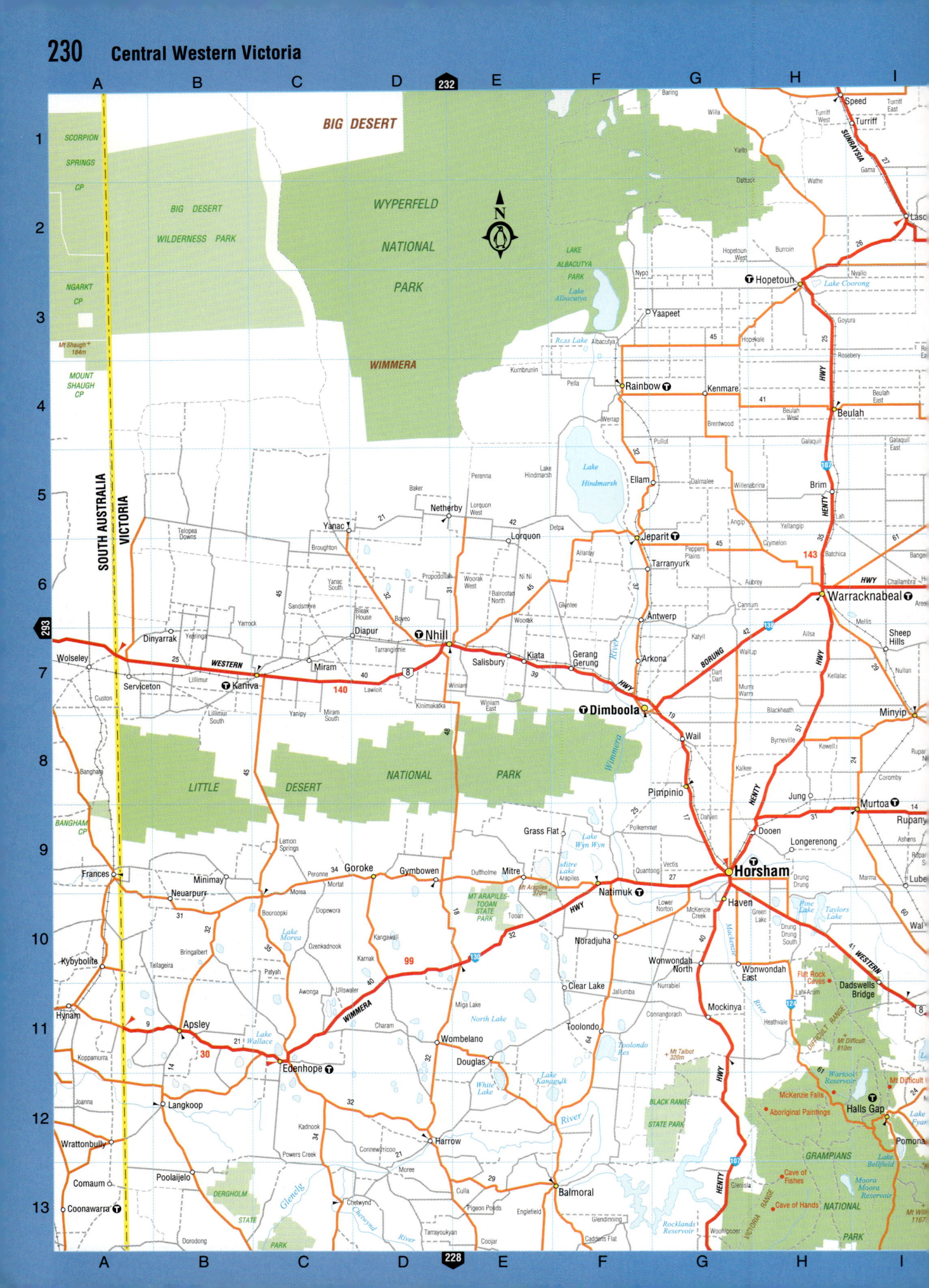

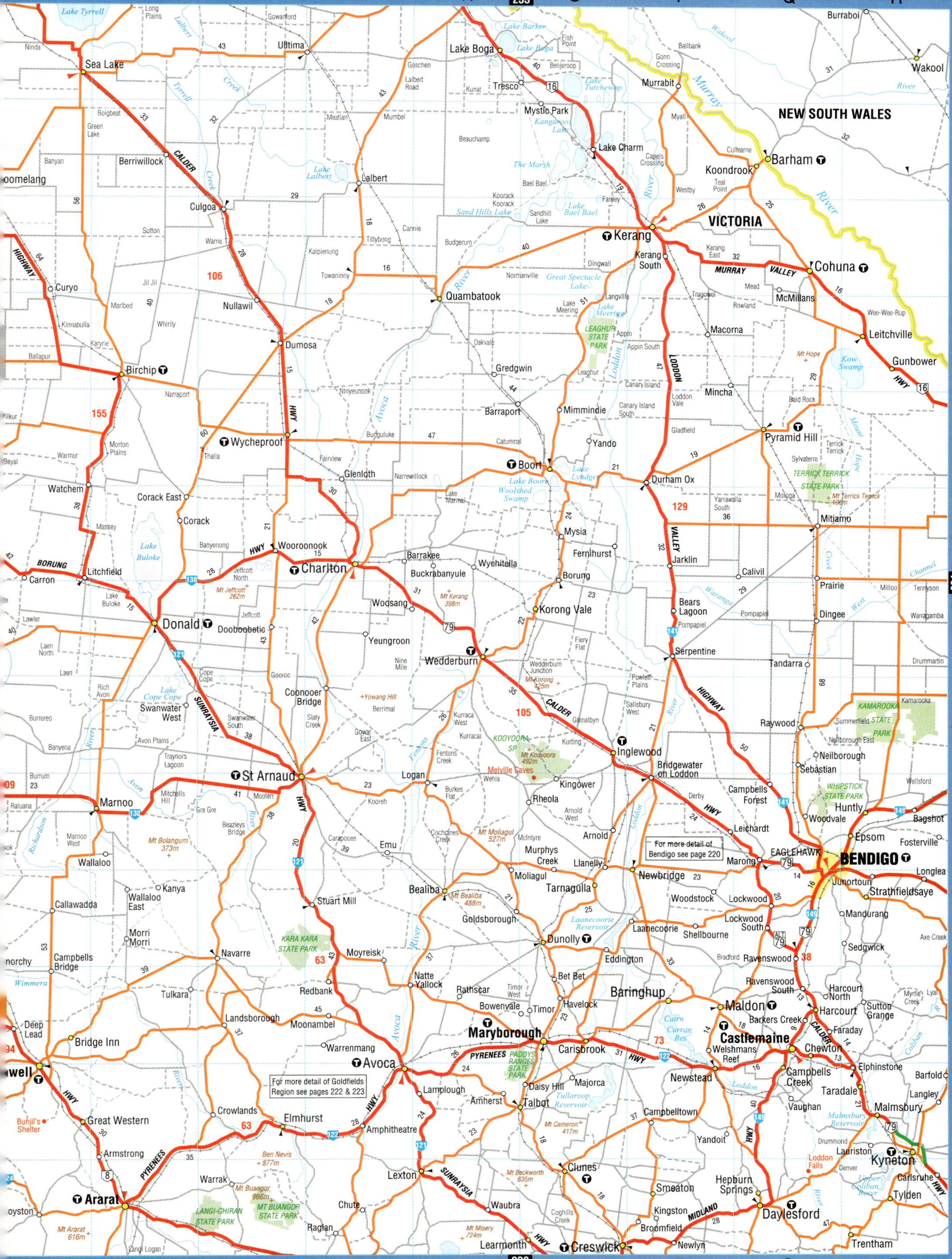
0 10 20 30 40 50 km
NEW SOUTH WALES
VICTORIA
Lake Tyrrell
Sea Lake
Ninda
Long Plains
Lalbert
Gowanford
Ultima
Tyrrell Creek
Boigbeat
Green Lake
Banyan
Berriwillock
Coomelang
Culgoa
CALDER
Sutton
Warne
Curyo
HIGHWAY
Kinnabulla
Karyrie
Marlbed
Jil Jil
Whirily
Nullawil
Dumosa
Ballapur
Birchip
Narraport
Wilkur
Warmur
Morton Plains
Beyal
Watchem
Wycheproof
Thalia
Corack East
Corack
Massey
Lake Buloke
Banyenong
Wooroonook
Jeffcott North
Mt Jeffcott 262m
Carron
BORUNG
Litchfield
Lake Buloke
Lawler
Donald
Dooboobetic
Jeffcott
Laen North
Laen
Rich Avon
Lake Cope Cope
Cope Cope
Swanwater West
SUNRAYSIA
Swanwater South
Burrereo
Banyena
Avon Plains
Traynors Lagoon
Burrum
Avon River
Mitchells Hill
Marnoo
Raluana
Marnoo West
Mt Bolangum 373m
Wallaloo
Richardson
Kanya
Wallaloo East
Callawadda
Morri Morri
Campbells Bridge
Wimmera
Navarre
Tulkara
Deep Lead
Bridge Inn
Landsborough
Moonambel
Stawell
Great Western
Bunjil's Shelter
Armstrong
PYRENEES
Warrak
Mt Buangor 966m
LANGI-GHIRAN STATE PARK
MT BUANGOR STATE PARK
Ararat
Mt Ararat 616m
Langi Logan
Moyston
Crowlands
Elmhurst
Ben Nevis 877m
Amphitheatre
Lexton
Chute
Raglan
Waubra
Avoca
Warrenmang
Redbank
KARA KARA STATE PARK
Moyreisk
Stuart Mill
St Arnaud
Moolerr
Gre Gre
Beazleys Bridge
Carapooee
Emu
Coonooer Bridge
Slaty Creek
Gooroc
Charlton
Barrakee
Buckrabanyule
Wychitella
Woosang
Mt Kerang 398m
Yeungroon
Nine Mile
Wedderburn
Yowang Hill
Berrimal
Gowar East
Kurraca West
Kurraca
Fentons Creek
Logan
Kooreh
Burkes Flat
Cochranes Creek
Mt Moliagul 527m
Bealiba
Mt Bealiba 488m
Goldsborough
Natte Yallock
Rathscar
Timor West
Bowenvale
Timor
Maryborough
Carisbrook
PADDYS RANGES STATE PARK
Daisy Hill
Majorca
Amherst
Talbot
Tullaroop Reservoir
Mt Cameron 417m
Mt Beckworth 635m
Clunes
Coghills Creek
Mt Misery 724m
Learmonth
Creswick
Lamplough
Quambatook
Tittybong
Cannie
Towaninny
Kalpienung
Lalbert
Lake Lalbert
Meatian
Mumbel
Goschen
Lalbert Road
Lake Boga
Tresco
Kunat
Fish Point
Benjeroop
Lake Barker
Lake Tutchewop
Mystic Park
Kangaroo Lake
Beauchamp
The Marsh
Bael Bael
Kooraack Kooraack
Sand Hills Lake
Sandhill Lake
Lake Bael Bael
Budgerum
Lake Charm
Capels Crossing
Fairley
Kerang
Kerang South
Dingwall
Normanville
Great Spectacle Lake
Lake Meering
Langville
LEAGHUR STATE PARK
Appin
Appin South
Oakvale
Gredgwin
Leaghur
Canary Island
Canary Island South
Barraport
Mimmindie
Yando
Ninyeunook
Catumnal
Boort
Lake Boort
Woolshed Swamp
Lake Lyndger
Lake Marmal
Narrewillock
Glenloth
Fairview
Burgulluke
Mysia
Fernihurst
Borung
Korong Vale
Fiery Flat
Wedderburn Junction
Mt Korong 425m
KOOYOORA SP
Mt Kooyoora 492m
Melville Caves
Kurting
Glenalbyn
Salisbury West
Powlett Plains
Inglewood
Kingower
Wehla
Rheola
Arnold West
Arnold
McIntyre
Murphys Creek
Moliagul
Llanelly
Tarnagulla
Laanecoorie Reservoir
Dunolly
Eddington
Bet Bet
Havelock
Baringhup
Cairn Curran Res
Maldon
Laanecoorie
Gonn Crossing
Murrabit
Murray River
Ballbank
Wakool
Myall
Westby
Teal Point
Koondrook
Barham
Cullearne
Burraboi
Wakool
Kerang East
MURRAY VALLEY
Cohuna
Tragowel
Mead
Macorna
McMillans
Wee-Wee-Rup
Leitchville
Gunbower
Kow Swamp
Mt Hope
Mincha
Bald Rock
Loddon Vale
Gladfield
Durham Ox
Pyramid Hill
Terrick Terrick
Sylvaterre
TERRICK TERRICK STATE PARK
Mt Terrick Terrick 196m
Mologa
Yarrawalla South
Mitiamo
LODDON
VALLEY
Jarklin
Calivil
Prairie
Milloo
Tennyson
Channel
Bears Lagoon
Pompapiel
Dingee
Warragamba
Serpentine
Tandarra
Drummartin
Raywood
Kamarooka
KAMAROOKA STATE PARK
Summerfield
Neilborough East
Neilborough
Sebastian
Wellsford
WHIPSTICK STATE PARK
Huntly
Woodvale
Bagshot
Epsom
Fosterville
Bridgewater on Loddon
Campbells Forest
Derby
Leichardt
For more detail of Bendigo see page 220
Marong
EAGLEHAWK
BENDIGO
Longlea
Junortoun
Strathfieldsaye
Newbridge
Woodstock
Lockwood
Lockwood South
Shelbourne
Mandurang
Axe Creek
Sedgwick
Bradford
Ravenswood
Ravenswood South
Harcourt North
Harcourt
Myrtle Creek
Sutton Grange
Barkers Creek
Faraday
Castlemaine
Welshmans Reef
Chewton
Newstead
Campbells Creek
Elphinstone
Barfold
Langley
Taradale
Vaughan
Malmsbury
Malmsbury Reservoir
Campbelltown
Yandoit
Drummond
Lauriston
Kyneton
Loddon Falls
Denver
Upper Coliban Reservoir
Carlsruhe
Tylden
Smeaton
Hepburn Springs
Kingston
Broomfield
MIDLAND
Daylesford
Newlyn
Trentham
For more detail of Goldfields Region see pages 222 & 223
233
229
234
J K L M N O P Q R
1 2 3 4 5 6 7 8 9 10 11 12 13

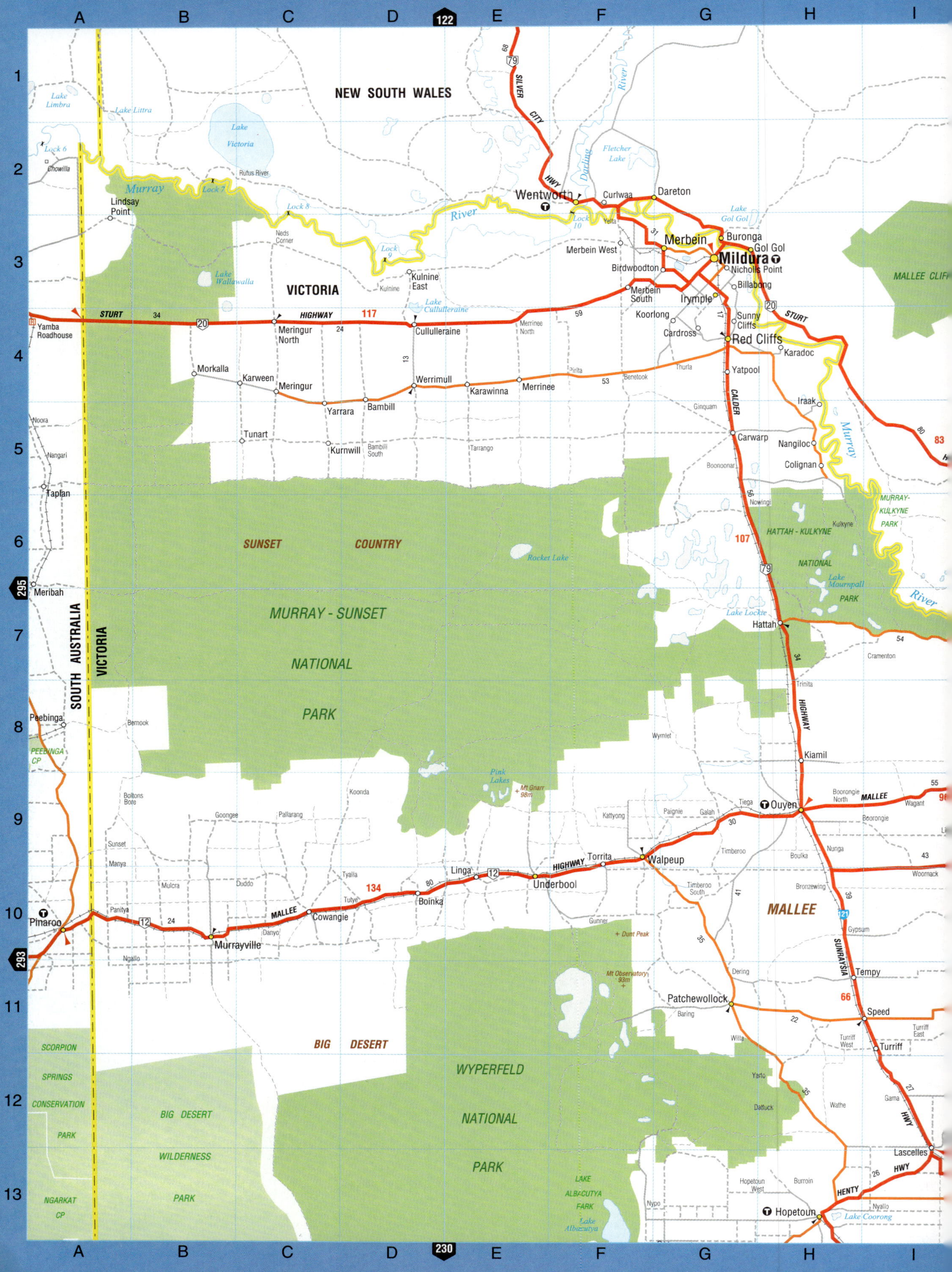

NEW SOUTH WALES
VICTORIA
SOUTH AUSTRALIA
Lake Limbra
Lake Littra
Lake Victoria
Lock 6
Chowilla
Rufus River
Murray
Lock 7
Lindsay Point
Lock 8
River
Neds Corner
Lock 9
Lake Wallawalla
Kulnine East
Kulnine
Lake Cullulleraine
SILVER CITY HWY
Darling
River
Fletcher Lake
Wentworth
Curlwaa
Dareton
Lock 10
Yelta
Lake Gol Gol
Buronga
Gol Gol
Merbein
Merbein West
Mildura
Nichols Point
Birdwoodton
Billabong
Merbein South
Irymple
Koorlong
Sunny Cliffs
Cardross
Red Cliffs
Karadoc
STURT HIGHWAY
117
Yamba Roadhouse
Meringur North
Cullulleraine
Merrinee North
Morkalla
Karween
Meringur
Werrimull
Karawinna
Merrinee
Pirita
Benetook
Thurla
Yatpool
Yarrara
Bambill
Ginquam
CALDER HIGHWAY
Iraak
Noora
Nangari
Tunart
Kurnwill
Bambill South
Tarrango
Carwarp
Nangiloc
Colignan
Boonoonar
Taplan
Nowingi
MURRAY-KULKYNE PARK
SUNSET COUNTRY
Rocket Lake
107
HATTAH - KULKYNE NATIONAL PARK
Kulkyne
Lake Mournpall
Meribah
MURRAY - SUNSET NATIONAL PARK
Lake Lockie
Hattah
Cramenton
Trinita
Peebinga
Bernook
PEEBINGA CP
Wymlet
Kiamil
Pink Lakes
Mt Gnarr 98m
Boltons Bore
Koonda
Goongee
Pallarang
Kattyong
Paignie
Galah
Tiega
Ouyen
Boorongie North
MALLEE
Wagant
Boorongie
Sunset
Manya
Timberoo
Walpeup
Torrita
Boulka
Nunga
Woomack
Mulcra
Duddo
Tyalla
Linga
HIGHWAY
Underbool
Timberoo South
Bronzewing
134
Tutye
Boinka
Panitya
Pinaroo
Cowangie
MALLEE
Danyo
Murrayville
Ngallo
Gunner
Dunt Peak
Gypsum
SUNRAYSIA
Tempy
Mt Observatory 93m
Dering
Patchewollock
Baring
66
Speed
Turriff East
Turriff West
Turriff
Willa
SCORPION SPRINGS CONSERVATION PARK
BIG DESERT
BIG DESERT WILDERNESS PARK
WYPERFELD NATIONAL PARK
Yarto
Datluck
Wathe
Gama
HWY
Lascelles
NGARKAT CP
LAKE ALBACUTYA PARK
Lake Albacutya
Nypo
Hopetoun West
Hopetoun
Burroin
HENTY HWY
Yaapeet
Lake Coorong
MALLEE CLIFFS

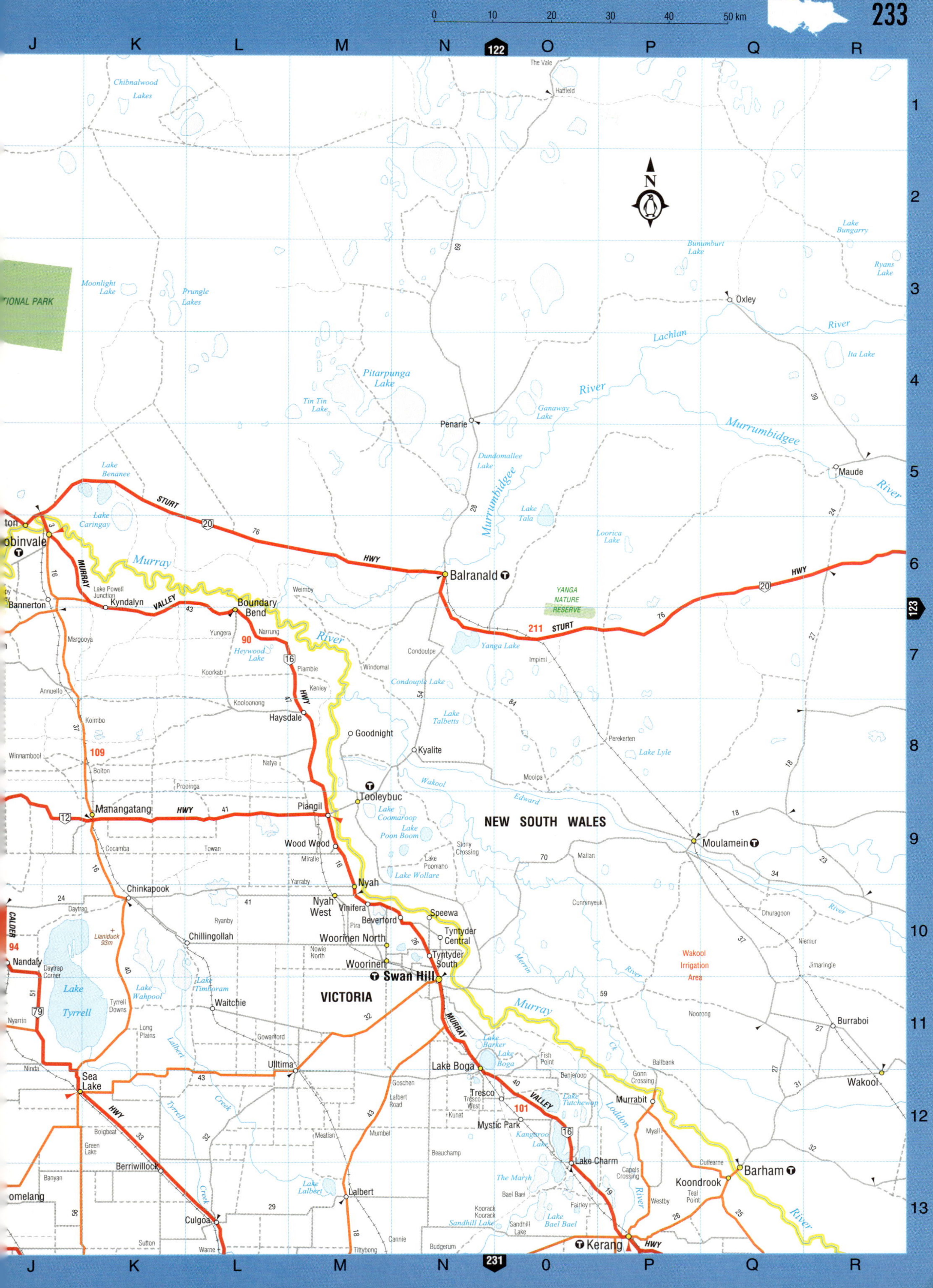
0 10 20 30 40 50 km
J K L M N O P Q R
122
231
123
1 2 3 4 5 6 7 8 9 10 11 12 13
NEW SOUTH WALES
VICTORIA
The Vale
Hatfield
Chibnalwood Lakes
Moonlight Lake
Prungle Lakes
Pitarpunga Lake
Tin Tin Lake
Penarie
Oxley
Lachlan
River
Lake Bungarry
Bunumburt Lake
Ryans Lake
Ita Lake
Ganaway Lake
Murrumbidgee
Maude
Dundomallee Lake
Lake Tala
Loorica Lake
Lake Benanee
Lake Caringay
STURT
HWY
Balranald
YANGA NATURE RESERVE
Yanga Lake
Robinvale
Murray
MURRAY
VALLEY
Lake Powell Junction
Kyndalyn
Bannerton
Boundary Bend
Margooya
Yungera
Narrung
Heywood Lake
Piambie
Kenley
Koorkab
Annuello
Kooloonong
Haysdale
Koimbo
Winnambool
Bolton
Natya
Goodnight
Kyalite
Condoulpe
Windomal
Condoulpe Lake
Lake Talbetts
Impimi
Perekerten
Lake Lyle
Moolpa
Wakool
Edward
Prooinga
Manangatang
Tooleybuc
Piangil
Lake Coomaroop
Lake Poon Boom
Moulamein
Wood Wood
Miralie
Towan
Cocamba
Stony Crossing
Lake Poomaho
Lake Wollare
Mallan
Yarraby
Nyah
Nyah West
Vinifera
Pira
Chinkapook
Daytrap
Ryanby
Speewa
Beverford
Tyntyder Central
Tyntyder South
Chillingollah
Woorinen North
Nowie North
Woorinen
Swan Hill
Cunninyeuk
Dhuragoon
Niemur
Jimaringle
Wakool Irrigation Area
CALDER
Nandaly
Daytrap Corner
Lianiduck 93m
Lake Tyrrell
Lake Wahpool
Lake Timboram
Tyrrell Downs
Waitchie
Nyarrin
Long Plains
Gowanford
Lalbert
Nootong
Burraboi
Lake Barker
Lake Boga
Fish Point
Ballbank
Gonn Crossing
Benjeroop
Lake Tutchewop
Murrabit
Wakool
Ninda
Sea Lake
Ultima
Goschen
Lalbert Road
Tresco
Tresco West
Kunat
Mystic Park
Kangaroo Lake
Loddon
Myall
Boigbeat
Green Lake
Meatian
Mumbel
Beauchamp
Lake Charm
Capels Crossing
Cullearne
Barham
Koondrook
Teal Point
Westby
Berriwillock
Banyan
Lake Lalbert
The Marsh
Bael Bael
Kooroc Kooroc
Sandhill Lake
Sandhill Lake
Lake Bael Bael
Fairley
Culgoa
Sutton
Warne
Tittybong
Cannie
Budgerum
Kerang
Creek
Tyrrell
Merran
Ck

234 North Central Victoria

0 10 20 30 40 50 km
J K L M N O P Q R
123
Rand
Berrigan
Daysdale
Walbundrie
Culcairn
Morven
Holbrook
Savenake
203
Coreen
Walla Walla
RIVERINA
Rennie
Oil Tree Lagoon
Brocklesby
Burrumbuttock
Gerogery
Gerogery West
Woomargama
TABLE TOP NAT RES
Lowesdale
Buraja
Balldale
NEW SOUTH WALES
Jindera
Barooga
Cobram
Murray River
Mulwala
Corowa
Howlong
Lake Mulwala
Yarrawonga
MURRAY
Bundalong
Wahgunyah
Rutherglen
Brimin
Albury
Wodonga
Lake Hume
Talgarno
Katamatite
Bundalong South
Esmond
133
Barnawatha
Bethanga
Granya
Chiltern Valley
Chiltern
HUME FWY
Bandiana
Ebden
Bonegilla
Jarvis Ck
Georges Ck
Darbyshire
Old Tallangatta
Wilby
Tungamah
Peechelba
Springhurst
VICTORIA
CHILTERN STATE PARK
Barandudu
Tallangatta
Boorhaman
PILOT RANGE
Kiewa
Tangambalanga
MURRAY VALLEY HWY
128
St James
Lake Rowan
73
Wooragee
Allans Flat
Dookie
WARBY RANGE STATE PARK
Eldorado
Woolshed
Yackandandah
Osbornes Flat
Kergunyah
Devenish
Thoona
Wangaratta
Beechworth
Silver Creek
87
Goorambat
Tarrawingee
Stanley
Gundowring
Oxley
Everton
Tallandoon
Glenrowan
Lake Mokoan
Milawa
Markwood
Dederang
Eskdale
Gapsted
77
Mudgegonga
Benalla
Winton
Docker
Bobinawarrah
Whorouly
Whorouly South
Myrtleford
Rosewhite
Mitta Mitta
Greta
Meadow Creek
Baddaginnie
Moyhu
Carboor
Merriang
Ovens
Havilah
REEF HILLS PARK
Molyullah
Eurobin
Mullindolingong
Edi
Nug Nug
MOUNT BUFFALO NATIONAL PARK
Porepunkah
Tawonga
136
Warrenbayne
Tatong
King Valley
Myrrhee
Bright
Tawonga Gap
Mount Beauty
Tawonga South
Swanpool
Whitfield
Cheshunt
Dandongadale
Wandiligong
Buckland
Smoko
Kiewa Hydro Electric Scheme
Strathbogie
MOUNT SAMARIA STATE PARK
Lake Nillahcootie
Powers Lookout
McKay Creek Power Station
Falls Creek Alpine Village
Harrietville
ALPINE NATIONAL PARK
Tolmie
Lake William Hovell
BOGONG HIGH PLAINS
Barjarg
Hotham Heights Alpine Village
Merton
Bonnie Doon
Kanumbra
Mansfield
Dinner Plain Alpine Village
GREAT DIVIDING RANGE
Merrijig
Mirimbah
Mt Stirling Ski Area
DARGO HIGH PLAINS
Alexandra
FRASER NATIONAL PARK
Lake Eildon
EILDON STATE PARK
Piries
Goughs Bay
Mt Buller Alpine Village
Eildon
Thornton
Macs Cove
Howqua
Snobs Creek
Rubicon
Jamieson
For more detail of Alpine Region see pages 224 & 225
HOWITT PLAINS
Taggerty
CATHEDRAL RANGE STATE PARK
Kevington
Buxton
Marysville
Gaffneys Creek
Crooked River
Dargo
A1 Mine Settlement
Narbethong
YARRA RANGES NATIONAL PARK
Woods Point
Waterford
Lake Tarli Karng
226
227
236

236 North Eastern Victoria

0 10 20 30 40 50 km
115
Cabramurra
Tumut Pond Reservoir
Adaminaby
Anglers Reach
Old Adaminaby
KOSCIUSKO
NATIONAL
PARK
RANGE
Lake Eucumbene
O'Neill Lagoon
Eucumbene
Mt Jagungal 2061m
Buckenderra
SNOWY
MOUNTAINS
Mt Flinders 1484m
Bredbo
Mt Dowling 1198m
MONARO
HWY
Bunyan
Murrumbidgee
Numeralla
Mt McInally Mtn 1085m
Peakview
Countegany
Tuross Falls
Bald Mtn 1469m
Bendethera Caves
DEUA
NATIONAL
PARK
Bendethera Mtn 997m
Bergalia
Bodalla
Nerrigundah
Eurobodalla
Dalmeny
Wagonga
Narooma
Belowra
Cooma
Cootralantra Lake
Kiah Lake
Lake Jindabyne
Guthega
Smiggin Holes
Perisher Blue
Alpine Village
Jindabyne
Berridale
Buckleys Lake
Dalgety
Moonbah
Lake Jillamatong
Beloka
Maffra
Numbla Vale
Paupong
Ingebyra
Rock Flat
HIGHWAY
Nimmitabel
WADBILLIGA
NATIONAL
PARK
Mt Kydra 1236m
Brogo Dam
Wandella
Central Tilba
Tilba Tilba
Corunna Lake
Cobargo
WALLAGA LAKE NP
Bermagui
Bermagui South
Quaama
BIAMANGA NATIONAL PARK
Brogo
Bunga
Wapengo
MIMOSA ROCKS
NATIONAL
PARK
Tanja
BEMBOKA
NATIONAL
PARK
Bemboka
Numbugga
Bega
Tathra
Kalaru
BOURNDA
NATIONAL
PARK
Beards Lake
Bungarby
Gunning Grach
Mt Cooper 1018m
Maclaughlin
Ando
Morgans Crossing
Bimbaya
Kameruka
Candelo
TATAWANGALO
NATIONAL
PARK
PRINCES
Wolumla
Tura Beach
Merimbula
Pambula
Pambula Beach
SOUTH
PACIFIC
OCEAN
Wallace Craigie Lookout
Mulligans Mtn 908m
Jimenbuen
Mt Rix 988m
Bukalong
Bibbenluke
Cathcart
Mt Darrah
Byadbo Mtn 1237m
Mt Alexander 1075m
Rodney
Tombong
Adams Pk
Bombala
Rocky Hall
Wyndham
Lochiel
Griegs Flat
COOLANGUBRA NATIONAL PARK
Tingaringy
NEW SOUTH WALES
VICTORIA
Carrowidgin
Maharatta
Burragate
YOWAKA NATIONAL PARK
Nethercote
Eden
BEN BOYD
NATIONAL
PARK
Ambyne
Tubbut
Deddick
McKillops Bridge
Delegate River
Delegate
Craigie
Mila
BONDI GULF NATURE RES
White Rock Mtn 1093m
GENOA NATIONAL PARK
Platts
Twofold Bay
East Boyd
Boydtown
Haydens Bog
Delickhora
Mt Delegate 1308m
Bendoc
Quinburra
Rockton
Pericoe
Towamba
Kiah
SNOWY RIVER
NATIONAL
PARK
Mt Bowen 1320m
Bonang
Bonang West
MT IMLAY NATIONAL PARK
Mt Imlay 886m
Wonboyn Lake
Mt Canterbury 1039m
Buldah
Kowat
Coopracamba 958m
COOPRACAMBRA
NATIONAL
PARK
Narrabarba
Green Cape
Brown Mtn 1010m
ERRINUNDRA
NATIONAL
PARK
Waalimma Mtn 722m
Mt Jersey 759m
Goongerah
Chandlers Creek
Wroxham
NADGEE
NATURE
RESERVE
Weeragua
Errinundra
Combienbar
Mt Kaye 1002m
Wangarabell
Timbillica
Mt Nagha 543m
For more detail of South Coast see page 113
Mt Ellery 1291m
Martins Creek
GIPPSLAND
Noorinbee North
VALLEY
Genoa
Gipsy Point
Fairhaven
Lake Barracoota
Cape Howe
Sardine Creek
Noorinbee
Mt Kuark 917m
Club Terrace
LIND NP
CANN
Karlo Creek
ALFRED NATIONAL PARK
Mallacoota
Mallacoota Inlet
Gabo Island
Mt Buck 507m
Tonghi Creek
Cann River
Murrungowar
CROAJINGOLONG
NATIONAL
PARK
Orbost
Brodribb River
Cabbage Tree Creek
Bellbird Creek
Mt Cann 530m
Thurra
Little Rame Head
Tabbara
Mt Everard 371m
Lake Corringle
Lake Curlip
Bemm River
CROAJINGOLONG NATIONAL PARK
Tamboon
Wingan Inlet
Marlo
Corringle
Point Ricardo
Cape Conran
Pearl Point
Sydenham Inlet
Tamboon Inlet
Point Hicks (Cape Everard)
Rame Head
TASMAN SEA
J K L M N O P Q R
1 2 3 4 5 6 7 8 9 10 11 12 13

South Australia

SOUTH AUSTRALIA

Festival State

The festivals of South Australia provide an excellent chance for people to discover a community at its liveliest. Given the number and variety of festivals – the Adelaide Festival of Arts, the Barossa Valley Vintage Festival, Schutzenfest, the Greek Glendi Festival and the Cornish Kernewek Lowender – it seems South Australians enjoy making the most of life.

This energetic spirit also seems to indicate that South Australians have triumphed over what might seem to be a rather depressing statistic: it is the driest State in the driest continent, two-thirds is near-desert and eighty-three per cent receives an annual rainfall of less than 250 millimetres. But these facts are easily forgotten when you visit the lush green Barossa Valley or explore the beauty of the Flinders Ranges.

South Australia's initial settlement began as the result of one man's idea for creating a model colony. Edward Gibbon Wakefield believed that the difficulties of other Australian colonies were caused by the ease with which anyone could obtain land. He claimed that if land was sold at two pounds an acre, only men of capital could buy; those who could not would provide a supply of labour, and the money generated would encourage investment and the development of resources. In 1834 he decided to test his ideas in the Gulf St Vincent area. Lieutenant-Colonel Light was dispatched as Surveyor-General to select a site. Despite financial difficulties in its early days, South Australia went on to lead Australia (and sometimes the world) in many social reforms.

In the 1990s South Australia's economy remains traditionally agrarian yet secondary industry provides nine out of ten jobs. Olympic Dam is one of the world's biggest copper mines and probably the biggest uranium mine. Leigh Creek coalfields supply the fuel for the State's power needs. South Australia also mines most of the world's opals. Coober Pedy, the main opal-mining town, produces eighty-five per cent of Australia's opals.

The gulf lands of South Australia enjoy a Mediterranean climate while the further north you go, the hotter and more inhospitable the temperatures become. Adelaide, the capital, with its average annual rainfall of 585 millimetres, enjoys a mid-summer average maximum temperature of about 28°C and a mid-winter average maximum of 15°C. Seventy-two per cent of the population lives here, making South Australia the most urbanised of all the States. Adelaide inherited its orderly and pleasant layout from its first Surveyor-General, Colonel Light, and many of its attractive original stone buildings have survived. The rolling hills of the Mount Lofty Ranges make a picturesque backdrop.

The Stuart Highway is completely sealed, making it possible to drive from Port Augusta to central Australia on an all-weather road. Before negotiating other roads in the north and west of the State – the desert regions – certain precautions should be taken (see: Outback Motoring). If you feel intrepid, the opal towns of Coober Pedy and Andamooka are fascinating. Temperatures climb to more than 40°C in Coober Pedy during summer (hence much of the town was built underground), so ensure you choose a cool period for your trip.

NOT TO BE MISSED in South Australia

- **Adelaide Hills** – historic towns, wineries, galleries and beautiful scenery
- **Barossa wine region** – Australia's most famous wine-producing area
- **Coorong National Park** – one of the best natural bird sanctuaries in Australia
- **'Copper Triangle' towns (Kadina, Moonta, Wallaroo)** – rich mining history
- **Innes National Park** – impressive coastal scenery and wildflowers in spring
- **Kangaroo Island** – unique scenery, pristine vegetation and native fauna
- **Mount Gambier** – caves and crater lakes, particularly the beautiful Blue Lake
- **Victor Harbor** – coastal resort town; take the horse-drawn tram to Granite Island
- **Whalers Way (Port Lincoln)** – stunning cliff-top drive near Port Lincoln
- **Wilpena Pound** – extraordinary geological formation in the Flinders Ranges

Golden vines provide a picturesque sight in the Adelaide Hills

Richly coloured hills in the Painted Desert, near Coober Pedy in central South Australia

The spectacular Flinders Ranges have passable roads, although some are unsealed. Wilpena Pound and Arkaroola are the main resort bases. The Heysen Trail (commemorating the South Australian painter Sir Hans Heysen) is a well-defined hiking trail that reaches from Cape Jervis almost to Quorn, with extensions into the Flinders Ranges.

Both the Yorke and Eyre Peninsulas have attractive, unspoilt coastlines. Port Lincoln, on the Eyre Peninsula, is a popular base for game fishing and on the Yorke Peninsula the towns of Wallaroo, Moonta and Kadina – known collectively as Little Cornwall – are well worth a visit.

South of Adelaide is Victor Harbor, the south coast's largest town. A little further on is Coorong National Park, renowned for its prolific birdlife, near the mouth of the Murray River at Lake Alexandrina. Here the river completes its 2600-kilometre course. A trip along the Riverland section of the Murray reveals historic towns, bountiful citrus orchards and extensive vegetable crops – all maintained by irrigation from the Murray. The

CALENDAR OF EVENTS

Note: The information given here was accurate at the time of printing. However, as the timing of events held annually is subject to change and some events may extend into the following month, it is best to check with the local tourism authority or event organisers to confirm the details. The calendar is not exhaustive. Most towns and regions hold sporting competitions, arts and craft exhibitions, agricultural and flower shows, music festivals and other such events annually. Details of these events are available from local tourism outlets.

JANUARY
Public holidays: New Year's Day; Australia Day. **Adelaide:** Sheffield Shield cricket; Schutzenfest German festival; Blessing of the waters (at Glenelg). **Ardrossan:** Ardrossan Alive outdoor music festival (biennial, odd-numbered years). **Hahndorf:** Founders Day. **Kingston S.E.:** Yachting regatta; Lobster fest. **Loxton:** Apex fisherama. **Milang:** Milang to Goolwa freshwater yacht race. **Murray Bridge:** State championship swimming. **Penola:** Vignerons Cup horse race. **Port Germein:** Festival of the crab. **Port Lincoln:** Tunarama festival. **Port MacDonnell:** Regatta day; Oz Rock music festival. **Port Vincent:** Gala day; Yacht race. **Robe:** Beer can regatta. **Streaky Bay:** Perlubie Beach sports and race day; Family fish day contest. **Tanunda:** Oompah festival. **Tumby Bay:** Fishing competition. **Wallaroo:** Regatta. **Whyalla:** Australian amateur snapper fishing championship; National jet ski titles.

FEBRUARY
Adelaide: Womadelaide music festival. **Aldinga Beach:** Historic bike race; Multicultural festival. **Berri:** Rodeo; Speedboat spectacular (subject to river condition). **Coonalpyn:** Trash farming field day (biennial, even-numbered years). **Goolwa:** Goolwa to Milang freshwater classic yacht race. **Kingscote:** Kangaroo Island racing carnival. **Loxton:** Mardi Gras. **Mount Compass:** Compass Cup cow race. **Peterborough:** Rodeo. **Port Lincoln:** Lincoln week regatta. **Tailem Bend:** Gumi racing festival. **Waikerie:** International food fair.

MARCH
Adelaide: Adelaide festival of arts (biennial, even-numbered years); Fringe festival (runs parallel to Adelaide festival); 'Come Out' youth arts festival (biennial, odd-numbered years); Glendi Greek festival. **Goolwa:** Wooden boat festival (biennial, odd-numbered years). **Kapunda:** Celtic music festival (weekend before Easter). **Kingscote:** Racing carnival. **Lucindale:** Field days. **Millicent:** Radiata festival week. **Mintaro:** Paddys market, food and bric-a-brac. **Mount Barker:** Power of the past (vintage cars). **Port Pirie:** Street go-kart grand prix. **Streaky Bay:** Race meeting. **Tanunda:** Essenfest. **William Creek:** Race meeting and gymkhana (weekend before Easter).

EASTER
Public holidays: Good Friday; Easter Monday. **Andamooka:** Easter family fun day and White Dam walk. **Barmera:** Lake Bonney yachting regatta. **Barossa Valley:** Vintage festival (biennial, odd-numbered years). **Berri:** Carnival. **Clare:** Easter races. **Cobdogla:** Art and craft fair. **Coober Pedy:** Opal festival. **Kadina:** Bowling carnival. **Oakbank:** Easter racing carnival. **Waikerie:** Horse and pony club Easter gymkhana. **Whyalla:** Sportfishing convention.

South Australia

lakes and lagoons at the river's mouth abound with birdlife and offer excellent fishing as well as seasonal duck-shooting. Mount Gambier, near the southern Victorian border, is the commercial centre of the south-east; it has Australia's largest pine forest and the beautiful Blue Lake.

The fame of South Australia's wine regions extends well beyond Australian shores. The Barossa, McLaren, Riverland, Clare Valley, Langhorne Creek, Adelaide Hills and Coonawarra wine regions – all have distinct specialities determined by soil and climate. In the famous Barossa Valley region, there are more than forty wineries. The valley was originally settled by German Lutherans who planted orchards, olive groves and vineyards, and built charming towns and wineries very much in Germanic style. To explore this area, particularly around the time of the Vintage Festival (every odd-numbered year), is to discover a region and lifestyle unique in Australia.

South Australia offers a quality of grandeur and individuality quite different from that of other States.

CLIMATE GUIDE

ADELAIDE

	J	F	M	A	M	J	J	A	S	O	N	D
Maximum °C	29	29	26	22	19	16	15	16	18	21	24	27
Minimum °C	17	17	15	13	10	9	8	8	9	11	13	15
Rainfall mm	20	21	24	44	68	72	67	62	51	44	31	26
Raindays	4	4	5	9	13	15	16	16	13	11	8	6

VICTOR HARBOR REGION

	J	F	M	A	M	J	J	A	S	O	N	D
Maximum °C	24	24	23	21	19	16	15	16	18	20	22	23
Minimum °C	16	16	15	12	10	8	8	8	9	11	12	14
Rainfall mm	22	20	23	43	62	71	74	67	55	46	28	23
Raindays	4	4	6	10	14	15	16	16	14	11	8	6

BAROSSA VALLEY

	J	F	M	A	M	J	J	A	S	O	N	D
Maximum °C	29	29	26	22	17	14	13	14	17	20	24	27
Minimum °C	14	14	12	9	7	5	4	5	6	8	10	12
Rainfall mm	18	19	24	42	61	52	66	63	58	50	28	22
Raindays	5	3	5	9	13	12	16	16	13	11	8	6

WILPENA REGION

	J	F	M	A	M	J	J	A	S	O	N	D
Maximum °C	31	31	27	24	17	14	13	15	20	24	27	29
Minimum °C	16	16	13	9	6	4	3	3	5	9	11	14
Rainfall mm	34	25	20	19	51	57	67	50	33	35	14	25
Raindays	3	3	2	3	8	8	9	7	5	6	4	4

APRIL
Public holiday: Anzac Day. **Laura:** Folk fair.

MAY
Public holiday: Adelaide Cup Day. **Adelaide:** Adelaide Cup racing carnival. **Aldgate:** Autumn Leaves festival. **Burra:** Antique and decorating fair. **Clare:** Gourmet weekend. **Hawker:** Horseracing carnival. **Mannum:** Houseboat hirers' open days. **Naracoorte:** Swap meeting; Young riders equestrian event. **Port Pirie:** Street go-kart grand prix. **Roxby Downs:** Horse races. **Seppeltsfield:** Hot air balloon regatta. **Stansbury:** Sheepdog trials. **Yorke Peninsula: (Kadina/Moonta/Wallaroo):** Kernewek Lowender (Cornish festival, biennial, odd-numbered years).

JUNE
Public holiday: Queen's Birthday. **Barmera:** South Australian country music festival and awards. **Gawler:** Three-day equestrian event.

JULY
Morgan: Fun run, walk cyclathon. **Willunga:** Almond blossom festival. **Woomera:** 4th of July celebrations.

AUGUST
Barossa Valley: Gourmet weekend. **Cleve:** Eyre Peninsula field days (biennial, even-numbered years). **Strathalbyn:** Collectors, hobbies and antique fair. **Yacka:** Sheepdog trials.

SEPTEMBER
Adelaide: Royal Adelaide show; Bay to Birdwood run (vintage car rally; biennial, even-numbered years). **Balaklava:** Agricultural show. **Beltana:** Picnic race meeting and gymkhana. **Ceduna:** Agricultural show. **Hawker:** Art exhibition. **Kimba:** Agricultural show. **Moonta:** Agricultural show. **Paskeville:** Yorke Peninsula field days (biennial, odd-numbered years). **Port Pirie:** Blessing of the fleet. **Robe:** Blessing of the fleet. **Stirling:** Food and Wine Affair.

OCTOBER
Public holiday: Labour Day. **Adelaide:** SA football league finals. **Andamooka:** Opal festival. **Barmera:** Agricultural show. **Barossa Valley:** Music festival. **Bordertown:** Clayton Farm vintage field day. **Ceduna:** Oyster-Fest. **Coober Pedy:** Horse races. **Edithburgh:** State windsurfing speed trials; Gala day. **Hawker:** Henley-on-Arkaba fun day. **Kingscote:** Agricultural show. **Marree:** Outback ball (biennial, even-numbered years). **McLaren Vale:** One Continuous Picnic; Wine bushing festival. **Naracoorte:** Show. **Port Pirie:** Festival of country music. **Strathalbyn:** Glenbarr Scottish festival. **Victor Harbor:** Folk festival. **Yorketown:** Picnic races and gymkhana.

NOVEMBER
Adelaide: Christmas pageant. **Berri:** Art, craft and fine food fair. **Gawler:** Country music festival; Sutch is Light (lighting of Australia's tallest Christmas tree). **Hahndorf:** Blumenfest (festival of flowers). **Kapunda:** Antique and craft fair. **Keith:** Market day. **Mount Gambier:** Blue Lake festival. **Murray Bridge:** Big River Challenge festival.

DECEMBER
Public holidays: Christmas Day; Boxing Day; Proclamation Day. **Adelaide:** Proclamation Day celebrations (at Glenelg). **Barmera:** Christmas pageant and fireworks. **Clare:** Clare Valley summer festival. **Jamestown:** Christmas festival. **Loxton:** Christmas Magic. **Naracoorte:** Street-traders party; Carols by candlelight. **Renmark:** Christmas pageant; Rowing regatta. **Streaky Bay:** Carols by the sea.

ADELAIDE
The Elegant City

The Rotunda in Elder Park with St Peter's Cathedral in the background

NOT TO BE MISSED in Adelaide

- **Adelaide Casino** – enjoy stylish gambling in a restored railway station
- **Adelaide Festival Centre** – hub of the famous Adelaide Festival of Arts
- **Art Gallery of South Australia** – unique collection of Aboriginal artifacts
- **Botanic Gardens** – take a free, guided tour of these beautiful formal gardens
- **Central Market** – fresh produce market in the centre of the city
- **Cleland Wildlife Park** – well-displayed native fauna in a bushland setting
- **Explorer Tram** – efficient and fun way to tour the attractions of the city
- **Glenelg** – take the tram to this historic, seaside resort town
- **Lights Vision lookout** – excellent views of city's broad streets and spacious parks
- **St Peter's Cathedral** – one of Australia's finest cathedrals

SOUTH AUSTRALIA

Adelaide, a gracious, well-planned city, is set on a narrow coastal plain between the rolling hills of the Mount Lofty Ranges and the blue waters of Gulf St Vincent. Surrounded by parkland, Adelaide combines the vitality of a large modern city (population around one million) with an easy-going Australian lifestyle.

Thanks to the excellent planning and foresight of Colonel Light, the first Surveyor-General, Adelaide is laid out on a grid pattern, its wide streets allowing easy access for locals and visitors alike. Adelaide is the only major world city completely surrounded by parklands. These parklands feature children's playgrounds, sports fields, barbecues, and tables and chairs under shady trees. The beautiful, formal **Botanic Gardens** on the north-east side of the city have 16 hectares of Australian and imported plants, and artificial lakes where children can feed ducks and swans; free guided tours are available. While there, do not miss the **Palm House**, an extensive glasshouse brought out from Germany in 1871. In the north-east corner is the **Bicentennial Conservatory,** considered the largest in the southern hemisphere, housing exotic tropical plants from all over the world. Two serpentine viewing paths on upper and lower levels have wheelchair access. At **Rymill Park** on the east side there is a children's boating lake with rowing boats for hire. Near the eastern end of South Terrace are the **Himeji Gardens**, a blend of traditional Japanese lake, mountain and dry gardens. The gate is modelled on that of a temple, and a water bowl is provided for visitors to purify themselves by washing their hands and mouths. At **Veale Gardens** to the south of the city there are fountains, rockeries and formal rose gardens. Flanagan's Riverfront Restaurant is set

Adelaide Arcade, one of the city's historic buildings

in parkland and overlooks the waters of the River Torrens near the weir, north of North Terrace.

Near the tree-lined boulevard of **North Terrace** on the edge of the city centre there are some fine colonial buildings. These include **Holy Trinity Church**, the oldest church in South Australia. The foundation stone was laid by Governor Hindmarsh in 1838, and the clock was made by Vulliamy, clockmaker to the English King William IV. Near this western end of North Terrace is the **Adelaide Gaol**, last used in 1988, and now open for inspection each Sunday. Also on North Terrace are the grand **Newmarket Hotel**, built 1884, and the **Lion Arts Centre**, home to the Mercury Cinema and the Jam Factory Craft and Design Centre.

The historic Adelaide Railway Station building, also in North Terrace, has been magnificently restored and now houses the elegant **Adelaide Casino**. The casino is part of the Adelaide Plaza, which includes the **Adelaide Convention Centre** and **Exhibition Hall**, and the luxurious **Hyatt Regency Adelaide Hotel**.

On the corner of King William Road is the present **Parliament House**. Nearby is **Government House**, the oldest building in Adelaide.

The **State Library**, on the corner of Kintore Avenue, holds many major collections. In the Mortlock Wing, volumes on South Australia share space with Donald Bradman's trophies in a beautifully restored Victorian building. Behind the Library is the **Migration Museum**, the first museum to tell the stories of Australia's migrants. Close by, in the former armoury, is the **Police Museum**. Back on North Terrace, the **South Australian Museum** and the **Art Gallery of South Australia** rub shoulders. The museum holds the world's largest collection of Aboriginal artifacts and features this in a range of exhibits. The collections of the Art Gallery give one of the best overviews of Australian art available. It also houses important collections of sculptures, paintings and decorative arts from around the world.

The **University of Adelaide** is also on North Terrace. Walk through the attractively landscaped grounds to see the blend of classic and contemporary architecture, and the **Museum of Classical Archaeology** where you can view some 500 objects, many dating back to the third millennium BC. **Elder Hall**, with its spectacular pipe organ, is a fine concert venue.

Ayers House, headquarters for the National Trust of South Australia, is at the eastern end of North Terrace. Sir Henry Ayers bought the property in 1855 and it became one of the major venues for social functions during Ayers' seven terms as Premier of the State. A charming nineteenth-century residence with slate roof and shuttered bay windows, Ayers House today has an elegant formal restaurant as well as an informal bistro which extends into a courtyard, enabling visitors to enjoy the historic surroundings while dining. The National Aboriginal Cultural Institute **Tandanya** is on the corner of Grenfell Street and East Terrace.

Back in the heart of the city on King William Street is **Edmund Wright House,** another important reminder of Adelaide's heritage. Built in 1878, the building with its elaborate Renaissance facade is used for civil weddings. Other historic buildings in the city include the **Adelaide Town Hall** in King William Street, with its formal portico entrance and graceful tower, the **General Post Office** and the **Treasury Buildings** on the corner of Victoria Square.

In North Adelaide there are many fine old colonial buildings, from delightful stone cottages to stately homes and grand old hotels with lacework balconies and verandahs. **St Peter's Cathedral** in King William Road is one of Australia's finest cathedrals and is a fitting backdrop to the beautiful **Pennington Gardens**. There is an excellent view from **Light's Vision** on Montefiore Hill. A bronze statue of Colonel Light overlooks the city with its broad streets and spacious parks.

The **River Torrens** flows through many of Adelaide's parks. The banks are landscaped, lined with gums and willows, and perfect for a lazy picnic lunch. Walking and cycling trails wind through some of the city's scenic parklands and along the riverbanks. A delightful way of travelling to the **Adelaide Zoological Gardens** is provided by a fleet of *Popeye* motor launches which cruise the river. The zoo has a large collection of animals and reptiles, and is noted for its variety of Australian birdlife. There is a walk-through aviary sheltering many species of unusual land and water birds, and a nocturnal house designed to display those animals and birds that are most active at night. The zoo is located in a beautiful setting featuring magnificent trees (including exotic species), rock beds and rose gardens.

Also situated on the curving banks of the Torrens is the world-renowned **Adelaide Festival Centre**, hub of the

ACCOMMODATION

HOTELS

Adelaide Hilton
233 Victoria Sq., Adelaide
(08) 8217 2000

Country Comfort Inn
226 South Tce, Adelaide
(08) 8223 4355

Hindley Parkroyal
65 Hindley St, Adelaide
(08) 8231 5552, (1800) 82 2633

Hyatt Regency Adelaide
North Tce, Adelaide
(08) 8231 1234

Terrace Intercontinental Adelaide
150 North Tce, Adelaide
(08) 8461 1111

FAMILY AND BUDGET

Adelaide Paringa Motel
15 Hindley St, Adelaide
(08) 8231 1000, (1800) 08 2202

Austral Hotel
205 Rundle St, Adelaide
(08) 8223 4660

YMCA
76 Flinders St, Adelaide
(08) 8223 1611

MOTEL GROUPS: BOOKINGS

Best Western 131779
Flag 13 2400
Travelodge 1800 22 2446

This list is for information only; inclusion is not necessarily a recommendation.

The famous Glenelg tram

SOUTH AUSTRALIA

biennial Adelaide Festival of Arts, held every even-numbered year. This streamlined, modern building contains a 2000-seat lyric theatre, drama and experimental theatres, and an imposing amphitheatre which is ideal for outdoor entertainment. The building has been acclaimed as one of the finest performing venues in the world. The Southern Plaza incorporates a spectacular environmental sculpture by German artist O. H. Hajek. There are also some fine contemporary tapestries and paintings hung inside the building. Group tours can be arranged, and restaurant and bar facilities are available. The Festival Centre has walkways linking it to King William Road, Parliament House, Adelaide Railway Station, the Casino and the Hyatt Regency hotel. Nearby is an attractive old band rotunda located in **Elder Park**.

Adelaide has a bustling shopping complex centred around **Rundle Mall**. With over 820 shops, Rundle Mall is the largest pedestrian shopping mall in the southern hemisphere. The paved area has trees and a fountain, modern sculpture, fruit and flower stalls, and seats where you can sit and watch the passing parade. Buskers and outdoor cafes add to the cosmopolitan atmosphere. In the surrounding arcades and streets are shops ranging from major department stores to tiny specialist boutiques. **King William Street** is lined with impressive bank and insurance buildings, while **Hindley Street** has clusters of restaurants, cafes, continental food shops, nightclubs and Aussie pubs. A bonus for shoppers is the free Bee-line bus service which operates in the inner-city area.

Make a trip to **Melbourne Street** in North Adelaide for some of the city's most exclusive shops; **Unley Road** for exclusive boutiques; **Magill Road** for antiques and second-hand treasures; the **Parade** at Norwood for all of the above plus great delis, coffee shops, home design stores and bookshops. **King William Road** at Hyde Park has several stylish specialty shops and boutiques. Some shops in **Glen Osmond Road** at Eastwood offer a wide variety of top-label fashions at reduced prices.

A fascinating shopping experience is a visit to the **Central Market** behind the Hilton hotel, with its stalls stacked high with fresh produce (open Tuesday, and Thursday to Saturday; tours available). Nearby arcades sell clothing, wine and spirits; this area is also home to Adelaide's **Chinatown** with its many food stalls, restaurants and colourful shopping complex. The east end of the city around **Rundle Street** has experienced a rebirth, with busy coffee houses, pubs, restaurants and a host of absorbing craft shops and boutiques. The **East End Markets** have become Rundle Street's focus on Friday, Saturday and Sunday, selling everything from fresh fish, meat and vegetables to clothing and jewellery.

In Norwood the **Orange Lane Market** (open Saturday and Sunday) features second-hand goods, home-made produce, local crafts and stalls. The **Brickworks Market and Leisure Complex** at Thebarton (open Friday to Sunday) sells produce and bric-a-brac, and is part of a 6-hectare complex featuring an amusement park. Other popular markets featuring fresh produce and a variety of other goods are the **Junction Markets** on Prospect Road, Kilburn (open Saturday and Sunday), and the **Reynella Markets** at 255 Old South Road, Reynella (open Friday to Sunday). At Port Adelaide the **Fisherman's Wharf**, located at the end of Commercial Road, sells produce and quality bric-a-brac; and at the **North Arm Fish Market**, on Moorhouse Road, fresh fish can be bought direct from the boats; both are open Sundays. Some of these markets are also open on public holidays and during school holidays; check opening times with the South Australian Travel Centre, (08) 8212 1505.

Adelaide is renowned for its restaurants. The city is credited with being the birthplace of modern Australian cuisine. Some of the best restaurants are tiny and crowded, with fast service and super-cheap prices. Others are set in historic buildings, serving international-class cuisine in gracious surroundings. **Hindley Street** offers a wide range of cosmopolitan eating. **Gouger Street**, near the Central Market, is known as $10 street – if you can't get a good meal for less than $10, you're in the wrong street – it is particularly noted for its good seafood cafes, and South Australian seafood is definitely worth sampling. **O'Connell Street** has an array of friendly cafes.

Adelaide also has some fine old pubs. Some are friendly 'locals', others incorporate restaurants, wine bars and dance floors. The **Old Lion Hotel** in North Adelaide is a handsome 1880s bluestone building with a first-class restaurant, a sheltered courtyard and popular disco. It is typical of the boutique-style hotel where beer is brewed on the premises; there are a number of these hotels within the inner-city area.

Take a leisurely tour around the city's attractions in a replica of a road-registered tram. The tram has on-board commentary. Board or alight the **Explorer Tram** as many times as you wish at any of the stopping points; the tram returns to any given point approximately every 2½ hours.

The longest guided busway system in the world, **Trans Adelaide's O-Bahn**, runs north-east from the city centre. It travels beside the River Torrens in its own landscaped park from Adelaide to a major shopping centre at **Tea Tree Plaza**, and there are stations at **Klemzig** and **Paradise**. Walking paths and cycling tracks follow the busway track to Tea Tree Plaza, and offer views over reservoirs, foothills and the city.

Not to be missed in Adelaide are the marvellous beaches, stretching right along the coastline with wide sandy shores and clear blue waters. Most are only a short drive from the city centre. **Glenelg**, the best known, can be reached by taking the famous 1929

Glenelg tram from Victoria Square to the foreshore in Glenelg. Spoil yourself by dining at the **Ramada Grand Hotel**, or stroll down Jetty Road to the shopping centre. The **Magic Mountain Waterslide and Amusement Centre** provides entertainment. Restaurants abound, and Greek food here is a specialty. Grand old homes and guest houses along the foreshore are a reminder of Glenelg's days as a seaside resort for the wealthy. The first settlers came ashore here in 1836 and proclaimed the colony of South Australia under a gum tree. The **Old Gum Tree** remains, with a commemorative plaque. **HMS *Buffalo*** played a significant part in South Australia's early settlement and the replica of the vessel at Glenelg is, appropriately, a setting for a maritime museum and restaurant.

Other beaches include **Brighton**, **West Beach**, **Henley**, **Grange** and **Semaphore**. Many beaches have sailboards and catamarans for hire, while the jetties are used for promenading, swimming and fishing. **Fort Glanville** at Semaphore is the oldest fortress in South Australia. The **Semaphore to Fort Glanville Tourist Railway** runs south along the seafront for more than 2 kilometres, from the Semaphore Jetty to Fort Glanville and the nearby caravan park; it operates daily during school holidays, and on all public holidays and Sundays during the summer months. Further south, near Hallett Cove, is the **Hallett Cove Conservation Park**, established to preserve the remnants of glacial features that probably occurred 270 million years ago.

Adelaide's suburbs have much to offer the visitor. A short drive west towards the suburb of **Grange** is **Sturt's Cottage** built in 1840, and home of Captain Charles Sturt, the famous pioneer and explorer. Managed by the Charles Sturt Memorial Museum Trust, the cottage with its period furniture and many of Sturt's belongings recalls the early days of South Australia.

In **Wayville**, just south-west of the city, the **Investigator Science and Technology Centre** with its hands-on 'gizmos' provides fun for the family; it is located in the International Pavilion, Wayville Showgrounds (enter from Rose Terrace). Also at the showgrounds in early September, the **Royal Adelaide Show** brings the country to the city.

Port Adelaide has several imposing buildings, a reminder of the port's heyday in the 1880s. Noteworthy are the police station and court house, town hall, shipping and transport building, and Ferguson's bond store. Visitors to the **Port Dock Station Railway Museum** can ride miniature steam trains. The **Lipson Street Museum** has a large collection of locomotives, rolling stock, platform displays, a theatrette and an operating HO-gauge model railway. Also located in Lipson Street is the **South Australian Maritime Museum**, complete with lighthouses and ships. A few blocks away is the **South Australian Historical Aviation Museum** in Mundy Street. There are a variety of cruises and fishing trips available from Port Adelaide.

At **St Kilda**, further north, is the **Australian Electric Transport Museum** where you can take trips on restored trams. A guided walk along the 1.7 km boardwalk of the **St Kilda Mangrove Trail** is an experience not to be missed.

Near the suburb of **Rostrevor**, east of the city, the **Morialta Conservation Park** has a ruggedly beautiful gorge and many walking tracks. **Brownhill Creek Recreation Park** with its giant pine and gum trees in a quiet valley setting is ideal for barbecues and picnics. **Belair National Park** has picnic grounds, bushland, a children's playground and the former summer residence of the Governor. The renowned **Cleland Wildlife Park** displays kangaroos, koalas, wombats and other native fauna in their natural surroundings.

Cowell Jade, at **Unley**, sells jewellery and carvings made from local jade. The **South Australian Society of Model and Experimental Engineers** headquarters, in the nearby suburb of **Millswood**, has field days (open to visitors) twice a month. For magnificent views of Adelaide, take a trip to **Windy Point Lookout** or to the summit of **Mount Lofty**. At night, the lights of the city are particularly impressive.

For the sports enthusiast, Adelaide offers horseracing at **Victoria Park**, **Morphettville** and **Cheltenham**; greyhound-racing at **Angle Park**; tennis, squash, swimming and golf. Pools, water-slides, fountains, river rapids, waterfalls, and gym, spa and sauna facilities are a feature of the **Adelaide Aquatic Centre** in North Adelaide. The **City Golf Links** in North Adelaide command splendid views of the city. **Adelaide Oval**, on King William Road, is a venue for interstate and international cricket matches, while the **Memorial Drive Tennis Courts** have played host to international players since 1929. Memorial Drive is also used for outdoor concerts and performances by visiting entertainers. The **Ice Arena** in Thebarton has skating and the world's first indoor artificial ski slope. For kart racing enthusiasts, **KartMania** has safe, supervised race tracks at Richmond and Gepps Cross.

As well as the diversions the city itself offers, Adelaide is an excellent base for tours of the surrounding hills and nearby wine regions.

For further information on Adelaide, contact the South Australian Travel Centre, 1 King William St, Adelaide; (08) 8212 1505, Freecall 1800 882 092, fax (08) 8303 2231.

ADELAIDE ON FOOT

There are a variety of walking tours around Adelaide and its suburbs.

- **Art in public places:** Self-guide walk highlighting indoor and outdoor works of art.
- **Botanic Gardens: 1.** Guided walk; free of charge. **2.** Self-guide walk concentrating on water features within gardens.
- **Marion: 1.** Self-guide village walk. **2.** Self-guide Sturt Creek Linear Park Walk.
- **North Adelaide:** Self-guide heritage walk.
- **Port Adelaide:** Self-guide heritage walk.
- **St Kilda:** Various guided walks through mangrove area near town; bookings essential; charge applies.

Pamphlets are available for the self-guide walks. For further information, contact the South Australian Travel Centre, 1 King William St, Adelaide; (08) 8212 1505.

TOURS from Adelaide

Vineyards at Seppeltsfield, in the Barossa Valley

One of Adelaide's greatest assets is its proximity to a number of fascinating regions. Vineyards and wineries, rolling hills and quaint villages, seaside resorts and beautiful wildlife reserves are all within an easy drive of South Australia's capital.

Barossa Valley

50 km from Adelaide via the Sturt Highway

A must for visitors to Adelaide is the Barossa, Australia's premier wine-producing region. Located north-east of Adelaide, the Barossa boasts more than forty wineries and a multitude of historic buildings, galleries, cafes and restaurants. Visit Gawler, Lyndoch, Tanunda, Nuriootpa and Angaston, detouring at will to smaller villages and visiting the tasting facilities at the wineries; make sure the driver is happy to forgo this pleasure! Alternatively, extend your visit and stay overnight at the many and varied accommodation outlets in the area. The major festival in the region is the Barossa Valley Vintage Festival which starts on Easter Monday each odd-numbered year. In August the Barossa Classic Gourmet Weekend offers visitors the opportunity to sample and enjoy fine wines and gourmet food. The award-winning Barossa Music Festival is held in October. **See also:** Festival Fun; Vineyards and Wineries; and individual town entries in A–Z listing.

Clare Valley

135 km from Adelaide via the Sturt Highway and Highway 32 (Highway 83 optional north of Tarlee)

The Clare Valley produces superb wines and the region is known internationally for its riesling. Driving north through Kapunda, Australia's first mining town, you will pass some of the State's richest pastoral country, noted for its stud sheep. The wine towns begin at Auburn and continue to Watervale, Sevenhill and Clare. The area is noted for its prize-winning table wines. Sevenhill Cellars winery was started by two Jesuit priests in 1851 and still operates today. Slightly further afield, there are several fine colonial buildings, such as the magnificent Martindale Hall at Mintaro (open daily except Christmas Day and Good Friday), which was used in the film *Picnic at Hanging Rock*. The area also has many charming parks and picturesque picnic spots. **See also:** Vineyards and Wineries; and individual town entries in A–Z listing.

McLaren region

42 km from Adelaide via the South Road

Another trip for wine-lovers is to the vineyards of the McLaren region. There are more than 50 wineries in the area, often in picturesque bush settings. Most are well signposted and have wine tastings and cellar-door sales. Hardy's Reynella, Chapel Hill, Seaview and Wirra Wirra are some of the names to recognise. Your return trip could include a visit to the nearby beaches of Moana, Port Noarlunga and Christies. **See also:** Vineyards and Wineries; The Fleurieu Peninsula; and individual town entries in A–Z listing.

Adelaide Hills and Hahndorf

28 km from Adelaide via the South Eastern Freeway

See: The Adelaide Hills.

Fleurieu Peninsula

112 km from Adelaide to its furthest point via the South Road

See: The Fleurieu Peninsula. On the return trip do not miss historic Strathalbyn first settled in 1839, on the banks of the River Angas. Milang, 20 km to the south-east, is on the shores of Lake Alexandrina. Take your camera – the birdlife is fascinating. **See also:** individual town entries in A–Z listing.

National Motor Museum

Birdwood, 43 km from Adelaide via the North-East Road

The National Motor Museum (open daily) houses the most important motor vehicle collection in Australia. Veteran vintage and classic cars, and motorcycles number over 300 and the grounds are a perfect venue for a picnic. At Gumeracha, west of Birdwood, is the Toy Factory, where you can climb the largest wooden rocking horse in the world. Drive back to Adelaide through Mount Torrens to the small town of Lobethal, which was founded in the 1840s. The Archives and Historical Museum houses a remarkable exhibit: the old Lobethal College, complete with shingled roof, which was built in 1845; open Sunday afternoons. Fairyland Village at Lobethal has fourteen chalets, each depicting a fairytale or a nursery rhyme; open daily. There is a scenic route through Basket Range and Norton Summit back to Adelaide.

The Adelaide Hills are scenically delightful, particularly in spring and autumn

The Adelaide Hills

The Adelaide Hills, only half an hour's drive from the city, are a scenic blend of gently rolling mountains, market gardens, vineyards and orchards with historic towns and farm buildings nestled in valleys. Cleland Wildlife Park in the **Cleland Conservation Park** on the slopes of Mount Lofty displays native birds and animals in a bush setting. The Gorge Wildlife Park at Cudlee Creek houses a large, privately-owned wildlife collection.

Just off the main highway are the townships of Stirling, with its beautiful trees and historic homes; Aldgate, nestled in a picturesque valley; and Bridgewater with its historic water wheel (1860), now part of the restored mill that houses the winemaking and maturation plant for Petaluma's premium sparkling wines. The lookout at the summit of Mount Lofty (726 m) offers spectacular views of Adelaide. Festivals in this section of the hills include the Autumn Leaves festival held in May at Aldgate and at Stirling, the Food and Wine Affair held in September.

Hahndorf is probably the best known town in the area. Settled by Silesian and Prussian refugees in 1839, its main street is lined with magnificent old elms and chestnut trees. Most of the buildings have been restored and the town has a leisurely, old-world feel about it. The Hahndorf Academy and Art Gallery has a permanent exhibition of paintings by Sir Hans Heysen, who lived in the town for many years and depicted the area's beauty so well. A local German heritage museum is upstairs from the art gallery. The bakeries here sell delicious *apfelstrudel*, cheesecake and Black Forest cake, and small shops offer interesting local handicrafts and home-made preserves. Other attractions include a model train village, a clock museum and a strawberry farm. The heritage of the town is celebrated with several festivals: Schutzenfest, held in Bonython Park, Adelaide each January; and in Hahndorf, Founders Day, also in January; and Blumenfest, the festival of flowers held in November. Two of South Australia's oldest townships, Nairne and Mount Barker, lie to the east and south-east of Hahndorf. Mount Barker showgrounds is the venue each March for Power of the Past (vintage cars, engines and motorcycles).

In the town of Oakbank the Easter racing carnival, Australia's biggest picnic race meeting, is held with great fanfare every Easter. North of Oakbank, the township of Forest Range is surrounded by apple orchards. There is an interesting archive and historical museum at nearby Lobethal. At Woodside, Melba's Chocolate Factory and Heritage Park is a popular attraction. From Hahndorf, the back road passes through winding hills and farmland to the old goldmining town of Echunga. The Warrawong Sanctuary at Mylor is a leader in the preservation of rare and endangered animals and is open to the public. At **Belair National Park** there are walks, a wildlife park, Old Government House and a native plant nursery.

For more information, contact the Adelaide Hills Tourist Information Centre, 41 Main St, Hahndorf; (08) 8388 1185. **See also:** Vineyards and Wineries; Festival Fun; and National Parks for those parks indicated by bold type. **Map reference:** 288 D10

Festival Fun

Because good food and wine go hand in hand with festivities, it seems appropriate that South Australia is both the nation's wine capital and home to some of Australia's major festivals. During the year, a wide variety of festivals is held throughout South Australia, ranging from the cultural extravaganza of the Adelaide Festival to carnivals in several country towns.

Each even-numbered year in March, Adelaide becomes the cultural centre of Australia as it hosts the **Adelaide Festival of Arts.** During this time the city is like a giant magnet, drawing throngs of people from interstate and overseas. Hotels are often booked months ahead; restaurants, taxi services and retailers do a roaring trade.

Since it started in 1960, the Adelaide Festival has grown from a modest 51 performances to over 300, with as many as 30 competing for attention in one day. The Festival includes concerts, carnivals and street-theatre. The cosmopolitan atmosphere and the world-renowned guest artists have made this festival an outstanding international event.

The **Fringe Festival** runs parallel to the Adelaide Festival. What started as a rejected performers' way of being on show during the Festival is now an integral part of its colour and excitement, and attracts large numbers in its own right. The Fringe offers a treasure trove of cheaper (often free) performances, some experimental, as well as well-known acts.

Performing at the Adelaide Festival of Arts

Although performances in theatre, dance, musical recitals, opera and ballet are emphasised, neither the Festival nor the Fringe are confined solely to the performing arts. There are exhibitions, lectures, a writers' week, an artists' week celebrating the visual arts, poetry readings and outdoor activities to coincide with this three-week-long cultural feast.

The focal point of the festival is the Adelaide Festival Centre, which stands on 1.5 hectares on the banks of the River Torrens, just 2 minutes' walk from the commercial heart of the city. The Festival Centre is also the permanent home of the South Australia Theatre Company, which presents at least 10 major productions annually.

When the Festival is not on, Adelaide visitors and residents still use the parks and gardens surrounding the centre, and the two restaurants and terrace-style cafe, which are open 6 days a week, are very popular.

Each odd-numbered year in March, the Festival Centre organises a youth arts festival, **Come Out,** which focuses its attention on the arts for children and young people.

Also each odd-numbered year the popular music festival **Womadelaide** is held in the Botanic Gardens during the last weekend in February.

The **Barossa Valley Vintage Festival,** in Australia's premier wine-producing district just one hour's drive from Adelaide, is also held in odd-numbered years. The mellow autumn weather and picturesque towns of the Barossa Valley draw large crowds to this event, which is traditionally a thanksgiving celebration for a successful harvest. The seven-day festival, which starts on Easter Monday, is strictly *gemütlichkeit* — happy and friendly. There is music and dancing, good food, wine-tasting, a vintage fair, float processions and traditional dinners like the *weingarten* — a big feast featuring German folk songs. The grand finale

The Barossa Classic Gourmet Weekend combines the pleasures of wine, food and music

takes the form of a spectacular fair held at the oval in Tanunda Park, where dancers in colourful national costumes dance around an 18-metre-high maypole, while food and wine are served in the marquees surrounding the oval. The **Barossa Classic Gourmet Weekend** in August combines the pleasures of wine, food and good music over two days. Another major festival in the region is the award-winning **Barossa Music Festival**, held in October.

During the long weekend in May the Clare Valley wineries host the **Gourmet Weekend**, which includes tastings and a progressive Sunday luncheon around the wineries.

McLaren Vale is the venue for **One Continuous Picnic**, held on the October long weekend; wineries and restaurants provide opportunities to sample the vintages of the McLaren region. The **McLaren Vale Wine Bushing Festival** follows at the end of October, a time of fun and festivity with craft exhibitions, parades, picnics and formal balls to celebrate the new vintage.

South Australia is a State of many cultures, which accounts for the many ethnic festivals held every year. The largest of these is **Schutzenfest**, held in Adelaide. Traditionally a shooting festival to raise funds for various charities, it has grown into the biggest German-style beer festival held outside Germany. Bonython Park is transformed into a bustling carnival with 'oompah' music, imported German beer, German folk dancers in national costume and restaurants serving platters of *sauerbraten* and *apfelstrudel*. The hot, thirsty month of January is ideal for drinking steins of ice-cold beer while listening to brass bands and waiting for a variety of *würst* to be served at your table.

In March, the Greek community organises the **Glendi Festival** to coincide with the Greek National Day. In May, every odd-numbered year, the colourful **Kernewek Lowender** (Cornish family festival) is held, centred around Kadina, Moonta and Wallaroo on the scenic Yorke Peninsula. Quaint old miners' cottages, abandoned mining installations and many museums remind visitors of the heyday of copper mining. There is music, Cornish dancing, a pasty-making competition and a wheelbarrow race.

For two weeks in June, Barmera is the country music capital of the State, when visitors from all over Australia attend the **Country Music Festival**.

Other South Australian festivals include the **Tunarama Festival** at the fishing port and resort of Port Lincoln, held every Australia Day holiday in January. Australia's only festival dedicated to a fish, it features competitions, displays, a street procession, sports, a fireworks spectacular and the famous tuna-tossing event; there is fun for the whole family in a gala atmosphere on the beautiful Tasman Terrace foreshore. In April the people of Laura, a small town in the lower Flinders Ranges, organise a **Folk Fair** that attracts thousands of visitors.

Each Easter Monday, the Great Eastern Steeplechase, part of the **Oakbank Easter Racing Carnival** is raced at Oakbank racecourse. This carnival is billed as the largest picnic meeting in the southern hemisphere and leads up to the running of the famous **Adelaide Cup** in May at Morphettville racecourse.

One special event for children and adults is the November **Christmas Pageant** in the city streets of Adelaide. Floats depicting well known nursery rhymes and fairytale characters thrill all those who line the streets to welcome Father Christmas to South Australia.

Information on festivals can be obtained from the South Australian Travel Centre, 1 King William St, Adelaide; (08) 8212 1505. **See also:** individual town entries in A–Z listing.

Music is an inherent part of the seven day Barossa Valley Vintage Festival

SOUTH AUSTRALIA from A to Z

A scenic drive near Beachport, south-east of Adelaide

Aldinga Pop. 3541

MAP REF. 288 A13, 289 F4, 290 B6, 293 B3, 295 K10

A small town 45 km S of Adelaide, near the Fleurieu Peninsula. **Of interest:** St Ann's Anglican Church (1866). Uniting Church (1863). **In the area:** At Aldinga Beach, 4 km SW: good swimming, surfing, diving and fishing; Gnome Caves, children's attraction; Historic Bike Race and Multicultural Festival, both held in Feb. Bush trails through Aldinga Scrub Conservation Park; leaflets available. Offshore, Aldinga Aquatic Reserve: rare reef formation and good diving. Lookout, views of Gulf St Vincent; 10 km SW. Lookout, views of Myponga Reservoir; 20 km SW. At Port Willunga Beach, 3 km NW, ruins of *Star of Greece* (1888) visible at low tide. Maslin Beach, Australia's first nude bathing beach; 6 km N. McLaren Vale, centre of wine-growing region with over 50 wineries; 12 km NE. Begonia Farm, 25 km S; open Oct.–Apr. **Tourist information:** Aldinga Bay Holiday Village, Esplanade, Aldinga Beach; (085) 56 5019. **Accommodation:** 3 B&B, 1 cara./camp. park. **See also:** The Fleurieu Peninsula; Vineyards and Wineries.

Andamooka Pop. 471

MAP REF. 296 G4

Andamooka is surrounded by opal fields and is located about 600 km N of Adelaide, to the west of the salt pan Lake Torrens. The road to Andamooka from the turnoff at Roxby Downs is now sealed. The town is off the beaten track, conditions are harsh in summer, the weather is severe and water is precious. Many people live in dugouts to protect themselves from the extreme heat. Visitors need to obtain a precious-stone prospecting permit from the Mines Department in Adelaide before staking out a claim and trying their luck. Looking for opals on mullock dumps left by miners requires permission from the owners of the claim. There are tours of the area, including underground mine tours and showrooms with opals for sale. **Of interest:** Duke's Bottle Home, made entirely of empty beer bottles. In Main St: Andamooka Press, working printing museum in underground house, open daily; Andamooka Gems and Trains, mineral specimens and model railway; and quaint 1930s miners' cottages, next to creek bed. Art and craft market, 1st Sun. each month. Easter: Family fun day and White Dam walk. Oct.: Opal festival. **In the area:** Roxby Downs, 30 km W, service town for nearby Olympic Dam where copper, gold, silver and uranium are mined; tours of mining operations available. At Woomera, 120 km SW, Heritage Centre and Missile Park with displays of rockets and aircraft. **Tourist information:** Opal Creek Showroom, Main St; (086) 72 7193. **Accommodation:** 1 hotel, 1 motel, 1 B&B, 2 cara. parks.

Angaston Pop. 1819

MAP REF. 288 G4, 292 I5, 295 M8

Angaston is in the highest part of the Barossa Valley; within 79 km of the coast, it is 361 m above sea level. The town is named after prominent 1830s Barossa Valley settler, George Fife Angas. **Of interest:** Angas Park Fruit Co., Murray St, produces dried fruit and nuts; open daily. For local art and craft: Angaston Galleria, Murray St, and Bethany Arts and Crafts, Washington St. A Clothes Revival, clothes of yesteryear and collectables; Murray St. **In the area:** Saltram Wine Estates, 2 km W. Magnificent view of Barossa Valley from Mengler's Hill Lookout, 8 km SW. Yalumba Winery, 2 km S. Collingrove Homestead (1850), 7 km SE, National Trust property once owned by Angas pioneering family; viewing and accommodation available (meals only by prior arrangement). Henschke's Wines, 10 km SE. Mountadam Winery at Eden Valley, 19 km SE. At Springton, 27 km SE: Springton Gallery, Grand Cru Estate, Robert Hamilton & Son Winery, Herbig Tree, Herbig Homestead Heritage Centre (open by appt) and Merindah Mohair Farm (open daily). Yookamurra Sanctuary, 54 km NE, local wildlife and plant species; guided walks and tours (check opening times); accommodation available, bookings essential. **Tourist information:** Angaston Galleria, 18 Murray St; (085) 64 2648. **Accommodation:** 2 hotels, 1 motel, 7 B&B. **See also:** Vineyards and Wineries.

Ardrossan Pop. 1008

MAP REF. 295 J7

Ardrossan, 148 km NW of Adelaide, is the largest port on the east coast of Yorke

Peninsula. An important outlet for wheat, barley and dolomite, it is an attractive town with excellent crabbing and fishing from the jetty. **Of interest**: Ardrossan and District Historical Museum, Fifth St. The stump jump plough was invented here in the late 1800s; restored plough on display on cliffs at end of First St in East Tce. Jan.: Ardrossan Alive, outdoor music festival (odd-numbered years). **In the area**: Salt and dolomite mines. BHP Lookout, 2 km S. For keen divers, *Zanoni* wreck off coast, 20 km SE; permission required to dive. Clinton Conservation Park, 40 km N. **Tourist information**: Ardrossan Caravan Park, Park Tce; (08) 8837 3262. **Accommodation**: 2 hotel/motels, 2 cara./camp. parks.

Arkaroola Pop. 10

MAP REF. 291 G3, 297 M3

Arkaroola is a remote village settlement, founded in 1968, in the northern Flinders Ranges, about 660 km N of Adelaide. This privately-owned property of 61 000 ha has been opened as the Arkaroola-Mt Painter Sanctuary, a flora and fauna sanctuary. The area's rugged outback country is crossed by incredible quartzite ridges, deep gorges and rich mineral deposits, and is a haven for birdlife and rare marsupials. **Of interest**: Astronomical Observatory (check viewing times). Mineral and Fossil Museum. Outdoor Pastoral and Mining Museum. Pioneer cottage. **In the area**: At nearby Gammon Ranges National Park: extensive wilderness areas; ruins of Cornish-style smelters (1861) and scenic waterholes at Bolla Bollana, 12 km NW; Weetootla Gorge, permanent springs, 31 km SW. Italowie Gap, 42 km SW; 4WD vehicles required; recommended for experienced bushwalkers only. Nooldoonooldoona Water Hole, 12 km NW. Famous Mt Painter, 10 km N; further 20 km N, breathtaking views from Freeling Heights, overlooking Yudnamutana Gorge. Siller's Lookout over Lake Frome (a salt lake), 16 km N. Big Moro Gorge (with rock pools), 59 km S; may require 4WD. Chambers Gorge (with Aboriginal rock carvings), 98 km S. Marked walking trails; self-guide pamphlets from Tourist information. Ridgetop Tour, spectacular 4WD trip across Australia's most rugged mountains. Scenic flights and guided tours available. **Tourist information**: Visitors Information Centre; (086) 48 4848. **Accommodation**: 3 motels, 1 hostel, 1 cara./camp. park. **See also**: The Flinders Ranges; National Parks.

Balaklava Pop. 1439

MAP REF. 295 K6

Balaklava, in a picturesque setting on the banks of the River Wakefield, 91 km N of Adelaide, was named after a famous battle in the Crimean War. **Of interest**: National Trust Museum, May Tce, has relics of district's early days of European settlement; check opening times. Country Crafters for local craft, 30 George St. Court House Gallery and Shop, community art gallery; Edith Tce. Urlwin Park Agricultural Museum, Short Tce. Lions Club Walking Trail along Wakefield River and through town; brochure available at Country Crafters (see Tourist information). Sept.: Agricultural show. **In the area**: Devils Gardens, 7 km NE on Auburn Rd, and The Rocks Reserve, 10 km E; both with picnic facilities. Beachside town of Port Wakefield, 26 km W at head of Gulf St Vincent. **Tourist information**: Country Crafters, 30 George St; (08) 862 2070. **Accommodation**: 2 hotels, 1 cara./camp. park.

Barmera Pop. 1859

MAP REF. 295 P7

The sloping shores of Lake Bonney make a delightful setting for the Riverland town of Barmera, 214 km NE of Adelaide. Lake Bonney is ideal for swimming, water-skiing, sailing, boating and fishing. The surrounding irrigated land is given over mainly to vineyards, but there are also apricot and peach orchards, and citrus groves. Soldier settlement after World War I marked the beginning of today's community-oriented town. **Of interest**: Donald Campbell Obelisk, Queen Elizabeth Dr, commemorates Campbell's attempt on world water-speed record in 1964. Rocky's Country Hall of Fame, Barwell Ave. Bonneyview Wines, Sturt Hwy, has gallery, restaurant and picnic facilities; open daily. Easter: Lake Bonney yachting regatta. June: South Australian country music festival and awards. Oct.: Agricultural show. Dec.: Christmas pageant and fireworks. **In the area**: At North Lake, 10 km NW, ruins of Napper's Old Accommodation House (1850) preserved by National Trust. Loch Luna Game Reserve, 16 km NW; wetlands cruise available by appt, contact Barmera Travel Centre (see Tourist information). At Overland Corner, 19 km NW on Morgan Rd: hotel (1859), now also National Trust museum; and self-guide historical walking trail. Near Monash, 8 km NE, Wein Valley Estate Winery. Highway Fern Haven, 5 km E on Sturt Hwy, rare ferns in tropical setting; open daily. At Cobdogla, 5 km W: Irrigation Museum with the only working Humphrey Pump in the world, photos and memorabilia of Loveday Internment Camp (brochure available for self-guide drive to remains of camp site, 3 km SW), as well as steam rides, historic displays and picnic areas (check opening times); Cobdogla Coloured Wool, spinning demonstrations, lamb-feeding and coloured fleeces; Chambers Creek for canoeing and prolific birdlife; Art and craft fair at Easter. Moorook Game Reserve, 16 km SW, includes Wachtels Lagoon with birdlife and walking trail. Nearby, Yatco Lagoon abounds with a variety of birdlife. **Tourist information**: Barmera Travel Centre, Barwell Ave; (085) 88 2289. **Accommodation**: 2 motels, 1 hotel/motel, 1 B&B, 3 cara./camp. parks.

Beachport Pop. 443

MAP REF. 293 F10

First settled as a whaling station in the 1830s, Beachport is a quiet little town 51 km S of Robe. Rivoli Bay nearby provides safe swimming beaches as well as shelter for lobster boats. One of the State's longest jetties stretches out into the waters of Rivoli Bay and is very popular with anglers. **Of interest**: Old Wool and Grain Store, now National Trust Museum with whaling, shipping and local history exhibits; Railway Tce. At Artifacts Museum, McCourt St, Aboriginal heritage. Centenary Park in town centre has barbecues, tennis, playgrounds and skateboard track. Heritage walk, maps available from National Trust Museum; other walking trails, maps available from District Council. **In the area**: Lake George, 4 km N: waterbirds, windsurfing and fishing. Beachport Conservation Park, between Lake George and the Southern Ocean: Aboriginal shell middens and walking trails (self-guide leaflets available). Bowman Scenic Drive from base of lighthouse to Woolleys Rock (5km N) for spectacular views of Southern

Ocean; on the way, swimming in Pool of Siloam, a lake with high salt content and reputed therapeutic benefits. Woakwine Cutting, 10 km N on Robe Rd, extraordinary drainage project, with observation platform and machinery exhibit. Canunda National Park, 40-km stretch of spectacular sand dunes and virgin bushland, with fascinating flora and fauna, and scenic self-guide walks (leaflets available from Tourist information); 20 km S, accessed from Southend and Millicent. **Tourist information:** District Council, McCourt St; (087) 35 8029. **Accommodation:** 1 hotel, 1 motel, 2 cara./camp. parks.

Berri Pop. 3733

MAP REF. 295 Q7

The commercial centre of the Riverland region, Berri is 227 km NE of Adelaide. Once a wood-refuelling stop for paddle-steamers and barges which plied the Murray River, the town was first proclaimed in 1911. This is fruit- and vine-growing country, dotted with peaceful picnic and fishing areas. **Of interest:** Water Tower Lookout (17 m), Fiedler St, for panoramic views of river and town. River crossings on Riverland's only twin ferries crossing Murray River; vehicular, 24-hr service, free of charge. Nearby, sculpture and cave memorial to Jimmy James, Aboriginal tracker. Houseboats, canoes for hire. Feb.: Rodeo; Speedboat spectacular (subject to river condition). Easter: Carnival. Nov.: Art, craft and fine food fair. **In the area:** Large range of dried fruit and confectionery at Angas Park Kiosk, 3 km W on Sturt Hwy. Berri Estates winery and distillery, largest winemaking facility in Australia; 13 km W on Sturt Hwy, near town of Glossop. Murray River National Park, 10 km SW, features Kia Kia Nature Trail for bushwalkers. Martin's Bend, 2 km E, popular for water-skiing and picnicking. Berrivale Orchards, 4 km N on Sturt Hwy, has educational audiovisual on Riverland's history and various stages in processing of fruit; open Mon.–Fri., Sat. a.m. Wilabalangaloo flora and fauna reserve, 5 km N, off Sturt Hwy: walking trails, spectacular scenery, museum and paddlewheeler; check opening times. Rollerama roller-skating centre nearby. Monash, 12 km NW on Morgan Rd; nearby, Wein Valley Estate Winery. **Tourist information:** 24 Vaughan Tce; (085) 82 1655. **Accommodation:** 1 hotel/motel, 3 motels, 1 hostel, 1 cara./camp. park.

Blinman Pop. 30

MAP REF. 291 E6, 297 K6

Blinman, 478 km N of Adelaide and 30 km from the magnificent Flinders Ranges National Park, was a thriving copper-mining centre from 1860 to 1890. **Of interest:** Several historic buildings including hotel (1869), post office (1862) and police station (1874); all in main street. **In the area:** Great Wall of China, ironstone-capped ridge; 10 km S on Wilpena Rd. Further south, beautiful Aroona Valley and ruins of old Aroona Homestead; nearby Mt Hayward and Brachina Gorge. Scenic Parachilna Gorge, between Blinman and Parachilna; nearby, the Blinman Pools, fed by a permanent spring. Scenic drive east through Eregunda Valley then north-east to Chambers Gorge with its rock pools and Aboriginal carvings; then north-west, to view spectacular Big Moro Gorge off Arkaroola Rd (track may require 4WD). **Tourist information:** Hawker Motors, cnr Wilpena and Cradock Rds, Hawker; (086) 48 4014. **Accommodation:** 1 hotel/motel, 1 cara./camp. park.

Bordertown Pop. 2235

MAP REF. 293 H6

Bordertown is a quiet town on the Dukes Hwy, 274 km SE of Adelaide. Growth was stimulated after 1852 when it became an important supply centre for the goldfields of western Victoria. Today the area is noted for wool, cereals, meat and vegetable production. **Of interest:** Robert J.L. Hawke, former Australian Prime Minister, was born here and his childhood home, in Farquhar St, has been renovated and includes memorabilia; open Mon.–Fri. Town parks offer picnic facilities. **In the area:** Bordertown Wildlife Park, Dukes Hwy: native birds and animals, including pure white kangaroos. Historic Clayton Farm, 3 km S: vintage farm machinery and thatched buildings; open p.m. Sun.–Fri. Clayton Farm vintage field day, held Oct. long weekend. At Mundulla, 10 km SW: Mundulla Hotel (1884), a National Trust building with restaurant, tearooms and craft shop. At Padthaway, 42 km SW: an 1882 homestead houses Padthaway Estate winery; meals and accommodation available. Picnic areas among magnificent red gums and stringybarks at Padthaway Conservation Park nearby. Bangham Conservation Park, 30 km SE, near the town of Frances. **Tourist information:** Council Chambers, 43 Woolshed St; (087) 52 1044. **Accommodation:** 1 hotel, 1 hotel/motel, 3 motels, 1 cara./camp. park.

Burra Pop. 1191

MAP REF. 295 L5

Nestled in Bald Hills Range, 154 km N of Adelaide, Burra, a former copper-mining centre, is one of the country's best preserved mining towns. The district of Burra Burra (Hindi for 'great great') is now famous for stud merino sheep, and Burra is the market town for surrounding farms. *Breaker Morant* was filmed here. Copper was discovered in 1845 and extracted to the value of almost $10 million before the mine closed in 1877. **Of interest:** Passport key-hire system allows visitors to walk or drive around 11 km of heritage buildings, museums, mine shafts and lookout points (details from Tourist information). Daily 2-hr bus tours of town and its mining history; bookings essential. Burra Creek miners' dugouts, alongside Blyth St, where over 1500 people lived during the boom; 2 dugouts preserved. Cemetery, off Spring St. Heritage and cemetery walks; details from Tourist information. Burra Mine Open Air Museum, off Market St: 'Enginehouse Museum' built in 1858 and reconstructed 1986 near archaeological excavation of 30-m entry tunnel to Morphett's Shaft, ore dressing tower, powder magazine; spectacular views of open-cut mine and town. Market Square Museum, opposite Tourist information office. Malowen Lowarth Museum, in old miner's cottage; Kingston St. In Bridge Tce: underground cellars of old Unicorn Brewery; and Paxton Square Cottages (1850), 33 two-, three- and four-roomed cottages built for Cornish miners, now restored as visitor accommodation. In Burra North: police lockup and stables (1849), Tregony St; Redruth Gaol (1857), off Tregony St; and Bon Accord Mine buildings (1846), Railway Tce, now a museum complex. Picturesque spots alongside Burra Creek for swimming, canoeing and picnicking. May: Antique and decorating fair. **In the area:** Chatswood Farm Gallery, 14 km S at

Brachina Gorge, near Blinman, one of the scenic attractions in the Flinders Ranges

Hanson. Wineries in the Clare Valley, about 30 km SW (inquire at tourist information). Scenic 90-km Dares Hill Drive, begins 30 km N near Hallett. Burra Gorge, 27 km E. **Tourist information:** 2 Market Sq.; (08) 8892 2154. **Accommodation:** 4 hotels, 1 motel, 15 B&B, 1 cara./camp. park.

Ceduna Pop. 2753

MAP REF. 303 N9

Near the junction of the Flinders and Eyre Hwys, Ceduna is the last major town before you cross the Nullarbor from east to west. It is the ideal place to check your car and stock up with food and water before the long drive. Ceduna is set on Murat Bay with its sandy coves, sheltered bays and offshore islands. It is an ideal base for a beach holiday, offering swimming, fishing, water-skiing, windsurfing and boating. The port at Thevenard, 3 km SW, handles bulk grain, gypsum and salt. The fishing fleet is noted for its large whiting hauls. Snapper, salmon, tommy ruff and crab are other catches. There was a whaling station on St Peter Island in the 1850s. According to map references in Swift's *Gulliver's Travels*, the tiny people of Lilliput might well have lived on St Peter Is. (visible from Thevenard) or the Isles of St Francis. **Of interest:** Old Schoolhouse National Trust Museum, Park Tce: pioneering items and artifacts from atomic testing at Maralinga; open Mon.–Sat. Half and full day tours of town, including oyster tours, available; contact Tourist information for details. Sept.: Agricultural show. Oct.: Oyster-Fest. **In the area:** Oestmann's Fish Factory at Thevenard Boat Haven; open daily, tours available. At Denial Bay, 13 km W: McKenzie Ruins, site of original settlement; and oyster farm. Picnicking and safe fishing at Denial Bay and Davenport Creek, west of town, and Decres Bay, Laura Bay and Smoky Bay, all south-east (boat charter for diving and fishing available at Ceduna). Southern right whales can be seen June–Oct. along coast west of Ceduna; tours available. At Penong, 73 km W: Penong Woolshed museum with local crafts for sale (open 10–4 daily); and Goanywea camel day-rides and safaris (May–Oct.). Amazing sand dunes and excellent surf at Cactus Beach, 94 km W. Caves, western side of Nullarbor; guided tours only, book at Tourist information. Telstra Earth Station, 37 km NW; guided tours available. Spectacular coastline includes prominent headland at Point Brown, 56 km SE. **Tourist information:** Gateway Tourist Centre, 58 Poynton St; (086) 25 2780. **Accommodation:** 1 hotel/motel, 3 motels, 5 cara./camp. parks. **See also:** The Eyre Peninsula.

Clare Pop. 2575

MAP REF. 295 K5

Set in rich agricultural and pastoral country, this charming town was first settled by Europeans in 1842; it was named after County Clare in Ireland. The area is famed for its prize-winning table wines. Wheat, barley, honey, stud sheep and wool are other important regional industries. The first vines were planted by Jesuit priests at Sevenhill in 1848; today Sevenhill Cellars still produces table and sacramental wines. **Of interest:** National Trust museum housed in old police station (1850), cnr Victoria Rd and Neagles Rock Rd; open Sat., Sun. and holidays. Stately Wolta Wolta Homestead (1846), West Tce, built by pastoralist John Hope and still owned by Hope family; homestead rebuilt after Ash Wednesday fires; open Sun. 10–1. Lookouts at Billy Goat Hill, from Wright St, and Neagles Rock, Neagles Rock Rd. Maynard Memorial Park, Pioneer Ave, picnic/barbecue facilities. Historic town walk; self-guide leaflets available. Easter: Clare Easter races. May: Gourmet weekend. Dec.: Clare Valley summer festival. **In the area:** Over 20 wineries in the area (most open for inspection and cellar-door sales; check opening times). Wineries around Clare: Tim Adams' Wines, Jim Barry Wines, Tim Knappstein Wines, Eldredge Wines, Leasingham Wines, Wendouree Cellars and Duncan Estate Winery; wineries in Polish Hill River district (12 km SE) include: Pike's Polish Hill River Estate, Paulett Wines and The Wilson Vineyard; at Mintaro, 19 km SE: Mintaro Cellars and Reilly's Cottage; at Sevenhill, 7 km S: Sevenhill Cellars established 1851, monastery buildings, including historic St Aloysius Church, Stringy Brae Wines, Waninga Wines, Skillogalee Wines, Jeanneret Wines and Mitchell Winery; around Penwortham, 10 km S: Penwortham Wines and Pearson Wines; around Watervale, 12 km S: Clos Clare, Crabtree of Watervale, Stephen John Wines, Black Opal-Quelltaler Vineyards (also wine museum), Rosenberg Cellars and Horrocks Winery; around Auburn, 26 km S: Taylors Wines and Grosset Wines. Also at Mintaro: historic Martindale Hall (featured in the film *Picnic at Hanging Rock*); accommodation

The unique landscape of The Breakaways, near Coober Pedy

and dining (closed Christmas Day and Good Friday); slate quarry, operational since 1856 (not open for tours). Also at Auburn: birthplace of poet C.J. Dennis in 1876; many historic buildings (accommodation available in some), maintained by National Trust (self-guide walking-tour leaflets available). At Blyth, 13 km W: flora and fauna in Padnainda Reserve; Medika Gallery, originally a Lutheran church (1886), specialising in Australian bird and flower paintings (open daily). Scenic drive 12 km S to Spring Gully Conservation Park (not well signposted) featuring rare red stringybarks. Spring-farm Galleries, Springfarm Rd, 6 km SE. Bungaree Station Homestead (1841), historic merino sheep station 12 km N, with knitting yarns, original patterns and hand-knitted Bungaree jumpers available for sale from Station Store; tours and accommodation available. Geralka Rural Farm, a working farm 25 km N of Clare; tours available. **Tourist information:** 229 Main North Rd; (08) 8842 2131. **Accommodation:** 1 hotel, 2 hotel/motels, 3 motels, 3 B&B, 1 cara./camp. park. **See also:** Festival Fun; Vineyards and Wineries.

Cleve   Pop. 738

MAP REF. 294 F5

Surrounded by rich farming country, this inland town on the Eyre Peninsula was settled in 1853 by Europeans. **Of interest:** Old Council Chambers Museum, Third St; contact District Council for appt. Aug.: Eyre Peninsula field days (even-numbered years). Oct.: Agricultural show. **In the area:** Yeldulknie Conservation Park, 5 km N. Hincks and Bascombe Well Conservation Parks (located 35 and 90 km W respectively). Enjoy scenic drive along escarpment of Cleve-Cowell Hills. Arno Bay, 24 km SE, and Cowell, 42 km E; both have excellent swimming beaches and jetties that are popular with anglers. **Tourist information:** District Council, 13 Main St; (086) 28 2004. **Accommodation:** 1 hotel/motel, limited cara./camp. facilities.

Coffin Bay   Pop. 343

MAP REF. 294 C8

A picturesque holiday town and fishing village located on the shores of a beautiful estuary 51 km NW of Port Lincoln; sailing, water-skiing, swimming and fishing are popular here. The coastal scenery in this area is magnificent. Oysters cultivated in Coffin Bay are among the best in the country. The bay's unusual name was bestowed by Matthew Flinders in 1802 to honour his friend Sir Isaac Coffin. **Of interest:** Oyster Farm, The Esplanade; also renowned for its lobster. Oyster Walk, a 6-km foreshore walkway from the caravan park to beyond Crinolin Point; leaflet available from Tourist information. Charter boats and boat hire available. **In the area:** Coffin Bay National Park and Kellidie Bay Conservation Park surround township, wildflowers abundant in spring. Farm Beach and nearby 'Anzac Cove', location for film *Gallipoli*. Yangie Trail drive, 10 km S, via Yangie Bay lookout (magnificent coastal views to Point Avoid). Further 50 km N, scenic stretch of Flinders Hwy between Mount Hope and Sheringa. At Koppio, 45 km NW: Blacksmith's museum and Kurrabi Lodge tea gardens. **Tourist information:** Beachcomber Agencies, The Esplanade; (086) 85 4057. **Accommodation:** 1 motel, 1 cara./camp. park. **See also:** The Eyre Peninsula.

Coober Pedy   Pop. 2491

MAP REF. 301 R11

In the heart of South Australia's outback, 845 km N of Adelaide on the Stuart Hwy, is the opal-mining town of Coober Pedy. This is the last stop for petrol between Cadney Homestead (151 km N) and Glendambo (252 km S) on the Stuart Hwy. The name Coober Pedy is Aboriginal for 'white fellows in a hole' – many of the town's inhabitants live in dugouts (at a constant 24°C underground) for protection from the severe summer temperatures, often reaching 45°C, and the cold winter nights. There is also a complete lack of timber for building. The countryside is desolate and harsh, and the town has reticulated water provided from a bore 23 km N. Opals were discovered here in 1915; today there are thousands of mines in the area. **Of interest:** Working mines and demonstrations of opals being cut and polished. Jewellery and polished stones for sale. On eastern edge of town: Big Winch Lookout, Italian Club Rd; and Old Timers Mine, Crowders Gully Rd, a mine museum and interpretive centre with self-guide walks. On Hutchison St: Umoona underground mine and museum, underground mine tours; underground churches, including St Peter and St Pauls; Desert Cave, an international underground hotel complete with shopping complex. Underground Catacomb Church, Catacomb Rd. Underground Pottery, west of town, features local pottery. Guided tours of mines and town available. Easter: Opal festival. Oct.: Coober Pedy races. **In the area:** Opal fields pocked with diggings; beware of unprotected mine shafts. Avoid entering any field area unless escorted by someone who knows the area. For safety reasons, visitors to the mines are advised to join a tour. Trespassers on claims can be fined a minimum of $1000. **The Breakaways**, 30 km N, colourful 40-sq. km reserve featuring unique landscape and good views; it has been used as a backdrop in many films and commercials; return via road passing part of the dog fence, a 9600-km fence stretching across Australia built to protect sheep properties in the south from wild dogs. **Arckaringa Hills**, 234 km N, richly coloured hills in an area known as the **Painted Desert**; also renowned for its flora and fauna. **William Creek**, 170 km E: hotel; race meeting and gymkhana, held weekend before Easter. **Tourist information:** Council Offices, Hutchison St; (086) 725298. **Accommodation:** 1 hotel, 1 hotel/ motel, 8 motels, 1 B&B, 3 hostels, 4 cara./camp. parks. **See also:** The Outback.

Coonalpyn　　　　　　　　Pop. 266

MAP REF. 293 F4, 295 O12

This tiny town on the Dukes Hwy, 180 km SE of Adelaide, is a good base to explore the Mt Boothby (30 km SW) and Carcuma (20 km NE) Conservation Parks, to see grey kangaroos, echidnas, emus and mallee fowl in their natural environment. Between Nov. and Apr., advisable to check bushfire danger and fire restrictions before entering parks; contact Department of Environment and Natural Resources, (087) 57 2261 or (018) 82 9780. **Of interest:** Mural depicting town's history in pedestrian subway under trainline. Daisy Patch Nursery, native plants; Richards Tce. Scenic 26-km loop drive. Feb.: Trash farming field day (even-numbered years). **Tourist information:** Coonalpyn Stores, Dukes Hwy; (085) 71 1020. **Accommodation:** 1 hotel, 1 cara./camp. park.

Coonawarra　　　　　　　　Pop. 40

MAP REF. 228 A2, 230 A13, 293 I10

The European settlement of Coonawarra goes back to 1890 when John Riddoch subdivided 2000 acres of his vast landholding for the development of orchards and vineyards. Although the vines flourished and excellent wines were made, demand was not high until a resurgence of interest in the 1950s and 1960s, and the region became recognised as an important winegrowing area. The terra rossa soil and dedicated viticulturalists and winemakers combine to produce award-winning white and red table wines. **Of interest:** Art gallery at Chardonnay Lodge, Penola Rd. **In the area:** Wineries, most open for tastings and cellar-door sales, including (from N to S): The Ridge Wines, Rymill Wines, Penley Estate, Redmans Wines, Brands Laira, Wynns Coonawarra Estate, Rouge Homme, Zema Estate, Mildara Wines, Majella Wines, St Mary's Vineyard (15 km E), Katnook Estate, Highbank Wines, Leconfield Coonawarra, Bowen Estate, Balnaves of Coonawarra, Hazelgrove winery, Hollick Wines, Wetherall Wines, Parker Estate, Penfolds and Ladbroke Grove Wines. **Tourist information:** 27 Arthur St, Penola; (087) 37 2855. **Accommodation:** 1 motel. **See also:** Vineyards and Wineries.

Cowell　　　　　　　　Pop. 695

MAP REF. 294 G5

A small, pleasant township 108 km S of Whyalla, Cowell is on the almost landlocked Franklin Harbour. One of the world's major jade deposits is in the district. The sandy beach at Cowell is safe for swimming; fishing is excellent. Oyster farming is a local industry and fresh oysters can be purchased year-round from various outlets. **Of interest:** Old post office and attached residence (1888), Main St, now Franklin Harbour National Trust Historical Museum. On Lincoln Hwy: open-air agricultural museum; and the Cowell Jade Motel, for its displays of local jade jewellery and sales; open daily. Smithy's Shell House, Warnes St. Boats available for hire. **In the area:** Entrance Island, in Franklin Harbour. Franklin Harbour

The Yorke Peninsula

Yorke Peninsula was put on the map by the discovery of rich copper-ore deposits in 1861 and the influx of thousands of miners, including so many from Cornwall that the **Wallaroo–Moonta–Kadina** area became known as Little Cornwall. Today, it is one of the world's richest wheat and barley regions.

The drive down the highway on the east coast is mainly within sight of the sea. Many of the east-coast towns have excellent fishing from long jetties once used for loading grain ships. Beach, surf and rock fishing are excellent, as is crabbing.

The west coast of Yorke Peninsula is lined with safe swimming beaches and excellent coastal scenery. **Port Victoria**, the last of the windjammer ports, was once the main port of call for sailing ships transporting grain. Further north, Moonta's old stone buildings give it a sense of history and the Moonta mines tell of its mining heyday.

Innes National Park with its diverse hinterland, birdlife and impressive coastal scenery is on the southern tip of the Peninsula. Visit the site of a once-flourishing township, Inneston. Pondalowie Bay is a must for surfers. Rocky cliff tops and windswept headlands provide vantage points for views across Investigator Strait.

For further information, contact the Yorke Peninsula Visitor Information Centre, 51 Taylor St, Kadina; (08) 8821 2093. **See also:** National Parks, and individual entries in A–Z listing for those parks and towns indicated by bold type. **Map reference:** 294 H8

Historic miner's cottage, Moonta

Conservation Park, south of Cowell, has good fishing spots. Swimming and excellent fishing locations abound, including around Gibbon Point, 15 km S. Arno Bay, 48 km S: popular holiday resort, sandy beaches and jetty for fishing. **Tourist information:** Council Offices, Main St; (086) 29 2019. **Accommodation:** 2 hotels, 1 motel, 1 B&B, 2 cara./camp. parks. **See also:** The Eyre Peninsula.

Crystal Brook   Pop. 1282

MAP REF. 295 J3

Once part of a vast sheep station, this town, 25 km SE of Port Pirie, is now a major centre for the sheep, beef and cereal industries of the region. **Of interest:** National Trust Museum, Brandis St: local history collection in first two-storeyed building in town, original butcher's shop and bakery, and underground bakehouse. Crystal Crafts, Bowman St, for local craft. Picnicking in creekside parks. Aug.: Agricultural show. **In the area:** Bowman Park, 5 km E, surrounds ruins of Bowman family property Crystal Brook Run (1847); excellent native fauna; open daily. Heysen Walking Trail runs through Bowman Park. Gladstone, 21 km NE, set in rich rural country in Rocky River Valley: tours of Gladstone gaol (1881); Trend Drinks Factory, home of Old Style Ginger Beer, tours available. Laura, boyhood town of C.J. Dennis, author of *The Songs of a Sentimental Bloke*, 32 km N: cottage crafts; art galleries; historic buildings (self-guide walking-tour leaflet available at Biles Art Gallery, Herbert St; open Sat., Sun. and public holidays); Folk fair at Beetaloo Valley and Reservoir (west of Laura) in Apr. Near Wirrabara, 50 km N, scenic walks through pine forests. Redhill, 25 km S: riverside walk, museum, craft shop and antique shop. Koolunga, 10 km E of Redhill: cottage industries (potters and painters) and picnic areas. Salt lakes around Snowtown, 50 km S. Nearby on Lochiel–Ninnes Rd, lookout with superb views of inland lakes and countryside. Yacka, 40 km SE, has sheepdog trials in Aug. **Tourist information:** District Council Offices, Bowman St; (086) 36 2150. **Accommodation:** Crystal Brook, 2 hotels, 1 cara./camp. park. Bowman Park, 1 hostel.

Edithburgh   Pop. 453

MAP REF. 294 I10

Located on the foreshore at the south-eastern tip of the Yorke Peninsula, Edithburgh overlooks Gulf St Vincent

SOUTH AUSTRALIA

The Eyre Peninsula

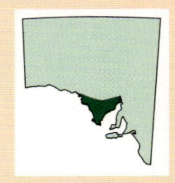

The Eyre Peninsula is a vast region stretching from Whyalla in the east to the Western Australian border in the west, and, in a north-south direction, from the Gawler Ranges to Port Lincoln. Spencer Gulf borders the eastern edge of the Peninsula, along which are located a number of small coastal towns featuring sheltered waters, safe swimming, white sandy beaches and excellent fishing from either shore or boat. The peaceful resort towns of **Cowell**, Arno Bay and Port Neill are charming. Cowell has the added attraction of being one of the world's major sources of black and green jade.

Whyalla is the second largest city in South Australia and acts as an important gateway to Eyre Peninsula. Located near the top of Spencer Gulf, this bustling, industrially-based city also offers a wide range of attractions for the visitor.

The southern Eyre Peninsula includes the tourist resort towns of **Tumby Bay,** famous for fishing and the beautiful Sir Joseph Banks Group of islands; the jewel in the crown, the city of **Port Lincoln,** nestled on blue Boston Bay; and **Coffin Bay,** with its magnificent sheltered waters.

In stark contrast to the sheltered waters of Spencer Gulf, the west coast is exposed to the full force of the Southern Ocean and offers some of the most spectacular coastal scenery to be found in Australia. This coast is punctuated by a number of bays and inlets and, not surprisingly, several resort towns have flourished where shelter can be found from precipitous cliffs and pounding surf. **Elliston**, Venus Bay, Port Kenny, **Streaky Bay,** Smoky Bay and **Ceduna** all offer the visitor a diverse range of coastal scenery, good fishing and other water-related activities. The only known mainland breeding colony of sea lions, and Murphy's Haystacks, windworn granite inselbergs over 1500 million years old, are both south of Streaky Bay.

Ceduna provides a vital service and accommodation facility for traffic across Australia, and acts as a gateway information centre for visitors approaching the region from the west.

The western side of Eyre Peninsula is exposed to the full force of the Southern Ocean

The hinterland of Eyre Peninsula encompasses the picturesque Koppio Hills in the south, the vast grain-growing tracts of the central region and the eternal beauty of the Gawler Ranges in the north.

The Nullarbor, the western corridor into the region, is a vast treeless plain, bordered in the south by towering limestone cliffs that drop sheer to the pounding Southern Ocean. Here schools of southern right whales can be seen along the coastline between June and October on their annual breeding migration. Sightings of these beautiful creatures occur regularly and are on the increase.

For more information on the area, contact the Eyre Peninsula Tourism Association, Jobomi House, Liverpool St, Port Lincoln; (086) 82 4688. **See also:** individual entries in A–Z listing for those towns indicated by bold type. **Map reference:** 294 C6.

and Troubridge Island. **Of interest:** Native Flora Park (17½ ha), Ansty Tce. Edithburgh Museum, Edith St, has historical maritime collection; check opening times. Bakehouse Arts and Crafts, Blanche St, for local crafts. Town jetty, end of Edith St, built in 1873. Natural tidal pool, excellent for swimming. Offshore skindiving. Nature walks, south to Sultana Point and north to Coobowie; brochures available from Anchorage Motel, O'Halloran Pde. Oct.: State windsurfing speed trials; Gala day. **In the area:** Nearby Sultana Point, 2 km S, for boating, fishing and swimming. Scenic drive south-west along coast to Innes National Park. Coobowie, 5 km N, a popular coastal resort. Tours to Troubridge Island Conservation Park; ½ hour by boat. **Tourist information:** Newsagency and Deli, Blanche St; (08) 8852 6230. **Accommodation:** 1 hotel, 3 motels, 1 B&B, 1 cara./camp. park. **See also:** The Yorke Peninsula.

Elliston   Pop. 242

MAP REF. 294 B5

Nestled in a small range of hills on the shore of Waterloo Bay, Elliston is a pleasant coastal town and the centre for a cereal-growing, mixed-farming and fishing community. Known for its rugged and scenic coastline, excellent fishing and safe swimming beaches, Elliston is a popular holiday destination. **Of interest:** Town hall mural, an art history of town and district; Main St. **In the area:** Just north of town: clifftop walk at Waterloo Bay; and good surfing near Anxious Bay. Talia Caves, 40 km N. Lock's Well Beach and Sheringa Beach to south, for surf fishing. Scenic drives north and south of town offer superb views of magnificent coastline; good views also from Cummings Monument Lookout, just off hwy near Kiana, 52 km S. Flinders Is., 35 km offshore; limited accommodation. **Tourist information:** District Council, Beach Tce; (086) 87 9177. **Accommodation:** 1 hotel/motel, 1 motel, 2 cara./camp. parks. **See also:** The Eyre Peninsula.

Gawler   Pop. 13 835

MAP REF. 288 D5, 295 L8

Settled by Europeans in 1839, Gawler, 40 km NE of Adelaide, is the centre for a thriving agricultural district and also the gateway to the famous Barossa Valley. **Of interest:** Historic buildings: Gawler Mill, Bridge St, and old telegraph station, Murray St (open Sun. or obtain key from Tourist information). Old Eagle Foundry, King St, now a B&B; also open to tourists. Para Para (1862), Penrith Ave, historic residence; not open. Anglican Church, has interesting pipe organ; open Sun. or by appt, contact Tourist information. Walking tour of Church Hill district (adjacent to Murray St), a State Heritage Area. Self-guide walking and driving tours; leaflets from Tourist information. Dead Man's Pass Reserve, end Murray St: picnic facilities and walking trails. June: Three-day equestrian event. Aug.: Agricultural show. Nov.: Country music festival; Sutch is Light (lighting of Australia's tallest Christmas tree in late Nov.) **In the area:** Restored Willaston post office, 2 km N. Astronomical Society of SA's observatory at Stockport, 30 km N, has public viewing nights; check at Tourist information. Scholz Park Museum at Riverton, 54 km N. Wellington Hotel at Waterloo, 76 km N (near Manoora), once Cobb & Co. staging point. **Tourist information:** 2 Lyndoch Rd; (085) 22 6814. **Accommodation:** 1 hotel, 1 motel, 3 B&B, 2 cara./camp. parks.

Goolwa   Pop. 3018

MAP REF. 289 I7, 290 G12, 293 C3, 295 L11

Goolwa is a rapidly growing holiday town 12 km from the mouth of the Murray River near Lake Alexandrina. Once a key port in the golden days of the riverboats, the area has a strong tradition of shipbuilding, trade and fishing. Today, the lakes area is ideal for boating, fishing and aquatic sports, and popular with birdwatchers and photographers. Southern right whales visit the bay July–Sept. **Of interest:** Historic buildings: distinctive railway superintendent's house (1852), known as 'the round-roofed house'; and RSL Club, in former stables of Goolwa Railway (1853); both in B.F. Laurie Lane, off Cadell St. In Cadell St, display of first horse-drawn railway carriage used in SA between Goolwa and Port Elliott from 1854. Cockle Train, steam-train rides between Goolwa and Victor Harbor; check at Tourist information. National Trust Museum, Porter St, housed in former blacksmith's shop dating from 1870s. Next door, in original but rebuilt cottage, Goolwa Print Room. Both hotels, the Goolwa in Cadell St and the Corio in Railway Pl., date from 1850s. Signal Point Interpretative Centre, The Wharf, computerised display of river and district before European settlement, and the impact of local development. Feb.: Goolwa to Milang freshwater classic yacht race. Mar.: Wooden boat festival (odd-numbered years). **In the area:** Excellent fishing. Bird sanctuary east of Goolwa, has swans, pelicans and other waterfowl, also bird hide. Nearby, the Barrages, desalination points that prevent salt water from reaching the Murray River. MV *Aroona*, PS *Mundoo* and MV *Coorong Pirate* cruise to mouth of the Murray, the Coorong, the Barrages and the Lower Murray. Hindmarsh Is. (via ferry) lookout, for view of Murray mouth. Malleebrae Woolshed, 2 km N: wool displays, shearing videos and art and craft (open by appt). Scenic flights available; airport 5 km N. At Currency Creek, 8 km N: Canoe Tree; Tonkin's Currency Creek Winery (with restaurant and fauna park); creekside park and walking trail. Tooperang Trout Farm, 20 km NW. **Tourist information:** Old Library Bldg, cnr Cadell St and Goolwa Tce; (085) 55 1144. **Accommodation:** 4 motels, 3 cara./camp. parks. **See also:** The Fleurieu Peninsula.

Hawker   Pop. 345

MAP REF. 291 D10, 297 J9

This outback town in the centre of the northern Flinders Ranges is 369 km N of Adelaide. Once a railway town, it is now the centre of a unique area that attracts visitors from both Australia and overseas to marvel at the colouring and grandeur of the many ranges that make up the Flinders. **Of interest:** Museum at Hawker Motors, cnr Wilpena and Cradock Rds. Historic buildings: post office (1882), Hawker Hotel (1882) and old railway-station complex (1885). Scenic flights and 4WD tours available. May: Horseracing carnival. Sept.: Art exhibition. Oct.: Henley-on-Arkaba fun day. **In the area:** Moralana Scenic Drive, 42 km N, joins roads to Wilpena and Leigh Creek. Further north, Arkaroo Rock, with paintings by Adnajamathana tribe; nearby Rawnsley Bluff, majestic southern rampart of Wilpena Pound. Merna Mora Station, 46 km N; station holidays available. Walking trail and scenic lookout at Jarvis Hill, 5 km SW. Rock paintings at

Yourambulla Caves, 11 km S. Historic Kanyaka ruins, south off main road to Quorn. Ruins at Wilson, Hookina, Wonoka and Willow Waters; check directions at Hawker before departure. **Tourist information**: Hawker Motors, cnr Wilpena and Cradock Rds; (086) 48 4014. **Accommodation:** 1 hotel/motel, 1 motel, 2 cara./camp. parks. **See also:** The Flinders Ranges; National Parks.

Innamincka Pop. 14

MAP REF. 299 Q7, 500 H10

This tiny settlement, 1027 km NE of Adelaide, is built around a hotel and trading post on the Strzelecki Track, and is on the banks of the Cooper Creek. Motorists intending to travel along the Track should ensure road conditions are suitable by phoning the Northern Roads Condition Hotline on (08) 11633 before departing; also read the section on Outback Motoring. There are no supplies or petrol between Lyndhurst and Innamincka. **Of interest:** Picturesque Cullyamurra Waterhole on Cooper Creek, 10 km NE: Aboriginal carvings and excellent fishing. Rebuilt Australian Inland Mission hostel, now houses National Parks office. Local tours and boat hire available. **In the area:** Various memorials to explorers Burke and Wills near Innamincka; famous 'Dig Tree' is best known, 40 km across border in Qld. Coongie Lakes, a haven for wildlife, 103 km NW (road conditions can vary considerably; 4WD recommended). **Tourist information:** Hawker Motors, cnr Wilpena and Cradock Rds, Hawker; (086) 48 4014. **Accommodation:** 1 hotel/motel. **See also:** The Outback.

Jamestown Pop. 1359

MAP REF. 295 L3, 297 K13

Jamestown is a well-planned country town 205 km N of Adelaide. The surrounding country produces stud sheep and cattle, cereals, dairy produce and timber. **Of interest:** Heritage murals, Ayre St. Railway Station Museum, Irbin St; open Sun. and by appt. Parks ideal for picnicking along banks of Belalie Creek; banks floodlit at night. Oct.: Agricultural show. Dec.: Christmas festival. **In the area:** Scenic drive through Bundaleer Forest Reserve, 9 km S, towards New Campbell Hill for panoramic views of plains towards Mt Remarkable and The Bluff. Around Spalding, 34 km S: series of open waterways with picnic areas and trout fishing opportunities; Geralka Rural Farm, 49 km S, working commercial farm; tours available. At Gladstone, 29 km SW: railway yards for train enthusiasts; tours of gaol (1881); and tours of Trend Drinks Factory, home of Old Style Ginger Beer. Appila Springs, scenic picnic spot 8 km from Appila, 24 km NW. **Tourist information:** Jamestown Country Retreat Caravan Park, 103 Ayre St; (086) 64 0077. **Accommodation:** 3 hotels, 1 hotel/motel, 1 cara./camp. park.

Kadina Pop. 3536

MAP REF. 294 I6

The largest town on Yorke Peninsula, Kadina is the chief commercial centre for the region. The town's history includes the boom copper-mining era during the 1800s and early 1900s, when thousands of Cornish miners flocked to the area; the community is still proud of its ancestry. **Of interest:** Historic hotels: Wombat and Kadina, both in Taylor St; and Royal Exchange, Digby St, with its iron lace balconies and shady verandahs. National Trust Kadina Heritage Museum complex includes Matta House (1863), home of manager of Matta Matta Copper Mine; agricultural machinery; blacksmith's shop; printing museum; old Matta mine; and the Kadina Story, a display depicting the history of Kadina and Wallaroo. Banking and Currency Museum, a unique private museum; 3 Graves St (check opening times). Wallaroo Mines site, open for signposted self-guide walking tour. Creative Activities Network, personalised learning experiences of hiking, gardening, historical walks, sailing, etc. with local residents; available throughout region; contact Tourist information. Easter: Bowling carnival. May: Prize-winning Kernewek Lowender, a Cornish festival, held in conjunction with Wallaroo and Moonta (odd-numbered years). Aug.: Agricultural show. **In the area:** Moonta, 18 km SW and Wallaroo, 10 km W; both of interest. Yorke Peninsula field days at Paskeville (19 km SE) in Sept. (odd-numbered years). **Tourist information:** Yorke Peninsula Visitor Information Centre, 51 Taylor St; (08) 8821 2093. **Accommodation:** 3 hotels, 2 motels, 1 B&B, 1 cara./camp. park. **See also:** Festival Fun; The Yorke Peninsula.

Kapunda Pop. 1979

MAP REF. 288 E3, 295 L7

Kapunda is situated 80 km N of Adelaide on the edge of the Barossa Valley. Copper was discovered here in 1842 and Kapunda became Australia's first mining town. At one stage the population rose to 5000 and there were 16 hotels in town. A million pounds' ($2m) worth of copper was dug out before the mines closed in 1878. **Of interest:** Historic buildings: Ford House, an 1860s general store with unusual vaulted iron roof. Kapunda Museum (1870s); and Bagot's Fortune, mine interpretation centre with mining history displays; both in Hill St. High School's main building on South Tce, off Clare Rd, formerly residence of famous cattle king Sir Sidney Kidman. 'Map Kernow' (Son of Cornwall), 8-m tall bronze statue at southern entrance to town, end of Main St. Heritage trail and historic mine walking trail (maps available from Tourist information). Mar.: Celtic music festival (weekend before Easter). Nov.: Agricultural show; Antique and craft fair. **In the area:** Pines Reserve, nature reserve and wildlife; 6 km NW. Historic local stone buildings at Tarlee; 16 km NW. Scholz Park Museum (open by appt) and heritage-listed railway station (not open) at Riverton; 30 km NW. Scenic drive 26 km NE through sheep, wheat and dairy country to Eudunda; walks and scenic lookouts. **Tourist information:** 5 Hill St; (085) 66 2902. **Accommodation:** 1 hotel, 1 cara./camp. park.

Keith Pop. 1176

MAP REF. 293 G6, 295 P13

Keith is a farming town on the Dukes Hwy, 241 km SE of Adelaide, in the centre of the former Ninety Mile Desert, now called Coonalpyn Downs. The area has been transformed from infertile pasture to productive farming by the use of plant nutrition and modern farming methods. **Of interest:** Buildings in Heritage St: former Congregational Church (1910), with 11 locally made leadlight windows depicting the town's life and pioneering history, and The Old Manse; both classified by National Trust. Nov.: Market day, local arts and crafts. **In the area:** Mount Rescue Conservation Park, a vast expanse of sandplain with heath, pink gums and an abundance of native

Vineyards and Wineries

South Australia produces about 50 per cent of the wines and 65 per cent of the brandy made in Australia. In the equable dry climate of the southern and eastern regions of the State, kilometres of vineyards stretch over valleys, plains and hillsides. The State has seven distinct grape-growing regions: the Barossa, McLaren, Clare Valley, Riverland, Adelaide Hills, Coonawarra and Langhorne Creek. New areas emerging include the Lower Eyre Peninsula, Kangaroo Island and around Padthaway.

The **Barossa,** encompassing Barossa Valley and Eden Valley, Australia's most famous wine-producing area, is located about 55 kilometres north-east of Adelaide. It is a warm and intimate place of charming old towns, with vineyards spreading across undulating hills in well-tended, precise rows. Visitors can appreciate the beauty of the region from a hot-air balloon and afterwards enjoy a champagne breakfast.

The Barossa Valley was named in 1837 by Colonel Light in memory of Barrosa in Spain, where he fought a decisive battle in 1811. The recorded spelling 'Barossa' was an error that was never rectified. The district was settled in 1839 by English and Germanic settlers. Today the Barossa has a distinctive culture and atmosphere that derives from this Germanic concentration in the mid-nineteenth century and is evidenced in the vineyards, the stone buildings, the restaurants, the bakeries and the Lutheran churches that dot the region.

The Barossa produces brandy, dry and sweet table wines, and fortified styles of wine. Some of the most famous wineries of the Barossa are Yalumba, Orlando, Penfolds and Seppelts. Some wineries are still run by members of the same families that established them last century. Others have been taken over by big international companies, but the distinctive qualities of the wine remain. There are many medium-size wineries making excellent wines, such as Wolf Blass, Peter Lehmann, Grant Burge, Basedows and Krondorf, and many boutique wineries specialising in producing quality wines, including Bethany, Barossa Settlers, Henschke, Elderton, Rockford and St Hallett.

The **McLaren** region, which is particularly suitable for red wines, is on Fleurieu Peninsula, just south of Adelaide. Nestled in the gentle folds of the Mount Lofty Ranges with a westerly view to

Grape picking, in the McLaren region on the Fleurieu Peninsula

the sea lies the township of McLaren Vale, the centre of this winegrowing area. There are more than fifty wineries in the region, among them Chapel Hill, Hardy's Reynella, James Haselgrove, Seaview and Wirra Wirra, and they range from very large to very small. In most of the wineries, the person at the cellar door is the person who makes the wine — meet your maker at McLaren!

The vineyards of the **Clare Valley** are about 130 kilometres north of Adelaide and produce fine table wines, specialising in semillon, shiraz and riesling. There are twenty-eight wineries in the Clare Valley, most of which are small family-owned operations. Two of the better-known wineries are Taylors and Leasinghams.

Near the Victorian border is the **Riverland** region, famous for a wide range of products from top-quality table wines to ouzo and brandy. The well-known wineries include Kingston Estate at Kingston-on-Murray and Angove's near Renmark.

There are vineyards scattered throughout the **Adelaide Hills.** Wineries include Karl Seppelts Grand Cru Estate and Gumeracha Cellars. This area is noted especially for its riesling. Closer to Adelaide are Petaluma and Stonyfell Wineries.

Many vineyards at **Coonawarra** in the far south-east produce award-winning white and red table wines from a small area of unique, rich, volcanic soil; examples are Wynns, Mildara, Redmans, Hazelgrove, Rymill and Rouge Homme.

The **Langhorne Creek** region is around 70 kilometres south of Adelaide, resting between the foothills of the Mount Lofty Ranges and Lake Alexandrina. It is a rapidly expanding wine region and produces mostly red wines, with Bleasdale Vineyards being the best-known winery.

The **Lower Eyre Peninsula** region is one of the State's newest. Located around Port Lincoln and North Shields are the two major wineries in this area: Boston Bay Wineries and Delacolline Estate. **Kangaroo Island** established its first vineyard in 1987 and produces grapes for red wine. There is no winery on the island. There are no wineries in the **Padthaway** region either; 16 vineyards in this area produce grapes for both red and white wines, particularly chardonnay.

Most of the South Australian wineries are open for inspection, tastings and cellar-door sales.

For further information about hours of inspection and winery tours, contact the South Australian Travel Centre, 1 King William Street, Adelaide; (08) 8212 1505. **Map references:** 290, for McLaren region; 292, for Barossa region.

'Larry Lobster', Kingston S.E.

SOUTH AUSTRALIA

wildlife, 16 km N. Old Settlers Cottage (1894), 2 km NE on Emu Flat Rd. Ngarkat Conservation Park, 25 km NE, variety of flora and fauna. Mt Monster Conservation Park, 10 km S, scenic views and diverse wildlife. **Tourist information:** Council Chambers, 43 Woolshed St, Border-town; (087) 52 1044. **Accommodation:** 1 hotel/ motel, 1 motel, 1 cara./camp. park.

Kimba   Pop. 682

MAP REF. 294 F3, 296 E13

A small town on the Eyre Hwy, Kimba is at the edge of the outback. This is sheep- and wheat-growing country. **Of interest:** Historical museum, Eyre Hwy, features Pioneer House (1908), school and blacksmith's shop. The Big Galah, Eyre Hwy. Locally mined and crafted jade, including rare black jade, at adjacent Gem Shop. Sept.: Agricultural show. **In the area:** Sturt Desert Pea nursery on Eyre Hwy, 1 km W. Walking trail 1 km NE of town, goes ½ km through bushland to White's Knob lookout (360° views). Lake Gilles Conservation Park, 20 km NE, habitat for mallee fowl. Caralue Bluff, 20 km SW, rock climbing, flora and fauna. Pinkawillinie Conservation Park, 45 km W. Gawler Ranges, north-west, vast wilderness area; check road conditions and read Outback Motoring. **Tourist information:** Kimba Halfway Across Australia Gem Shop, Eyre Hwy; (086) 27 2112. **Accommodation:** 1 hotel/motel, 1 motel, 1 cara./camp. park.

Kingscote   Pop. 1443

MAP REF. 294 I12

The largest town on Kangaroo Island, 120 km SW of Adelaide, Kingscote was the first official European settlement in the State (1836). There is a vehicular ferry from Cape Jervis (1 hour), a passenger ferry from Glenelg and an air service from Adelaide. **Of interest:** Cairn on foreshore marks State's first post office. Hope Cottage, National Trust Folk Museum; Centenary Ave. St Alban's Church, stained-glass windows and pioneer memorials. Town's cemetery is oldest in State. Rock pool and Brownlow Beach for swimming. Fishing from jetty for squid, tommy ruff, trevally, garfish and snook. Christo's Wagon Rides, Clydesdale-drawn wagon rides in summer; from The Esplanade. Feb.: Racing carnival. Oct.: Agricultural show. **In the area:** Jumbuck shearing demonstrations, Birchmore Rd; 17 km S. Eucalyptus oil distillery, Willsons Rd; 20 km S, off South Coast Rd. American River, a fishing village, about 50 km E. Penneshaw, on the north-east coast of Dudley Peninsula, where vehicular ferry arrives from Cape Jervis; Folk Museum in former Old Penneshaw School. Dudley, Cape Hart and Pelican Lagoon Conservation Parks on peninsula. Antechamber Bay, about 20 km SE of Penneshaw, excellent for bushwalking, fishing and swimming. On western end of island, Flinders Chase National Park, sanctuary for some of Australia's rarest wildlife; Cape Borda Lighthouse, north-west; Remarkable Rocks and Admirals Arch, south-west. Guided tours available for Seal Bay, Kelly Hill Caves, Cape Borda and Cape Willoughby Lighthouses. Penguin tours at Kingscote and Penneshaw. **Tourist information:** Department of Environment and Natural Resources, 37 Dauncey St; (0848) 2 2381. **Accommodation:** 2 hotels, 4 motels, 1 hostel, 1 B&B, 2 cara./camp. parks. **See also:** Kangaroo Island.

Kingston S.E.   Pop. 1425

MAP REF. 293 F8

Located at the southern end of the Coorong National Park on Lacepede Bay, Kingston S.E. is a farming and fishing town, and seaside resort. The multitude of shallow lakes and lagoons in the area are a haven for birdlife and a delight for naturalists and photographers. **Of interest:** Unusual analemmatic sundial, adjacent to Apex Park, in East Tce. Historic post office (1867), Holland St. National Trust Pioneer Museum (1872), Cooke St. Cape Jaffa Lighthouse (built 1860s, dismantled and re-erected in 1970s); Marine Pde. Fresh lobsters in season (Oct.–Apr.). Giant 'Larry Lobster' at entrance to town, Princes Hwy. Jan.: Lobster Fest; Yachting regatta. **In the area:** Butchers Gap Conservation Park, 6 km SW, has walking trails; contact Tourist information for pamphlets. Scenic drive west to Cape Jaffa, a small fishing village. The Granites, unique rock formations; 18 km N. Mt Scott Conservation Park, 20 km E. Jip Jip Conservation Park, 50 km NE. **Tourist information:** The Big Lobster, Princes Hwy; (087) 67 2555. **Accommodation:** 3 motels, 1 hostel, 1 cara./camp. park. **See also:** The Coorong.

Lameroo   Pop. 567

MAP REF. 293 H3, 295 Q11

A quiet little settlement 212 km E of Adelaide on the Mallee Hwy. **In the area:** Baan Hill Reserve, 20 km SW, a natural soakage area surrounded by sandhills and scrub; picnic facilities. Ngarkat Conservation Park, 25 km S. Byrne Homestead (1898), built of pug and pine; 3 km SE along Yappara Rd (contact Tourist information to gain entry). Billiatt Conservation Park, 37 km N. **Tourist information:** Council Offices, Railway Tce North; (085) 76 3002. **Accommodation:** 1 hotel/motel.

Leigh Creek   Pop. 1378

MAP REF. 291 D4, 297 J4

Located in the Flinders Ranges, Leigh Creek is the second-largest town north of Port Augusta. The economy is based on the large open-cut coalfield. The open-cut eventually consumed the original township, about 13 km N, and in 1982 residents moved to the new township. The extensive development and tree-planting scheme that followed transformed the new site into an attractive oasis. **In the area:** Viewing area for coal workings, 3 km from turnoff to coalfields, north on Hawker-Marree

Hwy; free tours on Sat. (Mar.–Oct.) and school holidays. Copley Hotel, 6 km N. Lyndhurst and Marree, 38 km and 119 km N, respective end points of Strzelecki and Birdsville Tracks. At Lyndhurst, unique gallery of sculptures by well-known talc-stone artist 'Talc Alf'; open to visitors. A further 5 km N of Lyndhurst, are the Ochre Pits, where Aborigines used to dig for ochre. Aroona Dam, 4 km W, in steep-sided valley with richly coloured walls; scenic picnic area near gorge. Gammon Ranges National Park, wilderness area; 64 km E. 'Almost ghost' town of Beltana 25 km S, declared an historic reserve; picnic race meeting and gymkhana in Sept. Sliding Rock Mine ruins, 60 km S; access track rough in places. Lakes Eyre, Frome and Torrens, all dry salt pans which occasionally fill with water; Desert Parks Pass required for Lake Eyre National Park (see National Parks for contact numbers and addresses). As with all outback driving, care must be taken; check road conditions with Northern Roads Condition Hotline on (08) 11633 before departure. **Tourist information:** The Town Centre, Electricity Trust of SA; (086) 75 4216. **Accommodation:** 1 motel, 1 cara./camp. park. **See also:** The Flinders Ranges; National Parks.

Loxton   Pop. 3322

MAP REF. 295 Q7

Known as the Garden City of the Riverland region, Loxton is 251 km NE of Adelaide. The surrounding irrigated land supports thriving citrus, wine, dried-fruit, wool and wheat industries. The area was first named Loxtons Hut, after a boundary rider from the Bookpurnong Station built a primitive pine and pug hut here. The largest war-service settlement scheme in the State was carried out here. **Of interest:** Loxton District Historical Village, on riverfront, with over 30 re-created buildings, and machinery and implements from late 1880s to mid-1900s; open daily except Christmas Day. Nearby, pepper tree planted by Loxton over 110 years ago. Art galleries and craft shops, for local paintings and handcrafts. Canoes available for hire. Jan.: Apex Fisherama. Feb.: Mardi Gras. Oct.: Agricultural show. Dec.: Christmas Magic. **In the area:** Excellent wines at Australian Vintage, Bookpurnong Rd (to Berri) in Loxton North. Picnic on banks of river at Habels Bend, 3 km NW. Kia Kia Nature Trail, for bushwalkers, in Murray River National Park; 10 km NW. Lock 4 and Moore's Woodlot (60 000 trees watered and fertilised by factory and town waste); 14 km N. Houseboats for hire at Kingston O.M., 40 km N. Unique wood sculpture display, 1½ km SE on Paruna Rd; open by appt (contact Tourist information). **Tourist information:** Bookpurnong Tce; (085) 84 7919. **Accommodation:** 1 hotel/motel, 1 B&B, 1 hostel, 1 cara./camp. park.

Lyndoch   Pop. 956

MAP REF. 288 E6, 292 C9, 295 L8

At the southern end of the Barossa Valley and a 40-min drive from Adelaide, Lyndoch is one of the oldest towns in the State. Early industry was farm-oriented, and four flour mills operated in the area. The Para River was used to operate a water mill in 1853. Vineyards were established early, but the first winery was not set up until 1896. **Of interest:** SA Museum of Mechanical Music, Barossa Valley Hwy; open daily. **In the area:** Wineries, most open for tastings and cellar-door sales, include to the north of town: Kies Estate Cellars, Burge Family Winemakers, Charles Cimicky Wines and Chateau Yaldara Estate; east of town: Kellermeister Wines and Barossa Settlers; south of town: Twin Valley Estate; west of town: Wards Gateway Cellar. At Rowland Flat, 5 km SE: Jenke Vineyards, Rovalley Estate, Orlando Wines and LiebichWein. Old School Gallery, local art; 9 km W. Goldfields Walk, 10 km W; brochure available at Tourist information. Barossa Reservoir and Whispering Wall, an acoustic phenomenon allowing messages whispered at one end to carry audibly to the other end, 140 m away; 8 km SW. Kersbrook, 22 km S: historic buildings and trout farm. **Tourist information:** Kies Estate Cellars, Barossa Valley Way; (085) 24 4110. **Accommodation:** 1 motel, 5 B&B, 1 cara./camp. park. **See also:** Vineyards and Wineries.

McLaren Vale   Pop. 1469

MAP REF. 288 A13, 289 F4, 290 C5, 293 B2, 295 K10

Centre of the McLaren winegrowing region, in which about 50 wineries flourish, McLaren Vale is 42 km S of Adelaide. Winemaking really began in 1853 when Thomas Hardy bought Tintara Vineyards. Today, Hardy's Tintara is the largest winery operating in the area; note huge Moreton Bay fig tree in grounds. **Of interest:** Historic buildings: Hotel McLaren, Main Rd; Congregational Church and Salopian Inn, Willunga Rd. Almond Train, variety of local almond produce housed in restored railway carriage; Main Rd. Oct.: One Continuous Picnic; Wine bushing festival. **In the area:** Many historic buildings are now restaurants, wineries, tearooms and galleries. Most wineries open for tastings and cellar-door sales; contact Tourist information. McLaren Vale Olive Grove, 3 km N: olive growing, crushing and bottling, and sales; open daily, tours available. Old Noarlunga, historic village 8 km NW. Scenic drive through wine region; starts ½ km W on Main Rd. **Tourist information:** The Cottage, Main Rd; (08) 8323 8537. **Accommodation:** 2 motels, 10 B&B, 1 cara./camp. park. **See also:** Festival Fun; Vineyards and Wineries.

Maitland   Pop. 1066

MAP REF. 294 I7

Maitland is a modern, well-planned town in the heart of Yorke Peninsula, and the centre for this rich agricultural area. Wheat, barley, wool and beef cattle are the main primary industries. Parks surround the town centre and provide both locals and visitors with many pleasant picnic spots. **Of interest:** St John's Anglican Church (1876), with stained-glass depicting Biblical stories in Australian settings; cnr Alice and Caroline Sts. Lions Bicycle Adventure Park, off Elizabeth St. Maitland National Trust Museum, in former school, has displays on local history (check opening times); cnr Gardiner and Kilkerran Tces. The Artist's Window, Robert St, local art and craft for sale. Self-guide nature and history trail; information and leaflets available from District Council, Elizabeth St. Apr.: Agricultural show. **In the area:** The 'copper triangle' towns of Moonta, Kadina and Wallaroo, 35 km N. Coastal town of Balgowan, 15 km W, popular with anglers. **Tourist information:** Yorke Peninsula Visitor Information Centre, 51 Taylor St, Kadina; (08) 8821 2093. **Accommodation:** 2 hotels. **See also:** The Yorke Peninsula.

SOUTH AUSTRALIA

National Parks

Nowhere else in Australia can wildlife be seen in such close proximity and in such profusion as in the parks of South Australia. To protect its valuable native animals and plants, and to conserve the natural features of the landscape, this State has set aside over 20 per cent of its total area as national, conservation and recreation parks, and regional and game reserves.

In addition to 17 national parks, the South Australian Department of Environment and Natural Resources also manages 211 conservation parks, 13 recreation parks, 10 game reserves and 7 regional reserves. The main criteria for each category, as stated in the National Parks and Wildlife Act of 1972, are as follows:

National parks. Areas with wildlife or natural features of national significance.

Conservation parks. Areas for the preservation and conservation of native flora and fauna representative of South Australia's natural heritage, although historical features may also be included in these parks.

Recreation parks. Areas for outdoor recreation in a natural setting.

Game reserves. Areas suitable for the management and conservation of native game species, usually duck and quail. Hunting of some species during restricted open seasons.

Regional reserves. A category established in 1988 which protects, at present, seven areas within South Australia considered to contain important wildlife and natural features, but where natural resources, such as minerals, may be needed in the future.

The range of climatic zones in South Australia enables visitors to enjoy these parks throughout the year; coastal parks are cool in summer and autumn, while mountain areas are ideal to visit in winter and spring.

In the south-east of the State

A unique, successful experiment of familiarising people with native fauna is evidenced at Cleland Wildlife Park in the centre of the larger **Cleland Conservation Park,** located on the slopes of Mount Lofty overlooking Adelaide. Here visitors are able to walk freely among the animals, which are housed in a natural bush setting in conditions similar to their native habitat.

Within Adelaide's southern suburbs is **Belair National Park,** which offers self-guide walks,

The Cazneaux Tree, near Wilpena in the Flinders Ranges National Park.

forested hills, spectacular views, parrots, wildflowers, an adventure playground, tennis courts, picnic facilities and the opportunity to tour Old Government House.

The Coorong, one of the State's finest national parks and of international importance, is 185 kilometres from Adelaide, south of the mouth of the mighty Murray River. From the Aboriginal word *karangh,* meaning 'narrow neck', Coorong is a series of saltwater lagoons fed by the Murray and separated from the sea by Younghusband Peninsula. In the park are six island bird sanctuaries, prohibited to the public, but which can be viewed through binoculars. These islands house rookeries of pelicans, crested terns and silver gulls. More than 280 species of birds have been recorded in the Coorong. The ocean beach is a favourite haunt of anglers. You can take the pleasant drive along the coast road beside the waterway, stopping to camp or picnic. At dusk, kangaroos and wombats can be seen feeding on the grassed open areas.

Bool Lagoon Game Reserve is on the southern flat plains of South Australia, near Naracoorte. The lagoon's natural cycle of flooding and drying out is perfect for breeding of waterbirds. In spring, when the water is deepest, the thousands of black swans that crowd the lagoon are spectacular. In summer and autumn, when the water is shallow, waterfowl and waders flock to feed on the rich plant life. Bool Lagoon is also the largest permanent ibis rookery in Australia. Dense thickets of paperbark and banks of reeds in the reserve's central reaches provide a safe breeding ground. A network of boardwalks provides access to wildlife without disturbing the natural environment.

The **Naracoorte Caves** are preserved in a small conservation park, now a World Heritage Area, in the south-east of the State. These impressive caves enclose a wonderland of stalagmites, stalactites, shawls, straws and other calcite formations. Four of the limestone caves, including Blanche Cave, the first to be discovered (1845), are open for inspection through guided or adventure tours. A tour through the museum set up in Victoria Fossil Cave shows visitors skeletons of such extinct animals as giant browsing kangaroos, a hippopotamus-sized wombat and a marsupial lion.

In the north of the State

The Flinders Ranges, extending for 430 kilometres, contain three national parks. **Mount Remarkable National Park** lies in a rugged and densely vegetated area of the southern Flinders Ranges. Mount Remarkable itself rises to 995 metres, and provides spectacular views over the surrounding country. The rock is red quartzite and glows a beautiful red at sunset. Two creeks flow through the park, providing water for river red gums, white cypress pines and brilliant wildflowers in spring. Alligator Gorge, the weathered red cliffs of which are a photographer's delight, and Mambray Creek, have a number of well-marked walking tracks.

The **Flinders Ranges National Park,** with its total area of 94 908 hectares, is one of the major national parks in Australia. The Wilpena section, in the south of the park, comprises the famed Wilpena Pound and the Wilpena Pound Range, covering an area of 10 000 hectares. The Pound is one of the most extraordinary geological formations in Australia. Developed in the Cambrian period, it is a vast oval rock bowl, ringed with sheer cliffs and jagged rocks, and with a flat floor covered with trees and grass. A homestead dating back to 1889 still stands. Native rock paintings at Arkaroo Rock indicate that this was a significant area in Aboriginal mythology. Twenty-five kilometres north of Wilpena is the Oraparinna section of the park. The 68 500 hectares of this section were a sheep station last century, at one time maintaining more than 20 000 sheep.

Further north the **Gammon Ranges National Park,** an arid, isolated region of rugged ranges and deep gorges, provides visitors with the experience of an extensive wilderness area. The mountains sparkle with exposed formations of quartz, fluorspar, hematites and ochres, making the region a gem-hunter's paradise (fossicking not permitted in geological sites). The Gammon Ranges are a sanctuary for many species of native fauna, including the western grey kangaroo, the big red kangaroo, the grey euro or hill kangaroo and the yellow-footed rock wallaby. Nearby, the remote settlement of Arkaroola offers motel accommodation and a serviced camping ground.

Further north, in the State's arid lands, over 8 million hectares have been set aside to protect the unique desert environment. Some of the parks and reserves in this vast desert area require a Desert Parks Pass from the Department of Environment and Natural Resources. These parks include Lake Eyre National Park, Witjira National Park, Innamincka Regional Reserve and Simpson Desert Conservation Park. Passes can be obtained from either the Adelaide Information Centre (77 Grenfell St, Adelaide, 5000; (08) 8204 1910) or from 60 Elder Tce, Hawker, 5434; (086) 48 4244. The pass is valid from the date of purchase; it allows twelve months' bush camping in Lake Eyre National Park, Witjira National Park, Innamincka Regional Reserve and Simpson Desert Conservation Park and Regional Reserve. The Desert Parks Pass also entitles you to free camping in Flinders Ranges and Gammon Ranges National Parks. The pass is part of the *Desert Parks South Australia Handbook* which also includes detailed information and maps on each park and reserve, and is available from the Department's offices in Adelaide and at Hawker as described above.

Lake Eyre, the central feature of the park of the same name, is one of the world's greatest salinas or salt lakes, found 16 metres below sea level. Contrarily, it is the hub of a huge internal drainage system while being located in the driest part of the Australian continent. In this area vegetation is sparse, but after heavy rains when the area floods, the ground is carpeted with colourful wildflowers, and the animal and bird populations attracted by the plant rejuvenation, rise accordingly. Care needs to be taken when visiting this area; 4WD vehicles are preferred for access to the park and campers must be fully self-sufficient.

Witjira National Park, 170 kilometres north of Oodnadatta, is an area of vast desert landscapes, gibber plains, sand dunes, salt pans and mound springs, upwellings of the Great Artesian Basin. Visitors may explore this extremely arid environment from the park's oasis, Dalhousie Springs.

The **Innamincka Regional Reserve** covers much of the flood prone country around the Cooper and Strzelecki Creeks up to the Queensland border. These arid wetlands, which comprise a series of semi-permanent overflow lakes, hold many surprises for bird-watchers.

The **Simpson Desert Conservation Park,** for the more adventurous park visitor, consists of spectacular red sand dunes, which in places can run parallel for hundreds of kilometres, as well as salt lakes, flood-out plains, hummock grasslands, gibber desert, gidgee woodland, tablelands and mesas.

In the south-west of the State

On the south-west tip of Yorke Peninsula is the 10 000-hectare **Innes National Park,** where the

National Parks

The Great Australian Bight forms the southern boundary of the Nullarbor National Park

SOUTH AUSTRALIA

ground is blanketed with wildflowers in spring and birdwatching is a favourite pastime. As well as native bushland and magnificent coastal scenery, there is good fishing at the beaches. Walking trails lead to the coast and to the historic ruins of Inneston (1913). This small settlement once housed miners who dug for gypsum, used for plaster and chalk; for many years nearly every schoolchild in Australia was taught with the aid of blackboard chalk mined here and shipped from Stenhouse Bay. Camping and accommodation are available.

Flinders Chase National Park, encompassing most of the western end of Kangaroo Island, protects pristine natural vegetation including forests, mallee and stunted coastal plants. Bushwalkers can enjoy trails along rivers to secluded beaches, or follow the rugged coastline to observe the full force of the Southern Ocean. Lighthouses and keepers' cottages provide cultural interest; visitors may see kangaroos, koalas, fur seals, echidnas and platypuses. **Seal Bay Conservation Park,** also on Kangaroo Island, allows visitors the unique opportunity to see Australian sea lion breeding colonies. The adjoining **Cape Gantheaume Conservation Park** is a wilderness area attracting experienced bushwalkers. A twelve-month pass for Kangaroo Island is available from the Department of Environment and Natural Resources office at 37 Dauncy St, Kingscote (PO Box 39, Kingscote 5223); (0848) 22 381, and enables access to all parks on the island where an entrance fee is charged.

The Eyre Peninsula, bordered to the north by the Eyre Highway, contains a number of parks. Coffin Bay National Park and Lincoln National Park feature wilderness areas and spectacular coastal scenery. Both these national parks provide excellent opportunities for bush camping, birdwatching and bushwalking. **Coffin Bay National Park** is 50 kilometres west of Port Lincoln and takes in all of Coffin Bay Peninsula. The western coastline faces the Great Australian Bight while the eastern part has sheltered sandy beaches and islands. Inquire locally about safe swimming.

Lincoln National Park, a 15-kilometre drive south of Port Lincoln, occupies a large part of Jussieu Peninsula and is surrounded by small islands. At its northern tip, on Stamford Hill, the Flinders Monument commemorates exploration by Matthew Flinders in 1802. From this hill visitors can enjoy spectacular views of the surrounding area.

Diverse bird habitats are provided at **Lake Gilles Conservation Park,** also on Eyre Peninsula, by the salt lakes and the dry mallee and western myall vegetation.

In the west of the State

Situated along the Eyre Highway in the far west corner of the State, the **Nullarbor National Park** offers spectacular views of the Great Australian Bight. The park itself is entirely desert, with patches of mallee scrub and some ground cover of bluebush and saltbush; it is renowned for its unique desolate, eerie beauty. The Nullarbor Plain's substratum of limestone has been eroded to form one of the largest underwater cave systems in the world, popular with experienced potholers and cave divers. Access to the caves is only available through arrangement with the Far West office of the Department of Environment and Natural Resources (11 McKenzie St, Ceduna; (086) 25 3144). The caves provide almost the only shelter for animals. Most species, including a large population of hairy-nosed wombats, are nocturnal.

Many of South Australia's national parks charge camping and entrance fees. For further information on camping restrictions, entry permits and fees, and general advice on visiting the State's national parks, contact the South Australian Department of Environment and Natural Resources Information Centre, 77 Grenfell St, Adelaide 5000 (GPO Box 1047, Adelaide 5001); (08) 8204 1910.

Mannum
Pop. 2025

MAP REF. 288 I9, 293 D1, 295 M9

Mannum, 82 km E of Adelaide, is one of the oldest towns on the Murray River. Picturesque terraced banks overlook the river. Wool, beef and cereals are produced in the region and the town is the starting point for the Adelaide water-supply pipeline. The *Mary Ann*, the first paddle-steamer on the Murray, left Mannum in 1853 and the first steam car was built in town in 1894 by David Shearer. **Of interest:** Mary-Ann Reserve, a popular recreation reserve on banks of Murray, has lookout tower, and picnic and barbecue facilities; also PS *River Murray Princess*. Historic Leonaville homestead, River Lane (1883), built by town's first private developer, Gottlieb Schuetze. PS *Marion* built in 1897, located in Arnold Park, Randell St. Twin ferries to eastern side of river and scenic upriver drive. Lookout, off Purnong Rd to east. River cruises available weekends in summer. May: Houseboat hirers open days. **In the area:** Excellent scenic drive from Wongulla to Cambrai; begins 20 km N. Award-winning Choni Leather, 10 km NW on Palmer Rd. Kia Marina, largest river marina in State (boats and houseboats available for hire); 8 km NE. Water sports at Walker Flat, 26 km NE. Scenic drive north-east along road to Purnong, runs parallel to a bird sanctuary for 15 km. Mannum Waterfalls Reserve, 10 km S, for picnics and scenic walks. **Tourist information:** PS *Marion* in Arnold Park, Randell St; (085) 69 1303. **Accommodation:** 1 motel, 3 B&B, 2 cara./camp. parks.

Marree
Pop. 85

MAP REF. 296 I1

Marree is a tiny outback town 645 km N of Adelaide at the junction of the legendary Birdsville and Oodnadatta Tracks. There are remnants of date palms planted by the Afghan traders who drove their camel trains into the Outback in the 1800s. Desolate saltbush country surrounds the town, now a service centre for the vast properties of the north-east of the State and for travellers. Oct.: Outback ball (even-numbered years). **In the area:** For motorists attempting the Birdsville and Oodnadatta Tracks care must be taken, as with all outback driving. These tracks are unsealed with sandy patches. Heavy rain in the area can cut access for several days. Motorists are advised to ring the Northern Roads Condition Hotline on (08) 11633 for information before departing; read section on Outback Motoring. On the Birdsville Track, fuel available only at Marree, Mungerannie Roadhouse (204 km N) and Birdsville. On the Oodnadatta Track, fuel available only at Marree, William Creek (202 km NW) and Oodnadatta. Lake Eyre National Park, 90 km N, accessible via Marree and Muloorina Station; Desert Parks Pass required (see National Parks for information). Ruins of railway sidings from original Ghan line to Alice Springs, at Curdimurka Siding and Bore; about 90 km W. Bubbler Mound Springs and Blanche Cup Mound Springs, 130 km W. Further 6 km W Coward Springs: extensive pond formed by warm water bubbling to the surface; old date palms, remnants of old plantation; and prolific birdlife. **Tourist information:** Hawker Motors, cnr Wilpena and Cradock Rds, Hawker; (086) 48 4014. **Accommodation:** 1 hotel. **See also:** The Outback.

Melrose
Pop. 205

MAP REF. 295 J2, 297 J12

Melrose is the oldest town in the Flinders Ranges, a quiet settlement at the foot of Mt Remarkable, 268 km N of Adelaide. **Of interest:** Historic buildings: old police station and court house (1862), Stuart St, now a National Trust Museum; ruins of Jacka's Brewery (former flour mill, 1877), Lambert St; North Star Hotel (1854), Nott St; and Mt Remarkable Hotel (1857), Stuart St. Melrose Inn (1857), Nott St; National Trust property, not open to the public. Serendipity Gallery, Stuart St. Heritage walk available. Pleasant walks and picnic spots along creek. Scenic views from War Memorial and Lookout Hill, Joe's Rd. Further on, Cathedral Rock. **In the area:** Walking trail (allow 5 hrs return) from town to top of Mt Remarkable (956 m); superb views. Mt Remarkable National Park, 2 km W. M. Woolford's sheep property at Murraytown, 3 km SW; visitors welcome. Near Murray Town, 14 km S: scenic lookouts at Box Hill, Magnus Hill and Baroota Nob; scenic drive west through Port Germein Gorge. Booleroo Steam Traction Preservation Society's Museum, Booleroo Centre, 15 km SE; open by appt. **Tourist information:** Council Offices, Stuart St; (086) 66 2014. **Accommodation:** 1 hotel, 1 cara./ camp. park.

Meningie
Pop. 818

MAP REF. 293 D4, 295 M12

Meningie is set on the edge of the freshwater Lake Albert and the northern tip of the vast salt pans of the Coorong National Park, 159 km from Adelaide. It is a farming area, and more than 40 professional anglers are employed on the lakes and the Coorong; fishing is a major industry in the town. The area abounds with a variety of birdlife including ibis, pelicans, cormorants, ducks and swans. Sailing, boating, water-skiing and swimming are popular. **In the area:** Camp Coorong, 12 km S, Aboriginal museum and cultural centre; Aboriginal food tours available, inquire at Tourist information. The Coorong, south and west: inland waterways, islands, ocean beach and wildlife. Scenic drive west following Lake Albert, adjacent to Lake Alexandrina, the largest permanent freshwater lake in the country (50 000 ha). Poltalloch Homestead, 30 km NW, one of the oldest in the region; accommodation and tours available, contact Tourist information. Further west, channel between lakes is crossed by free ferry service at Narrung. **Tourist information:** Melaleuca Centre, 76 Princes Hwy; (085) 75 1259. **Accommodation:** 1 hotel, 2 motels, 3 B&B, 1 cara./camp. park. **See also:** The Coorong.

Millicent
Pop. 5118

MAP REF. 293 G11

A thriving commercial and industrial town 50 km from Mt Gambier, Millicent is in the middle of a huge tract of land reclaimed in the 1870s. Today rural and fishing industries contribute to the area's prosperity, with pine forests supporting a paper mill and a sawmill. **Of interest:** On northern edge of town, gum trees surround a fine swimming lake and picnic area. Award-winning National Trust Museum and Admella Gallery, housed in original primary school (1873); Mt Gambier Rd. Shell Garden, Williams Rd, unusual display surrounded by fuchsias, ferns and begonias; open mid Aug.–mid June. Mar.: Radiata festival week. **In the area:** Tantanoola, 21 km SE, home of famous 'Tantanoola Tiger' (a Syrian wolf shot in the 1890s); 'tiger' now stuffed and displayed in the Tantanoola Tiger Hotel.

Naracoorte Caves, a World Heritage area, south-east of Naracoorte

Underground caves in Tantanoola Caves Conservation Park, fascinating limestone formations; 20 km SE on Princes Hwy, open daily. Also at Caves, Trevor Peters' 4-ha terraced cottage garden and restored National Trust cottage; open Sept.–Apr. (check opening times). Scenic pine-forest drive to Mount Burr, 10 km NE. National Trust Woolshed (1863) at Glencoe, 29 km E; tours available, contact Tourist information. Massive sand dune system and fascinating flora and fauna in Canunda National Park, 27 km W; accessed from Millicent and Southend; scenic self-guide walks (leaflets available). **Tourist information:** 1 Mt Gambier Rd; (087) 33 3205. **Accommodation:** 1 hotel/motel, 2 motels, 2 cara./camp. parks.

Minlaton   Pop. 796

MAP REF. 294 I9

Minlaton is a prosperous town serving the nearby coastal resorts of Yorke Peninsula. The town, 209 km W of Adelaide, was originally called Gum Flat because of the giant eucalypts in the area. Pioneer aviator Harry Butler, pilot of the Red Devil, a 1916 Bristol monoplane, was born here. **Of interest:** In Main St: Harry Butler Memorial; Fauna park; and National Trust Museum, check opening times. **In the area:** Gum Flat Homestead Gallery, pioneer homestead with local artists' work; 1 km E. At Port Vincent, 25 km E: good swimming, yachting and water-skiing; yacht race in Jan. Gipsy Waggon holidays at Brentwood, 14 km SW. Scenic Port Rickaby and Bluff Beach, 16 km NW. **Tourist information:** Council Offices, Main St; (08) 8853 2102. **Accommodation:** 1 hotel/motel, 1 cara./camp. park.

Mintaro   Pop. 80

MAP REF. 295 L5

The township nestles among rolling hills and rich agricultural land, 19 km SE of Clare. Classified as a Heritage Town, Mintaro is a timepiece of early colonial architecture. Many of the buildings display the fine slate for which the district is world-renowned; the quarry opened in 1854. **Of interest:** Early colonial buildings, 18 with heritage listings. Two historic cemeteries. Mar.: Paddys market, food and bric-a-brac. **In the area:** Magnificent classical architecture of Martindale Hall (1880), 3 km SE; location for film *Picnic at Hanging Rock*; open daily (check times); overnight accommodation and dining available. Clare, 19 km SE; over 20 wineries nearby. **Tourist information:** Town Hall, 229 Main North Rd, Clare; (08) 8842 2131. **Accommodation:** 1 hotel.

Moonta   Pop. 2723

MAP REF. 294 I6

The towns of Moonta, Kadina and Wallaroo form the corners of the area known as the 'Copper Triangle' or 'Little Cornwall'. Moonta is a popular seaside resort 163 km NW of Adelaide, with pleasant beaches and good fishing at Moonta Bay. A rich copper-ore deposit was discovered here in 1861 and soon thousands of miners, including many from Cornwall, flocked to the area. The mines were abandoned in the 1920s with the slump in copper prices and rising labour costs. **Of interest:** Stone buildings, charming Queen Square and picturesque town hall opposite the Square in George St. All Saints Church (1873), cnr Blanche and Milne Tces. Galleries include the Pug 'n' Dabble, George St. Prize-winning Cornish festival called Kernewek Lowender, is held in conjunction with nearby towns of Kadina and Wallaroo in May (odd-numbered years). Sept.: Agricultural show (odd-numbered years). **In the area:** Moonta Mines, a State Heritage Area, on Arthurton Rd, about 2 km SE: Moonta Mines National Trust Museum (old primary school), Cornish miner's cottage (1870) furnished in period style, pump house, shafts, tailings heaps and ruins of mines offices. On weekends and public and school holidays, Moonta Mines Railway takes visitors from Moonta Mines National Trust Museum through mines area. **Tourist information:** Town Hall, George St; (08) 8825 2622. **Accommodation:** 2 hotels, 1 motel, 4 B&B, 2 cara./camp. parks. **See also:** Festival Fun; The Yorke Peninsula.

Morgan   Pop. 446

MAP REF. 295 N6

Once one of the busiest river ports in the State, Morgan is a quiet little township on the Murray River, 164 km NE of Adelaide. **Of interest:** Self-guide heritage trail covers historic sites: the impressive wharves (1877), standing 12 m high, constructed for the riverboat industry; customs house and court house near railway station, reminders of town's thriving past. Picnic/barbecue facilities, with children's play area, near customs house. Mo's Pottery, Eighth St. Glass Space Studio and Gallery, cnr Second and Ninth Sts. Dockyards on Oval Rd; tours by appt. Port of Morgan

Historic Museum in old railway buildings on riverfront, off High St; open by appt. PS *Mayflower* (1884), still operating; details from museum's caretaker. Houseboats available for hire. July: Fun run, walk cyclathon. **In the area:** Morgan Conservation Park, across river. Fossicking for fossils near township. White Dam Conservation Park, 9 km NW. Engineering and Water Supply Pumping Station, 2 km E on Renmark Rd; tours by appt. Nor-West Bend private museum, 8 km E on Renmark Rd; open by appt. Overnight horse trail rides; book at Nor-West Bend. Riverland Camel Farm and Trail Ride, 13 km E on Renmark Rd; day and overnight trips available. **Tourist information:** Morgan Roadhouse, Fourth St; (085) 40 2205. **Accommodation:** 1 hotel, 1 hotel/motel, 1 motel, 1 cara./camp. park.

Mount Gambier   Pop. 21 153

MAP REF. 293 H12

In 1800 Lieutenant James Grant, sighted an extinct volcano and named it Mount Gambier. The city is on the slopes of the volcano, in the centre of the largest softwood pine plantations in the country. Surrounded by rich farming, horticulture, viticulture and dairy country, Mount Gambier is 460 km SE of Adelaide. The Hentys built the first dwelling in the area in 1841 and by 1850 there was a weekly postal service to Adelaide. The white Mount Gambier stone used in most of the buildings, together with many fine parks and gardens, make an attractive environment. **Of interest:** Historic buildings: town hall (1862), Commercial St; post office (1865), Bay Rd; and many old hotels. Heritage walks leaflets from Tourist information. Open caves: Cave Garden, Bay Rd; Umpherston Cave, Jubilee Hwy East; and Engelbrecht Cave, water-filled cave or sinkhole, Jubilee Hwy. Old Court House Law and Heritage Centre, National Trust museum; Bay Rd, open daily. Lewis' Museum, Pick Ave; open daily. The *Lady Nelson* Tourist and Interpretive Centre, Jubilee Hwy East, has full-scale replica of *Lady Nelson* as part of centre's structure. Dimjalla Park, fun park with barbecue areas; Jubilee Hwy East. Riddoch Art Gallery, in complex of 19th century buildings; Commercial St East. Nov.: Blue Lake festival. **In the area:** On the outskirts of town: crater lakes, particularly Blue Lake (197 m at its deepest) which changes from dull grey to brilliant blue each Nov. then reverts at end of summer; scenic 5 km drive offers lookouts, wildlife reserve, picnic areas and boardwalks; Pumping Station at Blue Lake, daily tours down through pumping station to lake level; and tours of timber mills, inspection of treatment process including pines being felled, trimmed and sawn ready for loading; contact the *Lady Nelson* Centre for details. Animal and Reptile Park, animal nursery and native gardens; 10 km N, off Penola Rd. Tarpeena Fairy Tale Park, 22 km N on Penola Rd. Glencoe Woolshed (1863), 23 km NW, National Trust building; open Sun. p.m. or by appt. Splendid Tantanoola Caves, 30 km W; tours available. Chant's Place flora and fauna park at Kongorong, 25 km SW. Haig's Vineyard, 4 km S. Mount Schank, 12 km S, excellent views of surrounding district. Glenelg River cruises from Nelson (Vic.), 36 km SE; tours of spectacular Princess Margaret Rose Caves. **Tourist information:** *Lady Nelson* Tourist Information and Interpretive Centre, Jubilee Hwy East; (087) 24 1730. **Accommodation:** 5 hotels, 1 hotel/motel, 21 motels, 3 B&B, 6 cara./camp. parks.

Murray Bridge   Pop. 12 725

MAP REF. 288 I12, 293 D2, 295 M10

Murray Bridge is South Australia's largest river town. The South Eastern Fwy provides access to Adelaide, 80 km away. First settled in the 1850s, it was a centre for the bustling riverboat traders. Murray Bridge overlooks a broad sweep of the Murray River. Water sports, river cruises and excellent accommodation make Murray Bridge a perfect holiday spot. **Of interest:** Captain's Cottage Museum, Thomas St. In Jervois Rd: Butterfly House; and Puzzle Park, a fun-park for adults as well as children. Cottage Box chocolate factory, Wharf Rd; open daily. Riverside reserves: Sturt Reserve, offers fishing, swimming, picnic and playground facilities; Hume Reserve, Hume Rd; and Long Island Reserve, Long Island Rd. Sims Park, for views of town; Lookout Dr. Charter and regular cruises on MV *Barrangul* and MV *Bridge Explorer*; chartered cruises on PS *Proud Mary*; contact Tourist information. Jan.: State championship swimming. Nov.: Big River Challenge festival, includes speedboat racing, water-skiing events and land-based sporting challenges. **In the area:** Monarto Zoological Park, 10 km W off Old Princes Hwy, an open-range zoo with many endangered species; open Sun. and public and school holidays. Willow Glen Wines, 10 km S on Jervois Rd. Riverglen Marina, 11 km S, has houseboats available for hire. Earthworks Pottery, 9 km NE, on Karoonda Rd. Talyala Emu Farm, 6 km N on Mannum Rd; open daily. Mypolonga, 14 km N, centre for surrounding beautiful citrus and stone-fruit orchard area and rich dairying country. At Avoca Dell, 5 km upstream: boating, water-skiing, mini-golf and picnic facilities. Thiele Reserve, east of river, good for water-skiing. Other riverside reserves located at Swanport, 5 km SE; and White Sands, 6 km S. Lookouts: White Hill, west on Princes Hwy; and east at new Swanport Bridge. **Tourist information:** Community Information and Tourist Centre, 3 South Tce; (085) 32 6660. **Accommodation:** 2 hotels, 4 motels, 1 B&B, 1 hostel, 5 cara./camp. parks.

Naracoorte   Pop. 4711

MAP REF. 293 H9

Situated 330 km SE of Adelaide, Naracoorte dates from the 1840s. The area is world-renowned for its limestone caves. Beef cattle, sheep, grains and grapes are the main local primary industries. **Of interest:** Sheep's Back wool museum, art gallery and tourist information, in former flour mill (1870); MacDonnell St. Naracoorte Museum and Snake Pit, museum collection and live snakes; Jenkins Tce (closed mid-July to end Aug.). Mini Jumbuk Factory, Smith St, for woollen products. Restored locomotive on display in Pioneer Park. Regional Art Gallery, Smith St. Jubilee Park and Swimming Lake, off Park Tce. May: Swap meeting; Young riders equestrian event. Oct.: Agricultural show. Dec.: Street-traders party; Carols by candlelight. **In the area:** Tiny Train Park, trains and mini-golf; 3 km S. World Heritage-listed Naracoorte Caves, in Conservation Park, 12 km SE: Victoria Fossil Cave, has unique fossilised specimens of Ice Age animals including giant kangaroos and giant wombats; Blanche Cave and Alexandra Cave have spectacular stalagmites and stalactites; bat viewing in new interpretive centre; tours daily. Bool Lagoon Wetlands 17 km S, haven for ibis and species of numerous waterbirds; guided boardwalks and bird-hide. Coonawarra wine region, located 40 km S. Padthaway and Keppoch wine districts, about 40 km NW. **Tourist information:** The Sheep's Back, MacDonnell St; (087) 62 1518. **Accommodation:** 3 hotels, 1 hotel/ motel, 4 motels, 5 B&B, 2 cara./camp. parks. **See also:** National Parks.

Nuriootpa Pop. 3321

MAP REF. 288 F4, 292 G4, 295 M7

The Para River runs through the town of Nuriootpa, its course marked by fine parks and picnic spots. The town is the commercial centre of the Barossa Valley. **Of interest:** Coulthard Reserve, off Penrice Rd. Coulthard House, pioneer settler's home; Murray St (not open). Luhrs Pioneer German Cottage, Light Rd. St Petri Church, First St. **In the area:** Wineries, south of town: Elderton Wines, Tarac Distillers, Penfolds Wines, Kaesler Farm; west of town: Heritage Wines, Gnadenfrei Estate, Seppelts Wines, Greenock Creek Cellars; north-east of town: The Willows Vineyard, Wolf Blass Wines, Stockwell Wines; south-east of town: Barossa Cottage Wines, Saltram Wine Estates; also other wineries in Barossa Valley. Most wineries are open for tastings and cellar-door sales. Hot Air Balloon Regatta in May at Seppeltsfield, 6 km W. **Tourist information:** Barossa Valley Visitors Centre, 68 Murray St, Tanunda; 1800 81 2662 or (085) 63 0600. **Accommodation:** 1 hotel, 1 motel, 1 cara./camp. park. **See also:** Vineyards and Wineries.

Old Noarlunga Pop. 2000

MAP REF. 288 A12, 289 F3, 290 B4, 293 B2, 295 K10

A small, historic village in the McLaren winegrowing region, Old Noarlunga is 32 km S of Adelaide on the Fleurieu Peninsula. **Of interest:** Church of St Philip and St James (1850), Church Hill Rd. Uniting Church, Malpas St. Old Jolly Miller Hotel (1850), now Noarlunga Hotel, Patapinda Rd. Market Square, site of first public market 1841. Leaflet for self-guide walking tour available. **In the area:** Port Noarlunga and Christies Beach, 10 km NW, and Moana and Maslin Beaches, 3 km and 6 km S; all offer good swimming and fishing. About 8 km N of Port Noarlunga, Hallett Cove has tracks left by glaciers millions of years ago. Lakeside Leisure Park at Hackham, 4 km N. At McLaren Vale, 5 km SE, some 50 vineyards and wineries. At Myponga, 27 km S: several historic buildings; Myponga Reservoir, barbecue and picnic facilities. **Tourist information:** Noarlunga Hotel, Patapinda Rd; (08) 8386 2061. **Accommodation:** None.

Oodnadatta Pop. 180

MAP REF. 298 B6

A tiny but famous outback town 1050 km NW of Adelaide, Oodnadatta is an old railway town with a well-preserved sandstone station (1890), now a museum. It is believed that the name Oodnadatta originated from an Aboriginal term meaning 'yellow blossom of the mulga'. Fuel and supplies available. May: Race meeting and gymkhana. **In the area:** Witjira National Park, gateway to Simpson Desert, 180 km N: hot thermal ponds at Dalhousie Springs; nearby, Dalhousie ruins (of early pastoral station); camping and accommodation at Mt Dare Homestead and at Dalhousie Springs; Desert Parks Pass required (see National Parks for information). The Oodnadatta Track runs from Marree through Oodnadatta and joins Stuart Hwy at Marla, 200 km W. Painted Desert, scenic drive; 100 km SW. **Tourist information:** Pink Roadhouse, Ikaturka Tce; (086) 70 7822 or 1800 80 2074. **Accommodation:** 1 hotel, 1 cara./camp. park.

Paringa Pop. 588

MAP REF. 122 A7, 295 Q6

Paringa, 4 km from Renmark, is the eastern gateway to the Riverland region. **Of interest:** Paringa Suspension Bridge (1927). Bert Dix Memorial Park, adjacent to Paringa Bridge. The Black Stump, root system of river red gum estimated to be about 500–600 years old; Murtho Rd. Houseboat marina, Lock 5 Rd; houseboats available for hire. **In the area:** Off Murtho Rd: Headings Lookout tower, 12 km N, excellent views of surrounding irrigated farmland and river cliffs; Murtho Forest Reserve, 15 km N, picnic and limited camping facilities. On Lock 5 Rd: SA Water Corporation Lock 5 and Weir, 2 km SW; Margaret Dowling National Trust Park, area of natural bushland; 3 km SW. Dunlop Big Tyre spans Sturt Hwy at Yamba Roadhouse, 12 km SE; also fruit fly inspection point (no fruit allowed into South Australia). Scenic drive, 36 km E into Victoria, to see spring blossoms at Lindsay Point Almond Park. **Tourist information:** Council Offices, Murtho Rd; (085) 95 5102. **Accommodation:** 1 hotel/motel, 1 cara./camp. park.

Penola Pop. 1147

MAP REF. 228 A2, 293 I10

The oldest town in the south-east of the State, Penola, 50 km N of Mount Gambier, has fine examples of slab and hewn-timber cottages erected in the 1850s. Several famous names are associated with Penola. Poets Adam Lindsay Gordon, John Shaw Neilson and Will Ogilvie all spent time here. The first school in Australia catering for children regardless of income or social class was established here in 1866 by Mother Mary MacKillop, recently beatified. The stone classroom in which she taught is on the corner of Portland St and Petticoat Lane. **Of interest:** In Petticoat Lane: heritage buildings, and art and craft shops. Self-guide heritage walk; details from Tourist information. John Riddoch Interpretive Centre in former Mechanics Institute: history of area and audiovisual, poetry recitals; Arthur St. Hydro-carbon display centre, features hands-on and static displays of oil process; at Tourist information, Arthur St. Market (bric-a-brac) last Sat. each month. Jan.: Vignerons Cup. June: Festival. **In the area:** Yallum Park Homestead (1880), historic homestead built by John Riddoch, founder of Coonawarra wine industry; 8 km W. Signposted walk at Penola Conservation Park, 10 km W. Coonawarra, 10 km N, has 15 wineries; most open for tastings and cellar-door sales. **Tourist information:** Arthur St; (087) 37 2855, (018) 84 9909. **Accommodation:** 2 hotels, 1 hotel/motel, 1 cara./camp. park.

Peterborough Pop. 2138

MAP REF. 295 L2, 297 K12

Peterborough is an old railway town 250 km N of Adelaide, surrounded by grain-growing and pastoral country. It is the principal town on the Port Pirie to Broken Hill railway line. **Of interest:** Historic narrow-gauge steam-train journeys to Orroroo or Eurelia; check

Kangaroo Island

Only 120 kilometres southwest of Adelaide, Kangaroo Island, the third largest Australian island, shows nature in its wildest and purest form. A walk through bush or along coastal cliffs may provide glimpses of koalas, echidnas or, of course, kangaroos; there are also several species of birds and wildflowers.

Visitors may fly to the island from Adelaide (Air Kangaroo Island, Emu Airways, Albatross Airlines and Kendell Airlines) or go by ferry. The ferry *Super Flyte* takes passengers from Glenelg to Kingscote (Sept. to Apr.). The vehicular ferries *Philanderer III* and *The Navigator*, and the passenger ferry *Valerie Jane* operate from Cape Jervis to Penneshaw. Tours are available and hire vehicles include cars, mopeds and bicycles. A bus service operates between Kingscote and the airport. A shuttle bus operates twice daily between Penneshaw and Kingscote. Kangaroo Island's waters offer excellent fishing; game-fishing charters are available and fishing equipment can be hired.

At the four main towns, **Kingscote**, American River, Parndana and Penneshaw, there is a range of accommodation from hotels and motels, through flats and cottages, to camping, cabins and bed-and-breakfasts. Many farms also provide bed and breakfast accommodation.

American River, nestled in a pine-fringed bay, is ideal for fishing, scuba diving and canoeing. Pelican Lagoon is a sanctuary for birds and fish. Penneshaw overlooks the passage separating the island from the mainland. Little (fairy) penguins promenade on the rocks here at night.

The coastline of the island varies from the several kilometres of safe swimming beach at Emu Bay in the north to the rugged cliffs and roaring surf of the south. However, in the south, D'Estrees Bay's wide deserted beach is ideal for fishing, collecting shells and exploring; there is an old whaling station at Point Tinline. **Cape Gantheaume** and **Seal Bay Conservation Parks** are located on this exposed southern coast. Seal Bay has a permanent colony of Australian sea lions. New Zealand fur seal colonies are found at Cape Gantheaume and Cape du Couedic, and leopard seals are occasional visitors. Also on the south coast are limestone formations in the caves at Kelly Hill Conservation Park. At Cape Borda, on the north-west tip of the island, is one of the most picturesque of Australia's old lighthouses; there are guided tours daily, arranged through the Department of Environment and Natural Resources at Cape Borda. Other attractive spots along the northern coast include the rugged rocks at Harveys Return; Western River Cove with its idyllic white beach; a superb protected bay at Snelling Beach; and Stokes Bay, where a secret tunnel leads to the beach. On the west coast, which is dominated by the soaring eucalypt forests of the **Flinders Chase National Park,** are two of the island's natural wonders: Admirals Arch, a huge arch where on sunny afternoons stalactites can be seen in silhouette; and the Remarkable Rocks, huge, unusually shaped granite boulders.

For further information and for a pass that covers all entry fees for the national parks, and tours, contact the Kangaroo Island Tourist Information Centre, 37 Dauncey St, Kingscote, (0848) 2 2381. **See also**: National Parks for those parks indicated by bold type; and entry for Kingscote in A–Z listing. **Map references:** 289 A10, 294 F11.

Australian sea lions, Seal Bay

times. Rann's Museum, 144 Moscow St, exhibits historic railway equipment and farm implements; open daily. The Gold Battery, an ore-crushing machine; end Tripney Ave (open by appt). Saint Cecilia, Callary St, gracious home (with splendid stained glass) once a bishop's residence; accommodation, dining and murder-mystery nights. In Queen St: Ley's Museum, exhibition of antiques (open daily); and Victoria Park, with picnic facilities and children's playground. Feb.: Rodeo. **In the area:** Terowie, old railway town with historic buildings; 24 km SE. At Ororoo, 37 km NW: historic buildings, Yesteryear Costume Gallery with display of fashion from 1850s; nearby, scenic walk among Aboriginal carvings along Pekina Creek; and panoramic views from Black Rock Peak, east. At Magnetic Hill, 8 km W of Black Rock, a vehicle with the engine turned off rolls uphill! **Tourist information:** Main St; (086) 51 2708. **Accommodation:** 2 hotels, 2 hotel/ motels, 1 motel, 1 hostel, 1 cara./camp. park.

Pinnaroo Pop. 645

MAP REF. 122 A11, 232 A10, 293 I3, 295 R10

This little township on the Mallee Hwy is only 6 km from the Victorian border. **Of interest:** Australia's largest cereal collection (1300 varieties), Pinnaroo Institute, Railway Tce Sth; weekdays only, obtain key from Council Offices. Historical Museum in railway station, Railway Tce Sth. Working printing museum, South Tce. Nearby, animal park and aviary with native birds. Farm-machinery museum at showgrounds, Homburg Tce. **In the area:** Walking trail in Karte Conservation Park; 30 km NW, on Karte Rd. Gum Family Collection, farm machinery; 25 km N at Kombali Homestead. Peebinga Conservation Park, 42 km N, on Loxton Rd. In Scorpion Springs Conservation Park, walking trail at Pine Hut Soak; 28 km S. Ngarkat Conservation Park, 48 km S, popular with birdwatchers. Pertendi walking trail, 49 km S. **Tourist information:** Council Offices, Day St; (085) 77 8002. **Accommodation:** 2 hotels, 1 motel, 1 B&B, 1 cara./camp. park.

Port Augusta Pop. 14 595

MAP REF. 291 A12, 296 I11

A thriving industrial city at the head of Spencer Gulf and in the shadow of the Flinders Ranges, Port Augusta is the most northerly port in South Australia. It is 317 km from Adelaide and is a vital supply centre for the outback areas of the State and the large sheep stations of the district. Port Augusta is an important link on the Indian–Pacific railway and a stopover for the famous Ghan train to Alice Springs, which departs from Adelaide. The city has played an intrinsic role in the State's development since the State Electricity Trust built a series of major power stations here. Fuelled by coal from the huge open-cut mines at Leigh Creek, the stations generate more than a third of the State's electricity. **Of interest:** Multi award-winning Wadlata Outback Centre, Flinders Tce, introduction to the sights and sounds of the outback. Homestead Park Pioneer Museum, Elsie St: large photographic collection, picnic areas, blacksmith's shop, old steam train and crane, and rebuilt 130-year-old pine-log Yudnappinna Homestead. Royal Flying Doctor Service Base, Vincent St, open weekdays. School of the Air, Power Cres.; tours during school-term time. Curdnatta Art and Pottery Gallery in town's original railway station, Commercial Rd; check opening times. Self-guide heritage walk includes: town hall (1887), Commercial Rd; court house (1884) with cells built of Kapunda marble, cnr Jervios St and Beauchamp's Lane; and St Augustine's Church (1882), Church St, with magnificent stained glass. Scenic views and picnic facilities in parks adjacent to: McLellan Lookout, Whiting Pde, site of Matthew Flinders landing in 1802; and Water Tower Lookout (1882), Mitchell Tce. Matthew Flinders Lookout, end of McSporran Cres., provides excellent view of Gulf and Flinders Ranges. Nearby are the new Australian Arid Lands Botanic Gardens. **In the area:** Scenic drive north-east to splendid Pichi Richi Pass, historic Quorn, and Warren and Buckaringa Gorges; or see the same sights by train on the Pichi Richi Railway, a 33-km round trip operating from Quorn from Easter to Nov. Tours of Northern power station, 4 km E, on weekdays. Winninowie Conservation Park, 30 km SE. Hancocks Lookout, 38 km SE towards Wilmington, provides excellent views of surrounding country including Port Augusta and Whyalla; turnoff road dangerous when wet. Mt Remarkable National Park features rugged mountain terrain, magnificent gorges and abundant wildlife; 63 km SE. Historic Melrose, 65 km SE, oldest town in Flinders Ranges. **Tourist information:** Wadlata Outback Centre, Flinders Tce; (086) 41 0793. **Accommodation:** 7 hotels, 9 motels, 1 hostel, 3 cara./camp. parks.

Port Broughton Pop. 681

MAP REF. 295 J4

A small port on the extreme north-west coast of Yorke Peninsula, Port Broughton is 169 km from Adelaide. On a protected inlet, the town is a major port for fishing boats and is renowned for its deep-sea prawns. **Of interest:** Safe swimming beach along foreshore. Historical Museum (old school building), Harvey St, and Cottage Museum, Kadina Rd, contain much of town's history. In Harvey St, Shandelé porcelain dolls made and on display. Historic walking trail. Charter boats and dinghies available for hire. **In the area:** Fisherman's Bay, 10 km N: popular fishing, boating and holiday spot. Heritage copper-mining towns of Moonta, Wallaroo and Kadina, 47 km S. Clare Valley and surrounding wine districts, 100 km E. **Tourist information:** Yorke Peninsula Visitor Information Centre, 51 Taylor St, Kadina; (08) 8821 2093. **Accommodation:** 1 hotel, 1 hotel/motel, 2 cara./camp. parks.

Port Elliot Pop. 1203

MAP REF. 289 H8, 290 F12, 293 C3, 295 L11

Only 5 km NE of Victor Harbor, Port Elliot is a charming, historic coastal town with the main focus on scenic Horseshoe Bay, the town's beach. The town was established in 1854, the same year Australia's first public horse-drawn railway operated between Goolwa and Port Elliot. **Of interest:** Along The Strand: National Trust historical display at railway station (1911); council chamber (1879); police station (1853); and St Jude's Church (1854). Spectacular views from Freeman's Knob at end of The Strand. Port Elliot Art Pottery, Main Rd. Guided walks of town available; contact Tourist information. **In the area:** Crows Nest Lookout, breathtaking views of coast; 6 km N. Middleton Winery, 11 km NE via Middleton. **Tourist information:** Dodd & Page Land Agents, 51 The Strand; (085) 954 2029. **Accommodation:** 2 hotels, 1 motel, 1 cara./camp. park.

Commercial fishing fleet moored at Lincoln Cove, Port Lincoln

Port Lincoln

Pop. 11 345

MAP REF. 294 D8

Port Lincoln, originally considered as a possible site for the State's capital, is attractively sited on the clear waters of Boston Bay, which is three times the size of Sydney Harbour. The port, 250 km due west of Adelaide across St Vincent and Spencer Gulfs, was reached by Matthew Flinders in 1802 and settled by Europeans in 1839. With its sheltered waters, Mediterranean climate, scenic coastal roads and attractive farming hinterland, Port Lincoln is a popular tourist resort. It is also the base for Australia's largest tuna fleet and an important export centre for wheat, wool, fat lambs, live sheep, frozen fish, lobster, prawns, abalone and tuna. The coastline is deeply indented, offering magnificent scenery, sheltered coves, steep cliff faces and impressive surf beaches. **Of interest:** Boston Bay for swimming, water-skiing, yachting and excellent fishing. Mill Cottage Museum (1867) and Settler's Cottage Museum; both in picturesque Flinders Park. Old Mill lookout, Dorset Place, offers views of town and bay. Lincoln Hotel (1840), oldest hotel on Eyre Peninsula; Tasman Tce. Axel Stenross Maritime Museum, north end of town. Nearby, First Landing site. Rose-Wal Memorial Shell Museum in grounds of Eyre Peninsula Old Folks Home. Arteyrea Gallery, Washington St, community art centre. Barbed Wire and Fencing Equipment Museum; open by appt. M.B. Kotz Collection of Stationary Engines, Baltimore St. Lincoln Cove, off St Andrews Tce: marina, leisure centre, holiday charter boats and base for commercial fishing fleet. Boat charter available for game fishing, diving, day fishing and island cruises. Yacht charter available. Regular launch cruises of Boston Bay and Boston Island. *Dangerous Reef Explorer* available for group charter to Dangerous Reef, off Boston Island, home for large sea lion colony, an underwater marine viewing platform and a commercial tuna farm. Apex Wheelhouse, original wheelhouse from tuna boat *Boston Bay*; adjacent to Kirton Point Caravan Park, Hindmarsh St. Jan.: Tunarama festival, (Australia Day holiday) celebrates opening of tuna season. Feb.: Lincoln week regatta. **In the area:** Several pleasant parks close to town. Vast natural reserves abounding in wildlife, within a day's outing. Winter Hill Lookout, 5 km NW on Flinders Hwy. Greenpatch Farm, 15 km NW, has native animals and bird-feeding; open Wed.–Sun. and school holidays. Coffin Bay, 49 km NW: lookout; Coffin Bay Oyster Farm for fresh oysters and other seafood; Oyster Trail; boat hire; and nearby Coffin Bay National Park. Boston Bay Winery, 6 km N on Lincoln Hwy, and Delacolline Estate Winery, Whillas Rd; sales on weekends or by appt. Karlinda Collection, adjacent to post office at North Shields, 16 km N: shells, marine life and Deepwater Trawl Fish Exhibit. At Poonindie, 20 km N, church (1850) with two chimneys. Award-winning Quandong Farm, 45 km N, has orchids, quandong seedlings and trees; open Tues. for tours or by appt. At Koppio, 38 km N: Koppio Smithy Museum (open Tues.–Sun.); Kurrabi Lodge, local crafts (open Tues.–Sun.); Tod Reservoir museum with heritage display and nearby picnic area. Tumby Bay, 48 km N, small beach resort. At Lincoln National Park, 20 km S: wildlife, extensive network of walking trails including access to Flinders Monument on Stamford Hill for panoramic views, cliff-top walk to impressive coastal scenery and Flinders Tablet in Memory Cove, a plaque in memory of crew members lost in seas nearby during Flinders' 1802 epic voyage (gate key and entry pass required; contact National Parks office at Port Lincoln). Whalers Way, a privately owned scenic clifftop tourist drive on southernmost tip of Eyre Peninsula: stunning coastal scenery from Flinders Lookout; permit required, contact Tourist information. On road to Whalers Way: Constantia Designer Craftsmen, world-class furniture factory and showroom (guided tours available); and historic Mikkira sheep station, open winter. Offshore islands for boating enthusiasts: Boston and Thistle Islands have accommodation; Thistle and Wedge Islands (both privately owned), popular with bluewater sailors and anglers. **Tourist information:** Eyre Travel, Civic Centre, Tasman Tce; (086) 82 4577. **Accommodation:** 3 hotels, 7 motels, 2 cara./camp. parks. **See also:** Festival Fun; The Eyre Peninsula.

Port MacDonnell

Pop. 677

MAP REF. 293 H13

Port MacDonnell is 28 km S of Mount Gambier. It is a quiet fishing town that was once a thriving port. The rock-lobster fishing fleet here is the largest in the State. **Of interest:** Maritime Museum, Meylin St, features salvaged artifacts from shipwrecks and photographic history of town. Jan.: Regatta day; Oz Rock music festival. **In the area:** 'Dingley Dell' (1862, but restored) home of poet Adam Lindsay Gordon, now a museum; 2 km W. Cape Northumberland Lighthouse on dramatic coastline west of town. Devonshire teas at Ye Olde Post Office Tea Rooms at Allendale East, 6 km N. Walking track to summit of Mt Schank, 10 km N, crater of extinct volcano; picnic facilities available. Nearby Mt Schank Fish Farm has fresh fish and yabbies for sale. Heading east, good surf fishing at Orwell Rocks. Sinkholes for experienced cave divers at Ewens Ponds, 7 km E, and Picaninnie Ponds Conservation Parks, 20 km E. **Tourist information:** Council Offices, 7 Charles St; (087) 38 2207. **Accommodation:** 1 hotel, 1 motel, 2 cara./camp. parks.

Port Pirie Pop. 14 110

MAP REF. 295 J3, 296 I13

Huge grain silos and smelters' chimneys dominate the skyline of Port Pirie, 227 km N of Adelaide on Spencer Gulf. Situated on the tidal Port Pirie River, the city is a major industrial and commercial centre. The first European settlers came in 1845; wheat farms and market gardens were established around the sheep industry in the region. Broken Hill Associated Smelters began smelting lead in 1889 and today the largest lead smelters in the world treat thousands of tonnes of concentrates annually from the silver, lead and zinc deposits at Broken Hill, NSW. Wheat and barley from the mid-north of the State are exported and there is a thriving fishing industry. Port Pirie is also a vital link in the road and rail routes to Alice Springs, Darwin, Port Augusta and Perth. Wheat farms, rolling hills and the ocean are all close by. Swimming, water-skiing, fishing and yachting are popular sports on the river. **Of interest:** Regional Tourism and Arts Centre: local and touring exhibitions, and craft shop; Mary Elie St. National Trust Museum Buildings, Ellen St, includes Victorian pavilion-style railway station; open daily. Historic residence 'Carn Brae', Florence St, features antique exhibits and a collection of over 2500 dolls; open daily. On waterfront: loading and discharging of Australian and overseas vessels. Tours of Pasminco Metals BHAS smelting works; details from Tourist information. Northern Festival Centre in Memorial Park, venue for local and national performances; Gertrude St. May: Street go-kart grand prix. Sept.: Blessing of the fleet and associated festivals, celebrate role of Italians at turn of century in establishing local fishing industry. Oct.: Festival of country music. **In the area:** Weeroona Island: good fishing, holiday area accessible by car; 13 km N. Port Germein, beach resort 24 km N: wooden jetty said to be longest in southern hemisphere; Festival of the crab in Jan. Southern reaches of beautiful Flinders Ranges are within 50 km; further east, ruggedly beautiful Telowie Gorge, lined with giant red river gums. **Tourist information:** Regional Tourism and Arts Centre, Mary Elie St; (086) 33 0439. **Accommodation:** 2 hotels, 1 hotel/motel, 4 motels, 3 cara./camp. parks.

Port Victoria Pop. 313

MAP REF. 294 H7

A tiny township on the west coast of Yorke Peninsula, Port Victoria was once the main port for sailing ships carrying grain from the area. **Of interest:** Geology trail; booklet available from Tourist information. Swimming and jetty fishing, from original 1888 jetty; end of Main St. National Trust Maritime Museum on jetty; check opening times. Wardang Island, Aboriginal reserve, 10 km off coast; permission required from Point Pearce Community Council. **In the area:** Conservation Islands are breeding areas for several bird species. Underwater Maritime Heritage Trail for scuba divers in waters around Wardang Island, visits to 8 wrecks; self-guide leaflet available. **Tourist information:** Yorke Peninsula Visitor Information Centre, 51 Taylor St, Kadina; (08) 8821 2093. **Accommodation:** 1 hotel/motel, 2 cara./camp. parks. **See also:** The Yorke Peninsula.

Quorn Pop. 1056

MAP REF. 291 B12, 296 I10

Nestled in a valley in the Flinders Ranges, 331 km N of Adelaide, Quorn was established as a railway town on the Great Northern Railway in 1878. Built by Chinese and British workers, the line was closed in 1957; part of the line through Pichi Richi Pass has been restored as a tourist railway taking passengers on the scenic 33-km round trip. **Of interest:** Historic buildings; historic walk leaflet available. In Railway Tce.: Quorn Mill (1878), originally a flour mill, now motel and restaurant; Quornucopia Galley; railway station, departure point for Pichi Richi Railway (operates Easter to end Nov.). Nairana Craft Centre, First St. **In the area:** Colourful rocky outcrops of Dutchman's Stern, 6 km W; walking trails in area. Junction Gallery, 16 km N on Yarrah Vale Rd. Warren Gorge, popular with climbers; 22 km N. Buckaringa Gorge, 32 km N: rock wallabies can be seen at dusk; picnic and camping areas. Kanyaka Homestead, ruins of historic sheep station; 42 km NE. Nearby, Kanyaka Death Rock, overlooks permanent waterhole, once an Aboriginal ceremonial ground. Towns of Bruce and Hammond, 22 km and 38 km SE respectively: 1870s architecture; and at Hammond, unusual museum and restaurant in original bank building. Scenic drive 50 km S to Devil's Peak, Pichi Richi Pass, Mt Brown Conservation Park and picturesque Waukarie Creek, 16 km away; walking trails in area. **Tourist information:** 3 Seventh St; (086) 48 6419. **Accommodation:** 2 hotels, 2 hotel/motels, 1 motel, 7 B&B, 1 cara./camp. park.

Renmark Pop. 4256

MAP REF. 295 Q6

Renmark is at the heart of the oldest irrigation area in Australia, 260 km NE of Adelaide on the Sturt Hwy. In 1887 the Chaffey brothers from Canada were granted 250 000 acres to test their irrigation scheme. Today lush orchards and vineyards thrive with the water piped from the Murray River. There are canneries, wineries and fruit-juice factories. Wheat, sheep and dairy cattle are other local industries. **Of interest:** Historic Renmark Hotel, community-owned and run. National Trust Museum 'Olivewood', former Chaffey homestead; cnr Renmark Ave (Sturt Hwy) and 21st St. Display of old hand-operated wine-press, Renmark Ave. One of the Chaffeys' original wood-burning irrigation pumps on display outside Renmark Irrigation Trust Office, original Chaffey Bros. office; Murray St. PS *Industry* (1911), now floating museum moored behind Tourist information. Rivergrowers Ark packing shed, sales of local products; Renmark Ave, near 19th St; group tours available. Zenith Art Gallery, Murtho St; Ozone Art Gallery, Murray Ave. Houseboats for hire. Oct.: Agricultural show. Dec.: Christmas pageant; Rowing regatta. **In the area:** Renmano Winery, 5 km SW on Sturt Hwy. Unique collection of fauna, particularly reptiles, at Bredl's Wonder World of Wildlife, 7 km SW on Sturt Hwy; open daily. Ruston's Roses, 3000 varieties, 7 km SW off Sturt Hwy; open

The Flinders Ranges

Moralana Scenic Drive, south of Wilpena Pound, one of many scenic drives in the ranges

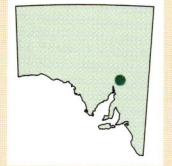

The Flinders Ranges are part of a mountain chain which extends for 430 kilometres from its southern end (between Crystal Brook and Peterborough) to a point 160 kilometres east of Marree. The most spectacular peaks and valleys are in three areas: the first in the **Melrose–Wilmington** area; the second, north-east of **Port Augusta;** and the third, east of **Leigh Creek.** The Flinders, while similar in scale to many of Australia's mountain ranges, are totally different in both colouration and atmosphere. There is a unique quality in the contrast of the dry, stony land and richly lined rock faces – the characteristics of a desert range – with the rich vegetation of the river red gums, casuarinas, native pines and wattles that clothe the valleys and cling to hillsides and rock crevices. In spring, after rain, the display of wildflowers is sometimes breathtaking, carpeting the whole region with masses of reds, pinks, yellows, purples and white. The wildflowers, together with the natural beauty of the rock shapes, pools, caves and twisted trees, make the Flinders Ranges a favourite haunt of photographers and artists. Many paintings by Sir Hans Heysen embody the shape and spirit of the ranges.

The Flinders is served by good roads. A pleasant trip, which will take in the best of the scenery, is the drive north-east from Port Augusta through the Pichi Richi Pass to **Quorn** and **Hawker,** and from there on the loop road to Parachilna, circling the Wilpena Pound area. But it is better to stay and explore the unique quality of the Flinders, this fascinating region, preferably on foot or by vehicle. There are kilometres of signposted tracks in the ranges, but as it is still only too easy to lose your way, it is important to be equipped with a good map and to follow a planned route. Drivers should avoid using the secondary roads after rain; they can be treacherous when wet.

The best-known feature of the Flinders Ranges is Wilpena Pound, an elevated basin covering about 50 square kilometres and encircled by sheer cliffs, which are set in a foundation of purple shale and rise through red stone to white-topped peaks. The only entrance is a narrow gorge, through which a creek sometimes flows. The external cliffs rise to over 1000 metres, but inside is a gentle slope to the floor of the plain. The highest point in the Pound is St Mary's Peak, at 1165 metres, which dominates the northern wall and provides a magnificent view over the mountains. Within the Pound are low, rounded hills and folded ridges, grasslands and pine-clad slopes that descend to the gums along Wilpena Creek. It is a wonderland of birdlife: rosellas, galahs, red-capped robins, budgerigars and wedgetailed eagles are common here. Bushland possums and endangered yellow-footed wallabies can also be seen.

There is a resort at **Wilpena,** catering for levels of accommodation from camping to modern motel. In this central section of the ranges are Warren Gorge, Buckaringa Gorge, Brachina Gorge, Yourambulla Cave with its Aboriginal drawings, the Hills of Arkaba, considered the most beautiful spur in this region, Bunyeroo and Aroona Valleys and the **Flinders Ranges National Park.**

Other features in the Flinders that are spectacular include, in the central section: Stokes Hill Lookout and the Great Wall of China, a long rocky escarpment; in the northern section: Mount Chambers and Chambers Gorge, which can be reached by vehicle or on foot.

The far northern region of the ranges also invites exploration. The 61 000-hectare privately-run property **Arkaroola** is a sanctuary situated in rugged outback country featuring quartzite razorback ridges over elongated valleys, once the sea bed of a great continental shelf, the legacy that remains is rippled rock with embedded marine fossils. There is a profusion of wildlife: emus, ducks, parrots, cockatoos, galahs, marsupial mice possums and yellow-footed rock wallabies – all abound in large numbers. Accommodation and camping is available at Arkaroola. Nearby is **Gammon Ranges National Park.**

From the heavily timbered slopes in the southern ranges, through picturesque gorges and rolling plains to the arid ranges of the north, the Flinders offer a variety of experiences. In addition to its unique flora and fauna, and its rugged beauty, the region contains an important Aboriginal heritage and traces of early pioneering days.

For further information on the area, contact Flinders Ranges and Outback of South Australia Regional Tourism, PO Box 666, Adelaide 5001; (08) 8373 3430. **See also:** National Parks and individual entries in A–Z listing for those parks and towns indicated by bold type. **Map reference:** 291.

Oct.–May. Angove's winery and distillery, Bookmark Ave, 5 km SW. Danggali Conservation Park, vast area of mallee scrub, bluebush and black oak woodland, and wildlife; 60 km N. **Tourist information:** Tourist and Heritage Centre, Murray Ave; (085) 86 6704. **Accommodation:** 1 hotel/motel, 4 motels, 1 B&B, 1 hostel, 3 cara./camp. parks. **See also:** Festival Fun.

Robe   Pop. 730

MAP REF. 293 F9

A small, historic town on Guichen Bay, 336 km S of Adelaide, Robe is a fishing port and holiday centre. The rugged, windswept coast has many beautiful and secluded beaches. Lagoons and salt lakes surround the area and wildlife abounds; penguins appear on the beach in the evening in summer. In the 1850s, Robe was a major wool port. During the gold rush, 16 500 Chinese disembarked there and travelled overland to the goldfields to avoid the Victorian Poll Tax. **Of interest:** National Trust buildings, and art and craft galleries; especially in Smillie and Victoria Sts. Historic Interpretation Centre in Library building, Victoria St: displays and tourist information including leaflets on self-guide heritage walks and drives. Old Customs House Museum (1863), Royal Circus; check opening times. Karatta House, summer residence of Governor Sir James Fergusson in 1860s; off Christine Dr. (not open). Caledonian Inn (1858), accommodation and meals; Victoria St. Crayfish fleet anchors in Lake Butler (Robe's harbour); fresh crays and fish Oct.–Apr. Jan.: Beer can regatta. Sept.: Blessing of the fleet. **In the area:** Long Beach (17 km long), 2 km N. Lakeside (1884), historic home, accommodation and caravan park; Main Rd, 2 km SE. Waterskiing on adjacent Lake Fellmongery. Narraburra Woolshed, sheep and wool activities; 14 km SE. Beacon Hill, panoramic views; 2 km S. Little Dip Conservation Park, 13 km S, features a complex moving sand-dune system, salt lakes, freshwater lakes and abundant wildlife. The Obelisk at Cape Dombey, 3 km W. **Tourist information:** Robe Library, Victoria St; (087) 68 2465. **Accommodation:** 2 hotels, 6 motels, 8 B&B, 3 cara./camp. parks.

Roxby Downs   Pop. 1999

MAP REF. 296 F4

A modern, newly established township built to accommodate the employees of the Olympic Dam mining project, Roxby Downs is 85 km N of Pimba, which is just off Stuart Hwy, 555 km N of Adelaide. A road from Roxby Downs

SOUTH AUSTRALIA

The Coorong

The Coorong National Park curves along the southern coast of South Australia for 145 kilometres, extending from the mouth of the Murray River in the north almost to the township of Kingston S.E. in the south. A unique area, it has an eerie isolation, a silence broken only by the sounds of any of the 280 species of native birds wheeling low over the scrub and dunes, and the pounding of waves from the Southern Ocean.

The Coorong proper is a shallow lagoon, a complex system of low-lying salt pans and clay pans. Never more than 3 kilometres wide, the lagoon is divided from the sea by the towering white sandhills of Younghusband Peninsula, known locally as the Hummocks. One of the best natural bird sanctuaries in Australia, the Coorong is home for giant pelicans, cormorants, ibis, swans and terns.

Access to the Park is gained by leaving the Princes Highway at Salt Creek and following the old road along the shore. Noonameena, Mark Point and Long Point in the northern section can be accessed from the turnoff at Meningie. Explore the unspoiled stretches of beach where the rolling surf washes up gnarled driftwood and beautiful shells. Year-round access to the beach is from a point further south known as 'the 42 mile'; the final 1.3 kilometres is suitable for 4WD or walking. The coastal scenery is magnificent.

For those who wish to explore in comfort, **Meningie** in the north and the fishing port of **Kingston S.E.** in the south have a range of accommodation and can be used as touring bases. Camping is permitted in the Coorong National Park; however, in the Younghusband Peninsula section, it is allowed in designated areas only. Permits may be obtained from local commercial outlets (look for the pelican logo), from self-registration points in the Park or from the Coorong Shop in Meningie. The area is rich in history as well as being a naturalists' haven; pick up the *Coorong Tattler* for details. Fishing, boating and walking are popular.

For further information, contact the Department of Environment and Natural Resources office, Meningie; (085) 75 1200. **See also:** National Parks; and entries for Kingston S.E. and Meningie in A–Z listing. **Map references:** 293 E5, 295 N13.

Coorong National Park protects a unique landscape and bird sanctuary

joins the Oodnadatta Track just south of Lake Eyre South, 125 km N of Roxby. **In the area:** Olympic Dam Mining Complex, 15 km N; daily tours of mining operations available mid Mar.–mid Nov. Heritage Centre and Missile Park, 90 km S at Woomera. **Tourist information:** Council Offices, Richardson Place; (086) 71 0010. **Accommodation:** 1 motel, 1 cara./camp. park.

Stansbury Pop. 513

MAP REF. 294 I9

Situated on the lower east coast of Yorke Peninsula, Stansbury was originally known as Oyster Bay because the bay was once one of the best oyster beds in the State. In days gone by, ketches shipped grain across the gulf from Stansbury to Port Adelaide. A popular holiday resort, the town has scenic views of Gulf St Vincent. The bay is excellent for water sports, including diving and water-skiing. May: Sheepdog trials. **Of interest:** School House Museum, in first Stansbury school (1878); North Tce. Jetty fishing. **In the area:** Lake Sundown, 15 km NW: one of many salt lakes in area; and photographer's delight at sunset. **Tourist information:** Yorke Peninsula Visitor Information Centre, 51 Taylor St, Kadina; (08) 8821 2093. **Accommodation:** 1 hotel, 2 motels, 2 cara./camp. parks.

Strathalbyn Pop. 2623

MAP REF. 289 I4, 290 I7, 293 C3, 295 L10

An inland town with a Scottish heritage, on the Angas River, Strathalbyn is 58 km S of Adelaide and a designated heritage township. The picturesque Soldiers Memorial Gardens follow the river through the town, offering shaded picnic grounds. **Of interest:** National Trust Museum, in old police station and court house; Rankine St. St Andrew's Church (1848), Alfred Pl. Old Provincial Gas Company (1868), now Gasworks Restaurant; South Tce. Antique and craft shops. Aug.: Collectors, hobbies and antique fair. Oct.: Glenbarr Scottish festival; Agricultural show. **In the area:** Lakeside resort town of Milang, 20 km SE; heritage trail around this old riverboat town available. Langhorne Creek, 15 km E: centre for winegrowing district; museum in town. Lookout, 7 km SW, views over town and district. Pottery at Paris Creek, near Meadows, 15 km NW. Iris gardens, 2 km W of Meadows; open Oct.–Mar. Jupiter Creek Goldfields, old gold diggings; 35 km NW. **Tourist information:** Old Railway Station, South Tce; (085) 36 3212. **Accommodation:** 2 hotels, 3 B&B, 1 cara./camp. park.

Streaky Bay Pop. 957

MAP REF. 303 P12

Streaky Bay, 727 km NW of Adelaide, is an excellent holiday resort, fishing port and agricultural centre for the cereal-growing hinterland. Matthew Flinders, the explorer, named the bay for the streaking effect caused by seaweed in its waters. The town is almost surrounded by small bays and coves, pleasant sandy beaches and spectacular towering cliffs. Crayfish and many species of fish abound, and fishing from boat or jetty is good. **Of interest:** At Tourist information: fishing information and interesting shark replica. Restored Engine Centre, Alfred Tce, has exterior historic murals. Old School House Museum, Montgomery Tce. Hospital Cottage (1864), first building in Streaky Bay. St Canutes Catholic Church, Poochera Rd. Jan.: Family fish day contest; Perlubie Beach sports and race day. Mar.: Race meeting. Dec.: Carols by the sea. **In the area:** Magnificent coastal scenery and rugged cliffs. Point Labatt Conservation Park, 55 km SE, has only permanent colony of sea lions on Australian mainland. Half-day tourist drive (map available): to diving and snorkelling areas, sea lions and Murphy's Haystacks, 2 sculptural groups of ancient pink granite rocks; 40 km SE off Flinders Hwy. Port Kenny, 62 km SE on Venus Bay; excellent fishing. Further 12 km S, fishing village of Venus Bay; nearby, breathtaking views from Needle Eye Lookout. Spectacular limestone caves at Talia, 88 km SE. Bairds Grave Monument, 25 km S. Felchillo Oasis: including quandong park (where fruit is grown) and wildlife sanctuary; 9 km NE. **Tourist information:** 13–15 Alfred Tce; (086) 26 1126. **Accommodation:** 1 hotel/motel, 1 motel, 1 B&B, 1 hostel, 1 cara./camp. park. **See also:** The Eyre Peninsula.

Swan Reach Pop. 230

MAP REF. 295 N8

Swan Reach is a quiet little township on the Murray River, about 100 km E of Gawler. Picturesque river scenery and excellent fishing make it an increasingly popular holiday resort. **In the area:** Swan Reach (11 km W) and Ridley (5 km S) Conservation Parks. Punyelroo, 7 km S, offers fishing, boating and water-skiing. Yookamurra Sanctuary, 21 km NW: conservation project, including eradication of feral animals and restocking with native animals; guided walks; overnight accommodation, bookings essential. The Murray Plains Museum, 45 km NW; open by appt. Nildottie, nearby junction of Rivers Marne and

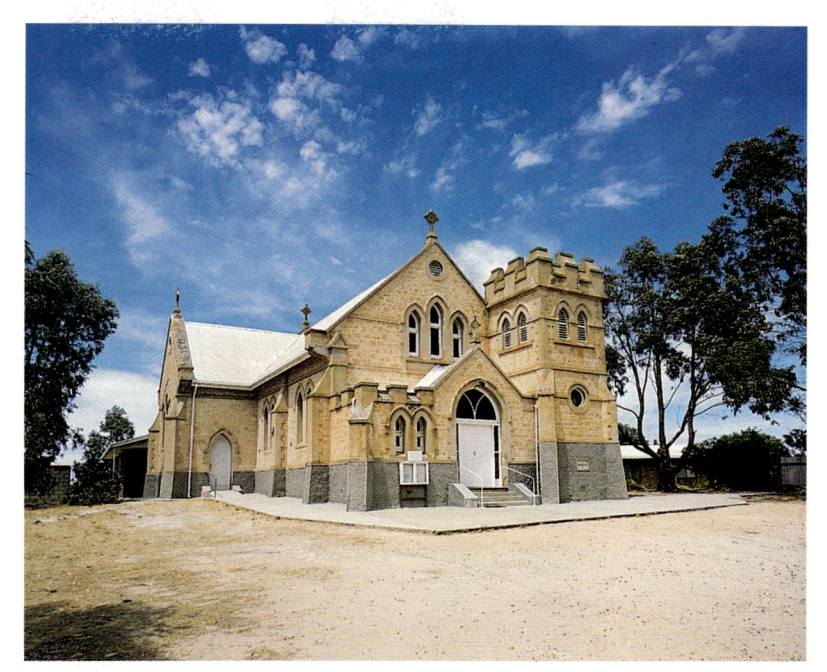

St Canutes Catholic Church, an historic church in Streaky Bay

Murray; 14 km S. Water sports at Walker Flat, 26 km S. **Tourist information:** Swan Reach Supermarket, Anzac Ave; (085) 70 2036. **Accommodation:** 1 hotel, 1 cara./ camp. park.

Tailem Bend   Pop. 1502

MAP REF. 293 E3, 295 N10

Once a railway-workshop town, now a service centre situated at the junction of the Dukes, Mallee and Princes Hwys, 107 km SE of Adelaide, Tailem Bend has excellent views across the Murray as the river bends sharply towards Wellington. Feb.: Gumi racing festival. **In the area:** Scenic drive via vehicular ferry across river to Jervois (visit the cheese factory), then 11 km S to Wellington, where river meets lake. At Wellington, restored court house complex (1864): cells, stables, post and telegraph office, courtyard and kiosk. Historic old woolshed, SE on Dukes Hwy, on left approaching Cooke Plains. Old Tailem Town Pioneer Village, 5 km N; open daily. **Tourist information:** 87–89 Railway Tce; (085) 72 3537. **Accommodation:** 2 hotels, 1 motel, 2 cara./camp. parks.

Tanunda   Pop. 3087

MAP REF. 288 F5, 292 F6, 295 L8

The town of Tanunda is the heart of the Barossa wine region. It was the focal point for early German settlement, growing out of the village of Langmeil, established in 1843, part of which can be seen in the western areas of town. **Of interest:** Fine examples of Lutheran churches. Historical museum, former post and telegraph office (1865), Murray St: collections specialising in German heritage; Color Studio for local art and craft. New Barossa Wine and Visitor Centre, a wine interpretation centre; 66 Murray St. Award-winning Kev Rohrlach Collection, displays range from pioneering heritage to satellites; Barossa Valley Way, Tanunda Nth; open daily. Story Book Cottage and Whacky Wood, for children; Oak St. Barossa Kiddypark, Menge St, family funpark with rides. Jan.: Oompah Fest. Mar.: Essenfest. **In the area:** Local wineries, to the north: Basedow Wines, Old Barn Wines, Veritas Winery, Richmond Grove Barossa Winery, Stanley Bros. Winery, Peter Lehmann Wines, Chateau Dorrien Wines and Tolley Pedare Winery; to the south: Turkey Flat Vineyards, Lanzerac Estate Wines, St Hallet Wines, Grant Burge Wines, Rockford Wines, Charles Melton Wines and Krondorf Wines. Bethany, first German settlement in Barossa, 4 km S: pretty village with creekside picnic area, pioneer cemetery, attractive streetscapes and two wineries (High Wycombe Wines and Bethany Wines). Norm's Coolie Sheep Dogs, 2 performances weekly (Wed. and Sat.); south off Barossa Valley Way. The Keg Factory, makers of kegs, barrel furniture, and wine racks; St Hallet Rd. At

SOUTH AUSTRALIA

The Fleurieu Peninsula

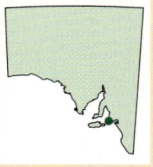

Starting 22 kilometres south of Adelaide, the Fleurieu Peninsula region stretches from O'Halloran Hill for about 90 km to Cape Jervis on the west coast, and east around the vast fresh waters of Lake Alexandrina, where the Murray River meets the sea.

The ocean scenery varies from magnificent cliff faces and roaring surf to wide, sandy beaches and sheltered bays and coves. Maslin Beach is renowned as Australia's first nude bathing beach. Cape Jervis, located at the tip of the Peninsula, commands a clear view across Backstairs Passage to Kangaroo Island.

McLaren Vale, the centre of the McLaren wine-producing region, has over 50 wineries. Some are in historic buildings with attached restaurants; most are open for tastings and cellar-door sales.

Inland there are historic buildings, particularly at **Willunga,** where public buildings vie with small cottages for the visitor's attention. The almond orchards around here are a marvellous sight, especially when they bloom at the end of winter. Late July to early August is Almond blossom festival time. Ideal for keen walkers as well as those looking for a quiet picnic spot are a number of conservation parks. There is a scenic drive around Myponga Conservation Park.

Victor Harbor is one of South Australia's most popular beach resorts. Either walk or take the historic horse-drawn tram along the causeway to Granite Island to see the colony of little (fairy) penguins. Spend time in **Port Elliot** to take in its history and perhaps take a ride to Goolwa on the Cockle Train, a steam train restored from the original line opened in 1854; for operating times inquire at Tourist information.

Rapid Bay, on the west coast of the Peninsula

There is superb fishing at **Goolwa.** Once a busy port, it is now the starting point for paddle-steamer cruises up the Murray, and cruises to Hindmarsh Island and the Barrages.

For further information on the area, contact the Victor Harbor Tourist Information Centre, 10 Railway Tce, Victor Harbor; (085) 52 5821 or (085) 52 5738. **See also:** individual entries in A–Z listing for those towns indicated by bold type. **Map references:** 289 E7, 290 A11, 293 B4.

Kersbrook, 40 km s: historic buildings; and trout farm. **Tourist information:** Barossa Wine and Visitors Centre, 66 Murray St; 1800 81 2662 or (085) 63 0600. **Accommodation:** 1 hotel, 1 hotel/motel, 2 motels, 18 B&B, 1 cara./camp. park. **See also:** Festival Fun; Vineyards and Wineries.

Tintinara   Pop. 316

MAP REF. 293 F5, 295 O12

A quiet little town 206 km SE of Adelaide in the Coonalpyn Downs. **In the area:** Historic buildings at Tintinara Homestead, 9 km W. Mt Boothby Conservation Park, 20 km W. Mt Rescue Conservation Park features sandplains with heath, native fauna, and Aboriginal campsites and burial grounds; 15 km E. **Tourist information:** Heart of the Park Tourist and Craft Shop, Becker Tce; (087) 57 2220. **Accommodation:** 1 hotel, 1 motel, 1 B&B, 1 cara./camp. park.

Tumby Bay   Pop. 1147

MAP REF. 294 E7

Tumby Bay is a pretty coastal resort 49 km N of Port Lincoln on the east coast of the Eyre Peninsula. The town is well-known for its long crescent beach and white sand. Lawns and picnic/barbecue facilities are found along the foreshore. **Of interest:** C. L. Alexander National Trust Museum, in old wooden schoolroom; West Tce; open Fri. and Sat. p.m. Police station (1871), Tumby Tce. Two jetties, one more than 100 years old. Jan.: Fishing competition. **In the area:** Rock and surf fishing. At Lipson Cove, 10 km NE, visitors can walk across to Lipson Island at low tide. Rugged, beautiful scenery and fishing at Poonta and Cowley's Beaches, 15 km NE; catches include snapper, whiting and bream. At Port Neill, 42 km NE: grassed foreshore for picnics; safe swimming beach; Vic and Jill Fauser's Museum (open daily); and Port Neill Lookout, 1 km N, for spectacular views. Fishing, sea lions, dolphins and birdlife at Sir Joseph Banks Group of islands, off coast; charter tours available. Trinity Haven Scenic Drive leads south along coast. Island Lookout for spectacular views; 3 km S. At Thuruna, excellent fishing; 10 km S. Koppio, about 40 km SW through attractive fertile countryside: National Trust-classified Smithy Museum, open Tues.–Sun.; and Tod Reservoir Museum. Near Wanilla, 60 km SW, wildflowers in spring. **Tourist information:** Hales Minimart, 1 Bratten Way; (086) 88 2584. **Accommodation**: 2 hotels, 1 motel, 1 cara./camp. park. **See also:** The Eyre Peninsula.

Victor Harbor   Pop. 5930

MAP REF. 289 G8, 290 E13, 293 B4, 295 L11

A popular coastal resort town and regional 'capital' of the Fleurieu Peninsula, Victor Harbor is 84 km S of Adelaide. Established in the early days of whaling and sealing (1830s), the town overlooks historic Encounter Bay, protected by Granite Island. **Of interest:** Historic buildings: original Congregational Church (1869), Victoria St; Mount Breckan (1879), Renown Ave; Adare House (1852), The Drive; Old Customs House (1867), now a National Trust Museum, Flinders Pde; St Augustine's Church (1869), Burke St; Telegraph Station Art Gallery, in former telegraph station (1866); Coral St. Davies Shoe Store, one of the longest family-owned shoe stores in the State; Railway Tce (no longer in operation). Whale-watching, from May–Sept. SA Whale Centre, educative displays to aid conservation of the 25 species of whale and dolphin in southern Australian waters; Railway Tce. Oct.: Folk and music festival. **In the area:** Granite Island, joined to mainland by 630 m causeway; walk or take horse-drawn tram (built 1894); chairlift (operates school holidays and weekends) offers magnificent views of land and sea; little (fairy) penguin rookeries on the island. The Bluff (Rosetta Head), facing Encounter Bay; worth 100-m climb for views. Waitpinga Beach, 17 km SW. Deep Creek Conservation Park, 50 km SW: spectacular flora and fauna; rugged cliffs; section of Heysen Trail for walking. Alongside Talisker Conservation Park, site of historic silver-lead mine; old mine buildings and diggings. At tip of Fleurieu Peninsula, Cape Jervis, 70 km SW, panoramic views to Kangaroo Island. Spring Mount Conservation Park, 14 km NW. Glacier Rock at Inman Valley, 19 km NW, shows effect of glacial erosion; said to be the first recorded discovery of glaciation in Australia. To north: Hindmarsh and Inman Rivers, good fishing and peaceful picnic spots. Greenhills Adventure Park, 3.5 km N on banks of Hindmarsh River. Urimbirra Wildlife Park, 5 km N. Opposite, Nangawooka Flora Reserve with over 1200 species of Australian plants. At Mt Compass, 24 km N: pottery; nearby, strawberry and blueberry farms, begonia farm and nursery, and Tooperang Trout Farm. The Steam Ranger, a restored, tourist railway service, operates between Victor Harbor and Goolwa, via Port Elliot. Hindmarsh Valley Falls, 15 km NE, has pleasant walks and spectacular waterfalls. **Tourist information:** 10 Railway Tce; (085) 52 5738. **Accommodation:** 2 hotels, 9 motels, 6 B&B, 1 hostel, 4 cara./camp. parks. **See also:** The Fleurieu Peninsula.

Waikerie   Pop. 1748

MAP REF. 295 O6

Waikerie, the citrus centre of Australia, is surrounded by an oasis of irrigated vegetable gardens, orchards and vineyards in mallee-scrub country in the Riverland. Situated 170 km NE of Adelaide, the town has beautiful views of the river gums and sandstone cliffs along

Horse-drawn tram, a popular attraction at Victor Harbor

the Murray River. The name means 'many things that fly': the river and lagoons teem with birdlife, and the mallee scrub is a haven for parrots and other native birds. **Of interest:** Co-op Fruit-packing House, the largest in Australia; Sturt Hwy. Lions Park, on riverfront, with children's playground and picnic/barbecue facilities. Harts Lagoon, a wetland area for birds with bird hides for viewing; Ramco Rd. Houseboat hire available. Feb.: International food fair. Easter: Horse and pony club gymkhana. **In the area:** The Orange Tree, fruit products and river-viewing platform; 2 km E on Sturt Hwy. Area internationally acclaimed as a glider's paradise; joy rides and courses available at Gliding Club 4 km E, off Sturt Hwy. Devlin's Pound, part of river where Devlin's ghost sighted; 11 km E. Holder Bend Reserve and Maize Island Conservation Park, 6 km NE. Crystallised gypsum fossils are found in abundance at Broken Cliffs on northern side of river near Lock 2, close to Taylorville. Brookfield Conservation Park, 11 km W, home of southern hairy-nosed wombat. At Blanchetown, 42 km W: first of Murray River's 6 SA locks; lookout at Blanchetown Bridge; floating restaurant. **Tourist information:** The Orange Tree, Sturt Hwy; (085) 41 2332. **Accommodation:** 1 motel, 1 hotel/motel, 1 cara./camp. park.

Wallaroo Pop. 2465

MAP REF. 294 I6

Situated 154 km NW of Adelaide, Wallaroo is a key shipping port for Yorke Peninsula, exporting barley and wheat. Processing of rock phosphate is another major industry here. The safe beaches and excellent fishing in this historical area make it a popular tourist resort. In 1859 vast copper-ore deposits were discovered. A smelter was built, thousands of Cornish miners arrived and Wallaroo and surrounding areas boomed until the 1920s, when copper prices dropped and the industry slowly died out. The nearby towns of Moonta and Kadina form part of the trio known as 'Little Cornwall', and the area still has many reminders of its colourful past. **Of interest:** Several charming old Cornish-style cottages in district. At cemetery, Moonta Rd, grave of Caroline Carleton, author of 'Song of Australia'. National Trust Wallaroo Heritage and Nautical Museum in town's original post office (1865), maritime exhibits; Jetty Rd. Historical walks, brochure available at museum or town hall, guided tours on Sun. Historic buildings: old railway station, Owen Tce; and in Jetty Rd, customs house (1862) and Hughes chimney stack (1865), which contains over 300 000 bricks and is more than 7 m square at its base. Wallaroo–Kadina Tourist Train operates from Wallaroo railway station, John Tce; second Sun. each month and during school holidays. Jan.: Regatta. May: Prize-winning Kernewek Lowender, Cornish festival held in conjunction with Moonta and Kadina (odd-numbered years). **In the area:** Nearby, fascinating towns of Moonta and Kadina. Wallaroo Mines site in Kadina, open for signposted self-guide walking tour; 10 km E. Bird Island, 10 km S, good crabbing. **Tourist information:** Yorke Peninsula Visitor Information Centre, 51 Taylor St, Kadina; (08) 8821 2093. **Accommodation:** 1 hotel, 1 hotel/motel, 2 motels, 3 cara./camp. parks. **See also:** Festival Fun; The Yorke Peninsula.

Whyalla Pop. 25 526

MAP REF. 294 I2, 296 H13

Whyalla, northern gateway to Eyre Peninsula, has grown from a small settlement known as Hummock Hill in 1901 to the largest provincial city in the State and an important industrial centre based on steel. It is famous for its heavy industry, particularly the enormous BHP iron and steel works, and ore mining in the Middleback Ranges. A shipyard operated from 1939–78, and the largest ship ever built in Australia was launched here in 1972. Whyalla is a modern city with safe beaches, good fishing and boating, and excellent recreational facilities. The area enjoys a sunny Mediterranean-type climate. **Of interest:** At Whyalla Maritime Museum, Lincoln Hwy: the largest permanently land-locked ship in Australia, the former 650-tonne corvette *Whyalla*; and a collection of models, including one of the biggest 'OO' gauge model railways in Australia, housed in the Tanderra Building; open daily 10–4. Mount Laura Homestead Museum (National Trust), Ekblom St; check opening times. Whyalla Art Gallery, Darling Tce. Foreshore redevelopment: attractive beach, jetty for recreational fishing, landscaped picnic and barbecue area, and marina with boat-launching facilities. Hummock Hill lookout, Queen Elizabeth Dr. Flinders Lookout, Farrel St. Ada Ryan Gardens, mini-zoo and picnic facilities under shady trees; Cudmore Tce. Guided tours of BHP steel works Mon. and Wed.; bookings at Tourist information (for safety reasons, visitors must wear long-sleeve top, trousers and closed footwear). Large, arid area wildlife and reptile sanctuary, south-east on Lincoln Hwy, near airport; open daily, bookings essential. Whyalla Tourist Drive, brochure from Tourist information. Jan.: Australian amateur snapper fishing championship. **In the area:** Port Bonython, 20 km E. Point Lowly, 34 km E: Point Lowly Lighthouse (1882), oldest building in area (not open); scenic coastal drive through Fitzgerald Bay to Point Douglas. Whyalla Conservation Park, 10 km N off Lincoln Hwy, near Port Bonython turnoff. At Iron Knob, 53 km NW: iron-ore quarries (tours available), Mining Museum, and Iron Knob Mineral and Shell Display. **Tourist information:** Lincoln Hwy; (086) 45 7900, 1800 08 8589. **Accommodation:** 4 hotels, 2 hotel/motels, 4 motels, 2 B&B, 2 cara./camp. parks. **See also:** The Eyre Peninsula.

Willunga Pop. 1164

MAP REF. 288 B13, 289 F4, 290 C6, 293 B3, 295 K10

An historic town that was surveyed in 1839, Willunga was named from the Aboriginal word *willa-unga*, meaning 'the place of green trees'. The town is just south of the McLaren winegrowing region and is Australia's major almond-growing centre. **Of interest:** Historic pug cottages and fine examples of colonial architecture. National Trust police station and court house (1855), Main St. Anglican church, with Elizabethan bronze bell; St Andrews Tce. Delabole Quarry (1842) operated for 60 years, now National Trust site. July: Almond blossom festival. **In the area:** Cowshed Gallery at Yundi, 9 km E. Mt Magnificent Conservation Park, 12 km SE: western grey kangaroos in bushland, scenic walks, picnic areas and good views from the summit. Kyeema Conservation Park, 14 km NE, variety of birdlife, good hiking and camping. Strawberry farm, 4 km N. **Tourist information:** The Cottage, Main Rd, McLaren Vale; (08) 8323 8537 **Accommodation:** 1 hotel, 4 B&B.

The Outback

Motorists contemplating travel in the outback should prepare their vehicles well and familiarise themselves with expected conditions before setting out.

The outback of South Australia covers almost 60 million hectares and is one of the most remote areas of the world; conditions are harsh, the climate extreme and distances are daunting.

The countryside is usually dry, barren and dusty, but freak rains and heavy floods can transform the land. Dry creek beds and waterholes fill, wildflowers bloom and birdlife flocks to the area. The enormous salt **Lake Eyre** has rarely been filled since Europeans first saw the desert.

The main road to the Northern Territory, the Stuart Highway, is a sealed road. From **Port Augusta** to **Alice Springs** the road covers a distance of 1243 kilometres. Turn off the highway to visit **Woomera**, the mining town of **Roxby Downs**, Olympic Dam and the opal-mining town of **Andamooka**.

Petrol, food and supplies are available at Port Augusta, Pimba, Glendambo, Coober Pedy, Cadney Homestead, Marla and Kulgera just over the Northern Territory border.

The notorious Birdsville Track starts at **Marree**, once a supply outpost for Afghan camel traders, and follows the route originally used to drove cattle from south-west Queensland to the railhead at Marree. The track skirts the fringes of the Simpson Desert, with its giant sand dunes, and the desolate Sturt's Stony Desert. Artesian bores line the route, pouring out 64 million litres of salty boiling water every day. The road is well maintained; however, care should be taken during and after heavy rains. *Petrol and supplies are available at Marree and Mungerannie, and at Birdsville over the Queensland border.*

The Oodnadatta Track runs from Marree to **Oodnadatta** and continues to join the Stuart Highway at Marla, 200 kilometres west. *Fuel available only at Marree and William Creek.*

The Strzelecki Track begins at Lyndhurst; a harsh, dusty road, it stretches 494 kilometres to the almost deserted outpost of **Innamincka**, with *no stops for petrol or supplies.*

Motorists intending to travel in the outback should be prepared and well equipped. Many of the roads in the outback are unsealed with sandy patches. Heavy rain can cut access for several days. Motorists are advised to ring the Northern Roads Condition Hotline on (08) 11633 for information before departure.

For further information on the area, contact Flinders Ranges and Outback of South Australia Regional Tourism, PO Box 666, Adelaide 5001, (08) 8373 3430. **See also:** Outback Motoring; and individual entries in A–Z listing for those towns indicated by bold type. **Map references:** pages 296–301.

Remote outback scene in northern South Australia

Wilmington
Pop. 250

MAP REF. 291 C13, 295 J1, 297 J11

A tiny settlement formerly known as Beautiful Valley, Wilmington is 290 km N of Adelaide in the Flinders Ranges. **Of interest:** Police station (1880), now a private residence, and old coaching stables (1880) at rear of Wilmington Hotel; both Main St; early 20th-century billiard rooms, Main St; open by appt. Butter Factory (1898), adjacent to school, off Main St. Beautiful Valley Aussie Relics Museum, Main North Rd; check opening times. **In the area:** Many scenic drives. Hancock's Lookout, 8 km W, at beginning of Horrocks Pass off road to Port Augusta, for views of Spencer Gulf. Mount Remarkable National Park, 13 km S: crystal-clear mountain pools, dense vegetation and abundant wildlife; Mambray Creek and spectacular Alligator Gorge in park. Historic Melrose, 24 km S, oldest town in Flinders Ranges. Booleroo Steam and Traction Preservation Society's Museum (open by appt), Booleroo Centre, 48 km SE. Hammond, historic railway town; 26 km NE. At Carrieton, 56 km NE: historic buildings; Aboriginal carvings, 5 km along Belton Rd; and scenic drive to deserted Johnberg. **Tourist information:** Wilmington Deli, Main St; (086) 67 5117. **Accommodation:** 1 hotel, 2 cara./camp. parks.

Wilpena
Pop. 20

MAP REF. 291 E8, 297 K7

Wilpena, 429 km N of Adelaide, consists of a motel and caravan park outside Wilpena Pound. The Pound, part of the Flinders Ranges National Park, is a vast natural amphitheatre surrounded by colossal peaks that change colour depending on the light. The only entrance is through a narrow gorge and across Sliding Rock. In 1900 a wheat farmer built a homestead inside the Pound, but a flood destroyed the log road and the farm was abandoned. Organised tours, 4WD tours and scenic flights available. **In the area:** Bushwalking and mountain climbing in surrounding countryside. Numerous walking trails in Wilpena Pound, including one to St Mary's Peak, the highest point (1165 m) in the Pound. Aboriginal rock carvings and paintings at Arkaroo Rock on slopes of Rawnsley Bluff, south, and at Sacred Canyon, south-east. At Rawnsley Park station, 20 km S on Hawker Rd, demonstrations of sheep-drafting and shearing Sept.–Oct. Appealinna Homestead (1851), ruins of house built of flat rock from creek bed; 16 km N off Blinman Rd. Scenic drives: Stokes Hill Lookout, 2 km NE; Bunyeroo and Brachina Gorges, Aroona Valley, 5 km NW; Moralana Scenic Drive, 25 km S; Wangarra Lookout, 10 km SW. **Tourist information:** Wilpena Pound Motel; (086) 48 0004. **Accommodation:** 1 motel, 2 cara./ camp. parks. **See also:** The Flinders Ranges.

Woomera
Pop. 1600

MAP REF. 296 F6

Established in 1947 as a site for launching British experimental rockets, Woomera was, until 1982, a prohibited area to visitors. The town, 490 km NW of Adelaide, is still administered by the Defence Department. **Of interest:** Missile Park and Heritage Centre, displays of rockets, aircraft and weapons. Guided tours of old rocket launch area Mar.–Oct. Old Guard Gate, opal sales; Old Pimba Rd. Breen Park picnic area. July: 4th of July celebrations. **In the area:** Roxby Downs, 78 km N, service centre for Olympic Dam mining operations; tours of mining operations available. Andamooka opal field, 107 km NE; tours available. **Tourist information:** Wadlata Outback Centre, Flinders Tce, Port Augusta; (086) 41 0793. **Accommodation:** 1 hotel, 1 cara./camp. park.

Wudinna
Pop. 573

MAP REF. 294 C3, 296 B13

Wudinna is a small settlement on the Eyre Hwy, 571 km NW of Adelaide. The township is the gateway to the timeless Gawler Ranges and has become an important service point for Eyre Peninsula. Wilderness safaris available. **In the area:** Mt Wudinna, second largest granite outcrop in southern hemisphere, 10 km NE: at summit (261 m), scenic views; at base, recreation area. Nearby, Turtle Rock, turtle-shaped ancient granite rock. Signposted tourist drives to all major rock formations. Prolific wildlife and wildflowers in spring. At Minnipa, 37 km NW: Grain Research centre; Pildappa Rock (wave rock); and recreation area at Tcharkuldu Hill. Darkes Memorial, 50 km W. **Tourist information:** District Council of Lehunte, Burton Tce; (086) 80 2002. **Accommodation:** 1 hotel/motel, 1 motel, 1 cara./camp. park.

Yankalilla
Pop. 408

MAP REF. 289 D7, 293 B3, 295 K11

A growing settlement just inland from the west coast of Fleurieu Peninsula, Yankalilla is 35 km W of Victor Harbor. **Of interest:** In Main St: Uniting Church (1878); Bungala House, gifts and pottery; craft shops with leatherwork, woodwork and gumnut creations; Yankalilla Hotel, country-style counter meals; and historical museum. **In the area:** Seaside town of Normanville, 4 km W. Bay Tree Farm, herbs, flowers, afternoon teas in farm setting; Cape Jervis Rd, Second Valley, 14 km SW. Cape Jervis, departure point for vehicular ferries to Kangaroo Island; 35 km S. Glacier Rock, 500 million year old Cambrian quartzite; 22 km E. Steep hillsides and gullies, and western grey kangaroos at Myponga Conservation Park, 9 km NE. At Myponga, 14 km NE: begonia farm, open to public Oct.–Apr.; Myponga Reservoir, ideal for family barbecues or picnics. **Tourist information:** Council Offices, Main St; (085) 58 2048. **Accommodation:** Yankalilla, 1 hotel. Normanville, 1 motel, 2 cara./camp. parks.

Yorketown
Pop. 738

MAP REF. 294 I9

The principal town at the southern end of Yorke Peninsula, Yorketown's shopping centre services the surrounding cereal-growing district. Yorketown is surrounded by extensive inland salt lakes (some are pink), which are still worked. Oct.: Picnic races and gymkhana. **In the area:** Innes National Park, 77 km SW: rugged coastal scenery and peaceful hinterland; and Inneston, historic mining town in park, managed as historic site by the Department of Environment and Natural Resources. Surfing at Daly Head, 50 km W. South of Daly Head, Blowhole. Many shipwrecks along this section of coast. At Corny Point, on north-western tip of Peninsula, 55 km NW: lighthouse, lookout, camping and fishing. Toy Factory, locally-crafted wooden toys; 5 km NE. **Tourist information:** Yorke Peninsula Visitor Information Centre, 51 Taylor St, Kadina; (08) 8821 2093. **Accommodation:** 1 hotel, 1 hotelmotel, 1 cara./camp. park. **See also:** The Yorke Peninsula.

South Australia

Location Map

Other Map Coverage
Central Adelaide 282
Adelaide Approach & Bypass Routes 283
Adelaide & Southern Suburbs 284
Northern Suburbs, Adelaide 286
Adelaide Region 288
McLaren Region 290

Flinders Ranges 291
Barossa Valley 292

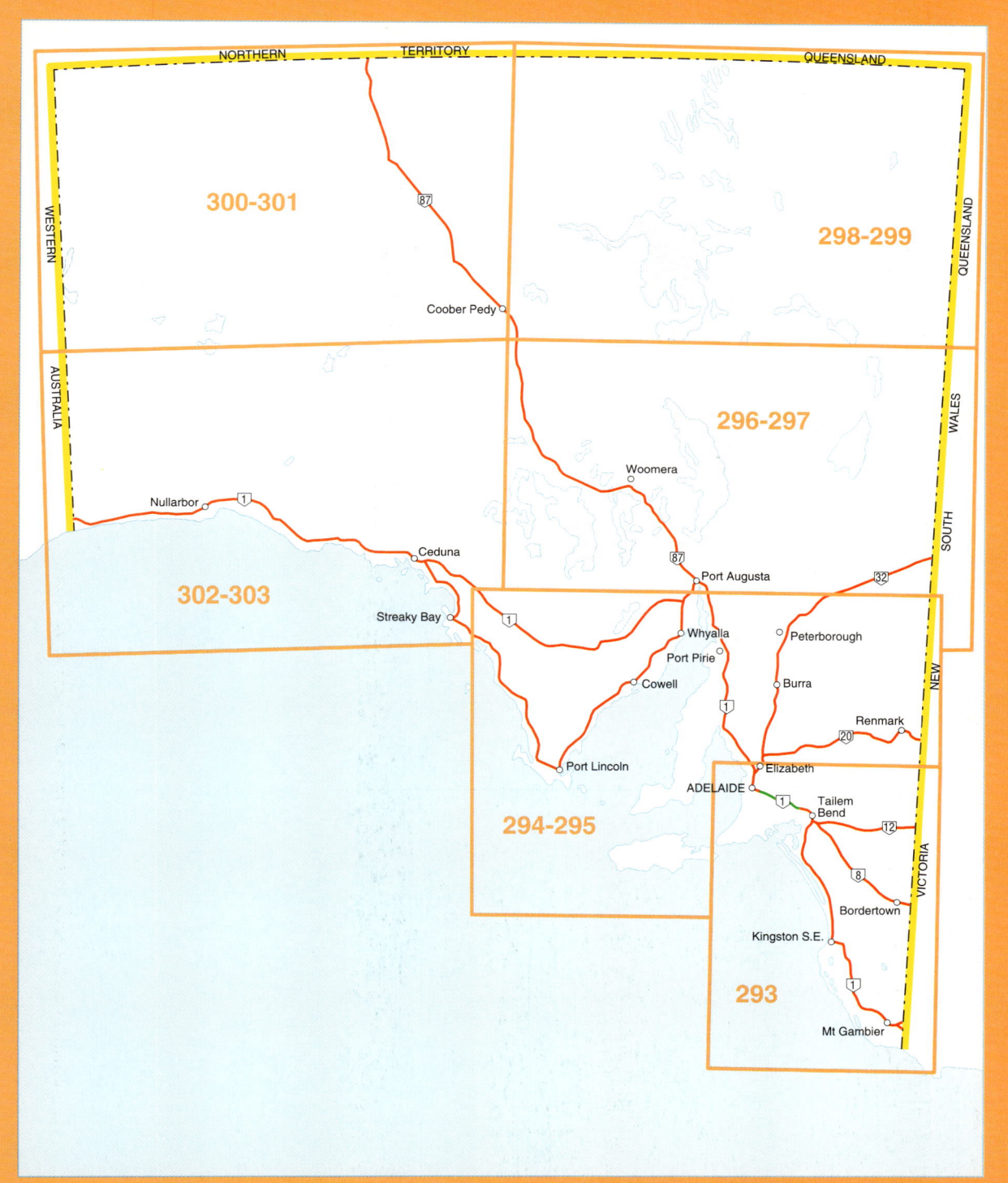

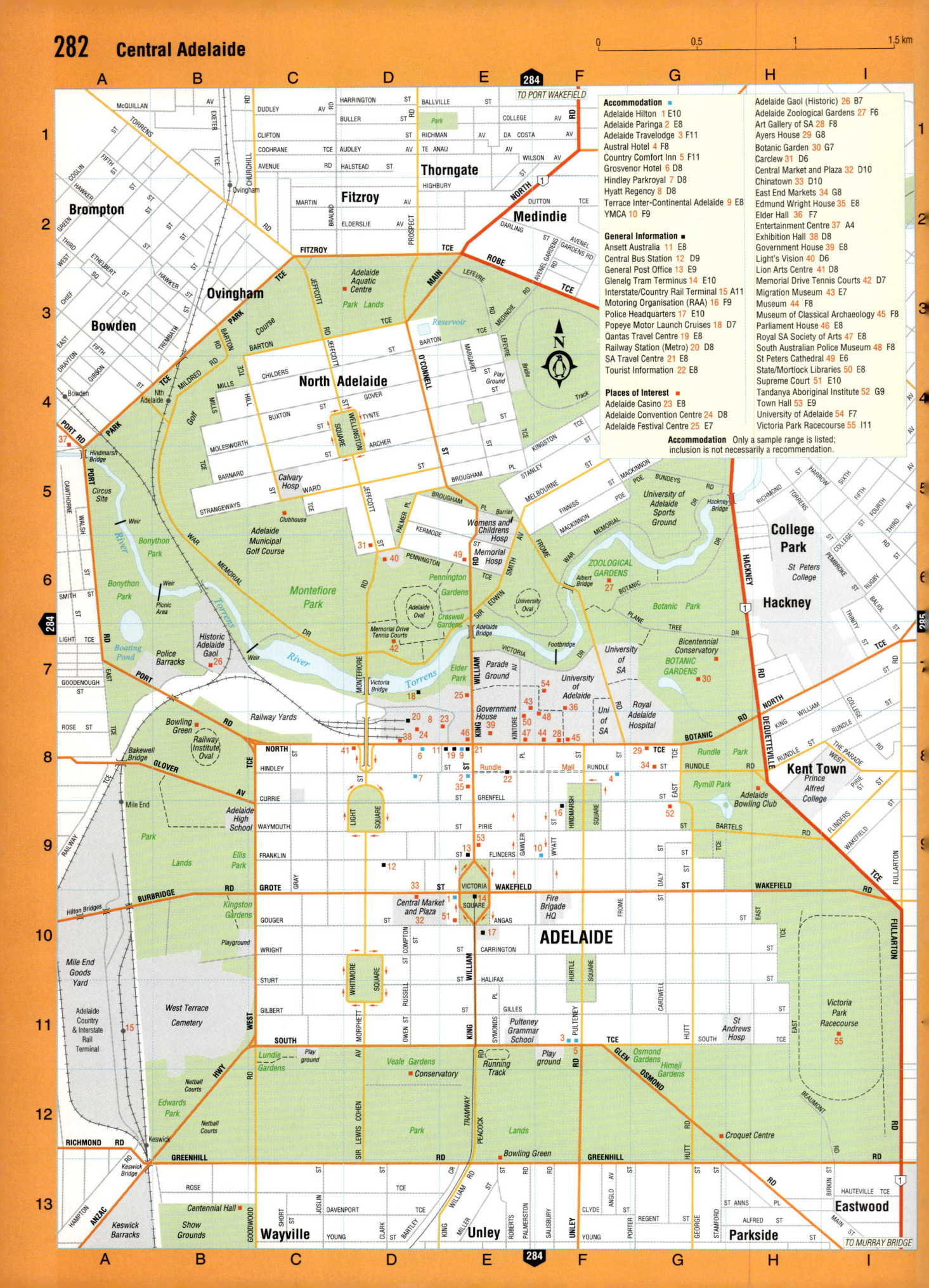

282 Central Adelaide

Accommodation
- Adelaide Hilton 1 E10
- Adelaide Paringa 2 E8
- Adelaide Travelodge 3 F11
- Austral Hotel 4 F8
- Country Comfort Inn 5 F11
- Grosvenor Hotel 6 D8
- Hindley Parkroyal 7 D8
- Hyatt Regency 8 D8
- Terrace Inter-Continental Adelaide 9 E8
- YMCA 10 F9

General Information
- Ansett Australia 11 E8
- Central Bus Station 12 D9
- General Post Office 13 E9
- Glenelg Tram Terminus 14 E10
- Interstate/Country Rail Terminal 15 A11
- Motoring Organisation (RAA) 16 F9
- Police Headquarters 17 E10
- Popeye Motor Launch Cruises 18 D7
- Qantas Travel Centre 19 E8
- Railway Station (Metro) 20 D8
- SA Travel Centre 21 E8
- Tourist Information 22 E8

Places of Interest
- Adelaide Casino 23 E8
- Adelaide Convention Centre 24 D8
- Adelaide Festival Centre 25 E7
- Adelaide Gaol (Historic) 26 B7
- Adelaide Zoological Gardens 27 F6
- Art Gallery of SA 28 G8
- Ayers House 29 G8
- Botanic Garden 30 G7
- Carclew 31 D6
- Central Market and Plaza 32 D10
- Chinatown 33 D10
- East End Markets 34 G8
- Edmund Wright House 35 E8
- Elder Hall 36 F7
- Entertainment Centre 37 A4
- Exhibition Hall 38 D8
- Government House 39 E8
- Light's Vision 40 D6
- Lion Arts Centre 41 D8
- Memorial Drive Tennis Courts 42 D7
- Migration Museum 43 E7
- Museum 44 F8
- Museum of Classical Archaeology 45 F8
- Parliament House 46 E8
- Royal SA Society of Arts 47 E8
- South Australian Police Museum 48 F8
- St Peters Cathedral 49 E6
- State/Mortlock Libraries 50 E8
- Supreme Court 51 E10
- Tandanya Aboriginal Institute 52 G9
- Town Hall 53 E9
- University of Adelaide 54 F7
- Victoria Park Racecourse 55 I11

Accommodation Only a sample range is listed; inclusion is not necessarily a recommendation.

Approach & Bypass Routes ADELAIDE 283

Thick roads represent recommended approach and bypass routes.

284 Adelaide & Southern Suburbs

0 1 2 3 4 5 km
J K L M N O P Q R
287
288
1 2 3 4 5 6 7 8 9 10 11 12 13
Northfield
Oakden
Strathmont Training Centre
Hillcrest Hospital
Research Centre
Gilles Plains
Hope Valley Reservoir
Highbury
Clearview
Enfield Cemetery and Crematorium
Department of Agriculture
Hillcrest
Dernancourt
Windsor Gardens
Greenacres
Athelstone
Castambul
Broadview
Hampstead Gardens
Thorndon Park Reservoir
Paradise
BLACK HILL CONSERVATION PARK
Sefton Park
Manningham
Klemzig
Campbelltown
Newton
Vale Park
Montacute
Collinswood
Walkerville
Marden
Felixstowe
Rostrevor
Medindie Gardens
Royston Park
Glynde
Hectorville
Payneham
Woodforde
MORIALTA CONSERVATION PARK
St Peters
College Park
Evandale
Firle
Tranmere
Cherryville
Maylands
St Morris
Magill
Trinity Gardens
Hackney
Kensington Gardens
Stepney
Marble Hill
Marble Hill National Trust Reserve
Norton Summit
Teringie
Auldana
Beulah Park
Orange Lane Market
Rosslyn Park
Norwood
Kent Town
Kensington
Skye
Erindale
Marryatville
Leabrook
Wattle Park
Rose Park
Heathpool
Toorak Gardens
FERGUSON CP
HORSNELL GULLY CONSERVATION PARK
Giles Park
Stonyfell
Ashton
Reserve
Burnside
Dulwich
Tusmore
Eastwood
Glenside
Linden Park
Hazelwood Park
Greenhill Recreation Park
Parkside
Frewville
Beaumont
Chambers Gully Reserve
Greenhill
Glenunga
Uraidla
Summertown
St Georges
Fullarton
Carey Gully
Malvern
Waterfall Gully
CLELAND CONSERVATION PARK
Mount Osmond Golf Course
Glen Osmond
Highgate
Myrtle Bank
Mount Osmond
Old Toll House
Urrbrae
Leawood Gardens
Kingswood
Netherby
Waite Agricultural Research Institute
Mt Lofty 727m
Lookout
Eagle On The Hill
Springfield
Torrens Park
Mitcham
Piccadilly
MOUNT LOFTY BOTANIC GARDENS
Mount Lofty Golf Course
Brownhill Creek Recreation Park
National Trust Reserve
Belair
Pinera
Stirling
Crafers
Crafers West
THE KNOLL CP
Mount Lofty
Arbury Park
Carripook
BELAIR NP
Old Government House
Glenalta
Long Gully
Stirling Sports Park
Reserve
Aldgate
Jibilla
National Park
Upper Sturt
Madurta
Heathfield
Cemetery
Blackwood
SOUTH EASTERN FREEWAY
Torrens River
First Creek
Second Creek
Fourth Creek
Brownhill Creek
Deep Creek

286 Northern Suburbs, Adelaide

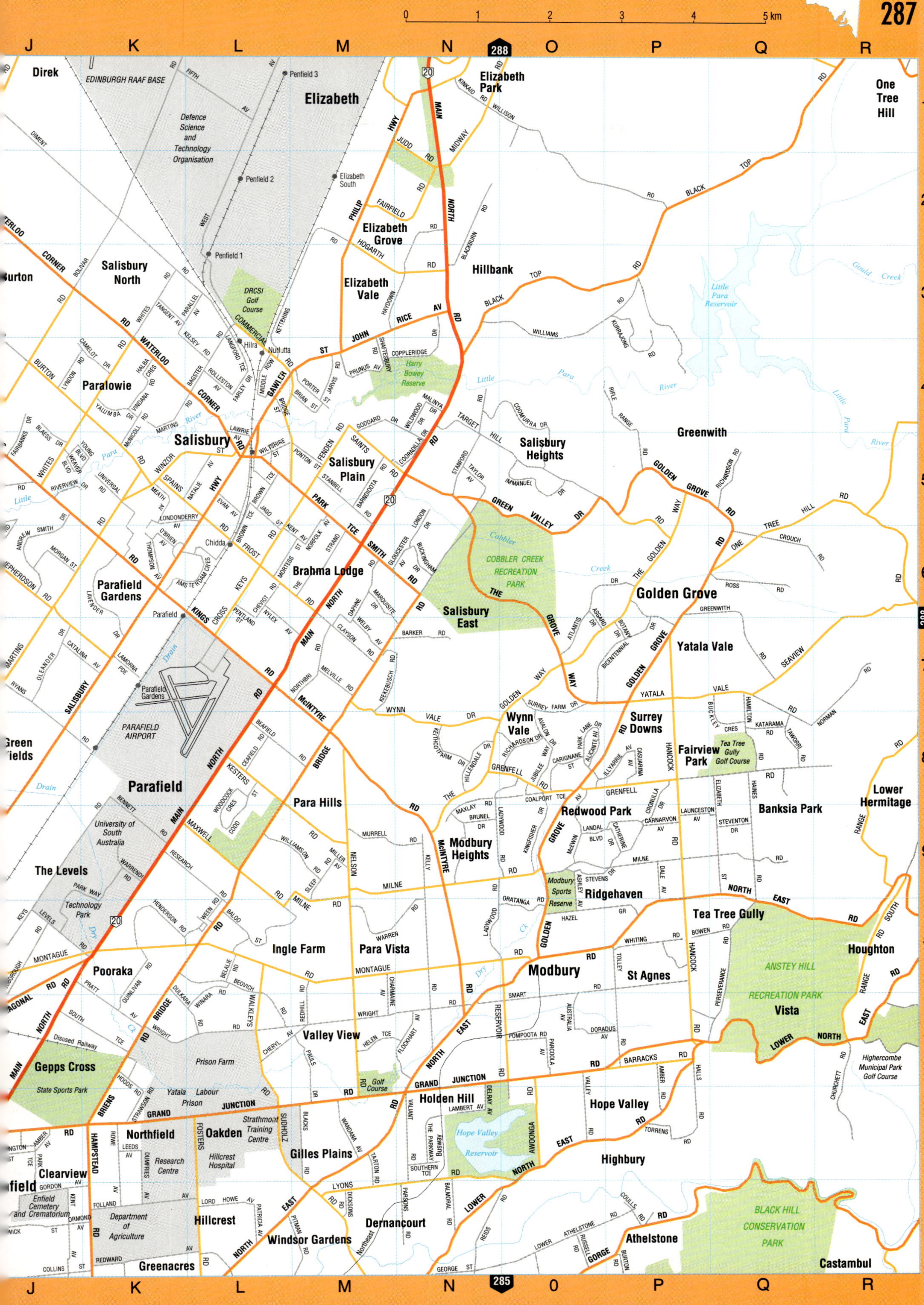
0 1 2 3 4 5 km
J K L M N O P Q R
288
1 2 3 4 5 6 7 8 9 10 11 12 13
Direk
EDINBURGH RAAF BASE
Defence Science and Technology Organisation
Penfield 3
Penfield 2
Penfield 1
Elizabeth
Elizabeth South
Elizabeth Park
One Tree Hill
Elizabeth Grove
Elizabeth Vale
Hillbank
Salisbury North
DRCSI Golf Course
Hilra
Nurlutta
Paralowie
Harry Bowey Reserve
Little Para Reservoir
Gould Creek
Little Para River
Salisbury
Salisbury Plain
Salisbury Heights
Greenwith
Chidda
Brahma Lodge
COBBLER CREEK RECREATION PARK
Cobbler Creek
Parafield Gardens
Salisbury East
Golden Grove
Parafield
Yatala Vale
Parafield Gardens
PARAFIELD AIRPORT
Wynn Vale
Surrey Downs
Fairview Park
Tea Tree Gully Golf Course
Green Fields
Parafield
Para Hills
Redwood Park
Banksia Park
Lower Hermitage
University of South Australia
Modbury Heights
The Levels
Technology Park
Modbury Sports Reserve
Ridgehaven
Tea Tree Gully
Ingle Farm
Para Vista
Houghton
Pooraka
Modbury
St Agnes
ANSTEY HILL RECREATION PARK
Vista
Valley View
Gepps Cross
State Sports Park
Prison Farm
Yatala Labour Prison
Golf Course
Holden Hill
Highercombe Municipal Park Golf Course
Hope Valley
Northfield
Oakden
Strathmont Training Centre
Hope Valley Reservoir
Clearview
Research Centre
Hillcrest Hospital
Gilles Plains
Highbury
Enfield Cemetery and Crematorium
Department of Agriculture
Hillcrest
Dernancourt
Windsor Gardens
Athelstone
BLACK HILL CONSERVATION PARK
Greenacres
Castambul
285

0 5 10 15 20 km
Brownlow
Neales Flat
Giles Corner
Hamilton
Owen
Alma
Tarlee
NORTH
Hansborough
Pinery
MOUNT
Allendale North
Bagot Well
Frankton
Barabba
Stockport
Bethel
Mt Rufus 547m
Hamley Bridge
Linwood
Kapunda
Kapunda Museum
Stonefield
Bald Hill
Dutton
Koonunga
Fords
LOFTY
Mallala
Hawker Hill 442m
Truro
STURT HWY
Belvidere 391m
Red Banks
Wasleys
Freeling
Stockwell
For more detail of Barossa Valley see page 292
Templers
Greenock
Daveyston
Nuriootpa
Moculta
Paterson Hill 300m
Seppeltsfield
BAROSSA VALLEY
Wineries
Shea-Oak Log
RANGES
Mt Karinya 444m
Angaston
Roseworthy
Kev Rohrlach Collection
Tanunda
Barossa Historical Museum
Mengler Hill
Kangaroo Flat
Bethany
Towitta
PORT WAKEFIELD RD
Rosedale
Concordia
Keyneton
Two Wells
Lewiston
Gawler
BAROSSA VALLEY HWY
Kaiserstuhl 599m
Rowland Flat
Sedan
Sandy Creek
Lyndoch
KAISERSTUHL CP
SANDY CREEK CP
Peggys Hill 491m
Mons Hill 471m
Gawler River
Kies Hill
Pewsey Vale Peak 629m
Whispering Wall
Eden Valley
Port Gawler
PORT GAWLER CONSERVATION PARK
Virginia
Barossa Res
Williamstown
Cambrai
PARA WIRRA RECREATION PARK
HALE CP
For more detail of Adelaide Suburbs see pages 284 - 287
ELIZABETH
Mt Colin
Waterloo Corner
Mt Crawford 562m
Springton
St Kilda
South Para Reservoir
Warren Reservoir
WARREN CP
Little Para Reservoir
Bare Hill 344m
Mt Pleasant 542m
Burns 502m
Cookes Hill 309m
Sanderston
Angas Valley
SALISBURY
OUTER HARBOR
Torrens Reach
Kersbrook
Mt Gould 530m
Forreston
Mt Pleasant
Scotts Hill 473m
Largs Bay
Millbrook Reservoir
Inglewood
Gumeracha
Birdwood
Punthari
MODBURY
Houghton
Chain Of Ponds
Tungkillo
Apamurra
Cudlee Creek
PORT ADELAIDE
Palmer
ENFIELD
WEST LAKES
Kangaroo Ck Reservoir
Castambul
BLACK HILL CP
Mt Torrens 533m
Mt Torrens
MONTACUTE CP
ADELAIDE
Fendlers Hill 473m
Lobethal
Cowirra
MAGILL
MORIALTA CP
Murrays Hill 415m
Mannum
HENLEY BEACH
Charleston
Norton Summit
Forest Range
Lenswood
Mt Beavor 503m
Ashton
ADELAIDE AIRPORT
Uraidla
Woodside
Harrogate
Rockleigh
Pondė
Caloote
CLELAND CP
ADELAIDE HILLS
GLENELG
MITCHAM
Balhannah
Oakbank
Bruckunga
Tepko
Mt Lofty 726m
Whalleys Hill 357m
Glenelg - Kingscote Passenger Ferry
Crafers
Verdun
Shephards Hill 450m
BRIGHTON
BELAIR NP
Stirling
Hahndorf
Nairne
MARION
STURT GORGE REC PARK
Mylor
Littlehampton
HALLETT COVE
HALLETT COVE CP
Happy Valley Reservoir
SCOTT CREEK CP
Mt Barker
Kanmantoo
Monarto
MORPHETT VALE
Chandlers Hill 307m
Clarendon
Mt Bold
Mt Bold Reservoir
Echunga
Wistow
Callington
SOUTH EASTERN FREEWAY
Monarto South
Murray Bridge
ONKAPARINGA RIVER REC PARK
Yaroona
Hackham
Kangarilla
Flaxley
Swanport
Mt Panorama 359m
MOUNT LOFTY RANGES
MONARTO CONSERVATION PARK
Old Noarlunga
Meadows
Macclesfield
Moana
Mt Wilson 408m
Hartley
Paris Creek
Woodchester
FERRIES MCDONALD CONSERVATION PARK
Brinkley
McLaren Vale
Wineries
Maslin Beach
For more detail of McLaren Region see page 290
Port Willunga
Aldinga
Willunga
KYEEMA CP
Bletchley

Adelaide Region, South 289

290 McLaren Region

WINERIES:
- Aldinga Bay Vineyards 1 B6
- Andrew Garrett Winery 2 C5
- Beresford/Bosanquet Wines 3 D2
- Chalk Hill Wines 4 C5
- Chapel Hill Winery 5 C4
- Coriole Vineyards 6 C4
- Curtis Wines 7 D5
- D'Arenberg Wines 8 C5
- Dennis of McLaren Vale Wines 9 C5
- Dyson Wines 10 B5
- Fern Hill Estate 11 D5
- Hardy's Tintara Wines 12 C5
- Hardy's Reynella Winery 13 C3
- Haselgrove Wines 14 D5
- Hillstowe Wines 15 C5
- Horndale Wines 16 D2
- Hugo Winery 17 E5
- Ingoldby Wines 18 D5
- Kay Bros. Amery Vineyards 19 D4
- Luong Rice Winery 20 C5
- Maglieri Wines 21 E4
- Manning Park 22 C5
- Marienberg Wines 23 C5
- Maxwell Wines 24 C5
- Merrivale Wines 25 C5
- Middlebrook Winery 26 D5
- Middleton Estate Winery 27 F10
- Mount Hurtle/Geoff Merrill 28 D3
- Noon's Winery 29 D6
- Norman's Wines 30 E3
- Old Clarendon Winery 31 E3
- Oliverhill Winery 32 C4
- Petaluma's Bridgewater Mill 33 G1
- Pirramimma Wines 34 C5
- Richard Hamilton Winery 35 C6
- Ryecroft Vineyards 36 D5
- St Francis Wines 37 C3
- Scarpantoni Estate Wines 38 D5
- Seaview Winery 39 C4
- Shottesbrooke Vineyards 40 D5
- Stevens Cambrai Vineyards 41 D5
- Tanami Red Wines 42 C5
- Tatachilla Winery 43 C5
- Tinlins Winery 44 D5
- Tonkins Currency Creek Winery 45 G10
- Torresan Happy Valley Winery 46 D2
- Wirilda Creek Winery 47 D5
- Wirra Wirra Vineyards 48 D5
- Woodstock Winery 49 D5

SCENIC DRIVES: There are many scenic drives in the area; all clearly sign-posted.

HEYSEN TRAIL: This famous 1500 km walking trail begins near Cape Jervis and ends in the Flinders Ranges. The section shown on the map is recommended for day treks. The trail is marked with orange triangles on the tops of pine posts.

TOURIST INFORMATION:
Goolwa (Cadell St)
Strathalbyn (South Tce)
Victor Harbor (Railway Tce)

HINDMARSH FALLS: Spectacular after heavy rain. A short, steep walk leads from the car park to the base of the falls located in a narrow, thickly vegetated valley.

GRANITE ISLAND: Home for many fairy penguins and linked by a causeway to the foreshore at Victor Harbor. Visitors can walk across or take Australia's only horse-drawn tram.

Flinders Ranges

THE FLINDERS RANGES: An ancient range of rugged mountains with spectacularly steep ridges of rock and tree-lined gorges. Sheer ruggedness, wild scenery, plentiful wildlife, unique flora and vestiges of long Aboriginal and short European occupation - all combine to make this region one of the greatest natural attractions in the country. Autumn, winter and spring are the best seasons to visit.

RIDGE TOP TOUR: Described as one of the most spectacular tours in Australia, this 4WD circuit of the ranges, from Arkaroola, offers breathtaking views of the ancient landscape.

GAMMON RANGES NATIONAL PARK: The granite peaks of the Gammon Ranges rear up between the great salt lakes of Lake Frome and Lake Torrens. The Park is renowned for its untamed wilderness; it is drier, wilder and lonelier than the Flinders Ranges National Park. To see the best of the Park, it is necessary to bushwalk, as roads do not penetrate far into the Park.

WARNING: Bushwalking over the rugged terrain in this region is often very demanding. Bushwalkers should carry ample water, food, map and matches or lighter. In hot conditions, ensure that you drink 1 litre of water per person per hour. A wide-brimmed hat, protective clothing and sturdy footwear are also essential. Someone should be informed of details of route and expected return time. A booklet 'Bushwalking in the Flinders Ranges' is available at the Flinders Ranges Nationaal Park Headquarters.
Driving in this region, particularly the northern section requires caution. While most major roads are sealed, many are not. Dust, corrugations and water are the main hazards. It is imperative that motorists obtain full information before proceeding on their journey. If you are off the main roads, check you have informed someone of your route, destination and arrival time; ensure you have adequate essential supplies. **Always** remain with your vehicle if it breaks down.

FLINDERS RANGES NATIONAL PARK: Incorporates most of the central Flinders Ranges. The Park offers a wide range of outdoor recreational activities, rugged mountain scenery, peaceful tree-lined gorges, abundant wildlife and a seasonal wealth of wildflowers.

TOURIST INFORMATION:
Hawker (cnr Wilpena and Cradock Rds)
Melrose (Main Street)
Port Augusta (Wadlata Outback Centre, Flinders Terrace)
Quorn (3 Seventh Street)

KANYAKA RUINS: This once gracious homestead dates back to the 1850s, when it supported around 70 families. Drought and poor seasons forced the owners off the land. Today restoration and interpretive signposting provides visitors with an interesting insight into the past.

292 Barossa Valley

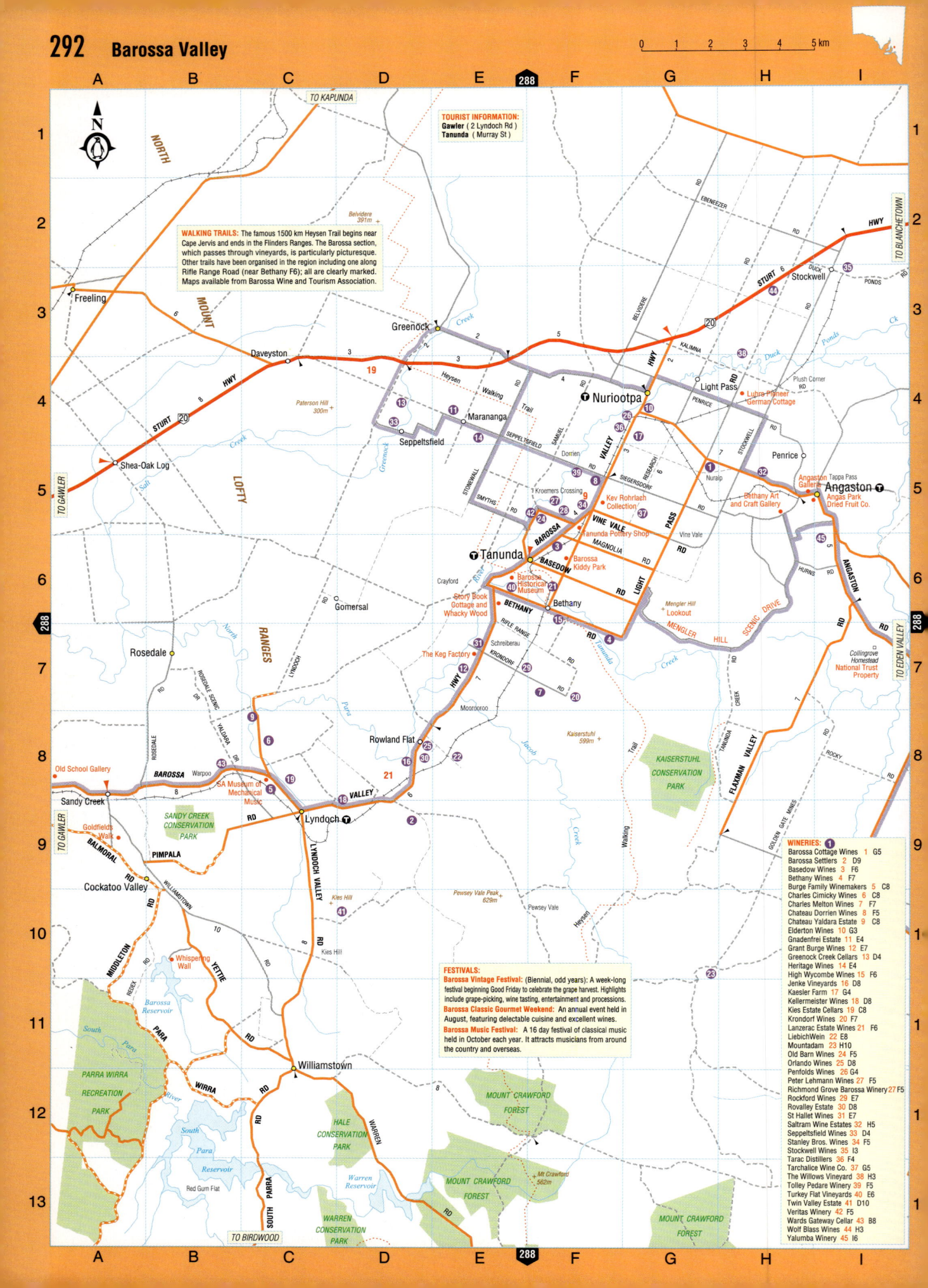

WALKING TRAILS: The famous 1500 km Heysen Trail begins near Cape Jervis and ends in the Flinders Ranges. The Barossa section, which passes through vineyards, is particularly picturesque. Other trails have been organised in the region including one along Rifle Range Road (near Bethany F6); all are clearly marked. Maps available from Barossa Wine and Tourism Association.

TOURIST INFORMATION:
Gawler (2 Lyndoch Rd)
Tanunda (Murray St)

FESTIVALS:
Barossa Vintage Festival: (Biennial, odd years) A week-long festival beginning Good Friday to celebrate the grape harvest. Highlights include grape-picking, wine tasting, entertainment and processions.
Barossa Classic Gourmet Weekend: An annual event held in August, featuring delectable cuisine and excellent wines.
Barossa Music Festival: A 16 day festival of classical music held in October each year. It attracts musicians from around the country and overseas.

WINERIES:
Barossa Cottage Wines 1 G5
Barossa Settlers 2 D9
Basedow Wines 3 F6
Bethany Wines 4 F7
Burge Family Winemakers 5 C8
Charles Cimicky Wines 6 C8
Charles Melton Wines 7 F7
Chateau Dorrien Wines 8 F5
Chateau Yaldara Estate 9 C8
Elderton Wines 10 G3
Gnadenfrei Estate 11 E4
Grant Burge Wines 12 E7
Greenock Creek Cellars 13 D4
Heritage Wines 14 E4
High Wycombe Wines 15 F6
Jenke Vineyards 16 D8
Kaesler Farm 17 G4
Kellermeister Wines 18 D8
Kies Estate Cellars 19 C8
Krondorf Wines 20 F7
Lanzerac Estate Wines 21 F6
LiebichWein 22 E8
Mountadam 23 H10
Old Barn Wines 24 F5
Orlando Wines 25 D8
Penfolds Wines 26 G4
Peter Lehmann Wines 27 F5
Richmond Grove Barossa Winery 27 F5
Rockford Wines 29 E7
Rovalley Estate 30 D8
St Hallet Wines 31 E7
Saltram Wine Estates 32 H5
Seppeltsfield Wines 33 D4
Stanley Bros. Wines 34 F5
Stockwell Wines 35 I3
Tarac Distillers 36 F4
Tarchalice Wine Co. 37 G5
The Willows Vineyard 38 H3
Tolley Pedare Winery 39 F5
Turkey Flat Vineyards 40 E6
Twin Valley Estate 41 D10
Veritas Winery 42 F5
Wards Gateway Cellar 43 B8
Wolf Blass Wines 44 H3
Yalumba Winery 45 I6

South Eastern South Australia

294 South Central South Australia

0 20 40 60 80 100 km

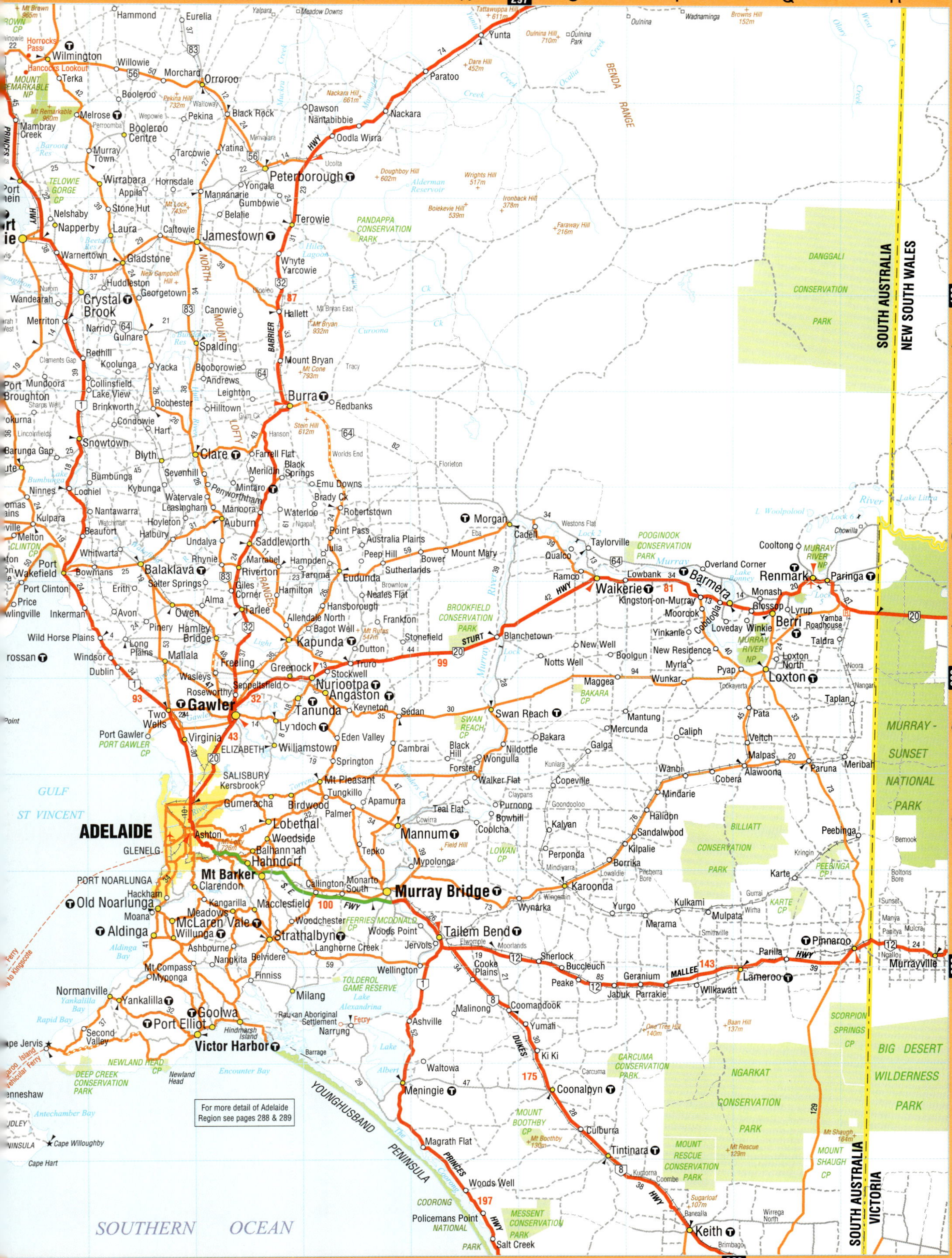

J K L M N O P Q R

296 Central South Australia

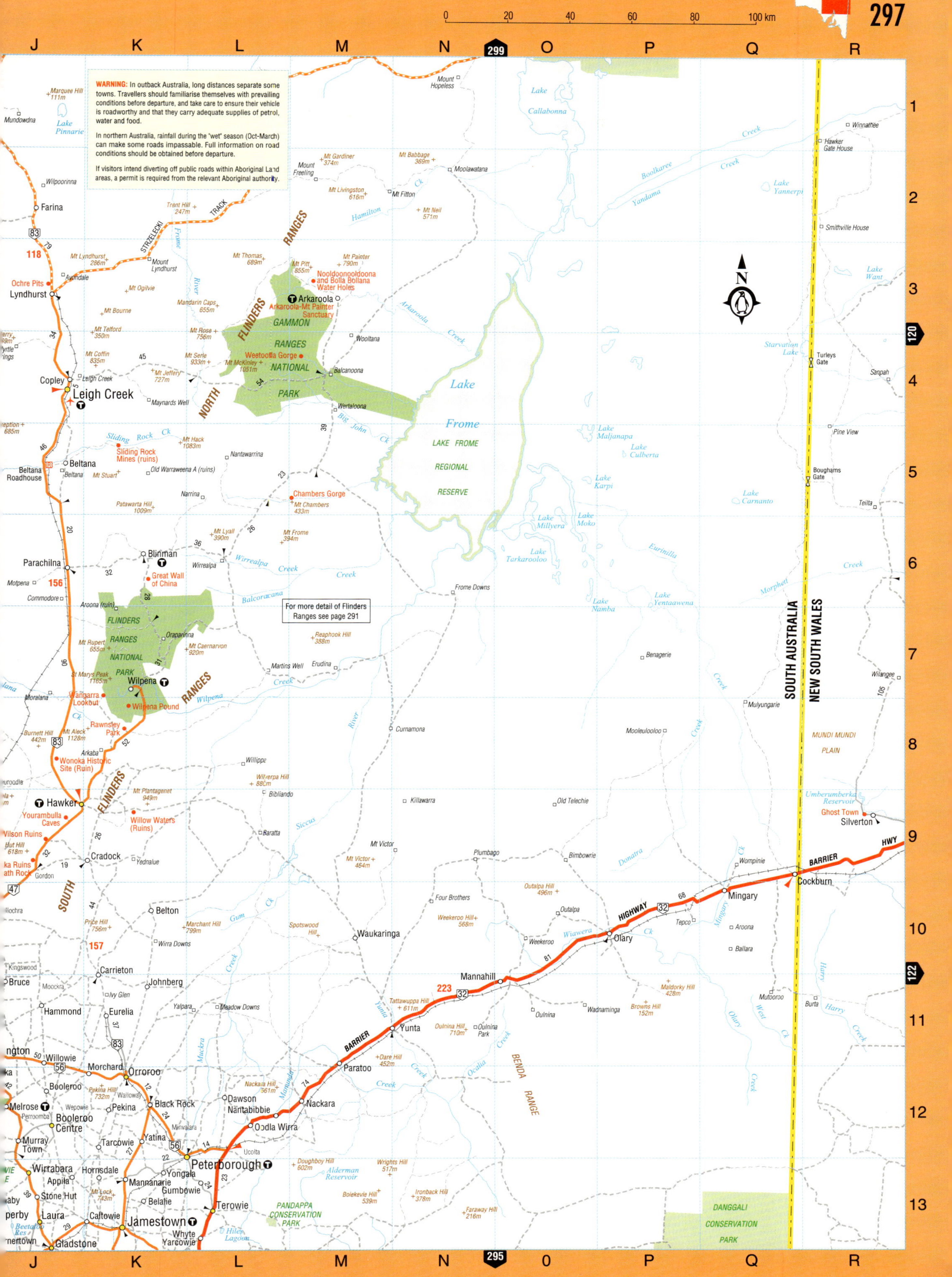

0 20 40 60 80 100 km
J K L M N 299 O P Q R
1 2 3 4 5 6 7 8 9 10 11 12 13
120
122
295
WARNING: In outback Australia, long distances separate some towns. Travellers should familiarise themselves with prevailing conditions before departure, and take care to ensure their vehicle is roadworthy and that they carry adequate supplies of petrol, water and food.
In northern Australia, rainfall during the 'wet' season (Oct-March) can make some roads impassable. Full information on road conditions should be obtained before departure.
If visitors intend diverting off public roads within Aboriginal Land areas, a permit is required from the relevant Aboriginal authority.
For more detail of Flinders Ranges see page 291
SOUTH AUSTRALIA
NEW SOUTH WALES
Lake Callabonna
Lake Frome
LAKE FROME REGIONAL RESERVE
GAMMON RANGES NATIONAL PARK
FLINDERS RANGES NATIONAL PARK
NORTH FLINDERS RANGES
SOUTH FLINDERS
BENDA RANGE
MUNDI MUNDI PLAIN
DANGGALI CONSERVATION PARK
PANDAPPA CONSERVATION PARK
STRZELECKI TRACK
BARRIER HIGHWAY
BARRIER HWY
Mount Hopeless
Marquee Hill 111m
Mundowdna
Lake Pinnarie
Wilpoorinna
Farina
Trent Hill 247m
Mount Freeling
Mt Gardiner 374m
Mt Babbage 369m
Moolawatana
Mt Livingston 616m
Mt Fitton
Mt Neil 571m
Hamilton
Mt Lyndhurst 286m
Mount Lyndhurst
Mt Thomas 689m
Mt Pitt 855m
Mt Painter 790m
Nooldoonooldoona and Bolla Bollana Water Holes
Arkaroola
Arkaroola-Mt Painter Sanctuary
Ochre Pits
Lyndhurst
Avondale
Mt Ogilvie
Mandarin Caps 655m
Mt Bourne
Mt Telford 350m
Mt Rose 756m
Wooltana
Arkaroola Creek
Mt Coffin 835m
Mt Serle 933m
Weetootla Gorge
Mt McKinley 1051m
Balcanoona
Copley
Leigh Creek
Mt Jeffery 727m
Maynards Well
Wertaloona
Big John Ck
Sliding Rock Ck
Sliding Rock Mines (ruins)
Mt Hack 1083m
Nantawarrina
Beltana
Beltana Roadhouse
Mt Stuart
Old Warraweena A (ruins)
Narrina
Patawarta Hill 1009m
Chambers Gorge
Mt Chambers 433m
Mt Lyall 390m
Mt Frome 394m
Parachilna
Blinman
Great Wall of China
Wirrealpa
Wirrealpa Creek
Balcoracana Creek
Motpena
Commodore
Aroona (ruin)
Frome Downs
Oraparinna
Mt Rupert 655m
Mt Caernarvon 920m
Reaphook Hill 388m
Martins Well
Erudina
St Marys Peak 1165m
Wilpena
Wilpena Creek
Wangarra Lookout
Wilpena Pound
Moralana
Rawnsley Park
Burnett Hill 442m
Mt Aleck 1128m
Arkaba
Wonoka Historic Site (Ruin)
Curnamona
Willippa
Wilcherpa Hill 880m
Bibliando
Mt Plantagenet 949m
Hawker
Yourambulla Caves
Willow Waters (Ruins)
Killawarra
Old Telechie
Baratta
Siccus
Wilson Ruins
Hut Hill 618m
Cradock
Yednalue
Mt Victor
Mt Victor 464m
Plumbago
Bimbowrie
Donatra
Gordon
Belton
Four Brothers
Outalpa Hill 496m
Outalpa
Weekeroo Hill 568m
Price Hill 756m
Marchant Hill 799m
Spotswood Hill
Waukaringa
Weekeroo
Wiawera
Olary
Wirra Downs
Kingswood
Carrieton
Bruce
Moockra
Johnberg
Mannahill
Ivy Glen
Hammond
Eurelia
Yalpara
Meadow Downs
Tattawuppa Hill 611m
Yunta
Oulnina
Wadnaminga
Oulnina Hill 710m
Oulnina Park
Browns Hill 152m
Maldorky Hill 428m
Willowie
Morchard
Orroroo
Dare Hill 452m
Paratoo
Booleroo
Pekina Hill 732m
Walloway
Melrose
Wepowie
Pekina
Black Rock
Dawson
Nackara Hill 561m
Nackara
Nantabibbie
Perroomba
Booleroo Centre
Oodla Wirra
Murray Town
Tarcowie
Yatina
Minvalara
Ucolta
Wirrabara
Hornsdale
Yongala
Peterborough
Doughboy Hill 602m
Alderman Reservoir
Wrights Hill 517m
Appila
Mannanarie
Gumbowie
Mt Lock 743m
Stone Hut
Belalie
Boiekevie Hill 539m
Ironback Hill 378m
Faraway Hill 216m
Laura
Caltowie
Terowie
Jamestown
Whyte Yarcowie
Hiles Lagoon
Beetaloo Res
Gladstone
Winnathee
Hawker Gate House
Lake Yannerpi
Bookaree Creek
Yandama Creek
Smithville House
Lake Want
Starvation Lake
Turleys Gate
Sanpah
Pine View
Lake Maljanapa
Lake Culberta
Lake Karpi
Boughams Gate
Lake Carnanto
Teilta
Lake Millyera
Lake Moko
Eurinilla
Lake Tarkarooloo
Lake Namba
Lake Yentaawena
Morphett Creek
Benagerie
Wilangee
Mulyungarie
Mooleulooloo
Umberumberka Reservoir
Ghost Town
Silverton
Wompinie
Cockburn
Mingary
Tepco
Aroona
Ballara
Mutooroo
Burta
Harry Creek
Olary Creek
West Ck

298 North Eastern South Australia

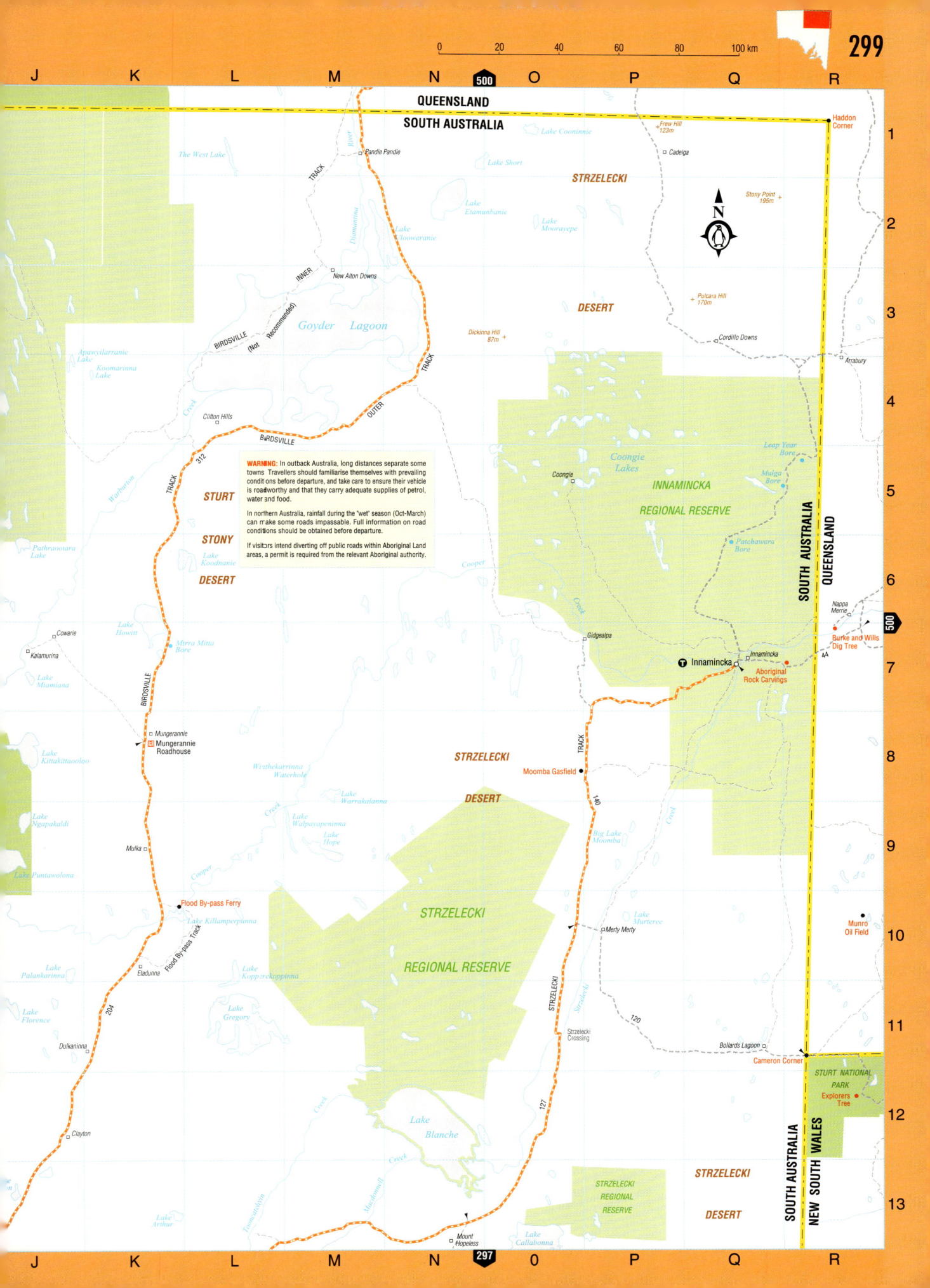

WARNING: In outback Australia, long distances separate some towns. Travellers should familiarise themselves with prevailing conditions before departure, and take care to ensure their vehicle is roadworthy and that they carry adequate supplies of petrol, water and food.

In northern Australia, rainfall during the 'wet' season (Oct-March) can make some roads impassable. Full information on road conditions should be obtained before departure.

If visitors intend diverting off public roads within Aboriginal Land areas, a permit is required from the relevant Aboriginal authority.

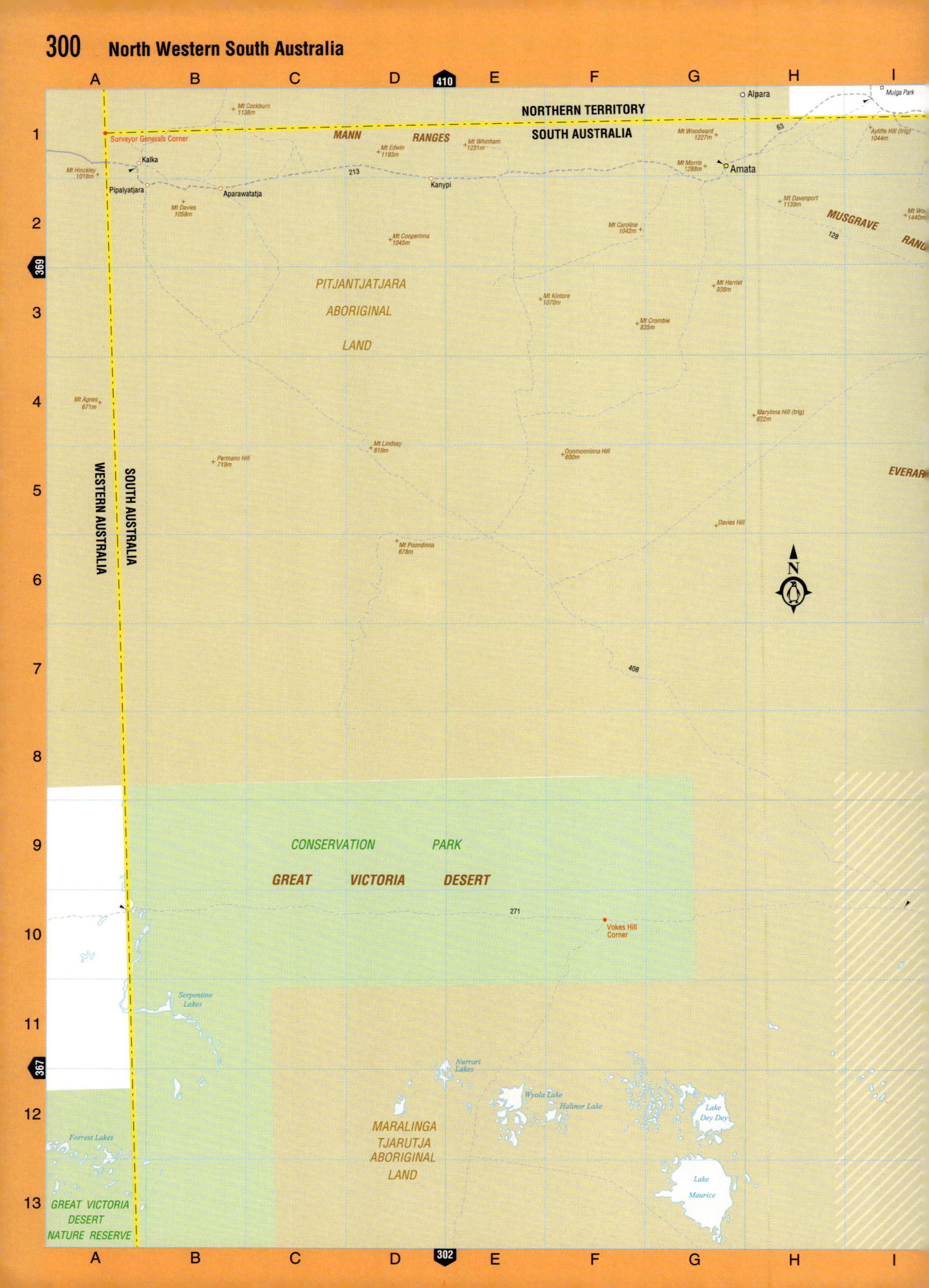

300 North Western South Australia

Map grid references A–I (columns) and 1–13 (rows).

Borders and regions:
- NORTHERN TERRITORY / SOUTH AUSTRALIA (northern border)
- WESTERN AUSTRALIA / SOUTH AUSTRALIA (western border)
- PITJANTJATJARA ABORIGINAL LAND
- MARALINGA TJARUTJA ABORIGINAL LAND
- GREAT VICTORIA DESERT CONSERVATION PARK
- GREAT VICTORIA DESERT NATURE RESERVE
- MANN RANGES
- MUSGRAVE RANGES
- EVERARD (Ranges)

Settlements:
- Surveyor Generals Corner
- Kalka
- Pipalyatjara
- Aparawatatja
- Kanypi
- Amata
- Alpara
- Mulga Park
- Vokes Hill Corner

Mountains / Hills (with elevations):
- Mt Hinckley 1018m
- Mt Cockburn 1138m
- Mt Davies 1058m
- Mt Edwin 1193m
- Mt Whinham 1231m
- Mt Woodward 1227m
- Mt Morris 1288m
- Ayliffe Hill (trig) 1044m
- Mt Davenport 1139m
- Mt Wo... 1440m
- Mt Cooperinna 1045m
- Mt Caroline 1042m
- Mt Kintore 1070m
- Mt Harriet 938m
- Mt Crombie 835m
- Mt Agnes 671m
- Marylinna Hill (trig) 622m
- Mt Lindsay 819m
- Permano Hill 719m
- Oonmoolinna Hill 600m
- Mt Poondinna 678m
- Davies Hill

Lakes:
- Forrest Lakes
- Serpentine Lakes
- Nurrari Lakes
- Wyola Lake
- Halinor Lake
- Lake Dey Dey
- Lake Maurice

Route numbers: 410, 369, 367, 302, 213, 128, 63, 271, 408

Compass: N

301

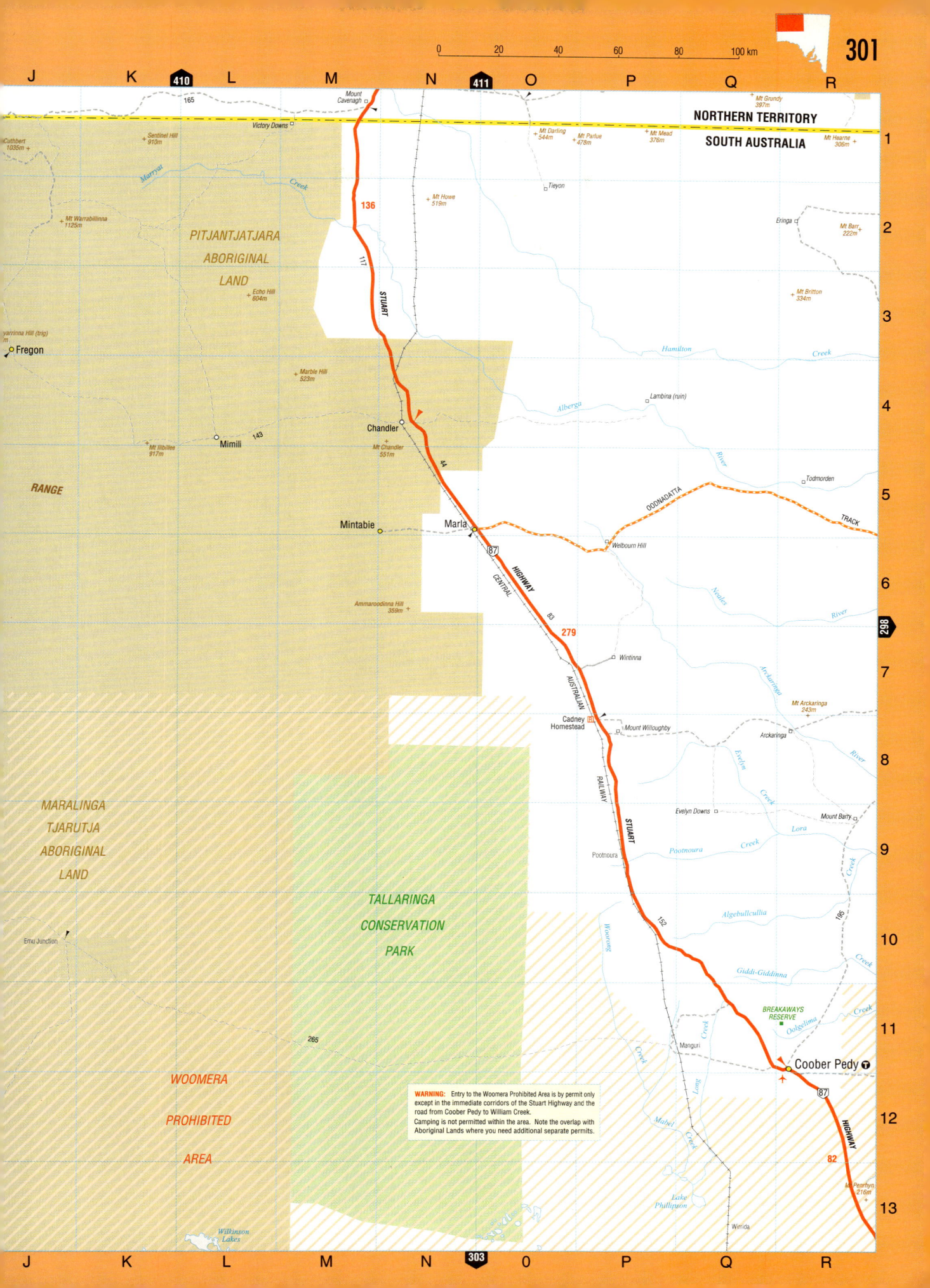

Map — Stuart Highway, South Australia / Northern Territory border region

NORTHERN TERRITORY / SOUTH AUSTRALIA

Scale: 0 — 20 — 40 — 60 — 80 — 100 km

Places and features

- Mount Cavenagh
- Victory Downs
- Mt Grundy 397m
- Mt Darling 544m
- Mt Parlue 478m
- Mt Mead 376m
- Mt Hearne 306m
- Cuthbert 1035m
- Sentinel Hill 910m
- Mt Howe 519m
- Tieyon
- Eringa
- Mt Barr 222m
- Mt Warrabillinna 1125m
- PITJANTJATJARA ABORIGINAL LAND
- Echo Hill 604m
- Mt Britton 334m
- yarrinna Hill (trig)
- Fregon
- Marble Hill 523m
- Hamilton Creek
- Marryat Creek
- Mt Ilbillee 917m
- Mimili
- Chandler
- Mt Chandler 551m
- Alberga River
- Lambina (ruin)
- Todmorden
- RANGE
- Mintabie
- Marla
- Welbourn Hill
- OODNADATTA TRACK
- Ammaroodinna Hill 359m
- STUART HIGHWAY
- CENTRAL AUSTRALIAN RAILWAY
- Wintinna
- Naules River
- Arckaringa Creek
- Mt Arckaringa 243m
- Cadney Homestead
- Mount Willoughby
- Arckaringa
- Evelyn Creek
- MARALINGA TJARUTJA ABORIGINAL LAND
- Evelyn Downs
- Mount Barry
- Lora Creek
- Pootnoura
- Pootnoura Creek
- TALLARINGA CONSERVATION PARK
- Emu Junction
- Woorong
- Algebullcullia
- Giddi-Giddinna Creek
- BREAKAWAYS RESERVE
- Oolgelima
- Manguri
- Coober Pedy
- WOOMERA PROHIBITED AREA
- Mabel Creek
- Lake Phillipson
- Wirrida
- Mt Pearhyn 216m
- Wilkinson Lakes

WARNING: Entry to the Woomera Prohibited Area is by permit only except in the immediate corridors of the Stuart Highway and the road from Coober Pedy to William Creek. Camping is not permitted within the area. Note the overlap with Aboriginal Lands where you need additional separate permits.

Highway markers: 410, 411, 87, 298, 303

Distances (km): 136, 117, 44, 83, 279, 152, 196, 265, 82

302 South Western South Australia

- GREAT VICTORIA DESERT NATURE RESERVE
- WESTERN AUSTRALIA / SOUTH AUSTRALIA
- CONSERVATION PARK
- MARALINGA TJARUTJA ABORIGINAL LAND
- OOLDEA RANGE
- Maralinga
- NULLARBOR PLAIN
- TRANS AUSTRALIA RAILWAY
- Deakin, Hughes, Denman, Cook, Fisher, O'Malley, Watson, Ooldea
- NULLARBOR REGIONAL RESERVE
- NULLARBOR NATIONAL PARK
- Eucla, Border Village, EYRE HIGHWAY
- Lookout, Lookouts, Lookouts, Lookout
- 293, 89, 55, 42, 94
- Nullarbor Roadhouse
- HEAD OF BIGHT
- YALATA ABORIGINAL LAND
- Yalata Roadhouse
- GREAT AUSTRALIAN BIGHT

303

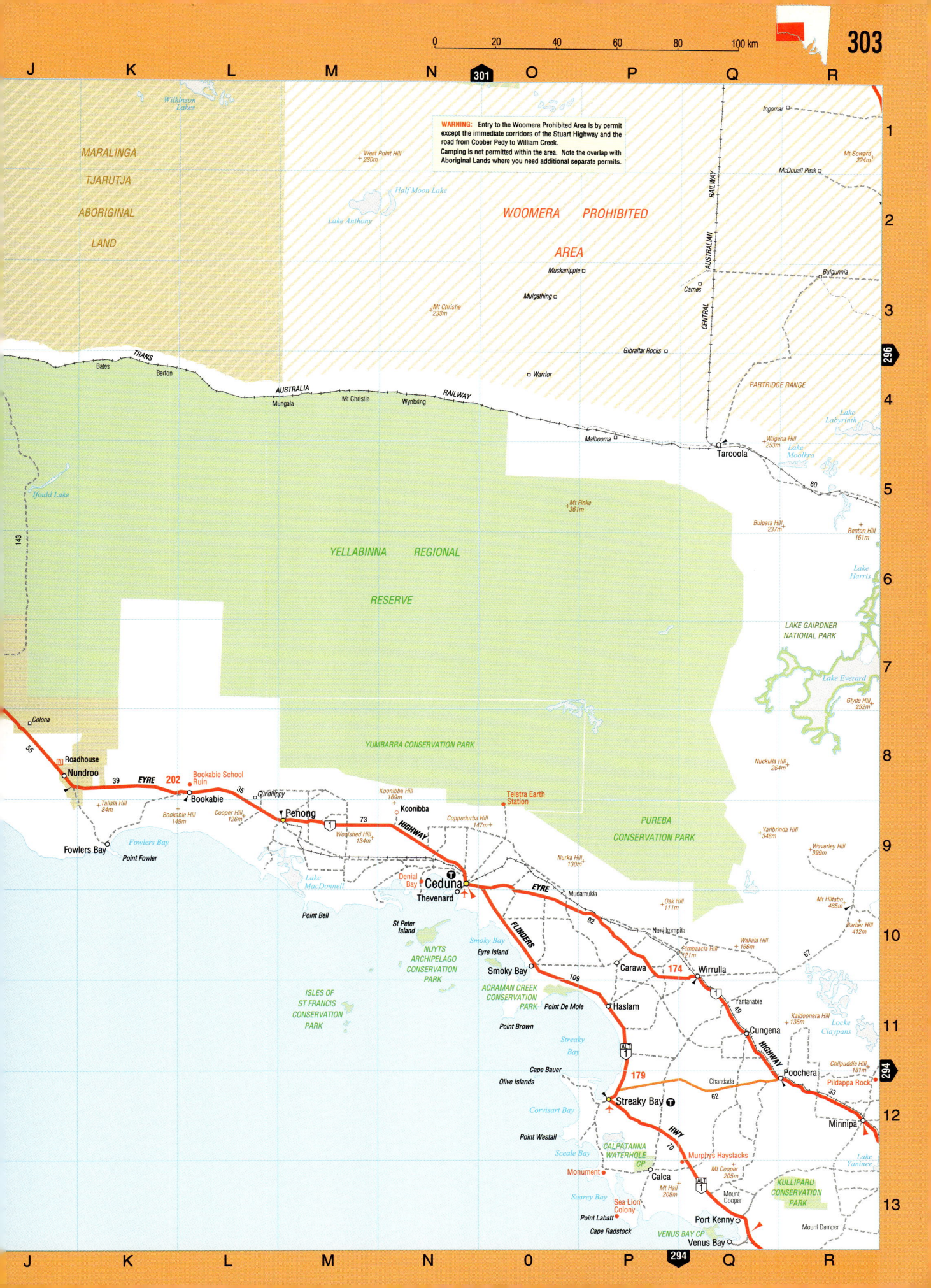

Western Australia

WESTERN AUSTRALIA

The Wildflower State

Western Australia, the largest of the Australian States and territories, covering roughly one-third of the Australian continent, has less than one-tenth of the nation's population. For the traveller, the contrast in scenery is just as great.

Even a casual glance at a map of Australia will quickly reveal that a motor touring holiday in Western Australia requires a great deal of thought and advance planning. For one thing, just getting there from the eastern States involves travelling huge distances, so fly/drive or MotoRail facilities are well worth investigation; and, given that it is almost one-third the size of the whole of Australia, unless you have unlimited time and energy, touring by road will only get you to certain sections. The south-west region is relatively easily and pleasantly covered by car, but to travel the unique north and north-east requires more time and careful planning. Once you have settled your method of travel, you will find an amazing State waiting to be explored.

Despite the fact that the Dutch had mapped the western coastline of Australia as early as the sixteenth century, it was not until 1826 that a British party from Sydney landed at King George Sound (Albany) and then only for fear of possible French colonisation. Three years later Perth, the first non-convict settlement in the country, was founded by Captain James Stirling. Due mainly to the ruggedness and sheer size of the land, the West remained pretty much as it had always been until 1892, when gold was discovered at Coolgardie and the first economic boom for the region began. Today it is an immensely rich mineral State, its thriving economy still growing.

The beautiful city of Perth has the best climate of any Australian capital with a midwinter average maximum temperature of 18°C, a year-round average maximum of 21°C and an average of almost eight hours of sunshine a day. The climate in the north of the State is tropical, and as you travel south the climate becomes sub-tropical and then temperate.

It is easy to assume from a map that Perth is a coastal city; in fact, it is 19 kilometres inland, up the broad and beautiful Swan River, home of the black swan. A city of over one million people, Perth is large enough to offer excitement and variety, yet compact enough to be seen quite easily. King's Park, 404 hectares of natural bushland, is only a short drive from the city centre, and nearby ocean beaches offer the visitor year-round swimming and surfing.

Nearby Rottnest Island is small and sandy and only 20 kilometres off the coast of Fremantle. Regular air and ferry services from Perth will take you to this popular holiday island, where even the surrounding sea has been declared a sanctuary. Reefs and shipwrecks attract skin-divers to this area.

The southern corner of this State is aptly described as the garden of Western Australia. Hardwood forests of massive karri and jarrah trees soar

NOT TO BE MISSED
in Western Australia

- **Broome** – once the world's leading pearling centre, now a beautiful holiday destination and gateway to the spectacular West Kimberleys
- **Dales Gorge** – breathtaking gorge in Karijini National Park
- **Hotham Valley Tourist Railway** – for sightseeing combined with the romance and nostalgia of train travel
- **John Forrest National Park** – stunning wildflower displays in spring
- **Kalgoorlie** – for its flamboyant architecture from the gold-boom days
- **Margaret River** – for magnificent coastal and river scenery, caves and craft outlets – and excellent wine
- **Nambung National Park** – a moonscape of coloured quartz studded with limestone pillars, some 4 metres high
- **Shark Bay** – where wild dolphins swim daily into the shallows at Monkey Mia
- **Valley of the Giants** – a beautiful drive; allow time to take the Tree Top Walk through the giant stands of karri and tingle trees
- **Wildflowers** – a brilliant display across the State each spring

Banksia in full bloom in the south of the State

WESTERN AUSTRALIA

The scenic Great Ocean Drive, near Esperance

above the hundreds of different species of wildflowers that bloom from September to November. Great surfing beaches and coastal panoramic views add to the attractions of the south-west region, with such popular locations as Margaret River, Busselton, Yallingup and Albany. The Margaret River region is a must, whether or not you are interested in wine. The region is fertile and beautiful, and the vineyards flourish on the rich loam that is perfect for grape-growing. At the end of a day's drive you can sample some notable results of these conditions.

North-east of this well-vegetated corner, and 596 kilometres from Perth, is the one-time gold-boom area around Kalgoorlie-Boulder, surrounded by ghost towns such as Coolgardie and Broad Arrow. South of Kalgoorlie-Boulder the modern town of Kambalda owes its prosperity to nickel. Further east you reach the Nullarbor Plain; further north are the Great Victoria and Gibson Deserts.

Along the Brand Highway, 424 kilometres north of Perth, is Geraldton, situated on the coast where you can sample freshly caught crays. Between August and October, the roadsides between Perth and Geraldton are ablaze with wildflowers. Further north you can see a splendid range of flora and fauna in Kalbarri National Park and explore the spectacular coastal gorges and cliffs. Magnificent beaches, excellent fishing and coral reefs are the main attractions along the coast north of Geraldton. At Monkey Mia on Shark Bay, wild dolphins come close to the shore to be fed. Carnarvon, renowned for its

CALENDAR OF EVENTS

Note: The information given here was accurate at the time of printing. However, as the timing of events held annually is subject to change and some events may extend into the following month, it is best to check with the local tourism authority or event organisers to confirm the details. The calendar is not exhaustive. Most towns and regions hold sporting competitions, regattas and rodeos, art, craft and trade exhibitions, agricultural and flower shows, music festivals and other events annually. Details of these events are available from local tourism outlets.

JANUARY
Public holidays: New Year's Day; Australia Day. **Perth:** Hopman Cup (tennis, contd); Perth Cup (horseracing); Vines golf classic. **Beverley:** Cross-country gliding regatta. **Busselton:** Festival of Busselton; Performing arts beach festival. **Esperance:** Sailboard classic; Turf racing (contd). **Geraldton:** Windsurfing classic. **Harvey:** Australia Day breakfast. **Hopetoun:** Summer festival. **Mandurah:** Festival. **Narrogin:** State gliding championships. **Rockingham:** Cockburn yachting regatta.

FEBRUARY
Perth: Chinese New Year festival; Festival of Perth. **Albany:** Great southern wine festival. **Boyup Brook:** Country music awards. **Esperance:** Offshore angling classic. **Katanning:** Triathlon. **Margaret River:** Leeuwin Estate concert; Wine and food festival.

MARCH
Public holiday: Labour Day. **Perth:** Festival of Perth (contd). **Augusta:** Dragon boat racing. **Brookton:** Old time motor show (biennial, even numbered years). **Bunbury:** Aqua spectacular; Show. **Busselton:** Blue-water classic (fishing). **Denmark:** International Australian jugglers' festival. **Kalbarri:** Sport fishing classic. **Mount Barker:** Field Day wine festival. **Pemberton:** King karri karnival. **Wagin:** Woolorama.

EASTER
Public holidays: Good Friday; Easter Monday. **Dongara:** Horse races. **Donnybrook:** Apple festival. **Guilderton:** King of the river. **Karratha:** Pilbara pursuit jetboat classic. **Lancelin:** Beach buggy championships. **Nannup:** Music festival.

APRIL
Public holiday: Anzac Day. **Perth:** National Trust Heritage Week. **Beverley:** Art exhibition. **Broome:** Rotary dragon boat classic. **Kununurra:** Dam to dam regatta.

MAY
Boyup Brook: Autumn art affair. **Carnarvon:** Tropical festival; Fremantle–Carnarvon yacht race. **Eucla:** Golf day. **Fremantle:** Fremantle–Carnarvon yacht race. **Gingin:** British Car Day. **Kununurra:** Ord River festival. **Toodyay:** Moondyne (colonial and convict) festival.

JUNE
Public holiday: Foundation Day. **Perth:** Western Australia Week (week-long celebration of foundation of State). **Cossack:** Fair and yachting regatta. **Geraldton:** Batavia celebrations; Foodfest. **Kambalda:** Sky diving gathering. **Karratha:** Festival. **Kununurra:** Ord River festival (contd). **Manjimup:** 15 000 Motocross. **Wagin:** Foundation Day.

JULY
Perth: Perth marathon. **Denmark:** Winter festival. **Derby:** Boab festival; Country music festival. **Exmouth:** Gala week; Arts and crafts show. **Fitzroy Crossing:** Rodeo. **Halls Creek:** Agricultural show. **Kununurra:** Ord River festival (contd). **Marble Bar:** Cup race weekend. **Onslow:** Bougainvillea festival. **Wickham:** Cossack–Wickham fun run.

AUGUST
Perth: City to surf fun run. **Beverley:** Agricultural show. **Broome:** Shinju Matsuri (Festival of the pearl); Opera under the stars. **Dampier:** Game-

succulent prawns, is an industrial fishing port at the mouth of the Gascoyne River. Ningaloo Marine Park protects the 260-kilometre coral reef near Coral Bay. Nearby, the town of Exmouth is world famous for its year-round fishing, particularly game-fishing.

The Pilbara region has some of the country's most spectacular gorges in Karijini (Hamersley Range) National Park. This is where Western Australia's second economic boom began, with the exploitation of the dramatic Hamersley Range, which is literally a mountain of iron. The Range stretches for 320 kilometres, yet from the air seems dwarfed by endless stretches of red sand.

At the State's very top is the Kimberley region, with the spectacular King Leopold Range in the west and Purnululu (Bungle Bungle) National Park in the east. The region's economy is based on diamond mining, as well as the more traditional cattle industry. A visit to this remote, dramatic region with its gorges and rivers is a unique experience – in keeping with many areas of Australia's largest State.

CLIMATE GUIDE

PERTH

	J	F	M	A	M	J	J	A	S	O	N	D
Maximum °C	30	31	29	25	21	19	18	18	20	22	25	27
Minimum °C	18	19	17	14	12	10	9	9	10	12	14	17
Rainfall mm	8	12	19	45	123	184	173	136	80	54	21	14
Raindays	3	3	4	8	14	17	18	17	14	11	6	4

ALBANY REGION

	J	F	M	A	M	J	J	A	S	O	N	D
Maximum °C	25	25	24	22	19	17	16	16	17	19	21	24
Minimum °C	14	14	13	12	10	8	8	7	8	9	11	12
Rainfall mm	27	24	28	63	102	103	124	106	82	78	48	25
Raindays	8	9	11	14	18	19	21	21	18	15	13	10

KALGOORLIE VALLEY

	J	F	M	A	M	J	J	A	S	O	N	D
Maximum °C	34	32	30	25	20	18	17	18	22	26	29	32
Minimum °C	18	18	16	12	8	6	5	5	8	11	14	17
Rainfall mm	22	28	19	19	28	31	26	20	15	16	18	15
Raindays	3	4	4	5	7	8	9	7	5	4	4	3

DERBY REGION

	J	F	M	A	M	J	J	A	S	O	N	D
Maximum °C	36	35	35	35	33	31	30	32	35	36	37	37
Minimum °C	26	26	25	22	19	16	14	16	20	23	25	26
Rainfall mm	182	155	110	32	22	10	6	1	0	2	17	84
Raindays	12	10	8	2	1	1	1	0	0	0	2	6

fishing classic. **Halls Creek:** Races. **Karratha:** FeNaCLNG festival. **Katanning:** Prophet Mohammad's birthday. **Mullewa:** Wildflower show. **Newman:** Fortescue festival. **Pingelly:** Art and tulip festival. **Port Hedland:** Spinifex spree. **Roebourne:** Royal show; Roebourne Cup and Ball. **Tom Price:** Nameless festival. **Walyunga National Park** (near Mundaring): Avon Descent (white-water raft race) festival. **Wyndham:** Top of the West festival.

SEPTEMBER
Public holiday: Queen's Birthday. **Perth:** Football league finals; Kings Park wildflower festival; Perth royal show; Rally Australia. **Augusta:** Spring flower show. **Boyup Brook:** Country music weekend. **Broome:** Shinju Matsuri (Festival of the pearl, contd). **Carnamah:** Agricultural show. **Coolgardie:** Camel races; Coolgardie Day. **Corrigin:** Agricultural show. **Cossack:** Art awards, Art Ball. **Cranbrook:** Wildflower show. **Denmark:** Festival of the classics. **Kalgoorlie:** Kalgoorlie Cup; Spring festival. **Kojonup:** Wildflower and country festival. **Kukerin:** Tracmach vintage fair. **Mingenew:** Lions expo (includes Wildflower display). **Mullewa:** Wildflower show (contd). **Nannup:** Discovery weekend. **Ravensthorpe:** Wildflower display. **Southern Cross:** Agricultural show. **Toodyay:** Folk festival. **York:** Jazz festival.

OCTOBER
Perth: Spring in the (Swan) Valley festival; Kings Park wildflower festival (contd). **Augusta:** Spring flower show (contd). **Boyup Brook:** Blackwood River marathon relay to Bridgetown. **Bridgetown:** Blackwood Classic (powerboat race); Finish of Blackwood River marathon relay. **Busselton:** West Coast golf open. **Esperance:** Agricultural show. **Eucla:** Eucla shoot. **Geraldton:** Festival of Geraldton. **Harvey:** Agricultural show. **Jilakan Rock** (near Kulin): Picnic race day. **Kukerin:** Tracmach vintage fair (contd). **Leonora:** Art prize. **Merredin:** Vintage car festival (biennial, odd-numbered years). **Morawa:** Music spectacular. **Narrogin:** Spring festival; Texpo (modern farming displays). **Northcliffe:** Mountain bike championship. **Three Springs:** White Rock Stakes wheelbarrow race. **Walpole:** Wildflower week. **Yallingup:** October festival.

NOVEMBER
Albany: Perth–Albany ocean yacht race. **Beverley:** Duck race (with plastic ducks). **Bridgetown:** Blues at Bridgetown. **Broome:** Mango festival. **Bunbury:** Bunbury Fest. **Dongara:** Blessing of the fleet. **Donnybrook:** Celebration time. **Dunsborough:** Down south dive classic. **Exmouth:** Gamex, world-class game-fishing. **Fitzroy Crossing:** Barra Bash (barramundi fishing competition). **Fremantle:** Festival. **Jurien:** Expo and Blessing of the fleet. **Kalbarri:** Blessing of the fleet. **Kalgoorlie:** Goldfields mining expo. **Mount Barker:** Vintage motor-bike hill climb. **Northam:** Avon Valley country music festival. **Rockingham:** Rocky spring festival. **Wickepin:** Art and craft show (biennial, even-numbered years). **Wyndham:** Hang gliding competition.

DECEMBER
Public holidays: Christmas Day; Boxing Day. **Perth:** Australian derby; Christmas pageant; Hopman Cup (tennis). **Cervantes:** Slalom carnival (windsurfing). **Derby:** Kimberley Boxing Day sports. **Esperance:** Turf racing. **Katanning:** Caboodle. **Lancelin:** Ledge Point ocean race (windsurfing). **Rockingham:** Christmas regatta. **Yallingup:** Malibu competition.

PERTH
A Friendly City

The beautiful Kings Park overlooks the city

WESTERN AUSTRALIA

With a Mediterranean-type climate and a river setting, Perth is made for an outdoor lifestyle. Within easy reach of the city lie clean surf beaches, rolling hills, tranquil forests and well-kept parklands. The Swan River winds through Perth and suburbs, widening to lake size at Perth and Melville Waters; and the Canning River provides another attractive waterway through the southern suburbs.

The city centre, 19 kilometres upstream from the port of Fremantle, is on the Swan River and surrounded by a series of gardens, parks and reserves, including the magnificent 404-hectare Kings Park. The green slopes of Mount Eliza in Kings Park contrast dramatically with Perth's skyline, and the serene blue hills of the Darling Range can be seen in the distance.

Perth was founded by Captain James Stirling in 1829, but the progress of the isolated Swan River Settlement, made up entirely of free settlers, was slow; it was not until the first shipment of convicts arrived in 1850 that the colony found its feet. The convicts were soon set to work building roads, bridges and fine public buildings, and in 1856 Perth was proclaimed a city. Gold discoveries in the State in the 1880s gave Perth another boost, and more recently, the huge diamond finds in the Kimberley and the reopening of goldmines in the Kalgoorlie-Boulder region have stimulated new growth.

The capital has a population of just over 1.2 million, many of whom live in the pleasant suburbs that stretch north and south. Perth is cosmopolitan, home to significant numbers of people born in Britain, New Zealand, Italy, the Netherlands, Malaysia, Vietnam and the Philippines, and there is a substantial Greek community. In addition, of a total Aboriginal population of 42 000 in the State, almost 12 000 live in the capital.

The city centre is compact, and easy to explore. Travel by bus or train within the city's **Free Transit Zone** (FTZ), day or night, seven days a week. A free 10-minute bus service, the **City Clipper**, circles the city during the day; other Clipper services connect the city with East and West Perth, and Northbridge. A fun way to discover the city is on the **Perth Tram**, a wooden replica of the city's first trams. You can break your journey at any point and rejoin later.

Most of Perth's shops and arcades are in the blocks bounded by St Georges Terrace and William, Wellington and Barrack Streets, centring around **Hay Street Mall**, **Raine Square Shopping Plaza**, and **Murray Street Mall** and **Forrest Place Mall**. Perth's shopping and business area is linked by pedestrian malls, overpasses and underground

NOT TO BE MISSED
in Perth

- **Ferry trip** – along the Swan River to the fascinating port town of Fremantle
- **Kings Park** – a huge bushland reserve offering magnificent views of the city and splendid wildflower displays in spring
- **Lake Monger** – to see black swans and other species of water bird
- **London Court** – to watch knights on horseback joust above one entrance while St George and the dragon do battle over the other
- **Market** – at weekends in Fremantle, has a unique atmosphere created by the ornate gold-rush-era architecture
- **Northbridge** – for its cosmopolitan restaurants and art galleries
- **Perth Mint** – the closest most people get to a fortune
- **Perth Tram** – a fun way to discover the city and its attractions
- **Scitech Discovery Centre** – for impressive hands-on science and technology displays
- **Underwater World** – to meet sharks and other marine creatures face to face

walkways, enabling access, unhampered by motor vehicles. Perth's unique **London Court**, an Elizabethan-style arcade, runs from Hay Street Mall to St Georges Terrace. At the Hay Street entrance, four knights on horseback joust above a replica of Big Ben every 15 minutes, while St George and the Dragon do battle above the clock over the St Georges Terrace entrance. Perth's decorative **Town Hall** on the corner of Hay and Barrack Streets was built by convicts between 1869 and 1879.

Stately **St Georges Terrace**, Perth's financial and professional heart, is worth strolling down for its historic buildings, cheek by jowl with towering modern glass giants. Start at the western end, where you will see **Parliament House**; when Parliament is not sitting, there are guided tours Monday to Friday. Nearby is the mellow brickwork of **Barracks Arch** (all that remains of the Tudor-style Pensioner Barracks built in 1863).

Continuing along St Georges Terrace you come to the charming **Cloisters** (1858), a former boys' school that has been integrated with the modern complex behind. The ecclesiastical-looking building nearby is the Old Perth Boys' School, now the National Trust giftshop and cafe. The **Palace Hotel**, a grand old Victorian iron-lace balconied hotel, has been modified as a banking chamber and forms an impressive exterior facade for Perth's second largest building, the Bankwest Tower. Located further along the terrace is an ornate Victorian church – **Trinity Church Chapel** – and the arched entrance to London Court. The impressive **Treasury Building** on the corner of Barrack Street overlooks **Stirling Gardens**, part of the **Supreme Court Gardens** and a popular picnic spot for shoppers and city workers. The **Orchestral Shell**, within the gardens, is the venue for various concerts and Carols by Candlelight. **St George's Cathedral** and the **Deanery** are two other interesting old buildings at this end of St Georges Terrace. On the opposite side is one of Perth's oldest buildings, the **Old Court House** (1836), and the turrets of the Gothic-style **Government House** in its lush private gardens.

Further along is the modern **Perth Concert Hall**, which seats 1900 and is used for everything from hard rock to opera. Inside, a restaurant, a tavern and a cocktail bar cater for music lovers.

Decoration above entrance to London Court

At the eastern end of Hay Street is the **Perth Mint**, where a spectacular viewing gallery provides views of pure gold bars being poured and moulded.

Just north of the city centre in Northbridge is the attractive **Perth Cultural Centre** complex. Nationally and internationally renowned artworks are on display in the **Art Gallery of Western Australia**. Nearby is the **Alexander Library**, and the original Perth Gaol (1856) within the modern complex of the **Western Australian Museum**. A blue whale skeleton, Aboriginal artifacts and a stuffed native bird display are among the exhibits.

A visit to the Cultural Centre could be combined with a meal at one of the many reasonably priced restaurants in this area, as cosmopolitan **Northbridge** is also the centre of the city's nightlife. Numerous hotels, nightclubs and piano bars offer a variety of live entertainment and dancing until dawn.

At the City West shopping complex in West Perth are the **Omni Theatre** and the award-winning **Scitech Discovery Centre**. The specially constructed theatre presents visitors with real adventure experiences, and the centre has a hands-on science and technology display. **It's a Small World**, in Parliament Place, West Perth, has a fascinating collection of miniatures ranging from historic miniature railways to push-button animation.

Just west of the city centre, in Havelock Street, is the **Old Observatory**, now the headquarters for the National Trust; four of its rooms are open to the public. The new **Perth Observatory**, at Bickley, has a substantial display centre and night tours are available, bookings essential. **Kings Park** is one of Perth's major attractions. Within this huge natural bushland reserve there are landscaped gardens and walkways, lakes, children's playgrounds, lookouts and the **Botanic Gardens** on **Mount Eliza Bluff**, where a blaze of Western Australian wildflowers is to be seen in spring. You can drive by car through the park or hire a bicycle, stopping at the many scenic lookouts over the city and river; or you can wander on foot along the many walking trails right to the top of Mount Eliza. Within the park the magnificently sited **War Memorial** also offers splendid views of the city.

Other city parks include **Hyde Park**, with its waterbirds, ornamental lake and English trees, and the beautiful **Queens Gardens**, with a replica of London's Peter Pan statue. Just north-west of the city centre is **Lake Monger**, a favourite picnic spot that is also the home of black swans, ducks and other varieties of birds. **Matilda Bay**, on the Swan River, offers grassed areas and ample shade, with stunning views of the Swan River and

ACCOMMODATION

HOTELS
Burswood Resort Hotel
Great Eastern Hwy, Victoria Park
(09) 362 7777

Hyatt Regency
99 Adelaide Tce, Perth
(09) 225 1234

Parmelia Hilton
14 Mill St, Perth
(09) 322 3622

Sheraton Perth Hotel
207 Adelaide Tce, Perth
(09) 325 0501

FAMILY AND BUDGET
All Seasons Freeway Hotel
55 Mill Point Rd, South Perth
(09) 367 7811

Jewell House YMCA Private Hotel
180 Goderich St, Perth
(09) 325 8488

MOTEL GROUPS: BOOKINGS
Flag 13 2400
Best Western 13 1779
Quality Pacific 1800 090 600
Travelodge 1800 222 446

This list is for information only; inclusion is not necessarily a recommendation.

Perth city skyline. The **Swan River Estuary Marine Park** includes three areas: Alfred Cove, Pelican Point and Milyu. South-west of the city centre is **Wireless Hill Park**, a natural bushland area with a grassed picnic and play ground area; a **Telecommunications Museum**, housed in the original Wireless Station; and three viewing towers.

The **Swan River foreshores**, on both the city side and South Perth, provide pleasant walking and cycling trails. Bicycles can be hired just off Riverside Drive near the Causeway.

A pleasant way to visit **Perth's Zoo**, with its magnificent garden environment and nocturnal house, is to catch a ferry from the Barrack Street Jetty. The trip can be combined with a visit to the **Old Mill**, on the South Perth foreshore. This picturesque whitewashed windmill, built in 1838, now houses an interesting collection of early colonial relics.

Further north along the coast at Sorrento is **Hillarys Boat Harbour**. A day can easily be spent here, enjoying the atmosphere and variety of **Sorrento Quay** or experiencing the thrill of **Underwater World**, where you are transported through a submerged acrylic tunnel on moving walkways to see the enormous variety of underwater life. From September to November, charter boats at the harbour offer visits to see whales basking between Perth and Rottnest Island.

Swimming and surfing are part of the joy of Perth and several beautiful Indian Ocean beaches – including **Cottesloe**, **Swanbourne** (a nude bathing beach), **City**, **Scarborough**, **Trigg** and **Port** – are within easy reach of the city.

There are many other places of interest around Perth, including the historic port of **Fremantle**, which underwent a complete facelift in preparation for the America's Cup challenge in 1987. In Fremantle you can relive the past by strolling along the streets of terraced houses, or visiting the city's magnificent historic buildings and the many galleries, museums and craft workshops. Relax at one of the many alfresco cafes in **South Terrace**, home also for the National Trust-classified **Fremantle market**, open every weekend and well worth a visit. The **Fremantle Tram** offers various hourly tours around the city's attractions.

The **University of Western Australia**, with its Mediterranean-style buildings and landscaped gardens in the riverside suburb of Crawley, is also worth seeing. The university's **Fortune Theatre** has been built as a replica of Shakespeare's Fortune Theatre in Elizabethan London.

At nearby **Subiaco**, a popular shopping and market area an easy train ride from the city, you will find the Aboriginal art gallery **Indiginart** in Hay Street; there is another, the **Creative Native Gallery**, in King Street in the city and in High Street, Fremantle. **Adventure World** in the southern suburb of Bibra Lake offers among its attractions a wildlife park, animal circus, rides and Australia's largest swimming-pool, and is open from October to April. **Cables Water Ski Park** at Spearwood features cable tows for water skiing, a water slide and mini golf.

Perth's sporting facilities are excellent, with two major racecourses, **Ascot** and **Belmont Park**; night pacing at **Gloucester Park** (the famous WACA cricket ground is near here); greyhound racing at **Cannington**; and speedcar and motorcycle racing at the **Claremont Showgrounds**. Major athletics meetings, rugby and soccer matches are held at **Perry Lakes Stadium**, and Australian Rules football finals at **Subiaco Oval**. Hockey is played at the **Commonwealth Hockey Stadium**, the first Astroturf stadium in Australia. The **Superdrome** hosts several international sporting events.

Perth offers the visitor a wide range of entertainment. The modern **Perth Entertainment Centre** (home of the Perth Wildcats basketball team), in Wellington Street, seats 8000. At the **Burswood Casino**, across the river at Rivervale, you can try your luck at the tables, or enjoy the five-star splendour of the hotel. Another resort complex is **Raddison Observation City Resort Hotel** on the coast at Scarborough. Perth also offers an excellent range of accommodation to suit all requirements.

During February and March, the **Festival of Perth** combines the visual arts, theatre, music and film. A festive occasion occurs every weekend on the Art Gallery and Museum Concourse where handcrafted items can be purchased at the **Galleria Art and Craft Market** and at the **Station Street Markets** at Subiaco with its range of bric-a-brac, live entertainment and a garden courtyard providing a colourful atmosphere. Other weekend markets include the **Scarborough Fair Markets**, with specialty stalls and a food hall; **Stock Road Markets** at Spearwood, undercover markets with a circus theme; **Gosnells Railway Markets**, with its old-world charm; **Canning Vale Sunday Markets**, one of the biggest undercover markets; **Subiaco Pavilion Markets**, held in a stylishly restored warehouse; and, at Midland, the **Military Markets** include a wildlife sanctuary, and the **Sunday Markets** are held in an open carpark.

For further information on Perth and Western Australia, contact the Western Australian Tourist Centre, Albert Facey House, cnr Forrest Place and Wellington St, Perth; (09) 483 1111 or 1800 812 808.

PERTH ON FOOT

There are many walking tours around Perth and its suburbs. The W.A. Heritage Committee, as part of Australia's 1988 Bicentenary, established a state-wide network of heritage trails; the Perth Heritage Trails listed below are part of this network.

- **Guntrips Walking Tours:** 2-hour guided walks including the Cultural Walk around the city and the Western Walk which takes in Kings Park; bookings essential.
- **Heritage Walk:** 2-hour guided walk of central business district; bookings essential.
- **Perth Walking Tours:** guided 2-hour walks concentrating on architecture, history and heritage; bookings essential.
- **Perth Heritage Trails:** self-guide heritage trails around central Perth; East Perth; Northbridge; West Perth; Subiaco; Jolimont; Shenton Park; and foreshore.
- **Subiaco Guided Walks:** Historic homes, Rokeby Road and City Square; bookings essential.

For brochures for the self-guide walks and for further information, contact the Western Australian Tourist Centre, cnr Forrest Place and Wellington St, Perth; (09) 483 1111.

TOURS from Perth

With the Indian Ocean surf beaches beckoning from the west, the peaceful Darling Range on the east and the Swan River meandering through Perth from Fremantle to the Swan Valley vineyards, there are many enjoyable trips within easy reach of Perth.

Ferry Cruises

From the Barrack Street Jetty, ferries leave regularly to Fremantle, Rottnest Island and Swan Valley. Other cruises will take you to the historic riverside home Tranby. From Wednesday to Saturday nights, in season, you can have dinner aboard a vessel that leaves the Barrack Street Jetty in the early evening and returns at midnight. Daily ferry services to Rottnest Island, Perth's popular hideaway and once the site of the infamous Rottnest Native Prison, also leave from Hillarys Boat Harbour and from Fremantle. **See**: Rottnest Island.

Fremantle

19 km from Perth via the Stirling or Canning Highways

A visit to this fascinating old port can make an interesting round trip by car if you return via the opposite side of the river. Fremantle is also easily accessible by bus, train and boat. Just 10 minutes from Fremantle is Adventure World, a fun park featuring a wide variety of entertainment. Adventure World is open most weekends, and daily except Christmas Day and Good Friday, between 1 October and 28 April. **See**: Entry for Fremantle in A–Z listing.

Serpentine Dam

54 km from Perth via the South Western Highway

Picnic beside the Serpentine Dam, which is set among peaceful hills and beautiful landscaped gardens of wildflowers.

Pinjarra

84 km from Perth on the South Western Highway

See: Entry for Pinjarra in A–Z listing.

Vineyards at Houghtons Winery in the Swan Valley

Pioneer Village, Armadale

29 km from Perth via the Albany Highway

Pioneer Village is a reconstruction of the days of the gold rush when every town boasted a blacksmith and a coaching-house. Nearby is Araluen Botanic Park, with its beautiful gardens and waterfalls. Close to Armadale, Tumbulgum Farm features a farm show, an Aboriginal cultural show and Showcase WA, which offers WA-made products for purchase. At nearby Gosnells, the Cohunu Koala Park has a wide range of Australian fauna.

York

97 km from Perth via the Great Southern Highway

See: Entry for York in A–Z listing.

Historic Guildford in the Swan Valley

18 km from Perth via Guildford Road or the Great Eastern Highway

On the way, visit the Craft Centre at Mount Lawley, and the rail museum in Bassendean. At Guildford, the old court house and gaol in Meadow Street houses, a folk museum, and nearby, is the Village Potters gallery. A 40-kilometre heritage trail starts at the Success Hill Reserve and retraces the steps of Captain Stirling on his 1827 search for a site for the new settlement. Just north-east of Guildford in Ford Street, West Midland, is Woodbridge, a gracious mansion overlooking the river, beautifully restored and furnished by the National Trust. Whiteman Park, 7 km north of Guildford, has train and tram rides, and the Trade Village, where trades people ply traditional skills. There are numerous wineries in the area, including the historic Houghtons Wines. Craft shops, galleries and antique shops also abound.

John Forrest National Park

28 km from Perth on the Great Eastern Highway

This huge bushland park in the Darling Range features walking trails, streams, waterfalls and a safe swimming pool for children. Three kilometres east of the park is the old Mahogany Inn (1837), now the oldest residential inn in Western Australia. At weekends enjoy a Devonshire tea.

Mundaring Weir

42 km from Perth via the Great Eastern Highway

This water catchment area, which provides water for the goldfields over 500 kilometres away, is surrounded by picnic areas. The O'Connor Museum explains the construction and operation of this complex water scheme. Kalamunda History Village is nearby.

Walyunga National Park

35 km from Perth via Guildford Road and the Great Northern Highway

The Avon River flows through this beautiful bushland park, renowned for its wildflower display in spring. It is a popular picnic spot and there are signposted walking trails. Each year in August, the Avon Descent, a major white-water canoeing event is held here.

Rottnest Island

Commodore Willem de Vlamingh referred to Rottnest Island as a 'terrestrial paradise' when he landed there in 1696, and holidaymakers still flock to the island to enjoy its peace, beauty and unique holiday atmosphere. A low, sandy island, just 20 kilometres north-west of Fremantle, Rottnest is a public reserve. Only 11 kilometres long and about 5 kilometres wide, it has an attractive coastline, with many small bays and coves, sparkling white beaches and turquoise waters. Vlamingh named it Rottnest, or Rat's Nest, for the island's marsupial resident, the quokka, which he believed to be a type of rat.

The Rottnest Hotel, completed in 1864, was originally the summer residence of the governors of Western Australia. Now commonly known as the Quokka Arms, it is a good place to stay, or just to enjoy a relaxing drink in the beer garden. Rottnest Lodge Resort has modern convention facilities in an informal setting. Other accommodation includes units, cabins, hostels and a camping area.

There is no lack of things to do on Rottnest Island. Cars are not permitted (which contributes to the wonderful sense of peace), but you can hire a bicycle and explore the island. You may even catch a glimpse of peacocks and pheasants, which were introduced at the turn of the century. Special 2-hour coach tours of the island are conducted twice daily. A train operates several times daily except Christmas Day, on a 7-kilometre route from the historic settlement area to the Oliver Hill Battery. Oliver Hill Lookout, located next to the battery, offers views across the salt lakes to the mainland. Other lookouts on the island include Vlamingh Lookout, near the hotel and the highest point of the circular 1-km trail known as the Vlamingh Memorial Heritage Trail; and Jeannies Lookout, popular with photographers. There are tennis courts, a 9-hole golf course and bowling facilities. You can hire a boat, dinghy or canoe, play mini-golf or go trampolining; or you can just laze on the beach in the sunshine. Scuba diving is available; contact the Dive, Surf and Ski Shop.

The *Underwater Explorer*, a glass-bottomed pleasure cruiser, leaves regularly from Main Jetty, giving glimpses of shipwrecks, reefs and a startling array of fish. Ferries operate daily services to Rottnest from Barrack Street Jetty in Perth and also from Fremantle and Hillarys Boat Harbour. There are daily flights from Perth. As all wildlife on Rottnest is protected, no pets and no guns of any description, including spear guns, are allowed on the island. In the interests of their health and survival, please do not feed the quokkas.

For further information, contact the Rottnest Visitor Centre, Henderson Ave; (09) 372 9752.

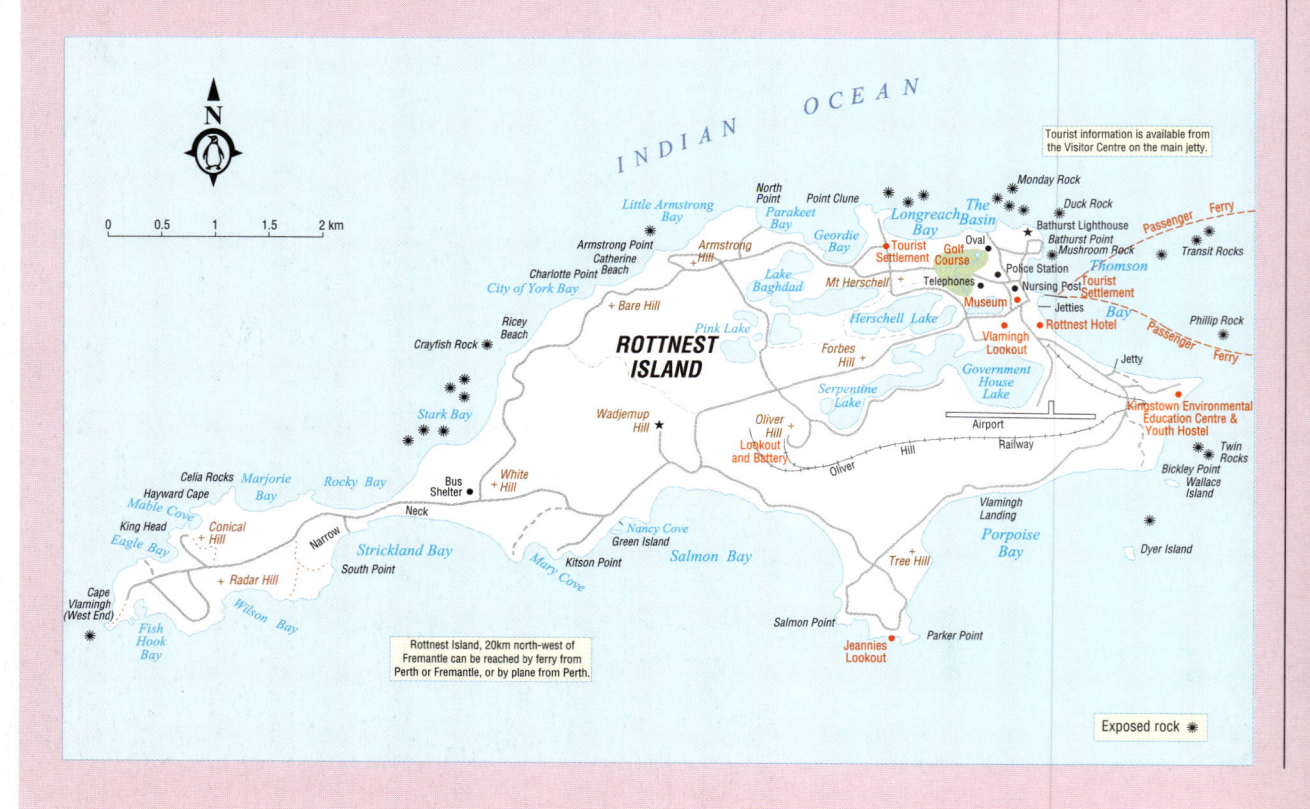

The island's resident marsupial, the quokka

WESTERN AUSTRALIA from A to Z

Albany
Pop. 18 826

MAP REF. 361 N12, 364 H13, 366 F12

Picturesque Albany is the state's oldest town. On the edge of King George Sound and the magnificent Princess Royal Harbour, the town is 406 km s of Perth. Albany dates back to 1826, when a military post was established to give the English a foothold in the West. Whaling was important in the 1840s; in the 1850s Albany became a coaling station for steamers bound from England. As WA's most important holiday centre, it offers visitors a wealth of history and a variety of coastal, rural and mountain scenery. Its harbours, weirs and estuaries provide excellent fishing. **Of interest:** Colonial Buildings Historic Walk; self-guide brochure from Tourist information. Old Post Office-Intercolonial Communications Museum, cnr Stirling Tce and Spencer St. Victorian shopfronts in Stirling Tce. Outlet for Alkoomi Wines, Lower Stirling Tce. In Residency Rd: Residency Museum (1850s), originally home of Resident Magistrates, now houses historical and environmental exhibits; Old Gaol and Museum (1851) has two gaols in one. Vancouver Arts Centre, Vancouver St. House of Gems, Frenchman Bay Rd. Outlet for Galafrey Wines, Proudlove Pde. Old Farm (1836), Middleton Rd, Strawberry Hill, site of first Government farm in WA. Faithfully restored Patrick Taylor Cottage (1832), Duke St, has extensive collection of period costume and household goods. Extravaganza Gallery, next to Esplanade Hotel, Middleton Beach, features vintage and veteran cars, art and craft. Princess Royal Fortress (commissioned 1893) on Mt Adelaide, Albany's first federal fortress. Mt Adelaide Forts Heritage Trails, starting cnr Apex Dr. and Forts Rd; self-guide leaflets from Tourist information. On Princess Royal Dr.: the *Amity*, a full-scale replica of brig that brought Major Lockyer and convicts to establish Albany in 1826; Amity Crafts, for local art and craft. Anzac Light Horse Memorial statue, near top of Mt Clarence, off Marine Dr.; spectacular view from here and from John Barnesby Memorial Lookout at Mt Melville. Feb.: Great southern wine festival. Nov.: Perth–Albany ocean yacht race. **In the area:** Swimming and fishing at: Jimmy Newhill's Harbour, 20 km s; Frenchman Bay, 25 km s; Emu Point, 8 km NE; Oyster Harbour, 15 km NE. *To the north*: Jolly Barnyard family farm (3 km); O'Dome deer farm (6 km); Porongurup National Park (37 km) featuring huge granite peaks and easy walking tracks to peaks providing splendid views; Stirling Range National Park (80 km) for climbing and bushwalking, breathtaking scenery, brilliant wildflowers in spring, some unique to area. *To the west towards Denmark*: West Cape Howe National Park (30 km) one of south coast's most popular parks for walking, fishing, swimming and hang-gliding, and has one of best lookouts on coast; Torbay Head in park is southernmost point in WA. Care should be taken when exploring the coast, king waves can be dangerous and have been known to rush in unexpectedly, with fatal consequences. *To the south*: Shell Museum (10 km) open Sun.–Fri.; Torndirrup National Park (17 km) for spectacular coastal views; The Gap and Natural Bridge (18 km); the Blow Holes (19 km). *To the south-east*: Camp Quaranup (20 km), site of old quarantine station, historical walk south on Geake Point; Cheyne's Beach Whaling Station (25 km) ceased operation 1978, in its heyday, the Station's chasers took up to 850 whales per season; now Albany Whaleworld. *To the east*: Locomotion tourist railway complex (15 km), for train rides, historic trams, art, craft, tearooms and accommodation; Willowie Game Park (30 km); Nanarup (20 km) and Little Beach (40 km) have sheltered waters; Two Peoples Bay Marron Reserve (20 km); Two Peoples Bay Nature Reserve (40 km). **Tourist information:** Old Railway Station, Proudlove Pde; (098) 41 1088. **Accommodation:** 5 hotels, 9 motels, 15 B&B, 2 hostels, 10 cara./camp. parks. **See also:** The Great Southern.

Historic Old Farm at Strawberry Hill, Albany

Augusta
Pop. 838

MAP REF. 357 C13, 359 D12, 364 B11, 366 B11

Set on the slopes of the Hardy Inlet, the town of Augusta overlooks the mouth of the Blackwood River, the waters of

Flinders Bay and rolling, heavily wooded countryside. Augusta is one of the oldest settlements in WA and a popular holiday town. Jarrah, karri and pine forests supply the district's 100-year-old timber industry. **Of interest:** In Blackwood Ave: Historical Museum; Lumen Christi Catholic Church. Crafters Croft, Ellis St, for art and craft. Mar.: Dragon boat racing. Sept.-Oct.: Spring flower show **In the area:** Picturesque coastline; excellent swimming and surfing. Good fishing in river and ocean. Marron (freshwater lobster) caught in season; marron fishing licence required, available from post office, Blackwood Ave. Augusta–Busselton Heritage Trail; details from Tourist information. Cruises on Blackwood River and Hardy Inlet available. Hillview Lookout and golf course, both offering panoramic views; 6 km NW. Jewel Cave, famous for its colourful limestone formations, and Moondyne Cave, for guided adventure tours; both 8 km NW. Alexandra Bridge, 10 km N, a charming picnic spot with towering jarrah trees and beautiful wildflowers in spring. Boranup Maze, 18 km N. Boranup Lookout, 19 km N; also pleasant picnic spot. Lake Cave and Mammoth Cave, both 30 km N. The Landing Place, 3 km S, where first European settlers landed in area. Whale Rescue Memorial, to people who helped save a large pod of pilot whales beached here in 1986; 4 km S. Matthew Flinders Memorial, 5 km S. Cape Leeuwin, 8 km SW, most southwesterly point of Australia and where Indian and Southern Oceans meet; at Cape, lighthouse (1895) and water wheel. **Tourist information:** Leeuwin Souvenirs, Blackwood Ave; (097) 58 1695, or Augusta-Margaret River Tourist Bureau, cnr Tunbridge Rd and Bussell Hwy, Margaret River; (097) 57 2911. **Accommodation:** 1 hotel/motel, 1 motel, 1 hostel, 4 cara./camp. parks.

Australind   Pop. 4407

MAP REF. 357 G4, 364 C8, 366 C10

The popular holiday town of Australind is located 11 km NE of Bunbury on the Leschenault Estuary. Fishing, crabbing, swimming and boating on the estuary and the Collie River are the main attractions. **Of interest:** In Paris Rd: Henton Cottage (1841); restored Church of St Nicholas (1842), thought to be smallest church in WA. Rock and Gem Museum, Old Coast Rd; check opening times. **In the area:** Cemetery, 2 km N, has pioneer graves and beautiful wildflowers in season. Kemerton Industrial Park (SCM Chemicals), 15 km N, has guided tours; contact Tourist information. Pleasant beach towns to the north: Binningup (26 km) and Myalup (30 km). **Tourist information:** Harvey Tourist and Interpretative Centre, South Western Hwy, Harvey; (097) 29 1122. **Accommodation:** 2 B&B, 3 cara./camp. parks.

Balladonia   Pop. 10

MAP REF. 367 L8

Balladonia is on the Eyre Hwy, 191 km E of Norseman. At this point, the road crosses gently undulating dryland forest through the Fraser Range. Visitors can see claypans typical of the region and old stone fences built by pioneer farmers in the 1800s. In July 1979, debris from the US Skylab fell to earth near the town. **In the area:** Wildflowers in spring. Balladonia Station Homestead (1886), off north side of highway behind old telegraph station, 22 km E, has a gallery of paintings depicting local history; open by appt. Newmans Rocks, 50 km W on Eyre Hwy. **Tourist information:** Balladonia Hotel/Motel; (090) 39 3453. **Accommodation:** 1 hotel/motel, 1 cara./camp. park (limited facilities). **See also:** Crossing the Nullarbor.

Beverley   Pop. 818

MAP REF. 364 F4, 366 D8

On the Avon River, 130 km E of Perth, is the town of Beverley. **Of interest:** Delightful picnic spots beside Avon River. Aeronautical Museum, Vincent St, shows development of aviation in WA and includes biplane built in 1929 by local aircraft designer Selby Ford. In Hunt Rd: Dead Finish (1872), one of oldest buildings in town and once a hotel in town centre but with the coming of the railway in 1886 the town centre moved nearer the station (open Sun. or by arrangement with Tourist information); Barry Ferguson's Garage, has display of old hand-operated machinery (open normal trading hours). Jan.: Cross-country gliding regatta. Apr.: Art exhibition. Aug.: Agricultural show. Nov.: Duck race (with plastic ducks). **In the area:** The Avon Ascent, a self-guide drive tour of the Avon Valley; leaflet from Tourist information. Magnificent view from top of Seaton Ross Hill, Beverley Rd, on northern outskirts of town. Restored St Paul's Church (consecrated 1862), opposite original town site, 5 km NW. Avondale Discovery Farm, 6 km W. Restored church, St John's in the Wilderness (consecrated 1895), 27 km SW. Farm Fresh Yabby Company, 8 km SE; check opening times. County Peak (362 m), 35 km SE, offers bushwalking, picnic area, spectacular views from summit. Yenyening Lakes Nature Reserve, 36 km SE, for picnics and water-skiing (if adequate water). **Tourist information:** Aeronautical Museum, Vincent St; (096) 46 1555. **Accommodation:** 2 hotels, 1 cara./camp. park.

Boyup Brook   Pop. 584

MAP REF. 360 E2, 364 E9, 366 D11

A small town near the junction of Boyup Creek and the Blackwood River, Boyup Brook is a centre for the district's sheep, dairy-farming and timber industries. Blackboys, huge granite boulders, shaded pools, charming cottages and farms are scenic features. **Of interest:** Pioneers Museum, Jayes Rd. Sandy Chambers Art Studio, Gibbs St, for artworks; outside are aviaries and camels. Stagline Woollen Clothing, Henderson St. Flax Mill, on Blackwood River off Barron St. Haddleton Flora Reserve, Arthur River Rd. Pioneer Garden, Kojonup Rd, has picnic/barbecue facilities. Carnaby Collection of beetles and butterflies at Tourist information. Bicentennial Walk Trail; details at Tourist information. Feb.: Country music awards. May: Autumn art affair. Sept.: Country music weekend. Oct.: Blackwood River marathon relay (running, canoeing, horseriding, cycling, swimming to Bridgetown). **In the area:** Visits to farms (wheat, sheep, pig, goat, deer and angora); Boyup Brook Flora Drive; details at Tourist information. Glacial rock formations at Glacier Hill, 18 km S. Wineries: Scotts Brook, 18 km SE, open by appt; Blackwood Crest, Kulikup, 40 km NE. Harvey Dickson Country Music Centre, 5 km NE; open by appt only. Gregory Tree, blazed by explorer Captain Gregory in 1845; 15 km NE. School and teacher's house (1900) at Dinninup, 21 km NE. At Wilga, 22 km NW, vintage engines and old timber-mill. Stormboy Jumpers, 20 km W on Jayes Rd, for locally-produced woollen goods; make appt at Tourist information. **Tourist information:** cnr Bridge and Able Sts; (097) 65 1444.

Camel riding on Cable Beach, near Broome

Accommodation: 1 hotel, 1 B&B, 1 hostel, 1 cara./camp. park. **See also:** The Great Southern.

Bremer Bay   Pop. 250

MAP REF. 366 G11

Bremer Bay, a popular holiday destination 181 km NE of Albany, was named in 1849 by Surveyor-General John Septimus Roe in honour of the captain of HMS *Tamar*, Sir Gordon Bremer. The town was built around the Old Telegraph Station at the mouth of Wellstead Estuary (named after John Wellstead, who settled in the area in the 1850s). **Of interest:** Fishing, boating, scuba diving and water-skiing. Rammed-earth buildings, including hotel/motel, Franton Way; church in John St, overlooking estuary. **In the area:** Fitzgerald River National Park, 17 km N. Military museum at Jerramungup, 90 km NW. **Tourist information:** Roadhouse, Gnombup Tce; (098) 37 4093. **Accommodation:** 1 hotel/motel, 1 B&B, 1 cara./camp. park. **See also:** The Great Southern.

Bridgetown   Pop. 2017

MAP REF. 360 C3, 364 D10, 366 D11

Bridgetown is a quiet spot in undulating country in the south-west corner of WA. Here the Blackwood River, well stocked with marron and trout, curves through some of the prettiest country in the State. The first European settlers arrived in 1857 and the first apple trees were planted soon after. **Of interest:** In Hampton St: Bridgetown Pottery; Brierley Jigsaw Gallery (at Tourist information); Gentle Era craft shop; St Paul's Church (1911), with paintings by local artists; Memorial Park, a peaceful picnic location. Bridgedale (1862), on South Western Hwy near bridge and overlooking river, constructed of local clay and timber by first European settler John Blechynden; restored by National Trust, check opening times. Also on South Western Hwy, Blackwood River Park for picnics and walks along river. Kalara Park Stud, Doust St; open by appt. Market, 2nd Sun. each month at Blackwood River Park. Oct.: Blackwood Classic, a 250-km power-boat event; Blackwood River marathon relay, (running, canoeing, swimming, horseriding and cycling) the 58.3 km course between Bridgetown and Boyup Brook. Nov.: Blues at Bridgetown. **In the area:** Wildflowers and apple blossom in season, begins Oct. Apple-orchard packing sheds worth a visit; contact Tourist information. Geegelup Heritage Trail (52 km) retraces history of agriculture, mining and timber; details from Tourist information. Scenic drives through rolling green hills, orchards and valleys into noted karri and jarrah timber country; contact Tourist information. Fine views: Sutton's Lookout, off Phillip St; Hester's Hill, 5 km N. Greenbushes Historical Park, 18 km N, has displays of tin-mining industry. Art and craft outlets at Ballingup, 28 km N, including Old Cheese Factory Art and Craft Centre. Bush walking and picnicking at Bridgetown Jarrah Park, 15 km W and also at Karri Gully, a further 5 km W. **Tourist information:** Hampton St; (097) 61 1740. **Accommodation:** 2 hotels, 1 hotel/motel, 6 B&B, 1 cara./camp. park. **See also:** The South-west.

Brookton   Pop. 576

MAP REF. 364 F5, 366 D8

An attractive town 137 km SE of Perth, near the Avon River in the heart of fertile farming country, Brookton was founded in 1884 when the Great Southern Railway line was opened. **Of interest:** In Robinson Rd: Old Police Station Museum, inquire at Tourist information; St Mark's Anglican Church (1895); Old Railway Station, houses Tourist information, and art and craft shop. Lions Picnic Park, off Corrigin Rd, at eastern entrance to town. Mar.: Old time motor show (even-numbered years). **In the area:** Nine Acre Rock, 12 km E on Brookton–Kweda Rd, one of the largest natural granite outcrops in the area; nearby remnants of pioneer Jack Hansen's home. Yenyening Lakes Nature Reserve, 35 km NE, has picnic/barbecue facilities. Boyagin Rock, 18 km SW, a reserve with picnic ground. **Tourist information:** Old Railway Station, Robinson Rd; (096) 42 1316. **Accommodation:** 2 hotels, 1 cara./camp. park.

Broome   Pop. 8906

MAP REF. 370 G9

Situated on the coast at the southern tip of the Kimberley, Broome enjoys wide beaches, turquoise water and a warm climate with plenty of sunshine. Closer to Bali than to Perth, and with an international airport, the town is lively and cosmopolitan. The discovery of pearling grounds off the coast in the 1880s led to the foundation of Broome township in 1883. By 1910 Broome was the world's leading pearling centre. However, the industry began to suffer when world markets collapsed in 1914. With increasing tourism, Broome is again rapidly expanding. **Of interest:** Many old buildings; self-guide heritage trail (2 km) introduces buildings and places of interest; contact Tourist information for brochure. Chinatown, including Pearl Emporiums, reminder of Broome's early multicultural mix. Historical Society Museum, in Old Customs House, Saville St. Library, Haas St. Captain Gregory's House, Carnarvon St; not open to public.

Several art galleries. In Hamersley St: Bedford Park, relics of Broome's history. Court house (former Cable House). Crocodile Park, Cable Beach Rd. Shell House, Guy St, contains one of largest shell collections in Australia. Sun Pictures, Carnarvon St, opened 1916 and believed to be oldest operating outdoor theatre in world. On Port Dr.: Chinese Cemetery; Japanese Cemetery (graves of early Japanese pearl divers). Pioneer Cemetery in Apex Park. Market, each Sat. at court house. Apr.: Rotary dragon boat classic. Aug.: Opera under the stars. Aug.–Sept.: Shinju Matsuri (Festival of the Pearl) recalls Broome's heyday. Nov.: Mango festival. **In the area:** Beaches, ideal swimming spots and prized by collectors for beautiful shells. Good fishing all year. Staircase to the Moon: natural phenomenon, visible at most full moons during dry season (Apr.–Oct.); caused by moonlight reflecting off exposed mudflats at extreme low tides; best seen from southern end of Dampier Tce (dates and times from Tourist information). Hovercraft *Spirit of Broome* visits local beaches. Safaris, cruises, scenic flights, short tours. Charter boats: 6- to 10-day Kimberley expeditions to coral reefs, Roley Shoals, Prince Regent River and waterfalls at Kings Cascades. Day tours: Lombadina Mission, 200 km NE; Cape Leveque, 220 km NE. Cable Beach, 3 km NW, is 22 km long, named after underwater cable that links Broome to Java. At Gantheaume Point, 5 km SW, giant dinosaur tracks, believed to be 130 million years old, can be seen when tide is out. Broome Bird Observatory, Roebuck Bay, 18 km E. Willie Creek Pearl Farm, 35 km N, tours available. **Tourist information:** cnr Bagot St and Great Northern Hwy; (091) 92 2222. **Accommodation:** 5 hotels, 1 hotel/motel, 2 hostels, 4 cara./camp. parks. **See also:** The Kimberley.

Bunbury   Pop. 24 003

MAP REF. 357 F4, 364 C8, 366 C10

Bunbury, 'Harbour City', is the second largest urban area in WA and serves as the major port, commercial and regional centre for the south-west. Situated 185 km S of Perth on the Leschenault Estuary, at the junction of the Preston and Collie Rivers, it is one of the State's most popular tourist areas, with a warm temperate climate, beautiful beaches and the Darling Range in the distance. Originally called Port Leschenault, Bunbury was settled by Europeans in 1838, and the whalers who anchored in Koombana Bay provided a market for the pioneer farmers. Today the port is the main outlet for the thriving timber industry, mineral sands and the produce of the fertile hinterland. **Of interest:** Heritage trails, contact Tourist information. Drive along breakwater to Koombana Bay, with its modern harbour facilities. King Cottage (1880), Forrest Ave, an historical museum; open Sun. Tree-lined pathways lead to Boulter's Lookout, Haig Cres., for views of city, suburbs, hills and farmland. Lighthouse, Ocean Dr., a notable landmark, painted in black and white checks, has lookout at base. Marlston Hill Lookout, Apex Dr., was original site of lighthouse. Art Gallery, cnr Victoria and Carey Sts. Centenary Gardens, cnr Wittenoom and Prinsep Sts in city centre, a peaceful picnic spot. Grassed foreshore of estuary has picnic/barbecue facilities, playground and boat ramp. Miniature railway, Forrest Park, Blair St. Excellent beaches; surf club at Ocean Beach. Koombana Bay, Koombana Dr., for water-skiing and boating; Dolphin Discovery Centre, for chance to swim with dolphins under ranger guidance. Good fishing for bream, flounder, tailor and whiting in bay, and deep-sea fishing. Succulent blue manna crabs in season in estuary. Great variety of birdlife in bush near waters of inlet. Big Swamp Wildlife Park, Prince Phillip Dr. Historic wooden jetty in outer harbour, popular for fishing and crabbing. Mar.: Show; Aqua spectacular. Nov.: Bunbury Fest. **In the area:** Gelorup Museum, 12 km S. St Mark's (1842), Picton, 5 km SE, oldest church in WA, restored, retains some of original timber structure. Boyanup Transport Museum, 20 km SE. Church of St Nicholas (1842), 11 km N, at Australind, thought to be smallest church in WA. Off Old Coast Road: Spring Hill Homestead (1855), 26 km N (not open to public); scenic drive, with good crabbing and picnic spots on way. **Tourist information:** Old Railway Station, Carmody St; (097) 21 7922. **Accommodation:** 9 hotels, 8 motels, 3 B&B, 2 hostels, 4 cara./camp. parks. **See also:** The South-west.

Busselton   Pop. 8936

MAP REF. 357 D7, 359 F3, 364 B9, 366 C10

First settled by Europeans in the 1830s, and one of the oldest towns in WA, Busselton is a pleasant seaside town at the centre of a large rural district. Situated 228 km S of Perth, on the shores of Geographe Bay and the picturesque Vasse River, the town is a popular holiday destination. Inland are jarrah forests for the local timber industry, dairy and beef cattle farms, and vineyards. Fishing is important, particularly crayfish and salmon in season. **Of interest:** Prospect Villa (1855), Pries Ave, a two-storey colonial building (now motel). Opposite, Ballarat Engine, first steam locomotive in WA. St Mary's (1844), Peel Tce, oldest stone church in State. Villa Carlotta (1897), Adelaide St, boarding school for 50 years, now guest house. Jetty, on beachfront near Queen St, longest timber jetty (2 km) in Australia; partially destroyed by Cyclone Alby in 1978, still popular with anglers. Near jetty on beachfront: Oceanarium; Nautical Lady Entertainment Centre with its Jetty Point tower, nautical museum and small train which runs along the jetty. Old Court House Arts Centre, Queen St. In Peel St: Old Butter Factory Museum, on riverbank, displays old butter- and cheese-making equipment; Vasse River Parkland, with barbecue/picnic facilities. In Layman Rd: Wonnerup House (1859), a National Trust Museum and fine example of colonial Australian architecture furnished in period style; restored old school and teacher's house, built of local timber. Archery Park and Minigolf, Bussell Hwy. Bay has good sheltered beaches for swimming. Western coast ideal for surfing. Jan.: Festival of Busselton; Performing arts beach festival. Mar.: Blue-water classic (fishing). Oct.: West Coast golf open. **In the area:** Woodcrafts; locally produced gourmet items; several protea nurseries. Scenic drive west for excellent views of rugged coast at Eagle Bay, 30 km; Sugar Loaf Rock, 35 km; and Cape Naturaliste, 39 km. Wildflower, scenic, canoe and 4WD tours; whale-watching cruises and flights (Oct.–Dec.); Augusta–Busselton Heritage Trail; details from Tourist information. Orchid farm at Vasse, 9 km W. Wildwood Pottery, 16 km W. Quindalup Fauna Park, 20 km W, has birds, fish, tropical butterflies and native mammals. Bannamah Wildlife Park; and Country Life Farm with hayrides, boat rides and children's farm; both 26 km W. At Yallingup, 32 km W, surfing and sheltered rock pool; nearby Yallingup Caves.

Western Wildflowers

Kangaroo paw, the floral emblem of Western Australia

The sandplains, swamps, flats, scrub and woodlands of south-western Australia light up with colour in spring as the 'wildflower State' puts on its brilliant display. The plains can become carpeted, almost overnight, with the gold of everlastings or feather flowers, or the red and pinks of boronia and leschenaultia. The banksia bushes throw up their red and yellow cylinders along the coast and in the woodlands, grevilleas spill their flowers down to the ground and orchids proliferate. Flowering gums on the south coast become a mass of red and the felty kangaroo paws invade the plains. Lilies, banksias, parrot bush, flame peas, feather flowers and native foxgloves – all are displayed in a magnificent abundance.

There are over 9000 named species and 2000 unnamed species of wildflowers in Western Australia, giving the State one of the richest floras in the world. Around 75 per cent of them are unique to the region, although they may have family connections with other plants of northern or eastern Australia. Isolation by the barrier of plain and desert that separates the west from the eastern States has caused plants on both sides to pursue their own evolution; some families of plants are unique to the west.

On even a short trip to Perth, visitors can see a wide variety of Western Australian wildflowers. At King's Park close to the city, wildflower species give a brilliant display between August and October. Visitors in any part of the south-west at that time will see wildflowers all around them. Often, however, it is in the State's national parks that the full beauty of massed wildflowers is best seen. Only 25 kilometres east of Perth on the Great Eastern Highway is **John Forrest National Park**, on the edge of the Darling Range escarpment. On these undulating hills and valleys the undergrowth of the jarrah forest is rich in flowering plants; red and green kangaroo paw, swamp river myrtle, blue leschenaultia and pink calytrix are the most common. Fifty kilometres north of Perth is **Yanchep National Park**, a place of coastal limestone and sandy plains, covered with wildflowers. There are many places further north that are worth visiting; one such is **Kalbarri National Park**, 670 kilometres north of Perth, at the mouth of the Murchison River. The park contains magnificent flowering trees and shrubs of banksia, grevillea and melaleuca, while the ground beneath is covered with many species, such as leschenaultia, twine rushes and sedges.

Prolific displays of wildflowers can also be found throughout the wheat belt, forests and sandplains of the south-west. Dryandra Woodland, a few kilometres from Narrogin in the south-west, has magnificent woodlands of wandoo and powderbark, with brown mallet and bush thickets. An important sanctuary for the mallee fowl and numbat, this forest contains a number of species of dryandra.

Another interesting area of Western Australia is **Stirling Range National Park**, 450 kilometres south of Perth and near the Porongurup Range. The Stirlings are very jagged peaks that rise above flat farmlands. The scenery is magnificent and wildflowers abound, many unique to the region. There are banksias here, as well as dryandra, cone bushes, cats paws and a number of mountain bells, which have red or pink flower heads. The bare granite domes and the boulders of the Porongurup Range tower over slopes of flowering trees such as *Banksia grandis* and creepers such as the native clematis.

There are many coastal parks around Albany. **Torndirrup National Park** is an area of coastal hills and cliffs, and such scenic features as the Gap, the Blowhole and the Natural Bridge. In the stunted, windswept coastal vegetation there are many wildflowers, including the endemic giant-coned *Banksia praemorsa* and the Western Australian Christmas tree with its brilliant orange flowers.

Twenty-five kilometres east of Albany is the peaceful and beautiful Two Peoples Bay Nature Reserve, which has thickets of mallee, banksia and peppermint, together with many flowering shrubs and plants. Along the coast west of Albany is **Walpole–Nornalup National Park**, where dense karri forest mingles with red tingle, jarrah, marri, casuarina and banksia, and many wildflowers including the tree kangaroo paw, the potato orchid and the babe-in-cradle orchid.

Although most wildflowers occur in the south-west of the State, northern areas also have displays peculiar to climatic changes and times of rainfall. While enjoying Western Australia's brilliant native flora, visitors should remember that wildflowers are protected under the State's *Native Flora Protection Act.*

For further information on national parks and wildflower display areas, contact the Western Australian Tourist Centre or the Department of Conservation and Land Management, 50 Hayman Rd (GPO Box 104), Como WA 6152; (09) 334 0333. **See also:** National Parks for those parks indicated by bold type.

Coastline near Carnarvon

WESTERN AUSTRALIA

Over 30 wineries in Willyabrup Valley, 30 km SW, and around town of Margaret River, 47 km SW; most open for tastings and cellar-door sales, contact Tourist information. Whistle Stop, a miniature railway, on Vasse Hwy, 11 km SE. Bunyip Craft Centre, 7 km E. **Tourist information**: Civic Centre Complex, Southern Dr.; (097) 52 1288. **Accommodation:** 4 hotels, 7 motels, 13 B&B, 1 hostel, 12 cara./camp. parks. **See also:** The South-west.

Caiguna   Pop. 10

MAP REF. 367 N8

Caiguna is the first stop for petrol and food after the long drive from Balladonia, 182 km W. This section of the Eyre Hwy is one of the longest straight stretches of sealed road in the world. **In the area:** South of town, Nuytsland Nature Reserve has sheer cliffs fronting the Southern Ocean. Afghan Rocks, 14 km E, natural freshwater dams, used as resting place by camel drivers in 1890s. **Tourist information:** John Eyre Motel; (090) 39 3459. **Accommodation:** 1 motel, 1 cara./camp. park. **See also:** Crossing the Nullarbor.

Carnamah   Pop. 367

MAP REF. 366 C5

Carnamah is a small, typically Australian country town, 290 km N of Perth. Wheat and sheep are the local industries. **Of interest:** Historical Society Museum, McPherson St, displays old farm machinery reflecting agricultural heritage. Sept.: Agricultural show. **In the area:** Several old goldmining and ghost towns 40–50 km E; area rich in minerals and popular with gemstone enthusiasts. MacPherson Homestead (1880), 1 km E, grounds open to the public; house open by appt. Water colour at Yarra Yarra Lakes, 2 km W, ranges in colour from red to green to blue; many varieties of migratory birds collect here; wildflowers in surrounding area in season. Lake Indoon, 61 km SW, for water-skiing. Perenjori area, 58 km NE, and Tathra National Park, 50 km SW, renowned for variety of wildflowers in spring. **Tourist information:** Shire Offices, McPherson St; (099) 51 1055. **Accommodation:** 1 hotel/motel, 1 cara./camp. park.

Carnarvon   Pop. 6901

MAP REF. 365 B8

Carnarvon, at the mouth of the Gascoyne River, 904 km N of Perth, is the commercial centre of the Gascoyne region. The district was seen in 1616 by Dirk Hartog. Another explorer, Willem de Vlamingh, landed at Shark Bay in 1697. Pioneers arrived in 1876; by the 1880s there were a number of European settlers in the region. Today, sheep and beef cattle are important industries, and the Gascoyne River has been tapped for irrigation for the extensive tropical fruit and vegetable plantations. The Overseas Telecommunications Commission earth station (no longer operating) and Radio Australia base are at nearby Browns Range. The USA National Aeronautics and Space Administration (NASA) operated here from 1964–74. Carnarvon has warm winters and takes on a tropical appearance when the bougainvilleas and hibiscus bloom. **Of interest:** The main street, c.1880s is 40 m wide, built to enable camel trains to turn; it is now divided by a row of trees. Jubilee Hall (1887), Francis St. Pioneer Park, Olivia Tce. Tropical Bird Park, Angela St. Rotary Park, North West Coastal Hwy. May: Tropical festival; Fremantle–Carnarvon yacht race. **In the area:** Excellent fishing for snapper or groper, game-fishing for marlin or sailfish; charter boats available. On Babbage Island, 5 km off Carnarvon, museum at lighthouse keeper's cottage; historic light-rail trips available, contact Tourist information. Prawning factory, 6 km off Binning Rd; tours in season, usually mid-Apr.–late Oct.; contact Tourist information. One Mile Jetty, 5 km NW, almost 1500 m long; closed to public. Pelican Point, 8 km NW, for picnics and swimming. Westoby Plantation, 4 km E; tours available. Mammoth 157-m diameter reflector ('the Big Dish'), 8 km E, offers views of area from platform of dish. Rocky Pool, deep billabong, for swimming; 55 km E along Gascoyne Rd. Munro's Banana Plantation, 10 km N via hwy and South River Rd, has freshpicked fruit and vegetables for sale in season; tours available Mon.–Sat. Department of Agriculture Research Station, 3 km from South River Rd turnoff; book at Tourist information. Bibbawarra artesian bore, 16 km N, where hot water surfaces at 70°C; picnic area nearby. Miaboolya Beach, 22 km N, has good fishing, crabbing and swimming. Blowholes, 70 km N, where water dramatically forced 20 m into air; about 1 km S, a superb sheltered beach with oysters on rocks, but beware of king waves and tides. Cairn commemorating loss of HMAS *Sydney* in 1942; just north of blowholes. A further 30 km N, excellent fishing at Cape Cuvier. **Tourist information:** Robinson St; (099) 41 1146. **Accommodation:** 5 hotel/motels, 7 cara./camp. parks.

Cocklebiddy

Pop. 11

MAP REF. 367 O8

This tiny settlement is on the Eyre Hwy, between Madura and Caiguna, 310 km from the SA border. **In the area:** Cocklebiddy Cave, just north-west, for experienced speleologists only (directions at Wedgetail Inn). To the south, a dirt track leads to the Escarpment, for magnificent views of Southern Ocean; from here 4WD necessary to reach Eyre Bird Observatory; and Post Office Historical Society Museum in old telegraph station building, guided tours available (24 hrs notice required), contact Tourist information. **Tourist information:** Wedgetail Inn; (090) 39 3462. **Accommodation:** 1 hotel/motel, 1 cara./camp. park (limited facilities). **See also:** Crossing the Nullarbor.

Collie

Pop. 7684

MAP REF. 364 D8, 366 C10

Collie, the centre of the State's only coal-producing region, plays an integral part in WA's development. Set in dense jarrah forest, 202 km S of Perth near the winding Collie River, the town has an abundance of attractive parks and gardens. Fine views on the drive into Collie from the South Western Hwy. **Of interest:** In Throssell St: tourist coal mine, guided tours daily; Historical and Mining Museum, in old Roads Board buildings, displays history of area and of coal industry; Steam Locomotive Museum; old police station (1926); post office (1898); art gallery at Shire Office, has collection of local art. Old court house, cnr Wittenoon and Pendleton Sts. Impressive All Saints' Anglican Church, built in Norman style; Venn St. Soldiers Park, Steer St, on banks of Collie River, has shady trees and lawns, ideal for picnics. Suspension bridge over river, River Ave. Minninup Pool, off Mungalup Rd, set in bushland; wildflowers in season. **In the area:** Scenic drive to Collie River, 5 km W. Wellington Dam and Honeymoon Pool, 15 km W, in heart of Collie River Irrigation Scheme,

The South-west

The south-west corner of Western Australia is a lush green land. Its gently rolling hills are crossed by rivers winding through deep-sided valleys. The soils are fertile and the farms prosperous. Along the coast there are beautiful bays, and inland, majestic towering karri and jarrah forests. The countryside is dotted with orchards and many wildflowers in season; Western Australia is one of the richest areas of flora in the world.

Pinjarra, 84 kilometres south of Perth, is one of the State's oldest districts. It has interesting historic buildings and makes a good base for touring the surrounding area.

Near **Harvey** there is fine agricultural land and the undulating farms stretch to the foothills of the Darling Range. North-west of Harvey is Yalgorup National Park (one of only three sites in Western Australia with stromatolites), where the lakes attract a wide variety of birdlife.

The coast of the south-west is fascinating: an unusual mixture of craggy outcrops and promontories, sheltered bays with calm waters and beaches pounded by rolling surf. In the course of a day at Cape Leeuwin it is possible to see the sun rising over one ocean and setting over another. The length of the coast, together with the many rivers and estuaries, makes the south-west an angler's paradise. The Murray, Harvey and Brunswick Rivers and their tributaries are only some of the streams annually stocked with trout.

The main port for the south-west, **Bunbury** rests on Geographe Bay looking out over the Indian Ocean. It is a perfect holiday town. One of the oldest towns in the State, **Busselton**, sited on the Vasse River, has a wealth of pioneer houses, many restored and open to the public.

Margaret River on the river of the same name, offers beaches, caves, magnificent scenery and world-class wineries. The **Leeuwin-Naturaliste National Park** combines a scenic rugged coast with magnificent wildflowers and the tall timbers of karri and jarrah forests.

Yallingup is known for its excellent surf and spectacular limestone caves. Dripping water has created strange shapes in the limestone, with magic colours reflected in the glittering underground water.

Bridgetown, **Donnybrook** and Greenbushes are small townships tucked away in green, hilly country and pretty apple orchards. Goldmining flourished briefly here at the turn of the century. **Manjimup** and **Pemberton** are world famous for the source of their timber, the karri and jarrah trees. Here some of the world's tallest trees reach straight up, often to 80 and 90 metres. The Pemberton, Scott, Warren and Brockman National Parks are nearby, and were introduced to protect the unique environment.

For further information contact the tourist information centres listed for those towns indicated by bold type. **Map reference:** for Margaret River, 359.

Limestone caves at Yallingup

popular attractions offering fishing, and bushwalking and grassy picnic spots on shore. Muja Power Station, 24 km SE; tours available, contact Tourist information. View Muja open-cut mines from viewing platform, 28 km SE. (*Muja* is Aboriginal word for bright yellow Christmas tree that grows in area.) **Tourist information:** Throssell St; (097) 34 2051. **Accommodation:** 5 hotels, 1 hotel/motel, 2 motels, 1 cara./camp. park.

Coolgardie   Pop. 1063

MAP REF. 366 I6

The old goldmining town of Coolgardie is 550 km east of Perth and 39 km SW of Kalgoorlie-Boulder. After Arthur Bayley and William Ford found alluvial gold at Fly Flat in 1892, Coolgardie grew to a boom town of 15 000 people, 23 hotels, six banks and two stock exchanges in just 10 years. The main street was wide enough for camel trains to turn, splendid public buildings were erected and ambitious plans were made. Sadly, the gold soon petered out. By 1985 there were only 700 people in the town; however, with an increase in tourism, the population of this pleasant town is increasing. **Of interest:** Series of historic markers placed around town, documenting historic points of interest; index to all markers located in Bayley St, next to Tourist information. Historic buildings in Bayley St include Goldfields Exhibition building (1898), most comprehensive prospecting museum in WA; post office (1898); old gaol; Denver City Hotel (1898), with handsome verandahs; Ben Prior's Open-air Museum, displaying wagons, horse- and camel-drawn vehicles. Railway Station (1896), Woodward St, now a museum with transport exhibition and display of famous Varischetti mine rescue. Warden Finnerty's house (1895), McKenzie St, striking example of early Australian architecture and furnishings. Adjacent, C.Y. O'Connor Dedication, a fountain and water course in memory of O'Connor who masterminded the Coolgardie Water Scheme. St Anthony's Convent, Lindsay St, now boarding school. Gaol Tree, Hunt St, used for restraining prisoners in early gold-rush days. Lions Bicentennial Lookout, near southern end of Hunt St. Lindsay's Pit Lookout, over open-cut gold mine; Ford St. Sept.: Coolgardie Day; Camel races. **In the area:** Eastern Goldfields Heritage Trail; details from Tourist information. Cemetery, 1 km W, evokes harsh early days of gold rush. Camel farm, 4 km W. Kurrawang Emu Farm, 20 km E. Rowte's Lagoon, 65 km N, for water sports. Further 20 km, Ora Banda, an historic goldmining town. **Tourist information:** Bayley St; (090) 26 6090. **Accommodation:** 1 hotel, 3 motels, 2 cara./camp. parks. **See also:** The Goldfields.

Coral Bay   Pop. 726

MAP REF. 365 B5

The Ningaloo Coral Reef system approaches the shore at Coral Bay, 150 km S of Exmouth. Unspoilt expanses of white beaches offer good swimming, snorkelling, boating and fishing. **In the area:** Ningaloo Marine Park, just off beach. Good views of reef from glass-bottomed boats. Diving equipment hire available. Numerous shipwreck sites at Pt Cloates, 8 km N; also ruins of Norwegian Bay whaling station (1915). **Tourist information:** Bayview Holiday Village, Robinson St; (099) 42 5932. **Accommodation:** 1 hotel/motel, 2 cara./camp. parks.

Corrigin   Pop. 725

MAP REF. 364 H5, 366 E8

Rich farming country surrounds Corrigin, 230 km SE of Perth. **Of interest:** In Kunjin St: folk museum; miniature railway, inquire at Tourist information. RSL monument, Gayfer St, is a Turkish mountain gun from Gallipoli. Art and craft shop, Walton St. Sept.: Agricultural show. **In the area:** Dog cemetery, 5 km W. Good views from observation tower, 3 km W, on Wildflower Scenic Drive, (well signposted). Gorge Rock, 20 km SE, for picnics. **Tourist information:** Shire Offices, Lynch St; (090) 63 2203. **Accommodation:** 1 hotel, 1 motel, 1 cara./camp. park.

Cossack   Pop. 1 & 1 dog

MAP REF. 365 G1, 368 A1

Cossack, once called Tien Tsin, has had a chequered history. Located at the mouth of the Harding River, it was the first port in the north-west and serviced the nearby town of Roebourne, as well as being the centre of a gold rush and the location for a turtle-product factory. Pearling in WA began at Cossack before moving to Broome in the 1890s. Cossack was also a centre for the Pilbara's developing pastoral and mining industries. Today it is a ghost town, but almost completely restored. **Of interest:** Historic buildings, all open Apr.–Christmas: in Pearl St, court house (now museum), bond store (now tearoom), and post and telegraph office; in Perseverance St, police quarters (budget accommodation all year). Cemetery, off Perseverance St, headstones reflect town's colourful past. Fishing, crabbing and swimming; boat hire available. June: Fair and yachting regatta. Sept.: Art awards, Art Ball. **In the area:** Wickham, 8 km SW, a modern company town. Point Samson, 18 km N, a popular seaside resort. **Tourist information:** Roebourne Tourist Bureau, Queen St, Roebourne; (091) 82 1060. **Accommodation:** 1 hostel. **See also:** The Pilbara.

Cranbrook   Pop. 306

MAP REF. 361 L6, 364 H11, 366 E11

In the 1800s sandalwood was exported from Cranbrook to China, where it was used as incense. Today this attractive town, near the foothills of the Stirling Range, 320 km SE of Perth, is a sheep and wheat centre. Sept.: Wildflower show. **In the area:** Frankland Heritage Trail; details from Tourist information. Gateway to Stirling Arch, Salt River Rd, a picnic area with native garden. Sukey Hill Lookout, 5 km E, off Salt River Rd. Stirling Range National Park, 15 km SE. High-quality table wines produced in Frankland district, 50 km W. Lake Poorrarecup, 55 km SW, for swimming and water skiing; picnic facilities, playground and camping on foreshore. **Tourist information:** Shire Offices, Gathorne St; (098) 26 1008. **Accommodation:** 1 hotel, 1 B&B, 1 cara./camp. park.

Cue   Pop. 394

MAP REF. 365 H13, 366 E1, 368 B13

Cue, 650 km NE of Perth on the Great Northern Hwy, grew up as a boom town, an important centre for the Murchison goldfields. Today its well-kept stone buildings are a testimony to those frenzied days. **Of interest:** National Trust-classified buildings in Austin St: bandstand built over well, water from which was said to have started a typhoid epidemic; impressive government offices. Former Masonic Lodge (1899), Dowley St, built largely of corrugated iron. **In the area:**

Dolphins at Monkey Mia, near Denham

Gemstone fossicking; heritage trail; and a number of Aboriginal art sites; contact Tourist information. Day Dawn, 5 km W, original town site on gold reef; town disappeared when reef died out in 1930s. Big Bell, 30 km W, large mine opened in 1989 (access restricted). Walga Rock, 50 km W, a monolith 1.5 km long and 5 km around base (second largest in Australia) with largest gallery of Aboriginal rock paintings in WA; details from Tourist information. Wilgie Mia Red Ochre Mine, 64 km NW, mined by Aborigines 30 000 years ago. **Tourist information:** Apr.–Oct.: Robinson St, (099) 63 1216; Nov.–May: Shell Garage, Northern Hwy, (099) 63 1051. **Accommodation:** 2 hotels, 1 cara./camp. park.

Dampier Pop. 1810

MAP REF. 365 G1

A model town with modern facilities, Dampier lies on King Bay, facing the unique islands of the Dampier Archipelago. Hamersley Iron Pty Ltd established the town as a port for ore mined from two of the world's richest iron-ore deposits, Tom Price and Paraburdoo. The town's deepwater port with its export facilities loads over 400 million tonnes of ore yearly. Salt is harvested from ponds near the port. **Of interest:** Jurat Reserve, Haig Close. Tours of the Hamersley Iron port facility, available Mon.–Fri.; bookings (091) 44 4600. Boating, sailing, fishing, diving, windsurfing and swimming. Game-fishing, charter boat hire; contact Tourist information for details. Aug.: Game-fishing classic. **In the area:** North West Shelf Gas Project on Burrup Peninsula 8 km NW, has Visitors Centre open weekdays, except public holidays. Aboriginal rock carvings on Burrup Peninsula; details from Tourist information. Hearsons Cove, 6 km S, popular tidal swimming beach and picnic area. Pilbara Railway Historical Society Museum, 10 km SE, home of *Pendennis Castle* steam locomotive; open Sun. **Tourist information:** 4548 Karratha Rd, Karratha; (091) 44 4600. **Accommodation:** 2 motels, 1 cara./camp. park. **See also:** The Hamersley Range; The Pilbara.

Denham Pop. 943

MAP REF. 365 B10

Two peninsulas form the geographical feature of Shark Bay, 833 km from Perth. Denham is the most westerly town in Australia and the main centre of the Shark Bay region. Dirk Hartog, the Dutch navigator, landed on an island at the entrance to Shark Bay in 1616. Pearling developed as the main industry and the population was a mixture of Malays, Chinese and Europeans. Until recently, Shark Bay was known only for its excellent fishing, but today it is renowned for the wild dolphins, which come inshore to be fed at Monkey Mia. **Of interest:** Shark Bay Fisheries, Dampier Rd; check opening times at Tourist information. Pioneer Park, Hughes St. **In the area:** Shark Bay Heritage Trail, contact Tourist information. Town Bluff; interesting guided walk south along beaches. Catamaran *MV Explorer* offers variety of cruises. Safaris and coach tours available. Boat trips to historic Dirk Hartog Island, weekends; also charter flights; homestead and backpackers' accommodation available on island. Francois Peron National Park, 7 km N, includes Peron homestead with its famous 'hot tub' containing hot artesian water. Eagle Bluff, 20 km S, habitat of sea eagle. Nanga Bay Resort, 50 km S, huge sheep station with motel units, restaurant, tourist facilities, sailboards, dinghy hire on beach and charter fishing. Shell Beach, 50 km S, 110-km stretch of unique Australian coastline comprising countless tiny shells. Zuytdorp Cliffs, 160 km S and extending further south to Kalbarri, striking scenery, 4WD access only. On shores of Hamelin Pool, 100 km SE: historic displays in Flint Cliff Telegraph Station and Post Office Museum (1894); stromatolites ('living rocks') in nature reserve. Spectacular coastal scenery at Steep Point, westernmost point on mainland; 260 km W by road (4WD only). **Tourist information:** 83 Knight Tce; (099) 48 1253. **Accommodation:** 1 hotel/motel, 1 motel, 2 hostels, 4 cara./camp. parks.

Denmark Pop. 1586

MAP REF. 361 K12, 364 G13, 366 E12

The attractive 100-year-old coastal town of Denmark, 54 km W of Albany, is at the foot of Mt Shadforth, overlooking the tranquil Denmark River. The town offers good fishing, sandy white beaches and scenic drives through farming country and karri forests. The dense hardwood forests supply timber for local mills. **Of interest:** Kurrabup Aboriginal Art Gallery, South Coast Hwy. Mitchell St: Historical Museum, Cottage Industries Shop. Strickland St: Denmark Gallery. Alpaca stud and tourist farm, Scotsdale Rd. Jassi Skincraft, Glenrowan Rd, off Mt Shadforth Scenic Drive. In Holling Rd: Rambling Rose Crafts; Berridge and Thornton Parks, both along riverbank, offering shaded picnic areas. Craft gallery and wine sales at Old Butter Factory, North St. Mt Shadforth Lookout, top of Mohr Dr., for magnificent views. Mar.: International Australian jugglers'

National Parks

The national parks of Western Australia are tourist attractions in themselves: their spectacular displays of wildflowers create a paradise for photographers and a wonderland for bushwalkers and campers. Western Australia has more than 9000 named species and 2000 unnamed species of wildflowers, growing undisturbed in their natural surroundings. One quarter of these species cannot be found anywhere else and they lure admirers from all over the world. The best months to see them are from August to October. This is also the best time for camping trips and bushwalking.

Thistle Cove, one of many magnificent bays protected by Cape Le Grand National Park

Around Perth
There are many national parks around Perth well worth a visit. At **Nambung National Park**, 230 kilometres north of Perth on the coast, unusual rock formations are to be found. Here a moonscape of coloured quartz is studded with fantastic limestone pillars ranging in size from stony 'twigs' to 4 metre high columns. This is the unique Pinnacle Desert, a favourite subject for photographers. **Yanchep National Park**, about 50 kilometres north of Perth on a belt of coastal limestone, has forests of massive tuart trees. Islands on Loch McNess, within the park, are waterfowl sanctuaries. Yanchep is also famed for its underground limestone caves and spring wildflowers.

Some 80 kilometres north-east of Perth is **Avon Valley National Park**; its most popular attractions are upland forests and river valleys, as well as beautiful wildflowers in season. The highest point in the park is Bald Hill, which provides panoramic views of the Avon River. After winter rains, a tributary of the Avon, Emu Spring Brook, spills 30 metres down in a spectacular waterfall.

A cluster of national parks to the east of Perth includes **John Forrest National Park**, which was Western Australia's first proclaimed national park. With the Darling Escarpment within its boundaries, the park features granite outcrops, dams and waterfalls, creeks and rock pools. Other nearby national parks are **Kalamunda**, **Greenmount**, **Gooseberry Hill** and **Lesmurdie Falls**, all within 20–25 kilometres of Perth. The Bibbulmun Track, a walk trail that links Forest, east of Perth, to the area once occupied by the Bibbulmun people of the south coast, begins its 650-kilometre route in Kalamunda National Park.

Proclaimed as the State's first flora and fauna reserve in 1894, **Serpentine National Park** is about 60 kilometres south of Perth and a firm favourite of day trippers who picnic at the falls area in the park. Jarrah and marri forests, and wildflowers in spring, are some of the park's attractions.

In the south of the State
Leeuwin-Naturaliste National Park extends along the rugged south-west coast. There are over 100 limestone caves in the area, some containing fossils of marsupials, no longer found on the mainland. The park is home to rare ospreys and rufous bristlebirds, as well as the more common sea birds. Whales can occasionally be seen offshore.

Along the lower south-west coast of the State is **Walpole–Nornalup National Park**, 15 861 hectares of wilderness in which creeks gurgle under tall eucalypts, rivers meander between forested hills and inlets rich in fish create a haven for anglers and boating enthusiasts. A network of roads and walking tracks, through forests of karri and tingle, attracts bushwalkers and birdwatchers.

About 100 kilometres east is **West Cape Howe National Park**, the spectacular coastline of which includes the gabbro cliffs of West Cape Howe and the granite of Torbay Heads, fronting the cold waters of the Southern Ocean. Extensive coastal heath, swamps, lakes and karri forest cover the inland area, and the park is popular with anglers, bushwalkers, rock climbers and hang-gliders.

The South Western Highway bisects **Shannon National Park**, 358 kilometres south of Perth. Within the park is the former timber-milling town site of Shannon. The remainder of the park consists of towering karri and jarrah forests, surrounding the Shannon River.

Stirling Range National Park, 450 kilometres south-east of Perth, is one of Australia's outstanding

Purnululu National Park in the north of the State

reserves. Surrounded by a flat, sandy plain, the Stirling Range rises abruptly to over 1000 metres, its jagged peaks veiled in swirling mists. The cool, humid environment created by these low clouds contributes to the survival of 1000 flowering plant species, some of which, like the mountain bells, are found nowhere else in the world.

Brilliant displays of wildflowers are also a feature of the nearby **Porongurup National Park**, where the granite domes of the Porongurup Ranges are clothed in a forest of karri trees.

Spectacular coastal scenery is the main attraction of the **Torndirrup National Park** on the Flinders Peninsula, 460 kilometres south of Perth. Also on the south coast are other outstanding parks, including **Cape Le Grand National Park**, with its magnificent bays and beaches, protected by granite headlands, located 40 kilometres east of Esperance.

Two other parks are near Esperance, both to the west of the town. **Stokes National Park** hugs the coastline around Stokes Inlet and features long sandy beaches and rocky headlands backed by sand dunes and low hills. Stokes Inlet and its associated lakes support a rich variety of wildlife. Inland from Stokes lies **Peak Charles National Park**. A walk to the ridge of this ancient granite peak allows sweeping views of its companion, Peak Eleanora, and over the dry sandplain heaths and salt-lake systems of the surrounding country.

One of the loveliest sections of the south coast of Western Australia is **Fitzgerald River National Park**, through which the rugged Barren Range (named by Matthew Flinders) stretches from west to east. The park's 330 000 hectares comprise gently undulating sandplains, river valleys, precipitous cliff edges, narrow gorges, and beaches for swimming and rock fishing. The park contains many rare species of flora and fauna.

In the north of the State

North of Geraldton, the visitor will discover the wild beauty of ancient landscapes, unsurpassed at **Kalbarri National Park**. Its 182 000 hectares encompass the lower reaches of the Murchison River, which winds its way through spectacular gorges to the Indian Ocean. Sea cliffs in layers of multi-coloured sandstone loom over the crashing white foam at Red Bluff.

Cape Range National Park, near Exmouth, is cut by deep gorges but arid for most of the year, Yardie Creek being the only permanent water. Vegetation is sparse, except around the creek and after cyclonic storms have flooded the area. Kangaroos are common and fairly tame, and there are over 80 species of reptiles in the park.

In the Pilbara, 1400 kilometres north of Perth, is **Karijini National Park**, in the Hamersley Range and part of a massive block of weathered rock over 450 kilometres long. Within this huge, spectacular park are many well-known gorges, including Dales Gorge, its strata in horizontal stripes of blue, mauve, red and brown dating back almost 2000 million years. Further north, still in the Pilbara, **Millstream-Chichester National Park** encompasses almost 200 000 hectares of clay tablelands and sediment-capped basalt ranges. At Millstream, on the Fortescue River, natural freshwater springs have created an oasis in arid country. In contrast, there are the Chichester Ranges: rolling hills, hummocks of spinifex, white-barked snappy gums on the uplands, and pale coolibahs along the usually dry watercourses.

In the far north of Western Australia are the national parks of the Kimberley region. The largest of these parks, **Geikie Gorge**, has an area of 3136 hectares and is 20 kilometres north-east of Fitzroy Crossing. The multi-coloured cliffs are reflected in the placid waters of the Fitzroy River, which flows through the gorge. The area is too rugged for extensive walking, but organised boat trips go up the river through the gorge, enabling visitors to see one of Australia's most beautiful waterways.

Other nearby national parks are **Windjana Gorge** and **Tunnel Creek**, both north-west of Geikie Gorge.

Tunnel Creek is a permanent watercourse that flows underground for 750 metres. It is possible to walk through the high, wide tunnel to a small river beach beyond; some deep wading may be necessary, and carry a torch.

South of Lake Argyle is the spectacular **Purnululu National Park**, with its tiger-striped, beehive-shaped domes, deep gullies and unique palms. Because of the fragility of internal roads in wet conditions, this park is closed from approximately 1 January to 1 April.

Mirima National Park, only 2.5 kilometres east of Kununurra, has features typical of the Kimberley: banded sandstone outcrops similar to those of the Bungle Bungle massif, boab trees, red soil dotted with eucalypts, and black kites circling overhead. Aboriginal rock paintings are also a feature of the park.

For further information on Western Australia's national parks, contact the Department of Conservation and Land Management, 50 Hayman Rd (GPO Box 104), Como, WA 6152; (09) 334 0333.

festival. July: Winter festival. Sept.: Festival of the classics. **In the area:** Scotsdale Rd–McLeod Rd Tourist Drive; and Denmark Timber, Mokare and Wilson Inlet Heritage Trail; details from Tourist information. Twelve wineries in Denmark-Mount Barker-Albany region, 15 km E. Meelia Strawberry Farm; Eden Gate Blueberry Farm; both 25 km E. Picturesque Albany, 54 km E, has rich history and beautiful beaches. Jonathan Hook Ceramics, Lantake Rd, 5 km NW. Mt Romance Emu Farm, 40 km NW, has showroom of emu-oil products. Wildflower Farm, 6 km W. Tinglewood Wines, 8 km W. Wynella Living Museum, 15 km W. Bartholomew's Meadery, 20 km W. Spiral Studio Pottery, 25 km W. Parry's Beach, 25 km W, for fishing (salmon in season). Majestic Merino Wool Craft Shop, 38 km W. Misty Creek Marron Farm, 40 km W. Valley of the Giants, 45 km W, massive karri and tingle trees best seen from Tree Top Walk. Boating, fishing, bushwalking and scenic drives around Nornalup, 50 km W, and Walpole, 66 km W, adjacent to Walpole-Nornalup National Park. Lookout from top of Monkey Rock, 10 km SW. Sheltered swimming at Greens Pool and William Bay at William Bay National Park, 17 km SW. Michael Cartwright Art Studio, 7 km S. Ocean Beach, 8 km S, for surfing. **Tourist information:** Strickland St; (098) 48 2055. **Accommodation:** 2 hotel/motels, 1 motel, 3 B&B, 4 cara./camp. parks. **See also:** The Great Southern.

Derby   Pop. 3022

MAP REF. 362 B9, 371 J7

Derby is an administrative centre for several Aboriginal communities and a hinterland rich in pastoral and mineral wealth. Located near King Sound, 220 km NE of Broome, the town is an ideal base for exploring the outback regions of the Kimberley. Roads have been greatly improved, including the Gibb River Rd, spanning the 667 km from Derby to the junction of the Great Northern Hwy between Wyndham and Kununurra. However, as rain usually closes the road Nov.– Mar., check local conditions before setting out. **Of interest:** In Loch St: Botanic Gardens; Old Derby Gaol; Wharfinger House museum, with photographic display. In Clarendon St: Raintree Craft Shop; Royal Flying Doctor Service. Ngunga Craft Shop, Stanley St. July: Country music festival; Boab festival (rodeo, mardi gras, mud football). Boxing Day: Kimberley sports. **In the area:** Charter boats to various locations including Buccaneer Archipelago and Walcott Inlet. Charter flights over Kimberley coast and Cockatoo and Koolan Islands. Pigeon Heritage Trail, from Derby to Windjana Gorge and Tunnel Creek National Park; details from Tourist information. Prison Tree, 7 km S, boab (or baobab) tree reputedly used as prison in early days. Close by, Myall's Bore, a 120-m-long cattle trough. Fitzroy River empties into King Sound, 48 km S. Tours available to: spectacular Windjana Gorge, 145 km E in Windjana Gorge National Park (4WD access only); remarkable Tunnel Creek in Tunnel Creek National Park (4WD access only), 184 km E, where colonies of flying foxes can be seen if you wade through tunnel with torch; also Pigeon's Cave, hideout of Aboriginal outlaw active in 1890s. King Leopold Ranges, 200 km E. Sir John Gorge, 350 km E (4WD access only). Lennard Gorge, 190 km NE (4WD access only). Barnett River Gorge, 340 km NE (4WD access only). Mitchell Plateau, 580 km NE via Gibb River Rd and Kalumburu Rd, features spectacular Mitchell Falls, King Edward River and Surveyor's Pool; in this remote region, visitors must be entirely self-sufficient (read section on Outback Motoring before departure). **Tourist information:** 1 Clarendon St; (091) 91 1426. **Accommodation:** 2 hotels, 1 hostel, 1 cara./camp. park. **See also:** The Kimberley.

Dongara   Pop. 1677

MAP REF. 366 B4

Dongara and the nearby town of Port Denison are quiet towns on the coast 359 km N of Perth. Dongara has beaches, reef-enclosed bays and an abundance of delicious rock lobster. There is good fishing in the waters around Port Denison. **Of interest:** Historic buildings in Waldeck St: Anglican rectory (1882) and church (1884), and old police station (1870); on Brand Hwy: Royal Steam Flour Mill (1894), Russ Cottage (1870) and St Dominicks Rd. Main street, Moreton Tce, shaded by huge 85-year-old Moreton Bay fig trees. In cemetery, Dodd St, headstones date from 1874. Heritage Trail from Old Mill to historic Priory Lodge; brochure from Tourist information. Easter: Horse races; market at old police station, Easter Sat. Nov.: Blessing of the fleet. **In the area:** Fisherman's Lookout, near Leander Point, Port Denison, for panoramic views of harbour. Holiday towns south-west of Eneabba: Leeman, 38 km, and Green Head, 50 km. Western Flora Caravan Park, 60 km S, noted for its wildflowers in bushland and river setting. At Eneabba, 81 km SE, mineral sand mining with large concentrations of rutile. Greenough, historic hamlet, 40 km NW. **Tourist information:** Old Police Station Building, 5 Waldeck St; (099) 27 1404. **Accommodation:** 1 hotel/motel, 1 motel, 1 hostel, 5 cara./camp. parks.

Donnybrook   Pop. 1570

MAP REF. 357 H6, 364 C8, 366 C10

The township of Donnybrook, the home of the Granny Smith apple, is at the heart of the oldest apple-growing area in WA, 210 km S of Perth. Gold was found here in 1897, but mined for only four years. Donnybrook stone has been used in construction State-wide. **Of interest:** On South Western Hwy, Anchor and Hope Inn (1865), once staging post for mail coaches. Rotary Lookout, Trigwell St East. Arboretum, junction Irishtown Rd and South Western Hwy. Trigwell Place, near river at southern end of town on South Western Hwy, has picnic/barbecue facilities, playground. Easter: Apple festival. Nov.: Celebration time. **In the area:** Scenic drives; details from Tourist information. Glen Mervyn Dam, 30 km NE, on-shore picnic/barbecue facilities. At Balingup, 30 km SE: Old Cheese Factory, now art and craft centre; Tinderbox, sells herbs and herbal remedies; further 2 km, Golden Valley Tree Park. **Tourist information:** 'Old' Railway Station, South Western Hwy; (097) 31 1720. **Accommodation:** 2 hotels, 1 motel, 2 B&B, 2 hostels, 1 cara./camp. park. **See also:** The South-west.

Dumbleyung   Pop. 292

MAP REF. 364 H8, 366 E10

Dumbleyung lies in the central south of WA, 217 km E of Bunbury and 224 km N of Albany. **Of interest:** Craft and Tourist Shop, Absolon St. **In the area:** Historic Schools Heritage Trails and scenic drives; details from Tourist information. Lake Dumbleyung, 10 km W via

Wind generators at windfarms supply some of Esperance's electricity

Rollands–Lake King Hwy, where Donald Campbell established new world water-speed record in 1964; for swimming, boating and birdwatching. At Kukerin, 39 km E: Wheatbelt Wildflower Drive, includes Tarin Rock Nature Reserve; Tracmach vintage fair held in Sept.-Oct. **Tourist information:** Shire Offices, Harvey St; (098) 63 4012. **Accommodation:** 1 hotel, 1 cara./camp. park.

Dunsborough Pop. 656

MAP REF. 357 C7, 359 C2, 364 B9, 366 B10

Dunsborough is a quiet town on Geographe Bay, west of Busselton, popular because of its beaches. **Of interest:** Greenacres Shell Museum, off Naturaliste Tce. Hutchings Antique Museum, Newbury Rd. Bush Cottage Crafts, Commonage Rd. Moonshine Brewery and Rivendell Gardens, both in Wildwood Rd. Nov.: Down south dive classic. **In the area:** Good beaches: Meelup, 5 km N; Eagle Bay, 8 km N; Bunker Bay, 12 km NW. Scuba diving, snorkelling and canoeing. 4WD, wildflower, winery, craft and Pemberton tours available; details from Tourist information. Bannamah Wildlife Park, 2 km W. Torpedo Rock, 10 km W. Yallingup Caves and surfing beach, 8 km SW. Canal Rocks, 15 km SW. Shearing Shed, 15 km SW on Wildwood Rd, has shearing demonstrations and wool craft sales; check opening times. Several wineries situated in the south-west; contact Tourist information. Sugarloaf Rock, 12 km NW. Cape Naturaliste Lighthouse and Museum, 13 km NW, open daily except Wed.; several walking tracks in area. **Tourist information:** Shop 3, Naturaliste Tce; (097) 55 3299. **Accommodation:** 1 hotel, 5 B&B, 1 hostel, 2 cara./camp. parks.

Dwellingup Pop. 383

MAP REF. 356 D11, 364 D6, 366 C9

This small town, 24 km SE of Pinjarra and 109 km from Perth, was rebuilt after being destroyed in the 1961 bushfire. The road into town offers panoramic views of the Indian Ocean and Peel Inlet. The impressive jarrah forests nearby supply the local timber mill. Bauxite is mined in the area. **Of interest:** In Marrinup St: country-style meals in Community Hotel; photographic exhibition at Tourist information. Forest Heritage Centre, Acacia Rd, has timber-related exhibits. Forest Ranger Tour, a steam-train ride operated by Hotham Valley Tourist Railway between Pinjarra and Dwellingup, and return (May-Oct.) Etmilyn Forest Tramway, old-style steam train from railway station into jarrah forest; check times. **In the area:** Scarp Lookout, 7 km S; further 3 km, Scarp Pool, a popular recreational area. Lane Pool Reserve, 10 km S, large recreational area in jarrah forest. Loop walk, starts 3 km SW and passes scenic Marrinup Falls. Oxley Dam and Falls, located 7 km SW. **Tourist information:** Marrinup St; (09) 538 1108. **Accommodation:** 1 hotel, 1 B&B.

Esperance Pop. 7066

MAP REF. 367 J10

Wide sandy beaches, scenic coastline and the offshore islands of the Recherche Archipelago are all attractions near Esperance, on the south coast of WA. The town, 720 km from Perth via Wagin, is the port and service centre for the productive agricultural and pastoral hinterland. In 1863, the first permanent European settlers came to this area. The town boomed during the 1890s as a port for the goldfields. From the 1950s, when scientists realised that the heath plains could become fertile pasture and farming country, the town's development began in earnest. **Of interest:** Municipal Museum, James St, displays old machinery, furniture and farm equipment; also display of Skylab, which fell to earth over Esperance in 1979. Public Library, Windich St, collection of books on history of Esperance. Art and craft centre at Old Cannery, Norseman Rd. Mermaid Marine Leather, Wood St, produces and sells fine fashion leathers from discarded fish skins. Charter boats and dive instruction at Esperance Diving Academy, 56 The Esplanade. Fishing and seal watching from Tanker Jetty. five-km waterfront walk and cycle pathway. Beach-fishing excursions, motorcycle tours and horseriding available. Jan.: Sailboard classic. Feb.: Offshore angling classic. Oct.: Agricultural show. Dec.-Jan.: Turf racing. **In the area:** Great Ocean Dr., 39-km loop road along spectacular coastline, passes Windfarms, supplier of 14 per cent of town's electricity, Salmon Beach (5 km W), Twilight Cove (12 km W) and Ten Mile Lagoon (16 km W); map available from Tourist information. Whale watching (June–Nov.) as Southern Right whales visit coastal bays and protected waters in area to calve. Rotary Lookout, or Wireless Hill, 2 km W, for panoramic views of bay, town and Recherche Archipelago. Pink Lake, 5 km W, a pink saltwater lake. Picnic Cove, 12 km W, a sheltered swimming beach. Views of bay and islands from Observatory Point and Lookout, 17 km W. Monjingup Lake Reserve, 20 km W. Dalyup River Wines, 42 km W, open weekends and public holidays. Recherche Archipelago (Bay of Isles), 105 small unspoiled islands provide haven for seals and sea lions. three-hour launch cruises around Gull, Button, Charlie, Woody and other islands

Round House, Fremantle, Western Australia's oldest building

available daily; landing permitted only on Woody Island. Full-day cruises to Woody Island (25 min. by boat); island developed as tourist attraction, overnight camping facilities. Cape Le Grand National Park, 56 km E, features spectacular coastline, attractive beaches (Lucky Bay, Hellfire Bay and Thistle Cove), scenic walks and beautiful wildflowers in spring for which the region is famous; also features Whistling Rock, a rock shaped by the elements that 'whistles' when certain winds blow, and magnificent view from Frenchmans Peak. Cape Arid National Park, 120 km E, for fishing and camping; 4WD routes. Helms Arboretum, 15 km N. Telegraph Farm, 21 km N on South Coast Hwy, has proteas, deer, buffalo and native animals; farm tours available. Speddingup Wildflower Sanctuary, 35 km N, offers guided walks through magnificent wildflowers in season. **Tourist information:** Tourist Bureau, Museum Village, Dempster St; (090) 71 2330. **Accommodation:** 3 hotels, 11 motels, 2 B&B, 2 hostels, 7 cara./camp. parks. **See also:** Crossing the Nullarbor; National Parks.

Eucla Pop. 30

MAP REF. 302 A8, 367 R7

Eucla is just 12 km from the WA-SA border, on the Eyre Hwy. There is a quarantine checkpoint for westbound travellers at Norseman; visitors should ensure they are not carrying fruit, vegetables, honey, used fruit and produce containers, plants or seeds. May: Golf day. Oct.: Eucla shoot. **In the area:** Bureau of Meteorology Weather Station, 1 km S. Cross on escarpment overlooking ocean and sand-covered ruins of old telegraph station and former town site, 5 km S, dedicated to all Eyre Hwy travellers; cross is illuminated at night. Highway westward from Eucla descends to coastal plain via Eucla Pass. Midway down Pass (about 200 m), track to left leads to old town site and ruins among sand dunes. Nine-hole golf course, 7 km N. Weebubby Cave, 12 km N; for experienced cavers only. **Tourist information:** Motor Hotel; (090) 39 3468. **Accommodation:** 1 hotel/motel, 1 cara./camp. park. **See also:** Crossing the Nullarbor.

Exmouth Pop. 3128

MAP REF. 365 C3

Exmouth is one of the newest towns in Australia and was founded in 1967 as a support town for the US Naval Communications station, which is the main source of employment in the area. The town has modern sporting and community facilities. Excellent year-round fishing and nearby beaches have made Exmouth a major tourist destination. The town is situated on the north-eastern side of North West Cape, which is the nearest point in Australia to the continental shelf, so there is an abundance of fish and other marine life in the surrounding waters. **Of interest:** Exmouth House of Dolls, Craft St. Ocean Exhibits Museum, Pellew St. July: Gala week; Arts and crafts show. Nov.: Gamex (world-class game-fishing). **In the area:** Turtle-nesting, Nov.–Jan.; coral-spawning, Mar.; whale sharks, Mar.–July; humpback whales and manta rays, July–Nov. Swimming, snorkelling and fishing. Safari tours of Cape; dive courses and dive trips; Lightfoot Heritage Trail – details from Tourist information. In Cape Range National Park, south of town: Shothole Canyon, a spectacular gorge easily accessed via Shothole Canyon Rd and linked by walking trail to Charles Knife Canyon; Yardie Creek Gorge, with its deep blue water and multi-coloured rock; Milyering Visitor Centre, 52 km SW; abundant wildlife, picnic spots, scenic lookouts and walking trails. Prawn fishery, 23 km S; tours available in season, May–Oct. Ningaloo Marine Park, 14 km W of Cape, largest fringing coral reef in Australia; 500 fish species identified and 220 reef-building coral species; daily coral-viewing trips from Exmouth and Coral Bay. Charter fishing at Bundegi Beach jetty, 14 km N. Panoramic views from Vlaming Head Lighthouse, 17 km N; guided tours available. Wreck of SS *Mildura*, 100 m off-shore. **Tourist information:** Payne St; (099) 49 1176. **Accommodation:** 2 motels, 2 hostels, 5 cara./camp. parks.

Fitzroy Crossing Pop. 1119

MAP REF. 362 G11, 371 L9

In the Kimberley, where the road north crosses the Fitzroy River, is the settlement of Fitzroy Crossing, 260 km inland from Derby. Once a sleepy little hamlet, the last few years have seen unprecedented growth of the town as a result of Aboriginal settlement, mining by BHP at Cadjebut, 80 km SE, and an increase in the number of visitors to the nearby Geikie Gorge National Park. July: Rodeo. Nov.: Barra Bash (barramundi fishing competition). **In the area:** Between Dec. and Mar., check road conditions, as area is prone to flooding. Picturesque waterholes support abundance of fish and other wildlife. Magnificent Geikie Gorge, 20 km NE in Geikie Gorge National Park, has rich variety of wildlife, including plentiful sawfish, barramundi, stingrays (adapted to fresh water) and freshwater crocodiles; best seen by boat, daily boat trips available May–Nov. Fitzroy River Lodge tourist complex, on Great Northern Hwy. **Tourist information:** Flynn Drive; (091) 91 5355. **Accommodation:** 1 hotel, 1 motel, 1 hostel, 3 cara./camp. parks. **See also:** National Parks.

Fremantle Pop. 27 000

MAP REF. 352 B11, 356 B5, 358, 364 C4

The largest port in the State and western gateway to Australia, Fremantle is a bustling city 19 km s of Perth. It is a city of contrasts, with galleries and museums, beautiful sandy white beaches and many historic buildings, a reminder of the city's heritage. Captain Charles Fremantle arrived in May 1829 to 'take possession' of 'the whole of the west coast of New Holland', and was followed one month later by Captain James Stirling, who brought a small group to found the first Australian colony made up entirely of European free settlers. The engineer C. Y. O'Connor, who began the Goldfields Water Scheme, was responsible for building the harbour that turned Fremantle into an important port. The city has become home to many more recent immigrants. With its old-world charm and colourful cosmopolitan culture, Fremantle is one of the most fascinating port cities in the world. **Of interest:** Various tram tours available, some with meals; contact Tourist information. Many coffee shops and restaurants in South Terrace's 'Cappuccino Strip'. Pavement cafes and excellent restaurants. *Near the waterfront:* Round House (1830), end of High St, oldest building in WA, a 12-sided structure constructed as gaol; Whalers Tunnel (1837), connects High St to original shipping beach; Joan Campbell's Bathers Beach Gallery, near The Round House, in converted boatshed; in Cliff St, Maritime Museum (1860s), fine example of colonial Gothic architecture and Port Authority Building, Fremantle's tallest building offering panoramic views from roof viewing area; Boat Museum, on Victoria Quay, not far from Maritime Museum, STS *Leeuwin*, traditional square rigger; weekend, day and half-day tours available Sept.–Dec.; The Docks complex, souvenir shops and cafe/gallery, Victoria Quay; in Beach St, Wildflower Factory; Nature's Gem House; adjacent to Marine Tce and the Esplanade, modern Challenger Harbour marina facilities, developed for first Australian defence of the America's Cup, yachting's most prestigious trophy; Fremantle's largest fishing fleet, which works Australia's most valuable fishing grounds (mainly lobster), and its considerable Italian community, give city a Mediterranean flavour; nearby, Success Yacht Harbour, headquarters of 100-year-old Fremantle Sailing Club; Kailis' Fish Market and cafe, and Fremantle Crocodile Park, at Fishing Boat Harbour; Georgian style Old Customs House (1853); cnr of Clifton and Phillimore Sts; in Phillimore St, Chamber of Commerce (1912), Old Fremantle Fire Station (1908). *In the central business district:* Spare Parts Puppet Theatre, Short St, permanent puppet display, regular performances; The Bannister Street Craftworks in old warehouse, Bannister St, for excellent crafts; Henry St Station, huge model railway; quaint old building, 5 Mouat St, originally housed German Consulate and shipping offices; Film and Television Institute, Adelaide St; in Henderson St, award-winning Warders' Quarters, Georgian terrace, and Fremantle Markets with seafoods, crafts, antiques, clothing, souvenirs (open Fri.–Sun.); St John's Church and Square (1882); Town Hall (1887) in Kings Sq., cnr William and Adelaide Sts; Sail & Anchor Hotel, South Tce, Australia's first pub brewery, serves specialty beers. *On the outskirts of the city centre:* Former Fremantle Gaol (1851–9), The Tce via Fairbairn St, forbidding building of local stone (open to visitors); adjacent Fremantle Prison Museum, displays recording of penal system in WA; War Memorial Park, commanding excellent views; magnificent Samson House (1900), cnr Ellen and Ord Sts, guided tours; Shell Museum, Beach St; Fremantle Museum and Arts Centre, Finnerty St, has musical performances in courtyard during summer; history of WA's electricity and gas at Energy Museum, Parry St; East Fremantle Heritage Trail, contact Tourist information for brochure. May: Fremantle–Carnarvon yacht race. Nov.: Festival. **In the area:** Swimming at Port, Leighton and South Beaches. Ferries to Rottnest Island, 20 km w, from wharf daily; charter boats to Rottnest also available. Tourist attractions nearby: Adventure World, 8 km SE; Cohunu Koala Park, 19 km SE; Pioneer Village, 29 km SE.

Tourist information: Town Hall Shop, King Sq., High St; (09) 430 2346. **Accommodation:** 15 hotels, 2 hotel/motels, 1 motel, 11 B&B, 3 hostels, 3 cara. parks.

Gascoyne Junction Pop. 34

MAP REF. 365 D8

Located 170 km E of Carnarvon, at the junction of the Gascoyne and Lyons Rivers, this town is the administration centre for the surrounding region. The old-fashioned pub is a good rest stop before the many scenic attractions of the Kennedy Ranges National Park, 60 km N. **Tourist information:** Junction Hotel; (099) 43 0504. **Accommodation:** 1 hotel.

Geraldton Pop. 24 361

MAP REF. 366 A3

The key port and administration centre for the midwest region, Geraldton is 424 km N of Perth on Champion Bay. A year-round sunny climate and a mild winter, make it one of the State's most popular holiday destinations. The flourishing city has interesting museums, excellent accommodation, white, sandy beaches and good fishing. Rich agricultural land surrounds Geraldton and the district is noted for beautiful spring wildflowers and picturesque countryside. The Houtman Abrolhos Islands, so named in the 16th century, lie 64 km off the coast and are used mainly as a base for rock-lobster fishing. **Of interest:** Heritage trail, contact Tourist information. In Cathedral Ave: Queens Park Theatre, surrounded by gardens; St Francis Xavier Cathedral, designed by Mons. John C. Hawes, architect of some fine buildings in and around Geraldton. On Marine Tce: Sir John Forrest Memorial; Geraldton Museum (includes maritime display building and old railway building), features relics from shipwrecks off coast. Art Gallery, cnr Durlacher St and Chapman Rd. Old Gaol Craft Centre, Bill Sewell Complex, Chapman Rd. Tourist Lookout and Wishing Well on Waverley Heights, Brede St. Point Moore Lighthouse (1878), Willcock Dr. Excellent fishing; town's breakwater is good location. At Fisherman's Wharf in season, Nov.–June, watch huge hauls of lobster being unloaded. Jan.: Windsurfing classic. June: Batavia celebrations; Foodfest. Oct.: Festival of Geraldton. **In the area:**

For good fishing: Sunset Beach, 6 km N; Drummond Cove, 10 km N; mouth of Greenough River, 10 km S. Banks of Greenough River, favourite place for picnics; safe swimming for children in river. Greenough hamlet, 24 km S, a National Trust-restored village preserved to look as it did in 1880s; guided tours available. Ellendale Bluffs and Pool, 45 km SE, a permanent waterhole at base of steep rock face. Mill's Park Lookout, 15 km NE on Waggrakine Cutting, offers views over Moresby Range and coastal plain towards Geraldton. Chapman Valley, 35 km NE, a farming district noted for its brilliant wildflowers in spring. Kalbarri, 164 km N, surrounded by beautiful Kalbarri National Park. **Tourist information:** Bill Sewell Complex, cnr Bayley St and Chapman Rd; (099) 21 3999. **Accommodation:** 14 hotel/motels, 2 hostels, 7 cara./camp. parks.

Gingin Pop. 473

MAP REF. 364 C2, 366 C7

Situated 83 km N of Perth and 30 km from the coast, Gingin is mainly a centre for mixed farming and horticulture. An interesting day trip from Perth, it offers alternative return trips touring coastal centres or inland via the scenic Chittering Valley. The town is built around a loop of Gingin Brook, which rises from nearby springs and flows strongly all year. **Of interest:** Town has village-like atmosphere. Fine examples of traditional Australian architecture: in Weld St, St Luke's Anglican Church (1860s), Granville (1871), Uniting Church (1868), and Dewar's House (1886); in Brockman St, Philbey's Cottage (1906). May: British Car Day. **In the area:** At Bullsbrook, 30 km S: The Maze; Bullsbrook Antiques and Cottage Crafts. Golden Grove Citrus Orchard, at Lower Chittering, 30 km SE. At Bindoon, 24 km E: Neroni Wines; Chittering Valley Estate; Kay Road Art and Craft Gallery. Sewell Leisure Park, 44 km NE, offers golf, rides, flora, fauna and picnic/barbecue facilities. **Tourist information:** Shire Offices, 7 Brockman St; (09) 575 2211. **Accommodation:** 1 hotel/motel, 1 cara./camp. park.

Guilderton Pop. 385

MAP REF. 364 B2, 366 C7

Located at the mouth of the Moore River, 94 km from Perth, Guilderton is both a popular day trip and a holiday destination. There is excellent fishing in both river and sea, and safe swimming for children. Many Dutch relics have been found here, possibly from the wreck of the *Vergulde Draeck* (the Gilt Dragon) in 1656. Easter: King of the river. **In the area:** Seabird, 20 km N, a small but growing fishing village with safe beach. Ledge Point, 28 km N, a community built around fishing industry. **Tourist information:** Caravan Park, 2 Dewar St; (09) 577 1021. **Accommodation:** 1 cara./camp. park.

Halls Creek Pop. 1305

MAP REF. 363 N11, 371 P9

In the heart of the Kimberley, 2832 km from Perth, at the edge of the Great Sandy Desert, is Halls Creek, site of WA's first gold find in 1885. Between 1885-7, 10 000 men came to the Kimberley fields in search of gold then gradually drifted away, leaving 2000 on the diggings. Today mineral exploration is still carried out and the pastoral industry is supported by steady beef prices. **Of interest:** Arts Centre, Duncan Rd, features Aboriginal art and artifacts, and jewellery made from Halls Creek gold. Russian Jack Memorial, Thomas St, honours early European settlers. July: Agricultural show. Aug.: Races. **In the area:** Aerial tours and 4WD safaris; contact Tourist information. China Wall, 16 km SE, a natural quartz formation; nearby, picnic spot above creek. Fishing, swimming and picnicking at Ruby Queen Mine, and Sawpit Gorge; both 40 km SE. Prospecting at Old Halls Creek, 16 km E, also mud-brick ruins of original settlement. Caroline Pool, near old town site off Duncan Rd, for swimming Oct.–May. Wolfe Creek Meteorite Crater, almost 1 km wide, 49 m deep and second largest meteorite crater in world; 148 km S. Purnululu (Bungle Bungle) National Park, 165 km NE. **Tourist information:** Memorial Park, Great Northern Hwy; (091) 68 6262. **Accommodation:** 1 hotel, 1 motel, 1 cara./camp. park. **See also:** The Kimberley.

Harvey Pop. 2597

MAP REF. 357 H2, 364 C7, 366 C10

The thriving town of Harvey is set in some of the finest agricultural country in Australia, 139 km S of Perth. Bordered by the Darling Range and the Indian Ocean, the fertile plains make perfect dairying country. The town's irrigation storage dams, with their recreation areas, have become popular tourist attractions. **Of interest:** Historical Society Museum, in old railway station (1914); Harvey St (open p.m. 1st, 3rd, 5th Sun. each month). Tourist information, South Western Hwy, has dairy industry displays, Moo Shoppe and local craft sales. Stirling Cottage, behind Tourist information, replica of 1880s home of May Gibbs (author of *Snugglepot and Cuddlepie*). Internment Camp Memorial Shrine, South Western Hwy, built by prisoners of war in 1940s; obtain key from Tourist information. Jan.: Australia Day breakfast. Oct.: Agricultural show. **In the area:** Weir, 3 km E, off Weir Rd. Scenic drive around north-west side of Stirling Dam, 17 km E, leads to Harvey Falls and Trout Ladder. Hoffmans Mill, 25 km NE, has picnic and camping facilities. Logue Brook Dam, 15 km NE, for swimming, water-skiing and trout fishing. At Yarloop, 15 km N: historic steam-age Workshops Museum (closed Tues.); heritage trail, details from museum. Yalgorup National Park, 35 km NW. Myalup and Binningup Beaches, 25 km W off Old Coast Rd, are wide and sandy, ideal for swimming, fishing and boating. Emu Tech Farm, Old Coast Rd, Myalup, has restaurant and picnic area. Kemerton Industrial Park (SCM Chemicals), 20 km S; group tours available, contact Tourist information. **Tourist information:** South Western Hwy; (097) 29 1122. **Accommodation:** 1 hotel, 1 motel, 1 cara./camp. park. **See also:** The South-west.

Hopetoun Pop. 206

MAP REF. 366 H11

Hopetoun is a peaceful holiday town overlooking the Southern Ocean. The town is 59 km S of Ravensthorpe and offers rugged but beautiful coastal scenery and year-round wildflowers. Once called Mary Anne Harbour, the town has a colourful history. **Of interest:** White-sand beaches, sheltered bays, excellent fishing. Chatterbox Craft, Veal St, for local art and craft. Jan.: Summer festival. **In the area:** Dunn's Swamp, 5 km N, for picnics, bushwalking and birdwatching. Fitzgerald River National Park, 10 km W, includes the Barrens, a series of rugged mountains, undulating sandplains and steep narrow gorges; Hamersley Inlet, in park, is a scenic picnic and camping spot. Take care fishing from rocks – king waves can roll in unexpectedly and take lives. **Tourist information:** Going Bush Information Shop, Morgan St, Ravensthorpe; (098) 38 1277. **Accommodation:** 1 hotel, 1 motel, 1 cara./camp. park.

Hyden   Pop. 150

MAP REF. 366 F8

Hyden is 351 km east of Perth, in the semi-arid eastern wheat area of WA. **In the area:** Fascinating rock formations, especially Wave Rock, 4 km E, a 2700 million-year-old granite outcrop rising 15 m, like a giant wave about to break; at Wave Rock: wildlife park; coffee shop; caravan park with chalets; Pioneer Town, with collection of Australiana; and lace collection (from 1600) at Visitors Centre. Other rock formations within walking distance of Wave Rock: Hippo's Yawn, The Falls and The Breakers. Aboriginal rock paintings at Mulka's Cave, 18 km N of Wave Rock. Nearby, The Humps, another unusual granite formation. **Tourist information:** Wave Rock Visitors Centre, Wave Rock Rd, 4 km E of town; (098) 80 5182. **Accommodation:** 1 hotel/motel, 1 cara./camp. park.

Jurien   Pop. 603

MAP REF. 366 B6

Located on the shores of a sheltered bay between Perth and Geraldton, Jurien is a lobster-fishing centre. The town is also a growing holiday destination because of its magnificent safe swimming beaches, excellent climate and reputation as an angler's paradise. Jurien boat harbour, a 17-ha inland marina, has excellent facilities for boating enthusiasts. **Of interest:** Tours of rock-lobster processing factory, Roberts Rd, in fishing season. Nov.: Expo and Blessing of the fleet. **In the area:** Spectacular sand dunes along coast. Cockleshell Gully, 31 km N, has great diversity of flora and fauna. Stockyard Gully National Park, 50 km N (4WD access only), has walk through 300-m Stockyard Gully Tunnel along winding underground creek; torch necessary, guided tours available. At Cervantes, 55 km S, Slalom carnival (windsurfing) held in Dec. Nearby, Nambung National Park, featuring The Pinnacles, thousands of spectacular

The Great Southern

Two Peoples Bay, east of Albany

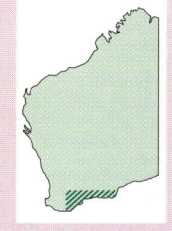

The Great Southern, also known as the Rainbow Coast, is bounded by a rugged coastline and the roaring Southern Ocean. During the winter months spectacular rainbows regularly occur. The coast gives way to an amazingly beautiful hinterland with rivers winding through forests, gentle valleys and ancient mountain ranges.

The district has an important historical heritage. **Albany** was the first town in Western Australia, established two and a half years before the Swan River colony. Major Edmund Lockyer landed here in 1826 to claim the western half of the continent as British territory.

Albany is the unofficial capital of the area, and retains a charming English atmosphere from the colonial days. The town looks out over the magnificent blue waters of Princess Royal Harbour in King George Sound. Albany has a number of fine old homesteads, museums and galleries. There are numerous scenic drives around the coast to the Gap, the Natural Bridge and the Blowholes. There are also stretches of golden sand and secluded bays. The fishing is superb. **Denmark**, a holiday destination, lies on the banks of the tranquil Denmark River, and the little village of Nornalup nestles near the Frankland River. Near Nornalup is the awe-inspiring Valley of the Giants.

The Great Southern has a thriving new viticulture industry, with the vineyards around **Mount Barker** producing award-winning wines. Mount Barker itself is the gateway to the Stirling and Porongurup mountain ranges, both within the confines of national parks. The Porongurup Range has granite peaks dominating giant hardwood trees, and a maze of wildflowers and creepers. There are many easy climbs, rewarded by splendid views; Castle Rock, Howard's Peak and Devil's Slide are three of the most popular.

The high, jagged peaks of the Stirling Range (the highest is Bluff Knoll at 1037 metres) tower over virgin bushland. From a distance, with the changing light, the vegetation varies from heathery shades to blues and reds. The peaks can sometimes be seen shrouded in mist, and on occasions even tipped with snow. There are more than 100 bird species in the **Stirling Range National Park** and native animals are plentiful. Look also for the beautiful wild orchids, Stirling banksia and mountain bells.

Small towns, including Tambellup with its colonial buildings, and thriving towns such as **Katanning, Kojonup**, Gnowangerup and Jerramungup are all surrounded by peaceful rural farmland.

For further information contact the Albany Tourist Bureau, Railway Station, Proudlove Pde, Albany; (098) 41 1088. **See also:** Entry for Stirling Range National Park in National Parks; and individual entries in A–Z listing for those towns indicated by bold type. **Map reference:** for Albany region, 360, 361.

Early Australian architecture in Hannan St, Kalgoorlie

calcified spires around 30 000 years old, scattered over 400 ha of multi-coloured sand; guided coach tours daily; check road conditions before leaving Jurien if taking coastal track; main signposted route further inland recommended. Waddi Farms, Koonah Rd, off Brand Hwy, Badgingarra, 60 km SE, has wildflowers, emu farm, native gardens, shop and restaurant. **Tourist information:** Shire Offices, Bashford St; (096) 52 1020. **Accommodation:** 1 hotel/motel, 4 B&B, 1 cara./camp. park.

Kalbarri   Pop. 1521

MAP REF. 365 C13, 366 A2

This popular holiday town is between Geraldton and Carnarvon, 661 km N of Perth. The town's picturesque setting on the Murchison River estuary, its year-round sunny climate and the spectacular gorges of the river running through the Kalbarri National Park attract a growing number of tourists. Kalbarri is also noted for excellent fishing and the brilliance of more than 500 wildflower species. **Of interest:** The Wildflower Centre, off Ajana Rd, has wide range of Kalbarri wildflowers. In Grey St: Doll and Marine Museum; Fantasy Land; Gemstone Mine. In Porter St: Kalbarri Entertainment Centre; bicycle hire. Mar.: Sport fishing classic. Nov.: Blessing of the fleet. **In the area:** Majestic coastal gorges and precipitous red cliffs dropping to Indian Ocean. *River Queen* ferry cruises, camel safaris, coach, 4WD, motorbike and abseiling adventure tours, canoe safaris and joy flights available; contact Tourist information. Kalbarri National Park, a large area of magnificent virgin bushland surrounding town, includes Kalbarri Big River Ranch, 3 km E, for horseriding; spectacular Murchison River gorges, 11 km E; abundance of wildlife and native flora; no camping. Meanarra Lookout, 7 km SE. Red Bluff, for swimming, fishing and rock climbing; Rainbow Jungle and Tropical Bird Park; cairn at Wittecarra Creek, marking site of first permanent landing of Europeans in Australia (two Dutchmen sent ashore for their part in *Batavia* mutiny in 1629) – all 4 km S. The Loop and Z Bend lookouts, 30 km NE. **Tourist information:** Allen Community Centre, Grey St; (099) 37 1104. **Accommodation:** 1 hotel/motel, 2 motels, 1 hostel, 4 cara./camp. parks.

Kalgoorlie-Boulder   Pop. 25 016

MAP REF. 366 I6

At the heart of WA's largest goldmining area is the city of Kalgoorlie-Boulder, 597 km E of Perth and centred on the famous Golden Mile, reputed to be the richest square mile in the world. Over 1300 tonnes of gold have been mined from this small area. Paddy Hannan found gold in 1893; by 1902 the population was 30 000, with 93 hotels operating. Fortunes were made overnight; the impressive stone buildings and magnificent wide streets recall the town's boom past. Miners set up their tents on the Golden Mile near the Great Boulder Mine, and this camp became the town of Boulder. One of the greatest difficulties facing the miners in this semi-desert area was lack of water. Determination and the brilliant scheme of engineer C. Y. O'Connor saved the day. A pipeline was completed in 1903, carrying water an incredible 563 km from a reservoir near Perth. Goldmining continues with renewed vigour now that gold prices have risen. The Kalgoorlie-Boulder region is also an important pastoral district for high-quality wool. **Of interest:** Heritage walk along Hannan St, booklet available from Tourist information. Fine examples of early Australian architecture: in Hannan St, Exchange, Palace and Australia Hotels; Government buildings; Kalgoorlie Post Office. Distinctive Kalgoorlie Town Hall (1908), has impressive staircase, paintings by local artists. Also in Hannan St: Museum of the Goldfields and British Arms Hotel (1899), has display recalling heyday of gold-rush boom; statue of Paddy Hannan; Goldfields Aboriginal Art Gallery. Paddy Hannan's Tree, Outridge Tce, marks site of first gold find in Kalgoorlie. School of Mines Museum, Egan St, includes world-class display of most minerals found in WA. At Hannans North Historical Mining Complex, Broad Arrow Rd, underground and surface tours, and gold-pouring demonstrations available. Super Pit Lookout, off Eastern Bypass Rd. In Burt St: Boulder Town Hall (1908), has regular art exhibits; Eastern Goldfields Historical Museum, in Boulder railway station. Picturesque Cornwall Hotel (1898), Chesapeake St. Royal Flying Doctor Base, Killarney St, serves one of largest areas in Australia; tours available weekdays. Hammond Park, Lyall St, a wildlife sanctuary with small lake and scale model of Bavarian castle. Mt Charlotte Reservoir and Lookout, off Sutherland St; reservoir is storage for Kalgoorlie's vital fresh-water supply.

The Loop Line, a tourist railway line around the Golden Mile; timetable at Tourist information. Sept.: Kalgoorlie Cup; Spring festival. Nov.: Goldfields mining expo. **In the area:** City is an ideal base for visiting old goldmining towns in district, some now ghost towns and all within a day's drive, and all active again: Coolgardie, 37 km SW; Broad Arrow, 38 km N; Ora Banda, 54 km NW; Kookynie, 200 km N; Leonora-Gwalia, 235 km N. WA's only two-up school, 7 km N of Kalgoorlie, on eastern side of road to Menzies. Kurrawang Emu Farm, 18 km W, also features Aboriginal artifacts; tours available (closed Sun.). **Tourist information:** 250 Hannan St, Kalgoorlie; (090) 21 1966. **Accommodation:** 17 hotels, 19 motels, 6 cara./camp. parks. **See also:** Crossing the Nullarbor; The Goldfields.

Kambalda Pop. 4259

MAP REF. 367 J7

Kambalda's goldmining history lasted from 1897 to 1906, during which time 30 000 ounces of gold were produced. When the gold petered out, so did the town. In 1966, however, rich nickel deposits were discovered and the town has since boomed. Today Kambalda, 634 km E of Perth, consists of two well-planned centres (Kambalda and Kambalda West), 6 km apart, and is noted for its environmental protection policy. **Of interest:** Several pleasant picnic areas in centre of town. Red Hill Lookout, off Gordon Adams Rd, offers excellent views of area, including vast Lake Lefroy (510 sq. km.). June: Sky diving gathering. **In the area:** Land yachting on salt bed of lake. Defiance Open Cut Gold Mine Lookout, 20 km S; obtain entry permit from town's Western Mining office. **Tourist information:** Emu Rocks Rd, Kambalda West; (090) 27 1446. **Accommodation:** 1 hotel, 1 cara./camp. park. **See also:** The Goldfields.

Karratha Pop. 11 325

MAP REF. 365 G1

This clean, modern town was established on Nickel Bay in 1968 as a result of the continuing development of the Hamersley Iron Project. There was a lack of suitable land for expansion at Dampier and a need for a new regional centre. The town grew even faster when Woodside Petroleum developed the immense offshore gas reserve on the North West Shelf, and Karratha now has the best facilities in the north-west. Karratha's warm winter temperatures make it a good place to escape the southern cold. **Of interest:** Largest shopping centre outside Perth, Welcome Rd. Excellent views from TV Hill Lookout, Millstream Rd. Easter: Pilbara pursuit jetboat classic. June: Festival. Aug.: FeNaCLNG festival. **In the area:** Scenic flights, day tours and safari tours of Pilbara outback; contact Tourist information for details. Jaburara Heritage Trail, 3.5 km W on Main Rd, includes Aboriginal rock carvings. Chichester Range Camel Trail and Millstream-Chichester National Park, 124 km S. **Tourist information:** 4548 Karratha Rd; (091) 44 4600. **Accommodation:** 2 motels, 1 hostel, 3 cara./camp. parks. **See also:** The Hamersley Range; The Pilbara.

Katanning Pop. 4139

MAP REF. 361 L1, 364 H9, 366 E10

A thriving town 186 km N of Albany, Katanning's well-planned streets have some impressive Federation buildings. The countryside is given over to grain-growing and pastoral activities, and is noted for its fine merino sheep. **Of interest:** Old Mill Museum (1889), cnr Clive St and Austral Tce, features outstanding display of vintage roller flour-milling process. Majestic Kobeelya mansion (1902), Brownie St, a country retreat now owned by Baptist Church; open by appt. All Ages Playground, Clive St, has miniature steam railway. Old Winery ruins, Andrews Rd, being restored. In Dore St: largest country-based sheep-selling facility in WA; regular sales on Thurs. throughout year, ram sale in Aug. Metro Meats meatworks, Wagin Rd; guided tours by appt, contact Metro Meats or Tourist information. Feb.: Triathlon. Aug.: Prophet Mohammad's birthday. Dec.: Caboodle. **In the area:** Katanning–Piesse Heritage Trail, details from Tourist information. Lakes surrounding town are excellent for swimming, boating and water-skiing. Stirling Range National Park, 80 km S. Work of local woodcarver John Davis whose subjects include native birds, at Gnowangerup, 60 km SE. **Tourist information:** Flour Mill, cnr Austral Tce and Clive St; (098) 21 2634. **Accommodation:** 3 hotels, 2 motels, 1 hostel, 2 cara./camp. parks. **See also:** The Great Southern.

Kojonup Pop. 1023

MAP REF. 361 J2, 364 G9, 366 E11

Situated on the Albany Hwy, 154 km NW of Albany, Kojonup takes its name from the Aboriginal word 'kodja', meaning 'stone axe'. In 1837, when surveying the road from Albany to the newly established Swan River settlement, Alfred Hillman was guided to the Kojonup Spring by local Aborigines. Later a military outpost was set up on the site, and this marked the beginning of the town. **Of interest:** Kojonup Spring and picnic area, Spring St. Military Barracks Museum (1845), Barracks Pl.; open Sun. p.m. Elverd's Cottage (1850s), Soldier Rd, has display of pioneers' tools and implements. Sundial in Hillman Park, Albany Hwy. Walsh's Cattle Complex, Broomehill Rd, has regular cattle sales. Sept.: Wildflower and country festival. **In the area:** Variety of flora (includes more than 60 orchid species) and fauna (especially birds). Outlets for locally made jarrah furniture, hand-turned blackboy articles, woollen jumpers. Yeedabirrup Rock, 10 km E, one of many granite monoliths in area. Tours and farmstay at Kalpara Farm; details from Tourist information. **Tourist information:** Benn Pde; (098) 31 1686. **Accommodation:** 1 hotel, 1 hotel/motel, 1 motel, 1 B&B, 1 cara./camp. park. **See also:** The Great Southern.

Kondinin Pop. 312

MAP REF. 364 I5, 366 F4

The small settlement of Kondinin is 278 km SE of Perth. There are sheep studfarms in the surrounding area. **Of interest:** Craft Shop, Gordon St, has local craft. **In the area:** Kondinin Lake, 8 km W, for water-skiing and yachting after a rainy winter. **Tourist information:** Craft Shop, Gordon St; (098) 89 1130. **Accommodation:** 1 hotel, 1 motel, 1 cara./camp. park.

Kulin Pop. 321

MAP REF. 364 I6, 366 F9

A centre for the sheep and grain farms of the district, Kulin lies 283 km SE of Perth. The eucalypt species *Eucalyptus macrocarpa* is spectacular feature of local flora. **In the area:** Several species of native orchids. Jilakin Rock and Lake, 18 km E, a salt lake with salt plants and wildflowers in spring; Jilakan Rock picnic race day, 15 km E, held in Oct. Buckley's Breakaway (pit with coloured hollows caused by granite decomposing to kaolin), 58 km E; also unusual coloured rock formations and wildflowers in area. Hopkins Nature Reserve, 20 km NE, an important flora conservation area. **Tourist information:** Kulin Woolshed, Johnston St; (098) 80 1275. **Accommodation:** 1 hotel/motel, 1 cara./camp. park.

Kununurra Pop. 4061

MAP REF. 363 P2, 371 Q5

Kununurra is situated alongside Lake Kununurra on the Ord River. Adjoining is the magnificent Mirima (Hidden Valley) National Park. The town supports several industries, including agriculture and mining, and is the major centre for the Argyle Diamond Mine (the largest diamond mine in the world) and the Ord River Irrigation area. **Of interest:** Apr.: Dam to dam regatta. May–July: Ord River festival (float parade, mardi gras, art and craft exhibitions, famous Ord Tiki Race and water-ski display). **In the area:** Kununurra is major starting point for flights and ground tours to: remarkably coloured and shaped Bungle Bungles in the south; Argyle Diamond Mine in the south-west (access only via tour); Mitchell Plateau and Kalumburu in the north-west Kimberley. Minibus tours of local attractions, charter flights and bushcamping; details at Tourist information. Sales of pink diamonds from the Argyle Diamond Mine, and other gems, at various outlets. Good fishing; barramundi, a prized catch. Mirima (Hidden Valley) National Park, 2 km E. Both 2 km N: Warringarri Aboriginal Arts; Kelly's Knob Lookout, for views of surrounding irrigated land. Melon Farm, Ivanhoe Rd, 8 km N and Banana Farm, River Farm Rd, 9 km N, for tasting and sales, daily May–Oct. Top Rockz Gallery, 10 km N, exhibits gemstones and precious metals; open Apr.–Sept. Ivanhoe Crossing, 13 km N, for fishing. Middle Springs, 30 km N, and Black Rock Falls, 32 km N; best in wet season. Cruises on Lake Kununurra and upstream into the Everglades and rugged gorges; teeming birdlife to be seen. El Questro Station, 100 km W, features Aboriginal rock art, rugged scenery, hot springs, fishing and boating; camping and accommodation available. Sleeping Buddha (Elephant Rock), 10 km S. Pandanus Wildlife Park; Zebra Rock Gallery; both 16 km S. Scenic Lake Argyle, 72 km S in Carr Boyd Range, one of largest constructed lakes in southern hemisphere; created by Ord River Dam which transformed mountain peaks into rugged islands. **Tourist information:** Coolibah Dr.; (091) 68 1177. **Accommodation:** 2 hotels, 2 motels, 5 cara./ camp. parks. **See also:** The Kimberley; The Ord River.

Kwinana Pop. 13 517

MAP REF. 356 B7, 364 C4, 366 C8

Kwinana, 20 km S of the port of Fremantle, is a major industrial centre, containing the BP Oil Refinery and Alcoa's Alumina Works. Kwinana Industrial Complex, built on Cockburn Sound, one of the world's finest natural harbours, was begun in 1951. The town is surrounded by pockets of bush and wetland, providing numerous opportunities for recreation. **Of interest:** Group tours of local industries, contact Tourist information. At Kwinana Beach: hull of the wrecked SS *Kwinana*; jet skiing. **In the area:** Spectacles Wetlands, on McLachlan Rd, 5 km NE. At seaside resort city of Rockingham, 10 km S, cruises to offshore islands, Point Peron (7 km W) and Penguin Island (10 km SW). Lookout over coast and town on Chalk Hill, western outskirts of town. **Tourist information:** Shire Offices, cnr Gilmore Ave and Sulphur Rd; (09) 419 2222. **Accommodation:** 1 hotel/motel.

Lake Grace Pop. 596

MAP REF. 366 F9

A pleasant country town with first-class service facilities, situated 252 km N of Albany in the peaceful rural countryside of the central south wheat belt, Lake Grace derives its name from the shallow lake just west of the settlement. **Of interest:** Wildlife sanctuary, South Rd. Restored Inland Mission hospital, Stubbs St, last in WA. Old railway buildings under restoration. **In the area:** Roe Heritage Trail, retraces part of J.S. Roe's explorations in 1848; details from Tourist information. Lookout, 5 km W. **Tourist information:** Lake Grace Newsagency, Stubbs St; (098) 65 1029. **Accommodation:** 1 hotel, 3 motels, 1 cara./camp. park.

Lake King Pop. 29

MAP REF. 366 C9

A crossroads centre with a tavern and store, Lake King is a stopping place for visitors travelling across arid country and through Frank Hann National Park to Norseman. **Of interest:** Interdenominational community church. **In the area:** Wildflowers in season. Lake King, 5 km W, and Lake Pallarup, 15 km S. Pioneer well at Pallarup, 18 km S. Mt Madden cairn and lookout, 25 km SE, also picnic area. Frank Hann National Park, 35 km E, cross-section of heath flora of inland sandplain east of wheat belt. Park is traversed by Lake King–Norseman Rd, a formed gravel all-weather road; check road conditions before departure. No visitor facilities or supplies available between Lake King and Norseman. Hollands Track, early goldfields access route. **Tourist information:** Morgane St, Ravensthorpe; (098) 38 1163. **Accommodation:** 1 hotel/motel, 1 cara. park.

Lancelin Pop. 531

MAP REF. 364 B1, 366 B7

This quiet little fishing town on the shores of Lancelin Bay is 127 km N of Perth. A natural breakwater extends from Edward Island to Lancelin Island, providing a safe harbour and a perfect breeding ground for fish. There are rock lobsters to be caught on the offshore reefs outside the bay. Long stretches of white sandy beach provide an ideal swimming area for children. Lancelin is becoming known as the sailboard mecca of WA and affords a colourful spectacle each Dec. with large numbers of international and interstate windsurfers taking part in the Ledge Point ocean race. **Of interest:** Large off-road area for dune buggies at northern end of town. Easter: Beach buggy championships. **In the area:** Whale-watching, Oct.–Mar. Track (4WD only) leads 55 km N to Nambung National Park; check road conditions before setting out. **Tourist information:** 102 Gingin Rd; (096) 55 1100. **Accommodation:** 1 hotel, 1 motel, 2 cara./camp. parks.

Laverton Pop. 1197

MAP REF. 367 J3

Laverton, situated 360 km NE of Kalgoorlie, is a modern satellite town

Crossing the Nullarbor

The trip from Adelaide to Perth along the Eyre Highway is one of Australia's great touring experiences. It is far from monotonous, with breathtaking views of the Great Australian Bight from the road in many places. There is nothing quite like a long straight road stretching as far as the eye can see.

If you are planning a return journey, it is well worth considering driving one way and putting the car on the train for the return. Train bookings need to be made well in advance, even at off-peak times. **(See:** Planning Ahead.)

The Eyre Highway is bitumen for its entire length. The highway is well signposted, with indications of the distance to the next town with petrol and other services.

If the journey is undertaken at a sensible pace, it can be surprisingly relaxing, especially during the quieter times of year. The standard of accommodation along the way is good and reasonably priced, with a friendly atmosphere in the bars and dining rooms of the large motel/roadhouses that are strategically situated along the highway. Many friendships have been made during the trip across the Eyre Highway as the same carloads of travellers meet at stopping-places each night.

The highway has certain hazards, including breakaways on the shoulders in places, requiring caution when drivers are overtaking; and kangaroos especially at dusk or after rain. Overtaking also can be hazardous in damp conditions when the spray from the vehicle in front completely cuts visibility ahead. On the other hand, the semitrailer drivers are usually courteous and signal when it is safe to overtake.

The setting sun can make driving somewhat unpleasant for drivers travelling in a westerly direction. Also, do not forget the time changes you will encounter on the way! **(See also:** Time Zones.)

Above all, it is most important to have a safe, reliable car. The settlements along the highway are mainly motels and roadhouses; you could have a long wait for mechanical or medical help.

The journey proper begins at **Port Augusta**, 330 kilometres north-east of Adelaide, at the head of Spencer Gulf. Port Augusta is a provincial city that services a vast area of semi-arid grazing and wheat-growing country to the north and west. As you head out of the city on the Eyre Highway, you see

The Eyre Highway links Port Augusta in South Australia and Norseman in Western Australia

the red peaks of the Flinders Ranges soaring above the sombre bluebush plains; these are the last hills of any size for 2500 kilometres. Through the little towns of **Kimba** and Kyancutta the scenery can vary from mallee scrub to wide paddocks of wheat. This area was once called Heartbreak Plains, a reminder of the time when farmers walked off their land in despair, leaving behind crumbling stone homesteads that today dot the plains.

The highway meets the sea at **Ceduna**, a small town of white stone buildings and limestone streets set against a background of blue-green sea. The waters of the Great Australian Bight here are shallow and unpredictable, but they yield Australia's best catches of its most commercially prized fish, whiting. On the outskirts of Ceduna is a warning sign about the last reliable water. This marks the beginning of the deserted, almost treeless land that creeps towards the Nullarbor Plain. The highway stays close to the coast, and alongside there is always a little scrub and other vegetation.

The name 'Nullarbor' is a corruption of the Latin words meaning 'no trees' and the name is apt. Geologists believe that the completely flat plain was once the bed of a prehistoric sea, which was raised by a great upheaval of the earth.

West of Ceduna the traveller will find **Penong**, a town of 100 windmills, and the breathtaking coastal beauty around Point Sinclair and Cactus Beach. Then on to Nundroo and south to the abandoned settlement of Fowlers Bay, once an exploration depot for Edward John Eyre and now a charming ghost town best known for its fishing. At the Yalata Roadhouse, run by the Yalata Aboriginal Community, there are genuine artifacts for sale at reasonable prices. Between Nullarbor and Border Village are five of Australia's most spectacular coastal lookouts, over giant ocean swells pounding the towering limestone cliffs that make up this part of the Great Australian Bight. From June to October there is the chance of spotting the majestic southern right whale on its annual migration along the southern part of the continent. Fuel, refreshments and accommodation are all available at Penong, Nundroo, Nullarbor and Border Village.

The stone ruins of an Aboriginal mission remain at **Cocklebiddy**. The road continues until it reaches the first real town in over 1200 kilometres, **Norseman**, an ideal stopping-place.

From here you turn north to **Kalgoorlie-Boulder** or south to **Esperance** on the coast. At Kalgoorlie-Boulder you will see one of the longest-established and most prosperous goldmining centres in Western Australia. Set in vast dryland eucalypt forest, the town is picturesque in frontier style. Esperance, on the other hand, offers coastal scenery including long, empty beaches. Nearby, wildflowers spread across the countryside in spring.

As you travel west from Kalgoorlie-Boulder, the undulating forest and wildflower scrub continue for a further 250 kilometres until the road reaches the wheat- and wool-growing lands surrounding the towns of **Southern Cross** and **Merredin**. The farmland becomes increasingly rich as it rises into the Darling Range, the beautiful, wooded mountain country that overlooks Perth. At the end of this long journey Perth glitters like a jewel on the Indian Ocean – a place of civilisation and style, of beaches, waterways and greenery.

See also: Entries in the South Australian A–Z listing or in the Western Australian A–Z listing for those towns indicated by bold type.

WESTERN AUSTRALIA

surrounded by numerous old mine workings. The nickel mining and goldmining in the area has recently ceased. With an annual rainfall of around 200 mm, summers are hot and dry; Apr.–Oct. is the recommended time to travel. From Laverton to Ayers Rock (1200 km), all roads are unsealed, and the following points should be noted:
- Permit required to divert from the Laverton–Yulara Rd; obtained from Aboriginal Planning Authority in Perth or Alice Springs.
- Water is scarce.
- Supplies at Laverton. Fuel, supplies and accommodation at Warburton and Warakurra Roadhouse. Petrol, supplies and accommodation at Tjirrkarli Roadhouse, 320 km NE of Laverton.
- Check on road conditions before departure at the Laverton Police Station or at Shire Offices. Roads can be hazardous when wet.

Tourist information: Desert Pea Caravan Park, Weld Dr. **Accommodation:** 1 hotel, 1 cara./camp. park. **See also:** The Goldfields.

Leonora   Pop. 1194

MAP REF. 366 I3

A busy mining centre 243 km N of Kalgoorlie, Leonora has a typical Australian country-town appearance, with wide streets and verandahed shopfronts. The town is the centrepoint of, and railhead for, the north-eastern goldfields, with mining of gold, copper and nickel at Laverton, 120 km NE, and Leinster, 134 km NW. Most of surrounding country is flat mulga scrub, but there are brilliant wildflowers in Aug. and early Sept. after good rains. Oct.: Art prize. **In the area:** Three major gold producers, including famous Sons of Gwalia. Town of Gwalia, 2 km S: museum capturing miners' lifestyle; 1 km heritage trail. Small goldmining town of Menzies, 110 km S. Kookynie, 92 km SE, a ghost town with old mine workings; Grand Hotel offers warm welcome. Malcolm, 20 km E; good picnic spot alongside Malcolm Dam. **Tourist information:** Shire Offices, Tower St; (090) 37 6044. **Accommodation:** 2 hotels, 1 motel, 1 cara./camp. park. **See also:** The Goldfields.

Madura   Pop. 15

MAP REF. 367 P8

The Hampton Tablelands form a backdrop to Madura, 195 km from the WA-SA border, on the Eyre Hwy. The settlement dates back to 1876 when horses for the Indian Army were bred here. Now it is surrounded by private sheep stations. **In the area:** Blowholes at The Pass, 1.5 km N. **Tourist information:** Madura Pass Oasis Motel; (090) 39 3464. **Accommodation:** 1 motel, 1 cara./camp. park. **See also:** Crossing the Nullarbor.

Mandurah   Pop. 23 343

MAP REF. 356 B9, 364 C5, 366 C9

The popular holiday destination of Mandurah is on the coast, 72 km S of Perth. The Murray, Serpentine and Harvey Rivers meet here, forming the vast inland waterway of Peel Inlet and the Harvey Estuary. The river waters and the Indian Ocean offer excellent conditions for yachting, boating, swimming, water-skiing and fishing, and the town becomes a mecca for tourists in holiday periods. **Of interest:** Hall's Cottage, Leighton Rd, a small whitewashed cottage built in 1845 by two of the colony's earliest European settlers. Christ Church (1870), cnr Pinjarra Rd and Sholl St, features hand-carved furniture. Community Museum, in old school building (1898), Pinjarra Rd (open Tues. and Sun.). Kerryelle's Collectors Museum, Gordon Rd. Boat hire and cruises on inlet and river. Dolphins sometimes seen in estuary. Waters attract abundance of birdlife. King Carnival Amusement Park, in Hall Park. Jan.: Festival. **In the area:** Pleasant picnic areas near numerous storage dams in nearby Darling Range; boating and swimming at Waroona and Logue Brook Dams. Good beaches and a pottery at Halls Head, just over old traffic bridge. Bavarian Castle Fun Park, Old Coast Rd, 2 km S. Further south, Dawesville Channel between inland waterways and ocean; good fishing from bridge. Handcrafted sculptures depicting Australian folklore and characters at Bouvard Coast Studio, Henry Rd, Melros; 15 km SW. Lakes Clifton and Preston, 45 km S, two long, narrow lakes running parallel to coast. Houseboat hire at South Yunderup, 12 km SE. Wineries at Cape Bouvard, Mt John Rd, 22 km S (weekends only); Peel Estate, Fletcher Rd, Baldivis, 20 km N. Hamel Forestry Department Nursery, 42 km SE. Western Rosella Bird Park, 5 km E, native birds in natural settings. Also 5 km E, local art and craft market, Sat., Sun., Mon. and public holidays. Durango Gallery, Amarillo Dr., Karnup, 14 km N. **Tourist information:** 5 Pinjarra Rd; (09) 535 1155. **Accommodation:** 2 hotels, 5 motels, 7 B&B, 11 cara./camp. parks.

Manjimup   Pop. 4353

MAP REF. 360 D6, 364 D10, 366 D11

Fertile agricultural country and magnificent karri forests surround Manjimup, 307 km S of Perth. This is the commercial centre of the State's south-west, and one of its most diversified horticultural regions: there is a flourishing timber industry, quality fresh fruit (it is WA's largest apple-growing area) and vegetables are grown for the State and Asian markets, and wine, wool and dairying also contribute to the local economy. **Of interest:** Manjimup Regional Timber Park, cnr Edward and Rose Sts, a major tourist attraction, includes Visitors Centre; Blacksmith's Shop; Timber Museum, display on development of timber industry in WA; original sawmill steam loco; Age of Steam Museum; Historical Hamlet; Fire Tower Lookout; gallery and tearooms, picnic/barbecue facilities; timber tours. WA Chip and Pulp (Paper Wood Co.) mill, Eastbourne Rd; guided tours available. Yallambee Gem Museum, Chopping St. June: 15 000 Motocross. **In the area:** Abseiling, rockclimbing, bushcraft, horse-drawn picnic excursions, forest discovery tours, safari tours available; contact Tourist information. Diamond Tree Fire Tower, 9 km S, a 51-m karri tree in use 1941–74; nearby, children's adventure trail and picnic/barbecue area. Piano Gully Wines, 10 km S. Bunnings Diamond Woodchip Mill, 12 km S; guided tours available. Nyamup, an old mill town redeveloped as a tourist village; 20 km SE. Southern Wildflowers farm, Quinninup, 33 km SE. King Jarrah, 4 km E, a 47-m-high tree estimated to be 600 years old; heritage trail begins here, contact Tourist information. Pioneer cairn, 9 km NE. Pioneer cemetery, 10 km NE. The 19-km round trip to Dingup, north-east of Manjimup, passes through farmland and forest; at Dingup, church (1896); historic house (1870). Constable Wines, Graphite Rd, 8 km W. One Tree Bridge, 22 km W, a single karri tree felled in 1904 to cross Donnelly River; pleasant walk along river edge to the Four Aces, four

Boranup Beach, south of Margaret River

magnificent karri trees, 300–400 years old. Donnelly River Holiday Village, 28 km W, features abundant wildlife and horseriding. Swimming at Fontys Pool, 10 km SW, originally dammed in 1925 for irrigation; picnicking in landscaped surrounds. Collect your own walnuts and chestnuts in season (Apr.–May) at Fontanini's Nut Farm, located next to Fonty's Pool. Warren National Park, 40 km SW, good for bushwalking and picnics. **Tourist information:** cnr Rose and Edward Sts; (097) 71 1831. **Accommodation:** 2 hotels, 4 motels, 3 cara./camp. parks. **See also:** The South-west.

Marble Bar   Pop. 383

MAP REF. 368 D2

Widely known as the hottest town in Australia because of its consistently high temperatures, Marble Bar lies 200 km SE of Port Hedland (last 90 km is unsealed). The town takes its name from the unique bar of red jasper that crosses the Coongan River, 4 km W of town. Alluvial gold was discovered at Marble Bar in 1891, and in 1931 at Comet Mine. Today the major industries are goldmining and pastoral production. Marble Bar is a typical WA outback town. **Of interest:** Government buildings (1895), General St, built using locally quarried stone. State Battery site (1910), Newman–Tabba Rd; not open to public. July: Cup race weekend. **In the area:** Beautiful scenery, especially in winter and after rain, when spinifex is transformed into flowering plants; rugged ranges, rolling plains, steep gorges, deep rock pools and many scenic attractions. Jasper deposit at Marble Bar Pool, 4 km W. Nearby, Chinaman's Pool, an ideal picnic spot. Flying Fox Lookout, 6 km SW, spectacular when river is running. Corunna World War II RAAF Base, 40 km SE; worth a visit. Old goldmines at Nullagine, 111 km SE. Good swimming at Coppin's Gap, 68 km NE; Kitty's Gap, further 6 km. **Tourist information:** BP Garage, 1 Francis St; (091) 76 1041. **Accommodation:** 1 hotel/motel, 1 motel, 1 cara./camp. park. **See also:** The Pilbara.

Margaret River   Pop. 1725

MAP REF. 357 C10, 359 C7, 364 A10, 366 B11

Margaret River is a pretty township nestled on the side of the Margaret River near the coast 280 km from Perth. The area is noted for its world-class wines, magnificent coastal scenery, excellent surfing beaches and spectacular cave formations. **Of interest:** Historic steam train in Rotary Park, Bussell Hwy; starting point for heritage walks, details from Tourist information. On Bussell Hwy: Old Settlement Craft Village; Margaret River Gallery; Margaret River Pottery. Melting Pot Glass Studio, Boodjidup Rd. 1885 Inn and restaurant, Farrelly St; formerly 1885 homestead. Feb.: Award-winning Leeuwin Estate concert; Wine and food festival. **In the area:** Wineries at Cowaramup, 10 km N, Willyabrup, 20 km N, and Margaret River; Leeuwin Estate Winery, 8 km S, has restaurant with contemporary Australian paintings and picnic/barbecue facilities. Eagles Heritage, has large collection of birds of prey; 5 km S. Bellview Shell Museum, Witchcliffe, 6 km S. Boranup Gallery, Caves Rd, Boranup; 20 km S. Trout fishing and marron delicacies at Margaret River Marron Farm, 9 km SE. Pioneer Settlers Memorial, 14 km SE. The Berry Farm and Winery, 15 km SE. Canoe hire available, 22 km SE. Cheese outlets on Bussell Hwy: Fonti's and Margaret River Cheese Factory, 4 km N; Adinfern Farm, 7 km N. At Cowaramup, 10 km N: Antique-a-Brac; Excentrix; Cowaramup Pottery; Silverthread Gallery. Gunyulgup Gallery, Caves Rd, near Yallingup, 39 km N. Ellensbrook Homestead (1853–5), National Trust property, 15 km NW. Prevelly, on coast 8 km W; Greek Chapel at Prevelly Park. Mammoth Cave, 21 km SW, features fossil remains of prehistoric animals; 4 km on is Lake Cave. Other coastal areas worth visiting include Gracetown, 15 km NW; Redgate, 10 km S; Hamelin Bay, 34 km S. Augusta–Busselton, Margaret River and Hamelin Bay Heritage Trails; details from Tourist information. **Tourist information:** cnr Tunbridge Rd and Bussell Hwy; (097) 57 2911. **Accommodation:** 1 hotel, 4 motels, 10 B&B, 2 hostels, 4 cara./camp. parks.

Meekatharra   Pop. 1414

MAP REF. 365 I11, 368 C12

Meekatharra lies 768 km NE of Perth on the Great Northern Hwy. Gold, copper and other minerals are mined, and there are huge sheep and cattle stations in the area. Meekatharra was once important as the railhead for cattle that had travelled overland from the Northern Territory or the East Kimberley. **Of interest:** State Battery relics, Main St. School of the Air, High St; open to public during school term. Old court house, Darlot St. **In the area:** Old goldmining towns, relics of mining equipment, mine shafts; several mines, including Peak Hill and Nannine, have reopened. Peace Gorge (The Granites), 5 km N. Bilyuin Pool, 88 km NW, for swimming. Mt Gould, 156 km NW; nearby, restored

The Goldfields

The land that boasted the first goldmining boom in Western Australia is almost as forbidding as that of the far north-west. This is the vast region to the east of Perth that contains the famous towns of Kalgoorlie-Boulder, Coolgardie, Norseman, Kambalda, Leonora, Gwalia and Laverton, with Kalgoorlie-Boulder the main centre.

The western gold rush began in 1892 with strikes around **Coolgardie**. The town sprang up from nowhere and enjoyed a boisterous but short life. With great optimism diggers flocked to the area. In 1900 there were 15 000 people, today Coolgardie has a population of 1063. The grand old court house, built at the height of the boom, is used now as a museum and has a record of life on the fields as it once was.

In 1893 Irishman Paddy Hannan made a bigger strike of gold at Kalgoorlie. The area became known as the Golden Mile, reputedly the richest square mile in the world. Kalgoorlie and its twin town Boulder boasted a population of 30 000 in 1902.

The modern **Kalgoorlie-Boulder** is a prosperous goldmining centre, producing 70 per cent of the gold mined in Australia. At Hannans North Historical Mining Complex visitors can don a hard hat and cap lamp, and go below the surface, where guides explain the hardships endured by the miners in their search for gold. To the south is **Kambalda**, a new boom town, founded on rich nickel deposits.

Most of the towns north of Kalgoorlie are alive again as a result of the current goldmining operations. Deep underground mines are being replaced by massive open-cuts, which create their own adjacent table top mountains of overburden. The little town of Menzies is a shadow of its former self. The renovated, stately old Gwalia Hotel just outside **Leonora** is one of the few buildings left in what was once one of the State's most prosperous gold-mining centres.

Kanowna once boasted a population of 12 000. Now all that remains is old and new mine workings, and historic markers describing what used to be. Siberia, Broad Arrow, Niagara and Bulong are the exotic names of some of the towns that flourished and died in a few short years. Nevertheless, mining is once again active in most of these areas.

See also: individual entries in A–Z listing for those towns indicated by bold type.

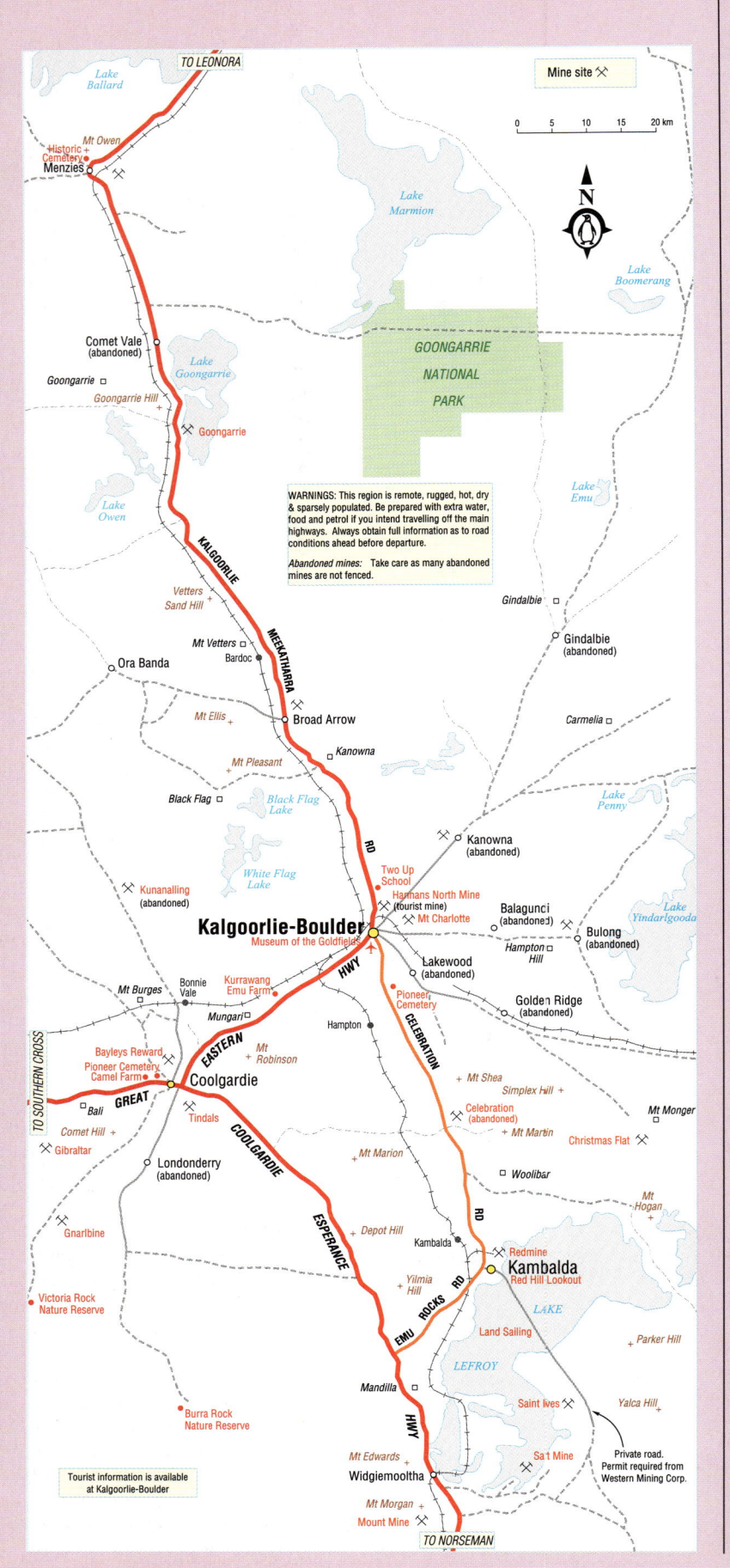

police station. Yagahong Hill, 40 km SE. **Tourist information:** Shire Offices, Main St; (099) 81 1002. **Accommodation:** 2 hotels, 2 motels, 1 cara./camp. park.

Merredin   Pop. 3068

MAP REF. 364 I2, 366 F7

A main junction on the important Kalgoorlie–Perth railway line, this important wheat centre is situated 259 km E from Perth. During the late 1800s, Merredin grew up as a shanty town as miners stopped on their way to the goldfields. The town has excellent parks and recreation facilities. **Of interest:** Cummins Theatre (1926), Bates St, oldest theatre outside Perth. Military Museum, East Barrack St, has World War II collection; also departure point for Merredin Peak Heritage Trail (self-guide drive or walk) featuring wildflowers in season, and a number of sites of historical and geological interest; details from Tourist information. Old Railway Station Museum, Great Eastern Hwy. CBH wheat storage and transfer depot, Gamenya Ave, is largest horizontal storage depot in southern hemisphere, with a capacity of 220 000 tonnes. Oct.: Vintage car festival (odd-numbered years). **In the area:** Pumping Station No. 4 (1902), 3 km W, designed by C. Y. O'Connor, a fine example of early industrial architecture; station closed 1960 to make way for electrically driven stations. Folk Museum, Kellerberrin, 55 km W. Durakoppin Wildlife Sanctuary, 27 km N of Kellerberrin, and Gardner Flora Reserve, 35 km SW. Totadgin Dam Reserve, 16 km SW; Totadgin Rock has wave formation similar to Wave Rock. At Bruce Rock, 50 km SW: museum, craft centre and Australia's smallest bank. Good views from summit of Kokerbin Rock, 90 km SW. Picnics and bushwalking near Hunts Dam, 5 km N. Lake Chandler, 45 km N. Mangowine Homestead, Nungarin, 56 km NW, a National Trust property. Museum, at Koorda, 140 km NW, several wildlife reserves in vicinity. **Tourist information:** Barrack St; (090) 41 1668. **Accommodation:** 2 hotels, 3 motels, 2 cara./camp. parks. **See also:** Crossing the Nullarbor.

Mingenew   Pop. 357

MAP REF. 366 B4

The little town of Mingenew is in the wheat district of the mid-west, 378 km N of Perth. **Of interest:** Museum, Victoria St, in small, original school building, displays pioneer relics. Views of surrounding wheat-growing area from Mingenew Hill Lookout and Pioneer Memorial, off Mingenew–Mullewa Rd. Sept.: Lions expo (includes wildflower display). **In the area:** Picnic spots at Depot Hill, 15 km W. Dongara, 53 km W, has superb beaches and excellent fishing. At Coalseam Conservation Park, 32 km NE: the State's first coal shafts, Irwin Gorge, riverbed rocks for rockhunters and wildflowers in spring. **Tourist information:** Post Office building, Midland St; (099) 28 1081. **Accommodation:** 1 hotel, 1 cara./camp. park.

Morawa   Pop. 624

MAP REF. 366 C4

Renowned for its grain harvests, Morawa is in the mid-west, 394 km N of Perth. The surrounding area is renowned for its wildflowers in spring. **Of interest:** In Prater St: Historical Museum, open by appt; St David's Anglican Church. Holy Cross Catholic Church, Davis St. Jo's Taxidermy, Winfield St. Oct.: Music spectacular. **In the area:** Koolanooka Springs Reserve, ideal for picnics, and Koolanooka Hills mine site, 24 km E. Bilya Rock Reserve, 4 km W, with 20-min. walk around rock. **Tourist information:** Shire Offices, Prater St; (099) 71 1004. **Accommodation:** 1 hotel/motel, 1 cara./camp. park.

Mount Barker   Pop. 1520

MAP REF. 361 M9, 364 H12, 366 E12

Mount Barker is a quiet, friendly town in the Great Southern district of WA. It is 360 km from Perth, with the Stirling Ranges to the north and the Porongurups to the east. Mt Barker was discovered by Europeans in 1829 and settlers arrived in the 1830s. Vineyards in the area, though relatively new, are producing some top-quality wines. **Of interest:** Historic police station and gaol (1868), Albany Hwy, now museum (open Sat., Sun. and school holidays). Banksia Farm, western outskirts of town (cnr Pearce and Marmion Sts). Heritage trail, 30 km drive through town and surrounds; contact Tourist information for map. Mar.: Field Day wine festival. Nov.: Vintage motorbike hill climb. **In the area:** Wineries, contact Tourist information for details. Lookout on summit of Mt Barker, 5 km SW, pinpointed by 168-m-high television tower, has excellent views of Stirling Ranges across to Albany, worth the drive. St Werburgh's Chapel (1872), 12 km SW, a small mud-walled chapel, privately-owned, overlooking Hay River Valley. Craft at Narrikup Country Store, 16 km S. Porongurup National Park, 24 km E, features granite peaks, karri forests and brilliant seasonal wildflowers. Tall peaks, picturesque plains and over 1000 species of native flora at Stirling Range National Park, 80 km NE. Historic town of Kendenup, 16 km N, location of WA's first gold find. Lake Poorrarecup, 50 km NW; area also noted for orchids and brown and red boronia, which bloom Sept.–Nov. **Tourist information:** 57 Lowood Rd; (098) 51 1163. **Accommodation:** 1 hotel, 1 hotel/motel, 1 motel, 1 cara./camp. park. **See also:** The Great Southern.

Mount Magnet   Pop. 1076

MAP REF. 366 E2

The goldmining town of Mount Magnet, a popular stopping-place for motorists driving north to Port Hedland, is 562 km from Perth on the Great Northern Hwy. The surrounding land is used for pastoral farming. There are spectacular wildflowers in the area in spring. **In the area:** Tourist drive (37 km) includes working open-cut gold mine, The Granites and various ghost towns; obtain map from Tourist information. Fossicking for gemstones, but take care as there are dangerous old mine shafts in the area. The Granites, 7 km N, has Aboriginal rock art and picnic spot nearby. Ghost town, Lennonville, 11 km N. Near Sandstone, 166 km E: The Brewery, an historic constructed cave formerly used for beer storage; London Bridge, a rock formation. **Tourist information:** Hepburn St; (099) 63 4172. **Accommodation:** 2 hotel/motels, 1 cara./camp. park.

Mullewa   Pop. 739

MAP REF. 366 B3

Gateway to the Murchison goldfields, Mullewa is 99 km from Geraldton. **Of interest:** Kembla Zoo, Stock Rd. In Maitland Rd: Our Lady of Mount Carmel Church; Monsignor John C. Hawes Priesthouse Museum. Water Supply Reserve, Lovers Lane, features native plants. Mons. Hawes Heritage Trail, details from Tourist information. Aug.–Sept.: Wildflower show. Sept.: Agricultural show. **In the area:** Scenic drive, contact Tourist information. Waterfalls after heavy rain, 5 km N, near airport. Tallering Peak and Gorge, 58 km N, has spectacular wildflowers in spring. Bindoo Hill Glacier Bed, 40 km NW. Tenindewa Pioneer Well (1900s), 18 km W, a stone-lined well. Butterabby grave site, 18 km S, burial-place of Aborigines hanged there after clash with European settlers. St Mary's Agricultural School, 40 km SE near Tardun. The Woolly Baa Baa at Tallering Station, 40 km NE, has gallery, sheepskin and wool products, and accommodation and camping; open Apr.–Oct. **Tourist information:** Jose St (May–Nov.) or Shire Offices, Maitland Rd; (099) 61 1007. **Accommodation:** 1 hotel, 1 hotel/motel, 1 cara./camp.park.

Mundaring   Pop. 1542

MAP REF. 356 E4, 354 D3, 366 C8

Mundaring is situated on the Great Eastern Hwy, 34 km E of Perth. The picturesque Mundaring Weir, 8 km S of town, is the source of water for the eastern goldfields. The original dam was opened in 1903, and the original pumping station was used until 1955. The attractive hilly bush setting makes the weir a popular picnic spot in summer. **Of interest:** Eastern Hills Showcase, Hartung St, collection of WA arts and crafts in magnificent 1890s home. Fred Jacoby Park, Mundaring Weir Rd, has picnic/barbecue facilities. Sculpture Park, Jacoby St, with sculptures by WA artists. **In the area:** Several heritage trails, including Farming Heritage Trail and John Forrest Heritage Trail; contact Tourist information. Lake Leschenaultia, 12 km NW, for swimming and canoeing; walks, camping and picnic/barbecue facilities, and miniature scenic railway on shore. Walyunga National Park, 30 km NW, a beautiful bushland park and location for Avon Descent, a major white-water canoeing event held each August. Old Mahogany Inn (1842), 3 km W, WA's oldest residential inn. Mount Olive Stained Glass Studio, 6 km W. Quatre Sessions Heritage Rose Garden, 9 km W, one of state's largest private collections. At Darlington, 10 km W: Darling Estate Winery, Nelson Rd; open Thurs.–Sun.; Brook Studio, open Fri.–Sun. John Forrest National Park, 26 km W, on high point of Darling Range, picnic spot beside natural pool at Rocky Pool. The C. Y. O'Connor Museum (1880s), 8 km S, housed in former pumphouse building, features models of Eastern Goldfields water supply. Further 15 km along road, near Kalamunda: Kalamunda National Park; History Village, a collection of historic buildings (open Sat.–Thurs.). Carosa Vineyard, 7 km S at Mt Helena; open Sat. and Sun. **Tourist information:** Shire Offices, 7000 Great Eastern Hwy; (09) 290 6666. **Accommodation:** 1 hotel/ motel, 1 hostel, 1 cara. park.

Mundrabilla   Pop. 11

MAP REF. 367 Q8

A tiny settlement on the Eyre Hwy where travellers can break the journey across the continent. There is a bird and animal sanctuary behind the motel. **Tourist information:** Roadhouse; (090) 39 3465. **Accommodation:** 1 motel, 1 cara./camp. park.

Nannup   Pop. 472

MAP REF. 357 G10, 360 A4, 364 C10, 366 C11

Nannup is a quiet, friendly town in the Blackwood Valley, 290 km S of Perth. The surrounding countryside is lush, gently rolling pasture alongside jarrah and pine forests. **Of interest:** In Brockman St: old police station (1922); Arboretum. In Warren Rd: art and craft centre; Bunnings Timber Mill, largest jarrah sawmill in State (guided tours available Mon., Wed. and Fri.); Robz Art Gallery and Nannup Temptations and Crafty Creations, for local art and craft including jarrah goods. Gemstone Museum, closed Wed. Easter: Music festival. Sept.: Discovery weekend. **In the area:** Walking trails, scenic drives of jarrah forest and pine plantations, and Nannup Heritage Trail; details from Tourist information. Blackwood River for canoeing and trout fishing. Barrabup Pool, 10 km W. Tathra Wines, 14 km NE. **Tourist information:** 4 Brockman St; (097) 56 1211. **Accommodation:** 1 hotel/motel, 1 B&B, 1 hostel, 2 cara./camp. parks.

Narrogin   Pop. 4638

MAP REF. 364 G6, 366 E9

The centre of prosperous agricultural country, Narrogin is 189 km SE of Perth on the Great Southern Hwy. Sheep, pigs and cereal farms are the main primary industries. Its name is derived from an Aboriginal word meaning waterhole. **Of interest:** Memorabilia at Old Butter Factory, on Great Southern Hwy, southern outskirts of town. Court House Museum (1894), Egerton St, originally a school, later district court house; open Tues., Sat. or by appt. Foxes Lair, Williams Rd, has 5 ha of natural bushland. Lions Lookout, Kipling St, for panoramic views. Restoration Group Museum, Federal St, displays cars, stationary engines and other machinery; open 3rd Sun. each month, or by appt. Centenary Park has pathway marked with 100 commemorative tiles relating to local history designed by local artists. Jan.: State gliding championships. Oct.: Spring festival; Texpo (modern farming displays). **In the area:** South Central Wheatbelt Heritage Trail, details from Tourist information. Yilliminning and Birdwhistle Rocks, 11 km E, unusual rock formations. Albert Facey's homestead, 40 km E, has a mini-zoo and local craft displays. Dryandra Woodland, 30 km NW, features walking trails and fauna including numbats and mallee fowl. **Tourist information:** 23 Egerton St; (098) 81 2064. **Accommodation:** 3 hotels, 2 motels, 1 cara./camp. park.

New Norcia   Pop. 73

MAP REF. 364 D1, 366 C6

In 1846 Spanish Benedictine monks established a mission at New Norcia, 132 km N of Perth in an attempt to help the local Aboriginal population. The handsome Spanish-inspired buildings come as a surprise, surrounded by paddocks and distant bushland. The settlement is in the secluded Moore Valley, and wheat, wool and other farm products are produced. New Norcia is owned by the Benedictine Community and is still operating as a monastery. **Of interest:** Heritage trail (2 km) includes inspection of oldest operating flour mill in WA (1879) (mill also has interpretive display), abbey church, cemetery, hotel (1927), Bishops Well, Rosendo Salvado Statue and historic olive press; brochure from Tourist information. Benedictine Community's Museum and art gallery, Great Northern Hwy, has priceless collection of religious art, both Australian and European, and Roman, Egyptian and Spanish artifacts; many gifted by

Queen Isabella of Spain; museum displays history of monk's involvement with local indigenous population; shop sells local food products and souvenirs. Group accommodation for up to 250 in old convent and college buildings (advance bookings required). Walking tours of monastery buildings avaiable; details from Tourist information. **In the area:** At Mogumber, 24 km SW, one of the State's highest timber and concrete bridges. Historic hotel at Bolgart, 49 km SE. Piawaning, 31 km NE, has magnificent stand of eucalypts just north of town. **Tourist information:** Museum and art gallery, Great Northern Hwy; (096) 54 8056. **Accommodation:** 1 hotel, 1 guest house (attached to monastery).

Newman
Pop. 5627

MAP REF. 368 D6

This town was built by Mt Newman Mining Co. for employees involved in the extraction of iron ore. Mt Newman ships its ore from Port Hedland, and the two towns are connected by a 426-km railroad. In 1981 responsibility for the town was handed over to the local shire. With the upgrading of the highway and improved tourist facilities in the town, Newman has become a popular stopping-place. **Of interest:** Tours (Mon.–Sat.) of Mt Whaleback mine, Newman Dr., largest iron ore open-cut mine in world. BHP Iron Ore Silver Jubilee Museum and Gallery, cnr Fortescue Ave and Newman Dr. Mining and pastoral museum, behind Tourist information. Radio Hill Lookout, off Newman Dr., for good views over town; walking trail and climb from museum to lookout. Aug.: Fortescue festival. **In the area:** Ophthalmia Dam, 15 km N, for swimming; picnic/barbecue facilities on shore. Good views from Mt Newman, 20 km N. Kalgans Pool, 51 km NW; day trip, 4WD access only. Eagle Rock Falls, 69 km NW, has permanent pools and picnic spots nearby; road to falls may require 4WD. Aboriginal rock carvings, rock pools and waterholes at Wanna Munna, 70 km W, and Punda (4WD only), 75 km NW. **Tourist information:** cnr Fortescue Ave and Newman Dr.;

The Pilbara

In the Pilbara there are over 3000 speakers of 28 Aboriginal languages belonging to one language 'family'. It is still common among Aboriginal people in the area to speak two or three languages, with some people able to use more. In the Port Hedland area the traditional language was Kariyarra; today you will also hear Ngarla, Nyarual Martuwangka and Nyangurnarta being spoken.

The iron ore boom in the area has created employment opportunities in this land of sand spinifex, mulga scrub and massive red mountains. Model mining-company towns have sprung up. Gardens, swimming pools, golf courses and communal activities help compensate for the isolation and harsh climate.

Dampier, on King Bay, is a modern iron-ore company town, with a major salt industry nearby. Offshore is the Woodside North West Shelf Gas Project, which is the largest single resource development undertaken in Australia; it includes a 1500-kilometre pipeline. Another side to the town is the Dampier Archipelago, comprising 42 islands of which 25 are incorporated into flora and fauna reserves. Fishing, diving, swimming, boating, camping and bushwalking allowed around and on several of these outcrops.

Roebourne, the oldest town in the north-west, has been a centre for the pastoral, copper and pearling industries. The old pearling port of **Cossack** is nearby. Inland on the Fortescue River,

Iron ore mined at Tom Price being railed to the coast for export

lush ferns, palms and lilies grow near the deep pools at Millstream, the source of water for many Pilbara towns. The **Millstream-Chichester National Park** is also well worth a visit. To the south, the fishing village of **Onslow** and its offshore islands is the perfect holiday retreat.

Karratha is a modern town and regional centre, as is **Wickham**. Wickham's port at Cape Lambert has the tallest and second-longest jetty in Australia, standing 18.5 metres above water and 3 kilometres long. At **Port Hedland**, streamlined port facilities cope with more tonnage than any other port in the country. Ore mined inland at **Tom Price**, **Newman**, Paraburdoo and other centres is railed on giant trains to the ports for export.

Fishing in the Port Hedland area is good, with many world records being set. Swimming in the sea can be dangerous, because sharks, sea snakes and poisonous stone fish frequent the waters; always make local enquiries before you swim.

Port Hedland also offers the visitor historic sites, exhibition centres, interesting flora and fauna, and sporting facilities. Tom Price affords easy access to the magnificent gorges in the **Karijini** (Hamersley Range) **National Park**. And, of course, there is **Marble Bar**, considered to be the hottest place in Australia and keeping alive the tradition of the great Australian outback.

Despite great improvements to the main roads – many are sealed – they are still liable to deterioration, and can have long stretches of rough and dangerous surface. It is wise to check local road conditions before setting out.

For further information contact the Tom Price Tourist Bureau, Central Rd, Tom Price; (091) 88 1112. **See also:** National Parks and individual town entries for those parks and towns indicated by bold type; and Outback Motoring. **Map reference:** 365 I3, 368 B4.

(091) 75 2888. **Accommodation:** 1 motel, 2 cara./ camp. parks. **See also:** The Hamersley Range; The Pilbara.

Norseman   Pop. 1398

MAP REF. 367 J8

Norseman, 195 km S of Kalgoorlie, is the last large town on the Eyre Hwy for travellers heading east towards SA. Gold put Norseman on the map in the early 1890s, and the richest quartz reef in Australia is still being mined today. The town is steeped in goldmining history, with colossal tailings dumps a reminder. The area is popular with amateur prospectors and gemstone collectors; gemstone fossicking permits are available from Tourist information. **Of interest:** Historical Collection, Battery Rd, includes mining tools and household items. Post Office (1896), cnr Prinsep and Ra Sts. Heritage trail (33 km), following original Cobb & Co. route, including descent into a 'decline'; details from Tourist information. In Roberts St: statue, commemorates horse called Norseman, who allegedly pawed the ground and unearthed a nugget of gold, thus starting a gold rush in area; Norseman Tourist Reception Centre, with visitor facilities, day parking and picnic area. Beacon Hill, Mines Rd, offers good views of surrounding salt lakes (spectacular at sunrise and sunset). **In the area:** Dundas Rocks, 22 km S, are 550 million years old; excellent picnic area and old Dundas town site nearby. Bromus Dam, 32 km S, freshwater dam with picnic area nearby. Peak Charles, 50 km S then 40 km off hwy; energetic climbers are rewarded with magnificent views. Gemstone leases on Eyre Hwy and off Kalgoorlie Hwy; details from Tourist information. Five km east of town: Old mines, Jimberlana Dyke, reputedly one of oldest geological areas in world; also Mt Jimberlana with walking trail to summit and views. Buldania Rocks, 28 km E, has picnic area and beautiful wildflowers in spring. To south-west, Frank Hahn National Park, 50 km E of Lake King township, traversed by Lake King–Norseman Rd; if travelling this road, check road conditions before departure and note that there are no visitor facilities or supplies available between Norseman and Lake King. **Tourist information:** 68 Roberts St; (090) 39 1071. **Accommodation:** 2 hotels, 2 motels, 1 hostel, 1 cara./camp. park. **See also:** Crossing the Nullarbor; The Goldfields.

Northam   Pop. 6560

MAP REF. 356 H2, 364 E3, 366 D7

The regional centre of the fertile Avon Valley at the junction of the Avon and Mortlock Rivers, Northam is an attractive rural town. On the Great Eastern Hwy, 99 km E of Perth, it is an important supply point for the farms of the eastern wheat belt. Northam is also a major railway centre and the main depot for the Goldfields Water Scheme, which takes water as far east as Kalgoorlie. WA's largest military training camp is on the outskirts of town. **Of interest:** In Wellington St: Old Police Station (1866), court house (1896), town hall (1897), and Avon Valley Arts Society art and craft shop. Flour Mill (1871), Newcastle St. In Fitzgerald St: Old Railway Station Museum, and Shamrock Hotel (1886), fully renovated. Large swinging bridge over Avon River behind Tourist information. Weir across river, near Peel Tce bridge, forms lake that has a colony of white swans and many other species of native birdlife. Morby Cottage (1836), Old York Rd, built by the Morrells, a pioneer family. National Trust-classified Sir James Mitchell House (1905), cnr Duke and Hawes Sts. Historic town walk, Northam–Katrine Heritage Trail and Farming Heritage Trail; details from Tourist information. Nov.: Avon Valley country music festival. **In the area:** Hot-air ballooning (in cooler months), horseriding and canoeing. Blue Gum Camel Farm, offers camel- and trail-riding in picturesque bushland surroundings; near Spencer Brook Rd at Clackline, 19 km SW. Muresk Agricultural College, 10 km S, former early farming property. At Dowerin, 58 km NE: museum, craft centre, Hagbooms Lake. In spring, wildflowers abound near Wubin, 190 km N. **Tourist information:** 138 Fitzgerald St; (096) 22 2100. **Accommodation:** 4 hotels, 1 motel, 3 B&B, 1 cara./camp. park.

Northampton   Pop. 786

MAP REF. 366 A3

Northampton nestles among gentle hills in the valley of Nokarena Brook, 48 km N of Geraldton. Inland there is picturesque country with vivid wildflowers in spring. The drive west leads to the coast, with beaches for swimming and fishing. **Of interest:** In Hampton Rd: Chiverton House Folk Museum; open Thurs.–Sun.; Bowerbird Collection, a private collection of memorabilia; open Tues.–Sun; St Mary's Convent and Church, designed by Mons. Hawes. Gwalla church site and cemetery, Gwalla St. Miners' cottages (1860s), Brook St. **In the area:** Wildflower tours in spring, contact Tourist information. Alma Schoolhouse, 12 km N. Near coast at Port Gregory, 47 km NW: Lynton Station, including ruins of labour-hiring depot for convicts, dating from 1800s; Lynton House, (not open), a squat building with slits for windows, probably erected as protection from hostile Aborigines; Sanford House. Hutt Lagoon, near Port Gregory, turns pink in light of midday sun. At Horrocks Beach, 20 km W: pleasant bays, sandy beaches and good fishing. **Tourist information:** Nagle Centre, Hampton Rd; (099) 34 1488. **Accommodation:** 2 hotels, 1 hotel/motel, 1 hostel, 1 cara./camp. park.

Northcliffe   Pop. 190

MAP REF. 360 C9, 364 D12, 366 D12

Magnificent virgin karri forests surround the little township of Northcliffe, 31 km S of Pemberton in the extreme south-west corner of the State. Unique flora and fauna is to be found in this area. **Of interest:** In Wheatley Coast Rd: Pioneer Museum, has historical relics and photographs; at Tourist information, rock and mineral collection, Aboriginal Interpretation Room and photographic folio of native flora and birds; Northcliffe Art and Craft. Off Wheatley Coast Rd, South West Timber Trekking Company, offers horseriding along forest tracks. Adjacent to town, Forest Park, has Hollow Butt Karri and Twin Karri walking trails, and picnic areas. Fishing, Warren River. Oct.: Mountain bike championship. **In the area:** Sandy beaches and good fishing. Mt Chudalup, 20 km S, a giant granite outcrop with walking trail to summit for views. Point D'Entrecasteaux, 27 km S; cliffs popular with climbers. Windy Harbour and Salmon Beach, 29 km S. Bibbulmun Track links the three national parks: D'Entresteaux (5 km S), Warren (20 km NW), and Shannon, (30 km E). Boorara Tree (once used as fire lookout) and Lane-Poole Falls, 18 km SE. **Tourist information:** Adjacent to Pioneer Museum, Wheatley

Karri forest near Pemberton

Coast Rd; (097) 76 7203. **Accommodation:** 1 hotel, 1 cara./camp. park.

Onslow Pop. 881

MAP REF. 365 D3

Onslow, on the north-west coast of the State, is important as the base for the gas and oil fields off the coast. The town was originally at the mouth of the Ashburton River, but was moved to Beadon Bay after constant cyclones caused the river to silt up. The remains of the old town site can still be seen. Onslow was a bustling pearling centre and in the 1890s gold was discovered. During World War II, US, British and Dutch submarines refuelled here, and the town was bombed twice. In 1952 it was the mainland base for Britain's nuclear experiments at Monte Bello Islands. **Of interest:** Heritage trail, contact Tourist information for brochure. July: Bougainvillea festival. **In the area:** Excellent fishing. Native fauna, including emus, red kangaroos, sand goannas, and a variety of birdlife. The Sturt desert pea and Ashburton pea are among the many wildflowers that bloom in spring in the area. **Tourist information:** Shire Offices, Second Ave; (091) 84 6001. **Accommodation:** 1 hotel/motel, 2 cara./camp. parks.

Pemberton Pop. 934

MAP REF. 360 C7, 364 D11, 366 C11

The town of Pemberton, 335 km s of Perth, is nestled in a quiet valley, surrounded by towering karri forests. This lush forest area has some of the tallest hardwood trees in the world, and, in spring, brilliant flowering bush plants. Pemberton is known as a centre for high-quality woodcraft. **Of interest:** Craft outlets include Pemberton Arts and Craft, Broadway Ave; Warren River Arts and Craft and Peter Kovacsy Studio in Jamieson St; Fine Woodcraft Gallery, Dickinson St. In Brockman St: Karri Visitors Centre, includes museum, with collection of historic photographs and authentic forestry equipment, and Karri Forest Discovery Centre; Pemberton Sawmill, guided tours available Mon.–Fri. Pemberton Tramway, tramcars based on 1907 Fremantle trams operate daily through tall-forest country between Pemberton and Northcliffe; depart from railway station, Railway Cres. Forest Industry tours into logging and regrowth areas; walking trails; scenic bus tours; 4WD adventure tours, 2 hours to overnight; and horseriding, including pub crawl; contact Tourist information for details. On Pump Hill Rd: Forest Park and Pool, offers walking trails and picnic spots; Trout and Marron Hatchery, supplies WA rivers and dams; daily tours available. Mar.: King karri karnival. **In the area:** Fishing in local rivers; inland fishing licence required for trout and marron, contact Tourist information. Wineries: Warren Vineyard, Dickinson St; Gloucester Ridge, Burma Rd; Mountford Wines, Bamess Rd; Salitage, Vasse Hwy; winery tours available, contact Tourist information. Gloucester Tree, signposted off Brockman St, tallest fire lookout in world, (over 60 m high with 150 rungs spiralling upwards); open for climbing during daylight hours. Moon's Crossing, 18 km SE, for picnics; 4WD access in winter. The Cascades, 8 km s, for picnics, bushwalking and fishing. Brockman Saw Pit, 13 km s, restored to show how timber was sawn in 1860s. Further south at Windy Harbour: sandy beaches, rugged coast and good fishing. King Trout Farm, 8 km SW. Warren National Park, 9 km SW, includes some of best accessible virgin karri forest, also Marianne North Tree; (tree was subject of painting by artist). Swamp Willow Farm on Hawke Rd near park, 12 km SW, for local wood-craft. Deep Forest Arabian Stud Farm, 13 km W on Green Rd off Vasse Hwy. Eagle Springs marron farm, 18 km W. Nearby, Beedelup National Park, features falls, suspension bridge, magnificent wildflowers in spring and a giant karri tree with a hole cut through it. Donnelly River Wines, 35 km NW. Marron and dairy farm, 1 km N. Big Brook Dam and Arboretum, 7 km N. Founders Forest, 10 km N on Smiths Rd, has karri trees over 120 years old. Piano Gully Vineyard, 24 km NE, off South Western Hwy. **Tourist information:** Karri Visitors Centre, Brockman St; (097) 76 1133. **Accommodation:** 1 hotel/motel, 2 motels, 2 B&B, 1 hostel, 1 cara./camp. park. **See also:** The South-west.

Perenjori Pop. 250

MAP REF. 366 C4

Located on the Wubin–Mullewa Hwy (known as 'Wildflower Way'), 352 km NE of Perth, Perenjori lies on the fringes of the Murchison goldfields and the great sheep stations of the west. **Of interest:** Historical Museum behind Tourist information, Fowler St; open June–Oct. Arts and Crafts Centre, Russell St. **In the area:** Wildflowers in season, July–Sept. Many scenic drives, brochures at Tourist information. Salt lakes, including Mongers Lake (lookout near lake), 50 km NE; Yarra Yarra Lakes, 58 km SW near Three Springs; variety of waterbirds to be seen. Perenjori–Rothsay Heritage Trail (180 km), recalls early goldmining days; details from Tourist information. For fossickers, many gemstones in this mineral-rich region. Many gold mines in surrounding area; care should be taken, as unfenced pits make the area dangerous. Aboriginal Stones at Damperwah Soak, 40 km NE (4WD access only). **Tourist information:** Fowler St; (099) 73 1105. **Accommodation:** 1 hotel, 1 cara./camp. park.

Pingelly   Pop. 763

MAP REF. 364 F5, 366 D9

On the Great Southern Hwy, 154 km SE of Perth, Pingelly is part of the central southern farming district. The cutting of sandalwood was once a local industry, but today the land is given over to sheep and wheat. **Of interest:** In Parade St: Community Craft Centre; Court House Museum. Apex Lookout, Stone St, for fine views of town and country. Aug.: Art and tulip festival. **In the area:** Moorumbine Heritage Trail, details from Tourist information. Historic St Patrick's Church (1873), Moorumbine, 10 km E. Tuttanning Flora and Fauna Reserve, 21 km E. Yealering Lake and picnic ground, 58 km E. County Peak Lookout, 30 m N. Boyagin Rock Picnic Ground and Reserve, 26 km NW. Christmas Tree Well picnic area, 80 km NW. Dryandra Reserve, 40 km SW, an ecological oasis with unique flora and fauna including the numbat, WA's fauna emblem; timber also produced. **Tourist information:** Shire Offices, 17 Queen St; (098) 87 1066. **Accommodation:** 1 hotel, 1 motel, 1 cara./camp. park.

Pinjarra   Pop. 1779

MAP REF. 356 C10, 364 C6, 366 C9

Pinjarra is a pleasant drive 84 km S of Perth, along the shaded South Western Hwy. The town has a picturesque setting on the banks of the Murray River in one of the earliest established districts in WA. The Alcoa Refinery, north-east of town on the South Western Hwy, is the largest alumina refinery in Australia. Pinjarra is a good base for exploring the area. **Of interest:** In Henry St: St John's Church (1862), Heritage Rose Garden, Liveringa (1874), Old School (1896), and Teacher's House. Edenvale (1888), George St. **In the area:** Heritage trail; details from Tourist information. Forest Range Tour, an old-style steam train from Pinjarra to Dwellingup and return run by Hotham Valley Tourist Railway (May–Oct.); departs West Rail Station, off South Western Hwy. Swimming at Scarp Pool, 20 km SE. Marrinup Falls, 3-km walk from Scarp Rd, Dwellingup, 24 km SE. Alcoa Scarp Lookout, 14 km E, for good views of coastal plain and surrounding farming area. Athlone Angora Stud and Goat Farm, 16 km E. Alcoa Refinery, 4 km NE; bus tours available. At North Dandalup, 10 km NE: Whittakers Mill, for bushwalking, camping and barbecues. Award-winning Tumbulgum Farm, 38 km N at Mundijong, features native and farm animals, Aboriginal culture and farm shows, and WA products sales. Yalgorup National Park on coast. Old Blythewood (1860s), 4 km S, a former post office, coaching inn and family home; check opening times. Lake Navarino Forest Resort and Waroona Dam, 33 km S, for watersports, fishing, walking and horseriding. **Tourist information:** Murray Tourist Centre (in Edenvale stately home), George St; (09) 531 1438. **Accommodation:** 4 hotels, 1 motel, 7 cara./camp. parks. **See also:** The South-west.

Point Samson   Pop. 180

MAP REF. 365 G1, 368 A1

Point Samson was named in honour of Michael Samson, who accompanied the district's first settler, Walter Padbury, on his 1863 journey. The town was established in 1910 as the major port for the Roebourne district, replacing Cossack, where the harbour had silted up after a cyclone. The port was very active for many years, but today the town supports a small fishing industry and its extremely attractive setting has made it a popular beach destination. **Of interest:** Beach is protected by a coral reef; good swimming, fishing and skindiving. Honeymoon Cove, Johns Creek Rd, for swimming and picnicking. Nearby at John's Harbour, jetty and boat ramp. Trawlers Tavern, Point Samson Rd, for local seafood. **In the area:** Excellent fishing in tidal rivers and offshore; coast renowned for its game-fishing. Emma Withnell Heritage Trail; details from Tourist information. Sam's Creek, 1 km N, a fishing boat harbour. Samson Reef can be explored at low tide. **Tourist information:** Point Samson Fisheries, Point Samson Rd; (091) 87 1414. **Accommodation:** 1 cara./camp. park.

Port Hedland   Pop. 11 344

MAP REF. 368 C1, 370 B13

Port Hedland's remarkable growth has been due to the iron-ore boom, which started in the early 1960s. The town was named after Captain Peter Hedland, who reached the harbour in 1829. Today Port Hedland handles the largest tonnage of any Australian port. Iron ore from some of the world's biggest mines is loaded on to the world's biggest ore carriers. The 2-km-long trains operated by BHP Iron Ore arrive six times daily. Salt production is another major industry, with about 2 million tonnes exported per annum. **Of interest:** Observation Tower, at Tourist information, Wedge St. Lions Park, Hunt St, has pioneer relics. Royal Flying Doctor Base, Richardson St; 11.15 a.m. Mon.–Fri. BHP mine tours; daily Mar.–Sept., 4 times a week Oct.–Feb.; book at Tourist information. Don Rhodes Mining Museum, Wilson St. At Two Mile Ridge, opp. fire brigade in Wilson St, Aboriginal carvings in limestone ridge (open Mon.–Fri.). Historic St Matthew's Church (1917), Edgar St, now art gallery and exhibition centre. Old Port Hedland cemetery, Stevens St, has graves of early gold prospectors, and Japanese pearl divers. Aug.: Spinifex spree. **In the area:** Stairway to the Moon, natural wonder created when full moon rises over shoreline at low tide; best seen alongside caravan park at Cooke Point, details from Tourist information. Picnic, fish and swim safely at Pretty Pool, next to Cooke Point caravan park. (Poisonous stone fish frequent coast, especially Nov.–Mar.; make local inquiries before swimming in sea.) At Cargill Salt, 8 km S, giant cone-shaped mounds of salt awaiting export. Whale-watching trips June–Oct. Excellent fishing; charter boat hire. Birdlife is abundant in district; watch for bustards, eagles, cockatoos, galahs, ibises, pelicans and parrots. **Tourist information:** 13 Wedge St; (091) 73 1650. **Accommodation:** 6 hotel/motels, 1 hostel, 3 cara./camp. parks. **See also:** The Pilbara.

Ravensthorpe   Pop. 392

MAP REF. 366 H10

Ravensthorpe, situated 533 km SE of Perth, is the centre of the old Phillips

River goldfield. Copper mining was also important here, reaching a peak in the late 1960s; the last copper mine shut in 1978. Many old mine shafts can be seen around the district. Wheat and sheep are the local industries. **Of interest:** Historic buildings: Anglican Church, Dunn St; 'the Big House', old mine manager's house, Carlisle St; in Morgan St, Dance Cottage (museum), Palace Hotel and restored Commercial Hotel (now Community Centre). Also in Morgan St, Rangeview Park, features plant species from Fitzgerald River National Park. Sept.: Wildflower display, features over 600 species from Fitzgerald River National Park. **In the area:** Catlin Creek Heritage Trail and short scenic drives; details from Tourist information. Rock-collecting; check locally to avoid trespass. Ravensthorpe Range, 3 km N, and Mt Desmond, 10 km SE, for views. WA Time Meridian at first rest bay west of town. Fitzgerald River National Park, 46 km S, now Biosphere Reserve for UNESCO. Old copper smelter, 2 km E. **Tourist information:** Community Centre, Morgan St; (098) 38 1277. **Accommodation:** 1 hotel/motel, 1 motel, 1 cara./camp. park.

Rockingham

Pop. 36 675

MAP REF. 356 B7, 364 C4, 366 C8

At the southern end of Cockburn Sound, 45 km S of Perth, Rockingham is a coastal city and seaside resort. Begun in 1872 as a port, the harbour fell into disuse with the opening of the Fremantle inner harbour in 1897. Today its magnificent golden beaches and protected waters are Rockingham's main attraction. **Of interest:** Museum, Kent St, features local history exhibits. Lookout at Point Peron, Point Peron Rd. In Civic Bvd.: Art Gallery; Art and Craft Centre. Sun. markets, Flinders Lane. Jan.: Cockburn yachting regatta. Nov.: Rocky Spring festival. Dec.: Christmas regatta. **In the area:** Old Rockingham Heritage Trail and Rockingham–Jarrahdale Heritage Trail; free tour of Alcoa's bauxite mine and reforestation areas at Jarrahdale, details from Tourist information. Penguin Island, with a colony of little (fairy) penguins. Garden

The Hamersley Range

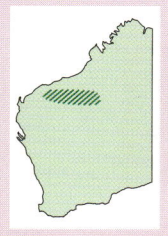

Stretching over 300 kilometres through the heart of the mineral-rich Pilbara, the Hamersley Range forms a wild and magnificent panorama. The mountains slope gently up from the south to the flat-topped outcrops and Western Australia's highest peak, Mt Meharry. In the north they rise majestically from golden spinifex plains.

Although the main activity in the area is centred on the mining towns of **Tom Price**, Paraburdoo, **Newman** and others, visitors will find many other areas of interest. Spectacular gorges have been carved by watercourses. Precipitous walls of rock are layered in colours from reddish brown to green, and blue to pink in the changing light. The gorges are up to 50 metres deep, and at their base are sometimes only one metre wide. Others have wide, crystal-clear pools. Lush green vegetation thrives and the gorges are cool oases in the harsh climate.

Tom Price is a good base from which to explore the beauty of the Hamersley Range. The breathtaking Dales Gorge, approached through Yampire Gorge, is 45 kilometres long. Crystal-clear pools and the splendid Fortescue Falls are found here. The small but intriguing Rio Tinto Gorge, and Hamersley Gorge with its folded bands of coloured rock, are also quite beautiful.

One particularly enchanting oasis in the Hamersley Range area is **Millstream-Chichester**

Iron stone rocks and spinifex in the Hamersley Range

National Park, on the Fortescue River, inland from Roebourne. Thousands of birds flock to this delightful spot, where ferns, lilies, palms and rushes grow in abundance. There are two long, deep, natural pools. The springs produce over 36 million litres of water a day from an underground basin, which is piped to Roebourne, Dampier, Karratha, Wickham and Cape Lambert. In contrast to the **Karijini (Hamersley Range) National Park**, the scenery in the Millstream-Chichester National Park varies from magnificent views over the coastal plain to the deep permanent river pools of tropical Millstream. This attractive spot offers excellent swimming conditions and pleasant camping areas.

The Hamersley Range is rugged, exciting country, and is enticing and often beautiful. Keep in mind, however, that you are travelling in remote areas. Read the section on Outback Motoring before departure. Old roads are being improved and new ones constructed in an effort to open up one of the oldest areas in the world.

For further information contact Tom Price Tourist Bureau, Central Rd, Tom Price; (091) 88 1112. **See also:** National Parks and individual town entries for those parks and towns indicated by bold type. **Map references:** 365 G3, 368 A4.

Island, home to HMAS *Stirling*, naval base; access by private boat during the day, or by bus tour from Perth weekly; causeway link to mainland closed to public. Offshore coral reefs and wrecks, popular with dive enthusiasts; diving excursions and various cruises available, contact Tourist information. Shoalwater Bay Islands Marine Park, 6 km NW, extends from just south of Garden Island to Becher Point in Warnbro; cruises of park available, and swim with the dolphins and seals tours Oct.–June, depart from Mersey Point Jetty. Near Lake Richmond, 4 km S, walks, freshwater flora and fauna, and domed stromalites. Marapana Wildlife World, 7 km S, State's first drive-through deer and wildlife park. Seal Island cruises from Safety Bay, 10 km S. Wineries: Baldivis Estate, 15 km SE; Peel Estate, 17 km SE. Scenic drive 48 km SE to Serpentine Dam, WA's major water conservation area; noted for its brilliant wildflowers, gardens and bushland; nearby, Serpentine Falls. WA Water Ski Park, 5 km NE, constructed water-ski complex. At suburb of Karnup: Pioneer Pottery, Fletcher Rd; self-guide Nature Reserve Environmental Walk; contact Tourist information. On northern outskirts, The Granary, displays depicting history of grain industry; free guided tours, by appt only. **Tourist information:** 43 Kent St; (09) 592 3464. **Accommodation:** 2 hotels, 2 motels, 10 B&B, 4 cara./camp. parks.

Roebourne
Pop. 1213

MAP REF. 365 G1, 368 A2

Named after John Septimus Roe, the State's first surveyor-general, Roebourne was established in 1864 and is the oldest town on the north-west coast.

The Kimberley

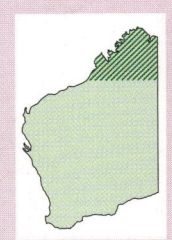

Until relatively recently the Kimberley region in the far north of Western Australia was only for hardened pioneers and prospectors. Now the National Highway puts it on Australia's travel map and it can offer both excitement and adventure. In addition, the 40 tonne, 18 metre ketch-rigged motor yacht *Opal Shell* cruises along the Kimberley coast out of Derby.

There are two seasons in the Kimberley. The long dry period in winter brings delightful weather, while the green season brings higher temperatures, with monsoonal rains usually falling between December and March.

On the west side, the gateway to the Kimberley is the old pearling town of **Broome**. In the boisterous days of the early 1900s the pearling fleet numbered some 400 luggers with 3000 crewmen. Today cosmopolitan Broome is rapidly expanding into one of Western Australia's most popular tourist destinations. There are many points of interest, including a set of dinosaur tracks believed to have been embedded in limestone 130 million years ago, and Buccaneer Rock, said to be the place where Dampier was wrecked in 1699.

Further north-east is **Derby**, on King Sound near the mouth of the Fitzroy River, a centre for the beef cattle industry of the Fitzroy Valley and the King Leopold Ranges. Just 7 kilometres south of the town is a centuries-old boab tree. Shaped like an inverted wineglass and 14 metres in diameter, it is hollow and is reputed to have been used as a cell for prisoners.

A group of boab trees, near Kununurra

Derby is a useful base for excursions to Windjana Gorge and Tunnel Creek in the Napier Range, and Geikie Gorge near the town of **Fitzroy Crossing**, which is a centre for local Aboriginal communities and also has excellent accommodation and camping facilities. The river gorges here are among the most colourful and spectacular in northern Australia.

The old gold settlement of **Halls Creek**, 16 kilometres from the site of the present town, was the scene of the first gold rush in Western Australia in 1885. Scores of diggers perished of hunger and thirst, and very little gold was found.

Nearby is the meteorite crater at Wolfe Creek, the second largest in the world, with an average depth of 50 metres. The meteorite is believed to have struck the earth about one million years ago. Also near Halls Creek is the China Wall, a natural white quartz outcrop above a placid creek.

The most northerly town and safe port harbour in Western Australia is **Wyndham**, the terminus of the Great Northern Highway and now also the port for the Ord River irrigation area as well as for the east Kimberley cattle stations. A 100-kilometre route from Wyndham to **Kununurra** winds through spectacular ancient gorge country. Kununurra, a lively town with excellent facilities, is the base for Lake Argyle, Hidden Valley National Park and **Purnululu (Bungle Bungle) National Park**. South of Lake Argyle is the Argyle diamond mine, the world's largest. Kununurra is then linked to Darwin by the National Highway.

For further information contact the Kununurra Tourist Bureau, Coolibah Drive, Kununurra; (091) 68 1177. **See also:** Entry for Purnululu National Park in National Parks, and individual entries in A–Z listing for those towns indicated by bold type. **Map references:** 362, 363, 371 L6.

It was developed as the capital of the north-west and was at one time the administrative centre for the whole area north of the Murchison River. As the centre for the early mining and pastoral industries in the Pilbara, it was connected to the pearling port of Cossack, and later to Point Samson, by tramway, for the transport of passengers and goods. Although now overshadowed by the iron-ore and other industries, Roebourne has retained its special character. **Of interest:** Old stone buildings (some National Trust-classified): police station, Queen St; post office (1887), Shell St; in Hampton St, hospital (1887), and court house; Holy Trinity Church (1894), Withnell St; in Roe St, Union Bank (1889, now Shire library), and Victoria Hotel, last of town's five original pubs. Old Roebourne Gaol (1886), Queen St, now art and craft centre. Good views from Mt Welcome, Fisher Dr. Aug.: Royal show; Roebourne Cup and Ball. **In the area:** Emma Withnell Heritage Trail (52 km) includes towns of Wickham and Cossack, ending at Point Samson. Fishing at Cleaverville, 25 km N. Millstream, 150 km S, former camel watering holes, now offer safe swimming in freshwater springs; walking trails nearby; old homestead now tourist information centre. **Tourist information**: Old Gaol, Queen St; (091) 82 1060. **Accommodation:** 1 hotel/motel, 1 cara./camp. park. **See also**: The Pilbara.

Southern Cross Pop. 982

MAP REF. 366 G7

A small, flourishing town on the Great Eastern Hwy, 368 km E of Perth, Southern Cross is the centre of a prosperous agricultural and pastoral area, and a significant gold-producing area. The town and its wide streets were originally designed to allow camel trains to turn around, and it was named after stars and constellations. **Of interest:** First court house in eastern goldfields (1893), Antares St, now a history museum. Other historic buildings: post office (1891), Antares St; Railway Tavern (1890s), Spica St. Restored Palace Hotel, Orion St. Sept.: Agricultural show. **In the area:** Wildflowers on sandplains in spring. Goldmining activities at Marvel Loch, 35 km S; Bullfinch, 36 km N. Hunt's Soak, 7 km N, a picnic area. Koolyanobbing, 52 km N, built for miners extracting iron ore, now virtually a ghost town since closure in 1983; recently, mining of rich iron ore has recommenced. Interesting rock formations with adjacent areas ideal for picnics at Frog Rock (30 km S), and Baladji Rock (50 km NW). **Tourist information:** Shire Offices, Antares St; (090) 49 1001. **Accommodation:** 3 hotels, 1 motel, 1 cara./camp. park. **See also:** Crossing the Nullarbor.

Three Springs Pop. 473

MAP REF. 366 C4

Sir John Forrest named Three Springs, which is 170 km SE of Geraldton. WA's finest talc, exported for use in the ceramics industry, is mined here from an open-cut mine 13 km E. **Of interest:** At southern town entrance, information bay and path through living display of stunning wildflowers. Heritage walk, details from Tourist information. Oct.: White Rock Stakes wheelbarrow race. **In the area:** Cockatoo Canyon, 6 km W. Emu Farm, 14 km W on Eneabba Rd. Eneabba, 58 km SW, a major mineral sands mining centre. Yarra Yarra Lake system, 5 km S, attracts many migratory birds. Wildflower drives (best Aug.–Nov.), details from Tourist information. Pink Lakes, 6 km E. Old copper-mine ruins, 7 km NW. Blue Waters, 18 km NW near Arrino, a picnic area amid river gums. **Tourist information:** Commercial Hotel, Thomas St; (099) 54 1041. **Accommodation:** 1 hotel/motel.

Tom Price Pop. 3634

MAP REF. 365 H4, 368 B5

The huge iron ore deposit now known as Mt Tom Price was discovered in 1962, after which the Hamersley Iron Project was established. The construction of a mine, two towns (Dampier and Tom Price) and a railway between the towns followed, all of which was achieved in a remarkably short period of time. The proximity of town to the spectacular Karijini (Hamersley Range) National Park, and a chance to tour open-cut mining operation, make the town a popular stopping-place. Aug.: Nameless festival. **In the area:** In Karijini National Park, 38 km E: Dales Gorge, with permanent waterfalls; Kalamina Gorge and Pool, the most accessible gorge; Joffre, Hancock, Weano and Red Gorges join below Oxer Lookout; Hamersley Gorge, with permanent pools for swimming and coloured folds in rock. *To the north-east is Wittenoom, no longer habitable as there is still a significant health risk from microscopic asbestos fibres created by the milling process at the asbestos mine which was closed in 1966. Some mine tailings potentially dangerous especially around old Wittenoom township and Wittenoom Gorge. When entering and exiting national park via Yampire Gorge Road keep car windows closed, observe warning signs and avoid tailings heaps.* Kings Lake, 2 km W, constructed lake; nearby, park with picnic/barbecue facilities. Views of remarkable scenery around Tom Price from Mt Nameless lookout, 6 km W, via walking trail or 4WD track. Aboriginal carvings, 10 km S; details from Tourist information. **Tourist information:** Central Rd; (091) 88 1112. **Accommodation:** 1 hotel, 1 motel, 1 cara./camp. park. **See also:** The Hamersley Range; The Pilbara.

Toodyay Pop. 604

MAP REF. 356 G1, 364 E2, 366 D7

The historic town of Toodyay, nestled in the Avon Valley, has many charming old buildings recalling its pioneering days. Situated 85 km NE of Perth, the town is surrounded by picturesque farming country and, to the west, virgin bushland. **Of interest:** Classified by the National Trust as an historic town, Toodyay has many buildings of historic significance in or near Stirling Tce, particularly Stirling House (1908), now art gallery, and Toodyay Antiques shop. Connor's Flour Mill (1870s), an imposing structure now housing tourist centre which has displays and a steam engine in working order. Old Newcastle Gaol Museum (1865), Clinton St, and police stables (1870), opposite, built by convicts with random rubble stone. Duidgee Park, Harper Rd, popular picnic spot on banks of river. Pelham Reserve Lookout, Duke St. May: Moondyne (colonial and convict) festival. Sept.: Folk festival. **In the area:** Windmill Hill Cutting, 6 km SE, deepest railway cutting in Australia. Northam, 27 km SE. Coorinja Winery, 4 km S, begun 1870; open Mon.–Sat. for tastings and sales. Century-old, 18 span, wooden Ringa Railway Bridge (1888), 6 km S. Hoddywell Archery Park, 8 km S. Nearby Avon River Weir, sanctuary for swans; grassy riverbank is delightful picnic spot. Emu farm, 15 km SW. White Gum Flower Farm, 9 km SW, just off road to Perth, with native and exotic flowers under cultivation. Trout farm, 12 km SW, offers fishing and sales. Cobbler Pool Animal Park, 15 km SW, animal nursery in picturesque riverside setting. Avon Valley National Park, 25 km SW, for spectacular scenery and seasonal wildflowers. Cartref Park, 16 km NW, 2 ha of English gardens and landscaped native plants; prolific birdlife. **Tourist information:** Connor's Mill, Stirling Tce; (09) 574 2435. **Accommodation:** 2 hotels, 1 hotel/motel, 2 cara./camp. parks.

Wagin Pop. 1293

MAP REF. 364 G8, 366 E10

The prosperous rural countryside that surrounds Wagin supports grain crops and pastures for livestock, especially sheep. Located 177 km E of Bunbury, Wagin's development has been tied to its important location as a railway-junction town. **Of interest:** Wagin Historical Village, Kitchener St, has collection of early pioneer artifacts set in 20 authentic old buildings. Fine Victorian buildings and shopfronts in Tudhoe and Tudor Sts. Heritage trail; details from Tourist information. Giant Ram (7 m high), Arthur Rd. Adjacent, park with ponds and waterfalls. Great Southern Gamebirds, Ware St, exhibits many native bird varieties. Regular trotting meets at Trotting Grounds, Kitchener St. Mar.: Woolorama, attended by sheep farmers from around the nation, attracting crowds of over 25 000. June: Foundation Day. **In the area:** Corralyn Emu Farm, 4 km N. Mt Latham, 6 km W, for bushwalking and views from summit. Puntapin, 6 km SE, a rock formation used as water-catchment area; wildflowers abound in spring. Lake Norring, 13 km SE, for swimming, sailing and water-skiing. At Dumbleyung, 30 km E; historic tavern; nearby, Lake Dumbleyung, for water sports. **Tourist information:** Shire Offices, Arthur Rd; (098) 61 1177; Wagin Historical Village, Showgrounds, Kitchener St; (098) 61 1232. **Accommodation:** 3 hotels, 2 motels, 1 cara./camp. park. **See also:** The Great Southern.

Walpole Pop. 290

MAP REF. 360 G12, 364 F13, 366 D12

Walpole is literally where the forest meets the sea. Surrounded by the Walpole-Nornalup National Park where a variety of trees grow, including karri, jarrah and the giant red tingle (*Eucalyptus jacksouii*), unique to the area. The region is known for its wildflowers in season as well as its wildlife. **Of interest:** Pioneer Cottage in Pioneer Park, South Coast Hwy, opened 1987 to commemorate district pioneers; cottage follows design of early pioneer homes, but not intended as a replica. Daily ferry trips on Nornalup Inlet, depart jetty off Boronia Ave. Bibbulmun Track (530 km), leading south from Kalamunda, 30 km E of Perth, ends at Walpole. Oct.: Wildflower week. **In the area:** Coalmine Beach Heritage Trail; details from Tourist information. Knoll Drive, 3 km E. Valley of the Giants, 16 km E, with huge tingles and karris; best seen from Tree Top Walk. Circular Pool, on Frankland River, 11 km NE. Tingle trees, off Hilltop Rd, 8 km SE; especially one huge specimen. Mt Frankland, 29 km N. Fernhook Falls, 32 km NW. For bushwalkers, Nuyts Wilderness area, 7 km W, and other walking trails. Ocean, river and inlet for anglers. Peaceful Bay, 28 km SE. **Tourist information:** Pioneer Cottage, Pioneer Park; (098) 40 1111. **Accommodation:** 1 hotel/motel, 1 B&B, 1 hostel, 3 cara./camp. parks.

Wanneroo Pop. 6745

MAP REF. 356 B3, 366 C8

Just a short drive from Perth, the district around Wanneroo stretches along 50 km of constantly changing coastline. **Of interest:** Botanic Golf, Burns Beach Rd, tee off at a botanical garden. Dizzy Lamb Park, cnr Carabooda and Wanneroo Rds, a family theme park. On West Coast Hwy at Hillarys Boat Harbour: Sorrento Quay, a marine centre and retail complex; Underwater World, with submerged tunnel, touch pool and Microworld display; whale-watch tours (Sept.–Nov.). In Prindiville Dr., Wangara: Gumnut World, a craft outlet, also pioneer village on site; Wanneroo Weekend Markets, huge market in carnival-like atmosphere. In Wanneroo Rd: Conti Estate Wine Cellars and Restaurant. Regular meetings with international competitors at Wanneroo Motor Racing Circuit. **In the area:** Lake Joondalup, 1 km W; Lake Jandabup, 4 km E; Lake Gnangara, 7 km SE. Vineyards: Faranda, 2 km S; Conti Estate, 4 km S; Hartridge, 10 km NW. At Yanchep National Park, 27 km NW: Gloucester Lodge Museum with local history exhibits; historic Yanchep Inn. **Tourist information:** Gumnut World, 30 Prindiville Dr., Wangara; (09) 409 6699. **Accommodation:** 1 motel, 1 B&B, 3 cara./camp. parks.

Wickepin Pop. 245

MAP REF. 364 G6, 366 E9

Wickepin dates back to the 1890s, when the first European settlers came to the district. The town is 214 km SE of Perth in farming country. **Of interest:** Good examples of Edwardian architecture in Wogolin Rd. The town has become well known following the publication of Albert Facey's autobiography *A Fortunate Life*. Nov.: Art and craft show (even-numbered years). **In the area:** Albert Facey Heritage Trail; details from Tourist information. Albert Facey's Homestead, 15 km S. Toolibin Lake reserve, 20 km S, has wide variety of waterfowl. Malyalling Roc, 15 km NE. Tiny town of Yealering, and Yealering Lake, 30 km NE. Sewell's Rock Nature Reserve, 44 km NE via Yealering, ideal for picnics and nature walks. **Tourist information:** Wickepin Newsagency and Milkbar, 28 Wogolin Rd; (098) 88 1070. **Accommodation:** 1 hotel, 1 cara./camp. park.

Wickham Pop. 1973

MAP REF. 365 G1

Construction of Wickham, 49 km N of Karratha, was begun in 1970 by the Cliff's Robe River Iron Associates. Today the town is still company-owned and operated, now by Robe River Iron Associates. Wickham is the sister town to Pannawonica; iron ore mined at Pannawonica is processed here before being exported from nearby Cape Lambert. **Of interest:** Tours of processing plant and port operations; depart from Robe River Visitors Centre, Wickham Dr., Mon.–Fri. Boat Beach, off Walcott Dr. Lookout at Tank Hill, for views of town. July: Cossack–Wickham fun run. **In the area:** At Cape Lambert, 10 km NW, tallest and second-longest open-ocean wharf in Australia. Point Samson, 9 km W, popular beach holiday town. Roebourne, 10 km S, oldest town in north-west. Cossack, 8 km SE, restored town, once pearling port. **Tourist information:** Roebourne Tourist Bureau, Queen St, Roebourne; (091) 82 1060. **Accommodation:** Limited budget accommodation. **See also:** The Hamersley Range; The Pilbara.

Williams
Pop. 371

MAP REF. 364 F7, 366 D9

This historical town enjoys a picturesque setting on the banks of the Williams River, 161 km SE of Perth. **Of interest:** Williams Hotel (1870). Old gravestones in cemetery, on northern outskirts of town. **In the area:** Dryandra State Forest, 25 km N. **Tourist information:** Williams Hotel, Albany Hwy; (098) 85 1016. **Accommodation:** 1 hotel, 1 motel, 1 cara./ camp. park.

Wyndham
Pop. 860

MAP REF. 363 N1, 371 P4

Wyndham is the most northerly town and safe port harbour in WA. The town consists of two main areas: the original town site of Wyndham Port, situated on Cambridge Gulf, and Wyndham East ('Three Mile'), on the Great Northern Hwy, the residential and shopping area. In 1985 the meatworks, representing Wyndham's main industry, closed. Today Wyndham is a service town for the pastoral industry, mining exploration, tourism and nearby Aboriginal communities. Port now handles live cattle shipment to South East Asia. **Of interest:** Self-guide cycle tours; heritage walk; contact Tourist information. Historic buildings in Port Town historic precinct, main street (Great Northern Hwy): Port Post Office, now tourist information centre; old Shire Hall, now Boab Art and Craft Gallery; Durack's Wool Store; court house, now historic museum; Anthon's Landing. Warriu Park Aboriginal Monument in town centre. Port display next to Marine and Harbours Offices, near wharf. Crocodile-spotting from wharf. Crocodile Farm, Great Northern Hwy, Wyndham Port; daily feeding. Three Mile Caravan Park, off Great Northern Hwy, has huge boab tree, 1500–2000 years old. Aug.: Top of the West festival. Nov.: Hang gliding competition. **In the area:** Self-guide drive, contact Tourist information. To south-west on King River Rd: Aboriginal rock paintings (18 km); prison tree 2000–4000 years old, (22 km); check road conditions. Horse treks from Diggers Rest Station, 33 km W. Alligator Airways Resort, Drysdale River, 80 km NW. Five Rivers Lookout, 5 km N atop Bastion Range, for spectacular views of Kimberley landscape, mountain ranges, Cambridge Gulf, Wyndham Port and rivers. Afghan cemetery, 1 km E. Abundant wildlife at Marlgu Billabong, 7 km E, part of Parry Lagoons, 70 sq. km of wetlands. The Grotto, 36 km E (2 km off road), a rock-edged waterhole, estimated to be 100 m deep, offering a cool, shaded oasis and safe year-round swimming. Sealed road leading to Wyndham passes through splendid gorge country. El Questro Station, 100 km S: vast cattle station,

The Ord River

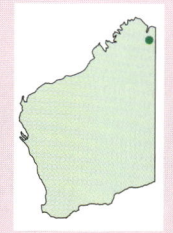

The development of the Ord River Scheme was a far-sighted move to develop the tropical north of Western Australia. During the wet season, the rivers of the Kimberley become raging torrents and at times the Ord River empties more than 50 million litres a second into the sea. With the end of the wet season, the rich seasonal pastures die and the land becomes dry again. The Ord River Dam was built to harness this tremendous wealth of water for agriculture.

The Kimberley Research Station found the black alluvial soil of the plains to be suitable for a variety of tropical crops. Between 1960 and 1963 the Diversion Dam at Kununurra was built to divert water from the river into supply channels. Lake Argyle, is the main storage reservoir. It is the largest constructed lake in Australia. This vast expanse of water is dotted with islands that were once peaks rising above the surrounding valleys. The water of the Ord is now capable of irrigating 72 000 hectares of land. A third of the projected irrigation area will be along the Keep River Plain in the Northern Territory.

The area is becoming increasingly attractive to tourists. Surrounding Lake Argyle are rugged red slopes, a haven for native animals, such as the bungarra lizard, the brush-tailed wallaby and the euro. There are lake cruises, bushwalks and a picnic area.

The original Durack homestead from Argyle Downs Station is also to be found here; once the residence of the cattle-pioneering Durack family, the homestead was moved to its present site to prevent it being covered by the waters of the lake as it filled. It is a fascinating memorial to the early settlers of the district.

Lake Argyle, south of Kununurra

The town of **Kununurra** was established in the 1960s as the residential and administrative centre of the Ord River Scheme.

For further information contact the Kununurra Tourist Bureau, Coolibah Drive, Kununurra; (091) 68 1177. **See also:** individual town entry for Kununurra in A–Z listing; The Kimberley.

Motor Museum, Avon Tce, York

Yalgoo
Pop. 80

MAP REF. 366 D3

Yalgoo lies 216 km E of Geraldton along an excellent road and is surrounded by typical Australian outback country. Alluvial gold was discovered in the 1890s. Small traces of gold are still found in the district, which encourages fossicking by locals and visitors. **Of interest:** Court House Museum, Gibbons St. Restored Dominican Convent Chapel, Henty St. **In the area:** Abundant native wildlife in the area and prolific wildflowers in season (July–Sept.). Joker's Tunnel, 12 km SE on Paynes Find Rd, carved through solid rock by early prospectors, named after Joker mining syndicate. **Tourist information:** Shire Offices, 15 Shamrock St; (099) 62 8042. **Accommodation:** 1 hotel/motel, 1 cara./camp. park.

includes Emma Gorge, just over 1 km walking track from parking area to gorge; Veil Waterfall for swimming; other touring options and accommodation available; details from Tourist information. **Tourist information:** Old Post Office building, O'Donnell St, Wyndham Port; (091) 61 1054. **Accommodation:** 1 hotel, 1 hotel/motel, 1 B&B, 1 cara./camp. park. **See also:** The Kimberley.

Yallingup
Pop. 150

MAP REF. 357 B7, 359 C2, 364 A9, 366 B10

Yallingup is known for its excellent surf, with the Australian Surf Championships held in the area. Its caves were a well-known attraction before the turn of the century. **Of interest:** Caves House Hotel, off Caves Rd, built by government as holiday hotel in 1903. Early visitors arrived from Busselton via horse and buggy along dirt road, a journey of 2 hours. Hotel was rebuilt in 1938 after fire, using locally milled timber; now has award-winning accommodation and restaurant. Oct.: October festival. Dec.: Malibu competition. **In the area:** Gunyulgup Gallery, 8 km S. Goanna Gallery and Bush Cottage Market, 8 km SE, for local art and craft. Shearing Shed, Wildwood Rd, 10 km SE, has shearing demonstrations and wool-shop; check opening times. Rivendell Gardens, 10 km SE, pick-your-own strawberries in season. Yallingup Caves, 2 km E. Canal Rocks and Smith's Beach, 5 km SW, offer good fishing, surfing, swimming and spectacular scenery. Wineries: Hunts Foxhaven Estate, 3 km S, open by appt; Wildwood, 5 km S; Cape Clairault Wines, 10 km S; Willyabrup Valley district, 20 km S; Margaret River area, 40 km S; Happ's Vineyard and Pottery, 8 km SE; Moonshine Brewery and Abbey Vale Vineyards, 11 km SE, further 8 km, Bootleg Brewery. **Tourist information:** Shop 3, Naturaliste Tce, Dunsborough; (097) 55 3299. **Accommodation:** 1 hotel, 4 B&B, 3 cara./camp. parks. **See also:** The South-west.

Yanchep
Pop. 1577

MAP REF. 356 A1, 364 C2, 366 C7

Yanchep is within easy driving distance from Perth, 51 km to the south. **In the area:** Yanchep National Park, 15 km E, covering 2799 ha of natural bushland; in park: Gloucester Lodge Museum; Crystal Cave, startling limestone formations; launch cruises on freshwater Loch McNess (Sun.). Wild Kingdom, 3 km NE, halfway between Yanchep and Two Rocks, a wildlife park and zoo. Marina at Two Rocks, 6 km NW. Wreck of *Alkimos*, south of Yanchep, said to be guarded by ghost. Picturesque Gnangara Lake, 30 km SE, with picnic facilities onshore. **Tourist information:** Information Office, Yanchep National Park; (09) 561 1004. **Accommodation:** 1 hotel/motel.

York
Pop. 1562

MAP REF. 356 I4, 364 F3, 366 D8

Founded in 1830, and the oldest inland town in WA, York is set on the banks of the Avon River in the fertile Avon Valley, 97 km from Perth. The town has a wealth of historic buildings, carefully preserved. **Of interest:** Heritage trails, contact Tourist information. In Avon Tce: Old gaol, court house, police station – all built of local stone in 1895; Settlers' House (1850), restored two-storey mud-brick building, now offering old-world accommodation; Castle Hotel and Imperial Inn, fine examples of early coaching inns; Romanesque town hall (1911), has impressive dimensions; Mill Gallery; Loder Antiques; Motor Museum, Australia's best collection of veteran, classic and racing cars (and some bicycles and motorcycles); Talking Points Antique Toy Train Museum, open Sun. and by appt; Sandalwood Yards and Tipperary School, old sandalwood storage area and now site of relocated school (1874); on southern outskirts; historic Balladong Farm, has old buildings and equipment, and domestic animals. Old railway station (1886), Railway Rd, has railway museum. In Brook St: old hospital, with original shingle roof; Residency Museum (1843), displaying colonial furniture and early photographs. Old-world costumes at The Needle and I, cnr Georgiana and Macarthy Sts. Fine churches: Holy Trinity (consecrated 1858), Suburban Rd; St Patrick's (1886), South St; Uniting Church (1888), Grey St. De Ladera Alpaca Farm, North Rd. Archery Park, Thorn St; open Fri.–Sun. Suspension Bridge (originally 1906) across river in Low St. Picnic/barbecue facilities at Avon Park in Low St, and at Railway Park, Railway Rd. Sept.: Jazz festival. **In the area:** Lookout, 3 km N; follow signs from Castle Hotel to Pioneer Dr. and then to Mt Brown. Picnic area in bush setting overlooking river at Gwanbygine Park, 10 km S. Near Quairading, 64 km E, Toapin Weir and panoramic views from Mt Stirling. **Tourist information:** 105 Avon Tce; (096) 41 1301. **Accommodation:** 1 hotel, 3 hotel/motels, 1 motel, 4 B&B, 1 cara./camp. park.

Western Australia

Location Map

Other Map Coverage
Central Perth 350
Perth Approach & Bypass Routes 351
Perth & Southern Suburbs 352
Northern Suburbs, Perth 354
Perth & Northern Region 356
Southern Region, Perth 357
Fremantle 358
Margaret River Region 359
Albany Region 360
Kimberley Region 362

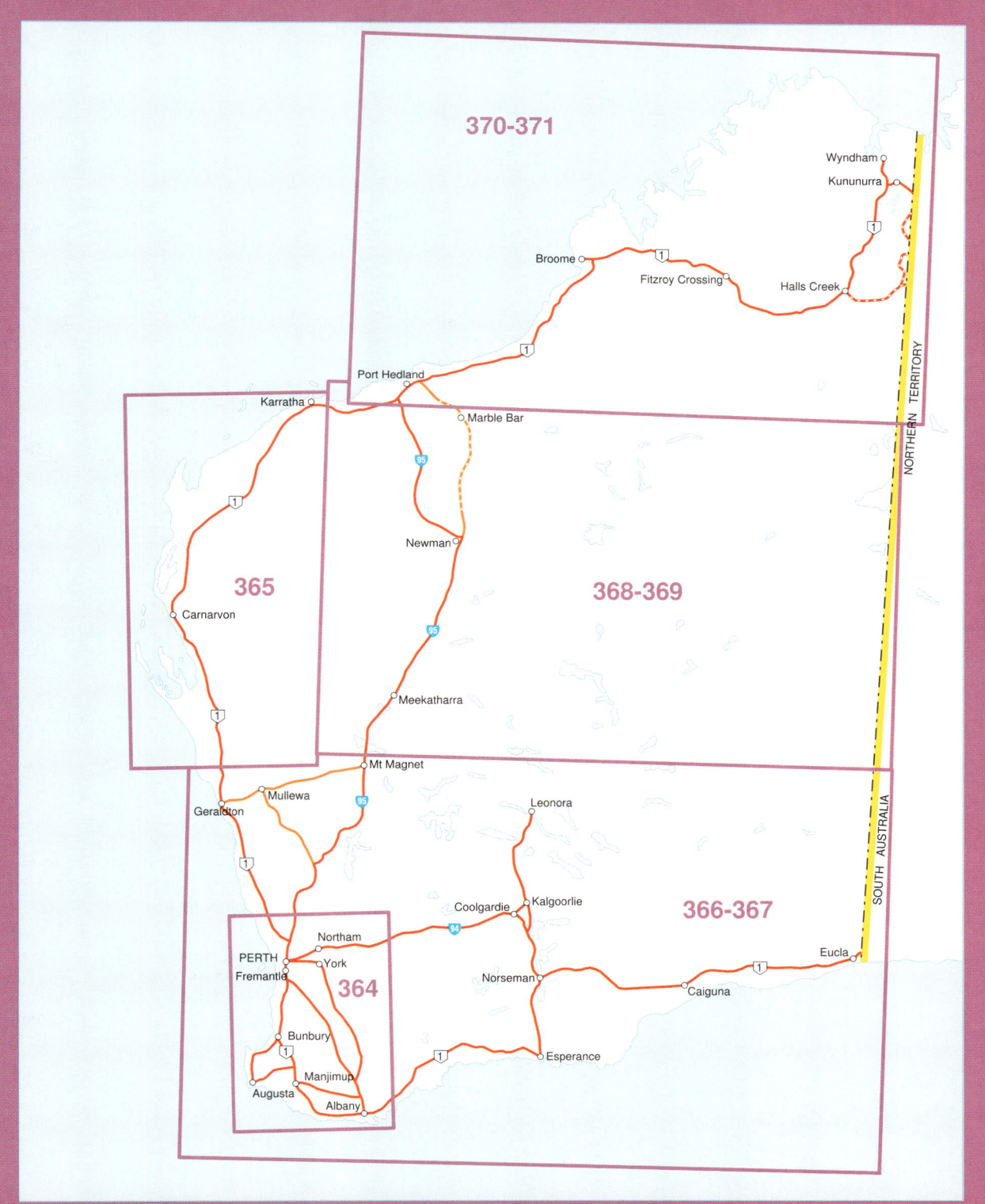

350 Central Perth

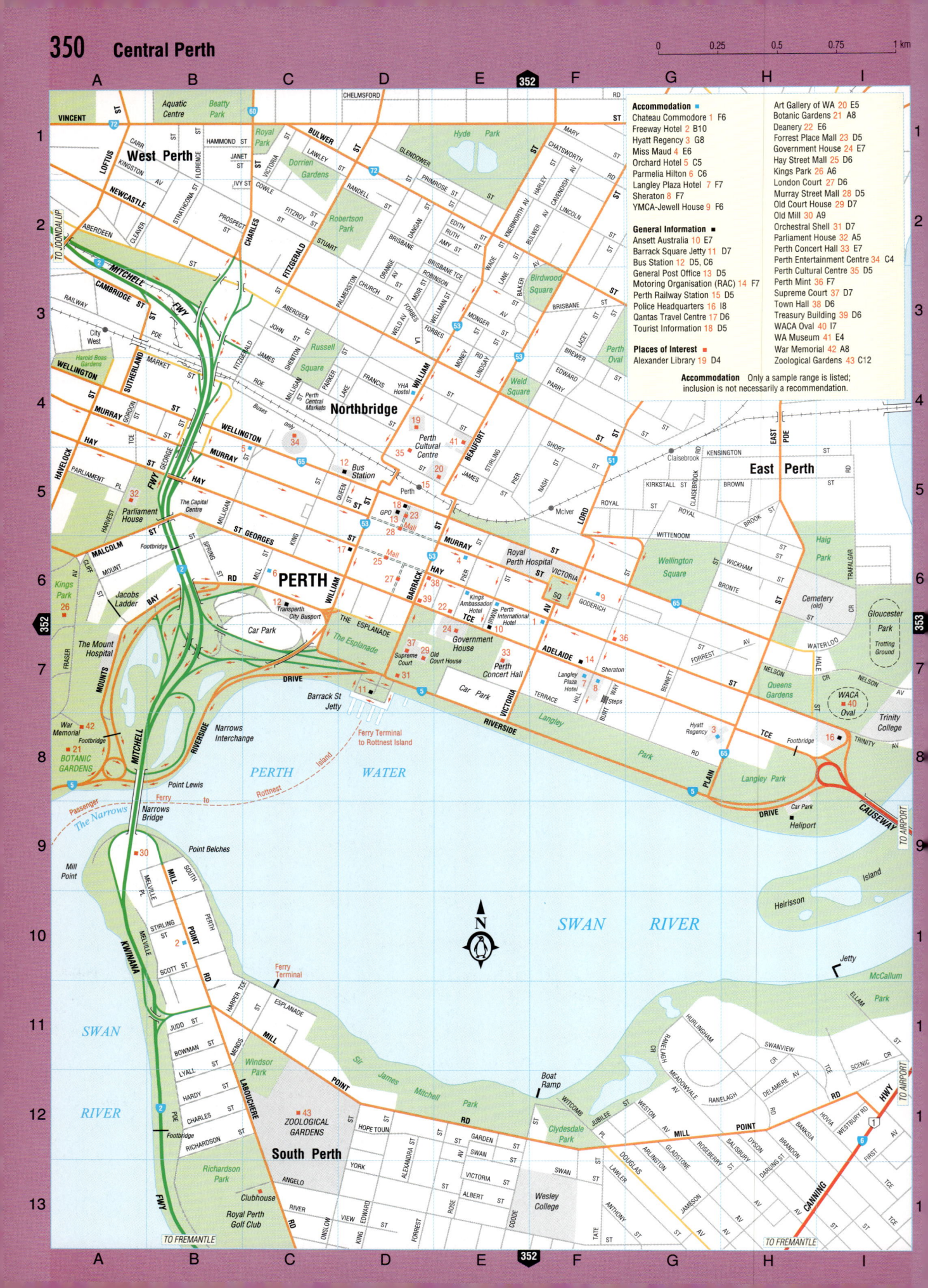

Accommodation ■
- Chateau Commodore 1 F6
- Freeway Hotel 2 B10
- Hyatt Regency 3 G8
- Miss Maud 4 E6
- Orchard Hotel 5 C5
- Parmelia Hilton 6 C6
- Langley Plaza Hotel 7 F7
- Sheraton 8 F7
- YMCA-Jewell House 9 F6

General Information ■
- Ansett Australia 10 E7
- Barrack Square Jetty 11 D7
- Bus Station 12 D5, C6
- General Post Office 13 D5
- Motoring Organisation (RAC) 14 F7
- Perth Railway Station 15 D5
- Police Headquarters 16 I8
- Qantas Travel Centre 17 D6
- Tourist Information 18 D5

Places of Interest ■
- Alexander Library 19 D4
- Art Gallery of WA 20 E5
- Botanic Gardens 21 A8
- Deanery 22 E6
- Forrest Place Mall 23 D5
- Government House 24 E7
- Hay Street Mall 25 D6
- Kings Park 26 A6
- London Court 27 D6
- Murray Street Mall 28 D5
- Old Court House 29 D7
- Old Mill 30 A9
- Orchestral Shell 31 D7
- Parliament House 32 A5
- Perth Concert Hall 33 E7
- Perth Entertainment Centre 34 C4
- Perth Cultural Centre 35 D5
- Perth Mint 36 F7
- Supreme Court 37 D7
- Town Hall 38 D6
- Treasury Building 39 D6
- WACA Oval 40 I7
- WA Museum 41 E4
- War Memorial 42 A8
- Zoological Gardens 43 C12

Accommodation Only a sample range is listed; inclusion is not necessarily a recommendation.

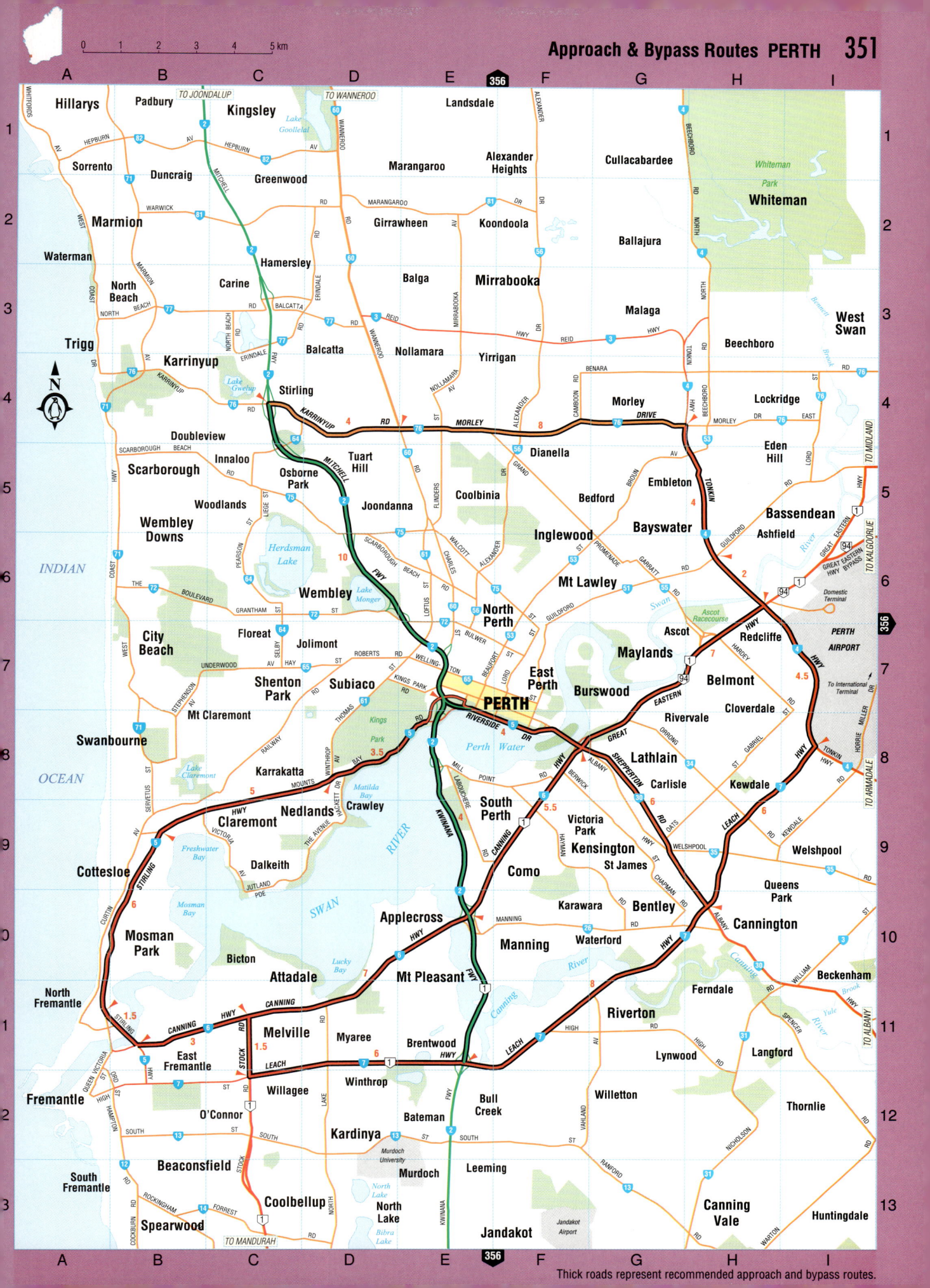

Approach & Bypass Routes PERTH 351

Thick roads represent recommended approach and bypass routes.

352 Perth & Southern Suburbs

353

354 Northern Suburbs, Perth

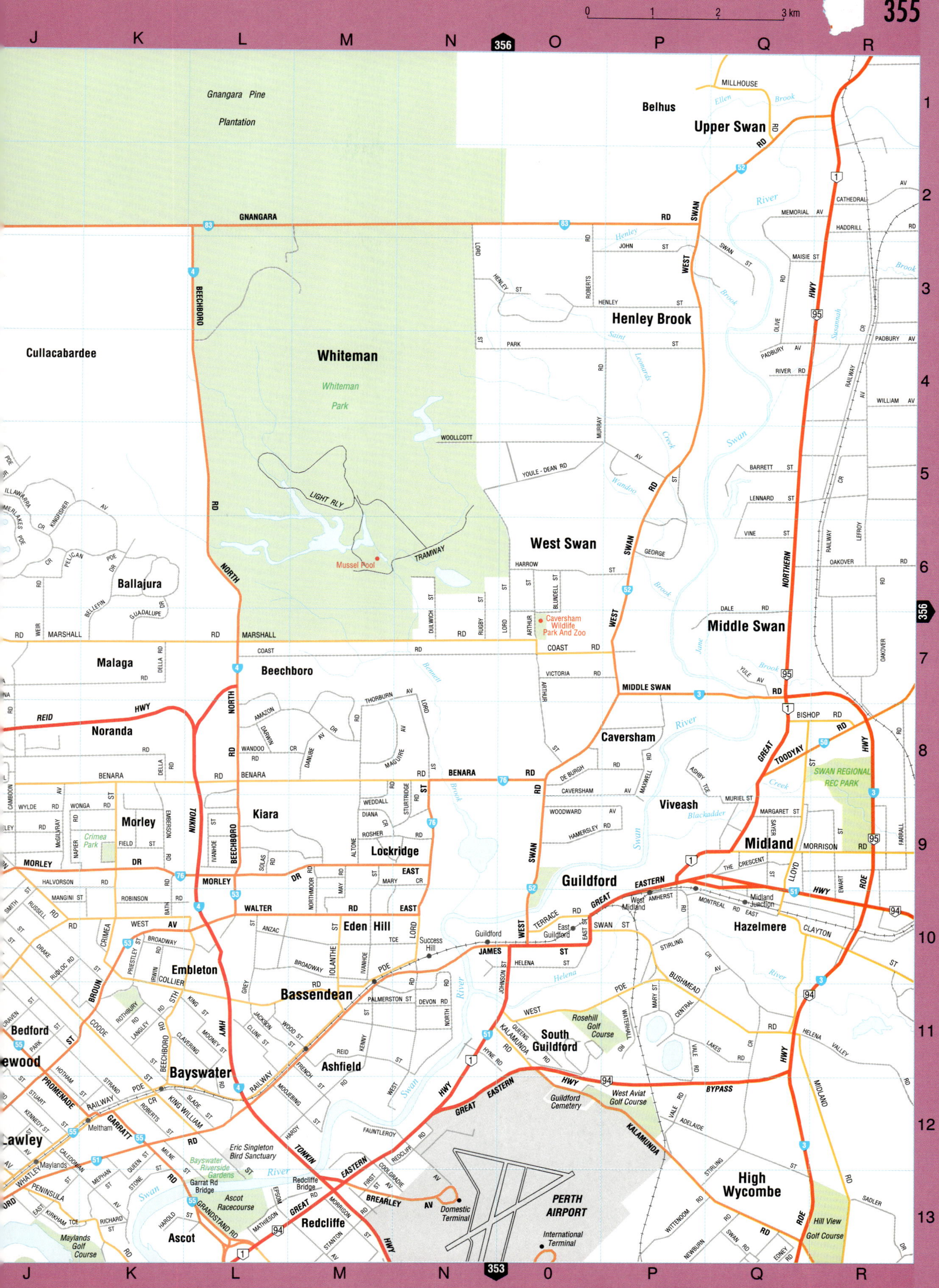
0 1 2 3 km
J K L M N O P Q R
356
1 2 3 4 5 6 7 8 9 10 11 12 13
353
Gnangara Pine Plantation
Belhus
Upper Swan
Cullacabardee
Whiteman
Whiteman Park
Henley Brook
West Swan
Ballajura
Malaga
Beechboro
Noranda
Morley
Kiara
Lockridge
Caversham
Viveash
Middle Swan
Midland
Guildford
Hazelmere
Eden Hill
Embleton
Bassendean
Bedford
Bayswater
Ashfield
South Guildford
High Wycombe
Redcliffe
Ascot
Maylands
Mussel Pool
Caversham Wildlife Park And Zoo
Crimea Park
Swan Regional Rec Park
Rosehill Golf Course
West Aviat Golf Course
Guildford Cemetery
Eric Singleton Bird Sanctuary
Bayswater Riverside Gardens
Ascot Racecourse
Maylands Golf Course
Hill View Golf Course
PERTH AIRPORT
Domestic Terminal
International Terminal
Garrat Rd Bridge
Redcliffe Bridge
Success Hill
West Midland
Midland Junction
East Guildford
Meltham
GNANGARA RD
BEECHBORO RD NORTH
MARSHALL RD
REID HWY
TONKIN HWY
GREAT NORTHERN HWY
WEST SWAN RD
MIDDLE SWAN RD
GREAT EASTERN HWY
GREAT EASTERN HWY BYPASS
ROE HWY
TOODYAY RD
BENARA RD
MORLEY DR
WALTER RD
KALAMUNDA RD
LIGHT RLY
TRAMWAY
Swan River
Helena River
Ellen Brook
Henley Brook
Jane Brook
Blackadder Creek

356 Perth & Northern Region

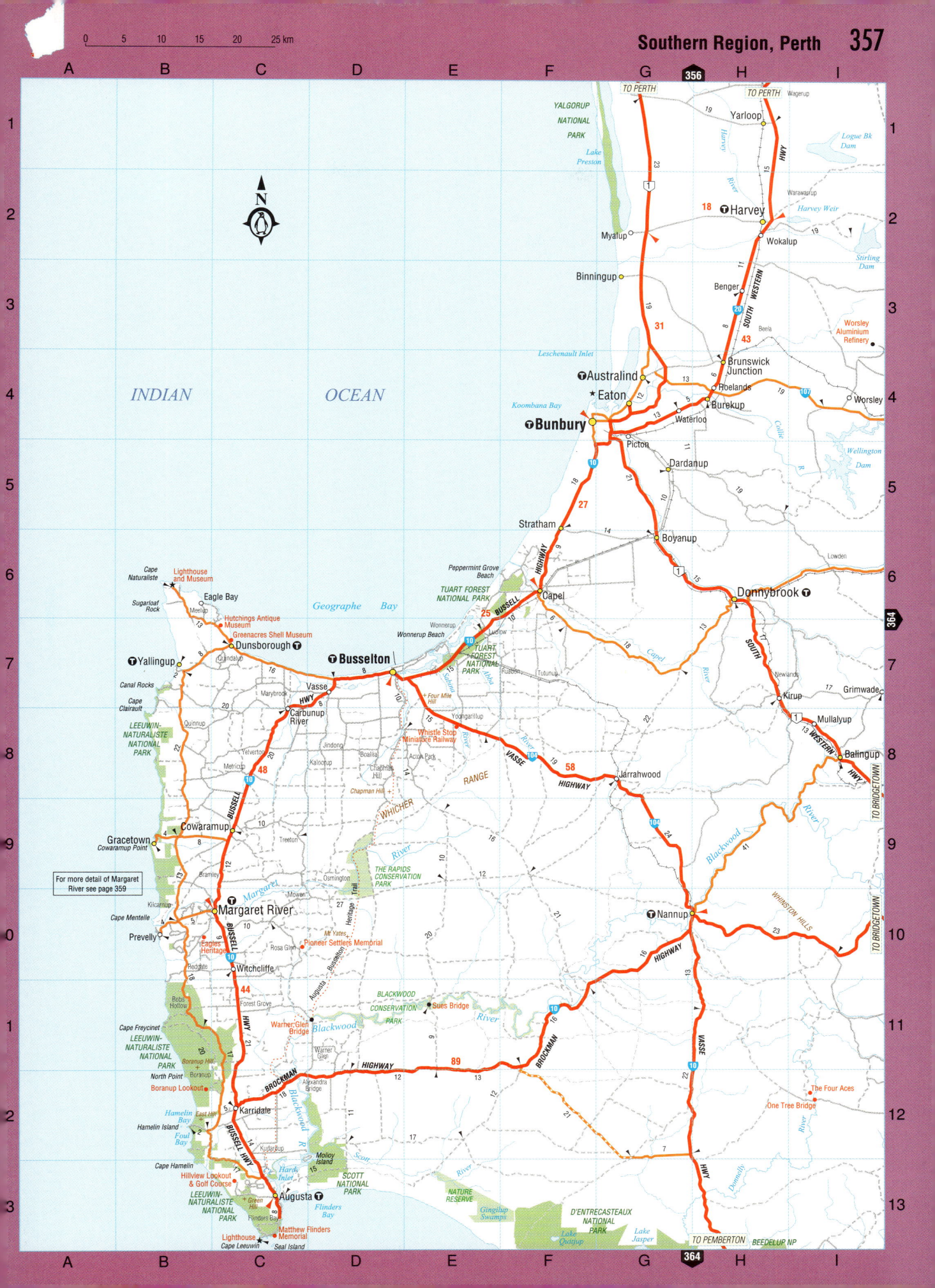

Southern Region, Perth 357

358 Fremantle

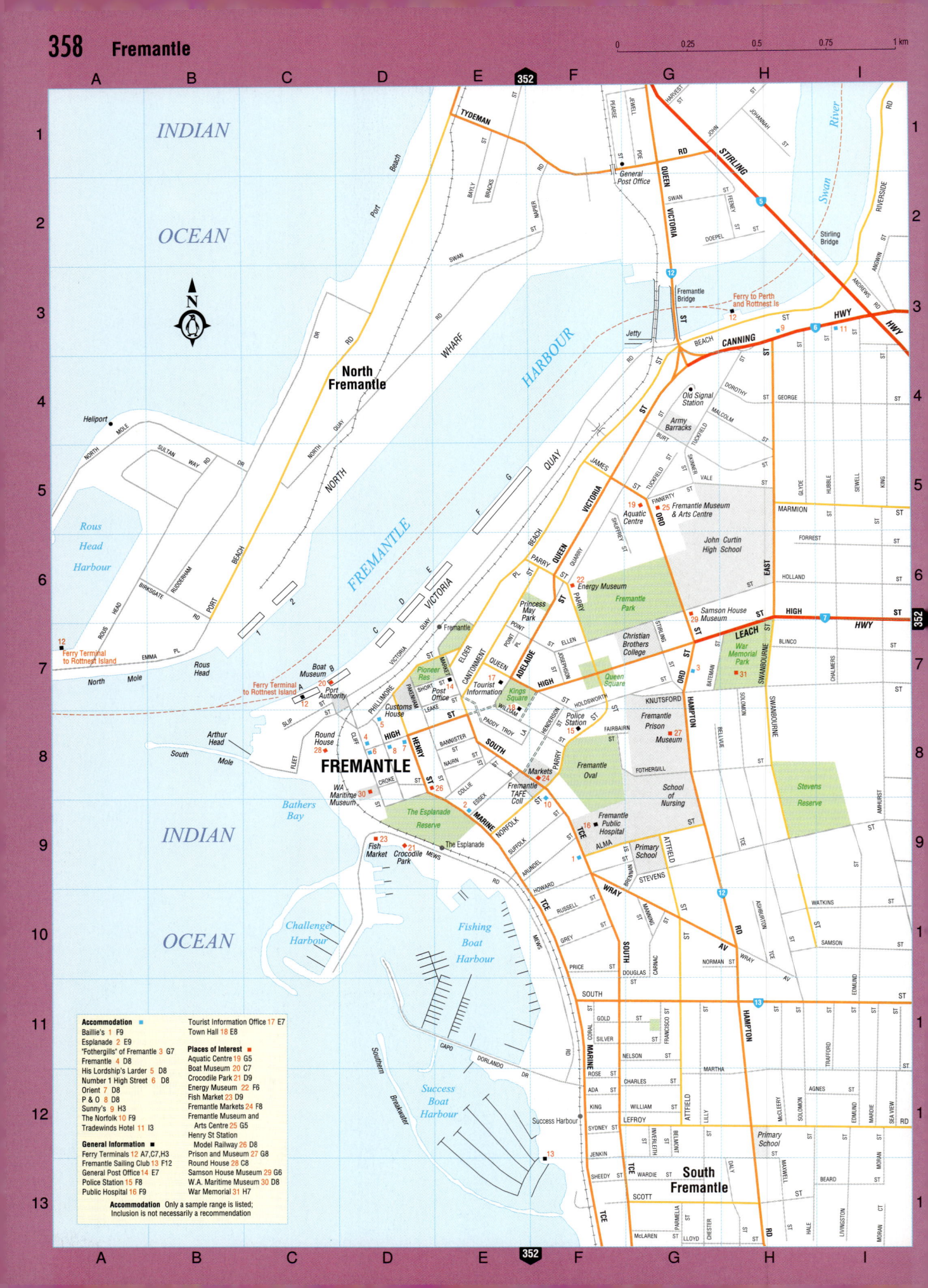

Accommodation
- Baillie's 1 F9
- Esplanade 2 E9
- "Fothergills" of Fremantle 3 G7
- Fremantle 4 D8
- His Lordship's Larder 5 D8
- Number 1 High Street 6 D8
- Orient 7 D8
- P & O 8 D8
- Sunny's 9 H3
- The Norfolk 10 F9
- Tradewinds Hotel 11 I3

General Information
- Ferry Terminals 12 A7, C7, H3
- Fremantle Sailing Club 13 F12
- General Post Office 14 E7
- Police Station 15 F8
- Public Hospital 16 F9
- Tourist Information Office 17 E7
- Town Hall 18 E8

Places of Interest
- Aquatic Centre 19 G5
- Boat Museum 20 C7
- Crocodile Park 21 D9
- Energy Museum 22 F6
- Fish Market 23 D9
- Fremantle Markets 24 F8
- Fremantle Museum and Arts Centre 25 G5
- Henry St Station Model Railway 26 D8
- Prison and Museum 27 G8
- Round House 28 C8
- Samson House Museum 29 G6
- W.A. Maritime Museum 30 D8
- War Memorial 31 H7

Accommodation Only a sample range is listed; Inclusion is not necessarily a recommendation.

Margaret River Region

WINERIES:
- Amberley Estate 1 C3
- Ashbrook Estate 2 C5
- Brookland Valley Vineyard 3 B5
- Cape Clairault Wines 4 C4
- Cape Mentelle 5 C7
- Chateau Xanadu 6 C7
- Cullens Willyabrup Wines 7 C5
- Driftwood Estate 8 B4
- Eagle Bay Estate 9 C2
- Evans and Tate 10 C5
- Fermoy Estate 11 C5
- Freycinet Estate 12 C8
- Gralyn 13 C5
- Green Valley Vineyard 14 C9
- Happ's Vineyard 15 C5
- Hay Shed Hill Winery 16 C5
- Hunts Foxhaven Estate 17 B3
- Leeuwin Estate 18 C8
- Lenton Brae 19 C5
- Moonshine Brewery 20 C3
- Moss Brothers 21 C4
- Mosswood 22 C5
- Pierro 23 C5
- Redgate 24 C8
- Ribbon Vale Estate 25 C5
- Rivendell Vineyard 26 C3
- Rosabrook Estate 27 C7
- Sandalford Wines 28 C5
- Thornhill Wines 29 E8
- Treeton Estate 30 D5
- Vasse Felix 31 C5
- Wildwood 32 C3
- Willespie 33 C5
- Woodlands 34 C5
- Woody Nook 35 C5
- Wrights 36 C5

FISHING: The length of the coast, together with the many rivers and estuaries make the region an angler's paradise. Many of the rivers and streams are stocked annually with trout.

TUART FOREST NATIONAL PARK: The park is home to a variety of animals, including the Western Ringtail Possum, an endangered species. The park also protects the state's largest remaining area of Tuart Forest. Tuart, a species of hardwood, only grows on coastal limestone, and hence is unique to the limestone coast of south-western Western Australia.

AUGUSTA-BUSSELTON HERITAGE TRAIL: This trail, which runs from Augusta to Vasse, basically retraces the original track, which, in the 1830s, linked these two towns.

TOURIST INFORMATION:
- Busselton (Civic Centre Complex, Southern Drive)
- Dunsborough (Naturaliste Tce)
- Margaret River (Cnr Tunbridge Rd and Bussell Hwy)
- Augusta (Blackwood Ave)

LEEUWIN-NATURALISTE NATIONAL PARK: This narrow strip of protected coastline combines a scenic coast with magnificent wildflowers and the tall timbers of Karri and Jarrah Forests.

CAVES: There are over 350 caves in this region, lying along the Leeuwin-Naturaliste ridge; only some of the caves are open to the public. They include Mammoth Cave, Jewel Cave, Lake Cave and Yallingup Cave - all of which have guided tours daily in summer. Moondyne Cave is an "adventure cave" open to the public; tour guide provided.

SURFING: The sheltered bays and excellent beaches that dot the coastline of the Yallingup-Margaret River region offer ideal surfing conditions.

CAPE LEEUWIN: From the cape it is possible to see the sun rising over one ocean and setting over another.

360 Albany Region

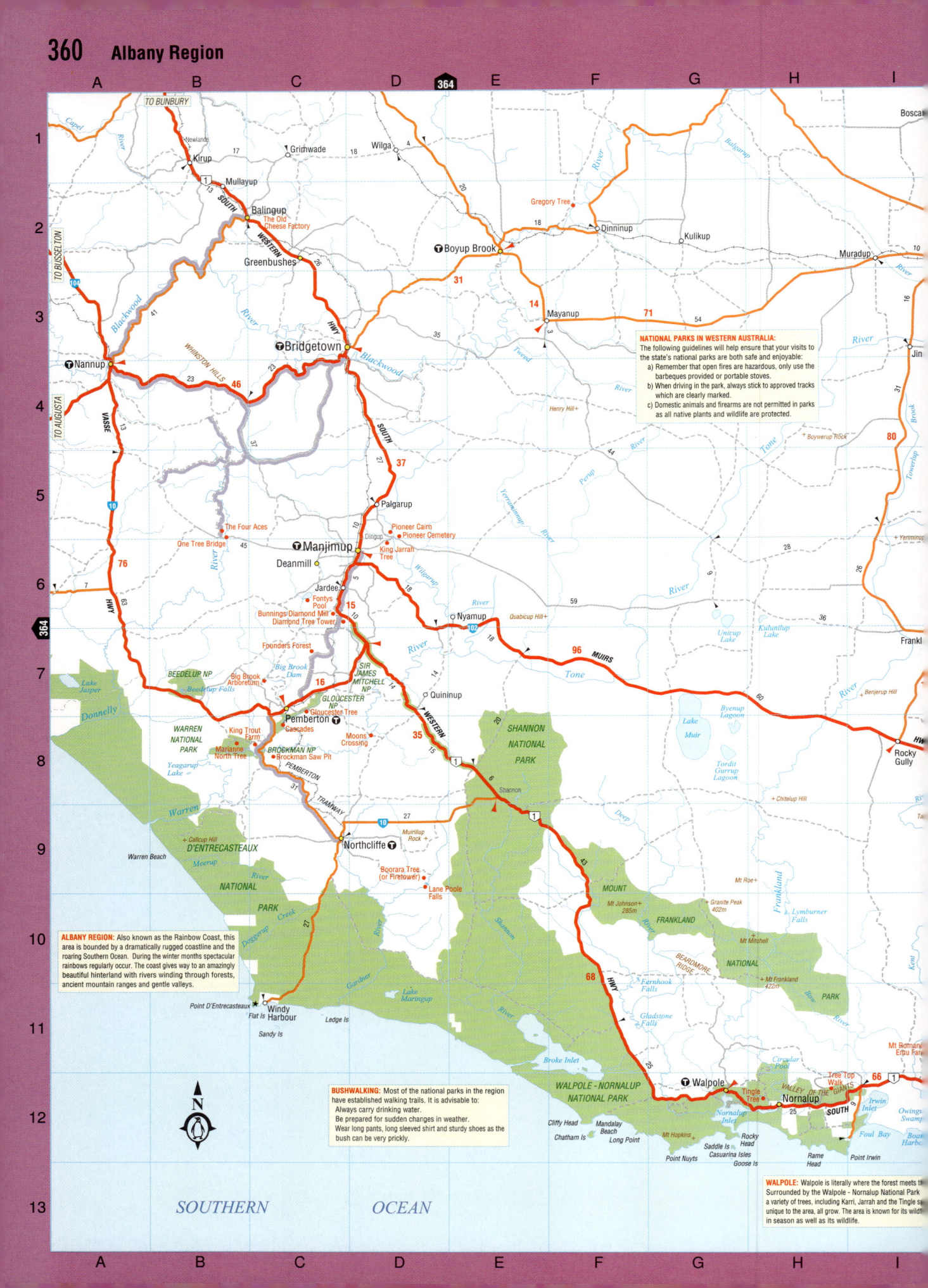

ALBANY REGION: Also known as the Rainbow Coast, this area is bounded by a dramatically rugged coastline and the roaring Southern Ocean. During the winter months spectacular rainbows regularly occur. The coast gives way to an amazingly beautiful hinterland with rivers winding through forests, ancient mountain ranges and gentle valleys.

NATIONAL PARKS IN WESTERN AUSTRALIA: The following guidelines will help ensure that your visits to the state's national parks are both safe and enjoyable:
a) Remember that open fires are hazardous, only use the barbeques provided or portable stoves.
b) When driving in the park, always stick to approved tracks which are clearly marked.
c) Domestic animals and firearms are not permitted in parks as all native plants and wildlife are protected.

BUSHWALKING: Most of the national parks in the region have established walking trails. It is advisable to:
- Always carry drinking water.
- Be prepared for sudden changes in weather.
- Wear long pants, long sleeved shirt and sturdy shoes as the bush can be very prickly.

WALPOLE: Walpole is literally where the forest meets the Surrounded by the Walpole - Nornalup National Park a variety of trees, including Karri, Jarrah and the Tingle unique to the area, all grow. The area is known for its wildl in season as well as its wildlife.

SOUTHERN OCEAN

WINERIES:

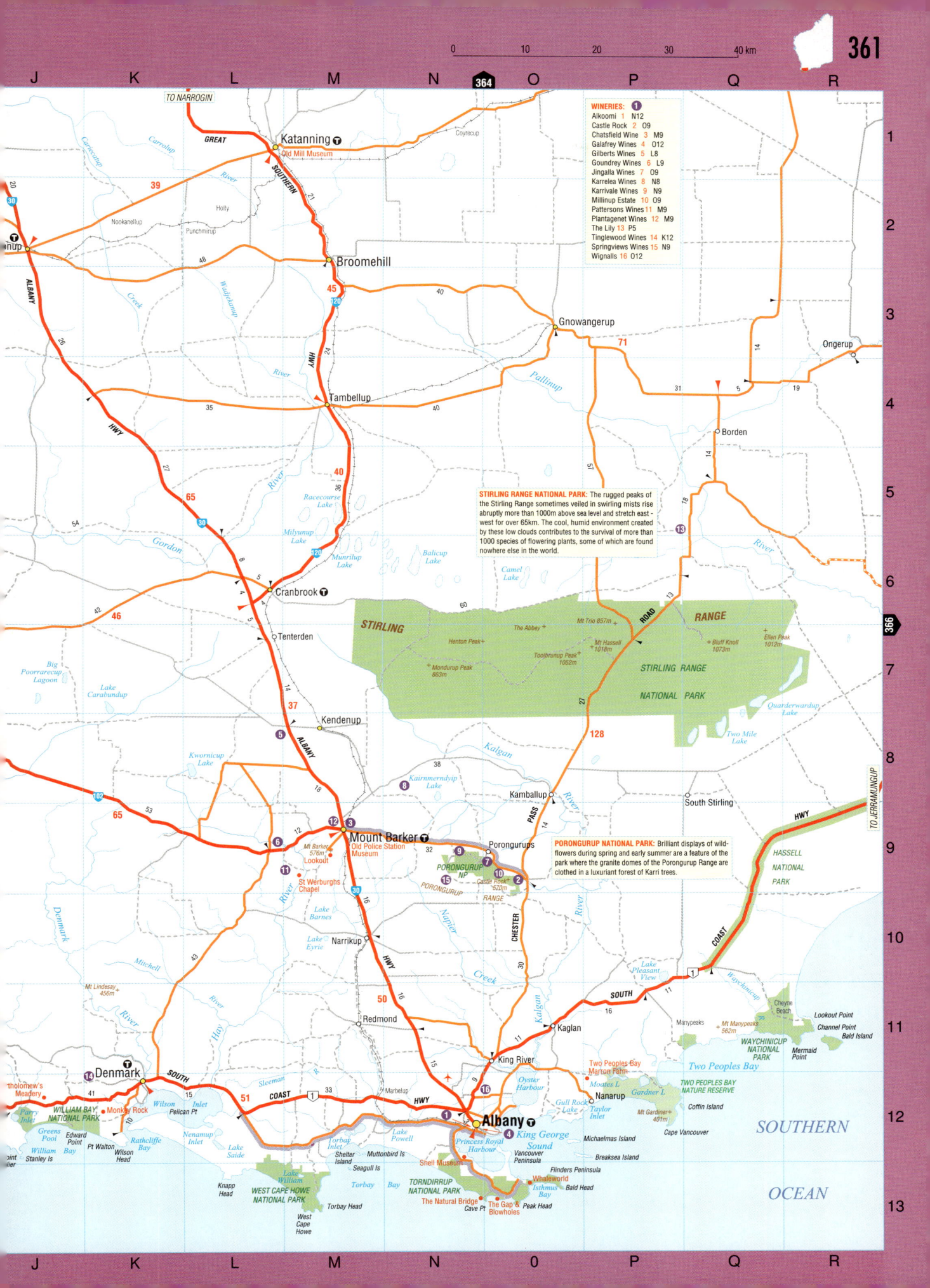

Winery	No.	Grid
Alkoomi	1	N12
Castle Rock	2	O9
Chatsfield Wine	3	M9
Galafrey Wines	4	O12
Gilberts Wines	5	L8
Goundrey Wines	6	L9
Jingalla Wines	7	O9
Karrelea Wines	8	N8
Karrivale Wines	9	N9
Millinup Estate	10	O9
Pattersons Wines	11	M9
Plantagenet Wines	12	M9
The Lily	13	P5
Tinglewood Wines	14	K12
Springviews Wines	15	N9
Wignalls	16	O12

STIRLING RANGE NATIONAL PARK: The rugged peaks of the Stirling Range sometimes veiled in swirling mists rise abruptly more than 1000m above sea level and stretch east-west for over 65km. The cool, humid environment created by these low clouds contributes to the survival of more than 1000 species of flowering plants, some of which are found nowhere else in the world.

PORONGURUP NATIONAL PARK: Brilliant displays of wildflowers during spring and early summer are a feature of the park where the granite domes of the Porongurup Range are clothed in a luxuriant forest of Karri trees.

361

362 Kimberley Region

TOURIST INFORMATION:
- Derby (1 Clarendon St)
- Fitzroy Crossing (Flynn Dr)
- Halls Creek (Great Northern Hwy)
- Kununurra (Coolibah Dr)
- Wyndham (O'Donnell St, Wyndham Port)

GIBB RIVER ROAD: Built to carry large road trains for beef being transported from isolated stations to the ports of Derby and Wyndham. Road conditions vary and it is advisable to check before departure.

TUNNEL CREEK NATIONAL PARK: Provides an opportunity to explore a creek as it tunnels through a mountain range. The tunnel contains permanent pools of water and for those with a torch, prepared to walk through cold water, the walk through is fascinating.

WINDJANA GORGE NATIONAL PARK: Consists of a gorge formed by the Lennard River as it snakes its way through a 350-million year old reef of ancient limestone. The river only flows for short periods but isolated pools support an abundance of fish and birds. A number of interesting walks exist with trail-side signs interpreting features in the gorge.

GEIKIE GORGE NATIONAL PARK: Formed by centuries of water eroding through an ancient limestone reef. The gorge contains permanent fresh water and supports a variety of animal life, including freshwater crocodiles. Cruise trips up the gorge are available.

363

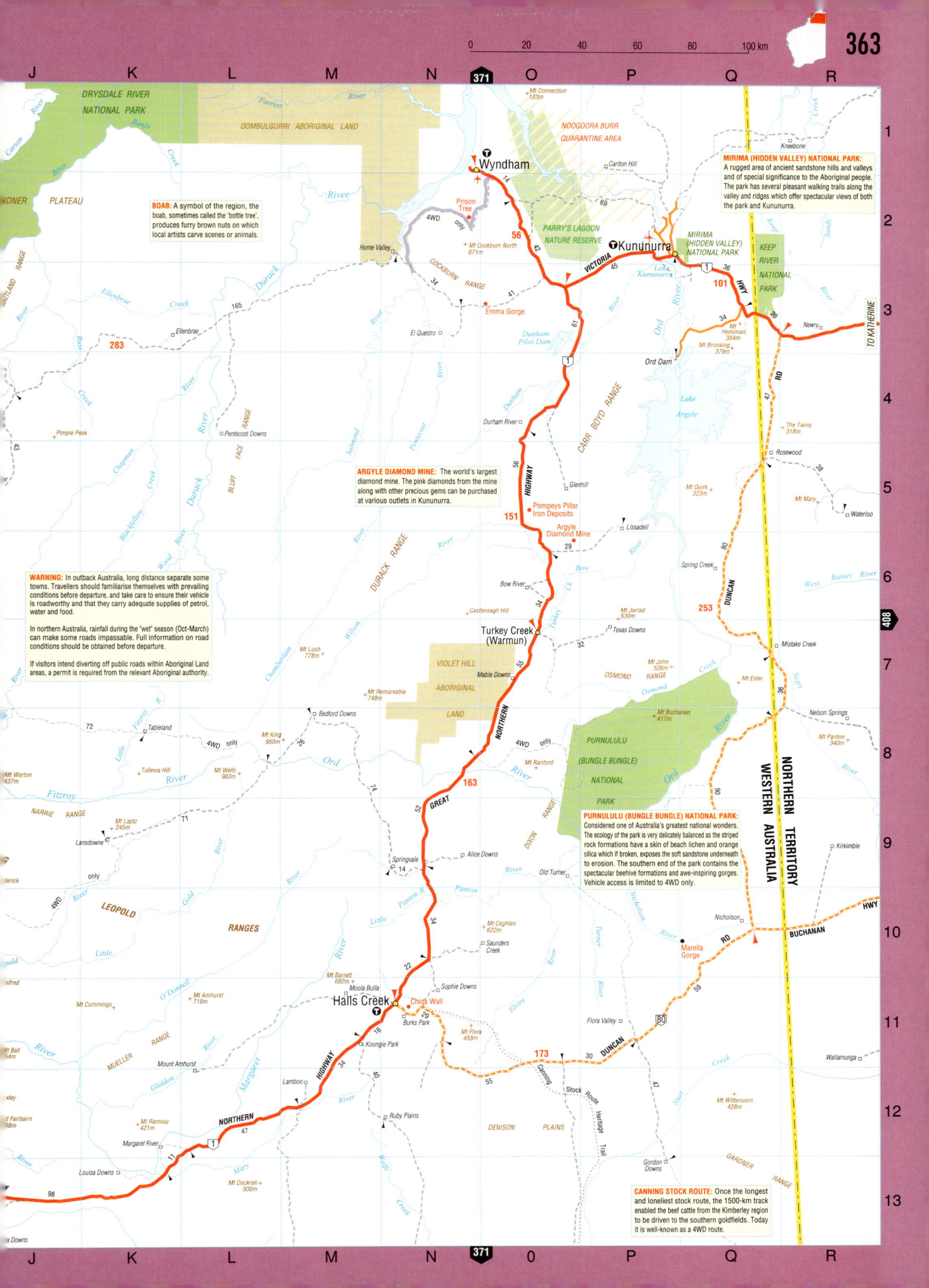

MIRIMA (HIDDEN VALLEY) NATIONAL PARK: A rugged area of ancient sandstone hills and valleys and of special significance to the Aboriginal people. The park has several pleasant walking trails along the valley and ridges which offer spectacular views of both the park and Kununurra.

BOAB: A symbol of the region, the boab, sometimes called the 'bottle tree', produces furry brown nuts on which local artists carve scenes or animals.

ARGYLE DIAMOND MINE: The world's largest diamond mine. The pink diamonds from the mine along with other precious gems can be purchased at various outlets in Kununurra.

WARNING: In outback Australia, long distance separate some towns. Travellers should familiarise themselves with prevailing conditions before departure, and take care to ensure their vehicle is roadworthy and that they carry adequate supplies of petrol, water and food.

In northern Australia, rainfall during the 'wet' season (Oct-March) can make some roads impassable. Full information on road conditions should be obtained before departure.

If visitors intend diverting off public roads within Aboriginal Land areas, a permit is required for the relevant Aboriginal authority.

PURNULULU (BUNGLE BUNGLE) NATIONAL PARK: Considered one of Australia's greatest wonders. The ecology of the park is very delicately balanced as the striped rock formations have a skin of beach lichen and orange silica which if broken, exposes the soft sandstone underneath to erosion. The southern end of the park contains the spectacular beehive formations and awe-inspiring gorges. Vehicle access is limited to 4WD only.

CANNING STOCK ROUTE: Once the longest and loneliest stock route, the 1500-km track enabled the beef cattle from the Kimberley region to be driven to the southern goldfields. Today it is well-known as a 4WD route.

364 South Western Western Australia

Central Western Western Australia 365

366 Southern Western Australia

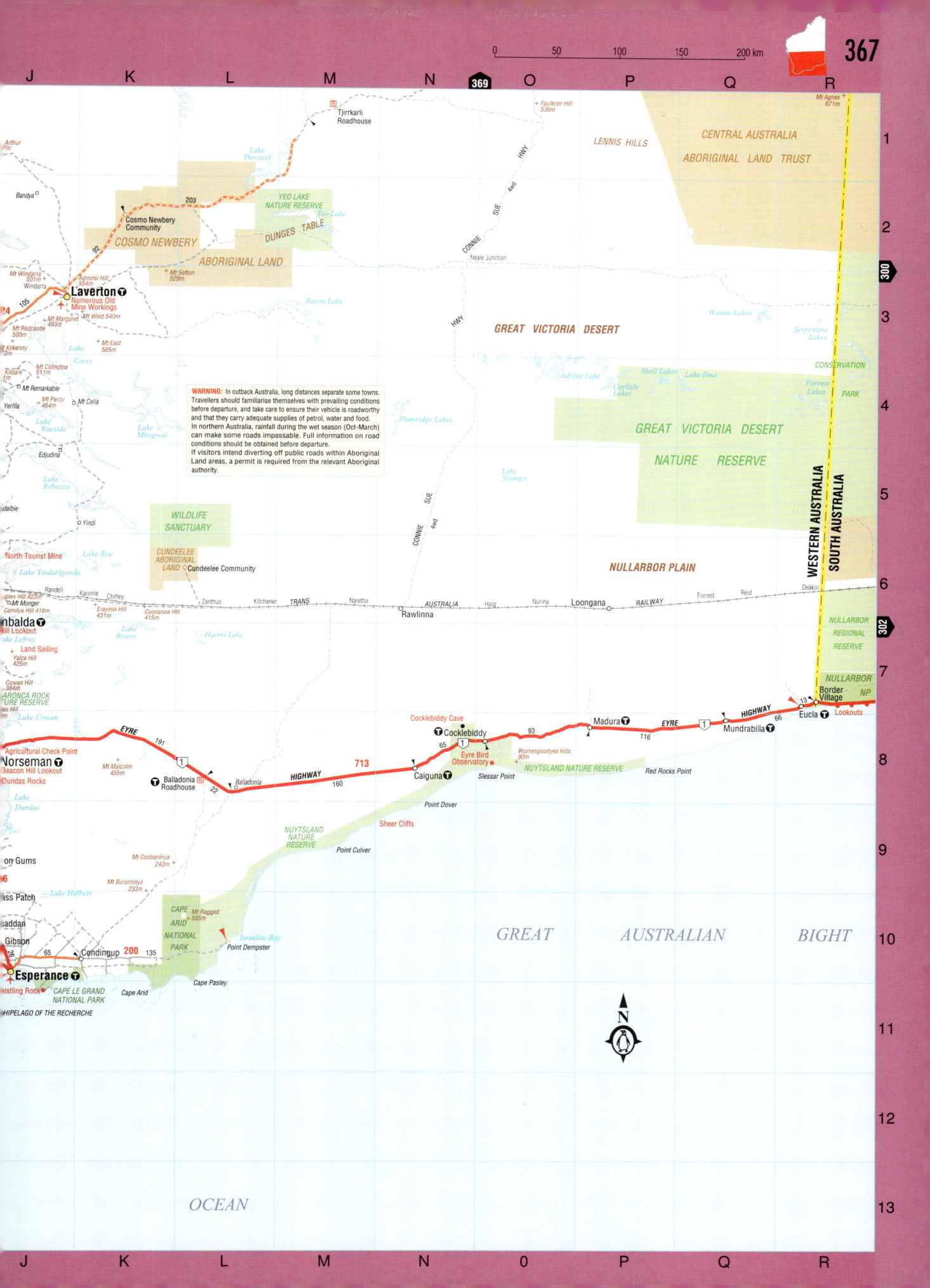

WARNING: In outback Australia, long distances separate some towns. Travellers should familiarise themselves with prevailing conditions before departure, and take care to ensure their vehicle is roadworthy and that they carry adequate supplies of petrol, water and food.
In northern Australia, rainfall during the wet season (Oct-March) can make some roads impassable. Full information on road conditions should be obtained before departure.
If visitors intend diverting off public roads within Aboriginal Land areas, a permit is required from the relevant Aboriginal authority.

368 Central Western Australia

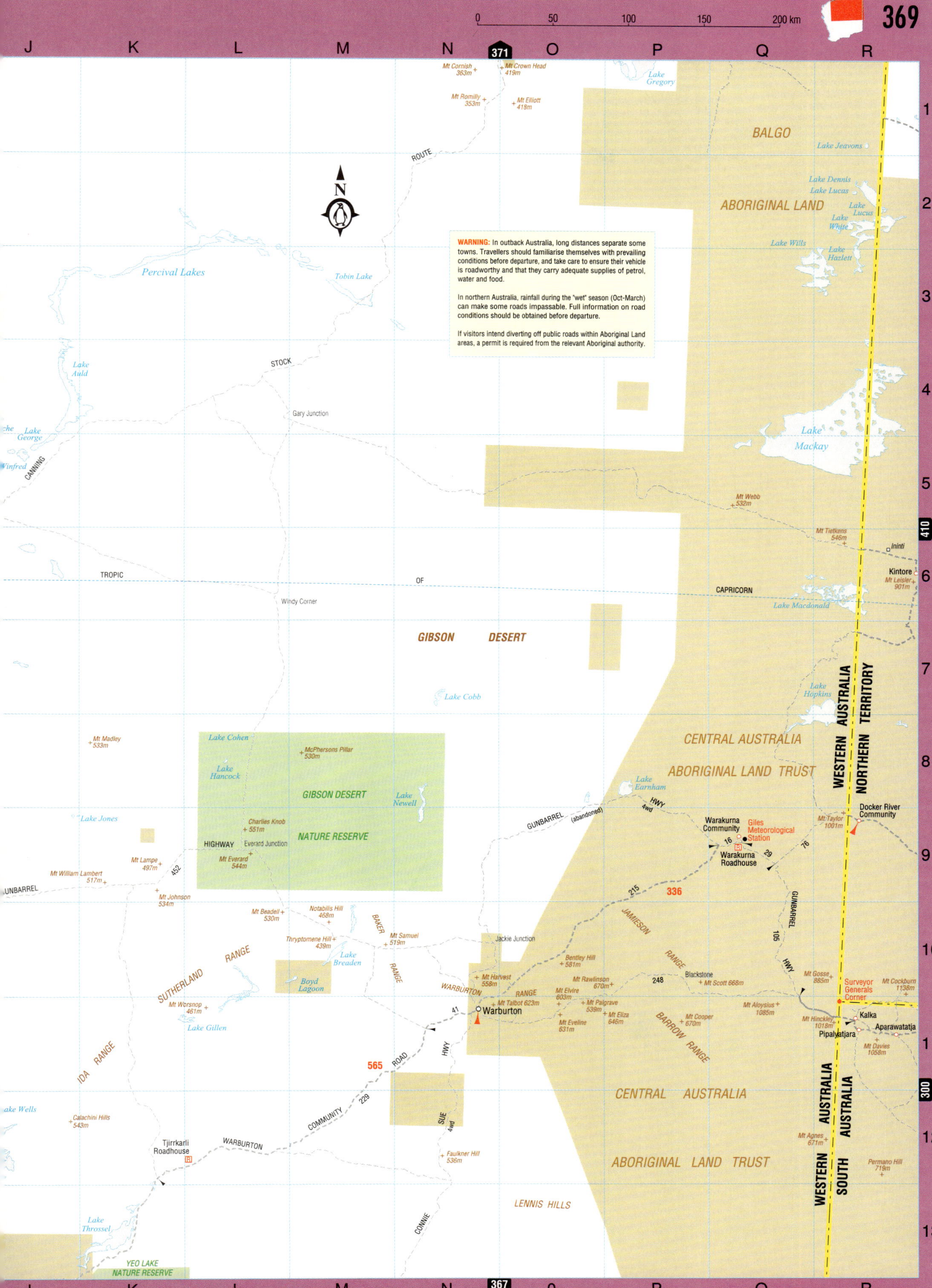
0 50 100 150 200 km
J K L M N 371 O P Q R
WARNING: In outback Australia, long distances separate some towns. Travellers should familiarise themselves with prevailing conditions before departure, and take care to ensure that their vehicle is roadworthy and that they carry adequate supplies of petrol, water and food.
In northern Australia, rainfall during the 'wet' season (Oct-March) can make some roads impassable. Full information on road conditions should be obtained before departure.
If visitors intend diverting off public roads within Aboriginal Land areas, a permit is required from the relevant Aboriginal authority.
Mt Cornish 363m
Mt Crown Head 419m
Mt Romilly 353m
Mt Elliott 419m
Lake Gregory
BALGO
ABORIGINAL LAND
Lake Jeavons
Lake Dennis
Lake Lucas
Lake White
Lake Wills
Lake Hazlett
ROUTE
STOCK
Percival Lakes
Tobin Lake
Lake Auld
Lake George
CANNING
Gary Junction
Lake Mackay
Mt Webb 532m
Mt Tietkens 546m
Ininti
Kintore
Mt Leisler 901m
TROPIC
OF
CAPRICORN
Windy Corner
Lake Macdonald
GIBSON DESERT
Lake Cobb
Lake Hopkins
WESTERN AUSTRALIA
NORTHERN TERRITORY
CENTRAL AUSTRALIA
ABORIGINAL LAND TRUST
Mt Madley 533m
Lake Cohen
McPhersons Pillar 530m
Lake Hancock
GIBSON DESERT
NATURE RESERVE
Lake Newell
Lake Earnham
HWY 4wd
Lake Jones
Charles Knob 551m
HIGHWAY
Everard Junction
GUNBARREL
(abandoned)
Warakurna Community
Giles Meteorological Station
Warakurna Roadhouse
Mt Taylor 1001m
Docker River Community
Mt Lampe 497m
Mt Everard 544m
Mt William Lambert 517m
Mt Johnson 534m
336
JAMIESON
RANGE
GUNBARREL HWY
Mt Beadell 530m
Notabilis Hill 468m
BAKER
RANGE
Mt Samuel 519m
Thryptomene Hill 439m
Lake Breaden
Jackie Junction
Bentley Hill 581m
Blackstone
Mt Scott 668m
Mt Gosse 885m
Surveyor Generals Corner
Mt Cockburn 1138m
SUTHERLAND RANGE
Boyd Lagoon
Mt Harvest 558m
WARBURTON
RANGE
Mt Talbot 623m
Mt Rawlinson 670m
Mt Elvire 603m
Mt Palgrave 539m
Mt Eliza 646m
Mt Eveline 631m
BARROW RANGE
Mt Cooper 670m
Mt Aloysius 1085m
Mt Hinckley 1018m
Kalka
Pipalyatjara
Aparawatatja
Mt Davies 1058m
Mt Worsnop 461m
Lake Gillen
Warburton
HWY
ROAD
565
IDA RANGE
CENTRAL AUSTRALIA
ABORIGINAL LAND TRUST
Calachini Hills 543m
COMMUNITY
SUE 4wd
Tjirrkarli Roadhouse
WARBURTON
Faulkner Hill 536m
Mt Agnes 671m
WESTERN AUSTRALIA
SOUTH AUSTRALIA
Permano Hill 719m
LENNIS HILLS
CONNIE
Lake Throssel
YEO LAKE
NATURE RESERVE
410
300
J K L M N 367 O P Q R
1 2 3 4 5 6 7 8 9 10 11 12 13

370 Northern Western Australia

371

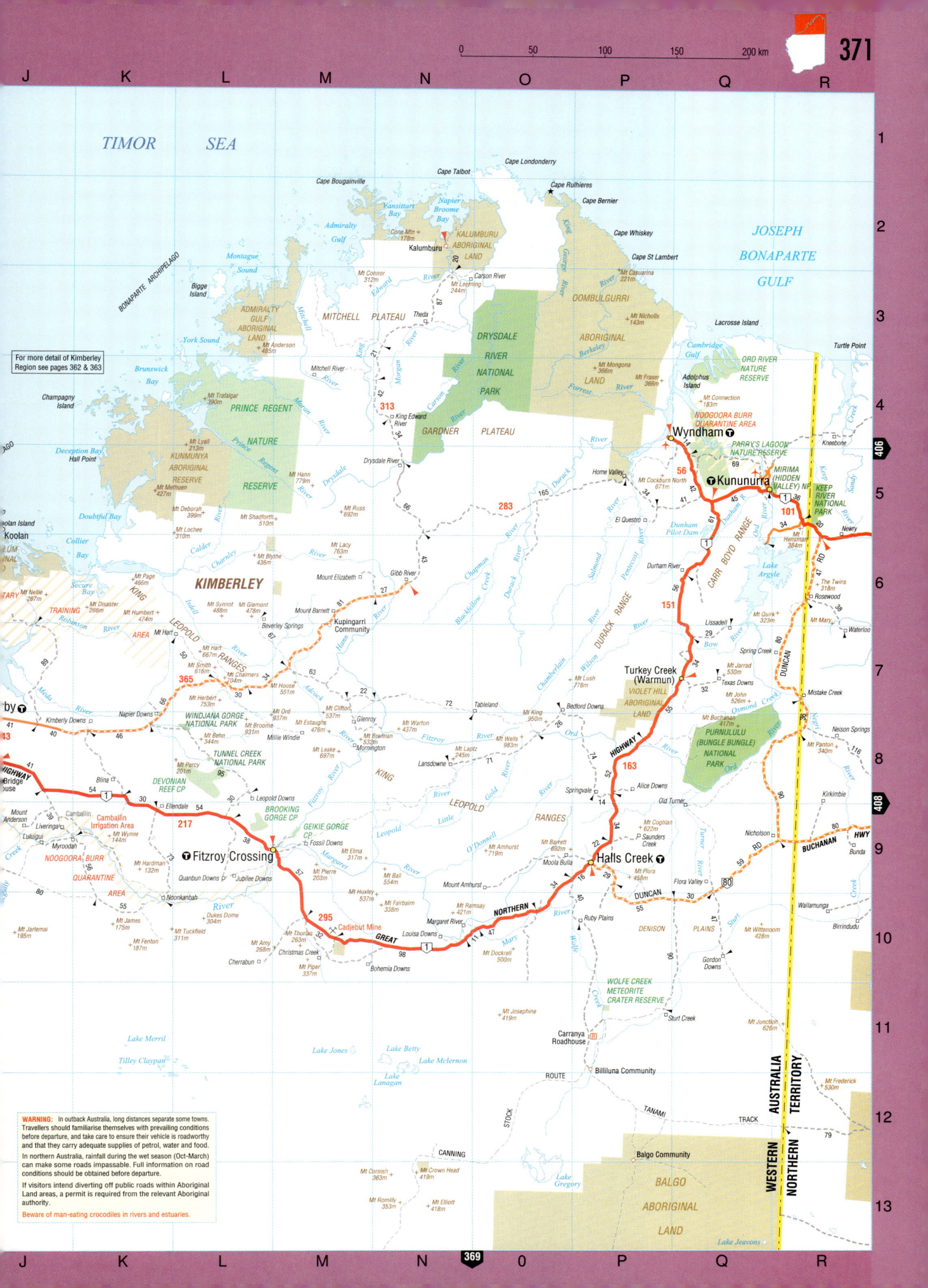

WARNING: In outback Australia, long distances separate some towns. Travellers should familiarise themselves with prevailing conditions before departure, and take care to ensure their vehicle is roadworthy and that they carry adequate supplies of petrol, water and food.

In northern Australia, rainfall during the wet season (Oct-March) can make some roads impassable. Full information on road conditions should be obtained before departure.

If visitors intend diverting off public roads within Aboriginal Land areas, a permit is required from the relevant Aboriginal authority.

Beware of man-eating crocodiles in rivers and estuaries.

For more detail of Kimberley Region see pages 362 & 363

Northern Territory

NORTHERN TERRITORY

Outback Australia

Northern Territory

There are only three main highways that take motorists into the Northern Territory: the Barkly Highway from Mount Isa in Queensland, the Stuart Highway from South Australia and the Victoria Highway from the extreme north-east of Western Australia.

Given the enormous distances involved, you may well decide to fly, either to Darwin or to Alice Springs, and then hire a car to travel around the area. Alternatively, airlines, coach companies and many tour operators offer day and extended coach tours, coach camping tours, and adventure and safari trek tours, all of which allow you to discover this unique, relatively uninhabited and exciting Territory in experienced hands.

Six times the size of Great Britain, the Northern Territory has a population similar to that of Newcastle in New South Wales. Among numerous places of interest it boasts the famous Red Centre, the world's largest monolith Uluru (Ayers Rock), and many of the best Aboriginal rock art sites in the continent.

The first, unsuccessful, attempt to settle this huge, forbidding region was not on the mainland at all, but on Melville Island in 1824. It was not until 1869 that a town called Palmerston, later to become Darwin, was established. Originally the Territory was part of New South Wales, when that State's western boundary extended to the 129th east meridian. Later, the Territory was annexed to South Australia and it did not come under Commonwealth control until 1911. In July 1978 the Territory attained self-government.

In terms of monetary value, the Territory's main industry is mining. Gold, bauxite, manganese ore, copper, silver, iron ore and uranium – all contribute to this industry. The tourist industry ranks second, and beef cattle farming is significant, even though sixteen hectares or more are often required to support one animal.

The dry season, between May and October, is a good time to visit; and 'dry' means dry – during the wet season Darwin has an average annual rainfall of 1500 millimetres, while only 25 millimetres falls in the dry season. In the wet season the rain falls mainly in the afternoon and overnight. July is the Territory's coolest month when temperatures in Darwin range between 20° and 30° C. In 'the Alice' (as Alice Springs is affectionately known) the average maximum in August is 22.5° C, cooling at night to around zero.

The Northern Territory's two main centres, Darwin and Alice Springs, are more than 1500 kilometres apart. Darwin, at the 'Top End', with a population of about 78 000, was largely rebuilt after Cyclone Tracy in 1974. It is known for its relaxed lifestyle and beautiful beaches, and makes a perfect jumping-off spot for exploring the Top End region.

If, however, you are going it alone by car, you should research your trip before setting out; read the section on Outback Motoring and bear in mind that the dry season is definitely the most pleasant weather for touring.

NOT TO BE MISSED in the Northern Territory

- **East Alligator River** – take a cruise on this spectacular river in Kakadu National Park with an Aboriginal guide
- **Glen Helen Gorge** – where the mighty Finke River squeezes between sandstone walls
- **Kings Canyon** – with its soaring 300-metre sandstone walls and views of valley below
- **Larapinta Trail** – explore the magnificent West MacDonnell Ranges on foot
- **Litchfield National Park** – superb scenery and waterfalls in this beautiful untouched wilderness area
- **Nitmiluk (Katherine Gorge)** – is in fact 13 gorges through which Katherine River flows
- **Territory Wildlife Park** – drive south from Darwin to see excellent displays of native fauna exhibited in natural bushland
- **Ubirr** – outstanding rock art galleries in Kakadu National Park
- **Uluru (Ayers Rock)** – at sunset for incredible colour changes on this massive monolith
- **Window on the Wetlands Visitor Centre** – for an overview of the conservation value of the wetlands

Rainbow Valley, south-west of Alice Springs

NORTHERN TERRITORY

Keep River National Park, south-west of Katherine on the Northern Territory border

Always make full enquiries about conditions before leaving sealed roads. The Stuart, Arnhem, Victoria and Barkly Highways are now all-weather roads, sealed for their entire length. Even so, any driving at night should be undertaken with care because of the danger from wildlife and cattle wandering across the road.

East of Darwin is the spectacular Kakadu National Park. The section of Arnhem Land east of Kakadu can be explored by extended coach tour or adventure tour. Many Aboriginal lands require entry permission from an Aboriginal Land Council. These lands belong to the Aborigines; their land is sacred to them and should be respected by visitors.

South of Darwin is Katherine with its spectacular gorge, on the southern fringe of Arnhem Land. Freshwater crocodiles are common in the Katherine River, so its beauty is best viewed from either bank. From Katherine, the Stuart Highway continues south to Alice Springs. The major town along the way is Tennant Creek, which is 104 kilometres north of the Devil's Marbles. The marbles are a random pile of huge, balancing granite boulders, some of which are almost perfect spheres. An Aboriginal

CALENDAR OF EVENTS

Note: The information given here was accurate at the time of printing. However, as the timing of events held annually is subject to change and some events may extend into the following month, it is best to check with the local tourism authority or event organisers to confirm the details. The calendar is not exhaustive. Most towns and regions throughout the Territory hold sporting competitions; regattas; rodeos; art, craft and trade exhibitions; agricultural and flower shows; music festivals and other events annually. Details of these events are available from local tourism outlets.

JANUARY
Public holidays: New Year's Day; Australia Day.

EASTER
Public holidays: Good Friday; Easter Monday. **Borroloola:** Barramundi fishing classic. **Wauchope:** Outback Go Kart Classic.

APRIL
Public holiday: Anzac Day. **Alice Springs:** Racing carnival; Country music festival.

MAY
Public Holiday: May Day. **Darwin:** Arafira sports festival (biennial, odd-numbered years); Fred's Pass rural show including 'Litchfield Gift' (foot race). **Alice Springs:** Alice Craft Acquisition; Bangtail Muster. **Mataranka:** Back to the Never Never festival; Never Never art show (sometimes in June). **Tennant Creek:** Cup Day (horseracing); Go Kart Grand Prix.

JUNE
Public holiday: Queen's Birthday. **Darwin:** Greek Glenti festival. **Adelaide River:** Bush race meeting. **Alice Springs:** Finke Desert race. **Batchelor:** International skydiving and parachuting championships (sometimes held in July). **Katherine:** Barunga sport and cultural festival; Katherine Cup; Canoe marathon.

JULY
Darwin: Agricultural show (regional public holiday); Darwin Cup carnival. **Alice Springs:** Camel Cup; Agricultural show. **Katherine:** Agricultural show (regional public holiday). **Tennant Creek:** Agricultural show (regional public holiday).

AUGUST
Public holiday: Picnic Day. **Darwin:** Beer Can regatta; Festival of Darwin; Darwin rodeo. **Alice Springs:** Yuendumu Aboriginal sports carnival; Rodeo. **Borroloola:** Agricultural show; Rodeo. **Jabiru:** Wind festival. **Mataranka:** Rodeo. **Tennant Creek:** Goldrush folk festival.

SEPTEMBER
Darwin: National Aboriginal Week. **Daly Waters:** Rodeo. **Katherine:** Flying fox festival. **Tennant Creek:** Desert harmony festival. **Timber Creek:** Races. **Wauchope:** Wimbledon at Wauchope.

OCTOBER
Alice Springs: Henley-on-Todd regatta.

NOVEMBER
Alice Springs: Corkwood festival (art, craft, music and dance).

DECEMBER
Public holidays: Christmas Day; Boxing Day.

legend says that they are eggs laid by the mythical Rainbow Serpent.

Many people outside Australia think of Alice Springs as one of the most important towns in Australia. Certainly it has been immortalised on film and in snapshots countless times. No other town, or even tiny settlement, is nearer to the geographic centre of the country. In 1872 Alice Springs was simply a repeater station for the Overland Telegraph Service; today it is not only the centre for the outback cattle industry, but also a lively tourist centre with a permanent population of approximately 25 000.

Uluru (Ayers Rock), 450 kilometres to the south-west in Uluru-Kata Tjuta National Park, is the world's biggest monolith: one huge rock, 9 kilometres in circumference and rising 348 metres above the plain on which it stands. Traditionally the Aborigines made the rock part of their sacred rituals. The mythology of the cave paintings at its base is explained on tours conducted by park guides.

The magnificent Kata Tjuta (The Olgas) and, closer to the Alice, the prehistoric palms at Palm Valley, the dramatic Kings Canyon, Standley Chasm and Ormiston Gorge – all add their own character to the wonders of the Northern Territory.

Kata Tjuta (the Olgas)

CLIMATE GUIDE

DARWIN

	J	F	M	A	M	J	J	A	S	O	N	D
Maximum °C	32	31	32	33	32	31	30	31	32	33	33	33
Minimum °C	25	25	24	24	22	20	19	21	23	25	25	25
Rainfall mm	406	349	311	97	21	1	1	7	19	74	143	232
Raindays	21	20	19	9	2	0	1	1	2	7	12	16

ALICE SPRINGS REGION

	J	F	M	A	M	J	J	A	S	O	N	D
Maximum °C	36	35	32	28	23	20	19	22	27	31	33	35
Minimum °C	21	21	17	13	8	5	4	6	10	15	18	20
Rainfall mm	36	42	37	14	17	15	16	12	9	21	26	37
Raindays	5	5	3	2	3	3	3	2	2	5	6	5

West MacDonnell Ranges

DARWIN
A Relaxed City

The city of Darwin with State Square in the foreground

NOT TO BE MISSED
in Darwin

- **Aqascene** – hand-feed fish at high tide
- **Australian Pearling Exhibition** – for fascinating history of pearling in northern Australia
- **Crocodylus Park** – a safe way to get close to these reptiles
- **Darwin Botanic Gardens** – take the Significant Tree Walk through these splendid tropical gardens
- **Deckchair Cinema** – relax in a deckchair under the stars and see a film (dry season only)
- **East Point Reserve** – excellent recreational area and home to Darwin's Military Museum and a colony of wallabies
- **Indo Pacific Marine** – for an insight into the wonders of the tropical ocean floor
- **Mindil Beach Markets** – art and craft markets, food stalls and free entertainment (dry season only)
- **Museum and Art Gallery** – fine collection of Aboriginal artifacts and fascinating Cyclone Tracy exhibit
- **The Tour Tub** – fun way to travel around the city's major attractions

The first coastal town established in the Northern Territory was Palmerston in 1864. Located at the mouth of the Adelaide River, it was quickly abandoned after a disastrous wet season in 1865.

Another expedition, led by Surveyor-General George Goyder, established a base at Adam Bay about 50 kilometres east of present-day Darwin. After surveying the area, he recommended that Port Darwin, which had been discovered in 1839 and named after Charles Darwin, would be the best place for a new settlement. The new site was also officially called Palmerston, but the locals referred to it as Port Darwin in order to distinguish it from the original settlement. The name was officially changed to Darwin in 1911 when the Federal Government took control of the Territory.

At first Darwin's development was hampered by its isolation. During

World War II, however, the Stuart Highway was completed, linking Darwin with the railhead at Alice Springs; but even when the town had recovered from the bomb damage of the war, growth was still slow.

The modern Darwin's prosperity is based largely on tourism and the mineral wealth of the Territory. Over the last 20 years the city has developed as a thriving capital that is Australia's gateway to Asia and a strategic defence location for the whole continent.

Life for the early citizens was hard and changed very little until World War II. Graziers and agriculturalists struggled to cope with the violent climatic changes. Gradual development saw the population grow to 45 000 by 1974, when Cyclone Tracy destroyed most of the city. Now the figure has pushed past 78 000, which says something for either the hardiness of its people or the desirability of the rebuilt city as a place to live, or perhaps a bit of both. With Broome, in Western Australia, Darwin is one of Australia's most multicultural settlements, embracing people of 70 racial and cultural backgrounds. Chinese people have always formed a major part of the city's population and, in more recent years, Timorese and South-East Asian refugees have arrived in Darwin and many have stayed. Quite large contingents of armed-forces personnel are also stationed at various bases around Darwin.

In the city there is very little or no rain between May and October, when the average Top End maximum temperature is 32°C. From November to April, maximum Top End temperatures average 33°C with high relative humidity; make sure you take light summer clothing on your holiday! However, Darwin is always good for sailing, swimming, water-skiing or enjoying the sunshine.

The city's business district is much like any other similar-sized city, but with a relaxed and tropical atmosphere all its own. Modern air-conditioned shopping centres serve Darwin's suburbs, which are in two main sections, divided by the international airport.

City sightseeing is conveniently done from air-conditioned motor coaches that make regular tours. The **Tour Tub** is another way to get around the city's attractions. It departs daily from the Smith Street Mall and visitors can hop on or off at their leisure. The city's main attractions are the splendidly tropical 34-hectare **Darwin Botanic Gardens**; the surviving historic buildings, churches, and memorials; the **Reserve Bank**; **State Square** which includes **Parliament House** and the **Supreme Court**; Darwin's busy **harbour** area; and, on the Esplanade overlooking the harbour, the **Beaufort Darwin Centre**, including a world-class hotel and the **Entertainment Centre**. A lookout on the Esplanade commemorates the fiftieth anniversary of the bombing of Darwin in 1942. Day, half-day and one-hour cruises around the harbour are available, contact Tourist information.

The elegant colonial architecture of **Government House** is near the southern end of the Esplanade and **Old Admiralty House**, an interesting tropical-style building, is further north.

Christ Church Cathedral was completed and consecrated in March 1977. It incorporates the porch from its predecessor, which was a garrison church during World War II and came under fire from Japanese bombers, but was eventually destroyed by Cyclone Tracy. The new cathedral features a stained glass window in memory of the trawlermen lost at sea during the cyclone. The altar, weighing 2.5 tonnes, was hewn from a jarrah log believed to be more than 400 years old. At the **Civic Centre**, not far from the cathedral, is the 'Tree of Knowledge', an ancient, spreading banyan tree. There are several other interesting places of worship in Darwin, particularly the **Chinese Temple**, where visitors are welcome to inspect the interior.

One of Darwin's most historic hotels, the **Old Victoria** in the Smith Street Mall, has been converted to a modern shopping complex, at the same time retaining its colonial character with punkahs to cool the Balcony Bar.

For those with cultural interests, the city boasts a theatre group that welcomes visitors' participation in its workshops held in **Brown's Mart**, another historic building. The **Beaufort Centre** includes a 1000-seat theatre for the performing arts. Cinemas are located in Mitchell Street and at Casuarina, and the **Deckchair Cinema** is at the Darwin Wharf Precinct.

Several art galleries, including some which feature the work of Aboriginal artists, can be visited in the city area. The **Museum and Art Gallery of the Northern Territory** located at Bullocky Point, houses important collections of Aboriginal, Balinese and New Guinean artifacts, works by Australia's most famous painters, and the Cyclone Tracy gallery which encapsulates the experience and aftermath of the cyclone.

At the entrance to the Darwin Wharf Precinct is **Indo Pacific Marine** with its brilliant coral displays and the **Australian Pearling Exhibition**, which features static, audiovisual and live displays on pearl farming. At the end of the Esplanade, at Doctors Gully off Daly Street, **Aquascene** provides the opportunity to hand-feed the ocean fish, which come in to the jetty; for feeding times, call 8981 7837. At Burnett Place on the outskirts of the city centre is the **Myilly Point** Heritage Precinct, headquarters for the National Trust. The Trust building houses an information centre and gift shop.

The **MGM Grand Darwin** is a few metres from the shores of **Mindil Beach**. This large complex offers luxury accommodation, restaurants and discos,

ACCOMMODATION

HOTELS
Beaufort Hotel
The Esplanade, Darwin
(08) 8982 9911

MGM Grand Darwin
Gilruth Ave, Mindil Beach
(08) 8946 2666

Novotel Atrium Darwin
100 The Esplanade, Darwin
(08) 8941 0755

The Plaza Hotel, Darwin
32 Mitchell St, Darwin
(08) 8982 0000

FAMILY AND BUDGET
Hotel Darwin
10 Herbert St, Darwin
(08) 8981 9211

Poinciana Inn
84 Mitchell St, Darwin
(08) 8981 8111

Top End Hotel
Cnr Daly and Mitchell Sts, Darwin
(08) 8981 6511

YWCA, Banyan View Lodge
119 Mitchell St, Darwin
(08) 8981 8644

MOTEL GROUPS: BOOKINGS
Best Western 13 1779
Flag 13 2400
Travelodge 1800 22 2446

This list is for information only; inclusion is not necessarily a recommendation.

Darwin

The splendidly tropical Darwin Botanic Gardens

sporting, gambling and convention facilities. The **Mindil Beach Sunset Market** operates on the foreshore from May to September; watch the setting sun while browsing through the food, art and craft stalls.

The **East Point Military Museum** at **East Point Reserve** displays artillery, war planes and other militaria close to the gun turrets that were constructed during World War II. The reserve is a popular recreational area with extensive walking and cycling paths, picnic areas, safe, year-round swimming in Lake Alexander and a colony of wallabies. Darwin boasts of its beautiful sunsets and East Point Reserve is one of the best viewing places. Nearby **Fannie Bay** is the site where Ross and Keith Smith landed their Vickers Vimy aircraft in 1919, completing the first flight from the UK to Australia. One of the most beautiful spots in the world to have had a prison, Fannie Bay also has some fine beaches. The former gaol, now the **Fannie Bay Gaol Museum**, features various displays including one on Cyclone Tracy.

For 'croc-spotting' in the city, **Crocodylus Park** is located at the end of McMillans Road, near the airport. The park is a research base and public education forum featuring videos, a museum, crocodile feeding and tours. Further north past the airport is **Casuarina Coastal Reserve**, an area which includes a long, white sandy beach, dunes, mangrove and monsoon vine thickets, patches of rainforest, World War II artillery observation posts and a registered Aboriginal Sacred Site, Old Man Rock. Darwin's best-known annual event is probably the Beer Can Regatta, held each August. The competing boats and other floating craft are constructed out of cans, and it is a day with lots of family fun.

Darwin's restaurants offer an excellent choice of cuisine, and there are also wine bars that offer varied menus and pleasant settings for lunch and dinner.

To the north of the city area, Darwin's suburbs have been virtually rebuilt since 1974. The tropical climate has encouraged a lush regrowth and the gardens are a feast of beautiful bougainvilleas, hibiscus and alamanders.

Sporting interests are well served in Darwin. There is a golf course, a motor sports complex, a racecourse at Fannie Bay, and facilities for tennis, squash, bowls (lawn and tenpin) and football (Aussie Rules, Rugby and Soccer). Swimming pools are located on Ross Smith Avenue, and at Casuarina and Nightcliff. Box jellyfish are common in the waters off Darwin between October and May, so swimming in the sea during this period is not recommended.

Darwin is the natural jumping-off point for touring the Top End. The pressure on luxury hotels and motels is often great and a range of alternative, less luxurious accommodation has developed, offering affordable alternatives. Many caravan parks in Darwin have permanent residents, so it is worth booking ahead.

For further information on Darwin, contact the Darwin Region Tourism Association, 33 Smith St Mall (PO Box 4392, Darwin 0801); (08) 8981 4300.

DARWIN ON FOOT

Darwin is a compact and well-designed city and most areas can be comfortably explored on foot. The following are some of the walking tours available around Darwin and its suburbs.

- **Darwin Botanic Gardens** – 3 self-guide walks through different environments; pamphlets available from Information Centre at Geranium Street entrance to gardens

- **Historical Stroll** – self-guide walk highlighting historical side of central city; route contained in Visitors Guide *Darwin and the Top End Today*

Darwin tourism authorities have prepared a series of pamphlets *Darwin: discovering our city* for self-guide walks around the city and suburbs. They include:

- **The City** – highlighting history, administrative buildings and major cultural centres

- **East Point** – recreational area with Military Museum and wallaby colony

- **The Esplanade** – stroll through foreshore park with its lookouts, memorial sites and heritage features

- **Northern Suburbs** – featuring recreational, sporting, cultural and scenic attractions

- **The Wharf** – features maritime precinct combining working port and tourist attractions

Pamphlets for the self-guide walks are available from the Darwin Region Tourism Association, 33 Smith Street Mall, Darwin; (08) 8981 4300.

TOURS from Darwin

Fogg Dam, a wildlife sanctuary 65 kilometres south-east of Darwin

In the 'dry', many tours of places of interest are accessible, by bus or conventional vehicle. Safaris by air and 4WD take sporting enthusiasts to less accessible areas for sightseeing, shooting and fishing. The best time to go bush is May to September.

Harbour cruises

Ferries depart daily from the Cullen Bay Marina on the western side of the city to Mandorah on the Cox Peninsula, an ideal place for a relaxed day on the beach, swimming or fishing. Cruises on the harbour provide a delightful way to see the city shores. Various cruises are available; sunset cruises are popular. There is also a wide range of fishing tours available around various locations in Darwin Harbour.

Air tours

Several tours by air from Darwin are available, including day or weekend excursions, and fishing and shooting trips. A three-day air tour into Western Australia, including a jungle cruise at Lake Kununurra, the Hidden Valley, the Carr Boyd Ranges, Lake Argyle and the Ord River, makes a most enjoyable trip if you can spare the time.

Howard Springs Nature Park

31 km from Darwin via the Stuart Highway

There is safe swimming here in a spring-fed pool surrounded by monsoon forest. Avid birdwatchers can spot 50 or more species in a few hours; varieties of reptiles abound. Picnic areas and a kiosk are provided.

Fogg Dam

65 km from Darwin via the Arnhem Highway

Fogg Dam was built in the late 1950s to service the short-lived rice growing plantations near Humpty Doo. Since then, the area has served as a wildlife sanctuary. A sunrise or sunset tour of this area offers an excellent opportunity to view animals and birds on the move between their feeding grounds and where they sleep. Not only is Fogg Dam a likely spot to see the Top End's birdlife, but you will also see many wallabies. The nearby swamps are the haunt of the elegant jabiru. Other birds in abundance are the pelican, egret, galah, cockatoo and kitehawk. A sign-posted trail and boardwalk provide access through patches of monsoon rainforest and paperbark swamp. The tour route then goes on to the Marrakai Plains where many species of birds can also be seen. Millions of dollars were lost in this area when the rice irrigation scheme at Humpty Doo failed. Nearby is Gows Reptile Farm, which has the largest range of snakes in Australia (250 species), as well as many lizards. Further along the highway on the top of Beatrice Hill is the Window on the Wetlands Visitor Centre providing an excellent overview of the conservation value of the wetlands.

Crocodile Farm, a large commercial crocodile farm, 40 kilometres south-east of Darwin

Cruises on the Adelaide River

64 km from Darwin via the Arnhem Highway
For a look at nature as you have never seen it, take a river cruise on which you will see jumping crocodiles from the safety of an air-conditioned vessel.

Kakadu National Park

250 km from Darwin via the Arnhem Highway
World Heritage-listed Kakadu is rich in natural and cultural heritage. Apart from abundant wildlife, the scenery here is dramatic and there are many fine examples of ancient Aboriginal rock art at sites throughout the park. The drive is fascinating, and can be topped off by a cruise on the East Alligator River. You would be unlucky not to see crocodiles, as well as wallabies, and the birdlife is prolific; however, sightings of buffalo are becoming rare. The Arnhem Highway is sealed all the way to Jabiru, and you could do the trip in your own car or a hired vehicle. Approximately 100 kilometres south of Jabiru are the Jim Jim Falls, accessible only by 4WD. There are many good camping spots on Jim Jim Creek and other billabongs. The safari guides have local knowledge and can show you far more than if you explore this area on your own. **See also**: Aboriginal Art; The Top End; National Parks.

Eastern Arnhem Land

304 km from Darwin via the Arnhem Highway
The 9.4 million hectares of eastern Arnhem Land, one of Australia's most fascinating wilderness areas, lie to the east of Kakadu. It is an ancient land that changes from broken mountains to vast plains, irrigated by constantly flowing rivers. An entry permit is required, which tourist agencies arrange through Aboriginal Land Councils. It is best visited as part of an organised tour.

Crocodile Farm

40 km from Darwin via the Stuart Highway
Australia's first and largest commercial crocodile farm has over 7000 crocodiles, that range in length from just a few centimetres to 4 metres. There are feeding displays and tours daily. Be adventurous and try some farm-raised crocodile delicacies.

Territory Wildlife Park at Berry Springs

56 km from Darwin via the Stuart Highway
A wildlife park of international standard, located in more than 400 hectares of bushland at Berry Springs, the Territory Wildlife Park is designed to display only animals native and feral to the Northern Territory. The exhibits are all connected by a 4-kilometre link road and include open-moated enclosures, with kangaroos, wallabies, dingoes, bustards, buffalo and banteng; a naturally occurring lagoon where native birds can be viewed from a hide; an aquarium that features an acrylic walk-through tunnel for underwater viewing of large freshwater fish; a series of aviaries that display birds in natural habitats; a walk-through rainforest aviary; and the second largest nocturnal house in the world, artificially moonlit, where visitors can see about 50 species of mammal, bird and reptile. The park is a project of the Parks and Wildlife Commission of the Northern Territory. Adjacent to the Territory Wildlife Park is the Berry Springs Nature Park, which features a spring-fed swimming area. The park is ideal for a picnic.

NORTHERN TERRITORY
from A to Z

Adelaide River   Pop. 356

MAP REF. 402 E8, 406 E7

A small settlement set in pleasant country 112 km SE of Darwin on Stuart Hwy, Adelaide River was the location for 30 000 Australian soldiers during World War II. **Of interest:** On Stuart Hwy: Motor Cycle Haven, a collection of motor cycles and memorabilia; historic railway station (1888) has displays of local history. June: Bush race meeting. **In the area:** War cemetery, just north of town. Litchfield National Park, a picturesque wilderness area featuring spectacular waterfalls, bushwalks and prolific wildlife; main entrance via Batchelor on sealed road. Daly River township, 114 km SW; great fishing, local Aboriginal arts and crafts, native flora and fauna in surrounding area. Organised tours available to Daly River Aboriginal Land Trust area, 100 km west of Daly River. **Accommodation:** 1 hotel/motel, 1 cara./camp. park.

Aileron   Pop. 50

MAP REF. 410 I6

A rest stop on Stuart Hwy, Aileron is 139 km N of Alice Springs. **Of interest:** At Roadhouse: Aboriginal art, native wildlife, Sunday roast lunch, playground and picnic/barbecue facilities. **In the area:** Ryans Well Historical Reserve, 7 km SE. **Accommodation:** 1 hotel/motel, 1 hostel.

Alice Springs   Pop. 20 448

MAP REF. 405 K3, 411 J8

Alice Springs is at the heart of the Red Centre, almost 1500 km from the nearest capital city, and is a base for many tourist attractions including Uluru (Ayers Rock). Small irrigated areas support dairy and fruit-growing enterprises, but the main produce in the region is beef cattle from huge runs. More than 350 000 visitors a year pass through this modern, well-maintained town set in the heart of the MacDonnell Ranges. 'The Alice' offers a variety of accommodation and restaurants, an international casino, sports grounds, an Olympic swimming pool and an 18-hole golf course. There is a wide variety of shops and a number of art galleries specialising in Aboriginal art. The Todd River, which runs through the town, is dry except after heavy rains; for the annual Henley-on-Todd regatta in Oct. the boats are carried or fitted with wheels. Between May and Sept. days are warm and nights can be cold. For the rest of the year daytime temperatures rise into the high 30s but nights are milder. Rains, usually brief, can come at any time of year. The town site was seen by William Whitfield Mills in 1871, when he was surveying a route for the Overland Telegraph Line. He named the Todd River after the SA Superintendent of Telegraphs, Sir Charles Todd, and a nearby waterhole Alice Springs after Lady Todd. The first settlement was at the repeater station, built for transmitting messages across the continent. In 1860 John McDouall Stuart had passed about 50 km W of the site. He named Central Mt Sturt after Captain Sturt, who had commanded an earlier expedition, however the SA Government renamed the mountain in Stuart's honour. Pastoralist John Ross also helped look for a route for the telegraph line. Until 1880 the repeater station was the only reason for the existence of a handful of people in this remote area, then the Government sent surveys north seeking suitable sites for railheads. The township of Stuart, 3.2 km from the telegraph station, was gazetted in 1880, but the railway remained unbuilt. Regular supply was maintained by the expensive and slow camel train from Port Augusta. Even the discovery of gold at Arltunga, 113 km NE of the settlement, did little to develop Stuart. The Federal Government took control of NT from SA in 1911; from that time the township developed slowly. The Australian Inland Mission stationed Sister Jane Finlayson there in 1916 and the growing needs of the area led to the establishment of Adelaide House nursing hostel in 1926. The railway was completed in 1929. The service became known as *The Ghan*, after the Afghan camel drivers it had replaced. As the township grew there

The Old Telegraph Station, just north of Alice Springs

The Red Centre

The first priority for most tourists in the Red Centre is Uluru (Ayers Rock). About 450 kilometres south-west of the Alice, the world's greatest monolith rises majestically 348 metres above a wide, sandy floodplain covered in spinifex and desert oak. The rock is 9 kilometres in circumference and, with the movement of the sun during the day, it changes colour through shades of fiery red, delicate mauve, blues, pinks and browns. When rain falls it veils the rock in a torrent of silver.

Yulara, about 20 minutes' drive north of Uluru, is a self-contained township; it has accommodation, a supermarket, and other shops and services. Ayers Rock Resort at Yulara offers a range of accommodation: the top-class Sails in the Desert Hotel, the Outback Pioneer Hotel and Lodge, the Desert Gardens four-star resort, Spinifex Lodge, Emu Walk self-contained serviced apartments, and well-equipped camping grounds. With its prize-winning design, Yulara does not intrude into the landscape but blends into the ochre colours of the desert. If you can, allow for a stay of at least two days, this will give you time to explore Uluru and see a sunrise and a sunset there, and to visit Kata Tjuta (The Olgas) – the two most famous attractions in **Uluru-Kata Tjuta National Park.**

An excellent way to familiarise yourself with the region is to spend an hour or so at the Yulara Visitors Centre. Displays depict the geology, history, flora and fauna of the region and there is a spectacular collection of photographs. Audiovisual shows are held regularly. Excellent displays of Aboriginal culture and arts are also available at the Uluru-Kata Tjuta Cultural Centre on the road to Uluru. This splendidly designed building is in the shape of two snakes.

According to Aboriginal legends, Uluru and Kata Tjuta were created and given their distinctive forms during the Tjukurpa or creation period. At the base of Uluru there are cave paintings and carvings made thousands of years ago by members of the Loritja and Pitjanjatjara tribes. It is not difficult to appreciate that this is a sacred place of ancient times, particularly for its traditional owners.

Do not attempt the 1.6-kilometre climb of Uluru unless you are fit and well, and have a good head for heights, or if the weather is hot – the track is exposed and steep, and casualties are common. The climb follows a religious track, and the Anangu (the traditional owners) prefer visitors to take some of the other discovery walks in the park and near the rock itself. Taking the 9-kilometre circuit walk around the base of Uluru, you will see rock art, the Mutitjulu (Sound Shell), a cavity as smooth as if formed by the sea, and the Taputji (Kangaroo Tail), a 160-metre strip of stone. Tours include the Mala Walk, the Edible Desert Walk (Aboriginal bush tucker) and the Liru Walk, conducted by Aboriginal guides.

Some 50 kilometres to the west are Kata Tjuta (The Olgas), a cluster of rounded, massive rocks equally mysterious. They too are dramatic and vividly coloured. The tallest dome of Kata Tjuta, Mount Olga, is 546 metres above the oasis-like Valley of the Winds that runs through the rock system. Ernest Giles, who first saw Mount Olga named it after the Queen of Spain.

Accommodation, meals and tours from Yulara to the unusual flat-topped Mount Conner are available; bookings at Yulara. Curtin Springs cattle station and roadside inn is on the Lasseter Highway, 82 kilometres east of Yulara.

A good way to see many of the tourist attractions in the Red Centre is to start from **Alice Springs**. You can take advantage of the coach tours that operate from there, or take your own vehicle. A few tourist destinations require 4WD; check before you set out. The Mereenie Loop Road links Glen Helen to Kings Canyon and enables visitors to travel from Alice Springs to Uluru (Ayers Rock) via the West MacDonnell Ranges, Glen Helen and Kings Canyon. It allows most of the attractions to the west and south of Alice Springs to be incorporated in a circular route without major backtracking. As the Loop Road passes through Aboriginal land, a permit is required.

The Alice Springs Telegraph Station Historical Reserve is only 3 kilometres north of Alice Springs. The original Alice Springs settlement's stone buildings have been restored by the Parks and Wildlife Commission of the Northern Territory and furnished with artifacts from early this century. There is also an historic display. Guided tours are available half-hourly. The 570-hectare reserve offers bushwalking, picnicking and wildlife observation. A small waterhole, the original water source for the settlement, from which Alice Springs obtained its name, is nearby. The telegraph station was built to link Port Augusta to Darwin, the link continuing by submarine cable to Java. Completed in 1872, the line was used until 1932, when operations were transferred to the site at the corner of Parsons Street and Railway Terrace in Alice Springs. The telegraph station site then housed an Aboriginal Mission, The Bungalow, which closed in 1963.

An interesting day tour from Alice Springs is to visit the attractions of the **West MacDonnell National Park.** The beautiful Standley Chasm, 50 kilometres west, is managed by the Angkerle Aboriginal Corporation. This colourful cleft in the West MacDonnells is only 5 metres wide. At midday when the sunlight reaches the floor of the chasm, turning the walls a blazing red, it is a memorable sight. On the way, Simpsons Gap, 18 kilometres west of Alice Springs, can be visited at

Uluru (Ayers Rock), the star attraction in the Red Centre

the same time and has walking access. A sealed bike track links Alice Springs and Simpsons Gap.

Further west, about 133 kilometres from Alice Springs on the Finke River, are Glen Helen and Ormiston Gorges. Their colours were captured by the famous Aboriginal artist Albert Namatjira; they also lend themselves to photography, as does the sunrise on Mount Sonder to the west. **Glen Helen** Homestead is an accommodation base for the West MacDonnells, or a day tour is available from Alice Springs.

A 4WD day tour from Alice Springs will also take you to Palm Valley and the Finke River Gorge, 155 kilometres south-west. The Finke River is one of the oldest watercourses in the world and to walk along its bed is an unforgettable experience. Palm Valley, with its rock pools, cycad palms and *Livistona* palms unique to the area, is yet another of the wonders of the Centre. The plant life has such a prehistoric appearance that to enter the valley is like taking a trip back in time. These two attractions can also be visited by taking a two-day tour from Alice Springs. Also well worth a visit is the restored Mission at **Hermannsburg**, 125 kilometres west of Alice Springs, on the way to Palm Valley – arrive for their splendid morning tea, lunch or afternoon tea.

Kings Canyon, 330 kilometres south-west of Alice Springs in **Watarrka National Park**, is one of the most interesting and scenic areas of the Centre. The climb to the rim of the canyon is fairly arduous, but well worth the effort. Even more spectacular views can be obtained by crossing via the small, railed Cotterills Bridge, near the old, nerve-racking tree-trunk bridge. The Lost City and the Garden of Eden are superb sights here. The Kings Canyon Resort and Kings Creek Camping Ground provide accommodation in this area.

East of Alice Springs in the East MacDonnell Ranges are Corroboree Rock, which is of significance to the Eastern Arrernte Aborigines; the scenic Trephina Gorge; N'Dhala Gorge, which has a variety of flora and ancient rock engravings; and Ruby Gap Nature Park, a picturesque area only accessible to high-clearance 4WD.

The Arltunga Historical Reserve, 110 kilometres east of Alice Springs, beyond Trephina Gorge, preserves memorabilia of the goldmining era in the region. Little evidence remains of the shanty town that grew up after 1887 when alluvial gold was found. You can explore the stone ruins, scattered workings, gravestones and go down a mine. At the Visitors Centre there are historical exhibits, with a gaol and restored police station 2 kilometres away.

There is a private camping ground next to the reserve and the hotel offers meals and has antiques on display. Fossicking in the area is good. **Ross River** Homestead, 88 kilometres east of Alice Springs, offers a range of outback experiences and comfortable accommodation.

Thirty-five kilometres south of Alice Springs are the ancient Ewaninga Rock Carvings or petroglyphs. Signs along a short walk explain Aboriginal use of this area.

A turning off the Stuart Highway about 140 kilometres south-west of Alice Springs leads to the Henbury meteorite craters. The Henbury craters are believed to have been formed several thousand years ago when a falling meteor broke into pieces and hit the earth. The largest of the 12 craters is 180 metres wide and 15 metres deep; while the smallest is 6 metres wide and only a few centimetres deep.

For further information about the attractions of the Red Centre, contact the Central Australian Tourism Industry Association, Centrepoint Building, cnr Gregory Tce and Hartley St, Alice Springs; (08) 8952 5199. **See also:** National Parks and A–Z listing for those parks and towns indicated by bold type. **Map reference:** 404–5.

The Mereenie Loop Road

The Mereenie Loop Road links **Glen Helen** to **Kings Canyon** in the far south-west. The road is mainly gravel or dirt but can be used by conventional vehicles throughout most of the year. As a section of the road passes through Aboriginal Land, a permit is required; these are obtainable in **Alice Springs** (contact Tourist information). This link enables visitors to travel from Alice Springs to Uluru (Ayers Rock) via the West MacDonnell Ranges, Glen Helen and Kings Canyon, without major backtracking.

Heading west from Alice Springs and along Namatjira Drive, this route passes the major attractions of the **West MacDonnell National Park**, including Simpsons Gap, Standley Chasm, Ellery Creek Big Hole and Serpentine and Ormiston Gorges, before reaching Glen Helen. An alternative route to approach Glen Helen is to continue on Larapinta Drive via **Hermannsburg** and, if travelling by 4WD, to divert to Finke River Gorge and Palm Valley in **Finke Gorge National Park**.

After Glen Helen, the route leads south-west, joining the Mereenie Loop Road, and down the escarpment to Kings Canyon in **Watarrka National Park**. Towards the Glen Helen end of this stretch it is possible to divert to

Valley of the Domes, Kings Canyon

Tnorala (Gosse Bluff), a spectacular crater formed 130 million years ago; a separate permit is required to enter the Tnorala Conservation Reserve and can be obtained from Mereenie Tour Pass outlets.

From Watarrka visitors can travel via the Ernest Giles Road, Luritja Road and Lasseter Highway to **Yulara** and **Uluru-Kata Tjuta National Park**. A minimum of two days should be allowed for the journey. Hotel-style accommodation is available at Glen Helen Homestead, Kings Canyon Resort and Yulara, or there are numerous camping facilities along the route. Various informative Aboriginal cultural tours are available at certain landmarks along the way. Contact Tourist information for details. **See also:** National Parks and A–Z listing for those parks and towns indicated by bold type; Aboriginal-operated Tours. **Map references:** 404 A5, 410 F9.

NORTHERN TERRITORY

was too much confusion between Stuart and Alice Springs, only 3 km apart, so the name Stuart was dropped. **Of interest:** Heritage Walk, contact Tourist information. In Todd Mall: Flynn Memorial Church, in memory of founder of Royal Flying Doctor Service; Adelaide House, originally hospital now museum housing pedal-radio equipment used by Flynn and other memorabilia; various outlets for Aboriginal art and artifacts. Aboriginal Art and Culture Centre, Todd St. Royal Flying Doctor Service base, Stuart Tce; tours daily. In Hartley St: Panorama 'Guth', 360° landscape painting of Central Australia; Minerals House, featuring geological and mineral displays (open Mon.–Fri.). Old Stuart Gaol, Parsons St. Strehlow Research Centre, collection of artifacts of Arrernte people; cnr Larapinta and Memorial Dr. Technology, Transport and Communications Museum, Memorial Dr. In Larapinta Dr.: Araluen Arts Centre, focal point for performing and visual arts; Diarama Village, includes Aboriginal Dreamtime Caves depicting Aboriginal myths and legends. At the northern end of town: Anzac Hill, West Tce, for excellent views of town. School of the Air, open school days a.m.; Head St. Across the river: Lasseter's Casino, Barrett Dr.; Olive Pink Flora Reserve, Australia's only arid-zone botanic garden; cnr Barrett Dr. and Causeway. Apr.: Racing carnival; Country music festival. May: Bangtail muster. June: Finke Desert race. July: Camel Cup; Agricultural show. Aug.: Yuendumu Aboriginal sports carnival; Rodeo. Oct.: Henley-on-Todd regatta. Nov.: Corkwood festival (art, craft, music and dance). **In the area:** Great variety of tours of varying duration covering scenic attractions, Aboriginal culture and specialist interests; experience these by bus or coach, limousine, 4WD safari, Harley-Davidson motorcycle, camel, horse, aircraft, helicopter or hot-air balloon. *To the north:* Old Telegraph Station (3 km), an historic reserve with original stone buildings and equipment. *To the north-east:* Gemtree (140 km), fossicking for garnet or zircon. *To the east:* Frontier Camel Farm (7 km) features camel rides, reptile house and museum displays highlighting importance of camels and their Afghan masters to the area; nearby, Mecca Date Gardens, Australia's first commercial date farm; Alice Springs Winery, NT's only commercial winery (11 km); Emily Gap (13 km) and Jessie Gap (18 km) Nature Parks; Corroboree Rock Reserve (48 km) has signposted walk explaining significance of rock to Eastern Arrernte people; Trephina Gorge Nature Park (80 km); N'Dhala Gorge Nature Park (98 km), ancient Aboriginal rock engravings and flora; Ross River Homestead (88 km), historic homestead offering bush activities and accommodation; Arltunga Historical Reserve (110 km), former goldmine with historic sites and restored buildings. *To the south:* Old Timers' Museum (5 km) features exhibits of 1890s era; Ghan Preservation Society rail museum at MacDonnell Siding (10 km) features the *Old Ghan* which runs on 23.5 km of private line between MacDonnell Siding and Ewaninga (trip includes meal at siding stop); Ewaninga Rock Carvings Conservation Reserve (39 km), an Aboriginal cultural site with rock engravings; Chambers Pillar Historical Reserve (149 km) includes 50-m high rock pillar which served as a landmark feature for the Centre's early pioneers and explorers. *To the south-west:* Pitchi Richi Sanctuary (2 km), open-air museum displaying William Ricketts clay sculptures; Palm Valley in Finke Gorge National Park (130 km) has unique *Livistona* palms (4WD access only); Virginia Camel Farm (93 km) offers camel rides and trail rides; Henbury Meteorite Craters Conservation Park (147 km); Kings Canyon in Watarrka National Park (323 km), spectacular scenery; Uluru-Kata Tjuta National Park (450 km) includes Uluru (Ayers Rock) and Kata Tjuta (the Olgas). *To the west:* Grave site of Rev. John Flynn (5 km); Simpsons Gap (18 km); Standley Chasm (50 km); Ellery Creek Big Hole (93 km); Serpentine Gorge (104 km); Ochre Pits (119 km), natural quarry once mined by Aborigines; Ormiston Gorge (132 km); Glen Helen Gorge (133 km); Redbank Gorge (170 km, 4WD access only); Hermannsburg (125 km); Tnorala (Gosse Bluff) meteor crater (210 km, permit required); most of these attractions are in the West MacDonnell National Park, so too is the famous Larapinta Trail, a well-marked walking track that winds through the West MacDonnell Ranges. A sealed bicycle path links Alice Springs to Simpsons Gap. The Mereenie Loop Road linking Glen Helen and Kings Canyon enables visitors to travel from Alice Springs to Uluru via the West MacDonnell Ranges and Kings Canyon; permit required, inquire at Tourist information. **Tourist information:** Centrepoint Building, cnr Gregory Tce and Hartley St; (08) 8952 5800. **Accommodation:** 2 hotels, 16 motels, 6 cara./camp. parks. **See also:** Aboriginal Art; The Red Centre.

Barkly Homestead Pop. 20

MAP REF. 409 N11

Barkly Homestead is a comfortable fuel or accommodation stop on the junction of Barkly and Tablelands Hwys, 185 km E from the junction of Stuart and Barkly Hwys. **Accommodation:** 1 motel, 1 cara./camp. park.

Barrow Creek Pop. 30

MAP REF. 411 J4

Located on the Stuart Hwy, 283 km N of Alice Springs, Barrow Creek was originally a water stop for cattle-droving. **Of interest:** Old Telegraph Station (1872). **Tourist information:** Barrow Creek Hotel; (08) 8956 9753. **Accommodation:** 1 hotel/motel, 1 cara./camp. park.

Batchelor Pop. 635

MAP REF. 402 D7, 406 E7

Former town for Rum Jungle mine (now closed), Australia's first uranium mine, Batchelor is now the gateway to Litchfield National Park. **Of interest:** Mini-replica of Karlstein Castle of Bohemia. Scenic flights, parachuting and gliding, at airport. June (or July): International skydiving and parachuting championships. **In the area:** Rum Jungle Lake, 10 km W, ideal for swimming. Litchfield National Park, 40 km W, a wilderness area with rivers, spectacular waterfalls (Wangi, Sandy Creek, Florence and Tolmer), bushwalks, fauna, magnetic termite mounds, pockets of scenic rainforest, secluded waterholes and well-equipped camping grounds. **Tourist information:** Rum Jungle Motor Inn, Rum Jungle Rd; (08) 8976 0123. **Accommodation:** 1 motel, 1 cara./camp. park.

Borroloola Pop. 594

MAP REF. 407 O13, 409 O3

A small settlement on the banks of the McArthur River and once one of the larger and more colourful frontier

The Top End

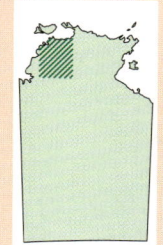

Darwin is a major tourist destination with its warm weather, excellent beaches and abundance of fish, but its real attraction is as a base for exploring the wild and fascinating country at the 'Top End'. Here you see wide billabongs covered with lilies, clouds of geese wheeling above the trees, crocodiles sunning themselves on waterside rocks, plunging waterfalls, rows of pillar-like termite mounds, spectacular cliff and rock features, and caves and cliffs bearing the Aboriginal rock art of the past.

A number of reserves preserve the features of the region and make them accessible to travellers. The most spectacular of these, in an area fast becoming one of the top natural tourist attractions in Australia, is **Kakadu National Park**, in the vast and wild country along the East and South Alligator Rivers.

Kakadu has World Heritage status; it is considered to be of outstanding worth for both its natural features and its cultural significance. Situated 250 kilometres from Darwin, it encompasses an area of 1 307 300 hectares (almost 20 000 square kilometres). Owned by the Aboriginal people, the park is leased to the Australian Nature Conservation Agency (ANCA) to manage for all visitors to enjoy.

Kakadu contains a wealth of archaeological and rock-art sites that provide insights into Aboriginal culture. The park's traditional owners are willing to share their knowledge and understanding of their land so that visitors will appreciate the importance of Kakadu and share responsibility for its protection.

Kakadu is unique in that it encompasses an entire river catchment, the South Alligator River system, and within it are found all the major habitat types of the Top End. The park is rich in vegetation, ranging from pockets of rainforest through dwarf shrubland to open forest and swamps. The abundant wildlife includes many animals unique to the area, such as the banded pigeon, the rock possum and a species of rock wallaby. Features in the park include Yellow Waters, a spectacular wetlands area with prolific birdlife, particularly in the dry season, and Ubirr and Nourlangie Rock, where there is Aboriginal rock art. A spectacular point in the park is the Jim Jim Falls, 215 metres high and with a sheer drop of 152 metres of water pouring (in the wet season) over a rugged escarpment (4WD access only).

Ubirr, a major rock-art site in Kakadu National Park

North of the Jim Jim Falls is the East Alligator River, a well-known fishing ground where barramundi can be caught and where the river reaches wind through spectacularly beautiful country. Visits to some isolated locations in the park are subject to a permit system to limit visitor numbers, because of the sensitive nature of those areas.

As crocodiles are present in the park, swimming is not recommended and those who fish from the banks of rivers or from boats should take care.

Visit the Bowali Visitor Centre on the Kakadu Hwy just before Jabiru and obtain a copy of the *Visitor Guide*, an excellent publication full of helpful information. Accommodation in the park consists of hotels, caravan parks, a youth hostel, and private and national park camping grounds. Facilities are available for the disabled. Fuel, food and provisions may be obtained at Jabiru township, Border Store, Kakadu Holiday Village and Cooinda. Visitors over sixteen years of age pay a park use fee (valid for fourteen days).

Spectacular **Litchfield National Park** is just a 2-hour drive south from Darwin. It offers stunning sandstone formations, magnetic termite mounds, four major waterfalls and year-round swimming. There are delightful short walks, camping sites within the park and, for the adventurous, a 4WD trail is open during the dry season.

Small parks close to Darwin are Berry Springs, 65 kilometres south, and Howard Springs, 35 kilometres south-east. Berry Springs is noted for its warm water, pleasant and safe swimming, and its birdlife. Adjacent to Berry Springs is the Territory Wildlife Park, where visitors can see animals and birds of the area in a bush setting; shuttle trains and guided tours are available. At Howard Springs the pool is surrounded by rainforest; again, the park abounds in birds and other wildlife.

Along the Stuart Highway, 354 kilometres south-east of Darwin, are the town of **Katherine** and the spectacular **Nitmiluk (Katherine Gorge) National Park**. Here the clear river flows between the brilliantly coloured walls of the gorge, which reach a height of 60 metres. A boat tour through the gorge is guaranteed to be a highlight of any holiday.

A further 110 kilometres south-east of Katherine is **Elsey National Park**, which includes the Mataranka Pool Reserve, where thermal springs are surrounded by lush tropical forest and the water is permanently at body temperature.

Four-wheel drive wildlife safaris can be arranged in Darwin; an ideal way to see the country and experience something of life in the Top End. There are major roads to all these Top End attractions. However, if you are contemplating an unguided tour of the region, it is vital to recognise that, should you stray into unknown areas, you may experience difficulties; so plan carefully. **See also:** Outback Motoring.

For further information on Kakadu, contact Park Manager, Kakadu National Park, PO Box 71, Jabiru NT 0886; (08) 8938 1100. A *Visitor Guide* to the park is available from the ANCA: GPO Box 636, Canberra ACT 2601; and GPO Box 1260, Darwin NT 0800; or from Park Headquarters. For further information on the Top End contact the Darwin Region Tourism Association, 33 Smith St Mall (PO Box 4392, Darwin 0801); (08) 8981 4300. **See also:** National Parks and individual town entries in A–Z listing for those parks and towns indicated by bold type. **Map references:** 402–3, 406–7.

Aboriginal Art

Art is one of the essential elements in Aboriginal culture, often using symbols to communicate ideas that cannot be expressed in any other way. Rich and complex beliefs embodied in the Dreaming are expressed in art with many layers of meaning in a variety of contexts, from the sacred and secret realm of ceremony to the more public domain. Aboriginal art takes many forms from the enduring rock engravings and paintings to the more ephemeral forms including body decoration, and bark and ground paintings.

There is an enormous diversity from region to region, for example in the desert regions, ground paintings are common, whereas in Arnhem Land bark paintings are made. Rock art is the oldest surviving type of Aboriginal art and is widely distributed throughout the continent. The most extensive and possibly the oldest rock art in the world can be found in the Victoria River District and Arnhem Land and also in the Kimberley in north-western Western Australia and the sandstone country of the Quinkin Reserves around Laura in far north Queensland. Simple engraved lines are found in caves in south-eastern Australia and the Nullarbor Plain, and engravings and petroglyphs ranging from simple designs to cryptic symbols are distributed across the continent from Sydney through southern Australia to the Pilbara in Western Australia.

Aboriginal contemporary artists continue the cultural traditions that are thousands of years old. Regional variation includes work in traditional ochres on bark or paper, acrylics on canvas and sculptural objects. In recent years there has been a flowering of traditional and contemporary themes applied to ceramics, fabrics and prints.

The following includes some of the places where rock art can be seen, as well as the major Aboriginal galleries and shops where paintings and artifacts can be viewed or purchased.

At the Top End

Western Arnhem Land, which includes Kakadu National Park, is the major rock art area in the Top End. Kakadu has representation of all the diverse rock art styles to be found in western Arnhem Land and the two most accessible sites for visitors are Ubirr and Nourlangie Rock. Some of the sites have been carbon-dated at 60 000 years, and others go back even earlier. The earliest images include imprints of hands and plants. Some of the most spectacular sites in western Arnhem Land can be seen via the number of exclusive safari camps; contact Tourist information for details.

Eastern Arnhem Land has an outstanding tradition of bark painting. Traditionally bark painting was transient and the designs were secret or sacred. The designs are complex and identify ancestral beings and their relationship to each other and the landscape against a background of intricate crosshatching. The production of bark paintings for sale involved the use of non-secret designs and techniques that preserved both bark and pigments. Eastern Arnhem Land has numerous art and craft centres in remote communities that can be accessed by special charters; contact Tourist information for details.

Aboriginal Galleries and Shops
Darwin: Ampiji, Darwin Airport • Framed the Darwin Gallery, Cnr Geranium St and Stuart Hwy • Raintree Aboriginal Art Gallery, Shop 1, 18 Knuckey St • Riji Dij, Shop 3, Anthony Plaza • Shades of Ochre Aboriginal Art Gallery, 17 Anthony Plaza, Smith Street Mall.
Kakadu National Park: Bowali Visitor Centre, Kakadu Hwy • Warradjan Cultural Centre, Cooinda Rd, Yellow Waters.
Katherine: Creative Native Art Gallery, Shop 2, Lot 4, Katherine Tce • Mimi Aboriginal Arts and Crafts, Shop 9, Southgate Complex, Lindsay St.

In Central Australia

Ground painting is a widespread practice in central Australia, particularly among the Warumungu people. The paintings are used for storytelling and ceremonial purposes, and the designs, based on significant landscape features and mythological creatures, are painted on prepared earth usually with ochre, and the background filled with dots. The Walpiri practise sand drawing and use it as a means of communication by using a form of graphic notation, for example a straight line represents a spear, and the children learn to read the designs by frequently watching the storytelling. Recently these ground-art designs have formed the design basis for artists working with ceramics, fabrics and acrylic paints on canvas.

Aboriginal Galleries and Shops
Alice Springs: Aboriginal Art and Culture Centre, 86 Todd St • Aboriginal Desert Art Gallery, 87 Todd Mall • Aboriginal Dreamtime Gallery, 71 Todd St • Arunta Art Gallery and Book Shop, 70 Todd St • CAAMA Shop, Yeperenye Shopping Plaza and Alice Springs Airport • Mbantua Gallery, Gregory Tce • The Original Dreamtime Art Gallery, 63 Todd Mall • Papunya Tula Artists Pty Ltd, 78 Todd St • VAST Art Gallery, cnr Todd St and Gregory Tce • Waraumpi Arts, Shop 7, Gregory House.
Tennant Creek: Anyinginyi Arts and Crafts.
Yulara: Mulgara Gallery, Foyer of Sails in the Desert Hotel, Ayers Rock Resort • Uluru-Kata Tjuta Cultural Centre, within park on road to Uluru.

For further information about Aboriginal art sites and Aboriginal galleries and shops: in the Top End, contact Darwin Region Tourism Association, 33 Smith St Mall; (08) 8981 4300; in central Australia, contact Central Australian Tourism Industry Association, Centrepoint Building, cnr Gregory Tce and Hartley St, Alice Springs; (08) 8952 5199.

'X-ray' art at Nourlangie Rock in Kakadu National Park

towns, Borroloola is now very popular with fishing enthusiasts. **Of interest:** Fishing charter available, contact Tourist information. Museum in old police station (1886), Robinson Rd; obtain key from Tourist information. Self-guide heritage walk. Scenic flights over town and Sir Edward Pellew Islands available. Easter: Barramundi fishing classic. Aug.: Agricultural show; Rodeo. **In the area:** Cape Crawford, 113 km SW, base for seeing Bukalava Rock Formations (60 km E), mass of chasms winding through ancient sandstone formations (in very remote area, guide recommended); and Lost City, accessible only by helicopter and visitors must be accompanied by a guide. **Tourist information:** McArthur River Caravan Park, Robinson Rd; (08) 8975 8734. **Accommodation:** 1 hotel, 1 cara./camp. park.

Daly Waters   Pop. 298

MAP REF. 408 I3

Situated 4 km N of the junction of Stuart and Carpentaria Hwys, Daly Waters became the first international refuelling stop for Qantas during World War II. **Of interest:** Historic hotel (1930), Stuart St. Sept.: Rodeo. **In the area:** Airport museum, 1 km NE, off Stuart Hwy at Old Daly Waters aerodrome. Tree, 1 km N, reputedly marked with the letter S by explorer John McDouall Stuart. **Tourist information:** Daly Waters Hotel, Stuart St; (08) 8975 9927. **Accommodation:** 1 hotel, 1 motel, 1 cara./camp. park.

Dunmarra   Pop. 30

MAP REF. 408 I4

This stopping-place on the Stuart Hwy is 8 km S of the Stuart and Buchanan Hwys junction, and 361 km N of Tennant Creek. **Of interest:** Historic photograph collection at Wayside Inn. **Tourist information:** Wayside Inn; (08) 8975 9922. **Accommodation:** 1 motel, 1 cara./camp. park.

Elliott   Pop. 423

MAP REF. 409 J6

Elliott is on the Stuart Hwy, 254 km N of Tennant Creek. Go-kart racing twice yearly. **In the area:** Unusual milky white water (thought to be caused by gum leaves) at Lake Woods, NT's largest lake located 13 km SW. **Tourist information:** Elliott Hotel, Stuart Hwy; (084) 69 2069. **Accommodation:** 1 hotel/motel, 2 cara./camp. parks.

Glen Helen   Pop. 20

MAP REF. 404 E3, 410 H8

On Namatjira Drive, 132 km W of Alice Springs, Glen Helen is an excellent base for exploring the superb scenery in the surrounding area. **Of interest:** At Glen Helen Gorge, 300 m E, walk along Finke River bed, between towering cliffs. Helicopter flights to surrounding areas including Mt Sonder available. Award-winning Glen Helen Homestead offers accommodation and restaurant. **In the area:** In West MacDonnell National Park: Ormiston Gorge, 12 km NE, the 'jewel of the MacDonnell Ranges'; Ochre Pits, 21 km E, natural ochre quarry once mined by Aborigines for painting and ceremonial decoration; Serpentine Gorge, 35 km E, narrow winding gorge with beautiful scenery, wildlife and walking trails; Ellery Creek Big Hole, 45 km E, large waterhole with high red cliffs and sandy creek fringed with river redgums; further east towards Alice Springs are Standley Chasm and Simpsons Gap; Redbank Gorge, 24 km NW, accessible by 4WD only. Famous Larapinta Walking Trail winds through heart of West MacDonnell Ranges; it currently extends 80 km and can be walked in total (registration necessary) or in part (some sections are overnight walks). Restored Aboriginal mission at Hermannsburg, 25 km SE. Mereenie Loop Rd links Glen Helen to Kings Canyon in far south west; permit required. **Tourist information:** Glen Helen Homestead, Namatjira Dr.; (08) 8956 7489. **Accommodation:** 1 hotel/motel, 1 hostel.

Hermannsburg   Pop. 422

MAP REF. 404 F5, 410 H9

This isolated Aboriginal community, 132 km W of Alice Springs, occupies the site of a former church mission station. For many years it was the home of the famous painter Albert Namatjira. **Of interest:** Strehlow's House (1897), now a gallery housing watercolour paintings by Aboriginal artists of the Hermannsburg school. Remains of church mission station, including schoolhouse (1896) and tannery (1941). Museum in the Old Colonists House (1885) displays historic items from missionary era. **In the area:** Monument to Albert Namatjira on Larapinta Dr., 8 km E. Cultural tours and camping at Wallace Rockhole Aboriginal community, 50 km SE. Finke River Gorge National Park, 20 km S (4WD access only), features amazing rock formations: 'amphitheatre', 'sphinx' and 'battleship'. Red cabbage palms (*Livistona mariae*), in nearby Palm Valley (4WD access only), found nowhere else in world. Tnorala (Gosse Bluff) meteorite crater, 35 km W; permit required, contact Tourist information. **Tourist information:** Kata-Anga Tearooms; (08) 8956 7402. **Accommodation:** None.

Glen Helen Homestead, an accommodation base for the West MacDonnells

NORTHERN TERRITORY

The spectacular Katherine Gorge, near Katherine

Jabiru — Pop. 1731

MAP REF. 401 H5, 403 P4, 406 H6

A mining town within the Kakadu National Park, 280 km from Darwin on Arnhem Hwy, Jabiru's services are designed to limit the effect of the town on the surrounding World Heritage National Park. **Of interest:** Gagudju Crocodile Hotel, Flinders St, 250-m crocodile shaped building; design was approved by the Gagudju people, to whom the crocodile is a totem. Kakadu Frontier Lodge and Caravan Park, Jabiru Dr., laid out in traditional Aboriginal circular motif. Jabiru Olympic Swimming Pool, Civic Dr., largest in NT; also 9-hole golf course. Fishing and safari tours available. Aug.: Wind festival. **In the area:** Tourist walk (1.5 km) from town centre through bush to Bowali Centre, an Aboriginal cultural centre. Nourlangie Rock, 25 km SE, has significant Aboriginal rock art featuring prominently around its base. Yellow Waters near Cooinda, 45 km SE, a landlocked billabong with prolific flora and fauna, particularly waterbirds; best seen by a cruise in flat-bottomed boat, available near Gagudju Cooinda Lodge. Nearby, Warradjah Cultural Centre, built in shape of a Warradjah (pig-nosed turtle), offering displays and Aboriginal craft gallery. Further south, Jim Jim Falls and Twin Falls (both 4WD access only), the two largest falls in park after rains (Nov.–Apr.). North of Jabiru is another renowned Aboriginal rock-art site, Ubirr, in Kakadu National Park, with galleries featuring a range of styles; ranger-guided walks and tours available. Ranger Uranium Mine, 6 km E, daily tours May–Oct. (information from Kakadu Air Services at Jabiru Air Terminal). At airport, scenic flights available over unique Kakadu territory – see virtually inaccessible sandstone formations standing 400 m above vast floodplains, seasonal waterfalls, wetland wilderness, remote beaches and ancient Aboriginal rock art sites. **Tourist information:** 6 Tasman Plaza; (08) 8979 2548. **Accommodation:** 1 hotel, 1 cara./camp. park. **See also:** The Top End.

Katherine — Pop. 7064

MAP REF. 406 G10

The multicultural town of Katherine on the southern side of the Katherine River is 320 km SE of Darwin, by a ruler-straight stretch of bitumen. Katherine River was named after a daughter of one of the sponsors of John McDouall Stuart, who first saw it in 1862. Katherine's economic mainstays are the Mt Todd goldmine, tourism and the Tindal RAAF airbase, 27 km SE. Sited in some of NT's most promising agricultural and grazing country, it is the centre of scientific experiments designed to improve the beef-cattle industry. **Of interest:** Katherine Museum, Gorge Rd. Railway Station Museum, Railway Tce. School of the Air, Giles St; open weekdays a.m. O'Keefe House, one of oldest houses in town; Riverbank Dr. Heli tours, scenic flights, 4WD safaris, barramundi fishing tours, horse trail-rides available, contact Tourist information. June: Burunga sport and cultural festival; Katherine Cup; Canoe marathon. July: Agricultural show. Sept.: Flying fox festival. **In the area:** Katherine Gorge (named Nitmiluk by the Aboriginal people) in Nitmiluk National Park, 29 km NE, with ancient rock walls dotted with caves and with both faces above floodline decorated with Aboriginal paintings, thousands of years old; numerous reptile and amphibian species; kangaroos and wallabies in hundreds crowd in to drink in higher reaches of gorge. The best way to see the gorge is by flat-bottomed boat; you can hire a canoe and camp in the gorge overnight, or take a guided tour; cruises run daily (book at Ranger Centre); (no motorboats allowed in gorge May–Oct.); weather is hot Nov.–Mar., but there is little humidity for the remaining months of the year, when it is warm during the day and cool at night. Also in park, Edith Falls, 62 km N, for bushwalking, picnicking and camping. Oldest remaining homestead in NT, historic Springvale Homestead (1879) built by Alfred Giles, 8 km W on Shadforth Rd; Aboriginal Corroboree performed here each Mon., Wed. and Sat. Rowlands Dairy, 12 km W on Florina Rd, where 600–1200 cows milked daily; tours weekdays. Nearby, Wildlife Park. Cutta Cutta Caves, 26 km SE; cave tours daily. Elsey National Park near Mataranka Homestead, 115 km SE, features thermal pool believed to have therapeutic powers. National Trust-classified Old Gallon Licensed Store Gallery (1847), 2 km E on Giles St, marks original site of township; now displays and sells work of local artists. Manyallaluk (formerly Eva Valley Station), 100 km NE, combines Aboriginal culture with magnificent scenery of wilderness park. **Tourist information:** Cnr Stuart Hwy and Lindsay St; (08) 8972 2650. **Accommodation:** 2 hotel/motels, 7 motels, 3 hostels, 8 cara./camp. parks. **See also:** Aboriginal Art; The Top End.

Kings Canyon — Pop. 50

MAP REF. 410 F9

Kings Canyon, an enormous natural amphitheatre with 100-m sheer rock faces is the main feature of Watarrka National Park, 325 km SW of Alice

Aboriginal Lands

In the Northern Territory, Commonwealth and Northern Territory laws do not permit people to enter Aboriginal land unless they have been issued with a permit.

It should be noted that as a general rule, Land Councils have been asked by traditional owners not to issue entry permits for unaccompanied tourist travel. This does not affect visitors travelling on organised tours on to Aboriginal land where tour bookings include the necessary permit.

When making an application for entry to any Aboriginal land, applicants must state the reason for entry, dates and duration of intended stay, names of persons travelling, and itinerary and routes to be used while on these lands. Permits can be issued only after consultation and approval of the traditional owners and relevant Aboriginal communities. Processing permit applications can take two to six weeks. It is the right of traditional owners of Aboriginal land to refuse entry permits.

All public roads that cross Aboriginal lands are exempt from the permit requirements; the exemption covers the immediate road corridor only. If travellers are unsure about the status of roads on which they are driving, they should seek advice from the Land Councils before departure. If there is a likelihood of a need to enter Aboriginal land for any reason, including fuel, travellers should seek permits from the relevant Land Councils. Some towns within Aboriginal land are also exempt from the provisions.

A pass is required to travel on the spectacular Mereenie Loop Road, which links Glen Helen with Kings Canyon and passes through Aboriginal homeland. Passes may be obtained from the CATIA office in Alice Springs, or from Hermannsburg, Glen Helen or Kings Canyon. Intending travellers also receive an information brochure.

A number of tourist ventures operate on Aboriginal land; they include tourist camps and outlets for artworks and artifacts. For details contact Northern Territory Tourist Commission, 67 Stuart Hwy, Alice Springs; (08) 8951 8555.

The relevant land councils to whom applications for permits and any inquiries must be directed in writing, are:

Alice Springs and Tennant Creek Regions:
Central Land Council Permits
25 Stuart Hwy, PO Box 3321
Alice Springs NT 0871
(08) 8951 6320

Darwin, Nhulunbuy and Katherine Regions:
Northern Land Council
9 Rowling St, PO Box 42921
Casuarina NT 0811
(08) 8920 5100

Melville and Bathurst Islands:
Tiwi Land Council
PO Box 38545
Winnellie NT 0821
(08) 8947 1838

Nguiu Community Council
Bathurst Island (via Darwin)
NT 0822
(08) 8978 3966

Pirlangimpi Community Council
Bathurst Island NT 0822
(08) 8978 3988

Tnorala (Gosse Bluff), a spectacular crater on Aboriginal land near Glen Helen

Historic Elsey Cemetery, near Mataranka

Springs. Kings Canyon Resort is situated at the edge of the park and provides a convenient base to explore the region. Aboriginal tours and scenic flights available. **In the area:** 6-km circuit walk of Kings Canyon, features boardwalk through prehistoric cycads in lushly vegetated Garden of Eden; unusual rock formations, particularly The Lost City; and views across the canyon. Also within park, Carmichael Crag (3 km N) displays majestic colours, particularly at sunset. Mereenie Loop Rd to Glen Helen; permit required. **Tourist information:** Kings Canyon Resort; (08) 8956 7442. **Accommodation:** 1 resort, 1 cara./camp. park.

Kulgera   Pop. 25

MAP REF. 410 I13

Kulgera is a rest stop about 20 km from the SA border on the Stuart Hwy. The town's name is Aboriginal for 'place of weeping eye', named for 45 m-high rocks with an intermittent trickle of water down the sides. **Of interest:** Kulgera Homestead museum and animal park. **Tourist information:** Kulgera Hotel, Stuart Hwy; (08) 8956 0973. **Accommodation:** 1 hotel/motel, 1 cara./camp. park.

Larrimah   Pop. 20

MAP REF. 406 I12, 408 I2

Larrimah is located on the Stuart Hwy, 90 km N of Daly Waters. **Of interest:** Historical museum, Mahoney St; train rides to ghost town of Birdum. Green Park, Stuart Hwy, has crocodiles and buffaloes. **Tourist information:** Green Park Tourist Complex, Stuart Hwy; (08) 8975 9937. **Accommodation:** 1 hostel, 2 cara./camp. parks.

Mataranka   Pop. 180

MAP REF. 406 I11

This small settlement is 110 km SE of Katherine. **Of interest:** On Stuart Hwy: Stockyard Gallery, for NT artists' works including leather sculpture; Territory Manor, daily feeding of barramundi. May: Back to the Never Never festival; Never Never art show at Stockyard Gallery (sometimes held in June). Aug.: Rodeo. **In the area:** Elsey National Park, 5 km E, featuring thermal pool, popular for swimming, surrounded by rainforest with walking tracks. Nearby, Mataranka Homestead Tourist Resort, offering camping, horse riding, scenic flights, river cruises, barramundi fishing and canoe hire; also replica of Elsey Homestead. Elsey Cemetery, 20 km S, graves of outback pioneers immortalised by Mrs Aeneas Gunn (who lived at Elsey Station Homestead 1902–3) in *We of the Never Never*; nearby, stone cairn marking site of original Elsey Station Homestead. **Tourist information:** Stockyard Gallery, Stuart Hwy; (08) 8975 4530. **Accommodation:** 1 hotel, 3 motels, 1 hostel, 5 cara./camp. parks. **See also:** The Top End.

Noonamah   Pop. 8

MAP REF. 402 E4, 406 E6

Noonamah is on the Stuart Hwy, 38 km S of Darwin. **In the area:** Over 7000 crocodiles at Crocodile Farm, just north of town; feeding displays and tours available. Howard Springs Nature Park, 22 km NW, for safe swimming, bird watching and picnicking. On Cox Peninsula Rd: Berry Springs Nature Park (14 km SW), safe swimming in spring-fed pool surrounded by monsoon forest; alongside, Territory Wildlife Park, exhibiting native fauna in 400-ha bushland setting viewed via walking trails or motorised, open train. Majestic Orchids, 16-ha orchid growing area, 7 km SW. Berry Springs Nature Park on Darwin River Dam Rd. Manton Dam, 20 km S, ideal for water sports and picnicking on foreshore. **Tourist information:** Hotel; (08) 8988 1054. **Accommodation:** 1 hotel/motel. (Please check availability as accommodation section being renovated at time of going to press).

Pine Creek   Pop. 437

MAP REF. 401 A13, 402 I13, 406 F8

On the Stuart Hwy, 90 km NW of Katherine, Pine Creek experienced a brief gold rush in the 1870s; today the town is experiencing a resurgence following the reopening of goldmining operations. **Of interest:** Numerous historic buildings. Miners Park, Main Tce, displays historic mining machinery. Railway Station museum, off Main Tce; check opening times. Museum and Library, Railway Tce. Mine Lookout, off Moule St. Restored steam ore crusher at Gun Alley Gold Mining, Gun Alley. Gold panning tours and scenic drive available. **In the area:** Gold fossicking (licence required). Copperfield recreation Dam, 6 km SW, foreshore ideal for picnics. Umbrawarra Gorge, 22 km SW, for swimming, rock climbing and walking. Edith Falls, 50 km SW in north-western end of Nitmiluk National Park, for swimming and bushwalking. The Rock Hole, 65 km NE via Kakadu Hwy, a secluded waterhole (4WD access only). Gunlom (Waterfall Creek), 110 km NE via Kakadu Hwy, beautiful falls and permanent waterhole in Kakadu National Park. Douglas Hot Springs Nature Park, 92 km NW, features thermal springs. Further 16 km (4WD access only), Butterfly Gorge, named for

Aboriginal-operated Tours

For over 60 000 years the Aboriginal people have developed a unique understanding of the relationship between the physical and spiritual world. Today many Aborigines work professionally to share their knowledge with visitors. There is a wide range of Aboriginal-operated tours available throughout the Northern Territory, each offering the Aboriginal perspective of their particular area. For further information on Aboriginal-operated Tours in the Northern Territory contact the Northern Territory Holiday Information HELPLINE; 1800 62 1336.

AT THE TOP END

Location	Tour name	Features
DARWIN Frontier Hotel	Indigenous Bungul	• traditional Aboriginal dance performance while you dine
KAKADU NATIONAL PARK	Guluyambi Aboriginal Cultural Cruise	• 1½ hour cruise along East Alligator river • spectacular contrasting scenery • landscape interpreted by Aboriginal guide
	Magela Cultural and Heritage Tours	• journeys through the more remote and restricted areas of the park as guests of Bunidji people • small groups only
EASTERN ARNHEM LAND	Davidson's Safaris	• award-winning wilderness experience • operates all seasons • includes airboat or cruise boat over wetlands to extensive rock-art galleries
	Dreamtime Safari	• exclusive, luxury camp • Talabon people demonstrate traditional dance, arts and crafts, and storytelling
	Inkiyu Scenic Educational and Cultural Tours	• half-day tours to spectacular Mikinj Valley • experienced Aboriginal guide • small groups
	The Arnhemlander Aboriginal Cultural Tour	• visit rock-art sites, Mikinj Valley • learn bush skills, food gathering and preparation • visit Injalak Arts and Crafts centre at Oenpelli • most tours accompanied by an Aboriginal guide
	Umorrduk Safaris	• exclusive safari camp • rock art galleries • interpretation of land, history and mythology of Aboriginal culture
KATHERINE Springvale Station Homestead (8 km W)	Aboriginal Corroboree	• traditional Aboriginal dance performance • historic homestead
Manyallaluk community (100 km NE)	Manyallaluk Aboriginal Cultural Tours	• various tours from one-day cultural experience to extended bushwalks led by Aboriginal guide along Nitmiluk (Katherine Gorge) • award-winning enterprise • caravan-park facility
Nitmiluk National Park (30 km N)	Travel North	• 2½ hour Aboriginal-guided bush tour • learn bush skills, food gathering and bush medicine
IN CENTRAL AUSTRALIA	Akalyte Antheme Tour Guide Services	• range of short and extended tours • specialises in personally designed private tours
	Desert Tracks	• tours vary from 1 to 8 days • specialise in small groups visiting Aboriginal land and learning from local people
	Rod Steinert Tours	• visit to bush campsite • learn boomerang and spear throwing, bush tucker, bush survival skills • purchase art and craft
	Vast Visual Arts and Specialist Tours	• personally designed art, culture and nature tours
ALICE SPRINGS Strehlow Research Centre	Strehlow Research Centre	• display revolves around Arrernte people and their association with Strehlow and the European community
Pitchi Richi Sanctuary (3 km SW)	Pitchi Richi Cultural Experience	• Ricketts collection of Aboriginal clay sculptures • billy tea and damper, boomerang throwing, whip cracking and storytelling
Hermannsburg (123 km SW)	Hermannsburg Tour	• first Aboriginal mission in NT
Wallace Rockhole (west)	Rockhole Tour	• historical artworks • camping facilities
Oak Valley (100 km S)	Oak Valley Tours	• day tour • ancient rock art • learn culture and lifestyle
Watarrka National Park (323 km SW)	Kurparu Tours	• Kings Canyon through eyes of Aboriginal guide • various cultural and walking tours available
Uluru-Kata Tjuta National Park	Anangu Tours	• local Aboriginal (Anangu) guides offer insights into their history, knowledge and lifestyle

National Parks

Ghost gum in West MacDonnell National Park

There are more than 90 parks, reserves and protected areas in the Northern Territory. The major ones are grouped in three sections. One group is at the Top End, close to Darwin, the second around Katherine, and the third at the southern end, around Alice Springs in central Australia.

At the Top End

At the Top End of the Territory are several impressive national parks, including the splendid **Kakadu National Park**, leased by the traditional Aboriginal owners to the Australian Nature Conservation Agency. Here the visitor can see Aboriginal rock-art and the magnificent scenery of Arnhem Land, go bushwalking or take a boat cruise through wetlands. On the way to this park, do not miss the Territory Wildlife Park, where you can see native fauna in a bush setting.

The popular **Litchfield National Park** is only 100 kilometres south of Darwin. Numerous waterfalls cascade from the sandstone plateau of Tabletop Range and create beautiful swimming holes for year-round swimming. Monsoonal rainforests contrast with treeless, black soil plains where magnetic termite mounds dot the landscape. Tjaynera Falls (Sandy Creek) and the Lost City with its fascinating sandstone formation, are on 4WD tracks. Swimming, photography, wildlife observation and bushwalking are all popular activities.

Gurig National Park, on the Cobourg Peninsula, can be reached by 4WD but a permit is necessary for this Aboriginal land. This isolated park is rich in Aboriginal culture as well as containing lonely ruins of early European attempts at settlement. A wilderness lodge, Seven Spirit Bay (not in the park), overlooks Coral Bay and can only be reached from Darwin by air. The complex offers a true wilderness experience. Fishing, sailing, a trip to historic ruins at Victoria Settlement, and exploration of the area's natural environment are available.

Around Katherine

Located 29 kilometres north-east of Katherine is **Nitmiluk (Katherine Gorge) National Park**. This fascinating river canyon, with its abundant wildlife and Aboriginal rock paintings, can be seen from a walking track, canoe or tour boat. When the river flows peacefully in the dry season (May–October), anglers make good catches of barramundi and other fish in the gorge's deep pools. **Elsey National Park**, 100 kilometres south-east of Katherine, and located alongside the Roper River, includes Mataranka Hot Springs, a refreshing swimming area believed to have therapeutic powers.

On the Victoria Highway to the west of Katherine lie **Gregory National Park**, one of the largest parks in the Territory, and **Keep River National Park**. Both feature tropical and semi-arid plant life, and spectacular range and gorge scenery. Significant Aboriginal sites and evidence of early European settlement and pastoral history are also features. Boat tours are available at Timber Creek on Victoria River.

South of Tennant Creek is **Devils Marbles Conservation Reserve**. The spherical boulders in the park were formed by the weathering of granite outcrops on a wide quartz plain. According to Aboriginal legend, they are eggs laid by the Rainbow Serpent. The Devils Marbles are particularly attractive at sunset, when they glow a deep red. There are no marked walking tracks in the reserve, but the flatness of the plain and the sparse vegetation allow easy walking.

Around Alice Springs

Best-known of all the parks in the Centre is World Heritage-listed **Uluru-Kata Tjuta National Park**, which contains the monolith Uluru (Ayers Rock) and Kata Tjuta (The Olgas) rising abruptly from the surrounding plains. The area is of vital cultural and religious significance to the Anangu (the traditional owners), whose ancestors have lived in the area for at least 30 000 years.

An easy way to explore Uluru's attractions is either by undertaking the Circuit Walk or joining a guided coach tour around the 9-kilometre rock base to see significant traditional sites, such as the Mutitjulu Cave containing elaborate Aboriginal paintings, and Kantju Gorge. The climb to the 348-metre summit is strictly for those with a good head for heights. It should not be attempted by anyone who is unfit or unwell, or in hot weather; casualties are common. The traditional owners, the Anangu community, encourage visitors to seek alternatives to the climb.

Further west, the great domes of Kata Tjuta are separated by deep clefts, many of which hold sweet water and support abundant wildlife. The name Kata Tjuta means 'many heads'. There are several walks such as Valley of the Winds, and Olga Gorge which take from one to four hours to complete. Keep to the marked tracks.

In the **West MacDonnell National Park** lie the MacDonnell Ranges, the land of the Arrernte Aboriginal people and a paradise for photographers and artists. Cutting through the ranges are spectacular gorges offering some of the finest scenery in Australia: crimson and ochre rock walls bordering deep blue pools, and slopes covered with spring wildflowers. In this park are a number of highlights. Close to Alice Springs is Simpsons Gap, only 18 kilometres west and best seen on foot. There are several walking tracks as well as ranger-guided tours, through rocky gaps and along steep-sided ridges overlooking huge gums and timbered creek flats. A bicycle path linking Alice Springs to Simpsons Gap provides a different way to see this part of the MacDonnell Ranges. Other well-known scenic spots include Ormiston Gorge and Pound, where fish bury themselves in the mud as a string of waterholes shrink to puddles, then wait for the rains to fill them again. The deepest part of Ormiston Creek is a magnificent permanent pool the Arrernte believe to be inhabited by a great watersnake. At the far end of the gorge, the walls are curtained by a variety of ferns and plants, including the lovely Sturt's desert rose and the relic *Macrozamia*.

Finke Gorge National Park, a scenic wilderness straddling the Finke River, includes the picturesque Palm Valley. This valley is a refuge for cycad palms and the ancient *Livistona mariae*, estimated to be about 5000 years old. The park is particularly rugged and visitors who do not join tours are advised to use a 4WD.

Between Finke and Uluru lies **Watarrka National Park**, its main attraction being the beautiful Kings Canyon. Waterholes, rock formations and abundant wildlife provide excellent photographic and bushwalking opportunities.

Note: In national parks and reserves and other areas, it is essential to heed local advice on the dangers of swimming. The saltwater crocodile (found mainly in river estuaries) is highly dangerous. The freshwater or Johnstone's crocodile (found in billabongs and rivers) is regarded as harmless though it has been known to attack humans.

For more information about the Territory's parks and reserves, contact the Parks and Wildlife Commission of the Northern Territory, PO Box 496, Palmerston NT 0830, (08) 8999 5511. For Kakadu and Uluru, contact the Australian Nature Conservation Agency (ANCA), GPO Box 636, Canberra ACT 2601, (06) 250 0200, or PO Box 1260, Darwin NT 0801, (08) 8981 5299. **See also:** The Top End. **Note** detailed map of Kakadu National Park on page 401.

Jim Jim Falls, accessible only by 4WD, in Kakadu National Park

Remains of gold-mining town in Arltunga Historical Reserve, near Ross River

large numbers of butterflies which settle in its rock crevices. **Tourist information:** Diggers Rest Motel, 32 Main Tce; (08) 8976 1442. **Accommodation:** 1 hotel/motel, 1 cara./camp. park.

Renner Springs Pop. 19

MAP REF. 409 J8

A roadside stop on the Stuart Hwy, Renner Springs is 161 km N of Tennant Creek. The water source for the springs is unknown. Picnic/barbecue facilities available. **Accommodation:** 1 hotel/motel, 1 cara./camp. park.

Ross River Pop. 30

MAP REF. 405 O2, 411 K8

At Ross River is Ross River Homestead, a ranch-style outback resort 85 km E of Alice Springs. **In the area:** Scenic walking tracks at Trephina Gorge, 17 km NW. N'Dhala Gorge, 11 km SW, features Aboriginal rock engravings and ancient fossil deposits. Arltunga Historical Reserve, 25 km E, old gold-mining town with stone ruins, scattered workings and gravestones; police station and gaol have been restored and Visitor Centre displays local history. Further east, Ruby Gap Gorge (4WD access only) on Hale River. **Tourist information:** Ross River Homestead, Ross Hwy; (08) 8956 9711. **Accommodation:** 1 hostel, 1 cara./camp park.

Tennant Creek Pop. 3480

MAP REF. 409 K10

According to legend, the town of Tennant Creek was founded when a beer wagon carrying building supplies broke down at the site. The town is 507 km N of Alice Springs, on the Stuart Hwy. Gold and copper deposits account for its development today. The town is a thriving centre for the Barkly Tablelands. **Of interest:** Civic Centre, Peko Rd, houses art, gem and mineral collection. National Trust Museum in historic Tuxworth Fullwood House, Schmidt St, features photographic collection and displays of early mine buildings and equipment; open May–Sept., check times. Travellers Rest Area in Purkiss Reserve, Ambrose St, has picnic area and swimming pool nearby. Tours of goldmining areas; scenic drives; heritage walk; information available from Tourist information. May: Cup Day (horseracing), Go Kart Grand Prix. July: Agricultural show. Aug.: Goldrush folk festival. Sept.: Desert harmony festival with local artists, craftspeople, musicians and performers. **In the area:** Gold Stamp Battery and Museum, Peko Rd, 1 km E, features one of the two 10-stamp batteries still operational in Australia; tours daily. Just past the Battery, lookout offers views of town and surrounding area. Juno Horse Centre, 10 km E, for horseriding. Nobles Nob, 16 km E, once richest open-cut goldmine of its size in world. Mary Ann Dam, 5 km NE, for water sports. Telegraph Station, 12 km N; tours available. Three Ways Roadhouse, junction of Stuart and Barkly Hwys, 25 km N; nearby, John Flynn Memorial. Attack Creek Historical Reserve, 73 km N, site of encounter between John McDouall Stuart and local Aborigines. Devils Pebbles, 16 km NW, miniatures of Devil's Marbles (huge 'balancing rocks' found 103 km S). **Tourist information:** Shop 1, Coach Transit Centre, Paterson St; (08) 8962 3388. **Accommodation:** 1 hotel/motel, 3 motels, 2 hostels, 2 cara./ camp. parks.

Ti Tree Pop. 50

MAP REF. 410 I5

A rest stop on the Stuart Hwy, Ti Tree is 194 km N of Alice Springs. **Of interest:** Art gallery displaying local art at roadhouse. Ti Tree Park, with picnic area and playground. **In the area:** Central Mt Stuart Historical Reserve, 8 km N, includes monument at base of mountain marking the spot as the centre of Australia. **Tourist information:** Roadhouse, Stuart Hwy; (08) 8956 9741. **Accommodation:** 1 motel, 1 cara./camp. park.

Timber Creek Pop. 100

MAP REF. 406 D13, 408 D2

Timber Creek is located 290 km SW of Katherine on Victoria Hwy. **Of interest:** National Trust Museum, off Hwy, has displays of historical artifacts; open Apr.–Aug. Boat tours, cruises, fishing tours and scenic flights available; inquire at Tourist information. Conservation Commission Headquarters, Victoria Hwy, provides road and park information for visitors travelling into Gregory or Keep River National Parks. Sept.: Timber Creek races (horseracing). **In the area:** Gregory National Park, 15 km W, features Limestone Gorge, Aboriginal and European heritage sites and boab trees. Keep River National Park, 175 km W, features rugged scenery, Aboriginal rock art and wildlife; most trails are accessible by 4WD only. For both parks, check with Conservation Commission for details regarding access. Jasper Gorge, scenic gorge with permanent waterhole, 48 km SW. **Tourist information:** Timber Creek Hotel, Victoria Hwy;

Fishing for barramundi on the lower Daly River, south of Darwin

Fishing in the Territory

Whether you are fishing in salt or freshwater, the Territory provides some of the best fishing in Australia. The coast has sheltered bays, estuaries, mangrove-lined creeks, offshore reefs and islands, and much of the fishing is easily reached from population centres. The inland has huge areas of wetlands, with rivers, billabongs and flood plains to be explored. In these outback environments the barramundi is king. Many visitors go on an inland camping and fishing tour with an experienced guide so that they can enjoy the camping life and get to the fishing spots with someone who knows where to go. Note that it is a rule of the north that you retain fish only for the table, and catch and release the others.

Some of the best blue-water fishing in Australia is available straight out of Darwin. You can fish from the shore or wharves of the city; explore the coastal estuaries, mangroves and sandbars; venture along the coast or to the offshore reefs by boat; or organise a charter to go game fishing. The fishing on the east coast of Arnhem Land, based on the Gove Peninsula and Groote Eylandt, is legendary, but as access is difficult these great tropical waters remain scarcely touched. Nhulunbuy on the Gove Peninsula is the starting point. The popular fish are giant trevally, queenfish (leatherskin), mackerel, cobia and the occasional tuna. Black jewfish and fingermark (golden snapper) are taken from the harbour wharves, and sweetlip, coral trout and stripey are around the reefs.

Essentially freshwater fishing in the Territory is best just after the wet, and at the end of the dry when the receding waters and increasing water temperatures mobilise the fish into an aggressive feeding pattern. The freshwater fishing around Darwin is both easily reached and varied, with several dams and lakes adding to the possibilities. In Darwin itself there are many operators of guided fishing tours. To the east of Darwin lies Kakadu National Park which contains several major angling rivers. Fishing is prohibited in parts of the park, however the areas where anglers are welcome fish well. The Mary and Adelaide Rivers' wetlands, the McArthur River at Borroloola and the Victoria River west of Katherine are popular places for catching barramundi. Fishing inland waters away from major population centres is not for the inexperienced. Much of the Territory is rugged and during the wet season the country can only be traversed on the few sealed highways and a couple of all-weather gravel roads.

Anglers should watch out for saltwater crocodiles in the tidal estuary waters and inland waters, and observe basic safety measures. Cleaning fish close to the waterline or wading in the water for long periods are not advised.

For further information on fishing in the Territory, contact the Darwin Region Tourism Association, 33 Smith Street Mall, Darwin; (08) 8981 4300.

(08) 8975 0722. **Accommodation:** 2 hotels/motels, 2 cara./camp. parks. **See also:** National Parks

Victoria River — Pop. 6

MAP REF. 406 E12, 408 E2

Victoria River is a rest stop located where the Victoria Hwy crosses the mighty Victoria River. Scenic bushwalks in area, particularly Joe's Creek Walk, 10 km W. **Tourist information:** Roadhouse, Victoria Hwy; (08) 8975 0744. **Accommodation:** 1 hotel/motel, 1 cara./camp. park.

Wauchope — Pop. 7

MAP REF. 409 K13, 411 K2

Wauchope is on the Stuart Hwy, 113 km S of Tennant Creek. Easter: Outback Go Kart Classic. Sept.: Wimbledon at Wauchope. **In the area:** Devil's Marbles, a collection of large, precariously balanced granite boulders; 8 km N. Old Wolfram Mines, 15 km E (4WD only). **Tourist information:** Wauchope Well Hotel, Stuart Hwy; (08) 8964 1963. **Accommodation:** 1 hotel/motel, 1 cara./camp. park.

Yulara — Pop. 2169

MAP REF. 404 E10, 410 E11

Situated on outskirts of Uluru-Kata Tjuta National Park, this town is the location for the world-class Ayers Rock Resort, offering full visitor facilities and comfortable air-conditioned accommodation in all price brackets (advance bookings are essential). **Of interest:** Visitors Centre has displays and information on national park. Tours available include Aboriginal Desert Culture Tour; Uluru Experience Night Sky Show, which offers night-sky viewing and narration of Aboriginal and European legends relating to the night sky; book tours at Tourist information or reception in accommodation areas. **In the area:** On approach road to Uluru, Uluru-Kata Tjuta Cultural Centre, designed in shape of two snakes, has displays of Aboriginal culture and arts. Uluru (Ayers Rock), 20 km SE, Australia's famous sandstone monolith, has Aboriginal rock-art sites; spectacular at sunrise and sunset; guided tour around base of Uluru highlighting its Aboriginal significance. Kata Tjuta (The Olgas), 50 km W, rock formations; highlights are Valley of Winds walk, views and flora and fauna. **Tourist information:** Visitors Centre; (08) 8956 2240. **Accommodation:** 3 hotels, hostel units, apartments, cara./camp. ground. **See also:** The Red Centre.

Devil's Marbles, north of Wauchope

The Gove Peninsula

The Gove Peninsula, named after W.H.J. Gove, an Australian airman killed in the area during World War II, is situated at the far north-east end of Arnhem Land. The whole of the peninsula is set aside as Aboriginal Land.

The peninsula offers white sandy beaches, inland waterways and abundant flora and fauna. Excellent deep-sea and reef fishing, and snorkelling and scuba diving on the reefs formed on submerged shipwrecks. The main centres are Yirrkala and Nhulunbuy. Nine kilometres west of Nhulunbuy, near Dundas Point, is Melville Bay, which the explorer Matthew Flinders described as the best natural harbour on the Gulf of Carpentaria.

Nhulunbuy was built as a service town for the bauxite mine and alumina concentration plant. Today it is the administrative centre for the Arnhem Land region. Nearby, Namabara Arts and Crafts has Aboriginal works for sale.

Yirrkala, formerly a mission, is near Mount Dundas. Today it is a residential base for many of the Aborigines in the area and home to the Yirrkala Arts and Crafts Museum. The museum has an extensive collection of locally crafted Aboriginal art including bark paintings and intricate basket weavings. Its name became familiar during the struggle by its people to win title to their land. The *Aboriginal Land Rights (Northern Territory) Act* was finally assented to on 16 December 1976. It represents to the people of Yirrkala the culmination of years of struggle to win recognition for their claims to land on which their people have lived for many thousands of years. The Yirrkala area is noted for Aboriginal carvings of birds and fish.

The easiest way to visit Nhulunbuy is by air. If you plan to explore by 4WD and without a tour guide, a permit is required from the Northern Land Council. Accommodation in Nhulunbuy is available at the Gove Peninsula Motel, a short walk from the town centre; the Hideway Safari Lodge, budget accommodation near the airport; and the Walkabout Arnhem Land Resort Hotel on the beachfront.

For further information contact the Darwin Region Tourism Association, 33 Smith St Mall, Darwin; (08) 8981 4300.

Northern Territory

Location Map

Other Map Coverage
Central Darwin 398
Darwin & Northern Suburbs 399
North Eastern Suburbs, Darwin 400
Kakadu National Park 401
Darwin Region 402
The Red Centre 404

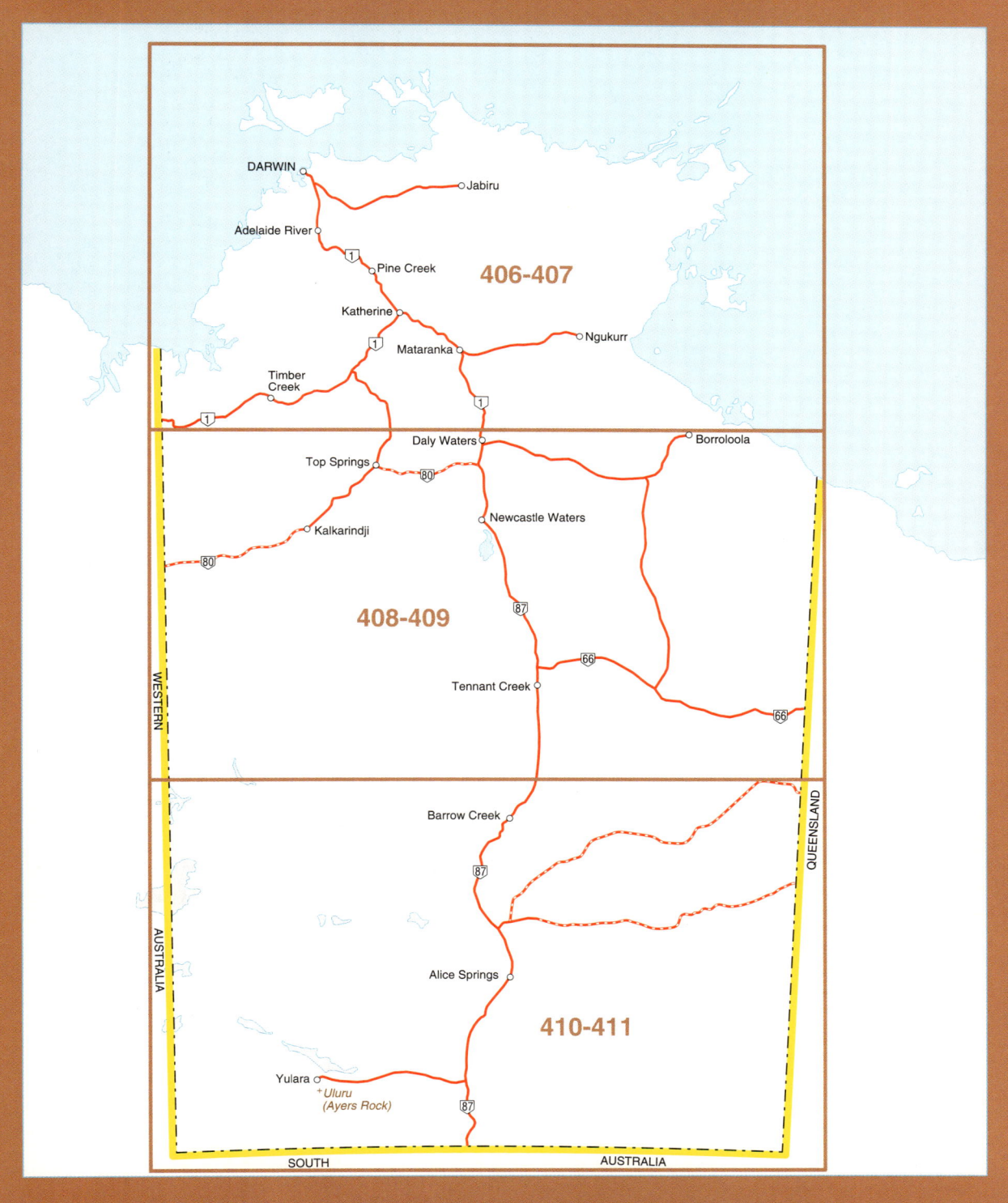

398 Central Darwin

Accommodation
- Beaufort International Hotel 1 B8
- Darwin Motor Inn 2 C7
- Hotel Darwin 3 E10
- Mirambeena Tourist Resort 4 D7
- Novotel Atrium 5 C9
- Plaza Hotel 6 E10
- Poinciana Inn 7 C8
- Top End Frontier 8 B7
- YHA Backpackers International 9 D9
- YWCA 10 B7

General Information
- Ansett Australia 11 F10
- Bus Terminal 12 F10
- Darwin Harbour Ferries 13 I11
- Darwin Region Tourism Assoc 14 E9
- Darwin Transit Centre (coach) 15 D9
- Fishermans Wharf Ferry Terminal 16 I7
- Garuda Indonesia Airlines 17 F9
- General Post Office 18 E8
- Malaysia Airlines 19 E9
- Motoring Organisation (AANT) 20 D8
- NT Tourist Commission 21 E10
- Police Station 22 E10
- Qantas Travel Centre 23 F10

Places of Interest
- Aquascene 24 A7
- Aviation Museum 25 D3
- Beaufort Darwin Centre 26 C8
- Botanical Gardens 27 C1
- Browns Mart 28 F10
- Chinese Temple 29 F9
- Christchurch Cathedral 30 F10
- Civic Centre 31 G10
- Government House 32 F11
- Holtze Memorial Cottage 33 C1
- Indo Pacific Marine \ Australian Pearling Exhibition 34 I11
- Lyons Cottage Museum 35 D10
- Mindil Beach Market 36 A1 (May to October)
- Old Admiralty House 37 D10
- Overland Telegraph Memorial 38 F11
- Parliament House, NT Library, Supreme Court 39 F11
- Performing Arts Centre 40 C8
- Reserve Bank 41 F10
- Tree of Knowledge 42 G10
- Wharf Precinct 43 H12
- Victoria Hotel 44 E10

Accommodation Only a sample range is listed; inclusion is not necessarily a recommendation.

Darwin & Northern Suburbs 399

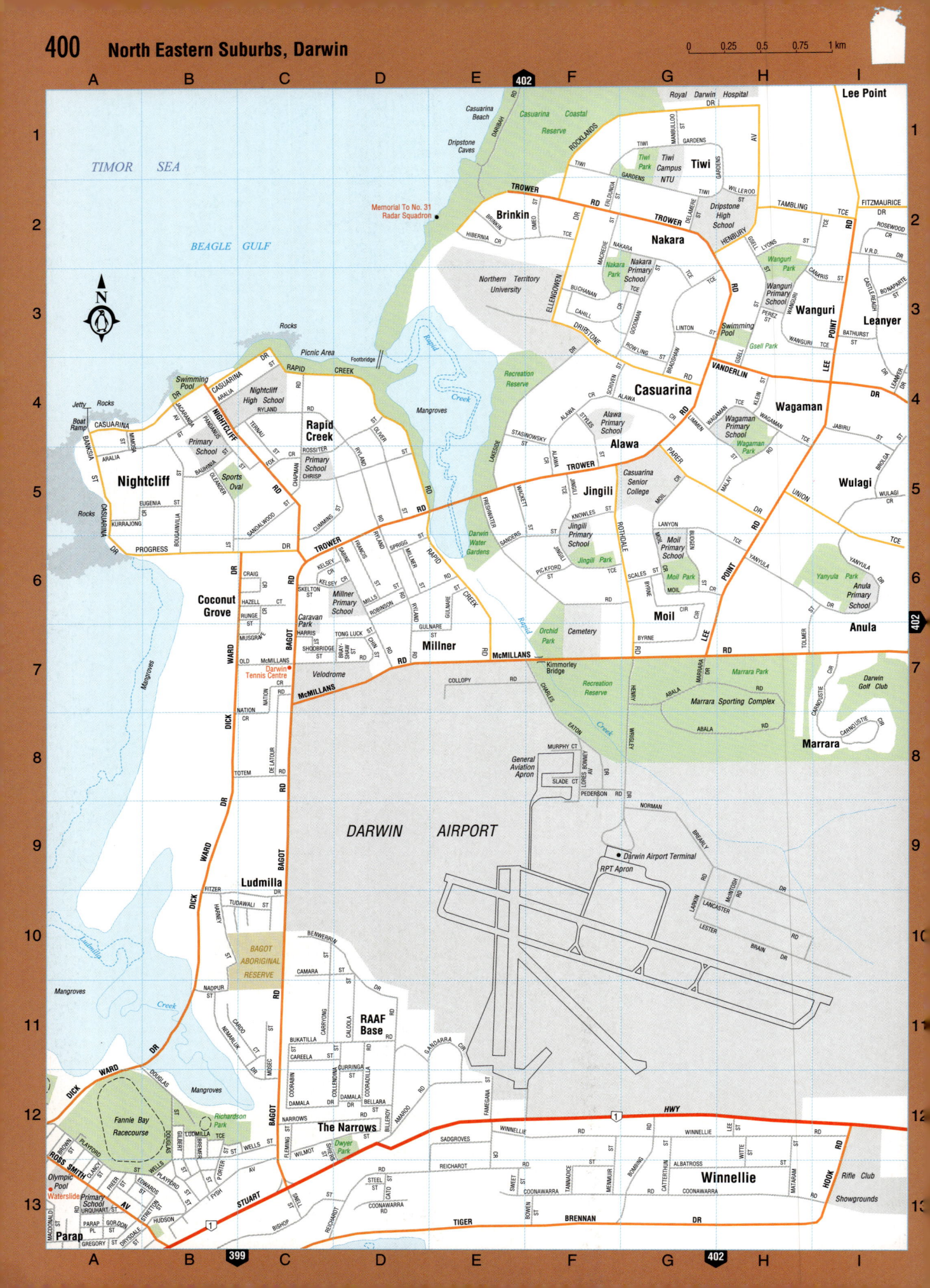

400 North Eastern Suburbs, Darwin

Kakadu National Park

WARNINGS: Freshwater and saltwater (estuarine) crocodiles are present in the Park. Both species can be dangerous, particularly the saltwater crocodile which may be found in both saltwater and freshwater.
- Do not swim or paddle in natural waterways.
- Do not allow children to play near the water's edge.

BOATING: Boat tours available; details provided at Park Headquarters. Boat ramps provided throughout the Park.
When boating:
- Take safety equipment including life jackets, safety light and oars.
- Do not overload boat.
- Carry extra fuel in tidal areas as making way against tidal flow can double fuel consumption.
- Beware of mudbanks, snags and shifting sandbanks.
- If stranded, stay with your boat until help arrives; remember, crocodiles inhabit the waters.
- When planning a long trip, advise ranger of your destination, estimated return time and number of people on board.

CAMPING: Camping grounds are provided throughout the Park. Permits are required for camping outside designated camping grounds and can be obtained at Park Headquarters.

FISHING: Fishing is permitted using lures. Northern Territory bag limits apply. Cast nets, traps, live bait, spear guns and crab pots are not permitted. East of the Kakadu Highway, fishing is permitted only in specific areas.

ART SITES: Kakadu contains a wealth of archaeological and rock art sites which provide insights into Aboriginal culture and the environmental changes witnessed through generations.
The various styles of rock art that can be seen include the stick-like mimi figures (believed to be the oldest), x-ray style paintings which show the internal structure of animals and contact art which began with the arrival of non-Aboriginal people. The principle sites are at Ubirr and Nourlangie Rock.
- Do not touch the paintings.
- Keep to walking tracks and behind fences.

PROTECTING THE PARK:
- Drive carefully and keep to roads and carparks.
- Pets are prohibited.
- Fires to be lit only in fireplaces provided.
- Use litter bins for rubbish.
- All animals and plants in the Park are protected.
- Avoid damage to rock paintings and other sacred sites.

FURTHER INFORMATION: Park Headquarters, P.O. Box 71, Jabiru NT 0886; (089)79 9101. The Park Headquarters, open daily, has displays providing interesting information about the Park; brochures and leaflets are available.

WALKING TRACKS: Numerous marked tracks of various lengths and degrees of difficulty have been constructed enabling visitors to view both the natural wonders of the Park and the richness of Aboriginal art.
Rangers conduct guided walks in the dry season; details are available at Park Headquarters.
- Wear comfortable shoes and a hat.
- Walk in the cooler hours of the day.
- Carry a litre of water for every hour you intend to walk.
- Keep to the marked tracks.
- Do not walk alone.
- If you get lost, do not wander, sit in the shade and wait for help.
- Obtain a camping permit if bushwalking for more than one day.

WARNINGS: In outback Australia, long distances separate some towns. Travellers should familiarise themselves with prevailing conditions before departure, and take care to ensure their vehicle is roadworthy, and that they carry adequate supplies of petrol, water and food.
In northern Australia, rainfall during the 'wet' season (October to March) can make some roads impassable. Full information on road conditions should be obtained before departure.
If visitors intend diverting off public roads within Aboriginal Land areas, a permit is required from the relevant Aboriginal authority.

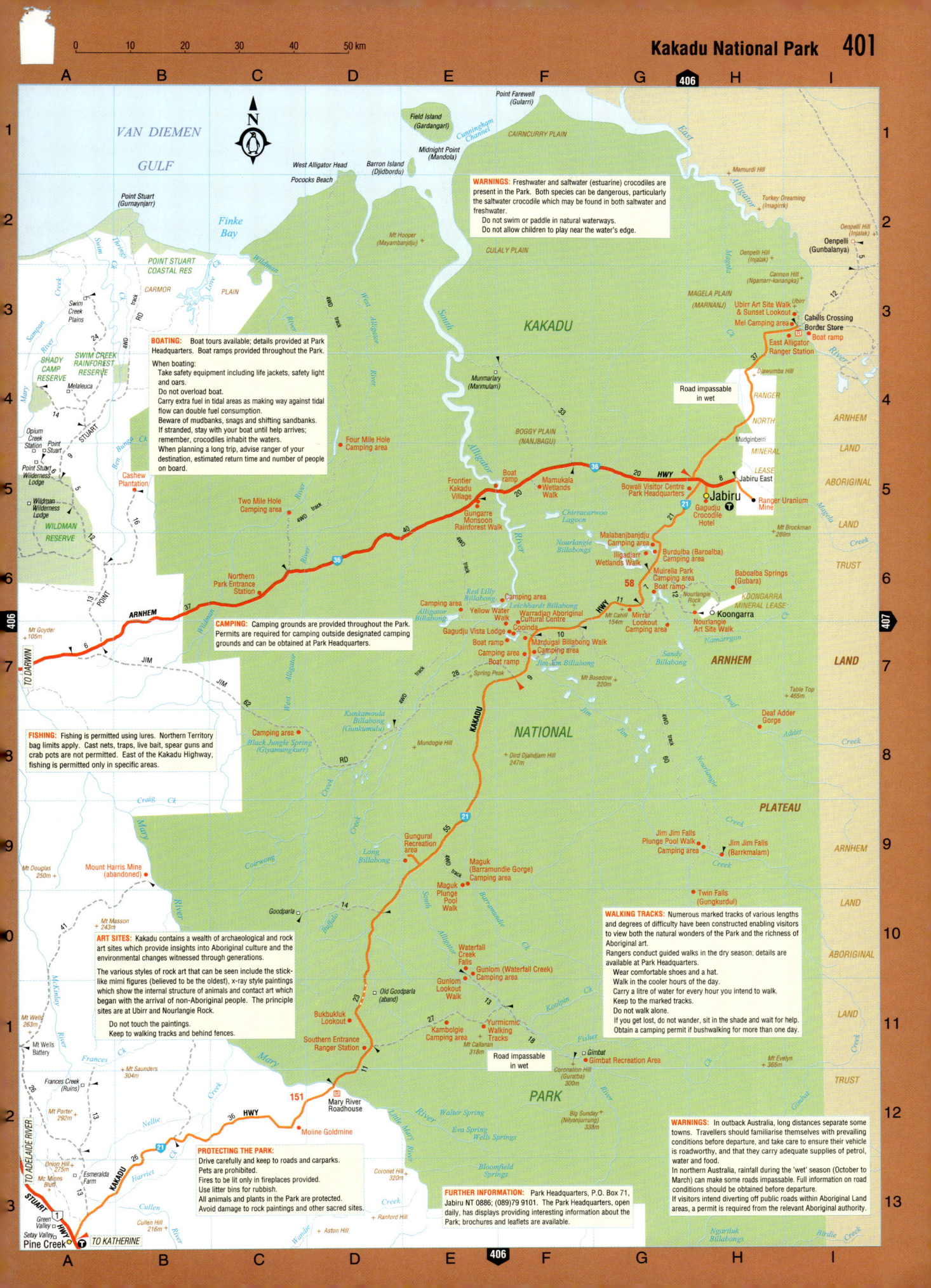

402 Darwin Region

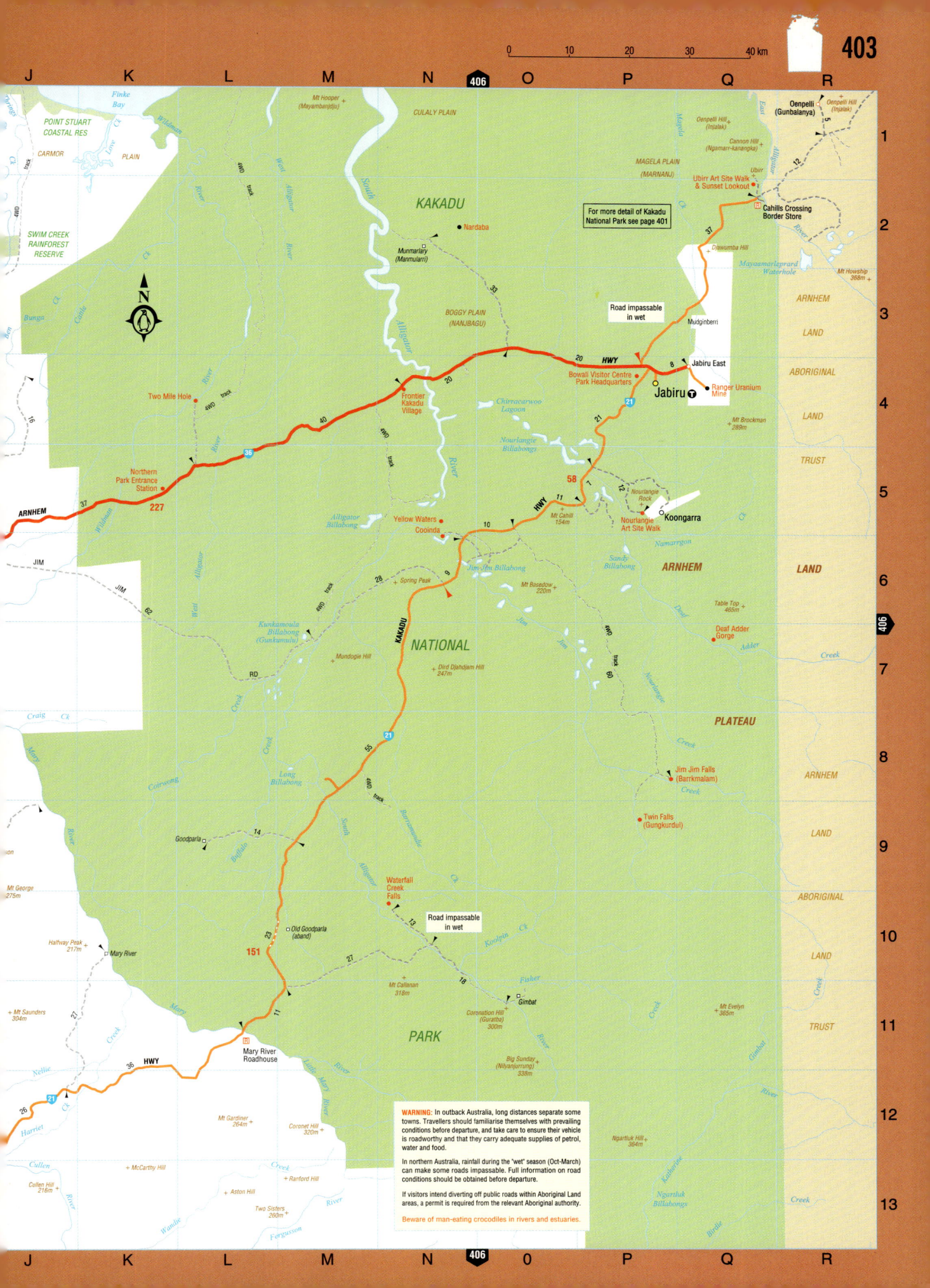

WARNING: In outback Australia, long distances separate some towns. Travellers should familiarise themselves with prevailing conditions before departure, and take care to ensure their vehicle is roadworthy and that they carry adequate supplies of petrol, water and food.

In northern Australia, rainfall during the 'wet' season (Oct-March) can make some roads impassable. Full information on road conditions should be obtained before departure.

If visitors intend diverting off public roads within Aboriginal Land areas, a permit is required from the relevant Aboriginal authority.

Beware of man-eating crocodiles in rivers and estuaries.

404 The Red Centre

STANDLEY CHASM: This impressive chasm in the West MacDonnells is only five metres wide. It is a memorable sight at midday when the sunlight reaches the floor of the chasm, transforming the colour of the walls to a blazing red.

PALM VALLEY: With its rock pools, cycad palms and *Livistona* palms unique to the area, Palm Valley is yet another of the incredible sights of the Centre. The valley's plant life has such a "prehistoric" appearance, to enter the area seems like taking a trip back in time.

KINGS CANYON: One of the most interesting and scenic areas of the Centre. Spectacular views can be obtained by crossing the wooden staircase bridge to the north wall. The Lost City and the Garden of Eden are of particular note.

HENBURY METEORITE CRATERS: Believed to have been formed several thousand years ago when a falling meteor broke into pieces and hit the earth. The largest of the twelve craters is 180 metres wide and 15 metres deep. The smallest is 6 metres wide and only a few centimetres deep. This area is a haunt of the ferocious-looking, but harmless, bearded dragon lizard.

INSET: ULURU - KATA TJUTA NATIONAL PARK

To ULURU (Ayers Rock) Erldunda to Ayers Rock - 260km. See inset for more detail.

405

MACDONNELL NATIONAL PARK: Walking within the park enable visitors to view the [spectac]ular rock outcrops, ridges and huge, stately [g]ums. Rock wallabies inhabit the area.

ARLTUNGA HISTORICAL RESERVE: This has been set aside to preserve memorabilia of the gold-mining era in the region. Explore the stone ruins, scattered workings, gravestones and the mine. The police station and gaol have been restored and a Visitors Centre displays historical exhibits.

ROSS RIVER HOMESTEAD: Provides a place to base yourself for exploration of the East MacDonnells. This ranch-style homestead resort features a range of outback experiences in comfortable surroundings. The historic pub bar has an interesting display of antiques.

ALICE SPRINGS: The gateway to the Northern Territory's biggest single tourist attraction, Uluru (Ayers Rock). A modern and well-maintained town in the heart of the MacDonnell Ranges, the 'Alice' as it is affectionately called, offers a wide variety of accommodation and restaurants, a casino, art galleries including some specialising in Aboriginal art and historic buildings. Heavitree Gap, a significant Aboriginal site and the Mecca Date Garden with its flourishing date palms, are south of the town.

EWANINGA ROCK CARVINGS: The origins of these carvings are lost in time. More correctly known as petroglyphs, the carvings are considered to be the work of an extremely old culture, since present-day Aborigines do not understand their meaning. The rock carvings form part of the Ewaninga Rock Carvings Conservation Reserve.

TOURIST INFORMATION:
- Alice Springs (Hartley Street)
- Glen Helen (Glen Helen Lodge, Namatjira Drive)
- Ross River (Ross River Homestead, Ross Hwy)

WARNING: In outback Australia, long distances separate some towns. Travellers should familiarise themselves with prevailing conditions before departure, and take care to ensure their vehicle is roadworthy and that they carry adequate supplies of petrol, water and food.

If visitors intend diverting off public roads within Aboriginal Land areas, a permit is required from the relevant Aboriginal authority.

CHAMBERS PILLAR: Named in 1860 by the explorer John McDouall, this 50 metre high rock pillar has served as a landmark feature for the Centre's explorers and pioneers.

ULURU NATIONAL PARK

Uluru-Kata Tjuta National Park is surrounded by Aboriginal Land which requires a permit to enter. The Aboriginal owners have leased Uluru to the Australian Nature Conservation Agency, whose officers are responsible for the day to day management of the park. Rangers offer a variety of tours within the Park including the Liru Walk which gives visitors an insight into the richness and variety of bush foods.

CLIMBING THE ROCK: The climb should be attempted only by the fit and healthy. At the top beware of strong gusts of wind. Keep to the chain and painted lines on the way to the cairn.

WALKING TRACKS: Walking tracks at the rock enable views of the rock and surrounding bush while protecting vegetation from the impact of many thousands of visitors. Keep to the tracks at all times, carry plenty of water and protect yourself from the sun.

KATA TJUTA (THE OLGAS): Walking tracks at the Olgas vary in length and difficulty. The route through Olga Gorge is very difficult and should be attempted by experienced climbers only. Carry plenty of water, a park map and food. Wear adequate clothing and footwear. Never underestimate the difficulty of the terrain or the climate.

ART SITES: The pigments used in the rock paintings found within the park are water based and hence susceptible to damage from moisture including human hands.

MARUKA AND CRAFTS GALLERY: The gallery specialises in craft works of the local Aborigines and is located near the Park entrance station.

ACCOMMODATION AND VISITORS INFORMATION: A range of accommodation is available ranging from camping to a 5-star hotel. The Visitors Centre has detailed information on attractions in the area.

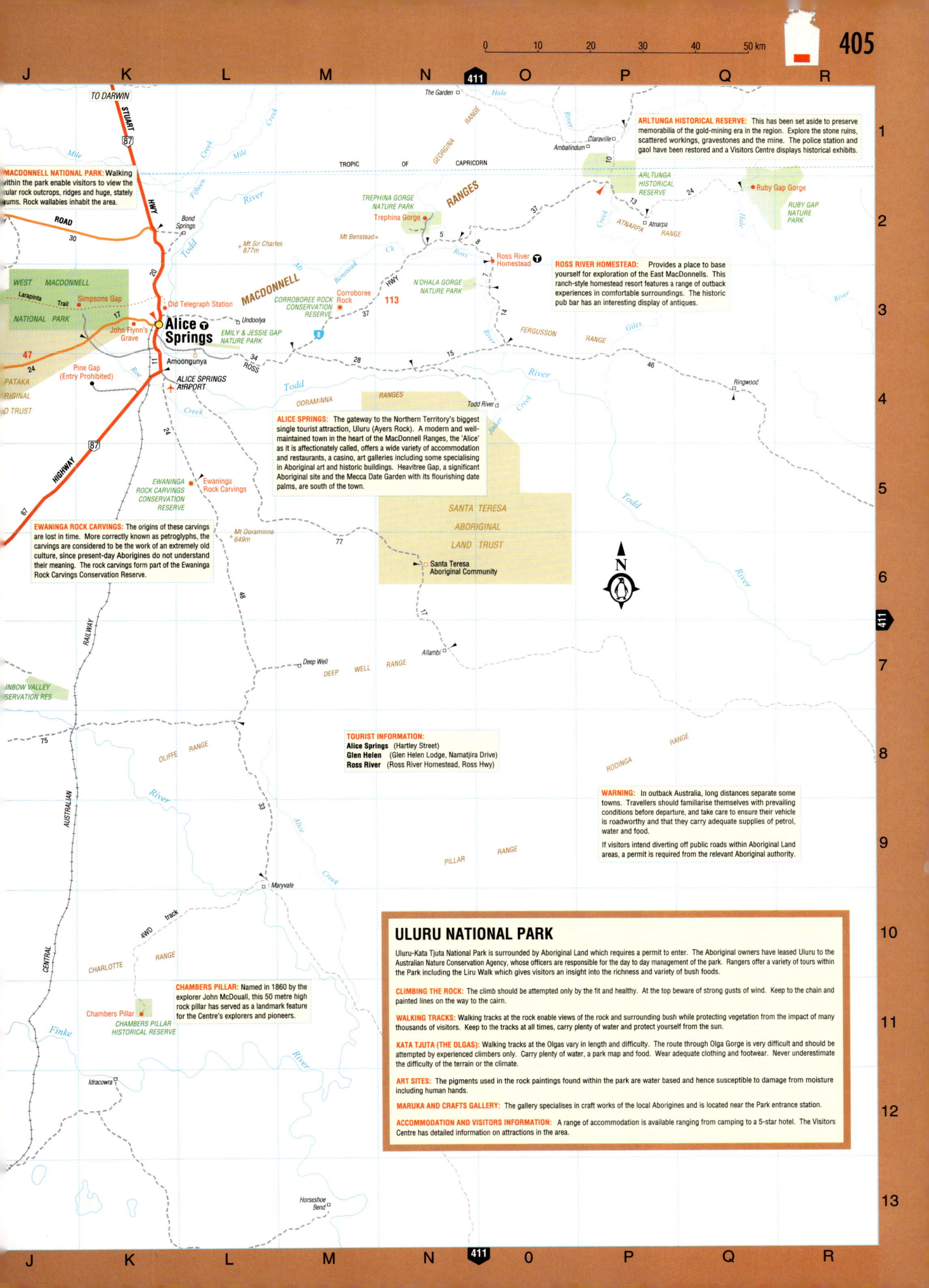

406 Northern Northern Territory

407

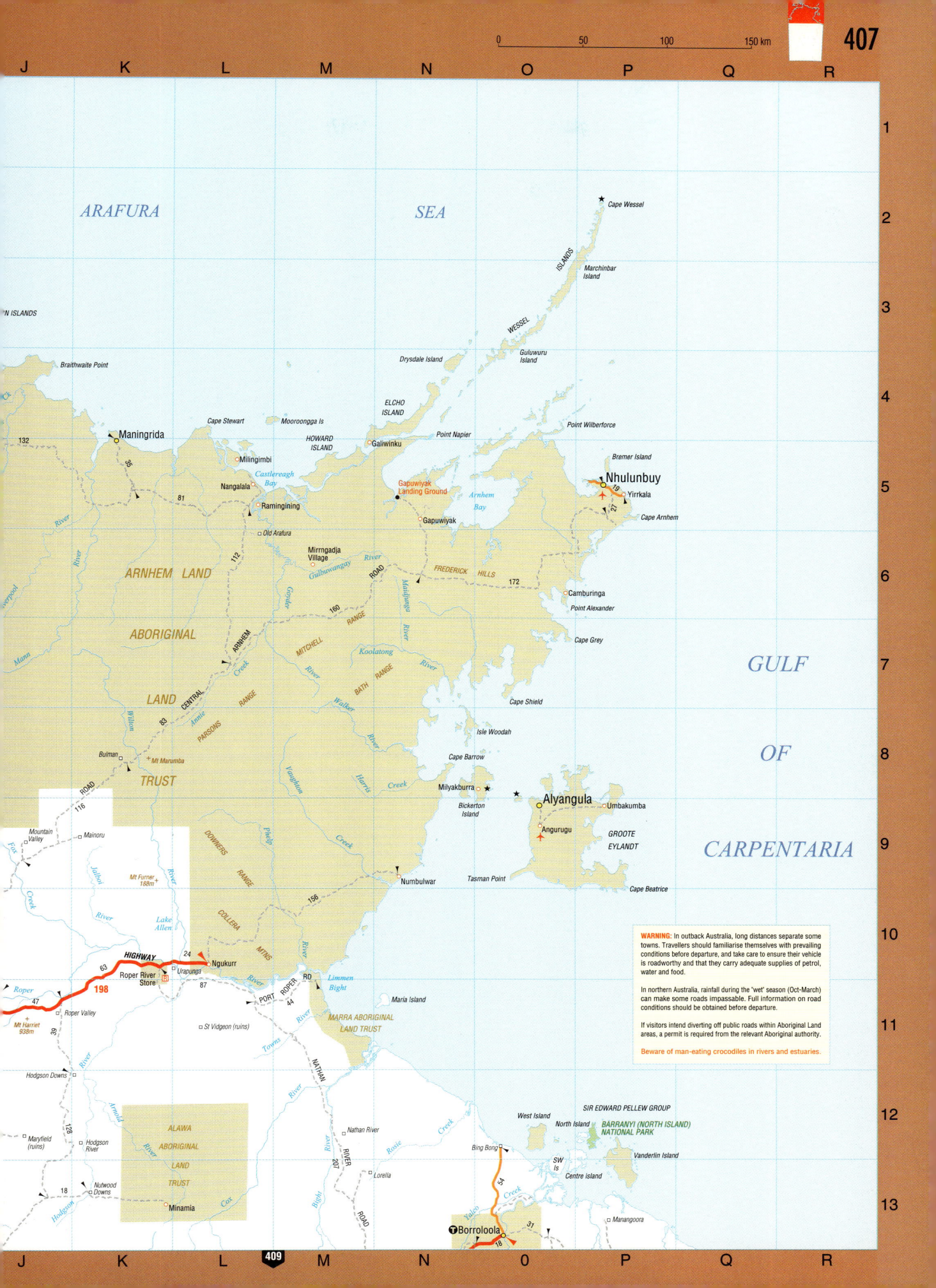

Map of Arnhem Land and Gulf of Carpentaria region

ARAFURA SEA

GULF OF CARPENTARIA

Locations and features

- Cape Wessel
- Marchinbar Island
- WESSEL ISLANDS
- Braithwaite Point
- Maningrida
- Cape Stewart
- Mooroongga Is
- Drysdale Island
- Guluwuru Island
- ELCHO ISLAND
- HOWARD ISLAND
- Galiwinku
- Point Napier
- Point Wilberforce
- Bremer Island
- Nhulunbuy
- Yirrkala
- Mlingimbi
- Nangalala
- Castlereagh Bay
- Ramingining
- Gapuwiyak Landing Ground
- Arnhem Bay
- Gapuwiyak
- Cape Arnhem
- Old Arafura
- Mirrngadja Village
- FREDERICK HILLS
- ARNHEM LAND ABORIGINAL LAND TRUST
- Gulbuwangay River
- ARNHEM ROAD
- MITCHELL RANGE
- Koolatong River
- Camburinga
- Point Alexander
- Goyder River
- Annie Creek
- CENTRAL PARSONS RANGE
- Walker River
- BATH RANGE
- Cape Grey
- Bulman
- Mt Marumba
- Wilton River
- Vaughton
- Harris Creek
- Cape Shield
- Isle Woodah
- Cape Barrow
- Milyakburra
- Bickerton Island
- Alyangula
- Umbakumba
- Mountain Valley
- Mainoru
- Phelp River
- Angurugu
- GROOTE EYLANDT
- Fox Creek
- Jalboi River
- Mt Furner 188m
- DOWNERS RANGE
- COLLERA MTNS
- Numbulwar
- Tasman Point
- Cape Beatrice
- Roper River
- Lake Allen
- HIGHWAY
- Urapunga
- Ngukurr
- ROPER RD
- PORT ROPER
- Limmen Bight
- Maria Island
- Roper River Store
- Roper Valley
- Mt Harriet 938m
- St Vidgeon (ruins)
- MARRA ABORIGINAL LAND TRUST
- Hodgson Downs
- Towns River
- Maryfield (ruins)
- Hodgson River
- ALAWA ABORIGINAL LAND TRUST
- Nathan River
- Rosie Creek
- SIR EDWARD PELLEW GROUP
- West Island
- North Island
- BARRANYI (NORTH ISLAND) NATIONAL PARK
- Nutwood Downs
- Cox River
- Lorella
- Bing Bong
- SW Is
- Vanderlin Island
- Minamia
- Bight River
- NATHAN RIVER ROAD
- Centre island
- Manangoora
- Borroloola
- Calvert Creek

WARNING: In outback Australia, long distances separate some towns. Travellers should familiarise themselves with prevailing conditions before departure, and take care to ensure their vehicle is roadworthy and that they carry adequate supplies of petrol, water and food.

In northern Australia, rainfall during the 'wet' season (Oct-March) can make some roads impassable. Full information on road conditions should be obtained before departure.

If visitors intend diverting off public roads within Aboriginal Land areas, a permit is required from the relevant Aboriginal authority.

Beware of man-eating crocodiles in rivers and estuaries.

Scale: 0 – 50 – 100 – 150 km

408 Central Northern Territory

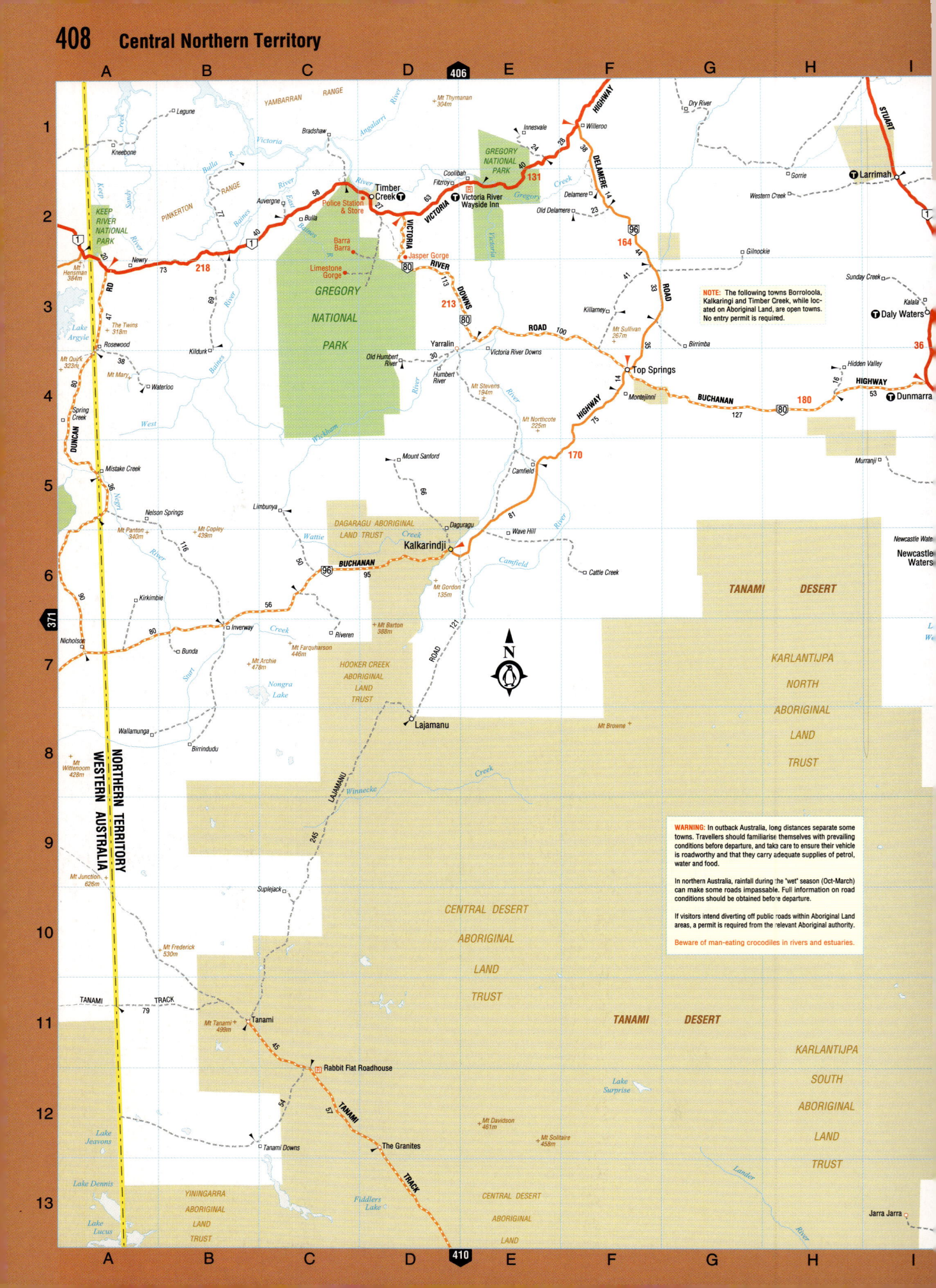

0 50 100 150 km

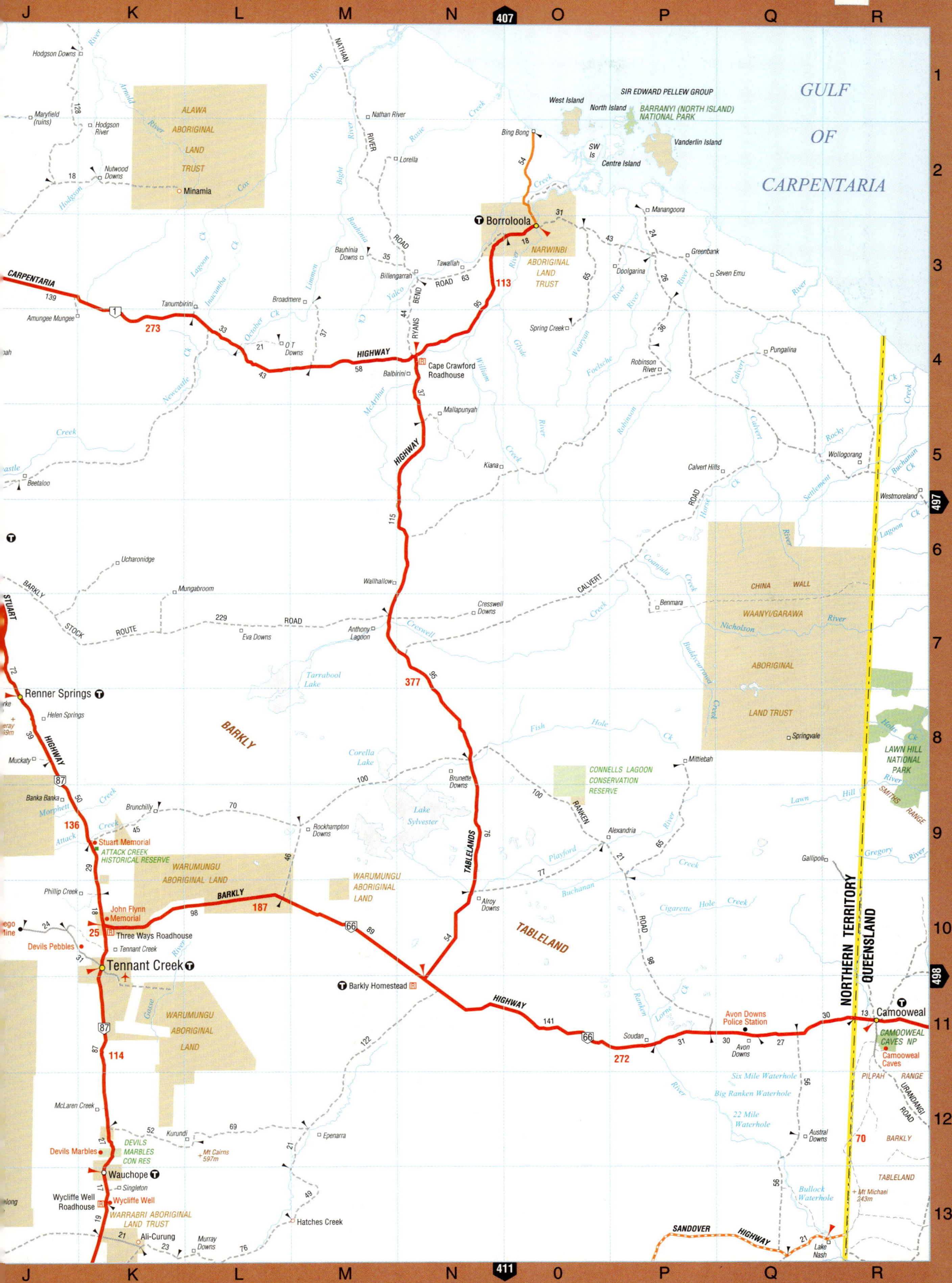

410 Southern Northern Territory

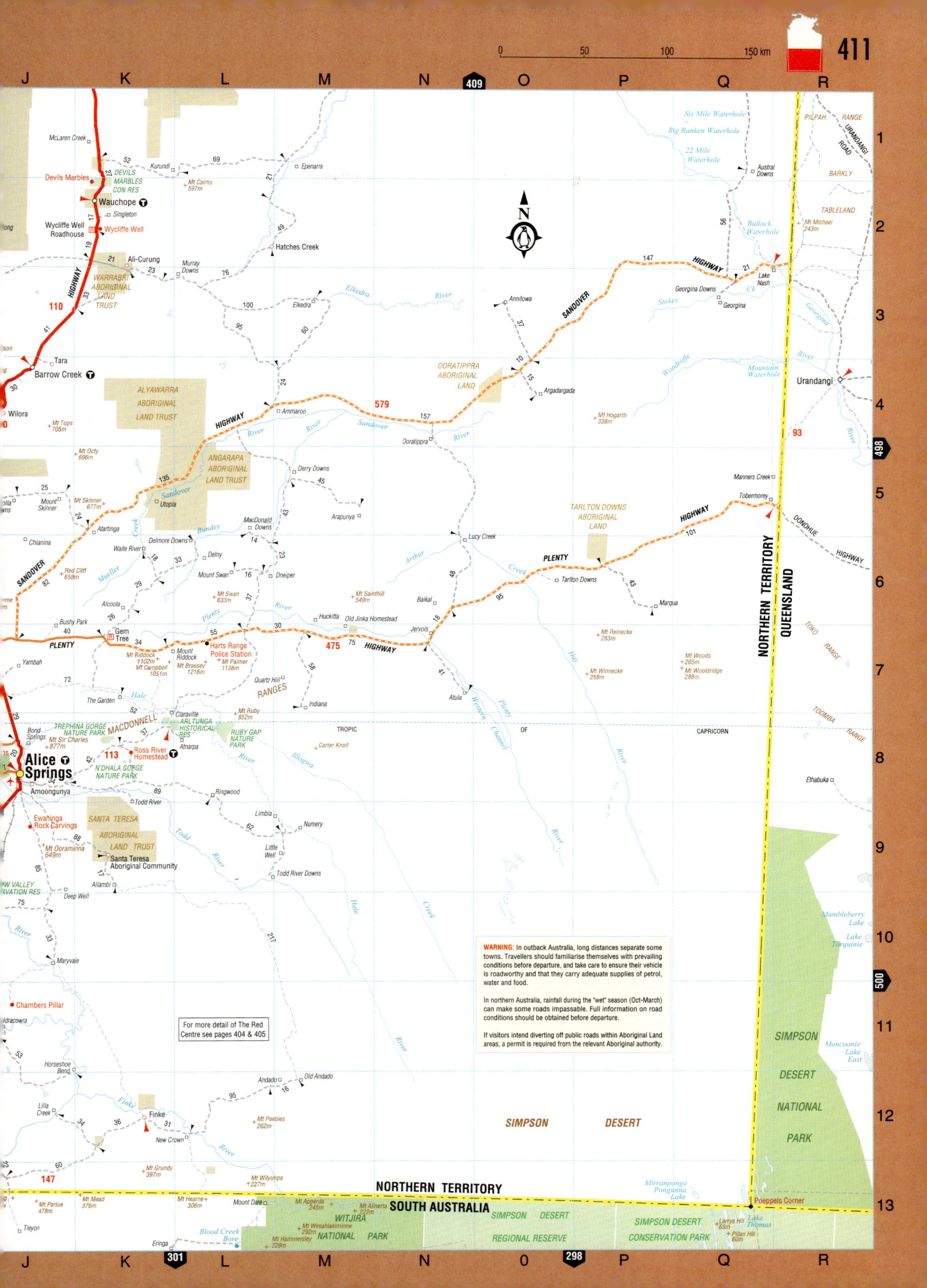

Queensland

Sunshine State

QUEENSLAND

Queensland

To visitors from other States, as well as to many Queenslanders, the Sunshine State is holiday country, evoking dreams of long, golden days, tropical islands set in jewel-blue seas and the chance to relax outdoors. The first settlers in the tropical north, however, were there for grimly practical reasons.

In 1821 Sir Thomas Brisbane, then Governor of New South Wales, sent John Oxley, his Surveyor-General, to explore the almost unknown country north of the Liverpool Plains. Oxley's task was to find a suitable site for a penal settlement and he decided on Moreton Bay. In 1824 troops and convicts arrived at Redcliffe, but a lack of fresh water and the hostility of the Aborigines persuaded them to move south and they decided to settle at the present site of Brisbane. By 1859 the settlement was well established and the free settlers were urging separation from New South Wales; on 10 December of that year, the state of Queensland was proclaimed.

Having gained legislative independence, the population of just 23 000 then set about achieving economic independence. Fortunately the new State was well endowed with excellent farming land, and wool and beef production were soon established on the western plains and tablelands. It was not long before sugar production, worked by 'kanaka' labour from the Pacific Islands, became much more important, and it is still significant.

As well as being blessed with fertile land that produces grain, sugar, dairy produce, wool, mutton, beef, cotton, peanuts and timber, Queensland has immensely rich mineral deposits, and the vast Mount Isa mining complex in the west produces copper, lead and zinc in enormous quantities.

Over the years, Queensland has been developing another, very different, form of industry – tourism. Its attraction as a holiday destination is very much due to its climate.

In the west, the climate is similar to that of the arid Red Centre, with fierce daytime heat, but on the coast the temperature rarely exceeds 38°C and for seven months or so of the year the weather is extremely pleasant. If you are unused to high humidity, however, the period from December to April can be uncomfortably damp.

Four geographic and climatic regions run north to south, neatly dividing the State. In the west is the Great Artesian Basin, flat and hot. Parched and bare during drought, it becomes grassy after rain, thanks to a complex system of boreholes that distribute water through channels and allow grazing. The tablelands to the east are undulating and sparsely timbered, broken up by slow, meandering rivers. The backbone of Queensland is the Great Dividing Range – most spectacular in its extreme north and south, where it comes closest to the coast. Although the coastal region is the area most popular with visitors, Queensland's hinterland is lushly beautiful and its national parks, with many species of flora and fauna unique to the State, total more than one million hectares.

The State's highway and road system is good in the south-east and in areas close to the larger northern towns, but elsewhere roads tend to be

NOT TO BE MISSED
in Queensland

- **Carnarvon National Park** – beautiful park with magnificent gorge and significant Aboriginal art
- **Darling Downs** – an area of beauty and prosperity – rural Australia at its best
- **Gemfield towns of Anakie, Rubyvale and Sapphire** – for fossicking (with a licence!)
- **Gold Coast hinterland** – spectacular scenery in Numinbah Valley and at Springbrook
- **Great Barrier Reef** – best seen by boat; your own, a charter boat or a cruise boat
- **Kuranda Scenic Railway** – spectacular train ride from Cairns to Kuranda; return via Skyrail Rainforest Cableway
- **Noosa National Park** – beautiful coastal park offering memorable views and walks
- **Scenic drive through Mapleton, Flaxton, Montville and Maleny** – one of the best in south-east Queensland
- **The Gulflander train** – train ride between Normanton and the old gold-mining town of Croydon
- **Theme parks on the Gold Coast** – Dreamworld, Movie World and Seaworld – fun for all the family

Green Island, a resort island on the Great Barrier Reef

Coastal edge of Daintree National Park in northern Queensland

narrow and poorly graded, and conditions deteriorate during drought or heavy rain.

The two main towns of the tropical northern region are Townsville and Cairns. The more northerly Cairns is a fashionable holiday centre and makes an excellent base for deep-sea fishing and for exploring the region, with its lush sugar plantations, mountainous jungle country and the wilds of the Cape York Peninsula. The Atherton Tableland is a rich volcanic area west of Cairns, with superb lakes, waterfalls and fern valleys. Stretching along this coastline are some of Queensland's famed islands: Lizard, north of Cooktown, Green, including Fitzroy, Dunk, Bedarra, Hinchinbrook, Orpheus and Magnetic. Further south are the beautiful Whitsunday Islands and Great Keppel, North West, Heron, Lady Musgrave, Lady Elliot, and Fraser islands. If you are planning an island holiday, make sure your choice fits in with your idea of a tropical paradise. Many islands are extensively developed for tourism; others remain relatively untouched. Beyond, and

CALENDAR OF EVENTS

Note: The information given here was accurate at the time of printing. However, as the timing of events held annually is subject to change and some events may extend into the following month, it is best to check with the local tourism authority or event organisers to confirm the details. The calendar is not exhaustive. Most towns and regions throughout the State hold sporting competitions; regattas and rodeos; art, craft, and trade exhibitions; agricultural and flower shows; music festivals and other events annually. Details of these events are available from local tourism outlets.

JANUARY
Public holidays: New Year's Day, Australia Day. **Georgetown:** Race meeting. **Redcliffe:** Blessing of the fleet. **Warwick:** Antique and collectables fair (sometimes held in Feb.).

FEBRUARY
Chinchilla: Melon festival (biennial, odd-numbered years). **Killarney:** Agricultural show. **Redcliffe:** Seafood festival. **Yeppoon:** Surf lifesaving championships.

MARCH
Gold Coast: IndyCar Australia racing spectacular (at Surfers Paradise). **Stanthorpe:** Apple and grape harvest festival (biennial, even-numbered years); Rodeo.

EASTER
Public holidays: Good Friday; Easter Monday. **Brisbane:** Brisbane–Gladstone yacht race. **Airlie Beach:** Regatta. **Bundaberg:** Country music roundup. **Burketown:** World barramundi handline-rod fishing championships. **Charters Towers:** Rodeo. **Emerald:** Sunflower festival. **Eromanga:** Rodeo. **Gladstone:** Harbour festival (includes finish of Brisbane–Gladstone yacht race). **Miles:** Museum display. **Roma:** Easter in the country. **St George:** Family fishing competition. **Tin Can Bay:** Easter festival.

APRIL
Public holiday: Anzac Day. **Allora:** 500 Endurance motor race. **Ipswich:** Heritage week. **Kilkivan:** Great horse ride. **Kingaroy:** Peanut festival (biennial, odd-numbered years, drought permitting). **Mooloolaba:** Finish of Sydney–Mooloolaba yacht race. **Mount Isa:** Country music festival. **Rockhampton:** Good Earth expo. **Stanthorpe:** Opera at sunset.

MAY
Public holiday: Labour Day. **Brisbane:** Winter racing carnival begins; International festival of music (biennial, odd-numbered years). **Beaudesert:** Rodeo. **Cardwell:** Country and western music festival. **Charters Towers:** Country music festival. **Childers:** Agricultural show. **Chinchilla:** Rotary May Day carnival. **Eromanga:** Race day. **Fraser Island:** Fishing expo. **Gatton:** Heavy horse field day. **Ingham:** Australian-Italian festival. **Julia Creek:** Campdraft. **Kuranda:** Folk festival. **Mareeba:** Dimbulah festival. **Maryborough:** Best of Brass. **Mount Morgan:** Golden Mount festival. **Normanton:** Show, rodeo and gymkhana. **Richmond:** Rodeo. **Town of Seventeen Seventy:** 1770 Commemorative festival. **Taroom:** Agricultural show. **Thursday Island:** Cultural festival.

JUNE
Public holiday: Queen's Birthday. **Biloela:** Country and western muster. **Blackall:** Race meeting. **Caboolture:** Agricultural show; Medieval festival. **Cardwell:** Coral Sea memorial. **Charters Towers:** Annual vintage car restorers' swap meet. **Cloncurry:** Agricultural show. **Cooktown:** Discovery festival. **Coolangatta:** Wintersun. **Croydon:** Rodeo. **Emerald:** Wheelbarrow derby. **Gayndah:** Orange festival (biennial, odd-numbered years). **Georgetown:** Race meeting. **Landsborough:** William Landsborough Day. **Longreach:** Hall of Fame race meeting. **Mallanda:** Pro-rodeo. **Monto:** Dairy festival (biennial, even-numbered years). **Mossman:** Bavarian festival. **Muttaburra:** Landsborough flock ewe show. **Nindigully:** 5-hour enduro (for motor bikes). **Noosa:** Aqueous festival of arts. **Normanton:** Show, rodeo and gymkhana. **Port Douglas:** Village carnivale. **Quilpie:** Diggers races. **Strathpine:** Pine Rivers heritage festival. **Taldora Station:** Saxby roundup. **Tin Can Bay:** Seafood and leisure festival. **Whitsunday:** Festival of sail.

JULY
Burketown: Rodeo and races. **Caboolture:** St

protecting them from the South Pacific, is the outer Great Barrier Reef, the world's largest and most famous coral formation.

South of the Reef is the Sunshine Coast. This scenic coastal region, with its leisurely pace and its wide variety of natural attractions and sporting facilities, offers an alternative to the more commercialised Gold Coast. Bribie Island and the Glass House Mountains are nearby.

Brisbane, Australia's third-largest capital city, is built on both sides of the Brisbane River. The city is easy-going, and its parks and gardens are lush with subtropical plants. It has a year-round average of 7½ hours of sunshine a day. The Gold Coast, 75 kilometres to the south, is the heart of holiday country. Luxuriously developed, it offers a wide range of accommodation, glittering nightlife, golden beaches and constant sun. Inland is rich agriculturally, mainly wheat and dairy farming, its setting a sharp contrast with the tropical north or the mining areas of Mount Isa.

The Sunshine State is a diverse place indeed.

CLIMATE GUIDE

BRISBANE

	J	F	M	A	M	J	J	A	S	O	N	D
Maximum °C	29	29	28	27	24	21	21	22	24	26	27	29
Minimum °C	21	21	20	17	14	11	10	10	13	16	18	20
Rainfall mm	169	177	152	86	84	82	66	45	34	102	95	123
Raindays	14	14	15	11	10	8	7	7	7	10	10	11

COOLANGATTA REGION

	J	F	M	A	M	J	J	A	S	O	N	D
Maximum °C	28	28	27	25	23	21	20	21	22	24	26	26
Minimum °C	20	20	19	17	13	11	9	10	12	15	17	19
Rainfall mm	184	181	213	114	124	122	96	103	49	108	137	166
Raindays	14	15	16	14	10	9	7	9	9	11	11	13

MACKAY VALLEY

	J	F	M	A	M	J	J	A	S	O	N	D
Maximum °C	30	29	28	27	24	22	21	22	25	27	29	30
Minimum °C	23	23	22	20	17	14	13	14	16	20	22	23
Rainfall mm	293	311	303	134	104	59	47	30	15	38	87	175
Raindays	16	17	17	15	13	7	7	6	5	7	9	12

CAIRNS REGION

	J	F	M	A	M	J	J	A	S	O	N	D
Maximum °C	31	31	30	29	28	26	26	27	28	29	31	31
Minimum °C	24	24	23	22	20	18	17	18	19	21	22	23
Rainfall mm	413	435	442	191	94	49	28	27	36	38	90	175
Raindays	18	19	20	17	14	10	9	8	8	8	10	13

Peters arts and crafts festival. **Chinchilla:** Polocrosse carnival. **Cleveland:** Flinders Day (re-enactment of landing on Coochiemudlo Island). **Cooktown:** Laura-Cape York Aboriginal dance festival (biennial, odd-numbered years). **Emu Park:** Service of Remembrance. **Esk:** Picnic races. **Gold Coast:** International marathon (at Southport). **Hughenden:** Dinosaur festival (biennial, even-numbered years). **Innisfail:** Agricultural show. **Ipswich:** Medieval fair and markets. **Karumba:** Karumba Kapers. **Mackay:** Rodeo. Festival of the arts. **Mareeba:** Rodeo. **Mission Beach:** Cassowary festival. **Nebo:** Rodeo. **Pomona:** King of the Mountain festival. **Rainbow Beach:** Fishing Classic.

Rockhampton: Bauhinia arts festival. **Sarina:** Visual arts festival. **Texas:** Agricultural show. **Townsville:** Australian festival of chamber music.

AUGUST
Public holiday: Brisbane Show Day. **Brisbane:** Brisbane international film festival; Royal Brisbane National Show (the Ekka); Spring Hill fair. **Atherton:** Maize festival. **Boulia:** Rodeo and gymkhana. **Bowen:** Art, craft and orchid expo. **Charters Towers:** Great gold rush. **Cloncurry:** Merry Muster rodeo. **Cunnamulla:** Opal festival. **Emerald:** Gemfest. **Eulo:** World lizard racing championships. **Hervey Bay:** Whale festival. **Mount Isa:** Rodeo. **Quilpie:** Diggers races. **Richmond:** Rodeo.

Rockhampton: Rocky round up. **Sarina:** Agricultural show. **Yeppoon:** World cooeeing festival.

SEPTEMBER
Brisbane: Warana festival. **Airlie Beach:** Fun race. **Beaudesert:** Mini royal agricultural show. **Birdsville:** Races. **Boonah:** Fassifern German festival. **Bundaberg:** Bundy in Bloom festival. **Caloundra:** Art and craft show. **Clermont:** Rodeo. **Comet:** Show and camp draft. **Cominya:** Boss camel races. **Dunk Island:** Billfish Classic. **Emerald:** Music spectacular. **Herberton:** Tin Festival. **Kynuna:** 'Surf' carnival. **Laidley:** Chelsea festival week. **Longreach:** Starlight stampede (biennial, even-numbered years). **Mackay:** Sugartime festival. **Maryborough:**

Heritage festival. **Miles:** Back to the Bush (includes wildflower festival). **Noosa:** Jazz party. **Port Douglas:** Regatta. **Quilpie:** Agricultural show. **Redcliffe:** First Settlement festival. **Redland Bay:** Strawberry festival. **Tambo:** Spring flower festival. **Taroom:** Leichhardt festival. **Thangool:** Arts festival. **Toowoomba:** Carnival of flowers. **Tully:** Flower show. **Winton:** Outback festival (biennial, odd-numbered years). **Yeppoon:** Pineapple festival.

OCTOBER
Brisbane: Colonial George Street festival. **Ayr:** Water festival. **Biggenden:** Rose festival (biennial, odd-numbered years). **Bowen:** Coral Coast festival. **Cairns:** Fun in the Sun festival.

Charleville: Booga Woongaroo (mulga tree) festival. **Crows Nest:** Crows Nest day; Worm races. **Dalby:** Harvest festival. **Emu Park:** Octoberfest. **Gatton:** Potato festival. **Georgetown:** Race meeting. **Goondiwindi:** Spring festival. **Gympie:** Gold Rush festival. **Hervey Bay:** Hervey Bay to Fraser Island sailboard marathon. **Ingham:** Maraka festival. **Innisfail:** Harvest festival. **Jundah:** Race carnival. **Laidley:** Festival of performing arts. **Logan:** Street parade. **Maroochydore:** Mapleton yarn festival. **Mission Beach:** Aquatic festival; Sailing regatta. **Nanango:** Pioneer festival. **Noosa:** Beach car classic, triathlon. **Ravenshoe:** Torimba forest festival. **Ravenswood:** Halloween ball.

Warwick: Rose and rodeo city festival. **Yandina:** Spring flower and ginger festival.

NOVEMBER
Esk: Eskibition. **Georgetown:** Race meeting. **Goondiwindi:** Rodeo. **Home Hill:** Harvest festival. **Killarney:** Rodeo. **Kynuna:** Rodeo. **Logan:** River festival and raft race. **Townsville:** Pacific festival. **Whitsunday:** Game-fishing championships; Annual spawning of the coral.

DECEMBER
Public holidays: Christmas Day; Boxing Day. **Karumba:** Fisherman's ball. **Pittsworth:** Great Australian team truck pull. **Tin Can Bay:** Robert Pryde memorial surf classic. **Whitsunday:** Festival of sail.

BRISBANE
A Subtropical City

The Brisbane River winds its way through the city

The best place from which to see the layout of Brisbane is the lookout on **Mount Coot-tha**, located 8 kilometres south-west of the city centre and easily distinguished by its television towers. Brisbane sprawls over the series of small hills below, with the Brisbane River wandering lazily through the suburbs and city, and out into **Moreton Bay**, 32 kilometres downstream. Surprisingly little use is made of the river for public transport, and most riverside houses back on to rather than face it. **Moreton and Stradbroke Islands** look like a protective mountain range against the Pacific Ocean, far to the east. On a good day, you can see the rugged mountains behind the Gold Coast to the south, and northward, the strange **Glass House Mountains** just south of the Sunshine Coast. Brisbane's best-known building, the **City Hall**, is now lost among the cluster of high-rise office buildings that dominate the skyline.

Although Brisbane is an international tourist destination, the city still does not bustle like the larger southern capitals. The suburban architecture, except for the newer, western areas, is predominantly the traditional galvanised iron-roofed timber house on stumps which residents think sensible and visitors find quaint. While some of these houses may be lacking in paint, this is more than made up for by colourful subtropical trees and shrubbery.

The city started inauspiciously as a convict settlement as far removed from Britain, and even from Sydney, as possible. In 1799 Matthew Flinders sailed into Moreton Bay on the sloop *Norfolk*. In 1823 John Oxley, then Surveyor-General, on board the cutter *Mermaid* sailed up the river that flowed into the bay and called it 'the Brisbane', after the Governor of New South Wales, Sir

NOT TO BE MISSED
in Brisbane

- **City Botanic Gardens** – lush tropical vegetation in a riverside setting
- **City Hall** – architecturally interesting building with an 85-metre clocktower
- **City Sights tour** – for a scenic round-up of the major attractions from tram-style coaches
- **Cultural Centre** – museum, art gallery, library and theatres; all in one building
- **Earlystreet Historical Village** – fine collection of early-Queensland buildings
- **Lone Pine Koala Sanctuary** – take a ferry ride to this famous koala sanctuary
- **Mt Coot-tha Lookout** – for superb views of Brisbane and surrounding area
- **Newstead House** – Brisbane's premier historic house with period furnishings and exhibits
- **South Bank Parklands** – a beach, cruise ships, rainforest and butterfly house – in the city
- **Sunday markets at Riverside Centre and at South Bank Parklands** – for art and craft

Thomas Brisbane. The first troops and convicts arrived in 1824 on the brig *Amity*. Soon, the original settlement at Redcliffe was abandoned, mainly because of a lack of fresh water, and barracks were built on the present site of the city centre, previously investigated by Oxley. The penal settlement was closed in 1839 and the region was opened for free settlement in 1842.

Today Brisbane is a busy city with a modern and extensive public transport system; a wide selection of restaurants, beautiful entertainment and nightlife; parks and gardens which thrive in the subtropical climate; and a population of over 1.3 million.

Among several interesting historic buildings is the **Observatory** or **Old Windmill** on Wickham Terrace, overlooking the city. Built in 1828, the mill proved unworkable, so convicts were pressed into service to crush the grain on a treadmill. In 1934 a picture of the mill was the first television image transmitted in Australia; it was sent to Ipswich, 33 kilometres away.

The restored **Commissariat Stores**, at North Quay below the old **State Library** building, were built by convicts in 1829. The **Treasury Building** at the top of Queen Street, an impressive Italian Renaissance structure built of local grey sandstone, was commenced in 1888 and is now the site for the **Conrad Treasury Casino**. The nearby **Lands Administration Building** is a boutique hotel. **Newstead House**, a charming building overlooking the river at Breakfast Creek, was built in 1846 by Patrick Leslie, the first settler on the Darling Downs. He sold it to his brother-in-law Captain John Wickham, RN, resident of the Moreton Bay colony, and it was the centre of official and social life in Brisbane until the first Government House was built in 1862. Newstead House is Brisbane's oldest house and has been restored to illustrate a bygone past. **Old Government House**, a classic colonial building with additions made between 1882 and 1895, was also the original University. It now forms part of the **Queensland University of Technology** complex at the bottom of George Street and is the home of the National Trust of Queensland. Nearby, is **Parliament House** designed by Charles Tiffin in a 'tropical Renaissance' style and opened in 1868. The **Parliament House Annexe** (irreverently called the Taj Mahal) is a modern tower block behind Parliament House overlooking the river. The exclusive **Queensland Club** is diagonally opposite Parliament House and was built during the 1880s.

The **General Post Office** in Queen Street was built between 1871 and 1879 on the site of the female convict barracks. The small church behind the Post Office in Elizabeth Street and beside **St Stephen's Catholic Cathedral** is the third oldest building in Brisbane, having been dedicated in 1850. The **Customs House** at Petrie Bight at the bottom of Queen Street was built in 1884; recently refurbished, it includes an art gallery, bookshop and cafe. The **Deanery**, built in 1849, behind **St John's Anglican Cathedral** in Ann Street, became a temporary residence for the first Governor of Queensland, Sir George Bowen. The proclamation announcing Queensland as a separate colony was read from its balcony on 10 December, 1859. It became the residence of the Dean of Brisbane in 1910. Further south along Ann Street is **All Saints' Church**, which dates from 1861.

Earlystreet Historical Village is a fine collection of Queensland buildings located at 75 McIlwraith Avenue, Norman Park, east of the city centre. Among the buildings are reconstructions of Stromness, one of the first houses at Kangaroo Point, and the ballroom and billiard-room of Auchenflower House. The village is open daily and afternoon teas are served on Sundays.

To the north of the city in Bowen Hills, another building open to the public is **Miegunyah**, a traditional Queensland house with verandahs and ironwork. Located in Jordan Terrace, it is home to the Queensland Women's Historical Society.

There are very few terrace houses in Brisbane, but a row at the **Normanby Junction** has been lovingly restored and incorporates two restaurants. A similar development has occurred on **Coronation Drive**. Brisbane's more impressive houses, including the famous old 'Queenslanders', are scattered throughout the inner-city suburbs. Many small cottages in the **Spring Hill**, **Paddington** and **Red Hill** areas are being restored. The **Regatta Hotel** on the river at Coronation Drive is worth a visit, and the famous **Breakfast Creek Hotel** has a popular outdoor area serving excellent steaks and beer 'off-the-wood'.

The main city department stores are located in **Queen Street**, which, between Edward and George Streets, is a mall containing four large shopping complexes, boutiques, entertainment centres, the major department stores, restaurants and taverns. Most shops in the city are open seven days a week and for late-night shopping on Fridays. Three of the city's most popular markets are the kilometre-long stretch of Sunday craft markets at the **Riverside Centre** in Eagle Street; the **South Bank Markets**, held on Friday nights, Saturdays and Sundays; and the Saturday markets in **Brunswick Street**, Fortitude Valley.

For the sports enthusiast, Brisbane's famous '**Gabba**' ground at Woolloongabba hosts cricket and football matches, and greyhound racing. There

---

ACCOMMODATION

HOTELS
Brisbane Hilton
190 Elizabeth St, Brisbane
(07) 3231 3131

Hotel Conrad
130 William St, Brisbane
(07) 3306 8888

Hotel Grand Chancellor
Wickham Tce, Spring Hill
(07) 3831 4055

Novotel Brisbane
200 Creek St, Brisbane
(07) 3309 3309

Sheraton Brisbane Hotel and Towers
249 Turbot St, Brisbane
(07) 3835 3535

The Heritage Hotel
Cnr Edward and Margaret Sts, Brisbane
(07) 3221 1999

FAMILY AND BUDGET
Albert Park Inn
551 Wickham Tce, Spring Hill
(07) 3831 3111

Kingsford Hall Private Hotel
114 Kingsford Smith Dr., Hamilton
(07) 3862 1317

Queensland Countrywomen's Association Club
89–95 Gregory Tce, Spring Hill
(07) 3831 8188

Sly Fox Travellers Hotel
73 Melbourne St, South Brisbane
(07) 3844 0022

Story Bridge Motor Inn
321 Main St, Kangaroo Point
(07) 3393 1433

MOTEL GROUPS: BOOKINGS
Best Western 13 1779
Flag 13 2400
Travelodge (008) 22 2446

This list is for information only; inclusion is not necessarily a recommendation.

are four horseracing venues at Albion Park, Doomben, Eagle Farm and Bundamba. The **ANZ Stadium** at Nathan and the Chandler aquatic centre, indoor sports hall and velodrome were all built for the 1982 Commonwealth Games. The ANZ Stadium is now the home of the rugby-league premiers, the Brisbane Broncos. Rugby-union headquarters are at the **Ballymore Stadium** at Herston.

The **King George Square** facing the **City Hall** is a popular spot for watching the world go by. The **Anzac Memorial** and **Eternal Flame** is located opposite **Central Railway Station** with its towering backdrop, the Sheraton Brisbane Hotel and Towers.

Across Victoria Bridge lies **South Bank Parklands**, 16 hectares of redeveloped and landscaped parklands with walking and bicycle paths, a constructed beach, a series of canals where the South Ships cruise, and several restaurants. The Gondwana Rainforest Sanctuary, the Butterfly and Insect House and Our World Environment Display are special features within the parklands.

For the art lover, the **Queensland Art Gallery**, part of the **Queensland Cultural Centre**, is on the southside riverbank. This impressive gallery includes significant Australian, British and European collections. The Cultural Centre also houses an auditorium, the award-winning **Queensland Performing Arts Complex** with three theatres, along with the **State Library of Queensland** and the **Queensland Museum**. The **Civic Art Museum** in the City Hall, the **Museum of Contemporary Art** at South Brisbane and the **University of Queensland Art Museum** at St Lucia are excellent. Private galleries include the Philip Bacon Gallery at New Farm; the Ray Hughes Gallery at Red Hill; the Victor Mace Gallery at Para Galleries at South Brisbane, which specialises in Queensland artists; and in the central city: the New Central Galleries, the Town Gallery, the Don McInnes Galleries, Barry's Gallery and two Aboriginal galleries. In Fortitude Valley, the Potter's Gallery has pottery by local artists for sale and the Fireworks Gallery in Ann Street features Aboriginal art. The **Leichhardt Street** area of Spring Hill has developed as a centre for arts and crafts enthusiasts.

Brisbane's annual Warana Festival, a feast of art, craft and cultural activities, occurs in late September and draws large crowds to the city. Also held annually are the Royal National Show (known as The Ekka) held at Herston in August and the Spring Hill Fair (usually on the second weekend in September) in the streets of Spring Hill. The Biennial International Festival of Music begins in late May every odd-numbered year. The Brisbane International Film Festival is held in August and the Queensland Winter Racing Carnival – sport, racing, and visual and performing arts – spans May and June. The **Brisbane Convention and Exhibition Centre** located on the corner of Glenelg and Merrivale Streets in South Brisbane is also the venue for a variety of exhibitions.

Queensland University is on a superb site on the river at St Lucia. It is built mainly from Helidon freestone. A second university, **Griffith**, is in beautiful bush country in the southern suburb of Nathan. **Queensland University of Technology** is located on several campuses throughout Brisbane.

The present **Government House** at Bardon was built in 1865 for Johann Heussler, who brought German farmworkers to the State; it became the official residence for the State Governor in 1920.

The old Queensland Museum is an ornate building on the corner of Bowen Bridge Road and Gregory Terrace. The **Science Centre** in George Street has hands-on interactive displays. The main Post Office in Queen Street has a museum of telegraphic material. The **Queensland Maritime Museum** in Stanley Street, South Brisbane, incorporates the old South Brisbane dry dock. Nearby are the popular **Riverside Esplanade walking and bicycle paths** leading to Kangaroo Point, with access to picnic areas.

The **City Botanic Gardens** next to Parliament House are magnificent. **New Farm Park**, which is close to the city via Fortitude Valley, has 12 000 rose bushes, jacaranda trees that blossom in October and November, and poinciana trees flowering in November and December.

Brisbane is famous for its seafood, and several good restaurants allow you the opportunity to come to grips with the awesome Queensland mudcrab, Moreton Bay bugs, tiger prawns, delicious reef fish and barramundi. Some of the popular venues are Pier Nine Oyster Bar and Restaurant at Eagle Street Pier; Michael's Riverside Restaurant at the Riverside Centre in Eagle Street; Rumpoles in Turbot Street; Muddie's in Edward Street; the Milano Italian Restaurant in the Queen Street Mall; Oxley's Wharf Restaurant on the river at Milton; and the exotic Cat's Tango in St Lucia. **Chinatown** in Fortitude Valley offers distinctive shopping and dining.

Because of its vast size (the Brisbane City Council controls an area of 12 200 hectares), the city's public transport network is extensive. Council buses take most of the load, while modern electric air-conditioned trains run to many areas. An excellent pocket map is produced by the Metropolitan Transit Authority. **City Sights** tours operate narrated tours of the major attractions in colourful tram-style coaches collecting passengers at city sights stops every half-hour. Small ferries operate from the city to Kangaroo Point, East Brisbane, New Farm Park and South Bank. Golden Mile operates river and bay cruises from North Quay, and Mirimar Cruises offer cruises to Lone Pine Koala Sanctuary. The City Ferry Cruise, operated by the Brisbane City Council, leaves the Edward Street ferry terminal near the Botanic Gardens, travelling downstream

BRISBANE ON FOOT

A series of self-guide heritage trails has been prepared by the Brisbane City Council. In addition to the central business district, heritage trails exist for Brisbane's riverfront, Fortitude Valley, Toowong Cemetery and some of the older residential suburbs including Hamilton, New Farm, Paddington and Wynnum-Manly. Pamphlets are available from the Brisbane Visitors and Convention Bureau information centres.

- **City streets:** 2-hour guided walk conducted each Tues. and Thurs.; bookings essential.
- **Historic buildings:** 1 or 2-hour guided walking tours; bookings essential.

For further information contact the Brisbane Visitors and Convention Bureau, City Hall, King George Square; (07) 3221 8411.

to Breakfast Creek and upstream to Queensland University. The paddle-wheeler *Kookaburra Queen* cruises the river daily and is a good place to dine in the evening.

Several of Brisbane's attractions lie just outside the city area. There are good views from the surrounding hills particularly from **Bartley's Hill Lookout** at Hamilton. The **Historical Observation Tower** at the Boardwalk in Newstead, a 33-metre tower, affords outstanding views of the city. The *Southern Cross*, Sir Charles Kingsford Smith's Fokker tri-motor aircraft, is on display at Brisbane Airport in Airport Drive. Just across the river is **Fort Lytton**, a garrison built in 1880 and opened to visitors in 1989. Brisbane's **Lone Pine Koala Sanctuary**, is 11 kilometres away at Fig Tree Pocket. **Samford Alpine Adventureland** at Samford, 21 kilometres from the city, offers grass-skiing, a 700-metre bobsled, and swimming and picnic areas. **Amazons Aquatic Adventureland** at Jindalee, 12 kilometres from the city, has family water-slide entertainment and picnic areas. **Brisbane Forest Park** at The Gap, 12 kilometres from the city, provides 'bushranger' and wildlife tours in its 25 000 hectares of bushland. Tours of the Castlemaine Perkins brewery are available; contact Tourist information.

The **Australian Woolshed**, fourteen kilometres north-west of the city, features trained rams, sheep-shearing demonstrations and tame koalas and kangaroos. At Kallangur, north of Brisbane, **Alma Park Zoo** exhibits native and exotic species of fauna, and has beautiful gardens.

For further information on Brisbane, contact the Brisbane Visitors and Convention Bureau, City Hall, King George Square; (07) 3221 8411, or visit the BVCB Information Booth in the Queen Street Mall.

Mount Coot-tha

Located only 8 kilometres from Brisbane's city centre, Mt Coot-tha offers city dwellers an attractive breathing space. Brisbane's newest Botanic Gardens are in the foothills of Mt Coot-tha. The tropical display house, in the form of a futuristic-looking dome, has a superb display of tropical plants and is open daily. The arid-zone garden and cactus house are nearby. The gardens also include a lagoon and pond, a demonstration garden, ornamental trees and shrubs, areas of Australian and tropical rainforest, and a large collection of Australian native plants.

View from the summit of Mount Coot-tha

Situated in the Botanic Gardens is the Sir Thomas Brisbane Planetarium. The largest planetarium in the country, it accommodates 144 people and was named after the 'founder of organised science in Australia'. When Sir Thomas was Governor of New South Wales, he set up an astronomical observatory in 1821 at Parramatta. His observations resulted in the publication of *The Brisbane Catalog of Stars*. Various programmes are shown at the Planetarium's Star Theatre. A representation of the night sky is projected on to the interior of the dome and the movements of the sun, moon and stars are described as they occur. Additional projectors are used to produce special effects in order to demonstrate more unusual phenomena in the sky. Programmes are shown in both the afternoon and evening, Wednesday to Sunday, with an additional afternoon show at weekends. Children under six are not admitted. The planetarium complex also contains an observatory that is used by members of the public, by prior arrangement, to view the day or night sky.

There are many picnic and barbecue areas at Mt Coot-tha, including a particularly attractive spot for walks at the J.C. Slaughter Falls. The Mount Coot-tha Summit Restaurant on Sir Samuel Griffith Drive is open daily for lunches, and morning and afternoon teas, and visitors can dine at the restaurant at the Mount Coot-tha Lookout. There is also a coffee shop and gift shop at the lookout. The view from the summit is superb, across the city and Moreton Bay, and sometimes as far as the Lamington Plateau in the south and the Glass House Mountains in the north.

Perhaps the best view of all from Mt Coot-tha is at night when the lights of the city of Brisbane are spread out before you – a breathtaking sight. Even if you have only one evening in Brisbane, it is worth making the short trip to the lookout to take in this memorable scene.

For further information, contact the Brisbane Visitors and Convention Bureau, City Hall, King George Square; (07) 3221 8411. **Map references:** 462 D13, 464 D1.

TOURS from Brisbane

Spring Bluff station at Toowoomba, 127 kilometres west of Brisbane

There is a variety of things to see and do around Brisbane. Most tours can be done in one day, but some are more suited to an overnight stop.

The Brisbane forest parks concept is being developed as breathing space for the city, and many new national parks have been declared in the surrounding area. As well as visiting the beaches, take advantage of these parks – they are well worth a visit.

Redcliffe

41 km from Brisbane via Gympie Road

Drive to Redcliffe via Petrie and a detour to the North Pine Dam. The Redcliffe Peninsula is almost completely surrounded by the waters of Moreton Bay. The sandy beaches are safe for swimming and the fishing is good. High on the volcanic red cliffs there are spectacular views far across Moreton Bay to Moreton and Stradbroke Islands, famous for their natural surroundings and mountainous sand dunes. The Redcliffe jetty is a favourite spot for local anglers. **See also:** Entry for Redcliffe in A–Z listing.

Bribie Island

65 km from Brisbane via Bruce Highway

See: Fraser and Moreton Bay Islands.

Wynnum-Manly and Redland Bay

35 km from Brisbane via Routes 23, 30 and 44

You will not have to drive far to enjoy the bayside suburbs of Wynnum and Manly, south-east of Brisbane on the shores of Moreton Bay. Manly has five marinas and is the headquarters of the Royal Queensland Yacht Squadron. Continue on to Redland Bay, a peaceful holiday town. The area is famed for its market gardens and the Strawberry festival (on the first Saturday of each September). Wayside stalls sell fruit and flowers at weekends. Boats can be hired all along this coast, so that you can do your own exploring, go fishing or visit the islands of Moreton Bay. **See also:** Entry for Redland Bay in A–Z listing.

The Gold Coast

70 km from Brisbane via the Pacific and Gold Coast Highways

See: City of the Gold Coast.

Gold Coast Hinterland

70 km from Brisbane via the Pacific Highway and Nerang

If possibly you are bored by the Gold Coast, simply drive west. The nearby McPherson Ranges have some of Australia's finest scenery.

Mount Tamborine

75 km from Brisbane via the Pacific Highway

Mount Tamborine, some 30 kilometres from Oxenford, is a retreat from the bustle of Brisbane. Here walking tracks lead through the rainforest, where palms, staghorns, elkhorns, ferns and orchids grow in profusion, to waterfalls and lookouts. There are picnic and barbecue facilities here and in the nearby Tamborine National Park. **See also:** National Parks.

Lamington National Park

112 km from Brisbane via the Mt Lindesay or Pacific Highways, and Canungra

Lamington National Park is one of the wildest and finest in Queensland. On a plateau at the top is O'Reilly's Guest House, and it is worth making this a full weekend's trip, though an advance booking should be made. A maze of walking tracks and an elevated treetop walkway allow you to see the area's many attractions. But if walking is not for you, you can just sit in the sun, breathe in the refreshing mountain air and admire the superb scenery or feed the birds. The subtropical rainforest has an abundance of wildlife, which has been protected for many years. You can walk from O'Reilly's to Binna Burra Lodge, a distance of 22 kilometres. It is a much longer trip by road. Binna Burra Lodge is a good base from which to enjoy the great variety of walks in the area, but a sensible pair of shoes is a must. Bring a jumper too – it can get cold even in summer. If you plan to spend a weekend wilderness camping in the mountains, a permit is necessary and can be obtained from the Chief Ranger at Binna Burra. Information is available in Canungra about the many walks and places of interest on the way. Those who prefer more comfort can stay overnight at the Binna Burra Lodge, but book in advance. **See also:** National Parks.

Toowoomba

127 km from Brisbane via the Warrego Highway

A comfortable distance from Brisbane for a day trip, this drive takes you past some small towns and old farmhouses. Stop at Marburg on the way to admire the old timber pub with its latticed verandah. Toowoomba's most popular tourist attraction is its parks and gardens with their magnificent deciduous trees including oaks, elms, plane trees and poplars. The gardens are best seen during September when the city has its Carnival of flowers. The carnival is usually held during the last week of September, and includes a procession, dancing and entertainment in the streets. The Blue Arrow Drive around the city, laid out by the city council, is a must for visitors. You could return to Brisbane via the New England and Cunningham Highways. **See also:** Entry for Toowoomba in A–Z listing.

The Jondaryan Woolshed Historical Museum and Park

176 km from Brisbane via the Warrego Highway

The Jondaryan Woolshed, between Oakey and Bowenville, was built in 1859, with space for 88 blade shearers to handle some 200 000 sheep a season. Now an ideal outing for all the family, it has been developed as a working memorial to the early pastoral pioneers. As well as the Woolshed, you can visit the blacksmith's shop, the one-roomed schoolhouse and the dairy. There is also a fascinating collection of old agricultural machinery. Open every day except Good Friday and Christmas Day; conducted tours operate daily.

The Bunya Mountains

250 km from Brisbane via Brisbane Valley and D'Aguilar Highways

This three-hour drive is often spectacular, but hairpin bends make the journey unsuitable for cars towing caravans or trailers. Because there is so much to see along the way, it would be wise to stay overnight either camping or at a hotel. On the way, Savages Crossing is a good place for a picnic. Bellevue Homestead at Coominya is worth a detour as it is a major National Trust project, the homestead having been moved from its original site, rebuilt and restored. Further on, stop to see the Koomba Falls and King House at Maidenwell. There are many more places to visit on the way to the mountains and all are fully signposted. Most of the area is set aside as the Bunya Mountains National Park; there are two major camping sites in the park and bushwalkers will enjoy the excellent graded tracks. If you have time and do not want to camp, continue on to Kingaroy, the peanut-growing area, where there is plenty of accommodation. **See also:** National Parks.

Mount Glorious

45 km from Brisbane via Waterworks Road

One of the more interesting short drives from Brisbane is through mountainous country due west of the city to Mount Glorious, via Mount Nebo, and then back via Samford. From Mount Glorious it is possible to extend this drive to take in the delights of Lake Wivenhoe, only 15 kilometres further on. There are spectacular views of the mountainous Brisbane Forest Park. Stop at McPhee's and Jolly's Lookouts before arriving at the pretty town of Mount Nebo. Hear bellbirds and whipbirds in the Manorina section of D'Aguilar National Park. At Mount Glorious, in the Maiala section of the same park, there are many long and short self-guide walks through the lush rainforest. Local Aboriginal history is recorded on a bush trail at Bellbird Grove in Brisbane Forest Park. At the information centre for the park (60 Mount Nebo Rd, The Gap; (07) 3300 4855), you can see exhibits of Queensland's native freshwater fish at the Walkabout Creek aquatic study centre, and then dine in the restaurant that is located upstairs.

The Sunshine Coast

100 km from Brisbane to its nearest point via the Bruce Highway

See: Sunshine Coast.

Beerwah and Buderim past the Glass House Mountains

100 km from Brisbane via the Bruce Highway and the Glass House Mountains Tourist Road

When travelling past the Glass House Mountains, you will see the ten spectacular trachyte peaks named by Captain Cook as he sailed up the coast in 1770. The sun shining on the rockfaces reminded him of glasshouses in his native Yorkshire. Further north from Beerwah is the Queensland Reptile and Fauna Park, reputed to be one of the best such parks in Australia. Here venomous snakes, including taipans, and lizards of all sizes, can be seen. The 2-hectare Crocodile Environment Park has guided tours enabling visitors to see crocodiles and alligators in their natural surroundings. Continue on through Landsborough to Buderim. Visit the Pioneer Cottage, one of Buderim's earliest houses (it contains many of its original furnishings from last century), the art galleries and the Festive Markets. **See also:** Entries for Buderim and Landsborough in A–Z listing.

The Big Pineapple complex

96 km from Brisbane via the Bruce Highway

Seven kilometres south of Nambour, the Big Pineapple complex is the largest and most popular tourist attraction on the Sunshine Coast. On the pleasant drive along the Bruce Highway you will pass colourful roadside stalls offering tropical fruit at prices that amaze the southern visitor. The Big Pineapple itself is a 16-metre replica of a pineapple, with a top-floor observation deck offering views of the plantation of tropical fruit below. There are two floors of audiovisual displays, a restaurant and a tropical-fruit market. Ride on a sugar-cane train through more than 40 hectares of pineapple, mango, avocado and sugar cane plantations. The attractive animal farm is fun for children. The Nutmobile will take you to the Magic Macadamia, a giant nut replica. Here the complete process, from cracking the nut to the final product, is revealed.

The Gold Coast

The Gold Coast, Australia's premier holiday destination, consists of 70 kilometres of coastline boasting 42 kilometres of golden, unpolluted beaches stretching from Southport in the north to Coolangatta in the south, with a lush subtropical backdrop in the Gold Coast hinterland – the 'green behind the gold'.

Only one hour's drive south of Brisbane, this international resort city offers a multitude of constructed and natural attractions, and, of course, superb surfing beaches – Main Beach, Surfers Paradise, Broadbeach, Mermaid Beach, Miami, Burleigh Heads, Tallebudgera, Palm Beach, Currumbin, Tugun, Kirra and Coolangatta.

With almost 300 days of sunshine each year – an average winter maximum of 21°C and an average summer maximum of 28°C – it is no wonder that the Gold Coast region is the country's holiday playground, attracting more than three million visitors annually.

Accommodation caters for all budgets, ranging from international five-star-plus hotels and resorts to hotels, motels, apartments, guest houses, caravan parks, camping grounds and backpackers' hostels. It is estimated there are more than 35 000 rooms with more than 55 000 beds available on the Gold Coast. A variety of theme parks, sporting facilities, restaurants, shops, nightlife and entertainment, guarantee to satisfy all tastes. The Gold Coast is said to have the largest number of restaurants per square kilometre in Australia.

With its towering skyline, beachfront esplanade, glitz and glamour, Surfers Paradise is the hub of the central Gold Coast region, while the Gold Coast hinterland is a subtropical hideaway with numerous national parks and reserves complete with massive trees, spectacular views, cascading waterfalls and bush walks only 30 minutes from the hustle and bustle of the city.

Moving west from the coastline into the hinterland, the terrain climbs steadily to 1000 metres and breathtaking scenery in the Numinbah Valley and at Springbrook. Highlights here include Canyon Lookout, with views of Goomoolahra Falls; Lyre Bird Ridge Pottery; the 190-metre Purlingbrook Falls; Winburra Lookout; and the Hinze Dam.

In the Numinbah Valley on the southern Queensland border is the Natural Arch, a spectacular waterfall which plummets through a stone archway into a rock pool below. This picturesque area is an excellent spot for picnics, barbecues and bush walks.

Tamborine Mountain's rainforests and Lamington National Park provide the backdrop to Beaudesert Shire. The more adventurous are easily tempted into tackling the rugged ranges and gorges of Lamington National Park, the largest preserved natural subtropical rainforest in Australia, with 160 kilometres of walking tracks.

At **Oxenford:** Award-winning Warner Bros Movie World, based on the famous Hollywood movie set, is a theme park and part of a fully operational movie set. Close by is Wet 'n' Wild, Australia's largest aquatic fun park.

Monorail at Sea World, a major attraction on the Gold Coast

The Gold Coast   423

The Gold Coast Highway separates the high-rise buildings and the beach at Surfers Paradise

At **Coomera:** To the north is Dreamworld, a theme park offering 11 'themed worlds' including an interactive tiger attraction, Tiger Island, and fun rides for all the family. Nearby is the exclusive Sanctuary Cove residential resort, which incorporates the Hyatt Hotel, two golf courses and a marina. The links-style Hope Island Golf Club is one of the Gold Coast's newest international golf courses. Just south is Cable Ski World and Pine Ridge Environmental Park at Coombabah.

At **Southport:** Sea World, on The Spit at Main Beach, is the largest marine park in the southern hemisphere. Its world-class attractions include performing dolphins, a monorail, a skyway, water-ski ballet, helicopter rides, a replica of the *Endeavour*, the Old Fort, a corkscrew rollercoaster, and for a journey into the unknown, board a 'lifeboat' and enter the Bermuda Triangle. It adjoins the Sea World Nara Resort. Also on The Spit overlooking the Broadwater is Fisherman's Wharf, a complex of specialty shops, outdoor cafes and restaurants. The Gold Coast's major cruise boats operate from its jetties. Mariner's Cove is also along the Broadwater with its marina, shopping and restaurants, and Marina Mirage, an upmarket shopping and boating complex, is opposite the Sheraton Mirage Hotel. Visitors can enjoy a variety of water sports on the Broadwater.

At **Surfers Paradise:** Attractions include Ripleys Believe It or Not Museum, Hoyts cinema complex, resort shopping, restaurants, many international hotels, numerous nightclubs and the sport of 'people watching'. The Gold Coast Arts Centre is near Surfers at Bundall.

At **Broadbeach:** The Pacific Fair Shopping Resort is on the Nerang River. Conrad Jupiters, Australia's largest casino, is linked by monorail to the Oasis Shopping Resort and the Pan Pacific Hotel. Cascade Park and Gardens on the Nerang River is ideal for picnicking. View the area by an open-cockpit flight in a Tiger Moth plane.

At **Mermaid Beach:** A huge cinema complex is located near family restaurants and a variety of specialty restaurants.

At **Miami:** The Miami Hotel features live music and dancing, food and beer.

At **Burleigh Heads:** Burleigh Knoll Conservation Park, Burleigh Head National Park and Fleay's Wildlife Park are all worth a visit.

Inland at **Mudgeeraba** are the Gold Coast War Museum, Skirmish, Movie Militaria and Balloon Down Under for balloon rides over the Gold Coast.

At **Tallebudgera:** Tally Valley art and craft markets, and the Playroom rock venue.

At **Currumbin:** Feed the thousands of lorikeets that flock to the Currumbin Sanctuary daily. The Chocolate Expo Factory is opposite. Visit Olson's Bird Gardens, the Currumbin Rock Pool, and the Cougal section of Springbrook National Park. On the way, visit Schusters Lookout and further south-west Arthur Freeman Lookout – both offer superb views over Currumbin Valley.

At **Coolangatta:** Foyster Mall links the main street with the beachfront; Rollerland, roller-skating rink; and the lighthouse at Point Danger.

At **Tweed Heads:** Across the border from Coolangatta, visit the Minjungbal Aboriginal Culture Centre.

For further information contact the Gold Coast Tourism Bureau, 64 Ferry Ave, Surfers Paradise; (07) 5592 2699. There are information centres at Cavill Mall, Surfers Paradise, (07) 5538 4419, and Beach House, Marine Pde, Coolangatta, (07) 5536 7765. **See also:** entries for Coolangatta, Currumbin, Southport and Tweed Heads in A–Z listing. **Map references:** 483 O13, 485, 491 R10.

QUEENSLAND from A to Z

Airlie Beach, on the beautiful Whitsunday Coast

Airlie Beach — Pop. 2524

MAP REF. 493 K3

Airlie Beach, part of the town of Whitsunday, is the centre of the thriving Whitsunday coast. Located 20 km from the Bruce Hwy at Proserpine, Airlie overlooks the Whitsunday Passage and islands, and has its own beach and marina. From Airlie and Shute Harbour passengers can travel to the outer reef and reef-fringed islands. It is a holiday town offering several major resorts with all facilities, top-grade holiday accommodation and a large range of activities and services for visitors. Community market each Sat. on foreshore. Easter: Regatta. Sept.: Fun race. **In the area:** Neighbouring Shute Harbour and islands of Whitsunday Passage. Fishing trips to nearby coastal wetlands and crocodile safaris available. Conway National Park, renowned for its natural beauty and habitat of the rock wallaby and many species of butterfly; 5 km SE. **Tourist information:** Beach Plaza, The Esplanade; (079) 46 6673. **Accommodation:** 1 hotel, 4 motels, 7 hostels, 6 cara./camp. parks.

Allora — Pop. 950

MAP REF. 482 E12, 491 N10

North of Warwick just off the Toowoomba road, the picturesque town of Allora is in a prime agricultural area. **Of interest:** Historical museum, Drayton St. Apr.: 500 Endurance motor race. **In the area:** Historic National Trust-classified Talgai Homestead (c. 1860), 6 km W, offers meals and accommodation. Goomburra State Forest, 35 km E, in the western foothills of the Great Dividing Range. Main Range National Park, 50 km E, part of the Scenic Rim, a crescent of national parks and mountains around Brisbane, has extensive walking tracks through dense rainforest, camping and picnic areas. **Tourist information:** 49 Albion St (New England Hwy), Warwick; (076) 61 3122. **Accommodation:** Limited.

Aramac — Pop. 326

MAP REF. 492 C10, 499 Q10

This small pastoral town is 67 km N of Barcaldine. Originally called Marathon, it was renamed by explorer William Landsborough as an acronym of Sir Robert Ramsay Mackenzie, Colonial Secretary in 1866 and Premier of Qld (1867–8). **Of interest:** Tramway Museum housing old engines and rolling stock, McWhannell St. **In the area:** Lake Dunn, 68 km NE, for swimming, fishing and birdwatching. **Tourist information:** Shire Offices, Gordon St; (076) 51 3311. **Accommodation:** 1 hotel, 1 cara./camp. park.

Atherton — Pop. 5206

MAP REF. 489 C12, 495 M7

Atherton is the agricultural hub of the Atherton Tableland. This farming town is 100 km SW of Cairns on the Kennedy Hwy and is surrounded by a patchwork of dense rainforest that abounds in varied birdlife and tropical vegetation. The fertile basalt soil, the gently undulating terrain and abundant rainfall have made the region the centre of the dairy and grain-growing industries that are still the major income-earners. The area bounded by the towns of Atherton, Kairi and Tolga is particularly suited to growing tomatoes, avocados, potatoes, peanuts, maize and other grains. **Of interest:** Chinese Joss House and Old Post Office Gallery, Herberton Rd. Mineralogical Museum, Main St, has a constructed underground attraction comprising tunnels and chambers, and displays of minerals and gemstones. **In the area:** Picturesque Atherton Tableland (surrounding area), one of oldest land masses in Australia, features rainforest-fringed volcanic crater lakes, spectacular waterfalls and fertile farmlands. Bushwalking at Halloran Hill, 3 km E; Baldy Mountain, 10 km SW; Wongabel State Forest, 8 km SE. At Tolga, 5 km N: woodworks, peanut factory and craft. Mareeba, 32 km N, centre of tobacco and tropical-fruit area. At Herberton, 19 km SW: Foster's Winery; Historical Village with more than 30 restored buildings. Mt Hypipamee National Park, 26 km S, includes sheer-sided explosion crater 124 m deep. At Malanda, 25 km SE: Pro-rodeo held in June; signposted rainforest walk at edge of town into Malanda Falls Conservation Park nearby. McHugh Road Lookout, 20 km S of Malanda. Beautiful crater lakes, Lakes Eacham and Barrine, in Crater Lakes National Park 25 km E; cruises available on Lake Barrine. Historic Yungaburra, 13 km E. The Curtain Fig Tree, 2.5 km SW of Yungaburra, renowned for its spectacular aerial roots in curtain formation. Lake Tinaroo, 15 km NE, for swimming, fishing, water-skiing and sailing; houseboats available for hire. **Tourist information:** Cnr Mabel and Vernon Sts; (070) 91 4222. **Accommodation:** 5 motels, 3 B&B, 1 hostel, 4 cara./camp. parks. **See also:** Atherton Tableland; The Far North.

Ayr   Pop. 8637

MAP REF. 492 H1, 495 Q13

This busy sugar town on the north side of the Burdekin delta is surrounded by intensively irrigated sugarcane fields, the most productive in Australia. The Burdekin River Irrigation Scheme, the lifeblood of the area, is the largest land and water conservation scheme in the State. **Of interest:** Ayr Nature Display, Wilmington St, fine collection of butterflies and beetles. Burdekin Cultural Complex, Queen St, includes 530-seat theatre, library and activities centre; distinctive 'Living Lagoon' in theatre forecourt. Oct.: Water festival. **In the area:** At Home Hill, Ayr's sister town on opposite side of Burdekin River, Inkerman Sugar Mill at foot of Burdekin Bridge; open during crushing season June–Dec. Alva Beach, 18 km N, for beach walks, birdwatching, swimming and fishing; market 3rd Sun. of each month. Australian Institute of Marine Science at Cape Bowling Green, 20 km N. Hutchings Lagoon, 5 km SW, for watersports and on-shore picnics. Mt Kelly Orchids, 16 km SW, for magnificent orchid displays, sales and Devonshire teas; open by appt. Scenic drives in area, contact Tourist information. **Tourist information:** 161 Queen St; (077) 83 2888. **Accommodation:** 4 hotels, 7 motels, 3 cara. parks.

Babinda   Pop. 1268

MAP REF. 489 H13, 495 N7

A swimming-hole and picnic area known as The Boulders is a feature of interest 10 km W of this small sugar town, which is 57 km S of Cairns in the Wooroonooran National Park. In the park are the State's two highest mountains, Mt Bartle Frere (1615 m) and Mt Bellenden Ker (1582 m), and the Josephine Falls. **Of interest:** Deeral Cooperative, Nelson Rd, makes footwear and Aboriginal artifacts. **In the area:** Deeral, 14 km N, departure point for cruises through rainforest and the saltwater-crocodile haunts of the Mulgrave and Russell Rivers. **Tourist information:** Far North Qld Promotion Bureau, cnr Grafton and Hartley Sts, Cairns; (070) 51 3588. **Accommodation:** Limited.

Barcaldine   Pop. 1530

MAP REF. 492 C11, 499 Q11

A pastoral and rail town, Barcaldine is 108 km E of Longreach. All the streets are named after trees. **Of interest:** Beta Farm Outback and Wildlife Centre, cnr Pine and Bauhinia Sts: 8 settlers' buildings including woolskin buyer's residence housing large doll collection and Cobb & Co. office now studio and art gallery, old shearing sheds with plant and press, and hand-reared wildlife. Historical Folk Museum, cnr Gidyes and Beech Sts. 'Tree of Knowledge', ghost gum in Oak St, the meeting-place for 1891 shearers' strike, which resulted in the formation of the Australian Labor Party. Australian Workers' Heritage Centre, Ash St: buildings containing tributes to Australia's workers in landscaped oasis around Burnsy's Billabong. Several National Trust-classified buildings: masonic lodge, Beech St; Anglican Church, Elm St; and Shire Hall, Ash St. During months Mar.–Oct.: mini steam-train rides on last Sun. of each month; market at Tourist information, Oak St, 1st Sun. of each month. **In the area:** Marraroo Gallery, 1 km W, unique Qld colonial and Aboriginal contemporary works. Wondae Deer Farm, 1 km W, a walk-through park with hand-feeding of animals and Kiddies Corner. Botanical walk, 9 km S, through variety of bushland. North Delta Station, 32 km E, outback station at work, also prolific birdlife and bushwalking; accommodation available. Red Mountain scenic drive from Richmond Hills station 55 km E. **Tourist information:** Oak St; (076) 51 1724. **Accommodation:** 6 hotels, 4 motels, 2 cara./camp. parks.

Bargara   Pop. 2703

MAP REF. 491 O2

This popular surf beach, 15 km E of Bundaberg, is patrolled by one of Qld's top surf clubs. Nearby beaches include Neilson Park and Kelly's. **In the area:** Mon Repos Conservation Park, 3 km N, largest and most accessible mainland loggerhead turtle rookery in Australia; giant sea turtles come ashore to lay their eggs Nov.–Mar. In 1912 Bert Hinkler, engineering apprentice, flew to a height of 9 m in his home-made glider off Mon Repos beach, marking the start of his distinguished aviation career. **Tourist information:** Cnr Bourbong and Mulgrave Sts, Bundaberg; (071) 52 2333. **Accommodation:** 1 hotel/motel, 5 motels, 3 cara./camp. parks.

Beaudesert   Pop. 4028

MAP REF. 483 L12, 491 P10

Beaudesert is a major market town on the Mount Lindesay Hwy, 66 km SW of Brisbane, near the NSW border. A road west leads to the Cunningham Hwy, and the road east leads to the Gold Coast via Tamborine. The district is noted for dairying, agriculture and beef cattle. **Of interest:** Historical Museum, Brisbane St. Popular Beaudesert race meetings. May: Rodeo. Sept.: Mini royal agricultural show. **In the area:** Rice's Honey Bee Farm, Mt Lindesay Hwy just north of town. Woollahra Farmworld, Gleneagle; 8 km N. Bigriggen Park, 30 km SW and Dartington Park, 12 km S, both recreation areas with picnic/barbecue facilities. Lamington National Park, 40 km S, subtropical rainforest with excellent graded walking tracks. At Tamrookum, 24 km SW, fine example of a timber church; guided tours by appt, contact Tourist information. Mt Barney National Park, 55 km SW, good hiking and camping. Unique flora and good

The hotel at Birdsville provides a resting place for travellers

views of Gold Coast at Tamborine Mountain, 35 km E. Nearby, dig for your own thunder eggs at Thunderbird Park, Cedar Creek. **Tourist information:** Historical Museum, 54 Brisbane St; (07) 5541 1284. **Accommodation:** 3 hotels, 3 motels, 1 cara. park.

Beenleigh Pop. 16 388

MAP REF. 481 P13, 483 N10, 491 Q9

Midway between Brisbane and the Gold Coast, Beenleigh is now almost a satellite town of Brisbane. The Beenleigh Distillery on the Albert River has been producing rum from local sugar since 1884. Rocky Point Sugar Mill, 20 km E, is Australia's only privately-owned mill. **In the area:** Coomera, 20 km S: several family attractions including Dreamworld family fun park; Movie World theme park; Wet 'n' Wild aquatic fun park. **Tourist information:** Visitors and Convention Bureau, City Hall, King George Square, Brisbane; (07) 3221 8411 **Accommodation:** 2 motels, 3 cara./camp. parks.

Biggenden Pop. 686

MAP REF. 491 N4

This agricultural centre is located near Mt Walsh National Park and The Bluff, 100 km SE of Bundaberg. Oct.: Rose festival (odd-numbered years). **In the area:** Mt Walsh National Park, 8 km S, wilderness park popular with experienced bushwalkers. Coalstoun Lakes National Park, 3 km SW, protects two volcanic crater lakes. Magnetite mine, 5 km SW; tours available. Mt Woowoonga, 20 km NW, forestry reserve with bushwalking and picnic/barbecue facilities. Chowey Bridge (1905), 20 km NW, concrete arch railway bridge (1 of 2 surviving in Aust.); picnic facilities nearby. Silver Bell Novelty Farm, 2 km N on Old Coach Rd, has buildings and collections; open by appt. **Tourist information:** Commercial Hotel/Motel, 2 Victoria St; (071) 27 1230. **Accommodation:** 1 hotel, 1 hotel/motel, 1 cara./camp. park.

Biloela Pop. 6200

MAP REF. 491 K1, 493 N13

This modern, thriving town in the fertile Callide Valley is at the crossroads of the Burnett and Dawson Hwys, 142 km S of Rockhampton. The name is Aboriginal for 'white cockatoo'. Underground water provides irrigation for lucerne, cotton and sunflower crops. **Of interest:** Greycliffe Homestead, Gladstone Rd; open by appt. Primary Industries Exhibition, Dawson Hwy, theme park combining display of hi-tech farming techniques with scenes of rural life. June: Country and western muster. **In the area:** Callide Dam, 5 km NE, for good boating, fishing and swimming. Nearby, Callide open-cut coal mine and power station, and lookout. Cotton Ginnery, 2 km N, tours Mar.–July; video offseason. Lyle Semgreen Gems at Jambin, 32 km NW, open by appt. At Wowan, 75 km NW, Scrub Turkey Museum housed in old butter factory. Baralaba Historical Village, 100 km NW. Bindiggin, 46 km W at Banana, has displays of dolls, bottles and rocks. Mt Scoria, 14 km S, solidified volcano core. Thangool, 10 km SE, renowned for its race days; Arts festival held in Sept. **Tourist information:** Callide St; (079) 92 2405. **Accommodation:** 2 hotels, 6 motels, 4 cara./camp. parks. **See also:** Capricorn Region.

Birdsville Pop. 102

MAP REF. 500 E5

The well-known Birdsville Track starts here on its long path into and across SA. In the 1870s the first settlers arrived in Birdsville, nearly 2000 km by road west of Brisbane, and at the turn of the century it was a thriving settlement with three hotels, three stores, several offices and a doctor. When the toll on cattle crossing the border near the town was abolished after Federation in 1901, prosperity declined and the population diminished. **Of interest:** Museum, McDonald St, features Australiana, domestic artifacts and working farm equipment. In Adelaide St: ruins of Royal Hotel, reminder of Birdsville's boom days; Birdsville Hotel, a hive of activity during Birdsville Races (held first weekend in Sept.) as population swells to about 3000. Hotel is an important overnight stop for tourists travelling down the Track, west across the Simpson Desert (4WD country), north to Mount Isa or east to Brisbane. *Travel in this area can be hazardous, especially in the wet season (approx. Oct.–Mar.). Supplies of food and water should always be carried, as well as petrol, oil and spare parts. Motorists are advised to ring the Northern Roads Condition Hotline on (08) 11633 for information before departing down the Track, and to advise police if heading west to Simpson Desert National Park; read section on Outback Motoring.* The famous Flynn of the Inland founded the first Australian Inland Mission at Birdsville; there is still a well-equipped medical outpost, Adelaide St. Birdsville's water comes from a 1219 m-deep artesian bore; water is almost at boiling point and four cooling ponds bring it to a safe temperature. Electricity is supplied by two diesel-run generators. **In the area:** Waddi trees, 20 km N. Big Red, a huge sand dune; 40 km W. **Tourist information:** Brooklands Store, Arthur St; (076) 56 3241. **Accommodation:** 1 hotel/motel, 1 cara./camp. park. **See also:** The Channel Country.

Blackall   Pop. 1578

MAP REF. 492 D13, 499 R13, 501 R1

Centre of some of the most productive sheep and cattle country in central Qld, Blackall has many sheep and cattle studs in its vicinity. In 1892 the legendary Jackie Howe set the almost unbelievable record of shearing 321 sheep with blade shears in less than 8 hours, at Alice Downs Station, 25 km N. Blackall sank the first artesian bore in Qld in 1885. **Of interest:** Jackie Howe statue, located at junction of Short and Shamrock Sts. Also in Shamrock St: petrified tree stump, millions of years old; Major Mitchell Memorial clock. Self-guide historic walk; property tours to view shearing; contact Tourist information for details. June: Race meeting. **In the area:** Steam-driven Blackall Wool Scour (1906), 4 km N on Clematis St; guided tours daily (Apr.–Nov.). Idalia National Park, 100 km SW, renowned as habitat of the rare yellow-footed rock wallaby. **Tourist information:** Short St; (076) 57 4637. **Accommodation:** 4 hotels, 3 motels, 2 cara./camp. parks.

Blackwater   Pop. 6760

MAP REF. 493 K11

This major mining town is 190 km W of Rockhampton on the Capricorn Hwy. The name comes from the discolouration of the local waterholes caused by ti-trees. Coal mined in the area is railed to Gladstone. The town's population is made up of workers of many nationalities and it displays what is claimed to be the most varied collection of national flags this side of the United Nations. Cattle is the traditional industry. **In the area:** Utah coal mine, 35 km S; tours available, bookings necessary. Expedition Range (732 m), 139 km SW near Springsure, discovered by Ludwig Leichhardt. At Comet, 30 km E, show and camp draft each Sept. Rainbow Falls in Blackdown Tableland National Park, 50 km SE, also picnic/barbecue facilities at Horseshoe Lookout and Mimosa Creek camping area. **Tourist information:** Clermont St, Emerald; (079) 82 4142. **Accommodation:** 3 motels, 2 cara./camp. parks. **See also:** The Capricorn Region.

Boonah   Pop. 2100

MAP REF. 483 J12, 491 P10

Eighty-six km SW of Brisbane between Warwick and Ipswich, Boonah is the main town in the Fassifern district, a highly productive agricultural and pastoral area. Its location was noted as a 'beautiful vale' by the explorer and colonial administrator Captain Logan in 1827, and by the explorer Allan Cunningham in 1828. Sept.: Fassifern German festival. **In the area:** At Templin, 5 km N, Historical Village; open Sun.–Thurs. Moogerah Peaks National Park, 12 km W. Lake Moogerah, 20 km SW, for water sports. In Main Range National Park, Cunninghams Gap lookout, 35 km W; walking tracks from lookout. Park is part of the Scenic Rim, a ring of mountains and national parks around Brisbane: scenic drives, bushwalking, trail-riding, rock-climbing, skydiving, water sports, picnic spots, recreation facilities, camping and accommodation. Coochin Coochin, historic homestead, 14 km S; not open to public. **Tourist information:** Shire Offices, High St; (074) 63 1599. **Accommodation:** 2 hotels, 1 motel, 1 cara./camp. park.

Boulia   Pop. 281

MAP REF. 498 F9

Situated near the Burke River, 360 km W of Winton, 295 km S of Mt Isa and 242 km E of the NT border, Boulia is the capital of the Channel Country. **Of interest:** Town's oldest house, Stone Cottage (1880s), now a museum displaying Aboriginal artifacts and historic relics of region; Pituri St. In Herbert St: The Red Stump, warning travellers of dangers of Simpson Desert; artificial 'Min Min' light. Koree Yuppiree Tree, near Boulia State School, thought to be last known corroboree tree of Pitta Pitta community. Varied birdlife around river. Aug.: Rodeo and gymkhana. **In the area:** Mysterious Min Min light, first reportedly sighted near ruins of Min Min Hotel (130 km E). Cawnpore Hills, 140 km E, offer good views from summit. Diamantina Gates National Park, 150 km SE. *Travel by road in wet season is not possible*; **See:** Outback Motoring. **Tourist information:** Shire Offices, Herbert St; (077) 46 3188. **Accommodation:** 1 hotel/motel, 1 cara./camp park. **See also:** The Channel Country.

Bowen   Pop. 8312

MAP REF. 493 J2

A relaxed town exactly halfway between Mackay and Townsville, Bowen was named after the State's first Governor. The town was established in 1861 on the shores of Port Denison and was the first settlement in north Qld. It boasts

Horseshoe Bay, a popular swimming area near Bowen

Mystery craters, south-west of Bundaberg

an excellent climate with an average of 8 hours' sunshine daily. Bowen region is famous for its tomatoes, and particularly for its mangoes (in season Nov.–Jan.). **Of interest:** Signposted Golden Arrow tourist route starts at Salt Works, Don St. Twelve historical murals in central city area. Historical Museum, Gordon St. Aug.: Art, craft and orchid expo. Oct.: Coral Coast festival. **In the area:** Excellent small bays (connected by walking tracks) for fishing, snorkelling and swimming; within 7 km of town. At Delta, 7 km N, coffee plantation. Collinsville coal mines, 82 km SW. **Tourist information:** Shire Offices, Herbert St; (077) 86 1866. **Accommodation:** 3 hotels, 5 motels, 3 hostels, 7 cara./camp. parks.

Buderim Pop. 7499

MAP REF. 483 N1, 486 G9, 491 Q7

Buderim is a delightful town just inland from the Sunshine Coast, high on the fertile red soil of Buderim Mountain, and between the Bruce Hwy and Mooloolaba on the coast. It is a popular residential and retirement area. **Of interest:** In Burnett St: Blue Marble and Fine Art Images galleries; Buderim Festive Markets, in Old Ginger Factory. Pioneer timber cottage (1876), one of Buderim's earliest houses, faithfully restored and retaining many original furnishings; Ballinger Rd. **In the area:** Buderim Forest Park, Quorn Close (just north of town) features waterfalls and walking tracks; wheelchair access to lower end, entry from Lindsay Rd. Rainforest walks at Foote Sanctuary, north-eastern end of town. Self-guide Forest Glen–Tanawha Tourist Drive includes Super Bee honey factory; Forest Glen Sanctuary (deer and native fauna); Moonshine Valley Winery, wines made from local tropical fruits. **Tourist information:** Cnr Aerodrome Rd and Sixth Ave, Maroochydore; (074) 79 1566. **Accommodation:** 2 motels, 2 cara./camp. parks.

Bundaberg Pop. 38 074

MAP REF. 491 O2

Bundaberg, 368 km N of Brisbane, is the southernmost access point to the Great Barrier Reef and an important provincial city in the centre of the fertile Burnett River plains. The district is known for its sugar (the area's main crop), timber, beef production and, in more recent years, tomatoes, avocados and small crops. Sugar has been grown in the area since 1866. Raw sugar is exported from an extensive storage and bulk terminal facility at Port Bundaberg, 16 km NE. Industry sidelines include the distilling of the world famous Bundaberg Rum, refined sugar production, and the manufacture and export of advanced Austoft cane-harvester equipment. Bundaberg is a city of parks and botanical gardens; its wide streets lined with poincianas provide a brilliant display in spring. The Burnett River flows through the city dividing it in two. Several famous Australians have called Bundy home: aviator Bert Hinkler, in 1928 the first man to fly solo from England to Australia; singer Gladys Moncrieff; cricketer Don Tallon; and rugby league star Mal Meninga. **Of interest:** Alexandra Park and Zoo on river bank, Quay St: free zoo, band rotunda, cacti garden and children's playground. In Bourbong St: Whaling Wall, a 6-storey-high whale mural; Boyd's Antiquatorium, considered best Edison Gramophone collection in Australia. In East Bundaberg: Bundaberg Rum Distillery, Avenue St, offers guided tours daily to see Famous Aussie Spirit being made. Schmeider's Cooperage and Craft Centre, demonstrations of ancient art of barrel-making; Alexandra St. Across the river in North Bundaberg: Botanical Gardens (Mt Perry Rd) include Hinkler House Memorial Museum (repository of aviation history), railway (steam-train rides around lakes), Bundaberg Historical Museum, and Sugar Museum in Fairymead House; Tropical Wines and Sunny Soft Drinks (unique tropical-fruit wine) also Mt Perry Rd; Banio's Horseriding Centre, 120 ha of picturesque riverside country, Patterson's Rd. Easter: Country music roundup. Sept.: Bundy in Bloom festival. **In the area:** Surfing beaches at Neilson Park and Kelly's Beach (near Bargara, 15 km NE); Moore Park (21 km NW) and Elliott Heads (18 km SE); fishing at Burnett Heads, Elliott Heads, Bargara and Moore Park. Hummock Lookout, 7 km NE, for excellent views over city, canefields and coast. Bauers Gerbera Nursery, 10 km NE on road to Bargara Beach. Turtles (Nov.–Feb.) at Mon Repos Conservation Park, 14 km NE. Tours to see migrating humpback whales, mid-Aug.–mid-Oct. Poseidon Seashells, displays and sales of coral, seashells and local shellcraft; Rickets Rd, Burnett Heads. Sharon Gorge, 12 km SW, features rainforest and walkway to Burnett River. Unexplained mystery, 25 km SW: 35 strange craters said to be 25 million years old. Pennyroyal Herb

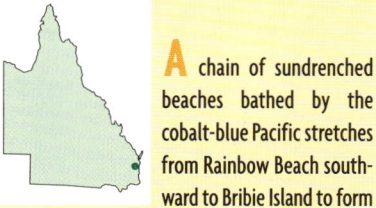

The Sunshine Coast

A chain of sundrenched beaches bathed by the cobalt-blue Pacific stretches from Rainbow Beach southward to Bribie Island to form Queensland's Sunshine Coast. This scenic coastal region, with its average winter temperature of 25°C, its leisurely pace and its wide variety of natural attractions and sporting facilities, offers an attractive alternative to the more commercialised Gold Coast.

While huge waves thunder on to white sand beaches to provide year-round surfing, the calmer waters of protected beaches ensure safe swimming, boating and water-skiing. Rivers and streams alive with fish lure the angler, and the foreshores of forest-fringed lakes become perfect picnic spots for the family.

The Sunshine Coast is blessed with many wonders of nature. The coloured sands of Teewah in the Cooloola section of **Great Sandy National Park**, between Tewantin and Rainbow Beach, rise in multi-coloured cliffs to over 200 metres. Geologists consider that these sandcliffs are over 40 000 years old and claim the main colouring is either the result of oxidisation or the dye of vegetation decay. However, an Aboriginal legend relates that the colours come from a rainbow serpent killed by a boomerang when it came to the rescue of a young woman. Another marvel of nature, the Glass House Mountains, were formed by giant cores of long-extinct volcanoes.

The **Noosa** area, at the northern end of the region, has facilities for fishing, boating and golf. Poised on the edge of Laguna Bay is the resort area of Noosa Heads, with its 2280-hectare Noosa National Park. This coastal park contains a network of walking tracks that wind through rainforests, giving spectacular ocean views of such unusual rock formations as Hell's Gates, Paradise Caves, Lion's Rock, Devil's Kitchen and Witches' Cauldron. The park also houses an animal sanctuary and there are coastal lakes inhabited by elegant black swans, pelicans, ducks and cranes.

The southernmost town of the Sunshine Coast is **Caloundra**, meaning 'the beautiful place', where Aborigines once came down from the hills to feast on seafood.

The hinterland of the Sunshine Coast is like a huge cultivated garden, covered with pineapples,

The Big Pineapple complex, south of Nambour

sugarcane, ginger and citrus, dotted with dairy farms and enclosing within its folds cascading waterfalls, lush rainforests and bubbling streams. Looming majestically behind this garden of plenty is the Blackall Range, a world apart with art and craft galleries, Devonshire-tea places, comfortable hotels and a feeling of 'olde England'. The scenic drive through the towns of Mapleton, Flaxton, Montville and Maleny is one of the best in southeast Queensland. The **Blackall Range National Park** is a must for nature lovers. The park includes the 80-metre Kondalilla Falls which drop into a valley of rainforest. The Mapleton Hotel offers authentic country-pub hospitality and panoramas from the traditional Queensland verandah. Visit the miniature English village with its castles, churches, thatched cottages and inns. A number of art and craft cottages surround Montville's Village Green. Take in the view from the picture window at the De'Lisle Gallery while being surrounded by works of art from the Sunshine Coast's best artists. Mary Cairncross Park, at the southern end of the range, gives breathtaking views of the coast and the Glass House Mountains. **Nambour** is conveniently located, just off the Bruce Highway, for trips to the mountains of the Blackall Range or to the beach.

Just 7 kilometres south of Nambour is the Big Pineapple complex, a working plantation of pineapples and macadamia nuts, and home of the Big Pineapple.

The Sunshine Coast has accommodation to suit all tastes and budgets, from beachfront caravan parks through to luxury 5-star international hotels; and if you enjoy dining out, there are dozens of fine restaurants in the area.

For more information on the Sunshine Coast, contact Tourism Sunshine Coast Ltd, 126 Alexandra Pde, Alexandra Headland; (008) 07 2041. **See also:** National Parks and individual town entries for those parks and towns indicated by bold type. **Map references:** 483 O1, 486, 491 Q7.

Turtle Bay, a beautiful beach east of Cairns

Farm, 6 km S: gardens, nursery and sales. Dreamtime Reptile Reserve, 8 km S on Childers Rd. Avocado Grove, 10 km S, subtropical gardens. Cruises to Lady Musgrave Island, a true coral cay, on either MV *Lady Musgrave* (departs Bundaberg Port) or by seaplane with, Bundaberg Seaplane Tours. Flights available to Lady Elliot Island resort. **Tourist information:** Cnr Mulgrave and Bourbong Sts; (071) 52 2333. **Accommodation:** Many hotels, 33 motels, 8 cara./camp. parks.

Burketown   Pop. 200

MAP REF. 497 E8

The centre of rich beef country, Burketown is 230 km W of Normanton. The Gulf of Carpentaria is accessible by boat from Burketown. The town is near the Albert River and on the dividing line between the wetlands to the north and the beginning of the Gulf Savannah grass plains to the south. In Sept. and Oct. visitors can witness the unusual meteorological phenomenon locally known as Morning Glory: a tube-like cloud formation that rolls across the sky. **Of interest:** 100-year-old bore, which issues boiling water. Burketown Hotel (1860s), originally customs house, oldest building in the Gulf. Burketown to Normanton telegraph line. Original post office. Easter: World barramundi handline-rod fishing championships. July: Rodeo and races. **In the area:** Original Gulf meatworks just north of town. Cemetery, 2 km N, for insights into town's historic past. Nicholson River wetlands, 17 km W, breeding grounds for crocodiles, and variety of fish and birdlife. Escott Lodge, 17 km W, operating cattle station; camping and accommodation are available. Lawn Hill National Park, 180 km SW, renowned for its rare vegetation, contains World Heritage-listed Riversleigh Fossil Field, an outstanding paleontological area. Landsborough Tree, 5 km E, blazed by explorer in 1862 when searching for Burke and Wills. Leichhardt Falls, 71 km SE: picturesque area, walks and flowing falls in rainy months. **Tourist information:** Burke Shire Council; (077) 45 5100. **Accommodation:** 1 hotel/motel, 1 cara./camp. park. **See also:** Gulf Savannah.

Burrum Heads   Pop. 770

MAP REF. 491 P3

This pleasant holiday resort on the foreshore of Hervey Bay, 45 km N of Maryborough off Bruce Hwy, offers excellent fishing. **In the area:** Fishing villages of Buxton and Walkers Point on north side of Burrum River. Magnificent surf beach at Woodgate, 90 km N (5 km N by boat). Nearby, Burrum Coast National Park, accessible from Woodgate, features walking tracks, including boardwalk; prolific birdlife; picnic spots; and camping areas. **Tourist information:** Phillips Travel, 45 Burrum St; (071) 29 5211. **Accommodation:** 1 hotel/motel, 2 cara./camp. parks.

Caboolture   Pop. 12 716

MAP REF. 483 M4, 491 P8

A major dairying centre just off the Bruce Hwy, 46 km N of Brisbane, Caboolture is noted for its butter, yoghurt and cheese. The area is also rich in Aboriginal history and relics. Market at Showground each Sun. June: Agricultural show; Medieval festival. July: St Peters arts and crafts festival. **In the area:** Caboolture Historical Village, faithfully restored; 2 km N on Beeburum Rd. Glass House Mountains, 22 km N. Popular fishing towns of Donnybrook and Toorbul (20 and 22 km NE), and Beachmere on Deception Bay (13 km SE). Abbey Museum, traces growth of Western civilisation; 9 km E on road to Bribie Island. Bribie Island, 23 km E, for family day-trips, picnic areas, fishing and safe swimming. **Tourist information:** Hasking St; (074) 95 3122. **Accommodation:** 3 hotels, 3 motels, 2 cara./camp. parks.

Cairns   Pop. 64 463

MAP REF. 488, 489 F8, 495 N6

This modern, colourful, coastal city is capital of the tropical Far North. The cosmopolitan esplanade traces the bay foreshore, and parks and gardens abound with colour and tropical trees and plants. Cairns' location is superb: the Great Barrier Reef to the east, the mountain rainforests and plains of the Atherton Tableland to the west, and palm-fringed beaches to the north and south. Cairns is one of the great, black-marlin fishing locations and offers easy access to the Great Barrier Reef for anglers, snorkelling enthusiasts, scuba divers and visitors wishing to see the coral from glass-bottomed boats. **Of interest:** Cairns Red Explorer bus from Lake St, 9 stops at attractions in and around city. National Trust-listed Regional Gallery, cnr Shields and Abbott Sts. Cairns Museum, cnr Lake and Shields Sts, displays of Aboriginal, gold-rush, timber and sugar-cane history. Game-fishing boats moor at Marlin Marina, Marlin Jetty, Trinity Wharf and The Pier; end of Spence St. Reef Hotel Casino complex, Wharf St.

Historical complex Freshwater Connection, also departure point for 100-year-old Kuranda Scenic Railway trip through Barron Gorge to rainforest village of Kuranda, 34 km NW. Wetland areas including the Esplanade; opportunities for birdwatching. Flecker Botanic Gardens, Collins Ave, features plants used by Aborigines, exotic trees and shrubs, and 200 varieties of palms. Walking track links gardens to Centenary Lakes Parkland. Tanks Centre, near Botanic Gardens, multipurpose centre in revamped World War II oil storage tanks. Jack Barnes Bicentennial Mangrove Boardwalk, Airport Ave. Rainforest walk to top of Mt Whitfield; in park opposite airport. Royal Flying Doctor Service Visitor Centre, Junction St, Edge Hill. Doll and Bear Museum, Mayers St, Manunda. Rusty's Bazaar, Grafton and Sheridan Sts, markets with local craft, homemade produce, plants, and new and secondhand goods; open Fri. p.m., Sat. and Sun. a.m. Markets at the Pier, Sat. and Sun. July: Agricultural show. Oct.: Fun in the Sun festival. **In the area:** Bulk sugar terminal has guided tours during crushing season (June–Dec.); Cook St, Portsmith, south of city centre. Marlin Coast, 26 km of spectacular coastline, extends from Machans Beach (10 km N) to Ellis Beach. Holloways Beach, 11 km N, popular seaside spot. Wild World and Outback Opal Mine, 22 km NW. Skyrail Rainforest Cableway, spectacular gondola ride through rainforest to Kuranda; departs from Caravonica Lakes Station, Smithfield; 11 km NE; (return via Scenic Railway or vice versa). Bushwalking, hiking, whitewater rafting and camping in delightful rural settings of Barron and Freshwater Valleys, north and south of Cairns; attractions include the Crystal Cascades, Barron Gorge hydro-electric power station and Copperlode Dam (Lake Morris). Reef and islands can be explored by private charters, daily cruises and by air (seaplane and helicopter). Longer cruises to resort islands and reef on catamarans *Coral Princess*, *Reef Escape* and *Kangaroo Explorer*. Access to nearby Green, Fitzroy and Frankland Islands on cruise vessels. Cairns also offers easy access to wilderness areas of Atherton Tableland, Daintree, Cape Tribulation, Cape York and Gulf Savannah regions. Safaris (4WD) to Cape York and Gulf Savannah. **Tourist information:** Cnr Grafton and Hartley Sts; (070) 51 3588. **Accommodation:** Many hotels and motels from 5-star, international-standard to family and budget; 12 cara./camp. parks. **See also:** The Far North; Cape York.

Caloundra Pop. 22 094

MAP REF. 483 N2, 486 I13, 491 Q7

This popular holiday spot on the Sunshine Coast is 96 km N of Brisbane via a turnoff from the Bruce Hwy. The main beaches are Kings, Shelly, Moffat, Dicky, Golden and Bulcock. The main shipping channel to Brisbane is just offshore. Pumicestone Passage (State marine park) to the south, between Bribie Island and the mainland, has sheltered waters for fishing, boating, water-skiing and sailboarding. **Of interest:** Queensland Air Museum at airport, Pathfinder Dr.; open Wed., Sat., Sun. and school holidays. Teddy Bear World, Bowman Rd, includes museum, waterslide and mini-golf. Scenic flights available from airport. Market each Sun. at Corbould Park Racetrack. Sept.: Art and craft show. **In the area:** Scenic drives: north along coastal strip; west to Blackall Range; south-west to Glass House Mountains. Wreck of SS *Dicky* (1893), Dicky Beach, 3 km N. Currimundi Lake Conservation Park, 4 km N. Pt Cartwright Lookout, 18 km N. Opals Down Under and House of Herbs, Bruce Hwy, 15 km NW. Aussie World incorporating Ettamogah Pub, Bruce Hwy, 16 km NW; Landborough Historical Museum, 17 km SW. Queensland Reptile Park at Beerwah, 23 km SW. Glass House Mountains, 29 km SW. **Tourist information:** Caloundra Rd; (074) 91 0202. **Accommodation:** 2 hotels, 13 motels, 12 cara./camp. parks. **See also:** Sunshine Coast.

Camooweal Pop. 234

MAP REF. 409 R11, 498 B2

On the Barkly Hwy, 188 km NW of Mount Isa, Camooweal is the last Qld town before crossing the NT border, 13 km W. **Of interest:** On Barkly Hwy: Shire Hall (1922–3) and Freckleton's Store; both National Trust-classified. Ellen Finlay Park, Morrison St. **In the area:** Cemetery, 1 km E on hwy, headstones tell local history. Caves in Camooweal Caves National Park, 25 km S; challenge to experienced potholers. **Tourist information:** Post Office, Barkly Hwy; (077) 48 2110. **Accommodation:** 1 hotel, 1 motel, 1 cara. park.

Cannonvale Pop. 2402

MAP REF. 493 K3

Cannonvale is the first of three seaside resorts along the Shute Harbour Rd from the Proserpine turnoff, and is a suburb of the town of Whitsunday. Located 3 km from Airlie Beach, Cannonvale is fast becoming a vital centre for service and manufacturing businesses in the region. **Of interest:** Wildlife Park, Shute Harbour Rd. **In the area:** Airlie Beach and Shute Harbour, neighbouring resorts to south. Conway National Park, 10 km S. Tours to Whitsunday Islands. **Tourist information:** Beach Plaza, The Esplanade, Airlie Beach; (079) 46 6673. **Accommodation:** 1 hotel, 1 motel, 1 hostel, 3 cara./camp. parks.

Cardwell Pop. 1294

MAP REF. 495 N10

From Cardwell, 58 km N of Ingham, there are beautiful views of Rockingham Bay and Great Barrier Reef islands in region. Local fishing and snorkelling is excellent. Channel is sheltered area for houseboats. **Of interest:** Museum (part of library), Victoria St. In Marine Pde: departure point for cruises to nearby islands including Hinchinbrook Island (4-day walk available); houseboat and yacht hire, bookings at Tourist information. National Parks Office, Victoria St, information about local national parks and Great Barrier Reef Marine Park. May: Country and western music festival. June: Coral Sea memorial. **In the area:** Scenic drives in Cardwell Forest (spectacular coastal scenery), and Kirrama Range, 9–10 km N, on Kennedy Rd. Murray Falls in State Forest Park, 20 km NW; also camping and picnic area. Dalrymple Gap walking track (10 km), 20 km S, between Damper Creek Bridge on Bruce Hwy and Abergowrie State Forest; permission required from Cardwell or Ingham Forestry offices. **Tourist information:** Hinchinbrook Travel, 13 Victoria St; (070) 66 8539. **Accommodation:** 1 hotel, 6 motels, 2 hostels, 5 cara./camp. parks.

Charleville Pop. 3513

MAP REF. 490 B6

Charleville marks the terminus of the

QUEENSLAND

City Hall in Charters Towers, with its classic Australian architecture

Westlander rail service and is at the centre of a rich pastoral district carrying some 800 000 sheep and 100 000 cattle. Charleville's river, the Warrego, was explored by Edmund Bourke in 1847, and in 1862 William Landsborough camped nearby when searching for Burke and Wills. By the late 1890s Charleville was a frontier town with its own brewery, 10 hotels and 500 registered bullock teams. Cobb & Co. had a coach-building factory here in 1893. The last coach on Australian roads ran to Surat in 1923. A monument 19 km N of the town marks the spot where Ross and Keith Smith landed with engine trouble on the first flight from London to Sydney in 1919. Amy Johnson also landed here in 1920. Qantas started flights from Charleville in 1922. The town is the heart of Mulga Country; the mulga ('the life-giving trees') provide welcome shade and in times of drought are cut down for sheep fodder. **Of interest:** In Alfred St: Historic House Museum in restored Qld National Bank building (1880), features amazing 5-m-long 'vortex gun' used in unsuccessful rainmaking experiments in 1902, Cobb & Co. coach and craft shop. Outback Queensland Skywatch at Meteorological Bureau at airport, features powerful telescopes outside and guided 'Adventure Through the Night Sky' in the evenings. 'Weary Willie' swagman statue, Wills St. National Parks and Wildlife Service Research Centre, Park St. Royal Flying Doctor Base and Visitors Centre, southern end of town. Nature walk on banks of Warrego River, northern end of town. Oct.: Booga Woongaroo (mulga tree) festival. **In the area:** Tree blazed by explorer Landsborough in 1862, 16 km S; guide required. **Tourist information:** Town Hall Building, Wills St; (076) 54 3057. **Accommodation:** 3 hotels, 1 hotel/motel, 3 motels, 2 cara./camp. parks.

Charters Towers　　Pop. 9016

MAP REF. 492 E2

This peaceful and historic city once had a gold-rush population of some 30 000. Between 1872 and 1916, Charters Towers produced ore worth 25 million pounds ($50m). On 25 December 1871 an Aboriginal boy named Jupiter made the first strike while looking for horses that had bolted during a thunderstorm. He brought some gold-laden quartz back to his employer, Hugh Mosman, who rode to Ravenswood to register his claim, and the gold rush was on. The Government rewarded Mosman, who adopted and educated Jupiter. Charters Towers is located 135 km inland from Townsville in hot, dry country, on the road and rail line to Mount Isa. Cattle-raising is the main industry in the area; four large goldmines are operating, the result of another gold boom. **Of interest:** Much classic Australian architecture with verandahs and lacework still remains, particularly facades in Mosman and Gill Sts. Historic homes: Ay-Ot-Lookout (1886), Hodgkinson St; Pfeiffer House (1880), Paull St. In Mosman St: Zara Clark Museum, for local history; souvenir centre in restored Stock Exchange. Buckland's Hill lookout, Fraser St. Easter: Rodeo. May: Country music festival. June: Annual vintage car restorers' swap meet. Aug.: Great Charters Towers gold rush. **In the area:** Towers Hill, 1.5 km W along Mosman St, has old mine shafts and ammunition bunkers from World War II. Mount Leyshon goldmine, 24 km S. Burdekin Falls Dam, 150 km SE; nearby camping, and accommodation. Old Venus gold treatment battery, 5 km E; guided tours available. Ravenswood, 88 km E, small mining town. Big Bend, 40 km NW, contains fossilised coral (part of ancient reef). Great Basalt Wall, 4 million year-old solidified lava wall extending 100 km; 80 km NW. **Tourist information:** Downstairs Post Office, 15–17 Gill St; (077) 87 1280. **Accommodation:** 5 hotels, 3 hotel/motels, 6 motels, 1 hostel, 3 cara./camp. parks. **See also:** The Far North.

Childers　　Pop. 1473

MAP REF. 491 O3

Childers is a picturesque sugar town, 53 km S of Bundaberg. Much of it was destroyed by fire in 1902; today it is a National Trust town. **Of interest:** Historic Childers, self-guide town walk taking in many historic buildings including: Old Butcher's Shop (1896), North St; Grand Hotel and Federal Hotel, Churchill St; also in Churchill St, Gaydon's Building (1894), now a Pharmaceutical Museum, art gallery and tourist centre; Royal Hotel, Randall St; Historic Complex, Taylor St, includes school, cottage and locomotive. May: Agricultural show. **In the area:** Burrum Coast National Park, 45 km E. Craft at Cane Cutters' Cottage, Apple Tree Creek, 5 km N. Isis Central Sugar Mill, Cordalba, 10 km N; tours July–Nov. **Tourist information:** Pharmaceutical Museum, Churchill St; (071) 26 1994. **Accommodation:** 4 hotels, 4 motels, 1 hostel, 2 cara./camp. parks.

Fraser and Moreton Bay Islands

Wreck of the *Maheno*, on Fraser Island

Fraser Island

If you like sand, sea, sailing, fishing and plenty of peace and quiet, Fraser Island is your ideal holiday place. Fraser is the largest sand island in the world, 123 kilometres long, and the largest island on Australia's east coast. It acts as a breakwater, protecting the coast from Bundaberg to well south of Maryborough, and forms the eastern shores of Hervey Bay. Ideal for sailing, it also attracts hundreds of anglers each year for the tailor season.

Fraser's remote and abundant sand dunes are particularly attractive to those with 4WD or beach buggies, but the island is large enough to prevent them becoming intrusive. Apart from its long stretches of beautiful beach, Fraser Island has a unique area of freshwater lakes and tangled rainforests. There are over 40 lakes on the island, all of them above sea level, and the dense forests surrounding them attract a wide range of bird and animal life. On the northern end of the island are the 32-kilometre sweep of Marloo Bay and the main surf beach – a rarity on Queensland islands, as those further north are sheltered from the surf by the Barrier Reef.

An odd feature of the island is its ever-shifting creeks, which may run parallel to the ocean for several kilometres, then spill through a dune, carving a new course through the sand to the sea.

The island is accessible by air from Brisbane or Hervey Bay, or by barge from Hervey Bay, Inskip Point (Rainbow Beach) and Mary River Heads.

Kingfisher Bay Resort Village is at North White Cliffs, on the western side of the island opposite Mary River Heads. The following accommodation is on the ocean side of Fraser Island: Happy Valley, Eurong, Dilli Village and Cathedral Beach Camping Park. Korawinga Lodge at Eurong has time-share units. All these holiday centres offer family accommodation. Day tours leave daily from Hervey Bay and Rainbow Beach. A permit is required to camp or to take a 4WD on to the island. For further information on Fraser Island, contact Maryborough Information Centre; (071) 21 4111. **Map references:** 483 P5, 491 Q3.

Moreton Bay Islands

Bribie Island is a largely residential island, 69 kilometres north of Brisbane, reached via a turnoff on the Bruce Highway and a 1-kilometre bridge across Pumicestone Passage. Bribie is about 31 kilometres long, the northern tip being opposite Caloundra on the Sunshine Coast. Matthew Flinders landed on the southern tip in 1799. Part of the island is a wildlife sanctuary. There are two townships: Bongaree on the mainland side and Woorim on the surf side. The island offers excellent fishing, boating, crabbing and bushwalking. Accommodation available includes 2 hotel/motels, 2 motels and 6 cara./camp. parks. For further information on Bribie Island, contact the Bribie Island Information Centre; (07) 3408 9026. **Map references:** 483 N4, 486 I13.

Moreton Island, predominantly national park, is a remarkable wilderness island only 35 kilometres east of Brisbane. Apart from rocky headlands, the island is mostly huge sandhills, native scrub and banksias, and freshwater lakes, which attract over 125 species of birds. A lighthouse at the northern tip, built in 1857, still guides ships into Brisbane. There are very few roads on the island, but cars (mostly 4WD) use the tracks and the magnificent 40-kilometre beach. Mt Tempest (280 m) is probably the highest permanent sandhill in the world. The resort of Tangalooma is on the leeward side and nearby, wild dolphins come to be fed each night as soon as the tide is high enough. Other activities include sand tobogganing, water sports and bushwalking. There are several campsites in the park (permit required). The island is reached by plane from Brisbane or barge from Brisbane or Redcliffe. For further information on Moreton Island, contact the Information Centre; (07) 3260 7823. **Map references:** 483 P5, 491 Q8.

North Stradbroke Island, or 'Straddie', is a 32-kilometre-long unspoiled island east of Brisbane across Moreton Bay, noted for being the home of the Aboriginal poet and activist Oodgeroo Noonuccal (Kath Walker), who died in 1993. It is popular for fishing, surfing, horseriding, canoeing, snorkelling, bike riding, 4WD tours and weekend stays. The small settlements of Dunwich, with its historic cemetery nearby, and Amity Point are on the leeward side, and Point Lookout is the vantage-point for watching the annual migration of whales, beginning in June. Point Lookout has the only hotel on the island. Nearby, the Captain Cook Memorial is near the beginning of the North Gorge Scenic Walk along the headland. Dunwich started as a quarantine station for Brisbane in 1828. Straddie is a sanctuary for many unique species of flora and fauna. The 500-hectare Blue Lake National Park offers scenic walks through coastal woodland, and a variety of wildlife. Take a vehicular ferry or water taxi from Cleveland; the ferry journey takes an hour, while a water taxi takes about 20 minutes. Accommodation includes 4 resorts/hotels, 4 hostels and 10 cara./camp. parks. For further information on North Stradbroke Island, contact the Information Centre; (07) 3409 9555. **Map references:** 483 Q8, 491 R9.

South Stradbroke Island was separated from North Stradbroke Island by a cyclone in 1896, and the channel between them is called Jumpinpin. South Stradbroke stretches south to Southport on the Gold Coast, the protected Broadwater being a well-used boating playground. The island, a natural reserve, is almost uninhabited and there are no vehicles on the island. Day cruises operate from Southport and a ferry operates from Runaway Bay. Accommodation is limited to one resort. For further information, contact South Stradbroke Island Resort; (07) 5577 3311. **Map references:** 483 O11, 485 F1, 491 Q10.

Chillagoe
Pop. 502

MAP REF. 495 K7

Chillagoe, once a thriving town where copper, silver, lead, gold and wolfram were mined, is now a small outback town where the recent development of tourism, international-standard marble mines and the Red Dome goldmine have returned the town to some of its former glory. **Of interest:** Local museum, for history of town including display of relics from old mining days. **In the area:** Rugged limestone outcrops and magnificent caves in Chillagoe-Mungana Caves National Park, 8 km S; guided tours available. **Tourist information:** Post Office, cnr Queen and Cathedral Sts; (070) 94 7163. **Accommodation:** 1 hotel, 1 hotel/motel, 1 motel, 1 cara./camp. park.

Chinchilla
Pop. 3152

MAP REF. 491 K7

Chinchilla is a prosperous town in the western Darling Downs, 354 km NW of Brisbane on the Warrego Hwy. Ludwig Leichhardt named the area in 1844 from Jinchilla, the local Aboriginal name for cypress pines. Grain-growing is the traditional industry, as well as cattle, sheep, pigs, timber and, more recently, grapes, cotton and watermelons. **Of interest:** Historical Museum, Villiers St, features working steam engines and slab cottage (1880s). Newman's Collection of Petrified Wood, Boyd St. Fishing on Charley's Creek and Condamine River. Feb.: Melon festival (odd-numbered years). May: Rotary May Day carnival. July: Polocrosse carnival. **In the area:** Cactoblastis Memorial Hall, dedicated to the insect introduced to eradicate the prickly pear cactus; at Boonarga, 8 km E. Fossicking for agate and petrified wood and palm at Magic Stone, 18 km W on Warrego Hwy. **Tourist information:** Warrego Hwy; (076) 68 9564. **Accommodation:** 1 hotel/motel, 4 motels, 3 cara./camp. parks.

Clermont
Pop. 2727

MAP REF. 492 H9

Centre of a fertile region which breeds cattle and sheep, and grows wheat, sorghum, safflower and sunflower as well as hardwood timber, Clermont is 350 km SW of Mackay, just off the Gregory Hwy. Nearby is the Blair Athol open-cut mine, the largest seam of steaming coal in the world. About 170 houses were built in 1982 in Clermont for coal workers. The town, which takes its name from Clermont in France, was established over 120 years ago (the first inland settlement in the tropics) after the discovery of gold. At first the settlement was at Copperfield, but was moved to the present site on higher ground after a major flood. Remnants of the gold rushes can still be seen. Sept.: Rodeo. **In the area:** Clermont and District Historical Museum, 4 km NW on road to Charters Towers. Copperfield Store museum, 5 km S, in original shop from copper-mining era. Copperfield Chimney, 8 km SW, chimney from copper-mining days. Theresa Creek Dam, 17 km SW; picnics and bush walks nearby. **Tourist information:** Capella St; (079) 83 1406. **Accommodation:** 4 hotel/motels, 2 motels, 1 cara./camp. park.

Cleveland
Pop. 9270

MAP REF. 483 O8, 491 Q9

Centre of the Redland region, 35 km SE of Brisbane, Cleveland was nearly the capital for the new colony of Qld; however, when Governor Gipps and his official party arrived for an inspection, the tide was out and the trudge over the mudflats created a less than favourable impression. **Of interest:** Cleveland Point Heritage Trail (brochure available from Tourist information) includes: court house (1853) in Paxton St, built by Francis Bigge for timber-getters, became first police station and court house, now restaurant; lighthouse (1864) in Shore St, wooden structure restored and relocated, and holder of Australian record for length of tenancy by one attendant (fifty years by James Froy); restored Grand View Hotel (1849) in North St, built by Francis Bigge in anticipation of influx of holidaymakers when Cleveland was named capital of Qld, later known as Bigge's Folly (main bar exhibits murals depicting historic events). Redlands Museum, at Showgrounds in Smith St, has Cobb & Co. coach, maritime exhibits and blacksmith's forge on display; open Fri.–Sun. Cleveland is departure point for barges and water taxis to North Stradbroke Island. Bayside markets each Sun. July: Flinders Day. **In the area:** Ormiston House (1862) open Sun. p.m. Mar.–Nov., overlooking bay at Ormiston 5 km NW; its builder, Captain Louis Hope, pioneered the State's sugar industry at this location. Whepstead Manor (1874), located at Wellington Point 7 km N, historic Queenslander-style home in beautifully landscaped grounds; now operates as a restaurant and function centre. **Tourist information:** 152 Shore St; (07) 3821 0057. **Accommodation:** 3 hotel/motels, 4 motels.

Clifton
Pop. 805

MAP REF. 482 E11, 491 N10

Located between Toowoomba and Warwick, Clifton is the centre of a rich grain-growing and dairying area. **Of interest:** Historic buildings: Club Hotel (1889), King St; Church of St James and St John (1890s), cnr Tooth St and Meara Pl. **In the area:** Tours of peanut factory, 5 km E. Arthur Hoey Davis (Steele Rudd), author of *On Our Selection*, grew up at East Greenmount, 10 km N. At Nobby, 8 km N: Burial site of Sister Kenny, renowned for her unorthodox method of treating poliomyelitis; Sister Kenny Memorial building, contains memorabilia; Rudd's Pub (1893) has a museum in part of hotel's dining room. **Tourist information:** Shire Offices, King St; (076) 97 3299. **Accommodation:** Limited.

Cloncurry
Pop. 2309

MAP REF. 498 G4

Located in the Gulf Savannah region, Cloncurry is an important mining town, 124 km E of Mount Isa, with an interesting history. In 1861, John McKinlay of Adelaide, leading an expedition to search for Burke and Wills, reported distinctive traces of copper in the area. Six years later, pioneer pastoralist Ernest Henry discovered the first copper lodes. A rail link to Townsville was built in 1908. During World War I, Cloncurry was the centre of a copper boom and in 1916 it was the largest source of copper in Australia, with four smelters operating. Following the war, Copper prices slumped and the burgeoning pastoral industry, which had developed in the surrounding area, took its place. In 1920 a new Qantas air service linked Cloncurry to Winton. In 1928 the town became the base for the famous Royal Flying Doctor Service (RFDS). In 1974 a rare type of pure 22-carat gold, resembling crystallised straw, was discovered, and is now used for making jewellery.

Captain Cook statue overlooking Endeavour River, Cooktown

The region is mainly cattle country, and Cloncurry is a major railhead for transporting stock. **Of interest:** John Flynn Place, Daintree St, includes Fred McKay Art Gallery and RFDS Museum, cultural centre, outdoor theatre and Cloncurry Gardens. Cloncurry-Mary Kathleen Memorial Park, McIlwraith St, features four buildings from abandoned uranium mining town of Mary Kathleen, re-erected and used to display items of historic interest and a rock, mineral and gem collection. Cloister of Plaques (RFDS memorial), Uhr St. Court house (1884), Shaeffe St. Afghan Cemetery, Henry St. Chinese Cemetery, Flinders Hwy. In Sir Hudson Fyshe Dr.: old Qantas hangar at aerodrome; saleyards, cattle sales each Wed. Market, 1st Sat. each month at Florence Park. June: Agricultural show. Aug.: Merry Muster rodeo. **In the area:** Rotary Lookout, 2 km W near Normanton Rd turnoff, Mt Isa Hwy; for views. Burke and Wills cairn near Corella River, 43 km W. Ruins of Great Australia Copper Mine, 2 km S. Kuridala ghost town, 88 km SE; amethyst fossicking a further 8 km, signposted. Walkabout Creek Hotel at McKinlay, 105 km SE, location for film *Crocodile Dundee*. Ruins of old goldmining town of Mount Cuthbert, 10 km from Kajabbi (77 km NW). **Tourist information:** Cloncurry-Mary Kathleen Memorial Park, McIlwraith St; (077) 42 1361. **Accommodation:** 4 hotels, 4 motels, 1 cara. park. **See also:** Gulf Savannah.

Cooktown   Pop. 1342

MAP REF. 495 L3

Captain James Cook beached the *Endeavour* here in 1770 to repair damage after running aground on a coral reef. Gold was discovered at the Palmer River in 1872 and by 1877 Cooktown was a booming, brawling gold-rush port with 37 busy hotels and a transient population of some 18 000 people a year, including 6000 Chinese. Cooktown today has three hotels and the town's main industry is tourism. Located 240 km NW of Cairns, it is the departure point for Cape York Peninsula. The surrounding district is good agriculturally and the town is also supported by prawning, fishing and tin mining. **Of interest:** Cemetery, with graves of tutor, early immigrant and heroine Mrs Mary Watson, and the nearby Chinese Shrine to the many who died on the goldfields. Grassy Hill offers views across the reef, township and hinterland. James Cook Historical Museum (est. 1945) has collection tracing town's two centuries of history, and an anchor from the *Endeavour*. Cooktown Museum, featuring maritime history of area; also shell collection. June: Discovery festival (long weekend), with re-enactment of Cook's landing. July: Laura-Cape York Aboriginal dance festival (odd-numbered years). **In the area:** Bicentennial National Trail (5000 km) for walkers and horse riders, runs from Cooktown to Healesville in Vic. Endeavour River National Park, just north of town. Lakefield National Park, 58 km NW; rivers, lagoons and swamps provide habitat for a great variety of wildlife and are crucial areas for crocodile conservation. Offshore, Lizard Island, 90 km NE, offers resort, national park and secluded beaches. Beautiful sandstone escarpments at Split Rock and Gu-Yalangi rock art sites, 12 km S of Laura (166 km W of Cooktown), perhaps the largest Aboriginal art site in Australia; guided tours of hundreds of cave paintings, best seen May–Nov. **Tourist information:** Port Douglas and Cooktown Tourist Information Centre, 23 Macrossan St, Port Douglas; (070) 99 5599. **Accommodation:** 3 hotels, 6 motels, 3 cara./camp. parks. **See also:** Atherton Tableland.

Coolangatta   Pop. part of Gold Coast

MAP REF. 119 Q1, 485 I10, 491 Q11

Coolangatta is the most southerly of Qld's coastal towns, with its twin town of Tweed Heads located across the border in NSW. June: Wintersun. **In the area:** Coolangatta Airport, Bilinga, services Gold Coast for domestic flights, charters, joy flights and tandem skydiving. Tom Beaston Outlook (Razorback Lookout), behind Tweed Heads, for excellent views. **Tourist information:** Beach House, Marine Pde; (07) 5536 7765. **Accommodation:** 3 hotels, 4 motels. **See also:** City of the Gold Coast.

Crows Nest   Pop. 1154

MAP REF. 482 F5, 491 N8

This small town, 45 km N of Toowoomba, acquired its name from Jim Crow, an Aborigine from the Kabi-Kabi community who once made his home in a hollow tree near what is now the police station. A memorial in Centenary Park commemorates this. **Of interest:** John French VC Memorial Library, William St. In Thallon St: Carbethon Folk Museum and Pioneer Village; Salts Antiques, open weekends. Oct.: Crows Nest day; Worm races. **In the area:** Authentic split-timber and shingle pioneer's hut north on Crows Nest–Cooyar Rd. Crows Nest National Park, 6 km E (look for sign to Valley of Diamonds): walking tracks to falls, picnic and camping facilities. Ravensbourne National Park, 25 km SE. **Tourist information:** Toowoomba and Golden West Tourist Association, 541

Rainbow lorikeets feeding at Currumbin Sanctuary

Ruthven St, Toowoomba; (076) 39 3797. **Accommodation:** 1 motel, 2 B&B, 1 cara./camp. park.

Croydon   Pop. 220

MAP REF. 494 F10

This Gulf town, 561 km SW of Cairns, is the eastern terminus for the Gulflander train service which leaves each Thurs. for Normanton. In town, many original buildings (1887–97), classified by National Trust and Australian Heritage Commission, have been restored to their former splendour and are a reminder of bygone days. **Of interest:** Old gaol, butcher shop, general store and hospital. Gaslights still stand on footpaths. Old court house and mining warden's office have original furnishings. Hospital Museum in old police station, Samwell St. Outdoor Museum, featuring a display of mining machinery from age of steam. Self-guide and guided walking tours of town; contact Tourist information. June: Rodeo. **In the area:** Working Mine Museum including battery stamper, 1 km N. Old cemetery, 1 km W, has historic graves. **Tourist information:** Shire Offices; (077) 45 6185. **Accommodation:** 1 hotel, 1 roadhouse, 1 cara./camp. park. **See also:** Gulf Savannah.

Cunnamulla   Pop. 1683

MAP REF. 490 A10, 501 R10

A western sheep town known for its friendliness and hospitality, Cunnamulla is near the Warrego River, 118 km N of the NSW border. It is the biggest wool-loading station on the Qld railway network, with some 2 million sheep in the area, plus beef cattle. Explorers Sir Thomas Mitchell and Edmund Kennedy were the first European visitors in 1846 and 1847 respectively, and by 1879 it had become a town with regular Cobb & Co. services. In 1880 a daring but disorganised villain, Joseph Wells, held up the local bank and tried to escape with the loot, but could not find his horse. Irate locals bailed him up in a tree, demanding justice and their money back. The tree, in Stockyard St, is still a landmark. **Of interest:** Historical Society display in Bicentennial Museum, John St. Yupunyah Tree, cnr Louise and Stockyard Sts. Centenary Park, Jane St, has picnic/barbecue facilities. Aug.: Opal festival. **In the area:** Wildflowers in spring; varied birdlife, particularly black swans, brolgas, pelicans and eagles. **Tourist information:** Centenary Park; (076) 55 1777. **Accommodation:** 2 hotels, 3 hotel/motels, 1 motel, 1 cara./camp. park.

Currumbin   Pop. part of Gold Coast

MAP REF. 485 G10, 491 Q10

Situated at the mouth of the Currumbin Creek, this part of the Gold Coast has many attractions for visitors. **Of interest:** Currumbin Sanctuary, 20-ha reserve owned by National Trust, features free-ranging animals in open areas, lorikeet feeding (twice-daily), walk-through rainforest aviary with pools and waterfalls, and rides through sanctuary on miniature railway. Opposite: Chocolate Expo Factory. **In the area:** Olson's Bird Gardens, 9 km W in Currumbin Valley, has large landscaped aviaries in subtropical setting. Section of Springbrook National Park, 22 km SW at end of Currumbin Creek Rd, scenic rainforest area ideal for bushwalking and picnicking. **Tourist information:** Beach House, Marine Pde, Coolangatta; (07) 5536 7765. **Accommodation:** 1 hotel, 8 motels. **See also:** City of the Gold Coast.

Daintree   Pop. 200

MAP REF. 489 A1, 495 M5

This unspoilt township lies in the heart of the Daintree River catchment basin surrounded by the McDowall Ranges, 115 km NW of Cairns. The area has abundant native plant life, birds and tropical butterflies. Australia's prehistoric reptile, the estuarine crocodile, can be seen in the mangrove-lined creeks and tributaries of the Daintree River. **Of interest:** Daintree Timber Museum. Local art and craft. A truly old-time local store. River cruises; vehicular ferry is one of last cable ferries in Australia. **In the area:** Daintree Butterfly Farm, 2 km E. Wonga-Belle Orchid Garden, 17 km SE, 3½ ha of lush gardens. Daintree Rainforest Environmental Centre, 11 km N via ferry, has a boardwalk through rainforest. Cape Tribulation, 35 km N, where rainforest meets reef, features crystal-clear creeks, forests festooned with creepers and vines, palm trees,

Great Barrier Reef

The Great Barrier Reef is a living phenomenon. Its coloured coral branches sit upon banks of limestone polyps that have been built up slowly over thousands of years from the seabed. The banks of coral are separated by channels of water, shaded from the delicate green of the shallows to the deepest blue. The reef area is over 1200 kilometres long, stretching from near the coast of western Papua New Guinea to north of Breaksea Spit, east of Bundaberg on the central Queensland coast. It is only between 15 and 20 kilometres wide in the north, but south of Cairns the reef area can extend up to 325 kilometres out to sea. The Great Barrier Reef was proclaimed a marine park in 1979 and a management programme was undertaken to balance the interests of scientists, tourists and fishing enthusiasts, and to preserve the reef for future generations. With over 700 islands scattered through the tropical sea, and the banks of reefs darkening the water, this sun-drenched, tropical paradise attracts thousands of visitors each year.

The coral presents an incredibly beautiful picture. Visitors can see it from semi-submersible vessels, which allow occupants to go underwater without getting wet, or from glass-bottomed boats; or, even better, they can swim around using snorkels or diving gear. The colours of purple, pink, yellow, white and red are intermixed and made more startling by the spectacular shapes of the coral. There are more than 340 varieties of identified coral, the most common being the staghorns, brain corals, mushroom corals, organ pipes and black corals. Spread among these are waving fields of soft coral, colourful anemones, sea urchins and sea slugs. Shellfish of all kinds, ranging from great clams to tiny cowries, cling to the reef while shoals of brightly coloured tropical fish – among them red emperors, coral trout, sweetlip, angel-fish, parrot-fish and demoiselles – glide and dart through the coral gardens. Multitudes of seabirds nest on the islands of the reef through spring and summer.

Three island resorts, Green Island, Lizard Island and Lady Elliot Island, are coral cays – actually part of the reef – and at low tide it is possible to walk on the coral ledges that surround them. Other resort islands are continental islands, having once been part of the mainland, and are generally more wooded and mountainous.

The Barrier Reef is Australia's most beautiful tourist attraction, and the best way to see it is by boat. If you do not have your own yacht, and the holiday budget will not stretch to chartering one, there are many excellent cruises available through the reef and its islands. Charter boats, scuba diving and fishing trips are also available.

The resort islands off the reef and the Queensland coast offer different styles of living to suit various tastes in holidays and entertainment. Their common denominator is their beautiful setting and a consistency of climate, broken only by the sudden and short-lived downpours of the monsoonal period from December to February. The period June to November is considered the best time to visit.

For further information on the islands of the Great Barrier Reef, contact the Queensland Government Travel Centre, cnr Adelaide and Edward Sts, Brisbane; (07) 3221 6111.

QUEENSLAND — Great Barrier Reef

Island	Features	Activities	Access	Accommodation
SOUTHERN REEF ISLANDS	The Southern Reef extends offshore from Bundaberg to Rockhampton.			
LADY ELLIOT ISLAND 80 km NE of Bundaberg	• small, sand covered coral cay • 19 major dive areas to view coral and marine life • significant bird rookeries • turtle nesting site	Birdwatching, turtle watching (turtles come ashore to lay eggs Nov.–Mar.; hatching can be seen late Dec.–May), diving, snorkelling, reef walking, island walking.	From Bundaberg, by plane. From Hervey Bay, by plane. From Caloundra, by plane.	Low-key resort ranging from budget to deluxe. Max. 100 people.
LADY MUSGRAVE ISLAND 105 km NNE of Bundaberg	• superb coral cay with navigable lagoon • underwater observatory • glass-bottomed boat • floating pontoon • semi-submersible submarine • prolific birdlife • turtle nesting site	Birdwatching, turtle watching (turtles come ashore to lay eggs Nov.–Mar.; hatching can be seen late Dec.–May), snorkelling, island walking.	From Bundaberg, by seaplane or catamaran. From Gold Coast, by seaplane.	Camping only; permit required (contact Gladstone office of Dept of Environment and Heritage; (079) 72 6055). Max. 50 people.
HERON ISLAND 72 km NE of Gladstone	• small coral cay • entire island is a national park • prolific flora and fauna • turtle nesting site	Birdwatching, turtle watching (turtles come ashore to lay eggs Nov.–Mar.; hatching can be seen late Dec.–May), diving, reef exploring.	From Gladstone, by catamaran or charter helicopter.	Resort. Max. 280 people.
NORTH WEST ISLAND 120 km E of Rockhampton	• uninhabited • second largest coral cay on reef • turtle nesting site • breeding site of common noddy and wedgetailed shearwater	Birdwatching, turtle watching (turtles come ashore to lay eggs Nov.–Mar.; hatching can be seen late Dec.–May).	From Gladstone, by charter boat.	Camping only; permit required (contact Gladstone office of Dept of Environment and Heritage; (079) 72 6055). Max. 150 people.
GREAT KEPPEL ISLAND 48 km NE of Rockhampton	• 30 km of white, sandy beaches • unspoiled tropical island scenery	Tennis, water-skiing, skindiving, parasailing, coral viewing, island cruises. 'Kids Klub' operates during school holidays.	From Rockhampton, by light plane. From Rosslyn Bay, by launch.	Wide range from cabins and tents to resort. Max. 500 people.
WHITSUNDAY ISLANDS	There are more than 80 islands in the magnificent Whitsunday Passage, most are uninhabited.			
BRAMPTON ISLAND 32 km N of Mackay	• national park and wildlife sanctuary • fine, white beaches • golf course	Water sports, reef cruises, snorkelling trail (with waterproof map), bushwalking, archery, golf.	From Mackay, by light plane or launch.	Resort. Max. 280 people.
LINDEMAN ISLAND 67 km N of Mackay	• Club Med resort • national park • prolific birds and butterflies • secluded sandy beaches • picturesque golf course • superb views from summit of Mt Oldfield	Water sports, bird and butterfly watching, bushwalking.	From Proserpine, by light plane. From Shute Harbour, Mackay or Hamilton Island, by plane or launch.	Club Med resort. Max. 440 people.

Island	Features	Activities	Access	Accommodation
HAMILTON ISLAND 16 km SE of Shute Harbour	• most complex island resort • extensive facilities including jet airport, school, bank and post office • 200-berth marina • fauna park • waterside village	Wide range of activities and entertainment including windsurfing, sailing, fishing, scuba diving, parasailing, tennis and squash; catamaran cruises.	Direct flight from Melbourne, Sydney, Brisbane, Cairns, Proserpine, Shute Harbour and Mackay. Also from Mackay, by launch.	Hotel resort offering wide range of accommodation. Max. 2000 people.
LONG ISLAND 9 km from Shute Harbour	• part of Conway National Park • excellent walking tracks leading to scenic lookouts • friendly scrub turkeys • fresh oysters	Bushwalking, fishing, resort activities.	From Shute Harbour or Hamilton Island, by launch or helicopter.	3 resorts: Island resort, action-packed location (max. 380 people); Palm Bay Hideaway for nature lovers (max. 50 people); Paradise Bay for keen anglers (max. 16 people).
SOUTH MOLLE ISLAND 8 km from Shute Harbour	• small, lightly timbered island with numerous inlets • splendid views of Whitsunday Passage from island's peaks • golf course • reef pontoon with fish observation chamber • platform for swimmers, snorkellers and scuba divers	Bushwalking, snorkelling, scuba diving, windsurfing, golf, squash.	From Shute Harbour, by launch or helicopter.	Resort. Max. 520 people.
DAYDREAM ISLAND 5 km from Shute Harbour	• luxurious resort on this small island of volcanic rock and coral • dense tropical foliage • spectacular coral gardens	Resort activities and facilities including tennis, gymnasium, water sports centre, diving, trips to outer reef and other islands.	From Shute Harbour, by launch or helicopter.	Resort. Max. 750 people.
WHITSUNDAY ISLAND 25 km E of Shute Harbour	• uninhabited • entire island is a national park • beautiful white silica beach, Whitehaven Beach	Bush and beach walking.	From Shute Harbour, by boat.	Camping only, permit required (contact Airlie Beach office of Dept of Environment and Heritage; (079) 46 7022). Max. 20 people.
HOOK ISLAND 20 km NE of Shute Harbour	• small low-key resort • breathtaking underwater observatory	Snorkelling, scuba diving, reef trips.	From Shute Harbour, by launch.	Wilderness Lodge with cabins, cottage and campsites. Max. 150 people.
HAYMAN ISLAND 25 km NE of Shute Harbour	• luxury resort • prolific birdlife • close to outer reef	Fishing, sightseeing trips, scenic flights, diving.	From major Australian cities, direct flight to Hamilton Island, then by launch to Hayman Island. From Airlie Beach, by water taxi.	Luxury resort. Max. 450 people.

Great Barrier Reef

Island	Features	Activities	Access	Accommodation
TROPICAL NORTH ISLANDS	This group of islands is located off the north coast of Queensland between Townsville and Cooktown. Generally speaking, the reef in this section is closer to the mainland than it is further south.			
MAGNETIC ISLAND 5 km NE of Townsville	• permanent population • national park • excellent walking tracks • beautiful beaches • buses and taxis available	Horseriding, snorkelling, parasailing, swimming, fishing; Harley tours.	From Townsville, by vehicular ferry, catamaran or water taxi.	Wide variety of hotels and accommodation from budget to deluxe.
ORPHEUS ISLAND 80 km N of Townsville	• small, volcanic island surrounded by coral reefs • island is a national park • prolific birdlife • nesting site for turtles	Birdwatching, turtle watching (turtles come ashore to lay eggs Nov.–Mar.; hatching can be seen late Dec.–May), island walks, fishing.	From Townsville or Cairns, by sea plane.	5-star resort (max. 74 people) or camping (max. 54 people) (camping permit required, contact Ingham office of Dept of Environment and Heritage; (077) 76 1700).
HINCHINBROOK ISLAND 5 km E of Cardwell	• small, low-key resort • island is a national park • mountains, tropical vegetation and waterfalls • sandy beaches and secluded coves on eastern side	Snorkelling, swimming, fishing.	From Cardwell, by launch.	Resort. Max. 50 people.
BEDARRA ISLAND 35 km NE of Cardwell	• exclusive resort • untouched tropical beauty • no day visitors	Bushwalking, swimming, windsurfing, sailing.	From Dunk Island, by launch.	One exclusive resort. Max. 32 people.
DUNK ISLAND 5 km SE of Mission Beach	• popular resort • island is a national park • extensive walking tracks through superb rainforest • prolific birdlife, butterflies and wild orchids	Bushwalking, birdwatching, nightwalks, parasailing, waterskiing, sailing.	From Townsville or Cairns, by plane. From Clump Point near Mission Beach, by launch. From South Mission Beach, by watertaxi.	Resort. Max. 360 people.
FITZROY ISLAND 30 km SE of Cairns	• low-key resort • magnificent flora and fauna • secluded sandy beaches • 360° views from lighthouse	Bushwalking, diving, snorkelling.	From Cairns, by catamaran.	Resort offering bunkhouses and cabins (max. 160 people). Also camping (max. 60 people).
GREEN ISLAND 27 km NE of Cairns	• popular with day-trippers • true coral cay • thick tropical vegetation • glass-bottomed boats • underwater observatory • theatrette with films on reef life	Reef viewing, bushwalking.	From Cairns, by catamaran.	Resort. Max. 90 people.
LIZARD ISLAND 95 km NE of Cooktown	• small, luxurious resort • national park • excellent reefs surround island • game-fishing offshore, especially marlin in season (Sept.–Nov.)	Reef viewing, fishing, bushwalking.	From Cairns, by plane.	Homestead-style resort (max. 80 people) or camping (max. 20 people). Permit required, contact Cairns office of Dept of Environment and Heritage; (070) 52 3096.

orchids, butterflies, cassowaries and bushwalks. Bloomfield Falls, 85 km N, via Cape Tribulation. **Tourist information:** Port Douglas and Cooktown Tourist Information Centre, 23 Macrossan St, Port Douglas; (070) 99 5599. **Accommodation:** 2 B&B, 1 cara./camp. park.

Dalby   Pop. 9385

MAP REF. 482 A4, 491 M8

Dalby is a pleasant, well planned country town at the crossroads of the Warrego, Bunya and Moonie Hwys, 84 km NW of Toowoomba on the Darling Downs. It is the centre of Australia's richest grain-growing area. Cattle, pigs, sheep, cotton and coal add wealth to the district. **Of interest:** Pioneer Park Museum, Black St: historic buildings, displays of household and agricultural items, and craft shop. Obelisk at crossing in Edward St marks spot where explorer Henry Dennis camped in 1841. Memorial cairn in Myall Creek picnic area pays homage to the cactoblastis, the Argentinian caterpillar that eradicated the dreaded prickly pear cactus in the 1920s. Cultural and Administration Centre, Drayton St, includes theatre, cinema, art gallery and restaurant. Self-guide heritage walk and self-guide drive tour available, contact Tourist information. Oct.: Harvest festival. **In the area:** Lake Broadwater Conservation Park, 29 km SW: boating and water-skiing on lake when full, 3-km walk, tower for bird-watching, picnic/barbecue facilities and camping. Bunya Mountains National Park, 60 km NE. Heritage-listed Jimbour House, 27 km N; grounds open daily except in wet weather. **Tourist information:** Thomas Jack Park, cnr Drayton and Condamine Sts; (076) 62 1066. **Accommodation:** 3 hotels, 1 hotel/motel, 5 motels, 2 cara./camp. parks. **See also:** Darling Downs.

Dirranbandi   Pop. 460

MAP REF. 118 C2, 490 G12

A small pastoral township and railhead near the Balonne River, Dirranbandi is located south-west of St George, close to the NSW border. **Of interest:** Railway Park, Railway St; in park, Railway Station Master's Office (1913) has magnificent jarrah wood floor (contact Newsagency to gain entry). Also in Railway St, Cafe-de-Lux, a reminder of days when most country towns had a Greek cafe. **In the area:** Cubbie Station, 33 km W, largest privately-owned cotton property in State; tours available, contact Tourist information. Old Bullamon Homestead (1860), 60 km SE, still has original shingle roof and canvas ceilings; tours by appt only. **Tourist information:** Caravan Park, 13 Railway St; (076) 25 8350. **Accommodation:** 1 motel.

Eidsvold   Pop. 587

MAP REF. 491 M3

The Eidsvold goldfield was extremely productive for 12 years from 1888 and still remains attractive to fossickers. The district is the State's best producer of quality beef cattle. **Of interest:** Historical Museum, features Knockbreak Homestead (1850s), George Schafer and Eric Schultz Collection of rocks and minerals, Noel Duncan Bottle Collection and local history displays, especially of goldmining. **In the area:** Waruma Dam, 48 km N via Burnett Hwy, for swimming, sailing and water-skiing. **Tourist information:** Historical Museum, Mt Rose St; (071) 65 1277. **Accommodation:** 1 hotel/motel, 1 motel, 1 cara./camp. park.

Emerald   Pop. 6557

MAP REF. 492 I11

An attractive town, 263 km W of Rockhampton at the junction of the Capricorn and Gregory Hwys, Emerald is the hub of the Central Highlands. The largest sapphire fields in the southern hemisphere are nearby. As well as the cattle industry, grain, oilseeds, soybeans and cotton are important. **Of interest:** Shady Moreton Bay fig trees line Clermont and Egerton Sts. National Trust-classified railway station (1901), Clermont St. Pioneer Cottage complex, Harris St. Pastoral College, Capricorn Hwy. Easter: Sunflower festival. June: Wheelbarrow derby. Aug.: Gemfest. Sept.: Music spectacular. **In the area:** Fossicking for gems, licence required. At Rubyvale, 60 km NE: Miner's Heritage Walk-in Mine, tours of underground sapphire mine and gemcutting displays; Bobby Dazzler Walk-in Mine, also has museum and shop; various gem outlets; 4WD tours of gemfields available. Gregory coalfields, 60 km N. At Capella, 51 km NW: Capella Pioneer Village, home to first settlement in area, Peak Downs Homestead. Lake Maraboon/Fairbairn Dam, 19 km S, for fishing and water sports; cruises of lake available. Tour historic schoolhouse, storehouse and slab homestead at Old Rainworth Fort, Springsure; 66 km S. Further south, Carnarvon National Park featuring deep sandstone gorge and sacred Aboriginal art sites. **Tourist information:** Clermont St; (079) 82 4142. **Accommodation:** 3 hotels, 6 motels, 6 cara./camp. parks. **See also:** The Capricorn Region.

Emu Park   Pop. 1919

MAP REF. 493 O10

On the way to this seaside resort, 45 km NE of Rockhampton, is St Christopher's Chapel. Built by the US Army in 1943, the chapel is on the Rockhampton–Emu Park Rd, 25 km SW of the town. Emu Park has excellent picnic spots and a safe beach. **Of interest:** Historical Museum, Hill St, features King O'Malley Memorial. Unusual 'singing ship' memorial to Captain Cook, who discovered the bay on voyage up east coast in May 1770 (sea breezes cause hidden organ pipes to make sounds). Bell Park, located on beach. Markets, 4th Sun. each month at Bell Park. July: Service of Remembrance, memorial to American troops. Oct.: Octoberfest. **In the area:** Great Keppel Island and nearby underwater observatory; tours daily. Other islands in Keppel group offer limited facilities including camping and day trips (permit required); contact Tourist information. Coral Life Marineland, 3 km NE at Kinka Beach; open weekends and school holidays. Koorana Crocodile Farm, Emu Park–Rockhampton Rd, 20 km W. **Tourist information:** Historical Museum, Hill St; (079) 39 6080. **Accommodation:** 2 motels, 1 cara./ camp. park.

Eromanga   Pop. 90

MAP REF. 501 M7

A centre for extensive oil exploration, 103 km W of Quilpie, Eromanga has a refinery producing around 1.5 million barrels of oil a year. Named from an Aboriginal word meaning 'hot windy plain', Eromanga is reputedly the furthest town from the sea in Australia. **Of interest:** Royal Hotel, Webber St, once Cobb & Co. staging post. Some original 19th-century buildings. Easter: Rodeo. May: Race day. **In the area:** Opal fields;

Boyne River at Gladstone, a prosperous seaside city

some leaseholders permit visitors, contact Mining Warden at Quilpie or police at Eromanga. **Tourist information:** Quilpie Shire Offices, Brolga St, Quilpie; (076) 56 1133. **Accommodation:** 1 cara./camp. park.

Esk
Pop. 882

MAP REF. 482 I5, 491 O8

Esk, in the Upper Brisbane Valley, is 99 km NW of Brisbane. It is one of the largest towns in the region. The Upper Brisbane Valley is renowned for its beautiful lakes and dams. **Of interest:** Numerous antique and local craft shops. July: Picnic races. Nov.: Eskibition (art and craft, and carnival). **In the area:** Lakes and dams: Lake Somerset (25 km NE) and Lake Wivenhoe (25 km E), the source of Brisbane's main water supply, and Atkinson Dam (30 km SE); all are popular swimming, fishing and boating spots. Lake Wivenhoe is State's main centre for championship rowing. At Coominya, 22 km SE: historic Bellevue Homestead; Boss camel races in Sept. Further north, some of the finest grazing country in Brisbane Valley; this is deer country, where progeny of a small herd of deer presented to the State by Queen Victoria in 1873 still roam the area. **Tourist information:** Shire Offices, 2 Redbank St; (074) 24 1200. **Accommodation:** 2 hotels, 3 motels, 1 cara./camp. park.

Eulo
Pop. 42

MAP REF. 501 Q11

Once the centre for opal mining in the area, Eulo is situated on the banks of the Paroo River, 68 km W of Cunnamulla. **Of interest:** Eulo Queen Hotel, Leo St, owes its name to Isobel Robinson (nee Richardson) who ran the hotel and virtually reigned over the opal fields at turn of century. Eulo Date Farm, western outskirts of town (open Aug.–Sept.). Aug.: World lizard racing championships, at Paroo Lizard Race Track, next to hotel. Destructo Cockroach Monument commemorates death of a champion racing cockroach. **In the area:** Fossicking area for visitors at Yowah, 87 km NW. Mud Springs, 7 km W. Thargomindah, 130 km W; inquire at Council Chambers for mud map to Burke and Wills Dig Tree site. Good fishing at Noccundra water hole 260 km W. Currawinya National Park, 60 km SW, for birdwatching and fishing. **Tourist information:** Centenary Park, Cunnamulla; (076) 55 1777. **Accommodation:** 1 hotel, 1 cara./camp. park.

Gatton
Pop. 5098

MAP REF. 482 H8, 491 O9

First settled in the 1840s, this agricultural town in the Lockyer Valley is located midway between Ipswich and Toowoomba, and 96 km W of Brisbane via the Warrego Hwy. Saw-milling, dairy cattle, small-crop farming and raising of beef cattle, pigs and calves, are the main activities of the area. May: Heavy horse field day. Oct.: Potato festival. **In the area:** Agricultural College, 5 km E, opened 1897. Helidon, 14 km W, noted for its freestone, used in many Brisbane buildings, and for its spa water. Grantham, 7 km SW, known for fresh fruit and vegetables; many roadside stalls offer local produce. **Tourist information:** Lake Apex Dr.; (074) 62 3430. **Accommodation:** 3 hotels, 1 hotel/motel, 1 motel, 3 cara./camp. parks. **See also:** Darling Downs.

Gayndah
Pop. 1750

MAP REF. 491 N4

Gayndah claims to be Qld's oldest town, having been founded in 1848. It is on the Burnett Hwy near the Burnett River, just over 100 km W of Maryborough. **Of interest:** Original school (1863), still in use. Several homesteads in district built in 1850s. Capper St, location for film *The Mango Tree*. Historical Museum, Simon St, includes Ban Ban Springs Homestead. June: Orange festival (odd-numbered years). **In the area:** Claude Warton Weir Recreation Area, 3 km W, for fishing and picnics. Natural springs at Ban Ban Springs, 26 km S, a popular picnic area. **Tourist information:** Grand Hotel, 2 Meson St; (071) 61 1200. **Accommodation:** 2 motels, 2 cara./camp. parks.

Georgetown
Pop. 310

MAP REF. 494 I10

Georgetown is a small town on the Gulf Developmental Rd to Croydon and Normanton. It was once one of many small goldmining towns on the Etheridge Goldfield. The area is now noted for its gemstones, especially agate and gold nuggets. Georgetown is also a trans-shipping centre for beef road-trains. New Year's Day, June, Oct. and Nov.: Race meetings. **In the area:** Gemfields at Agate Creek, 95 km S, and O'Briens Creek, 129 km NE. Tallaroo hot springs, 55 km E. Undara Volcanic National Park, 129 km E variety of birdlife **Tourist information:** Etheridge Shire Offices, St George St; (070) 62 1233. **Accommodation:** 1 hotel, 1 motel, 2 cara./camp. parks. **See also:** Gulf Savannah.

Gin Gin
Pop. 907

MAP REF. 491 N2

Some of Qld's oldest cattle properties are in the area around this pastoral town on the Bruce Hwy, 52 km SW of Bundaberg. The district is known as Wild Scotchman Country, after James McPherson, Qld's only authentic bushranger. **Of interest:** The Residence, Mulgrave St, former police sergeant's house now displaying district's pioneering memorabilia. **In the area:** Mystery Craters, 17 km NE, curious formation of 35 craters, about 25 million years old. Lake Monduran, 24 km NW, held back by Fred Haigh Dam (Qld's second largest), ideal for boating and picnics. Moonara Craft Spinning, 25 km W, daily demonstrations of spinning process. Currajong Gardens, 9 km S, indoor and outdoor plants featuring exotic and rare cacti. **Tourist information:** Richardsons Pharmacy and Gift Shop, 48 Mulgrave St; (071) 57 2184. **Accommodation:** 2 motels, 1 cara./camp. park.

Gladstone
Pop. 23 462

MAP REF. 493 P12

Matthew Flinders discovered Port Curtis, Gladstone's impressive deepwater harbour, in 1802, but it was not until the 1960s that its potential began to be utilised. As an outlet for central Qld's mineral and agricultural wealth, Gladstone, 550 km NW of Brisbane, is now one of Australia's most prosperous seaboard cities. Its harbour is one of Australia's busiest, handling more shipping tonnage per annum than Sydney. One reason for this growth is the opening up of the almost inexhaustible coal supplies in the hinterland. Another is that the world's largest single alumina plant is at Parsons Point where millions of tonnes of bauxite from Weipa on the Gulf of Carpentaria are processed annually into millions of tonnes of alumina, the halfway stage of aluminium. Comalco has built an aluminium smelter at Boyne Island. A large power station has been built in Gladstone to supply power to the refinery and smelter, as well as feeding into the State's electricity grid. Chemical processing is a new regional industry. Gladstone's most important tourist advantage is its proximity to the southern section of the Great Barrier Reef. The city is known for its mud crabs and prawns, and has won the State Tidy Towns Competition seven times. **Of interest:** In Goondoon St: historic Kullaroo House (1911); Radar Hill Lookout. Gladstone Regional Art Gallery and Museum, cnr Goondoon and Bramston Sts. Potter's Place, Dawson Hwy, art and craft gallery. Tondoon Botanic Gardens, has all native species (tours available at weekends); end Glenlyon St. Barney Point Beach and Friend Park, Barney St. Reg Tanna Park, Glenlyon St, includes Railway Dam. Waterfall, end Auckland St, is floodlit at night. Views of harbour and islands from Auckland Hill Lookout. Round Hill Lookout, Boles St, West Gladstone. Auckland Inlet offers anchorage alongside James Cook Park; finishing-line for annual Brisbane to Gladstone yacht race, highlight of 10-day Harbour festival held Easter. Marina, departure point for Barrier Reef cruises and harbour cruises. **In the area:** Tours of Gladstone Power Station, north of town. Curtis Island, also north, in Gladstone Harbour, is a family recreation area. Quoin Island Resort, 20 min. by ferry; day trippers welcome. Spectacular views from Mt Larcom summit, 33 km W. Port Curtis Historical Village, 26 km SW at Calliope River. Lake Awoonga, 30 km S, offers picnic and camping areas, water-based recreation, walking trail and varied wildlife. Historic town of Many Peaks, 80 km SE. Nearby towns of Boyne Island and Tannum Sands are linked by bridge; Boyne Island renowned for its beautiful foreshore parks, also Boyne Smelter on island has visitor information centre and guided tours; Tannum Sands offers long stretches of sandy beaches. Town of Seventeen Seventy holds 1770 Commemorative festival in May in honour of Captain Cook's first Qld landing. Various national parks in region, contact Tourist information. **Tourist information:** 56 Goondoon St; (079) 72 9922. **Accommodation:** 19 motels, 5 hotel/motels, 10 cara./camp. parks. **See also:** Gladstone Region.

Goondiwindi
Pop. 4331

MAP REF. 118 H2, 491 K11

This country town at the junction of five highways is near the picturesque MacIntyre River, which was discovered by explorer Allan Cunningham in 1827 and forms the State border. The Aboriginal word *goonawinna* means 'resting place of the birds'. The district's thriving economy is based on cotton, wheat, beef and wool, and a growing manufacturing sector. **Of interest:** Botanic Gardens of Western Woodlands (25 ha), access from Brennans Rd, 1 km NW. Statue of famous racehorse Gunsynd, the 'Goondiwindi Grey', in Apex Park, MacIntyre St. Customs House Museum, opposite park. Historic Victoria Hotel, Marshall St. Tours of Bulk Grains depot and cotton gin; by appt, in season. Oct.: Spring festival, coincides with flowering of jacarandas and silky oaks. Nov.: Rodeo. **In the area:** Boobera Lagoon, 20 km SW into NSW, wildlife sanctuary. **Tourist information:** Watertower, McLean St; (076) 71 2653. **Accommodation:** 2 hotels, 2 hotel/motels, 7 motels, 3 cara./camp. parks. **See also:** Darling Downs.

Gordonvale
Pop. 2658

MAP REF. 489 F10, 495 N7

This town is 24 km S of Cairns. **In the area:** Gillies Hwy, with 295 bends, leads west to Atherton. Goldsborough Valley State Forest, 6 km W (15 km off Gillies Hwy), for walking, swimming, canoeing and picnicking. Wooroonooran National Park, 10 km S, spectacular views from summit of Walsh's Pyramid. The Mulgrave Rambler, 15-km steam-train ride along cane railway system through canefields and rainforest; charter only. Spectacular Orchid Valley Farm, 15 km SW; tours available. Hambledon Sugar Mill at Edmonton, 16 km N. **Tourist information:** Far North Queensland Promotion Bureau, cnr Grafton and Hartley Sts, Cairns; (070) 51 3588. **Accommodation:** 4 hotels, 1 cara./camp. park.

Gympie
Pop. 10 791

MAP REF. 491 P6

The city of Gympie started with the 'Great Australian Gold Rush' in 1867, following the discovery of gold by James Nash. The field proved extremely rich, and some 4 million ounces had been found by the time the gold petered out in the 1920s. By then dairying and agriculture were well established and Gympie continued to prosper. Near the Mary River and 166 km N of Brisbane via the Bruce Hwy, Gympie is the major provincial city servicing the Cooloola region. It is an attractive city with its jacarandas, flowering silky oaks, cassias,

Rainbow Beach, near Gympie, famous for its coloured sands

poincianas and flame trees. **Of interest:** Woodworks Museum, Frazer Rd. Gympie Golden Gem, Bruce Hwy, gem display and sales. Self-guide heritage walk, contact Tourist information for details. Market, 2nd and 4th Sun. each month at Gympie South State School. Oct.: Gold Rush festival. **In the area:** Gold Mining Museum, Brisbane Rd, 5 km S; nearby, cottage of Andrew Fisher, first Queenslander to become Prime Minister (1908). Rock pools and excellent views at Mothar Mountain, 20 km SE. Cooloola section of Great Sandy National Park, 50 km E. Peaceful fishing resort of Tin Can Bay (55 km NE) and small resort of Rainbow Beach with its coloured sands, 77 km NE via vast pine forests. Ferry to Fraser Island operates from Inskip Point north of Rainbow Beach. Part of the Bicentennial National Trail (a 5000-km trail for walkers and horse riders) runs through Kilkivan, 50 km NW; Great horse ride held here each April. Goomeri, 25 km further W, known as 'clock town' because of unique memorial clock in town centre. Lake Borumba, for picnics and water sports, 50 km SW in picturesque Mary Valley. Nearby, Imbil Forest Drive through scenic pine-forest plantations. Mary Valley Scenic Way runs south between Gympie and Maleny, via Kenilworth. **Tourist information:** Bruce Hwy, Lake Alford; (074) 82 5444. **Accommodation:** 12 hotels, 7 motels, 4 cara./camp. parks.

Hervey Bay Pop. 22 205

MAP REF. 491 P3

Hervey (pronounced Harvey) Bay is the large area of water between Maryborough and Bundaberg that is protected by Fraser Island. It is also the name of a thriving city on its shore that comprises the pleasant strip of seaside resorts along its southern shore, some 34 km NE of Maryborough. An ideal climate makes the area popular, and during the winter months there is an influx of visitors from the south. Hervey Bay is actively promoted as 'Australia's family aquatic playground'. As there is no surf, swimming is safe even for children. Fishing is the main recreation. Boats may be hired and yabbies caught for bait. **Of interest:** In Pialba: Village Pottery, Old Maryborough Rd, open for tour of manufacturing process; Hervey Bay Tourist and Visitors Centre, Old Maryborough Rd, displays model village and ships, and woodwork; paintings at Wide Bay Gallery, Main St; Nature World Wildlife Park, features koalas, other marsupials, lorikeets, crocodiles and other reptiles. In Scarness: Hervey Bay Historical Society Museum, Zephyr St, recalls pioneer days. In Torquay: Golf 'n' Games, Cypress St, with 18-hole mini-golf and 120-m water-slide. At Urangan: cairn in Pulgul St at Dayman Point commemorates landing by Matthew Flinders in 1799 and the Z-Force commandoes who trained there on the *Krait* in World War II; 1-km long pier, off The Esplanade, used by anglers; Neptune's Aquarium, Pulgul St, has performing seals and sharks; Vic Hislop's Shark Show. Humpback whales visit Hervey Bay early Aug.–mid-Oct. on their annual migration; viewing cruises available, contact Tourist information for details. Day trips to Fraser Island. Sun. markets at Urangan and Nikenbar. Aug.: Whale festival. Oct.: Hervey Bay to Fraser Island sailboard marathon. **In the area:** Hervey Bay Marine Park, 40 km N. Quiet seaside resorts at Toogoom and Burrum Heads, 15 km NW. Go-kart track, 2 km W. Historic Brooklyn House at Howard, 25 km W. **Tourist information:** 63 Old Maryborough Rd, Pialba; (071) 24 4050. **Accommodation:** 4 hotel/motels, 18 motels, 20 caravan parks.

Home Hill Pop. 3197

MAP REF. 492 H1, 495 Q13

Sister town to Ayr, Home Hill is on the south side of the Burdekin River, 84 km SE of Townsville. The towns are joined by a high-level bridge as the river is liable to flood. **Of interest:** Tours of Inkerman Sugar Mill, Seventh Ave, during crushing season Mon.–Fri. (June–Dec.). Ashworths, Eighth Ave, rock shop, museum, and art and craft. Nov.: Harvest festival. **In the area:** Groper Creek, 16 km W, for fishing and catching giant mud crabs; nearby, camping, caravan and picnic areas. **Tourist information:** Ashworths, Eighth Ave; (077) 82 1177. **Accommodation:** 3 hotels, 1 motel, 2 cara./camp. parks.

Hughenden Pop. 1592

MAP REF. 492 A4, 499 O4

An expedition led by Frederick Walker was the first to pass by this spot near the Flinders River, while searching for the Burke and Wills expedition in 1861. Two years later a cattle station was established by Ernest Henry, and Hughenden came into existence. The town is on the Townsville–Mount Isa rail line and the Flinders Hwy, 243 km SW of Charters Towers, and is a major centre for the wool and cattle industry in the region. **Of interest:** Explorers' Tree, Stansfield St East, on east bank of Station Creek, a coolibah tree blazed by Walker, and again by William Landsborough in 1862 when he passed through the area on a second Burke and

Gladstone Region

Heron Island, a popular resort island offshore from Gladstone

Gladstone is only a 6-hour drive north of Brisbane and offers the closest major southern access to the Great Barrier Reef. Reef trips depart daily from Gladstone's marina and regularly from the Town of Seventeen Seventy. **Lady Musgrave Island** is accessed from Town of Seventeen Seventy. With its gracious palm-studded city centre, Gladstone faces the harbour and offers accommodation ranging from international hotels to caravan parks, as well as restaurants serving the region's famous mud crabs. Gladstone, the outlet for central Queensland's mineral and agricultural wealth, is a world-class port.

The hinterland west of Gladstone features national parks, lush rainforests and an historical village, and is ideal for trail riding, camping, walking, fishing and four-wheel driving.

Located south of the city and nestled in the delta of the picturesque Boyne River, Boyne Island, which is noted for its beautiful foreshore parks, is linked by a bridge to its twin beachside community, Tannum Sands. Safe, patrolled swimming beaches provide year-round swimming. In an easy blend of scenery and industry, a major smelter on the island produces a quarter of Australia's aluminium output.

Further south, the Agnes Water and Town of Seventeen Seventy area is well-known for its natural springs, palm groves, pockets of wilderness, rare birds and other animals, and plants. The beaches with their crystal-clear waters are virtually unaltered since Captain Cook landed here in 1770.

Heron Island, a world-famous coral cay resort, is on the Barrier Reef just off Gladstone. Wilson Island, another beautiful coral cay, offers camping holidays in comfortable seclusion. Locally based helicopters, and a host of vessels moored in the Gladstone marina, enable visits to this tropical paradise. Most of the islands are national parks and offer diverse flora, birdlife, and fish and marine life. A large charter-boat fleet departs regularly for fishing and diving trips or to take campers to the reef islands.

For further information contact Gladstone Area Promotion and Development Ltd, 56 Goondoon St, Gladstone; (079) 72 9922. **See also:** Great Barrier Reef for those islands indicated by bold type; entry for Gladstone in A–Z listing. **Map reference:** 493 P12.

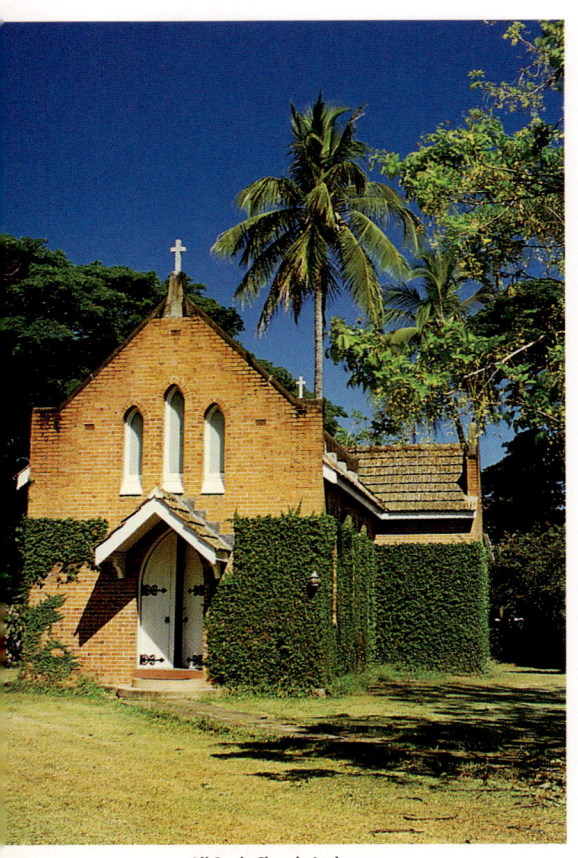

All Souls Church, Ingham

Wills expedition. Dinosaur Display Centre, Gray St, houses 14-m replica of Muttaburrasaurus, most complete dinosaur fossil found in Australia. July: Dinosaur festival (even-numbered years). **In the area:** At Prairie, 44 km E on Flinders Hwy: mini-museum; historical relics at Cobb & Co. Yards. Porcupine National Park, 62 km N, features mini 'Grand Canyon'. Gemstone fossicking at Cheviot Hills, 200 km N; contact Tourist information. **Tourist information:** Shire Offices, 34 Gray St; (077) 41 1288. **Accommodation:** 1 hotel, 2 hotel/motels, 2 motels, 2 cara./camp. parks.

Ilfracombe   Pop. 350

MAP REF. 492 A11, 499 P11

This town, 27 km E of Longreach on the Matilda Hwy, was developed in 1891 as a transport nucleus for Wellshot Station, the largest sheep station in the world (in terms of stock numbers) at that time; the head station was itself the size of a town. The first Qld motorised mail service departed from Ilfracombe in 1910. **Of interest:** Folk Museum, on hwy, includes Oakhampton Craft Cottage (local crafts in historic cottage) and three parks with various outdoor displays. Opposite, historic Wellshot Hotel. Langenberger House, Mitchell St, an early settler's house (rare example of outback living conditions of the era). **Tourist information:** Shire Offices, Devon St; (076) 58 2233. **Accommodation:** 1 hotel, 1 cara./camp. park.

Ingham   Pop. 5075

MAP REF. 495 N11

A major sugar and sightseeing town near the waterways of the Hinchinbrook Channel, Ingham is on the Bruce Hwy, 110 km NW of Townsville. The town has a strong Italian and Spanish Basque cultural background. **Of interest:** Macknade Mill, Halifax Rd, oldest sugar mill still operating on original site. Victoria Sugar Mill, Forrest Beach Rd, largest in southern hemisphere; guided tours in crushing season, June–Nov. Daintree market, 1st Sun. each month. May: Australian-Italian festival. Oct.: Maraka festival. **In the area:** Cemetery, 5 km E, interesting Italian mausoleums. Forrest Beach, 20 km E, 16 km of sandy beach overlooking Palm Group of islands, stinger net swimming enclosures installed in summer. Taylor's Beach, 24 km NE, popular family seaside spot. Hinchinbrook and Orpheus resort islands offshore. Lucinda, 27 km NE on banks of Herbert River, excellent base for fishing holidays. Lumholtz National Park, 40 km NW, features 303-m Wallaman Falls, spectacular scenery, and excellent camping, swimming and picnic spots. Mt Fox, extinct volcano, 65 km SW. Jourama Falls in Paluma Range National Park, 25 km S. Spectacular view from McClelland's Lookout, 48 km S off Bruce Hwy. **Tourist information:** Bruce Hwy; (077) 76 5211. **Accommodation:** 7 hotels, 2 motels, 3 B&B, 1 hostel, 2 cara./camp. parks.

Inglewood   Pop. 1007

MAP REF. 119 K1, 491 L11

An early hostelry called Brown's Inn grew into the town of Inglewood, in the south-western corner of the Darling Downs, 108 km SW of Warwick. In the surrounding area beef cattle and sheep are raised, and lucerne, grain and fodder crops are irrigated from Coolmunda Dam, 20 km E, which attracts boating enthusiasts as well as many pelicans and swans. **Tourist information:** Cnr Albert and Elizabeth Sts; (076) 52 1444. **Accommodation:** 2 motels, 3 cara./camp. parks.

Injune   Pop. 394

MAP REF. 490 G5

This small cattle and timber town, 89 km N of Roma, is the southern gateway to the Carnarvon National Park. Explorer Ludwig Leichhardt called the region 'ruined Castle Valley'. **In the area:** Carnarvon National Park, 154 km N: Carnarvon Gorge, major Aboriginal art sites at Art Gallery and Cathedral Cave, spectacular sandstone scenery with gorges and escarpments, and several walking tracks. Carnarvon Gorge Oasis Lodge adjacent to park. **Tourist information:** Kookas Travel, Bowen St, Roma; (076) 22 1333. **Accommodation:** 1 hotel, 1 motel, 1 cara./camp. park.

Innisfail   Pop. 8520

MAP REF. 495 N8

Innisfail is a prosperous, colourful town on the banks of the North and South Johnstone Rivers, 88 km SE of Cairns. Sugar has been grown here since the early 1880s and its contribution to the area is celebrated with a 9-day gala Harvest festival held early Oct. Besides the growing of sugarcane, bananas, paw-paws and other tropical and rare fruit, beef cattle are raised, and the town has a prawn and reef fishing fleet. **Of interest:** Local history museum, Edith St. Chinese Joss House, Owen St. Cane Cutter Monument, Fitzgerald Espl. Warrina Lakes and Botanical Gardens, Charles St. Several lovely parks with riverside picnic facilities. July: Agricultural show. Oct.: Harvest festival. **In the area:** Flying Fish Point and Ella Bay, 5 km N, for swimming and camping. Bramston Beach, palm-fringed shoreline, 23 km N. Johnstone River Crocodile Farm, 8 km NE. Qld's highest peak Mt Bartle Frere (1611 m), 25 km NW; track to summit. Johnstone River Gorge, via Palmerston Hwy, 18 km W, has walking tracks to several waterfalls. Wooroonooran National Park, 30 km W; road leads to Atherton Tableland. Australian Sugar Museum at Mourilyan, 7 km S. Etty Bay, 15 km S, beach and picnic area. Innisfail is excellent base for exploration of quieter lagoons and islands (including Dunk) of Great Barrier Reef. **Tourist information:**

Cassowary Coast Development Bureau, Bruce Hwy, Mourilyan; (070) 61 6448. **Accommodation:** 2 hotels, 7 motels, 1 hostel, 4 cara./camp. parks.

Ipswich   Pop. 65 346

MAP REF. 483 K9, 491 P9

In 1827 a convict settlement was established alongside the Bremer River to quarry limestone and convey it down the river to Brisbane for building. In 1842 the settlement, called Limestone, opened to free settlers and in 1843 it was renamed Ipswich. The town is a major industrial centre, with coalmining, earthenware works, sawmills, abattoirs and foundries. **Of interest:** Numerous heritage buildings including St Pauls Anglican Church (1859), Brisbane St; Claremont (1858), Milford St, open 1st Sun. in month; Gooloowan (1864), Quarry St; Ginn Cottage, Ginn St; and Ipswich Grammar School (1863), Burnett St. Regional Art Gallery, cnr Limestone St and D'Arcy Doyle Pl. Self-guide historic walks, contact Tourist information. Showground market each Sun. Country markets, 1st Sun. each month. Apr.: Heritage week. July: Medieval fair and markets. **In the area:** North-east: College's Crossing (7 km), Mt Crosby (12 km) and Lake Manchester (22 km) – all popular swimming and picnic spots. Outback Emu Farm, 6 km N. At Rosewood, 20 km W: St Brigid's Church, largest wooden church in South Pacific; steam-train rides, last Sun. each month. At Swanbank Power Station, 12 km SE, steam trains run by Qld Pioneer Steam Railway Co-op; Apr.–Dec., check times. Restored historic homestead Wolston House at Wacol, 16 km E. **Tourist information:** Cnr Brisbane St and d'Arcy Doyle Pl.; (07) 3281 0555. **Accommodation:** 3 hotel/motels, 6 motels, 3 B&B, 1 hostel, 5 cara./camp. parks.

Isisford   Pop. 150

MAP REF. 492 A13, 499 P13, 501 O1

Established in 1877 by travelling hawkers William and James Whitman, Isisford is 116 km S of Longreach. First called Wittown, the town was renamed in 1880 to recall the ford in the nearby Barcoo River and the proximity of Isis Downs Station Homestead. **Of interest:** Bicentennial Museum, Centenary Dr. **In the area:** Huge (largest in Australia) semicircular, prefabricated shearing shed, (1913), at Isis Downs Station, 20 km E; visits by appt; (076) 58 8203. Oma Waterhole, 16 km W, popular spot for fishing and water sports. **Tourist information:** Shire Offices, St Marys St; (076) 58 8277. **Accommodation:** 2 hotels, 1 cara./camp. park.

Julia Creek   Pop. 572

MAP REF. 499 J4

A small cattle and rail township named after the niece of Donald MacIntyre, the first European settler in the area. Located on the Flinders Hwy, Julia Creek is 134 km E of Cloncurry. A sealed road runs north to Normanton in the Gulf Savannah. The town is an important cattle-trucking centre. **Of interest:** McIntyre Museum, Burke St. May: Campdraft. **In the area:** Saxby roundup held each June at Taldora Station, an isolated area 230 km N; access via Julia Creek. **Tourist information:** Shire Offices, Julia St; (077) 46 7166. **Accommodation:** 1 hotel, 1 hotel/motel, 1 motel, 1 cara./camp. park. See also: Gulf Savannah.

Jundah   Pop. 100

MAP REF. 501 M2

Jundah (an Aboriginal word for 'women'), 219 km SW of Longreach, was gazetted as a town in 1880. For 20 years the area was important for opal mining, but lack of water eventually caused the mines to close. **Of interest:** Barcoo Historical Museum, Perkins St. Oct.: Race carnival. **In the area:** Jundah Opal Fields, 27 km NW. Welford National Park, 20 km S. **Tourist information:** Shire Offices, Dickson St; (076) 58 6133. **Accommodation:** 1 hotel, 1 cara./camp. park.

Karumba   Pop. 708

MAP REF. 494 B8, 497 H8, 501 O1

Karumba, 69 km NW of Normanton, is at the mouth of the Norman River and is the centre of the prawning industry in the Gulf of Carpentaria. A barramundi fishing industry and live-cattle industry also operate from the town. **Of interest:** Slipway once used by the Sydney-to-England Empire Flying Boats Service. Boat hire and accommodation at Karumba Point. Old cemetery, 2 km NW, on road to Karumba Point, a small settlement 6 km NW. July: Karumba Kapers. Dec.: Fishermen's ball. **In the area:** Town is surrounded by flat wetlands extending 30 km inland, habitat of saltwater crocodiles and many species of birds, including brolgas and cranes. Karumba is easiest point of access to the Gulf. Charter vessels for fishing and exploration of the Gulf and Norman River. *The Ferryman*, cruises on Norman River. **Tourist information:** Shire Offices, Haig St, Normanton; (077) 45 1166. **Accommodation:** 1 hotel/motel, 4 cara./camp. parks. See also: Gulf Savannah.

Kenilworth   Pop. 257

MAP REF 491 P7

West of the Blackall Range, through the Obi Obi Valley, is Kenilworth. The town is famous for its Kenilworth Country Foods hand-crafted cheeses. This enterprise began when the local cheese factory closed and six employees mortgaged their homes to start the venture. **Of interest:** Kev Franzi's Photo Workshop and Movie Museum, Eumundi Rd. **In the area:** Little Yabba Creek, 8 km S, a good picnic spot where bellbirds often heard. Lake Borumba 32 km NW, for picnics and watersports. Nearby, Imbil Forest Dr. through scenic forests and farmlands to Gympie. **Tourist information:** Cnr Sixth Ave and Aerodrome Rd, Maroochydore; (074) 79 1566. **Accommodation:** 1 hotel, 1 motel, camping facilities.

Killarney   Pop. 827

MAP REF. 119 N1, 491 O11

This attractive small town is on the banks of the Condamine River, 34 km SE of Warwick, and very close to the NSW border. Feb.: Agricultural show. Nov.: Rodeo. **In the area:** Noteworthy mountain scenery. Dagg's and Brown's waterfalls, 1–2 km S. Cherrabah Homestead Resort, 7 km S, offers horseriding, golf, sailing and bushwalking. Queen Mary Falls in Main Range National Park, 7 km E; native birds fed daily at kiosk. **Tourist information:** 49 Albion St (New England Hwy), Warwick; (076) 61 3122. **Accommodation:** 1 cara./camp. park, 1 resort.

Kingaroy   Pop. 6672

MAP REF. 491 N6

This prosperous agricultural town is known for its peanuts and is the home of Sir Johannes (Joh) Bjelke-Petersen, the

The Far North

Elinjaa Falls, near Millaa Millaa on the Atherton Tableland

Sitting in a lush, tropical garden through dusk and into evening, and dining superbly on king prawns and Queensland mud crabs, you will find it hard to believe you are at 'the end of the line' – **Port Douglas** is the most northerly of the easily accessible coastal towns of Queensland. This Port Douglas scene typifies the beauty of coastal Queensland; the restaurant looks down from a forest-covered hill that looms over the small town and the 7 kilometres of ocean beach. By day the dense tropical forest is revealed in showers of coloured flowers against the intense green. The lavish rainforest and the rush of sparkling mountain streams are lasting impressions for the traveller in the north – a region larger than most European countries and considered by many to be the most diversely beautiful and exciting part of Australia.

Cairns, 1832 kilometres from Brisbane, is the stepping-stone to a variety of sightseeing excursions. A major city for tourism, Cairns is often known as the 'capital of Far North Queensland'. Nestling beside Trinity Bay, this scenic city is an ideal base for visiting the surrounding tourist attractions. From Cairns you can relax on a launch cruise that takes you to see the wonders of the Great Barrier Reef or explore uninhabited islands. Aerial tours from Cairns take you over the Great Plateau, with its lush tablelands and spectacular waterfalls.

The pleasant climate in winter and early spring is one of the main attractions of this city. Visitors can enjoy snorkelling or other water sports, while anglers flock to Cairns from September to December to catch the big black marlin. Cairns itself is a picturesque city. Delicate ferns, tropical shrubs and fragrant flowers thrive in the Botanical Gardens, where a walking track joins the Centenary Lakes Parkland, created in 1976 to mark the city's hundredth anniversary. Two lakes, one saltwater and the other freshwater, provide a haven for wildlife among native trees and shrubs. You can also see orchids growing to perfection in orchid nurseries, which form the basis of one of Cairns' important export industries.

There are dozens of places around Cairns, all within easy driving distance on good roads, that will claim the traveller's attention. Port Douglas is only one of them. The 60-kilometre journey north from Cairns passes through a magnificent stretch of coastal scenery as the Cook Highway winds past white coral beaches, through archways of tropical forest and past the islands that dot the blue northern waters. Despite its increasing popularity with tourists, Port Douglas still retains some of its fishing-village atmosphere.

Just north of Port Douglas (and remember to stop at the cemetery that contains the graves of many pioneer settlers who were lured north by the Palmer River gold rush) is the sugar town of **Mossman**. During the months July to October, sugarcane farmers once created raging fires to prepare the cane for harvesting; nowadays, however, cane is more often harvested green. These days the cane cutter is seldom seen, having exchanged a machete for a seat on an ingenious machine that cuts the cane and throws it, in a shower of short sticks, into the hopper that trails behind. Sugar-growing is a major industry of the north, and the waving fields of cane wind through the mountains for hundreds of kilometres down the lush coastal plain.

Near Mossman is one of those perfect places that seem so plentiful in the north, the Mossman River Gorge. A short walk under the dense green canopy of the rainforest leads to the boulder-strewn river, which rushes in a series of cascades through the jungle-sided gorge. It is a place to picnic, to swim or simply to bask in the rays of the North Queensland sun.

There are many such places, particularly on the edge of the Atherton Tableland, where the mountains have thrown up fascinating geological oddities and where waterfalls spill. For example, near **Atherton** township there are two volcanic lakes, Barrine and Eacham, where walking tracks through the rainforest give beautiful water views and a chance to see the abundant wildlife, including parrots, waterfowl, turtles, platypuses, goannas and many marsupials. Nearby is Tinaburra, a popular tourist settlement alongside Tinaroo Dam. On the Yungaburra–Malanda road is the amazing and much-photographed Curtain Fig Tree. The rich dairy country around Malanda, 14 kilometres south-east of Atherton, supplies milk for what is known as the longest milk run in the world: to Weipa, Mount Isa, Darwin, and into Western Australia.

South-west of Malanda is Mount Hypipamee National Park, where visitors can walk beneath huge rainforest trees, past staghorn ferns and orchids, along Dinner Creek to the falls and up to the crater, a funnel of sheer granite walls that fall away into dark and forbidding water. Ten kilometres away from the Malanda Falls, where water cascades over a fern-swathed precipice into a delightful swimming pool, is the huge Curtain Fig Tree, which has resulted from a strangling fig taking over its host tree, climbing higher and higher and throwing down showers of roots to support its massive structure. There are dozens of other waterfalls in this area. Near **Millaa Millaa** is Falls Circuit, where the Millaa Millaa, Zillie, Mungalli and Elinjaa waterfalls are sited amid a magnificent panorama of rainforest mountains and plains.

There are four main highways linking the tablelands with the coast; all are magnificent scenic routes. Undoubtedly, however, the most novel and popular way of getting up to the tableland is by the scenic railway to **Kuranda**, built to serve the Herberton tin mine in the 1890s and now regarded as one of the most difficult feats of engineering in Queensland. The track climbs 300 metres in 20 kilometres to traverse the Barron Gorge, and part of it runs over a viaduct along the edge of a 200-metre precipice. The lovely old carriages of the train have rear platforms with decorative iron railings where travellers can stand and take in the superb view uninterrupted. The Kuranda railway station, festooned in tropical plants, ferns and orchids, is a much-photographed stop before the descent to Cairns. More recently the Skyrail Rainforest Cableway has been constructed between Smithfield, near Cairns, and Kuranda providing visitors an alternative: a spectacular gondola ride through the rainforest.

The Atherton and Evelyn Tablelands are areas of volcanic land at altitudes between 600 and 1000 metres, mild in climate and supporting dairying, maize and tobacco-farming. Gradually the tablelands change to dry, rough country, where tin, copper, lead and zinc were once mined. Beyond the main tableland settlement of Atherton is the fascinating mining town of Herberton, with its Historical Village, Tin festival each September, local museum called the Tin Pannikan and old houses proclaiming its boom days of the late nineteenth century. Ravenshoe, on the Kennedy Highway, is noted for its gemstones and fine timbers grown and milled in the area (the Torimba forest festival is held each October); and further west, Mount Garnet, an old mining town where tourists can pan the tailings.

Four-wheel drive tours of the region with an Aboriginal guide are available. Visitors are educated on the local Aboriginal sites, Dreamtime legends and native flora; details are available at Port Douglas Dive Centre. Near Mission Beach, join the Giramay Walkabout where members of the Giramay Aboriginal group share with visitors the beauty of the Murray Falls area, as well as their knowledge of the environment.

For further information on the Far North, contact the Far North Qld Promotion Bureau Ltd, cnr Grafton & Hartley Sts, Cairns; (070) 51 3588. For more information on the Atherton Tableland, contact the Atherton Tableland Promotion Bureau, cnr Mabel and Grafton Sts, Atherton; (070) 91 4222. **See also:** individual entries in A–Z listing for those towns indicated by bold type. **Map references:** 489, 495.

Atherton Tableland – its European history

A century ago the Atherton Tableland was unknown to Europeans until an aptly named prospector, James Venture Mulligan, led several expeditions south-west from Cooktown between 1874 and 1876, having previously discovered the spectacular Palmer River goldfields in 1873. The northern Aboriginal groups bitterly resented the miners' intrusion, and during the 1860s and 1870s there were many skirmishes between new settlers and Aborigines, and several massacres.

In 1874 Mulligan named the Hodgkinson and St George Rivers, and Mount Mulligan, north of the tobacco town of Dimbulah. He returned in 1875 and found a beautiful river flowing north. This was the Barron River, which eventually flows east to the Pacific coast. Mulligan travelled up the Barron and camped at Granite Creek, where Mareeba now stands. He travelled over rich basaltic plains, now the tobacco fields on the Kuranda road, until stopped by dense, impenetrable forest near what is now Tolga. He marvelled at huge cedar and kauri trees, but skirted the forest and camped near the site of Atherton. Nearby he discovered the Wild River and traces of tin. However, as the nearest ports were Cooktown and Cardwell, some 500 kilometres away, Mulligan considered the area too isolated for tin mining.

Mulligan later found extensive gold strikes as he prospected the valley. The Hodgkinson gold rush started as soon as he reported his find, most of the diggers coming from Cooktown and the Palmer River. The towns of Kingsborough and Thornborough quickly sprang up in 1876 between Mt Mulligan and Mareeba, and in two years the population was approximately 10 000.

This caused an unusual situation, the interior being opened up before a direct route to the coast had been discovered and a port founded. During 1876 several difficult tracks were cut down the steep, densely jungled coastal ranges towards Port Douglas and Trinity Bay. The latter eventually became Cairns. Some epic hauls up the range were recorded: in 1881, 80 bullocks hauled up the complete battery for the Great Northern tin mine at Herberton. An impressive monument at the foot of the Cairns–Kuranda road, the Kennedy Highway, commemorates the trailblazers.

The railway line from Cairns to Kuranda, on the edge of the Tableland, is only 34 kilometres long but took four years to build, cost 20 workers their lives, and has 15 tunnels. It was completed in 1888, and the prosperity of the Atherton Tableland, and Cairns, was assured.

In April 1877 John Atherton settled at the junction of Emerald Creek and the Barron River, and formed Emerald End station. When he found alluvial tin in the headwaters of the creek, he reputedly yelled 'Tinhurroo' to his mate – hence the name of the area, Tinaroo. Atherton led others to major tin lodes on the Wild River, discovered by Mulligan four years earlier. Mining commenced and the town of Herberton came into existence. The Tate River field was also an important find, and tin proved to be more influential in the development of the area than the short-term excitement of gold.

In 1880 Atherton built a wide-verandahed shanty at Granite Creek, a popular camping spot halfway between Port Douglas and Herberton, and used by men flocking to the new field. This became Mareeba. Eventually the railway linked Herberton and Ravenshoe with Cairns.

Peanut silos behind the original Council Chambers at Kingaroy

former Premier of Qld. Peanuts, maize, wheat, soy and navy beans are grown, and specialised agricultural equipment is manufactured. Kingaroy is 233 km NW of Brisbane and its giant peanut silos are a distinctive landmark. Kingaroy claims the title 'Peanut Capital of Australia', and also 'Baked Bean Capital of Australia', with 75 per cent of Australia's navy beans grown in the district. **Of interest:** In Haly St: Kingaroy Bicentennial Heritage Museum; Tourist Information Centre, with videos on peanut and navy-bean industries; Garden of Rocks, landscaping with semi-precious stones and petrified wood. Apr.: Peanut festival (odd-numbered years, drought permitting). **In the area:** Mt Wooroolin scenic lookout, 3 km W. Bunya Mountains National Park, 56 km SW. **Tourist information:** Haly St (opp. silos); (071) 62 3199. **Accommodation:** 5 hotels, 6 motels, 2 cara./camp. parks.

Kuranda Pop. 616

MAP REF. 489 E7, 495 M6

This village in the rainforest at the top of the Macalister Range is best known to tourists who have taken the 34-km trip from Cairns on the 100-year-old Scenic Railway or the more recent Skyrail cableway. **Of interest:** Railway station with platforms adorned by lush ferns and orchids. Skyrail Rainforest Cableway, spectacular gondola ride through rainforest to Cairns; return via Scenic Railway, or vice versa. Wildlife Noctarium, displays rainforest animals normally active only at night. Australian Butterfly Sanctuary, over 2000 butterflies in forest setting; guided tours available. Award-winning Tjapukai Aboriginal Dance Theatre; performs daily. Heritage markets and Bird Sanctuary in rainforest setting. Guided tours of river and rainforest depart from riverbank below railway station. Markets Wed.–Fri. and Sun. May: Folk festival. **In the area:** Paradise in the Rainforest, offers scenic rides on tractor train. Wrights Lookout, 7 km SE, offers views of the Barron Falls, spectacular after heavy rain. **Tourist information:** Far North Queensland Promotion Bureau, cnr Grafton and Hartley Sts, Cairns; (070) 51 3588. **Accommodation:** 2 hotels, 3 motels, 1 cara./camp. park. **See also:** Atherton Tableland; The Far North.

Kynuna Pop. 18

MAP REF. 499 J6

On the Matilda Hwy, 161 km NW of Winton, Kynuna was established in the 1860s and was a staging point for Cobb & Co. coaches. **Of interest:** Kynuna's only hotel is the famous Blue Heeler with its 1-m high, illuminated, blue heeler statue on roof. Waltzing Matilda Exhibition, open Apr.–Sept., in tent opposite hotel. Sept.: 'Surf' carnival, inland version of Iron Man contest. Nov.: Rodeo. **In the area:** Combo Waterhole, scene of the events described in 'Waltzing Matilda', Banjo Paterson's famous song, 24 km SE on western side of old Winton–Kynuna Rd. **Tourist information:** Blue Heeler Hotel, Matilda Hwy; (077) 46 8650. **Accommodation:** 1 hotel/motel, 2 cara./camp. parks.

Laidley Pop. 2315

MAP REF. 482 H9, 491 O9

Laidley, 75 km from Brisbane, is between Ipswich and Gatton, in the Lockyer Valley. It is the principal town in a rural area of the Greater Brisbane Region regarded as 'Queensland's country garden'. **Of interest:** Das Neumann Haus (1893), William St, an historic house with tourist centre and art gallery. Regular country markets each month. Sept.: Chelsea festival week. Oct.: Festival of performing arts. **In the area:** Laidley Pioneer Village, 1 km S, features original buildings from old township. Adjacent, Narda Lagoon, flora and fauna sanctuary; longest suspension footbridge in southern hemisphere crosses over lagoon. Lake Dyer, 1 km W; picnic/barbecue facilities nearby. Lake Clarendon, 17 km NW. Scenic drives; leaflets from Tourist information. **Tourist information:** Cnr William and Patrick Sts; (074) 65 3241. **Accommodation:** 2 hotels, 1 motel, 1 B&B.

Landsborough Pop. 1150

MAP REF. 483 M2, 486 E13, 491 P7

Landsborough is just off Glass House Mountains Tourist Dr., 9 km SW of the Caloundra turnoff from the Bruce Hwy. **Of interest:** In Maleny St: Historical museum; De Maine Pottery. Collectorama, a bottle, gemstone and shell museum; Glass House Mountains Tourist Dr. June: William Landsborough Day. **In the area:** Queensland Reptile and Fauna Park, 4 km S. Dularcha National Park, 5 km NW. Big Kart Track, 5 km N. **Tourist information:** Museum, Maleny St; (074) 941 755. **Accommodation:** 1 motel, 2 cara./camp. parks.

Logan

Pop. 132 000

MAP REF. 483 M9, 491 Q9

Captain Patrick Logan, one of the founders and first Commandant of the Moreton Bay Penal Settlement, first discovered the area now known as Logan. On 21 August 1862 he reported sighting a 'very considerable river which empties itself into the Moreton Bay. I have named it the Darling.' This river later became the Logan River, an acknowledgment by Governor Darling of Logan's 'zeal and efficient service'. The region was named after Logan when it was declared a shire in 1978; it became a city in 1981. Midway between Brisbane and the Gold Coast, Logan is Qld's fastest growing city. Enjoying close proximity to both Brisbane and the Gold Coast (a little more than half an hour from each), it has a strong economic base. **Of interest:** Mayes Cottage (1871), Mawarra St, a National Trust Building, once home of early pioneers. Daisy Hill Forest Park (430 ha), Daisy Hill Rd, offers bushwalking, horseriding, and viewing koalas and other wildlife. Kingston Butter Factory Community Art Centre, Milky Way, off Kingston Rd. Logan Hyperdome, off Pacific Hwy, largest shopping complex under one roof in Australia. Oct.: Street parade. Nov.: River festival and raft race. **Tourist information:** 4195 Pacific Hwy, Loganholme; (07) 3801 3400. **Accommodation:** 4 motels, 11 cara./camp. parks.

Longreach

Pop. 3607

MAP REF. 492 A11, 499 O11

Longreach has a relatively small population, but there are 800 000 sheep and 20 000 beef cattle in the area. It is the most important and prosperous town in the central west of the State. On the Thomson River, this friendly, modern town is some 700 km by road or rail west of Rockhampton. It was here in 1870 that Harry Redford, better known as Captain Starlight, with four mates rounded up 1000 head of cattle and drove them 2400 km into SA over wild unmapped country that only 10 years before had been the downfall of Burke and Wills. There Starlight sold the cattle. Since they did not belong to him, he was arrested in Adelaide and brought back to Qld to be put on trial at Roma. Despite the evidence, the jury found him not guilty, probably because of the pioneer philosophy that if you are daring enough to carry out that sort of deed, you deserve to get away with it! The events were the basis for Rolf Boldrewood's novel *Robbery Under Arms*. Although Qantas (**Q**ueensland **A**nd **N**orthern **T**erritory **A**ir **S**ervices) actually started in Winton, it soon moved its base to Longreach and began regular operations. The same hangar used then became Australia's first aircraft factory and the first of 6 DH-50 biplanes was assembled in 1926. The world's first Flying Surgeon Service started from Longreach in 1959. **Of interest:** Broad streets and several historic buildings: Uniting Church (1892), Galah St, built for Grazier's Association; court house (1892), Eagle St; post office (1902), cnr Duck and Galah Sts; railway station (1916), Sir Hudson Fysh Dr. Old machinery displayed at Powerhouse Museum, Swan St. Arts and Crafts, Ibis St; open p.m. Mar.–Oct. On Capricorn Hwy: Stockman's Hall of Fame and Outback Heritage Centre, featuring exhibition hall, theatre with audio-visuals, library and resource centre; nearby, Banjo's Outback Theatre and Pioneer Shearing Shed (open Mar.–Oct.); School of Distance Education (tours during term); Longreach Pastoral College (free tours daily). Qantas Park, Eagle St. Qantas Founders Outback Museum at airport, Matilda Hwy. Jackson's Weapon Museum, Cassowary St. Pamela's Doll Display and Syd's Outback Collection Corner, Quail St. Cobb & Co. coach rides around town. *Yellowbelly Express* and Billabong Boat Cruises, for cruises on Thomson River. Tourist Promotion Assoc. Markets, 2nd Sun. Apr.–Sept. June: Hall of Fame race meeting. Sept.: Starlight stampede (even-numbered years). **In the area:** Oakley Station, 10 min. N, tours available of this sheep and cattle station. Group tours available to quarter-horse stud at Longway Station, 16 km N. Folk Museum at Ilfracombe, 27 km E. Toobrack Station, 68 km S, 96-year-old homestead; open daily, also offers accommodation and camping. **Tourist information:** Qantas Park, Eagle St; (076) 58 3555. **Accommodation:** 3 hotels, 2 hotel/motels, 5 motels, 1 hostel, 2 cara./camp. parks.

Lucinda

Pop. 784

MAP REF. 495 O11

Lucinda, the port for Ingham's sugar, has the world's longest offshore sugar-loading jetty. The conveyor belt, 5.76 km long, loads 2000 tonnes of sugar an hour. Charter boats leave the Dungeness harbour for fishing, cruising and trips to the islands. **In the area:** Unique Italian cemetery, 3 km N. Wallaman Falls, 303-m-high single fall, 80 km S in Lumholtz National Park. **Tourist information:** Bruce Hwy, Ingham; (077) 76 5211. **Accommodation:** 1 hotel/motel, 1 cara./camp. park.

Stockman's Hall of Fame and Outback Heritage Centre at Longreach

The Herb Garden at Montville, near Maleny

Mackay
Pop. 40 250

MAP REF. 493 L5

Mackay is often called the sugar capital of Australia, producing one-third of the nation's sugar crop. Five mills operate in the area, and the bulk-sugar loading terminal is the world's largest. Sugar was first grown in 1866, a mill was built and in the same year Mackay became a town. It became a major port in 1939 when a breakwater was built, making it one of Australia's largest artificial harbours. The nearby Hay Point coal-loading terminals handle the output from the Central Qld coalfields. Gazetted in 1918, Mackay is now a progressive tropical city. Besides sugar and coal, the town's economy depends on beef cattle, dairying, timber, grain, seafood and the growing of tropical fruit. Tourism is a growth industry, with the islands of Brampton, Lindeman and Hamilton, and the Great Barrier Reef accessible from Mackay. **Of interest:** Self-guide heritage walk of historic buildings includes: Commonwealth and National Banks, town hall, court house, police station and customs house. Queens Park and Orchid House, Goldsmith St. Entertainment Centre, Gordon St. Replica of old Richmond sugar mill, Nebo Rd, houses Tourist information. Just north of town: Mt Bassett Weather Station and lookout; Mt Pleasant Reservoir and lookout. Numerous beaches: Harbour, Town, Blacks, Bucasia, Illawong, Lamberts and Shoal Point. Illawong Fauna Park at Illawong Beach. Cruises, fishing charters and scenic flights available. July: Festival of the arts. Sept.: Sugartime festival. **In the area:** Farleigh sugar mill, 15 km N; tours available during crushing season (July–Oct.). Cape Hillsborough National Park, 40 km N. Various lookouts off road to Eungella township. Eungella National Park, 84 km NW. Polstone Sugar Cane Farm, 15 km W; tours during July–Oct. Historic Greenmount Homestead, 20 km W, near Walkerston. Kinchant Dam, 20 km W of Walkerston. At Mirani, 30 km W, Juipera Walkabout, an educational walk with Aboriginal guide explaining use of plants; contact Mirani museum in Victoria St. Orchidways, orchid farm on Homebush Rd, 25 km S; closed Thurs. At Homebush: craft and art gallery; self-drive tour through historic Homebush area (pamphlet available at Tourist information). Lookout at Hay Point coal-loading-terminal, 30 km S. Cape Palmerston National Park, 80 km S; 4WD access only. **Tourist information:** The Mill, Nebo Rd; (079) 52 2677. **Accommodation:** 19 hotels, 29 motels, 10 cara./camp. parks.

Maleny
Pop. 789

MAP REF. 483 L2, 486 B11, 491 P7

A steep road climbs from the coast west to Maleny, 50 km SW of Maroochydore. The surrounding area is excellent dairy country. From Mary Cairncross Park, an area of thick rainforest south-east of town, there is a fine view of the Glass House Mountains to the south. These 10 spectacular trachyte peaks were named by Captain Cook as he sailed up the coast in 1770, for the sun shining on the rockfaces reminded him of glasshouses in his native Yorkshire. **Of interest:** Art and craft galleries. **In the area:** 28-km scenic drive north-east from Maleny through Montville and Flaxton to Mapleton (one of the best in south-east Qld); offering views of Sunshine Coast, Moreton Island, and nearby pineapple and sugarcane fields; museums, antique shops, fruit stalls, tea rooms and tourist attractions along the way. Montville, 17 km NE, has excellent potteries and art and craft galleries. At Flaxton, 3 km further N, miniature English village and clock museum. Kondalilla and Mapleton Falls in Main Range National Park, 7 km W of Montville. Lookout at Howell's Knob, 4 km W. Rainforest walks and spectacular views at Mary Cairncross Park, 7 km SE. **Tourist information:** Maroochy Tourist Information Centre, cnr Sixth Ave and Aerodrome Rd, Maroochydore; (074) 79 1566. **Accommodation:** 1 hotel, 3 motels, 1 cara./camp. park. **See also:** Sunshine Coast.

Mareeba
Pop. 6795

MAP REF. 489 C9, 495 M7

This town is at the centre of the main tobacco-growing region of Australia. Farms in the Mareeba-Dimbulah area are irrigated from Lake Tinaroo. Mining and cattle are also important industries. **Of interest:** Bicentennial Lakes, a park with plantings to encourage wildlife; Mason St. May: Dimbulah festival. July: Rodeo. **In the area:** Pinevale Ranch, 10 km E, offers day-horseriding. Granite Gorge, 12 km SW, off Chewko Rd. Mareeba Coffee Estates, 7 km W on Mareeba–Dimbulah road; inquire at Tourist information. Dirt and sealed road via Dimbulah crosses Great Dividing Range to Chillagoe (145 km W), old mining town with fine limestone caves nearby. **Tourist information:** Nata Travel, 150

Cape York

The Cape York Peninsula is a vast area as large as Victoria. There are more than 10 000 people living on the Cape. About half live in Weipa, and the rest in Aboriginal and Islander communities, isolated townships and scattered pastoral stations. Many of these are along the telegraph line which runs to the northern tip.

The first European exploration of Cape York was in the 1840s and the 1860s by the Jardine brothers, John Bradford, Robert Jack, and the ill-fated Edmund Kennedy and his famous Aboriginal guide Jacky Jacky. Little has changed since then. Vegetation varies from gums and anthills in the south to swamps and rainforests in the north. Many areas of the Cape are national parks and a sanctuary for much of Australia's unique flora and fauna. Further information on the national parks in the area and permits for camping may be obtained from the Department of Environment and Heritage, McLeod St, Cairns; (070) 52 3096.

There are two distinct seasons: the wet and the dry. During the wet virtually all road transport stops as there are almost no sealed roads or bridges in the area. The only movement during this season is by regular flights with Flight West and Sunstate airlines; both run scheduled daily flights to Cape York Airport. Some 50 kilometres further along a dirt track leads to the northernmost area of Cape York. The local Aboriginal place name for this area is Pajinka. Situated 400 metres from the very tip of the peninsula, on traditional Aboriginal land, is the comfortable Pajinka Wilderness Lodge providing cabin-style rooms with private amenities. Adjacent to the lodge is the Pajinka camping ground. Both are owned and operated by the Injinoo Aboriginal Community.

All Aboriginal and Islander communities are self-sufficient and may be visited, but *it is essential that a permit be obtained in writing beforehand.* The main communities are Lockhart River and Portland Roads on the east coast; Bamaga at the tip; and Edward River, Weipa South and Aurukun on the Gulf. The Ang-Gnarra Aboriginal Corporations at Laura offer a guide and ranger service to visitors. Details at the caravan park.

The Cape is the ideal place to go exploring. A reliable and well-equipped 4WD vehicle, preferably with a winch, is essential for this area. It is possible to drive north from Cairns or Mareeba to Bamaga through Laura and Coen. The Royal Automobile Club of Queensland provides an excellent map and information sheet; it is essential reading before an expedition north is planned. *Conditions on the track are unpredictable and the RACQ or police at Cairns should be contacted before heading north.*

June to November are the recommended travel months. At the peak of the season over one hundred vehicles travel northern Cape roads daily. The narrow, rough and blind roads are difficult, and a motorist travelling fast has no chance of avoiding an oncoming car. There are many accidents in this area each year. Drivers are advised to travel slowly and exercise particular care. The Laura, Kennedy, Stewart, Archer, Wenlock and Dulhunty Rivers must be forded. The Jardine River provides the main source of water for the local communities. In order to maintain this natural asset, it is requested that motorists do no attempt to cross the river at any point other than the ferry crossing. During good, dry conditions it is possible to take a conventional car, with care, north to Coen and west to Weipa.

Weipa, on the Gulf of Carpentaria, has the world's largest deposits of bauxite. Comalco offers conducted tours of the bauxite mining operation. Direct access to Weipa is by regular Ansett flights from Cairns.

Permits are required to enter the Injinoo area north of the Dulhunty River; these can be obtained on board the Jardine River ferry, or by contacting the Injinoo Community Council; (070) 69 3252.

For further information on Cape York, contact the Far North Qld Promotion Bureau Ltd, cnr Grafton & Hartley Sts, Cairns; (070) 51 3588. **See also:** Entry for Weipa in A–Z listing. **Map references:** 494 F2, 496.

Cape York, the northernmost region in Queensland, is largely a wilderness area

Byrnes St; (070) 92 1811. **Accommodation:** 4 hotels, 2 motels, 3 cara./camp. parks. **See also:** Atherton Tableland; Cape York.

Maroochydore   Pop. 28 509

MAP REF. 483 N1, 486 H9, 491 Q7

A well-established and popular beach resort, Maroochydore is the business centre of the Sunshine Coast, 112 km N of Brisbane. **Of interest:** Famous surfing beaches. Maroochy River, with pelicans and swans, offers safe swimming. Cotton Tree, at river mouth, popular camping area. Replica of Captain Cook's ship *Endeavour*, David Low Way. Oct.: Mapleton yarn festival. **In the area:** Mooloolaba, 5 km S. River cruises up Maroochy River to Dunethin Rock through sugarcane fields. Bli Bli Castle, 10 km NE, a 'medieval' castle with dungeon torture chamber and doll museum. Nostalgia Town, 11 km NE, emphasises humour in history. **Tourist information:** Cnr Sixth Ave and Aerodrome Rd; (074) 79 1566. **Accommodation:** 2 hotels, 11 motels, 4 cara./camp. parks. **See also:** Sunshine Coast.

Maryborough   Pop. 20 790

MAP REF. 491 P4

Maryborough is a well-planned, attractive, provincial city, 3 hours' drive north of Brisbane and situated on the banks of the Mary River, which was discovered in 1842. In 1847 a wool store was established near the original town site. A village and port soon grew to handle the wool being produced inland. The settlement was officially proclaimed a port in 1859 and a municipality in 1861. Maryborough is promoted as the Heritage City and visitors are encouraged to take the Heritage Walk and drive through the suburbs to see the excellent architecture of a bygone era. The climate is dry subtropical with warm moist summers and mild winters, and several seaside resorts are nearby. **Of interest:** Fine examples of early colonial architecture: Baddow House, Queen St, furnished in period style; St Paul's bell tower (1887), Lennox St, with one of the last sets of pealing bells in Qld; Brennan & Geraghty's Store, also in Lennox St, property of National Trust. Historic displays at Bond Store Museum, Wharf St. Croydon Foundry Office, Ferry St, includes museum and tourist information centre. Fruit Salad Cottage Heritage Museum, Banana St. Pioneer gravesites and original township site in Alice St, Baddow; historic time gun outside city hall. Several parks: in Sussex St, Queen's Park, unusual domed fernery and waterfall; in Kent St, Elizabeth Park, rose gardens; on cnr Cheapside and Alice Sts, Anzac Park; Ululah Lagoon, near the golf links, off Lions Dr., a scenic waterbird sanctuary where black swans, wild geese, ducks and waterhens may be hand-fed. Houseboat hire available at 102 Steindl St, Granville. Heritage City Market each Thurs., Adelaide and Kent Sts. May: Best of Brass. Sept.: Heritage City festival. **In the area:** Hervey Bay, Rainbow Beach, Tin Can Bay, Burrum Heads and Woodgate seaside resorts. Also at Hervey Bay, tours to see humpback whale migration. Fraser Island, just off coast, World Heritage-listed sand island. Pioneer museum at Brooweena, 49 km W on Biggenden Rd. Teddington Weir, 15 km S. Tuan Forest, 24 km SE. **Tourist information:** 30 Ferry St; (071) 21 4111. **Accommodation:** 5 hotel/motels, 8 motels, 6 cara./camp. parks.

Mary Kathleen   Pop. Nil

MAP REF. 498 F4

Well known to many Australians because of the controversial issue of uranium mining, Mary Kathleen was once a small mining town on the Barkly Hwy between Mount Isa and Cloncurry. The area has now been returned to its natural state, leaving no trace of the former inhabitants. In late 1982 the mine was shut down and by the end of 1983 the houses were sold and moved to new areas. Four buildings have been re-erected in the Mary Kathleen Memorial Park at Cloncurry. **In the area:** Mount Frosty, 8 km W off Mt Isa Rd, popular swimming-hole (not recommended for children as hole is some 9 metres deep with no shallow areas); nearby, fossicking area for minerals and gemstones. **Tourist information:** Centenary Park, Marian St, Mount Isa; (077) 44 4250.

Miles   Pop. 1260

MAP REF. 491 K7

Ludwig Leichhardt passed through the Miles district (340 km W of Brisbane) on three separate expeditions. He named the place Dogwood Crossing, after the shrub that grows on the banks of the creek. In 1878 the western railway line reached Dogwood Crossing, and Cobb & Co. continued the journey to Roma. The town was renamed Miles after a local member of parliament. The area has always been good sheep country, but today the emphasis is on cattle, mainly Herefords, and wheat; tall silos dominate the surrounding plains. After the spring rains the wildflowers are magnificent. **Of interest:** Historical village, Warrego Hwy, 'pioneer settlement' with all types of early buildings, a war museum, and vehicles and implements on display. Easter: Museum display. Sept.: Back to the Bush (includes wildflower festival). **In the area:** Gorges, walks, wildlife and fishing. Historical display at Possum Park, 21 km N; caravans and camping available, and ex-airforce ammunition store with underground bunkers converted for accommodation. Myall Park Botanical Gardens at Glenmorgan, 100 km SW. **Tourist information:** Historical village, Warrego Hwy; (076) 27 1492. **Accommodation:** 3 hotels, 4 motels, 2 cara./camp. parks.

Millaa Millaa   Pop. 325

MAP REF. 495 M8

Located 75 km inland from Innisfail, Millaa Millaa is noted for the many spectacular waterfalls in the area. The town's main industry is dairying. **Of interest:** Eacham Historical Society Museum. **In the area:** Millaa Millaa Falls, Zillie Falls and Elinjaa Falls – all seen from 15-km gravel road that leaves and rejoins Palmerston Hwy east of town. Millstream Falls, 40 km SW. White-water rafting on Tully River, south of town. Lookout to west of town for excellent views of district. **Tourist information:** Rainforest Holiday Park, Palmerston Hwy; (070) 97 2290. **Accommodation:** 1 hotel, 1 cara./camp. park. **See also:** Atherton Tableland; The Far North.

Millmerran   Pop. 1159

MAP REF. 482 A10, 491 M10

This town on the Condamine River produces eggs, cotton, grain, vegetables, cattle and wool. **Of interest:** Historical Society Museum, Charlotte St. **In the area:** Ned's Corner, offering camp-oven meals, Australiana, yarns and poetry; 27 km N, open by appt. **Tourist information:** Toowoomba and Golden West Tourist Association, 541 Ruthven St,

Toowoomba; (076) 32 1988. **Accommodation:** 1 hotel, 1 motel, 1 cara./camp. park.

Miriam Vale   Pop. 447

MAP REF. 491 M1, 493 Q13

Situated on the Bruce Hwy, 150 km N of Bundaberg, this town is renowned for its mud-crab sandwiches. Watch for the Giant Crab. The twin towns of Town of Seventeen Seventy and Agnes Water lie 25 km E. Captain Cook, while on his voyage of discovery in Australian waters, made his first landing in Qld at the Town of Seventeen Seventy. Estuary and beaches provide ideal spots to get away from it all. Fishing is excellent. **Tourist information:** Discovery Coast Information Centre, Roe St; (079) 74 5428. **Accommodation:** 1 hotel, 1 motel, 1 cara./camp. park.

Mission Beach   Pop. 814

MAP REF. 495 N9

This quiet tropical 14-km-long beach with magnificent golden sand, close to Tully, is fringed by coconut palms and unique heritage rainforest. The Great Barrier Reef is close to shore. Day cruise and sailing trips to Dunk and surrounding islands (excluding Bedarra) can be taken from the jetty at Clump Point. A cairn at Tam O'Shanter Point commemorates the ill-fated 1848 Cape York expedition of Edmund Kennedy. Monster Markets, last Sun. each month (Easter–Nov.). July: Cassowary festival. Oct.: Aquatic festival; Sailing regatta. **In the area:** Art and craft galleries. Horseriding, boat and jetski hire, tandem parachuting, game and island reef fishing. Water taxis to Dunk Island. Guided and self-guide rainforest walks; scenic drives; calm water, guided, canoe trips; croc-spotting tours on Hull River – contact Tourist information. Giramay Walkabout and Clump Mountain Walk, Aboriginal cultural experiences; half or full-day. Railway station with its tropical-plant display at Tully, 24 km W. Nearby, Tully Sugar Mill, tours during crushing season (July–Oct.). Whitewater rafting and kayaking on Tully River, beginning in Tully Gorge, 70 km inland; also superb scenery and swimming in the top reaches of the river. **Tourist information:** Porters Promenade; (070) 68 7099. **Accommodation:** 1 hotel/ motel, 4 motels, 3 B&B, 7 cara./camp. parks.

Mitchell   Pop. 1101

MAP REF. 490 F6

This typical western country town, on the banks of the Maranoa River, lies on the Warrego Hwy between Roma and Charleville, and was named after Sir Thomas Mitchell, explorer and Surveyor-General of NSW, who visited the region in 1845. **Of interest:** Kenniff Court House, Cambridge St, features court-room display and local craft; operating artesian windmill in grounds. Also in Cambridge St, Nalingu Aboriginal Corporation for directions and/or guided tours of local Aboriginal community's cultural and heritage centre at Yumba, 3 km E. **In the area:** *There are no facilities north of town. For all tours north, sufficient petrol and supplies must be carried for return trip; read section on Outback Motoring.* Tourist road (mostly unsealed) leads north into Great Dividing Range; views of impressive sandstone formations, some with Aboriginal rock-art paintings. This region was former stronghold of local turn-of-century bushrangers, the Kenniff brothers; monument and statues erected at the site of their last stand, 7 km S. Carnarvon National Park, 256 km N; camping, walking tracks and two major Aboriginal art sites. Bird sanctuary and picnic/barbecue facilities near Neil Turner Weir, 3.5 km NW. **Tourist information:** Shire Offices, 100 Cambridge St; (076) 23 1133. **Accommodation:** 5 hotels, 2 motels, 2 cara./camp. parks.

Thursday Island

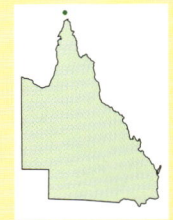

Situated 35 kilometres north-west off the tip of Cape York Peninsula in the Torres Strait, Thursday Island is a colourful outpost. Its population of around 2900 is made up of islanders, a minority of Europeans, Malays, Polynesians, Chinese and Japanese. At Rosie's Shop, at the corner of Douglas and Blackall Streets, a range of Torres Strait Islander and Aboriginal artifacts are available for purchase. The Harbours and Marine Department's Torres Strait Pilot Service operates from its harbour, once the base for 150 pearling luggers. Ferry and day cruises depart from the harbour and operate between Bamaga, Horn Island, Punsand Bay and Pajinka Wilderness Lodge. A Cultural festival is held each May.

View towards Thursday Island

For further information contact the Far North Qld Promotion Bureau Ltd, cnr Grafton & Hartley Sts, Cairns; (070) 51 3588. **Map reference:** 496 C2

National Parks

The diverse landscapes of Queensland's national parks lure visitors by the million each year. They are drawn not only to the endless stretches of sandy beaches and the magnificent Great Barrier Reef cays and islands off the coast, but also to the cooler mountains of the southern ranges, the inland plains and semi-arid areas, and the wilderness of Cape York.

Many parks and reserves are accessible by conventional vehicle, some require a 4WD. Their major attraction is the climate – beautiful one day, perfect the next! Certainly, daytime temperatures in the north and west can reach a searing 40°C or more in summer, and the monsoon period (November to March) brings the occasional cyclone and rainfall that can be measured in metres, but other than these extremes, the climate makes for pleasant visits and extended bushwalking, camping and other recreation-based activities are popular with visitors.

Great Sandy National Park on Fraser Island

In the south-east of the State

Around Brisbane, the crescent of national parks, or Scenic Rim, includes **Main Range**, **Mount Barney**, **Lamington** and **Springbrook** national parks. These offer Brisbane residents and visitors panoramic views, extensive walking tracks, picnic facilities and a range of recreational opportunities. Lamington attracts visitors by the thousands to its cool rainforest, rich in elkhorn and staghorn ferns and over 700 plant species, including orchids.

Tamborine National Park, in the Gold Coast hinterland attracts many day visitors from Brisbane and the Gold Coast to its varied rainforests, waterfalls and scenic lookouts. **Girraween National Park**, the 'Place of Flowers', located south of Stanthorpe and close to the New South Wales border, offers visitors the best floral displays in the State. This area is a photographer's paradise, while the park's massive granite outcrops provide a challenge for the rock climber.

Offshore in Moreton Bay, **Moreton Island National Park** is predominantly a wilderness area with vast tracts of sand dunes including Mt Tempest (280 m), which is probably the tallest permanent sand dune in the world. On the leeward side near the resort, wild dolphins make regular visits to be fed by visitors.

Bunya Mountains National Park, 250 kilometres north-west of Brisbane, was established to preserve the last remaining large community of bunya pine forest. It was here that Aborigines used to gather about every third year to feast on bunya nuts. Further east lie the **Glass House Mountains**, eroded volcanic plugs that rise suddenly from the landscape. First sighted by Captain Cook in 1770, four of these mountains are in the national park – Coonoorwin, Tibrogargan, Ngungun, and Beerwah.

Noosa National Park, 160 kilometres north of Brisbane, offers the visitor a wide variety of coastal scenery. Walking tracks lead to lookouts from which can be seen such unusual rock formations as Hell's Gates, Boiling Pot and Fairy Pool. Located further north off Hervey Bay is the world's largest sand island, Fraser Island. The northern third of the island is **Great Sandy National Park**. This and its Cooloola section on the mainland require 4WD vehicles for access; the Cooloola section offers excellent boating opportunities, particularly on the Noosa River.

Launches and charter vessels from several central Queensland ports will take visitors to Heron, Masthead, North West and Lady Musgrave Islands, all rich in coral and marine life and a paradise for snorkellers and scuba divers. The Southern Reef islands are outstanding rookeries of the loggerhead and green turtles, and the summer nesting-grounds for thousands of wedgetailed shearwaters and white-capped noddies. **Lady Musgrave Island** is a charming coral cay reached from Bundaberg and Town of Seventeen Seventy. Around the cay's edge, exposed to wind and salt spray, grows a vegetation fringe of casuarina and pandanus, which protects the shady pisonia forest on the inner part of the island. The sheltered lagoon is popular for sailing, snorkelling and reef-viewing in glass-bottomed boats.

Coastal parks around Bundaberg include Burrum Coast National Park, and Baldwin Swamp and Mon Repos conservation parks. **Burrum Coast National Park**, south of Bundaberg, covers 21 300 hectares and provides an essential habitat for wildlife; plant communities in the park include mangroves lining the Gregory and Burrum Rivers, wallum heathland, eucalypt and angophora forests, ti-tree swamps and small pockets of palm forest. Roads within the park are gravel or sand, and 4WD vehicles are recommended, although at times conventional vehicle access is possible. Situated only 3 kilometres east of Bundaberg and covering 40 hectares is the Baldwin Wetlands, containing the **Baldwin Swamp Conservation Park**. Walking tracks and a boardwalk allow observation of the park's wildlife. **Mon Repos Conservation Park**, 14 kilometres east of Bundaberg, is eastern Australia's largest mainland turtle rookery. The turtle season extends from November to March. Visitors to the information centre gain some basic knowledge of sea turtles and acceptable human interaction with them. This ensures that a visit to the rookery is an enlightening and enjoyable experience.

Eurimbula National Park is south-east of Gladstone, near the twin communities of Agnes Water and Town of Seventeen Seventy. Over 200 years ago Captain Cook and his crew chose this picturesque stretch of coast, with its broad sandy beaches between small rocky headlands, for their first landing in what is now Queensland. Botanically this is a key coastal area, preserving a complex array of vegetation, including some plants common in southern areas and others found in northern forests. Inland parks in this area include Auburn River and Cania Gorge national parks. **Auburn River National Park**, south-west of Mundubbera, protects an area of open eucalypt forest and dry scrub. The Auburn River flows through this 390-hectare park over a jumbled mass of pink granitic boulders. Over time, water erosion has sculptured the river's rock pools and cataracts. Vegetation along the river banks includes stunted figs, and bottle trees are common. Rainforest species occur in some areas and small lizards can be seen sunbaking on rocks near the water. North-west of Monto, **Cania Gorge National Park** features prominent sandstone cliffs up to 70 metres high, cave formations, dry rainforest on sheltered slopes and open eucalypt forest. This park protects a valuable scenic resource and provides an important wildlife habitat.

In the north-east of the State

Queensland's central and northern coastal islands range from large, steep continental types to coral cays, many of them lying between the mainland and the outer Great Barrier Reef. Several national park islands have been developed for tourism; these include **Hinchinbrook**, one of the world's largest national park islands with 39 900 hectares of wilderness and quiet beaches. More than 90 per cent of the 100 islands in the Whitsunday Group are national parks and six also have resorts. Sail-yourself yachts are a novel way to visit some of the more isolated spots.

Two well-known parks around Mackay are Eungella and Cape Hillsborough national parks. **Eungella National Park**, 83 kilometres west of Mackay, is the Aboriginal 'Land of the Clouds'. It is one of Queensland's wildest and most majestic parks, and the freshness under the canopy of rainforest makes it a perfect destination for a day trip. Many visitors, however, choose to camp by the Broken River, where the normally shy platypus

Lush rainforest and crystal-clear creeks, a feature of Daintree National Park

Causeway and mangroves at Cape Hillsborough National Park

QUEENSLAND

can be seen swimming casually in the creek waters. **Cape Hillsborough National Park**, 50 kilometres north-west of Mackay, often referred to as 'the island you can drive to', combines the beauty of an island with the accessibility of the mainland. Wildlife includes kangaroos, wallabies, possums, echidnas and numerous bird species.

Within a several-hundred-kilometre radius of Cairns are scores of national parks catering for all tastes. About 50 kilometres from Cairns is the Atherton Tableland, on which lie several national parks. Here visitors can follow walking tracks through spectacular rainforest at **Mt Hypipamee**, or visit the 65-metre-wide **Millstream Falls**, or the famous crater lakes of Eacham and Barrine in **Crater Lakes National Park**.

A north Queensland visit would not be complete without a train trip to Kuranda via **Barron Gorge National Park**, or a visit to the **Wooroonooran**, **Lumholtz** and **Daintree** national parks. This undeveloped mountainous country, with its scenic waterfalls and lush rainforest, should not be missed. **Chillagoe-Mungana Caves National Park**, three hours' drive from Cairns, is dominated by weird limestone outcrops, castle-like pinnacles that house a wonderland of colourful caves. Guided tours are conducted daily. Once Queensland's leading mineral producing area, it is still popular with fossickers.

Today Cape York Peninsula is like a magnet to tourists, even though the only aim of thousands of visitors may be simply to stand at its tip. The peninsula's vast and monotonous country is interspersed with surprising pockets of forest, broad vegetation-fringed rivers and occasional waterfalls – all the home of a wide variety of wildlife. **Jardine River**, **Mungkan Kandju** and **Iron Range** national parks are destinations for keen and experienced wilderness explorers. However, a growing number of visitors divert to **Lakefield**. Its fringing rainforest, paperbark woodland, open grassy plains, swamps and coastal mudflats leading to mangroves along Princess Charlotte Bay, all offer a variety of attractions for the most demanding visitor. Basic campsites are located along many watercourses.

In the north-west of the State

One of the most breathtakingly beautiful scenic reserves in Australia is **Carnarvon National Park**, 720 kilometres by road north-west of Brisbane. The Carnarvon Gorge section of this park, a dramatic, twisting chasm of soft sandstone gouged from vertical white cliffs, is a popular destination for campers. Formed walking tracks lead through forests of eucalypt, she-oaks, tall cabbage palms and relic macrozamia palms. Two major Aboriginal art sites, the Art Gallery and Cathedral Cave, contain rock paintings of great significance. Year-round limits on visitor numbers protect the ecology of the park.

In the remote north-west of Queensland, **Lawn Hill National Park** is an oasis on the edge of the Barkly Tableland. The road into the park is very rough in places, so 4WD travel is recommended, especially for caravanners. Lawn Hill Gorge has colourful cliffs rising 60 metres to the surrounding plateau. On the gorge walls are Aboriginal rock paintings, and middens also remain. Visitors can see these from the boardwalk and viewing platforms. The creek has permanent water and offers a habitat for tropical vegetation including cabbage tree palms and Leichhardt pines. The water attracts various bird species and reptiles, including freshwater crocodiles, tortoises and water monitors. There are over 20 kilometres of walking tracks in the park. World Heritage-listed Riversleigh Fosssil Field, site of unique fossil finds of previously unknown animals, is an extension to the park.

For more information about Queensland's national parks, including the requirement for camping permits, contact the Naturally Queensland Information Centre, 160 Ann St, Brisbane (PO Box 155, Brisbane Albert St 4002); (07) 3227 8185.

Monto
Pop. 1339

MAP REF. 491 M2

Monto, on the Burnett Hwy, 250 km inland from Bundaberg, is the centre of a rich dairying, beef cattle and agricultural district. June: Dairy festival (even-numbered years). **In the area:** Cania Gorge National Park, 25 km N, features spectacular sandstone formations. **Tourist information:** Three Moon Motel, 4 Flinders St; (071) 66 1777. **Accommodation:** 2 motels, 1 cara./camp. park.

Mooloolaba
Pop. part of Maroochydore

MAP REF. 483 N1, 486 I9, 491 Q7

Because of its excellent, clean, sandy beach and variety of restaurants and nightlife, Mooloolaba is popular for both family and young people's holidays. The Mooloolaba Esplanade, offering beachside resort shopping, rises to the bluff at Alexandra Headland. From the headland there are sweeping panoramic views up the beach to the Maroochy River and Mudjimba Island, with Mt Coolum creating an impressive backdrop. Alexandra Headland beach is a popular board-riding location. One of the safest anchorages on the eastern coast is at Mooloolaba Harbour. **Of interest:** Underwater World complex, on The Spit, includes the Oceanarium with its 80-m transparent tunnel for viewing three separate marine environments, the Wharf, and many restaurants and specialty shops. Harbour: finishing point for the annual Sydney-to-Mooloolaba yacht race in Apr.; also base for Sunshine Coast's main prawning and fishing fleet; and for pilot vessels guiding ships into Port of Brisbane. Yachting and game-fishing trips to near offshore reefs available. Paraflying off Mooloolaba Beach. **Tourist information:** Cnr Aerodrome Rd and Sixth Ave, Maroochydore; (074) 79 1566. **Accommodation:** 2 hotels, 10 motels, 3 cara./camp. parks.

Moranbah
Pop. 6525

MAP REF. 492 I7

Located just off the Peak Downs Hwy, 200 km SW of Mackay, this town services the huge open-cut coal mines of the expanding Bowen Coal Basin. Coking coal is railed to the Hay Point export terminal just south of Mackay. **Of interest:** Tours to Peak Downs Mine leave town square each Thurs. 10 a.m. **Tourist information:** Shire Offices, Goonyella Rd; (079) 41 7254. **Accommodation:** 1 hotel/motel, 1 motel, 2 cara./camp. parks.

Mossman
Pop. 1771

MAP REF. 489 B3, 495 M5

Mossman, the sugar town of the north, situated 78 km NW of Cairns on the Captain Cook Hwy, is surrounded by green mountains and fields of green sugarcane. June: Bavarian festival. **In the area:** Mt Demi (1159 m) towers over town. Popular beaches: Cooya, Newell and Wonga. Mossman Gorge, 9 km S, short walk through rainforest to picturesque cascades. Rex Lookout, 30 km SE, for stunning coastal views. A further 3 km S, Hartleys Creek Wildlife Reserve features crocodiles and other native fauna. Tropical fruit and restaurant in rainforest setting at High Falls Farm, Miallo, 15 km N. Wonga Belle Orchid Garden, 20 km N. Exotic jungle river cruises on Daintree River, 25 km N. Daintree National Park, 64 km NE, largest tract of tropical rainforest in Australia. **Tourist information:** Port Douglas and Cooktown Tourist Information Centre, 23 Macrossan St, Port Douglas; (070) 99 5599. **Accommodation:** 2 hotels, 2 motels, 1 cara./camp. park. **See also:** The Far North.

Mount Isa
Pop. 23 667

MAP REF. 498 E4

In 1923, John Campbell Miles discovered a rich silver-lead deposit on the western edge of the Cloncurry field. Today the progressive city of Mount Isa is the most important industrial, commercial and administrative centre in north-west Qld. The city is a company town, with Mount Isa Mines operating one of the largest silver-lead mines in the world. Copper and zinc are also mined and processed. Ore trains run 900 km E to Townsville for shipment. The city is an oasis of civilisation with excellent amenities and facilities in the otherwise hot and monotonous spinifex and cattle country surrounding it. **Of interest:** Surface and underground mine tours, advance bookings essential. Lead smelter stack, Australia's tallest free-standing structure (265 m). Riversleigh Interpretive Centre, Centenary Park, features displays of fossil discoveries in Riversleigh area 200 km NW and of early Aboriginal occupation. In Church St: John Middlin Mining Display and Visitors Centre; Frank Aston Underground Museum, opp. KMart. National Trust Tent House, Fourth Ave. Kalkadoon Tribal Centre and Cultural Keeping Place, Marian St. Mt Isa Potters Gallery, Alma St. Flying Doctor Service base, Barkly Hwy. School of Distance Education, Kalkadoon High School, Abel Smith Pde; open schooldays, tours a.m. City Lookout, Hilary St. Donaldson Memorial lookout and walking track, off Marian St. Apr.: Country music festival. Aug.: Rodeo (attracts rough-riders from all over Qld; population almost doubles during this time). **In the area:** Artificial Lake Moondarra, 15 km N, a wildlife sanctuary offering swimming, water sports and picnic/barbecue facilities nearby. Lake Julius and surrounds 100 km NE, features Aboriginal cave paintings, fishing, water-skiing, nature trails and abandoned goldmine. Air-charter companies provide flights to excellent barramundi fishing grounds near Birri Fishing Lodge at Birri Beach on Mornington Island and Sweers Island in Gulf of Carpentaria. Gunpowder Resort, 140 km NW, offers several activities ranging from bull-catching to water-skiing. Tours of World Heritage-listed Riversleigh Fossil Site, 200 km NW, an extension of Lawn Hill National Park, 500 km NW. Camooweal, 188 km NW on Barkly Hwy, last Qld town before crossing NT border. Mount Frosty, 53 km E, old limestone mine and swimming-hole, popular area for fossickers. Burke and Wills memorial cairn near Corella River, 90 km E. **Tourist information:** Riversleigh Interpretive Centre, Centenary Park, Marian St; (077) 44 4250. **Accommodation:** 4 hotels, 13 motels, 2 hostels, 8 cara. parks.

Mount Morgan
Pop. 2782

MAP REF. 493 N11

Located 32 km SW of Rockhampton, the crater of the Mount Morgan open-cut gold, silver and copper mine is the largest excavation in the southern hemisphere, measuring some 800 m across and 185 m deep. In the golden heyday of the mine, around 1910, the town had 14 000 people. Mine tours leave town 1 p.m. daily. **Of interest:** Museum, Morgan St. Court house and other historic buildings have National Trust classifications. At Railway Station, Burnett Hwy: restored 1904 steam engine and operational 5-stamp ore-crusher battery from old mine; fettler's trolley rides along 4-km track. May: Golden Mount festival. **In the area:** The Big Dam, 2.7 km N via William St, for boating. **Tourist information:** Railway Station, Burnett Hwy; (079) 38 2312. **Accommodation:** 3 hotels, 1 hotel/motel, 2 cara./camp. parks. **See also:** The Capricorn Region.

Mourilyan — Pop. 446

MAP REF. 495 N8

Mourilyan, located 7 km S of Innisfail, is the bulk-sugar outlet for sugar produced in the Innisfail area. **Of interest:** Australian Sugar Museum, Bruce Hwy. **In the area:** South-west on Old Bruce Hwy: tours of South Johnstone Sugar Mill (8 km) in season, July–Oct.; National Trust-classified Paronella Park (15 km), ruins of Spanish castle set in rainforest; suspension bridge, waterfall, and picnic and camping areas nearby. Etty Bay, 8 km E, quiet tropical beach. **Tourist information:** Australian Sugar Museum, Bruce Hwy; (070) 63 2306. **Accommodation:** 1 hotel.

Mundubbera — Pop. 1118

MAP REF. 491 M4

The citrus capital of the State, Mundubbera is on the Burnett Hwy, 410 km NW of Brisbane. **Of interest:** Big Mandarin Information Centre, also has local art and craft. Jones Weir, Bauer St. **In the area:** Golden Mile Orchard, 13 km W, open Apr.–Sept.; tours of packing sheds. Rare Neoceratodus (lungfish) found in Burnett River. Auburn River National Park, 40 km SW. Peanut, maize and bean crops on Gurgeena and Binjour Plateaus, to north-east. **Tourist information:** Big Mandarin Information Centre, Dalby–Durong Hwy; (071) 65 4549. **Accommodation:** 2 motels, 1 cara./camp. park.

Murgon — Pop. 2210

MAP REF. 491 N6

Murgon, known as the beef capital of the Burnett, is one of the most attractive towns in southern Qld. Settlement dates back to 1843 and the name comes from an Aboriginal word meaning 'lily pond'. Beef, dairying and mixed crops are the main industries. The town is 101 km inland from Gympie and 46 km N of Kingaroy. **Of interest:** Vic Rewald's Lapidary Display, semi-precious gemstone collection; Nutt St. Queensland Dairy Museum, Gayndah Rd. Adjacent, relocated Trinity Homestead, one of district's original buildings. **In the area:** Cherbourg Emu Farm at Cherbourg Aboriginal Community, 5 km SW, has walk-through enclosures, educational displays and sales of emu products and Aboriginal artifacts. Bjelke-Petersen Dam, 15 km SE, for water sports and fishing. Nature walk and scenic views in Jack Smith Scrub Conservation Park, 15 km NE; adjacent, Boat Mountain Conservation Park. **Tourist information:** 118 Lamb St; (071) 68 1984. **Accommodation:** 1 hotel/motel, 1 motel, 2 cara. parks.

Muttaburra — Pop. 195

MAP REF. 492 A9, 499 P9

Muttaburra, 119 km N of Longreach, was developed as a town in the late 1870s, the name being derived from an Aboriginal word meaning 'meeting of the waters'. **Of interest:** Joe Amatta Memorial Museum, in old hospital, Sword St; tours by appt, contact Tourist information. Behind museum, site of Shearers' Strike 1891. Replica of dinosaur, Edkins St. June: Landsborough flock ewe show. **In the area:** The area has many fossil remains as it was formerly part of an inland sea. The name Muttaburrasaurus was given to a previously unknown dinosaur, the fossilised bones of which were discovered here. Fishing and water-skiing in Landsborough River, 6 km S. Agate fossicking, 5 km W. **Tourist information:** Muttaburra Motors and Cafe, Edkins St; (076) 58 7140. **Accommodation:** 1 hotel, 1 cara./camp. park.

Nambour — Pop. 10 355

MAP REF. 483 M1, 486 E8, 491 P7

Nambour is a busy provincial town, 106 km N of Brisbane, just off the Bruce Hwy. The district was settled in the 1860s, mainly by disappointed miners from the Gympie goldfields, and sugar has been the main crop since the 1890s. Small locomotives pulling trucks of sugarcane trundle across the main street to Moreton Central Mill during the crushing season (July–Oct.). Pineapples and other tropical fruit are grown extensively. Nambour is the Aboriginal name for the red-flowering ti-tree that grows locally. **In the area:** Spectacular Glass House Mountains to south, and scenic Blackall Range to west. The Big Pineapple complex, home of the Big Pineapple and Macfarms macadamia nut factory, 7 km S. Moonshine Valley Winery, Forest Glen deer sanctuary and Super Bee honey factory, 10 km further S on Forest Glen–Tanawha Tourist Drive. Beach resorts of Maroochydore and Mooloolaba, 20 km E. **Tourist information:** The Big Pineapple complex, Bruce Hwy, Woombye; (074) 42 1333. **Accommodation:** 12 hotels, 8 motels, 2 cara./camp. parks. **See also:** Sunshine Coast.

Nanango — Pop. 2571

MAP REF. 491 N7

Gold was mined here from 1850 to 1900, but the area, 24 km SE of Kingaroy, now relies on beef cattle, beans and grain. The 1400-megawatt Tarong Power Station and Meandu Coal Mine, 18 km SW, are also of economic importance to the area. **Of interest:** Astronomical Observatory, Faulkners Rd. Market, 1st Sun. each month. Oct.: Pioneer festival. **In the area:** Berlin's Gem and Historical Museum, 17 km SW. Coomba Falls, near Maidenwell, 28 km SW. Bunya Mountains National Park, 84 km SW. Forest drive from Benarkin, 40 km SE. **Tourist information:** Shire Offices, 48 Drayton St; (071) 63 1307. **Accommodation:** 3 hotels, 3 motels, 2 cara./camp. parks.

Nebo — Pop. 160

MAP REF: 493 K6

Nebo is situated 100 km SW of Mackay on the Peak Downs Hwy. Beef cattle and grain-farming are the major industries. **Of interest:** Nebo Museum, Reynolds St. July: Rodeo. **Tourist information:** Shire Offices, 10 Reynolds St; (079) 50 5133. **Accommodation:** 1 hotel, 1 motel, 1 cara./camp. park.

Nerang — Pop. 10 174

MAP REF. 483 N12, 485 C5, 491 Q10

This town in the Gold Coast hinterland is 10 km from Southport. **In the area:** At Carrara, 5 km SE, weekend Hinterland country market. Hinze Dam on

Tea Tree Bay, near Noosa off Queensland's Sunshine Coast

Advancetown Lake, 8 km SW, good for swimming and sailing. Spectacular scenery in Numinbah Valley area, 15 km SW near Beechmont. Towards Springbrook, 42 km SW: Wunburra Lookout on Springbrook Plateau; Best of All View, off Repeater Station Rd; Purlingbrook Falls in Springbrook National Park. Natural Bridge section of Springbrook National Park, 38 km SW, popular picnic spot, walking tracks through scenic rainforest, lookout nearby, glow-worms in cave under bridge. Lookout near Mt Tamborine, 20 km NE, offers spectacular views to Gold Coast and north to South Stradbroke Island. **Tourist information:** Cavill Mall, Surfers Paradise; (07) 5538 4419. **Accommodation:** 2 hotels, 3 motels, 1 cara./camp. park.

Noosa Pop. 17 776

MAP REF. 486 H1, 491 Q6

Noosa extends from Tewantin to Sunshine Beach and includes Noosa Heads and the commercial area Noosa Junction. The most northerly of the Sunshine Coast resorts, it is noted for its natural scenery. A combination of the Noosa National Park, a protected main beach facing north, the Noosa River and lakes system, and Qld sunshine, has made a fashionable, relaxed resort with temperate weather and safe year-round swimming. Wildlife abounds in the area. There are excellent restaurants and accommodation, but without Gold Coast-style high-rise development. Tewantin, 6 km up river, was first settled in the 1870s as a base for timber-cutters. Noosaville, on the river between Tewantin and Noosa Heads, is a family-style resort. **Of interest:** At Tewantin: Noosa Regional Gallery, Pelican St; Big Shell, Gympie St; House of Bottles, Myles St. Selina Antiques, Sunshine Beach Rd, at Noosa Junction. Noosa National Park, between Noosa Heads and Sunshine Beach, features walks, surfing beach, rocky headlands, Cook's monument, Devils kitchen (blowhole), sandy coves, patches of rainforest and views of river and lakes from Laguna Lookout. June: Aqueous festival of arts. Sept.: Jazz party. Oct.: Beach car classic, triathlon. **In the area:** Camel rides on Noosa's north-shore beach. Horseriding through the bush. Within 20–40 km N: Stranded freighter *Cherry Venture* (accessible by 4WD); Noosa River Everglades (part accessible by car) – both accessible via boat tours from Noosaville; Cooloola section of Great Sandy National Park (accessible by 4WD). Coloured sands of Teewah in Cooloola section, multi-coloured sand cliffs that rise to over 200 metres; considered to be over 40 000 years old. Noosa Lakes system, navigable for 50 km into Great Sandy National Park, ideal for boating, sailing and windsurfing; houseboat hire available. Boreen Point, holiday and sailing centre near Lake Cootharaba, 21 km N of Tewantin. At Eumundi, 16 km SW, markets held each Sat. Dig for volcanic rocks at Thunder Egg Farm, 30 km SW. **Tourist information:** Hastings St roundabout, Noosa Heads; (074) 47 4988. **Accommodation:** 47 hotels/ motels, 3 cara./camp. parks. **See also:** Sunshine Coast.

Normanton Pop. 1189

MAP REF. 494 C8, 497 I8

Normanton, 151 km from Croydon, is the central town of the Gulf Savannah and is situated on a high, gravel ridge on the edge of the savannah grasslands that extend to the west and the wetlands that extend to the north. The town is also the terminus of the historic Normanton to Croydon railway, and the Normanton railway station is the home of the award-winning *Gulflander* tourist train. **Of interest:** Penitentiary, Haig St. Restored Bank of NSW building, Little Brown St. Town well, Landsborough St; no longer in use. June: Show, rodeo and gymkhana. **In the area:** Fishing and camping at Walkers Creek, 32 km NW, and Norman River at Glenore, 23 km S. Lakes on outskirts of Normanton attract jabirus, brolgas, herons and other birds. Shady Lagoons, 18 km E, for bush camping, bird watching and wildlife. Dorunda station, 170 km NE, cattle station offering barramundi and saratoga fishing in lake and rivers, and accommodation. Karumba, 69 km NW, prawn-fishing centre for Gulf region. Burke and Wills Cairn, 40 km SW. Bang Bang Jump Up rock formation, 106 km SW, a solitary hill on the surrounding flat plains; road goes over top, excellent views. **Tourist information:** Shire Offices, Haig St; (077) 45 1166. **Accommodation:** 3 hotel/motels, 1 motel, 1 cara./camp. park. **See also:** Cape York; Gulf Savannah.

Oakey Pop. 3425

MAP REF. 482 D6, 491 N9

On the Warrego Hwy, 29 km NW of Toowoomba, this town, the base for Australian Army Aviation, is surrounded by beautiful rolling hills and dark soil plains. **Of interest:** Bronze statue of racehorse Bernborough. Oakey Historical Museum, Warrego Hwy. Flypast Museum of Australian Army Flying, at army base, via Kelvinaugh St, has large collection of original and replica aircraft (some in flying condition), and aviation memorabilia. **In the area:** Acland Coal Mine Museum, 18 km N; closed Feb. Jondaryan Woolshed (1859), off Warrego Hwy, 22 km NW, memorial to pioneers of wool industry, includes huge woolshed and other buildings, shearing demonstrations, sheep dogs, billy tea and damper, and sales of goods at wool store; Australian heritage festival, at

Woolshed in Aug. **Tourist information:** Library, 64 Campbell St; (076) 91 1388. **Accommodation:** 4 hotels, 3 motels, 2 cara./ camp. parks.

Palm Cove Pop. 2800

MAP REF. 489 E7, 495 M6

Serene Palm Cove, 27 km NW of Cairns, offers visitors an inviting selection of world-class accommodation with an equally splendid range of boutiques, art galleries and souvenir shops – all set on a tropical beach. Dive and tour bookings to the Barrier Reef are available, as are pick-up services for a host of day tours to the Atherton Tableland and surrounding areas. There is also convenient access to Mossman and Port Douglas. **In the area:** On Captain Cook Hwy at Clifton Beach, 7 km S: Wild World, Australian Wildlife Showpark, features exotic range of flora and fauna; Outback Opal Mine, simulated mine with displays of Australia's most famous stone. Bungy tower in rainforest, McGregor Rd, Smithfield; 14 km S. **Tourist information:** Cnr Hartley and Grafton Sts, Cairns; (070) 51 3588. **Accommodation:** 12 motels, 3 resorts, 2 cara./ camp. parks.

Pittsworth Pop. 2110

MAP REF. 482 C9, 491 N9

Pittsworth is a typical Darling Downs town, situated 40 km SW of Toowoomba on the road to Millmerran. It is the centre of a rich grain and dairying district. Cotton is grown with the help of irrigation. The jacarandas and silky oaks in and around the town are a spectacular sight when they flower in late spring. **Of interest:** Some buildings listed by National Trust. Folk Museum, Pioneer Way, includes pioneer cottage, blacksmith's shop and early school. Dec.: Great Australian team truck pull. **Tourist information:** Sunkist Cafe, Yandilla St; (076) 93 1246. **Accommodation:** 1 hotel, 1 hotel/motel, 1 motel, 1 cara./camp. park.

Pomona Pop. 885

MAP REF. 486 B1

This small farming centre is in the northern hinterland of the Sunshine Coast, 33 km S of Gympie. Mt Cooroora (439 m) dominates the town. **Of interest:** Majestic Theatre, cinema museum and location for annual film festival. July: King of the Mountain festival, race attracting mountain runners from around world. **In the area:** Water sports at Lake Cootharaba, 18 km NE, a large, shallow saltwater lake on Noosa River near where Mrs Eliza Fraser spent time with Aborigines after wreck of *Stirling Castle* on Fraser Island in 1836. **Tourist information:** Noosa Information Centre, Hastings St roundabout, Noosa Heads; (074) 47 4988. **Accommodation:** 1 hotel.

Port Douglas Pop. 3660

MAP REF. 489 C4, 495 M5

Just 65 km NW of Cairns, along one of the most scenic coastal drives in Australia, Port Douglas offers the contrast of cosmopolitanism in a tropical, tree-covered mountain setting beside the Coral Sea. Once a small village, Port Douglas has become an international tourist destination. The town, off the main highway, is surrounded by lush vegetation and pristine rainforests. This setting, along with its proximity to the Great Barrier Reef, makes it an ideal holiday destination. **Of interest:** Ben Cropp's Shipwreck Museum, end of Macrossan St, in Anzac Park. Rainforest Habitat, Port Douglas Rd, displays flora and fauna in natural setting. Flagstaff Hill, end Murphy St, commands excellent views of Four Mile Beach and Low Isles. Tours available from town include: horse trail-riding, rainforest hiking, rainforest tours, 4WD safaris, coach tours to Cape Tribulation, Kuranda and Cooktown, reef tours to Outer Barrier Reef and Low Isles, and the *Lady Douglas* paddlewheel cruise. Market, each Sun. at Anzac Park. June: Village Carnivale. Sept.: Regatta. **In the area:** Sugar town of Mossman, 14 km N; picturesque Mossman Gorge, nearby. Daintree River rainforest cruises begin further 26 km NW. **Tourist information:** 23 Macrossan St; (070) 99 5599. **Accommodation:** 5 resorts, 32 motels, 1 hostel, 4 cara./camp. parks. **See also:** The Far North.

Proserpine Pop. 3034

MAP REF. 493 J3

A sugar town, Proserpine is close to Airlie Beach, Shute Harbour and the islands of Whitsunday Passage. **Of interest:** Bulk sugar mill, Hinschen St; tours during crushing season (July–Oct.). **In the area:** Conway National Park, 10 km SE, views across islands of Whitsunday Passage from vantage points within park. Lake Proserpine at Peter Faust Dam, 20 km W, offers boat hire, water-skiing, fishing and swimming. **Tourist information:** Bruce Hwy, Airlie Beach; (079) 45 3711. **Accommodation:** 5 hotels, 5 motels, 3 cara./camp. parks.

Quilpie Pop. 624

MAP REF. 501 O7

Quilpie, 217 km W of Charleville, was established as a centre for the large sheep and cattle properties in the area, but is better known as a boulder opal town. It takes its name from the Aboriginal word *quilpeta*, meaning 'stone curlew'. **Of interest:** Sales of opals at various outlets in town. Altar, font and lectern of St Finbarr's Catholic Church, Buln Buln St, made from opal-bearing rock. June and Aug.: Diggers races, at racecourse. Sept.: Agricultural show. **In the area:** Opal workings just outside town. Lake Houdrahan, 6 km N on river road to Adavale, popular recreation area. Duck Creek Opal Mine at Cheepie, 75 km E. **Tourist information:** Shire Offices, Brolga St; (076) 56 1133. **Accommodation:** 1 hotel/motel, 1 motel, 1 cara./camp. park. **See also:** The Channel Country.

Ravenswood Pop. 120

MAP REF. 492 G2

Ravenswood, friendly and 'not quite a ghost town', is 88 km E of Charters Towers via Mingela. One hundred years ago it was the classic gold-rush town. Visitors will find interesting old workings and perhaps a little gold along with the nostalgia. **Of interest:** Several restored historic buildings in town, including court house, shops and current ambulance centre. Oct.: Halloween ball. **In the area:** Burdekin Dam, 80 km SE, popular recreational area. **Tourist information:** Railway Hotel, Barton St; (077) 70 2144. **Accommodation:** 2 hotels, 1 motel/camping park, camping in showgrounds.

Redcliffe Pop. 39 073

MAP REF. 483 N6, 491 Q8

Redcliffe was the first European settlement in Qld. Matthew Flinders landed here in 1799 while exploring Moreton Bay and the spot was named for what he found: red cliffs. In 1824 John Oxley and Commandant Miller arrived with convicts and troops to set up the Moreton Bay penal colony, which was abandoned the following year in favour of Brisbane. The Aborigines called the place Humpybong, meaning 'dead houses', and the name is still used for the Redcliffe Peninsula, which comprises the towns of Woody Point, Margate, Clontarf, Scarborough and Redcliffe. The City of Redcliffe, 35 km N of Brisbane, was proclaimed in 1959 and is a fast-growing area and a satellite city of Brisbane. The 2.6-km bridge, which links the two cities, is known as the Houghton Hwy, which in 1979 replaced the old Hornibrook Hwy. Fishing and boating are popular pastimes. **Of interest:** Historical museum, Marine Pde. Self-guide heritage walks and drives of city; pamphlets available from Tourist information. Seawater lagoon at Redcliffe Point. Craft markets on beach each Sun. Jan.: Blessing of the fleet. Feb.: Seafood festival. Sept.: First Settlement festival. **In the area:** Scarborough is departure point for vehicular ferry to Moreton Island, where sand dunes are reputed to be highest in world; dolphin feeding at Tangalooma resort on western side of island. **Tourist information:** Mall, Sutton St; (07) 3284 5595. **Accommodation:** 6 hotels, 3 motels, 7 cara./camp. parks. **See also:** Tours from Brisbane.

Redland Bay   Pop. 2576

MAP REF. 483 O9, 491 Q9

Some 30 km SE of Brisbane on the shores of Moreton Bay, the famous red soil of this area grows excellent vegetables and strawberries, mainly for the Brisbane market. It is a popular Sunday afternoon drive from the city. Cleveland is the main centre of the Redland area, and beaches at Wellington Point, Victoria Point and Redland Bay offer safe swimming and boating. Sept.: Strawberry festival. **In the area:** Roseworld, 2 km S, exhibition gardens showing most varieties of roses. Koala Bushland National Park, Mt Cotton, 12 km SW, a fauna sanctuary with walking tracks and picnic/barbecue area. King Country Nursery at Thornlands, 10 km NW, in rainforest setting with picnic facilities. Cleveland, 15 km N, departure point for boats to North Stradbroke Island, while Redland Bay is departure point for Russell, Lamb, Macleay and Karragarra Islands. Off Victoria Point, 6 km N, Coochiemudlo Island, quiet but popular. Islands are all excellent places to picnic, swim and explore; full range of facilities and services. **Tourist information:** Redlands Tourism, 152 Shore St, Cleveland; (07) 3821 0057. **Accommodation:** 1 hotel/motel, 2 cara./camp. parks. **See also:** Tours from Brisbane.

Richmond   Pop. 631

MAP REF. 499 M4

This small town on the Flinders Hwy, 500 km SW of Townsville, serves the surrounding sheep and cattle properties. **Of interest:** In Goldring St: Restored Cobb & Co. coach; Marine Fossil Museum; Old Strand Theatre; display

Fishing in Queensland

The tropical climate, breathtaking scenery and variety of fishing combine to make the State a wonderful destination for the angler. The coast is the chief attraction with Cairns being world famous as a location for black marlin and other game-fishing. The Great Barrier Reef is closest to the coast north of Cairns and is easily fished on day trips either in your own boat or from a charter boat. Coral trout, red emperor and nannygai are here and, for those with an inclination for sportfishing, Spanish mackerel, giant trevally and marlin. Cairns is a major centre for charter boats going out to the Great Barrier Reef and deepwater game-fishing. Further north the remote regions of Cape York provide a frontier experience for those seeking barramundi, queenfish and giant trevally.

Around Brisbane the warm tropical currents provide a mix of temperate and tropical fish species, and estuary, beach, reef and offshore fishing are possible. Further north, the tailor at Hervey Bay are legendary, and the nearby Great Sandy Strait has a large variety of estuary species in the mangrove channels. Around Townsville the mangrove estuaries on the coastline are renowned for barramundi and mangrove jack. Just off the coast are the wonders of the Whitsundays surrounded by waters teeming with mackerel, queenfish, trevally and other species.

Inland fishing areas, particularly in the north, are situated at vast distances from population centres. In the south-east the stocking of impoundments has improved inland fishing; anglers can now fish for golden perch and Murray cod.

Heading out of Fitzroy Island for some light tackle sportfishing

Botanic Gardens at Rockhampton

of moon rocks (spherical fossil rocks of various sizes, feature of local landscape) in Lions Park. Aug.: Rodeo. **In the area:** The area is rich in fossils. **Tourist information:** Shire Offices, Goldring St; (077) 41 3277. **Accommodation:** 1 hotel, 1 hotel/motel, 2 motels, 1 cara. park.

Rockhampton   Pop. 55 768

MAP REF. 493 N10

Rockhampton is called the beef capital of Australia, with some 2.5 million cattle in the region. Gold was discovered at Canoona, 60 km NW of Rockhampton, in 1858; however, cattle became the major industry, with Herefords the main breed, since cross-bred with more exotic breeds to produce disease-resistant herds. Rockhampton straddles the Tropic of Capricorn. It is a prosperous city on the banks of the Fitzroy River and has considerable architectural charm. Many of the original stone buildings and churches remain, set off by flowering bauhinia and brilliant bougainvilleas. The city has several well-established secondary industries, including two of Australia's largest meat processing and exporting factories. **Of interest:** In Quay St, alongside river, National Trust-classified buildings: ANZ Bank (1864); customs house (1901). Heritage walk around city centre, contact Tourist information. Scattered around city are old Queensland houses carefully preserved. Botanic Gardens on Athelstane Range, via Spencer St, contain fine tropical displays, an orchid and fern house, a Japanese-style garden, monkeys, koala park and walk-in aviary. Cliff Kershaw Gardens, Bruce Hwy, features Braille Trail. Fitzroy River Barrage, Savage St, separates tidal saltwater from upstream freshwater. The Capricorn Spire (14 m) at Curtis Park, Gladstone Rd, marks exact line of Tropic of Capricorn. Rocky markets, Sat. and Sun. in Denison St. Apr.: Good Earth expo. July: Bauhinia arts festival. Aug.: Rocky round up. **In the area:** Dreamtime Cultural Centre, north on Bruce Hwy, largest Aboriginal and Torres Strait Islander cultural centre in Australia, features culture of Aborigines in Carnarvon Gorge area. Old Glenmore historic homestead, 5 km N, has displays and historic buildings. Rockhampton Heritage Village, Gangalook, 20 km N: heritage buildings with hall of clocks and pioneering tools, also steam engine; tours daily, special events last Sun. in month. St Christopher's Chapel, 20 km N, on Emu Park Rd, built by American servicemen. Olsen's Capricorn Caverns and Cammoo Caves, both limestone cave systems, 32 km N; guided tours. Historic mining town of Mount Morgan, 38 km W. Thunder-egg fossicking at Mt Hay Gemstone Tourist Park, 41 km W on Capricorn Hwy. Pleasant drive to top of Mt Archer, 6 km E. Great Keppel Island Resort, 13 km off Capricorn Coast; Underwater Observatory off Middle Island. Yeppoon and Emu Park beaches, 25–30 km NE. **Tourist information:** The Spire, Gladstone Rd; (079) 27 2055. **Accommodation:** 18 hotels, 8 hotel/motels, 32 motels, 1 hostel, 9 cara./camp. parks. **See also:** The Capricorn Region.

Roma   Pop. 5669

MAP REF. 490 H6

Roma is 261 km W of Dalby at the junction of the Warrego and the Carnarvon Hwys. It was named after the wife of Sir George Bowen, Qld's first Governor, and was first surveyed in 1862. The Mt Abundance cattle station was established in 1847, and sheep and cattle have been the area's economic mainstay ever since. The famous trial of Harry Redford, alias Captain Starlight, was held in Roma in 1872. In 1863 the SS *Bassett* brought vine cuttings to Roma and Qld's first wine-making enterprise began. Australia's first natural gas strike was made at Hospital Hill in 1900, and the gas from this source was used, briefly, to light the town. Further deposits were found periodically, and 'oil' (actually gas and condensate) caused excitement in the area in the early 1960s. Roma now supplies Brisbane with gas via a 450-km pipeline. **Of interest:** Oil rig, named Big Rig by locals, erected as landmark at eastern entrance to town on Warrego Hwy. Romavilla Winery, Injune Rd. Cultural Centre, cnr Bungil and Injune Rds, includes mural by local artists.

Darling Downs

The 72 500 square kilometres of black volcanic soil on the Darling Downs produce 90 per cent of the State's wheat, 50 per cent of its maize, 90 per cent of its oilseeds, two-thirds of its fruit and one-third of its tobacco, as well as oats, sorghum, millet, cotton, soybeans and navy beans. It is a major sheep, cattle and dairying area and the home of several famous bloodstock studs.

Allan Cunningham was the first European to ride across these fertile plains in 1827. The Darling Downs is rural Australia at its best, with a touch of England in the oaks, elms, plane trees and poplars of **Toowoomba's** parks, and the rose gardens of **Warwick** in the south. The climate is cooler and more bracing than in the rest of the State. Driving across the Downs with its neat strips of grainfields, lush pastures, patches of forest and national parks, and well-established homesteads, gives the visitor a lasting impression of beauty and quiet prosperity.

The Warrego Highway leads north-west from Toowoomba to the wheatfields and silos of **Dalby**, the hub of the Downs. Gowrie Mountain is a popular lookout. At Jimbour, 27 kilometres north of Dalby, stands the stately two-storey Jimbour House. On an elevated site with panoramic views of the Jimbour Plains, this historic home in landscaped gardens was constructed between 1874 and 1876, mainly from local materials, including cedar from the Bunya Mountains. Part of an earlier (1870) bluestone building still stands at the rear of the house.

The New England Highway, the main Sydney to Brisbane inland route, turns into the Cunningham Highway at Warwick, and descends from the Downs towards the coast through Cunninghams Gap, discovered in 1827. Main Range National Park has lovely rainforest, palms and native wildlife. An alternative inland route between Brisbane and Melbourne is the Newell Highway, which runs west from Warwick to **Goondiwindi** and then south into New South Wales through Moree and Narrabri. A less-used but scenic route is the Heifer Creek Way through the Lockyer Valley from near Greenmount East to **Gatton**.

For further information on the Darling Downs, contact the Southern Downs Tourist Association, 49 Albion St (New England Hwy), Warwick; (076) 61 3122. **See also:** individual entries in A–Z listing for those towns indicated by bold type. **Map reference:** 482 B6

Paddock patterns are an attractive sight in the Darling Downs

Shute Harbour, main departure point for the Whitsunday Islands

St George
Pop. 2512

MAP REF. 490 G10

Situated at a major road junction, St George is in the centre of a rich cotton-growing district. It is on the Balonne River, 118 km NW of Mungindi on the Carnarvon Hwy, and 286 km SW of Dalby on the Moonie Hwy. It is often referred to as the inland fishing capital of Qld as there are many fishing spots yielding Murray cod and yellowbelly, particularly in the Balonne River. As St George has a rainfall of only 500 mm a year, extensive irrigation is carried out by means of a dam and three weirs. Cotton-growing and harvesting is completely mechanised; planting is Oct. to Nov., harvesting Apr. to June. Wheat, barley, oats and sunflowers are also irrigated, and sheep and cattle are raised. **Of interest:** Balonne Creative Arts Group, Klinge Lane, for local craft. Riversands Winery, southern end of Alfred St. Carved emu eggs displayed at Balonne Sports store, Victoria St. Easter: Family fishing competition. **In the area:** Ostrich farming at Burra Boogie, 3 km W, off Balonne Hwy; open a.m. by appt only. Rosehill Aviaries, 64 km W, one of Australia's largest private collections of Australian parrots. Cotton Ginnery, 20 km S; open by appt from Apr.–June. Historic hotel (1863) at Nindigully, 44 km SE, has featured in commercials; motorbike riders arrive each June to tackle the Nindigully 5-hour enduro. Native flowers including Geraldton Wax at Gillebri flower farm, 24 km E; flower tours Aug.–Oct., by appt only; watch rockmelons being prepared and packed Nov.–Mar. Further 3 km, restored vintage tractor collection; open by appt. Ancient rockwell, hand hewn by Aborigines possibly thousands of years ago; 37 km E. Beardmore Dam, 20 km N for fishing and water sports; scenic picnic spots in surrounding parklands. **Tourist information:** Shire Offices, Victoria St; (076) 25 3222. **Accommodation:** 1 hotel, 3 hotel/motels, 2 motels, 3 cara./camp. parks.

Adjacent park has picnic facilities. Market, 3rd Sat. each month at Roma Fair, Wyndham St. Easter: Easter in the country. **In the area:** Largest inland cattle market in Australia, 4 km E on Warrego Hwy. Meadowbank Museum, 15 km W on Warrego Hwy. Carnarvon National Park, 251 km NW, features Carnarvon Gorge, Aboriginal cave paintings, varied scenery and walks; guided tours and accommodation available. **Tourist information:** Big Rig Site, Lower McDowall St; (076) 22 4355. **Accommodation:** 10 hotels, 8 motels, 1 cara./camp. park.

Sarina
Pop. 3094

MAP REF. 493 L6

In the sugar belt, Sarina lies 37 km S of Mackay on the Bruce Hwy. The area has many fine beaches, including Sarina, Campwin, Grasstree, Salonika, Halftide, and, to the south, Armstrong. Sarina produces molasses and ethyl alcohol as byproducts of the sugar industry. **Of interest:** Plane Creek Central Sugar Mill. CSR Distillery, Bruce Hwy, also produces Dundah, fertiliser for local sugarcane crops. Flea market, last Thurs. each month in Broad St. July: Visual arts festival. Aug.: Agricultural show. **In the area:** To the north: tours of Campwin Beach Prawn Farm (8.5 km); Prawn and Crab Hatchery, Grasstree Beach (13 km NE). Viewing gallery at Hay Point and Dalrymple Bay coal terminal complex (12 km N). **Tourist information:** Shire Offices, 65 Broad St; (079) 56 1444. **Accommodation:** 4 hotels, 3 motels, 3 cara./camp. parks.

Shute Harbour
Pop. 200

MAP REF. 493 K3

Shute Harbour, 36 km NE of Proserpine, is a suburb of the town of Whitsunday. It is also one of the largest marine passenger terminals in Australia, second only to Sydney's Circular Quay. **Of interest:** Jetty at Shute Harbour, best place to start exploring the 80 or more tropical islands in the beautiful Whitsunday waters including well-known Hayman, Daydream, South Molle, Hamilton and Lindeman Islands; variety of cruise boats depart daily; booking offices, souvenir and food outlets on main jetty. Boom-net riding available daily. Seaplane ride to Hardy's Lagoon on the outer Barrier Reef for snorkelling among the coral. Ex-America's Cup challenger *Gretel* takes day trips through the Whitsunday Islands. Day trips to the pontoon at Hardy Reef for swimming, scuba diving and snorkelling. The brigantine *Romance* offers five-night cruises off the islands and the reef. Sail and power vessels, varying sizes and classes, can be hired. Lions Lookout, Whitsunday Dr., for spectacular views. Heritage Doll Museum, Shute Harbour Rd, adjacent to Whitsunday Airport. **In the area:** Airlie Beach, 5 km N. Conway National Park, 15 km S. Great Barrier Reef and Whitsunday Islands. **Tourist information:** Beach Plaza, The Esplanade,

Airlie Beach; (079) 46 6673. **Accommodation:** 4 motels, 3 cara./camp. parks.

Southport
Pop. part of Gold Coast

MAP REF. 483 O12, 485 E5, 491 Q10

Towards the northern end of the Gold Coast strip, Southport is packed with attractions. It also serves as the commercial and administrative centre for the Gold Coast. **In the area:** At Main Beach on The Spit: Sea World, famous marine park; Marina Mirage, Mariner's Cove and Fisherman's Wharf – tourist complexes with speciality shops, restaurants, outdoor cafes and weekend entertainment. Other attractions of the Gold Coast and its hinterland. **Tourist information:** Cavill Mall, Surfers Paradise; (07) 5538 4419. **Accommodation:** Low and high-rise hotels and motels, self-contained apartments, cara./camp. parks. **See also:** City of the Gold Coast.

Stanthorpe
Pop. 4187

MAP REF. 119 M2, 491 N12

The main town in the Granite Belt and in the mountain ranges along the border between Qld and NSW, Stanthorpe, 225 km SW of Brisbane, came into being after the discovery of tin at Quartpot Creek in 1872. Silver and lead were discovered in 1880, but the minerals boom did not last. The area has produced excellent wool for more than a century, but is best known for its large-scale growing of apples, pears, plums, peaches and grapes. Stanthorpe is 915 m above sea level and is often the coolest part of the State. Spring is particularly beautiful with fruit trees and wattles in bloom. There are 90 varieties of wild orchids found in the area. **Of interest:** Museum, High St. Art Gallery and Library Complex, Weeroona Park, Marsh St. Mar.: Apple and grape harvest festival (even-numbered years); Rodeo. Apr.: Opera at sunset. **In the area:** Granite Belt wineries, most open for tastings and cellar-door sales: Old Caves, just north of town; Castle Glen at Summit, 10 km N; Heritage Wines at Cottonvale, 12 km NW; Mt Magnus at Pozieres, 14 km NW; Granite Cellars, Granite Country Estate, Stone Ridge, Felsberg, Mountview and Kominos, near Glen Alpin, 11 km S; Rumbalara at Fletcher, 14 km S; Ballandean Estate Golden Grove, Winewood, Bungawarra and Robinson's Family Winery, near Ballandean, 19 km S; Bald Mountain at Wallangarra, 30 km S. Girraween National Park, 32 km S, for camping, bushwalking, rock climbing and spectacular wildflowers in spring. Sundown National Park, 79 km SW, wilderness area; camping on Severn River in southwest of park. Sunworld Park at Eukey, 13 km SE, has displays of sun and wind-powered instruments. Storm King Dam, 26 km SE, for canoeing and water-skiing. Falls in Boonoo Boonoo National Park, 60 km SE. Mt Marlay, 2 km E, for excellent views. **Tourist information:** 61 Marsh St; (076) 81 2057. **Accommodation:** 5 hotels, 7 motels, 8 B&B, 1 hostel, 3 cara./camp. parks.

Strathpine
Pop. 10 108

MAP REF. 478 C3, 483 M6

Immediately behind Brisbane and to the north is the Pine Rivers region, a peaceful rural district that includes the forested areas and national parks closest to Brisbane. Taking advantage of this rural setting so close to the city are a number of art and craft industries. Each Sunday the oldest and largest country market is held at North Pine Country Park, Whiteside, 6 km NW of Strathpine; local artworks, food and produce are sold while buskers entertain and craft demonstrations are given. June: Pine Rivers heritage festival. **In the area:** Alma Park Zoo at Dakabin, 14 km N, features native and exotic animals, and a Friendship Farm for children. Lakeside Racing Circuit, 14 km N, venue for major events. Bunya Park Wildlife Sanctuary, Eatons Hill, 8 km SW, native animals in bush setting. Australian Woolshed at Ferny Hills, 16 km SW, for demonstrations of shearing, spinning and sheepdogs working; also bush dances with bush band. Brisbane Forest Park, via Ferny Hills. Mountains and national parks that form scenic rim around Brisbane. **Tourist information:** Shire Offices, 220 Gympie Rd; (07) 3205 0555. **Accommodation:** 2 hotels, 2 motels, 3 hostels, 1 cara./camp. park, 1 overnight camp. ground.

Tambo
Pop. 351

MAP REF. 490 B2

Tambo, 101 km SE of Blackall on the Matilda Hwy, was established in the mid-1860s. From a point where the town now stands, explorer Thomas Mitchell first saw the Barcoo River in 1846. **Of interest:** Old Post Office Museum; also produces Tambo Teddies, all-wool teddy bears. Court house (1888), now library. Sept.: Spring flower festival (includes ram racing). **In the area:** Ivanhoe Hills, just east of town, the highest point on the hwy west of Toowoomba. Salvator Rosa section of Carnarvon National Park, 120 km E; the area was named by Major Mitchell, who was reminded of landscapes painted by 17th-century artist; access to park via Dawson Development Rd and Cungelella Station (4WD recommended); permission to camp must be obtained from Department of Environment and Heritage; (079) 84 1716. **Tourist information:** Shire Offices, Arthur St; (076) 54 6133. **Accommodation:** 1 hotel, 1 hotel/motel, 1 motel, 1 cara./camp. park.

Taroom
Pop. 705

MAP REF. 491 J4

Taroom is on the banks of the Dawson River almost 300 km due W of Maryborough. Cattle-raising is the main industry. **Of interest:** Coolibah tree in main street, marked 'L.L.' by Ludwig Leichhardt on his 1844 trip from Jimbour House near Dalby to Port Essington (Darwin). Museum, Kelman St, features old telephone-exchange equipment, farm machinery and items of local history. May: Agricultural show. Sept.: Leichhardt festival. **In the area:** Rare Livistona palms near Leichhardt Hwy, 15 km N. Isla Gorge National Park, 55 km N. Robinson Gorge, 108 km NW. Reedy Creek Homestead, a cattle station, 115 km NW. **Tourist information:** Shire Offices, Yaldwyn St; (076) 27 3211. **Accommodation:** 1 hotel, 1 hotel/motel, 1 motel, 1 cara./camp. park.

Texas
Pop. 816

MAP REF. 119 K3, 491 M12

Quite the opposite in size to its USA namesake, Texas lies alongside the Dumaresq River and the Qld-NSW border, 55 km SE of Inglewood. **Of interest:** Historical Museum in old police station (1893). July: Agricultural show. **In the area:** Good fishing in Glenlyon Dam, 51 km SE. **Tourist information:** Ridgways general store, 40 High St; (076) 53 1245. **Accommodation:** 1 hotel/motel, 1 motel, 1 cara./camp. park.

Tin Can Bay, ideal for boating and fishing

Theodore
Pop. 502

MAP REF. 491 J2

Grain and cotton are the main crops around this town on the Leichhardt Hwy, 220 km N of Miles. Theodore was named after Edward Theodore, a Premier of Qld, and designed by Burley Griffin. **Of interest:** Theodore Hotel, The Boulevard; only cooperative hotel in Qld. Dawson Folk Museum, Second Ave. **In the area:** Fishing on Theodore Weir, southern outskirts of town. Isla Gorge National Park, 35 km SW. Cracow, 49 km SE, where gold was produced from famous Golden Plateau mine 1932–76. **Tourist information:** Theodore Hotel, The Boulevard; (079) 93 1244. **Accommodation:** 1 hotel, 1 cara./camp. park.

Thuringowa
Pop. 36 000

MAP REF. 495 P13

Thuringowa is a growing city surrounding the city of Townsville. It depends not only on its established grazing and sugar industries but on such diversification as tropical fruit plantations, including mango and pineapple, extensive mixed vegetable farming, the Qld Nickel Refinery at Yabulu and, increasingly, tourism. Some of north Qld's best beaches, stretching along more than 120 km of coastline, provide visitors with surfing and fishing. **In the area:** Woodstock, 33 km SW. At Alligator Creek, 18 km SE: Australian farm display; Billabong Sanctuary, Muntalunga Dr., a wildlife park. Haughton River Company's Invicta Sugar Mill at Giru, 27 km SE. Internationally recognised Australian Institute of Marine Science at Turtle Bay, on Cape Bowling Green, 97 km SE. **Tourist information:** Bruce Hwy, Townsville; (077) 78 3555. **Accommodation:** 3 hotels, 2 hotel/motels, 1 motel, 5 cara./camp. parks.

Tin Can Bay
Pop. 1355

MAP REF. 491 P5

Half an hour's drive north-east of Gympie takes travellers to Tin Can Bay and nearby Rainbow Beach. These two hamlets are popular fishing, prawning and crabbing areas; the quiet waters of Tin Can Bay are ideal for boating and fishing, while Rainbow Beach has good surfing. **Of interest:** Easter: Festival. June: Seafood and leisure festival. Dec.: Robert Pryde memorial surf classic. **In the area:** Fishing Classic at Rainbow Beach in July. Road south from Rainbow Beach (4WD) leads to coloured sands and beaches of Cooloola section of Great Sandy National Park. North, at Inskip Point, ferry to Fraser Island. At Carlo Point, 3 km E, cruising, fishing, swimming; houseboats and yachts for hire. **Tourist information:** Tin Can Bay Rd; (074) 86 4333. **Accommodation:** 1 hotel, 3 motels, 4 cara./camp. parks.

Toowoomba
Pop. 75 990

MAP REF. 482 F8, 491 N9

The garden city of Toowoomba has a distinctive charm and graciousness in its wide, tree-lined streets, colonial architecture and many fine parks and gardens. Toowoomba is 127 km W of Brisbane, on the rim of the Great Dividing Range. It began in 1849 as a village near an important staging post for teamsters and travellers, and was known as The Swamp. Aborigines pronounced the name 'T'wamp-bah'; this became 'Toowoomba'. Today it is the commercial centre for the fertile Darling Downs, with butter and cheese factories, sawmills, flour mills, tanneries, engineering and railway workshops, a modern iron foundry, clothing and shoe factories. It has an active cultural and artistic life. **Of interest:** Self-guide Russell St heritage walk. Cobb & Co. Museum, Lindsay St, traces history of horse-drawn vehicles. St Patrick's Cathedral (1880s), James St. St Luke's Anglican Church (1897), cnr Herries and Ruthven Sts. Parks include Lake Annand, MacKenzie St, for birdlovers; Laurel Bank, scented gardens; Botanic Gardens and adjacent Queens Park, Lindsay St; Waterbird Habitat, MacKenzie St. Ascot House (1870s), Newmarket St, serves teas and lunches. Royal Bull's Head Inn (1847), Brisbane St, fully restored by National Trust. Toowoomba Art Gallery, Linton Gallery and Gould Gallery, all in Ruthven St; Downs Gallery, Margaret St. Willow Springs Adventure Park, Spring St. Antique and craft shops. Sept.: Carnival of flowers. **In the area:** Self-guide scenic drives of varying lengths: 48-km circuit to Spring Bluff (old railway station at Spring Bluff has superb gardens) and Murphy's Creek; 100-km circuit to Heifer Creek, known as Valley of the Sun, provides spectacular scenery; 255-km circuit takes in Bernborough Centre, Jondaryan Woolshed, Cecil Plains Cotton Ginnery, Millmerran Museum and Pittsworth Folk Museum. Picnic Point, 5 km E, offers mountain views and waterfall. At Highfields, 15 km N: Orchid Park;

Capricorn Region

This rich and varied slice of Queensland stretches inland from Rockhampton and the Capricorn Coast out to Jericho, and straddles the Tropic of Capricorn. The area includes the Capricorn Coast, Rockhampton city and surrounds, the central highlands and the rural hinterlands, and is drained by the Fitzroy, Mackenzie, Comet, Nogoa and Dawson Rivers. The district was first opened up by gold- and copper-mining around **Emerald** in the 1860s, and the discovery of sapphires around Anakie. The original owners of the land have left their heritage in superb and mysterious rock paintings on the silent stone walls of the Carnarvon Ranges to the south. Cattle have been the economic mainstay since European settlement, but vast tracts of brigalow scrub were cleared after World War II to grow wheat, maize, sorghum and safflower. These days coal is dominant, with mainly American companies gouging out enormous deposits for local and Japanese markets. On a smaller scale, professional and amateur fossickers still find gems in the region with a great deal of enjoyment.

For a pleasurable tour of the region, drive west from **Rockhampton**, the commercial and manufacturing capital, along the Capricorn Highway. Detour to Blackdown Tableland National Park where there are waterfalls, rock pools and camping areas; the turnoff is between Dingo and Blackwater. (If camping in the park, you will need a permit; available on arrival at park except at busy school holiday periods when it is necessary to obtain a permit from the regional office of the Department of Heritage and Environment (079) 86 1964.) At Emerald turn south to Springsure, then east to **Biloela** on the Dawson Highway. Continue north on the Burnett Highway via **Mount Morgan** back to Rockhampton.

Mount Hay Gemstone Tourist Park, 41 kilometres west of Rockhampton, allows visitors to fossick for thunder eggs and rhyolite, which may be cut and polished at the factory in the park. Utah's Blackwater coalmine produces 4 million tonnes of coking coal and almost 3 million tonnes of steaming coal annually. Tours can be arranged.

Emerald is the main town in the central-highlands region, with the central-western railway continuing much further west to **Longreach** and the Channel Country. Clermont and the Blair Athol coalfields are 106 kilometres to the north-west. The gemfields of Anakie, Rubyvale, Sapphire, The Willows and Tomahawk Creek are west of Emerald, and are popular with tourists seeking a different holiday. (A fossicker's licence is necessary.)

Springsure, 66 kilometres south of Emerald, is one of Queensland's oldest towns, having been surveyed in 1854. It produces beef and grain. Nearby is the Old Rainworth Fort at Burnside, a fascinating piece of Australiana, where early farm equipment, wool presses and the like, are on display. It was built in 1853 from local stone.

Rolleston, 70 kilometres to the south-east, is the turnoff to the magnificent **Carnarvon National Park**, 103 kilometres further south. The park covers 28 000 hectares of rugged mountains, forests, caves and deep gorges, some of which are Australia's earliest art galleries; there are countless Aboriginal paintings and engravings, which in places extend in a colourful frieze for more than 50 metres.

The Callide open-cut mine is situated near Biloela, the principal town in the Callide Valley. The nearby Callide Power Station supplies the Rockhampton, Moura and Blackwater districts as well as Biloela.

What are known as the 'Snowy Mounts' are actually huge piles of salt in the Fitzroy River delta between Bajool and Port Alma. Underground salty water is pumped to the surface into pools called crystallisers, and the salt is harvested during October and November after solar evaporation.

For further information on the Capricorn Region, contact the Capricorn Information Centre, The Spire, Gladstone Rd, Rockhampton; (079) 27 2055. **See also:** National Parks and individual entries in A–Z listing for those parks and towns indicated by bold type. **Map reference:** 492-3.

Fossicking for sapphires near Emerald

Townsville on Cleveland Bay with Castle Hill in the background

QUEENSLAND

Danish Flower Art; Pioneer Museum. At Cabarlah, 20 km N: Telopea Gallery; Black Forest Hill Cuckoo Clock Centre. Acland Coal Mine Museum, near Oakey, 25 km NW. **Tourist information:** 541 Ruthven St; (076) 32 1988. **Accommodation:** 35 motels, 5 B&B, 1 hostel, 5 cara./camp. parks. **See also:** Tours from Brisbane; Darling Downs.

Townsville   Pop. 75 990

MAP REF. 487, 495 P12

In 1864 a sea captain named Robert Towns commissioned James Melton Black to build a wharf and establish a settlement on Cleveland Bay to service the new cattle industry inland. Townsville was gazetted in 1865 and declared a city in 1903. Today it is Australia's largest tropical city. There are many handsome historic buildings, particularly in the waterfront park area around Cleveland Bay. The city's busy port handles minerals from Mount Isa and Cloncurry; beef and wool from the western plains; sugar and timber from the rich coastal region; and its own manufacturing and processing industries. Townsville is the administrative, commercial, education and manufacturing capital of northern Qld. It is becoming a renowned centre for research into marine life and is the headquarters for the Great Barrier Reef Marine Park Authority. **Of interest:** The Strand with its tropical parks, waterfall and overhanging bougainvillea gardens. At the end of The Strand is the Rockpool, which provides year-round swimming. Sheraton Breakwater Casino-Hotel, Western Breakwater, end Flinders St. Great Barrier Reef Wonderland, Flinders St East: aquarium with touch-tank and walk-through transparent underwater viewing-tunnel, Omnimax theatre and Museum of Tropical Queensland; the complex is also a ferry terminal for services to Magnetic Island and for day cruises to the Great Barrier Reef. Billabong Sanctuary, entry from Muntalunga Dr., features koala feeding and crocodile shows. Perc Tucker Regional Art Gallery, Flinders Mall. Jezzine Military Museum, end The Strand. Copper refinery at Stuart; conducted tours available. Queen's Gardens, cnr Paxton and Gregory Sts. Botanic Gardens, Anderson Park, Kings Rd. Historic Flinders Street East. Castle Hill Lookout, off Stanley St. Town Common and Environmental Park, Pallarenda Rd, a coastline park with prolific birdlife. Maritime Museum, Palmer St, South Townsville. Contact Tourist information for information on: cruises to Cairns via resort islands and reef on luxury catamaran *Coral Princess*; reef day-trips and dive cruises; day sailing around Magnetic Island; daily connections to resort islands of Magnetic, Orpheus, Hinchinbrook and Dunk; day outback tours, rainforest and white-water rafting tours. Cotters Market, each Sun. at Flinders Mall. July: Australian festival of chamber music. Nov.: Pacific festival. **In the area:** Paluma Range National Park, 80 km NW. Bowling Green Bay National Park, 25 km S, off Bruce Hwy. Pangola Park (32 km S) at Spring Creek. Near Giru, 50 km SE: waterfalls, bush walks, swimming and picnic and camping facilities. Offshore, Magnetic Island with a resident population of more than 2000; two-thirds of island is national park featuring beaches, walks and wildlife. **Tourist information:** Flinders Mall; (077) 21 3660. **Accommodation:** 40 hotel/motels, 1 hostel, 11 cara./camp. parks. **See also:** The Far North.

Tully   Pop. 2715

MAP REF. 495 N9

Situated at the foot of Mt Tyson, Tully receives one of the highest annual rainfalls in Australia, averaging around 4200 mm annually. Major industries are sugarcane, bananas, tropical fruit, cattle and timber. **Of interest:** Beautiful railway station, with its profusion of tropical plants; Booth Hwy. Market, 2nd Fri. each month. Sept.: Flower show. **In the area:** White-water rafting, canoeing, and reef and island cruising. Popular picnic spot on Tully River near Cardstone, 44 km W. Fishing at Tully

Heads, 22 km SE; at Cardwell, 45 km S. Spectacular rainforests near Mission Beach and Clump Point (9 km NE), Bingil Bay (25 km NE), Tully River Gorge (44 km W) and Murray Falls (40 km SW). **Tourist information:** Bruce Hwy; (070) 68 2288. **Accommodation:** 1 motel, 1 hostel, 1 cara./camp. park.

Warwick   Pop. 10393

MAP REF. 119 M1, 482 F13, 491 N11

An attractive city on the Darling Downs, Warwick is 162 km SW of Brisbane on the Cunningham Hwy, and 73 km S of Toowoomba on the New England Hwy. The area was first explored by Allan Cunningham in 1827; in 1840 the Leslie brothers arrived from the south and established a sheep station at Canning Downs, and other pastoralists followed. The NSW government asked Patrick Leslie to select a site for a township, and in 1849 Warwick was surveyed and established. It was the first town, after Brisbane, in what became Qld. The railway line from Ipswich was opened in 1871 and Warwick became a city in 1936. In what seemed to be a minor incident in 1917, Prime Minister Billy Hughes was hit by an egg while addressing a crowd on the controversial conscription issue of the day. He asked a local policeman to arrest the man responsible but the policeman refused. The result was the formation of the Federal Police Force. Warwick is located alongside the willow-shaded Condamine River, 458 m above sea level, and calls itself 'the Rose and Rodeo city'. The surrounding rich pastures support famous horse and cattle studs, and produce some of Australia's finest wool and grain. Fruit, vegetables and timber grow well, and the area is noted for its dairy products and bacon. **Of interest:** Self-guide walk around historic buildings; map available from Tourist information. Pringle Cottage (1870), Dragon St, houses large historical photo collection, vehicles and machinery. Leslie Park in Palmerin St. Jubilee Gardens, cnr Alice and Helene Sts, features displays of roses. Warwick Regional Art Gallery, Albion St. In Jan. or Feb.: Antique and collectables fair. Oct.: Rose and rodeo city festival. **In the area:** Leslie Dam, 15 km W, for water sports. Main Range National Park, 45 km E via Killarney, and Carr's Lookout, a further 14 km. Goomburra State Forest, east of Allora, 26 km N. **Tourist information:** 49 Albion St (New England Hwy); (076) 61 3122. **Accommodation:** 13 hotels, 10 motels, 2 B&B, 3 cara./camp. parks. **See also:** Darling Downs.

Weipa   Pop. 2510

MAP REF. 496 B7

Located on the west coast of Cape York, the township of Weipa is the home of the world's largest bauxite mine. This small mining town provides a comprehensive range of services and facilities for travellers. **Of interest:** Guided tours of bauxite mine provide excellent coverage of whole mining process at Weipa. **In the area:** Tours of local areas, such as Rocky Point, Trunding, Nanum and Evans Landing, give insight into town's development and lifestyle. Number of fishing and camping areas near the town developed for well-equipped tourist. **Tourist information:** Cnr Grafton and Hartley Sts, Cairns; (070) 51 3588. **Accommodation:** Limited. **See also:** Cape York.

Whitsunday   Pop. 6093

MAP REF. 493 K3

The town of Whitsunday is one of Australia's fastest-growing tourist destinations. It includes the suburbs of Airlie Beach, Cannonvale and Shute Harbour, and depends on the tourism industry. Stretching along 15 km of the coastline, Whitsunday was gazetted in 1987. Offshore, Whitsunday Island (uninhabited), the largest in the group, was named by Captain Cook in 1770. June and Dec.: Festival of sail. Nov.: Game-fishing championships; Annual spawning of the coral. **In the area:** Scenic bush walks through areas behind town in Conway National Park. Coral-viewing and tours of Great Barrier Reef and Whitsunday Islands. Extensive half- and full-day mainland tours, taking in Cedar Creek Falls, rainforests and other major attractions. **Tourist information:** Beach Plaza, The Esplanade, Airlie Beach; (079) 46 6673. **Accommodation:** 5 resorts, 7 hotels, 14 motels, 9 hostels, 15 cara. parks.

Winton   Pop. 1156

MAP REF. 499 M8

Banjo Paterson wrote Australia's most famous song, 'Waltzing Matilda', on Dagworth Station near Winton in 1895. Combo Waterhole was then part of Dagworth, and the ballad had its first public airing in Winton on 6 April, 1895. The town is 174 km NW of Longreach on the Matilda Hwy. A major sheep area, Winton is also a large trucking centre for the giant road trains bringing cattle from the Channel Country to the railhead. In 1920 the first office of a company called Qantas was registered in Winton. The town's water supply comes out of deep artesian bores at a temperature of 83°C. **Of interest:** In Elderslie St: Historic Royal Theatre, open-air movie theatre and museum, one of the oldest still operating in Australia; swagman statue near swimming pool; Gift and Gem Shop with 'Opal Walk' set up inside; Qantilda Pioneer Place, a complex of seven buildings includes re-creation of the lounge room where Banjo Paterson finalised 'Waltzing Matilda' after he arrived from Dagworth Station, Qantas Room, old telephone exchange, radio display, Aboriginal artifacts, steam locomotive and railway carriage, vintage vehicles, and collection of 4000 bottles. Sept.: Outback festival (odd-numbered years). **In the area:** Aboriginal paintings and bora ceremonial grounds at Skull Hole, 40 km S. Opalton, 115 km S, historic ghost town; gemfields nearby. Combo Waterhole, 150 km NW via Matilda Hwy. Carisbrooke Station, 85 km SW, a working sheep station; Aboriginal cave paintings and scenic drives in surrounds; day tours and accommodation available. Lark Quarry Conservation Park, 110 km SW, features preserved tracks of dinosaur 'stampede'. **Tourist information:** Qantilda Pioneer Place, Elderslie St; (076) 57 1618. **Accommodation:** 4 hotels, 3 motels, 2 cara./camp. parks.

Wondai   Pop. 1156

MAP REF. 491 N6

This typical small country town in the South Burnett region is 15 km S of Murgon and 31 km N of Kingaroy. The surrounding area produces peanuts and a variety of grains; other industries include dairying, beef and pork production, timber milling and dolomite mining. **Of interest:** Museum with local history displays, Mackenzie St. Country market, 2nd Sat. each month. **In the area:** Gem-fossicking areas surround district. Boondooma Dam, 50 km NW near Proston, for water sports. **Tourist**

Channel Country

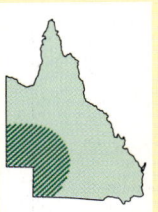

The remote Channel Country is an endless horizon of sweeping plains in the far west and south-west corner of the State. It seldom rains in the Channel Country itself, but after the northern monsoons the Georgina, Hamilton and Diamantina Rivers and Cooper Creek completely take over the country as they flood through hundreds of channels in their efforts to reach Lake Eyre. There is scarcely any gradient. After the 'wet without rain', the enormous quantities of water carried by these rivers usually vanish into waterholes, salt pans and desert sands; grass, wildflowers and bird and animal life miraculously appear, and cattle are moved in for fattening.

The region is sparsely populated except for large pastoral holdings and scattered settlements linked by essential beef-roads. The Diamantina Developmental Road runs south from Mount Isa through Dajarra and Boulia to Bedourie, then swings east across the many channels of the Diamantina River and Cooper Creek through Windorah to the railhead at Quilpie, then on to Charleville, a journey of some 1335 kilometres.

Boulia, proclaimed the capital of the Channel Country, was first settled by Europeans in 1877. It is 295 kilometres south of Mount Isa and 360 kilometres west of Winton. A friendly, relaxed town on the Burke River, its name comes from an Aboriginal word meaning 'clear water'. Burke and Wills filled their water-bags here. The first mail service was by horse from Cloncurry, and a telegraph station was established in 1884.

Bedourie, 191 kilometres further south, is the administrative centre for the Diamantina region, and has a store, school, police station, Flying Doctor medical clinic, roadhouse, motel and caravan park. It has ample artesian water, without the usual pungent smell, and swimming is popular.

South of Bedourie the Diamantina Developmental Road swings east for the partly sealed drive to Windorah. The name means 'place of large fish'. During drought the area is a dustbowl, during the monsoonal period, a lake. There is a good hotel in town and sheep-raising is the only industry.

A good but narrow sealed road leads 237 kilometres east to **Quilpie**, the eastern gateway to the Channel Country. Cattle, sheep and wool are transported by rail to the coast from here. The name derives from the Aboriginal word for the stone curlew, and all but one of the streets have birds' names. Opals have been found here since 1880. Although it is near the Bulloo River, the town's water supply is obtained from a near-boiling artesian bore.

Thargomindah, 193 kilometres south of Quilpie, is a small settlement on the eastern fringe of the Channel Country, 198 kilometres from Cunnamulla. Around the turn of the century Cobb & Co. was operating regularly to Cunnamulla, Hungerford, Charleville, Noccundra and Eromanga. Noccundra, 122 kilometres even further west, has a permanent population of 3, but they can put you up at the hotel and sell you fuel (leaded, unleaded and diesel). Waterholes on the nearby Wilson River are the places for yellow-belly and catfish, brolgas, pelicans, emus and red kangaroos.

The Kennedy Developmental Road from Winton to Boulia is sealed for most of its 256 kilometres. A welcome stop is the remote bush hotel at Middleton. Visitors are sure to be told about the Min Min light a totally unexplained phenomenon that often appears at night near the old Min Min hotel, some 130 kilometres from Boulia. One theory says it is an earthbound UFO that chases cars and then disappears.

The Eyre Developmental Road starts south of Bedourie and leads to **Birdsville**, the most isolated settlement in Queensland, and 11 kilometres from the South Australian border, with the Simpson Desert to the west. It is at the top end of the Birdsville Track to Marree in South Australia. The Birdsville Developmental Road runs north-east to join the Diamantina Developmental Road and east to Windorah. Betoota is the only stop on the lonely 394-kilometre drive from Birdsville to Windorah, and it can be truly welcome. Betoota has one building (a hotel) that basks in the centre of a very large, virtually featureless gibber plain. The hotel is open every day and sells fuel.

Visitors should realise that summer in the Channel Country can become unbearably hot. The best time to go is between April and October. The wildflowers in the area usually bloom in late August or early September.

For further information on the Channel Country, contact the Outback Qld Tourism Authority, Library Building, Shamrock St, Blackall; (076) 57 4255. **See also:** individual entries for those towns indicated by bold type in A–Z listing. **Map reference:** 498 D12.

Landscape close to the South Australian border

Rosslyn Harbour at the popular coastal town of Yeppoon

information: Shire Offices, Scott St; (071) 68 5155. **Accommodation:** 2 hotels, 1 hotel/motel, 1 motel, 1 cara./camp. park.

Yandina Pop. 707

MAP REF. 486 E6

Yandina lies 10 km N of Nambour on the Bruce Hwy and is the home of the world-famous Ginger Factory and Gingertown, where visitors may enjoy ginger goodies. The processing of the crop can be observed from the tower platform at the factory and the *Ginger Bell* paddlesteamer offers river cruises from the factory to a working ginger farm. **Of interest:** Carinya, historic homestead on Bruce Hwy at northern edge of town. The Queenslander, sells antiques and bric-a-brac. Oct.: Spring flower and ginger festival. **In the area:** Wappa Dam, just west of town. At Eumundi, 8 km N: markets each Sat. a.m., selling a range of goods; old and impressive Imperial Hotel, located near markets. **Tourist information:** Cnr Aerodrome Rd and Sixth Ave, Maroochydore; (074) 79 1566. **Accommodation:** 1 hotel, 1 cara./camp. park.

Yeppoon Pop. 7542

MAP REF. 493 O10

This popular coastal resort, 40 km NE of Rockhampton, lies on the shores of Keppel Bay. Yeppoon and the strip of beaches to its south – Cooee Bay, Rosslyn Bay, Causeway Lake, Emu Park and Keppel Sands – are known as the Capricorn Coast. Great Keppel Island Resort is 13 km offshore. Market, 1st Sun. each month. Feb.: Surf lifesaving championships. Aug.: World cooeeing festival. Sept.: Pineapple festival. **In the area:** Scenic drives, contact Tourist information. Cooberrie Park, 15 km N, a noted flora and fauna reserve. Further 17 km N, Byfield State Forest, home of extremely rare Byfield fern. Nearby, Waterpark Creek. Coral Life Marineland, 13 km S at Kinka Beach, unique living displays of coral and marine life; open weekends and school holidays. Catamaran service daily to Great Keppel Is. and nearby underwater observatory; twice weekly to Barren Island. **Tourist information:** Ross Creek Roundabout; (079) 39 4888. **Accommodation**: 2 hotels, 2 hotel/motels, 8 motels, 9 cara./camp. parks.

Yungaburra Pop. 807

MAP REF. 489 D12, 495 M7

On the edge of the Atherton Tableland, 13 km from Atherton and inland from Cairns, the town is known for its National Trust Historic Precinct listing. **Of interest:** Self-guide Historic Precinct Buildings Walk. Lake Eacham Hotel, Cedar St. Gem Gallery, Eacham Rd, offers mineral display and gem-fossicking information. Artists Galleries, cnr Gillies Hwy and Cedar St. Produce and craft markets, 4th Sat. each month on Gillies Hwy. **In the area:** Curtain Fig Tree, 2.5 km SW, spectacular example of strangler fig. The Seven Sisters, seven rolling hills, 2 km N. Tinaburra, 3 km N on the shores of Lake Tinaroo. Across the lake, The Chimneys, two chimneys from timber-milling days. Views of lake from Tinaroo Falls Lookout, 23 km NW. Spectacular views over Gillies Range from Heales Outlook Lookout, 16 km NE. Lakes Eacham (5 km E) and Barrine (10 km E), volcanic crater lakes. **Tourist information:** Curtain Fig Motel, 16 Gillies Hwy; (070) 95 3168. **Accommodation:** 1 hotel, 4 motels.

Gulf Savannah

The Gulf Savannah is a vast, remote, thinly populated region stretching east to the Undara Volcanic National Park, north from **Mount Isa** and **Cloncurry** to the mangrove-covered shores of the Gulf of Carpentaria, and west to the Queensland–Northern Territory border. The unfortunate Burke and Wills were the first European visitors, although the waters of the Gulf itself were first charted by Dutch navigators almost 400 years ago. The country is flat and open, and has more rivers than roads. April to October is the recommended time to see the Gulf country. During the monsoon period, generally November to March, rain may close the dirt roads and on rare occasions may flood the sealed roads from Cloncurry and **Julia Creek**. However, bird-migration patterns make this the best time for observing the spectacular birdlife. Motorists should realise that this is not 'Sunday-driving' country, although main roads have been upgraded, and should plan accordingly. The safest way to travel in the monsoon period is by air out of Cairns, Mount Isa or Karumba. The Gulf Savannah is, however, an ideal corner of Australia if you want to get away from it all.

The wide expanses of the Gulf Savannah region divide themselves into separate areas. The Eastern Savannah is easily reached via the Great Top Road (Gulf Developmental Road), which winds up the eastern face of the Dividing Range, passing above Cairns. As an alternative route to Georgetown, or for travellers with limited time to explore the outback, the Undara Loop is a leisurely 3-day round trip from Cairns through the Lynd Junction, Einasleigh and Forsayth to Georgetown.

Georgetown, 411 kilometres from Cairns, is the centre of the Etheridge Goldfield, where nuggets can still be found. Completing the loop back to Cairns takes the traveller to Tallaroo Hot Springs, Mt Surprise and Undara Volcanic National Park, where visitors can see the lava tubes, a geological phenomenon. The Savannahlander train operates twice weekly between Mt Surprise and Forsayth, and is not connected to any other service.

From Georgetown the traveller can head west 150 kilometres to **Croydon**, terminus of the railway from Normanton, an historic link established to service Croydon, a rich goldmining town of the last century. The railway between the two towns is not connected to any other system. It is used once a week by the Gulflander, the award-winning tourist train, which leaves Normanton every Wednesday and Croydon every Thursday. Many of Croydon's buildings have been classified by the National Trust and the Australian Heritage Commission.

Normanton is the central town of the whole Gulf Savannah, with a population of 1189, although in the gold days of 1891 it had a population of about 3000 people.

Karumba, 71 kilometres north-west of Normanton on the mouth of the Norman River, is the centre of the Gulf prawning industry and home to the barramundi fishing industry. Keen anglers from all over Australia come to Karumba to try their skills.

The Western Savannah has endless flat grassed plains stretching as far as the eye can see, while the wetlands around Karumba stretch across the top of the Western Savannah above Burketown and beyond to the border. Here rivers some 8 kilometres apart overflow their banks during the monsoons and form an unbroken sheet of water.

The town of **Burketown**, close to the Gulf, can be isolated for long periods during the wet. Explorer John Stokes termed the surrounding area the 'Plains of Promise', and today, like most of the Gulf region, it is cattle country. Barramundi fishing and birdwatching attract adventurers; a well-equipped 4WD vehicle is advisable in some areas, but is not essential for the majority of locations.

Lawn Hill National Park, the World Heritage-listed Riversleigh Fossil Field Section. The park is to the west of the Gregory Downs Hotel, a welcome watering-hole for the traveller. Within the park, 60-metre sheer sandstone walls form Lawn Hill Gorge with emerald green water at their base. The National Parks Service has established 20 kilometres of walking tracks to enable visitors to see this beautiful country safely.

When travelling on the sealed beef-road from Cloncurry to Normanton, motorists notice the Bang Bang Jump-up, a change in terrain height, 29 kilometres north of the Donors Hill Station turnoff.

Flight West operate regular flights from both Cairns and Mt Isa, and this is probably the best way to appreciate the vast beauty of the Gulf Savannah and its many sleepy, winding rivers.

The Gulf Savannah is a new frontier in Australia that is opening up to those in search of interesting but authentic educational and adventure experiences. To assist visitors, an organisation of Savannah Guides has been formed. These guides are professional interpreters who have lived in the Gulf Savannah for many years and are able to offer a wide range of knowledge concerning the wilderness environment. There are guide stations at: Tallaroo (at Tallaroo Station); Hells Gate (at Hells Gate Roadhouse); Undara Volcanic National Park (at Lava Lodge, Undara); Borroloola, NT (at McArthur River Caravan Park); Lawn Hill National Park (at Adels Grove); and Cape Crawford, NT (at Heartbreak Hotel).

For further information on the area, contact Savannah Guide Headquarters, 57 McLeod St, Cairns; (070) 31 7933. **See also:** Lawn Hill National Park entry in National Parks; individual entries in A–Z listing for those towns indicated by bold type. **Map references:** 494 C12, 497 I12.

Lawn Hill National Park is close to the Northern Territory border

Queensland

Location Map

Other Map Coverage
Central Brisbane 476
Brisbane Approach & Bypass Routes 477
Brisbane & Northern Suburbs 478
Southern Suburbs, Brisbane 480
Brisbane Region 482
Gold Coast Approach & Bypass Routes 484

The Gold Coast 485
The Sunshine Coast 486
Townsville 487
Cairns 488
Cairns Region 489

476 Central Brisbane

Accommodation ■
- Bellevue Hotel 1 E7
- Hotel Grand Chancellor 2 C2
- Gateway 3 C5
- Gazebo Terrace 4 C3
- Heritage Hotel 5 G6
- Hilton International 6 E5
- Hotel Conrad 7 E7
- Lennons Plaza Hotel 8 D6
- Parkroyal 9 F7
- Radisson 10 A4
- Ridge Hotel 11 E2
- Sheraton Brisbane Hotel 12 E3
- Story Bridge Motor Inn 13 I6
- Travel Lodge 14 B4

General Information ■
- Ansett Australia 15 D6
- Brisbane Transit Centre 16 B4
- Central Railway Station 17 E3
- General Post Office 18 F4
- Motoring Organisation (RACQ) 19 F4
- Police Headquarters 20 B4
- Qantas Travel Centre 21 F4
- River Cruises 22 D7/H2
- Roma Street Station 23 B3
- Tourist Information 24 E5/D5

Places of Interest ■
- Anzac War Memorial 25 E4
- Brisbane Cricket Ground 26 I13
- City Botanic Gardens 27 G8
- City Hall 28 D5
- City Plaza 29 D5
- Commissariat Stores 30 D7
- Customs House 31 G3
- Deanery 32 G3
- Observatory (Old Windmill) 33 D3
- Old Government House 34 F9
- Parliament House 35 E8
- Qld Art Gallery 36 B7
- Qld Cultural Centre 37 B7
- Qld Maritime Museum 38 E11
- Qld Museum 39 B7
- Qld University of Technology 40 F9
- State Library of Qld 41 B6
- Conrad Treasury Casino 42 D6

Accommodation Only a sample range is listed; inclusion is not necessarily a recommendation.

Approach & Bypass Routes BRISBANE 477

478 Brisbane & Northern Suburbs

479

MORETON BAY

Mud Island

For more detail of Central Brisbane see page 476

St Helena Island
ST HELENA ISLAND NATIONAL PARK

Juno Point
Jubilee Ck
Luggage Point
Port of Brisbane
Inner Bar Reach
FISHERMAN ISLANDS

Green Island

Myrtletown
Boat Passage
Whyte Island
Crab Ck
Oil Refinery
Bulwer Island
Fort Lytton National Park
Quarantine Station
Lytton
Oil Refinery
Pritchard St
Pinkenba
Brisbane Airport
International Terminal
Domestic Terminal
Meeandah
Bunour
Gibson Island
Aquarium Passage
Gosport St
Wynnum North
Elanora Park
Oyster Point
Darling Point
Eagle Farm
Royal Queensland Golf Club
Gateway Bridge
Sibley
Lindum
Crawfords
Wynnum Golf Course
Wynnum
Mountjoy Tce
Manly Boat Harbour
King Island
ENVIRONMENTAL PARK
Queensport
Hemmant Park
Hemmant
Kianawah
New Lindum Rd
Preston
Memorial Park
Manly
Wellington Point
Murarrie
Carmichael Park
Wynnum West
Fleming Rd
Wondall
Manly West
Lota
Fig Tree Point
Waterloo Bay
Erobin
Cannon Hill
Cemetery
Villanova College Sports Ground
Wakerley
Rickertt Rd
Green Camp Rd
Ransome
Mooroondu Point
Thorneside
Quarry Rd
Birkdale
Wellington Point
Geoff Skinner Reserve
Historic Ormiston House
Tingalpa
Eversholt
Thurston
Tilley
New Cleveland
Molle
Howeston Golf Course
Tingalpa Creek Reserve
Birkdale
Carina
Fursden
Meadowlands
D'Arcy
Clem Jones Centre
Carindale
Meadowlands Picnic Ground
London
Gumdale
The Plantation
Chelsea
John Frederick Park
Ormiston
Camp Hill
Belmont Hospital
Winstanley
Cleveland Rd
Belmont Rifle Range
Cannon Hill Rifle Range
Chandler (Sleeman) Sports Complex
Chandler
Finucane
Sturgeon
Northern Arterial

480 Southern Suburbs, Brisbane

0 1 2 3 4 5 km

J K L M N O P Q R

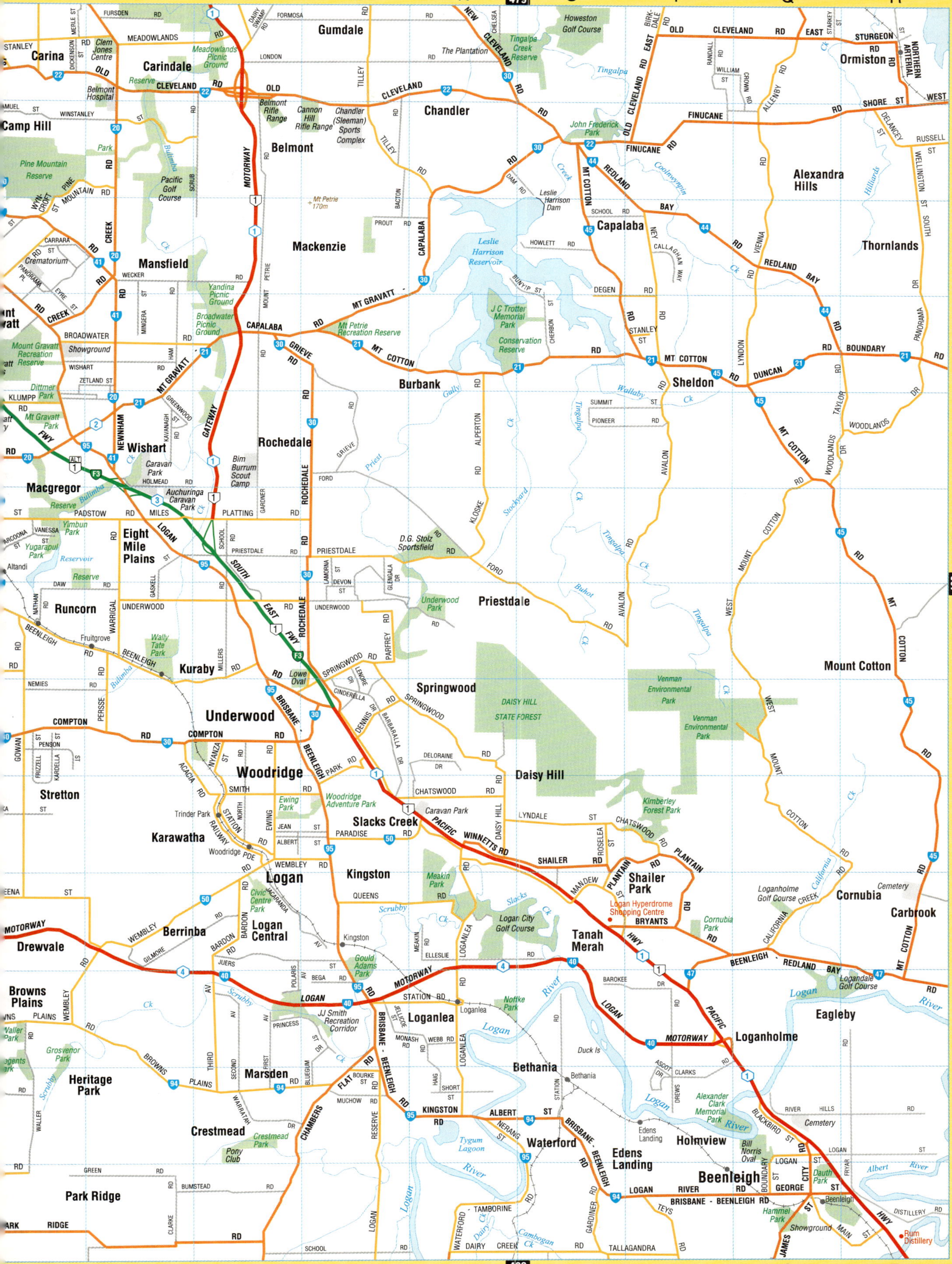

J K L M N O P Q R

1 2 3 4 5 6 7 8 9 10 11 12 13

482 Brisbane Region

0 10 20 30 km

J K L M N 491 O P Q R

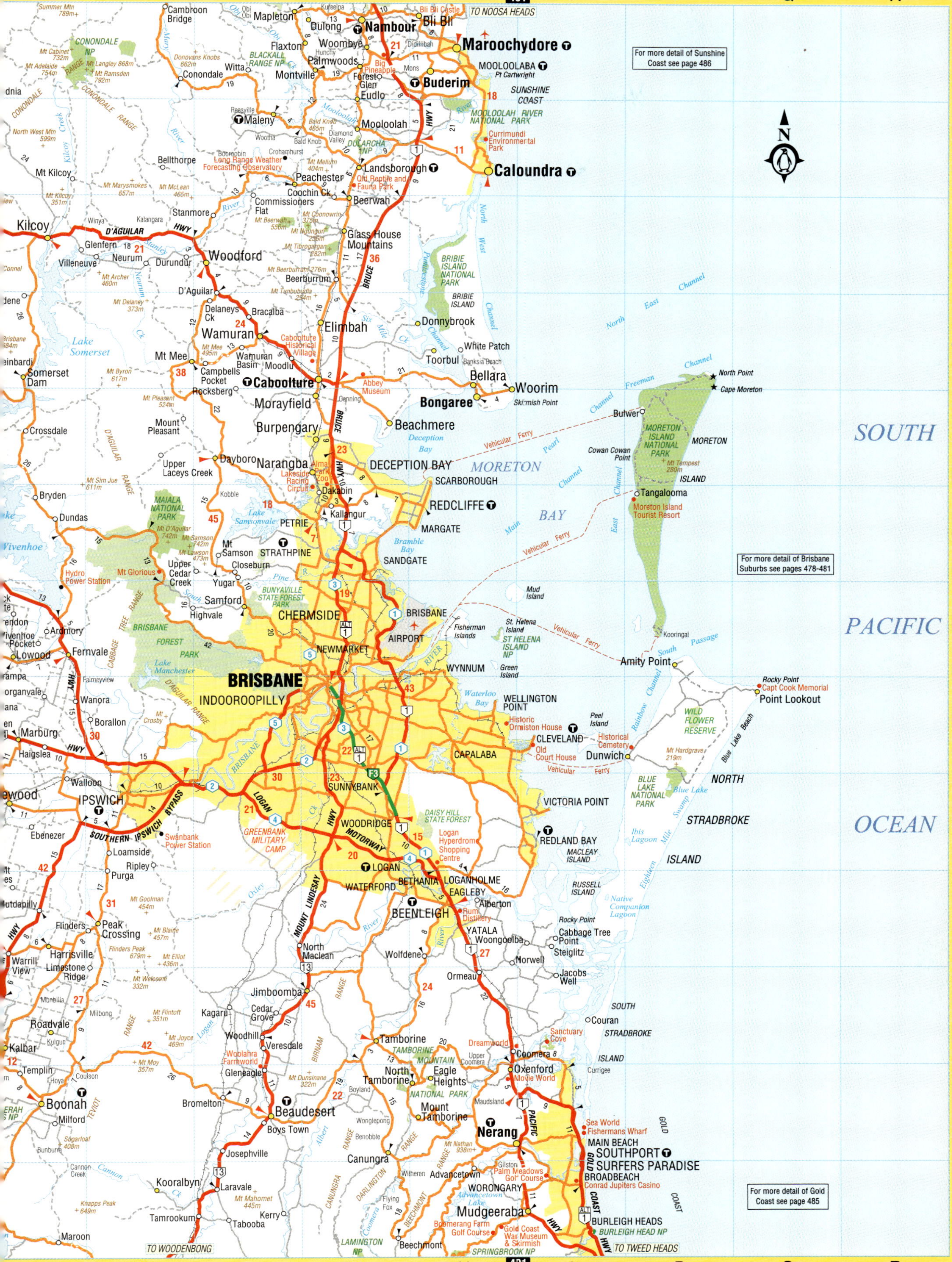

J K L M N 491 O P Q R

484 GOLD COAST Approach & Bypass Routes

Thick roads represent recommended approach and bypass routes.

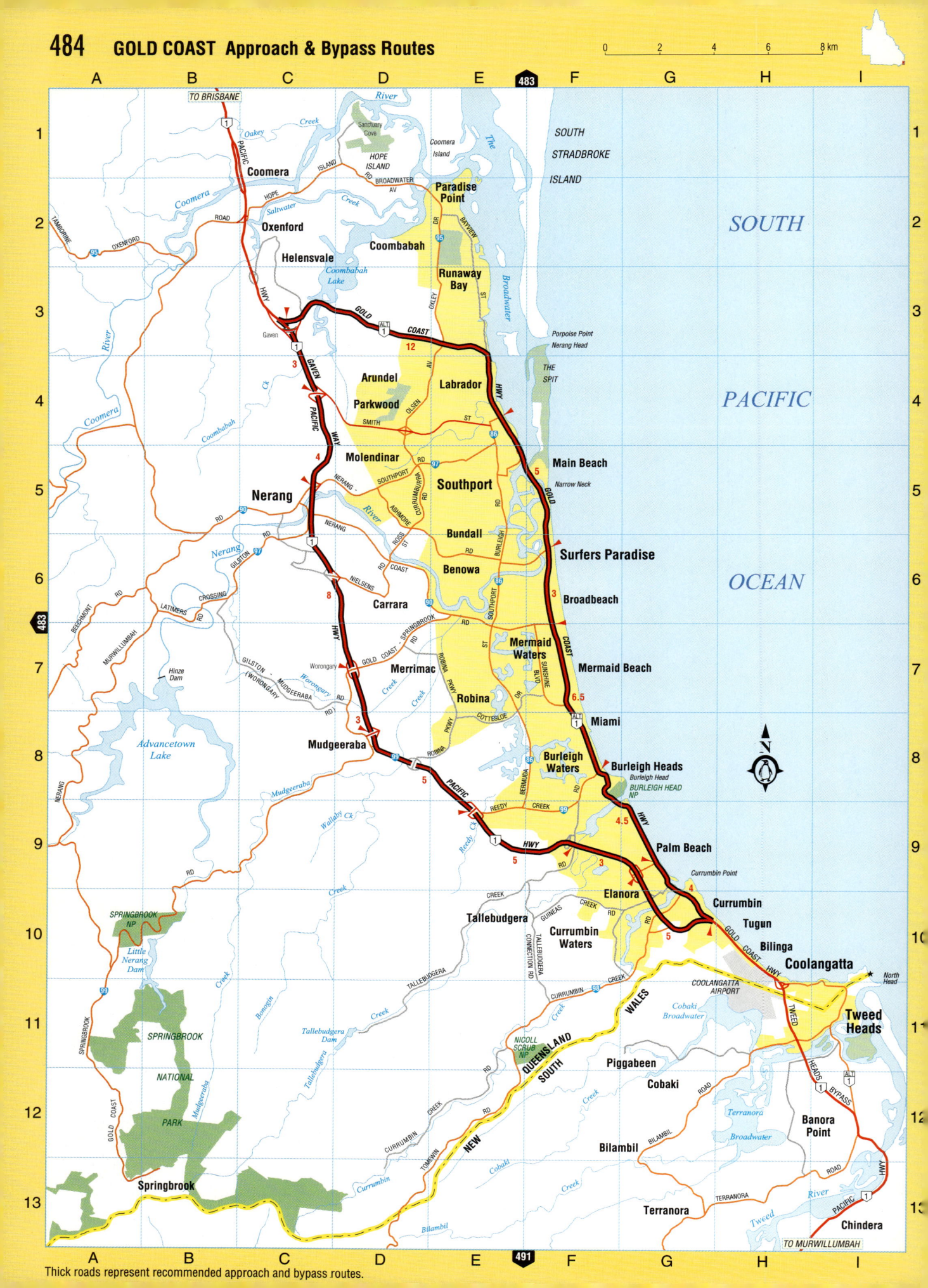

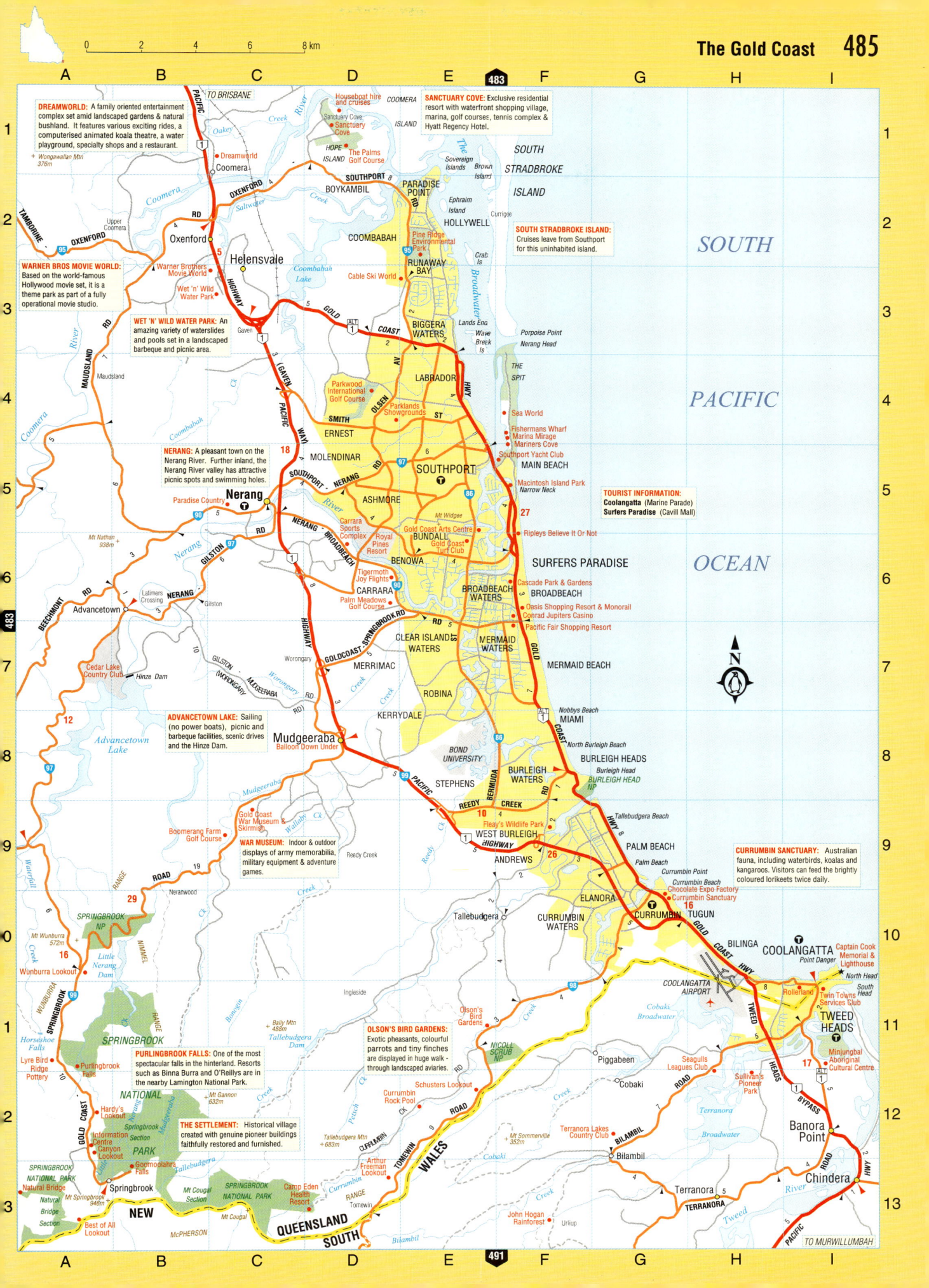

The Gold Coast 485

DREAMWORLD: A family oriented entertainment complex set amid landscaped gardens & natural bushland. It features various exciting rides, a computerised animated koala theatre, a water playground, specialty shops and a restaurant.

WARNER BROS MOVIE WORLD: Based on the world-famous Hollywood movie set, it is a theme park as part of a fully operational movie studio.

WET 'N' WILD WATER PARK: An amazing variety of waterslides and pools set in a landscaped barbeque and picnic area.

NERANG: A pleasant town on the Nerang River. Further inland, the Nerang River valley has attractive picnic spots and swimming holes.

SANCTUARY COVE: Exclusive residential resort with waterfront shopping village, marina, golf courses, tennis complex & Hyatt Regency Hotel.

SOUTH STRADBROKE ISLAND: Cruises leave from Southport for this uninhabited island.

TOURIST INFORMATION:
Coolangatta (Marine Parade)
Surfers Paradise (Cavill Mall)

ADVANCETOWN LAKE: Sailing (no power boats), picnic and barbeque facilities, scenic drives and the Hinze Dam.

WAR MUSEUM: Indoor & outdoor displays of army memorabilia, military equipment & adventure games.

CURRUMBIN SANCTUARY: Australian fauna, including waterbirds, koalas and kangaroos. Visitors can feed the brightly coloured lorikeets twice daily.

PURLINGBROOK FALLS: One of the most spectacular falls in the hinterland. Resorts such as Binna Burra and O'Reillys are in the nearby Lamington National Park.

OLSON'S BIRD GARDENS: Exotic pheasants, colourful parrots and tiny finches are displayed in huge walk-through landscaped aviaries.

THE SETTLEMENT: Historical village created with genuine pioneer buildings faithfully restored and furnished.

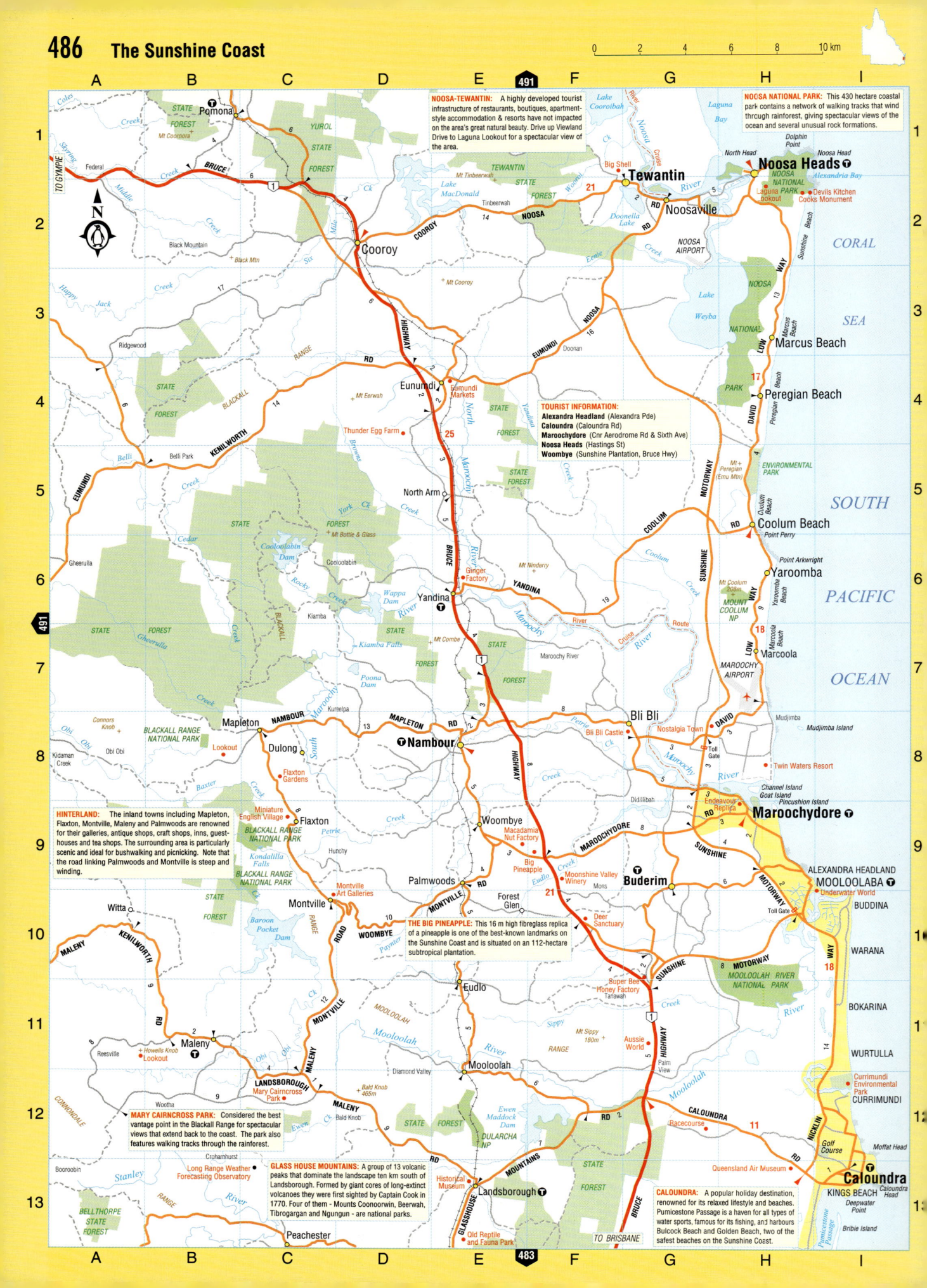

486 The Sunshine Coast

NOOSA-TEWANTIN: A highly developed tourist infrastructure of restaurants, boutiques, apartment-style accommodation & resorts have not impacted on the area's great natural beauty. Drive up Viewland Drive to Laguna Lookout for a spectacular view of the area.

NOOSA NATIONAL PARK: This 430 hectare coastal park contains a network of walking tracks that wind through rainforest, giving spectacular views of the ocean and several unusual rock formations.

TOURIST INFORMATION:
- Alexandra Headland (Alexandra Pde)
- Caloundra (Caloundra Rd)
- Maroochydore (Cnr Aerodrome Rd & Sixth Ave)
- Noosa Heads (Hastings St)
- Woombye (Sunshine Plantation, Bruce Hwy)

HINTERLAND: The inland towns including Mapleton, Flaxton, Montville, Maleny and Palmwoods are renowned for their galleries, antique shops, craft shops, inns, guesthouses and tea shops. The surrounding area is particularly scenic and ideal for bushwalking and picnicking. Note that the road linking Palmwoods and Montville is steep and winding.

THE BIG PINEAPPLE: This 16 m high fibreglass replica of a pineapple is one of the best-known landmarks on the Sunshine Coast and is situated on an 112-hectare subtropical plantation.

MARY CAIRNCROSS PARK: Considered the best vantage point in the Blackall Range for spectacular views that extend back to the coast. The park also features walking tracks through the rainforest.

GLASS HOUSE MOUNTAINS: A group of 13 volcanic peaks that dominate the landscape ten km south of Landsborough. Formed by giant cores of long-extinct volcanoes they were first sighted by Captain Cook in 1770. Four of them - Mounts Coonoowrin, Beerwah, Tibrogargan and Ngungun - are national parks.

CALOUNDRA: A popular holiday destination, renowned for its relaxed lifestyle and beaches. Pumicestone Passage is a haven for all types of water sports, famous for its fishing, and harbours Bulcock Beach and Golden Beach, two of the safest beaches on the Sunshine Coast.

Townsville 487

Accommodation 🔵
- Aquarius on the Beach 1 F2
- Hi Roller Motel 2 D9
- Reef Lodge 3 G3
- Seagulls Holiday Inn 4 D2
- South Bank Motor Inn 5 G4
- Townsville Plaza Hotel 6 F4
- Townsville Travelodge 7 G4
- YHA 8 G3

General Information ■
- Ansett Australia 9 G4
- Hospital 10 F3
- Motoring Organisation (RACQ) 11 F5
- Police Station 12 F4

Accommodation Only a sample range is listed; Inclusion is not necessarily a recommendation.

- Post Office 13 G4
- Qantas Travel Centre 14 G4
- Town Hall 15 F4
- Townsville Railway Station 16 F4
- Townsville Transit Centre 17 G4
- Tourist Information 18 G4

Places of Interest 🔴
- Art Gallery 19 G4
- Botanic Gardens 20 C8
- Sheraton Breakwater Casino 21 H3
- Castle Hill Lookout 22 E4
- Civic Theatre 23 F6
- Flinders Mall 24 G4
- Great Barrier Reef Wonderland 25 G3
- Jimmy's Lookout 26 B1
- Old Fort & Museum 27 E1
- St James Cathedral 28 G3

488 Cairns

Accommodation
- All Seasons Sunshine Tower 1 G8
- City Caravan Park 2 F8
- Hilton Hotel 3 I9
- Holiday Inn 4 H8
- Pacific Coast Guest House 5 H10
- Pacific International 6 I9
- Radisson Plaza 7 I9
- Tuna Towers 8 H8
- Youth Hostels 9 H9, H10

General Information
- Ansett Australia 10 H9
- Bus Station 11 I10
- Cairns and Far North Environment Centre 12 E7
- Cairns Railway Station 13 H10
- Hospital 14 G8
- Motoring Organisation (RACQ) 15 H9
- Police 16 H10
- Post Office 17 I10
- Qantas Travel Centre 18 H9
- Tourist Information 19 I9

Places of Interest
- Flecker Botanic Gardens 20 D6
- Hides of Cairns Hotel 21 H9
- Museum 22 H9
- Marlin Jetty 23 I9
- Royal Flying Doctor Service 24 C6
- The Pier 25 I9

Accommodation — Only a sample range is listed; inclusion is not necessarily a recommendation.

Cairns Region

DAINTREE NATIONAL PARK: A stunning combination of rainforest, reef and beach. The park encompasses the largest and one of the oldest tracts of tropical rainforest in Australia.

THE GREAT BARRIER REEF: The world's largest coral reef system is a living phenomenon that has World Heritage status. Despite its name, The Great Barrier Reef is not one reef but a complex of some 2500 reefs and 1000 islands, including 71 coral cays, that stretch from near the coast of western Papua to Breaksea Spit east of Gladstone. While most of the islands are uninhabited, a number have been developed as tourist resorts and they attract thousands of visitors each year.

MOSSMAN RIVER GORGE: A short walk under a dense green canopy of rainforest leads to the boulder-strewn Mossman River which rushes in a series of cascades through the gorge; an ideal location for picnicking and swimming.

TOURIST INFORMATION:
Atherton (cnr Mabel & Vernon Sts)
Cairns (cnr Grafton & Hartley Sts)
Port Douglas (23 Macrossan St)

GREEN ISLAND: A coral cay surrounded by beautiful patches of reef and crested with thick tropical vegetation. Visitors from Cairns frequent the island daily to view the Reef through glass-bottomed boats and to visit the underwater observatory.

FITZROY ISLAND: This island offers magnificent native flora and fauna and secluded sandy beaches. Accommodation ranging from villa-style to bunk-style, with communal amenities is available.

CURTAIN FIG TREE: This extraordinary tree is one of the most-frequently visited spots on the Tablelands. Located within a state forest park, the Curtain Fig Tree has resulted from a strangling fig taking over its host tree, climbing higher and higher and throwing down showers of roots to support its massive structure. Rainforest birds and animals frequent the park.

WOOROONOORAN NATIONAL PARK: Seventy nine thousand five hundred hectares of dense rainforest make this park a haven for a variety of reptiles and birds. Mt Bartle Frere and Mt Bellenden - the two highest mountains in the state - are within the park boundaries.

490 South Eastern Queensland

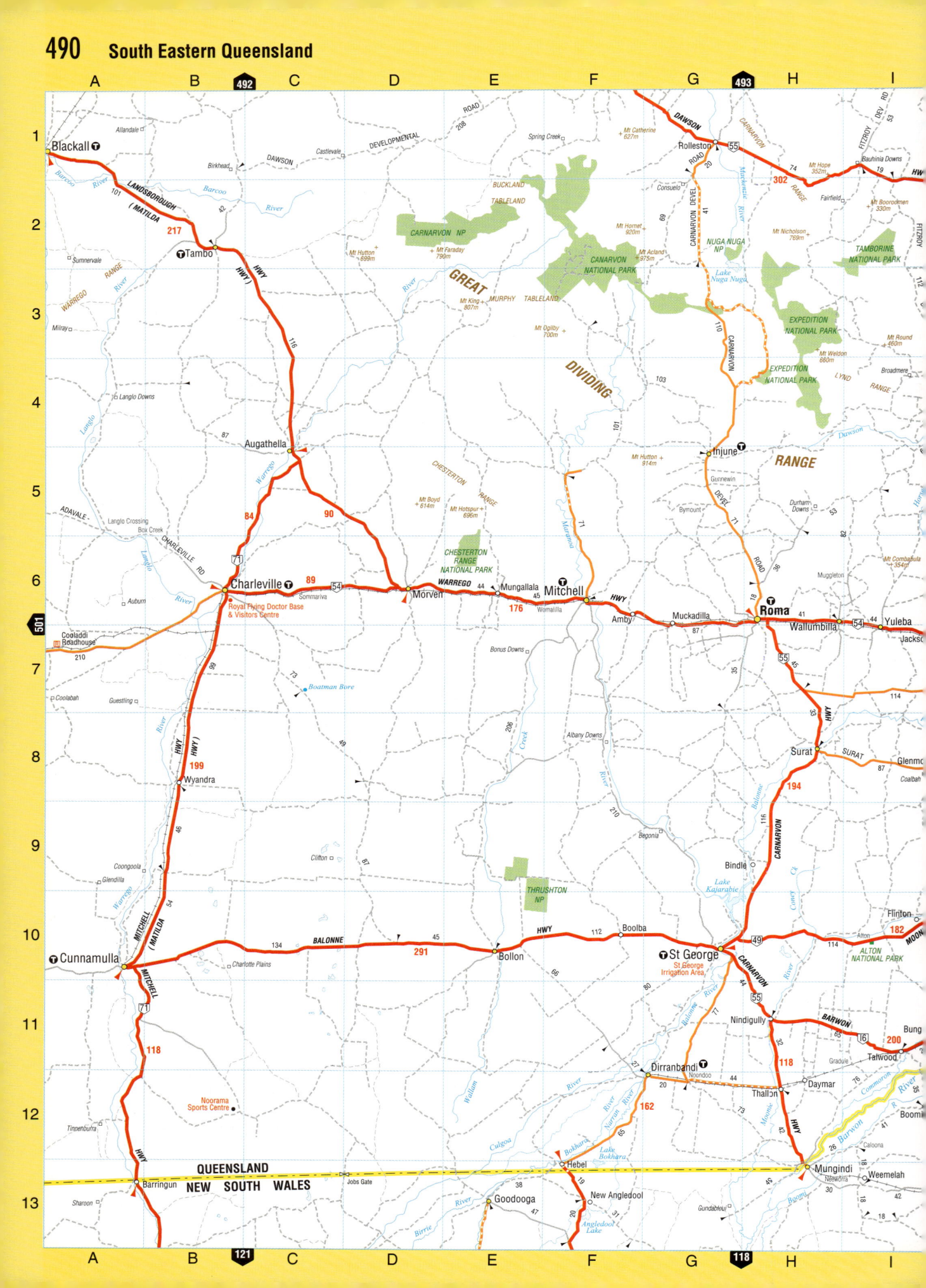

0 25 50 75 100 km

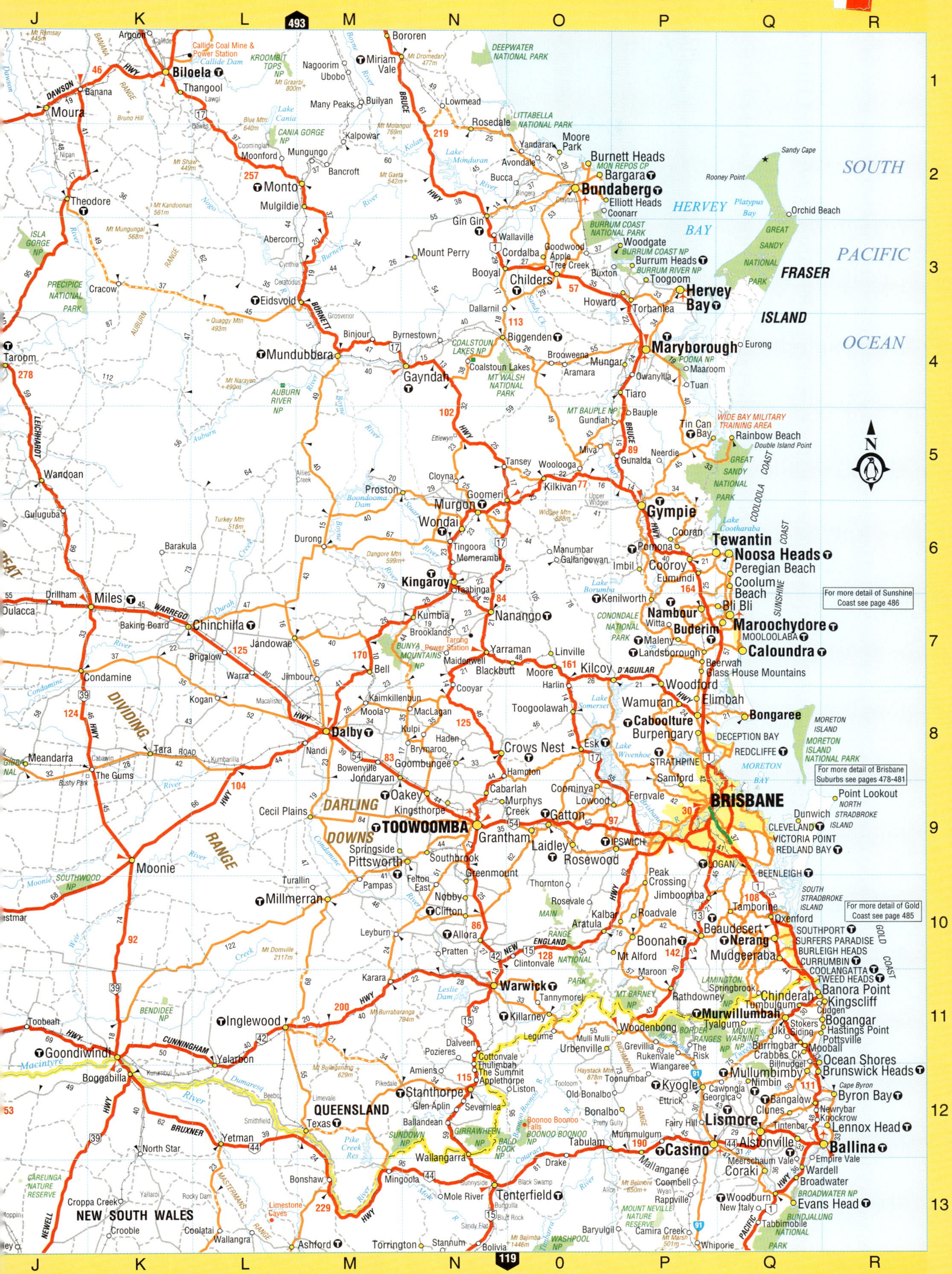

492 North Eastern Queensland

493

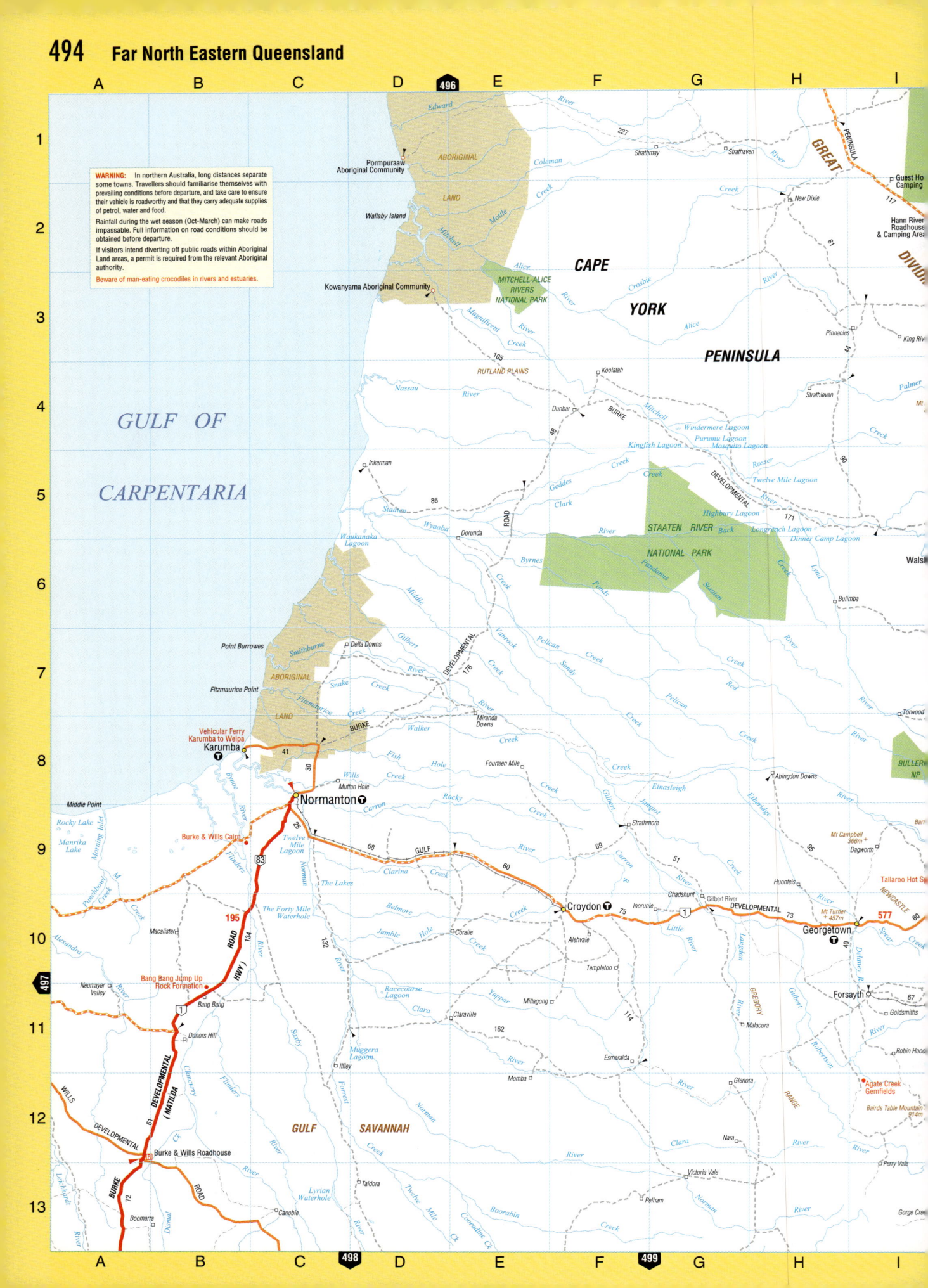

494 Far North Eastern Queensland

WARNING: In northern Australia, long distances separate some towns. Travellers should familiarise themselves with prevailing conditions before departure, and take care to ensure their vehicle is roadworthy and that they carry adequate supplies of petrol, water and food.

Rainfall during the wet season (Oct-March) can make roads impassable. Full information on road conditions should be obtained before departure.

If visitors intend diverting off public roads within Aboriginal Land areas, a permit is required from the relevant Aboriginal authority.

Beware of man-eating crocodiles in rivers and estuaries.

0 25 50 75 100 km
J K L M N O P Q R
496
499
492
1 2 3 4 5 6 7 8 9 10 11 12 13
CORAL SEA
GREAT BARRIER REEF
For more detail of Cairns Region see page 489
For more detail of Townsville see page 487
LIZARD ISLAND NP
Lizard Island
Flat Top Hill 107m
Saddle Hill 508m
Mt Stuckey (Numbargulme) 479m
STARCKE NP
Cape Flattery
MT WEBB NP
Glenrock
Cape Bedford
Hope Vale Aboriginal Community
Mt Piebald 417m
ENDEAVOUR RIVER NATIONAL PARK
Cooktown
MT COOK NP
Laura
Split Rock & Gu Yulangi Rock Art Sites
Helenvale
Rossville
CEDAR BAY NP
Mt Finnigan 1148m
Ayton
Lakeland
Wujal Wujal
DAINTREE NATIONAL PARK
Cape Tribulation
Palmer River Roadhouse
Maitland Downs
Daintree
Mt Alexandra 483m
Wonga
Miallo
Cooya Beach
Mossman Gorge
Mossman
Port Douglas
Trinity Bay
Oak Beach
Mount Carbine
Maryfarms
Julatten
Mount Molloy
Ellis Beach
Palm Cove
Smithfield
Kuranda
CAIRNS
Green Island
GREEN ISLAND NATIONAL PARK
Fitzroy Island
FITZROY ISLAND NATIONAL PARK
BARRON GORGE NP
Biboohra
Mareeba
Mareeba-Dimbula Irrigation Area
Edmonton
Gordonvale
Aloomba
Walkamin
Tinaroo Falls
Kairi
Tolga
Atherton
Yungaburra
Tinaburra
Fishery Falls
Deeral
RUSSELL RIVER NP
WOOROONOORAN NATIONAL PARK
Babinda
Bramston Beach
Herberton
Malanda
Miriwinni
EUBENANGEE SWAMP NP
Millaa Millaa Falls
Topaz
Flying Fish Point
Innisfail
Millaa Millaa
Tumoulin
Ravenshoe
Millstream Falls
Mourilyan
Mena Creek
Inarlinga
Silkwood
El Arish
Kurrimine Beach
Bingil Bay
Mission Beach
Dunk Island
FAMILY ISLANDS NP
Bedarra Island
Tully
Euramo
HULL RIVER NP
Tully Heads
EDMUND KENNEDY NP
Rockingham Bay
Kennedy
Cape Richards
Cape Sandwich
HINCHINBROOK ISLAND
HINCHINBROOK ISLAND NP
Cardwell
LUMHOLTZ NATIONAL PARK
Murray Falls
Abergowrie
Lannercost
Lucinda-Dungeness
Halifax
Cassady Beach
Pelorus Island (Yanooa)
Orpheus Island (Goolboddi)
ORPHEUS ISLAND NP
Trebonne
Ingham
Toobanna
Forrest Beach
Great Palm Island Aboriginal Community
Great Palm Island
PALUMA RANGE NATIONAL PARK
Jourama Falls
Extinct Volcano
Bambaroo
Balgal Beach
Rollingstone
McClellands Lookout
Magnetic Island
MAGNETIC ISLAND NP
Nelly Bay
Jalloonda
Bluewater
Pallarenda
TOWNSVILLE
Cape Bowling Green
BOWLING GREEN BAY NATIONAL PARK
Bowling Green Bay
Alligator Creek
Cungulla
Giru
Alva
Brandon
Ayr
Home Hill
Woodstock
Ross River Res
Chillagoe
CHILLAGOE MUNGANA CAVES NP
Chillagoe Limestone Caves
Dimbulah
Almaden
Petford
Watsonville
Irvinebank
Kalunga
Ootann
Mount Mulligan
Nychum
Mount Garnet
Innot Hot Springs
Nymbool
Koombooloomba Reservoir
FORTY MILE SCRUB NP
Mount Surprise
UNDARA VOLCANIC NATIONAL PARK
Einasleigh
The Lynd Junction
Oasis Roadhouse
Greenvale Nickel Mine
Greenvale
Blue Water Springs Roadhouse
O'Briens Creek Gemfields (Topaz)
Two Mile Dam
Walters Plains Lake
Lake Lucy
Saltern Lagoon
HANN TABLELAND NP
Lake Mitchell
CAPTAIN COOK HWY
BRUCE HWY
PALMERSTON HWY
KENNEDY HWY
GREGORY DEVELOPMENTAL ROAD
HERVEYS RANGE DEVELOPMENTAL ROAD

496 Cape York Peninsula

Far North Western Queensland 497

498 North Western Queensland

0 25 50 75 100 km

J K 494 L M N O P 495 Q R

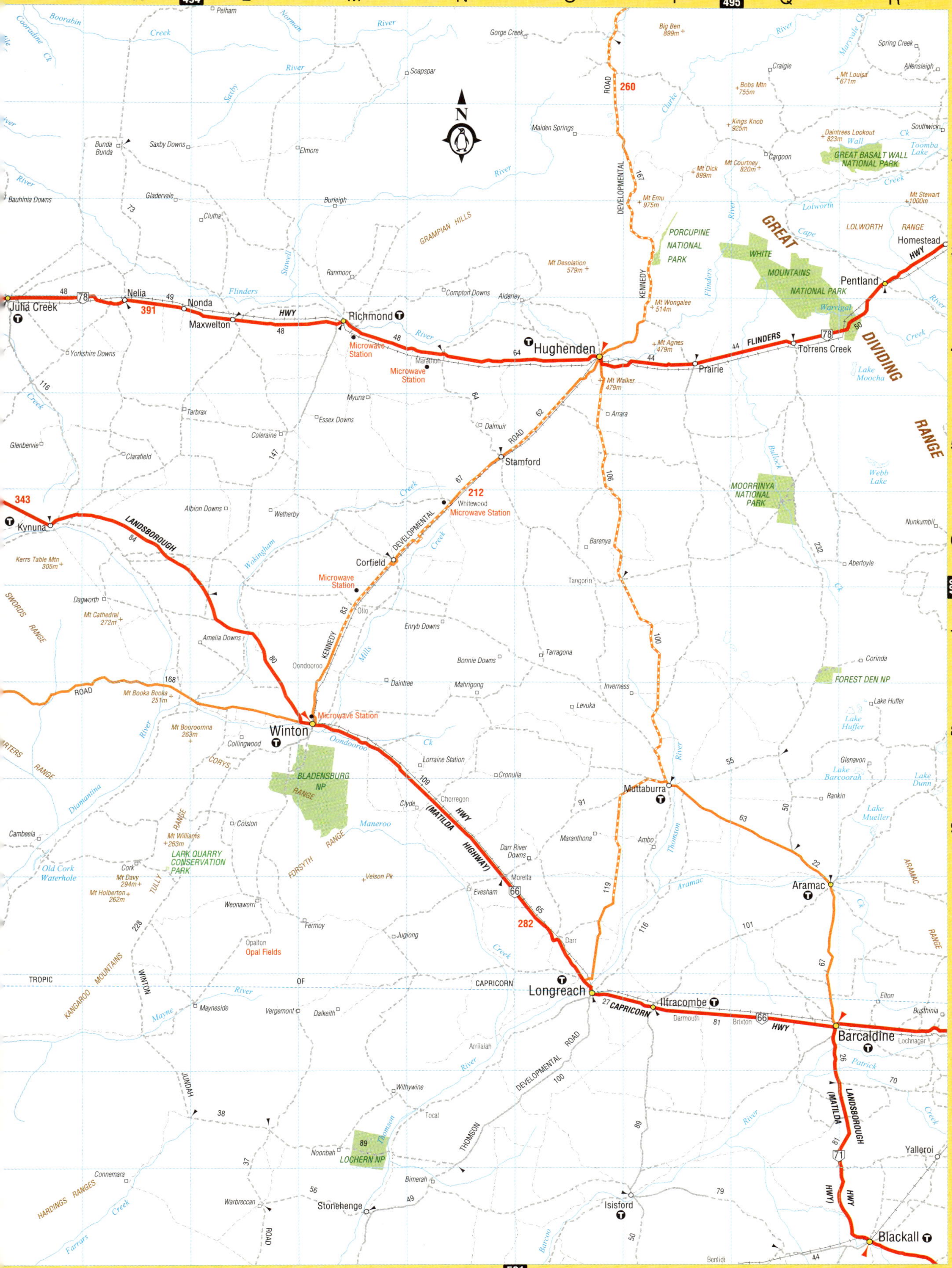

J K L M N 501 O P Q R

1 2 3 4 5 6 7 8 9 10 11 12 13

500 South Western Queensland

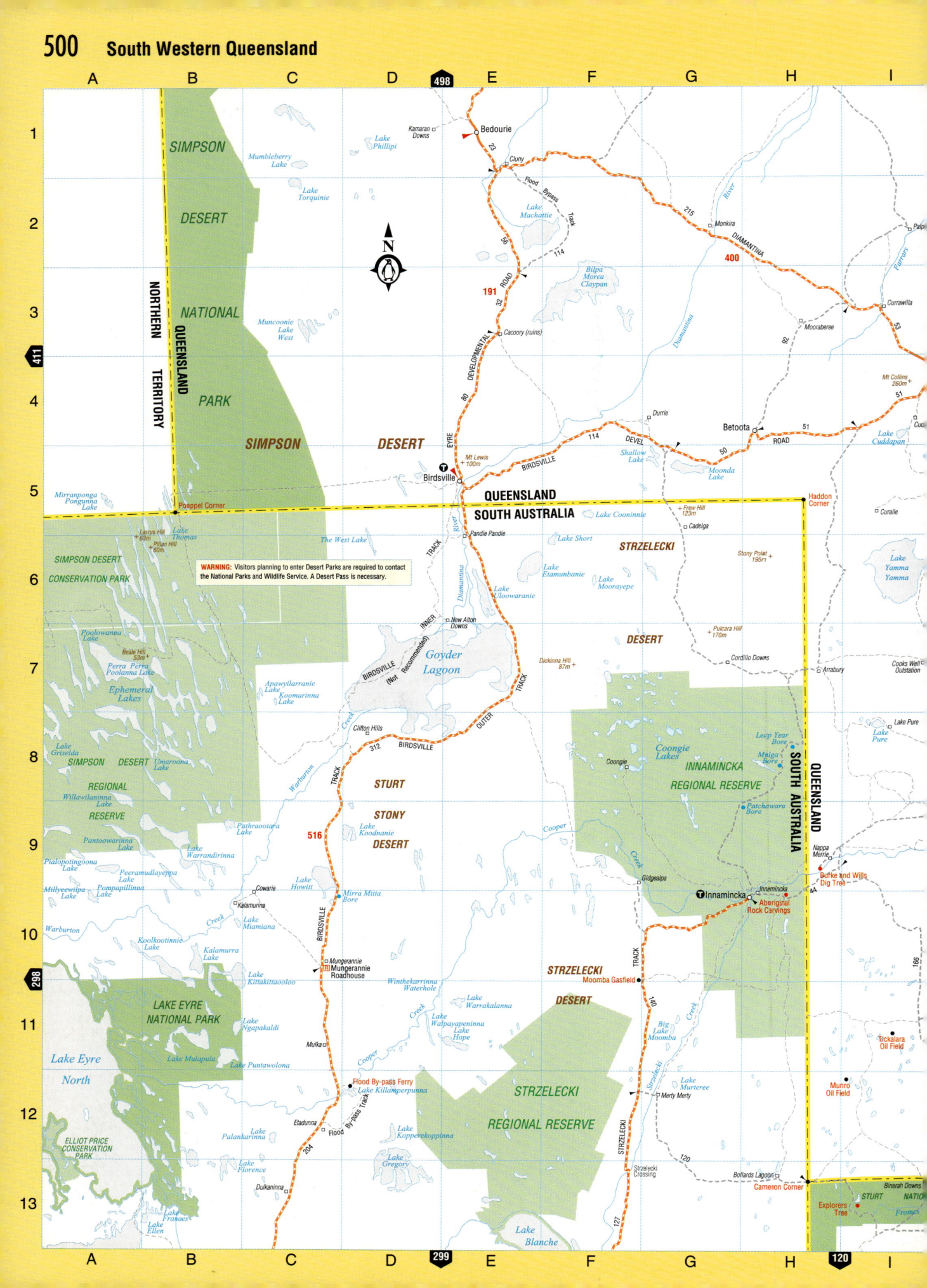

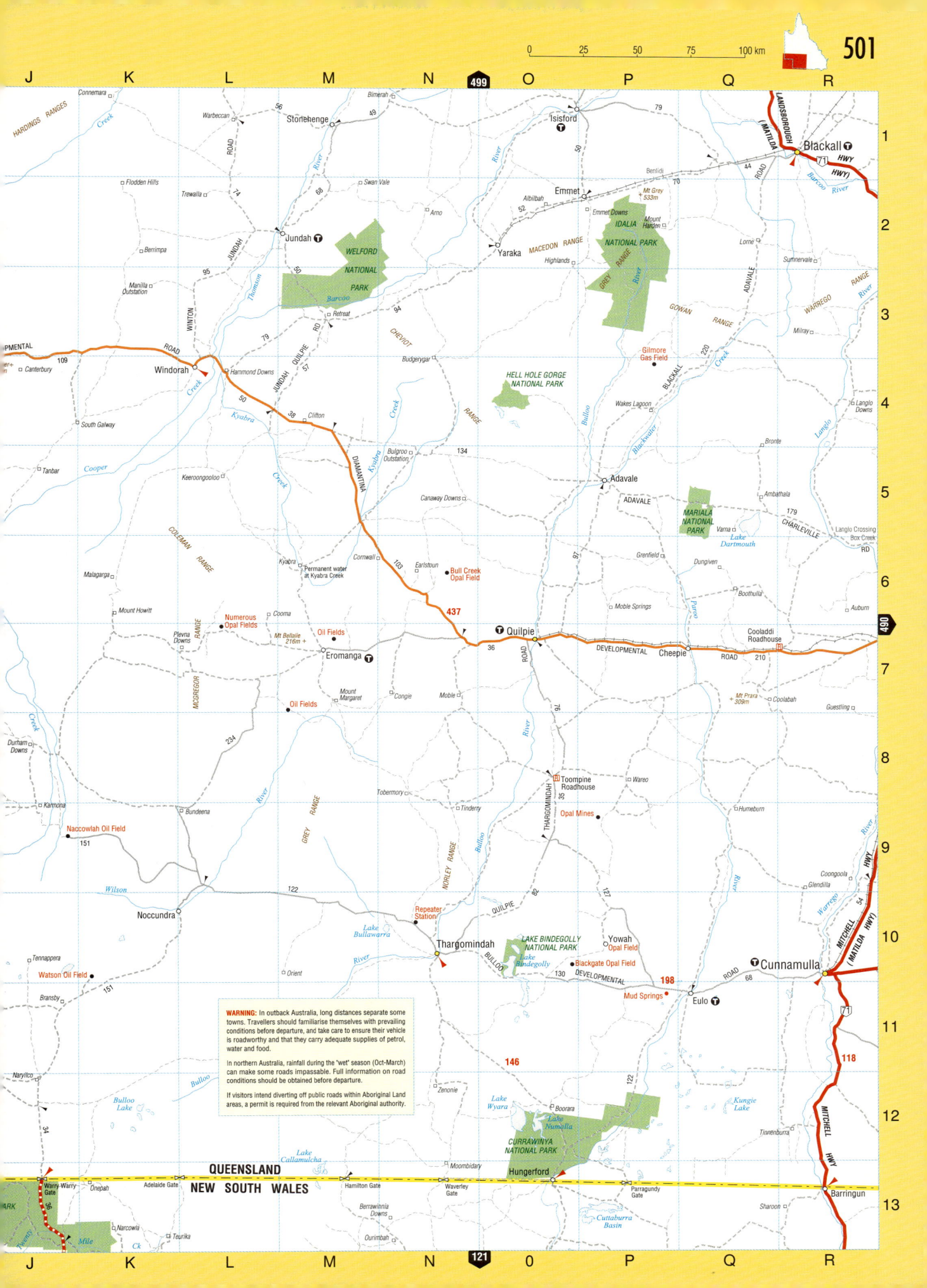

Tasmania

TASMANIA

Heritage Island

Tasmania has certainly won many more hearts than it can claim square kilometres. It has only 68 000 of the latter, but it crams into them its rugged west, a central plateau broken by steep mountains and narrow river valleys, and an eastern coastal region offering a soft pastoral beauty.

Tasmania's diverse charms have made it a popular tourist attraction for Australians from 'the mainland' for many years.

This dramatically beautiful island, however, has a far from beautiful early history. The first European to sight the island was Abel Tasman in 1642; it was later claimed by Captain Cook for the English and the British settlement dates from 1803. For the next fifty years it was maintained primarily as a penal colony, although prosperous settlements developed around Hobart and New Norfolk. The convicts did the hard labour and lived in brutal conditions at Port Arthur. The Tasmanian Aborigines, who resisted the takeover of their land, were treated even more harshly than the convicts.

Political separation from New South Wales was granted in 1825 and transportation of convicts ceased in 1853. Today the ruins of Port Arthur have taken on a mellow charm and Tasmania is an infinitely more hospitable place.

Tasmania was first called Van Diemen's Land; these days it is known as the 'heritage island', 'treasure island' or the 'apple isle'. Its economy is basically agricultural with the major growth area being in quality specialised food products. The Tasmanian hydro-electric system has a greater output than that of the Snowy Mountains Scheme; Tasmania's high rainfall helps this. The climate offers mild summers and cool winters, with much of the mountain regions receiving heavy winter snowfall. Mid-December to late January is very popular with tourists; late spring or autumn are also pleasant. Even the winter months offer good touring.

When planning a trip to Tasmania note the heavy booking for the *Spirit of Tasmania* ferry service between Melbourne and Devonport from December to March. Either book well in advance or consider a fly/drive holiday, which can be a relaxing and economic alternative. Tasmania's roads are well suited to relaxed meandering, many of them being winding and narrow. In a fortnight, however, you can happily complete what is virtually a round tour of the island.

Hobart, the capital of Tasmania, is built on either side of the Derwent River, and is dominated by Mount Wellington. The Wrest Point Hotel-Casino, Australia's first casino, with its lavish entertainment and International Convention Centre, is now competing for first place as the city's best-known landmark, towering over Hobart's many colonial buildings. All within easy reach are Port Arthur, Richmond with its beautiful bridge (the oldest in Australia) and the settlements of Bothwell and New Norfolk.

The Derwent Valley with its hop fields and apple orchards, lovely in blossom-time and in autumn, lies to the west. Further west is Lake Pedder;

NOT TO BE MISSED
in Tasmania

- **Arve Road Forest Drive** – for spectacular forest scenery including ancient huon pines
- **Bicheno** – old sealing and whaling town, now home port for crayfishing boats
- **Cataract Gorge Reserve** – Launceston's own piece of wilderness
- **Clarendon House** – one of the finest Georgian homes in the country
- **Coles Bay** – a beautiful unspoiled bay on the Freycinet Peninsula
- **Cradle Mountain-Lake St Clair National Park** – for excellent bushwalking in this famous mountain wilderness
- **Don River railway** – a scenic train trip along the banks of the river
- **Gordon River** – enjoy its beauty from a cruise boat
- **Newdegate Cave** – one of Australia's most beautiful limestone caves
- **Port Arthur** – said to be Australia's most significant heritage site
- **Richmond** – delightful, well-preserved Georgian village
- **Strahan Wharf Centre** – for fascinating history in a unique hands-on museum

Coles Bay, near Freycinet National Park

Dove Lake, Cradle Mountain-Lake St Clair National Park

the flooding of this area was a source of great controversy when it was made part of the hydro-electric scheme. The surrounding country makes up the Southwest National Park, Tasmania's largest and one which has been given World Heritage status. The Lyell Highway leads to Cradle Mountain-Lake St Clair National Park. Queenstown, surrounded by stark ochre-coloured mountains, is the largest settlement in this wild, forested region. Nearby coastal Strahan was once a mining boom-town and is the starting-point of the

CALENDAR OF EVENTS

Note: The information given here was accurate at the time of printing. However, as the timing of events held annually is subject to change and some events may extend into the following month, it is best to check with the local tourism authority or event organisers to confirm the details. The calendar is not exhaustive. Most towns and regions hold sporting competitions, art, craft, and trade exhibitions, agricultural and flower shows, music festivals and other events annually. Details of these events are available from local tourism outlets.

JANUARY
Public holidays: New Year's Day; Australia Day. **Hobart:** Summer festival; Hobart Cup; Taste of Tasmania. **Burnie:** New Year's Day athletic carnival. **Cygnet:** Huon folk festival. **Latrobe:** Australia Day carnival; Henley on the Mersey. **Latrobe-Port Sorell:** Summer festival. **Triabunna:** Spring Bay crayfish derby.

FEBRUARY
Hobart: Royal Hobart regatta. **Devonport:** Food and wine festival. **Evandale:** Village fair and national penny farthing championships. **Latrobe-Port Sorell:** Summer festival (contd). **Oatlands:** Rodeo. **Richmond:** Country music festival. **Scottsdale:** Golconda: Tasmanian circus festival. **Waratah:** Back to Waratah.

MARCH
Public holiday: Eight Hours Day. **Hobart:** Garden Week. **Campbell Town:** Highland games. **Cygnet:** Port Cygnet fishing carnival. **Devonport:** Harbours festival. **Fingal:** Fingal Valley festival (includes World coal shovelling and roof bolting championships). **Kingston:** Kingborough festival (includes road cycle race). **Longford:** Targa Tasmania. **New Norfolk:** Hop festival. **St Helens:** Tasmanian game-fishing classic. **Sheffield:** Steam Fest. **Westbury:** Maypole festival; St Patrick's Day festival.

EASTER
Public holidays: Good Friday; Easter Monday; Easter Tuesday. **Beauty Point:** Three Peaks race (yacht race to Hobart). **Deloraine:** Grand national steeplechase.

APRIL
Public holiday: Anzac Day. **Hobart:** Targa Tasmania (exotic car rally).

MAY
Hobart: City to Casino fun run (at Glenorchy). **Carrick:** Agfest.

JUNE
Public holiday: Queen's Birthday. **Hobart:** Tasmanian Celtic winterfest. **Campbell Town:** Show. **St Helens:** Suncoast jazz festival. **Scottsdale:** Arts and crafts exhibition.

JULY
Hobart: Brighton craft fair.

AUGUST
New Norfolk: Winter challenge.

SEPTEMBER
Hobart: Film festival; Tasmanian football league grand final; Tasmanian tulip festival. **Burnie:** Festival. **Sheffield:** Daffodil festival.

OCTOBER
Public holidays: Hobart Show Day (southern Tas. only); Launceston Show Day (northern Tas. only); Flinders Island Show Day (Flinders Island only); Burnie Show Day (Burnie only). **Hobart:** Royal Hobart agricultural show. **Burnie:** Rhododendron festival. **Derby:** River Derby. **Kingston:** Oliebollen festival. **Launceston:** Garden festival; Royal national show; Tasmanian poetry festival. **Richmond:** Village fair. **Ulverstone:** Show. **Wynyard:** Tulip festival.

NOVEMBER
Public holiday: Recreation Day (northern Tas. only). **Hobart:** North Hobart fiesta. **Campbell Town:** Country muster. **Deloraine:** Tasmanian cottage industries' exhibition and craft fair; Tasmanian trout fishing championships. **Ross:** Rodeo. **Scottsdale:** Agricultural show. **Sorell:** Taste of Sorell. **Stanley:** Tasmania Day. **Westbury:** Steam spectacular.

DECEMBER
Public holidays: Christmas Day; Boxing Day. **Hobart:** Christmas pageant; Summer festival; Sydney–Hobart/Melbourne–Hobart yacht race. **Eaglehawk Neck:** Port Arthur chopping carnival. **Latrobe:** Latrobe wheel race and Latrobe Gift. **Port Arthur:** Boxing Day woodchop; Absconders run. **Stanley:** Agricultural show. **Ulverstone:** Christmas mardi gras. **Zeehan:** King of the mountain fun run.

CLIMATE GUIDE

HOBART

	J	F	M	A	M	J	J	A	S	O	N	D
Maximum °C	22	22	21	18	15	13	12	13	15	17	19	20
Minimum °C	12	12	11	9	6	5	4	5	6	7	9	11
Rainfall mm	37	38	40	49	41	29	49	49	42	48	48	59
Raindays	9	8	10	11	13	11	13	15	14	13	14	13

LAUNCESTON REGION

	J	F	M	A	M	J	J	A	S	O	N	D
Maximum °C	23	23	21	17	14	11	11	12	14	16	19	21
Minimum °C	10	10	9	7	5	3	2	3	4	6	7	9
Rainfall mm	40	43	43	58	63	61	81	80	65	63	51	53
Raindays	8	7	9	11	13	13	16	16	13	13	11	10

CRADLE MOUNTAIN REGION

	J	F	M	A	M	J	J	A	S	O	N	D
Maximum °C	17	18	14	11	8	5	5	5	7	10	12	14
Minimum °C	6	7	6	4	2	0	0	0	-1	2	3	4
Rainfall mm	147	131	158	228	288	276	329	309	277	249	216	192
Raindays	16	14	18	20	21	21	24	23	22	21	19	19

BICHENO REGION

	J	F	M	A	M	J	J	A	S	O	N	D
Maximum °C	21	21	20	19	16	14	14	14	16	18	18	19
Minimum °C	12	13	12	10	9	7	6	6	8	8	10	11
Rainfall mm	47	61	60	63	63	66	54	51	43	56	55	70
Raindays	7	7	7	9	9	9	9	9	7	9	9	9

Gordon River cruises. North of Queenstown, the town of Zeehan is currently enjoying a mining revival with the reopening of the Renison Bell Tin Mine.

The north coast is yet another contrasting area. Burnie is one of the larger towns and Stanley is a classified historic town situated beneath the Nut, an unusual peninsula. East of Burnie, the Bass Highway hugs the coast as far as Devonport, the terminal of the Bass Strait passenger/vehicle ferry *Spirit of Tasmania* and the centre of an apple-growing area. Inland is Launceston, Tasmania's second largest city, situated on the Tamar River. Only minutes from the city centre is the beautiful Cataract Gorge. The nearby colonial villages of Evandale, Hagley, Westbury, Carrick, Perth, Longford and Hadspen are well worth a visit.

A mild climate, good surfing beaches and sheltered seaside towns add to the attraction of the east-coast region. St Helens, 160 kilometres east of Launceston, is the principal resort town. Try not to miss Bicheno, a picturesque old port and one-time whaling town. Further south, the Hazards, a red granite mountain range, towers up behind Coles Bay, at the entrance to the Freycinet National Park. Nearby Swansea offers top-class ocean and freshwater fishing.

A sense of Tasmania's history can be gained from studying graveyards and headstones: in St David's Park, in the centre of Hobart; on Maria Island; on the Isle of the Dead off Port Arthur; King Island; Flinders Island and Sarah Island in Macquarie Harbour; at National Trust properties; and in towns like Stanley, Richmond, Ross, Evandale and Corinna.

Whether you complete a round trip or only explore parts of this island State, it is very likely that, by the time you come to leave, Tasmania will have won yet another heart.

Richmond Bridge, the oldest bridge in Australia

HOBART
An Historic City

The city's skyline viewed from Mt Nelson

Hobart is Australia's second oldest and most southerly city. It is an enchanting city built around a beautiful harbour and under the spell of nearby majestic Mount Wellington. A strong seafaring flavour and sense of the past give Hobart an almost European air. This feeling is heightened in winter when Mount Wellington is snow-capped and temperatures drop to a crisp 4°C. The rest of the year Hobart has plenty of days with sparkling blue skies, but temperatures rarely exceed 25°C. It is Australia's second driest capital city.

NOT TO BE MISSED in Hobart

- **Battery Point** – former mariners' village with fascinating tiny houses
- **Cadbury Cruise** – take a sweet cruise to the chocolate factory
- **Constitution dock** – for watching the bustle of fishing boats and larger vessels
- **Derwent River ferry ride** – a pleasant means to see the city at a different angle
- **Ghost tour** – a spooky way to see the Penitentiary
- **Markets** – at Gasworks Shopping Village in Sullivans Cove each Sunday
- **Mount Wellington** – offers stunning views of the city and surrounds from summit
- **Naturally Tasmanian** – distinctive range of crafts from local craftspeople
- **Royal Tasmanian Botanical Gardens** – the horticultural jewel of the State
- **Salamanca Place** – for art galleries and restaurants in old merchant warehouses

Many of Hobart's beautiful colonial sandstone buildings were erected by the unfortunate convicts who formed the majority of the European settlers in 1803. In spite of its convict troubles, the small colony flourished. Hobart's deepwater harbour on the broad estuary of the Derwent River soon became a thriving seaport and by 1842 Hobart was proclaimed a city. The harbour is still Hobart's lifeblood and the port is always busy with yachts. The suburbs nestle right up to the lower slopes of **Mount Wellington** and the city's population of 217 900 spreads both sides of the graceful **Tasman Bridge**.

From the bridge you will see **Government House** and the **Royal Tasmanian Botanical Gardens** set in the **Queen's Domain**, a large parkland with sporting facilities and an adventure playground. In the lovely old Botanical Gardens are a playground, a Japanese garden and a restaurant that serves lunch and teas. Further along the Tasman Highway towards the city is the **Gasworks Shopping Village** with shops and restaurants in restored 19th century buildings near Sullivans Cove. Australia's only commercial whisky distillery is located here and is open daily for tours. On Sundays, bargains are to be found at the Sullivans Cove market.

In a matter of minutes you are in the heart of Hobart, which has escaped the usual pressures of modern city life. Parking is no problem. Visitors should note that most of the city streets are one-way.

Hobart's waterfront retains much of its early character and it is not hard to imagine it in the early whaling days when Hobart Town was a lusty, brawling seaport known to sailors all round the world. Foreign ships tie up almost in the centre of town, battered whalers are now replaced by fishing-trawlers at Victoria Dock. Wander around to **Constitution Dock**, a haven for the yachts during the annual Sydney to Hobart Yacht Race; here you can buy live seafood.

Just round the corner in Macquarie Street is the **Tasmanian Museum and Art Gallery**, which has a fine collection of Aboriginal artifacts, early prints and paintings, and convict relics. From here it is only a short stroll to the **Theatre Royal**, which was built in 1837 and is the oldest theatre in Australia. It is worth going inside to glimpse its charming dolls'-house-scale Georgian interior. Dame Sybil Thorndike rated it as the finest theatre she had played in outside of London. Not far from the Theatre Royal are the **Criminal Courts** and **Penitentiary Chapel**, both operated by the National Trust; guided tours are conducted daily.

Heading back towards the centre of the city, you will see Hobart's sandstone Italianate-style **Town Hall**, built on the site of the original **Government House**, on the corner of Macquarie and Elizabeth Streets.

Hobart has a wealth of beautiful Georgian buildings, mostly concentrated in **Macquarie and Davey Streets**. More than ninety of them have a National Trust classification. Built around 1846, the **Anglesea Barracks**, in Davey Street, is the oldest military establishment in Australia still used by the army. The **Cascade Brewery** in South Hobart, is over a century and a half old and offers conducted tours on weekdays.

Several modern complexes blend in with the older buildings without destroying the overall scale and atmosphere. The largest landmark is the tower of Australia's first hotel-casino, **Wrest Point**, built on a promontory in the suburb of Sandy Bay, just out of town. Back towards the waterfront is the famous **Salamanca Place**, which displays the finest row of early merchant warehouses in Australia. Dating back to the whaling days of the 1830s, the whole area has been sympathetically restored and the warehouses are now used as art and craft galleries, restaurants and a puppet theatre. A colourful open-air craft market, where almost anything is sold for almost any price, is held here each Saturday.

The steep **Kelly's Steps**, wedged between two old warehouses in Salamanca Place, lead to the heart of unique **Battery Point**, a former mariners' village, which has retained its nineteenth-century character. Battery Point has several quaint cottage tearooms and many excellent restaurants offering a variety of different cuisines.

This area is also Hobart's mecca for antique-hunters. Just round the corner is the **Van Diemen's Land Folk Museum**, with its interesting collection of colonial relics housed in Narryna, a gracious old town house, complete with a shady garden and an ornamental fountain. A short walk from here is the graceful old **St George's Anglican Church**, which was built between 1836 and 1847 and designed by two of Tasmania's most prominent colonial architects, John Lee Archer and James Blackburn. The **Tasmanian Maritime Museum**, in Secheron Road, has a collection of old seafaring relics and documents.

Back towards the city, **St David's Park**, with its beautiful old trees, is an ideal place for a rest. One side of this park was Hobart Town's first colonial burial ground; the pioneer gravestones, which date from 1804, make fascinating reading. Across the road, in Murray Street, is **Parliament House**, one of the oldest buildings in Hobart. Originally used as the Customs House, it was built by convicts between 1835 and 1841. Visitors may ask to see the tiny **Legislative Council Chamber**, which is exactly as it was when it was inaugurated. The ceiling has been painstakingly repainted in its original ornate pastel patterns and the benches refurbished in plush red velvet. The building was designed by the colonial architect John Lee Archer.

The **Allport Library and Museum of Fine Arts**, a library of rare books and a collection of antique furniture, china and silver, is also in Murray Street, in the **State Library**.

The main shopping area of Hobart is centred round the **Elizabeth Street Mall**, between Collins and Liverpool Streets. The **Cat and Fiddle Arcade and Square** is located between the Mall and Murray Street. Shoppers can relax in the modern square with its fountain and an animated mural which 'performs' on the hour. In the Mall, in addition to the hourly antics of the Cat and Fiddle Clock, entertainment is also provided by strolling buskers. Further along Elizabeth Street, in **Franklin Square**, you can play giant chess.

Hobart offers a sophisticated nightlife with the Wrest Point Hotel-Casino with its casino and revolving restaurant, and a range of licensed restaurants – from Japanese and Mexican to colonial-style. For a touch of old-world class you can sip cocktails in the drawing-room of **Lenna**, an Italianate former mansion (now a distinctive hotel-motel) in Battery Point, before dining in the lavishly decorated restaurant. Fresh seafood is a specialty of many of the city's restaurants. **Mures Fish Centre**, at Victoria Dock, offers a range of fish delights from takeaway to fisherman's basket (brimming with such delicacies as crayfish, mussels, squid and scallops). Hobart also has several interesting old pubs with a nautical flavour; a good example is the **Customs House Hotel** on the corner of Murray and Morrison Streets.

The suburbs of Hobart have much to offer the visitor. Nearby Sandy Bay is the site of both the **University of Tasmania** and the **Model Tudor Village**. Beyond this, just out of Taroona, is the convict-built **Shot Tower**, from which you can get a superb view of the Derwent estuary. As well as the original owner's house, built in 1835, the Shot Tower complex includes a small museum and tearooms, both housed in an 1855 building. **North Hobart**, only a few minutes from the centre of the city, is the gourmet's suburb, where a concentration of excellent restaurants and delicatessens have proliferated to the delight of residents and visitors alike. Slightly further north, and located in the suburb of New Town is **Runnymede**, a National Trust homestead. Beautifully restored, it commands

ACCOMMODATION

HOTELS
Hotel Grand Chancellor
1 Davey St, Hobart
(03) 6235 4535

Lenna of Hobart
20 Runnymede St, Battery Point
(03) 6232 3900

Wrest Point Hotel-Casino
410 Sandy Bay Rd, Sandy Bay
(03) 6225 0112

FAMILY AND BUDGET
Hobart Pacific Motor Inn
Kirby Crt, West Hobart
(03) 6234 6733

Hobart Tower Motel
300 Park St, New Town
(03) 6228 0166

Taroona Hotel
178 Channel Hwy, Taroona
(03) 6227 8748

MOTEL GROUPS: BOOKINGS
Best Western 13 1779
Flag 13 2400
Innkeepers 1800 03 0111

The above list is for information only; inclusion is not necessarily a recommendation.

an attractive view over New Town Bay and Risdon, where Hobart's first European settlement began. Further north, in the suburb of Goodwood, the **Derwent Entertainment Centre** stands beside the river and **Elwick Racecourse**. **Bellerive**, the ruins of an old fort at Kangaroo Bluff, was built to guard Hobart against a feared Russian invasion late last century. Some of Hobart's best beaches, including **Lauderdale**, **Cremorne** and **Seven Mile Beach**, are in this area. For surfers there is a wild ocean beach at **Clifton**.

There are dozens of scenic drives and lookouts around Hobart, with spectacular views from the pinnacle of **Mount Wellington** and from the old **Signal Station** on top of **Mount Nelson**. The **Waterworks Reserve** is an attractive picnic area close to town.

The hundreds of yachts moored near the prestigious **Royal Yacht Club** in Sandy Bay are evidence of one of Hobart's most popular sports. Other sports are well catered for with a public golf course at Rosny Park, racing and trotting at Glenorchy, and public squash courts at Sandy Bay, New Town and Bellerive. The Southern Tasmanian Tennis Association Courts are in Queen's Domain. Tasmania's cricket headquarters is at Bellerive.

Hobart offers a complete range of accommodation, from the modern Hotel Grand Chancellor or the Wrest Point Hotel-Casino to tiny Georgian cottage guest houses at Battery Point. Between these two extremes there are many hotels, motels and numerous guest houses, as well as caravan parks, holiday flats and cottages.

As a result of the popularity of colonial accommodation over the last few years, there are now over 150 properties, including host farms and colonial cottages, available for visitors. Host farms provide a wide variety of standard and type of service, and offer guests the opportunity to observe farm life or become involved in it. Colonial accommodation is provided in buildings or cottages established on their present sites before 1901. Although concessions are made to allow modern facilities to be incorporated, interiors are presented in colonial style by the use of genuine or reproduction furniture and other decoration.

Hobart offers the visitor an impressive State capital, rich in history, and only minutes away from a wide variety of natural attractions.

HOBART ON FOOT

There are many walking tours around Hobart, including:

- **Battery Point:** National Trust guided walk; leaves Franklin Square each Sat. morning; bookings essential
- **Battery Point and Sullivans Cove:** Self-guide walk; brochure available; small donation required
- **Old Penitentiary Chapel and Criminal Courts:** Guided ghost tours; bookings essential
- **Sullivans Cove:** Guided walk, departs Visitor Centre, Davey St; bookings essential

Brochures are available for the self-guide walk. For further information, contact the Tasmanian Travel and Information Centre, 20 Davey Street, Hobart; (03) 6230 8233.

For further information, contact the Tasmanian Travel and Information Centre, 20 Davey St; (03) 6230 8233.

Battery Point

A most delightful part of Hobart is the former maritime village **Battery Point**, perched between the city docks and Sandy Bay. Battery Point dates back to the early days of Hobart Town, when it became a lively mariners' village with fishermen's cottages, shops, churches, a village green and a riot of pubs with such evocative names as the Whalers' Return and the Neptune Inn. Miraculously, it has hardly changed since those days. To anyone strolling through its narrow, hilly streets – with enchanting glimpses of the harbour, yachts and mountains at every turn – it looks almost like a Cornish fishing village.

Quaint **Arthurs Circus** is built around the former village green, now a children's playground. A profusion of old-fashioned flowers – sweet william, honeysuckle, daisies and geraniums – grow in pocket-sized gardens.

Pubs such as the Knopwood's Retreat and the Shipwright's Arms add to the feeling that time has

Arthurs Circus

stood still. Knopwood Street and Kelly's Steps are reminders of two pioneer settlers: the Reverend Bobby Knopwood, Battery Point's first landowner, and the adventurer James Kelly, who owned a whaling fleet and undertook a daring voyage around Van Diemen's Land.

Battery Point gets its name from a battery of guns set up on the promontory in front of a small guardhouse in 1818. This soon became a signalling station and is now the oldest building in Battery Point.

Today the Point has many inviting restaurants and tearooms, and several antique shops to explore, but it is still mainly a residential area. Most of the houses are tiny dormer-windowed fishermen's cottages, with a few grander houses such as Secheron, Stowell, Narryna and Lenna. An attractive leaflet with a detailed map, *Let's Talk About Battery Point*, is available from the Tasmanian Travel and Information Centre, and the National Trust organises walking tours of the area, departing from the Wishing Well, Franklin Square, each Saturday morning.

For further information, contact the Tasmanian Travel and Information Centre, 20 Davey St, Hobart; (03) 6230 8233.

TOURS from Hobart

The charming town of Richmond has many historic buildings

A marvellous range of tourist attractions is within easy reach of Hobart. To appreciate its superb natural setting it is worth going on a scenic flight over the city and its surroundings, taking in the beautiful Derwent estuary, the patchwork fields of the Midlands, the Tasman Peninsula, and the spectacular lakes and mountains of central and south-western Tasmania. Flight bookings can be made at the Tasmanian Travel and Information Centre, Hobart, which can also arrange half-day and full-day coach tours.

Mt Wellington

22 km from Hobart via the Huon Road

The most popular short trip from Hobart is to the pinnacle of Mt Wellington, 1271 metres above the city, which commands panoramic views of both the D'Entrecasteaux Channel to the south and the Derwent Valley to the north. A novel way to see the views is the half-day tour 'Mt Wellington Downhill': transport to the summit and a thrilling bike ride back down.

Richmond

26 km from Hobart via the Eastern Outlet Road

See: Entry for Richmond in A–Z listing.

Cadbury's Chocolate Factory, Claremont

14 km from Hobart on the Brooker Highway

A visit to this beautifully sited model factory, the biggest chocolate and cocoa factory in Australia, is another popular short trip. Privately run coach tours leave Tuesday to Thursday and self-drive tours may be made Monday to Friday. A Cadbury Cruise operates Monday to Friday. Reservations are essential; bookings and information at the Tasmanian Travel and Information Centre, Hobart. The chocolate factory is usually closed for two weeks in September and from the end of December to mid-January.

New Norfolk

32 km from Hobart on the Lyell Highway

See: Entry for New Norfolk in A–Z listing.

Mt Field National Park and Russell Falls

72 km from Hobart via the Lyell Highway and Gordon River Road

The road from New Norfolk to Mt Field passes through some of the loveliest parts of the Derwent Valley. A nature walk leads to the magnificent Russell Falls, cascades that drop 32 metres into a gorge of rainforest and tree ferns, from near the park entrance. This large scenic wildlife reserve shelters many native birds and animals, including the elusive Tasmanian devil. **See also:** National Parks.

Lake Pedder and Lake Gordon

170 km from Hobart via the Lyell Highway and Gordon River Road

In clear weather, the road from Mt Field National Park to the township of Strathgordon is probably the most spectacular stretch of mountain highway in Australia. Unfortunately (from the visitor's point of view), there is very high rainfall in the area, which of course results in its unique natural topography. Motorists are advised to cancel trips on overcast days. Constructed Lakes Pedder and Gordon, part of the Hydro-Electric Commission's giant Gordon River power development, are liberally stocked with trout. The underground power station at the Gordon Dam can be inspected on regular tours. You can hire boats and fishing tackle from Strathgordon, where a chalet is available for overnight accommodation. Inquiries should be directed to the Tasmanian Travel and Information Centre in Hobart. **See also:** National Parks.

Tasman Peninsula and Port Arthur

100 km from Hobart via the Arthur Highway

There is so much to see on this fascinating trip that it would be well worth staying overnight at the narrow isthmus of Eaglehawk Neck, at Port Arthur or at Nubeena. Once guarded by a line of tethered dogs to prevent convicts escaping, Eaglehawk Neck is now a base for game-fishing charter boats. There are four unique coastal formations in the area: the spectacular Devil's Kitchen, the Blowhole, Tasman's Arch and the Tessellated Pavement. The old penal settlement of Port Arthur is Tasmania's number one tourist attraction. Other attractions in the area include Bush Hill, Remarkable Cave and Safety Cove. **See also:** A Convict Past; and entries for Port Arthur and Eaglehawk Neck in A–Z listing.

Huonville

37 km from Hobart via Huon Road and the Huon Highway

Huonville, just south-west of Hobart, is the centre of Tasmania's picturesque apple-growing district. You can take the scenic route from Hobart via the shoulder of Mt Wellington on the Huon Highway, returning via the Channel Highway and passing through the small town of Cygnet. The Channel Highway commands spectacular vistas of the coastline and rugged Bruny Island. **See:** Entry for Huonville in A–Z listing.

Hastings Caves

110 km from Hobart via the Huon Road and Huon Highway

These caves, 13 km from the small township of Hastings, are another popular attraction. There are regular guided tours of the only illuminated cave, Newdegate Cave, regarded as one of the most beautiful limestone caves in Australia. A natural thermal swimming-pool with an average temperature of 27°C is nearby. Motorists are warned that Dover is the last place to buy petrol when travelling south towards Recherche Bay. The Ida Bay Scenic Railway is another popular tourist attraction near Hastings. **See also:** Entry for Hastings in A–Z listing.

Lake Pedder, Southwest National Park, is renowned for its trout fishing

TASMANIA from A to Z

Old mine building, one of many brick ruins at Beaconsfield

Beaconsfield Pop. 1088

MAP REF. 541 J5, 545 K7

The ruins of several impressive brick buildings with Romanesque arches dominate this quiet town on the West Tamar Hwy, 46 km NW of Launceston. Formerly a thriving gold township (called Cabbage Tree Hill), the ruins are the remains of several buildings erected at the pithead of the Tasmanian Gold Mine in 1904. When the mine closed 10 years later after water seepage, more than 6 million dollars' worth of ore had been won from the reef. In 1804 a party of officers established a settlement north of the town, called York Town. **Of interest:** Grubb Shaft Museum, West St, in one of old mine buildings; restored miner's cottage and original Flowery Gully School alongside museum. **In the area:** York Town monument, 9 km N on Kelso–Greens Beach Rd. At Rowella, 15 km E, Holm Oak Vineyard. Auld Kirk (1843) at Sidmouth, 9 km SE; nearby, Batman Bridge, with its A-frame reaching 100 m above Tamar River. **Tourist information:** Tamar Visitor Centre, Main Rd, Exeter; (03) 6394 4454. **Accommodation:** None.

Beauty Point Pop. 1137

MAP REF. 541 K5, 545 K6

This popular fishing and yachting centre on the West Tamar Hwy, 48 km NW of Launceston, is the oldest deepwater port in the area and was constructed to serve the Beaconsfield goldmine. Today the town is home to the Australian Maritime College. Cargo is loaded at Bell Bay across the river. **Of interest:** Daily ferry service to George Town. Nearby Sandy Beach for safe swimming. Easter: Three Peaks yacht race. **In the area:** Two northern holiday towns: Kelso, 15 km NW, dates back to early York Town settlement; Greens Beach, 20 km NW, at mouth of Tamar River. Asbestos Range National Park, 25 km NW, 5-hour walking trail from Badger Head to Bakers Beach. Marion's Vineyard, Deviot, 12 km SE. **Tourist information:** Tamar Visitor Centre, Main Rd, Exeter; (03) 6394 4454. **Accommodation:** 2 hotels, 2 motels, 1 cara./camp. park.

Bicheno Pop. 705

MAP REF. 543 Q2, 545 Q12

A fishing port and holiday destination on the east coast, 195 km from Hobart, Bicheno offers surf, rock, sea and estuary fishing. The town's mild climate, outstanding fishing, fine sandy beaches located nearby and its picturesque setting make it one of Tasmania's most popular holiday resorts. Licensed seafood restaurants and a range of accommodation add to its appeal. Originally a sealing and whaling town from about 1803, it later became a coal-mining port in 1854. Today crayfishing is the main local industry. **Of interest:** On Tasman Hwy: Sea Life Centre, with aquarium and seafood restaurant; Dive Centre, offering diving instruction and charters. Foreshore walkway, from Redbill Point north of town, south to Blowhole. Lookouts at top of town's twin hills: Whalers Lookout, off Foster St, and National Park Lookout, off Morrison St; rock orchids, unique to east coast, spectacular sight here in Oct. and Nov. Grave of Aboriginal heroine Waubedebar, Lions Park, Burgess St. Adventure tours available, including scuba diving and mountain-bike riding. **In the area:** Little (fairy) Penguin Rookery, 6 km N; guided nightly tours only in season, contact Tourist information. East Coast Bird Life and Animal Park, 8 km N, exhibits Tasmanian devils and other native fauna. Lookout in Douglas Apsley National Park, 14 km NW. Freycinet National Park, 40 km S. Freycinet Vineyard, 18 km SW on Tasman Hwy. **Tourist information:** Bicheno Penguin Adventure Tours, Tasman Hwy; (03) 6375 1333. **Accommodation:** 2 hotel/motels, 2 hostels, 2 cara./camp. parks.

Boat Harbour Pop. 109

MAP REF. 544 F5

The clear water and rocky points of this attractive town make it an ideal spot for skindiving and spear fishing. Situated on the north-west coast, 31 km W of Burnie, it adjoins one of the richest agricultural areas in the State. **Of interest:** Shannondoah Cottage, Bass Hwy, for local craft, lunches and Devonshire teas. **In the area:** Boat Harbour Beach, 3 km N: safe swimming, marine life in pools at low tide, fishing, water-skiing and bushwalking. Sisters Beach, 5 km NW, for good fishing and swimming; nearby,

Birdland Native Gardens in Rocky Cape National Park, 19 km NW. **Tourist information:** Seaside Garden Motel, The Esplanade; (03) 6445 1111. **Accommodation:** 2 motels, 1 hostel, 1 cara./camp. park.

Bothwell — Pop. 396

MAP REF. 543 K5

This peaceful old country town in the beautiful Clyde River valley, 74 km NW of Hobart, has been proclaimed an historic village. It has 52 buildings either classified or recorded by the National Trust. Surveyed in 1824 and named by Lieutenant-Governor Arthur after the Scottish town, it is now the centre of sheep and cattle country. It is possible that the first golf in Australia was played at the nearby homestead of Ratho in the 1830s. This course still exists and is open to visitors with golf-club membership elsewhere. **Of interest:** Bothwell Grange (c. 1836), Alexander St, a guest house with tearooms and art gallery. Lamont Weaving Studio, Patrick St, has demonstrations, sales and tearoom. Peter Muere Woodturning, Queens St. St Luke's Church (1830), Dennistoun St. Georgian brick Slate Cottage (1836), High St, restored and furnished in style of day. **In the area:** Restored and operational Thorpe Water Mill, 2 km N on Interlaken Rd; tours by appt. Steppe Stones, 20 km N, a collection of 13 monoliths by sculptor Steven Walker, each representing an aspect of area's history and character. Excellent trout fishing at Arthurs Lake, 51 km N, Penstock Lagoon, 45 km NW, Great Lake, 56 km N, and Lake Echo, 48 km NW; all via Lakes Hwy. **Tourist information:** Council Offices, Alexander St; (03) 6259 5503. **Accommodation:** 1 cara./camp. park. **See also:** Scenic Island State.

Bridgewater — Pop. 8684

MAP REF. 538 H4, 543 L7

This town, only 19 km N of Hobart, is situated on the bank at the main northern crossing of the Derwent River. The causeway was built in the early 1830s by 200 convicts, who barrowed 2 million tonnes of stone and clay from the site. The original bridge was opened in 1849; the present one dates from 1946. **In the area:** At Granton, 1 km S across bridge: Old Watch House (1838), now a petrol station, was built by convicts to guard causeway and has smallest cell in Australia (50 cm square, 2 m high); Black Snake Inn (1833), also convict-built. Risdon Cove Historic Site, 15 km SE, site of original Hobart Town settlement. **Tourist information:** Council Offices, Tivoli Rd, Gagebrook; (03) 6263 0333. **Accommodation:** None.

Bridport — Pop. 1165

MAP REF. 541 R2, 545 N6

Bridport is a popular holiday and fishing town on the north-east coast, 85 km NE of Launceston. **Of interest:** Fine beaches, excellent river, sea and lake fishing. '2000 Plus' Information Centre, Main St. **In the area:** Bowood (1839), 8 km W, historic homestead near town; open Sun. or by appt. Views from Waterhouse Point and Ranson's Beach. Winegrowing at Piper's Brook, 18 km SW. **Tourist information:** '2000 Plus' Information Centre, Main St; or Motor Inn, Main St; (03) 6356 1238. **Accommodation:** 1 hotel, 1 hotel/motel, 1 hostel, 1 cara./camp. park.

Bruny Island — Pop. 520

MAP REF. 543 L11

Almost two islands, separated by a narrow isthmus, Bruny was named after the French Admiral Bruni D'Entrecasteaux, who surveyed the channel between the island and the mainland of Tasmania in 1792; the Aboriginal name for the island was Lunawannaaloona. Abel Tasman saw the island in 1642 but did not land. Other European visitors in the 18th century included Furneaux (1773), James Cook (1777) and William Bligh (1788, 1792). The first apple trees in Tasmania are said to have been planted here by a botanist with the Bligh expedition. **Of interest:** Bruny Island ferry departs from Kettering, on the mainland, several times daily. On isthmus between North and South Bruny: memorial to Truganini, Tasmania's last full-blood Aborigine who died in 1876; lookout, views of spectacular coastal scenery; boardwalk; and penguin and muttonbird viewing. *On South Bruny*: Bligh Museum, exhibits island's recorded history; Captain Cook's Landing Place, has model of Cook's ship; Mavista Falls, in scenic reserve; lookouts at Adventure and Cloudy Bays; lighthouse (1836) at Cape Bruny, second oldest in Australia; walking tracks to Mt Mangana and Mt Bruny. *On North Bruny*: Dennes Point beach, D'Entrecasteaux Channel, has picnic/barbecue facilities; at Variety Bay, remains of convict-built church on private property near airstrip, conducted tours available; at Barnes Bay, vault of William Lawrence (1839). Fishing. Camel tours. **Tourist information:** Bruny D'Entrecasteaux Visitor Centre, Ferry Rd, Kettering; (03) 6267 4494. **Accommodation:** 1 hotel, 2 cara./camp. parks.

Buckland — Pop. 228

MAP REF. 539 M2, 543 N7

A stained glass window depicting the life of John the Baptist and dating back to the 14th century is in the church in this tiny township, 64 km NE of Hobart. History links the window with Battle Abbey, England. The abbey was sacked by Oliver Cromwell in the 17th century, but the window was hidden before it could be destroyed. Two centuries later it was given to Rev. T.H. Fox, Buckland's first rector, by the Marquis of Salisbury. It is now set into the east wall of the Church of St John the Baptist, (1846) on the Tasman Hwy. Although the window has been damaged and restored several times in its long life, the original figure-work is intact. Also of interest is Ye Olde Buckland Inn, in Kent St, a 19th-century tavern and restaurant. **Tourist information:** Ye Olde Buckland Inn, Kent St; (03) 6257 5114. **Accommodation:** None.

Burnie — Pop. 20 505

MAP REF. 544 G6

The rapid expansion of Burnie, now Tasmania's fourth largest city, is based on one of the State's largest industrial enterprises, Australian Paper. Situated on the banks of Emu Bay, 148 km NW of Launceston, Burnie has a deepwater port, which serves the west coast mining centres. Other important industries include plants for the manufacture of titanium oxide pigments, dried milk, chocolate products and cheese. **Of interest:** Lactos cheese factory, Old Surrey Rd, has educational facility and sales outlet. Tours of Amcor (Mon.–Fri.), a paper mill; Marine Tce. Pioneer Village Museum, High St, includes reconstruction of Burnie's small tradesmen's shops c. 1900. Restored Burnie Inn, town's oldest remaining building, re-erected in Burnie Park.

The Hazards at Freycinet National Park, near Coles Bay

Glen Osborne, Aileen Cres., historic building, now a B&B. New Year's Day: Athletic carnival. Sept.: Festival. Oct.: Rhododendron festival. **In the area:** Views from Round Hill, 5 km E. Fern Glade, off Old Surrey Rd, 5 km W, for riverside walks and picnics. Emu Valley Rhododendron Gardens, off Cascade Rd, 6 km S. Annsleigh Gardens, 9 km S on Mount Rd. Guide Falls near Ridgley, 17 km S. Upper Natone Forest Reserve, 20 km S, for picnics. Scenic drive south-west via Somerset through Elliott to Yolla. Day tours available to Cradle Mountain, Gunns Plains, Leven Canyon and Fossil Cliffs. Pieman River cruises, contact Tourist information. **Tourist information:** Pioneer Village Museum, Civic Centre Precinct, Little Alexander St; (03) 6434 6111. **Accommodation:** 4 hotels, 2 hotel/motels, 5 motels, 2 B&B, 2 cara./camp. parks. **See also:** Scenic Island State.

Campbell Town   Pop. 820

MAP REF. 543 M2, 545 N12

Campbell Town, on the Midlands Hwy, 66 km SE of Launceston, is a national centre for selling stud sheep. The area's links with the wool industry go back to the early 1820s, when Saxon merinos were introduced to the Macquarie Valley, west of the town. Timber and stud beef are also important primary industries. The town and the Elizabeth River were named by Governor Macquarie for his wife, the former Elizabeth Campbell. **Of interest:** National Trust-classified buildings: St Michael's Church (1857) and Wesleyan Chapel (1846), no longer operational, King St; Balmoral Cottage (1840s), Bridge St; St Luke's Church (1839), The Grange (1840), now colonial accommodation, Campbell Town Inn (1840), Fox Hunters Return (1830s), now colonial accommodation, and convict-built Red Bridge (1837) – all in High St. Memorial to locally born Harold Gatty, first round-the-world flight navigator, High St. Mar.: Highland games. June: Show, oldest continuous Show in Australia. Nov.: Country muster. **In the area:** Trout fishing in local rivers and lakes, particularly Lake Leake, 30 km SE. Evansville Game Park, 30 km E. **Tourist information:** 105 High St; (03) 6381 1283. **Accommodation:** 2 hotels. **See also:** Scenic Island State.

Coles Bay   Pop. 120

MAP REF. 543 Q4, 545 Q13

This beautiful unspoiled bay, 39 km S of Bicheno on the Freycinet Peninsula, is a good base for visitors to the 70 000-ha Freycinet National Park. **In the area:** At Freycinet National Park: pleasant beaches, clear waters and heathland, ideal for swimming, fishing and bushwalking; abundant birdlife; variety of wildflowers, including 60 varieties of small ground orchid; rock climbing on 'The Hazards' and nearby cliffs; water-skiing, skindiving, canoeing and sailing; charter boat trips to Schouten Island available. **Tourist information:** Park Ranger; (03) 6257 0107. **Accommodation:** 1 lodge, 2 cara./camp. parks, basic camping ground in park. **See also:** National Parks.

Cygnet   Pop. 924

MAP REF. 538 F10, 543 K10

The centre of a fruit-growing district, 52 km SW of Hobart, the town was originally named Port de Cygne Noir (meaning Black Swan Port) by the French Admiral Bruni D'Entrecasteaux because of the number of swans in the bay. Jan.: Huon folk festival. Mar.: Port Cygnet fishing carnival. **In the area:** Boating, fishing, bushwalking, gem fossicking. Good beaches and boat-launching facilities at Randalls Bay, 14 km S, nearby Verona Sands, and Egg and Bacon Bay, 15 km S. Pelvereta Falls, 10 km N on Sandfly Rd. The Deepings, woodturners' workshop and sales, 10 km E at Nicholls Rivulet. Talune Wildlife Park and Koala Gardens, 6 km SE at Gardners Bay, has good picnic/barbecue facilities. Hartzview Vineyard and Wine Centre, 10 km SE. Unique Lymington lace agate sometimes found at Drip Beach, Lymington, 12 km SW. **Tourist information:** Talune Wildlife Park, Gardners Bay; (03) 6295 1775. **Accommodation:** 3 hotels, 2 hostels, 1 cara./camp. park.

Deloraine   Pop. 2098

MAP REF. 540 I11, 545 J9

Scenic Deloraine, with Bass Strait to the north and the Great Western Tiers to the south, is an ideal base for exploring the many attractions of northern Tasmania. The surrounding rich country-side is used mainly for dairying and mixed farming. **Of interest:** Walk along river bank, through parkland. Gallery 9, West Barrack St. Markets, 1st Sat. each month. Easter: Grand national steeplechase. Nov.: Tasmanian cottage industries' exhibition and craft fair; Tasmanian trout fishing championships. **In the area:** Ashgrove Farm, Elizabeth Town, 6 km NW, sells English-style cheeses. Lobster Falls, 15 km W, 2-hour return walk from roadside; Westmoreland Falls, further 10 km SW at Caveside. Trowanna Wildlife Park, 18 km W on Mole Creek Rd, has specially

Scenic Island State

Wineglass Bay, one of many pretty coves in Freycinet National Park

Wherever your holiday journey in Tasmania takes you, you will be sure to see magnificent scenery and to have many fascinating experiences along the way. Most travellers start their Tasmanian holiday in the north, where they have either taken their car off the ferry or have hired a car or mobile home for the journey south.

Probably the best way to see what Tasmania has to offer is to take the 'circle route', with as many diversions along the way as time permits to see and explore scenic or historic highlights. Such a tour of the island will take you through some of the most fascinating country that Australia has to offer. The incomparable wilderness of the west coast, the towering mountains of the central district, the gentle pastoral landscapes of the Midlands, the lavish orchard country around Launceston and the Huon Valley, the snug beaches, bays and villages of the east coast – are all relatively accessible on good roads.

You will soon find that not everything about Tasmania is small. Nurtured by the temperate climate, the trees are taller here than on the mainland (Tasmania has the world's tallest hardwood trees, some exceeding 90 metres); mountains vault to the skies from wild forest land. The great inland lakes in the mountains feed savage rivers, some of which are harnessed for the State's hydro-electric schemes. The hills and valleys are harshly carved by the weather and become gentle only in the rolling pastoral lands of the Midlands and the north.

In this romantic landscape, more reminiscent of Scotland than Australia, are set the remnants of a rich past of convict and colonial life – the prisons, churches, cottages and court houses, the barracks, mansions and homesteads from the earliest days of European settlement.

From **Devonport** the coast road to the west runs with the northern railway along the sea's edge. Along this road are the thriving towns of **Ulverstone**, **Burnie**, **Wynyard** and **Stanley**, and the striking headlands of Table Cape, Rocky Cape and the Nut. They are worth a special trip, as is a detour down the side road from **Penguin** to the peaceful mountain farmland of Gunns Plains and the Gunns Plains caves. The road from Forth into the vast wilderness areas of the magnificent **Cradle Mountain-Lake St Clair National Park** is also well worth a visit, but the turnoff to follow the circle route is at Somerset, and from there you head south down the Murchison Highway through the rich farmlands towards the increasingly mountainous country of the west coast. An interesting diversion leads to Corinna, once a thriving town but now virtually abandoned, on the beautiful Pieman River, not far from its mouth. A launch trip from Corinna travels through deeply-cut river gorges west to the Indian Ocean.

Back on the main road, the mountain scenery is unique and quite spectacular. The towns here developed as a result of their mineral wealth. **Zeehan** now has only a small population, but at the turn of the century there were more than 10 000 inhabitants when silver, lead and zinc mining was at its height. Many buildings of those days still stand. The larger town of **Queenstown** has grown up around the Mount Lyell copper mine, in a valley beneath bare, bleached hills, streaked and stained with the hues of minerals – chrome, purple, grey and pink. Nearby is **Strahan** on Macquarie Harbour, the only coastal town in the west. The harbour can be reached only by shallow-draught vessels through the notorious passage called Hell's Gates. Cruises are available through wilderness country along the Gordon River, past the ruins of the remote convict settlement on Sarah Island, or take a sea-plane flight over the **Franklin-Gordon Wild Rivers National Park**.

The road turns inland from these towns, avoiding the almost inaccessible south-west, and travels through the Franklin-Gordon Wild Rivers National Park, across the central highlands past Lake St Clair and down the Derwent River valley through the town of **New Norfolk**, centre of the Tasmanian hop-growing industry. This valley, beautiful in spring and brilliantly coloured with foliage in autumn, is of both scenic and historical interest. It was settled by Europeans in 1808, the site having been chosen by Governor Macquarie.

A detour from the Hobart road leads to the lovely old town of **Richmond,** one of the many historic towns the visitor bypasses if the circle route is followed. (Some of the others are **Ross, Oatlands, Campbell Town, Bothwell** and **Longford,** all set in the charming rolling countryside of the Midlands with their English trees framing or hiding the landowners' mansions.) Richmond is probably the best example of a historic town, with its old Georgian houses and cottages clustered together and its bridge, convict-built and the oldest free-stone bridge still in use in Australia. The gaol pre-dates Port Arthur as a penal settlement; two churches, a court house, a schoolhouse, a rectory, the hotel granary, a general store and a flour mill were all built in the 1820s and 1830s.

Hobart, Australia's second oldest and most southerly city, is attractively sited on either side of the Derwent River, with Mount Wellington looming behind. The port area at Salamanca Place, where the old bond stores and warehouses are sited, is a reminder of the days when the whaling fleet and the timber ships tied up at the wharf and sailors went out on the town. Battery Point with its barracks, workers' cottages and Arthur's Circus – its Georgian-style houses built around a circular green – is part of Hobart's beginnings. There is modern-day fun in Hobart, too, since the Wrest Point Hotel-Casino developed as Hobart's best-known entertainment complex.

In complete contrast, the grim but beautiful penal settlement of **Port Arthur** is not far from Hobart, on the Tasman Peninsula. Here, within the forbidding sandstone walls, visitors will feel some of the hopelessness and isolation of the thousands of convicts who passed through this settlement during its 47 years of existence.

South of Hobart is the scenic Huon Valley, particularly spectacular when the apple trees are in blossom. At the southern end of the route is Cockle Creek on Recherche Bay, where the South Coast walking track begins.

North on the circle route from Hobart, the Tasman Highway traverses the east coast, a region enjoying a mild and equable climate throughout most of the year and with a number of attractive seaside town. Most are on sheltered inlets but within easy reach of surf beaches and fishing grounds: towns like **Orford**, **Triabunna**, **Swansea**, **Bicheno**, **S**camander and **St Helens**.

Off the Tasman Highway near Bicheno is the **Freycinet National Park** on the Freycinet Peninsula. There are many walking tracks through this park, which is dominated by the Hazards, a red-granite mountain range.

The road cuts across the less developed farming country of the north and goes west to **Launceston**, the northern capital of Tasmania, 64 kilometres from the north coast at the junction of the North Esk, South Esk and Tamar Rivers. It is a smaller, more provincial city than Hobart, set in hilly countryside, and makes an excellent base from which to explore the rich coastal plain of the Tamar Valley and the mountain country to the north. Cataract Gorge, historic Franklin House and Entally House, and the hydro-electric station at Duck Reach, built in 1895, are all within easy reach of Launceston.

On to Devonport, where this description of the circle route began. Note that many of Tasmania's magnificent national parks are not far from the circle route highway. If time permits, detouring to visit them is well worthwhile.

For further information, contact the Tasmanian Travel and Information Centre, 20 Davey St, Hobart; (03) 6230 8233. **See also:** National Parks and individual town entries for those parks and towns indicated by bold type.

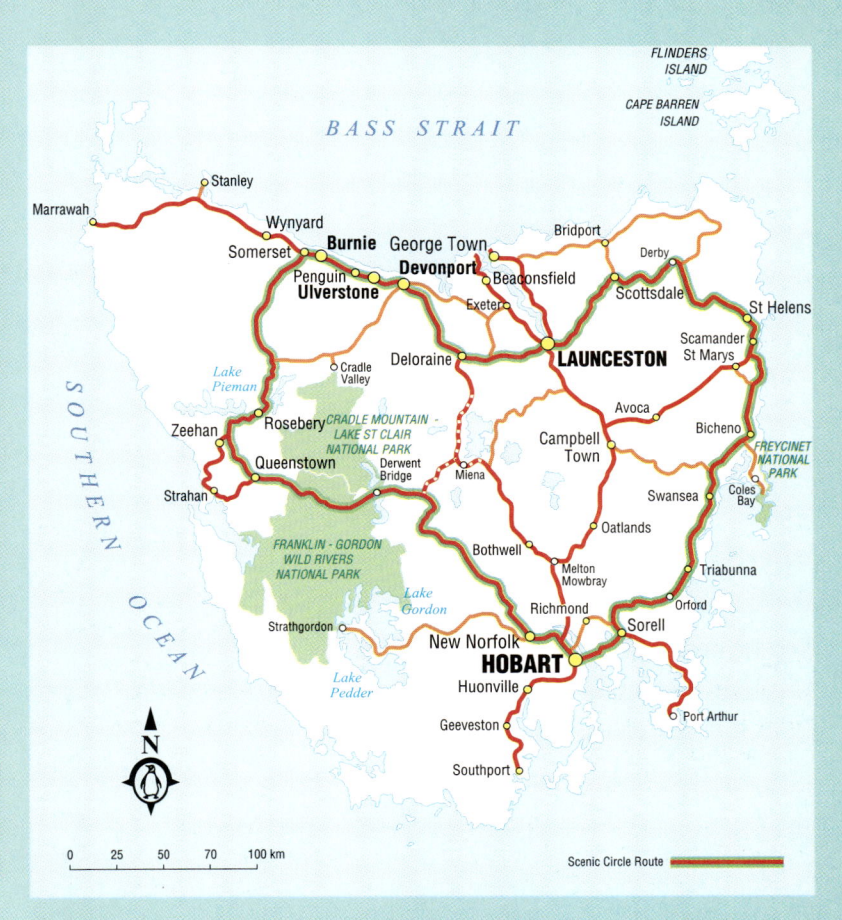

Lighthouse on Mersey Bluff, Devonport

designed noctarium for displaying nocturnal animals. Montana Falls, 9 km SW, small but pretty falls; 5–10 min. approach walk. Meander Falls in Meander Forest Reserve, 22 km SW, 5-hour return walk from carpark (not accessible if heavy snow); other walking tracks in reserve. Quamby Bluff, 20 km S, solitary mountain behind town; walking track to summit (6-hour return, medium difficulty) starts near Lake Hwy. Liffey Falls, 29 km S, 45 min. return walk from carpark. Scenic drive south to Central Highlands, through Golden Valley, to Great Lake, one of the largest high-water lakes in Australia. Dry's Bluff, part of Great Western Tiers; 40 km SE. Excellent trout fishing on lake and in Mersey and Meander Rivers. Heidi Cheese Farm, 6 km E at Exton, sells Swiss-style cheeses. **Tourist information:** 29 West Church St; (03) 6362 2046. **Accommodation:** 1 motel, 6 B&B, 2 hostels, 1 cara./camp. park. **See also:** Stately Homes.

Derby
Pop. 200

MAP REF. 545 O7

Derby is a former mining town on the Tasman Hwy, 34 km E of Scottsdale in the north-east. In its heyday, tin mining was a flourishing industry, but there has been a gradual swing to rural production, although tin is still worked. **Of interest:** Derby Tin Mine Museum, in old school (1897), has displays of local history, gemstones, minerals and tin panning. Reconstructed Shanty Town, surrounding museum, has original buildings from area: miner's cottage, newspaper office, mining assay office, butcher's shop, general store, blacksmith's shop and two cells from old Derby gaol. In Main St: Wallaby's Woodcraft, woodturning; Bank House Antiques and Craft, in old bank. Oct.: River Derby. **In the area:** Former tin-mining town of Branxholm, 12 km SW. Near Ringarooma, 24 km SW, lookouts at Mathinna Hill and Mt Victoria; scenic drives; Agricultural show held each Oct. **Tourist information:** Tin Mine Museum, Main St; (03) 6354 2262. **Accommodation:** 1 hotel, 1 camp. area.

Devonport
Pop. 22 660

MAP REF. 540 E5, 544 I6

As the terminal for the vehicular ferry *Spirit of Tasmania* from Melbourne, Devonport has become a busy industrial and agricultural-export town, as well as a major tourist centre. Devonport has its own airport, and is ideally suited as a visitor base for seeing scenic northern Tasmania. **Of interest:** Tiagarra, Tasmanian Aboriginal Culture and Art Centre, Bluff Rd, Mersey Bluff; Tasmanian Aboriginal rock engravings outside display area. Maritime Museum, Victoria Pde. National Trust-classified Home Hill, Middle Rd, home of former Prime Minister Joseph Lyons and Dame Enid Lyons; tours available. Scenic flights available, contact Tourist information. Feb.: Food and wine festival. Mar.: Harbours festival. **In the area:** Walking track (12 km) from town to Don, 6 km W. At Don, Don River Railway and Museum, scenic train rides weekends. Braddon's Lookout, 9 km W near Forth, has panoramic view of coastline. Tasmanian Aboretum (45 ha), 10 km S at Eugenana; also picnic area and walking tracks. **Tourist information:** Tasmanian Travel and Information, Devonport Showcase, 5 Best St; (03) 6424 4466. **Accommodation:** 4 hotels, 2 hotel/motels, 3 motels, 5 B&B, 2 hostels, 4 cara./camp. parks. **See also:** Scenic Island State.

Dover
Pop. 521

MAP REF. 538 E12, 543 K11

This attractive fishing port, south-west of Hobart, was once a convict station. The original Commandant's Office still stands, but the cells, which are underground just up from the wharf, can no longer be seen. From the late 1850s several large sawmills were built, with a large output of first-class timber. The main industries today are fruit-growing, fishing and Atlantic salmon fish-farming. Quaint old cottages and English trees give the town an old-world atmosphere. The three islands in the bay are called Faith, Hope and Charity. **Of interest:** Chartered fishing trips available, depart end Jetty Rd. **In the area:** Attractive scenery and unspoiled beaches, ideal for bushwalking and swimming. Several old graves on Faith Island. **Tourist information:** Church St, Geeveston; (03) 6297 1836. **Accommodation:** 1 hotel/motel, 1 B&B, 1 hostel, 1 cara./camp. park.

Dunalley
Pop. 306

MAP REF. 539 M6, 543 N9

This prosperous fishing village stands on the narrow isthmus connecting the Forestier Peninsula to the rest of Tasmania. The Denison Canal, spanned by a swing bridge, provides access to the east coast for small vessels. **Of interest:** Tasman Memorial, Imlay St, marks first landing by Europeans on 2 Dec. 1642; actual landing occurred to the north-east, near Cape Paul Lamanon. **In the area:** Just south, Bangor Farm, on Arthur Hwy, a conservation farm and home of Oyster Bay Aborigines, also site of Abel Tasman's landing; tours of farm with its middens, artifacts and nature reserves available, bookings essential; (03) 6253 5233. Collection of memorabilia in museum at Copping, 11 km N. **Tourist information:** Dunalley Hotel, 210 Arthur Hwy; (03) 6253 5101. **Accommodation:** 1 hotel.

Eaglehawk Neck
Pop. 150

MAP REF. 539 N8, 543 O9

In convict days this narrow isthmus, which separates the Tasman from the Forestier Peninsula, was guarded by a line of ferocious tethered dogs. Soldiers and constables also stood guard, to ensure that no convicts escaped from the notorious convict settlement at Port Arthur. The only prisoners to escape did so by swimming. The town today, in complete contrast, is a pleasant fishing destination. A charter tuna-fishing fleet operates from Pirate's Bay. **Of interest:**

A Convict Past

The infamous Port Arthur settlement ruins are the greatest historic tourist attraction in Tasmania. The fact that they were a place of incarceration for more than 12 000 prisoners has been blurred by time but it is still possible, particularly in bleak weather, for the ruins to create something of the atmosphere of hopelessness and misery that existed there about 160 years ago.

Port Arthur is on the Tasman Peninsula, which extends from the Forestier Peninsula south-east of Hobart, screening Pitt Water and the Derwent estuary from the Tasman Sea. Both peninsulas are very beautiful, with sweeping pastures, timbered areas, sheltered bays and towering cliffs.

Eaglehawk Neck is the isthmus between the two peninsulas. In the days of the penal colony, dogs were tethered in a tight line across the Neck to prevent escapes. The line was continually patrolled and guard posts were established in the nearby hills. No prisoner ever broke through this barrier, although some did swim to freedom. A major Port Arthur conservation project was completed in 1986. Among the ruins still standing are the church, penitentiary, guard tower, hospital and model prison. Buildings that have been restored include Exile Cottage, home of exiled Irish rebel William Smith O'Brien, the Commandant's House and the Junior Medical Officer's House. The restored former lunatic asylum is a museum and gift shop. Introductory walking tours of the site are conducted all year round, between 9.30 a.m. and 4 p.m.

The settlement was established by Governor Arthur in 1830 and, although transportation ceased in 1853, it was not abandoned until 1877. Many buildings were demolished by contractors and others were badly damaged by bushfires in 1895 and 1897. Today, nocturnal historical 'ghost tours' through the settlement are an unforgettable experience; they begin at 8.30 p.m. in winter and 9.30 p.m. during daylight saving. The site is open daily; an entrance fee allows visitors access to over 40 hectares of ruins and sites. An alternative way to experience Port Arthur is an audio tour, with 'Frank the Poet' recounting his experiences as a Port Arthur convict.

In Port Arthur Bay stands the Island of the Dead, with its 1100 convict, free settler, prison staff and military graves. As well as harbour cruises, a ferry makes regular trips to this unique island cemetery from Port Arthur.

For further information, contact Port Arthur Historic Site, Clougha, Port Arthur 7182; (03) 6250 2363. **See also:** Entries for Port Arthur and Eaglehawk Neck in A–Z listing.

Ruins at Port Arthur, Tasmania's infamous penal settlement

Evandale, an historic village near Launceston

Restored historic officers' quarters, next to Officers Mess, off Arthur Hwy. Dec.: Port Arthur chopping carnival. **In the area:** Tessellated Pavement, 1 km N. Unusual natural features 4 km E in Tasman Arch State Reserve, off Arthur Hwy: Tasman's Arch, Devil's Kitchen and Blowhole. Tasmanian Devil Park, a wildlife refuge centre, 12 km S. Fortescue Forest Reserve, south along coast from Waterfall Bay to Munro Bight, for water sports and picnics; coastal walking track from Waterfall Bay to Fortescue Bay. Good sailing in Eaglehawk Neck Bay. Port Arthur convict settlement, 21 km SW. **Tourist information:** Officers Mess, off Arthur Hwy; (03) 6250 3635. **Accommodation:** 1 hotel, 1 motel, 1 B&B. **See also:** A Convict Past; Tours from Hobart.

Evandale Pop. 772

MAP REF. 541 P12, 545 M9

This little township, 20 km from Launceston, has been proclaimed an historic village. Founded in 1829, some of its buildings date from 1809. Originally it was named Morven but was renamed in 1836 in honour of Tasmania's first Surveyor-General, G. W. Evans. Streetscapes remain unspoiled by progress and there are many buildings of historical and architectural significance. **Of interest:** Self-guide Heritage Walk from Tourism and History Centre, High St; brochure available. Also in High St: Solomon House (1836), now a cafe, also has accommodation; St Andrew's Anglican (1871) and Uniting (1839) Churches; Blenheim (1840s), now workshop with sales of stained glass. Clarendon Arms Hotel, Russell St, has mural depicting early history of area. The Art Cottage, Scone St, has variety of unusual bicycles for hire. Market, each Sun. at Falls Park, Russell St. Feb.: Village fair and national penny farthing championships. **In the area:** Clarendon (1836), 8 km S near Nile, a Georgian mansion designed in grand manner set in extensive formal gardens; also at Nile, historic inn. At Deddington, 24 km SE, chapel (1840), on private land, possibly designed by artist John Glover who bought land where town now stands; Glover's grave beside chapel. **Tourist information:** 18 High St; (03) 6391 8128. **Accommodation:** 2 hotels, 2 B&B. **See also:** Stately Homes.

Exeter Pop. 394

MAP REF. 541 L7, 545 L7

Exeter, 24 km NW of Launceston, serves a large fruit-growing area. **In the area:** To the north-east, former river towns of Gravelly Beach (5 km E) and Paper Beach (9 km E). Walking track (5 km return) from Paper Beach to Supply River; near mouth of Supply River, 10 km N off Gravelly Beach Rd, ruins of first water-driven flour mill in Tasmania, built 1825. Nearby, Marion's Vineyard. Five wineries in West Tamar area; Wine Centre in Main Rd. Notley Fern Gorge, Notley Hills, 11 km S, a 10-ha rainforest reserve with picnic/barbecue areas. Brady's Lookout, a rocky outcrop used by notorious bushranger Matthew Brady, 5 km SE in State Reserve. On Rosevears Dr. which begins just south of Exeter: historic Rosevears Hotel, first licensed 1831; Waterbird Haven, a wetlands habitat with treetop hide. At Rosevears, 6 km SE, monument to John Batman's ship *Rebecca*, in which he crossed Bass Strait to Yarra River; ship was built at the town's once busy shipyards. Further 2 km S, St Matthias Vineyard. Grindelwald Swiss Village, 10 km SE, a Swiss-architectural style village. **Tourist information:** Tamar Visitor Centre, Main Rd; (03) 6394 4454. **Accommodation:** Limited.

Fingal Pop. 428

MAP REF. 543 P1, 545 P10

Situated in the Esk Valley, 21 km inland from St Marys on the South Esk River, Fingal is the headquarters of the State's coal industry. The first payable gold in Tasmania was found in 1852 at The Nook, near Fingal. **Of interest:** Historic buildings: St Joseph's Church, Grey St; Masonic Lodge, Brown St. In Talbot St: St Peter's Church; Holder Bros. General Store; Fingal Hotel, with its collection of over 340 brands of Scotch whisky. On eastern outskirts, view coal-washing process at Cornwell Coal Company washery. Mar.: Fingal Valley festival, incorporating World coal shovelling championships and Roof bolting championships. **In the area:** Evercreech Forest Reserve, 30 km N, on road to Mathinna, features an 89-m white gum; also picnic/barbeque area and walking tracks. Mathinna Falls, 36 km N near Mathinna; picnic/barbecue area nearby. At Avoca, 27 km NE, historic buildings; town located in foothills of Ben Lomond. **Tourist information:** Fingal Hotel, Talbot St; (03) 6374 2121. **Accommodation:** 1 hotel. **See also:** Stately Homes.

Franklin Pop. 462

MAP REF. 538 E9, 543 K10

This timber milling town, 45 km SW of Hobart, was the site of the first European settlement in the Huon district in 1804. It was named after

Governor Sir John Franklin, who took up 259 ha on the banks of the Huon River. Timber milling has been an important local industry since the very early years. Orcharding and dairy farming are the other main industries. **Tourist information:** Huon River Jet Boats, Esplanade, Huonville; (03) 6264 1838. **Accommodation:** Limited. **See also:** Rural Landscapes.

Geeveston Pop. 826

MAP REF. 538 D10, 543 J10

This important timber town is the gateway to Tasmania's south-west World Heritage Area. **Of interest:** Forest and Heritage Centre, Church St, a tourist complex incorporating Gateway to South-West (Huon Hwy), Hartz Gallery (wilderness art and craft) and five forest walks. **In the area:** Arve Valley west of town contains world's tallest (87 m) hardwood trees. Waratah Lookout, Hartz Mountains National Park, 23 km SW off Arve Rd (pass needed to enter park, contact Tourist information). Arve Road Forest Drive, includes Arve River Picnic Area (10 km W); Big Tree Lookout (15 km W); Keoghs Creek Walk (15 km W); and Tahune Forest Reserve (27 km W); where camping, fishing and rafting allowed. Cruises on Huon River available from Port Huon, 4 km NE. **Tourist information:** Forest and Heritage Centre, Church St; (03) 6297 1836. **Accommodation:** 1 B&B.

George Town Pop. 5026

MAP REF. 541 K4, 545 K6

Situated at the mouth of the Tamar River, George Town was settled by Europeans in 1811, when it was named for King George III. Today it is a commercial centre, mainly as a result of the Comalco plant at Bell Bay and other industrial developments. **Of interest:** Self-guide Discovery Trail of region, brochure available at Tourist information. Monument on Esplanade commemorates an unintentional landing in 1804, when Lieut.-Col. William Paterson and his crew in HMS *Buffalo* ran aground during a storm. The Grove (c. 1838), cnr Elizabeth and Cimitiere Sts, now serves Devonshire teas and lunches. Daily ferry service to Beauty Point. Art and craft market, 2nd. Sun. each month. **In the area:** Comalco and BHP Temco plants, Bell Bay, 6 km S; tours available (Mon., Wed. and Fri.). At Hillwood, 24 km SE, apple orchards and a pick-your-own strawberry farm. Lefroy, 10 km E, ghost town of goldmining settlement with ruins, old diggings and cemetery. Several wineries to the east between Pipers River (23 km) and around Pipers Brook (30 km E), including Rochecombe, Delamere, Pipers Brook, Heemskerk, Dalrymple and Brook Eden; open for tastings and cellar-door sales (check times). At historic maritime village of Low Head, 5 km N: surf beach; river beach; Maritime Museum in Australia's oldest continuously used pilot station, opened 1803; nearby, lighthouse and little (fairy) penguin colony, viewed via guided tours at dusk, contact Tourist information. Day and weekend cruises to Bass Strait islands on SS *Furneaux Explorer* during summer months; departs end Anne St. Cruises to fur seal colony at mouth of Tamar River, inquire Tourist information. **Tourist information:** Main Rd; (03) 6382 1700. **Accommodation:** 2 hotels, 1 hotel/ motel, 2 motels, 3 B&B, 1 hostel, 1 cara./camp. park. **See also:** Stately Homes.

Gladstone Pop. 200

MAP REF. 545 P6

The small town of Gladstone is one of the few communities in the far northeast that still relies on tin mining. The district was once a thriving tin and goldmining area, with a colourful early history. Now many of these once substantial townships are ghost towns or nearly so. **In the area:** Geological formations south-west in area between Gladstone and South Mt Cameron. At Moorina, 30 km SW: gemstone fossicking park on Tasman Hwy; cemetery has graves of Chinese miners. Mt William National Park, 25 km E, has prolific flora and fauna, and excellent beaches. Historic lighthouse at Eddystone Point, 35 km E. **Tourist information:** Gladstone Hotel, Chaffey St; (03) 6357 2143. **Accommodation:** 1 hotel.

Hadspen Pop. 1334

MAP REF. 541 N11, 545 L9

The township of Hadspen, which was first settled in the early 1820s, has many historic buildings some of which offer accommodation and/or meals. **Of interest:** Row of Georgian buildings, Main Rd: Red Feather Inn (c. 1844); old coaching station; Hadspen Gaol (c. 1840); Church of the Good Shepherd, building of church commenced in 1858, funded by Thomas Reibey, who withdrew his support after a dispute with the bishop; church was completed in 1961, almost 50 years after Reibey's death. **In the area:** Entally House (1819), one of Tasmania's most famous historic homes, 1 km W on banks of South Esk River; magnificent collection of Regency furniture and fine silverware. Agfest held each May at Carrick, 5 km SW. **Tourist information:** Tasmanian Travel and Information Centre, cnr St John and Paterson Sts, Launceston; (03) 6336 3133. **Accommodation:** 1 hotel/motel, 1 cara./camp. park. **See also:** Stately Homes.

Hamilton Pop. 150

MAP REF. 538 D1, 543 J6

A classified historic town in a rural setting, Hamilton has retained many of its colonial buildings. **Of interest:** Glen Clyde House (c. 1840), Grace St, now craft gallery with works representing over 100 craft artists and tearooms. **In the area:** Meadowbank Lake, 10 km NW, a popular venue for picnics, boating, water-skiing and trout fishing. Sheep Centre, 4 km W, has sheep shearing and mustering demonstrations; pre-bookings only, contact Tourist information. Old MacDonalds Tourist Farm, 28 km SW, a children's adventure farm. **Tourist information:** Council Offices, Tarleton St; (03) 6286 3202. **Accommodation:** 1 hotel.

Hastings Pop. 20

MAP REF. 538 D13, 543 J12

This tiny town, about 100 km SW of Hobart on the Huon Hwy, attracts many tourists to its famous dolomite caves, local gemstones and nearby scenic railway. **In the area:** Hastings Forest Tour, self-drive with cassette guide available from Tourist information and other outlets, begins off Hastings Rd and heads north-west to Esperance River. At Hastings Caves, 13 km NW: tours of illuminated Newdegate Cave, swimming in thermal springs pool, streamside walks and picnic/barbecue facilities. Lune River, 2 km S, a haven for gem collectors. Beyond river, 2 km further S, Ida Bay Scenic Railway, originally built to carry dolomite, now carries passengers 7 km to Deep Hole and back; picnic facilities at

National Parks

Tasmania packs an incredible variety into a remarkably compact area. Even in a few days you can experience a surprising cross-section of the natural and cultural heritage that help make Tasmania unique. But the best of the island State, from wild rivers and deep forests to grand mountains and ancient cave shelters, is to be found in its national parks. The island's landscape is shaped by ice as much as by isolation. In the national parks you can find mountains, tarns and lakes carved out during the past Ice Ages, and a unique flora and fauna that survives from ancient times. The rainforests are clothed in trees that trace their origins back to the supercontinent of Gondwana. Nowhere else in Australia is there such rich and unusual flora and fauna.

The Parks and Wildlife Service of Tasmania manages the State's 14 national parks and also the many State reserves with their Aboriginal sites, caves, gorges, waterfalls, rivers and European historic sites that date back as far as 1803, when Europeans first arrived.

All parks are accessible year round, and a park entry fee applies in all national parks. Some tourists believe the highland parks are best seen in summer and autumn, when the weather is more reliable, when wildflowers bloom in profusion and when flowering trees and shrubs attract birdlife. Bushwalking in the parks is popular, however in the highland parks, there can be sudden storms even in summer. Bushwalkers are advised to be prepared for sudden changes in the weather.

In the south-west of the State

Mount Field, just 80 kilometres north-west of Hobart, is a popular tourist venue, offering a diversity of activities ranging from picnicking to overnight bushwalking. It also has the only developed skiing area in southern Tasmania. There are several waterfalls in the park, the best-known being Russell Falls, first seen by Europeans in 1856. Here the cascading water plunges in two stages into a forested valley where tree ferns filter sunlight and create a mosaic effect. The forest includes large myrtles, giant 250-year-old gum trees, sassafras, huge tree ferns, the unique horizontal scrub and a variety of mosses, ferns, lichens and fungi. There are many walks, including the aptly named Tall Trees Walk and a circuit walk that takes in Russell, Horseshoe and Lady Barron Falls.

A 2-hour drive from Hobart, through Geeveston to the south-west, brings visitors to the **Hartz Mountains National Park**. Most of the area is over 600 metres in altitude with Hartz Peak being 1255 metres high. There are basic facilities for the day visitor and no camping facilities, although camping is permitted. Bushwalking is popular with visitors to the park.

Tasmania's largest national park is **Southwest National Park**, which has 605 213 hectares of mainly remote wilderness country. Here there are dolerite- and quartzite-capped mountains, sharp ridges and steep valleys left by glaciers; the dense forests are made up of eucalypts, myrtles, sassafras and leatherwood, often covered with mosses, ferns and lichens, and tangled with pink-flowered climbing heath and bauera. Climbers will find a challenge in Federation Peak, Mount Anne and Precipitous Bluff, while anglers will be kept busy with trout fishing at Lakes Pedder and Gordon. A specially-built bird hide at Melaleuca can be used in summer to observe the rare and endangered orange-bellied parrot.

The 440 000-hectare **Franklin-Gordon Wild Rivers National Park** forms the central portion of Tasmania's World Heritage Area. The Franklin attracts wilderness adventurers from around the world to test its challenging rapids. Along the slightly more placid lower Gordon River are stands of 2000-year-old Huon pine. Unusual buttongrass vegetation, growing right to the edge of the water, stains it the colour of tea. The Lyell Highway, the road link between Hobart and the west coast, runs through the park. A number of excellent short walks lead off the highway to rainforests, waterfalls and spectacular lookouts.

In the central north of the state

Covering some of Tasmania's highest country is **Cradle Mountain-Lake St Clair National Park**. There is a visitor centre near the park entrance at Cradle Mountain, and a nature walk into the nearby rainforest. Cradle Mountain has a variety of fine bushwalks, including one of Australia's best-known walking routes, the 85-kilometre Overland Track, through forests of deciduous beech, Tasmanian 'myrtle', pandanus, King Billy pine and a wealth of wildflowers. Cradle Mountain Wilderness Lodge lies on the northern boundary of the national park. At the other end of the park, there is a new visitor centre which features displays on the history of the

Bushwalking in Cradle Mountain-Lake St Clair National Park

area. The tranquil Lake St Clair, with a depth of over 200 metres, occupies a basin gouged out by glaciers more than 20 000 years ago. Cruises operate daily, and a 5–8 day trek traverses the park, taking in Mt Ossa (Tasmania's highest mountain) and a range of highland lakes and waterfalls. There are several campsites and cabins, and luxury accommodation nearby.

Steep, jagged mountains create a natural amphitheatre at the **Walls of Jerusalem National Park** (51 800 hectares), and ancient forests of pencil pines ring tiny glacially-formed lakes, making the park very popular with bushwalkers. The park is not accessible for day trips.

In the north of the State

The central north coastal strip of **Asbestos Range National Park** is an important refuge for a wide variety of birds, as well as wombats, quolls and devils. Its islands off Port Sorell provide an important breeding area for little (fairy) penguins, and the tidal and mud flats are ideal feeding grounds for a variety of migratory seabirds. On the unspoiled beaches, white sands come to life with thousands of soldier crabs.

Further west along the coast, **Rocky Cape National Park** (3064 hectares) encompasses rugged coastline with small sheltered beaches backed by heath-covered hills. It is known for its rock shelters used for over 8000 years by Tasmanian Aborigines.

In the east of the State

Many of Tasmania's national parks are important wildlife reserves. One such park, the 13 899-hectare **Mount William National Park**, is a sanctuary for native animals, including the Forester kangaroo (Tasmania's only kangaroo), echidna, wombat, pademelon, Bennetts wallaby and Tasmanian devil. Spring brings a carpet of wildflowers to this park: red and white heaths, golden wattle and guinea flower. At Lookout Point, thousands of rock orchids cover the granite rocks. Sheltered bays and beaches complete this little-known but beautiful park.

Fifty kilometres south-east of Launceston is **Ben Lomond National Park**, one of Tasmania's two main ski fields offering both downhill and cross country skiing, with an alpine village, ski-tows, ski hire, a tavern with accommodation, and a public shelter.

A short distance north of Freycinet National Park is Tasmania's newest national park, **Douglas-Apsley** (16 080 hectares). Proclaimed in 1990, this park contains the State's last large dry sclerophyll forest and can be traversed along a 3-day north-south walking track. Here lightly forested ridges contrast with patches of rainforest and river gorges. Waterfalls and spectacular coastal views add to the grandeur of the area. As yet, facilities in the park are basic.

Freycinet National Park offers wide stretches of white sands, rocky headlands, granite peaks, quiet beaches and small coves, and an excellent choice of short and long walking tracks. Just north of the park is Moulting Lagoon, the breeding ground of the lovely black swan and a refuge for other waterfowl. Freycinet National Park also includes Schouten Island, separated from the Freycinet Peninsula by a kilometre-wide passage, and reached only by boat. Near the park is Coles Bay, a fishing and swimming destination with delightful coastal scenery and a range of accommodation.

Maria Island, off the east coast, is well worth a visit. You can get there either by light aircraft or by passenger ferry from the Eastcoaster Resort. On arrival, it seems as if you have stepped into another world, for on Maria Island no tourist vehicles are permitted. This island national park embraces magnificently coloured sandstone cliffs and is a refuge for over 80 species of birds. Forester kangaroos, emus and Cape Barren geese roam freely in this unspoiled landscape. Its intriguing history and historic buildings date back to the convict era which began in 1825.

In some of the many State reserves, limestone caves are a popular attraction. The cave interiors are dramatically lit to enhance the wonderland of limestone-derived calcite formations. The Hastings Caves, located 110 kilometres from Hobart, include a nearby thermal swimming pool with a year-round warm temperature. Lawns and picnic areas surround the pool and incorporate a sensory trail designed for wheelchair access and the visually impaired. In the north central region, King Solomon and Marakoopa Caves are popular destinations.

For further information on Tasmania's national parks, contact the Parks and Wildlife Service, 134 Macquarie Street, Hobart (GPO Box 44A, Hobart 7001); (03) 6233 6191.

both ends of track (check departure times at Tourist information). Cockle Creek, 41 km S, is start of extended South Coast Walking Track. Southport, 6 km SE, originally a fishing port in days of sealers and whalers, offers good fishing, swimming, surfing and bushwalking. **Tourist information:** Church St, Geeveston; (03) 6297 1836. **Accommodation:** None. **See also:** Tours from Hobart.

Hawley Beach — Pop. 1000

MAP REF. 540 G5, 545 J6

This popular seaside area near Port Sorell is well known for its good fishing, excellent beaches and safe swimming. **Of interest:** Historic Hawley House (1878), Main Rd, offers meals and accommodation. **Tourist information:** Shop 1, 70 Gilbert St, Latrobe; (03) 6426 2693. **Accommodation:** Limited.

Huonville — Pop. 1524

MAP REF. 538 F8, 543 K9

Huonville is a busy commercial centre serving the nearby townships, and is also the centre for the surrounding apple-producing area. As well as producing apples, the nearby Huon Valley is the State's cherry-growing centre and in summer roadside stalls and pick-your-own orchards sell cherries. Other stone fruits are also grown in the area. The valuable softwood now known as Huon pine was discovered in this district. **Of interest:** Model Train World, Main Rd. Horseback Wilderness Tours, Sale St. Pedal boat and aqua bike hire, Esplanade. **In the area:** River jet-boat rides over rapids to Glen Huon. Apple and Heritage Museum just out of Grove, 6 km NE. Possum's Country Market, 4 km N on Huon Hwy, for craft. Snowy Range Trout Fishery, Little Dennison River, 25 km NW. Scenic drives: west to Glen Huon, Judbury and Ranelagh; south east to Cygnet. Antique Motor Museum near Ranelagh, 5 km NW. Model Miniature Village and apple carvings at Glen Huon, 8 km W. At holiday town of Port Huon, 10 km SW, river cruises visit salmon farms on river. **Tourist information:** Huon River Jet Boats, Esplanade; (03) 6264 1838. **Accommodation:** 1 hotel. **See also:** Tours from Hobart.

Kettering — Pop. 295

MAP REF. 538 H9, 543 L10

This town on the Channel Hwy south of Hobart serves a large fruit-growing district. **Of interest:** Bruny Island ferry, leaves several times daily from Ferry Rd terminal; extra services during holidays. Oyster Cove Inn and marina, Ferry Rd. Variety of boats for hire; skippered cruises available. **In the area:** Bruny Island. At Snug, 8 km N, Mother's Favourites, for seafood; pleasant walks in Snug Falls Track area. Nearby, Coningham Beach, for good swimming and boating. Monument to French explorer Admiral Bruni D'Entrecasteaux, 21 km S at Gordon. **Tourist information:** Bruny D'Entrecasteaux Visitor Centre, Ferry Rd; (03) 6267 4494. **Accommodation:** 1 hotel/motel, 1 cara./camp. park.

Kingston — Pop. 12 907

MAP REF. 538 H7, 543 L9

Kingston, 12 km S of Hobart, is the administrative centre for the nearby area. **Of interest:** Display at Federal

TASMANIA

Rural Landscapes

Tasmania's homesick European settlers were amazingly successful in their attempts to tame their strange new antipodean home. They set about systematically clearing the more accessible lowlands of all traces of native bush, replacing it with neatly tilled fields fringed by hedgerows and the exotic trees familiar to them. Georgian farmhouses set in gardens with flower beds and borders completed the picture.

Tasmania's main pastoral district is the beautiful Midlands area between Brighton and Perth, noted for stock-raising and high-quality merino wool. This was one of the first farming areas established in Tasmania and its gently undulating plains are offset by mellow farmhouses, historic villages and a wealth of huge old English trees.

The historic township of **New Norfolk** is the centre of Tasmania's long-established hop-growing district, which is a main supplier of hops for Australian beer. This enchanting countryside is

Hops farms in the beautiful Derwent Valley

enhanced by quaint old oast houses, or hop-drying kilns. Apples and dairy products are produced in the Derwent Valley, which is also an important beef-raising and wool-growing district.

The Huon Valley, south of Hobart, the centre of Tasmania's famous apple-growing industry, is now the State's cherry-growing centre as well. During summer, roadside stalls and pick-your-own orchards in the area are popular with passing travellers.

Tasmania's richest and most highly productive farmland lies on the north-west coast, where the main industries are potato-growing and the raising of prime beef and dairy cattle.

See also: Entry for New Norfolk in A–Z listing.

Government's Antarctic research headquarters, southern outskirts on Channel Hwy; open Mon.–Fri. Mar.: Kingborough festival (includes road cycle race). Oct.: Oliebollen festival (relates to Dutch community). **In the area:** Scenic drives south through Blackmans Bay, Tinderbox and Howden; magnificent views of Droughty Point and Bruny Island from Piersons Point. Small blowhole at Blackmans Bay, 7 km S at reserve on Blowhole Rd; spectacular in stormy weather. Old shot tower, 3 km NE near Taroona; wonderful views of Derwent River estuary from top of tower. **Tourist information:** Council Offices, Channel Hwy; (03) 6229 5555. **Accommodation:** 2 hotel/motels.

Latrobe   Pop. 2551

MAP REF. 540 E6, 544 I7

Situated on the Mersey River, 9 km SE of Devonport, the Latrobe area was once the home of four main Aboriginal groups collectively known as the North Tribe. After European settlement Latrobe became a busy town with its own shipyards. Today it is the site of one of the biggest cycling carnivals in Australia, held at Christmas. **Of interest:** Many early buildings and shopfronts dating from 1840s, some National Trust-classified; self-guide walk, leaflet available from Tourist information. Court House Museum, Gilbert St, for local history. Bell's Parade, off Gilbert St along riverbank, has picturesque reserve and picnic areas. Sherwood Hall, historic timber structure, Bells Parade. Markets, each Sun. at Gilbert St and James St. Jan.: Latrobe-Port Sorell summer festival (continues into Feb.); Australia Day carnival; Henley on the Mersey. Dec.: Latrobe wheel race and Latrobe Gift. **In the area:** Shale Road Reserve, 3 km S, for picnics and water sports. Henry Somerset Orchard Reserve, 7 km S, has native orchids and other rare flora. **Tourist information:** Shop 1, 70 Gilbert St; (03) 6426 2693. **Accommodation:** 1 hotel, 1 motel, 2 B&B.

Launceston   Pop. 66 747

MAP REF. 541 N10, 545 L8

Although it is Tasmania's second-largest city and a busy tourist centre, Launceston manages to retain a relaxed, friendly atmosphere. Nestling in hilly country where the Tamar, North Esk and South Esk Rivers meet, Launceston is also at the junction of three main highways and has direct air links with Melbourne and Hobart. It is sometimes known as the Garden City because of its beautiful parks and gardens. **Of interest:** Yorktown Square, The Avenue, Quadrant Mall, Civic Square, and Prince's Square with its magnificent baroque fountain and fine surrounding buildings. Main shopping area around the Mall. Old Umbrella Shop, George St, a unique 1860s shop preserved by National Trust. Penny Royal World, Paterson St: a collection of buildings originally sited at Barton, near Cressy, and moved stone by stone to Launceston; includes tavern, museum, working water mill, corn mill, graceful windmill, accommodation and restaurants; linked by restored tramway to Penny Royal Gunpowder Mill at old Cataract quarry site; boat trips available on artificial lake. Parks include 5-ha City Park with Monkey Island and conservatory (Design Centre of Tasmania nearby displays contemporary art and craft), end of Cameron St; Royal Park, formal civic park on South Esk River; Zig Zag Reserve, leading to Cataract Gorge area. Queen Victoria Museum and Art Gallery, in Royal Park off Wellington St, with displays of Aboriginal and convict relics, Tasmania's mineral wealth, flora and fauna, early china and glassware, and colonial and modern art. Cruises on lower reaches of Tamar, on *Lady Stelfox*; departs from Ritchie's Mill Arts Centre, Bridge Rd. Boags Brewery, William St, has guided tours. Self-guide and guided walking tours, contact Tourist information. Oct.: Garden festival; Royal national show; Tasmanian poetry festival. **In the area:** One of Launceston's outstanding natural attractions, spectacular Cataract Gorge, 2 km W of city centre. Cataract Cliff Grounds Reserve, on north side of gorge, a formal park with lawns, European trees, peacocks and restaurant. Area linked to swimming pool and kiosk on south side by scenic chairlift and suspension bridge. Walks on both sides of gorge. Trevallyn Dam, 6 km W, an attractive picnic spot. Nearby, Australia's only hang-gliding simulator. Launceston Federal Country Club Casino, 7 km SW. Punchbowl Reserve and Rhododendron Gardens, 5 km SW, has native and European fauna in natural surroundings. Longford Wildlife Park, 20 km S; open Tues.–Sun. Waverley Woollen Mills, 5 km E, offers tours which include historic collection of plant machinery used to create the industry for which Launceston earned national reputation. Alpine Village in Ben Lomond National Park, 60 km SE; open during ski season. St Matthias' Church, Windermere, 15 km N. Tamar Valley wineries, 50 km NE. Guided tours throughout northern Tasmania; details from Tourist information. Three National Trust historic houses: Entally House, 13 km SW at Hadspen; Franklin House, 6 km S; Clarendon, near Nile, 28 km SE. **Tourist information:** cnr St John and Paterson Sts; (03) 6336 3133. **Accommodation:** 17 hotels, 12 motels, 1 cara./camp. park. **See also:** Anglers Paradise; Scenic Island State; Stately Homes.

Kings Bridge, Launceston

Lilydale `Pop. 333`

MAP REF. 541 P6, 545 M7

At the foot of Mt Arthur, 27 km from Launceston, the town of Lilydale has many nearby bush tracks and picnic spots. **In the area:** Lilydale Falls Reserve, 3 km N, has two oak trees grown from acorns from Windsor Great Park, planted here on coronation day of British King George IV, 12 May 1937. Scenic walks to top of Mt Arthur (1187 m). At Lalla, 4 km W: Walker Rhododendron Reserve; Appleshed, for local art and craft. Brown Mountain School of Bonsai, Brown Mountain Rd, Underwood, 11 km SW; open by appt. Ash tree plantation at Hollybank Forest Reserve, Underwood, 5 km S; picnic/barbecue areas. Bridestowe Lavender Farm, 26 km NE near Nabowla, has sales of lavender products; tours in flowering season, Dec.-Jan. **Tourist information:** Tasmanian Travel and Tourist Information Centre, cnr St John and Paterson Sts, Launceston; (03) 6336 3133. **Accommodation:** 1 hotel.

Longford `Pop. 2601`

MAP REF. 541 N13, 545 L9

Longford, 22 km S of Launceston, was established in 1813 when former settlers of Norfolk Island were given land grants in the area. Since then it has had two name changes; its previous names were Norfolk Plains and Latour. Now classified as a historic town, it serves a rich agricultural district. **Of interest:** Many historic buildings, some convict-built. In Wellington St: Christ Church (1839), has outstanding stained-glass window and pioneer gravestones; 'Car in window' at Country Club Hotel. Mar.: Targa Tasmania motor racing, classic and veteran car displays. **In the area:** Brickendon (1824), 2 km S, a homestead built by William Archer and still owned by descendants; tours by appt. Cressy, 10 km S, renowned for its fly-fishing at Brumbys Creek, especially in Nov. when mayflies hatch. At Perth, 5 km NE, historic buildings: Eskleigh, Jolly Farmer Inn, Old Crown Inn and Leather Bottell Inn. Longford Wildlife Park, 5 km N, a conservation area for fallow deer and Australian fauna and flora; also has picnic/barbecue areas and constructed lake. **Tourist information:** Council Offices, Smith St; (03) 6391 1303. **Accommodation:** 3 hotels, 1 cara./camp. park. **See also:** Scenic Island State; Stately Homes.

Mole Creek `Pop. 249`

MAP REF. 540 E12, 544 I9

This town, 74 km S of Devonport, serves an important farming and forestry district. It was named after the creek which curiously 'burrows' underground. The unique Tasmanian leatherwood honey from the blossom of the leatherwood tree, which grows only in the rainforests of the west coast of Tasmania, is processed here. Each summer, apiarists transport hives to the nearby leatherwood forests. **Of interest:** Honey Factory, Pioneer Dr., provides viewing of extraction and processing of honey; open Mon.–Fri. **In the area:** Guided tours of fine limestone caves: Marakoopa, 8 km W, also has glow worm display; and smaller but still spectacular King Solomons Cave further 8 km W. Trowunna Wildlife Park, 4 km E. Devils Gullet, 40 km SE, a natural lookout overlooking Fisher River Valley, in World Heritage area; reached by walking track (30-min. return). Popular day bushwalk in Walls of Jerusalem National Park, starts 45 km S. **Tourist information:** 29 West Church St, Deloraine; (03) 6362 2046. **Accommodation:** 1 hotel, 1 B&B, 1 cara./camp. park.

New Norfolk `Pop. 5822`

MAP REF. 538 F4, 543 K8

Colonial buildings set among English trees and hop fields dotted with oast houses give this classified historic town a decidedly English look; the countryside has often been compared to that of Kent in England. On the Derwent River, 33 km NW of Hobart, the town owes its name to the fact that displaced European settlers from the abandoned Norfolk Island settlement were granted land in this area. Although the New Norfolk district produces a majority of the hops used by Australian breweries, the chief industry today is paper manufacture. **Of interest:** At Historical Centre in Council Chambers, Circle St: genealogical and other records; also self-guide historic walk leaflets. Scenic lookouts: Peppermint Hill, off Blair St; Pulpit Rock and Four Winds Display Gardens, off Rocks Rd. Old Colony Inn (1835), Montague St, now museum with large antique dolls' house and original kitchen. On Lyell Hwy: Oast House, Tynwald Park, a hop museum and art gallery; Bush Inn (1815), claims oldest licence in Commonwealth, although contested by Launceston Hotel. Jet boat rides on Derwent River rapids leave from Bush Inn. St Matthew's Church (1823), Bathurst St, reputedly oldest church still standing in Tasmania; craft centre in adjoining Close. Mar.: Hop festival. Aug.: Winter challenge. **In the area:** Tours of Australian Newsprint Mill, 5 km E at Boyer; 24-hrs notice required. Famous Salmon Ponds, 11 km NW at Plenty,: hatchery where first brown and rainbow trout in southern hemisphere were bred in 1864; restaurant; museum. Meadowbank Vineyard, 20 km NW. Mt Field National Park, 40 km NW, features impressive Russell Falls. **Tourist information:** Council Offices, Circle St; (03) 6261 2777. **Accommodation:** 3 hotels, 1 motel, 3 B&B, 1 cara./camp. park. **See also:** Rural Landscapes; Scenic Island State; Stately Homes; Tours from Hobart.

Oatlands `Pop. 522`

MAP REF. 543 M5

This classified historic town on the shores of Lake Dulverton, 84 km N of Hobart, attracts both anglers (lake dries up in times of drought) and lovers of history. It was designated as a garrison town by Governor Macquarie in 1821 and surveyed in 1832. Many of the town's unique sandstone buildings were constructed in the 1830s and it is said that most residents live in historic houses. **Of interest:** Convict-built court house (1829), Campbell St. Holyrood House (1840), High St, has historic gardens. St Peter's Church (c. 1838), William St. Callington Flour Mill (1836), Mill Lane. Lake Dulverton Wildlife Sanctuary, Esplanade. Feb.: Rodeo. **In the area:** Trout fishing on Lake Sorell, 29 km NW, and adjoining Lake Crescent. **Tourist information:** Council Offices, 71 High St; (03) 6254 0011. **Accommodation:** 1 hotel, 4 B&B. **See also:** Rural Landscapes; Scenic Island State.

Orford `Pop. 502`

MAP REF. 539 N2, 543 O6

Views from this popular holiday town at the estuary of the Prosser River, on the Tasman Hwy, are dominated by Maria Island National Park, 20 km offshore. **Of interest:** Walk along Old Convict Rd follows northern bank of river; starts adjacent to Tourist information. **In the area:** River and sea fishing, and scuba diving. The Thumbs Lookout, 2 km S, overlooks Maria Island. Daily ferry service to Maria Island from Eastcoaster Resort, 4 km NE on Louisville Rd. On Maria Island, historic settlement of Darlington has camping and dormitory-style accommodation; walking trails across island. Wielangta Relic Rainforest Walk, 20 km S, a boardwalk through ancient pocket of rainforest. Church of St John the Baptist, 18 km SW at Buckland, a beautiful 14th-century stained-glass window.

Tourist information: Riverside Villas, Old Convict Rd; (03) 6257 1372. **Accommodation:** 1 hotel/motel, 1 motel, 1 cara./camp. park. **See also:** Scenic Island State.

Penguin   Pop. 2876

MAP REF. 540 A4, 544 H6

The Dial Range rises over this quiet town, named after little (fairy) penguins still found in rookeries nearby. **Of interest:** In Main St: St Stephen's Church and Uniting Church, both National Trust-classified. Hiscutt Park, off Crescent St, has working Dutch windmill and tulips in season. Penguin rookeries on eastern outskirts, tours available Dec.–early Mar. Old School Market, King Edward St, 2nd and 4th Sun. in month. **In the area:** Mt Montgomery, 5 km S, has magnificent view from summit. Mason's Fuschia Fantasy, 6 km S on West Pine Rd, with 750 varieties; open p.m. and Sat. Ferndean Wildlife Reserve, 6 km S, has

The Gourmet Island

Tasmania has a growing reputation for fresh produce and wine, and there is a wide variety of gourmet options available to the traveller. Vineyards and fresh food producers are dotted across the island. Take a basket, and stop at roadside stalls and farms to buy the best food and wine that Tasmania has to offer.

In the north of the island, travel the Tasmanian Wine Route from Launceston across the Tamar River to Bridport, returning via Lilydale. The highlight of this drive is the Pipers River wine region, noted for its good rieslings and, more recently, for its chardonnays and pinot noirs. Like all Tasmanian wine-growing areas, it is relatively new. In less than three decades it has become the State's premier wine region, and is now responsible for half of Tasmania's wine production. Most of the wineries, including Heemskerk, Delamere and Pipers Brook, encourage cellar-door sales.

West of Launceston is some of the finest dairy country in Australia. Heidi Cheese Farm makes preservative-free cheeses at Exton, on the highway to Deloraine. Their washed rind cheeses include a nutty Gruyere and the well-known Heidi Barrel.

Off the north-western coast is King Island which has built a strong reputation for its pure cream and double brie. The Island has some great cheeses which visitors can taste at the King Island Dairy, and has also gained a reputation for its crayfish and smoked meats.

Central Tasmania is famous for its trout fishing. Near Miena is the 'Land of Three Thousand Lakes', which provides the angler with the chance to catch fresh trout. For the less dedicated, there are a number of outlets in Tasmania which sell smoked trout. Besides trout, atlantic salmon is one of Tasmania's finest fish. A significant salmon-farming industry has developed on the south coast, and salmon can be purchased across the State, either fresh, cured or smoked. Salmon roe is also popular. Boat tours of the Huon River salmon farms leave daily from Port Huon.

The Huon Valley is Tasmania's apple and cherry-growing centre. During the summer months roadside stalls and pick-your-own orchards offer a variety of stone fruits to passing travellers. Fresh apricots are a particular favourite.

Cascade Premium Lager, with its distinctive Tasmanian tiger label, has become a highly-prized beer in recent years. Tours of the historic brewery in South Hobart are held on weekdays.

An unusual place to sample Tasmanian beers is the Pub in the Paddock at Pyengana, near St Helens. It is precisely that: a hotel located in the middle of a large empty paddock, where drinkers can share their Premium Lagers with the resident pig.

Between Launceston and Hobart are a number of small food producers, including Butlers Butchery in Campbell Town, which specialises in large 'stag snags' (venison sausages).

For an overview of gourmet Tasmania, visit The Taste of Tasmania festival in Hobart, held at Princes Wharf each January. The best of the island's food and wine is on show, from chargrilled seafood to deicious relishes and Tasmanian wines.

Historic Cascade Brewery, famous for its Premium Lager

picnic spot and walking tracks. Pioneer Park, 10 km SW at Riana, with gardens, walks and picnic facilities. Pindari Deer Farm, 15 km SW, has deer-handling demonstrations. Beyond South Riana (20 km SW), lies Gunns Plains, caves and hop fields. Scenic drive south-east to Ulverstone via coast road. **Tourist information:** Main St; (03) 6437 1421. **Accommodation:** 1 hotel, 2 B&B, 1 cara. park. **See also:** Scenic Island State.

Pontville Pop. 1125

MAP REF. 538 H3, 543 L7

Much of the freestone used in Tasmania's old buildings was quarried near this classified historic town. On the Midland Hwy, 27 km N of Hobart, Pontville was founded in 1830 and many of its early buildings remain. **Of interest:** Historic buildings on or adjacent to Midland Hwy include: St Mark's Church (1841); The Sheiling (built 1819, restored 1953), behind church; old post office; Crown Inn; and 'The Row', thought to have been built in 1824 as soldiers' quarters, now restored. **In the area:** Towns nearby with interesting historic buildings: Bagdad, 8 km N; Kempton, 11 km further N; Broadmarsh, 10 km W; Tea Tree, 5 km E. Brighton, 3 km S, an important military post; Agricultural show held each Nov. Bonorong Park Wildlife Centre, 5 km S. **Tourist information:** Council Offices, Tivoli Rd, Gagebrook; (03) 6263 0333. **Accommodation:** None.

Port Arthur Pop. 190

MAP REF. 539 N10, 543 N10

This historic town on the scenic Tasman Peninsula was one of Australia's most infamous penal settlements from the 1830s to the 1850s. Today it is still possible to sense the incredible hardships endured by the early convict population. **Of interest:** Port Arthur Historic Site: stabilised and restored ruins of the convict settlement, period houses, museum, and Heritage Nursery and Gallery; self-guide and guided walks available. Ghost Tours depart nightly from the Visitor Information Office. Dec.: Boxing Day woodchop; Absconders run. **In the area:** Daily cruises on harbour and to Isle of the Dead (1100 convict, military and civil graves). Historic and nature walk to nearby Stewarts Bay, brochures available from Tourist information. Steam-train rides available at the re-created milling settlement of Bush Mill, 1km N. Coal Mines Historic Site, 30 km NW, Tasmania's first operational mine. Remarkable Cave, 6 km S on coast, formed by wave action; check tides. Palmers Lookout, 3 km S, views of harbour and surrounding coastline. **Tourist information:** Visitor Information Office, Historic Site, Arthur Hwy; (03) 6250 2363. **Accommodation:** 2 hotel/motels, 1 hostel, 1 B&B, 1 cara./camp. park. **See also:** A Convict Past.

Port Sorell Pop. 1494

MAP REF. 540 G5, 545 J6

Sheltered by hills, this well-established holiday town at the estuary of the Rubicon River near Devonport has a mild climate. Named after Governor Sorell and established in 1822, it is the oldest township on the north-west coast. Unfortunately many of its old buildings were destroyed by bushfires early this century, after it had been almost deserted for the thriving new port of Devonport. **Of interest:** Swimming, fishing, boating and bushwalking. Views from Watch House Hill, off Meredith St, once site of old gaol, now bowling green. Asbestos Range National Park across estuary, a scenic park with numerous isolated beaches. Jan.-Feb.: Latrobe-Port Sorell summer festival. **Tourist information:** Shop 1, 70 Gilbert St, Latrobe; (03) 6426 2693. **Accommodation:** 2 cara./camp. parks. **See also:** National Parks.

Queenstown Pop. 3368

MAP REF. 542 E3, 544 E12

The discovery of gold and mineral resources in the Mt Lyell field last century led to the almost overnight emergence of Queenstown. It is a town carved out of the mountains that tower starkly around it. Mining was continuous in Queenstown from 1888 to 1994, and the field produced more than 670 000 tonnes of copper, 510 000 kg of silver and 20 000 kg of gold. Gold Mines of Australia resumed mining for copper, silver and gold at the end of 1995; tours of the mine are available. The town has modern shops and facilities, but its wide streets, remaining historic buildings and unique setting give it an old mining-town flavour. In certain lights, multi-coloured boulders on the bare hillsides surrounding the town reflect the sun's rays and turn to amazing shades of pink and gold. **Of interest:** Guided tours of Mt Lyell Mine depart from Tourist information; surface and underground mine tours. Galley Museum, cnr Sticht and Driffield Sts, displays history of west coast, photographs and memorabilia. Chairlift, from Penghana Rd, travels up hill to old silica and limestone quarries; magnificent views, particularly at sunset. **In the area:** Spectacular views from Lyell Hwy as it climbs steeply out of town. Original Iron Blow goldmine (1833), off Lyell Hwy at Gormanston, 6 km E. Ghost town of Linda, 9 km E. Mt Jukes Rd lookout, 7 km SW; road leads to old mining settlement of Lynchford, and Crotty Dam. Rafting on Franklin River, to the east and south of town. Mt Mullens and Franklin River scenic nature walk along old mining railway line between Queenstown and Zeehan, 37 km N. Lyell Tours, offer 4WD day or half-day tours south to Bird River rainforest area and Mt McCall. **Tourist information:** Mt Lyell Mine Tour Office, 1 Driffield St; (03) 6471 2388. **Accommodation:** 2 hotels, 2 hotel/motels, 3 motels, 1 cara./camp. park. **See also:** Scenic Island State; The West Coast.

Railton Pop. 996

MAP REF. 540 F8, 544 I8

This substantial country town south-east of Devonport owes its existence to the Goliath Portland Cement Company, representing one of Tasmania's major industries. Raw materials are taken from a quarry on the site and carried by an overhead conveyor to the crusher. **In the area:** Scenic drive through area known as Sunnyside to Stoodley Forest Reserve, 14 km S; at reserve, walking tracks and picnic/barbecue areas. **Tourist information:** Kentish Museum, 93 Main St, Sheffield; (03) 6491 1861. **Accommodation:** 1 hotel.

Richmond Pop. 754

MAP REF. 539 J4, 543 M7

Richmond, 26 km from Hobart, is the most important historic town in Tasmania. The much-photographed Richmond Bridge is the oldest surviving bridge in Australia (1823–25) and many of the town's buildings were constructed in the 1830s or even earlier. Some of these structures, including the bridge, were built by convicts under appallingly harsh conditions. Legend has it that the ghost of an overseer who was murdered by convicts still haunts the bridge. **Of interest:** Self-guide leaflet of town and area, contact Tourist information. Old Richmond Gaol (1825), Bathurst St, one of Australia's best-preserved convict prisons; guided tours available. St John's (1837), St John's Circle, oldest Catholic church in Australia still in use. St Luke's Church (1834–36), Torrens St, has fine timber ceiling. General store and former post office (1832), Bridge St, oldest postal building in Australia. Also in Bridge St: galleries featuring local art and craft, including Saddler's Court (c. 1848) and Peppercorn Gallery (c. 1850); restored Bridge Inn, one of town's oldest buildings, housing complex of shops; Old Hobart Town, a model of Hobart in early 1800s; Toy Museum; The Maze; Village Store (1836), one of oldest general stores still operating in Tasmania. Georgian mansion, Prospect House (1830s) off Hobart Rd, haunted by ghost of Mrs Buscombe; offers meals and colonial accommodation. Feb.: Country music festival. Oct.: Village fair. **In the area:** Scenic drive north through Campania (7 km) and Colebrook (19 km). Crosswinds Vineyard, 10 km NW. **Tourist information:** Saddler's Court Gallery, 48 Bridge St; (03) 6260 2132. **Accommodation:** 1 hotel, 1 cara./camp park. **See also:** Scenic Island State; Stately Homes; Tours from Hobart.

Rokeby
Pop. 3495

MAP REF. 537 O10, 539 J6, 543 M8

This old town on the eastern shore of the Derwent River was first settled in 1809. The first apples to be exported from Tasmania were grown here, as was the first wheat ever produced in Tasmania. Rokeby's rural character is now rapidly changing as housing developments occupy the farmland. **Of interest:** Historic cemetery, Rokeby Rd, contains graves of many First Fleeters. Historic buildings include

Stately Homes

One of Tasmania's attractions is its wealth of beautiful stately homes with a distinctly English air. You can dine in style in some, such as **Prospect House** in the historic town of Richmond, and stay in others.

Several of Tasmania's grand old mansions, such as **Malahide** and **Killymoon**, both on the Esk Highway near Fingal, are privately-owned and cannot be inspected, but many of the State's finest homesteads are open daily to the public.

Clarendon House, via Evandale, 27 kilometres from Launceston, is probably Australia's grandest Georgian mansion. Completed in 1838 for woolgrower James Cox and given to the National Trust in 1962, it has been meticulously restored.

Three other stately homesteads within reach of Launceston are Franklin House, just 6 kilometres south; Entally House at Hadspen, 18 kilometres from Launceston; and Brickendon in Longford.

Franklin House, another elegant Georgian mansion now owned by the National Trust, was built in 1838 for Mr Britton Jones, a Launceston brewer and innkeeper. In 1842 it became the W.K. Hawkes School for Boys.

Charming **Entally House**, the most historic of the Trust houses, was built in 1819. Set in superb grounds, Entally has a greenhouse, chapel and coach-house. It was opened to the public in 1950.

At Longford, the two-storeyed, shuttered **Brickendon**, with its graceful metal front porch, looks French, but long stretches of hawthorn hedges and many old chestnuts, oaks, ash and junipers make it seem part of an English landscape.

Prospect House, Richmond

The Grove in George Town, north of Launceston, is another privately-owned historic house open to visitors. Built in the 1820s, it has been painstakingly restored by the present owners, who dress in period costume to serve lunch and teas.

Home Hill in Middle Road, Devonport, the home of former Prime Minister Joseph Lyons and Dame Enid Lyons, was built by them in 1916. Now open to the public, the house and grounds are owned by the City of Devonport. The contents of the house are owned by the National Trust.

Privately-owned but operated by the Trust, the **White House**, in Westbury, near Deloraine, was built c. 1841 as a corner shop and residence. It stands on a corner of the town's Village Green and displays a collection of Staffordshire china.

Hobart has two historic houses open for inspection: the National Trust property **Runnymede**, in the suburb of New Town, and **Narryna** in Battery Point. Graceful Runnymede, built c. 1836, has been restored and furnished by the Trust. Narryna, a Georgian sandstone and brick townhouse with a walled courtyard, is set in an old-world garden shaded by elm trees. Also known as the Van Diemen's Land Memorial Folk Museum, it houses a significant collection of colonial artifacts.

The misleadingly named **Old Colony Inn** (1835) in New Norfolk was never used as an inn. It serves light lunches and Devonshire teas. Three rooms are set aside for antique objects, including an antique dolls' house. This beautiful old building, set in delightful grounds, has become one of Tasmania's most photographed tourist attractions.

For further information, contact the National Trust of Australia (Tasmania), 413 Hobart Rd, Franklin Village 7249; (03) 6344 6233.

The West Coast

The beautiful but inhospitable west coast, with its wild mountain ranges, lakes, rivers, eerie valleys and dense rainforests, is one of Tasmania's most fascinating regions. The majestic, untamed beauty of this coast is in complete contrast to the State's pretty pastures. The whole area has vast mineral wealth and a colourful mining history, reflected in its towns. The discovery of tin and copper in 1871 and 1883 started a rush to the west coast, booming at the turn of the century. **Queenstown**, the largest town, and the other main towns – **Zeehan**, **Rosebery** and **Strahan** – largely owe their existence to mining.

It was not until 1932 that a rough road was pushed through the mountainous country between Queenstown and Hobart. Fortunately, modern road-making techniques have improved the situation and today west coast towns are linked by the Murchison, Zeehan and Waratah Highways, and the Lyell Highway (the original road to Hobart) has been brought up to modern standards. In fact, the flooding of Lake Burbury has resulted in the re-routing of the highway, which now takes motorists across the lake itself, enhancing the spectacular entry to Queenstown. Driving round the west coast road circuit and seeing the superb mountain scenery and colourful towns of the area is an unforgettable experience. The only drawback is that the area is subject to exceptionally heavy rainfall, even in summer and autumn.

The little township of Zeehan, south-west of Rosebery, typifies the changing fortunes of mining towns. Following the rich silver-lead ore discoveries in 1882, its population swelled to 10 000 and the town boasted 26 hotels and the Gaiety Theatre, with seating for over 10 000, where Dame Nellie Melba sang. Many of these fine buildings from the boom period can still be seen, including the Gaiety Theatre at the Grand Hotel. Zeehan's West Coast Pioneers Memorial Museum, housed in the former School of Mines, is a popular tourist attraction.

One of the most spectacular views on any highway in Australia can be seen as you drive into Queenstown. As the narrow road winds down the steep slopes of Mt Owen, you can see the amazingly bare hills – tinged with pale pinks, purples, golds and greys – that surround the town. At the turn of the century, the trees from these hills were cut down to provide fuel for the copper smelters, and heavy rains eroded their topsoil, revealing the strangely hued rocks beneath.

The first European settlement on the west coast was established in 1821, when the most unruly convicts from Hobart were dispatched to establish a penitentiary on Sarah Island (Settlement Island) in Macquarie Harbour and to work the valuable huon pine forests around the Gordon and King Rivers. Sarah Island soon became a notorious prison and most of the unfortunate convicts who managed to escape died in the magnificent but unyielding surrounding bush. The horrors of that time are echoed in the name of the entrance to the harbour – Hell's Gates. Today the port of Strahan on Macquarie Harbour has thousands of visitors each year, many attracted to the spectacular Gordon River, one of Tasmania's largest and most remote wild rivers. Cruise boats make regular trips to Heritage Landing at the mouth of the river. On the return trip they stop along the way to allow visitors to see the old convict ruins on Sarah Island. Scenic flights departing from Strahan enable visitors to take in the beauty of more inaccessible areas. Another interesting trip from Strahan is to Ocean Beach, 6 kilometres from the town. This long, lonely stretch of beach, lashed by spectacular breakers, somehow typifies the magnificent wild west coast.

The magnificent scenic wilderness in Tasmania's remote south-west can be reached only by plane or boat. Flights with Par Avion leave Cambridge Airport near Hobart daily. Fishing, hiking and sailing are offered in this incredibly rugged area of Tasmania; also, sightings of the rare and endangered orange-bellied parrot are becoming more frequent.

See also: individual entries in A–Z listing for those towns indicated by bold type.

The landscape around Queenstown has a unique quality created by the bare hills that surround the town

Rokeby Court and Rokeby House, in Hawthorn Pl., and St Matthew's Church (1843), North Pde; some chairs in church's chancel were carved from wood from ship in Nelson's fleet; church's organ, brought from England in 1825 and first installed in what is now St David's Cathedral, Hobart, is still in use. **In the area:** Historic buildings at Bellerive, 8 km NW. Historic Centre at Rosny, 10 km NW. To the south, excellent surfing at Clifton Beach (9 km); boating and swimming at South Arm (22 km). **Tourist information:** Council Offices, 38 Bligh St, Rosny Park; (03) 6244 0600. **Accommodation:** Limited.

Rosebery　　　　Pop. 1637

MAP REF. 542 E1, 544 E10

Gold was discovered at Rosebery in 1893 in what is now called Rosebery Creek. Huge deposits of lead and zinc were also discovered in the area. Goldmining has long since been abandoned and the town now owes its existence to the zinc mining company Pasminco-EZ. **In the area:** Montezuma Falls, highest waterfall in State, 5 km SW; accessible by 4WD or walking track. Picturesque lake near Tullah, 12 km NE; nearby, historical Wee Georgie Wood Railway, check operating times. **Tourist information:** West Coast Pioneers Museum, Main St, Zeehan; (03) 6471 6225. **Accommodation:** 2 hotels, 1 cara./camp. park. **See also:** The West Coast.

Ross　　　　Pop. 282

MAP REF. 543 M3, 545 N12

One of the oldest and most beautiful bridges in Australia spans the Macquarie River at this classified historic township. The bridge, completed in 1836, was designed by colonial architect John Lee Archer and built by convicts. The convict stonemason Daniel Herbert received a free pardon in recognition for his 186 fine carvings on the bridge. Herbert's grave is in the old burial ground in Park St. Ross was established in 1812 as a military post for the protection of travellers who once stopped there to change coaches. Today it is still an important stopping-place on the Midland Hwy between Launceston and Hobart. The district is famous for its superfine wool. **Of interest:** Self-guide leaflet on town and area, contact Tourist information. Ruins of women's prison, off Bond St. Tasmanian Wool Centre, Church St, highlights area's links with wool industry. Avenue of English elms in Church St complements historic sandstone buildings, including Scotch Thistle Inn and Coach House, former coaching stop; old Ross General Store and Tea Room, now selling Tasmanian crafts and Devonshire teas. In Bridge St, old barracks building, restored by local National Trust; street leads to Ross Bridge (floodlit at night). Nov.: Rodeo. **In the area:** World-class fly-fishing for brown trout in Macquarie River. Some of State's best trout-fishing lakes – Sorell, Crescent, Tooms and Leake – are within hour's drive of town. **Tourist information:** Tasmanian Wool Centre, Church St; (03) 6381 5466. **Accommodation:** 1 hotel, 1 B&B, 1 cara./camp. park. **See also:** Scenic Island State.

St Helens　　　　Pop. 1145

MAP REF. 545 Q8

This popular resort on the shores of Georges Bay is renowned for its crayfish and scalefish. Three fish-processing plants in or near the settlement to handle the catch of the fishing fleet based in its harbour. **Of interest:** Bay beaches ideal for swimming, coastal beaches for surfing. Charter boats for deep-sea fishing, and dinghy hire for bay fishing, Tasman Hwy. Excellent fishing for bream and trout on Scamander River. Many local restaurants specialise in fish dishes. Mar.: Tasmanian game-fishing classic. June: Suncoast jazz festival. **In the area:** Bushwalks to view birdlife and wildflowers. Scamander, 19 km S, for swimming and fishing. Binalong Bay, 11 km NE, has good surf and rock fishing. At Pyengana, 28 km NW: St Columba Falls; Healey's Cheese Factory; the 'Pub in the Paddock', hotel in middle of empty paddock. Several coastal reserves in Bay of Fires district offer camping and good beach fishing. **Tourist information:** St Helens Secretariat, 20 Cecilia St; (03) 6376 1329. **Accommodation:** 2 hotel/motels, 1 motel, 3 B&B, 2 cara./camp. parks. **See also:** Scenic Island State.

St Marys　　　　Pop. 629

MAP REF. 545 Q10

The position of this small town, at the junction of the Tasman Hwy and the Esk Main Rd, makes it a busy thoroughfare. At the headwaters of the South Esk River system, St Marys is about 10 km inland. **In the area:** Small coastal township of Falmouth, 14 km NE, an early settlement of historical interest, with several convict-built structures, fine beaches, attractive rocky headlands and good fishing. Spectacular mountain and coast views to south through Elephant Pass, 4 km S. **Tourist information:** St Helens Secretariat, 20 Cecilia St, St Helens; (03) 6376 1329. **Accommodation:** 1 hotel.

Scamander　　　　Pop. 407

MAP REF. 545 Q9

This well-developed holiday town, midway between St Marys and St Helens, offers excellent sea and river fishing, and has good swimming beaches. **In the area:** Scenic walks and drives via forestry roads through plantations south of town. Scamander River, noted for bream fishing, trout in upper reaches. Beaches and lagoons at Beaumaris, 5 km N. Trout Creek Reserve, 10 km W, has fishing landing stage and picnic/barbecue facilities. **Tourist information:** St Helens Secretariat, 20 Cecilia St, St Helens; (03) 6376 1329. **Accommodation:** 1 hotel/motel, 1 cara./camp. park. **See also:** Scenic Island State.

Scottsdale　　　　Pop. 2020

MAP REF. 545 N7

Scottsdale, the major town in Tasmania's north-east, serves some of the richest agricultural and forestry country on the island. A large food-processing factory specialises in the deep-freezing of locally-grown vegetables. Feb.: Golconda: Tasmanian circus festival. June: Arts and crafts exhibition. Nov.: Agricultural show. **In the area:** Bridport, 23 km NW, a seaside holiday town. Bridestowe Lavender Farm near Nabowla, 13 km W, for sales of lavender products and tours in flowering season, Dec.-Jan. Sideling Lookout, 16 km W. South Springfield Forest Park, 20 km S. Mt Maurice Forest Reserve, 30 km S. **Tourist information:** Rose's Travel, 11 Alfred St; (03) 6352 2186. **Accommodation:** 2 hotels, 1 motel, 1 B&B, 1 cara./camp. park.

Sheffield　　　　Pop. 992

MAP REF. 540 D9, 544 I8

This town, located 30 km S of Devonport, stands at the foothills of

The Nut, Stanley

Mt Roland, in one of the most scenically attractive areas of the State. The town's economy is based on farming. **Of interest:** 36 murals on various buildings depict area's history; video explanation of murals, at Diversity, Main St. Kentish Museum, Main St, has local history and hydro-electric exhibits. Steam Museum, cnr Main and Spring Sts. Red Water Creek and Heritage Society runs steam train 1st weekend of month (departs cnr Spring and Main Sts) and daily around New Year; check times with Tourist information. Claude Road Hall markets, 3rd weekend in Mar., June, Sept. and Dec. Mar.: Steam Fest. Sept.: Daffodil festival. **In the area:** Lakes and dams of Mersey-Forth Power Development Scheme, 10 km W. Lake Barrington, created by scheme, a major recreation area; international rowing venue, 14 km SW. Lake Barrington Estate Vineyard, 10 km W, for tastings and sales. Devil's Gate Dam, 13 km NW, with unique semi-circular dam wall; spectacular scenery from viewing areas. Cradle Mountain-Lake St Clair National Park, 61 km SW for bushwalking, spectacular rainforest and mountain scenery, and flora and fauna. Forest walk, a pleasant walking track, 7 km E. **Tourist information:** Kentish Museum, 93 Main St; (03) 6491 1861. **Accommodation:** 1 hotel, 2 motels, 1 B&B, 1 cara./camp. park. **See also:** National Parks.

Smithton Pop. 3495

MAP REF. 544 C4

This substantial township is the administrative centre of Circular Head, which is renowned for its unique blackwood swamp forests and was the first European settlement in the far northwest. Smithton serves the most productive dairying and vegetable-growing area in the State, and is also the centre of one of Tasmania's most important forestry areas, with several large sawmills. Fishing is another important industry. **Of interest:** Lookout tower, Tier Hill, end of Massey St. **In the area:** Forestry Tasmania reserves throughout district offer wide range of recreational activities. Duck River and Duck Bay, 2 km N, for fishing and boating. Lacrum Dairy Farm, Mella, 6 km W, has milking demonstrations during summer, afternoon teas, cheese tastings and sales. Nearby, Wombat Tarn has picnic/barbecue area, lookout, bushwalks and playground. At Marrawah, 50 km SW, excellent surfing. Sumac Lookout, 4 km S on Sumac Rd, for views over Arthur River and surrounding eucalypt forest. Allendale Gardens, 13 km S at Edith Creek, offers rainforest walks and Devonshire teas. Seasonal scenic cruises on Arthur River, 70 km S; closed mid-June–1 Aug. At Rocky Cape National Park, 45 km E, Aboriginal caves and walks. **Tourist information:** Council Offices, Goldie St; (03) 6452 1265. **Accommodation:** 1 hotel, 1 motel.

Sorell Pop. 3199

MAP REF. 539 K5, 543 M8

Named after Governor Sorell, this town is 23 km E of Hobart. Founded in 1821, it played an important part in early colonial history by providing most of the grain for the State from 1816–60. It also supplied grain to NSW for more than 20 years. The area is still an important agricultural district, specialising in fat lambs. **Of interest:** In Somerville St, Historic Blue Bell Inn. Pioneer Park, Parsonage Pl., has picnic/barbecue facilities. Nov.: Taste of Sorell. **In the area:** Saddletramp Horseback Tours near Woodsdale 37 N, offers 1-hr to 7-day rides. Orani Vineyard, 3 km E. Bream Creek Vineyard, 22 km E. Popular beach areas around Dodges Ferry and Carlton Beach, 18 km S. **Tourist information:** Council Offices, Summerville St; (03) 6265 2201. **Accommodation:** 4 B&B.

Stanley Pop. 576

MAP REF. 544 D3

This quaint little village, nestling under a huge rocky outcrop called the Nut, is steeped in history. It was the site for the headquarters of the Van Diemen's Land (VDL) Company, set up in 1825 to establish a high-quality merino wool industry. Then its wharf handled whalers and sailing ships. Today these are replaced by a strong fleet of cray and other fishing boats, but little else has changed. The birthplace of Australia's only Tasmanian prime minister, the Hon. J. A. (Joe) Lyons, Stanley has been declared an historic town and for 5 of the last 7 years has won the State's Premier Tourist Town award. **Of interest:** Historic buildings in wharf area: bluestone bond store, Wharf Rd; former VDL Co. store, in Marine Park, designed by colonial architect John Lee Archer, who lived in township. Archer's own home, now Poet's Cottage, Alexander Tce, at base of the Nut; not open to public. Also in Alexander Tce, Lyons Cottage, birthplace of J. A. Lyons. Other historic buildings in Church St include: still-licensed Union Hotel (1849), with its nest of cellars and narrow stairways; Commercial Hotel (1842), now private residence; multi-award-winning Plough Inn (1850s), an authentic 19th century house museum, with fine Tasmanian craft. Next door, Discovery Centre Folk Museum. Chairlift, from Browns Rd to top of the Nut (152 m). Graves in burial ground on Browns Rd, dating from 1828, include those of John Lee Archer and explorer Henry Hellyer. Small colonies of little (fairy) penguins near wharf and cemetery, and on Scenic Drive. Nov.: Tasmania Day. Dec.: Agricultural show. **In the area:** Highfield Historic Site (1835), headquarters of VDL Co., 2 km N on Scenic Dr.: homestead, chapel, schoolhouse, barn, stables, workers' cottages and remains of barracks nearby; two arched gates remain of former deer park. Dip Falls, 40 km SE off hwy, via Mawbanna; nearby, Big Tree (giant eucalypt) and picnic area. Pelletising plant of Savage River Mines, Port Latta, 20 km SE, where ore is moved by conveyor to jetty for loading onto bulk ore ships. **Tourist information:** The Nut Chairlift, Browns Rd; (03) 6458 1286. **Accommodation:** 1 hotel, 1 motel, 2 B&B, 1 hostel, 1 cara./camp. park. **See also:** Scenic Island State.

Strahan
Pop. 597

MAP REF. 542 D3, 544 D12

This pretty little port on Macquarie Harbour on Tasmania's forbidding west coast is best known as the departure point for cruises to the Franklin-Gordon Wild Rivers National Park. Originally a Huon pine timber-milling town, its growth was boosted by the copper boom at the Mt Lyell mine. When the Strahan–Zeehan railway opened in 1892, it became a busy port. Today it is a popular holiday town and is used as a base by crayfish, abalone and shark fishing operators, but the use of the harbour is limited because of the formidable bar at Hell's Gates, the mouth of the harbour. **Of interest:** Award-winning Wharf Centre, The Esplanade, has historical display of Tasmania's south-west, from Aboriginal times to present. Adjacent, Morrison's Mill, one of few remaining Huon pine sawmills. Tuts Whittle Wonders, carvings from driftwood; Reid St. Excellent views of township and harbour from Water Tower Hill. Mineral and gemstone museum, Innes St. Seaplane flights over Gordon River and Frenchmans Cap, landing at Sir John's Falls; depart from The Esplanade. Wild River jet-boat rides; West Coast Yacht Charters, overnight to Gordon River and evening cruises; 4WD tours, including fishing tour; huon pine forestry tour; Henty Dunes Tour; Strahan Trail Rides; contact Tourist information. **In the area:** Ocean Beach, 6 km W, offers area for trail rides, and beach fishing; also has a muttonbird rookery; it is Tasmania's longest beach. Teepookana Forest Reserve, 15 km S, features Huon pines, walking tracks, viewing platform and historic bridge. At Henty Dunes, 12 km N on Strahan–Zeehan Hwy, spectacular, vast sand dunes, lagoon and picnic/barbecue areas. Cruises available include upstream along the Gordon River to Heritage Landing and infamous Sarah (or Settlement) Island, Tasmania's first and most brutal penal establishment; and across Macquarie Harbour to Hell's Gates. Strahan Wilderness 4WD tours, follow Old Abt Railway from Strahan towards Queenstown. **Tourist information:** Wharf Centre, The Esplanade; (03) 6471 7488. **Accommodation:** 2 hotels, 1 motel, 9 B&B, 1 hostel, 1 cara./camp. park. **See also:** Scenic Island State; The West Coast.

Swansea
Pop. 418

MAP REF. 543 P4, 545 P13

Swansea is a small town of historical interest on scenic Great Oyster Bay, in the centre of Tasmania's east coast. **Of interest:** Self-guide leaflet on town and area, contact Tourist information. Original council chambers (c. 1860), Noyes St; still in use. On Tasman Hwy: Bark Mill and Yesteryear Museum (c. 1885); restored wattlebark mill machinery; tearooms. In Franklin St: Morris' General Store (1838), run by Morris family for over 100 years; Community Centre (c. 1860), has museum with unusually large slate billiard table made for 1880 World Exhibition. Schouten House (c. 1846), Bridge St, once Swansea Inn, now restaurant and colonial accommodation. Meredith House (c. 1853), two-storeyed Georgian house, now offering colonial accommodation. **In the area:** Splendid views from Duncombes Lookout, 3 km S. Spikey Beach, 7 km S, with picnic area and excellent rock fishing. Mayfield Beach, 14 km S, for safe swimming, fishing and walking (track from camping area to Three Arch Bridge). Meetus Falls, 50 km NW. **Tourist information:**

The Bass Strait Islands

King Island and Flinders Island, Tasmania's two main Bass Strait islands, are ideal holiday spots for the adventurous. You can fish, swim, go bushwalking or skindive among the wrecks of the many ships that foundered off their shores last century. Each spring millions of muttonbirds make a spectacular sight as they fly in to nest in coastal rookeries on the islands.

King Island, at the western end of the strait, is a picturesque, rugged island with an unspoiled coastline of beautiful sandy beaches on the east and north coasts, contrasting with the forbidding cliffs of Seal Rocks and the lonely coast to the south. The lighthouse at Cape Wickham is the largest in Australia. There is a penguin colony on the breakwater at Grassy Harbour which can be visited at dusk. Once famous for its seal population and now almost extinct sea lions, the island's main industries today are dairy and beef products, kelp harvesting, fishing and sheep farming. King Island dairy and beef products have earned a reputation for their high quality. The King Island Dairy, on North Rd, is open Sunday to Friday. The unofficial capital is Currie, which has a kelp factory. Accommodation includes a hotel, 2 motels, numerous guest houses, several holiday flats and a caravan/camping park.

Flinders Island is renowned for its excellent fishing, its magnificent granite mountains and its gemstones, including the Killiecrankie 'diamonds', actually a kind of topaz. Strzelecki National Park, near the civic centre, Whitemark, provides challenging rock climbing. From Whitemark, 4WD tours are available to hills and remote beaches. The island is also popular with scuba divers, naturalists and photographers. Accommodation on the island includes 2 hotels, 1 guest house and several holiday houses. Flinders is one of more than 50 islands in the Furneaux Group that were once part of the land bridge linking Tasmania with the mainland.

In the 1830s the few surviving Tasmanian Aborigines were settled near Emita in an attempt to save them from extinction. All that remains of the settlement today is the graveyard and the chapel, Wybalenna, which has been restored by the National Trust. Nearby, there are historic displays relating to the Furneaux Islands in the museum.

Fishing is the main industry of the tiny community of Lady Barron to the south, a port village overlooking Franklin Sound and **Cape Barren Island**, the home of the protected Cape Barren goose.

For further information on King Island contact The Trend, Main St, Currie, King Island (for brochures); or for pre-arrival information, contact the King Island Tourist Development Association; 1800 64 5014. For information on Flinders Island, contact Council Offices, Davey St, Flinders Island; (03) 6359 2131. For information on Cape Barren Island, contact the Tasmanian Travel and Information Centre, 20 Davey St, Hobart; (03) 6230 8233.

Wine and Wool Centre, 96 Tasman Hwy; (03) 6257 8677. **Accommodation:** 1 hotel/ motel, 2 cara./camp. parks. See also: Scenic Island State.

Triabunna   Pop. 831

MAP REF. 539 O1, 543 O6

When Maria Island was a penal settlement, Triabunna, 86 km NE of Hobart, was a garrison town and whaling base. Today it is a centre for the scallop and abalone industries, with an important export wood-chipping mill just south of the town. **Of interest:** On The Esplanade: Bicentennial Park, with picnic/barbecue areas; National Trust-run Pioneer Park, featuring machinery exhibits. Charter fishing boats for hire. Jan.: Spring Bay crayfish derby. **In the area:** Daily ferry from Eastcoaster Resort at Louisville Point, 7 km S, to historic settlement of Darlington, Maria Island National Park. Local beaches for swimming, water-skiing and fishing. Working Horse Museum, 25 km N. **Tourist information:** Council Offices, cnr Vicary and Henry Sts; (03) 6257 3113. **Accommodation:** 1 hotel, 1 hotel/motel, 1 cara./camp. park. See also: National Parks; Scenic Island State.

Ulverstone   Pop. 9923

MAP REF. 540 B5, 544 H6

Situated 19 km W of Devonport, near the mouth of the Leven River, Ulverstone is a well-equipped tourist centre that was established as a town in 1852. Dairying, furniture making, and poultry and vegetable farming are the main industries of the area. **Of interest:** Shrine of Remembrance Clock Tower (1953), Reibey St. History Museum, Main St. On Beach Rd: Riverside Anzac Park, with children's playground and picnic/barbecue areas; Fairway Park, a wildfowl reserve, with giant water-slide. Footpath inscribed with excerpts of 75-year history of Royal Australian Navy leads from town centre to HMAS *Shropshire* Naval Memorial Park, Dial St. Numerous antique, and art and craft shops. Legion Park, Esplanade at West Ulverstone, has magnificent coastal position. Tobruk Park, Hobbs Pde. Boer War Memorial, Queens Gardens, Kings Pde. Weeda Copper, Eastland Dr., for hand-made local copperware. Lookout, eastern end of Upper Maud St. Oct.: Show. Dec.: Christmas mardi gras. **In the area:** Extensive beaches east and west of town, safe swimming for children. Good beach, river and estuary fishing. Miniature railway, 2 km E, check times. Goat Island Sanctuary, 5 km W; walking access to island at low tide only. Scenic views at Preston Falls, 19 km S. Castra Falls, 30 km S. Near Gunns Plains, 24 km SW: hop farm, with visitor centre and tours during harvest time (mid Mar.–mid Apr.); Gunderman Trail Rides, Wings Farm Park; Creative Wood and Floral Designs; Gunns Plains Store; caves featuring underground river and glow worms (guided tours). Walking tracks to viewing platform with spectacular views at Leven Canyon, 41 km SW; beyond, south-west of South Nietta, Winterbrook Rainforest Walk and Falls. **Tourist information:** Car Park Lane, (behind PO); (03) 6425 2839. **Accommodation:** 2 hotels, 3 motels, 2 B&B, 2 cara./camp. parks. See also: Scenic Island State.

Waratah   Pop. 360

MAP REF. 544 E8

This picturesque little settlement, set in mountain heathland 100 km N of Queenstown, was the site of the first mining boom in Tasmania. In 1900 it had a population of 2000 and Mount Bischoff was the richest tin mine in the world. The deposits were discovered in 1871 by James 'Philosopher' Smith, a colourful local character, and the mine closed in 1947, with dividends totalling 200 pounds for every one pound of original investment. Today the town is experiencing a revival of mining activity at nearby Hellyer Mine, operated by Aberfoyle. **Of interest:** Self-drive tour of town, leaflet available at Tourist information. In Smith St: Waratah Museum and Gift Shop; adjacent, Philosopher Smith's Hut, replica of miner's hut and features audio historical commentary; Atheneum Hall (c. 1887), has portrait of Smith; St James' Anglican Church (1880), first church in Tasmania to be lit by hydro power. Feb.: Back to Waratah. **In the area:** River and lake trout fishing. At Corinna, 66 km SW, a fascinating former goldmining town, cruises on Pieman River. **Tourist information:** Fossey River Information Bay, 8 km S on Murchison Hwy; or Council Offices, Smith St; (03) 6439 1231. **Accommodation:** 1 hotel, 1 B&B, 1 cara./camp. park. See also: The West Coast.

Westbury   Pop. 1292

MAP REF. 541 K11, 545 K9

A village green, said to be unique in Australia, gives this town, 35 km SW of Launceston, a decidedly English air. Situated on the Bass Hwy, Westbury was first surveyed in 1823 and laid out in 1828; it has several fine old colonial buildings. **Of interest:** Self-guide leaflet on town and area, leaflet available from Tourist information. In Village Green, King St: White House (c. 1841), comprising house, bakery, coachhouse, courtyard and stable complex; former police barracks (c. 1832), now an RSL Club; St Andrews Church. On Bass Hwy: Hedge maze; Gemstone and Mineral Display; Pearn's Steam World, a large collection of working steam traction engines. Tractor Shed, Veterans Row, a museum of old tractors and farm machinery; also scale model tractor exhibition. Market, 2nd Sun. each month at St Andrews Church. Mar.: Maypole festival, includes Morris dancing on Village Green; St Patrick's Day festival. Nov.: Steam spectacular. **In the area:** At Hagley, 5 km E, St Mary's Anglican Church, noted for fine east window donated by Lady Dry, wife of Sir Richard Dry, first Tasmanian-born premier. At Carrick, 10 km E, fine examples of Georgian and Victorian buildings. Trout fishing at Four Springs, 15 km NE. **Tourist information:** Old Bakehouse, 52 William St; (03) 6393 1140. **Accommodation:** 1 hotel, 2 B&B. See also: Stately Homes.

Wynyard   Pop. 4679

MAP REF. 544 F5

Situated within a short driving distance of many varied attractions, this small centre at the mouth of the Inglis River, west of Burnie, has become a well-developed tourist centre, offering a range of accommodation and sporting facilities. There are daily flights between nearby Burnie airport and Melbourne. The Waratah–Wynyard region is a prosperous dairying and mixed-farming district and the town has a large, modern dairy factory. **Of interest:** Table Cape Tulip Farm; open in season. Oct.: Tulip festival. **In the area:** Excellent fly-fishing for trout and sea fishing. Table Cape Lookout, 5 km N, for coastal and inland views. Oldest marsupial fossil in Australia found at Fossil Bluff, 7 km N; displayed at the Hobart Museum.

Boat Harbour, 11 km NW. **Tourist information:** cnr Hogg and Goldie St; (03) 6442 4143. **Accommodation:** 3 hotels, 1 hotel/motel, 1 motel, 4 B&B, 1 hostel, 2 cara./camp. parks. **See also:** Scenic Island State; National Parks.

Zeehan
Pop. 1132

MAP REF. 542 D1, 544 D11

Named after one of Abel Tasman's ships, this former mining town, situated 36 km NW of Queenstown, has had a chequered history and is now a National Trust-classified historic town. Silver-lead deposits were discovered here in 1882. By 1901, Zeehan had 26 hotels and a population of 10 000, making it Tasmania's third largest town. Just 7 years later mining began to decline and Zeehan became almost a ghost town. In the boom period between 1893 and 1908, 8 million dollars' worth of ore had been recovered. Now the town is again on an upward swing with the reopening of the Renison Bell tin mine. **Of interest:** Self-guide scenic drives of town and surrounding area, brochures available at Tourist information. Many 'boom' buildings in Main St, including Gaiety Theatre at the Grand Hotel, ANZ Bank, St Luke's Church, post office and court house (now art gallery). West Coast Pioneers Memorial Museum, in School of Mines building (1894), Main St, has mineral, historical, geological and biological collections. Beside museum, display of steam locomotives and rail carriages used on west coast. Frank Long Memorial Park, Dodd St; Long discovered silver-lead deposit here. Pioneer cemetery, southern outskirts of town. Dec.: King of the mountain fun run. **In the area:** Old mine workings at Dundas, 13 km E. Trial Harbour, 20 km W, a popular fishing area. Unsealed roads to both areas often in poor condition; check before departure. Fishing and boating on Lake Pieman, 50 km NW. Trout fishing on Henty River, 25 km S. **Tourist information:** West Coast Pioneers Memorial Museum, Main St; (03) 6471 6225. **Accommodation:** 2 hotels, 1 hotel/motel, 1 cara./camp. park. **See also:** Scenic Island State; The West Coast.

Angler's Paradise

Fish are biting all year round in Tasmania, which is why it is an angler's paradise by any standards. Tasmania is famous for three species of fish: trout in fresh water, bream in the estuaries and tuna off the coast.

One area alone contains hundreds of lakes and lagoons stocked with **trout** of world-class size. This is the undeveloped 'Land of Three Thousand Lakes'. You are more likely, however, to choose from the huge range of developed areas brimming with trout in the central highlands region, among them Great Lake, Bronte Lagoon, Lake Sorell and Arthurs Lake. Brumby Creek, located just 25 kilometres from Launceston between Cressy and Poatina, has a reputation as one of the great trout waters in the country.

Tasmania is well known world-wide for its 'sighted' fishing, that is fly-fishing to individual fish. Early in the season in particular, when lake levels are high, brown trout move into shallow water in the weedy lake margins, in search of food. Their tails are often visible above the water providing exciting fly-fishing at close range. In summer, especially in the Land of Three Thousand Lakes, it is possible for the angler wearing polarised glasses, to spot individual fish in bright light conditions and present flies to them.

Before the trout season closes in May, game fish begin to move down the mild east coast around March and anglers start hauling in the big ones: **bluefin tuna**, often weighing over 45 kilograms.

Trout fishing at Brumby's Creek, near Cressy

Then, as the bluefin leave in the midwinter months, large **Australian salmon** schools return to the estuaries and along the shoreline.

In spring, one of the great sport fish of Tasmania, the tasty **silver bream**, arrives in the river estuaries. Anglers regard this as one of the best fighting fish for its size.

January and February are peak inland trout-fishing months, and from February to March schools of Australian salmon swim close to the shoreline of Tasmania's many river estuaries, providing exciting fishing for the angler from the beach or rocks.

For further information on licence requirements, fees, bag limits, seasons and regulations for freshwater fishing contact the Inland Fisheries Commission, 127 Davey St, Hobart 7000; (03) 6223 6622. For sea fishing enquiries, contact the department of Primary Industries and Fisheries, Marine Resources Division, 1 Franklin Wharf, Hobart 7000; (03) 6233 6234.

Tasmania

Location Map

Other Map Coverage
Central Hobart 535
Hobart & Suburbs 536
Hobart Region 538
Launceston Region 540

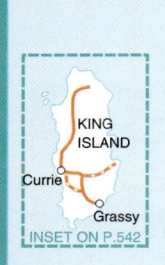

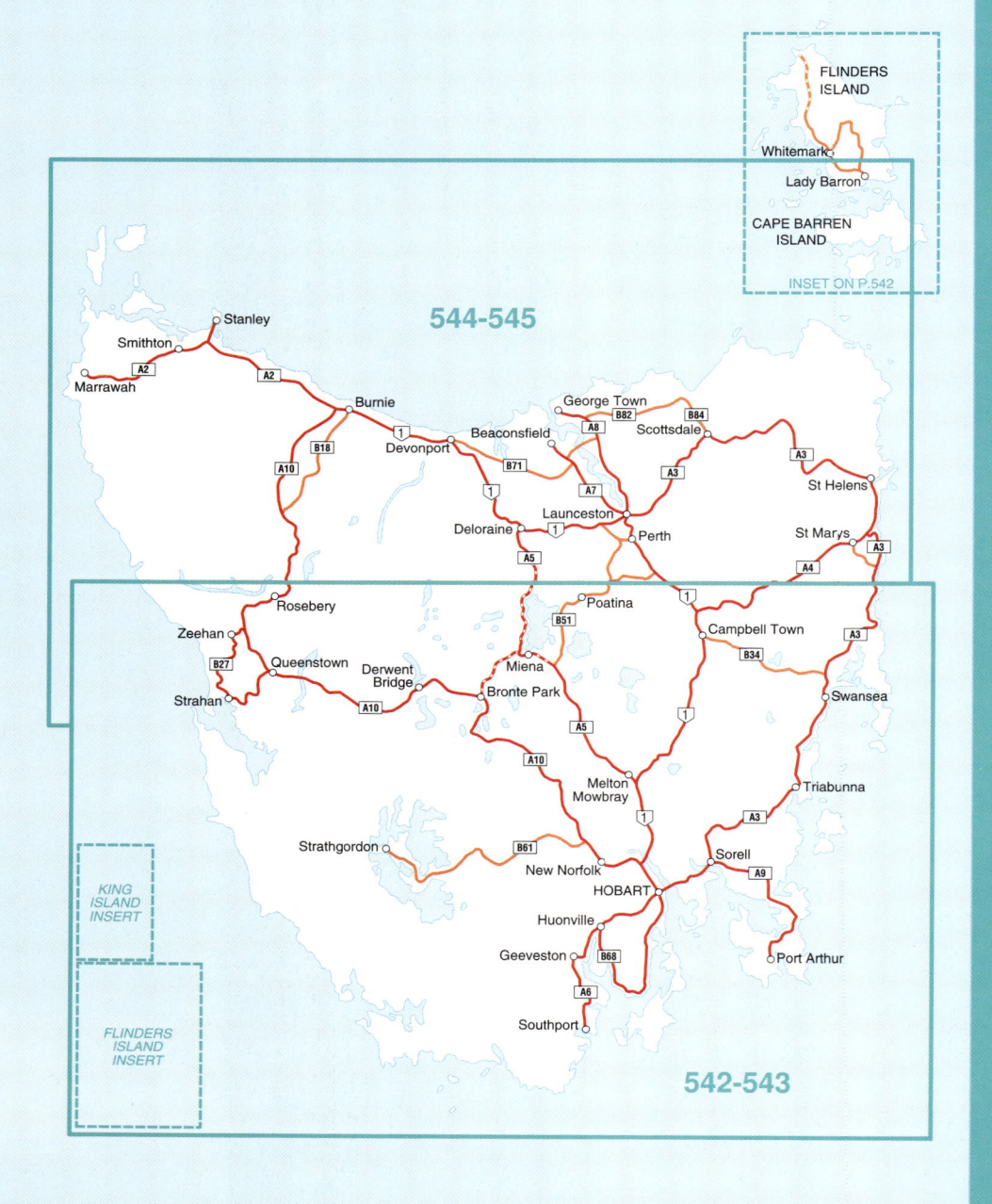

Central Hobart 535

Accommodation
- Barton Cottage 1 F13
- Colville Cottage 2 H13
- Country Comfort Hadleys Hotel 3 C7
- Hobart Macquarie 4 B9
- Hotel Grand Chancellor 5 F5
- Lenna of Hobart 6 H11
- Salamanca Inn 7 E10

General Information
- Ansett Australia 8 C6
- General Post Office 9 E6
- Harbour Cruises 10 F8
- Hobart Coaches Terminal 11 E3
- Hobart Transit Centre 12 A10
- Metro City Bus Terminus 13 D6
- Motoring Organisation (RACT)
  cnr Murray and Patrick Sts, Hobart
- Police Headquarters 14 D4
- Qantas Travel Centre 15 C6
- Tourist Information 16 E7

Places of Interest
- Cat and Fiddle Arcade 17 C6/7
- Cenotaph 18 H3
- Constitution Dock 19 F6
- Franklin Square 20 E7
- Gasworks Shopping Centre 21 E7
- Kellys Steps 22 G10
- Maritime Museum 23 I13
- National Trust Info. Office 24 E10
- Parliament House 25 E9
- Penitentiary Chapel/Criminal Courts (National Trust HQ) 26 C2
- Queen's Domain 27 E1
- Salamanca Place 28 F10
- St Davids Park 30 D9
- State Library/Allport Library and Museum of Fine Arts 29 A6
- Tasmanian Museum/Art Gallery 31 E6
- Theatre Royal 32 E4
- Town Hall 33 E6
- Van Diemen's Land Folk Museum (Narryna) 34 E12

Accommodation Only a sample range is listed; inclusion is not necessarily a recommendation.

536 Hobart & Suburbs

537

538 Hobart Region

0 5 10 15 20 km
543
TO SWANSEA
Triabunna
Woodstock
Okehampton
Cape Bougainville
Louisville
Eastcoaster Resort
Point Horne
Orford
Prosser Bay
Quarry Point
Shelly Beach
Spring Beach
Ferry
Isle Du Nord
Cape Boullanger
Darlington
Historical Settlement
Bishop and Clerk
Mt Maria 709m
MILITARY TRAINING AREA ENTRY PROHIBITED
Stonehurst
Mt Hobbs 823m
Levendale
Craigbourne Dam
Mt Bains 334m
Brown Mountain 792m
Brockley
Prosser River
Buckland
Historic Church
Sally Peak
Court Farm
Three Thumbs 549m
Whitemarsh
Runnymede
Campania
Campania House
Mt Morrison 469m
Byton Tops
Johnsons Point
Rheban
Carrickfergus Bay
Lachlan Island
Ringrove
MARIA ISLAND NATIONAL PARK
MERCURY PASSAGE
Earlham
Prosser Sugarloaf 647m
Mistaken Cape
Point Des Galets
Shoal Bay
Riedle Bay
Cockle Bay
Walking Track
MARIA ISLAND
Cape Maurouard
Cape Bernier
Cape Peron
Australia's Oldest Bridge
Park View
Richmond
Orielton
Pawleena
Nugent
Wattle Hill
Hillcrest
Mt Lord 279m
Penna
Gordon SL 415m
Kellevie
Bendes Hill 404m
Sorell
Midway Point
Forcett
ARTHUR HWY
TASMAN HWY
Bream Creek
Copping Museum
Marion Bay
HOBART AIRPORT
Pitt Water
Seven Mile Beach Protected Area
Cambridge
Lookout
Mt Rumney 378m
Lewisham
Seven Mile Beach
Tiger Head
Dodges Ferry
Carlton River
Park Beach
Carlton
Connellys Marsh
Blackman Bay
Cape Paul Lamanon
North Bay
Rokeby
Cape Frederick Hendrick
Lauderdale
Carlton Bluff
Primrose Point
Primrose Sands
Dunalley
Tasman Memorial
Denison Canal
Sandford
Frederick Henry Bay
Fulham Island
Dunalley Bay
Mt Forestier 320m
FORESTIER PENINSULA
Humper Bluff
Green Head
High Yellow Bluff
Cremorne
Sloping Island
Lime Bay
Smooth Island
Whitehouse Point
LIME BAY NATURE RESERVE
King George Island
Murdunna
Cape Surville
Cape Deslacs
Clifton Beach
Mt Stewart 130m
Norfolk Bay
Flinders Bay
FLINDERS BAY COASTAL RESERVE
Macgregor Peak 591m
North West Head
Coal Mines Historic Site
EAGLEHAWK BAY COASTAL RESERVE
TASMAN
Gwandalan
Cape Contrariety
Saltwater River
Deer Point
Lookout
Tessellated Pavement
Eaglehawk Bay
Dart Island
Eaglehawk Neck
Premaydena Point
Betsey Island
Mt Communication 344m
The Blowhole
Outer North Head
Premaydena
Taranna
Doo Town
Tasman Arch
Devils Kitchen
Koonya
Tasmanian Devil Park
TASMAN ARCH STATE RESERVE
Waterfall Bay
For more detail of Hobart Suburbs see pages 536 & 537
ROARING BEACH COASTAL RESERVE
Nubeena
O'Hara Bluff
STORM BAY
Wedge Bay
White Beach
TASMAN PENINSULA
Mt Koonya 488m
Oakwood
Thumb Point
Wedge Island
STEWARTS BAY STATE RES
The Bush Mill Steam Railway
SEA
Highcroft
Port Arthur
Port Arthur Historic Site
Mt Arthur
Fortescue Bay
Cape Hauy
Stormlea
Palmers Lookout
Port Arthur
PALMERS HILL LOOKOUT STATE RESERVE
CAPE RAOUL STATE RESERVE
CAPE PILLAR STATE RESERVE
Remarkable Cave
Salters Point
Munro Bight
West Arthur Head
Raoul Bay
Maingon Bay
Black Head
Cape Pillar
Cape Raoul
Tasman Island
N

540 Launceston Region

SPIRIT OF TASMANIA: Ferries passengers and cars across Bass Strait between Melbourne and Devonport. This powerful sea voyager offers all the facilities of an ocean cruise-liner, accommodating passengers seeking luxury to the budget-conscious backpacker.

ASBESTOS RANGE NATIONAL PARK: Lying between Greens Beach and Port Sorell, this scenic northern coastal park has numerous isolated beaches, sand dunes and grasslands covered in wildflowers. Mineral asbestos was mined last century at the northern point.

541

542 Southern Tasmania

0
10
20
30
40
50 km
545
J
K
L
M
N
O
P
Q
R
1
2
3
4
5
6
7
8
9
10
11
12
13
Liffey Falls
Liffey
Cressy
Blackwood Creek
Powranna
Storeys Creek
Rossarden
Fingal
Gray
Chain Of Lagoons
Poatina
Epping Forest
Cleveland
Conara Junction
Llewellyn Siding
Avoca
Ormley
Seymour
Long Point
DOUGLAS APSLEY NATIONAL PARK
Cramps
Campbell Town
Royal George
Lookout
MacLean Bay
Birdlife and Animal Park
Waubs Harbour
Sealife Park
Bicheno
Cape Lodi
Tods Corner PS
Flintstone
Miena
Wilburville
Shannon
Auburn
Goldsmith
Meetus Falls
Llandaff
Apslaw
Cranbrook
Lake Leake
Ross
Steppes
Waddamana
Lake Sorell
Interlaken
Tunbridge
Mount Morrison
Trefusis
Bark Mill
Swansea
Swanwick
Cape Tourville
Coles Bay
Sleepy Bay
The Hazards
Great Oyster Bay
Wineglass Bay
Promise Bay
Cape Forestier
FREYCINET NATIONAL PARK
FREYCINET PENINSULA
Cape Degerando
Hermitage
Victoria Valley
Osterley
Bothwell
Water Mill
Oatlands
Nala
Pawtella
Lemont
Little Swanport
Pontypool
Schouten Island
Cape Baudin
Cape Sonnerat
Cape Faure
Lower Marshes
Jericho
Parattah
Andover
Mt Seymour
Stonehenge
Apsley
Melton Mowbray
Stonor
Tiberias
Whitefoord
Tunnack
Baden
Rhyndaston
Woodsdale
MILITARY TRAINING AREA ENTRY PROHIBITED
Isle des Phoques
Grindstone Bay
Grindstone Point
Langloh
Hamilton
Hollow Tree
Kempton
Eldon
Colebrook
Levendale
Triabunna
Cape Bougainville
Orford
Louisville
Eastcoaster Resort
Shelly Beach
Spring Beach
Darlington
Historical Settlement
MARIA ISLAND NATIONAL PARK
Pelham
Elderslie
Bagdad
Buckland
Historic Church
Rheban
Gretna
Broadmarsh
Mangalore
Pontville
Campania
Runnymede
Glenora
Bushy Park
Plenty
Black Hills
Hayes
Dromedary
Magra
Boyer
Brighton
Bridgewater
Gagebrook
Granton
Old Beach
Rekuna
Australia's Oldest Bridge
Richmond
Orielton
Pawleena
Nugent
Riedle Bay
MARIA ISLAND
Shoal Bay
Cape Peron
Uxbridge
Moogara
Fellton
New Norfolk
Glenfern
Mt Lloyd
Lachlan
CLAREMONT
BERRIEDALE
Risdon Vale
Penna
Sorell
Wattle Hill
Kellevie
Midway Point
Lewisham
Bream Creek
Copping
Marion Bay
Collinsvale
GLENORCHY
LINDISFARNE
HOBART
BELLERIVE
HOWRAH
Cambridge
Seven Mile Beach
Dodges Ferry
Carlton
WELLINGTON PARK
Fern Tree
Rokeby
Lauderdale
Primrose Sands
Cape Frederick Hendrick
Denison Canal
Dunalley
Tasman Memorial
Mountain River
Crabtree
Lucaston
Judbury
Ranelagh
Longley
Neika
Leslie Vale
Sandfly
Grove
Taroona
Sandford
Kingston
Opossum Bay
Cremorne
Frederick Henry Bay
Green Head
Smooth Is
Lime Bay
Murdunna
FORESTIER PENINSULA
Cape Surville
Glen Huon
Huonville
Kaoota
Margate
Howden
Blackmans Bay
Clifton Beach
Coal Mines Historic Site
Saltwater River
Eaglehawk Neck
Lookout
Tessellated Pavement
The Blowhole
Tasman Arch
Devils Kitchen
Taranna
Franklin
Pelverata
Tinderbox
South Arm
Betsey Island
Premaydena
Koonya
Snug
Coningham
Dennes Point
Woodstock
Oyster Cove
Kettering
Barnes Bay
Storm Bay
Castle Forbes Bay
Port Huon
Geeveston
Cygnet
Nicholls Rivulet
Woodbridge
Birchs Bay
White Beach
Nubeena
Oakwood
TASMAN PENINSULA
The Bush Mill Steam Railway
Fortescue Bay
Cape Hauy
Wedge Island
Cairns Bay
Lymington
Waterloo
Surges Bay
Glendevie
Gardners Bay
Police Point
Garden Island Creek
Flowerpot
Middleton
NORTH BRUNY ISLAND
Highcroft
Stormlea
Port Arthur
Port Arthur Historic Site
Palmers Lookout
Remarkable Cave
CAPE RAOUL STATE RESERVE
Raoul Bay
Maingon Bay
Cape Raoul
CAPE PILLAR STATE RESERVE
Munro Bight
Cape Pillar
Tasman Island
Francistown
Surveyors Bay
Gordon
Verona Sands
Isthmus Bay
Cape Queen Elizabeth
Raminea
Strathblane
Dover
Lookout
Simpsons Bay
Lunawanna
Alonnah
Adventure Bay
Captain Cook's Landing Place
Cookville
Bligh Museum
Cape Connella
For more detail of Hobart Region see pages 538 & 539
Hastings
Lady Bay
Lune River
Ida Bay
Southport
Scenic Railway
Southport Lagoon
Great Taylors Bay
Cloudy Bay
SOUTH BRUNY ISLAND
Tasman Head
TASMAN
SEA
Lepreña
Recherche Bay
Catamaran
Cockle Creek
South East Cape
MIDLAND HWY
TASMAN HWY
ARTHUR HWY
HUON HWY
CHANNEL HWY
LYELL HWY
LAKE HWY
FINGAL VALLEY MAIN ROAD
ESK MAIN ROAD
D'ENTRECASTEAUX CHANNEL
MERCURY PASSAGE
DERWENT RIVER
N

544 Northern Tasmania

545

Index of Place Names

Place names that appear in this gazetteer are followed by a map page number and grid reference, and/or the text page number on which that place name occurs. A page number set in bold type indicates the main text entry for that place name.
Bairnsdale Vic. 227 P4, **158**, 181, 193
Bairnsdale – Place name
Vic. – State
227 P4 – Bairnsdale appears on this map page
158 – Main entry for Bairnsdale
181, 193 – Bairnsdale is mentioned on these pages

The alphabetical order followed in the index is that of 'word-by-word', where all entries under one word are grouped together. Where a place names consists of more than one word, the order is governed by the first and then the second word. For example:
Green Bay
Green River
Greenbank
Greens Beach
Greenwood Forest
Greg Greg
Gregafell

Names beginning with Mc are indexed as Mac and those beginning with St, as Saint.
The following abbreviations and contractions are used in the index:
ACT – Australian Capital Territory
JBT – Jervis Bay Territory
NSW – New South Wales
NT – Northern Territory
Qld – Queensland
SA – South Australia
St – Saint
Tas. – Tasmania
Vic. – Victoria
WA – Western Australia

A1 Mine Settlement Vic. 213 R4, 227 J2, 235 M13
Abbeyard Vic. 224 I8
Abbotsford NSW 94 I8
Abbotsford Vic. 209 L8
Abbotsham Tas. 540 C6, 544 H7
Abercorn Qld 491 M3
Aberdeen NSW 117 K2
Aberfeldy Vic. 227 J3
Abergowrie Qld 495 N10
Abermain NSW 108 C9, 109 H11, 117 M4
Abernethy NSW 108 C10, 117 M4
Acacia Ridge Qld 480 H7
Acacia Store NT 402 E5, 406 E6
Acheron Vic. 213 O2, 235 J11
Acland Qld 482 D5
Acton ACT 134 A3, 136 G9, 129
Acton Park WA 357 E8, 359 G4, 364 B9
Adaminaby NSW 114 H5, 115 D8, 138 E9, 237 L1, **44**
Adamsfield Tas. 542 H7
Adavale Qld 501 P5
Addington Vic. 212 B2, 223 K8
Adelaide SA 282 F10, 285 J7, 288 A9, 289 E1, 293 A2, 295 J9, **242–9**
Adelaide Hills SA 288 D10, 239, 241, **247**, 259
Adelaide Lead Vic. 223 K5
Adelaide River NT 402 E8, 406 E7, 380, **381**
Adelong NSW 115 B5, 116 D13, **44**
Adjungbilly NSW 115 C4, 116 E12
Advancetown Qld 483 N13, 485 B6
Adventure Bay Tas. 538 H13, 543 L11, 512
Aeroglen Qld 488 C4
Agery SA 294 I6
Agnes Vic. 227 J10
Agnes Banks NSW 101 K6
Agnes Water Qld 493 Q13, 445
Aileron NT 410 I6, **381**
Ailsa Vic. 230 H7
Ainslie ACT 136 H8
Aireys Inlet Vic. 212 E12, 219 C12, 229 P10, 157
Airlie Beach Qld 493 K3, **424**, 431, 466
Airly Vic. 227 N5

Airport West Vic. 208 H4
Aitkenvale Qld 487 A9
Akaroa Tas. 545 R8
Alawa NT 400 F5
Alawoona SA 293 H1, 295 Q8
Albacutya Vic. 230 F3
Albany WA 361 N12, 364 H13, 366 F12, **313**, 324, 329
Albany Creek Qld 478 C6
Albert NSW 116 B3, 121 R13, 123 R1
Albert Park SA 284 E3
Albert Park Vic. 209 K10, 147, 150
Alberton Qld 483 N10
Alberton SA 284 E2, 286 E13
Alberton Tas. 545 O8
Alberton Vic. 227 L9, 189, 203
Albion Qld 478 H10, 418
Albion Park NSW 112 G8
Albury NSW 123 Q13, 235 P4, 236 C1, **44**, 47, 66, 201
Alcomie Tas. 544 D5
Alderley Qld 478 F9
Aldersyde WA 364 G5
Aldgate SA 285 R13, 247
Aldinga SA 288 A13, 289 F4, 290 B6, 293 B3, 295 K10, **250**
Aldinga Beach SA 289 E5, 290 A6, 250
Alectown NSW 116 D4
Alexander Heights WA 354 H5
Alexander Morrison National Park WA 366 B5
Alexandra Vic. 213 O1, 235 J11, **157**
Alexandra Bridge WA 357 C12, 359 E10, 364 B10
Alexandra Headland Qld 486 H9, 459
Alexandra Hills Qld 481 Q2
Alexandria NSW 95 M12, 99 O2
Alford SA 294 I5
Alfords Point NSW 98 F8
Alfred Cove WA 352 E9
Alfred National Park Vic. 115 F13, 237 O11
Alfred Town NSW 115 A5, 116 C12, 123 R10
Algester Qld 480 H8
Ali-Curung NT 409 K13, 411 K2
Alice NSW 119 O4, 491 O13

Alice Creek Qld 482 D1
Alice Springs NT 405 K3, 411 J8, 373, 377, 381, 382, 383, **384**, 386, 389, 391
Alison NSW 108 B2
Allambee Vic. 213 Q11, 226 I7
Allambee South Vic. 213 Q12, 226 I8
Allambie Heights NSW 95 O3, 97 N13
Allanby Vic. 230 F6
Allandale NSW 109 H5
Allans Flat Vic. 235 P5, 236 B3, 202
Allansford Vic. 228 I9
Allanson WA 364 D8
Allawah NSW 99 K7
Allawah NSW 123 M6
Alleena NSW 116 A9, 123 Q6
Allenby Gardens SA 284 G5
Allendale East SA 293 H12, 271
Allendale North SA 288 E2, 295 L7
Allens Rivulet Tas. 538 G8
Allenvale Vic. 217 I10, 183
Allies Creek Qld 491 M5
Alligator Creek Qld 495 P13, 468
Allora Qld 482 E12, 491 N10, **424**, 471
Alma SA 288 B1, 295 L7
Alma Vic. 223 K4
Alma Park NSW 123 P12, 235 O1
Almaden Qld 495 K7
Almonds Vic. 235 L5
Alonnah Tas. 538 G12, 543 L11
Aloomba Qld 489 G11, 495 N7
Alpara NT 300 G1, 410 E13
Alpha Qld 492 F11
Alphadale NSW 119 Q3, 71
Alpine National Park Vic. 115 B11, 224 G8, 225 P5, 227 L1, 235 O12, 236 D6, 147, **175–6**, 177, 183, 184
Alstonville NSW 119 Q3, 491 Q12, **45**
Alton Qld 490 I10
Alton National Park Qld 490 I10
Altona Vic. 208 F10, 212 I7, 226 C4
Altona Meadows Vic. 208 E12
Alva Qld 492 H1, 495 Q13
Alvie Vic. 212 A10, 217 F5, 229 N8, 167
Alyangula NT 407 O9
Amaroo ACT 136 G2
Amata SA 300 G1, 410 E13

Ambrose Qld 493 O11
Amby Qld 490 F6
Ambyne Vic. 115 D11, 237 K8
American River SA 294 I12, 260, 269
Amherst Vic. 212 B1, 223 K6, 229 N1, 231 N12
Amiens Qld 119 M2, 491 N12
Amity Point Qld 483 P7, 433
Amoongunya NT 405 L4, 411 J8
Amosfield NSW 119 M2
Amphion WA 356 E11, 364 D6
Amphitheatre Vic. 222 H6, 229 M1, 231 M12
Anakie Qld 492 H11, 413, 469
Anakie Vic. 212 F7, 219 D3, 229 Q6, 173
Anakie East Vic. 212 F7, 219 E4
Anakie Junction Vic. 212 F7, 219 D3
Ancona Vic. 235 K10
Andamooka SA 296 G4, 239, **250**, 279, 280
Anderson Vic. 213 M13, 226 F9
Ando NSW 113 A7, 115 E10, 237 N6
Andover Tas. 543 M5
Andrews Qld 485 E9
Andrews SA 295 L4
Anduramba Qld 482 G4
Anembo NSW 115 F7, 135 I11, 138 I7
Angas Valley SA 288 I8
Angaston SA 288 G4, 292 I5, 295 M8, 246, **250**
Angip Vic. 230 G5
Angle Park SA 284 G1, 286 G12, 245
Anglers Reach NSW 114 G5, 115 D8, 138 D9, 237 K1
Anglers Rest Vic. 115 A11, 225 R9, 236 E8, 188
Anglesea Vic. 212 E12, 219 C11, 229 Q9, **157**, 187, 196, 204
Angleside Vic. 224 F3
Angourie NSW 119 Q5, 90
Angurugu NT 407 O9
Angus Place NSW 100 F3, 116 I6
Angustown Vic. 234 G8, 192
Anna Bay NSW 108 H3, 117 N4, 51, 76
Annandale NSW 95 K10, 99 M1
Annangrove NSW 101 M6
Annerley Qld 480 H3

Annuello Vic. 233 J7
Ansons Bay Tas. 545 R6
Anstead Qld 480 A6
Antill Ponds Tas. 543 L4, 545 M13
Antwerp Vic. 230 F6, 170, 203
Anula NT 400 I7
Anzac Village NSW 98 B5
Apamurra SA 288 H9, 293 D1, 295 M9
Aparawatatja SA 300 B2, 369 R11, 410 B13
Apollo Bay Vic. 217 G12, 229 N12, **157**, 187
Appila SA 295 K2, 297 J13
Appin NSW 101 L12, 112 G3, 117 K9
Appin Vic. 231 O4, 234 A3
Appin South Vic. 231 P4, 234 A3
Apple Tree Creek Qld 491 O3
Apple Tree Flat NSW 116 H4
Applecross WA 352 G8
Applethorpe Qld 119 M2, 491 N12
Apslawn Tas. 545 Q12
Apsley Tas. 543 L5
Apsley Vic. 230 B11, 293 I9
Araluen NSW 115 G6, 139 L6, 47, 132
Araluen North NSW 139 L6
Aramac Qld 492 C10, 499 Q10, **424**
Aramara Qld 491 O4
Arana Hills Qld 478 C9
Aranda ACT 136 E8
Arapiles Vic. 230 F9
Ararat Vic. 222 D8, 229 K2, 231 K13, 147, **157–8**, 162, 163, 177, 195, 197
Aratula Qld 482 I12, 491 O10
Arcadia NSW 96 D4
Arcadia Vic. 234 H7
Archdale Vic. 222 I2
Archer River Roadhouse Qld 496 D9
Archerfield Qld 480 G6
Archies Creek Vic. 213 N13, 226 G9
Ardath WA 364 I4
Ardeer Vic. 208 F7
Ardglen NSW 119 J13
Ardlethan NSW 116 A10, 123 Q7
Ardmona Vic. 234 H6
Ardmory Qld 483 J7
Ardno Vic. 228 A5, 293 I12
Ardross WA 352 G9
Ardrossan SA 295 J7, **250–1**
Areegra Vic. 230 I6
Areyonga NT 404 C6, 410 G9
Argalong NSW 138 B2
Argoon Qld 491 K1, 493 N13
Argyle Vic. 234 E9
Ariah Park NSW 116 B9, 123 Q7
Aringa Vic. 228 G9
Arkaroola SA 291 G3, 297 M3, 240, **251**, 263, 273
Arkona Vic. 230 F7
Armadale Vic. 209 M10, 145, 150
Armadale WA 356 C6, 364 C4, 366 C8, 311
Armatree NSW 118 D12
Armidale NSW 119 L9, **45**
Armstrong Vic. 222 D7, 229 K1, 231 K12
Armstrong Beach Qld 493 L6
Armytage Vic. 212 C10, 217 H6
Arncliffe NSW 99 L4
Arnhem Land NT 374, 380, 386, 389, 392, 395
Arno Bay SA 294 F5, 254, 256
Arnold Vic. 231 O9, 234 A8
Arnold West Vic. 231 O9, 234 A8
Arrawarra NSW 119 P7
Arrilalah Qld 499 N11
Arrino WA 366 C4
Artarmon NSW 95 L6
Arthur River Tas. 544 A5
Arthur River WA 364 F8
Arthurs Creek Vic. 213 L4
Arthurton SA 294 I7
Arthurville NSW 116 F3
Asbestos Range National Park Tas. 540 H4, 545 J6, 511, **521**, 526
Ascot Qld 478 H9
Ascot Vic. 212 C3, 223 L9
Ascot WA 353 K2, 355 K13
Ascot Park SA 284 G11
Ascot Vale Vic. 209 J7
Ashbourne SA 289 H5, 290 G7, 293 C3, 295 L10
Ashburton Vic. 209 N11
Ashbury NSW 94 I12, 99 K2
Ashcroft NSW 98 A3
Ashens Vic. 230 I9
Ashfield NSW 94 H11, 99 J1
Ashfield WA 355 M11
Ashford NSW 119 K4, 491 L13, **45**
Ashford SA 284 H8
Ashgrove Qld 478 F11
Ashley NSW 118 G4, 491 J13
Ashmore Qld 485 D5
Ashton SA 285 R7, 288 C10, 289 H1, 293 C1
Ashville SA 293 D3, 295 M11
Ashwood Vic. 209 O11
Aspendale Vic. 211 D7
Aspley Qld 478 F6
Asquith NSW 96 F8
Athelstone SA 285 P2, 287 P13
Atherton Qld 489 C12, 495 M7, **424–5**, 448, 449
Atherton Tableland Qld 489 D10, 414, 430, 448, 449, 458, 462
Athlone Vic. 213 O10, 226 H7
Athol Qld 482 D8
Athol Park SA 284 F1, 286 F12
Attadale WA 352 E9
Attunga NSW 119 J10
Attwood Vic. 208 I2
Aubigny Qld 482 C7
Aubrey Vic. 230 G6
Auburn NSW 94 D9
Auburn SA 295 L6, 246, 253, 254
Auburn Tas. 543 L3, 545 M12
Auburn River National Park Qld 491 L4, **457**, 460
Auchenflower Qld 478 E12, 480 E1
Auchmah Qld 482 B5
Audley NSW 98 H13, 101 N10
Augathella Qld 490 C5
Augusta WA 357 C13, 359 D12, 364 B11, 366 B11, **313–14**
Auldana SA 285 N6
Aurukun Aboriginal Community Qld 496 A9, 453
Austinmer NSW 101 M13, 112 H5
Australia Plains SA 295 M6
Australind WA 357 G4, 364 C8, 366 C10, **314**, 316
Avalon NSW 97 Q4, 101 P6, 104 H12
Avenel Vic. 234 H9
Avenue SA 293 G9
Avoca Tas. 543 N1, 545 O11, 518
Avoca Vic. 222 I5, 231 M12, **158**, 163, 197
Avoca Beach NSW 101 Q4, 104 H6
Avoca Vale Qld 482 H1

Avon SA 295 K7
Avon Plains Vic. 231 K8
Avon Valley National Park WA 356 E1, 364 D2, 366 C7, **322**, 346
Avondale NSW 108 F12, 117 M5
Avondale Qld 491 O2
Avondale Heights Vic. 208 H6
Avonmore Vic. 234 D7
Avonsleigh Vic. 213 M7, 216 C12, 226 F5
Awaba NSW 108 F10
Awonga Vic. 230 C11
Axe Creek Vic. 231 R10, 234 D9
Axedale Vic. 234 D8
Ayers Rock *see* Uluru
Ayers Rock Resort *see* Yulara
Ayr Qld 492 H1, 495 Q13, **425**, 444
Ayrford Vic. 229 J10
Ayton Qld 495 M4

Baan Baa NSW 118 H9
Baandee WA 364 H2
Baarmutha Vic. 235 O6, 236 A4
Babakin WA 364 I4
Babbage Island WA 318
Babinda Qld 489 H13, 495 N7, **425**
Bacchus Marsh Vic. 212 G5, 223 R13, 226 A3, 229 R4, **158**, 161
Back Creek Vic. 235 P5
Back Creek Tas. 541 N2, 545 L6
Back Plains Qld 482 D10
Back Valley SA 290 C12
Backwater NSW 119 M7
Baddaginnie Vic. 235 K7
Baden Tas. 543 M6
Badger Head Tas. 511
Badgerys Creek NSW 101 K9
Badgingarra WA 366 B6, 330
Badgingarra National Park WA 366 B6
Badja Mill NSW 139 J9
Badjaling WA 364 G4
Bael Bael Vic. 231 O2, 233 O13
Baerami NSW 117 J3
Bagdad Tas. 538 H2, 543 L7, 526
Bagnoo NSW 105 C8, 119 N12
Bagot Well SA 288 F2, 295 M7
Bagshot Vic. 231 R9, 234 D8
Bailieston Vic. 234 G8, 192
Bairnsdale Vic. 227 P4, 236 F13, **158**, 181, 193
Bajool Qld 493 O11
Bakara SA 295 O8
Baker Vic. 230 D5
Baker Gully SA 290 E4
Bakers Beach Tas. 540 G5, 511
Bakers Creek Qld 493 L5
Bakers Hill WA 356 G3, 364 E3
Bakers Swamp NSW 116 F4
Baking Board Qld 491 K7
Balaklava SA 295 K6, **251**
Balcatta WA 354 E8
Bald Hills Qld 478 E4
Bald Knob NSW 119 M6
Bald Knob Qld 483 L2, 486 D12
Bald Rock Vic. 231 Q5, 234 B3
Baldivis WA 334
Bald Rock National Park NSW 119 M3, 491 N12, 83
Baldry NSW 116 E4
Balfes Creek Qld 492 D2
Balfour Tas. 544 B7
Balga WA 354 G7
Balgal Beach Qld 495 O12

Balgo Community WA 371 P12
Balgowan SA 294 H7, 261
Balgowlah NSW 95 P5
Balgowlah Heights NSW 95 P6, 101 O8
Balgownie NSW 110 C4
Balhannah SA 288 D10, 289 I1, 290 H1, 293 C2, 295 L9
Balingup WA 357 I8, 360 C2, 364 D9, 366 C11, 315, 324
Balintore Vic. 212 B11, 217 F6
Balkuling WA 364 F4
Ball Bay Qld 493 K4
Balladonia WA 367 L8, **314**
Balladoran NSW 116 E1, 118 D13
Ballajura WA 355 K6
Ballalaba NSW 115 F6, 116 H13, 139 K5
Ballan Vic. 212 F4, 223 Q12, 229 Q4, 234 C13, **158**, 161
Ballandean Qld 119 M3, 491 N12, 467
Ballangeich Vic. 228 I8
Ballapur Vic. 231 J4
Ballarat Vic. 212 C4, 221, 223 M11, 229 O3, 234 A13, 141, 142, 147, 152, **159**, 161, 162, 163
Ballarat North Vic. 221 D3
Ballarat South Vic. 221 C8
Ballard Qld 482 F7
Ballark Vic. 212 D5, 223 N13
Ballaying WA 364 G8
Ballbank NSW 122 I11, 231 P1, 233 P11
Balldale NSW 123 P12, 235 N2
Ballendella Vic. 234 E5
Balliang Vic. 212 F6, 219 E2, 229 R5
Balliang East Vic. 212 G6, 219 F1
Ballidu WA 366 D6
Ballimore NSW 116 F2
Ballina NSW 119 Q3, 491 R12, **45**
Ballimore NSW 116 F2
Ballogan Vic. 222 E9
Balmain NSW 95 L9, 101 N8, 35, 38, 40
Balmattum Vic. 235 J8
Balmoral NSW 95 O7, 101 J13, 112 D4
Balmoral Qld 478 I11
Balmoral Vic. 228 F2, 230 F13, 168
Balnarring Vic. 213 K11, 215 L8, 226 D8, 155, 197
Balook Vic. 227 K8
Balranald NSW 122 H8, 233 N6, **45**
Balrootan North Vic. 230 E6
Balumbah SA 294 E3, 296 E13
Balup WA 356 E2, 364 D3
Balwyn Vic. 209 O8
Balwyn North Vic. 209 O7
Bamaga Qld 496 C3, 453
Bamawm Vic. 234 E5
Bamawm Extension Vic. 234 E5
Bambaroo Qld 495 O11
Bambill Vic. 122 B8, 232 D4
Bambill South Vic. 232 D5
Bamboo Creek WA 368 E2
Bambra Vic. 212 D11, 219 A10, 229 P9
Bamera SA 295 P7
Bamganie Vic. 219 A3
Banana Qld 491 J1, 493 N13, 426
Bancroft Qld 491 M2
Bandiana Vic. 123 Q13, 235 P4, 236 C2, 200
Bandon NSW 116 E6
Bandon Grove NSW 117 M2
Banealla SA 293 G5, 295 P13
Bangalow NSW 119 Q2, 491 Q12, **45–6**
Bangerang Vic. 230 I6
Bangham SA 230 A8, 293 I7
Bangholme Vic. 211 G7

Bangor NSW 98 F9
Bangor Tas. 541 O6, 545 L7
Banimboola Vic. 225 R2
Banks ACT 137 D13
Banksia NSW 99 L5
Banksia Beach Qld 483 N4
Banksia Park SA 287 Q9
Banksmeadow NSW 99 P5
Bankstown NSW 94 D13, 98 F3, 101 M9
Bannaby NSW 115 G2, 116 I10
Bannerton Vic. 122 F9, 233 J6
Bannister NSW 115 F3, 116 H10
Bannister WA 356 G11, 364 E6
Bannockburn Vic. 212 E8, 219 C5, 229 Q7
Banool Vic. 217 F9
Banora Point NSW 119 Q1, 485 I12, 491 Q11
Banyan Vic. 231 J2, 233 J13
Banyena Vic. 231 J8
Banyenong Vic. 231 L6
Banyo Qld 478 I6
Bar Beach NSW 106 E10
Barabba SA 288 B2
Baradine NSW 118 E10, 56
Barakula Qld 491 K6
Baralaba Qld 493 M13, 426
Baranduda Vic. 235 P4, 236 C2
Barcaldine Qld 492 C11, 499 Q11, **425**
Bardon Qld 478 E12, 418
Bardwell Park NSW 99 K4
Barellan NSW 123 P7
Barfold Vic. 229 R1, 231 R12, 234 D10
Bargara Qld 491 O2, **425**, 428
Bargo NSW 101 J13, 112 D4, 115 I2, 117 J9
Barham NSW 231 Q2, 233 Q13, 234 B1, **46**
Baring Vic. 230 G1, 232 G11
Baringhup Vic. 223 N4, 231 P11, 234 B10
Barjarg Vic. 224 B9, 235 L10
Bark Hut Inn NT 402 I6
Barkers Creek Vic. 223 Q5, 231 Q11, 234 C10
Barkly Vic. 222 G4
Barkly Homestead NT 409 N11, **384**
Barkstead Vic. 212 E3, 223 O10
Barmah Vic. 123 K13, 234 F3
Barmedman NSW 116 B9, 123 R7, 88
Barmera SA 249, **251**
Barmundu Qld 493 P13
Barnadown Vic. 234 D8
Barnawartha Vic. 123 P13, 235 O4, 236 A2, 202
Barnawartha North Vic. 235 O4, 236 B1
Barnes NSW 123 K13, 234 E3
Barnes Bay Tas. 538 I9, 543 L10, 512
Barongarook Vic. 212 B12, 217 G8
Barongarook West Vic. 212 A12, 217 F8
Barooga NSW 123 M13, 235 J3, **46**, 84, 167, 201
Baroota SA 295 J2, 296 I12
Barossa Valley SA 292, 239, 241, 246, 248, 250, 257, 259, 268
Barpinba Vic. 212 B9, 217 G4
Barraba NSW 118 I8, **46**, 69
Barrakee Vic. 231 M6
Barramunga Vic. 212 B13, 217 G10
Barranyi (North Island) National Park NT 407 P12, 409 P1
Barraport Vic. 122 H13, 231 N5
Barringo Vic. 212 H3
Barrington NSW 117 N1
Barrington Tas. 540 D8, 544 I7
Barrington Tops National Park NSW 117 M1, **59**, 61, 63, 80

Barringun NSW 121 N1, 490 A13, 501 R13
Barrogan NSW 116 F6
Barron Gorge National Park Qld 489 D8, 495 M7, **458**
Barrow Creek NT 411 J4, **384**
Barry NSW 116 G7, 119 K12
Barrys Reef Vic. 212 F3, 223 Q10
Bartle Frere National Park *see* Wooroonooran National Park
Barton ACT 134 D10, 136 H11, 137 F2
Barton SA 303 K4
Barton Vic. 222 B8
Barunga NT 406 H10
Barunga Gap SA 295 J5
Barwidgee Creek Vic. 225 J2, 235 O7, 236 B5
Barwite Vic. 224 D9
Barwo Vic. 234 G3
Barwon Downs Vic. 212 C12, 217 H8, 229 O10
Barwon Heads Vic. 212 G10, 219 G9, 226 A7, 229 R8, 187
Baryulgil NSW 119 O4, 491 P13
Basin Qld 483 L5
Basket Range SA 246
Bass Vic. 213 M13, 226 F9
Bass Hill NSW 94 C12, 98 E2
Bassendean WA 355 L11, 311
Batchelor NT 402 D7, 406 E7
Batchica Vic. 230 H6
Bateau Bay NSW 101 Q3, 104 H3
Batehaven NSW 139 N7
Bateman WA 352 G11
Batemans Bay NSW 115 H7, 139 N7, **47**, 55, 132
Bates SA 303 K4
Batesford Vic. 212 F9, 219 E6, 229 Q7, 173
Bathumi Vic. 235 L4
Bathurst NSW 100 B4, 116 H6, 31, **47**
Batlow NSW 115 B6, 116 D13, 138 A4, **47**
Batman Bridge Tas. 541 L6
Battery Point Tas. 535 F11, 536 H8, 538 I6, 506, 507, 508, 515, 527
Baulkham Hills NSW 94 C3, 96 B12
Bauple Qld 491 P5
Baw Baw National Park Vic. 227 K4, **176**, 196, 198
Bawley Point NSW 115 H6, 117 J13, 139 P5
Baxter Vic. 213 K10, 215 M2, 226 D7
Bayindeen Vic. 222 F8
Bayles Vic. 213 N10, 226 G7
Baynton Vic. 212 H1
Bayswater Vic. 210 C10
Bayswater WA 355 K11
Bayview NSW 97 P7, 104 H13
Beachmere Qld 483 M5, 430
Beachport SA 293 F10, **251–2**
Beacon WA 366 E6
Beacon Hill NSW 95 O2, 97 N12
Beaconsfield NSW 95 M13, 99 O3
Beaconsfield Tas. 541 J5, 545 K7, **511**
Beaconsfield Vic. 213 M8, 226 E6
Beaconsfield WA 352 C12
Beagle Bay WA 370 H7
Bealiba Vic. 223 J2, 231 N10
Bearbung NSW 118 E12
Beardmore Vic. 227 K4
Beargamil NSW 116 D5
Bearii Vic. 123 L13, 234 H3
Bears Lagoon Vic. 231 P7, 234 A6
Beatrice Hill NT 402 F4
Beauaraba Qld 482 D8
Beauchamp Vic. 231 N2, 233 N12

Beaudesert Qld 483 L12, 491 P10, **425–6**
Beaufort SA 295 J6
Beaufort Vic. 222 H9, 229 M3, **159**
Beaumaris Tas. 545 Q9, 529
Beaumaris Vic. 211 B5
Beaumont SA 285 L8
Beauty Point NSW 95 O6
Beauty Point Tas. 541 K5, 545 K6, **511**, 519
Beazleys Bridge Vic. 231 L9
Beckenham WA 353 N8
Beckom NSW 116 A9, 123 Q7
Bedarra Island Qld 495 N9, **440**
Bedford WA 355 J11
Bedgerebong NSW 116 C6
Bedourie Qld 498 E13, 500 E1, 472
Beeac Vic. 212 B10, 217 G5, 229 N8
Beebo Qld 119 J2, 491 L12
Beech Forest Vic. 217 F10, 229 N11
Beechboro WA 355 L7
Beechford Tas. 541 L2, 545 L6
Beechmont Qld 483 M13
Beechwood NSW 105 E7, 119 O12
Beechworth Vic. 235 O6, 236 A3, **159–60**, 186, 200
Beecroft NSW 94 F3, 96 D12
Beedelup National Park WA 357 H13, 360 B7, 341
Beela WA 357 H3, 364 C7
Beelbangera NSW 123 N7
Beenak Vic. 216 F12
Beenleigh Qld 481 P13, 483 M10, 491 Q10, **426**
Beerburrum Qld 483 M3
Beerwah Qld 483 M3, 491 P7, 421, 431
Bega NSW 113 F7, 115 G10, 237 Q6, **47**, 55
Beggan Beggan NSW 115 C3, 116 E10
Beilpajah NSW 122 I2
Belair SA 285 J13
Belair National Park SA 285 L12, 288 B11, 289 G1, 290 E1, 245, 247, **262**
Belalie SA 295 L3, 297 K13
Belaringar NSW 118 A13
Belbora NSW 117 O1
Belconnen ACT 135 E3, 136 E6, 138 G1
Beldon WA 354 B1
Belfield NSW 94 G12, 98 I2, 101 N9
Belford NSW 109 B1
Belgian Gardens Qld 487 C2
Belgrave Vic. 210 F13, 213 L7, 216 A12, 226 E5, 156, 172
Belhus WA 355 P1
Belka WA 364 I3
Bell NSW 100 H5
Bell Qld 482 C2, 491 M7
Bell Bay Tas. 541 K4, 545 K6, 511, 519
Bellambi NSW 110 H2, 112 H5
Bellara Qld 483 N4
Bellarine Vic. 212 H9, 214 A1, 219 H7, 226 B6
Bellarine Peninsula Vic. 219 F8, 141, 154, 173
Bellarwi NSW 116 A9, 123 Q7
Bellata NSW 118 G7
Bellbird NSW 108 B10, 109 C13
Bellbird Creek Vic. 237 L12
Bellbowrie Qld 480 A6
Bellbrae Vic. 212 F11, 219 D10, 229 Q9, 196
Bellbrook NSW 119 N10, 69
Bellellen Vic. 222 B5
Bellenden Ker Qld 489 H12
Bellenden Ker National Park *see*
Wooroonooran National Park
Bellerive Tas. 537 K6, 538 I5, 543 M8, 508, 529
Bellevue Hill NSW 95 P11, 99 R1
Belli Park Qld 486 B5
Bellimbopinni NSW 105 G2
Bellingen NSW 119 P8, **47–8**
Bellingham Tas. 541 O2, 545 M6
Bellmount Forest NSW 115 E4, 116 G11
Bellthorpe Qld 483 K2
Belltrees NSW 117 L1
Belmont NSW 108 G9, 117 M5
Belmont Qld 481 L2
Belmont Vic. 218 C13, 219 E7
Belmont WA 353 L3
Belmore NSW 94 G13, 99 J3
Belmunging WA 364 F3
Beloka NSW 114 H13, 115 D10, 237 L5
Belowra NSW 113 F2, 115 G8, 139 K11, 237 P2
Belrose NSW 95 M1, 97 L11
Beltana SA 291 D5, 297 J5, 261
Beltana Roadhouse SA 291 D5, 297 J5
Belton SA 291 E11, 297 K10
Belvidere SA 293 C3, 295 L10
Belyuen NT 402 B3, 406 D6
Bemboka NSW 113 D6, 115 F10, 237 P5
Bemboka National Park NSW 113 D5, 115 F10, 237 O5
Bemm River Vic. 237 M13, 189
Bemook Vic. 293 I1, 295 R9
Ben Boyd National Park NSW 113 G10, 115 G11, 237 Q8, **60**, 61
Ben Bullen NSW 100 F2, 116 I5
Ben Lomond NSW 119 L7
Ben Lomond National Park Tas. 545 O9, **521**, 523
Ben Nevis Vic. 222 F7
Bena NSW 116 A7, 123 Q4
Bena Vic. 213 O12, 226 G8, 180
Benalla Vic. 224 A2, 235 K7, 147, **160**
Benambra Vic. 115 A11, 236 F7, 189
Benandarah NSW 139 N6
Benaraby Qld 493 P12
Benarubra Vic. 188
Benarkin Qld 482 G2, 460
Bencubbin WA 366 E6
Bendalong NSW 115 I5, 117 J12, 139 Q3, 86
Bendemeer NSW 119 K10
Bendering WA 364 I5
Bendick Murrell NSW 115 C1, 116 E9
Bendidee National Park Qld 118 I1, 491 K11
Bendigo Vic. 220, 231 Q9, 234 C8, 142, **160**, 161, 163, **164**, 173, 197
Bendoc Vic. 115 D12, 237 L9
Bendolba NSW 117 M2
Beneree NSW 116 F6
Benetook Vic. 232 F4
Benger WA 357 H3, 364 C7
Bengworden Vic. 227 P5
Beni NSW 116 F2
Benjeroop Vic. 231 O1, 233 O12
Benlidi Qld 499 P13, 501 P1
Bennies Vic. 224 H9
Benobble Qld 483 M12
Benowa Qld 485 D6
Bentleigh Vic. 209 M13, 211 B1
Bentley NSW 119 P3
Bentley WA 353 K7
Benwerrin Vic. 212 D12, 217 I9, 229 P10

Berala NSW 94 D11, 98 G1
Berambing NSW 100 I5, 71
Berat Qld 482 F12
Beremboke Vic. 212 F6, 219 D1
Berendebba NSW 115 A1, 116 C8
Beresfield NSW 108 E7, 117 M4
Bergalia NSW 115 G8, 139 M9, 237 R1
Bermagui NSW 113 H4, 115 H9, 139 M13, 237 R4, **48**, 55
Bermagui South NSW 113 H5, 115 H9, 139 M13, 237 R4
Bernook Vic. 232 A8
Berowra NSW 96 H4
Berowra Heights NSW 96 I3, 104 D13
Berowra Waters NSW 96 G2, 104 C13, 46
Berrara NSW 115 I5, 117 J12, 139 Q3
Berri SA 295 Q7, **252**
Berridale NSW 114 I10, 115 D9, 138 E12, 237 L4, **48**
Berriedale Tas. 536 B2, 538 H5, 543 L8
Berrigan NSW 123 N12, 235 K1, **48**
Berrima NSW 112 B6, 115 H3, 117 J10, 29, 39, **48**, 49
Berrimah NT 402 D2
Berrimal Vic. 231 M8
Berrinba Qld 481 K10
Berringa Vic. 212 B6, 229 N5
Berringama Vic. 115 A9, 236 F3
Berriwillock Vic. 122 F12, 231 K2, 233 K13
Berry NSW 112 F11, 115 I4, 117 K11, **48**
Berrybank Vic. 212 A8, 217 F2, 229 M6
Berwick Vic. 213 M8, 226 E5
Bessiebelle Vic. 228 F8
Bet Bet Vic. 223 L3, 231 O11
Beta Qld 492 E11
Bete Bolong Vic. 237 J12
Bethanga Vic. 123 Q13, 235 Q4, 236 C2
Bethania Qld 481 O12, 483 M10
Bethany SA 288 F5, 292 F6, 276
Bethel SA 288 E2
Bethungra NSW 115 B4, 116 C11, 68
Betley Vic. 223 M3
Betoota Qld 500 H4, 472
Beulah Tas. 540 E10, 544 I8
Beulah Vic. 122 E13, 230 H4
Beulah East Vic. 230 I4
Beulah Park SA 285 L6
Beulah West Vic. 230 H4
Bevendale NSW 115 E3, 116 F10
Beverford Vic. 122 H10, 195
Beveridge Vic. 213 J3, 226 D1, 234 F12
Beverley SA 284 F4
Beverley WA 364 F4, 366 D8, **314**
Beverley East WA 364 F4
Beverley Park NSW 99 L7
Beverly Hills NSW 98 I5
Beverwood Vic. 233 N10
Bexhill NSW 119 Q3
Bexley NSW 99 K5, 101 N9
Bexley North NSW 99 J4
Beyal Vic. 231 J5
Biala NSW 115 E3, 116 G10
Biamanga National Park NSW 113 F5, 115 G10, 237 Q5
Biarra Qld 482 H5
Bibbenluke NSW 113 A8, 115 E11, 237 N7
Biboohra Qld 489 C8, 495 M6
Bibra Lake WA 310
Bicheno Tas. 543 Q2, 545 Q12, 503, 505, **511**, 515
Bicton WA 352 D8
Biddeston Qld 482 D7

Biddon NSW 118 D12
Big Pats Creek Vic. 213 O6, 216 H9
Bigga NSW 115 E1, 116 G8, 57
Biggara NSW 115 B9, 236 H3
Biggenden Qld 491 N4, **426**
Biggera Waters Qld 485 E3
Bilambil NSW 485 G12
Bilbarin WA 364 H4
Bilbul NSW 123 O7
Bilgola NSW 97 Q5
Bilinga Qld 485 H10
Billabong Vic. 122 D7, 232 G3
Billabong Roadhouse WA 365 C12, 366 A1
Billaricay NSW 364 I5
Billilingra Siding NSW 138 G9
Billiluna Community WA 371 P11
Billimari NSW 116 E7
Billinudgel NSW 119 Q2, 491 Q11, 52
Billys Creek NSW 119 O7
Biloela Qld 491 K1, 493 N13, **426**, 469
Bilpin NSW 101 J5, 117 J6
Bilyana Qld 495 N9
Bimbaya NSW 113 D7, 237 P6
Bimbi NSW 115 B1, 116 D8
Bimbimbie NSW 139 N8
Binalong NSW 115 D3, 116 E10
Binalong Bay Tas. 545 R8
Binbee Qld 492 I3
Binda NSW 100 A13, 115 F2, 116 G9, 57
Bindi NSW 115 B12, 236 G8
Bindi Bindi WA 366 D6
Bindle Qld 490 H9
Bindoon WA 364 D2, 366 C7, 328
Bingara NSW 118 I6, **48–9**, 69
Bingera Qld 491 O2
Bingil Bay Qld 495 N9, 471
Binginwarri Vic. 227 K9
Biniguy NSW 118 H5
Binjour Qld 491 M4
Binnaway NSW 118 F12
Binningup WA 357 G3, 364 C7, 314
Binnu WA 366 A2
Binnum SA 293 H8
Binya NSW 123 O7
Birchgrove NSW 95 L9
Birchip Vic. 122 F13, 231 K4, **164**
Birchs Bay Tas. 538 H10, 543 L10
Bird Island SA 278
Birdsville Qld 500 E5, 265, 279, **426–7**, 472
Birdwood NSW 105 B6, 119 N11
Birdwood SA 288 F8, 293 C1, 295 L9
Birdwoodton Vic. 122 D7, 232 G3
Birkdale Qld 479 P12
Birkenhead SA 286 D11
Birralee Tas. 541 J9, 545 K8
Birrego NSW 123 O10
Birregurra Vic. 212 C11, 217 H7, 229 O9, 167
Birriwa NSW 116 G2
Birrong NSW 94 D12, 98 F2
Bishopsbourne Tas. 541 M13, 545 L9
Bittern Vic. 213 K11, 215 M7, 226 E8
Black Bobs Tas. 542 I5
Black Forest SA 284 H9
Black Hill SA 293 E1, 295 N8
Black Hill Vic. 221 G4
Black Hills Tas. 538 F3, 543 K7
Black Mountain NSW 119 L8
Black Mountain Qld 486 B2
Black River Tas. 544 D4
Black Rock SA 295 L2, 297 K12
Black Rock Vic. 211 A4

Black Springs NSW 100 D8, 116 H8
Black Springs SA 295 L5
Black Swamp NSW 119 N4, 491 O13
Blackall Qld 490 A1, 492 D13, 499 R13, 501 R1, **427**
Blackall Range National Park Qld 483 L1, 486 C9, 429
Blackburn Vic. 209 Q9
Blackbutt Qld 482 G2, 491 O7
Blackdown Tableland National Park Qld 493 K11, 427, 469
Blackfellow Caves SA 293 G12
Blackheath NSW 100 H6, 102 C5, 117 J7, 42, 68
Blackheath Vic. 230 H8
Blackmans Bay Tas. 538 H8, 523
Blacksmiths NSW 108 G10
Blackstone WA 369 P10
Blacktown NSW 101 L7
Blackville NSW 118 H12
Blackwall Tas. 541 L7
Blackwarry Vic. 227 L8
Blackwater Qld 493 K11, **427**
Blackwood Vic. 212 F3, 223 Q10, 229 Q3, 234 C13, 158, 180
Blackwood Creek Tas. 543 K1, 545 K10
Blackwood National Park Qld 492 F5
Bladensburg National Park Qld 499 M8
Blair Athol Qld 492 H9
Blair Athol SA 284 I2, 286 I13
Blairgowrie Vic. 212 I11, 214 E8, 154
Blakehurst NSW 99 J8, 101 N10
Blakeville Vic. 212 F3, 223 P10
Blampied Vic. 212 D2, 223 O9
Blanchetown SA 295 N7, 278
Bland NSW 115 A1, 116 B8, 123 R6
Blandford NSW 119 J13
Blanket Flat NSW 115 E1, 116 G9
Blaxland NSW 101 J7, 103 P7
Blaxland Qld 482 B4
Blaxlands Ridge NSW 101 K5
Blayney NSW 116 G6, **49**
Bleak House Vic. 230 D6
Blenheim Qld 482 H9
Blessington Tas. 545 N9
Bletchley SA 288 F13
Blewitt Springs SA 290 D4
Bli Bli Qld 483 N1, 486 G8, 491 Q7
Blighty NSW 123 L12, 234 H1
Blinman SA 291 E6, 297 K6, **252**
Bloomsbury Qld 493 J4
Blow Clear NSW 116 B7, 123 Q5
Blowclear NSW 116 C5
Blue Lake National Park Qld 483 P9, 433
Blue Mountains NSW 100 I6, 102, 112 A1, 115 H1, 116 I8, 29, 42, 43, 68, 85
Blue Mountains National Park NSW 100 G8, 102 H3, 103 L2, 112 A1, 115 G1, 116 I8, 117 J7, 42, **58**, 68
Blue Water Springs Roadhouse Qld 495 M13
Bluewater Qld 495 O12
Blueys Beach NSW 117 P2
Bluff Qld 493 K11
Bluff Beach SA 294 H8, 266
Bluff Rock NSW 119 M4, 491 N13
Blumont Tas. 541 R5
Blyth SA 295 K5, 254
Boallia WA 357 D8, 359 F4, 364 B9
Boambee NSW 119 P8
Boat Harbour NSW 108 H3
Boat Harbour Tas. 544 F5, **511–12**, 532

Boat Harbour Beach Tas. 544 F5, 511
Boatswain Point SA 293 F9
Bobadah NSW 121 P13
Bobbin Head NSW 96 H6, 46
Bobin NSW 119 N13
Bobinawarrah Vic. 224 G2, 235 N7, 236 A5
Bobs Creek Vic. 224 D9
Bobs Hollow WA 357 B11, 359 B9, 364 A10
Bochara Vic. 228 F5
Bodalla NSW 113 H1, 115 H8, 139 M10, 237 R2, 73
Bodallin WA 366 F7
Boddington WA 356 G12, 364 E6
Bogan Gate NSW 116 C5
Bogangar NSW 119 Q1, 491 R11, 84
Bogantungan Qld 492 H11
Boggabilla NSW 118 I2, 491 K12
Boggabri NSW 118 H9, **49**
Bogolong NSW 116 D8
Bogong Vic. 225 O6, 185
Bogong Saddle Vic. 225 R5
Boho Vic. 235 J8
Boho South Vic. 235 K8
Boigbeat Vic. 231 K2, 233 K12
Boinka Vic. 122 C10, 232 D10
Boisdale Vic. 227 M5
Bokarina Qld 486 I11
Bolgart WA 364 E1, 339
Bolinda Vic. 212 I3
Bolivar SA 286 I5
Bolivia NSW 119 M4, 491 N13
Bolla Bollana SA 251
Bolton Vic. 233 K8
Boltons Bore Vic. 232 A9, 293 I2, 295 R10
Bolwarra NSW 108 C6
Bolwarra Qld 288 D9
Bolwarrah Vic. 212 E4, 223 O10, 229 P3, 234 B13
Bomaderry NSW 112 E12, 115 I4, 117 K11, 77
Bombala NSW 113 A9, 115 E11, 237 N7, **49–50**
Bombo NSW 112 H9
Bomera NSW 118 G12
Bonalbo NSW 119 O3, 491 P12
Bonang Vic. 115 D12, 237 L9, 189
Bonang West Vic. 115 D12, 237 K9
Bonbeach Vic. 211 D8
Bondi NSW 95 P11, 99 R1
Bondi Gulf National Park NSW 113 A11, 115 E12
Bondi Junction NSW 95 P11, 99 R2, 101 O9
Bondo NSW 115 C5, 116 E12, 138 C1
Bonegilla Vic. 123 Q13, 235 Q4, 236 C2
Boneo Vic. 213 J12, 214 G9
Bongaree Qld 483 N5, 491 Q8, 433
Bongeen Qld 482 B8
Bonnells Bay NSW 108 G11
Bonnet Bay NSW 98 H9
Bonnie Doon Vic. 235 K10, 157
Bonnie Rock WA 366 F6
Bonny Hills NSW 105 G9, 119 O12
Bonshaw NSW 119 K4, 491 M13
Bonville NSW 119 P8
Bony Mountain Qld 482 D12
Bonython ACT 137 C10
Booborowie SA 295 L4
Boobyalla Tas. 545 P5
Boodua Qld 482 E6
Bookabie SA 303 L8

Bookar Vic. 217 B4, 229 L7
Bookham NSW 115 D4, 116 E11
Bool Lagoon SA 293 H9
Boolaroo NSW 108 F9
Boolarra Vic. 213 R12, 227 J8
Boolba Qld 490 F10
Booleroo SA 291 C13, 295 K1, 297 J12
Booleroo Centre SA 295 K2, 297 J2
Boolgun SA 295 O7
Booligal NSW 123 K6
Boolite Vic. 231 J7
Boomahnoomoonah Vic. 235 L4
Boomerang Beach NSW 117 P2
Boomi NSW 118 F2, 490 I12
Boomleera NT 402 H11
Boonah Qld 483 J12, 491 P10, **427**
Boonah Vic. 217 I8
Boonarga Qld 434
Boondall Qld 478 H5
Boonoo Boonoo NSW 119 N3
Boonoo Boonoo National Park NSW 119 N3, 491 O12, 83, 467
Boonoonar Vic. 232 G5
Boorabbin National Park WA 366 H7
Booragoon WA 352 G10
Booral NSW 117 N3
Boorcan Vic. 217 B5, 229 K8
Boorhaman Vic. 235 M5
Boorindal NSW 121 O6
Boorolite Vic. 213 R1, 224 D11
Boorongie Vic. 232 I9
Boorongie North Vic. 232 H9
Booroobin Qld 483 L2, 486 A13
Booroopki Vic. 230 C10
Booroorban NSW 123 K9
Boorowa NSW 115 D2, 116 F10
Boort Vic. 122 H13, 231 O5, **164**
Boosey Vic. 235 J4
Booti Booti National Park NSW 117 P2, 62
Booyal Qld 491 N3
Boppy Mount NSW 121 O10
Borallon Qld 483 K8
Boralma Vic. 235 M5
Borambil NSW 116 I1
Boraning WA 364 E7
Boranup WA 357 B12, 359 C10, 364 A10, 335
Borden WA 361 Q4, 364 I10
Border Ranges National Park NSW 119 O1, 491 P11, **59**, 70, 71, 75
Border Village SA 302 B8, 367 R7
Bordertown SA 293 H6, **252**
Boree NSW 116 F6
Boree Creek NSW 123 P10
Boro NSW 115 G5, 116 H12, 139 K1
Boronia Vic. 210 D11
Boronia Heights Qld 480 I13
Boronia Park NSW 95 J7
Bororen Qld 491 M1, 493 P13
Borrika SA 293 F2, 295 O9
Borroloola NT 407 O13, 409 O3, **384**, **387**, 395, 474
Borung Vic. 231 O6
Boscabel WA 360 I1, 364 F9, 366 E10
Bostobrick NSW 119 O8, 61
Bostock Creek Vic. 217 B6
Boston Island SA 271
Botany NSW 99 O5, 101 O9
Botany Bay National Park NSW 99 P10, 101 O10, **58**
Bothwell Tas. 543 K5, 503, **512**, 515

Bouddi National Park NSW 101 P5, 104 G9, **59**, 63, 83, 90
Bouldercombe Qld 493 N11
Boulia Qld 498 F9, **427**, 472
Boulka Vic. 232 H9
Boundain WA 364 G6
Boundary Bend Vic. 122 G9, 233 L7
Bourke NSW 121 N5, **50**
Bournda National Park NSW 113 G8, 115 G10, 237 R6, 47, 82
Bow NSW 117 J2
Bowan Park NSW 116 F6
Bowden SA 282 A3, 284 H5
Bowen Qld 493 J2, **427–8**
Bowen Hills Qld 478 G10, 417
Bowen Mountain NSW 101 J5
Bowenfels NSW 100 F4
Bowenvale Vic. 223 K4, 231 O11, 184
Bowenville Qld 482 C5, 491 M8
Bower SA 295 N6
Boweya Vic. 235 L5
Bowhill SA 293 E1, 295 N9
Bowling Alley Point NSW 119 K12
Bowling Green Bay Qld 495 P13
Bowling Green Bay National Park Qld 492 G1, 495 R13, 470
Bowman Vic. 224 H1
Bowmans SA 295 K6
Bowna NSW 123 Q13, 235 Q3, 236 D1
Bowning NSW 115 D4, 116 F11
Bowral NSW 112 C6, 115 I3, 117 J10, 39, 49, **50**
Bowraville NSW 119 O9, 72
Bowser Vic. 235 M5
Box Creek Qld 490 A5, 501 R6
Box Hill Vic. 209 O8
Box Tank NSW 120 D12
Boxwood Vic. 235 J5
Boxwood Hill WA 366 F11
Boyanup WA 357 G6, 364 C8
Boyeo Vic. 230 D6
Boyer Tas. 538 G4, 543 K8, 524
Boykambil Qld 485 D2
Boyland Qld 483 M12
Boyne Island Qld 493 P12, 443, 445
Boys Town Qld 483 L12
Boyup Brook WA 360 E2, 364 E9, 366 D11, **314**
Bracalba Qld 483 L4
Bracken Ridge Qld 478 F4
Brackendale NSW 119 L11
Bracknell Tas. 545 K10
Braddon ACT 134 E2, 136 H8, 130
Bradford Vic. 231 P10, 234 B9
Bradvale Vic. 212 A6, 229 M5
Brady Creek SA 295 M6
Braefield NSW 119 J12
Braemar NSW 112 D6
Braemar Bay NSW 114 G6
Braeside Vic. 211 D5
Brahma Lodge SA 287 M6
Braidwood NSW 115 G6, 116 H13, 139 L4, **50**, 132
Bramfield SA 294 B5
Bramley WA 357 B9, 359 C6, 364 A9
Brampton Island Qld 493 L4, **438**, 452
Bramston Beach Qld 489 I13, 495 N8
Branch Creek Qld 478 A6
Brandon Qld 492 H1, 495 Q13
Branxholm Tas. 545 O7, 516
Branxholme Vic. 228 E6
Branxton NSW 109 E1, 117 M3

Brawlin NSW 115 B3, 116 D11
Bray Junction SA 293 F10
Bray Park Qld 478 B2
Braybrook Vic. 208 G7
Breadalbane NSW 115 F4, 116 H11
Breadalbane Tas. 541 O11, 545 M9
Break O Day Vic. 213 M2, 226 E1, 234 H12
Breakfast Creek NSW 115 D1, 116 E8
Breakfast Creek NSW 116 I4
Breakfast Creek Qld 478 H10, 417, 419
Breakwater Vic. 218 H12
Bream Creek Tas. 539 N5, 543 O8
Breamlea Vic. 212 G11, 219 F9, 226 A7, 229 R8, 196
Brecon SA 293 G6
Bredbo NSW 115 E8, 138 G8, 237 N1
Breelong NSW 116 F1, 118 D13
Breeza NSW 118 I11
Bremer Bay WA 366 G11, **315**
Brendale Qld 478 C4
Brentwood SA 294 H9, 266
Brentwood Vic. 230 G4
Brentwood WA 352 H10
Breona Tas. 543 J1, 545 J10
Bretti NSW 119 M13
Brewarrina NSW 121 Q5, **50**
Brewongle NSW 100 C5
Brewster Vic. 212 A3, 223 J10
Briagolong Vic. 227 N4, 236 C13, 183, 193
Bribbaree NSW 115 B1, 116 C9
Bribie Island National Park Qld 483 N3, 486 I13, 420, 429, 430, 431, **433**
Bridge Creek Vic. 224 C9
Bridge Inn Vic. 222 C4, 231 J11
Bridgeman Downs Qld 478 E5
Bridgenorth Tas. 541 M9, 545 L8
Bridgetown WA 360 C3, 364 D10, 366 D11, **315**, 319
Bridgewater SA 247
Bridgewater Tas. 538 H3, 543 L7, **512**
Bridgewater on Loddon Vic. 231 P9, 234 A7, 178, 197
Bridport Tas. 541 R2, 545 N6, **512**, 525, 529
Brigalow Qld 491 L7
Bright Vic. 225 L5, 235 P8, 236 C6, 147, **164–5**, 186
Brighton Qld 478 H2
Brighton SA 284 E13, 288 A11, 289 E2, 245
Brighton Tas. 538 H3, 543 L7, 526
Brighton Vic. 209 L13, 211 A1, 213 J7, 226
Brighton-Le-Sands NSW 99 M6, 101 N9
Brightwaters NSW 101 Q1
Brim Vic. 122 E13, 230 H5
Brimbago SA 293 H6, 295 P13
Brimboal Vic. 228 C3
Brimin Vic. 123 O13, 235 M4
Bringagee NSW 123 M8
Bringalbert Vic. 230 B10, 293 I8
Bringelly NSW 101 K9
Brinkin NT 400 E2
Brinkley SA 288 H13
Brinkworth SA 295 K5
Brisbane Qld 476, 478 F12, 491 P9, 413, **416–21**, 426, 463
Brisbane Ranges National Park Vic. 212 F6, 219 C2, 223 P13, 229 Q5, 158, 173
Brisbane Water National Park NSW 101 O4, 104 D9, 46, **59**, 63, 90
Brit Brit Vic. 228 E3
Brittons Swamp Tas. 544 C4
Brixton Qld 492 B11, 499 Q11
Broad Arrow WA 366 I5, 331

Broadbeach Qld 483 O13, 485 F6, 423
Broadbeach Waters 485 E6
Broadford Vic. 213 K1, 234 G11, **165**
Broadmarsh Tas. 538 G3, 543 L7, 526
Broadmeadows Vic. 209 J2
Broadview SA 285 J2
Broadwater NSW 119 Q3, 491 Q13
Broadwater Vic. 228 G7
Broadwater National Park NSW 119 Q4, 491 Q13, 61
Brocklehurst NSW 116 E2
Brocklesby NSW 123 P12, 235 O2
Brockman National Park WA 360 C8
Brodies Plains NSW 119 K6
Brodribb River Vic. 237 K12
Brogo NSW 113 F6, 115 G10, 237 Q5
Broke NSW 117 L4, 80
Broken Hill NSW 120 B12, 29, 31, **50–1**, 73, 272
Bromelton Qld 483 L12
Bromley Vic. 223 L3
Brompton SA 282 A2, 284 H5
Bronte NSW 95 P12, 99 R2
Bronte Park Tas. 542 I3, 544 I13
Bronzewing Vic. 232 H10
Brookfield NSW 108 C3
Brookfield Qld 480 B3
Brooklands Qld 482 E1, 491 N7
Brooklyn NSW 101 O5, 104 E11, 46
Brooklyn Vic. 208 F8
Brooklyn Park SA 284 F7
Brooks Creek NT 402 G10
Brookside Vic. 225 K5
Brookstead Qld 482 B9
Brookton WA 364 F5, 366 D8, **315**
Brookvale NSW 95 P3, 97 N13
Brookville Vic. 115 A12, 227 Q1, 236 F10
Broome WA 370 G9, 305, **315–16**, 344
Broomehill WA 361 M2, 364 H9, 366 E11
Broomfield Vic. 212 D2, 223 M9, 229 P2, 231 P13, 234 A12
Brooms Head NSW 119 Q6
Brooweena Qld 491 O4, 454
Broughton Vic. 230 C6
Broula NSW 116 E8
Broulee NSW 115 H7, 139 N8
Brown Hill Vic. 221 I4
Brownlow SA 288 I1, 295 M7
Brownlow Hill NSW 101 J10, 112 E1
Browns Plains Qld 481 J11
Browns Plains Vic. 235 O3, 236 A1
Bruarong Vic. 235 P6, 236 B4
Bruce ACT 136 E7, 127
Bruce SA 291 C12, 297 J11, 272
Bruce Rock WA 364 I3, 366 F8
Brucefield SA 294 I5
Brucknell Vic. 217 A8
Bruckunga SA 288 E10
Brungle NSW 115 C5, 116 D12, 138 A1
Brunkerville NSW 108 E10
Brunswick Vic. 209 K6
Brunswick Heads NSW 119 Q2, 491 Q12, **51**
Brunswick Junction WA 357 H4, 364 C7
Brunswick West Vic. 209 J6
Bruny Island Tas. 510, **512**
Brushgrove NSW 119 P5, 64, 72, 90
Bruthen Vic. 227 Q3, 236 G12, 189
Bryden Qld 483 J6
Brymaroo Qld 482 D5, 491 N8
Buangor Vic. 158
Buaraba Qld 482 H6

Buaraba Creek Qld 482 I7
Bucasia Qld 493 L5
Bucca Qld 491 O2
Buccarumbi NSW 119 N6
Buccleuch SA 293 F3, 295 O11
Buchan Vic. 115 B13, 236 I11, **165**, 189
Buchan South Vic. 115 B13, 236 H11, 165
Bucheen Creek Vic. 115 A9, 236 F4
Buckenderra NSW 114 H7, 115 D8, 138 D10, 237 L2, 44
Bucketty NSW 101 N1, 117 L5
Buckety Plain Vic. 225 P8
Buckingham SA 293 H6
Buckland Qld 482 F1
Buckland Tas. 539 M2, 543 N7, **512**
Buckland Vic. 225 K6, 235 P9, 236 B7
Buckleboo SA 294 E2, 296 D12
Buckley Vic. 212 E10, 219 C8
Buckleys Swamp Vic. 228 G6
Buckrabanyule Vic. 231 N6
Budawang National Park NSW 115 H5, 116 I13, 139 N4
Buddabaddah NSW 116 A1, 121 R11
Budderoo National Park NSW 112 E9, 49, **60**, 80
Buddigower NSW 116 A8, 123 Q6
Buddina Qld 486 I10
Buderim Qld 483 N1, 486 G9, 491 Q7, 421, **428**
Budgee Qld 482 F10
Budgee Budgee NSW 116 H3
Budgeree Vic. 227 J8
Budgeree East Vic. 227 J8
Budgerum Vic. 231 N3, 233 N13
Budgewoi NSW 101 Q2, 108 H13, 117 M5
Buffalo Vic. 226 I10
Buffalo River Vic. 224 I3
Buffalo River South Vic. 224 I5
Bugaldie NSW 118 E11
Bugilbone NSW 118 D7
Builyan Qld 491 M1
Bukalong NSW 113 A8, 115 E11, 237 N6
Bukkulla NSW 119 K5
Bulahdelah NSW 117 O3, **52**
Bulart Vic. 228 F4
Buldah Vic. 115 E12, 237 M9
Bulga NSW 105 A10, 117 L3, 119 N12
Bulgandramine NSW 116 D3
Bulgandry NSW 123 P12, 235 O1
Bulgobac Tas. 544 E9
Bulimba Qld 478 H11
Bull Creek SA 290 G6
Bull Creek WA 352 I10
Bulla Vic. 212 I5, 226 C3, 158
Bullaburra NSW 100 I7, 102 I8
Bullarah NSW 118 F5
Bullaring WA 364 H5
Bullarook Vic. 212 D4, 223 N10, 229 P3, 234 B13
Bullarto Vic. 212 F3, 223 P9
Bullarto South Vic. 212 F3, 223 P9
Bulleen Vic. 209 O6
Bullengarook Vic. 212 G4
Bullengarook East Vic. 212 G3
Bulleringa National Park Qld 494 I8
Bullfinch WA 366 G6, 345
Bullhead Creek Vic. 235 R6, 236 D4
Bulli NSW 101 M13, 112 H5, 117 K9
Bullio NSW 100 G13, 115 H2, 116 I9
Bullioh Vic. 235 R5, 236 E2, 195
Bullock Creek Qld 495 J8

Bullocks Flat NSW 68
Bullsbrook WA 356 D2, 364 D3, 328
Bullumwaal Vic. 115 A13, 227 P3, 236 F12
Buln Buln Vic. 213 P9, 226 H6
Buln Buln East Vic. 213 Q9, 226 I6
Bulwer Qld 483 P5
Bulyee WA 364 G5
Bumbaldry NSW 115 C1, 116 E8
Bumberry NSW 116 E6
Bumbunga SA 295 K5
Bunbartha Vic. 234 H5
Bunburra Qld 483 J12
Bunbury WA 357 F4, 364 C8, 366 C10, **316**, 319
Bundaberg Qld 491 O2, **428**, 430
Bundaburrah NSW 116 C7
Bundalaguah Vic. 227 M6
Bundall Qld 485 E6, 423
Bundalong Vic. 123 O13, 235 L3
Bundalong South Vic. 123 O13, 235 L4
Bundamba Qld 418
Bundanoon NSW 112 A9, 115 H3, 117 J10, 49, **52**, 77
Bundarra NSW 119 K7
Bundeena NSW 101 O11
Bundella NSW 118 H12
Bunding Vic. 212 E4, 223 P11
Bundjalung National Park NSW 119 Q4, 491 Q13, **59**, 61, 64, 67
Bundook NSW 117 N1, 119 M13
Bundoora Vic. 209 N3
Bundure NSW 123 N10
Bung Bong Vic. 223 J5
Bunga NSW 113 G6, 115 G10, 237 R5
Bungador Vic. 217 D8
Bungal Vic. 212 E5, 223 O13
Bungalow Qld 488 E12
Bungarby NSW 115 E10, 237 M6
Bungaree Vic. 212 D4, 223 N11, 229 P3, 234 B13, 161
Bungeet Vic. 235 L5
Bungendore NSW 115 F5, 116 H12, 135 I3, 139 J2, 79, 131, 132
Bungil Vic. 235 R3, 236 E1
Bungle Bungle National Park see Purnululu National Park
Bungonia NSW 115 G4, 116 I11
Bungowannah NSW 123 P13, 235 O3, 236 B1
Bungulla NSW 119 M4, 491 N13
Bungulla WA 364 H3
Bunguluke Vic. 231 M5
Bungunya Qld 118 G1, 490 I11
Bungwahl NSW 117 P3, 62
Buninyong Vic. 212 C5, 223 M12, 229 O4, 161, 162
Bunkers Hill Qld 482 D8
Bunnaloo NSW 123 K12, 234 E2
Bunnan NSW 117 K1
Buntine WA 366 D5
Bunya Qld 478 B7
Bunya Mountains National Park Qld 482 D1, 491 M7, 421, 441, 450, **456**, 460
Bunyah NSW 117 O2
Bunyan NSW 113 A1, 115 E8, 138 G10, 237 N2
Bunyip Vic. 213 O9, 226 G6
Buraja NSW 123 O12, 235 M2
Burbank Qld 481 M4
Burbong NSW 135 H4, 138 I3
Burcher NSW 116 B7, 123 R5

Burekup WA 357 H4, 364 C8
Burgooney NSW 123 P4
Burke & Wills Roadhouse Qld 494 A12, 497 G12
Burkes Flat Vic. 231 N9
Burketown Qld 497 E9, **430**, 474
Burleigh Head National Park Qld 483 O13, 485 F8, 423
Burleigh Heads Qld 483 O13, 485 F8, 491 Q10, 423
Burleigh Waters Qld 485 F8
Burnbank Vic. 212 A1, 223 J7
Burnett Heads Qld 491 O2, 428
Burnie Tas. 544 G6, 505, **512**, 514, 532
Burns WA 356 B3
Burns Beach WA 356 B2
Burns Creek Tas. 545 N9
Burnside Qld 469
Burnside SA 285 M7
Burnt Yards NSW 116 F7
Buronga NSW 232 G3, 88
Burpengary Qld 483 M5, 491 P8
Burra SA 295 L5, **252–3**
Burra Boogie Qld 466
Burraboi NSW 123 J11, 231 R1, 233 R11
Burracoppin WA 366 F7
Burradoo NSW 112 C7
Burraga NSW 100 B9, 115 F1, 116 H8
Burragate NSW 113 D10, 115 F11, 237 P8
Burramine Vic. 235 K3
Burramine South Vic. 235 K4
Burrandana NSW 116 B13, 123 R11
Burraneer NSW 99 L13
Burrawang NSW 112 D8, 115 I3, 117 J10
Burraway NSW 116 D1
Burrell Creek NSW 117 O1, 119 N13
Burren Junction NSW 118 E7
Burrereo Vic. 231 J8
Burrier NSW 112 C12
Burrill Lake NSW 115 I6, 117 J13, 139 P4
Burringbar NSW 119 Q2, 491 Q11
Burrinjuck NSW 115 D4, 116 E11
Burroin Vic. 230 H2, 232 H13
Burrowa-Pine Mountain National Park Vic. 115 A8, 236 F2, 168
Burrowye Vic. 115 A8, 236 E1
Burrum Vic. 231 J9
Burrum Coast National Park Qld 491 O3, 430, 432, **457**
Burrum Heads Qld 491 P3, **430**, 444, 454
Burrum River National Park Qld 491 P3
Burrumbeet Vic. 212 B3, 223 K9, 229 N3
Burrumboot Vic. 234 F7
Burrumbuttock NSW 123 P12, 235 P2
Burton SA 287 J3
Burwood NSW 94 H10
Burwood Vic. 209 O10
Burwood East Vic. 209 P10
Bushfield Vic. 228 I9
Bushy Park Tas. 538 D3, 543 J7
Bushy Park Vic. 227 M5
Busselton WA 357 D7, 359 F3, 364 B9, 366 C10, **316**, **318**, 319
Butchers Ridge Vic. 115 C12, 236 I9
Bute SA 295 J5
Butler Tanks SA 294 E6
Butlers Gorge Tas. 542 H4, 544 H13
Butmaroo NSW 139 J2
Butterfly Gorge National Park NT 406 F8
Buxton NSW 101 J12, 112 D3, 115 I2, 117 J9
Buxton Qld 491 P3, 430

Buxton Vic. 213 O3, 216 H1, 226 G1, 235 J12, 184
Byabarra NSW 105 D8, 119 O12
Byaduk Vic. 228 F6
Byawatha Vic. 235 N5
Byfield National Park Qld 493 O9
Byford WA 356 D7, 364 D4
Bylands Vic. 213 J2
Bylong NSW 116 I3
Bymount Qld 490 G5
Byrne Vic. 224 F3
Byrneside Vic. 234 G6
Byrneville Vic. 230 H8
Byrock NSW 121 P7
Byron Bay NSW 119 R2, 491 R12, 46, **52**
Bywong NSW 115 F5, 116 G12, 135 H2, 138 I1, 79

Cabarita NSW 94 H9
Cabarlah Qld 482 F7, 491 N9, 470
Cabawin Qld 491 K8
Cabbage Tree Creek Vic. 237 K12, 189
Cabbage Tree Point Qld 483 O10
Caboolture Qld 483 M4, 491 P8, **430**
Caboonbah Qld 482 I5
Cabramatta NSW 98 B2, 101 M8
Cabramurra NSW 114 C4, 138 B8, 237 J1
Caddens Flat Vic. 228 F2, 230 F13
Cadell SA 295 O6
Cadney Homestead SA 301 P8, 279
Cadoux WA 366 D6
Cahills Crossing Border Store NT 401 I3, 403 Q2, 406 H5
Caiguna WA 367 N8, **318**
Cairns Qld 488, 495 N6, 413, 414, **430–1**, 448, 449, 463
Cairns Bay Tas. 538 E10, 543 K10
Cairns North Qld 488 G6
Calala NSW 82
Calamvale Qld 480 I9
Calca SA 303 P13
Calder Tas. 544 F6
Caldwell NSW 123 J12, 234 D1
Calen Qld 493 K4
Calga NSW 101 O4, 104 C7
Calingiri WA 364 E1
Caliph SA 295 P8
Calivil Vic. 231 Q6, 234 B5
Callala Bay NSW 115 I4, 117 K11, 139 R1
Callawadda Vic. 222 C2, 231 J10
Calleen NSW 116 A7, 123 Q5
Callide Qld 491 K1, 493 N13
Callignee Vic. 227 K8
Callignee North Vic. 227 L8
Callington SA 288 F12, 293 D2, 295 M10
Calliope Qld 493 P12
Caloona NSW 118 F3, 490 I12
Caloote SA 288 I10
Caloundra Qld 483 N2, 486 I13, 491 Q7, 429, **431**
Caltowie SA 295 K3, 297 K13
Calulu Vic. 227 P4, 236 E13
Calvert Qld 482 I9
Calvert Vic. 222 B10
Calwell ACT 137 E11
Camballin WA 371 J9
Cambarville Vic. 213 P4
Camberwell NSW 117 L3
Camberwell Vic. 209 N9, 145
Cambewarra NSW 112 D11, 115 I4, 117 J11
Cambrai SA 288 I6, 295 M8

Cambrian Hill Vic. 212 C4, 223 L12
Cambridge Tas. 537 O4, 539 J5, 543 M8
Cambroon Bridge Qld 483 K1
Camburinga NT 407 O6
Camdale Tas. 544 G5
Camden NSW 101 K10, 112 F1, 115 I1, 117 K8, 43, **52**, 81
Camden Park SA 284 F10
Camellia NSW 94 D7
Camena Tas. 544 G6
Camira Qld 480 D10
Camira Creek NSW 119 P4, 491 P13
Cammeray NSW 95 M7
Camooweal Qld 409 R11, 498 B2, **431**, 459
Camooweal Caves National Park Qld 409 R11, 498 B2, **431**
Camp Hill Qld 479 J13, 481 J2
Campania Tas. 539 J3, 543 M7, 527
Campbell ACT 134 H6, 136 I10, 130
Campbell Town Tas. 543 M2, 545 N12, **513**, 515, 525
Campbellfield Vic. 209 K2
Campbells Bridge Vic. 222 C3, 231 J11
Campbells Creek Vic. 223 P5, 231 Q12, 234 C10
Campbells Forest Vic. 231 Q9, 234 B7
Campbells Pocket Qld 483 L4
Campbells River NSW 100 C9
Campbelltown NSW 101 L10, 112 G1, 117 K8, 43, **52-3**
Campbelltown SA 285 M3
Campbelltown Vic. 212 D1, 223 N6, 229 P1, 231 P12, 234 A11
Camperdown NSW 95 K11, 99 M1
Camperdown Vic. 217 C5, 229 L8, **165**, 204
Campsie NSW 94 H13, 99 J3
Camurra NSW 118 H5
Canada Bay NSW 94 H10
Canadian Vic. 221 H9
Canary Island Vic. 231 P4, 234 A3
Canary Island South Vic. 231 O5, 234 A4
Canbelego NSW 121 O10
Canberra ACT 115 E5, 116 F12, 135 I4, 136 G11, 137 E2, 138 G2, **125-32**
Candelo NSW 113 E8, 115 G10, 237 P6, 47
Cangai NSW 119 O5
Cania Gorge National Park Qld 491 L2, **457**, 459
Caniambo Vic. 235 J6
Canimble NSW 116 E7
Canley Heights NSW 98 A1
Canley Vale NSW 98 B1
Cann River Vic. 115 E13, 237 N11, **165**
Canna WA 366 C4
Cannawigara SA 293 H6
Cannie Vic. 231 M3, 233 M13
Canning Qld 483 M5
Canning Vale WA 353 K12
Cannington WA 353 L7, 356 C5
Cannon Qld 479 J11
Cannon Creek Qld 483 J13
Cannon Hill Qld 479 J11
Cannons Creek Vic. 213 M10, 215 Q3
Cannonvale Qld 493 K2, **431**
Cannum Vic. 230 G6
Canomodine NSW 116 F6
Canonba NSW 118 A12, 121 R9
Canoona Qld 464
Canowie Vic. 295 L4
Canowindra NSW 116 E7, **53**
Canterbury NSW 94 I12, 99 K2
Canterbury Vic. 209 O9

Canunda National Park SA 293 G11, 252, 266
Canungra Qld 483 M12
Capalaba Qld 481 O3, 483 N8
Cape Arid National Park WA 367 K10, 326
Cape Barren Island Tas. 542 A13, 545 Q2, 531
Cape Bridgewater Vic. 228 C9
Cape Clear Vic. 212 B6, 229 N5
Cape Crawford Roadhouse NT 409 N4
Cape Hillsborough National Park Qld 452, 457, **458**
Cape Horn Vic. 217 F12
Cape Jaffa SA 260
Cape Jervis SA 289 B9, 293 A4, 295 J11, 240, 280
Cape Le Grand National Park WA 367 J11, **323**, 326
Cape Melville National Park Qld 496 H12
Cape Palmerston National Park Qld 493 L6, 452
Cape Paterson Vic. 226 G10
Cape Range National Park WA 365 B3, **323**, 326
Cape Schanck Vic. 214 G11, 154
Cape Tribulation National Park *see* Daintree National Park
Cape Upstart National Park Qld 492 I1
Cape York Peninsula Qld 494 F2, 496 C10, 414, 431, **453**, 455, 458, 463
Capel WA 357 F6, 359 I1, 364 C8, 366 C10
Capella Qld 492 I10, 441
Capels Crossing Vic. 231 P2, 233 P13, 234 A1
Capertee NSW 100 E1, 116 I5
Capricorn Region Qld 492, **469**
Capricorn Roadhouse WA 368 E6
Captain Billy Landing Qld 496 D5
Captains Flat NSW 115 F6, 116 H13, 135 I8, 138 I5
Carabost NSW 115 A6
Caragabal NSW 116 C8
Caralue SA 294 E4
Caralulup Vic. 212 B1, 223 K6
Caramut Vic. 228 I6
Carapooee Vic. 231 M9, 192
Carapook Vic. 228 D4
Caravan Head NSW 98 I8
Carawa SA 303 P10
Carboor Vic. 224 G3, 235 N7, 236 A5, 198
Carboor Upper Vic. 224 G3
Carbrook Qld 481 R10
Carbunup River WA 357 C8, 359 D3
Carcoar NSW 116 G7, 49
Carcuma SA 293 F4, 295 O12
Cardiff NSW 108 F8
Cardigan Village Vic. 212 B3, 223 K10, 229 O3
Cardinia Vic. 213 M9, 226 F6, 180
Cardross Vic. 122 D7, 232 G4
Cardstone Vic. 470
Cardwell Qld 495 N10, **431**, 449, 471
Careel Bay NSW 97 Q4
Carey Gully SA 285 R9
Cargerie Vic. 212 D6, 219 B2, 229 P5
Cargo NSW 116 F7
Carina Qld 479 J13, 481 J1
Carinda NSW 118 A8
Carindale Qld 479 K13, 481 K1
Carine WA 354 D7
Caringbah NSW 99 K11
Carisbrook Vic. 223 M5, 231 O11, 234 A10

Carlingford NSW 94 E4
Carlisle WA 353 L5
Carlisle River Vic. 212 A13, 217 E9, 229 M10
Carlsruhe Vic. 212 G2, 229 R2, 231 R13, 234 D11, 180, 202
Carlton NSW 99 K7
Carlton Tas. 539 L6, 543 N8
Carlton Vic. 206 E2, 209 K8, 145, 151
Carlwood NSW 100 E6
Carmelicup WA 364 G8
Carmila Qld 493 L7
Carnamah WA 366 C5, **318**
Carnarvon WA 365 B8, 306, **318**
Carnarvon National Park Qld 490 D2, 413, 441, 446, 455, **458**, 466, 467, 469
Carnegie Vic. 209 N12
Carnegie Roadhouse WA 368 I10
Carngham Vic. 212 B4, 223 J11
Caroda NSW 118 I7
Carole Park Qld 480 D9
Caroline SA 228 A6, 293 I12
Caroling WA 364 G4
Caroona NSW 118 I12
Carpa SA 294 F5
Carpendeit Vic. 217 D7
Carpenter Rocks SA 293 G12
Carrajung Vic. 227 L8
Carrajung South Vic. 227 L8
Carramar WA 354 A4, 98 C1
Carranballac Vic. 222 F13
Carranya Roadhouse WA 371 P11
Carrara Qld 485 D6, 460
Carraragarmungee Vic. 235 N5, 236 A3
Carrathool NSW 123 M8
Carrick Tas. 541 M12, 545 L9, 505, 519, 532
Carrickalinga SA 289 D6
Carrieton SA 291 D12, 297 K11, 280
Carrington NSW 106 E4
Carroll NSW 118 I10
Carroll Gap NSW 118 I10
Carron Vic. 231 J6
Carrow Brook NSW 117 L2
Carrowidgin NSW 115 D11, 237 L8
Carrs Creek Junction NSW 119 P6
Carrum Vic. 211 D9
Carrum Downs Vic. 211 G10
Carseldine Qld 478 F5
Carss Park NSW 99 K8
Carwarp Vic. 122 D8, 232 G5
Cascade WA 366 I10
Cascades Tas. 536 E9
Cashmere Qld 478 A4
Cashmore Vic. 228 D9
Casino NSW 119 P3, 491 P12, **53**
Cassady Beach Qld 495 O11
Cassilis NSW 116 I1, 73
Cassilis Vic. 115 A12, 236 F9, 188
Castambul SA 285 Q2, 287 R13, 288 D9
Castella Vic. 213 M4, 216 C3
Casterton Vic. 228 C4, **165-6**, 204
Castle Cove NSW 95 N5
Castle Forbes Bay Tas. 538 E9, 543 K10
Castle Hill NSW 94 D1, 96 B11, 101 M7
Castle Hill Qld 487 D3
Castlemaine Vic. 223 P5, 231 Q11, 234 C10, 142, 161, 163, **166**, 173
Castlereagh NSW 46
Casuarina NT 400 G4, 402 C2, 378
Casula NSW 98 A6
Cataby Roadhouse WA 366 B6

Catamaran Tas. 543 J13
Catani Vic. 213 N10
Cathcart NSW 113 B8, 115 F11, 237 O7
Cathcart Vic. 222 C8
Cathedral Rock National Park NSW 119 M8, 45
Catherine Field NSW 101 K10
Catherine Hill Bay NSW 101 R1, 108 H11, 117 M5
Catherine Station Vic. 225 J8
Cathkin Vic. 213 N1
Cathundral NSW 116 C1, 118 B13
Cattai NSW 101 M5
Cattai National Park NSW 101 M5, 89
Catumnal Vic. 231 N5
Caulfield Vic. 209 M11
Cavan NSW 115 E4, 116 F11
Cavan SA 286 I10
Caveat Vic. 234 I10, 204
Cavendish Vic. 228 G3
Caversham WA 355 P8
Caveside Tas. 540 F13, 544 I9, 513
Cawdor NSW 101 K11, 112 E2
Cawdor Qld 482 E7
Cawongla NSW 119 P2, 491 Q12
Cecil Park NSW 101 L8
Cecil Plains Qld 491 M9
Cedar Bay National Park Qld 495 M4
Cedar Brush NSW 101 O1
Cedar Brush Creek NSW 101 O1
Cedar Grove Qld 483 L11
Cedar Party Creek NSW 105 B11, 119 N13
Ceduna SA 303 N9, **253**, 256, 333
Cement Creek Vic. 213 O5, 216 H8, 226 G3
Centennial Park NSW 95 O11, 99 Q1, 40
Central Castra Tas. 540 B7, 544 H7
Central Colo NSW 101 K4
Central McDonald NSW 101 M3
Central Mangrove NSW 101 O2, 104 B4
Central Tilba NSW 113 H3, 115 H9, 139 M12, 237 R3, 48, 75
Ceratodus Qld 491 L3
Ceres NSW 116 D2
Ceres Vic. 212 F9, 219 D7, 229 Q8, 173
Cervantes WA 366 B6
Cessnock NSW 108 B10, 109 E12, 117 M4, **53-4**
Chadstone Vic. 209 O12
Chain Of Lagoons Tas. 543 Q1, 545 Q10
Chain Of Ponds SA 288 D8
Chakola NSW 138 G10
Challambra Vic. 230 I6
Chambigne NSW 119 O6
Chandada SA 294 A1, 303 Q12
Chandler Qld 479 N13, 481 N2
Chandler SA 301 N4
Chandlers Creek Vic. 115 E12, 237 M10
Chandlers Hill SA 290 E3
Channel Country Qld 498 D12, 427, **472**
Chapel Hill Qld 480 D3
Chapman ACT 137 A5
Chapman Hill WA 357 D8, 359 F5, 364 B9
Chapple Vale Vic. 229 L11
Charam Vic. 230 D11
Charleston SA 288 E9
Charlestown NSW 108 G8, 117 M5
Charleville Qld 490 B6, **431-2**
Charley Creek Vic. 217 F10
Charleyong NSW 115 G5, 116 I12, 139 M2
Charleys Creek Vic. 212 A13

Charlotte Pass NSW 114 D12, 115 C9, 138 A12, 237 J4, 60, 65
Charlton NSW 121 Q5
Charlton Vic. 231 M6, **166**
Charnwood ACT 136 B3
Charringa Qld 489 G11
Charters Towers Qld 492 E2, **432**
Chatham Village NSW 98 A5
Chatsbury NSW 115 G3, 116 I10
Chatswood NSW 95 L5, 101 O8
Chatsworth NSW 119 Q5
Chatsworth Vic. 228 I6
Cheepie Qld 501 Q7, 462
Cheesemans Creek NSW 116 F5
Chelmer Qld 480 E3
Chelsea Vic. 211 D8, 213 K8
Chelsea Heights Vic. 211 F7
Cheltenham NSW 94 G3, 96 E12
Cheltenham SA 284 E2, 245
Cheltenham Vic. 211 C3
Chepstowe Vic. 212 A4, 222 I11
Cherbourg Aboriginal Community Qld 460
Chermside Qld 478 F7, 483 L7
Chermside West Qld 478 E7
Cherokee Vic. 212 H2
Cherrybrook NSW 96 D10
Cherryville SA 285 R5
Cheshunt Vic. 224 G6, 235 N9, 184, 198
Chesney Vale Vic. 235 L6
Chester Hill NSW 94 C11, 98 E1
Chesterton Range National Park Qld 490 E6
Chetwynd Vic. 228 C2, 230 C13
Chevoit Vic. 213 M1
Chewton Vic. 223 Q5, 231 Q11, 234 C10, 166
Cheyne Beach WA 361 Q11
Chidlow WA 356 F4, 364 D3
Chifley ACT 137 C5
Chifley NSW 99 Q6
Chifley WA 367 K6
Chigwell Tas. 536 B1
Childers Qld 491 O3, **432**
Childers Vic. 213 Q11, 226 I8, 203
Chillagoe Qld 495 K7, **434**, 452
Chillagoe-Mungana Caves National Park Qld 495 J7, 434–5, **458**
Chillingham NSW 119 Q1
Chillingollah Vic. 122 G10, 233 L10
Chiltern Vic. 123 P13, 235 O4, 236 A2, 160, **166–7**
Chiltern Valley Vic. 123 P13, 235 N4, 236 A2
Chinaman Wells SA 293 F10
Chinchilla Qld 491 K7, **434**
Chindera NSW 485 I13
Chinderah NSW 119 Q1, 491 Q11
Chinkapook Vic. 122 F10, 233 K10
Chintin Vic. 212 I3
Chipping Norton NSW 94 A13, 98 C4
Chirnside Park Vic. 210 D6
Chisholm ACT 137 F9
Chiswick NSW 95 J9
Chittering WA 364 D2
Chorregon Qld 499 N9
Christies Beach SA 289 E3, 246, 268
Christmas Creek Vic. 225 R6
Christmas Hills Tas. 544 C4
Christmas Hills Vic. 210 E1, 213 L5, 216 A5
Chudleigh Tas. 540 F12, 544 I9

Chullora NSW 94 E11, 98 G1
Church Point NSW 97 O5
Churchill Vic. 227 K8
Churchill Island National Park Vic. 213 L13, 215 Q12, 169
Churchill National Park Vic. 211 I3, 213 L7, 226 E5
Churchlands WA 352 D1, 354 D12
Chute Vic. 222 H8, 229 M2, 231 M13
City Beach WA 352 C3, 356 A4
Clackline WA 356 G2, 364 E3, 340
Clairview Qld 493 L7
Clandulla NSW 116 I4
Clapham SA 285 J11
Clare Qld 492 G1
Clare SA 295 K5, 246, **253–4**
Clare Valley SA 241, 246, 249, 253, 259, 270
Claremont Tas. 538 H4, 543 L8, 509
Claremont Vic. 224 F3
Claremont WA 352 D5
Clarence NSW 100 G4
Clarence Park SA 284 H9
Clarence Point Tas. 541 J4, 545 K6
Clarence Town NSW 108 D3, 117 N3, 61
Clarendon Qld 483 J7
Clarendon SA 288 B12, 289 G3, 290 E3, 293 B2, 295 K10
Clarendon Tas. 541 P13, 545 M10
Clarendon Vic. 212 D5, 223 N13
Clarendon Vale Tas. 537 O8
Clareville NSW 97 Q5
Clarinda Vic. 211 D2
Clarkefield Vic. 212 I3, 226 B2
Clarkes Hill Vic. 212 D3, 223 N10
Clarkfield Vic. 234 E13
Claude Road Tas. 540 D10, 544 H8
Clay Wells SA 293 G10
Clayfield Qld 478 H9
Claypans SA 293 E1, 295 N9
Clayton Qld 491 O2
Clayton Vic. 211 E2
Clear Island Waters Qld 485 D7
Clear Lake Vic. 230 F11
Clear Mountain Qld 478 A5
Clear Ridge NSW 116 B7, 123 R5
Clearview SA 285 J1, 287 J12
Cleaverville WA 345
Clematis Vic. 213 M7, 216 C13
Clements Gap SA 295 J4
Clemton Park NSW 94 H13, 99 J3
Clermont Qld 492 H9, **434**
Cleve SA 294 F5, **254**
Cleveland Qld 483 O8, 491 Q9, **434**, 463
Cleveland Tas. 543 M1, 545 M11
Clifton NSW 101 M12, 112 I4
Clifton Qld 482 E11, 491 N10, **434**
Clifton Beach Qld 489 E7, 462
Clifton Beach Tas. 539 J8, 543 M9, 529
Clifton Creek Vic. 227 Q3, 236 F12
Clifton Gardens NSW 95 O8
Clifton Hill Vic. 209 L7
Clifton Springs Vic. 212 H9, 219 G7, 226 A6, 170
Clinton Centre SA 295 J7
Clintonvale Qld 482 F12, 491 O10
Clonbinane Vic. 213 K2
Cloncurry Qld 498 G4, **434–5**, 454
Clontarf NSW 95 P6
Clontarf Qld 463
Closeburn Qld 483 L6
Clouds Creek NSW 119 N7

Cloudy Bay Tas. 512
Clovelly NSW 95 P13, 99 R3, 101 O9
Clovelly Park SA 284 G13
Cloven Hills Vic. 217 C4
Cloverdale WA 353 M4
Cloyna Qld 491 N5
Club Terrace Vic. 115 D13, 237 M11
Cluan Tas. 541 K13, 545 K9
Cluden Qld 487 H12
Clumber Qld 482 H12
Clunes NSW 119 Q3, 491 Q12
Clunes Vic. 212 C2, 223 L7, 229 O2, 231 O13, 234 A11, 161, 162, **167**
Clybucca NSW 105 H2, 119 O10
Clyde Vic. 213 L9
Clydebank Vic. 227 N6
Clydesdale Vic. 212 E1, 223 O6
Coal Creek Qld 482 I5
Coalcliff NSW 101 M12, 112 I4, 117 K9
Coaldale NSW 119 O5
Coalstoun Lakes Qld 491 N4
Coalstoun Lakes National Park Qld 491 N4, 426
Coalville Vic. 213 R10
Cobains Vic. 227 N6
Cobaki NSW 485 G12
Cobar NSW 121 N10, **54**
Cobargo NSW 113 G4, 115 G9, 139 L13, 237 Q4, 48
Cobark NSW 117 M1, 119 L13
Cobaw Vic. 212 H2
Cobbadah NSW 118 I8
Cobbannah Vic. 227 N3, 236 D12
Cobbitty NSW 101 K10, 115 I1, 117 K8
Cobbora NSW 116 G2
Cobden Vic. 217 B2, 229 K9, 165
Cobdogla SA 295 P7, 251
Cobera SA 293 G1, 295 P8
Cobram Vic. 123 M13, 235 J3, **167**, 201, 204
Cobrico Vic. 217 B6
Cobungra Vic. 225 Q11
Coburg Vic. 209 K5, 213 J5
Cocamba Vic. 233 K9
Cochranes Creek Vic. 231 N9
Cockaleechie SA 294 D7
Cockatoo Vic. 213 M7, 216 D13, 226 F5, 172
Cockatoo Valley SA 292 A9
Cockburn SA 120 A12
Cockle Creek Tas. 543 J13, 522
Cocklebiddy WA 367 O8, **319**, 333
Coconut Grove NT 400 B6
Cocoparra National Park NSW 123 O6, 64
Codrington Vic. 228 F9
Coen Qld 496 E11
Coffin Bay SA 294 C8, **254**, 256, 271
Coffin Bay National Park SA 294 C8, 254, **264**, 271
Coffs Harbour NSW 119 P8, **54**
Coghills Creek Vic. 212 C2, 223 L8, 229 O2, 231 O13, 234 A12
Cohuna Vic. 123 J12, 231 Q3, 234 C2, **167**
Coimadai Vic. 212 G4
Colac Vic. 212 B11, 217 G7, 229 N9, **167**
Colac Colac Vic. 115 A9, 236 G3
Colbinabbin Vic. 234 F7
Colbinabbin West Vic. 234 E7
Coldstream Vic. 210 G5, 213 M5, 216 B8, 226 E3, 152, 197
Cole Crossing SA 290 F8

Coleambally NSW 123 N9, **54**
Colebrook Tas. 538 I1, 543 M6, 527
Coledale NSW 101 M13, 112 H4
Coleraine Vic. 228 E4, **168**, 177, 204
Coles Bay Tas. 543 Q4, 545 Q13, 503, 505, **513**, 521
Coleyville Qld 482 I10
Colignan Vic. 122 E8, 232 H5
Colinroobie NSW 123 P8
Colinton NSW 135 F12, 138 G7
Colinton Qld 482 I3
Collarenebri NSW 118 D5
Collaroy NSW 95 Q1, 97 P11, 101 P7, 116 I2
Collaroy Plateau NSW 95 Q1, 97 P11
Collector NSW 115 F4, 116 H11
College Park SA 282 H6, 285 K5
Collerina NSW 121 P4
Collie NSW 118 C13
Collie WA 364 D8, 366 C10, **319–20**
Collie Burn WA 364 D8
Collie Cardiff WA 364 D8
Collier Range National Park WA 368 C8
Collingullie NSW 116 A12, 123 Q10, 86
Collingwood Vic. 209 L8
Collins Cap Tas. 538 G5
Collinsfield SA 295 K4
Collinsvale Tas. 538 G5, 543 L8
Collinsville Qld 492 I3, 428
Collinswood SA 285 J4
Collombatti Rail NSW 105 F2, 119 O10
Colly Blue NSW 118 H12
Colo NSW 101 L4
Colo Heights NSW 101 K3, 117 K6
Colo Vale NSW 112 D5, 115 I2, 117 J9
Colonel Light Gardens SA 284 I11
Colquhoun NSW 227 R4, 236 H13
Colton SA 294 B4
Comara NSW 119 N9
Comaum SA 228 A2, 230 A13, 293 I10
Combara NSW 118 C11
Combienbar Vic. 115 E13, 237 M10
Comboyne NSW 105 C10, 119 N12
Come-by-chance NSW 118 D8
Comerloy Road NSW 101 K5
Comet Qld 493 J11, 427
Commissioners Flat Qld 483 L3
Como NSW 98 H9
Como WA 352 I6
Compton Downs NSW 121 P6
Conara Junction Tas. 543 M2, 545 N11
Conargo NSW 123 L11
Concord NSW 94 H8
Concordia SA 288 D5
Condah Vic. 228 E6
Codrington Vic. 228 F9
Condamine Qld 491 J7
Condell Park NSW 94 C13, 98 F3
Conder ACT 137 D12
Condingup WA 367 K10
Condobolin NSW 116 A5, 123 Q3, **54**
Condoulpe NSW 122 H9, 233 N7
Condowie SA 295 K5
Congo NSW 115 H8, 139 N9
Congupna Vic. 234 I5
Conimbla National Park NSW 116 E7, 57
Coningham Tas. 543 L10, 522
Coniston NSW 110 C12
Conjola NSW 115 I5, 117 J12, 139 P3
Conmurra SA 293 G9
Connangorach Vic. 230 F11
Connells Point NSW 99 J7
Connemarra NSW 118 G12

Connewarre Vic. 212 F10, 219 E9
Connewirricoo Vic. 228 D1, 230 D12
Conondale Qld 483 K1
Conondale National Park Qld 483 J1, 491 O7
Conway National Park Qld 493 K3, 424, 431, 462, 466, 471
Coober Pedy SA 301 R11, 239, **254–5**, 279
Coochiemudlo Island Qld 463
Coochin Creek Qld 483 M3
Cooee Tas. 544 G5
Cooeeinbardi Qld 483 J4
Coogee NSW 95 P13, 99 R3
Cooinda NT 385, 388
Coojar Vic. 228 E2, 230 E13
Cook ACT 136 D8
Cook SA 302 E4
Cookamidgera NSW 116 D5
Cookardinia NSW 123 Q12, 67
Cooke Plains SA 293 E3, 295 N11
Cooks Gap NSW 116 H2
Cooks Hill NSW 106 E8
Cooktown Qld 495 L3, **435**, 449, 462
Cookville Tas. 538 H13, 543 L11
Coolabah NSW 121 P8
Coolac NSW 115 B4, 116 D11
Cooladdi Roadhouse Qld 490 A7, 501 R7
Coolah NSW 116 H1, 118 G13
Coolalie NSW 115 E3, 116 F11
Coolamon NSW 116 B11, 123 Q9
Coolana Qld 483 J8
Coolangatta NSW 112 F12, 84
Coolangatta Qld 485 H10, 491 Q11, 422, 423, **435**
Coolangubra National Park NSW 113 C10, 115 F11, 237 O7
Coolaroo Vic. 209 J1
Coolatai NSW 119 J4, 491 L13
Coolbellup WA 352 E12
Coolbinia WA 354 H11
Coolcha SA 293 E1, 295 N9
Coolgardie WA 366 I6, 305, **320**, 331, 336
Coolimba WA 366 B5
Coolongolook NSW 117 O2
Cooloola National Park *see* Great Sandy National Park
Cooloolabin Qld 486 C6
Cooltong SA 295 Q6
Coolum Beach Qld 486 H5, 491 Q6
Coolup WA 356 C11, 364 C6
Cooma NSW 113 A2, 115 E9, 138 G11, 237 M3, **54**, **56**
Cooma Vic. 234 G6
Coomalbidgup WA 366 I10
Coomandook SA 293 E3, 295 N11
Coombabah Qld 485 D2, 423
Coombah Roadhouse NSW 122 C3
Coombe SA 293 G5, 295 P13
Coombell NSW 119 P3, 491 P13
Coomberdale WA 366 C6
Coombogolong NSW 118 B8
Coomera Qld 483 N11, 485 C1, 423, 426
Coominglah Qld 491 L2
Coominya Qld 482 I7, 491 O9, 421, 442
Coomoora Vic. 212 E2, 223 P8
Coonabarabran NSW 118 F11, **56**, 75
Coonalpyn SA 293 F4, 295 O12, **255**
Coonamble NSW 118 C10, **56**
Coonarr Qld 491 O2
Coonawarra SA 228 A2, 230 A13, 293 I10, 241, **255**, 259, 268
Coonerang NSW 113 A2, 138 G13

Coongulla Vic. 227 L5
Coongulmerang Vic. 227 O4, 236 E13
Coonong NSW 123 O10
Coonooer Bridge Vic. 231 M8
Coopernook NSW 105 D12, 117 P1, 119 O13, 82
Coopers Creek Vic. 227 K5
Coopers Plains Qld 480 I6
Cooplacurripa NSW 119 M12
Coopracambra National Park Vic. 113 A13, 115 E12, 237 N10, 189
Cooran Qld 491 P6
Cooranbong NSW 108 F12, 117 M5
Cooranga North Qld 482 B1
Coorong National Park SA 293 E5, 295 N13, 239, 240, **262**, **274**
Coorow Vic. 366 C5
Cooroy Qld 486 D2, 491 P6
Coorparoo Qld 478 I13, 480 I1
Coorpan Qld 499 M6
Cooya Beach Qld 489 B3, 495 M5
Cooyal NSW 116 H3
Cooyar Qld 482 E3, 491 N7
Cooyar Creek Upper Qld 482 E3
Cope Cope Vic. 231 L7
Copeland NSW 117 N1, 63
Copeville SA 293 F1, 295 O9
Copley SA 291 D4, 297 J4
Copmanhurst NSW 119 O5
Copocabana NSW 104 H7
Coppabella Qld 493 J7
Copping Tas. 539 N5, 543 N8, 516
Coppins Crossing ACT 136 C9
Cora Lynn Vic. 213 N9, 226 G6
Corack Vic. 231 K6
Corack East Vic. 231 K6
Coradgery NSW 116 D4
Coragulac Vic. 212 A10, 217 F6
Coraki NSW 119 Q3, 491 Q13
Coral Bank Vic. 225 M3
Coral Bay WA 365 B5, **320**
Coral Ville NSW 105 E11, 117 P1, 119 O13
Coram Vic. 217 G8
Coramba NSW 119 P8
Corang NSW 115 G5, 116 I12, 139 N2
Corattum SA 293 H12
Cordalba Qld 491 O3, 432
Cordering WA 364 E8
Coree South NSW 123 M11
Coreen NSW 123 O12, 235 M2
Corfield Qld 499 M6
Corinda Qld 480 F5
Corindhap Vic. 212 C7, 217 H1, 229 O5
Corindi NSW 119 P7
Corinella Vic. 213 M12, 226 F8
Corinna Tas. 544 C9, 505, 514, 532
Corio Vic. 219 F6
Cornella Vic. 234 E8
Cornubia Qld 481 R10
Cornwall Tas. 545 Q10
Cornwallis NSW 101 K6
Corny Point SA 294 G9
Corobimilla NSW 123 O9
Coromby Vic. 230 I8
Coronation Beach WA 366 A3
Corop Vic. 234 F6
Cororooke Vic. 212 A11, 217 F6, 229 N8
Corowa NSW 123 O13, 235 M3, **56–7**, 201
Corra Linn Tas. 541 P11, 545 M9
Corrigin WA 364 H5, 366 E8, **320**
Corrimal NSW 110 F3, 112 H5
Corringle NSW 116 B7, 123 R5

Corringle Vic. 237 J13
Corroboree Park Tavern NT 402 G5
Corryong Vic. 115 B8, 236 G2, **168**, 189
Corunna NSW 113 H3, 139 M12
Cosgrove Vic. 235 J5
Cosmo Newbery Community WA 367 K2
Cossack WA 365 G1, 368 A1, **320**, 339, 342, 345, 346
Costerfield Vic. 234 F9
Cottesloe WA 352 B6. 356 B5
Cottles Bridge Vic. 213 L4, 226 E2, 234 H13, 197
Cottonvale Qld 119 M2, 491 N11, 467
Couangalt Vic. 212 H4
Cougal NSW 119 P1
Coulson Qld 483 J12
Coulta SA 294 C7
Countegany NSW 113 C1, 138 I11, 237 O2
Courabyra NSW 115 B7
Courada NSW 118 H7
Couran Qld 483 O11
Couta Tas. 544 B6
Coutts Crossing NSW 119 P6
Cow Flat NSW 100 B6
Cowabbie West NSW 116 A10, 123 Q8
Cowan NSW 96 I2, 101 N5, 104 D12
Cowandilla SA 284 G7
Cowangie Vic. 122 B10, 232 C10
Cowaramup WA 357 C9, 359 C6, 364 A9, 335
Coward Springs SA 265
Cowell SA 294 G5, 254, **255–6**, 256
Cowes Vic. 213 L12, 215 O11, 226 E9, **168**, 169
Cowirra SA 288 I9, 293 E1, 295 N9
Cowleys Creek Vic. 217 A9
Cowper NSW 119 P5
Cowra NSW 116 E8, **57**
Cowwarr Vic. 227 L6
Coyrecup WA 361 N1, 364 H9
Crabbes Creek NSW 119 Q2, 491 Q11
Crabtree Tas. 538 F7
Cracow Qld 491 K3, 468
Cradle Mountain-Lake St Clair National Park Tas. 540 A13, 542 F2, 544 F11, 503, 504, 514, **520**, 530
Cradle Valley Tas. 544 G9
Cradoc Tas. 538 E9, 543 K10
Cradock SA 291 D10, 297 K9
Crafers SA 285 O12, 288 C10, 289 H1, 290 F1
Crafers West SA 285 N12
Craigie NSW 115 E12, 237 M8, 50
Craigie Vic. 223 L5
Craigie WA 354 B2
Craigieburn Vic. 213 J4, 226 C2, 234 F13, 151
Cramenton Vic. 232 I7
Cramps Tas. 543 J2, 545 K11
Cranbourne Vic. 213 L9, 226 E6, 180
Cranbourne South Vic. 211 H13
Cranbrook Tas. 543 P3, 545 P12
Cranbrook WA 361 L6, 364 H11, 366 E11, **320**
Crater Lakes National Park Qld 489 E12, 425, **458**
Craven NSW 117 N2
Cravensville Vic. 115 A9, 236 F4
Crawley WA 352 F5, 310
Crayfish Creek Tas. 544 E4
Crayford SA 292 E6
Creek Junction Vic. 235 K9

Creek View Vic. 234 E7
Creighton Vic. 234 I8
Creighton Creek Vic. 234 I9
Cremorne NSW 95 N7
Cremorne Tas. 539 K7, 543 M9, 508
Cremorne Point NSW 95 N8
Crescent Head NSW 105 H4, 119 P11, 69
Cressbrook Lower Qld 482 I4
Cressy Tas. 543 L1, 545 L10, 523, 524
Cressy Vic. 212 B8, 217 G3, 229 N6
Crestmead Qld 481 K12
Creswick Vic. 212 C3, 223 M9, 229 O2, 231 O13, 234 A12, 161, 162, **168**
Crib Point Vic. 213 L11, 215 N8, 226 E8
Croajingolong National Park Vic. 115 F13, 237 P12, 143, 165, **175**, 183, 189
Croftby Qld 482 I13
Crohamhurst Qld 483 L2, 486 B13
Cromer NSW 95 P1, 97 N11
Cronulla NSW 99 M12, 101 O10
Crooble NSW 118 H4, 491 K13
Crooked River Vic. 227 N2, 235 Q13, 236 C10
Crookwell NSW 115 F2, 116 H10, **57**
Croppa Creek NSW 118 I4, 491 K13
Crossdale Qld 483 J5
Crossley Vic. 228 H9
Crossman WA 356 H12, 364 E6
Crow Mountain NSW 119 J8
Crowdy Bay National Park NSW 105 E12, 117 P1, 119 O13, 70, 82
Crowdy Head NSW 105 F12
Crower SA 293 G9
Crowlands Vic. 222 F6, 229 L1, 231 L12
Crows Nest NSW 95 M7
Crows Nest Qld 482 F5, 491 N8, **435–6**
Crows Nest National Park Qld 482 G5, 435
Crowther NSW 115 C1, 116 E9
Croxton East Vic. 228 H5
Croydon NSW 94 H11, 99 J1
Croydon Qld 494 F10, 413, **436**, 474
Croydon SA 284 G4
Croydon Vic. 210 C8, 213 L6
Croydon Hills Vic. 210 C7
Croydon Park NSW 94 H11, 99 J2
Croydon Park SA 284 G3
Crymelon Vic. 230 H6
Cryon NSW 118 D7
Crystal Brook SA 295 J3, **256**
Cuballing WA 364 G6, 366 E9
Cubbaroo NSW 118 E7
Cuckoo Tas. 545 N7
Cudal NSW 116 F6
Cuddell NSW 123 O9
Cudgee Vic. 228 I9
Cudgen NSW 119 Q1, 491 Q11
Cudgera Creek NSW 119 Q1
Cudgewa Vic. 115 A8, 236 G2
Cudgewa North Vic. 115 B8, 236 G2
Cudlee Creek SA 288 D9, 247
Cudmirrah NSW 115 I5, 117 J12, 139 Q3
Cue WA 365 H13, 366 E1, 368 B13, **320–1**
Culbin WA 364 F7
Culburra NSW 112 G13, 117 K11, **57**
Culburra SA 293 F5, 295 O12
Culcairn NSW 123 Q12, 235 Q1, **57**
Culfearne Vic. 231 P2, 233 P13, 234 B1
Culgoa Vic. 122 G12, 231 L3, 233 L13
Culla Vic. 228 E1, 230 E13
Cullacabardee WA 355 J4
Cullen Bullen NSW 100 F3, 116 I6
Cullendulla NSW 115 H7, 139 O6

Culler NSW 115 F4, 116 G11
Culloden Vic. 227 N4, 236 D13
Cullulleraine Vic. 122 C7, 232 D4
Cumberland Park SA 284 H10
Cumborah NSW 118 B6
Cummins SA 294 D7
Cumnock NSW 116 F4
Cundare Vic. 212 A9, 217 F4
Cundeelee Community WA 367 L6
Cunderdin WA 364 G3, 366 E7
Cundletown NSW 105 D13
Cungena SA 294 A1, 303 Q11
Cungulla Qld 495 Q13
Cunjurong Point NSW 139 Q3
Cunliffe SA 294 I6
Cunnamulla Qld 490 A10, 501 R10, **436**
Cunningar NSW 115 C3, 116 E10
Cunningham Qld 482 D12
Cunningham SA 294 I7
Cunninyeuk NSW 122 H10, 233 O10
Cuparra NSW 119 N13
Cuprona Tas. 544 G6
Curara WA 366 C3
Curban NSW 118 D12
Curdie Vale Vic. 229 J10
Curdimurka SA 298 G13, 265
Curl Curl NSW 95 Q4, 97 O13
Curlewis NSW 118 H11
Curlwaa NSW 122 D6, 232 F2
Currabubula NSW 119 J11
Currajong Qld 487 A6
Curramulka SA 294 I8
Currarong NSW 117 K12
Currawang NSW 115 F4, 116 H11
Currawarna NSW 116 A12, 123 Q10
Currawinya National Park Qld 121 J1, 501 O12, 442
Currency Creek SA 289 H7, 290 G11, 257
Currie Tas. 542 A9, 531
Currigee Qld 483 O12, 485 E2
Currimundi Qld 486 I12
Currowan Corner Upper NSW 115 H6, 116 I13, 139 N5
Currumbin Qld 485 G10, 423, **436**
Currumbin Waters Qld 485 F10
Curtin ACT 136 E12, 137 C3
Curtin Springs NT 410 F12
Curtinye SA 294 F3, 296 E13
Curtis Island National Park Qld 493 P10, 443
Curyo Vic. 122 F12, 231 J3
Custon SA 230 A7, 293 I7
Cuttabri NSW 118 F8
Cygnet Tas. 538 F10, 543 K10, 510, **513**, 522
Cygnet River SA 294 I12
Cynthia Qld 491 L3

D'Aguilar Qld 483 L4
D'Aguilar National Park Qld 421
D'Entrecasteaux National Park WA 357 F13, 359 H13, 360 B9, 364 C12, 366 C12, 340
Daceyville NSW 99 P4
Dadswells Bridge Vic. 230 I11
Dahlen Vic. 230 G9
Dahwilly NSW 123 K11
Daintree Qld 489 A1, 495 M5, **436**, **441**
Daintree National Park Qld 489 A2, 495 L5, **458**, 459
Daisy Dell Tas. 540 A12, 544 H9
Daisy Hill Qld 481 N9

Daisy Hill Vic. 212 B1, 223 K6, 229 N1, 231 O12
Dajarra Qld 498 E6
Dakabin Qld 483 M6, 467
Dalbeg Qld 492 G3
Dalby Qld 482 A4, 491 M8, **441**, 465
Dalgety NSW 114 I12, 115 D10, 138 E13, 237 L5
Dalkeith WA 352 E7
Dallarnil Qld 491 N3
Dalma Qld 493 N11
Dalmalee Vic. 230 G5
Dalmeny NSW 113 I2, 115 H8, 139 N11, 237 R2
Dalmorton NSW 119 N6
Dalton NSW 115 E3, 116 G11
Dalveen Qld 119 M2, 491 N11
Dalwallinu WA 366 D5
Dalwood NSW 109 H1
Daly River NT 402 B12, 406 D8, 381
Daly Waters NT 408 I3, **387**
Dalyston Vic. 226 F9
Dampier WA 365 G1, **321**, 339
Dandaloo NSW 116 C2
Dandaragan WA 366 C6
Dandenong Vic. 211 G5, 213 K8, 226 D5
Dandenong Ranges National Park Vic. 210 F10, 213 L6, 216 A11, 226 E4, 141, 144, 147, 153, **156**, 172, **174**
Dandenong South Vic. 211 H6
Dandongadale Vic. 224 I6, 235 O9, 236 A6
Dangarsleigh NSW 119 L9
Dangerfield NSW 117 L2
Dangin WA 364 G4
Danyo Vic. 232 C10
Dapto NSW 112 G7
Darby Falls NSW 115 D1, 116 F8
Darbyshire Vic. 235 R4, 236 E2
Dardadine WA 364 F7
Dardanup WA 357 G5, 364 C8
Dareton NSW 122 D6, 232 F2
Dargo Vic. 227 O2, 235 R13, 236 D11, 183, 193
Dark Corner NSW 100 E3, 116 I6
Darkan WA 364 E8
Darke Peak SA 294 E4
Darkwood NSW 119 O8
Darley Vic. 212 G5, 223 R12
Darling Downs Qld 482 B6, 413, **465**
Darling Point NSW 95 O10
Darlinghurst NSW 95 N10, 36, 39, 40
Darlington Tas. 539 P2, 543 P7, 532
Darlington Vic. 217 B3, 229 K7, 170
Darlington WA 338
Darlington Point NSW 123 N8
Darnick NSW 122 H2
Darnum Vic. 213 Q10, 226 I7, 203
Daroobalgie NSW 116 D6
Darr Qld 492 A10, 499 O10
Darra Qld 480 E7
Darraweit Guim Vic. 213 J3, 226 C1, 234 F12
Darriman Vic. 227 M9
Dart Dart Vic. 230 G7
Dartmoor Vic. 228 C6
Dartmouth Qld 492 B11, 499 P11
Dartmouth Vic. 115 A10, 225 R2, 236 E5
Darwin NT 398, 399, 402 C3, 406 D5, 373, **376–80**, 386, 391, 395
Dattuck Vic. 230 G2, 232 G12
Daveyston SA 288 E4, 292 C4
Davidson NSW 95 M1, 97 K11

Davies Creek National Park Qld 489 D9
Davis Creek NSW 117 L2
Daw Park SA 284 H11
Dawes Qld 491 L2
Dawesville WA 356 A10, 364 C6
Dawson SA 295 M2, 297 L12
Dawson Vic. 227 L5
Dawsons Hill NSW 117 L2
Daydream Island Qld **439**, 466
Dayboro Qld 483 L5
Daylesford Vic. 212 E2, 223 P8, 229 Q2, 231 Q13, 234 B12, 141, 142, 161, 162, 163, **168**, **170**
Daymar Qld 118 E2, 490 H12
Daysdale NSW 123 O12, 235 M1
Daytrap Vic. 233 J10
Daytrap Corner Vic. 233 J10
Dead Horse Gap NSW 114 C13, 138 A13
Deagon Qld 478 H4
Deakin ACT 134 A13, 136 F12, 137 E2, 130
Deakin WA 302 A5, 367 R6
Dean Vic. 212 D3, 223 N10, 229 P3, 234 B12
Deanmill WA 360 C6, 364 D10
Deans Marsh Vic. 212 D12, 217 I8, 229 O9, 183
Deception Bay Qld 483 M5, 491 Q8
Deddick Vic. 115 C11, 237 J8
Deddington Tas. 541 R13, 545 N10, 518
Dederang Vic. 225 M1, 235 Q6, 236 C4, 202
Dee Lagoon Tas. 542 I4
Dee Why NSW 95 Q2, 97 O12, 101 P7
Deep Creek Vic. 115 A11, 236 F7
Deep Lead Vic. 222 B4, 231 J11
Deepwater NSW 119 M5, 63
Deepwater National Park Qld 491 N1, 493 O13
Deer Park Vic. 208 E6
Deeral Qld 489 H12, 495 N7, 425
Delacombe Vic. 221 A10
Delamere SA 289 C8
Delaneys Creek Qld 483 L4
Delatite Vic. 213 R1, 224 D11, 235 L11
Delburn Vic. 213 R11, 227 J8
Delegate NSW 115 E11, 237 M8, 50, 189
Delegate River Vic. 115 D11, 237 L8
Dellicknora Vic. 115 D12, 237 K8
Deloraine Tas. 540 I11, 545 J9, **513**, **516**, 525, 527
Delta Qld 492 I2, 428
Delungra NSW 119 J6
Delvine Vic. 227 O5
Denham WA 365 B10, **321**
Denicull Creek Vic. 222 C8
Deniliquin NSW 123 L11, **57**, **61**
Denistone NSW 94 G5
Denman NSW 117 K3
Denman SA 302 D4
Denmark WA 361 K12, 364 G13, 366 E12, **321**, **324**, 329
Dennes Point Tas. 538 I9, 543 L10, 512
Dennington Vic. 228 H9
Denver Vic. 212 F2, 223 Q8, 229 Q2, 231 Q13, 234 C11
Depot Beach NSW 139 O6
Deptford Vic. 115 A13, 227 Q3, 236 F12
Derby Tas. 545 O7, **516**
Derby Vic. 231 P9, 234 B8
Derby WA 362 B9, 371 J7, **324**, 344
Dereel Vic. 212 C6, 229 O5

Dergholm Vic. 228 B3
Dering Vic. 232 G11
Deringulla NSW 118 F12
Dernancourt SA 285 M2, 287 M13
Derrinal Vic. 234 E9
Derrinallum Vic. 217 C2, 229 L6, **170**
Derriwong NSW 116 B5, 123 R3
Derwent Bridge Tas. 542 H3, 544 H13
Derwent Park Tas. 536 E3
Detention River Tas. 544 E4
Detpa Vic. 230 F5
Deua National Park NSW 139 K8, 237 P1, 73
Devenish Vic. 235 K5
Devils Marbles NT 392, 394, 396
Devlins Bridge Vic. 213 M3
Devoit Tas. 541 L6, 545 L7, 511
Devon Vic. 227 L9
Devon Meadows Vic. 215 P2
Devon Park Qld 482 D6
Devon Park SA 284 H4
Devondale Vic. 217 D11
Devonport Tas. 540 E5, 544 I6, 503, 514, 515, **516**, 526, 527
Dewars Pool WA 364 E2
Dharug National Park NSW 101 N3, 104 A9, 117 L6, 46, **59**, 89
Dhulura NSW 116 B12, 123 Q10
Dhuragoon NSW 123 J10, 233 Q10
Dhurringile Vic. 234 H7
Diamantina Gates National Park Qld 498 H11, 427
Diamond Beach NSW 117 P1
Diamond Creek Vic. 209 Q2
Diamond Valley Qld 483 M2, 486 D12
Dianella WA 354 I9
Diapur Vic. 230 D7
Dickson ACT 136 H7
Diddleum Plains Tas. 545 N8
Didillibah Qld 483 M1, 486 G9
Digby Vic. 228 D5
Diggers Rest Vic. 212 I4, 226 B3
Diggora Vic. 234 E6
Dilkoon NSW 119 P5
Dilston Tas. 541 N8, 545 L8
Dimboola Vic. 230 F7, **170**, 203
Dimbulah Qld 495 L7, 449
Dingabledinga SA 290 E6
Dingee Vic. 231 Q7, 234 C6
Dingley Vic. 211 E4
Dingo Qld 493 L11
Dingup WA 360 D5, 364 D10, 334
Dingwall Vic. 231 O3, 234 A2
Dinmont Vic. 217 F10, 229 N11
Dinner Plain Vic. 225 O9, 235 R10, 236 D8, 177, 182, 189
Dinninup WA 360 F2, 364 E9, 314
Dinoga NSW 118 I7
Dinyarrak Vic. 230 B7, 293 I6
Direk SA 287 J1
Dirk Hartog Island WA **321**
Dirranbandi Qld 118 C2, 490 G12, **441**
Dixie Vic. 217 A6
Dixons Creek Vic. 213 M4, 216 C5, 226 F2, 234 I13
Djuan Qld 482 F4
Dobbyn Qld 498 F1
Dobie Vic. 222 E8
Dobroyd Point NSW 95 J10
Docker Vic. 224 F2, 235 M7
Docker River Community NT 369 R9, 410 A11

Doctors Creek Qld 482 E4
Doctors Flat Vic. 115 A12, 227 Q1, 236 F10
Dodges Ferry Tas. 539 L6, 543 N8
Dolans Bay NSW 99 K12
Dolls Point NSW 99 M8
Don Tas. 540 D5, 544 I6, 516
Don Valley Vic. 213 N6, 216 E9
Donald Vic. 231 K7, **170**
Doncaster Vic. 209 P7
Doncaster East Vic. 209 Q7
Dongara WA 366 B4, **324**
Donnybrook Qld 430
Donnybrook Vic. 213 J4, 226 C2, 234 F13
Donnybrook WA 357 H6, 364 C8, 366 C10, 319, **324**
Donovans Landing SA 228 A7, 293 I12
Donvale Vic. 209 R7, 210 A8
Doo Town Tas. 539 O9
Dooboobetic Vic. 231 L7
Doodlakine WA 364 H2
Dooen Vic. 230 H9
Dookie Vic. 235 J5
Doolandella Qld 480 F9
Doomadgee Aboriginal Community Qld 497 D9
Doomben Qld 478 I9, 418
Doonan Qld 486 F3
Doonside NSW 43
Dooralong NSW 101 P1
Dopewora Vic. 230 C10
Dora Creek NSW 108 F11
Doreen NSW 118 F7
Dorodong Vic. 228 B2, 230 B13, 293 I10
Dorrien SA 292 F5
Dorrigo NSW 119 O8, **61**
Dorrigo National Park NSW 119 O8, 48, **59**, 61
Dorrington Qld 478 E10
Dorset Vale SA 290 F3
Double Bay NSW 95 O10, 40
Doubleview WA 354 C10
Doughboy NSW 115 G5, 116 H12, 139 K2
Douglas Qld 482 E6
Douglas Vic. 230 E11
Douglas Park NSW 101 K12, 112 F3
Douglas-Apsley National Park Tas. 543 P1, 545 Q11, 511, **521**
Dover Tas. 538 E12, 543 K11, **516**
Dover Heights NSW 95 Q10, 101 O8
Doveton Vic. 211 H5
Dowerin WA 364 F1, 340
Dowlingville SA 295 J7
Downer ACT 136 H6
Downside NSW 116 B12, 123 R10
Doyalson NSW 101 Q1, 108 H13
Drake NSW 119 N3, 491 O12, 83
Dreeite Vic. 212 A10, 217 F5
Drewvale Qld 481 J10
Drik Drik Vic. 228 C7
Drillham Qld 491 J7
Dripstone NSW 116 F4
Dromana Vic. 213 J11, 214 I7, 226 D8, 154, 155, 197
Dromedary Tas. 538 G3, 543 L7
Dropmore Vic. 234 I10, 204
Drouin Vic. 213 P9, 226 H6, **170**
Drouin South Vic. 213 P10, 226 H7
Drouin West Vic. 170, 199
Drumborg Vic. 228 D7
Drumcondra Vic. 218 D2
Drummartin Vic. 231 R7, 234 D6

Drummond Vic. 212 F1, 223 Q7, 229 Q1, 231 Q12, 234 C11, 180
Drummoyne NSW 95 J9
Drung Drung Vic. 230 H9
Drung Drung South Vic. 230 H10
Dry Creek SA 286 H11
Dry Creek Vic. 235 K10
Dryander National Park Qld 493 J2
Drysdale Vic. 212 H9, 219 H7, 226 B6, **170**, 191
Drysdale River National Park WA 363 K1, 371 O3
Duaringa Qld 493 M11
Dubbo NSW 116 E2, 31, **61**, 75
Dubelling WA 364 G4
Dublin SA 295 K7
Duchess Qld 498 F5
Duck Reach Tas. 515
Duckenfield NSW 108 D6
Duckmaloi NSW 100 E7
Duddo Vic. 232 C10
Dudinin WA 364 H6
Dudley Vic. 226 G10
Dudley Park SA 284 H3
Duffholme Vic. 230 E9
Duffy ACT 136 B13, 137 A3
Duffys Forest NSW 97 K7
Dulacca Qld 491 J7
Dularcha National Park Qld 483 M2, 486 E12, 450
Dullah NSW 116 A11, 123 Q9
Dulong Qld 486 C8
Dululu Qld 493 N12
Dulwich SA 285 K7
Dulwich Hill NSW 95 J12, 99 L2
Dumbalk Vic. 213 Q13, 226 I9
Dumberning WA 364 F7
Dumbleyung WA 364 H8, 366 E10, **324-5**, 346
Dumosa Vic. 122 G13, 231 L4
Dunach Vic. 212 B1, 223 L7
Dunalley Tas. 539 M6, 543 N9, **516**
Dunbogan NSW 105 G10, 119 O12
Duncraig WA 354 C5
Dundas NSW 94 D6
Dundas Qld 483 J6
Dundas Tas. 542 D1, 544 E11, 532
Dundas Valley NSW 94 E5
Dundee NSW 119 M5
Dundonnell Vic. 217 B1, 229 K6
Dundurrabin NSW 119 O7
Dunedoo NSW 116 G1
Dungog NSW 108 A1, 117 N3, **61**
Dungowan NSW 119 K11
Dunk Island Qld 495 O9, **440**, 455
Dunkeld NSW 100 B4, 116 H6
Dunkeld Vic. 228 H4, **170**, 177, 204
Dunluce Vic. 223 K3
Dunmarra NT 408 I4, **387**
Dunmore NSW 112 G9, 116 C4
Dunmore Vic. 228 G7
Dunneworthy Vic. 222 E6
Dunnstown Vic. 212 D4, 223 N11, 229 P3, 234 B13, 161
Dunolly Vic. 223 L3, 231 O10, **170-1**
Dunorlan Tas. 540 G11, 545 J8
Dunrobin Vic. 228 C4
Duns Creek NSW 108 C5
Dunsborough WA 357 C7, 359 C2, 364 B9, 366 B10, **325**
Duntroon ACT 136 I10, 137 G1
Dunwich Qld 483 P8, 491 Q9, 433

Durack Qld 480 F8
Dural NSW 96 B8
Duranillin WA 364 F8, 366 D10
Durdidwarrah Vic. 212 E6, 219 C2
Durham Lead Vic. 212 C5, 223 M13, 229 O4
Durham Ox Vic. 122 I13, 231 P5, 234 A4
Duri NSW 119 J11
Durong Qld 491 M6
Durran Durra NSW 115 G5, 116 I12, 139 L3
Durras NSW 115 H7, 139 O6
Durundur Qld 483 K3
Dutson Vic. 227 N7
Dutton SA 288 H3, 295 M7
Dutton Park Qld 480 G2
Duverney Vic. 212 B8, 217 G3
Dwarda WA 356 H11, 364 E6
Dwellingup WA 356 D11, 364 D6, 366 C9, **325**, 342
Dwyer Vic. 224 F4
Dwyers NSW 121 O6
Dynnyrne Tas. 536 G10
Dysart Qld 493 J9
Dysart Tas. 538 H1

Eagle Bay WA 357 B6, 359 C1, 364 A8
Eagle Farm Qld 479 J9, 418
Eagle Heights Qld 483 N12
Eagle Junction Qld 478 G9
Eagle On The Hill SA 285 M10
Eagle Point Vic. 227 Q5
Eagleby Qld 481 Q11, 483 N10
Eaglehawk Vic. 223 Q1, 231 Q9, 234 C8, 164
Eaglehawk Neck Tas. 539 N8, 543 O9, **516**, 517, **518**
Earlando Qld 493 J2
Earlston Vic. 235 J7
Earlville Qld 488 D12
Earlwood NSW 94 I13, 99 K3
East Boyd NSW 113 G11, 237 Q8
East Brisbane Qld 478 H12, 480 H1, 418
East Cannington WA 353 N7
East Fremantle WA 352 C10
East Gresford NSW 117 M3
East Haldon Qld 482 G10
East Hills NSW 98 E6
East Jindabyne NSW 114 G11
East Kurrajong NSW 101 L5
East Lynne NSW 139 O6
East Melbourne Vic. 206 I5, 146, 151
East Perth WA 350 H5, 352 I3
East Point NT 399 C2
East Sydney NSW 92 G9
East Victoria Park WA 353 J6
East Yolla Tas. 544 F6
Eastbourne NSW 114 G7
Eastern View Vic. 212 E12, 219 B12
Eastlakes NSW 99 O4
Eastville Vic. 223 N3
Eastwood NSW 94 G5
Eastwood SA 282 I13, 285 J8, 244
Eaton WA 357 G4, 364 C8
Eatons Hill Qld 478 C5, 467
Eatonsville NSW 119 O6, 64
Eba SA 295 N6
Ebden Vic. 235 Q4, 236 C2
Ebenezer NSW 101 L5, 79, 89
Ebenezer Qld 483 J9
Ebor NSW 119 N8, 61
Eccleston NSW 117 M2
Echuca Vic. 123 K13, 234 E4, 143, **171**, 197, 201

Echuca Village Vic. 123 K13, 234 F4
Echunga SA 288 D12, 289 I3, 290 H3
Ecklin South Vic. 217 A7
Eddington Vic. 223 M3, 231 O10, 234 A9
Eddystone Point Tas. 545 R6, 519
Eden NSW 113 F11, 115 G11, 237 Q8, 55, 61
Eden Hill WA 355 M10
Eden Hills SA 284 H13
Eden Park Vic. 213 K3
Eden Valley SA 288 G6, 295 M8, 250, 259
Edenhope Vic. 230 C11, **171**
Edens Landing Qld 481 O12
Edgcumbe Beach Tas. 544 E4
Edge Hill Qld 488 E6
Edgecliff NSW 95 O11, 99 Q1
Edgecombe Vic. 212 G1
Edgeroi NSW 118 G7
Edgewater WA 354 C1
Edi Vic. 224 F4, 235 N7
Edi Upper Vic. 224 G5
Edillilie SA 294 D7
Edith NSW 100 E8, 116 I7
Edith Creek Tas. 544 C5, 530
Edith River NT 406 F7
Edithburgh SA 294 I10, **256-7**
Edithvale Vic. 211 D7
Edmonton Qld 489 F10, 495 N7, 443
Edmund Kennedy National Park Qld 495 N9
Edwardstown SA 284 G11
Eganstown Vic. 223 O8
Egg Lagoon Tas. 542 A8
Eidsvold Qld 491 M3, **441**
Eight Mile Plains Qld 481 K6
Eildon Vic. 213 P2, 224 A12, 235 K11, **171-2**, 204
Einasleigh Qld 495 J10
Ejanding WA 364 F1
Ekibin Qld 480 H3
El Arish Qld 495 N9
Elaine Vic. 212 D6, 219 B1, 229 P5
Elands NSW 105 A10, 119 N12
Elanora Qld 485 F10
Elanora Heights NSW 97 O9, 101 O7
Elaroo Qld 493 J4
Elbow Hill SA 294 G5
Elcombe NSW 118 I6
Elderslie Tas. 538 F1, 543 K7
Eldon Tas. 543 M6
Eldorado Vic. 235 N5, 236 A3, 198
Electrona Tas. 538 H8
Elermore Vale NSW 108 F8
Elimbah Qld 483 M4, 491 P8
Elingamite Vic. 217 B7
Elizabeth SA 287 M1, 288 B7, 293 C1, 295 L8
Elizabeth Bay NSW 95 N10, 40
Elizabeth Beach NSW 117 P2
Elizabeth Grove SA 287 M2
Elizabeth Park SA 287 N1
Elizabeth Town Tas. 540 G10, 545 J8
Elizabeth Vale SA 287 M3
Ellalong NSW 108 C11, 117 L4
Ellam Vic. 122 D13, 230 G5
Ellangowan Qld 482 D11
Ellen Grove Qld 480 E9
Ellenborough NSW 105 C8, 119 N12
Ellendale Tas. 538 C2, 543 J7
Ellerslie Vic. 229 J8
Ellerston NSW 117 L1, 119 K13
Ellesmere Qld 482 E1

Elliminyt Vic. 212 B11, 217 F7, 229 N9
Ellinbank Vic. 213 P10, 226 H7
Elliott NT 409 J6, **387**
Elliott Tas. 544 F6
Elliott Heads Qld 491 O2, 428
Ellis Beach Qld 489 E6, 495 M6
Elliston SA 294 B5, 256, **257**
Elmhurst Vic. 222 G6, 229 L1, 231 L12
Elmore Vic. 234 E6
Elong Elong NSW 116 F2
Elphinstone Qld 482 E11
Elphinstone Vic. 223 R6, 231 R12, 234 C10
Elsey National Park NT 406 I11, 385, 388, 390, 392
Elsinore NSW 121 L10
Elsmore NSW 119 K6
Elsternwick Vic. 209 L12, 150
Eltham NSW 119 Q3
Eltham Vic. 209 Q4
Elwomple SA 293 E3, 295 N10
Elwood Vic. 209 K11
Embleton WA 355 K10
Emerald Qld 492 I11, **441**, 469
Emerald Vic. 213 M7, 216 C13, 226 F5, 156, **172**
Emerald Beach NSW 119 P7
Emerald Hill NSW 118 H10
Emerald Springs Roadhouse NT 402 H11
Emita Tas. 542 A11, 531
Emmaville NSW 119 L5, 63
Emmdale Roadhouse NSW 121 J10
Emmet Qld 501 P2
Empire Vale NSW 119 Q3, 491 Q13
Emu Vic. 222 I1, 231 M9
Emu Bay SA 294 H11
Emu Creek Qld 482 E10
Emu Creek Vic. 223 R2
Emu Downs SA 295 M5
Emu Junction SA 301 J10
Emu Park Qld 493 O10, **441**, 464, 473
Emu Plains NSW 43
Endeavour Hills Vic. 211 I4, 213 L8
Endeavour River National Park Qld 495 L3, 435
Eneabba WA 366 B5, 324, 345
Enfield NSW 94 H11, 99 J1
Enfield SA 285 J1, 287 J13, 288 B9
Enfield Vic. 212 C6, 223 L13, 229 O5
Engadine NSW 98 F12
Englefield Vic. 228 E2, 230 E13
English Town Tas. 545 N9
Enmore NSW 95 K12, 99 M2, 119 M9
Enngonia NSW 121 N2
Enoch Point Vic. 213 R3
Enoggera Qld 478 E10
Ensay Vic. 115 B12, 227 R1, 236 G10
Ensay South Vic. 115 A13, 227 Q1, 236 G10
Eppalock Vic. 234 D9
Epping NSW 94 G4
Epping Vic. 209 M1
Epping Forest Tas. 545 M11
Epsom Vic. 223 R1, 231 R9, 234 C8, 164
Eraring NSW 77
Ercildoun Vic. 212 B3, 223 J9
Erica Vic. 227 J5, 196
Erigolia NSW 123 O6
Erikin WA 364 H3
Erina NSW 101 P4, 104 G6
Erindale SA 285 M7
Erith SA 295 K7

Erldunda NT 404 H13, 410 I11
Ermington NSW 94 F7
Ernest Qld 485 D4
Erobin Qld 479 Q10
Eromanga Qld 501 M7, **441–2**
Erriba Tas. 540 B10, 544 H8
Erringibba National Park Qld 491 J8
Errinundra Vic. 115 D13, 237 L10
Errinundra National Park Vic. 115 D12, 237 L10, 189
Erskine Park NSW 101 L8
Erskineville NSW 95 L12, 99 N2
Esk Qld 482 I5, 491 O8, **442**
Eskdale Vic. 225 P1, 235 R6, 236 D4, 195
Esmond Vic. 123 O13, 235 L4
Esperance WA 367 J10, **325–6**, 333
Essendon Vic. 208 I5
Essington NSW 100 C7
Ethelton SA 284 C1, 286 C12
Etmilyn WA 356 E11
Eton Qld 493 K5
Ettalong NSW 101 P5, 104 G9
Ettamogah NSW 123 Q13, 235 P3, 236 C1
Ettrick NSW 119 P2, 491 P12
Euabalong NSW 123 P3
Euabalong West NSW 123 O3
Eubenangee Swamp National Park Qld 495 N8
Euchareena NSW 116 G4
Eucla WA 302 A8, 367 R7, **326**
Eucumbene NSW 114 G7, 115 D8, 138 D10, 237 K2
Eudlo Qld 483 M1, 486 E11
Eudunda SA 295 M6
Eugenana Tas. 540 D6, 516
Eugowra NSW 116 E6, **61**
Eujinyn WA 364 I3
Eukey Qld 467
Eulo Qld 501 Q11, **442**
Eumundi Qld 491 P6, 461, 473
Eumungerie NSW 116 E1, 118 D13
Eungai Creek NSW 119 O10
Eungella NSW 119 Q1, 75
Eungella Qld 493 J5, 452
Eungella National Park Qld 493 J4, 452, **457**
Eunumdi Qld 486 E4
Eurack Vic. 212 B9, 217 H4
Eurambeen Vic. 222 H9
Euramo Qld 495 N9
Euratha NSW 123 P6
Eureka Vic. 221 I8
Eurelia SA 291 D12, 295 K1, 297 K11
Euri Creek Qld 492 I2
Eurimbula National Park Qld 493 Q12, **457**
Euroa Vic. 234 I8, **172**, 204
Eurobin Vic. 225 K4, 235 P7, 236 B5, 186
Eurobodalla NSW 113 H1, 115 G8, 139 M11, 237 R2
Euroka NSW 102 C12
Eurong Qld 491 Q4
Eurongilly NSW 115 A4, 116 C11
Euston NSW 122 F8, 233 J6
Evandale SA 285 K5
Evandale Tas. 541 P12, 545 M9, 505, **518**, 527
Evans Head NSW 119 Q4, 491 Q13, **61**
Evans Plains NSW 100 B4
Evansford Vic. 212 B2, 223 K7
Evatt ACT 136 D4
Everard Junction WA 369 L9

Evergreen Qld 482 D4
Eversley Vic. 222 F7
Everton Vic. 224 H1, 235 N6, 236 A4
Everton Hills Qld 478 D8
Everton Park Qld 478 E8
Ewens Ponds SA 293 H13
Exeter NSW 112 B8, 52, 74
Exeter SA 286 C11
Exeter Tas. 541 L7, 545 L7, **518**
Exford Vic. 212 H5, 219 H1
Exmouth WA 365 C3, 307, **326**
Expedition National Park Qld 490 H3
Exton Tas. 541 J11, 545 K9, 516, 525
Eyre Peninsula SA 294 D6, 240, **256**

Fadden ACT 137 E8
Fairfield NSW 94 A10
Fairfield Qld 480 G2
Fairfield Vic. 209 M7, 151
Fairhaven Vic. 115 G13, 212 E12, 213 L11, 215 P7, 219 B12, 229 P10, 237 Q11
Fairholme NSW 116 B6, 123 R4
Fairley Vic. 231 O3, 233 O13, 234 A1
Fairlight NSW 95 P5
Fairneyview Qld 483 J8
Fairview Vic. 231 M5
Fairview Park SA 287 P8
Fairy Dell Vic. 234 E6
Fairy Hill NSW 119 P3, 491 P12
Fairy Meadow NSW 110 E6, 112 H6
Faith Island Tas. 516
Falls Creek NSW 115 I4
Falls Creek NSW 112 D13, 117 K11
Falls Creek Vic. 225 P7, 235 R9, 236 D7, 164, 176, 182, 185
Falmouth Tas. 545 Q9, 529
Family Islands National Park Qld 495 O9
Fannie Bay NT 399 D6, 378
Faraday Vic. 223 Q5, 231 Q11, 234 C10
Farina SA 291 C1, 297 J2
Farleigh Qld 493 K5
Farnborough Qld 493 O10
Farnham NSW 116 G4
Farrell Flat SA 295 L5
Farrer ACT 137 D6
Fassifern Valley Qld 483 J12
Faulconbridge NSW 101 J7, 103 M6
Fawcett Vic. 213 O1
Fawkner Vic. 209 K4, 213 J5
Federal Qld 486 A1
Feilton Tas. 538 E4, 543 K8
Felixstow SA 285 L4
Felton East Qld 491 N10
Felton South Qld 482 C10
Fentonbury Tas. 538 C2, 543 J7
Fentons Creek Vic. 231 N8
Fern Hill Vic. 212 G2, 223 R9
Fern Tree Tas. 536 D11, 538 H6, 543 L9
Fernbank Vic. 227 O5, 236 E13
Ferndale NSW 123 P11
Ferndale WA 353 L9
Ferndene Tas. 540 A5, 544 H6
Fernhill NSW 110 D4
Fernihurst Vic. 231 O6, 234 A5
Ferntree Gully Vic. 210 D12, 213 L7
Ferntree Gully National Park Vic. 156
Fernvale Qld 483 J7, 491 P9
Ferny Creek Vic. 210 E12
Ferny Grove Qld 478 B9
Ferny Hills Qld 478 C9, 467
Ferryden Park SA 284 G3
Fields Find WA 366 D4

Fiery Flat Vic. 231 O7, 234 A6
Fifield NSW 116 B4, 123 R2
Fifteen Mile School Vic. 224 E4
Fig Tree NSW 110 A11
Fig Tree Pocket Qld 480 D4, 419
Figtree NSW 112 G6
Finch Hatton Qld 493 J5
Findon SA 284 E5
Fine Flower Creek NSW 119 O5
Fingal Tas. 543 P1, 545 P10, **518**, 527
Fingal Bay NSW 108 I2, 51
Finke NT 411 K12
Finke Gorge National Park NT 404 F6, 410 H9, 383, 384, 387, 393
Finley NSW 123 M12, 234 I1, **61–2**
Finniss SA 289 I6, 290 H9, 293 C3, 295 L11
Firle SA 285 L5
Fish Creek Vic. 226 I10, 173
Fish Point Vic. 231 O1, 233 O11
Fisher ACT 137 B5
Fisher SA 302 G4
Fishermans Bend Vic. 209 J9
Fishery Falls Qld 489 G11, 495 N7
Fiskville Vic. 212 F5, 223 P12, 229 Q4
Fitzgerald Tas. 538 B3, 542 I7
Fitzgerald River National Park WA 366 G11, **323**, 328, 343
Fitzgibbon Qld 478 F4
Fitzroy SA 282 D2, 284 F4
Fitzroy Vic. 206 H4, 209 K8, 151
Fitzroy Crossing WA 362 G11, 371 L9, **326–7**, 344
Fitzroy Falls NSW 112 D9
Fitzroy Island National Park Qld 489 H9, 495 N7, 431, **440**
Fitzroy North Vic. 209 K7, 151
Five Dock NSW 95 J10
Five Ways NSW 116 A2, 121 Q12
Five Ways Vic. 215 Q1
Flaggy Rock Qld 493 L7
Flagstaff Gully Tas. 537 J5
Flagstone Creek Qld 482 G8
Flamingo Beach Vic. 227 O7
Flat Tops NSW 108 C2
Flaxley SA 288 D12, 289 I3, 290 H4
Flaxton Qld 486 C9, 413, 429, 452
Flemington Vic. 209 J7
Fletcher Qld 467
Fleurieu Peninsula SA 289 E7, 290 A11, 293 B4, 246, **276**
Flinders Qld 483 K10
Flinders Vic. 213 J12, 215 J11, 226 D9, 155
Flinders Bay WA 357 C13, 359 D13, 364 A11
Flinders Chase National Park SA 294 F12, 260, **264**, 269
Flinders Group National Park Qld 496 G11
Flinders Island SA 257
Flinders Island Tas. 505, **531**
Flinders Park SA 284 G5
Flinders Ranges National Park SA 291 D7, 297 K7, 239, 240, 249, **263**, 273, 280, 333
Flinton Qld 490 I10
Flintstone Tas. 543 J2, 545 K12
Floreat WA 352 D2, 354 D13
Florey ACT 136 C5
Florida NSW 121 O10
Florida WA 356 A10, 364 C6
Florieton SA 295 N5
Flowerdale Tas. 544 F5
Flowerdale Vic. 213 L2, 226 E1, 234 H12

Flowerpot Tas. 538 H11, 543 L10
Flowery Gully Tas. 541 K7, 545 K7
Flying Fish Point Qld 495 N8
Flying Fox Qld 483 M13
Flynn ACT 136 C4
Flynn Vic. 227 L7
Flynns Creek Vic. 227 K7
Fogg Dam NT 379
Footscray Vic. 208 I8, 226 C4
Forbes NSW 116 D6, **62**, 75
Forcett Tas. 539 L5
Fords SA 288 E3
Fords Bridge NSW 121 M4
Forest Tas. 544 D4
Forest Den National Park Qld 492 C7, 499 Q7
Forest Glen NSW 96 A2
Forest Glen Qld 483 M1, 486 E10
Forest Grove WA 357 C11, 359 D9, 364 B10
Forest Hill NSW 115 A5, 116 B12, 123 R10
Forest Hill Qld 482 H8
Forest Hill Vic. 209 R10, 210 A10
Forest Lake Qld 480 E9
Forest Range SA 288 D10, 289 I1, 247
Forest Reefs NSW 116 G6
Forestdale Qld 480 H12
Forester Tas. 545 O6
Forestville NSW 95 M3, 97 K13
Forge Creek Vic. 227 P5
Formartin Qld 482 B6
Forrest ACT 134 C12, 136 G12, 137 E2
Forrest Vic. 212 B13, 217 H9, 229 O10
Forrest WA 367 Q6
Forrest Beach Qld 495 O11
Forresters Beach NSW 101 Q4, 104 H4, 63
Forrestfield WA 353 Q5
Forreston SA 288 E8
Forsayth Qld 494 I11
Forster SA 293 E1, 295 N8
Forster Tuncurry NSW 117 P2, **62**
Fortescue Roadhouse WA 365 F2
Forth Tas. 540 D5, 544 H6, 514, 516
Fortitude Valley Qld 417, 418
Forty Mile Scrub National Park Qld 495 K9
Foster Vic. 227 J10, **173**
Fosterville Vic. 231 R9, 234 D8
Four Mile Creek Tas. 545 Q10
Fowlers Bay SA 303 K9, 333
Fox Ground NSW 112 F10, 117 K11, 62
Foxhow Vic. 217 F3
Framlingham Vic. 229 J8
Frampton NSW 115 B3, 116 C11
Frances SA 230 A9, 293 I8
Francistown Tas. 538 E12, 543 K11
Francois Peron National Park WA 365 B9, 321
Frank Hann National Park WA 366 H9, 332, 340
Frankford Tas. 541 J8, 545 K8
Frankland WA 360 I7, 364 F11, 366 E11
Frankland Island Qld 431
Franklin Tas. 538 E8, 543 K10, **518–19**
Franklin-Gordon Wild Rivers National Park Tas. 542 F5, 544 F13, 515, **520**, 531
Franklinford Vic. 212 E1, 223 O7
Frankston Vic. 211 D12, 213 K9, 215 K1, 226 D6, 154
Frankton SA 288 H2, 295 M7
Fraser ACT 136 C3

Fraser Island Qld 483 P5, 491 Q3, **433**, 444, 454, 456, 462, 468
Fraser National Park Vic. 213 P1, 235 K11, 142, 157, 172, **176**, 184
Frederickton NSW 105 G3, 119 O10
Freeburgh Vic. 225 M6
Freeling SA 288 D4, 292 A3, 295 L7
Freemans Reach NSW 101 L5, 117 K7
Freemans Waterhole NSW 108 E10
Freestone Qld 482 F12
Fregon SA 301 J3
Fremantle WA 352 B11, 356 A5, 358, 364 C4, 366 B8, 310, 311, **327**, 343
French Island Vic. 213 M11, 154
Frenchmans Vic. 222 G4
Frenchs Forest NSW 95 M2, 97 L12, 101 O7
Freshwater Creek Vic. 212 F10, 219 D9, 229 Q8
Frewville SA 285 K8
Freycinet National Park Tas. 543 Q4, 545 Q12, 505, 511, 513, 515, **521**
Frogmore NSW 115 D2, 116 F9
Fryerstown Vic. 212 F1, 223 Q6, 166
Fulham SA 284 D7
Fulham Vic. 227 M6
Fulham Gardens SA 284 D6
Fullarton SA 285 K9
Fullerton NSW 100 C12, 115 F2, 116 H9
Fumina Vic. 213 Q7
Furner SA 293 G10
Furracabad NSW 119 L6
Fyansford Vic. 212 F9, 219 E7, 229 Q7, 173
Fyshwick ACT 137 H2

Gadara NSW 138 A2
Gaffneys Creek Vic. 213 R4, 227 J2, 235 M13
Gagebrook Tas. 538 H4, 543 L7
Galah Vic. 232 G9
Galaquil Vic. 230 H4
Galaquil East Vic. 230 I4
Galga SA 293 F1, 295 O8
Galiwinku NT 407 M5
Gallanani Qld 482 I5
Gallangowan Qld 491 O6
Galong NSW 115 D3, 116 E10
Galston NSW 96 D6, 101 N6, 117 L7
Gama Vic. 230 I1, 232 I12
Gammon Ranges National Park SA 291 F3, 297 L3, 251, 261, **263**, 273
Gangalook Qld 464
Ganmain NSW 116 A11, 123 Q9
Gannawarra Vic. 234 B2
Gapsted Vic. 224 I2, 235 O7, 236 A4
Gapuwiyak NT 407 N5
Garah NSW 118 G4
Garbutt Qld 487 A4
Garden Island Creek Tas. 538 F11, 543 K11
Gardens of Stone National Park NSW 100 F1, 116 I5
Gardners Bay Tas. 538 F10, 543 K10, 513
Garema NSW 116 D7
Garfield Vic. 213 O9, 226 G6
Garibaldi Vic. 212 C5, 223 M13
Garigal National Park NSW 95 L1, 97 M9, 101 O7
Garland NSW 116 F7
Garra NSW 116 F5
Garran ACT 136 F13, 137 D4
Garrawilla NSW 118 G11

Garvoc Vic. 229 J9
Gary Junction WA 369 M4
Gascoyne Junction WA 365 D8, **327**
Gatton Qld 482 H8, 491 O9, **442**
Gatum Vic. 228 F3
Gaven Qld 485 C3
Gawler SA 288 D5, 295 L8, 246, **257**
Gawler Tas. 540 B5, 544 H6
Gayndah Qld 491 N4, **442**
Gaythorne Qld 478 E9
Gazette Vic. 228 G6
Geary's Gap NSW 130
Geebung Qld 478 G6
Geehi NSW 114 B11
Geelong Vic. 218, 226 A6, 152, **173**
Geelong East Vic. 218 I8
Geelong North Vic. 218 C1
Geelong South Vic. 218 F9
Geelong West Vic. 218 C5
Geeralying WA 364 F7
Geeveston Tas. 538 D10, 543 K10, **519**
Geikie Gorge National Park WA 362 H11, 371 M9, **323**, 326
Gelantipy Vic. 115 C12, 236 I9
Gellibrand Vic. 212 A13, 217 F9, 229 N10
Gelliondale Vic. 227 L10
Gem Tree NT 411 K7
Gembrook Vic. 213 N8, 216 E13, 226 F5, 172
Genoa Vic. 115 F13, 237 P11, 183
Genoa National Park NSW 113 B11, 115 F12, 237 O8
George Town Tas. 541 K4, 545 K6, 511, **519**, 527
Georges Creek Vic. 235 R4, 236 D2
Georges Hall NSW 94 B13, 98 D3
Georges Heights NSW 95 O7
Georges Plains NSW 100 B5, 116 H6
Georges River National Park NSW 98 E7, 101 M9
Georgetown Qld 494 I10, **442**, 474
Georgetown SA 295 K4
Georgica NSW 119 P2, 491 Q12
Gepps Cross SA 287 J11, 245
Geraldton WA 366 A3, 306, **327–8**
Gerang Gerung Vic. 230 F7
Gerangamete Vic. 212 B12, 217 H9, 229 O10
Geranium SA 293 G3, 295 P11
Germantown Vic. 225 M5
Gerogery NSW 123 Q12, 235 P2
Gerogery West NSW 123 Q13, 235 P2
Gerringong NSW 112 G10, 117 K11, **62**
Gerroa NSW 112 G11, 62
Geurie NSW 116 F3
Gheerulla Qld 486 A6
Gheringhap Vic. 212 F8, 219 D6
Ghin Ghin Vic. 213 M1
Giangurra Qld 489 G8
Gibraltar Range National Park NSW 119 M5, 63, 64
Gibson WA 367 J10
Gibsonvale NSW 123 P5
Gidgegannup WA 356 E3, 364 D3
Gidginbung NSW 115 A2, 116 B9, 123 R7, 83
Giffard Vic. 227 N8
Gilbert River Qld 494 G10
Gilberts SA 290 H10
Gilderoy Vic. 216 H11
Giles Corner SA 288 C1, 295 L7
Gilgai NSW 119 K6

Gilgandra NSW 118 D13, **62**
Gilgooma NSW 118 D9
Gilgunnia NSW 121 N13, 123 N1
Gilles Plains SA 285 L1, 287 L12
Gilliat Qld 498 I4
Gillieston Vic. 234 G5
Gillingarra WA 366 C6
Gillman SA 286 F11
Gilmore ACT 137 F9
Gilmore NSW 138 A2
Gilston Qld 483 N13, 485 B6
Gin Gin NSW 116 D1, 118 C13
Gin Gin Qld 491 N2, **443**
Gindie Qld 492 I11
Gingin WA 364 C2, 366 C7, **328**
Ginninderra ACT 136 E3, 130
Ginquam Vic. 232 G5
Gippsland Vic. 227 P6, 141, 142, 175, 180, 192, 193
Gippsland Lakes Vic. 141, **193**
Gipsy Point Vic. 115 G13, 237 P11, 183
Giralang ACT 136 E5
Girgarre Vic. 234 F6
Girilambone NSW 121 Q9
Girral NSW 116 A7, 123 Q5
Girraween National Park Qld 119 M3, 491 N2, 83, **456**, 467
Girrawheen WA 354 F6
Giru Qld 492 G1, 495 Q13, 468, 470
Gisborne Vic. 212 H3, 226 B2, 234 E13, **173**, 202
Gladesville NSW 94 I7, 101 N8
Gladfield Vic. 231 P5, 234 A4
Gladstone NSW 105 H3, 119 P10
Gladstone Qld 493 P12, 427, **443**, 445
Gladstone SA 295 K3, 297 J13, 256, 258
Gladstone Tas. 545 P6, **519**
Gladstone Region Qld 493 P12, **445**
Gladysdale Vic. 213 N6, 216 G10, 226 G4
Glamis NSW 119 M12
Glamorganvale Qld 483 J8
Glandore SA 284 G9
Glanmire NSW 100 C4
Glanville SA 286 C12
Glass House Mountains Qld 483 M3, 491 P7, 421
Glaziers Bay Tas. 538 E9
Glebe NSW 95 L10, 99 N1, 40
Glebe Tas. 535 E1, 536 G7
Glen Tas. 541 N5, 545 L6
Glen Alice NSW 117 J5
Glen Aplin Qld 119 M3, 491 N12, 467
Glen Broughton Qld 489 G9
Glen Creek Vic. 235 P6
Glen Davis NSW 80
Glen Elgin NSW 119 M5
Glen Esk Qld 482 I5
Glen Forbes Vic. 213 N12, 226 F9
Glen Geddes Qld 493 N10
Glen Helen NT 404 E3, 410 H8, 382, 383, 384, **387**, 389
Glen Huntly Vic. 209 N12
Glen Huon Tas. 538 E7, 543 K9, 522
Glen Innes NSW 119 L6, **63**, 69
Glen Iris Vic. 209 N10
Glen Martin NSW 108 D3
Glen Oak NSW 108 C4
Glen Osmond SA 285 L9
Glen Valley Vic. 225 R7
Glen Waverley Vic. 209 Q12, 210 A12, 213 K7
Glen William NSW 108 C2

Glen Wills Vic. 115 A11, 236 F7
Glenaire Vic. 217 E12
Glenaladale Vic. 227 O4, 236 D13
Glenalbyn Vic. 231 O8, 234 A7
Glenalta SA 285 K13
Glenariff NSW 121 P8
Glenaroua Vic. 213 J1
Glenarron Vic. 187
Glenbrae Vic. 212 A2, 223 J8
Glenbrook NSW 101 J7, 103 Q8, 42
Glenburn Vic. 213 M3, 216 C1, 226 F1, 234 I12
Glenburnie SA 228 A6, 293 I12
Glencoe NSW 119 L7
Glencoe SA 293 H11, 266
Glencoe West SA 293 H11
Glendalough WA 352 F1, 354 F12
Glendambo SA 296 C5, 279
Glendaruel Vic. 212 B2, 223 K8
Glenden Qld 492 I5
Glendevie Tas. 538 E11, 543 K10
Glendinning Vic. 228 F2, 230 F13
Glendon Brook NSW 117 L3
Gleneagle Qld 483 L12, 425
Glenelg SA 284 D11, 288 A10, 289 E1, 293 B2, 295 K9, 244
Glenelg North SA 284 D10
Glenfern Qld 483 J3
Glenfern Tas. 538 F5, 543 K8
Glenfyne Vic. 217 A7, 229 K9
Glengarry Tas. 541 K8, 545 K8
Glengarry Vic. 227 K6
Glengower Vic. 212 C1, 223 M7
Glengowrie SA 284 E11
Glenhaven NSW 96 A9, 101 M7
Glenhope Vic. 234 D10
Glenisla Vic. 228 G2, 230 G13
Glenlee Vic. 230 F6
Glenlofty Vic. 222 G5
Glenloth Vic. 122 G13, 231 M5
Glenluce Vic. 212 F1
Glenlusk Tas. 538 G5
Glenlyon Vic. 212 F2, 223 Q8
Glenmaggie Vic. 227 L5
Glenmore NSW 101 J10, 112 E1
Glenmore Vic. 212 F5, 223 Q13, 229 R4
Glenmorgan Qld 490 I8, 454
Glenora Tas. 538 D3, 543 J7
Glenorchy Tas. 536 D3, 538 H5, 543 L8, 508
Glenorchy Vic. 222 B3, 231 J11
Glenore Qld 461
Glenore Tas. 541 K12, 545 K9
Glenore Grove Qld 482 I8
Glenorie NSW 96 A2, 101 M6
Glenormiston Vic. 217 A5, 229 K8
Glenormiston North Vic. 217 A4
Glenpatrick Vic. 222 H6
Glenreagh NSW 119 P7
Glenrowan Vic. 224 D1, 235 M6, 160, **173**, **177**, 197, 198
Glenrowan West Vic. 224 D2
Glenroy NSW 100 G5
Glenroy SA 293 H10
Glenroy Vic. 208 I4
Glenshee Vic. 222 G6
Glenside SA 285 K8
Glenthompson Vic. 228 I4
Glenunga SA 285 K8
Glenvale Vic. 213 K3, 226 D2, 234 G13
Glenworth Valley NSW 101 O4, 104 B8
Glossodia NSW 101 K5

Glossop SA 295 Q7, 252
Gloucester NSW 117 N1, **63**
Gloucester National Park WA 360 C7
Glynde SA 285 L4
Gnangara WA 354 G1
Gnarming WA 364 I5
Gnarpurt Vic. 217 E3
Gnarwarre Vic. 212 E9, 219 C7, 229 Q8
Gneedingarra WA 365 B8
Gnotuk Vic. 217 B5
Gnowangerup WA 361 O3, 364 I10, 366 F11, 329, 331
Goangra NSW 118 C7
Gobarralong NSW 115 C4, 116 D12
Gobur Vic. 235 J10
Gocup NSW 138 A1
Godfreys Creek NSW 115 D1, 116 F9
Gogango Qld 493 M11
Gol Gol NSW 122 D7, 232 G3
Golconda Tas. 541 Q5, 545 M7
Gold Coast Qld 483 O13, 485, 491 R10, 415, 416, **422–3**, 467
Golden Beach Vic. 227 O7
Golden Grove SA 287 P6
Golden Point Vic. 223 Q5
Golden Valley Tas. 540 I13, 545 J9
Goldsborough Vic. 223 K2, 231 N10
Goldsmith Tas. 543 L3, 545 M12
Goldsworthy (Abandoned) WA 368 D1, 370 C13
Gollan NSW 116 G2
Golspie NSW 100 C13, 115 G2, 116 H9
Gomersal SA 292 C6
Gongolgon NSW 121 Q6
Gonn Crossing NSW 122 I11, 231 P1, 233 P12
Goobarragandra NSW 115 C6, 116 E13, 138 C3
Good Hope NSW 115 D4, 116 F11
Goodilla NT 402 F9
Goodmans Ford NSW 100 F13
Goodna Qld 480 C9
Goodnight NSW 122 H9, 233 M8
Goodooga NSW 118 A4, 121 R2, 490 E13
Goodwood Qld 491 O3
Goodwood SA 284 I9
Goodwood Tas. 536 E2, 508
Googa Googa Qld 482 G3
Goolgowi NSW 123 M6
Goolma NSW 116 G3
Goolmangar NSW 119 Q3
Gooloogong NSW 116 E7, 57
Goolwa SA 289 I7, 290 G12, 293 C3, 295 L11, 201, **257**, 276
Goomalibee Vic. 235 K6
Goomalling WA 364 F1, 366 D7
Goombungee Qld 482 E5, 491 N8
Goomeri Qld 491 O6, 444
Goon Nure Vic. 227 P5
Goondah NSW 115 D3, 116 F11
Goondiwindi Qld 118 H2, 491 K11, 75, **443**
Goondooloo SA 293 F1, 295 O9
Goongarrie WA 366 I5
Goongarrie National Park WA 366 I5
Goongee Vic. 232 B9
Goongerah Vic. 115 D12, 237 K10
Goonumbla NSW 116 D5
Gooram Vic. 235 J9
Goorambat Vic. 235 K6
Goorawin NSW 123 M5
Goornong Vic. 234 D7
Gooroc Vic. 231 L8

Gooseberry Hill National Park WA 356 D4, **322**
Goovigen Qld 493 N13
Goowarra Qld 493 L11
Gorae Vic. 228 D8
Gorae West Vic. 228 D8
Gordon ACT 137 D12
Gordon NSW 95 J3, 96 H13
Gordon SA 291 C11, 297 J9
Gordon Tas. 538 G11, 543 L11, 522
Gordon Vic. 212 E4, 223 O11, 229 Q3, 234 B13, 161
Gordonvale Qld 489 F10, **443**
Gore Hill NSW 95 K7
Gorge Rock WA 364 I5
Gormandale Vic. 227 L7
Gormanston Tas. 542 E3, 544 E12, 526
Gorokan NSW 101 Q2, 108 H13
Goroke Vic. 230 D9
Goschen Vic. 231 M1, 233 N12
Gosford NSW 104 F6, 117 L6, 40, **63**
Goshen Tas. 545 Q8
Gosnells WA 353 P13, 311
Gosse SA 294 G12
Goughs Bay Vic. 213 Q1, 224 C12, 235 L11
Goulburn NSW 115 G3, 116 H11, **63**
Goulburn River National Park NSW 116 H2, 73, 75
Goulburn Weir Vic. 234 G8
Goulds Country Tas. 545 P7
Gove Peninsula NT 395, 396
Gowanford Vic. 231 L1, 233 L11
Gowangardie Vic. 235 J6
Gowar Vic. 223 P5
Gowar East Vic. 231 M8
Gowrie ACT 137 E9
Gowrie Qld 482 E7
Gowrie Park Tas. 540 C11, 544 H8
Goyura Vic. 230 H3
Grabben Gullen NSW 115 F3, 116 G10
Gracemere Qld 493 N11
Gracetown WA 357 B9, 359 B6, 364 A9, 366 B11, 335
Graceville Qld 480 E4
Gradgery NSW 118 B11
Gradule Qld 118 E2, 490 H11
Grafton NSW 119 P6, **63–4**
Graham NSW 115 D1, 116 F9
Graman NSW 119 J5
Grampians National Park Vic. 222 A7, 228 H1, 230 H12, 141, 142, 165, 170, **176**, 177, 178, 195, **198**
Grange Qld 478 F9
Grange SA 284 C5, 245
Granite Flat Vic. 225 Q3
Granite Island SA 277
Grantham Qld 482 G8, 491 O9, 442
Granton Tas. 538 H4, 543 L8, 512
Grantville Vic. 213 N12, 226 F8
Granville NSW 94 C8
Granville Harbour Tas. 542 B1, 544 C10
Granya Vic. 123 R13, 235 R4, 236 E2
Grass Flat Vic. 230 F9
Grass Patch WA 367 J10
Grassdale Vic. 228 E5
Grassmere Vic. 228 I8
Grasstree Qld 493 L5
Grasstree Hill Tas. 538 I4
Grassy Tas. 542 A9
Gravelly Beach Tas. 541 L7, 545 L7, 518
Gravesend NSW 118 I5

Grawin NSW 118 A6
Grawlin Plains NSW 116 D6
Gray Tas. 543 Q1, 545 Q10
Grays Point NSW 98 I12
Graytown Vic. 234 F9, 186, 192
Gre Gre Vic. 231 K9
Great Barrier Reef Qld 489 F2, 493 M3, 495 N3, 413, 415, 430, **437–40**, 445, 446, 448, 452, 455, 463, 466
Great Basalt Wall National Park Qld 492 C2, 499 R2
Great Keppell Island Qld 493 O10, **438**, 441, 464
Great Northern Vic. 235 N3, 236 A1
Great Ocean Road Vic. 212 D13, 217 A10, 219 B12, 229 N12, 141, 142, 152, 157, 179, 181, 183, **187**
Great Palm Island Aboriginal Community Qld 495 O11
Great Sandy National Park Qld 491 Q5, 429, 444, **456**, 461, 468
Great Western Vic. 222 C6, 229 J1, 231 J12, 158, 195, 197
Gredgwin Vic. 122 H13, 231 N4
Green Fields SA 287 J8
Green Head WA 366 B5, 324
Green Hill Creek Vic. 212 A1, 222 I6
Green Hills SA 290 H4
Green Island National Park Qld 489 H7, 495 N6, 431, 437, **440**
Green Lake Vic. 230 H10
Green Lake Vic. 231 J2, 233 K12
Green Patch NSW 139 R2
Greenacre NSW 94 E12, 98 G2
Greenacres SA 285 K2, 287 K13
Greenbushes WA 360 C2, 364 D9, 319
Greendale Vic. 212 F4, 223 Q11, 229 Q3, 234 C13
Greenethorpe NSW 115 C1, 116 E8
Greenhill SA 285 O8
Greenhills WA 364 F3
Greenmount Qld 491 N10
Greenmount Vic. 356 D4
Greenmount WA 356 D4
Greenmount East Qld 482 E9, 434
Greenmount WA 356 D4, **322**
Greenock SA 288 E4, 292 E3, 295 L7
Greenough WA 366 A4, 324, 328
Greens Beach Tas. 541 J3, 545 K6, 511
Greens Creek Vic. 222 D3
Greensborough Vic. 209 P3, 213 K5
Greenslopes Qld 480 H2
Greenvale Qld 495 L12
Greenwald Vic. 228 C7
Greenway ACT 137 B9
Greenways SA 293 G10
Greenwell Point NSW 112 F12, 115 I4, 117 K11, 77
Greenwich NSW 95 L8
Greenwith SA 287 P5
Greenwood Qld 482 D6
Greenwood WA 354 D5
Greg Greg NSW 115 B8, 236 H1
Gregors Creek Qld 482 I3
Gregory WA 366 A3
Gregory National Park NT 406 C13, 406 E12, 408 C3, 408 E1, 392, 394
Greigs Flat NSW 113 F10
Grenfell NSW 115 B1, 116 D8, **64**
Grenville Vic. 212 C6, 229 O5
Gresford NSW 117 M3
Greta NSW 108 A8, 109 G3

Greta Vic. 224 E2, 235 M7
Greta South Vic. 224 D3
Greta West Vic. 224 D2
Gretna Tas. 538 E3, 543 K7
Grevillia NSW 119 O2, 491 P11
Grey Peaks National Park Qld 489 G10
Greymare Qld 482 D13
Griegs Flat NSW 237 Q8
Griffin Qld 478 F1
Griffith ACT 136 H12, 137 F3
Griffith NSW 123 N7, 31, **64**, 81
Grimwade WA 357 I7, 360 C1, 364 D9
Gringegalgona Vic. 228 E3
Gritjurk Vic. 228 E4
Grogan NSW 115 B2, 116 C9
Grong Grong NSW 116 A11, 123 P9
Grose Vale NSW 101 J6
Grosvenor Qld 491 M4
Grove Tas. 538 F7, 543 K9, 522
Grove Hill NT 402 H10
Grovedale Vic. 219 E7, 196
Grovely Qld 478 D9
Gruyere Vic. 210 I5, 213 M5, 216 C8
Gubbata NSW 123 P5
Guilderton WA 364 B2, 366 C7, **328**
Guildford NSW 94 B8
Guildford Tas. 544 F8
Guildford Vic. 212 E1, 223 P6, 166
Guildford WA 355 O9, 356 C4, 311
Gular NSW 118 C11
Gulargambone NSW 118 D11
Gulf Creek NSW 119 J7
Gulf Savannah Qld 494 C12, 497 I12, 430, 431, 442, **474**
Gulf of Carpentaria Qld 430, 447
Gulgong NSW 116 H2, **64**
Gullewa WA 366 C3
Gulliver Qld 487 A7
Gulnare SA 295 K4
Gulpa NSW 123 K12, 234 F1
Guluguba Qld 491 J6
Gum Creek SA 295 L5
Gum Lake NSW 122 F2
Gumble NSW 116 E5
Gumbowie SA 295 L2, 297 K13
Gumdale Qld 479 M12, 481 M1
Gumeracha SA 288 E8, 293 C1, 295 L9, 246
Gumlu Qld 492 H2
Gumly Gumly NSW 116 B12, 123 R10
Gunalda Qld 491 P5
Gunbar NSW 123 M6
Gunbar South NSW 123 M6
Gunbower Vic. 123 J13, 231 R4, 234 C3
Gundagai NSW 115 B5, 116 D12, **64**
Gundaring WA 364 G8
Gundaroo NSW 115 E4, 116 G11
Gundary NSW 139 M8
Gunderman NSW 101 N4
Gundiah Qld 491 P5
Gundillion NSW 115 F7, 139 K7
Gundowring Vic. 235 Q6, 236 C4
Gundowring Junction Vic. 225 M2
Gundowring North Vic. 235 Q6
Gundowring Upper Vic. 225 N1
Gundy NSW 117 L1
Gunebang NSW 123 P3
Gungahlin ACT 135 F2, 136 G2, 138 G1
Gungal NSW 117 J2, 73
Gunnary NSW 115 D2, 116 F9
Gunnedah NSW 118 H10, **64**, 66
Gunner Vic. 232 F10

Gunnewin Qld 490 G5
Gunning NSW 115 E4, 116 G11, 44, 47, **66**
Gunning Grach NSW 115 E10, 237 M6
Gunningbland NSW 116 C5
Gunns Plains Tas. 540 A7, 544 G7, 513, 514, 526, 532
Gunpowder Qld 498 E1
Gunyah Vic. 227 J9
Gurig National Park NT 406 G3, 392
Gurley NSW 118 G6
Gurrai SA 293 H2, 295 Q10
Gurrundah NSW 115 F3, 116 G10
Guthalungra Qld 492 I2
Guthega NSW 114 D11, 115 C9, 138 B12, 237 J4, 65
Guy Fawkes River National Park NSW 119 N7, 63
Guyong NSW 116 G6
Guyra NSW 119 L8, **66**
Guys Forest Vic. 115 A8, 236 F2
Gwabegar NSW 118 E9
Gwalia WA 366 I3, 334
Gwandalan NSW 101 R1, 108 H11
Gwandalan Tas. 539 L8, 543 N9
Gwelup WA 354 D8
Gwynneville NSW 110 C9
Gymbowen Vic. 230 D9
Gymea Bay NSW 98 I12
Gympie Qld 491 P6, **443–4**
Gypsum Vic. 232 H10

Haasts Bluff NT 404 A2, 410 G8
Haberfield NSW 95 J11, 99 L1
Hackett ACT 136 I7
Hackham SA 288 A12, 289 F3, 290 C4, 293 B2, 295 K10, 268
Hackney SA 282 H6, 285 K5
Haddon Vic. 212 B4, 223 K11, 229 O3
Haden Qld 482 E5, 491 N8
Hadspen Tas. 541 N11, 545 L9, 505, **519**, 523, 527
Hagley Tas. 541 K11, 545 K9, 505, 532
Hahndorf SA 288 D11, 289 I2, 290 H2, 293 C2, 295 L9, 247
Haig WA 367 O6
Haigslea Qld 483 J8
Hail Creek Qld 493 J5
Halbury SA 295 K6
Half Tide Qld 493 L5
Halfway Creek NSW 119 P7
Halfway Hill Roadhouse WA 366 B5
Halidon SA 293 G1, 295 P9
Halifax Qld 495 O11
Hall ACT 136 D2, 131
Hallett SA 295 L4
Hallett Cove SA 288 A11, 289 E2, 245, 268
Hallidays Point NSW 117 P2
Halls Creek WA 363 N11, 371 P9, **328**, 344
Halls Gap Vic. 228 I1, 230 I12, **177**, 195, 198, 204
Halls Head WA 356 A9, 364 C5, 334
Hallston Vic. 213 Q12, 226 I8
Halton NSW 117 M2
Hamel WA 356 C12, 364 C6
Hamersley WA 354 F7
Hamersley Range WA 365 G3, 368 A4, **343**
Hamersley Range National Park see Karijini National Park
Hamilton NSW 106 A6
Hamilton Qld 478 H10, 418, 419
Hamilton SA 288 E1, 295 L7

Hamilton Tas. 538 D1, 543 J6, **519**
Hamilton Vic. 228 F5, **177**, 204
Hamilton East NSW 106 C8
Hamilton Hill WA 352 C12
Hamilton Island Qld 493 K3, **439**, 452, 466
Hamilton South NSW 106 B9
Hamley Bridge SA 288 C2, 295 L7
Hamlyn Heights Vic. 218 B2
Hammond SA 291 C12, 295 K1, 297 J11, 272, 280
Hammondville NSW 98 C6
Hampden SA 295 M6
Hampshire Tas. 544 F7
Hampstead Gardens SA 285 K3
Hampton NSW 100 F6, 116 I7
Hampton Qld 482 F6, 491 N8
Hampton Vic. 211 A2
Hann River Roadhouse Qld 494 I2
Hann Tableland National Park Qld 489 A8, 495 L6
Hannahs Bridge NSW 116 H1
Hannan NSW 123 O5
Hansborough SA 288 G1, 295 M7
Hanson SA 295 L5, 253
Hansonville Vic. 224 E3
Hanwood NSW 123 N7, 64
Happy Valley Vic. 212 B5, 223 J13, 225 K3, 229 N4, 233 J6
Harbord NSW 95 Q4
Harcourt Vic. 223 Q4, 231 Q11, 234 C10, 166
Harcourt North Vic. 223 Q4, 231 Q11, 234 C10
Harden NSW 115 C3, 116 E10, 56, 74
Hardwicke Bay SA 294 H9
Harefield NSW 115 A4, 116 C12, 123 R10
Harford Tas. 540 G6, 545 J7
Hargrave Park NSW 98 A3
Hargraves NSW 116 H4
Harkaway Vic. 213 M8
Harlin Qld 482 I3, 491 O7
Harrietville Vic. 225 M8, 235 Q9, 236 C7, **177**
Harrington NSW 105 E13, 117 P1, 119 O13, 82
Harris Park NSW 94 C7
Harrismith WA 364 H6
Harrisville Qld 483 J10
Harrogate SA 288 F10
Harrow Vic. 228 D1, 230 D12, 171
Harrys Creek Vic. 235 J8
Harston Vic. 234 G6
Hart SA 295 K5
Hartley NSW 100 G5, 116 I6, **66**, 71
Hartley SA 288 F13
Hartley Vale NSW 100 G5
Hartz Mountains National Park Tas. 538 B10, 543 J10, 519, **520**
Harvey WA 357 H2, 364 C7, 366 C10, 319, **328**
Harwood NSW 119 Q5
Haslam SA 303 P11
Hassell National Park WA 361 Q9, 364 I12, 366 F12
Hastings Tas. 538 D13, 543 J12, 510, **519**, **522**
Hastings Vic. 213 L11, 215 N6, 226 E7, 155
Hastings Point NSW 119 Q1, 491 R11
Hat Head NSW 105 I3, 119 P10
Hat Head National Park NSW 105 I2, 119 P10, 69
Hatches Creek NT 409 M13, 411 L2

Hatfield NSW 122 H6, 233 O1
Hatherleigh SA 293 G11
Hattah Vic. 122 E9, 232 H7
Hattah-Kulkyne National Park Vic. 122 D8, 232 H6, **176**, 185, 189, 191, 201
Hatton Vale Qld 482 I8
Havelock Vic. 223 L4, 231 O11
Haven Vic. 230 G10
Havilah Vic. 225 L3, 235 P7, 236 B5
Hawker ACT 136 B7
Hawker SA 291 D10, 297 J9, **257–8**, 273
Hawkesbury Region NSW 101 M4, 104 C10, 117 K6, **46**
Hawkesbury Heights NSW 101 K6, 103 Q3
Hawkesdale Vic. 228 H7
Hawks Nest NSW 108 H1, 117 O4, 51
Hawley Beach Tas. 540 G5, 545 J6, **522**
Hawthorn SA 285 J10
Hawthorn Vic. 209 L9
Hawthorne Qld 478 I12
Hay NSW 123 K8, **66**
Haydens Bog Vic. 115 D12, 237 L8
Hayes Tas. 538 E4, 543 K7
Hayes Creek Roadhouse NT 402 G11, 406 E8
Hayman Island Qld **439**, 466
Haymarket NSW 92 D11
Haysdale Vic. 122 G9, 233 M8
Hazel Park Vic. 227 J10
Hazelbrook NSW 100 I7, 103 J8
Hazeldene Qld 483 J4
Hazeldene Vic. 213 L2, 226 E1, 234 H12
Hazelgrove NSW 100 E6
Hazelmere WA 355 Q10
Hazelwood Vic. 227 J7
Hazelwood Park SA 285 L8
Healesville Vic. 213 N5, 216 E6, 226 F3, 153, **177–8**, 197
Heath Hill Vic. 213 O10, 226 G7
Heathcote NSW 98 E13, 101 M11, 112 I1, 117 L8
Heathcote Vic. 234 E9, **178**, 197
Heathcote Junction Vic. 213 K2, 226 D1, 234 G12
Heathcote National Park NSW 98 E13, 101 M11, 112 H2
Heatherton Vic. 211 D3, 293 I11
Heathfield Vic. 228 B4
Heathmere Vic. 228 D8
Heathmont Vic. 210 C10
Heathpool SA 285 L7
Heathvale Vic. 230 H11
Heathwood Qld 480 F10
Hebden NSW 117 L3
Hebel Qld 118 B3, 490 F13
Hectorville SA 285 M4
Hedley Vic. 227 K10
Heidelberg Vic. 209 N5
Heidelberg West Vic. 209 N5
Heka Tas. 544 G7
Helensburgh NSW 101 M11, 112 I3, 117 L9, 89
Helensvale Qld 485 C3
Helenvale Qld 495 L3
Helidon Qld 482 G8, 442
Hell Hole Gorge National Park Qld 501 O4
Helling NT 406 G10
Hells Gate Roadhouse Qld 497 B8, 474
Hellyer Tas. 544 E4
Hemmant Qld 479 L10
Hendon SA 284 D3

Hendra Qld 478 H9
Henley NSW 95 J8
Henley Beach SA 284 C6, 288 A10, 245
Henley Brook WA 355 P3
Henrietta Tas. 544 F6
Hensley Park Vic. 228 G4
Henty NSW 116 A13, 123 Q11, **66–7**
Henty Vic. 228 D5
Hepburn Springs Vic. 212 E2, 223 P8, 229 Q2, 231 Q13, 234 B12, 141, 142, 163, 168
Herberton Qld 495 M8, 425, 449
Heritage Park Qld 481 J12
Hermannsburg NT 404 F5, 410 H9, 383, 384, **387**, 389, 391
Hermidale NSW 121 P10
Hermit Park Qld 487 E7
Hermitage Tas. 543 J4, 545 K13
Hernani NSW 119 N8
Herne Hill Vic. 218 A4
Heron Island Qld **438**, 445, 457
Herons Creek NSW 105 F9, 119 O12
Herrick Tas. 545 P6
Herston Qld 478 G11, 418
Hervey Bay Qld 491 P3, **444**, 454, 463
Hesket Vic. 212 H2
Hesso SA 296 H9
Hewetsons Mill NSW 119 N2
Hexham NSW 108 E7
Hexham Vic. 229 J7
Heybridge Tas. 544 G6
Heyfield Vic. 227 L5, 183, 194
Heytesbury Settlement Vic. 217 C8
Heywood Vic. 228 E8, 191
Hiamdale Vic. 227 L7
Hiawatha Vic. 203
Hidden Vale Qld 482 I9
Hidden Valley National Park see Mirima National Park
Hideaway Bay Tas. 538 E11
Higgins ACT 136 B6
High Camp Vic. 212 I1, 234 F11
High Range NSW 100 H13, 112 A5, 115 H2, 117 J9
High Wycombe WA 353 Q1, 355 Q13
Highbury SA 285 O1, 287 O12
Highbury WA 364 G7
Highclere Tas. 544 G6
Highcroft Tas. 539 M10, 543 N10
Higher McDonald NSW 101 M2
Highett Vic. 211 B3
Highfields Qld 482 F7, 468
Highgate SA 285 J9
Highgate WA 352 I2, 354 I13
Highgate Hill Qld 478 G13, 480 G1
Highlands Vic. 213 M1, 234 H10
Highton Vic. 218 A10, 219 E7
Highvale Qld 483 K7
Hilgay Vic. 228 D4
Hill End NSW 100 A1, 116 G5, 29
Hill End Vic. 213 R8, 226 I5
Hillarys WA 354 A3, 356 A3
Hillbank SA 287 N3
Hillcrest SA 285 L2, 287 L13
Hillcrest Vic. 212 B4, 223 K11
Hilldale NSW 108 A4
Hillgrove NSW 119 M9, 45
Hillman WA 364 F8
Hillsdale NSW 99 P5
Hillside Vic. 227 P4, 236 F13
Hillston NSW 123 M4
Hilltop NSW 101 J13, 112 D5, 115 I2, 117 J9

Hilltown SA 295 L5
Hillwood Tas. 541 M6, 545 L7, 519
Hilton SA 284 G7
Hilton WA 352 D12
Hinchinbrook Island National Park Qld 495 O10, 431, **440**, 446, **457**
Hindmarsh SA 284 G5, 276
Hindmarsh Valley SA 290 E11
Hines Hill WA 364 I2
Hinnomunjie Vic. 115 A11, 236 F8
Hinton NSW 108 D6
Hirstglen Qld 482 F10
Hobart Tas. 535 D6, 536 G7, 538 H6, 543 L8, 503, 505, **506–10**, 515, 525, 527
Hobbys Yards NSW 100 A7, 116 G7
Hoddle Vic. 226 I10
Hoddles Creek Vic. 213 N6, 216 F10, 226 F4, 198
Hodgson Vale Qld 482 E8
Holbrook NSW 123 R12, 235 R1, **67**
Holden Hill SA 287 N12
Holder ACT 136 C13, 137 A4
Holgate NSW 101 P4, 104 G5
Holland Park Qld 480 I3
Hollow Tree Tas. 543 K6
Holloways Beach Qld 489 F8
Holly WA 361 L2, 364 G9
Hollydeen NSW 117 K2
Hollywell Qld 485 E2
Holmview Qld 481 P12
Holmwood NSW 116 F5
Holsworthy Village NSW 98 B6
Holt ACT 136 A5
Holwell Tas. 541 J7, 545 K7
Home Hill Qld 492 H1, 495 Q13, 425, **444**
Homebush NSW 94 F10
Homebush Qld. 223 J5
Homebush Qld 452
Homebush Bay NSW 94 F9, 101 N8, 40
Homecroft Vic. 230 I6
Homerton Vic. 228 E8
Homestead Qld 492 D3, 499 R3
Homewood Vic. 213 M1
Honiton SA 294 I10
Hook Island National Park Qld 493 K2, **439**
Hope Forest SA 289 G5, 290 D7
Hope Vale Aboriginal Community Qld 495 L2
Hope Valley SA 287 O12
Hopetoun Vic. 122 E12, 230 H3, 232 H13, **178**
Hopetoun WA 366 H11, **328–9**
Hopetoun West Vic. 230 G2, 232 G13
Hopevale Vic. 230 G3
Hoppers Crossing Vic. 208 B11, 212 H6, 219 I3
Hordern Vale Vic. 217 E12
Hornsby NSW 95 P9, 101 N7
Hornsby Heights NSW 96 F7
Hornsdale SA 295 K2, 297 K13
Horrocks WA 366 A3
Horse Lake NSW 120 D12
Horsham SA 290 F5
Horsham Vic. 230 G9, **178**, 203
Horsley Park NSW 101 L8
Hoskinstown NSW 115 F6, 116 H13, 135 I5, 139 J3
Hotham Heights Vic. 225 N9, 235 Q10, 236 D8
Hotspur Vic. 228 D6
Houghton SA 287 R10, 288 D8
Houtman Abrolhos Islands WA 327

Hove SA 284 E13
Howard Qld 491 P3
Howard Springs NT 402 D3, 406 E5
Howard Springs National Park NT 402 D3
Howden Tas. 538 H8, 543 L9, 523
Howes Valley NSW 117 K4
Howley NT 402 G10
Howlong NSW 123 P13, 235 O3, 236 A1
Howqua Vic. 213 R2, 224 D12, 235 L11
Howrah Tas. 537 M7, 538 I5, 543 M8
Howth Tas. 544 G6
Hoya Qld 483 J12
Hoyleton SA 295 K6
Huddleston SA 295 K3
Hughenden Qld 492 A4, 499 O4, **444**
Hughes ACT 136 F13, 137 D3
Hughes SA 302 C5
Hull River National Park Qld 495 O9
Hume ACT 137 H7
Hume Park NSW 115 D4, 116 F11
Humevale Vic. 213 K3
Humpty Doo NT 402 E3, 406 E6, 379
Humula NSW 115 A6, 116 C13
Hunchy Qld 483 M1, 486 C9
Hungerford Qld 121 J1, 501 O13
Hunter Vic. 234 D6
Hunter Valley NSW 109, 29, 43, 81
Hunters Hill NSW 95 J7
Hunterston Vic. 227 L9
Huntingdale WA 353 N12
Huntly Vic. 231 R9, 234 C8
Huon Vic. 235 Q5, 236 C2
Huonville Tas. 538 F8, 543 K9, 510, **522**
Hurdle Flat Vic. 235 O6, 236 A4
Hurlstone Park NSW 94 I13, 99 K3
Hurstbridge Vic. 210 A1, 213 L5, 226 E3
Hurstville NSW 99 J6, 101 N9
Huskisson NSW 115 I5, 117 K12, 139 R1, **67**
Hutt WA 366 A2
Hyams Beach NSW 139 R2
Hyde Park Qld 487 D6
Hyde Park SA 284 I9, 244
Hyden WA 366 F8, **329**
Hynam SA 230 A11, 293 I9

Icy Creek Vic. 213 Q7
Ida Bay Tas. 543 J12
Idalia Qld 487 F10
Idalia National Park Qld 501 P2, 427
Iguana Creek Vic. 227 O4
Ilbilbie Qld 493 L6
Ilford NSW 116 I5
Ilfracombe Qld 492 A11, 499 P11, **446**, 451
Ilfraville Tas. 541 J4
Illabarook Vic. 212 B6, 229 N5
Illabo NSW 115 A4, 116 C11
Illalong Creek NSW 115 C3, 116 E11
Illawarra Vic. 222 B5
Illawarra Coast NSW 112 G3, 117 K12, **53**
Illawong NSW 98 G9
Illawong WA 366 B5
Illowa Vic. 228 H9
Iluka NSW 119 Q5, **67**, 72
Imanpa NT 404 D13
Imbil Qld 491 P6
Impimi NSW 122 H9, 233 O7
Inala Qld 480 F8
Inarlinga Qld 495 N8
Indented Head Vic. 212 I9, 214 C1, 219 I7, 226 B6

Indigo Vic. 235 N4, 236 A2
Indigo Upper Vic. 235 O5, 236 B3
Indooroopilly Qld 480 E2, 483 L8
Ingebyra NSW 115 C10, 237 J5
Ingham Qld 495 N11, **446**
Ingle Farm SA 287 L10
Ingleby Vic. 217 I6
Inglegar NSW 118 B12
Ingleside NSW 97 O7
Ingleside Qld 485 D11
Inglewood Qld 119 K1, 491 L11, **446**
Inglewood SA 288 D8
Inglewood Vic. 231 O8, 234 A7, **178**, 192
Inglewood WA 355 J11
Ingliston Vic. 212 F5, 223 Q12
Ingoldsby Qld 482 H9
Injinoo Qld 496 C3
Injune Qld 490 G5, **446**
Inkerman Qld 492 H1
Inkerman SA 295 J7
Inman Valley SA 289 E7, 290 B11, 277
Innaloo WA 354 D10
Innamincka SA 299 Q7, 500 H10, **258**, 279
Innes National Park SA 294 G10, 239, 255, **263**, 280
Inneston SA 255
Innisfail Qld 495 N8, **446–7**
Innot Hot Springs Qld 495 L8
Interlaken Tas. 543 L4, 545 L13
Inverell NSW 119 K6, **67**, 69
Invergordon Vic. 123 M13, 234 I4
Inverleigh Vic. 212 E9, 219 B6, 229 P7, **178**
Inverloch Vic. 226 G10, 153, **179**, 200
Invermay Tas. 541 O10
Invermay Vic. 221 E1
Iona Vic. 213 O9
Ipolera NT 404 D5, 410 G9
Ipswich Qld 483 J9, 491 P9, 417, **447**
Iraak Vic. 122 E8, 232 H5
Irishtown Tas. 544 D4
Irishtown Vic. 223 Q6
Iron Baron SA 294 H2, 296 G13
Iron Knob SA 294 H1, 296 G12, 278
Iron Range Qld 496 E8
Iron Range National Park Qld 496 E7, **458**
Irongate Qld 482 C8
Ironside Qld 480 F2
Irrewarra Vic. 212 B11, 217 G6
Irrewillipe Vic. 212 A12, 217 E8, 229 M9
Irvinebank Qld 495 L8
Irvingdale Qld 482 B4
Irymple Vic. 122 D7, 232 G3, 185
Isaacs ACT 137 E6
Isabella NSW 100 C9, 115 F1, 116 H8
Isabella Plains ACT 137 D10
Isisford Qld 492 A13, 499 P13, 501 O1, **447**
Isla Gorge National Park Qld 491 J3, 467, 468
Island Bend NSW 114 E10, 138 C11
Isle of the Dead Tas. 505, 517
Islington NSW 106 B5
Ivanhoe NSW 123 J2
Ivanhoe Vic. 209 M6
Ivory Creek Qld 482 I3
Iwupataka NT 404 I4, 410 I8

Jabiru NT 401 H5, 403 P4, 406 H6, 380, 385, **388**
Jabiru East NT 401 H5, 403 Q4, 406 H6
Jabuk SA 293 F3, 295 O11
Jack River Vic. 227 K9

Jackadgery NSW 119 O5
Jackeys Marsh Tas. 545 J10
Jackie Junction WA 369 N10
Jackson Qld 490 I7
Jacobs Well Qld 483 O11
Jacobs Well WA 364 G4
Jalloonda Qld 495 O12
Jallumba Vic. 230 F11
Jaloran WA 364 G7
Jamberoo NSW 112 G9, 117 K10, **67**
Jambin Qld 493 N13, 426
Jamboree Heights Qld 480 C6
Jamestown SA 295 L3, 297 K13, **258**
Jamieson Vic. 213 R2, 224 D13, 226 I1, 235 L12, 172, 183, 184, 185, 196
Jancourt Vic. 217 B7
Jancourt East Vic. 217 C7
Jandakot WA 352 I13, 356 C6
Jandowae Qld 491 L7
Jannali NSW 98 I10
Jardee WA 360 C6, 364 D11
Jardine River National Park Qld 496 C4, **458**
Jarklin Vic. 231 P6, 234 A5
Jarra Jarra NT 408 I13, 410 I2
Jarrahdale WA 356 D8, 364 D5, 343
Jarrahmond Vic. 237 J12
Jarrahwood WA 357 G8, 364 C9
Jarvis Creek Vic. 235 R4, 236 D2
Jaurdi WA 366 H6
Jeffcott Vic. 231 L7
Jeffcott North Vic. 231 L6
Jellat Jellat NSW 113 F7
Jemalong NSW 116 C6
Jennacubbine WA 364 E2
Jenolan Caves NSW 100 F8, 116 I7, 29
Jeogla NSW 119 M9
Jeparit Vic. 230 F6, **179**, 199
Jerangle NSW 115 F7, 135 I3, 138 I8
Jericho Qld 492 E11
Jericho Tas. 543 L5
Jericho Vic. 213 R5, 227 J3
Jerilderie NSW 123 M11, **67–8**, 75
Jerralang North Vic. 227 K8
Jerramungup WA 366 G11, 315, 329
Jerrawa NSW 115 E4, 116 G11
Jerrys Plains NSW 117 K3
Jerseyville NSW 105 I1, 119 P10
Jervis Bay JBT 115 I5, 139 R2, 67, 125, 132
Jervis Bay National Park JBT 139 R2
Jervis Bay National Park NSW 139 R2
Jervois SA 293 E3, 295 N10, 276
Jetsonville Tas. 545 N6
Jiggalong Community WA 368 F6
Jil Jil Vic. 231 K3
Jilliby NSW 101 P2, 104 D1, 117 M6
Jimaringle NSW 123 J11, 233 R10
Jimboomba Qld 483 M11, 491 P10
Jimbour Qld 491 M7, 465
Jimenbuen NSW 115 D10, 237 L6
Jindabyne NSW 114 G11, 115 D9, 138 C12, 237 K3, **68**
Jindalee Qld 480 C5, 419
Jindera NSW 123 P13, 235 J3, 236 B1, 57
Jindivick Vic. 213 P8, 226 H5
Jindong WA 357 D8, 359 E4, 364 B9
Jingalup WA 360 I3, 364 F10
Jingellic NSW 115 A8, 236 F1, 201
Jingili NT 400 F5
Jitarning WA 364 I6, 366 F9
Joadja NSW 112 A6, 115 H2, 117 J10
Joanna SA 228 A1, 230 A12, 293 I9

Joel Joel Vic. 222 E4
Joel South Vic. 222 E5
Johanna Vic. 217 E12, 229 M12
John Forrest National Park WA 356 D4, 305, 311, 317, **322**, 338
Johnberg SA 291 E12, 297 K11
Johns River NSW 105 E11, 119 O13
Johnsonville Vic. 227 Q4, 236 G13
Jolimont WA 352 E2
Jondaryan Qld 482 C6, 491 M8
Jones Gully Qld 482 F5
Joondanna WA 354 G11
Josbury WA 364 F7
Josephville Qld 483 L12
Joskeleigh Qld 493 O10
Joyces Creek Vic. 223 N5
Joyner Qld 478 B1
Jubilee Qld 478 E11
Jubuck WA 364 H5
Judbury Tas. 538 D7, 543 K9, 522
Jugiong NSW 115 C4, 116 E11, 64, 74
Julatten Qld 489 B5, 495 M6
Julia SA 295 M6
Julia Creek Qld 499 J4, **447**
Jumbuk Vic. 227 K8
Jumbunna Vic. 213 O12, 226 G9
Junction View Qld 482 G10
Jundah Qld 501 M2, **447**
Junee NSW 115 A4, 116 C11, 123 R9, **68**
Junee Reefs NSW 115 A3, 116 C11
Jung Vic. 230 H8, 178
Junortoun Vic. 223 R2, 231 R10, 234 C8
Jupiter Creek SA 290 G4
Jura WA 364 I3
Jurien WA 366 B6, **329–30**
Jurunjung Vic. 212 H4

Kaarimba Vic. 234 H4
Kadina SA 294 I6, 239, 240, 249, 255, **258**, 261, 266, 270, 278
Kadnook Vic. 228 C1, 230 C12
Kadungle NSW 116 C4
Kaglan WA 361 O11, 364 I12
Kaimkillenbun Qld 482 B3, 491 M8
Kain NSW 115 F7, 139 J6
Kainton SA 295 J6
Kairi Qld 489 D12, 495 M7, 424
Kajabbi Qld 498 F2
Kakadu National Park NT 401 F3, 403 N2, 406 G5, 373, 374, 380, 385, 386, 388, 390, 391, 392, 395
Kalamunda National Park WA 356 D5, **322**
Kalangadoo SA 293 H11
Kalangara Qld 483 K3
Kalannie WA 366 D6
Kalaru NSW 113 G8, 115 G10, 237 Q6
Kalbar Qld 483 J11, 491 P10
Kalbarri WA 365 C13, 366 A2, 328, **330**
Kalbarri National Park WA 365 C13, 366 A1, 306, 317, **323**, 328, 330
Kaleen ACT 136 F5
Kaleentha Loop NSW 122 F1
Kalgarin WA 366 F9
Kalgoorlie-Boulder WA 366 I6, 305, **330–1**, 333, 336
Kalimna West Vic. 227 R4, 236 G13
Kalinga Qld 478 G8
Kalka SA 300 A1, 369 R11, 410 B13
Kalkallo Vic. 213 J4, 226 C2, 234 F13
Kalkarindji NT 408 D6
Kalkee Vic. 230 G8

Kalkite NSW 114 G10, 138 D12
Kallangur Qld 483 M6, 419
Kallaroo WA 354 A2
Kallista Vic. 210 G12
Kaloorup WA 357 D8, 359 E4, 364 B9
Kalorama Vic. 210 G9
Kalpienung Vic. 231 M3
Kalpowar Qld 491 M2
Kalumburu WA 371 N2, 332
Kalunga Qld 495 M8
Kalyan SA 293 F1, 295 O9
Kamarah NSW 116 A9, 123 P7
Kamarooka Vic. 231 R8, 234 D7
Kambah ACT 137 B7
Kambalda WA 367 J7, 306, **331**, 336
Kamballup WA 361 O8, 364 I11
Kamber NSW 118 D12
Kameruka NSW 113 E8, 237 P6
Kamona Tas. 545 O7
Kanangra Boyd National NSW 115 H1
Kanangra Boyd National Park NSW 100 F8, 115 H1, 116 I8
Kanawalla Vic. 228 G4
Kancoona Vic. 225 M2
Kancoona South Vic. 225 M3
Kandos NSW 116 I4, 80
Kangaloon NSW 112 D7
Kangarilla SA 288 C12, 289 G3, 290 E4, 293 B2, 295 L10
Kangaroo Flat NSW 119 M11
Kangaroo Flat SA 288 C5
Kangaroo Ground Vic. 209 R2, 210 A3
Kangaroo Island SA 289 A11, 294 F11, 239, 259, **269**, 276, 277
Kangaroo Point Qld 476 H8, 478 H12, 417, 418
Kangaroo Valley NSW 112 D10, 115 I3, 77
Kangarooby NSW 116 E7
Kangawall Vic. 230 D10
Kangiara NSW 115 D3, 116 F10
Kaniva Vic. 230 C7, **179**
Kanmantoo SA 288 F11
Kanumbra Vic. 235 J10
Kanya Vic. 222 E1, 231 K10
Kanyapella Vic. 123 K13, 234 F4
Kanypi SA 300 D2, 410 C13
Kaoota Tas. 538 G7, 543 L9
Kapinnie SA 294 C6
Kapooka NSW 116 B12, 123 R10, 86
Kapunda SA 288 E3, 295 L7, 246, **258**
Karabeal Vic. 228 G4
Karadoc Vic. 122 E7, 232 H4
Karalundi WA 368 C11
Karanja Tas. 538 D3
Karara Qld 119 L1, 482 B13, 491 M11
Karatta SA 294 G13
Karawara WA 353 J7
Karawatha Qld 481 K9
Karawinna Vic. 122 C8, 232 E4
Kardinya WA 352 E11
Kareela NSW 98 I9
Kariah Vic. 217 C5
Karijini (Hamersley Range) National Park WA 365 I5, 368 B5, 307, **323**, 339, 343, 345
Karingal Vic. 211 F12
Karkoo SA 294 D6
Karlo Creek Vic. 115 F13, 237 O11
Karn Vic. 224 B4
Karnak Vic. 230 D10
Karnup WA 334, 344
Karonie WA 367 K6

Karoola Tas. 541 O6, 545 M7
Karoonda SA 293 F2, 295 O10
Karoonda Roadhouse Vic. 115 C12, 236 I9
Karrakatta WA 352 D5
Karratha WA **331**, 339
Karratha Roadhouse WA 365 G1
Karridale WA 357 C12, 359 C11, 364 B10
Karrinyup WA 354 C8
Kars Springs NSW 117 J1, 118 I13
Karte SA 293 H2, 295 Q10
Karuah NSW 108 F2, 117 N3
Karumba Qld 494 B8, 497 H8, **447**, 461, 474
Karween Vic. 122 B8, 232 C4
Karyrie Vic. 231 K4
Katamatite Vic. 123 M13, 235 J4, 204
Katandra Vic. 234 I5
Katanning WA 361 L1, 364 H9, 366 E10, 329, **331**
Kata Tjuta NT 404 B11, 382, 393, 396
Katherine NT 406 G10, 374, 385, 386, **388**, 391
Katoomba NSW 100 H7, 102 E9, 117 J7, 42, 43, 58, **68–9**
Kattyong Vic. 232 F9
Katunga Vic. 123 M13, 234 I3, 187
Katyil Vic. 230 G7
Kawarren Vic. 212 B12, 217 F8, 229 N10
Kayena Tas. 541 L5, 545 K7
Kealba Vic. 208 F5
Kedron Qld 478 G9
Keep River National Park NT 363 Q2, 371 R5, 406 A13, 408 A2, 392, 394
Keera NSW 119 J7
Keilor Vic. 208 G4
Keilor Downs Vic. 208 F4
Keilor East Vic. 208 H5
Keilor Park Vic. 208 H4
Keiraville NSW 110 A9
Keith SA 293 G6, 295 P13, **258**, 260
Kelfeera Vic. 224 C3
Kellac Vic. 230 H7
Kellalac Vic. 230 H7
Kellatier Tas. 544 F6
Kellerberrin WA 364 H3, 366 E7, 337
Kellevie Tas. 539 N5, 543 N8
Kelmscott WA 356 D6
Kelso NSW 100 B4
Kelso Tas. 541 J4, 545 K6, 511
Kelvin NSW 118 I10
Kelvin Grove Qld 478 F11
Kelvin View Vic. 235 J9
Kelvinhaugh Qld 482 D6
Kempsey NSW 105 G3, 119 O11, **69**
Kempton Tas. 538 H1, 543 L6, 526
Kendall NSW 105 E10, 119 O12, 70
Kendenup WA 361 M8, 364 H11, 337
Kenebri NSW 118 E9
Kenilworth Qld 483 L1, 491 P7, **447**
Kenley Vic. 233 M7
Kenmare Vic. 122 D13, 230 G4
Kenmore NSW 115 G3, 116 H10
Kenmore Qld 480 C3
Kenmore Hills Qld 480 B2
Kennedy Qld 495 N10
Kennedy Range National Park WA 365 D7, 327
Kennedys Creek Vic. 217 C10
Kennett River Vic. 217 I11, 229 O11
Kennys Creek NSW 115 D2, 116 F10
Kensington NSW 95 N12, 99 P2
Kensington SA 285 L6

Kensington WA 353 J5
Kensington Gardens SA 285 M6
Kent Town SA 282 H8, 285 J6
Kentbruck Vic. 228 C8, 191
Kenthurst NSW 96 A6
Kentlyn NSW 112 G1
Kentucky NSW 119 L9
Kenwick WA 353 P8
Keperra Qld 478 C9
Keppel Sands Qld 493 O10, 473
Keppoch SA 293 H8, 268
Kerang Vic. 122 I12, 231 P3, 233 P13, 234 A2, **179**, 201
Kerang East Vic. 231 P3, 234 B2
Kerang South Vic. 122 I12, 231 P3, 234 A2
Kergunyah Vic. 235 Q5, 236 C3
Kergunyah South Vic. 235 P6, 236 C4
Kernot Vic. 213 N12, 226 G8
Kerrabee NSW 117 J3
Kerrie Vic. 212 I2
Kerrisdale Vic. 213 L1, 234 H11, 204
Kerrs Creek NSW 116 G5
Kerry Qld 483 L13
Kerrydale Qld 485 D8
Kersbrook SA 288 E8, 293 C1, 295 L9, 261, 277
Keswick SA 284 H8
Kettering Tas. 538 H9, 543 L10, 512, **522**
Kevington Vic. 213 R3, 226 I1, 235 L12
Kew NSW 105 E10, 119 O12
Kew Vic. 209 M8
Kewarra Beach Qld 489 E7
Kewdale WA 353 M5
Kewell Vic. 230 H8
Keyneton SA 288 H5, 295 M8
Keysborough Vic. 211 F4
Keysbrook WA 356 C9, 364 D5
Khancoban NSW 114 A9, 115 B9, 236 H3, **69–70**
Ki Ki SA 293 F4, 295 O11
Kiah NSW 113 F12, 115 G12, 237 Q9
Kialla NSW 115 F3, 116 H10
Kialla West Vic. 234 H6, 194
Kiama NSW 112 H9, 117 K10, 53, **70**
Kiamba Qld 483 M1, 486 C6
Kiamil Vic. 122 E10, 232 H8
Kiandra NSW 114 D3, 115 C7, 138 C7, 84
Kianga NSW 113 I2, 139 N11
Kiara WA 355 L9
Kiata Vic. 230 E7, 170, 186
Kidaman Creek Qld 486 A8
Kidman Park SA 284 D6
Kielpa SA 294 E4
Kies Hill SA 292 C10
Kiewa Vic. 235 Q5, 236 C3
Kikoira NSW 123 P5
Kilburn SA 284 H2, 286 H13, 244
Kilcarnup WA 357 B10, 359 B7, 364 A10
Kilcoy Qld 483 J3, 491 P7
Kilcunda Vic. 213 M13, 226 F9, 200
Kilkenny SA 284 F3
Kilkerran SA 294 I7
Kilkivan Qld 491 O5, 444
Killabakh Creek NSW 105 B11, 119 N13
Killara NSW 95 K2, 97 J12
Killarney Qld 119 N1, 491 O11, **447**
Killarney Vic. 228 H9
Killarney Heights NSW 95 N4
Killawarra Vic. 235 L5
Killcare NSW 104 G8
Killcare Heights NSW 101 P5, 104 H8, 117 M6, 59

Killiecrankie Tas. 542 A11
Killora Tas. 538 H9, 543 L10
Kilmany Vic. 227 M6
Kilmany South Vic. 227 M6
Kilmore Vic. 213 J2, 234 F11, 165
Kilpalie SA 293 G2, 295 O9
Kilsyth Vic. 210 E8
Kimba SA 294 F3, 296 E13, **260**, 333
Kimberley, The WA 362, 363, 371 L6, 307, 308, **344**, 347
Kimberley Tas. 540 F9, 544 I8
Kimbriki NSW 117 O1, 119 N13
Kinalung NSW 120 D12
Kincaid Vic. 217 E11
Kinchega National Park NSW 120 D13, 122 D1, **60**, 73
Kinchela NSW 105 H2, 119 P10
Kinchella Creek NSW 105 H2, 119 P10
Kincumber NSW 101 P4, 104 G7, 117 M6
Kindred Tas. 540 C6, 544 H7
King Island Tas. 505, 525, **531**
King River WA 361 O11, 364 H13
King Valley Vic. 224 F5, 235 N8
Kingaroy Qld 491 N6, 421, **447**, **450**
Kinglake Vic. 213 M4, 226 E2, 234 H13
Kinglake Central Vic. 213 L3
Kinglake East Vic. 213 M4, 216 B2
Kinglake National Park Vic. 213 L3, 216 B1, 226 E1, 234 H12, **174**, 204
Kinglake West Vic. 213 L3
Kingoonya SA 296 B5
Kingower Vic. 231 O9, 178, 197
Kings Beach Qld 486 I13
Kings Camp SA 293 E9
Kings Canyon Resort NT 410 F9, 373, 382, 383, 384, **386**, 387, **388**, 389, 390, 393
Kings Creek Qld 482 E10
Kings Cross NSW 95 N10, 36, 40
Kings Meadows Tas. 541 O10
Kings Plains National Park NSW 119 K5
Kingsborough Qld 495 L6, 449
Kingsbury Vic. 209 M4
Kingscliff NSW 119 Q1, 491 R11, 84
Kingscote SA 294 I12, **260**, 269
Kingsdale NSW 115 G3, 116 H11
Kingsford NSW 95 N13, 99 P3, 101 O9
Kingsgrove NSW 99 J5
Kingsley WA 354 D4
Kingsthorpe Qld 482 E7
Kingston ACT 134 G13, 136 H11, 137 F2, 130
Kingston Qld 481 M10
Kingston Tas. 538 H7, 543 L9, **522–3**
Kingston Vic. 212 D2, 223 N8, 229 P2, 231 P13, 234 A12
Kingston Beach Tas. 538 I7
Kingston O.M. SA 295 P7, 261
Kingston S.E. SA 293 F8, **260**, 274
Kingsvale NSW 115 C2, 116 E10
Kingswood NSW 101 K8
Kingswood SA 285 J10, 291 C12, 297 J10
Kinimakatka Vic. 230 D7
Kinka Qld 493 O10
Kinnabulla Vic. 231 J4
Kintore NT 369 R6, 410 B7
Kioloa NSW 115 H6, 117 J13, 139 P6
Kiora NSW 139 M9
Kipper Qld 482 H5
Kirkstall Vic. 228 H8
Kirrawee NSW 98 I11
Kirup WA 357 H7, 360 B1, 364 C9
Kital Qld 482 F12

Kitchener NSW 108 C10
Kitchener WA 367 L6
Kithbrook Vic. 235 J9
Klemzig SA 285 L3, 244
Klimpton NSW 115 I4, 117 K11, 139 Q1
Knebsworth Vic. 228 F7
Knockrow NSW 119 Q3, 491 Q12
Knockwood Vic. 213 R3
Knorrit Flat NSW 117 O1, 119 M13
Knowsley Vic. 234 E9
Knoxfield Vic. 210 B13, 211 I1
Koallah Vic. 217 C6
Kobble Qld 483 L6
Kobyboyn Vic. 234 H10
Koetong Vic. 115 A8, 236 E2
Kogan Qld 491 L8
Kogarah NSW 99 L6
Koimbo Vic. 233 K8
Kojonup WA 361 J2, 364 G9, 366 E11, 329, **331**
Koloona NSW 119 J6
Kolora Vic. 217 A4
Kommamurra Qld 482 B4
Komungla NSW 115 G4, 116 H11
Konagaderra Vic. 212 I4
Kondinin WA 364 I5, 366 F9, **331**
Kongal SA 293 H6
Kongorong SA 293 H12, 267
Kongwak Vic. 213 O13, 226 G9
Konnongorring WA 364 F1
Konong Wootong Vic. 228 E3
Konong Wootong North Vic. 228 E3
Koo-wee-rup Vic. 213 M10, 226 F7, **179–80**
Kookynie WA 366 I4, 331, 334
Kookaburra NSW 105 B2, 119 N10
Koolan WA 362 B5, 371 J5
Koolewong NSW 104 F7
Kooloonong Vic. 233 L8
Koolunga SA 295 K4
Koolyanobbing WA 345
Koolywurtie SA 294 I8
Koombal Qld 489 G8
Koonda Vic. 232 D9, 235 J7
Koondah Qld 482 B2
Koondoola WA 354 I6
Koondrook Vic. 122 I12, 231 Q2, 233 Q13, 234 B1, 46, 179
Koongarra NT 401 H6, 403 P5
Koongawa SA 294 D3, 296 C13
Koonibba SA 303 N9
Koonoomoo Vic. 234 I2
Koonunga SA 288 F3
Koonwarra Vic. 213 P13, 226 H9
Koonya Tas. 539 M9, 543 N10
Koorack Koorack Vic. 231 N3, 233 N13
Kooralbyn Qld 483 K13
Kooralgin Qld 482 F2
Koorawatha NSW 115 C1, 116 E8
Koorda WA 366 E6, 337
Kooreh Vic. 231 M9
Kooringal Qld 483 P7
Koorkab Vic. 233 L7
Koorlong Vic. 122 D7, 232 G4
Kootingal NSW 119 K10
Kooyong Vic. 209 M9
Koppamurra SA 230 A11, 293 I9
Koppio SA 294 D7, 254, 271, 277
Korbel WA 364 I3
Koriella Vic. 213 O1
Korobeit Vic. 212 F4
Koroit Vic. 228 H9, **180**

Korong Vale Vic. 231 O7
Koroop Vic. 234 B2
Korora NSW 119 P8, 54
Korumburra Vic. 213 O12, 226 H8, **180**, 181
Korweinguboora Vic. 212 E3
Kosciusko National Park NSW 114 D2, 115 C6, 116 E13, 135 A10, 138 C5, 237 J2, 32, **60**, 65, 68, 69, 85, 168, 175
Kotta Vic. 234 D4
Kotupna Vic. 123 L13, 234 G4
Koumala Qld 493 L6
Kowanyama Aboriginal Community Qld 494 D3
Kowat Vic. 115 E12, 237 N10
Koyuga Vic. 234 F5
Krambach NSW 117 O1
Kringin SA 293 H2, 295 Q9
Kroemers Crossing SA 292 F5
Kroombit Tops National Park Qld 491 L1, 493 O13
Krowera Vic. 213 O12
Ku-Ring-Gai Chase National Park NSW 96 H8, 97 N3, 101 O6, 104 F11, 117 L7, 41, 46, **58**
Kudardup WA 357 C12, 359 D12, 364 B11
Kuitpo SA 290 E6
Kuitpo Colony SA 290 F7
Kukerin WA 364 H7, 366 F10, 325
Kulgera NT 410 I13, 279, **390**
Kulgun Qld 483 J11
Kulikup WA 360 G2, 364 E9, 314
Kulin WA 364 I6, 366 F9, **331–2**
Kulkami SA 293 G2, 295 P10
Kulkyne Vic. 232 H6
Kulnine Vic. 232 D3
Kulnine East Vic. 122 C7, 232 D3
Kulnura NSW 101 O2, 104 A2, 117 L5
Kulpara SA 295 J6
Kulpi Qld 482 D4, 491 N8
Kulwin Vic. 232 I9
Kulyalling WA 364 F5
Kumarl WA 367 J9
Kumbarilla Qld 491 L8
Kumbia Qld 491 N7
Kumorna SA 293 G5, 295 P13
Kunama NSW 115 B6
Kunat Vic. 231 N1, 233 N12
Kundabung NSW 105 G5, 119 O11, 69
Kungala NSW 119 P7
Kunghur NSW 119 P2
Kunjin WA 364 H5
Kunlara SA 293 F1, 295 O8
Kunnunoppin WA 364 H1
Kununurra WA 363 P2, 371 Q5, **332**, 344, 347
Kunwarara Qld 493 N9
Kupingarri Community WA 362 H6, 371 M7
Kuraby Qld 481 K7
Kuranda Qld 489 E7, 495 M6, 413, 431, 449, **450**, 462
Kureelpa Qld 483 M1, 486 C7
Kuridala Qld 498 G5, 435
Kuringup WA 364 I8
Kurmond NSW 101 K5
Kurnbrunin Vic. 230 E4
Kurnell NSW 99 P9, 101 O10, 41
Kurnwill Vic. 122 B8, 232 C5
Kurraca Vic. 231 N8
Kurraca West Vic. 231 N8
Kurrajong NSW 101 K5

Kurrajong Heights NSW 101 J5, 79
Kurralta Park SA 284 G9
Kurri Kurri NSW 108 C9, 117 M4
Kurrimine Beach Qld 495 N9
Kurting Vic. 231 O8, 234 A7
Kurumbul Qld 118 I2, 491 K12
Kuttabul Qld 493 K5
Kweda WA 364 G5
Kwinana WA 356 A7, 364 C4, 366 C8, **332**
Kwolyin WA 364 H3
Kyabram Vic. 234 G5, **180**, 201
Kyalite NSW 122 G9, 233 N8
Kyancutta SA 294 C3, 296 C13, 333
Kybeyan NSW 113 C3
Kybunga SA 295 K5
Kybybolite SA 230 A10, 293 I8
Kydra NSW 113 B4
Kyeamba NSW 115 A6, 116 C13, 123 R11
Kyeemagh NSW 99 M5
Kyndalyn Vic. 122 F9, 233 K7
Kyneton Vic. 212 G1, 229 R1, 231 R12, 234 D11, 166, 173, **180**
Kynuna Qld 499 J6, **450**
Kyogle NSW 119 P2, 491 P12, **70**
Kyotmunga WA 356 E1, 364 D2
Kyup Vic. 228 F4
Kyvalley Vic. 234 G5
Kywong NSW 123 P10

La Perouse NSW 99 P8, 101 O10, 58
Laanecoorie Vic. 223 N2, 231 P10, 234 A9
Laang Vic. 229 J9
Labertouche Vic. 213 O9, 226 G6, 199
Labrador Qld 485 E4
Lachlan Tas. 538 F5, 543 K8
Lacmalac NSW 138 B2
Lady Barron Tas. 542 B12, 545 R1, 531
Lady Bay Tas. 543 K12
Lady Elliot Island Qld 430, 437, **438**
Lady Julia Percy Island Vic. 190
Lady Musgrave Island Qld 493 I12, 430, **438**, 445, 457
Ladys Pass Vic. 234 E8
Ladysmith NSW 115 A5, 116 C12, 123 R10
Laen Vic. 231 J7
Laen North Vic. 231 J7
Laggan NSW 115 F2, 116 H9, 57
Lah Vic. 230 H5
Lah-Arum Vic. 230 H11
Laheys Creek NSW 116 G2
Laidley Qld 482 H9, 491 O9, **450**
Lajamanu NT 408 D8
Lake Vic. 233 O13
Lake Barrine National Park *see* Crater Lakes National Park
Lake Bathurst NSW 115 F4, 116 H13
Lake Biddy WA 366 G9
Lake Bindegolly National Park Qld 501 O11
Lake Boga Vic. 122 H11, 231 N1, 233 N11
Lake Bolac Vic. 222 C13, 229 J5, **180**
Lake Buloke Vic. 231 K7
Lake Burley Griffin ACT 134 C7, 136 F10, 137 D1, 125, 127, 128
Lake Cargelligo NSW 123 O4, **70**
Lake Cathie NSW 105 G9, 119 O12
Lake Charm Vic. 122 H12, 231 O2, 233 O13, 234 A1
Lake Clifton WA 356 A12
Lake Condon Vic. 228 E7
Lake Conjola NSW 115 I5, 117 J12, 139 Q3
Lake Cowal NSW 116 B7, 123 R5

Lake Eyre National Park SA 298 I8, 500 B11, 261, **263**, 265
Lake Gairdner National Park SA 296 C7, 303 R7
Lake Goldsmith Vic. 222 H11
Lake Grace WA 366 F9
Lake Hindmarsh Vic. 230 E5
Lake King WA 366 G9, **332**, 340
Lake Leake Tas. 543 O3, 545 O12
Lake Margaret Tas. 542 E2, 544 E11
Lake Marmal Vic. 231 N6
Lake Meering Vic. 231 O4
Lake Mountain Vic. 226 H2, 153, 182, 184
Lake Mundi Vic. 228 B4, 293 I11
Lake Poomaho NSW 122 H10, 233 N9
Lake Powell Junction Vic. 233 K6
Lake Rowan Vic. 235 K5
Lake Torrens National Park SA 291 A5, 296 I5
Lake Tyers Vic. 236 H13, 181
Lake View SA 295 K4
Lakefield National Park Qld 495 J2, 496 G13, 435, **458**
Lakeland Qld 495 K4
Lakemba NSW 94 G13, 98 I3
Lakes Entrance Vic. 227 R5, 236 H13, **180–1**, 193
Lakesland NSW 101 J12, 112 D2
Lal Lal Vic. 212 D5, 223 N12, 229 P4
Lalbert Vic. 122 G12, 231 M2, 233 M13
Lalbert Road Vic. 231 M1, 233 M12
Lalla Tas. 541 O6, 545 M7, 524
Lallat Vic. 231 J9
Lallat North Vic. 231 J8
Lalor Vic. 209 M2
Lameroo SA 293 H3, 295 Q11, **260**
Lamington National Park Qld 119 P1, 483 M13, 491 P11, 420–1, 422, 425, **456**
Lamplough Vic. 212 A1, 223 J6, 229 M1, 231 N12
Lancaster Vic. 234 G5
Lancefield Vic. 212 I2, 234 E11, **181**, 202
Lancelin WA 364 B1, 366 B7, **332**
Landsborough Qld 483 M2, 486 E13, 491 P7, **450**
Landsborough Vic. 222 F4, 231 L11
Landsdale WA 354 H3
Lane Cove NSW 95 K6, 101 N8
Lane Cove National Park NSW 94 I3, 95 J4, 96 F11, 101 N7, **58**
Lanena Tas. 541 L7, 545 L7
Lang Lang Vic. 213 N10, 226 F7
Langford WA 353 M9
Langhorne Creek SA 293 D3, 295 M10, 241, 259, 275
Langi Kal Kal Vic. 212 A3, 223 J9
Langi Logan Vic. 222 D9, 229 K2, 231 K13
Langkoop Vic. 228 B1, 230 B12, 293 I9
Langley Vic. 212 G1, 229 R1, 231 R12, 234 D11
Langlo Crossing Qld 490 A5, 501 R5
Langloh Tas. 543 J6
Langsborough Vic. 227 L10
Langtree NSW 123 M5
Langville Vic. 231 O4, 234 A2
Langwarrin Vic. 211 G13, 215 N1
Lankeys Creek NSW 115 A7, 123 R12
Lannercost Qld 495 N11
Lansdowne NSW 94 B12, 98 D2, 105 D12, 117 P1, 119 O13
Lansvale NSW 94 A11, 98 C1

Lapoinya Tas. 544 E5
Lapstone NSW 103 R9
Lara Vic. 212 G8, 219 F5, 226 A5, 229 R7, 173
Lara Lake Vic. 212 F8, 219 E5
Larapinta Qld 480 H10
Laravale Qld 483 L13
Largs Bay SA 286 C10
Largs North SA 286 D10
Larpent Vic. 212 A11, 217 F7, 229 M9
Larrakeyah NT 399 B10
Larras Lee NSW 116 F5
Larrimah NT 406 I12, 408 I2, **390**
Lascelles Vic. 122 E12, 230 I2, 232 I13
Latham ACT 136 B5
Latham WA 366 D5
Lathlain WA 353 K4
Latimers Crossing Qld 485 B6
Latrobe Tas. 540 E6, 544 I7, **523**
Lauderdale Tas. 537 Q9, 539 J6, 543 M9, 508
Laughtondale NSW 101 M4
Launceston Tas. 505, 515, **523**, 525, 527
Launching Place Vic. 213 N6, 216 E9, 226 F4
Laura Qld 495 K3, 435, 453
Laura SA 295 K3, 297 J13, 249, 256
Laurel Hill NSW 115 B7
Laurieton NSW 105 F10, 119 O13, **70**
Lauriston Vic. 212 F1, 223 R7, 229 R1, 231 R12, 234 C11
Lavers Hill Vic. 217 E11, 229 M11, 157, 175
Laverton Vic. 208 D11
Laverton WA 367 J3, **332**, 334
Lawgi Qld 491 L1
Lawler Vic. 231 J7
Lawloit Vic. 230 D7
Lawn Hill National Park Qld 409 R8, 497 B11, 430, **458**, 459, 474
Lawnton Qld 478 C2
Lawrence NSW 119 P5
Lawrence Vic. 212 C2, 223 M8
Lawrence Road NSW 119 P5
Lawrenny Tas. 543 J6
Lawson ACT 136 E5
Lawson NSW 100 I7, 102 I8, 117 J7
Layard Vic. 219 C9
Le Roy Vic. 227 K8
Leabrook SA 285 L7
Leadville NSW 116 H1
Leaghur Vic. 231 O4, 234 A3
Leam Tas. 541 M4
Leanyer NT 400 I3
Learmonth Vic. 212 B3, 223 K9, 229 O2, 231 O13
Learmonth WA 365 B4
Leasingham SA 295 L6
Leawood Gardens SA 285 N10
Lebrina Tas. 541 P5, 545 M7
Ledge Point WA 364 B1, 328
Lee Point NT 400 I1
Leederville WA 352 G1, 354 G13
Leeman WA 366 B5, 324
Leeming WA 352 I13
Leeton NSW 123 O8, **70–1**, 81
Leets Vale NSW 101 M4
Leeuwin-Naturaliste National Park WA 357 B11, 359 B9, 364 A9, 366 A11, 319, **322**
Leeville NSW 119 P3
Lefroy Tas. 541 M4, 545 L6

Legana Tas. 541 M8, 545 L8
Legerwood Tas. 545 O7
Legume NSW 119 N1, 491 O11
Leichardt Vic. 223 O1, 231 Q9, 234 B8
Leichhardt NSW 95 J11, 99 L1, 38
Leigh Creek SA 291 D4, 297 J4, **260–1**, 273
Leighton SA 295 L5
Leightonfield NSW 94 B11, 98 D1
Leinster WA 366 H2, 334
Leitchville Vic. 123 J13, 231 R4, 234 C3, 167
Leith Tas. 540 D5
Lemana Tas. 545 J9
Lemnos Vic. 234 I5
Lemon Springs Vic. 230 C9
Lemon Tree Passage NSW 108 G3, 117 N4, 51
Lemont Tas. 543 N5
Lenah Valley Tas. 536 D6
Leneva Vic. 235 P5, 236 B2, 202
Lennox Head NSW 119 R3, 491 R12, 45, **71**
Lenswood SA 288 D10
Leonards Hill Vic. 212 E3, 223 P9
Leongatha Vic. 213 P13, 226 H9, 180, **181**
Leongatha South Vic. 213 O13
Leonora WA 366 I3, 331, **334**, 336
Leopold Vic. 212 G10, 219 F8, 226 A7, 229 R8
Leppington NSW 101 L9
Leprena Tas. 543 J12
Leslie Manor Vic. 217 E4
Leslie Vale Tas. 538 H7, 543 L9
Leslies Bridge Qld 482 C10
Lesmurdie Falls National Park WA 353 R6, 356 D5, **322**
Lesueur National Park WA 366 B5
Lethbridge Vic. 212 E7, 219 C4, 229 Q6
Leumeah NSW 101 L10, 112 G1
Leura NSW 100 H7, 102 F8, 68
Levendale Tas. 539 K1, 543 M6
Lewis Ponds NSW 116 G6
Lewisham NSW 95 J12, 99 L2
Lewisham Tas. 539 L5, 543 N8
Lewiston SA 288 B5
Lexton Vic. 212 A2, 223 J7, 229 N2, 231 N13
Leyburn Qld 482 C11, 491 M10
Liawenee Tas. 543 J2, 545 J11
Licola Vic. 227 L3, 236 A12, 183
Lidcombe NSW 94 E10
Liddell NSW 117 L3
Lidsdale NSW 100 F4, 116 I6
Liena Tas. 540 C12, 544 H9
Lietinna Tas. 545 N7
Lietpar Vic. 232 I9
Liffey Tas. 543 K1, 545 K10
Light Pass SA 292 G4
Lightning Creek Vic. 225 R4
Lightning Ridge NSW 118 B5, **71**
Lileah Tas. 544 D5
Lilli Pilli NSW 99 K13
Lillicur Vic. 212 A1, 223 J6
Lillimur Vic. 230 B7
Lillimur South Vic. 230 B8
Lilydale Qld 482 G8
Lilydale Tas. 541 P6, 545 M7, **524**, 525
Lilydale Vic. 210 F6, 213 L6, 216 B8, 226 E3, 197
Lilyfield NSW 95 J10
Lima Vic. 224 A5
Lima East Vic. 224 A6

Lima South Vic. 224 B7
Limeburners Creek NSW 108 E3, 117 N3
Limekilns NSW 100 D2, 116 H5
Limerick NSW 100 A11, 115 F1, 116 G8
Limestone Vic. 213 N2, 234 I11
Limestone Ridge Qld 483 K11
Limevale Qld 119 K2, 491 M12
Lincoln National Park SA 294 E9, **264**, 271
Lincolnfields SA 295 J5
Lind National Park Vic. 115 E13, 237 M11
Linda Tas. 526
Lindeman Island Qld 493 K3, **438**, 452, 466
Linden NSW 101 J7, 103 L7
Linden Park SA 285 L8
Lindenow Vic. 227 P4, 236 E13
Lindfield NSW 101 K7
Lindisfarne Tas. 537 J4, 538 I5, 543 L8
Lindsay Vic. 228 A4, 293 I11
Lindsay Point Vic. 122 A7, 232 A3
Lindum Qld 479 L10
Linga Vic. 122 C10, 232 E10
Linley Point NSW 95 J7
Linthorpe Qld 482 C8
Linton Vic. 212 B5, 223 J12, 229 N4
Linville Qld 482 H2, 491 O7
Linwood SA 288 D3
Lipson SA 294 E7
Lipson Island SA 277
Lisarow NSW 101 P3, 104 F4
Lisle Tas. 541 Q6, 545 M7
Lismore NSW 119 Q3, 491 Q12, **71**
Lismore Vic. 217 E2, 229 M6
Liston NSW 119 M2, 491 O12
Litchfield Vic. 231 J6
Litchfield National Park NT 402 C8, 406 D7, 373, 381, 384, 385, 392
Lithgow NSW 100 G5, 116 I6, **71**
Littabella National Park Qld 491 O1
Little Bay NSW 99 Q7
Little Billabong NSW 123 R12
Little Desert National Park Vic. 230 B8, 293 I7, 170, **176**, 178, 179, 186, 203
Little Hard Hills Vic. 212 C6, 223 L13
Little Jilliby NSW 101 P2, 104 D1
Little Mulgrave Qld 489 E11
Little River Vic. 212 G7, 219 G4, 226 A5, 229 R6
Little Snowy Creek Vic. 225 O2
Little Swanport Tas. 543 O5
Little Topar Roadhouse NSW 120 D11
Littlehampton SA 288 E11, 289 I2, 290 I2
Liverpool NSW 98 A4, 101 M9, 117 K8, 43
Lizard Island National Park Qld 495 M1, 435, 437, **440**
Llandaff Tas. 543 P3, 545 Q12
Llandeilo Vic. 212 E4, 223 O11
Llanelly Vic. 223 M1, 231 O9, 234 A8
Llangothlin NSW 119 L7
Llewellyn Siding Tas. 543 N2, 545 N11
Llowalong Vic. 227 M5
Loamside Qld 483 K9
Lobethal SA 288 E9, 293 C1, 295 L9, 246
Loccota Tas. 542 B12, 545 Q1
Loch Vic. 213 O12, 226 G8, 180, 181
Loch Sport Vic. 227 P6, 189, 193, 194
Loch Valley Vic. 213 Q6
Lochaber SA 293 H8
Lochern National Park Qld 499 M12
Lochiel NSW 113 E10, 237 Q7
Lochiel SA 295 J6

Lochinvar NSW 108 B7, 117 M4, 72
Lochnagar Qld 492 D11, 499 R11
Lock SA 294 D4
Lockhart NSW 123 P10, **71**
Lockhart River Aboriginal Community Qld 496 E8, 453
Lockington Vic. 234 D5
Lockleys SA 284 E6
Lockridge WA 355 M9
Locksley NSW 100 D5, 116 H6
Locksley Vic. 234 H9
Lockwood Vic. 223 P2, 231 Q10, 234 B9
Lockwood South Vic. 223 P3, 231 Q10, 234 B9
Lockyer Qld 482 F7
Loddon Vale Vic. 231 P5, 234 A3
Loftus NSW 98 H11
Logan Qld 481 L10, 483 M10, 491 P9, **451**
Logan Vic. 231 N9
Logan Central Qld 481 L10
Loganholme Qld 481 Q11, 483 N10
Loganlea Qld 481 M11
Logie Brae NSW 123 M11
Loira Tas. 541 L7
Lombadina WA 370 H6
Londonderry NSW 101 K6
Londrigan Vic. 235 N5
Long Beach NSW 115 H7, 139 O7
Long Flat NSW 105 C7, 119 N12
Long Island Qld 439
Long Jetty NSW 101 Q3, 104 H3
Long Plains SA 295 K7
Long Plains Vic. 231 K1, 233 K11
Long Pocket Qld 480 F3
Longerenong Vic. 230 H9
Longford Tas. 541 N13, 545 L9, 505, 515, **524**, 527
Longford Vic. 227 N7
Longlea Vic. 231 R10, 234 D8
Longley Tas. 538 G7, 543 L9
Longreach Qld 492 A11, 499 O11, **451**
Longueville NSW 95 K8
Longwarry Vic. 213 O9, 226 G6
Longwood Vic. 234 I9, 172
Longwood East Vic. 234 I9
Lonnavale Tas. 538 C6, 543 J9
Loongana Tas. 544 G8
Loongana WA 367 P6
Loorana Tas. 542 A9
Lorinna Tas. 540 B12, 544 H9
Lorne NSW 105 D10, 119 O13
Lorne Vic. 212 D13, 219 A13, 229 P10, **181**, **183**, 187
Lorquon Vic. 230 E6
Lorquon West Vic. 230 E5
Lostock NSW 117 L2
Lota Qld 479 N11
Lotta Tas. 545 P7
Louisville Tas. 539 O1, 543 O6
Louth NSW 121 L7
Louth Bay SA 294 D8
Loveday SA 295 P7
Low Head Tas. 541 J3, 545 K6, 519
Lowaldie SA 293 F2, 295 O10
Lowan Vale SA 293 H6
Lowanna NSW 119 P8
Lowbank SA 295 P6
Lowden WA 357 I6, 364 D8
Lowdina Tas. 539 J2
Lower Acacia Creek NSW 119 N2
Lower Barrington Tas. 540 D7, 544 I7
Lower Beulah Tas. 540 E10, 544 I8

Lower Boro NSW 139 L1
Lower Bucca NSW 119 P7
Lower Chittering WA 328
Lower Creek NSW 119 N9
Lower Gellibrand Vic. 217 C11
Lower Glenelg National Park Vic. 228 B7, 191
Lower Hermitage SA 287 R8
Lower Heytesbury Vic. 217 A9
Lower Mangrove NSW 101 N4, 104 A8
Lower Marshes Tas. 543 L5
Lower Mookerawa NSW 116 G4
Lower Mount Hicks Tas. 544 F5
Lower Mount Walker Qld 482 I9
Lower Norton Vic. 230 G10
Lower Plenty Vic. 209 P5, 213 K5
Lower Quipolly NSW 118 I12
Lower Sandy Bay Tas. 536 I11
Lower Templestowe Vic. 209 P6
Lower Turners Marsh Tas. 541 N6, 545 L7
Lower Wilmot Tas. 540 C8, 544 H7
Lowes Mount NSW 100 D6
Lowesdale NSW 123 O12, 235 M2
Lowlands NSW 123 M3
Lowmead Qld 491 N1
Lowood Qld 483 J7, 491 P9
Lowther NSW 100 F6
Loxton SA 295 Q7, **261**
Loxton North SA 295 Q7
Loy Yang Vic. 227 K7
Loyetea Tas. 544 G7
Lubeck Vic. 222 A1, 230 I9
Lucas Heights NSW 98 D11
Lucaston Tas. 538 F7, 543 K9
Lucinda Qld 446, **451**
Lucinda-Dungeness Qld 495 O11
Lucindale SA 293 G9
Lucknow NSW 116 G6
Lucknow Vic. 227 Q4, 236 F13
Lucky Bay SA 294 G5
Lucyvale Vic. 115 A9, 236 F3
Luddenham NSW 101 K9
Ludlow WA 357 E7, 359 H2, 364 B9
Ludmilla NT 399 G2, 400 C9
Lue NSW 116 I3
Lugarno NSW 98 G7
Lughrata Tas. 542 A11
Luina Tas. 544 E8
Lulworth Tas. 541 N2, 545 L5
Lumholtz National Park Qld 495 M10, 446, 451, **458**
Lunawanna Tas. 538 G13, 543 L11
Lune River Tas. 543 J12
Lurg Vic. 224 C3
Lurg Upper Vic. 224 D3
Lurnea NSW 98 A4
Lutana Tas. 536 F3
Lutwyche Qld 478 G9
Lyal Vic. 231 R11, 234 D10
Lymington Tas. 538 F10, 543 K10, 513
Lymwood Tas. 542 A9
Lynchford Tas. 542 E3, 544 E12, 526
Lynchs Creek NSW 119 P2
Lyndhurst NSW 116 F7
Lyndhurst SA 291 D3, 297 J3, 261
Lyndhurst Vic. 211 H8, 213 L8, 226 E5
Lyndoch SA 288 E6, 292 C9, 295 L8, 246, **261**
Lyneham ACT 136 G7
Lynton SA 285 J12
Lynwood WA 353 L10
Lyons ACT 136 E13, 137 C4

Lyons Vic. 228 D7
Lyonville Vic. 212 F3, 223 Q9
Lyrup SA 295 Q7
Lysterfield Vic. 213 L7
Lytton Qld 479 M8

Maaoope SA 293 H10
Maaroom Qld 491 P4
Macalister Qld 491 L8
McAllister NSW 115 F3, 116 H10
Macarthur ACT 137 F8
MacArthur Vic. 228 F7, 177
Macclesfield SA 288 D12, 289 I3, 290 H5, 293 C2, 295 L10
Macclesfield Vic. 213 M7, 216 D12, 226 F4, 172
McCrae Vic. 213 J11, 214 H7, 155
McCullys Gap NSW 117 L2
McDowall Qld 478 D7
Macedon Vic. 226 A1, 234 D12, 202
McGillivray SA 294 I12
McGraths Hill NSW 101 L6
Macgregor ACT 136 A4
Macgregor Qld 481 J6
Machans Beach Qld 489 F8
McHarg Creek SA 290 F7
McIntyre Vic. 223 L1, 231 N9
Mackay Qld 493 L5, **452**
McKees Hill NSW 119 Q3
McKellar ACT 136 E5
Mackenzie Qld 481 L3
McKenzie Creek Vic. 230 G10
McKinlay Qld 498 I5, 435
McKinnon Vic. 209 M13, 211 B1
Macks Creek Vic. 227 L9
Macksville NSW 119 P9, **71–2**
MacLagan Qld 482 D3, 491 N8
McLaren Vale SA 288 A13, 289 F4, 290 C5, 293 B2, 295 K10, 249, 250, 259, **261**, 268, 276
McLaren Region SA 290, 241, 246, 259
Maclean NSW 119 P5, **72**
Macleod Vic. 209 N4
McLoughlins Beach Vic. 227 M9
McMahons Creek Vic. 213 P5, 226 H3
McMahons Reef NSW 115 C3, 116 E11
MacMasters Beach NSW 101 P4, 104 H7
McMillans Vic. 122 I12, 231 Q3, 234 B2
Macorna Vic. 122 I13, 231 P4, 234 B3
McPhail NSW 116 D3
Macquarie ACT 136 D7
Macquarie Fields NSW 101 L10
Macquarie Park NSW 94 H3, 96 G13
Macquarie Pass National Park NSW 112 F8
Macquarie Plains Tas. 538 E3
Macrossan Qld 492 F2
Macs Cove Vic. 213 R1, 224 D12, 235 L11
Madalya Vic. 227 K9
Maddington WA 353 P10, 356 D5
Madora WA 356 B9, 364 C5
Madura WA 367 P8, **334**
Mafeking Vic. 222 A9, 158
Maffra NSW 115 D10, 237 M5
Maffra Vic. 227 M5, **183**, 194
Maffra West Upper Vic. 227 M5
Maggea SA 295 O7
Magill SA 285 N5, 288 C9
Magnetic Island Qld 470
Magnetic Island National Park Qld 495 P12, **440**
Magpie Vic. 212 C4, 223 M11

Magra Tas. 538 F4, 543 K7
Magrath Flat SA 293 E5, 295 N12
Mahaikah Vic. 224 E8
Maharatta NSW 113 A10, 115 E11, 237 N8
Maiala National Park Qld 483 K6
Maianbar NSW 99 L13
Maiden Gully Vic. 223 Q1
Maidenwell Qld 482 E2, 491 N7, 421
Maidstone Vic. 208 I7
Mailors Flat Vic. 228 I9
Maimuru NSW 115 C2, 116 D9
Main Beach Qld 483 O12, 485 F5, 467
Main Lead Vic. 222 H9
Main Range National Park Qld 119 N1, 482 H13, 491 O10, 424, 427, 447, 452, **456**, 465, 471
Main Ridge Vic. 214 I9, 155, 197
Maindample Vic. 224 A10
Maitland NSW 108 C7, 117 M4, **72**
Maitland SA 294 I7, **261**
Major Plains Vic. 235 K6
Majorca Vic. 212 C1, 223 L6, 229 O1, 231 O12, 234 A10
Majors Creek NSW 115 G6, 116 H13, 139 K5
Majors Creek Vic. 234 F9
Malabar NSW 99 Q6
Malaga WA 355 K7
Malanda Qld 489 D13, 495 M7, 425, 448
Malbina Tas. 538 G4
Malbon Qld 498 G5
Malcolm WA 366 I3, 334
Maldon NSW 101 K12, 112 E3
Maldon Vic. 223 O4, 231 P11, 234 B10, 161, 163, 166, **183**
Maleny Qld 483 L2, 486 B11, 491 P7, 413, 429, **452**
Malinong SA 293 E3, 295 N11
Mallacoota Vic. 115 G13, 237 Q11, 175, **183**
Mallala SA 288 A3, 295 K7
Mallan NSW 122 I10, 233 O9
Mallanganee NSW 119 O3, 491 P12
Mallee Cliffs National Park NSW 122 E7, 232 I3
Malling Qld 482 D3
Mallum Vic. 224 B5
Malmsbury Vic. 212 F1, 223 R7, 229 R1, 231 R12, 234 C11, 166, 180
Malpas SA 293 H1, 295 Q8
Malua Bay NSW 115 H7, 139 O7, 47
Malvern SA 285 J9
Malvern Vic. 209 M11
Malyalling WA 364 G6
Mambray Creek SA 295 J2, 296 I12
Manangatang Vic. 122 F10, 233 K9
Manara NSW 122 G2
Mandagery NSW 116 D6
Mandalong NSW 101 P1, 108 F13
Mandorah NT 402 B2, 406 D5, 379
Mandurah WA 356 B9, 364 C5, 366 C9, **334**
Mandurang Vic. 223 Q2, 231 R10, 234 C9, 164
Mangalo SA 294 F4
Mangalore NSW 121 P11
Mangalore Tas. 538 H2, 543 L7
Mangalore Vic. 234 G9
Mangana Tas. 545 P10
Mangerton NSW 110 C11
Mangoplah NSW 116 B13, 123 Q11
Mangrove Creek NSW 101 N3, 104 A6
Mangrove Mountain NSW 101 O3, 104 A4

Manguri SA 301 Q11
Manildra NSW 116 F5
Manilla NSW 119 J9, 69, **72**
Maningrida NT 407 K5
Manjimup WA 360 D6, 364 D10, 366 D11, 319, **334–5**
Manly NSW 95 Q5, 101 P7, 117 L7, 35, 40, 41
Manly Qld 479 N10
Manly Vale NSW 95 O4
Manly West Qld 479 N10
Manmanning WA 366 D6
Mannahill SA 291 I12, 297 O11
Mannanarie SA 295 L2, 297 K13
Mannerim Vic. 212 H10, 214 A3, 219 H8
Mannering Bay NSW 101 Q1
Mannering Park NSW 101 Q1, 108 G12, 117 M5
Mannibadar Vic. 212 A6, 222 I13, 229 N5
Manning WA 352 I8
Manningham SA 285 K3
Manns Beach Vic. 227 L10
Mannum SA 288 I9, 293 D1, 295 M9, **265**
Manoora Qld 488 A9
Manoora SA 295 L6
Mansfield Qld 481 K3
Mansfield Vic. 224 C10, 235 L10, **183–4**, 197, 204
Mansfield Park SA 284 F1, 286 G13
Mantung SA 295 P8
Manumbar Qld 491 O6
Manunda Qld 488 D9, 431
Many Peaks Qld 491 M1, 443
Manya Vic. 232 A9, 293 I2, 295 R10
Manyana NSW 139 Q3
Manypeaks WA 361 P11, 364 I12
Mapleton Qld 483 L1, 486 C8, 413, 429
Mapoon Aboriginal Community Qld 496 B6
Marakoopa Tas. 524
Maralinga SA 302 H3
Marama SA 293 G2, 295 P10
Marananga SA 292 E4
Maranboy NT 406 H10
Marangaroo WA 354 G5
Marathon Qld 499 N4
Marbelup WA 361 N12, 364 H13
Marble Bar WA 368 D2, **335**, 339
Marble Hill SA 285 R6
Marburg Qld 483 J8, 421
Marchagee WA 366 C5
Marcoola Qld 483 N1, 486 H7
Marcus Beach Qld 486 H3
Marcus Hill Vic. 212 H10, 219 H9, 226 B7
Mardella WA 356 C8, 364 D5
Marden SA 285 K4
Mareeba Qld 489 C9, 495 M7, 425, 449, **452**, **454**
Marengo NSW 119 N7
Marengo Vic. 217 G12, 229 N12
Margaret River WA 357 C10, 359 C7, 364 A10, 366 B11, 305, 318, 319, **335**
Margate Qld 483 N6, 463
Margate Tas. 538 H8, 543 L9
Margooya Vic. 233 J7
Maria Island National Park Tas. 539 Q3, 543 P7, 505, **521**, 524, 532
Mariala National Park Qld 501 Q5
Maribyrnong Vic. 208 I6, 151
Marion SA 284 G13, 288 A11, 289 F2, 245
Marion Bay SA 294 G10

Markdale NSW 115 E2, 116 G9
Markwell NSW 117 O2
Markwood Vic. 224 G1, 235 N6, 236 A4
Marla SA 301 N5, 279
Marlbed Vic. 231 K4
Marlborough Qld 493 M9
Marlee NSW 105 A12, 117 O1, 119 N13
Marleston SA 284 G8
Marlo Vic. 237 J13, 189
Marma Vic. 230 I9
Marmion WA 354 B6
Marmor Qld 493 O11
Marnoo Vic. 231 K9
Marnoo West Vic. 231 J9
Marong Vic. 223 P1, 231 Q9, 234 B8
Maroochy River Qld 483 M1, 486 F7
Maroochydore Qld 483 N1, 486 H9, 491 Q7, **454**, 460
Maroon Qld 119 O1, 483 J13, 491 P11
Maroona Vic. 222 C10, 229 J3
Maroota NSW 101 M4
Maroubra NSW 99 Q5, 117 L8
Maroubra Junction NSW 99 Q5, 101 O9
Marp Vic. 228 B6
Marrabel SA 295 L6
Marradong WA 356 G12, 364 E6
Marramarra National Park NSW 96 E1, 101 N5, 104 A11, 46
Marrangaroo NSW 100 F4
Marrar NSW 116 B11, 123 R9
Marrara NT 400 H8
Marrawah Tas. 544 B4, 530
Marraweeny Vic. 235 J8
Marree SA 296 I1, 261, **265**, 279
Marrickville NSW 95 J13, 99 L3, 101 N9
Marrinup WA 356 D11, 364 D6
Marryatville SA 285 L7
Marsden NSW 116 B7, 123 R5
Marsden Qld 481 L12
Marsden Park NSW 101 L7
Marshall Vic. 212 F10, 219 E8, 226 A7, 229 R8
Marshdale NSW 108 B1
Martindale NSW 117 K3
Martins Creek NSW 108 B4
Martins Creek Vic. 115 C13, 237 K10
Martinsville NSW 108 E12
Marulan NSW 115 G3, 116 I11
Marulan South NSW 115 H4, 116 I11
Marungai Vic. 234 I4
Marvel Loch WA 366 G7, 345
Mary Kathleen Qld 435, **454**
Mary River Roadhouse NT 401 D12, 403 L11
Maryborough Qld 491 P4, **454**
Maryborough Vic. 223 L5, 231 O11, 163, **184**
Marybrook WA 357 C7, 359 D3, 364 A9
Maryfarms Qld 495 L5
Marysville Vic. 213 O4, 216 I3, 226 G2, 235 J13, **184**, 204
Maryvale NSW 116 F3
Maryville NSW 106 C4
Mascot NSW 95 L13, 99 N4
Maslin Beach SA 288 A13, 289 E4, 290 B5, 250, 268, 276
Massey Vic. 231 K6
Matakana NSW 123 N3
Mataranka NT 406 I11, **390**
Matcham NSW 101 P4, 104 G5, 63
Matheson NSW 119 L6
Mathiesons Vic. 234 F7

Mathinna Tas. 545 P9, 518
Mathoura NSW 123 K12, 234 F2, 57, 171, 201
Matlock Vic. 213 R5, 227 J3
Matong NSW 116 A11, 123 Q9
Matraville NSW 99 Q6
Maude NSW 123 J8, 233 R5, 66
Maude Vic. 212 E7, 219 C4, 229 Q6
Maudsland Qld 483 N12, 485 A4
Mawbanna Tas. 544 E5, 530
Mawson ACT 137 D6
Mawson WA 364 G4
Maxwelton Qld 499 L4
May Reef Vic. 234 D7
Mayanup WA 360 F3, 364 E9
Mayberry Tas. 540 D12, 544 I9
Maydena Tas. 538 A4, 542 I7
Mayfield East NSW 106 A2
Maylands SA 285 K5
Maylands WA 353 K3
Mayne Qld 478 G10
Mayrung NSW 123 L11
Mays Hill NSW 94 B7
Maytown Qld 495 J4
Mazeppa National Park Qld 492 G7
Mead Vic. 231 Q3, 234 B2
Meadow Creek Vic. 224 G3, 235 N7
Meadow Flat NSW 100 E4
Meadowbank NSW 94 G6
Meadows SA 288 D13, 289 H3, 290 G5, 293 C2, 295 L10
Meandarra Qld 491 J8
Meander Tas. 545 J10
Meandu Creek Qld 482 F1
Meatian Vic. 231 M2, 233 M12
Meckering WA 364 F3, 366 D7
Medindie SA 282 E2, 285 J5
Medindie Gardens SA 285 J4
Medlow Bath NSW 100 H6, 102 C7
Medowie NSW 108 F4
Meeandah Qld 479 J9
Meekatharra WA 365 I11, 368 C12, **335**, **337**
Meelon WA 356 C11, 364 D6
Meelup WA 357 B6, 359 C1, 364 A8
Meenar WA 364 F2
Meeniyan Vic. 226 I10, 181
Meerawa Qld 489 G11
Meerlieu Vic. 227 O5
Meerschaum Vale NSW 119 Q3, 491 Q13
Megalong NSW 100 G7, 102 B9
Megan NSW 119 O8
Melba ACT 136 C4
Melba Flats Tas. 542 D1, 544 D10
Melbourne Vic. 206, 209 K9, 213 J6, 226 D4, 141, **144–53**
Mella Tas. 544 C4
Mellis Vic. 230 I6
Melros WA 356 A10, 364 C6, 334
Melrose NSW 116 A4, 123 Q2
Melrose SA 295 J2, 297 J12, **265**, 270, 273, 280
Melrose Tas. 540 D6, 544 I7
Melrose Park NSW 94 G7
Melrose Park SA 284 H11
Melton NSW 295 J6
Melton Vic. 212 H5, 226 B3, 158
Melton Mowbray Tas. 543 L6
Melton South Vic. 212 H5, 219 H1
Melville WA 352 E10
Melville Forest Vic. 228 F3
Memana Tas. 542 B11

Memerambi Qld 491 N6
Mena Creek Qld 495 N8
Mena Park Vic. 212 A4, 222 I11
Menai NSW 98 F9
Menangle NSW 101 K11, 112 F2, 53
Menangle Park NSW 101 K11, 112 F1
Mendooran NSW 116 G1, 118 E13
Mengha Tas. 544 D4
Menindee NSW 120 E13, 122 E1, **73**
Meningie SA 293 D4, 295 M12, **265**, 274
Menora WA 354 H11
Mentone Vic. 211 C4
Menzies WA 366 I4, 334, 336
Menzies Creek Vic. 213 M7, 216 B12, 156, 172
Mepunga East Vic. 229 J10
Mepunga West Vic. 228 I9
Merah North NSW 118 F7
Merbein Vic. 122 D7, 232 G3
Merbein South Vic. 122 D7, 232 F3
Merbein West Vic. 122 D7, 232 F3
Mercunda SA 295 O8
Merebene NSW 118 E9
Meredith Vic. 212 E6, 219 C2, 229 P5, 173
Mereenie Loop Road NT 404 A5, 410 F9, **383**
Merewether NSW 106 C11, 108 G7
Meribah SA 122 A9, 232 A6, 293 I1, 295 R8
Merildin SA 295 L5
Merimal Qld 493 N10
Merimbula NSW 113 F9, 115 G11, 237 Q7, 55, **73**
Merinda Qld 492 I2
Meringandan Qld 482 E6
Meringo NSW 115 H8, 139 N9
Meringur Vic. 122 B8, 232 C4
Meringur North Vic. 122 B7, 232 C4
Merino Vic. 228 D5
Mermaid Beach Qld 485 F7, 423
Mermaid Waters Qld 485 E7
Mernda Vic. 213 K4, 226 D2, 234 G13
Merredin WA 364 I2, 366 F7, 333, **337**
Merriang Vic. 213 K3, 224 I2, 226 D2, 234 G13, 235 O7, 236 A5
Merriang South Vic. 224 I3
Merricks Vic. 213 K12, 215 L9, 155, 197
Merricks North Vic. 215 K8
Merrigum Vic. 234 G6
Merrijig Vic. 224 E11, 235 M10, 184
Merrimac Qld 485 D7
Merrinee Vic. 122 C7, 232 E4
Merrinee North Vic. 232 E4
Merriton SA 295 J4
Merriwa NSW 117 J2, **73**
Merriwagga NSW 123 M5
Merrygoen NSW 116 G1, 118 F13
Merrylands NSW 94 B8, 101 M8
Merrywinbone NSW 118 D6
Mersey Bluff Tas. 516
Merseylea Tas. 540 F9, 544 I8
Merton Tas. 536 C5
Merton Vic. 235 J10
Metcalfe Vic. 223 R5, 180
Methul NSW 116 A10, 123 Q8
Metricup WA 357 C8, 359 C4, 364 A9
Metung Vic. 227 R5, 236 G13, 158, 181, 193
Meunna Tas. 544 E6
Mia Mia Vic. 234 D10
Miallo Qld 489 B3, 495 M5, 459
Miami Qld 485 F8, 423

Miami WA 356 A10, 364 C5
Miandetta NSW 121 Q10
Michael Creek Qld 495 N11
Michelago NSW 115 E7, 135 F10, 138 G6
Mickleham Vic. 213 J4, 226 C2, 234 F13
Middle Cove NSW 95 M5
Middle Creek Vic. 222 F9, 229 L3
Middle Dural NSW 96 B4
Middle Indigo Vic. 235 O4, 236 A2
Middle Park Qld 480 C6
Middle Park Vic. 209 J10
Middle River SA 294 G12
Middle Swan WA 355 Q7
Middle Tarwin Vic. 226 H10
Middlemount Qld 493 K9
Middlepoint NT 402 F3
Middleton Qld 498 I8, 472
Middleton SA 289 H7, 290 F12
Middleton Tas. 538 G11, 543 L11
Middlingbank NSW 114 H8
Midge Point Qld 493 K4
Midgee Qld 493 N11
Midland WA 355 Q9, 356 D4, 310
Midway Point Tas. 539 K5, 543 M8
Miena Tas. 543 J2, 545 J12, 525
Miepoll Vic. 234 I7
Miga Lake Vic. 230 E11
Mil Lel Vic. 228 A5, 293 I12
Mila NSW 115 E12, 237 N8
Milabena Tas. 544 E5
Milang SA 293 C3, 295 L11, 246, 275
Milawa Vic. 224 G1, 235 N6, **184**, 197, 198
Milbong Qld 483 K11
Milbrulong NSW 116 A13, 123 P10
Milchomi NSW 118 D8
Mildura Vic. 232 G3, 143, **185**, 197, 201
Mile End SA 284 H7
Miles Qld 491 K7, **454**
Milford Qld 483 J12
Milguy NSW 118 H5
Milikapiti NT 406 D3
Miling WA 366 C6
Milingimbi NT 407 L5
Mill Park Vic. 209 N1
Millaa Millaa Qld 495 M8, 449, **454**
Millaroo Qld 492 G2
Millbrook Vic. 212 E4, 223 O11
Millers Point NSW 92 A2
Millfield NSW 108 B12, 117 L4
Millgrove Vic. 213 N6, 216 G9, 226 G3
Millicent SA 293 G11, **265–6**
Millie NSW 118 F6
Millmeran Qld 482 A10
Millmerran Qld 491 M10, **454–5**
Millner NT 400 D7
Milloo Vic. 231 R7, 234 C5
Millstream-Chichester National Park WA 365 H2, 368 A3, **323**, 339, 343
Millswood SA 284 I9, 245
Millthorpe NSW 116 G6, 49, 78
Milltown Vic. 228 E7
Millwood NSW 116 A12, 123 Q9
Milman Qld 493 N10
Milparinka NSW 120 C4, 83
Milperra NSW 98 D5, 101 M9
Miltalie SA 294 G4
Milton NSW 117 J13, 139 P4, 86
Milton Qld 478 F12, 418
Milvale NSW 115 B2, 116 D9
Milyakburra NT 407 O8

Mimili SA 301 L4
Mimmindie Vic. 122 H13, 231 O5
Mimosa NSW 116 B10, 123 R8
Mimosa Rocks National Park NSW 113 H6, 115 G10, 237 R5, 47, 48, 82
Minamia NT 407 K13, 409 K2
Minbrie SA 294 G4
Mincha Vic. 122 I13, 231 P4, 234 B3
Mindarie SA 293 G1, 295 P9
Minden Qld 483 J8
Mindiyarra SA 293 F2, 295 O9
Miners Rest Vic. 212 C3, 223 L10, 229 O3, 234 A13
Minerva Hills National Park Qld 492 I12
Mingay Vic. 217 D1, 297 Q10
Mingela Qld 492 F2
Mingenew WA 366 B4, **337**
Mingoola NSW 119 L3, 491 M13
Minhamite Vic. 228 H6
Minilya Roadhouse WA 365 B6
Minimay Vic. 230 B9, 293 I8
Mininera Vic. 222 D12, 229 K4
Minjilang NT 406 H2
Minlaton SA 294 I9, **266**
Minmi NSW 108 E8
Minnamurra NSW 112 H9
Minnie Water NSW 119 Q6
Minniging WA 364 F6
Minnipa SA 294 B2, 296 A12, 303 R12, 280
Minnivale WA 364 G1
Minore NSW 116 E2
Mintabie SA 301 N5
Mintaro SA 295 L5, 246, 253, **266**
Minto NSW 101 L10
Minvalara SA 295 L2, 297 K12
Minyip Vic. 230 I8
Miowera NSW 118 A12, 121 R10
Miralie Vic. 233 M9
Miram Vic. 230 C7
Miram South Vic. 230 C8
Miranda NSW 99 J11, 101 N10
Mirani Qld 493 K5, 452
Mirannie NSW 117 M2
Mirboo Vic. 213 R13, 227 J9
Mirboo North Vic. 213 R12, 226 I8, 181, 203
Miriam Vale Qld 491 M1, 493 Q13, **455**
Mirima (Hidden Valley) National Park WA 363 Q2, 371 R5, **323**, 332, 344
Mirimbah Vic. 224 F11, 235 N11
Miriwinni Qld 495 N8
Mirmgadja Village NT 407 M6
Mirrabooka WA 354 I8, 356 C4
Mirranatwa Vic. 228 H3
Mirrool NSW 116 A9, 123 Q7
Missabotti NSW 119 O9
Mission Beach Qld 495 N9, 449, **455**, 471
Mitcham SA 285 K11, 288 B10, 289 G1
Mitcham Vic. 209 R9, 210 A9
Mitchell ACT 136 H5
Mitchell Qld 490 F6, **455**
Mitchell Park SA 284 G13
Mitchell River National Park Vic. 227 O3, 236 D12, 158, **176**, 193
Mitchell-Alice Rivers National Park Qld 494 E3
Mitchells Hill Vic. 231 K9
Mitchellstown Vic. 234 F9
Mitchelton Qld 478 D9
Mitiamo Vic. 231 Q6, 234 C5

Mitre Vic. 230 E9
Mitta Mitta Vic. 225 Q2, 235 R7, 236 E5, 189
Mittagong NSW 112 C6, 115 I2, 117 J10, 39, 49, **73**
Mittons Bridge Vic. 213 L4
Mittyack Vic. 233 J9
Miva Qld 491 O5
Moama NSW 123 K13, 234 E4, 171
Moama SA 288 A13
Moana SA 289 E4, 290 B5, 293 B2, 295 K10, 246, 268
Mockinya Vic. 230 G11
Moculta SA 288 G4
Modbury SA 287 O10, 288 C8
Modbury Heights SA 287 N9
Modella Vic. 213 O10, 226 G7
Modewarre Vic. 219 C9
Moe Vic. 213 R10, 227 J7, **185**
Mogendoura NSW 139 M8
Moggill Qld 480 A8
Mogil Mogil NSW 118 D5
Moglonemby Vic. 234 I7
Mogo NSW 115 H7, 139 N7, 47, 73, 132
Mogriguy NSW 116 E2
Mogumber WA 364 D1, 339
Moil NT 400 G6
Moina Tas. 540 A11, 544 H8
Moira NSW 123 K13, 234 F4
Mokepilly Vic. 222 A5, 228 I1, 230 I12
Mokine WA 356 H2, 364 E3
Mole Creek Tas. 540 E12, 544 I9, **524**
Mole River NSW 119 M4, 491 N13
Molendinar Qld 485 D5
Molesworth Tas. 538 G4
Molesworth Vic. 213 N1, 234 I11
Moliagul Vic. 223 K1, 231 N10, 170, 171, 178
Molka Vic. 234 I8
Mollongghip Vic. 212 D3, 223 N10
Mollymook NSW 139 P4, 86
Mologa Vic. 231 Q6, 234 B4
Molong NSW 116 F5, **73**
Moltema Tas. 540 G10, 545 J8
Molyullah Vic. 224 D4, 235 L7
Mona Vale NSW 97 P7, 101 P6, 104 H13
Monarto SA 288 G11
Monarto South SA 288 G12, 293 D2, 295 M10
Monash ACT 137 D9
Monash SA 295 Q7, 251, 252
Monbulk Vic. 210 G12, 213 M7, 216 B11, 226 F4, 172
Monea Vic. 234 H9
Monegeetta Vic. 212 I3, 226 B1, 234 E12, 192
Monga NSW 139 M5
Mongans Bridge Vic. 225 N3
Mongarlowe NSW 115 G6, 116 I13, 139 M4
Monkey Mia WA 365 B10, 305, 306, 321
Mons Qld 483 M1, 486 F9
Montacute SA 285 Q4
Montagu Tas. 544 C4
Montagu Bay Tas. 536 I6
Montague Island NSW 48, 55, 76
Montana Tas. 540 H13, 545 J9
Montarra SA 290 D6
Monteagle NSW 115 C1, 116 E9
Monterey NSW 99 M7
Montgomery Vic. 227 N6
Montmorency Vic. 209 P4

Monto Qld 491 M2, **459**
Montrose Tas. 536 C3
Montrose Vic. 210 F9
Montumana Tas. 544 E5
Montville Qld 483 M1, 486 C10, 413, 429, 452
Mooball NSW 119 Q2, 491 Q11, 86
Moockra SA 291 D12, 297 J11
Moodlu Qld 483 L4
Moogara Tas. 538 D4, 543 J8
Moogerah Qld 482 I13
Moogerah Peaks National Park Qld 482 I12, 483 J12, 427
Moola Qld 482 C3, 491 M8
Moolap Vic. 219 F7
Moolerr Vic. 231 L9
Moolert Vic. 223 N5
Mooloolaba Qld 483 N1, 486 I9, 491 Q7, 454, **459**, 460
Mooloolah Qld 483 M2, 486 E12
Mooloolah River National Park Qld 483 N2, 486 H10
Moolpa NSW 122 H10, 233 O8
Moombooldool NSW 123 P7
Moombra Qld 482 I6
Moona Plains NSW 119 M10
Moonah Tas. 536 E4, 538 H5
Moonambel Vic. 222 H4, 231 M11, 158, 197
Moonan Flat NSW 117 L1, 119 K13, 80
Moonbah NSW 138 C13, 237 K4
Moonbi NSW 119 K10
Moondarra Vic. 227 J6
Moonee Beach NSW 119 P8
Moonee Ponds Vic. 208 I6
Mooney Mooney NSW 101 O5, 104 D10
Moonford Qld 491 L2
Moonie Qld 491 K9
Moonta SA 294 I6, 239, 240, 249, 255, 261, **266**, 270, 278
Moonta Bay SA 294 I6
Moora WA 366 C6
Moorabbin Vic. 211 B2
Mooralla Vic. 228 G3
Moore Qld 482 H2, 491 O7
Moore Creek NSW 119 J10
Moore Park NSW 95 N12, 99 P2
Moore Park Qld 491 O2, 428
Moore River National Park WA 364 C1, 366 C7
Moorebank NSW 98 B4
Moores Flat Vic. 223 J5
Mooreville Tas. 544 G6
Moorilda NSW 100 A6, 116 G7
Moorilim Vic. 234 H7
Moorina Tas. 545 P7, 519
Moorine Rock WA 366 G7
Moorland NSW 105 E12, 117 P1, 119 O13
Moorlands SA 293 E3, 295 N10
Moorleah Tas. 544 F5
Moormbool Vic. 234 F8
Moorngag Vic. 224 B5
Mooroobool Qld 488 A12
Moorooduc Vic. 213 K10, 215 L4
Moorook SA 295 P7
Moorooka Qld 480 G4
Moorookyle Vic. 212 D2, 223 N7
Mooroolbark Vic. 210 E7
Mooroopna Vic. 234 H6, 194
Moorooroo SA 292 E7
Moorowie SA 294 H10

Moorrinya National Park Qld 492 B5, 499 Q5
Moorumbine WA 364 G5, 342
Mootwingee National Park NSW 120 E8, 51, **60**, 88
Moppin NSW 118 G4, 491 J13
Moranbah Qld 492 I7, **459**
Morangarell NSW 115 A1, 116 C9
Morawa WA 366 C4, **337**
Morayfield Qld 483 M5
Morchard SA 291 D13, 295 K1, 297 K2
Mordialloc Vic. 211 C6, 213 J8
Morea Vic. 230 C10
Moree NSW 118 G5, **73**, 75
Moree Vic. 228 D1, 230 D13
Morella Qld 499 N10
Moreton Island National Park Qld 483 P5, 491 Q8, 416, 420, **433**, 452, **456**
Morgan SA 295 N6, 201, **266-7**
Morgans Crossing NSW 113 D7, 237 P6
Moriac Vic. 212 E10, 219 C8, 229 Q8, 173, 196
Moriarty Tas. 540 F6, 545 J7
Morisset NSW 101 Q1, 108 F12, 117 M5
Morkalla Vic. 122 B7, 232 B4
Morley WA 355 K9
Morningside Qld 478 I11
Mornington Tas. 537 L5
Mornington Vic. 213 K10, 215 J3, 226 D7, 154, 197
Mornington Peninsula Vic. 213 J12, 214 G10, 226 C8, 141, 153, **154-5**, 197
Mornington Peninsula National Park Vic. 212 I12, 213 J12, 214 D8, 219 H10, 226 B8, 154, 155, **174**
Morongla NSW 115 D1, 116 F8
Morpeth NSW 108 D6, 117 M4, 72
Morphett Vale SA 288 A12, 289 F3
Morphettville SA 284 F11, 245
Morri Morri Vic. 222 D2, 231 K10
Morrisons Vic. 212 E6, 219 C1
Mortat Vic. 230 C9
Mortchup Vic. 212 A5, 222 I12
Mortdale NSW 98 I6
Mortlake NSW 94 H8
Mortlake Vic. 229 J7
Morton National Park NSW 112 A11, 115 H4, 117 J11,139 O2, 49, 52, **60**, 74, 77, 80, 86
Morton Plains Vic. 231 K5
Morundah NSW 123 O9
Moruya NSW 115 H7, 139 M8, **73**
Moruya Heads NSW 115 H7, 139 N8
Morven NSW 123 Q12, 235 Q1
Morven Qld 490 D6
Morwell Vic. 227 J7, **185**, 196
Morwell National Park Vic. 227 J8, 185
Mosman NSW 95 O7, 101 O8, 35
Mosman Park WA 352 B7
Mosquito Creek NSW 118 I5
Mosquito Flat SA 290 F10
Moss Vale NSW 112 B7, 115 I3, 117 J10, 39, 49, **74**
Mossgiel NSW 123 J3
Mossman Qld 489 B3, 448, **459**, 462
Mossy Point NSW 115 H7, 139 N8
Moulamein NSW 122 I10, 233 P9, **74**
Moulyinning WA 364 I7
Mount Aberdeen National Park Qld 492 H2
Mount Adrah NSW 115 A5, 116 C12
Mount Alford Qld 482 I12, 491 P10

Mount Alfred Vic. 115 A8, 236 F1
Mount Barker SA 288 E11, 289 I2, 290 I3, 293 C2, 295 L10, 247
Mount Barker WA 361 M9, 364 H12, 366 E12, 329, **337**
Mount Barney National Park Qld 119 O1, 491 P11, 425, **456**
Mount Bauple National Park Qld 491 O5
Mount Baw Baw Vic. 213 R7, 227 J4, 182, 185
Mount Beauty Vic. 225 N5, 235 Q8, 236 D6, **185**
Mount Beckworth Vic. 212 B2, 223 K7
Mount Benson SA 293 F9
Mount Beppo Qld 482 I4
Mount Berryman Qld 482 H9
Mount Best Vic. 227 J9
Mount Bogong Vic. 185
Mount Blue Cow NSW 60, 65, 68
Mount Bruce SA 293 G10
Mount Bryan SA 295 L4
Mount Bryan East SA 295 M4
Mount Buffalo Vic. 164, 182
Mount Buffalo National Park Vic. 225 J4, 235 O7, 236 B5, **176**, 186
Mount Buller Vic. 224 G11, 235 N11, 172, 182
Mount Buller Alpine Village Vic. 183
Mount Burnett Vic. 172
Mount Burr SA 293 G11
Mount Bute Vic. 217 E1
Mount Carbine Qld 495 L5
Mount Carmel Vic. 234 E8
Mount Charlton Qld 493 K5
Mount Christie SA 303 M4
Mount Claremont WA 352 C3
Mount Colah NSW 96 F7
Mount Cole Vic. 222 F7
Mount Compass SA 289 G5, 290 E8, 293 B3, 295 K10, 277
Mount Cook National Park Qld 495 M3
Mount Coolon Qld 492 H5
Mount Coolum National Park Qld 483 N1, 486 H6
Mount Cooper SA 294 A3, 303 Q13
Mount Coot-tha Qld 478 D13, 480 D1, 416, **419**
Mount Cotton Qld 481 Q7, 463
Mount Cottrell Vic. 212 H6, 219 H2
Mount Damper SA 294 B3, 296 A13, 303 R13
Mount Dandenong Vic. 210 F10
Mount Darrah NSW 113 C8, 237 O7
Mount Darry Qld 482 D4
Mount David NSW 100 C8, 116 H7
Mount Direction Tas. 541 M6, 545 L7
Mount Donna Buang Vic. 226 G3, 182, 198
Mount Doran Vic. 212 D5, 223 N13, 229 P4
Mount Druitt NSW 101 L7
Mount Drysdale NSW 121 N9
Mount Duneed Vic. 212 F10, 219 E8, 196
Mount Ebenezer Roadhouse NT 404 E13, 410 H11
Mount Eccles Vic. 213 Q12, 226 H8
Mount Eccles National Park Vic. 228 F7, **176**, 177, 190
Mount Edwards Qld 482 I12
Mount Egerton Vic. 212 E5, 223 O12
Mount Eliza Vic. 215 K2
Mount Emlyn Qld 482 A11
Mount Emu Vic. 212 A5, 222 H12

Mount Evelyn Vic. 210 G7
Mount Fairy NSW 139 K1
Mount Field National Park Tas. 538 A2, 542 I7, 509, 510, **520**, 524
Mount Forbes Qld 483 J10
Mount Frankland National Park WA 360 F9, 364 F12, 366 D12
Mount Franklin Vic. 212 E2, 223 P8
Mount Gambier SA 293 H12, 239, 241, **267**
Mount Garnet Qld 495 L8, 449
Mount George NSW 117 O1, 119 N13
Mount Gravatt Qld 481 J4
Mount Hallen Qld 482 I6
Mount Hawthorn WA 354 G12
Mount Helen Vic. 223 M12, 229 O4
Mount Helena WA 356 E4, 364 D3
Mount Hope NSW 123 N2
Mount Hope SA 294 C6
Mount Horeb NSW 115 B5, 116 D12
Mount Hotham Vic. 225 N5, 235 Q10, 236 D8, 164, 165, 176, 177, 182, 189, 194
Mount Hunter NSW 101 K10, 112 E1, 425
Mount Hypipamee National Park Qld 449
Mount Imlay National Park NSW 113 D12, 115 F12, 237 P9
Mount Irvine NSW 100 I4
Mount Irving Qld 482 C7
Mount Isa Qld 498 E4, 413, 415, **459**
Mount Kaputar National Park NSW 118 I7, 46, **59**, 60, 75, 76
Mount Keira NSW 110 A9
Mount Keith WA 366 H1, 368 F12
Mount Kembla NSW 112 G6, 89
Mount Kilcoy Qld 483 J2
Mount Kosciusko NSW 114 C12, 115 C9, 65, 68
Mount Kuring-Gai NSW 96 G6
Mount Lambie NSW 100 E4
Mount Larcom Qld 493 O12
Mount Lawley WA 353 J1, 355 J12, 311
Mount Lewis NSW 94 E13, 98 G3
Mount Liebig NT 410 E7
Mount Lloyd Tas. 538 E5, 543 K8
Mount Lonarch Vic. 222 H7
Mount Macedon Vic. 212 H3, 226 B1, 234 E12, 173
Mount Magnet WA 366 E2, **337**
Mount Marshall Qld 482 E12
Mount Martha Vic. 213 J10, 215 J5, 155, 197
Mount Mary SA 295 N6
Mount McIntyre SA 293 H11
Mount Mee Qld 483 K4
Mount Mercer Vic. 212 C6, 229 O5
Mount Molloy Qld 489 B6, 495 M6
Mount Morgan Qld 493 N11, **459-60**, 464
Mount Moriac Vic. 212 E10, 219 C8, 229 Q8
Mount Muirhead SA 293 G11
Mount Mulligan Qld 495 L6
Mount Nebo Qld 483 K7, 421
Mount Nelson Tas. 536 G12
Mount Olive NSW 117 L3
Mount Ommaney Qld 480 C6
Mount Osmond SA 285 M9
Mount Ossa Qld 493 K4
Mount Ousley NSW 110 C6
Mount Perry Qld 491 N3
Mount Pleasant NSW 110 A6
Mount Pleasant Qld 483 K5
Mount Pleasant SA 288 G8, 293 D1, 295 M9

Mount Pleasant Vic. 221 E10
Mount Pleasant WA 352 G8
Mount Pritchard NSW 98 A2
Mount Rat SA 294 H8
Mount Remarkable National Park SA 291 B13, 295 J1, 296 I12, **262**, 265, 270, 280
Mount Richmond Vic. 228 D8
Mount Richmond National Park Vic. 228 D8, 191
Mount Rowan Vic. 212 C3, 223 M10
Mount St Gwinear Vic. 182, 185
Mount St Thomas NSW 110 B13
Mount Samson Qld 483 L6
Mount Schank SA 293 H12, 267
Mount Seaview NSW 119 M12
Mount Selwyn NSW 114 D4, 115 C7, 138 C8, 44, 60, 65, 84
Mount Seymour Tas. 543 M5
Mount Sibley Qld 482 E10
Mount Slide Vic. 213 M4, 216 C3
Mount Spec/Crystal Creek National Park *see* Paluma Range National Park
Mount Stirling Vic. 235 N10, 236 A8, 182
Mount Stirling Alpine Resort Vic. 184
Mount Stuart Tas. 536 E7, 538 H6
Mount Surprise Qld 495 J10
Mount Sylvia Qld 482 G9
Mount Tamborine Qld 483 N12
Mount Tarampa Qld 482 I7
Mount Taylor Vic. 227 P4, 236 F13
Mount Thorley NSW 117 L3
Mount Torrens SA 288 F9
Mount Tyson Qld 482 C7
Mount Victoria NSW 100 H6, 102 B3, 117 J7, 68
Mount Walker Qld 482 I10
Mount Wallace Vic. 212 F5, 219 D1, 223 P13, 229 Q4
Mount Walsh National Park Qld 491 N4, 426
Mount Warning National Park NSW 119 P1, 491 Q11, **59**, 75
Mount Waverley Vic. 209 P11
Mount Webb National Park Qld 495 L2
Mount Wedge SA 294 B4
Mount Wellington Tas. 538 H6, 543 L8, **509**
Mount Wells Battery NT 401 A11, 402 I11
Mount White NSW 101 O4, 104 C9, 117 L6
Mount Whitestone Qld 482 G9
Mount William National Park Tas. 545 R6, 519, **521**
Mount Wilson NSW 100 H5
Mountain River Tas. 538 G7, 543 K9
Moura Qld 491 J1
Mourilyan Qld 495 N8, 446, **460**
Moutajup Vic. 228 G4
Mowbray Tas. 541 O9, 545 L8
Mowbray Park NSW 101 J11, 112 D2
Mowen WA 357 C10, 359 D7, 364 B10
Moyhu Vic. 224 F3, 235 M7, 196
Moyreisk Vic. 222 I3, 231 M10
Moyston Vic. 222 B8, 229 J2, 231 J13
Muchea WA 356 C1, 364 D2
Muckadilla Qld 490 G6
Mudamukla SA 303 O10
Mudgee NSW 116 H3, **74**, 81
Mudgeeraba Qld 483 O13, 485 D8, 491 Q10, 423
Mudgegonga Vic. 225 K1, 235 P6, 236 B4
Mudginberri NT 401 H4, 403 Q3

Mudjimba Qld 486 H8
Muggleton Qld 490 H6
Mukinbudin WA 366 F6
Mulambin Qld 493 O10
Mulbring NSW 108 D9
Mulcra Vic. 232 B10, 293 I2, 295 R10
Muldu Qld 482 D5
Mulgildie Qld 491 M2
Mulgoa NSW 101 K8, 117 K8
Mulgrave Vic. 209 R13, 211 G1
Mullaley NSW 118 G11
Mullaloo WA 354 A1, 356 A3
Mullalyup WA 357 I8, 360 B2, 364 D9
Mullaway NSW 119 P7
Mullenderee NSW 139 N8
Mullengandra NSW 123 Q13, 235 Q3
Mullengudgery NSW 118 A13, 121 R11
Mullewa WA 366 B3, **337–8**
Mulli Mulli NSW 119 O2, 491 P11
Mullindolingong Vic. 225 N4, 235 Q8, 236
Mullion Creek NSW 116 G5
Mullumbimby NSW 119 Q2, 491 Q12, **74**
Mulpata SA 293 G2, 295 P10
Mulwala NSW 123 N13, 235 L3, **74**, 201, 204
Mumbannar Vic. 228 B6
Mumbel Vic. 231 M2, 233 M12
Mumbil NSW 116 F4
Mumblin Vic. 217 A7
Mummulgum NSW 119 O3, 491 P12
Munbilla Qld 483 J11
Mundaring WA 356 E4, 364 D3, 366 C8, **338**
Mundijong WA 356 D7, 364 D5, 342
Mundingburra Qld 487 B9
Mundoona Vic. 234 H4
Mundoora SA 295 J4
Mundrabilla WA 367 Q8, **338**
Mundubbera Qld 491 M4, **460**
Mundulla SA 293 H7, 252
Munetta SA 290 D8
Mungala SA 303 L4
Mungallala Qld 490 E6
Mungana Qld 495 J7
Mungar Qld 491 P4
Mungerannie Roadhouse SA 299 K8, 500 C10, 265, 279
Mungeribar NSW 116 D2
Mungery NSW 116 C3
Mungindi NSW 118 E3, 490 H13
Mungkan Kandju National Park Qld 496 D10, **458**
Munglinup WA 366 I10
Mungo National Park NSW 122 G5, 45, **60**, 88
Mungungo Qld 491 M2
Muniganeen Qld 482 E6
Munjina Roadhouse WA 368 C4
Munro NSW 227 N5
Munster WA 356 B6
Muntadgin WA 366 F7
Muradup WA 360 I2, 364 F9
Murarrie Qld 479 K11
Murchison Vic. 234 H7, 186, 192
Murchison WA 365 E12, 366 C1
Murchison East Vic. 234 H7
Murdinga SA 294 D5
Murdoch WA 352 G12
Murdunna Tas. 539 N7, 543 O9
Murga NSW 116 E6
Murgenella Settlement NT 406 H3
Murgheboluc Vic. 212 E9, 219 C6
Murgon Qld 491 N6, **460**

Murnnie Beach SA 294 H3
Murphys Creek Qld 482 F7, 491 N9, 468
Murphys Creek Vic. 223 L1, 231 O9
Murra Warra Vic. 230 G7
Murrabit Vic. 122 I11, 231 P1, 233 P12, 46, 179
Murramarang National Park NSW 139 O7, 47
Murrawal NSW 118 F12
Murray Bridge SA 288 I12, 293 D2, 295 M10, 201, **267**
Murray River National Park SA 122 A7, 295 Q7, 252, 261
Murray Town SA 295 J2, 297 J12, 265
Murray-Sunset National Park Vic. 122 B9, 232 C8, 293 I1, 295 R8, **176**, 189, 201
Murrayville Vic. 122 B11, 232 B10, 295 R10, 186
Murrindal Vic. 115 C13, 236 I10
Murrindindi Vic. 213 N2, 226 F1, 234 I12
Murringo NSW 115 C2, 116 E9, 90
Murroon Vic. 212 C12, 217 H8
Murrumba Qld 482 I5
Murrumbateman NSW 115 E4, 116 F11, 131
Murrumbeena Vic. 209 N12
Murrumburrah NSW 115 C3, 116 E10, **74**
Murrungowar Vic. 115 D13, 237 K12
Murrurundi NSW 119 J13, **74**
Murtoa Vic. 230 I9, **186**
Murwillumbah NSW 119 Q1, 491 Q11, **74–5**
Musk Vic. 212 E2, 223 P9, 168
Musk Vale Vic. 212 E2, 223 P9
Muskerry East Vic. 234 D8
Musselboro Tas. 545 N9
Muston SA 294 I12
Muswellbrook NSW 117 K2, **75**
Mutarnee Qld 495 O12
Mutdapilly Qld 483 J10
Muttaburra Qld 492 B9, 499 P9, **460**
Muttama NSW 115 B4, 116 D11
Muttonbird Island NSW 54
Myall Vic. 231 P2, 233 P12
Myall Lakes National Park NSW 117 O3, 52, **59**, 62
Myall Mundi NSW 116 C1
Myall Plains NSW 123 N11
Myalla Tas. 544 E5
Myalup WA 357 G2, 364 C7, 314
Myamyn Vic. 228 E7
Myaree WA 352 F10
Myaring Vic. 228 B5
Myers Flat Vic. 223 Q1
Mylestom NSW 119 P8
Mylor SA 288 D11, 289 H2, 290 G2, 247
Myola Qld 489 D7
Myola Vic. 234 E8
Mypolonga SA 293 D2, 295 N9, 267
Myponga SA 289 E6, 290 B9, 293 B3, 295 K11, 268, 280
Myponga Beach SA 289 D5
Myrla SA 295 P7
Myrniong Vic. 212 F4, 223 R12, 229 R4, 234 C13, 161
Myrrhee Vic. 224 E5, 235 M8
Myrtle Bank SA 285 K9
Myrtle Bank Tas. 541 Q7, 545 M7
Myrtle Creek Vic. 231 R11, 234 D10
Myrtle Scrub NSW 119 M11
Myrtleford Vic. 225 J2, 235 O7, 236 B5, **186**

Myrtletown Qld 479 L6
Myrtleville NSW 115 G3, 116 I10
Mysia Vic. 231 O6
Mysterton Qld 487 C8
Mystic Park Vic. 122 H11, 231 O2, 233 O12, 195
Mywee Vic. 234 I2
Mywybilla Qld 482 B7

Nabageena Tas. 544 C5
Nabawa WA 366 B3
Nabiac NSW 117 O2
Nabowla Tas. 541 R5, 545 N7, 524, 529
Nackara SA 295 M2, 297 M12
Nagambie Vic. 234 G8, **186**, 194, 197
Nagoorim Qld 491 M1, 493 P13
Nailsworth SA 285 J3
Nairne SA 288 E11, 247
Nakara NT 400 G2
Nala Tas. 543 M5
Nalangil Vic. 217 E6
Nalinga Vic. 235 J6
Nallama NSW 84
Nalya WA 364 G5
Namadgi National Park ACT 114 I1, 115 D6, 116 F13, 135 C9, 138 E4, 125, 132
Nambour Qld 483 M1, 486 E8, 491 P7, 429, **460**
Nambrok Vic. 227 M6
Nambucca Heads NSW 119 P9, **75**
Nambung National Park WA 366 B6, 305, **322**, 329, 332
Nana Glen NSW 119 P7
Nanango Qld 491 N7, **460**
Nanarup WA 361 P12, 364 I13
Nandaly Vic. 122 F11, 233 J10
Nandi Qld 491 M8
Nanga WA 356 D12, 364 D6
Nangalala NT 407 L5
Nangana Vic. 213 N7, 216 E11, 226 F4
Nangar National Park NSW 116 E6
Nangari SA 122 A8, 232 A5, 295 R8
Nangeenan WA 364 I2
Nangiloc Vic. 122 E8, 232 H5
Nangkita SA 289 H5, 290 F8, 293 C3, 295 L10
Nangus NSW 115 B5, 116 C12
Nangwarry SA 293 H11
Nanneella Vic. 234 F5
Nannine WA 335
Nannup WA 357 G10, 360 A4, 364 C10, 366 C11, **338**
Nanson WA 366 A3
Nantabibbie SA 295 M2, 297 L12
Nantawarra SA 295 K6
Nanutarra Roadhouse WA 365 E4
Napoleons Vic. 212 C5, 223 L12, 229 O4
Napperby SA 295 J3, 297 J13
Nar Nar Goon Vic. 213 N9, 226 F6
Nara Qld 482 E6
Naracoopa Tas. 542 B9
Naracoorte SA 293 H9, **267–8**
Naradhan NSW 123 O5
Naraling WA 366 B3
Narangba Qld 483 M5
Narara NSW 101 P3, 104 E5
Narbethong Vic. 213 N4, 216 G4, 226 G2, 235 J13
Nareen Vic. 228 D3, 168
Narellan NSW 101 K10, 112 F1, 52
Narembeen WA 366 F8
Naremburn NSW 95 M6

Naretha WA 367 M6
Nariel Vic. 115 B9, 236 G4
Naringal Vic. 229 J9
Narioka Vic. 234 G4
Narko Qld 482 D4
Narnu Bay SA 290 H12
Naroghid Vic. 217 B6
Narooma NSW 113 I2, 115 H9, 139 N11, 237 R2, 55, **75–6**
Narrabarba NSW 113 E13, 115 F12, 237 P10
Narrabeen NSW 97 O10, 101 O7
Narrabri NSW 118 G8, 75, **76**
Narrabri West NSW 118 G8
Narrabundah ACT 136 H13, 137 F4
Narracan Vic. 213 R11, 227 J7
Narrandera NSW 123 P9, 75, **76**, 81
Narraport Vic. 231 K5
Narrawa NSW 115 E2, 116 G10
Narrawa Tas. 540 B9, 544 H8
Narrawallee NSW 139 P3
Narraweena NSW 95 P2, 97 N12
Narrawong Vic. 228 E8
Narre Warren Vic. 213 L8
Narrewillock Vic. 231 M5
Narridy SA 295 K4
Narrien Range National Park Qld 492 G9
Narrikup WA 361 M10, 364 H12
Narrogin WA 364 G6, 366 E9, **338**
Narromine NSW 116 D2, **76**
Narrung SA 293 D3, 295 M11, 265
Narrung Vic. 233 L7
Narwee NSW 98 H5
Nashdale NSW 116 F6
Nathalia Vic. 123 L13, 234 H4, 187
Nathan Qld 480 I5, 418
Natimuk Vic. 230 F9, **186**, 203
National Park Tas. 538 C2, 543 J7
Natone Tas. 544 G6
Nattai NSW 100 I11, 112 C1, 117 J8
Nattai National Park NSW 100 I12, 112 B3, 115 H2, 117 J9
Natte Yallock Vic. 222 I3, 231 N11
Natural Arch National Park see **Springbrook National Park**
Natya Vic. 233 L8
Naval Base WA 356 A7
Navarre Vic. 222 F3, 231 L10
Navigators Vic. 212 D4, 223 N11, 229 P4
Nayook Vic. 213 P7, 170
Neale Junction WA 367 N2
Neales Flat SA 288 H1, 295 M7
Neath NSW 108 C9, 109 G11
Nebo Qld 493 K6, **460**
Nectar Brook SA 291 B13, 295 J1, 296 I12
Nedlands WA 352 E6
Neds Corner Vic. 232 C3
Needles Tas. 540 G12, 545 J9
Neerabup National Park WA 356 A2, 364 C3, 366 B8
Neerdie Qld 491 P5
Neerim NSW 213 P8, 226 H5
Neerim East Vic. 213 Q8
Neerim Junction Vic. 213 P7
Neerim South Vic. 213 P8, 226 H5, 170, 199
Neeworra NSW 118 E4, 490 H13
Neika Tas. 538 H7, 543 L9
Neilborough Vic. 231 Q8, 234 C7
Neilborough East Vic. 231 Q8, 234 C7
Neilrex NSW 118 F13
Nelia Qld 499 K4

Nelligen NSW 115 H6, 139 N6, 47
Nelly Bay Qld 495 P12
Nelshaby SA 295 J3, 297 J13
Nelson NSW 101 M6
Nelson Vic. 228 B7, 293 I13, 165, 191, 204
Nelson Bay NSW 108 H2, 117 O4, 51, **76**
Nelsons Plain NSW 108 E5
Nelungaloo NSW 116 D5
Nene Valley SA 293 H12
Nerang Qld 483 N12, 485 C5, 491 Q10, **460–1**
Neranwood Qld 485 B10
Nerrena Vic. 181
Nerriga NSW 115 H5, 116 I12, 139 N1
Nerrigundah NSW 113 G1, 115 G8, 139 L10, 237 Q2, 73
Nerrin Nerrin Vic. 229 K5
Nerrina Vic. 212 D4, 221 I4, 223 M11, 229 O3, 234 A13
Nerring Vic. 212 A3, 222 I10
Netherby SA 285 K10
Netherby Vic. 122 C13, 230 D5
Nethercote NSW 113 F11, 115 G11, 237 Q8
Netley SA 284 F8
Neuarpurr Vic. 230 B10, 293 I8
Neumgna Qld 482 F1
Neurea NSW 116 F4, 87
Neuroodla SA 291 C9, 297 J8
Neurum Qld 483 K3
Neutral Bay NSW 95 N8, 35
Neuve Qld 482 E5
Nevertire NSW 116 C1, 118 B13
Neville NSW 116 G7
Nevilton Qld 482 E10
New Angledool NSW 118 B4, 490 F13
New Brighton NSW 119 Q2
New England NSW 119 M7, **69**
New England National Park NSW 119 N9, 45, **59**, 61
New Farm Qld 478 H11, 418
New Gisborne Vic. 212 H3, 226 B1, 234 E12, 202
New Italy NSW 119 Q4, 491 Q13, 61
New Mollyann NSW 118 F12
New Norcia WA 364 D1, 366 C6, **338–9**
New Norfolk Tas. 538 F4, 543 K8, 503, 509, 515, **524**, 527
New Residence SA 295 P7
New Town Tas. 536 F6, 507, 527
New Well SA 295 O7
Newborough Vic. 213 R10, 227 J7
Newbridge NSW 100 A6, 116 G7, 49
Newbridge Vic. 223 N1, 231 P10, 234 A8
Newburn WA 353 O4
Newbury Vic. 212 F3, 223 Q9
Newcastle NSW 106, 117 N4, 29, 30, 40, **76–7**
Newcastle Waters NT 408 I6
Newcastle West NSW 106 D7
Newdegate WA 366 G9
Newell Qld 489 B3
Newell, The NSW 116 C7, 118 F10, 75
Newfield Vic. 217 A9, 229 K10
Newham Vic. 212 H2, 226 B1, 234 E12, 202
Newhaven Vic. 213 M13, 215 R13, 226 E9, 168, 169
Newington Vic. 221 D7
Newland SA 289 G8, 290 D13
Newlands WA 357 H7, 360 B1, 364 C9
Newlands Coal Mine Qld 492 I5
Newlyn Vic. 212 D3, 223 N9, 229 P2, 231 P13, 234 B12

Newman WA 368 D6, **339–40**, 343
Newmarket Qld 478 E10, 483 M7
Newmerella Vic. 237 J13
Newnes NSW 100 G1, 117 J5
Newnes Junction NSW 100 G4
Newnham Tas. 541 N9
Newport NSW 97 P6, 101 P6, 104 H12
Newport Vic. 208 H10
Newport Beach NSW 104 H12
Newry Vic. 227 M5
Newrybar NSW 119 Q3, 491 Q12
Newstead Qld 478 H10, 419
Newstead Tas. 541 O10
Newstead Vic. 212 E1, 223 O5, 231 P12, 234 B10, 166
Newton SA 285 N3
Newton Boyd NSW 119 N6
Newtown NSW 95 K12, 99 M2
Newtown Vic. 212 B5, 218 B8, 219 E7, 223 K12
Ngallo Vic. 232 A11, 293 I3, 295 R10
Ngapal SA 295 L6
Nguiu NT 406 D4
Ngukurr NT 407 L10
Ngunnawal ACT 136 F2
Nhill Vic. 230 D7, **186**
Nhulunbuy NT 407 P5, 395, 396
Ni Ni Vic. 230 E6
Niagara Park NSW 104 E5
Niangala NSW 119 K11
Nicholls ACT 136 F3
Nicholls Point Vic. 122 D7, 232 G3
Nicholls Rivulet Tas. 538 F10, 543 K10, 513
Nicholson Vic. 227 Q4, 236 G13
Nicoll Scrub National Park Qld 485 E11
Niddrie Vic. 208 H5
Niemur NSW 123 J10, 233 Q10
Nierinna Tas. 538 G8
Nietta Tas. 540 A9, 544 H8
Nightcap National Park NSW 119 P2, 59, 71, 75, 77
Nightcliff NT 400 A5, 402 C2, 378
Nildottie SA 293 E1, 295 N8, 275
Nile Tas. 545 M10, 518, 523
Nillahcootie Vic. 224 B9
Nilma Vic. 213 P10, 226 H7
Nimbin NSW 119 Q2, 491 Q12, **77**
Nimmitabel NSW 113 B5, 115 E10, 237 N5
Ninda Vic. 231 J1, 233 J12
Nindigully Qld 118 D1, 490 H11, 466
Nine Mile Vic. 231 M7
Ninnes SA 295 J6
Ninyeunook Vic. 231 M5
Nipan Qld 491 J2
Nippering WA 364 H8
Nirranda Vic. 229 J10
Nirranda South Vic. 229 J10
Nitmiluk National Park NT 406 G9, 385, 388, 390, 391, **392**
Nobby Qld 482 E10, 491 N10, 434
Noble Park Vic. 211 F4
Noccundra Qld 501 L10, 442, 472
Noggojerring WA 356 I1, 364 E2
Nollamara WA 354 H9
Nonda Qld 499 K4
Noojee Vic. 213 Q7, 226 I4, 170, 198
Nook Tas. 540 D8, 544 I8
Nookanellup WA 361 K2, 364 G9
Noonamah NT 402 E4, 406 E6, **390**
Noonbinna NSW 116 E8
Noondoo Qld 118 C2, 490 G12
Noora SA 122 A8, 232 A5, 295 R7

Nooramunga Vic. 235 K6
Noorat Vic. 217 A5, 229 K8, 165, 196
Noorinbee Vic. 115 E13, 237 N11
Noorinbee North Vic. 115 E13, 237 N11
Noorong NSW 122 I11, 233 P11
Noorongong Vic. 235 Q5, 236 D3
Noosa Heads Qld 486 H1, 491 Q6, 429, **461**
Noosa Junction Qld 461
Noosa National Park Qld 486 H2, 413, 429, **456**, 461
Noosaville Qld 486 G2, 461
Nora Creina SA 293 F10
Noradjuha Vic. 230 F10
Norah Head NSW 101 Q2, 108 I13
Norahville NSW 101 Q2, 108 I13
Noranda WA 355 K8
Nords Wharf NSW 101 R1, 108 H11
Norillee Qld 482 B7
Norlane Vic. 219 E6
Norman Park Qld 478 I12, 417
Normanhurst NSW 94 G1, 96 F11
Normanton Qld 494 C8, 497 I8, 413, **461**, 474
Normanville SA 289 D7, 293 B3, 295 K11, 280
Normanville Vic. 231 N3
Nornakin WA 364 H4
Nornalup WA 360 H12, 364 F13, 324
Norseman WA 367 J8, 333, **340**
North Adelaide SA 282 C4, 284 H5, 243, 244, 245
North Arm Qld 486 E5
North Avoca NSW 104 H6
North Beach SA 294 I5
North Beach WA 354 B8
North Bendigo Vic. 220 D1
North Berry Jerry NSW 116 B11, 123 R9
North Bondi NSW 95 Q11, 101 O8
North Bruny Island Tas. 538 I10, 510, **512**, 522
North Dandalup WA 356 C9, 364 D5, 366 C9, 342
North Fremantle WA 352 A9, 358 D4
North Haven NSW 105 F10, 119 O12
North Haven SA 286 D7
North Hobart Tas. 536 F6, 507
North Jindong WA 359 E4, 364 B9
North Lake WA 352 F13
North Lilydale Tas. 541 P6, 545 M7
North Maclean Qld 483 L10
North Melbourne Vic. 206 A3
North Motton Tas. 540 B6, 544 H7
North Perth WA 352 H1, 354 H13
North Richmond NSW 101 K5
North Rocks NSW 94 D4
North Rothbury NSW 108 A8, 109 E3
North Ryde NSW 94 I5
North Scottsdale Tas. 545 N6
North Shields SA 294 D8, 271
North Star NSW 118 I3, 491 K12
North Stradbroke Island Qld 483 Q8, 491 R9, **433**, 463
North Sydney NSW 95 M8, 101 O8, 34
North Ward Qld 487 E2
North West Island Qld 438
North Wollongong NSW 110 F8, 112 H6
North Yunderup WA 356 B10, 364 C5
Northam WA 356 H2, 364 E3, 366 D7, **340**
Northampton WA 366 A3, **340**
Northbridge NSW 95 M6
Northbridge WA 350 C4, 352 H2, 308, 309

Northcliffe WA 360 C9, 364 D12, 366 D12, 340–1
Northcote Vic. 209 L7
Northdown Tas. 540 F5, 545 J6
Northfield SA 285 K1, 287 K12
Northgate Qld 478 H7
Northmead NSW 94 C5
Northwood NSW 95 L7
Northwood Vic. 234 G10
Norton NSW 98 C4
Norton Summit SA 285 P6, 288 C10, 246
Norval Vic. 222 C7
Norwell Qld 483 N10
Norwin Qld 482 B7
Norwood SA 285 K6, 244
Notley Hills Tas. 541 L8, 545 K8, 518
Notting WA 364 I5
Notting Hill Vic. 209 P13, 211 E1
Notts Well SA 295 O7
Novar Gardens SA 284 E10
Nowa Hill NSW 115 I4, 117 J11
Nowa Nowa Vic. 236 H12
Nowendoc NSW 119 L12
Nowie North Vic. 233 M10, 195
Nowingi Vic. 232 G6
Nowley NSW 118 E7
Nowra NSW 112 E12, 115 I4, 117 K11, 53, **77**
Nowra Hill NSW 112 D13
Nubba NSW 115 B3, 116 D10
Nubeena Tas. 539 M10, 543 N10
Nudgee Qld 478 I5
Nudgee Beach Qld 478 I5
Nug Nug Vic. 225 J4, 235 O8, 236 B5
Nuga Nuga National Park Qld 490 G2
Nugent Tas. 539 M4, 543 N7
Nulkaba NSW 109 E10, 53
Nulla Vale Vic. 212 I1
Nullagine WA 368 E3, 335
Nullan Vic. 230 I7
Nullarbor, The SA 302 G7, 333
Nullarbor National Park SA 302 C7, 367 R7, **264**
Nullawarre Vic. 229 J10
Nullawil Vic. 122 G12, 231 L4
Numbla Vale NSW 114 I13, 115 D10, 237 L5
Numbugga NSW 113 E7, 115 F10, 237 P6
Numbulwar NT 407 N9
Numeralla NSW 113 C1, 115 F8, 138 H10, 237 O2
Numurkah Vic. 123 M13, 234 I4, 167, **186–7**
Nunamara Tas. 541 Q9, 545 M8
Nunawading Vic. 209 Q8
Nundah Qld 478 H8
Nundle NSW 119 K12, **77–8**, 82
Nundroo SA 303 J8
Nunga Vic. 232 H9
Nungarin WA 364 I1, 337
Nungurner Vic. 227 R5, 236 G13
Nunjikompita SA 303 P10
Nuraip SA 292 G5
Nurina WA 367 O6
Nurinda Qld 482 I3
Nuriootpa SA 288 F4, 292 G4, 295 M7, 246, **268**
Nurom SA 295 J3
Nurrabiel Vic. 230 G11
Nutfield Vic. 213 L4
Nutgrove Qld 482 E3
Nyabing WA 364 I8, 366 F10

Nyah Vic. 122 G10, 233 M10
Nyah West Vic. 122 G10, 233 M10
Nyallo Vic. 230 I3, 232 I13
Nyamup WA 360 E6, 364 E12, 334
Nyarrin Vic. 233 J11
Nyirripi NT 410 D6
Nymagee NSW 121 O12
Nymboida NSW 119 O7
Nymboida National Park NSW 119 N6
Nymbool Qld 495 L8
Nyngan NSW 121 R10, **78**
Nyora Vic. 213 O11, 226 G8, 180, 181
Nypo Vic. 230 F3, 232 F13

O'Connell NSW 100 C5, 47
O'Connor ACT 136 G8
O'Connor WA 352 D11
O'Malley ACT 137 E4
O'Malley SA 302 G4
O'Sullivan Beach SA 289 E3
Oak Beach Qld 489 D5, 495 M6
Oak Park Vic. 208 I4
Oakbank SA 288 D10, 289 I1, 290 I1, 247
Oakdale NSW 101 J11, 112 D1, 115 I1, 117 J8
Oakden SA 285 L1, 287 L12
Oakey Qld 482 D6, 491 N9, **461–2**, 470
Oakey Creek NSW 118 G12
Oaklands NSW 123 O11
Oaklands SA 294 I9
Oaklands Park SA 284 F12
Oakleigh Vic. 209 O13, 211 D1, 226 D4
Oakleigh East Vic. 209 O12
Oaks Tas. 541 L13, 545 L9
Oakvale Vic. 231 N4
Oakwood Tas. 539 N10, 543 N10
Oasis Roadhouse Qld 495 K11
Oatlands Tas. 543 M5, 515, **524**
Oatley NSW 98 I7
Ob Flat SA 293 H12
Oberne NSW 115 A6, 116 C13
Oberon NSW 100 E7, 116 I7
Obi Obi Qld 483 L1, 486 A8
Obley NSW 116 E4
Obx Creek NSW 119 O6
Ocean Grove Vic. 212 G10, 219 G9, 226 A7, 229 R8, **187**
Ocean Shores NSW 119 Q2, 491 Q12
Ockley WA 364 G6
Oenpelli (Gunbalanya) NT 401 I2, 403 R1, 406 I5
Officer Vic. 213 M9
Ogilvie WA 366 A3
Ogmore Qld 493 M9
Olangalah Vic. 217 G10
Olary SA 297 P10
Old Adaminaby NSW 114 G5, 115 D8, 138 D9, 237 K1
Old Bar NSW 117 P1
Old Beach Tas. 538 H4, 543 L8
Old Bonalbo NSW 119 O2, 491 P12
Old Junee NSW 115 A4, 116 C11, 123 R9
Old Noarlunga SA 288 A12, 289 F3, 290 B4, 293 B2, 295 K10, 261, **268**
Old Tallangatta Vic. 235 R4, 236 D2
Old Toongabbie NSW 94 B5
Old Warrah NSW 118 I12
Oldina Tas. 544 F6
Olgas, The see Kata Tjuta
Olinda NSW 116 I4
Olinda Vic. 210 F11, 213 M7, 216 B11, 226 E4, 156, 172

Olio Qld 499 M7
Olympic Dam Village SA 296 F4
Ombersley Vic. 212 C10, 217 I5
Omega NSW 112 G10
Omeo Vic. 115 A12, 236 F8, 181, **188–9**, 193
Ondit Vic. 212 B10, 217 G6
One Arm Point WA 370 I6
One Tree NSW 123 K7
One Tree Hill SA 287 R1
Ongerup WA 361 R3, 366 F11
Onslow WA 365 D3, 339, **341**
Oodla Wirra SA 295 M2, 297 L12
Oodnadatta SA 298 B6, 265, **268**, 279
Ooldea SA 302 I4
Ooma Creek NSW 116 D7
Ooma North NSW 116 D7
Oonah Tas. 544 F7
Oondooroo Qld 499 L7
Oonoonba Qld 487 G9
Oorindi Qld 498 H4
Ootann Qld 495 K8
Ootha NSW 116 B5, 123 R3
Opalton Qld 499 L10, 471
Ophir NSW 116 G5
Opossum Bay Tas. 538 I8, 543 M9
Ora Banda WA 366 I5, 320, 331
Orange NSW 116 G6, **78**
Orange Grove WA 353 Q8
Orangeville NSW 101 J10, 112 D1
Oranmeir NSW 115 F7, 139 K6
Orbost Vic. 237 J12, **189**
Orchid Beach Qld 491 Q2
Ord River WA 332, **347**
Orford Tas. 539 N2, 543 O6, 515, **524–5**
Orford Vic. 228 G8
Organ Pipes National Park Vic. 208 E1, 212 I5, 226 C3, **174**
Orielton Tas. 539 K4, 543 M7
Orient Point NSW 112 F12
Ormeau Qld 483 N11
Ormiston Qld 479 R13, 481 R1, 434
Ormiston Gorge National Park see West MacDonnell National Park
Ormley Tas. 543 O1, 545 O10
Ormond Vic. 209 M12, 211 B1
Orpheus Island National Park Qld 495 O11, **440**, 446
Orroroo SA 291 D13, 295 L1, 297 K12, 270
Orrvale Vic. 234 I6
Orton Park NSW 100 B4
Osborne SA 286 D8
Osborne Park WA 354 F11
Osbornes Flat Vic. 235 P5, 236 B3
Osbourne NSW 116 A13, 123 P11
Osmaston Tas. 541 J12, 545 K9
Osmington WA 357 D9, 359 E7, 364 B9
Osterley Tas. 543 J5
Otford NSW 101 M12, 112 I3
Ottoway SA 284 F1, 286 F12
Otway National Park Vic. 217 F12, 229 N12, 157, **175**, 181
Ourimbah NSW 101 P3, 104 E4, 63
Ournie NSW 115 B8, 236 G1
Ouse Tas. 543 J6
Outer Harbor SA 286 D6, 288 A8
Outtrim Vic. 213 O13, 226 G9
Ouyen Vic. 122 E10, 232 H9, **189**
Ovens Vic. 225 J3, 235 O7, 236 B5
Overland Corner SA 295 P6, 251
Overlander Roadhouse WA 365 C11

Ovingham SA 282 B3
Owanyilla Qld 491 P4
Owen SA 288 A1, 295 K7
Owens Gap NSW 117 K1
Oxenford Qld 483 N12, 485 C2, 491 Q10, 422
Oxford Falls NSW 95 O1, 97 N11
Oxford Park Qld 478 D9
Oxley ACT 137 C9
Oxley NSW 122 I7, 233 Q3, 66
Oxley Qld 480 E6
Oxley Vic. 224 F1, 235 M6, 184
Oxley Wild Rivers National Park NSW 119 M10, 45, 87
Oyster Bay NSW 98 I9
Oyster Cove Tas. 538 G9, 543 L10
Ozenkadnook Vic. 230 C10

Paaratte Vic. 217 A9
Pacific Palms NSW 117 P2
Packsaddle Roadhouse NSW 120 C7
Padbury WA 354 B3
Paddington NSW 95 N11, 99 P1, 101 O8, 38, 40
Paddington Qld 478 F12, 417, 418
Paddys River NSW 115 H3, 116 I10
Padstow NSW 98 G6
Padthaway SA 293 H7, 252, 259, 268
Page ACT 136 C6
Pages Flat SA 290 C8
Pagewood NSW 99 P5
Paignie Vic. 232 G9
Painswick Vic. 223 L2
Pakenham Vic. 213 M9, 226 F6, 180
Palana Tas. 542 A11
Palgarup WA 360 D5, 364 D10
Pallamallawa NSW 118 H5
Pallara Qld 480 G9
Pallarang Vic. 232 C9
Pallarenda Qld 495 P12
Pallarup WA 366 H10, 332
Palm Beach NSW 97 Q2, 101 P5, 104 H11, 40, 41
Palm Beach Qld 485 G9
Palm Cove Qld 489 E7, 495 M6, **462**
Palm Dale NSW 101 P3, 104 E3
Palm Grove NSW 101 P3, 104 D4
Palm Valley see Finke Gorge National Park
Palm View Qld 486 G11
Palmer SA 288 H9, 293 D1, 295 M9
Palmer River Roadhouse Qld 495 K4
Palmers Island NSW 119 Q5
Palmers Oaky NSW 100 D2
Palmerston ACT 136 G3
Palmerston NT 402 D3, 376
Palmerville Qld 495 J4
Palmwoods Qld 483 M1, 486 E9
Palmyra WA 352 D10
Paloona Tas. 540 D7, 544 I7
Paluma Range National Park Qld 495 N11, 446, 470
Pambula NSW 113 F10, 115 G11, 237 Q7, 55, 73
Pambula Beach NSW 113 F10, 115 G11, 237 Q7, 73
Pampas Qld 482 B9, 491 M10
Panania NSW 98 E5
Panitya Vic. 232 A10, 293 I2, 295 R10
Panmure Vic. 229 J9
Pannawonica WA 365 F3, 346
Panorama SA 285 J11
Pantapin WA 364 H3

Panton Hill Vic. 210 C1, 213 L5, 226 E3
Paper Beach Tas. 541 L6, 518
Pappinbarra NSW 105 C7, 119 N12
Papunya NT 410 G7
Para Hills SA 287 M9
Para Vista SA 287 M10
Paraburdoo WA 365 H5, 368 A6, 343
Parachilna NSW 297 J6
Parachilna SA 291 D6, 273
Paradise SA 285 N2, 244
Paradise Tas. 540 D10, 544 I8
Paradise Vic. 217 G12, 222 F2
Paradise Beach Vic. 227 O7
Paradise Point Qld 485 E2
Parafield SA 287 K8
Parafield Gardens SA 287 K6
Paralowie SA 287 K4
Parap NT 399 E6, 400 A13
Paraparap Vic. 219 D9
Paratoo SA 291 G13, 295 N1, 297 M11
Parattah Tas. 543 M5
Pardoo Roadhouse WA 370 D12
Parenna Tas. 542 A9
Parilla SA 293 H3, 295 Q10
Paringa SA 122 A7, 295 Q6, **268**
Paris Creek SA 288 D13, 289 I4, 290 H5
Park Holme SA 284 F11
Park Orchards Vic. 209 R7, 210 A7
Park Ridge Qld 481 J13
Parkers Corner Vic. 227 J5
Parkes ACT 134 D9, 136 G11, 137 F1
Parkes NSW 116 D5, 75, **78**
Parkham Tas. 540 H9, 545 J8
Parkhurst Qld 493 N10
Parkinson Qld 480 I10
Parkside SA 282 H13, 285 J8
Parkside Tas. 545 Q8
Parkville NSW 117 K1
Parkville Vic. 209 K7, 151
Parkwood Vic. 228 E4
Parndana SA 294 H12, 269
Parnella Tas. 545 R8
Parrakie SA 293 G3, 295 P11
Parramatta NSW 94 C6, 101 M8, 117 L7, 35, 43
Parramatta Park Qld 488 F9
Parrawe Tas. 544 E7
Paru NT 406 D4
Paruna SA 122 A9, 293 H1, 295 Q8
Parwan Vic. 212 G5, 223 R13, 226 A3, 229 R4
Pasadena SA 284 H12
Paschendale Vic. 228 D4
Pascoe Vale Vic. 209 J4
Paskeville SA 295 J6, 258
Pastoria Vic. 212 H1
Pata SA 295 Q8
Patchewollock Vic. 122 D11, 232 G11, 189
Pateena Tas. 541 N12, 545 L9
Paterson NSW 108 B5, 117 M3, 72
Patersonia Tas. 541 Q8, 545 M8
Patho Vic. 234 D3
Patonga NSW 101 O5, 104 F10
Patrick Estate Qld 483 J7
Patterson Lakes Vic. 211 E9
Patyah Vic. 230 C10
Paupong NSW 114 H13, 115 D10, 237 K5
Pawleena Tas. 539 K4, 543 N7
Pawtella Tas. 543 M5
Paxton NSW 108 B11, 117 M4
Payneham SA 285 L5
Paynes Crossing NSW 117 L4

Paynes Find WA 366 E4
Paynesville Vic. 227 Q5, **189**, 193, 194
Paytens Bridge NSW 116 D7
Peachester Qld 483 L2, 486 C13
Peak Charles National Park WA 366 I9, **323**
Peak Crossing Qld 483 K10, 491 P10
Peak Downs Qld 492 I8
Peak Hill NSW 116 D4, 78
Peak Hill WA 368 C10, 335
Peak View NSW 115 F8, 138 I10
Peake SA 293 F3, 295 O11
Peakhurst NSW 98 H6, 101 N9
Peakview NSW 237 O1
Pearce ACT 137 C5
Pearcedale Vic. 213 L10, 215 O3, 226 E7
Pearl Beach NSW 104 F9
Pearshape Tas. 542 A9
Peats Ridge NSW 101 O3, 104 B4, 117 L6
Pebbly Beach NSW 115 H6, 139 O6
Pebbly Beach Qld 489 D5
Pechey Qld 482 F6
Peebinga SA 122 A9, 232 A8, 293 I1, 295 R9
Peechelba Vic. 235 M4
Peechelba East Vic. 235 M4
Peel NSW 100 C3, 116 H6
Peelhurst WA 356 B9, 364 C5
Peelwood NSW 100 A11, 115 F1, 116 G8, 57
Peep Hill SA 295 M6
Pegarah Tas. 542 A9
Pekina SA 295 K2, 297 K12
Pelaw Main NSW 108 D9, 53
Pelham Tas. 538 F1, 543 K6
Pella Vic. 230 F4, 191
Pelverata Tas. 538 F8, 543 K9
Pemberton WA 360 C7, 364 D11, 366 C11, 319, **341**
Pembroke NSW 105 F7, 119 O12
Penarie NSW 122 H7, 233 N4
Penderlea NSW 114 E12
Pendle Hill NSW 94 A6
Penguin Tas. 540 A4, 544 H6, 514, **525–6**
Penguin Island WA 332, 343
Penna Tas. 539 K4, 543 M8
Pennant Hills NSW 94 G1, 96 E11
Penneshaw SA 295 J12, 260, 269
Pennington SA 284 E2, 286 E13
Pennyroyal Vic. 212 C12, 217 I8
Penola SA 228 A3, 293 I10, **268**
Penong SA 303 M9, 253, 333
Penrice SA 292 H5
Penrith NSW 101 K7, 117 K7, 43
Penrose NSW 115 H3, 117 J10
Penshurst NSW 98 I7
Penshurst Vic. 228 H6
Pentland Qld 492 C3, 499 R3
Penwortham SA 295 L5, 253
Peppermint Grove WA 352 C7
Peppers Plains Vic. 230 G6
Peppimenarti NT 406 C9
Peranga Qld 482 D4
Percydale Vic. 222 H5
Peregian Beach Qld 486 H4, 491 Q6
Perekerten NSW 122 I9, 233 P8
Perenjori WA 366 C4, **341–2**
Perenna Vic. 230 E5
Pericoe NSW 113 C11, 115 F12, 237 P8
Perisher NSW 114 E11, 115 C9, 138 B12, 60, 65, 68
Perkins Reef Vic. 223 O5

Peronne Vic. 230 C9
Perponda SA 293 F2, 295 O9
Perroomba SA 295 K2, 297 J12
Perry Bridge Vic. 227 O6
Perseverance Qld 482 G6
Perth Tas. 541 O12, 545 L9, 505, 524
Perth WA 350, 352 H3, 356 A5, 364 C4, 366 B8, 305, **308–11**, 333
Perthville NSW 100 B5, 116 H6
Petcheys Bay Tas. 538 E10
Peterborough SA 295 L2, 297 L13, **268**, **270**
Peterborough Vic. 217 A9, 229 K11, 187
Peterhead SA 286 C11
Petersham NSW 95 J11, 99 L1
Petersville SA 294 I7
Petford Qld 495 L7
Petrie Qld 478 C1, 483 L6
Petrie Terrace Qld 476 A2
Pewsey Vale SA 292 F10
Pheasant Creek Vic. 213 L3, 226 E1, 234 H13
Phillip ACT 136 F13, 137 D4
Phillip Bay NSW 99 Q7
Phillip Island Vic. 213 L13, 215 N12, 226 E9, 141, 153, 168, **169**
Phils Creek NSW 115 E2, 116 F9
Piallaway NSW 118 I11
Pialligo ACT 137 I2
Piambie Vic. 233 M7
Piangil Vic. 122 G10, 233 M9
Piawaning WA 366 D6, 339
Piccadilly SA 285 Q10
Pickertaramoor NT 406 D4
Picnic Point NSW 98 E7
Picola Vic. 123 L13, 234 G3
Picola North Vic. 123 L13, 234 G3
Picton NSW 101 J11, 112 E2, 115 I2, 117 K9, **78**
Picton WA 357 G4, 364 C8
Pier Millan Vic. 122 F10, 233 J10
Piesseville WA 364 G7
Pigeon Ponds Vic. 228 E2, 230 E13
Piggabeen NSW 485 G11
Piggoreet Vic. 212 B5, 223 K13, 229 N4
Pikedale Qld 119 L2, 491 M12
Pilbara, The WA 365 I3, 368 B4, 307, 331, **339**
Pilcherra Bore SA 293 G2, 295 P10
Pilchers Bridge Vic. 223 R3
Pile Siding Vic. 217 E10
Pillar Valley NSW 119 P6
Pilliga NSW 118 E8
Pillinger Tas. 542 E4
Pilot Hill NSW 138 A5
Pilton Qld 482 F10
Pimba SA 296 F6, 274, 279
Pimlico Qld 487 C7
Pimpimbudgee Qld 482 D2
Pimpinio Vic. 230 G8
Pinaroo SA 232 A10
Pindar WA 366 C3
Pine Creek NT 401 A13, 402 I13, 406 F8, **390**, **394**
Pine Hill Qld 492 G11
Pine Lodge Vic. 234 I5
Pine Point SA 294 I8
Pine Ridge NSW 118 I12
Pinelands Qld 482 F5
Pinery SA 288 A2, 295 K7
Pingaring WA 366 F9
Pingelly WA 364 F5, 366 D9, **342**

Pingrup WA 366 F10
Pinjarra WA 356 C10, 364 C6, 366 C9, 319, **342**
Pinjarra Hills Qld 480 B5
Pinkenba Qld 479 K8
Pinnaroo SA 122 A11, 293 I3, 295 R10, **270**
Pioneer Tas. 545 P6
Pipalyatjara SA 300 B2, 369 R11, 410 B13
Pipers Brook Tas. 541 O3, 545 M6, 519
Pipers Creek Vic. 212 G2
Pipers Flat NSW 100 E3
Pipers River Tas. 541 N4, 545 L6, 519, 525
Pira Vic. 233 M10
Piries Vic. 213 R1, 224 D11, 235 L11
Pirlta Vic. 232 F4
Pirron Yallock Vic. 212 A11, 217 E7, 229 M9
Pithara WA 366 D6
Pitt Town NSW 101 L6, 46, **78–9**
Pittong Vic. 212 A5, 222 I12
Pittsworth Qld 482 C9, 491 N9, **462**
Plain View Qld 482 D5
Plainland Qld 482 I8
Platts NSW 113 A11, 115 E12, 237 N8
Pleasant Hills NSW 116 A13, 123 P11
Pleasure Point NSW 98 D6
Plenty Tas. 538 E3, 543 K7, 524
Plenty Vic. 209 O2
Plush Corner SA 292 H4
Plympton SA 284 G9
Plympton Park SA 284 F10
Poatina Tas. 543 K1, 545 K11
Point Clare NSW 101 P4, 104 F7
Point Cook Vic. 208 D13
Point Leo Vic. 213 K12, 215 K10, 155
Point Lonsdale Vic. 212 H11, 214 A6, 219 H9, 226 B7, 152, 191
Point Lookout Qld 483 Q8, 491 R9, 433
Point Pass SA 295 M6
Point Piper NSW 95 P10
Point Samson WA 365 G1, 368 A1, 320, **342**, 346
Point Turton SA 294 H9
Pokataroo NSW 118 D5
Pokolbin NSW 108 A10, 109 A9, 53, 81
Police Point Tas. 538 E11, 543 K11
Policemans Point SA 293 E5, 295 N13
Polkemmet Vic. 230 F9
Pomborneit Vic. 217 D6, 229 M9
Pomborneit East Vic. 217 E6
Pomborneit North Vic. 217 D6
Pomona Qld 486 B1, 491 P6, **462**
Pomonal Vic. 222 A6, 228 I1, 230 I12
Pompapiel Vic. 231 Q7, 234 B6
Ponde SA 288 I10
Pondooma SA 294 G4
Pontville Tas. 538 H3, 543 L7, **526**
Pontypool Tas. 543 O5
Poochera SA 294 A1, 296 A12, 303 R12
Pooginagoric SA 293 H7
Poolaijelo Vic. 228 B2, 230 B13, 293 I10
Poole Tas. 545 Q5
Poona National Park Qld 491 P4
Pooncarie NSW 122 E4
Poonindie SA 294 D8, 271
Pooraka SA 287 K10
Pootilla Vic. 212 D4, 223 N10
Pootnoura SA 301 P9
Poowong Vic. 213 O11, 226 G8, 180
Poowong East Vic. 213 P11
Popanyinning WA 364 F6
Porcupine Flat Vic. 223 O4

Porcupine National Park Qld 492 A3, 499 P3, 446
Porcupine Ridge Vic. 212 E1, 223 P7
Porepunkah Vic. 225 L5, 235 P8, 236 C6, 165
Pormpuraaw Aboriginal Community Qld 494 D1, 496 A13
Porongurup National Park WA 361 N9, 364 H12, 313, **323**, 337
Porongurups WA 361 O9, 364 H12
Port Adelaide SA 286 E12, 288 A9, 244, 245
Port Albert Vic. 227 L10, **189**, 203
Port Alma Qld 493 O11
Port Arthur Tas. 539 N10, 543 N10, 503, 505, 510, 515, 516, 517, 518, **526**
Port Augusta SA 291 A12, 296 I11, **270**, 273, 279, 333
Port Bonython SA 294 I2, 296 I12
Port Broughton SA 295 J4, **270**
Port Campbell Vic. 217 A10, 229 K11, 165, 187, **189–90**
Port Campbell National Park Vic. 217 B11, 229 K11, 142, **175**, 187, 200
Port Clinton SA 295 J7
Port Davis SA 295 J3, 296 I13
Port Denison WA 366 B4, 324
Port Douglas Qld 489 C4, 495 M5, 448, 449, **462**
Port Elliot SA 289 H8, 290 F12, 293 C3, 295 L11, **270**, 276
Port Fairy Vic. 228 G9, 180, 187, **190**, 200
Port Franklin Vic. 227 J10, 173
Port Gawler SA 288 A6, 295 K8
Port Germein SA 295 J2, 296 I13, 272
Port Gibbon SA 294 G5
Port Hacking NSW 99 K13
Port Hedland WA 368 C1, 370 B13, 339, **342**
Port Hughes SA 294 I6
Port Huon Tas. 538 E10, 543 K10, 519, 522, 525
Port Julia SA 294 I8
Port Kembla NSW 112 H6, 117 K10, 29
Port Kenny SA 294 A3, 303 Q13, 256, 275
Port Latta Tas. 544 E4, 530
Port Lincoln SA 294 D8, 240, 249, **271**
Port Macdonnell SA 293 H13, **271–2**
Port Macquarie NSW 105 G7, 119 P12, 30, **79**
Port Melbourne Vic. 209 J10, 150
Port Minlacowie SA 294 H9
Port Neill SA 294 E6, 256, 277
Port Noarlunga SA 289 E3, 290 B3, 293 A2, 295 J10, 246, 268
Port Pirie SA 295 J3, 296 I13, **272**
Port Rickaby SA 294 H8, 266
Port Sorell Tas. 540 G5, 545 J6, 521, **526**
Port Stephens NSW 108 G2, 117 O4, **51**
Port Victoria SA 294 H7, 255, **272**
Port Vincent SA 294 I9, 266
Port Wakefield SA 295 J6, 251
Port Welshpool Vic. 227 K10, 200
Port Willunga SA 288 A13, 289 E4, 290 B6
Portarlington Vic. 212 H9, 219 I7, 226 B6, **190**
Porters Retreat NSW 100 D10, 115 G1, 116 H8
Portland NSW 100 E3, 116 I6
Portland Vic. 228 D9, **190–1**
Portland Roads Qld 496 F7, 453
Portsea Vic. 212 I11, 214 C7, 219 I10, 226 B8, 154, 155, 191

Portsmith Qld 488 G13, 431
Postmans Ridge Qld 482 F7
Potato Point NSW 113 I1, 139 N10
Pothana NSW 109 C1
Potts Point NSW 95 N10
Pottsville NSW 119 Q1, 491 R11, 84
Pound Creek Vic. 226 H10
Powelltown Vic. 213 O7, 216 H11, 226 G4, 198
Powers Creek Vic. 228 C1, 230 C12
Powlett Plains Vic. 231 P8, 234 A6
Powlett River Vic. 213 N13
Powranna Tas. 543 L1, 545 M10
Pozieres Qld 119 M2, 491 N11, 467
Prahran Vic. 209 L10, 145
Prairie Qld 492 B4, 499 P4, 446
Prairie Vic. 231 Q6, 234 C5
Pranjip Vic. 234 I8
Pratten Qld 482 D12, 491 N10
Precipice National Park Qld 491 J3
Premaydena Tas. 539 M9, 543 N10
Premer NSW 118 G12
Preolenna Tas. 544 E6
Preston Qld 482 F8
Preston Tas. 540 A7, 544 H7
Preston Vic. 209 L5
Pretty Gully NSW 119 N3, 491 O12
Prevelly WA 357 B10, 359 B8, 335
Price SA 295 J7
Priestdale Qld 481 N7
Primrose Sands Tas. 539 L6, 543 N9
Princetown Vic. 217 C11, 229 L11, 187
Priors Pocket Qld 480 B8
Priory Tas. 545 Q8
Prooinga Vic. 233 K8
Propodollah Vic. 230 D6
Proserpine Qld 493 J3, **462**
Prospect SA 284 I4
Prospect Tas. 541 N10
Prospect Hill SA 290 G6
Proston Qld 491 N5, 471
Puckapunyal Qld 234 G10, 194
Pudman Creek NSW 115 E3, 116 F10
Pularumpi NT 406 C3
Pullabooka NSW 116 C7
Pullenvale Qld 480 A5
Pullut Vic. 230 G4
Punchbowl NSW 94 F13, 98 H3
Punchmirup WA 361 L2, 364 G9
Punthari SA 288 I8
Pura Pura Vic. 217 B1, 229 L5
Puralka Vic. 228 B6, 293 I12
Purfleet NSW 117 P1
Purga Qld 483 K10
Purlewaugh NSW 118 F11
Purnim Vic. 228 I8
Purnong SA 293 E1, 295 N9
Purnululu (Bungle Bungle) National Park WA 363 P8, 371 Q8, 307, **323**, 344
Purrumbete South Vic. 217 C7
Putney NSW 94 H7
Pyalong Vic. 213 J1, 234 F10
Pyap SA 295 Q7
Pyengana Tas. 545 P8, 525, 529
Pygery SA 294 C2, 296 B13
Pymble NSW 95 J2, 96 H12, 101 N7
Pyramid Hill Vic. 122 I13, 231 Q5, 234 B4, **191**
Pyrmont NSW 95 L10, 40

Quaama NSW 113 F5, 115 G9, 237 Q4
Quairading WA 364 G4, 348

Quakers Hill NSW 101 L7
Qualco SA 295 O6
Quambatook Vic. 122 H12, 231 N4, 179
Quambone NSW 118 B10
Quamby Qld 498 G3
Quamby Brook Tas. 540 I13, 545 J9
Quandary NSW 116 B9, 123 R7
Quandialla NSW 115 A1, 116 C8
Quantong Vic. 230 F9
Queanbeyan NSW 116 G13, 135 G4, 138 H3, **79**
Queens Park WA 353 M7
Queenscliff NSW 95 P4
Queenscliff Vic. 212 H10, 214 B5, 219 I9, 226 B7, 152, 154, 170, **191**
Queensport Qld 479 J10
Queenstown SA 284 D2, 286 D13
Queenstown Tas. 542 E3, 544 E12, 504, 514, **526**, 528
Quellington WA 364 F3
Quilpie Qld 501 O7, 442, **462**, 472
Quinalow Qld 482 D4
Quinburra NSW 115 E12, 237 M9
Quindalup WA 357 C7, 359 C2, 364 A9
Quindanning WA 364 E7
Quininup WA 360 D7, 364 D11, 334
Quinns Rock WA 356 A2, 364 C3
Quinnup WA 357 B8, 359 C4, 364 A9
Quirindi NSW 119 J12, **79**
Quoiba Tas. 544 I7
Quorn SA 291 B12, 296 I10, 240, 270, **272**, 273
Quorrobolong NSW 108 C11

RAAF Base NT 399 I4, 400 D11
Rabbit Flat Roadhouse NT 408 C12, 410 C1
Raglan Qld 493 O11
Raglan Vic. 222 H8, 229 M2, 231 M13
Railton Tas. 540 F8, 544 I8, **526**
Railway Estate Qld 487 G6
Rainbow Vic. 122 D13, 230 F4, **191**
Rainbow Beach Qld 491 Q5, 429, 444, 454, 468
Rainbow Flat NSW 117 P1
Rainworth Qld 478 E12
Raleigh NSW 119 P8, 86
Raluana Vic. 231 J9
Ramco SA 295 O6
Raminea Tas. 538 E12, 543 K11
Ramingining NT 407 L5
Ramornee Bridge NSW 119 O6
Ramsay Qld 482 E9
Ramsgate NSW 99 L7
Ranceby Vic. 213 P12, 226 H8
Rand NSW 123 P12, 235 N1
Randell NT 367 J6
Randwick NSW 95 O12, 99 Q3
Ranelagh Tas. 538 E7, 543 K9, 522
Ranga Tas. 542 B12, 545 Q1
Rangemore Qld 482 D3
Rankins Springs NSW 123 O6
Rannes Qld 493 N12
Rannock NSW 116 B10, 123 Q8
Ransome Qld 479 N12
Rapid Bay SA 289 C8
Rapid Creek NT 400 C4
Rappville NSW 119 P4, 491 P13
Rathdowney Qld 119 P1, 491 P11
Rathmines NSW 108 G10, 117 M5
Rathscar Vic. 223 J4, 231 N11

Raukan Aboriginal Settlement SA 293 D3, 295 M11
Ravensbourne Qld 482 G6
Ravensbourne National Park Qld 482 G6, 435
Ravensdale NSW 101 O1
Ravenshoe Qld 495 M8, 449
Ravensthorpe WA 366 H10, **342**
Ravenswood Qld 492 G2, 432, **462**
Ravenswood Vic. 223 Q3, 231 Q10, 234 C9
Ravenswood South Vic. 223 Q4, 231 Q11, 234 C10
Ravensworth NSW 117 L3
Rawdon Vale NSW 117 M1
Rawlinna WA 367 N6
Rawson Vic. 227 J5, 196
Raymond Terrace NSW 108 E6, 117 N4, **79**
Raywood Vic. 231 Q8, 234 C7
Red Banks SA 288 B4
Red Centre, The NT 404, 405, 382–3
Red Cliffs Vic. 122 D7, 232 G4, 185, 201
Red Gum Flat SA 292 B13
Red Hill ACT 136 G13, 137 F3, 130
Red Hill Qld 478 F11, 417, 418
Red Hill Vic. 213 J11, 215 J8, 226 D8, 155, 197
Red Hill South Vic. 213 K11, 215 J8
Red Hills Tas. 540 H12, 545 J9
Red Jacket Vic. 227 J2
Red Range NSW 119 M6
Red Rock NSW 119 Q7
Redan Vic. 221 C10
Redbank Qld 480 A9
Redbank Vic. 222 H3, 225 N4, 231 M11, 197
Redbanks SA 295 M5
Redcastle Vic. 234 E8
Redcliffe Qld 483 N6, 491 Q8, 413, 417, 420, **462–3**
Redcliffe WA 353 M2, 355 M13
Redesdale Vic. 234 D10
Redfern NSW 95 M11, 99 O1, 38
Redgate WA 357 B10, 359 C8, 364 A10, 335
Redhead NSW 108 G9
Redhill SA 295 J4
Redland Bay Qld 483 O9, 491 Q9, **463**
Redmond WA 361 M11, 364 H12
Redpa Tas. 544 B4
Redwood Park SA 287 O9
Reedy Creek Qld 485 D9
Reedy Creek SA 293 F9
Reedy Creek Vic. 213 K2, 234 G11
Reedy Dam Vic. 230 I4
Reedy Flat Vic. 115 B12, 227 R1, 236 G10
Reedy Marsh Tas. 540 I10, 545 J8
Reefton NSW 116 B9, 123 R7
Reekara Tas. 542 A8
Reesville Qld 483 L2, 486 A11
Regans Ford WA 364 C1, 366 C7
Regatta Point Tas. 542 D3, 544 D12
Regency Park SA 284 H2, 286 H13
Regents Park NSW 94 D11, 98 G1
Reid ACT 134 F4, 136 H9, 128
Reid WA 367 Q6
Reid River Qld 492 F1
Reids Creek Vic. 235 O5
Reidsdale NSW 139 L5
Rekuna Tas. 538 I3, 543 M7
Relbia Tas. 541 O11, 545 M9
Remine Tas. 542 C2, 544 D11

Rendelsham SA 293 G11
Renison Bell Tas. 542 D1, 544 E10
Renmark SA 295 Q6, 201, 259, **272**, **274**
Renner Springs NT 409 J9, **394**
Rennie NSW 123 O12, 235 L2
Renown Park SA 284 H4
Research Vic. 209 R3, 210 A4
Reservoir Vic. 209 L4
Retreat Tas. 541 O4, 545 M6
Revesby NSW 98 F5, 101 M9
Reynella SA 244
Rheban Tas. 539 O3, 543 O7
Rheola Vic. 231 O9
Rhodes NSW 94 G7
Rhyll Vic. 213 L12, 215 P11, 226 E9, 169
Rhymney Reef Vic. 222 C7
Rhyndaston Tas. 543 M6
Rhynie SA 295 L6
Riachella Vic. 222 B2
Riana Tas. 544 G6, 526
Rich Avon Vic. 231 K8
Richardson ACT 137 E10
Richlands NSW 100 E13, 115 G2, 116 H9
Richlands Qld 480 E9
Richmond NSW 101 K6, 39, 43, 46, **79**
Richmond Qld 499 M4, **463–4**
Richmond SA 284 G7, 245
Richmond Tas. 539 J4, 543 M7, 503, 505, 515, **526–7**, 527
Richmond Vic. 209 L9, 151
Riddells Creek Vic. 212 H3, 226 B1, 234 E12
Ridgehaven SA 287 O9
Ridgelands Qld 493 N10
Ridgeway Tas. 536 E12, 538 H6
Ridgewood Qld 486 A3
Ridgley Tas. 544 G6, 513
Ridleyton SA 284 H4
Riggs Creek Vic. 235 J8
Ringa WA 356 G1, 364 E2
Ringarooma Tas. 545 O7, 516
Ringwood Vic. 210 B9, 213 L6, 226 E4
Ripley Qld 483 K9
Ripplebrook Vic. 213 O10, 226 G7
Risdon Tas. 536 G2, 508
Risdon Vale Tas. 536 I1, 538 I5, 543 L8
Riverhills Qld 480 C7
Riverland Region SA 259
Riverstone NSW 101 L6
Riverton SA 295 L6, 257, 258
Riverton WA 353 K9
Rivervale WA 353 L4, 310
Riverview NSW 95 K7
Riverwood NSW 98 H5
Rivett ACT 137 A4
Roadvale Qld 483 J11, 491 P10
Rob Roy Vic. 210 D1
Robe SA 293 F9, **274**
Robertson NSW 112 E8, 115 I3, 117 K10, 49, **79–80**
Robertson Qld 480 I5
Robertstown SA 295 M6
Robigana Tas. 541 L6, 545 L7
Robina Qld 485 E7
Robinvale Vic. 122 F8, 233 J6, **191**
Rochedale Qld 481 L5
Rocherlea Tas. 541 O9, 545 L8
Roches Beach Tas. 537 R7
Rochester SA 295 K5
Rochester Vic. 234 E6, **191–2**
Rochford Vic. 212 H2

Rock Flat NSW 113 A3, 115 E9, 138 G12, 237 N4
Rockbank Vic. 208 A4, 212 H5, 219 I1, 226 B3
Rockdale NSW 99 L5
Rockhampton Qld 493 N10, **464**, 469
Rockingham WA 356 B7, 364 C4, 366 C8, 332, **343–4**
Rocklea Qld 480 G5
Rockleigh SA 288 G10
Rockley NSW 100 B7, 116 H7, 47
Rocklyn Vic. 212 E3, 223 O9
Rockton NSW 237 N9
Rockvale NSW 119 M8
Rocky Cape Tas. 544 E5
Rocky Cape National Park Tas. 544 E4, 512, **521**, 530
Rocky Creek NSW 118 H7
Rocky Creek Qld 482 A11
Rocky Dam NSW 119 J4, 491 K13
Rocky Glen NSW 118 G11
Rocky Gully WA 360 I8, 364 F11
Rocky Hall NSW 113 C9, 115 F11, 237 O7
Rocky Hill Qld 482 F1
Rocky Plains NSW 114 G8, 138 D11
Rocky River NSW 119 K9
Rocky River SA 294 F13
Rodd Point NSW 95 J10
Rodney NSW 115 E11, 237 M7
Roebourne WA 365 G1, 368 A2, 339, **344–5**, 346
Roebuck Roadhouse WA 370 H8
Roelands WA 357 H4, 364 C8
Rogans Hill NSW 94 D1, 96 B11
Roger Corner SA 294 I9
Roger River Tas. 544 C5
Roger River West Tas. 544 C5
Rokeby Tas. 537 O10, 539 J6, 543 M8, **527**, **529**
Rokeby Vic. 213 P9, 226 H6
Rokewood Vic. 212 B7, 217 H1, 229 O6
Rokewood Junction Vic. 212 B6, 217 G1, 229 N5
Roland Tas. 540 C9, 544 H8
Rollands Plains NSW 105 E5, 119 O11
Rolleston Qld 490 G1, 493 J13
Rollingstone Qld 495 O12
Roma Qld 490 H6, 451, **464**, 466
Romsey Vic. 212 I2, 226 B1, 234 E12, **192**, 202
Rookhurst NSW 117 N1, 119 L13
Rookwood NSW 94 F11, 98 H1
Rooty Hill NSW 101 L7
Ropeley Qld 482 H9
Roper River Store NT 407 K10
Rosa Glen WA 357 C10, 359 D8, 364 B10
Rosanna Vic. 209 N5
Rose Bay NSW 95 P10, 40
Rose Bay Tas. 536 I6
Rose Park SA 285 K7
Rosebery NSW 95 M13, 99 O3
Rosebery Tas. 542 E1, 544 E10, 528, **529**
Rosebery Vic. 230 H4
Rosebery East Vic. 230 I3
Rosebrook NSW 108 B6
Rosebrook Vic. 228 H9
Rosebud Vic. 213 J11, 214 G8, 226 C8, 155
Rosebud West Vic. 214 G8
Rosedale NSW 114 I4, 115 D8, 138 E8
Rosedale NSW 139 N7
Rosedale Qld 491 N2
Rosedale SA 288 E5, 292 B7

Rosedale Vic. 227 L6
Rosegarland Tas. 538 E3
Rosehill NSW 94 D7
Roselands NSW 98 H4
Roseneath Vic. 228 B3
Rosenthal NSW 117 N3
Roses Tier Tas. 545 O9
Rosetta Tas. 536 B2
Rosevale Qld 482 I11, 491 O10
Rosevale Tas. 541 L9, 545 K8
Rosevears Tas. 541 M8, 545 K8, 518
Roseville NSW 95 K5
Rosewater SA 284 E1, 286 E13
Rosewhite Vic. 225 K3, 235 P7, 236 B5
Rosewood NSW 115 B7
Rosewood Qld 483 J9, 491 P9, 447
Roseworthy SA 288 D5, 295 L8
Roslyn NSW 115 F3, 116 H10
Roslynmead Vic. 234 D4
Rosny Tas. 536 I7
Rosny Park Tas. 537 J6, 508
Ross Tas. 543 M3, 545 N12, 505, 515, **529**
Ross Creek Vic. 212 C4, 223 L12
Ross River Homestead NT 405 O2, 411 K8, 383, **394**
Rossarden Tas. 543 O1, 545 O10
Rossbridge Vic. 222 C10, 229 J3
Rossi NSW 115 F6, 116 H13, 139 J4
Rosslea Qld 487 D9
Rosslyn Park SA 285 M6
Rossmore NSW 101 L9
Rossvale Qld 482 C8
Rossville Qld 495 L3
Rostrevor SA 285 N4, 245
Rostron Vic. 222 G1
Rothbury NSW 109 D6, 53
Roto NSW 123 M3
Rottnest Island WA 364 B4, 366 B8, 305, 311, **312**, 327
Rouchel Brook NSW 117 L2
Round Corner NSW 96 B9
Rowella Tas. 541 L5, 545 K7, 511
Rowena NSW 118 E6
Rowes Bay Qld 487 B1
Rowland Vic. 231 Q4, 234 B2
Rowland Flat SA 288 E5, 292 D8, 261
Rowsley Vic. 212 F5, 223 R13, 226 A3, 229 R4
Roxby Downs SA 296 F4, 250, **274–5**, 279, 280
Royal George Tas. 543 O2, 545 P11
Royal National Park NSW 98 G12, 101 N11, 112 I2, 117 L8, 41, **58**
Royal Park SA 284 D3
Royalla NSW 115 E6, 116 G13, 135 F7, 138 H4
Royston Park SA 285 K4
Rozelle NSW 95 K9
Ruabon WA 357 F7, 359 H3, 364 B9
Rubicon Vic. 213 P2, 226 H1, 235 K12
Ruby Vic. 213 P12, 226 H9, 180, 181
Rubyvale Qld 492 H11, 413, 441, 469
Rudall SA 294 E5
Rudall River National Park WA 368 H4
Ruffy Vic. 234 I10
Rufus River NSW 122 B6, 232 C2
Rugby NSW 115 E2, 116 F9
Rukenvale NSW 119 P2, 491 P11
Rules Point NSW 114 E1, 138 C6
Rumula Qld 489 B5
Runaway Bay Qld 485 E3
Runcorn Qld 481 J7

Running Creek Vic. 225 M2
Running Stream NSW 116 I5
Runnyford NSW 139 M6
Runnymede Tas. 539 K3, 543 M7
Runnymede Vic. 234 E7
Rupanyup Vic. 230 I9, 186
Rupanyup North Vic. 230 I8
Rupanyup South Vic. 230 I9
Rushcutters Bay NSW 95 N10, 40
Rushworth Vic. 234 G7, **192**
Russell ACT 134 H8, 136 I10, 137 G1
Russell Lea NSW 95 J9
Russell River National Park Qld 489 H12, 495 N7
Rutherglen Vic. 123 O13, 235 N4, 44, 57, **192**, 197, 198, 200
Ryanby Vic. 233 L10
Ryans Creek Vic. 224 D4
Rydal NSW 100 F5, 116 I6
Rydalmere NSW 94 D6
Ryde NSW 94 H6, 101 N8
Rye Vic. 212 I11, 214 F8, 226 C8, 155
Rye Park NSW 115 D3, 116 F10
Ryeford Qld 482 D11
Rylstone NSW 116 I4, **80**
Ryton Vic. 227 J9

Sabine Qld 482 D6
Sackville North NSW 101 L4
Saddleworth SA 295 L6
Safety Bay WA 356 B7, 364 C5
Safety Beach Vic. 213 J11, 214 I6
St Agnes SA 287 P10
St Albans NSW 101 M2, 117 L6
St Albans Vic. 208 E5, 212 I5
St Andrews Vic. 226 E2, 234 H13, 197
St Arnaud Vic. 231 L9, **192**, 195
St Clair NSW 117 L3
St Fillans Vic. 213 N4
St George Qld 490 G10, **466**
St Georges SA 285 L9
St Georges Basin NSW 115 I5, 117 K12, 139 Q2
St Germains Vic. 234 G5
St Helena Island National Park Qld 479 P6, 483 N7
St Helens Tas. 545 Q8, 505, 515, 525, **529**
St Helens Vic. 228 G8
St Ives NSW 95 K1, 96 I11
St Ives North NSW 97 J10
St James Vic. 235 K5
St James WA 353 K6
St Johns Park NSW 98 A1
St Kilda SA 286 G3, 288 B7, 245
St Kilda Vic. 209 K11, 213 J7, 150
St Kilda East Vic. 209 L11
St Lawrence Qld 493 L8
St Leonards NSW 95 L7
St Leonards Tas. 541 O10
St Leonards Vic. 212 I9, 214 C2, 219 I8, 226 B6, **192**
St Lucia Qld 480 F2, 418
St Marys NSW 101 L8
St Marys SA 284 H12
St Marys Tas. 545 Q10, **529**
St Morris SA 285 L5
St Patricks River Tas. 541 Q8, 545 M8
St Peter Island SA 253
St Peters NSW 95 L12, 99 N2
St Peters SA 285 K5
Sale Vic. 227 N6, **192**, 193, **194**
Salisbury NSW 117 M2

Salisbury Qld 480 H5
Salisbury SA 287 K5, 288 C8, 293 C1, 295 L9
Salisbury Vic. 230 E7
Salisbury East SA 287 N6
Salisbury Heights SA 287 O5
Salisbury North SA 287 K3
Salisbury Plain SA 287 M5
Salisbury West Vic. 231 O8, 234 A7
Sallys Flat NSW 116 H5
Salmon Gums WA 367 J9
Salt Ash NSW 108 G4, 76
Salt Creek SA 293 E6, 295 N13, 274
Salter Springs SA 295 L7
Saltwater River Tas. 539 L8, 543 N9
Samaria Vic. 224 C6
Samford Qld 483 L7, 491 P9, 419
San Remo Vic. 213 M13, 215 R13, 226 F9, 168, 169
Sanctuary Cove Qld 485 D1
Sanctuary Point NSW 115 I5, 117 K12, 139 R2
Sandalwood SA 293 G1, 295 P9
Sandergrove SA 289 I5, 290 I8
Sanderson NT 402 C2
Sanderston SA 288 H8
Sandfire Roadhouse WA 370 F12
Sandfly Tas. 538 G7, 543 L9
Sandford Tas. 537 R13, 539 J7, 543 M9
Sandford Vic. 228 D4
Sandgate Qld 478 H3, 483 M6
Sandhill Lake Vic. 231 O3, 233 O13
Sandigo NSW 123 P9
Sandilands SA 294 I8
Sandon Vic. 212 D1, 223 O6
Sandringham NSW 99 L8
Sandringham Vic. 211 A3, 213 J8
Sandsmere Vic. 230 C6
Sandstone WA 366 G2, 337
Sandy Bay Tas. 536 G9, 538 I6, 507, 508
Sandy Creek SA 288 D5, 292 A8
Sandy Creek Vic. 235 Q5, 236 D3
Sandy Creek Upper Vic. 235 Q6, 236 C4
Sandy Flat NSW 119 M4, 491 N13
Sandy Hill NSW 119 N3
Sandy Hollow NSW 117 J2
Sandy Point NSW 98 E7
Sandy Point Vic. 226 I11
Sangar NSW 123 N12, 235 L1
Sans Souci NSW 99 L8
Santa Teresa Aboriginal Community NT 405 N6, 411 K9
Sapphire NSW 119 K6
Sapphire Qld 492 H11, 413
Sapphiretown SA 294 I12
Sarah Island Tas. 505, 528
Sardine Creek Vic. 115 C13, 237 J11
Sarina Qld 493 L6, **466**
Sarina Beach Qld 493 L5
Sarsfield Vic. 227 Q4, 236 G13
Sassafras NSW 115 H4, 117 J11, 139 O1
Sassafras Tas. 540 G7, 545 J7
Sassafras Vic. 210 F11, 172
Sassafras East Tas. 540 G7, 545 J7
Savage River Tas. 544 D8
Savenake NSW 123 N12, 235 L2
Sawmill Settlement Vic. 224 F11
Sawtell NSW 119 P8, **80**
Sayers Lake NSW 122 G2
Scaddan WA 367 J10
Scamander Tas. 545 Q9, 515, 529, **529**

Scarborough NSW 101 M12, 112 I4, 117 K9
Scarborough Qld 483 N5, 463
Scarborough WA 354 B10, 356 A4, 366 C8, 310
Scarsdale Vic. 212 B5
Scheyville NSW 101 L5
Schofields NSW 101 L7
Schreiberau SA 292 E7
Schouten Island Tas. 513
Scone NSW 117 K1, **80**
Scoresby Vic. 210 B13, 211 H1
Scotland Island NSW 97 P5
Scotsburn Vic. 212 D5, 223 M12
Scott National Park WA 357 D13, 359 E12, 364 A11, 366 B11
Scotts Creek Vic. 217 B8, 229 K10
Scotts Head NSW 119 P9, 72
Scottsdale Tas. 545 N7, **529**
Scottsville Qld 492 I3
Scullin ACT 136 C6
Sea Elephant Tas. 542 B8
Sea Lake Vic. 122 F11, 231 J1, 233 J12
Seabird WA 364 B1, 328
Seacombe Vic. 227 O6
Seaford Vic. 211 E10, 213 K9
Seaforth NSW 95 O5
Seaforth Qld 493 K4
Seaham NSW 108 D5, 117 N4
Seal Rocks NSW 117 P3, 52, 62
Seaspray Vic. 227 N8, 194, 203
Seaton SA 284 D4
Seaton Vic. 227 L5
Seaview Vic. 213 P11, 226 H7
Sebastian Vic. 231 Q8, 234 C7
Sebastopol NSW 115 A3, 116 C10, 123 R8
Sebastopol Vic. 212 C4, 221 C13, 223 M11
Second Valley SA 289 C8, 293 A3, 295 J11
Sedan SA 288 I5, 295 M8
Sedgwick Vic. 223 Q3, 231 R10, 234 C9, 164
Sefton NSW 94 C11, 98 F1
Sefton Park SA 285 J3
Seisia Qld 496 C3
Selbourne Tas. 541 K10, 545 K8
Seldom Seen Roadhouse Vic. 115 C12, 236 I8
Sellheim Qld 492 E2
Sellicks Hill SA 290 B7
Semaphore SA 286 B11, 245
Semaphore Park SA 284 B2, 286 B13
Semaphore South SA 286 B12
Separation Creek Vic. 229 O11
Seppeltsfield SA 288 E4, 292 D4, 295 L8, 268
Serpentine Vic. 231 P7, 234 A6
Serpentine WA 356 C8, 364 D5
Serpentine National Park WA 356 D8, 364 D5, 366 C8, **322**
Serviceton Vic. 230 A7, 293 I7
Seven Hills Qld 479 J12
Seven Mile Beach Tas. 537 R6, 539 J6, 543 M8, 508
Seven Mile Beach National Park NSW 112 F11, 62
Sevenhill SA 295 L5, 246, 253
Seventeen Mile Rocks Qld 480 D6
Severnlea Qld 119 M2, 491 N12
Seville Vic. 210 I7, 213 M6, 216 C9, 226 F4, 197
Seymour Tas. 545 Q11
Seymour Vic. 234 G10, **194**, 197

Shackleton WA 364 H3
Shadforth NSW 116 G6
Shady Creek Vic. 213 Q9, 226 I6
Shailer Park Qld 481 P10
Shallow Crossing NSW 139 N5
Shannon Tas. 543 J3, 545 J12
Shannon WA 360 E8, 364 E11
Shannon National Park WA 360 E8, 364 E11, 366 D11, **322**, 340
Shannons Flat NSW 115 D7, 138 F8
Shannonvale Vic. 225 R8, 236 E7
Sharps Well SA 295 J5
Shay Gap (Abandoned) WA 368 E1, 370 D13
Shays Flat Vic. 222 F5
Shea-Oak Log SA 288 D4, 292 A5
Sheans Creek Vic. 235 J9
Shearwater Tas. 540 G5
Sheep Hills Vic. 230 I7
Sheffield Tas. 540 D9, 544 I8, **529–30**
Sheldon Qld 481 P4
Shelford Vic. 212 D8, 219 A5, 229 P6
Shellbourne Vic. 223 O3, 231 P10, 234 B9
Shelley Vic. 115 A8, 236 F2
Shelley WA 353 J9
Shellharbour NSW 112 H8, 117 K10, 53, **80**, 89
Shelly Beach Tas. 539 O2, 543 O7
Shenton Park WA 352 D3
Sheoaks Vic. 212 E7, 219 C3, 229 Q6
Shepherds Flat Vic. 212 E2, 223 O7
Shepparton Vic. 234 I6, **194**, 197
Shepperd Qld 482 E8
Sherbrooke Vic. 210 F12, 156
Sheringa SA 294 B5
Sherlock SA 293 F3, 295 O10
Sherwood Qld 480 E4
Shipley NSW 100 G6, 102 B7
Shirley Vic. 222 F10
Shoal Bay NSW 108 H1, 117 O4, 51, 76
Shoal Point Qld 493 L5
Shoalhaven Heads NSW 112 F12, 117 K11
Shooters Hill NSW 100 E9, 115 G1, 116 H8
Shoreham Vic. 213 K12, 215 K10, 226 D8, 155
Shorncliffe Qld 478 H3
Shotts WA 364 D8
Shute Harbour Qld 493 K3, 424, **466–7**
Sidmouth Tas. 541 L6, 545 K7, 511
Sidonia Vic. 212 H1
Silkwood Qld 495 N8
Silvan Vic. 210 H10, 213 M6, 216 C10, 226 F4, 156, 172
Silver Creek Vic. 235 O6, 236 B4
Silver Sands SA 289 E5, 290 B7
Silverdale NSW 101 J9, 115 I1, 117 K8
Silverton NSW 120 B11, 297 R9, 51
Silverwater NSW 94 E8
Simmie Vic. 234 F5
Simpson Vic. 217 C9, 229 L10
Simpson Desert National Park Qld 411 R11, 498 B13, 500 B1, 426
Simpsons Bay Tas. 538 H12, 543 L11
Singleton NSW 117 L3, **80**
Singleton WA 356 A9, 364 C5, 366 C9
Sinnamon Park Qld 480 D5
Sir James Mitchell National Park WA 360 D7
Sir Joseph Banks Group of Islands SA 256, 277
Sisters Beach Tas. 544 E5, 511
Sisters Creek Tas. 544 E5

Skehan Vic. 224 F1
Skenes Creek Vic. 217 G11, 229 O12, 157
Skenes Creek North Vic. 217 H11
Skipton Vic. 222 H13, 229 M4, **194–5**
Skye SA 285 N6
Skye Vic. 211 G11
Slacks Creek Qld 481 M9
Slaty Creek Vic. 231 M8
Smeaton Vic. 212 D2, 223 N8, 229 P2, 231 P13, 234 A12, 168
Smiggin Holes NSW 114 E11, 115 C9, 138 B12, 237 J4, 60, 65, 68
Smithfield NSW 491 L12
Smithfield Qld 119 K3, 489 E8, 495 M6, 431, 449
Smiths Gully Vic. 213 L4, 226 E2, 234 H13
Smithton Tas. 544 C4, **530**
Smithtown NSW 105 H2, 119 P10
Smithville SA 293 G2, 295 P10
Smoko Vic. 225 M6, 235 Q9, 236 C7
Smoky Bay SA 303 O10, 253, 256
Smythesdale Vic. 212 B5, 223 K12, 229 N4, 159
Snake Range National Park Qld 492 H12
Snake Valley Vic. 212 B4, 223 J11, 229 N4
Snapper Island National Park Qld 489 D2
Snobs Creek Vic. 213 P2, 224 A13, 235 K11
Snowtown SA 295 J5
Snowy Mountains, The NSW 114, **65**, 68, 69, 84
Snowy River National Park Vic. 115 C12, 237 J9, 165, **176**, 189
Snug Tas. 538 H9, 522
Snuggery SA 293 G11
Sodwalls NSW 100 F5
Sofala NSW 100 C1, 116 H5, 47
Soldiers Point NSW 108 G2, 51
Somers Vic. 213 K12, 215 M9, 226 D8, 155
Somersby NSW 101 O3, 104 D5
Somerset Tas. 544 G5, 514
Somerset Dam Qld 483 J4
Somerton NSW 118 I10
Somerton Park SA 284 E12
Somerville Vic. 213 K10, 215 M3, 226 E7
Sommariva Qld 490 C6
Sorell Tas. 539 K5, 543 M8, **530**
Sorrento Vic. 212 I11, 214 D7, 219 I10, 226 B8, 154, 155, 191
Sorrento WA 354 A5
South Arm Tas. 538 I8, 543 M9, 529
South Bank Qld 418
South Bindoon WA 364 D2, 538 H12
South Brisbane Qld 476 A9, 478 G12, 480 G1, 418
South Bruny Island Tas. 538 H12, 543 L12, **512**
South Coast, The NSW 113, 115, 135, **55**
South Forest Tas. 544 D4
South Fremantle WA 352 C12, 358 G13
South Guildford WA 355 O11
South Gundagai NSW 115 B5, 116 D12
South Heathcote Vic. 178
South Head NSW 40
South Hedland WA 368 C1, 370 B13
South Hobart Tas. 536 F9, 507, 525
South Kilkerran SA 294 I7
South Kumminin WA 364 I4, 366 F8
South Melbourne Vic. 206 B13, 209 K9, 149, 150
South Molle Island Qld **439**, 466
South Morang Vic. 209 O1, 213 K4
South Mount Cameron Tas. 545 P6

South Nanango Qld 482 F1
South Nietta Tas. 540 A9, 544 H8, 532
South Perth WA 350 C12, 352 H5, 310
South Riana Tas. 544 G7
South Springfield Tas. 545 N7
South Stirling WA 361 Q8, 364 I11
South Stradbroke Island Qld 483 O11, 485 F1, 491 Q10, **433**
South Townsville Qld 487 H5
South Turramurra NSW 94 H2, 96 F12
South West Rocks NSW 105 I1, 119 P10, 69
South Yaamba Qld 493 N10
South Yarra Vic. 209 L10, 144, 150
South Yunderup WA 356 B10, 364 C5, 334
Southbrook Qld 482 D8, 491 N9
Southend Qld 493 P12
Southend SA 293 G11
Southern Cross Vic. 228 H8
Southern Cross WA 366 G7, 333, **345**
Southern Highlands NSW 112, **49, 49**, 74
Southport Qld 483 O12, 485 E5, 491 Q10, 422, **423**, 467
Southport Tas. 543 K12
South-west, The WA 319
Southwest National Park Tas. 538 A5, 542 F9, 504, **520**
Southwood National Park Qld 491 J10
Spalding SA 295 L4, 258
Spalford Tas. 540 C6, 544 H7
Spargo Creek Vic. 212 E3, 223 P10
Spearwood WA 356 A6, 310
Speed Vic. 122 E11, 230 H1, 232 I11, 178
Speewa Vic. 122 H10, 233 N10
Spence ACT 136 D4
Spencer NSW 101 N4, 104 B9
Spicers Creek NSW 116 G3
Spit Junction NSW 95 O7
Spotswood Vic. 208 H9, 151
Sprent Tas. 540 B7, 544 H7
Spreyton Tas. 540 E6, 544 I7
Spring Beach Tas. 539 O2, 543 O7
Spring Bluff Qld 482 F7
Spring Creek Qld 482 E11
Spring Creek Upper Qld 482 F11
Spring Hill NSW 116 G6
Spring Hill Qld 476 C1, 478 G11, 417, 418
Spring Hill Vic. 212 F2, 223 Q8
Spring Ridge NSW 116 G2
Spring Ridge NSW 118 H12
Springbrook Qld 119 Q1, 485 A13, 413, 461
Springbrook National Park Qld 483 N13, 485 A11, 423, 436, **456**, 461
Springdale NSW 115 A3, 116 C10
Springfield SA 285 K10
Springfield Tas. 536 D5, 545 N7
Springfield Vic. 212 I2
Springhurst Vic. 235 N4
Springmount Vic. 212 D3, 223 M9
Springside Qld 482 C8, 491 M9
Springsure Qld 492 I12, 427, 441, 469
Springton SA 288 G7, 293 D1, 295 M8, 250
Springvale Vic. 211 F3, 213 K7
Springwood NSW 101 J7, 103 N5, 117 J7, 42
Springwood Qld 481 N8
Squaretop Qld 482 B3
Squeaking Point Tas. 540 G5
Staaten River National Park Qld 494 G6
Stafford Qld 478 F9
Stafford Heights Qld 478 E8

Stamford Qld 499 N5
Stanborough NSW 119 J7
Stanhope Vic. 234 G6
Stanley Tas. 544 D3, 505, 514, **530**
Stanley Vic. 235 O6, 236 B4, 160
Stanmore NSW 95 K11, 99 M1
Stanmore Qld 483 L3
Stannifer NSW 119 K6
Stannum NSW 119 M5, 491 N13
Stansbury SA 294 I9, **275**
Stanthorpe Qld 119 M2, 491 N12, **467**
Stanwell Qld 493 N11
Stanwell Park NSW 101 M12, 112 I3, 117 K9
Starcke National Park Qld 495 L1, 496 I13
Staughton Vale Vic. 212 F6, 219 E2
Stavely Vic. 222 A12, 228 I4
Staverton Tas. 540 C10, 544 H8
Stawell Vic. 222 C5, 231 J12, 162, 163, **195**
Steels Creek Vic. 213 M4, 216 B4, 226 E2, 234 H13
Steiglitz Vic. 212 E7, 219 D3, 229 Q5
Stenhouse Bay SA 294 G10
Stephens Qld 485 E8
Stephens Creek NSW 120 B11
Stepney SA 285 K6
Steppes Tas. 543 K3, 545 K13
Stieglitz Tas. 545 R8
Stirling ACT 136 C13, 137 B4
Stirling SA 285 P12, 288 C11, 289 H2, 290 F1, 247
Stirling Vic. 227 Q2, 236 G11
Stirling WA 354 E10
Stirling North SA 291 B12, 294 I1, 296 I11
Stirling Range National Park WA 361 P7, 364 H11, 366 F11, 313, 317, **322**, 329, 337
Stockdale Vic. 227 N4, 236 D13
Stockinbingal NSW 115 B3, 116 C10
Stockmans Reward Vic. 213 Q4
Stockport SA 288 C2, 257
Stockton NSW 106 G3, 108 G7
Stockwell SA 288 G4, 292 I3, 295 M7
Stockyard Qld 482 F8
Stockyard Gully National Park WA 329
Stockyard Hill Vic. 222 G11
Stokers Siding NSW 119 Q1, 491 Q11
Stokes SA 294 D7
Stokes Bay SA 294 H12, 269
Stokes National Park WA 366 I10, **323**
Stone Hut SA 295 K3, 297 J13
Stonefield SA 288 I3, 295 M7
Stonehaven Vic. 212 F9, 219 D7
Stonehenge NSW 119 L6
Stonehenge Qld 499 M13, 501 M1
Stonehenge Tas. 543 N5
Stones Corner Qld 480 H2
Stoneyford Vic. 217 D7, 229 M9
Stonor Tas. 543 M5
Stony Creek Vic. 226 I10
Stony Crossing NSW 122 H10, 233 N9
Stony Point Vic. 213 L11, 215 N8, 226 E8
Stonyfell SA 285 N7
Stoodley Tas. 540 E9, 544 I8
Store Creek NSW 116 G4
Storeys Creek Tas. 543 O1, 545 O10
Stormlea Tas. 539 M11, 543 N10
Stowport Tas. 544 G6
Stowport Upper Tas. 544 G6
Stradbroke Vic. 227 M8
Stradbroke West Vic. 227 M7

Strahan Tas. 542 D3, 544 D12, 504, 514, 528, **531**
Strangways Vic. 212 E1, 223 O6
Stratford NSW 117 N2
Stratford Qld 488 B3
Stratford Vic. 227 N5, 194
Strath Creek Vic. 213 L1, 234 H11, 165
Strathalbyn SA 289 I4, 290 I7, 293 C3, 295 L10, **275**
Strathallan Vic. 234 E5
Stratham WA 357 F5, 364 C8
Strathblane Tas. 538 D12, 543 K11
Strathbogie NSW 119 K5
Strathbogie Vic. 235 J9
Strathbogie South Vic. 235 J9
Strathdownie Vic. 228 B5, 293 I11
Stratherne WA 364 G5
Strathewen Vic. 213 L4
Strathfield NSW 94 G11, 98 I1, 101 N8
Strathfieldsaye Vic. 223 R2, 231 R10, 234 C9
Strathgordon Tas. 542 G7
Strathkellar Vic. 228 G5
Strathlea Vic. 212 D1, 223 N6
Strathmerton Vic. 123 M13, 234 I3, 167, 187
Strathmore Vic. 208 I5
Strathpine Qld 478 C3, 483 L6, 491 P8, **467**
Streaky Bay SA 303 P12, 256, **275**
Streatham Vic. 222 E13, 229 K4
Streton WA 364 H5
Stretton Qld 481 J9
Strickland Tas. 543 J5
Stroud NSW 117 N3, **80**
Stroud Road NSW 117 N2
Struan SA 293 H9
Strzelecki Vic. 213 P11, 226 H8
Strzelecki Crossing SA 299 O11, 500 F13
Strzelecki National Park Tas. 542 A12, 545 Q1, 531
Stuart Mill Vic. 222 H2, 231 M10
Stuart Park NT 398 F4, 399 G9
Stuart Town NSW 116 G4
Stuarts Point NSW 119 P10
Sturt National Park NSW 120 A2, 299 R12, 500 I13, **60**, 83
Subiaco WA 352 F3, 310
Sue City NSW 114 C3, 138 B7
Suggan Buggan Vic. 165
Sulphur Creek Tas. 540 A4, 544 H6
Summer Hill NSW 95 J11, 99 L2
Summerfield Vic. 231 Q8, 234 C7
Summerhill Tas. 541 N10
Summerholm Qld 482 I8
Summertown SA 285 P9
Summervale NSW 121 Q10
Summit Qld 467
Sumner Qld 480 C6
Sunbury Vic. 212 I4, 226 B2, 234 E13, 158
Sunday Creek Vic. 213 K1, 234 G11
Sundown National Park Qld 119 L3, 491 M12, 467
Sunny Cliffs Vic. 122 D7, 232 G4
Sunny Corner NSW 100 E3
Sunnybank Qld 480 I7, 483 M9
Sunnyside NSW 119 M4, 491 N13
Sunnyside Tas. 540 F9, 544 I8
Sunnyside Vic. 225 R7, 236 E7
Sunnyvale SA 294 I6
Sunset Vic. 232 A9, 293 I2, 295 R10
Sunshine Vic. 208 G7

Sunshine Coast Qld 483 O1, 486, 491 Q7, 415, 416, 421, **429**, 431, 452, 454, 459
Surat Qld 490 H8, 432
Surf Beach NSW 139 N7
Surfers Paradise Qld 483 O13, 485 F6, 491 Q10, 423
Surges Bay Tas. 538 E11, 543 K10
Surprise Bay Tas. 542 A9
Surrey Downs SA 287 P8
Surrey Hills Vic. 209 O9
Surry Hills NSW 95 M11, 99 O1, 40
Surveyors Bay Tas. 538 F12, 543 K11
Sussex Inlet NSW 115 I5, 117 K12, 139 Q2, 86
Sutherland NSW 98 H11, 101 M10
Sutherlands SA 295 M6
Sutton NSW 115 E5, 116 G12, 135 G2, 138 H1
Sutton Vic. 231 K3, 233 K13
Sutton Forest NSW 112 A8, 49, 74
Sutton Grange Vic. 223 R4, 231 R11, 234 C10
Swan Hill Vic. 122 H11, 233 N11, 143, 164, **195**, 197, 201
Swan Marsh Vic. 217 E7, 229 M9
Swan Reach SA 295 N8, **275–6**
Swan Reach Vic. 227 R4, 236 G13
Swanbourne WA 352 B4
Swanhaven NSW 115 I5, 117 J12, 139 Q2
Swanpool Vic. 224 B5, 235 L8
Swanport SA 288 I12, 267
Swansea NSW 108 G10, 77
Swansea Tas. 543 P4, 545 P13, 505, 515, **531–2**
Swanwater South Vic. 231 L8
Swanwater West Vic. 231 K8
Swanwick Tas. 543 Q4, 545 Q13
Sweetmans Creek NSW 108 A12
Swifts Creek Vic. 115 A12, 227 Q1, 236 G9, 189
Sydenham NSW 95 K12, 99 M3
Sydenham Vic. 208 D3, 165
Sydney NSW 92 E6, 95 M10, 101 O8, 117 L8, 29, **33–43**
Sydney Harbour National Park NSW 95 P7, 101 P8, **58**
Sylvania NSW 99 J9, 101 N10
Sylvania Heights NSW 99 J10
Sylvania Waters NSW 99 K9
Sylvaterre Vic. 231 Q5, 234 C4
Symonston ACT 137 H4

Taabinga Qld 491 N6
Tabbara Vic. 237 K12
Tabberabbera Vic. 227 O3, 236 E12
Tabbimoble NSW 491 Q13
Tabbita NSW 123 N6
Tabilk Vic. 234 G9
Table Top NSW 123 Q13, 235 Q3, 236 C1
Table Top Vic. 224 D9
Tabooba Qld 483 L13
Tabor Vic. 228 G6
Tabulam NSW 119 O3, 491 O12
Taggerty Vic. 213 O2, 226 G1, 235 J12, 157
Tahara Vic. 228 E5
Tahara Bridge Vic. 228 E5
Tahmoor NSW 101 J12, 112 E3
Taigum Qld 478 G4
Tailem Bend SA 293 E3, 295 N10, **276**
Takone Tas. 544 F6
Talawa Tas. 545 O8
Talbingo NSW 115 C6, 116 E13, 138 B4

Talbot–Thurla 577

Talbot Vic. 212 B1, 223 K6, 229 N1, 231 O12, 167
Talbot Brook WA 356 H5, 364 E4
Taldra SA 122 A7, 295 Q7
Talgai Qld 482 E11
Talgarno Vic. 123 Q13, 235 Q4, 236 D1
Talia SA 294 A4, 275
Tallageira Vic. 230 A10, 293 I8
Tallandoon Vic. 225 O1, 235 Q6, 236 D4
Tallangalook Vic. 224 A8
Tallangatta Vic. 235 Q5, 236 D2, 189, **195**
Tallangatta Valley Vic. 235 R5, 236 E3
Tallarook Vic. 234 G10, 204
Tallebudgera Qld 485 F10, 423
Tallebung NSW 123 P2
Tallimba NSW 116 A8, 123 Q6
Tallong NSW 115 H3, 116 I11
Tallygaroopna Vic. 234 I5
Talmalmo NSW 123 R13, 236 E1
Talwood Qld 118 F2, 490 I11
Tamarama NSW 95 Q12
Tamarang NSW 118 H12
Tambar Springs NSW 118 G11
Tambellup WA 361 M4, 364 H10, 329
Tambo Qld 490 B2, **467**
Tambo Crossing Vic. 115 B13, 227 Q2, 236 G11
Tambo Upper Vic. 227 R4, 236 G13
Tamboon Vic. 237 N13
Tamborine Qld 483 M11, 491 Q10
Tamborine National Park Qld 483 M11, 420, **456**
Tamboy NSW 117 O3
Taminick Vic. 235 L6, 177
Tamleugh Vic. 235 J7
Tamleugh North Vic. 235 J7
Tamleugh West Vic. 234 I7
Tammin WA 364 G3
Tamrookum Qld 483 L13, 425
Tamworth NSW 119 J11, 69, **82**
Tanah Merah Qld 481 O10
Tanami NT 408 B11
Tanawah Qld 486 F11
Tandarra Vic. 231 Q7, 234 C6
Tangalooma Qld 483 P6, 433, 463
Tangambalanga Vic. 235 Q5, 236 C3
Tangkam Qld 482 C7
Tangmangaroo NSW 115 D3, 116 F10
Tangorin Qld 492 A7, 499 O6
Tanilba Bay NSW 108 G3, 51
Tanja NSW 113 G7, 115 G10, 237 R5
Tanjil Bren Vic. 213 R7, 227 J4
Tanjil South Vic. 213 R9, 227 J6
Tankerton Vic. 213 L12, 215 P9, 226 E8
Tannum Sands Qld 493 P12, 443, 445
Tannymorel Qld 119 N1, 491 O11
Tansey Qld 491 N5
Tantanoola SA 293 G11, 265
Tantawangalo National Park NSW 113 C7, 115 F10
Tanunda SA 288 F5, 292 F6, 295 L8, 246, **276–7**
Tanwood Vic. 222 I4
Tanybryn Vic. 217 G11
Taperoo SA 286 D9
Taplan SA 122 A8, 232 A5, 295 R8
Tappa Pass SA 292 I5
Tara NSW 116 A10, 123 Q8
Tara NT 411 J4
Tara Qld 491 K8
Taradale Vic. 212 F1, 223 R6, 231 R12, 234 C11

Tarago NSW 115 F4, 116 H11
Tarago Vic. 213 P9
Taralga NSW 115 G2, 116 I9
Tarampa Qld 483 J7
Tarana NSW 100 E5
Tarana Quarry NSW 100 E5
Taranna Tas. 539 N9, 543 O10
Tarcombe Vic. 234 H10
Tarcoola SA 303 Q5
Tarcoon NSW 121 P6
Tarcowie SA 295 K2, 297 K12
Tarcutta NSW 115 A5, 116 C13
Tardun WA 366 C3, 338
Taree NSW 105 C13, 117 O1, 119 N13, **82**
Taren Point NSW 99 K10
Targa Tas. 541 R7, 545 M8
Tarilta Vic. 212 E1, 223 P6
Taringa Qld 480 E2
Tarlee SA 288 D1, 295 L7, 258
Tarlo NSW 115 G3, 116 I10
Tarlo River National Park NSW 115 G3, 116 I10
Tarnagulla Vic. 223 M2, 231 O10, 234 A8, 171
Tarneit Vic. 208 B9, 212 H6, 219 I2, 226 B4
Tarnma SA 295 L6
Tarnook Vic. 235 K7
Tarome Qld 482 I12
Tarong Qld 482 E1
Taroom Qld 491 J4, **467**
Taroona Tas. 536 H13, 538 I7, 543 L9, 507, 523
Tarpeena SA 293 H11
Tarra-Bulga National Park Vic. 227 K8, 143, 147, 181, 185, 189, 196, 202, 203
Tarragal Vic. 228 C9
Tarragindi Qld 480 H4
Tarraleah Tas. 542 I4
Tarranginnie Vic. 230 D7
Tarrango Vic. 232 E5
Tarranyurk Vic. 230 F6
Tarraville Vic. 227 L10, 189, 203
Tarrawanna NSW 110 D3
Tarrawingee Vic. 235 N6, 236 A4, 198
Tarrayoukyan Vic. 228 D2, 230 D13
Tarrenlea Vic. 228 E5
Tarrington Vic. 228 G5
Tarrion NSW 121 Q5
Tarwin Vic. 226 H10
Tarwin Lower Vic. 226 H10, 200
Tarwin Meadows Vic. 226 H10
Tarwonga WA 364 F7
Tascott NSW 104 F7
Tasman Peninsula Tas. 539 M10, 543 O10, 509, 510, 515
Tatawangalo National Park NSW 237 O6
Tatham NSW 119 P3
Tathra NSW 113 G8, 115 G10, 237 R6, 47, **82**
Tathra National Park WA 366 B6, 318
Tatong Vic. 224 C5, 235 L8
Tatura Vic. 234 H6, 194
Tatyoon Vic. 222 D11, 229 K3
Tawonga Vic. 225 N4, 235 Q8, 236 D6
Tawonga South Vic. 225 N5, 235 Q8, 236 D6
Tayene Tas. 545 N8
Taylors Arm NSW 119 O9, 72
Taylors Flat NSW 115 E2, 116 F9
Taylors Lakes Vic. 208 E3
Taylorville SA 295 O6
Tea Gardens NSW 108 H1, 117 O4, 51

Tea Tree Tas. 538 I3, 526
Tea Tree Gully SA 287 P10
Teal Flat SA 293 E1, 295 N9
Teal Point Vic. 231 P2, 233 P13, 234 B1
Tecoma Vic. 210 F13
Teesdale Vic. 212 D8, 219 B5, 229 P7
Telegraph Point NSW 105 F6, 119 O11
Telford Vic. 235 K4
Telita Tas. 545 O7
Telopea NSW 94 D5
Telopea Downs Vic. 230 B5
Temma Tas. 544 B6
Temora NSW 115 A2, 116 C10, 123 R8, **82–3**
Tempe NSW 95 K13, 99 M3
Templers SA 288 D4
Templestowe Vic. 209 Q6, 213 K6
Templin Qld 483 J12, 427
Tempy Vic. 122 E11, 232 H11
Ten Mile Vic. 213 R3
Ten Mile Hollow NSW 101 N3
Tenandra Vic. 118 D11
Tennant Creek NT 409 K10, 374, 386, **394**
Tennyson NSW 94 I8
Tennyson Qld 480 F4
Tennyson SA 284 C3
Tennyson Vic. 231 R7, 234 D5
Tenterden WA 361 L7, 364 H11
Tenterfield NSW 119 M4, 491 N13, 69, **83**
Tenthill Qld 482 G5
Tepko SA 288 H10, 293 D2, 295 M9
Terang Vic. 217 A6, 229 K8, **195–6**
Teridgerie NSW 118 E10
Teringie SA 285 O6
Terip Terip Vic. 234 I10
Terka SA 291 C13, 295 J1, 297 J12
Termeil NSW 115 H6, 117 J13, 139 O5
Terowie NSW 116 C3
Terowie SA 295 L3, 297 L13, 270
Terranora NSW 485 H13
Terrey Hills NSW 97 L8, 101 O6, 41
Terrick Terrick Vic. 231 Q5, 234 C4
Terrigal NSW 101 Q4, 104 H5, 117 M6, **83**
Terry Hie Hie NSW 118 H6
Tesbury Vic. 217 C6
Tewantin Qld 486 G2, 491 Q6, 429, 461
Tewinga NSW 119 O9
Tewkesbury Tas. 544 F6
Texas Qld 119 K3, 491 M12, **467**
Thalaba NSW 100 B13, 115 F2, 116 G9
Thalia Vic. 231 L5
Thallon Qld 118 E2, 490 H12
Thanes Creek Qld 482 C12
Thangool Qld 491 K1, 493 N13, 426
Tharbogang NSW 123 N7
Thargomindah Qld 501 N10, 442, 472
Tharwa ACT 135 E7, 138 G4
The Anchorage NSW 139 N9
The Basin Vic. 210 E11
The Bluff Qld 482 G5
The Brothers Vic. 115 A11, 236 G7
The Cascade Vic. 235 R5, 236 E3
The Caves Qld 493 N10
The Channon NSW 119 Q2
The Cove Vic. 229 J10
The Entrance NSW 101 Q3, 104 H2, 117 M6, **83**
The Entrance North NSW 101 Q3, 104 H2
The Gap NSW 40
The Gap Qld 478 C11, 419
The Gap Vic. 212 H4
The Gardens NT 398 C3, 399 D8

The Gardens Tas. 545 R7
The Glen Tas. 541 N5, 545 L7
The Granites NT 408 D12, 410 D2
The Gums Qld 491 K8
The Gurdies Vic. 213 N11, 226 F8
The Heart Vic. 227 N6
The Highlands Vic. 212 G5, 223 R12
The Hill NSW 106 F8
The Junction NSW 106 C9
The Lagoon NSW 100 B5
The Lakes National Park Vic. 227 Q5, **175**, 189, 193, 194
The Levels SA 287 J9
The Lynd Junction Qld 495 K11
The Monument Qld 498 F6
The Narrows NT 399 H5, 400 C12
The Oaks NSW 101 J11, 112 D1, 115 I1, 117 J8, 52
The Palms National Park Qld 482 F2
The Patch Vic. 210 H12, 213 M7
The Range SA 290 E6
The Risk NSW 119 P2, 491 P11
The Rock NSW 116 B13, 123 Q11, **83**
The Rocks NSW 92 D3, 33, 36, 38
The Sisters Vic. 229 J8
The Spit NSW 95 O6
The Summit Qld 119 M2, 491 N12
The Vale NSW 122 H5, 233 O1
Thebarton SA 284 G6, 244, 245
Theodore ACT 137 E11
Theodore Qld 491 J2, **468**
Theresa Park NSW 101 K10
Thevenard SA 303 N10, 253
Thirlmere NSW 101 J12, 112 D3, 115 I2, 117 J9, 78
Thirlmere Lakes National Park NSW 112 D3, 73, 78
Thirlstane Tas. 540 G6, 545 J7
Thirroul NSW 101 M13, 112 H5, 117 K9
Thistle Island SA 271
Thomas Plains SA 295 J6
Thomastown Vic. 209 M2, 213 K5, 226 D3
Thomson Vic. 218 H10
Thoona Vic. 235 L5
Thora NSW 119 O8, 48
Thornborough Qld 495 L6, 449
Thornbury Vic. 209 L6
Thorneside Qld 479 O11
Thorngate SA 282 D1
Thornlands Qld 481 R3, 463
Thornleigh NSW 94 F1, 96 E11
Thornlie WA 353 N11
Thornton NSW 108 D7
Thornton Qld 482 H10, 491 O10
Thornton Vic. 213 P2, 235 K11, 172
Thornville Qld 482 E3
Thorpdale Vic. 213 R11, 226 I7, 203
Thowgla Vic. 115 B8, 236 H3
Thowgla Upper Vic. 115 B9, 236 H3
Thredbo NSW 114 C13, 115 C10, 138 A13, 236 I5, 60, 65, 68, 132
Three Bridges Vic. 213 O7, 216 G11, 226 G4
Three Springs WA 366 C4, **345**
Three Ways Roadhouse NT 409 K10, 394
Thrington SA 294 I6
Thrushton National Park Qld 490 E10
Thuddungra NSW 115 B1, 116 D9
Thulimbah Qld 119 M2, 491 N12
Thulloo NSW 116 A7, 123 P5
Thuringowa Qld 495 P13, **468**
Thurla Vic. 232 G4

Thursday Island Qld 496 B2, **455**
Thuruna SA 277
Ti Tree NT 410 I5, **394**
Ti Tree Store & Police Station NT 410 I5
Tia NSW 119 M11
Tiaro Qld 491 P4
Tibbuc NSW 117 N1, 119 M13
Tiberias Tas. 543 M6
Tibooburra NSW 120 D3, **83**
Tichborne NSW 116 D5
Tickera SA 294 I5
Tidal River Vic. 227 J12, 188
Tiega Vic. 232 G9
Tieri Qld 493 J10
Tighes Hill NSW 106 B3
Tilba Tilba NSW 113 H3, 115 H9, 139 M12, 237 R3
Tilpa NSW 121 J8
Timbarra Vic. 115 B12, 236 H10
Timber Creek NT 406 D13, 408 D2, 392, **394, 396**
Timbertown NSW 79
Timberoo Vic. 232 G9
Timberoo South Vic. 232 G10
Timbillica NSW 115 G13, 237 P10
Timboon Vic. 217 A8, 229 K10, 165, 190
Timmering Vic. 234 F6
Timor Vic. 223 L4, 231 O11, 184
Timor West Vic. 223 K4, 231 N11
Tin Can Bay Qld 491 P5, 444, 454, **468**
Tinaburra Qld 489 D12, 495 M7, 448, 473
Tinamba Vic. 227 M5
Tinaroo Falls Qld 489 D11, 495 M7
Tinbeerwah Qld 486 E2
Tincurrin WA 364 H7
Tindal NT 406 G10
Tinderbox Tas. 538 I8, 543 L10, 523
Tingalpa Qld 479 L12
Tingaringy NSW 115 D11, 237 K7
Tingha NSW 119 K7, **83–4**
Tingoora Qld 491 N6
Tinonee NSW 105 B13, 117 O1, 119 N13
Tintaldra Vic. 115 B8, 236 H1, 168
Tintenbar NSW 491 Q12
Tintinara SA 293 F5, 295 O12, **277**
Tipton Qld 482 A6, 491 M9
Tiona NSW 62
Tirranaville NSW 115 G4, 116 H11
Tirranna Roadhouse Qld 497 E9
Tittybong Vic. 122 G12, 231 M3, 233 M13
Tiwi NT 400 G1
Tjirrkarli Roadhouse WA 367 M1, 369 L12, 334
Tocal NSW 72
Tocal Qld 499 N12
Tocumwal NSW 123 M12, 234 I2, 75, **84**, 167, 201
Togari Tas. 544 B4
Toggannoggera NSW 115 F6, 139 K6
Toiberry Tas. 541 M13, 545 L9
Tolga Qld 489 C12, 495 M7, 424, 425, 449
Tolmie Vic. 224 E8, 235 M9, 184
Tom Groggin NSW 114 A13
Tom Price WA 365 H4, 368 B5, 339, 343, **345**
Tomahawk Tas. 545 O5
Tomahawk Creek Vic. 217 E8
Tomakin NSW 139 N8
Tomalla NSW 117 M1, 119 L13
Tomaree National Park NSW 108 I2, 117 O4, 76
Tombong NSW 115 E11, 237 M7

Tomboye NSW 115 G5, 116 I12, 139 M2
Tomerong NSW 139 Q1
Tomewin Qld 485 D13
Tomingley NSW 116 D3
Tongala Vic. 234 F5
Tonganah Tas. 545 N7
Tonghi Creek Vic. 115 E13, 237 M12
Tongio Vic. 115 A12, 236 G9
Tongio West Vic. 115 A12, 236 F9
Tonimbuk Vic. 213 O8, 226 G5
Tooan Vic. 230 E10
Toobanna Qld 495 N11
Toobeah Qld 118 G1, 491 J11
Tooborac Vic. 234 F10
Toodyay WA 356 G1, 364 E2, 366 D7, **345–6**
Toogong NSW 116 E6
Toogoolawah Qld 482 I4, 491 O8
Toogoom Qld 491 P3, 444
Tookayerta SA 295 P8
Toolamba Vic. 234 H7
Toolangi Vic. 213 M4, 216 D3, 226 F2, 234 I13, 177
Toolern Vale Vic. 212 H4, 226 B2, 234 E13
Tooleybuc NSW 122 G10, 233 M9, **84**, 195
Toolibin WA 364 H7
Tooligie SA 294 D5
Toolleen Vic. 234 E8
Toolondo Vic. 230 F11
Toolong Vic. 228 G9
Tooloom NSW 119 N2, 491 O12
Tooloon NSW 118 C10
Tooma NSW 115 B8, 236 H1, 84
Toombul Qld 478 H8
Toombullup Vic. 224 E8, 235 M9
Toompine Roadhouse Qld 501 O8
Toongabbie Vic. 227 L6
Toongi NSW 116 E3
Toonumbar NSW 119 O2, 491 P12
Tooperang SA 290 F9
Toora Vic. 227 J10, 173, 200
Tooradin Vic. 213 M10, 215 R3, 226 F7, 180
Toorak Vic. 209 M10, 145, 150
Toorak Gardens SA 285 K7
Tooraweenah NSW 118 E12
Toorbul Qld 483 N4, 430
Toorongo Vic. 213 Q6
Tootgarook Vic. 214 F8
Tootool NSW 116 A13, 123 Q10
Toowong Qld 478 E13, 480 E2
Toowoomba Qld 491 N9, 421, 465, **468, 470**
Toowoon Bay NSW 101 Q3, 104 H3
Top End NT 402, 406, **385**
Top Springs NT 408 F4
Topaz Qld 495 M8
Torbanlea Qld 491 P3
Torndirrup National Park WA 361 N13, 364 I13, 366 F12, 313, 317, **323**
Toronto NSW 108 F10
Torquay Vic. 212 F11, 219 E10, 229 Q9, 187, **196**
Torrens ACT 137 D6
Torrens Creek Qld 492 B4, 499 Q4
Torrens Park SA 285 J11
Torrensville SA 284 G6
Torrington NSW 119 L4, 491 N13, 63, 83
Torrita Vic. 122 D10, 232 F9
Torrumbarry Vic. 123 J13, 234 D3
Tostaree Vic. 236 I13
Tottenham NSW 116 B2, 121 R12
Tottenham Vic. 208 G8

Tottington Vic. 222 F1
Toukley NSW 101 Q2, 108 H13, 117 M6, **84**
Tourello Vic. 212 C2, 223 L8
Towallum NSW 119 O7
Towamba NSW 113 D11, 115 F12, 237 P8
Towan Vic. 233 L9
Towaninny Vic. 231 M3
Tower Hill Tas. 545 P9
Tower Hill Vic. 228 H9
Towitta SA 288 I5
Town of Seventeen Seventy Qld 493 Q13, 443, 445, 455
Townsville Qld 487, 495 P12, 414, 463, **470**
Towong Vic. 115 B8, 236 H2, 168
Towong Upper Vic. 115 B8, 236 H2
Towradgi NSW 110 F5, 112 H5
Towrang NSW 115 G3, 116 I10
Tracy SA 295 M4
Trafalgar Vic. 213 R10, 226 I7, 203
Tragowel Vic. 231 P4, 234 B2
Trangie NSW 116 C1
Tranmere SA 285 M5
Tranmere Tas. 537 M9
Traralgon Vic. 227 K7, 185, 196, **196**
Traralgon South Vic. 227 K7
Trawalla Vic. 212 A3, 222 I9, 229 M3
Trawool Vic. 234 H10, 194
Trayning WA 364 H1, 366 E7
Traynors Lagoon Vic. 231 K8
Treasures Homestead Vic. 225 O11
Trebonne Qld 495 N11
Treeton WA 357 C9, 359 D6, 364 B9
Tremont Vic. 210 E12
Trenah Tas. 545 O8
Trentham Vic. 212 F3, 223 Q9, 229 R2, 231 R13, 234 C12, 170, 180, 202
Trentham East Vic. 212 G3, 223 R9
Tresco Vic. 122 H11, 231 N1, 233 O12
Tresco West Vic. 233 N12
Trevallyn NSW 117 M3
Trevallyn Tas. 541 N10, 545 L8
Trewalla Vic. 228 D9
Trewilga NSW 116 D4
Triabunna Tas. 539 O1, 543 O6, 515, **532**
Trida NSW 123 L3
Trida Vic. 213 P11
Trigg WA 354 B9
Trinita Vic. 232 H8
Trinity Beach Qld 489 E7
Trinity Gardens SA 285 L5
Trowutta Tas. 544 C5
Truganina Vic. 208 D9
Trundle NSW 116 C4
Trunkey NSW 100 A8, 116 G7
Trunkey Creek NSW 47
Truro SA 288 H3, 295 M7
Tuan Qld 491 P4
Tuart Forest National Park WA 357 E6, 359 H1
Tuart Hill WA 354 F10
Tubbul NSW 115 B2, 116 D9
Tubbut Vic. 115 D11, 237 K8
Tucklan NSW 116 G2
Tuena NSW 100 A10, 115 F1, 116 G8, 57
Tuggerah NSW 101 P3, 104 F2, 90
Tuggeranong ACT 135 E5, 137 B9, 138 G3
Tugun Qld 485 H10
Tulendeena Tas. 545 O7
Tulkara Vic. 222 E3, 231 K11
Tullah Tas. 544 F10, 529

Tullamarine Vic. 208 H3
Tullamore NSW 116 B3, 123 R1
Tullibigeal NSW 123 P4
Tulloh Vic. 212 B12, 217 G7
Tully Qld 495 N9, 455, **470–1**
Tully Heads Qld 495 N9, 470
Tumbarumba NSW 115 B7, **84**
Tumbi Umbi NSW 101 P3, 104 G3
Tumblong NSW 115 B5, 116 D12
Tumbulgum NSW 119 Q1
Tumby SA 294 E7
Tumby Bay SA 256, 271, **277**
Tummaville Qld 482 B10
Tumorrama NSW 115 C5, 116 E12, 138 B1
Tumoulin Qld 495 M8
Tumut NSW 115 C5, 116 D12, 138 A2, **84**
Tunart Vic. 122 B8, 232 C5
Tunbridge Tas. 545 M13
Tuncurry NSW 62
Tungamah Vic. 123 N13, 235 K4
Tungamull Qld 493 O10
Tungkillo SA 288 G8, 293 D1, 295 M9
Tunnack Tas. 543 M6
Tunnel Tas. 541 O5, 545 M7
Tunnel Creek National Park WA 362 F9, 371 L8, **323**, 324
Tura Beach NSW 113 G9, 115 G11, 237 Q7, 73
Turallin Qld 491 M10
Turill NSW 116 I2
Turkey Creek (Warmun) WA 363 O7, 371 Q7
Turlinjah NSW 139 M9
Turner ACT 136 G8
Turners Beach Tas. 540 C5, 544 H6
Turners Marsh Tas. 541 O7, 545 L7
Turondale NSW 100 B1, 116 H5
Tuross Head NSW 113 I1, 115 H8, 139 N10
Turramurra NSW 94 I1, 96 G11
Turrawan NSW 118 G8
Turrella NSW 99 L4
Turriff Vic. 122 E11, 230 I1, 232 I11, 178
Turriff East Vic. 230 I1, 232 I11
Turriff West Vic. 230 H1, 232 H11
Turtons Creek Vic. 213 R13, 173
Tusmore SA 285 L7
Tutunup WA 357 F7, 359 I3, 364 C9
Tutye Vic. 232 D10
Tweed Heads NSW 119 Q1, 485 I11, 491 Q11, **84**, 423, 435
Twelve Mile NSW 116 G3
Two Mile Flat NSW 116 G3
Two Rocks WA 364 C2
Two Wells SA 288 A5, 295 K8
Tyaak Vic. 213 K1, 234 G11
Tyabb Vic. 213 L10, 215 N5, 226 E7
Tyagarah NSW 119 Q2
Tyagong NSW 115 C1, 116 E8
Tyalgum NSW 119 P1, 491 Q11
Tyalla Vic. 232 D10
Tycannah NSW 118 G6
Tyenna Tas. 538 B3, 543 J7
Tyers Vic. 227 K6
Tyers Junction Vic. 227 J5
Tylden Vic. 212 G2, 223 R8, 226 A1, 229 R2, 231 R13, 234 D12, 202
Tyndale NSW 119 P5
Tynong Vic. 213 N9, 226 G6, 170, 180
Tyntyder Central Vic. 122 H10, 233 N10
Tyntyder South Vic. 122 H11, 233 N10
Typo Vic. 224 H7
Tyrendarra Vic. 228 E8

Tyrendarra East Vic. 228 F8
Tyringham NSW 119 N8
Tyrrell Downs Vic. 233 K11

Uarbry NSW 116 H1
Ubobo Qld 493 P13
Ubodo Qld 491 M1
Ucolta SA 295 M2, 297 L12
Uki NSW 119 Q1, 491 Q11
Ulamambri NSW 118 F11
Ulan NSW 116 H2
Ulinda NSW 118 F12
Ulladulla NSW 115 I6, 117 J13, 139 P4, **86**
Ullina Vic. 212 C2, 223 M7
Ullswater Vic. 230 C11
Ulltima Vic. 122 G11, 231 M1, 233 M12
Ulmarra NSW 119 P6, 64
Ulong NSW 119 P8
Ulooloo SA 295 L3
Ultimo NSW 92 B13, 95 M11, 99 O1
Ulupna Vic. 123 M13, 234 I3
Uluru NT 404 F12, 410 E12, 373, 375, 382, 393, 396
Uluru-Kata Tjuta National Park NT 404 C11, 410 E12, 375, 382, 383, 384, 391, 393
Ulva WA 364 I2
Ulverstone Tas. 540 C5, 544 H6, 514, **532**
Umbakumba NT 407 P9
Umbiram Qld 482 D8
Umina NSW 101 P5, 104 F9
Unanderra NSW 112 G6
Undalya SA 295 L6
Undara Volcanic National Park Qld 495 K10, 442, 474
Undera Vic. 234 H5
Undera North Vic. 234 H5
Underbool Vic. 122 C10, 232 E10
Undercliffe NSW 99 L4
Underdale SA 284 G6
Underwood Qld 481 L8
Underwood Tas. 541 P7, 545 M7, 524
Ungarie NSW 116 A7, 123 Q5
Ungarra SA 294 E6
Unley SA 282 E13, 285 J8, 245
Unley Park SA 285 J9
Upper Beaconsfield Vic. 213 M8, 226 F5
Upper Bingara NSW 118 I7, 49
Upper Blessington Tas. 545 N9
Upper Bowman NSW 117 M1, 119 L13
Upper Castra Tas. 540 B8, 544 H7
Upper Cedar Creek Qld 483 L6
Upper Colo NSW 101 K4
Upper Coomera Qld 483 N11, 485 A2
Upper Esk Tas. 545 O9
Upper Ferntree Gully Vic. 210 F13, 216 A12
Upper Freestone Qld 482 G13
Upper Gellibrand Vic. 212 B13, 217 G10
Upper Horton NSW 118 I7
Upper Kedron Qld 478 B10
Upper Koondah Qld 482 C2
Upper Laceys Creek Qld 483 K5
Upper Mangrove NSW 101 N2
Upper Mangrove Creek NSW 101 N2
Upper Manilla NSW 118 I9
Upper McDonald NSW 101 L2
Upper Mount Hicks Tas. 544 F6
Upper Myall NSW 117 O2
Upper Natone Tas. 544 G7
Upper Pappinbarra NSW 105 B5, 119 N11
Upper Plenty Vic. 213 K3, 226 D1, 234 G12

Upper Scamander Tas. 545 Q9
Upper Sturt SA 285 N13
Upper Swan WA 355 P1, 356 C3
Upper Tenthill Qld 482 G9
Upper Widgee Qld 491 O5
Upper Woodstock Tas. 538 F8
Upper Yarra Dam Vic. 213 P5
Upper Yarraman Qld 482 F2
Upwey Vic. 210 E13, 213 L7
Uraidla SA 285 Q8, 288 C10, 289 H1
Uralla NSW 119 L9, **86**
Urana NSW 123 O11
Urandangi Qld 411 R4, 498 B6
Urangeline East NSW 123 P11
Urania SA 294 I8
Uranno SA 294 D7
Uranquinty NSW 116 B12, 123 Q10
Urbenville NSW 119 O2, 491 O11
Urliup NSW 485 F13
Urrbrae SA 285 L10
Urunga NSW 119 P9, **86**
Uxbridge Tas. 538 D4, 543 J8

Vacy NSW 108 A5, 117 M3
Vale Park SA 285 K3
Vale View Qld 482 E8
Valencia Creek Vic. 227 M4, 236 C13, 183
Valla Beach NSW 119 P9
Valley Heights NSW 101 J7, 103 O6
Valley View SA 287 M11
Varley WA 366 G9
Vasey Vic. 228 F2
Vasse WA 357 D7, 359 E3, 364 B9, 316
Vaucluse NSW 95 P9, 40
Vaughan Vic. 212 E1, 223 P6, 229 Q1, 231 Q2, 234 C11, 166
Vectis Vic. 230 G9
Veitch SA 295 Q8
Ventnor Vic. 213 L12, 215 N11, 226 E9
Venus Bay SA 294 A3, 303 Q13, 256, 275
Venus Bay Vic. 226 H10
Verdun SA 288 D11, 289 H1, 290 H1
Veresdale Qld 483 L11
Vermont Vic. 209 R10, 210 A10
Verona Sands Tas. 538 F12, 543 K11, 513
Verran SA 294 E5
Victor Harbor SA 289 G8, 290 E13, 293 B4, 295 L11, 239, 240, 276, **277**
Victoria Gully Vic. 228 H4
Victoria Hill Vic. 482 D12
Victoria Park WA 353 J5
Victoria Point Qld 483 O9, 491 Q9, 463
Victoria Point Vic. 228 G3
Victoria River NT **396**
Victoria River Wayside Inn NT 406 E12, 408 E2

Wallace Rockhole Aboriginal Community NT 404 G6, 410 I9
Wallacedale Vic. 228 E6
Wallacia NSW 101 K8, 103 R13
Wallaga Lake National Park NSW 113 H4, 115 G9, 139 L13, 237 R4, 48
Wallaloo Vic. 222 D1, 231 K9
Wallaloo East Vic. 222 D1, 231 K10
Wallaman Falls National Park *see* Lumholtz National Park
Wallan Vic. 213 J3, 226 D1, 234 F12
Wallangarra Qld 119 M3, 491 N12, 467
Wallangra NSW 119 J4, 491 L13
Wallarobba NSW 108 A3
Wallaroo Qld 493 L11

Wallaroo SA 294 I6, 239, 240, 255, 261, 266, 270, **278**
Wallaville Qld 491 N3
Wallendbeen NSW 115 B3, 116 D10, 56
Wallerawang NSW 100 F4, 116 I6, 71
Walli NSW 116 F7
Wallinduc Vic. 217 F1
Wallingford Qld 482 C8
Wallington Vic. 212 G10, 219 G8, 187, 191
Walloon Qld 483 J9
Walloway SA 295 K2, 297 K12
Walls of Jerusalem National Park Tas. 542 H2, 544 H11, **521**, 524
Wallsend NSW 108 E8
Wallumbilla Qld 490 H6
Wallup Vic. 230 G7
Walmer NSW 116 F4
Walmer Vic. 223 P4
Walpa Vic. 227 P4, 236 E13
Walpeup Vic. 122 D10, 232 F9
Walpole WA 360 G12, 364 F13, 366 D12, 317, 324, **346**
Walpole-Nornalup National Park WA 360 F12, 364 E13, 366 D12, **322**, 346
Walsall WA 359 G4, 364 B9
Walsh Qld 494 I6
Waltowa SA 293 E4, 295 N11
Walwa Vic. 236 G1, 168, 201
Walyunga National Park WA 356 D3, 364 D3, 311, 338
Wamberal NSW 104 H5
Wambidgee NSW 115 B4, 116 D11
Wamboyne NSW 116 A7, 123 Q5
Waminda NSW 118 C7
Wammon NSW 123 O8
Wampoony SA 293 H7
Wamuran Qld 483 L4, 491 P8
Wamuran Basin Qld 483 L4
Wanaaring NSW 120 I4
Wanalta Vic. 234 F7
Wanbi SA 293 G1, 295 P9
Wandandian NSW 139 Q2
Wandearah SA 295 J4
Wandearah West SA 295 J4
Wandella NSW 113 F3, 115 G9, 139 K12, 237 Q3
Wandering WA 356 H11, 364 E6
Wandiligong Vic. 225 M6, 235 P8, 236 C6, 165
Wandilo SA 293 H11
Wandin Vic. **198**
Wandin North Vic. 210 H7, 213 M6, 216 C9, 226 F4
Wandin Yallock Vic. 210 I8, 213 M6, 216 C9
Wando Bridge Vic. 228 C3
Wando Vale Vic. 228 C3
Wandoan Qld 491 J5
Wandong Vic. 213 K2, 226 D1, 234 G12
Wandsworth NSW 119 L7
Wang Wauk NSW 117 O2
Wangara WA 354 G2
Wangarabell Vic. 115 F13, 237 O10
Wangaratta Vic. 235 M6, **196**, **198**, 200
Wangary SA 294 C8
Wangenella NSW 123 K10
Wangerrip Vic. 217 D11
Wangi Wangi NSW 108 G10, 117 M5, 77
Wangoon Vic. 228 I9
Wanguri NT 400 H3
Wanilla SA 294 D8, 277
Wanneroo WA 356 B3, 366 B8, **346**

Wanniassa ACT 137 D8
Wannon Vic. 228 E5
Wanora Qld 483 J8
Wantabadgery NSW 115 A5, 116 C12
Wantirna Vic. 210 B11
Wanwin Vic. 228 B7, 293 I12
Wapengo NSW 113 G6, 115 G10, 237 Q5
Wappinguy NSW 117 J2
Warakurna Community WA 369 Q9
Warakurna Roadhouse WA 369 Q9, 334
Waramanga ACT 137 B5
Warana Qld 486 I10
Waranga Vic. 234 G7
Waratah Tas. 544 E8, **532**
Waratah Bay Vic. 226 I11
Waratah North Vic. 226 I10
Warawarrup WA 357 I2, 364 D7
Warburton Vic. 213 O6, 216 H9, 226 G3, 152, 153, 197, **198–9**
Warburton WA 369 N11, 334
Wardang Island SA 272
Wardell NSW 119 Q3, 491 Q13
Wards River NSW 117 N2
Wareek Vic. 223 J4
Wareemba NSW 95 J9
Warge Rock NSW 116 C3
Wargela NSW 115 D3, 116 F10
Warialda NSW 118 I5, 69, **87**
Warialda Rail NSW 118 I5
Warilla NSW 112 H8, 80
Warkton NSW 118 F12
Warkworth NSW 117 L3
Warmga Qld 482 C2
Warmur Vic. 231 J5
Warncoort Vic. 217 G6
Warne Vic. 231 L3, 233 L13
Warneet Vic. 215 P3, 226 E7
Warner Qld 478 B4
Warner Glen WA 357 D11, 359 E10, 364 B10
Warners Bay NSW 108 F9
Warnertown SA 295 J3, 297 J13
Warooka SA 294 I9
Waroona WA 356 C12, 364 C6, 366 C9
Warpoo SA 292 B8
Warra Qld 491 L7
Warra Yadin Vic. 222 E7
Warrabah National Park NSW 119 J8, 72, 82
Warrabrook Vic. 228 G6
Warracknabeal Vic. 230 H6, **199**, 203
Warradale SA 284 E12
Warraderry NSW 116 D7
Warragamba NSW 101 J9, 117 J8
Warragamba Vic. 231 R7, 234 D6
Warragul Vic. 213 P10, 226 H6, 153, **199**
Warrah Creek NSW 119 J13
Warrak Vic. 222 F7, 229 L2, 231 L13
Warrall NSW 119 J11
Warrambine Vic. 212 C7, 217 I2
Warramboo SA 294 C3, 296 C13
Warrandyte Vic. 210 B5
Warrane Tas. 537 K6
Warranook Vic. 231 J9
Warrawee NSW 96 G10
Warrayure Vic. 228 G5
Warrell Creek NSW 119 P9
Warren NSW 118 B13, **87**
Warren Qld 493 N11
Warren National Park WA 360 B8, 335, 340, 341
Warrenbayne Vic. 235 K8

Warrenmang Vic. 222 H5, 231 M11
Warrentinna Tas. 545 O6
Warriewood NSW 97 P8
Warrill View Qld 483 J10
Warrimoo NSW 101 J7, 103 P6
Warringa Tas. 540 A7, 544 H7
Warrion Vic. 212 B10, 217 F5, 229 N8
Warrnambool Vic. 228 I9, 180, 187, 190, 199–200, 204
Warrong Vic. 228 H8
Warrow SA 294 C7
Warrumbungle National Park NSW 118 E11, 29, 56, **59**, 60, 62, 75
Warruwi NT 406 I3
Warup WA 364 F8
Warwick Qld 119 M1, 482 F13, 491 N11, 465, **471**
Warwick WA 354 E6
Warwick Farm NSW 98 B3
Washpool National Park NSW 119 N5, 491 O13, 63, 64
Wasleys SA 288 C4, 295 L7
Watarrka National Park NT 404 A8, 410 F9, 383, 384, 388, 391, 393
Watchem Vic. 231 J5
Watchman SA 295 K6
Waterfall NSW 101 M11, 112 I2, 117 L9
Waterfall Gully SA 285 N9
Waterford Qld 481 O12, 483 M10
Waterford Vic. 227 N2, 235 Q13, 236 D11
Waterford WA 353 J8
Waterford Park Vic. 213 K2
Waterhouse Tas. 545 O5
Waterloo SA 295 L6, 257
Waterloo Tas. 538 E10, 543 K10
Waterloo WA 357 G4, 364 C8
Waterloo Corner SA 286 H2, 288 B7
Waterman WA 354 B7
Watervale SA 295 L6, 246, 253
Wathe Vic. 230 H2, 232 H12
Watheroo WA 366 C6
Watheroo National Park WA 366 C5
Watson ACT 136 I6
Watson SA 302 H4
Watsonia Vic. 209 O4, 213 K5
Watsons Bay NSW 95 Q8, 101 O8
Watsons Creek NSW 119 J9
Watsons Creek Vic. 210 C2, 213 L5
Watsonville Qld 495 M8
Wattamolla NSW 101 N11
Wattamondara NSW 115 D1, 116 E8
Wattle Glen Vic. 209 R1, 210 A2, 213 L5
Wattle Grove NSW 98 B6
Wattle Grove Tas. 538 E10
Wattle Grove WA 353 Q7
Wattle Hill Tas. 539 L4, 543 N8
Wattle Hill Vic. 217 C12
Wattle Park SA 285 M7
Wattle Range SA 293 H10
Wattle Valley Vic. 234 G9
Wattleup WA 356 B6
Waubra Vic. 212 B2, 223 K8, 229 N2, 231 N13
Wauchope NSW 105 F8, 119 O12, 79, **87**
Wauchope NT 409 K13, 411 K2, **396**
Waukaringa SA 291 G11, 297 M10
Wauraltee SA 294 I8
Waurn Ponds Vic. 212 F10, 219 D8, 229 Q8, 173
Wave Hill NSW 121 O6
Wavell Heights Qld 478 G7
Waverley NSW 95 P12, 99 R2

Waverton NSW 95 M8
Wayatinah Tas. 542 I5
Waychinicup National Park WA 361 Q11
Waygara Vic. 236 I12
Wayville SA 282 C13, 284 I8, 245
Webbs NSW 116 D2
Webbs Creek NSW 101 M3
Webster Hill Vic. 217 G10
Wedderburn NSW 101 L11, 112 G2
Wedderburn Vic. 231 N7, **200**
Wedderburn Junction Vic. 231 O7
Weddin Mountains National Park NSW 115 B1, 116 D8, 64
Wedge Island SA 271
Wee Elwah NSW 123 L3
Wee Jasper NSW 115 D5, 116 F12, 138 D1, 90
Wee Waa NSW 118 F8, **87**
Wee-wee-rup Vic. 231 R4, 234 C2
Weeaproinah Vic. 217 F11
Weegena Tas. 540 F10
Weemelah NSW 118 F3, 490 I13
Weeragua Vic. 115 E13, 237 N10
Weetah Tas. 540 H10, 545 J8
Weetaliba NSW 118 G12
Weetangera ACT 136 C7
Weethalle NSW 123 P6
Weetulta SA 294 I7
Wehla Vic. 231 N9
Weimby NSW 122 G8, 233 M6
Weipa Qld 496 B7, 443, 453, **471**
Weipa South Qld 453
Weismantels NSW 117 N2
Weja NSW 116 A7, 123 P5
Welaregang NSW 115 B8, 236 H1
Welby NSW 112 C6
Weldborough Tas. 545 P7
Welford National Park Qld 501 M3, 447
Wellcamp Qld 482 E8
Wellingrove NSW 119 L6
Wellington NSW 116 F3, 31, **87–8**
Wellington SA 293 E3, 295 N10, 276
Wellington Point Qld 479 Q11, 483 N8, 434, 463
Wellsford Vic. 231 R9, 234 D7
Welshmans Reef Vic. 223 O5, 231 P11, 234 B10
Welshpool Vic. 227 K10, **200**
Welshpool WA 353 L6
Wembley WA 352 E2, 354 E13
Wembley Downs WA 354 C11
Wemen Vic. 122 E9, 233 J7
Wendouree Vic. 221 A3
Wengenville Qld 482 D1
Wentworth NSW 122 C6, 232 F2, **88**, 201
Wentworth Falls NSW 100 H7, 102 G8, 42, 68
Wentworthville NSW 94 B6
Wepowie SA 295 K2, 297 J12
Wereboldera NSW 138 A3
Werneth Vic. 212 B7, 217 G2
Werombi NSW 101 J10
Werona Vic. 212 D1, 223 N7
Werrap Vic. 230 F4
Werri Beach NSW 112 G10
Werribee Vic. 208 A12, 212 H7, 219 H3, 226 B4, 152
Werrikimbe National Park NSW 105 A4, 119 N11
Werrimull Vic. 122 C8, 232 D4
Werris Creek NSW 118 I11
Wesburn Vic. 213 N6, 216 G9

Wesley Vale Tas. 540 F5, 544 I7
West Beach SA 284 D8, 245
West Burleigh Qld 485 E9
West Cape Howe National Park WA 361 L13, 364 G13, 313, **322**
West Croydon SA 284 G4
West End Qld 478 F13, 480 F1, 487 C4
West Frankford Tas. 540 I8, 545 K7
West Haldon Qld 482 F10
West Hill National Park Qld 493 L7
West Hobart Tas. 536 F8
West Kentish Tas. 540 D9
West Lakes SA 284 C3, 288 A9
West Lakes Shore SA 284 C2, 286 C13
West MacDonnell National Park NT 404 F2, 405 J3, 410 H8, 382, 383, 384, 387, 393
West Midland WA 311
West Montagu Tas. 544 B4
West Moonah Tas. 536 D4
West Pennant Hills NSW 94 D2, 96 C12
West Perth WA 350 A1, 352 G3, 309
West Pine Tas. 544 G6
West Pymble NSW 94 I3, 96 G13
West Ridgley Tas. 544 F6
West Ryde NSW 94 G6
West Scottsdale Tas. 541 Q5, 545 M7
West Swan WA 355 O6
West Takone Tas. 544 E6
West Wallsend NSW 108 E9
West Wollongong NSW 110 B10
West Wyalong NSW 116 B8, 123 Q6, 75, **88**
Westbourne Park SA 284 I10
Westbrook Qld 482 E8
Westbury Tas. 541 K11, 545 K9, 505, 527, **532**
Westbury Vic. 213 R10, 227 J6
Westby Vic. 231 P2, 233 P13, 234 A1
Westcourt Qld 488 D11
Westdale NSW 119 J11
Westdale WA 356 H8, 364 E5
Western Creek Tas. 544 I10
Western District, The Vic. C5, 204
Western Flat SA 293 H7
Western Junction Tas. 541 P12, 545 M9
Westerway Tas. 538 C2, 543 J7
Westlake Qld 480 B6
Westleigh NSW 96 D10
Westmar Qld 491 J10
Westmead NSW 94 B6
Westmeadows Vic. 208 I1
Westmere Vic. 222 D13, 229 K5
Weston ACT 136 D13, 137 B4
Weston NSW 108 C9
Weston Creek ACT 135 E4, 136 B13, 138 G3
Westonia WA 366 F7
Westons Flat SA 295 O6
Westwood Qld 493 N11
Westwood Tas. 541 L11, 545 L9
Weymouth Tas. 541 O2
Whale Beach NSW 97 R3, 101 P6, 104 H11
Wharminda SA 294 E6
Wharparilla Vic. 234 E4
Wharparilla North Vic. 234 D4
Wheatsheaf Vic. 212 F2, 223 P8
Wheeler Heights NSW 95 P1, 97 N11
Wheelers Hill Vic. 209 R13, 210 A13, 211 G1
Wheeo NSW 115 F3, 116 G10
Whim Creek WA 365 H1, 368 B2
Whiporie NSW 119 P4, 491 P13

Whirily Vic. 231 K4
White Beach Tas. 539 L10, 543 N10
White Cliffs NSW 120 F8, **88**
White Flat SA 294 D8
White Gum Valley WA 352 C11
White Hills Tas. 541 P11, 545 M9
White Hills Vic. 223 R1, 164
White Mountains National Park Qld 492 B3, 499 Q4
White Patch Qld 483 N4
White Rock NSW 100 C4
White Rock Qld 489 F9
Whitefoord Tas. 543 M6
Whiteheads Creek Vic. 234 H10
Whiteman WA 355 M4, 356 C3
Whitemark Tas. 542 A12, 531
Whitemore Tas. 541 L13, 545 K9
Whiteside Qld 467
Whitewood Qld 499 N6
Whitfield Qld 488 B5
Whitfield Vic. 224 F6, 235 N8, 184, 198
Whitlands Vic. 224 F6
Whitsunday Qld 493 J3, 424, 431, 466, **471**
Whitsunday Islands National Park Qld 493 K2, **439**, 466
Whittlesea Vic. 213 K4, 226 D2, 234 G13
Whitton NSW 123 O8, **88**
Whitwarta SA 295 K6
Whoorel Vic. 212 C11, 217 I7
Whoroully South Vic. 236 A4
Whorouly Vic. 224 H2, 235 N7, 236 A5, 198
Whorouly East Vic. 224 I2
Whorouly South Vic. 224 H2, 235 N7
Whroo Vic. 234 G8
Whyalla SA 294 I2, 296 H13, **278**
Whyte Yarcowie SA 295 L3, 297 L13
Wialki WA 366 F6
Wiangaree NSW 119 P2, 491 P12
Wickepin WA 364 G6, 366 E9, **346**
Wickham NSW 106 C6
Wickham WA 365 G1, 320, 339, **346–7**
Wickliffe Vic. 222 B13, 229 J5
Widgiemooltha WA 366 I7
Widgiewa NSW 123 O10
Wilberforce NSW 101 L5, 117 K7, 46
Wilbursville Tas. 543 K3, 545 K12
Wilby Vic. 123 N13, 235 L4
Wilcannia NSW 120 G10, **88**
Wild Horse Plains SA 295 K7
Wiley Park NSW 98 I4
Wilga WA 360 D1, 364 D9, 314
Wilgul Vic. 212 A7, 217 F2
Wilkawatt SA 293 G3, 295 P11
Wilkur Vic. 231 J5
Willa Vic. 230 G1, 232 G11
Willagee WA 352 E10
Willalooka SA 293 G7
Willamulka SA 294 I5
Willandra National Park NSW 123 L3
Willare Bridge Roadhouse WA 362 B10, 371 J8
Willaring Vic. 222 D2
Willatook Vic. 228 G8
Willaura Vic. 222 B11, 229 J4
Willawarrin NSW 105 D1, 119 O10
Willawong Qld 480 G8
Willbriggie NSW 123 N8
Willenabrina Vic. 230 G5
Willetton WA 353 J10
William Bay National Park WA 361 J12, 364 G13, 324
William Creek SA 298 D11, 255, 265, 279

Williams WA 364 F7, 366 D9, **347**
Williamsdale NSW 135 F8, 138 G5
Williamsford Tas. 542 E1, 544 E10
Williamstown SA 288 E6, 292 C12, 293 C1, 295 L8
Williamstown Vic. 209 J11, 213 J7, 151
Williamtown NSW 108 F5, 117 N4
Willigulli WA 366 A3
Willina NSW 117 O2
Willochra SA 291 C11, 297 J10
Willoughby NSW 95 N5
Willow Grove Vic. 213 R9, 226 I6
Willow Tree NSW 119 J12
Willowie SA 291 C13, 295 K1, 297 J11
Willowmavin Vic. 213 J1, 234 F11
Willows Qld 492 H11
Willowvale Qld 482 F12
Willowvale Vic. 212 A6, 229 M5
Willung Vic. 227 M7
Willung South Vic. 227 L8
Willunga SA 288 B13, 289 F4, 290 C6, 293 B3, 295 K10, 276, **278**
Willyabrup WA 335
Wilmington SA 291 C13, 295 J1, 273, **280**
Wilmot Tas. 540 C9, 544 H8
Wilora NT 411 J4
Wilpena SA 291 E8, 297 K7, 273, **280**
Wilroy WA 366 C3
Wilson WA 353 K8
Wilson Island Qld 445
Wilsons Downfall Qld 119 M3
Wilsons Promontory Marine Reserve Vic. 227 K13
Wilsons Promontory National Park Vic. 227 J11, 141, 143, 147, 153, 173, **175**, 181, **188**
Wilsons Valley NSW 114 E10
Wilston Qld 478 F10
Wilton NSW 101 K12, 112 F3
Wiltshire Junction Tas. 544 D4
Wiluna WA 368 E11
Wimba Vic. 212 B13, 217 F10
Wimmera, The Vic. 230 D4, 203
Winchelsea Vic. 212 D10, 219 A8, 229 P8, **200**
Windang NSW 112 H7
Windarra WA 367 J3
Windellama NSW 115 G4, 116 I11
Windermere Tas. 541 M7, 545 L8, 523
Windermere Vic. 212 C3, 223 L10
Windeyer NSW 116 H4
Windjana Gorge National Park WA 362 E8, 371 L8, **323**, 324
Windomal NSW 122 G9, 233 M7
Windorah Qld 501 L4, 472
Windowie NSW 138 A2
Windsor NSW 101 K6, 117 K7, 39, 43, 46, 79, **88–9**
Windsor Qld 478 G10
Windsor SA 295 K7
Windsor Gardens SA 285 L2, 287 L13
Windurong NSW 118 D12
Windy Corner WA 369 L6
Windy Harbour WA 360 C11, 364 D12
Wingala NSW 95 Q3, 97 O13
Wingamin SA 293 F2, 295 O10
Wingeel Vic. 212 C9, 217 I3, 229 O7
Wingello NSW 115 H3, 116 I10
Wingen NSW 117 K1, 119 J13, 74, 80
Wingfield SA 286 G12
Wingham NSW 105 B13, 117 O1, 119 N13, **89**

Winiam Vic. 230 D7
Winiam East Vic. 230 E7
Winjallok Vic. 222 G2
Winkie SA 295 Q7
Winkleigh Tas. 541 K7, 545 K7
Winmalee NSW 101 J7, 103 O4
Winnaleah Tas. 545 O6
Winnambool Vic. 233 J8
Winnap Vic. 228 C6
Winnellie NT 399 G6, 400 G13, 402 C2
Winnindoo Vic. 227 L6
Winninowie SA 291 B13, 295 J1, 296 I11
Winnunga NSW 116 A7, 123 Q5
Winslow Vic. 228 I8
Winston Hills NSW 94 B4
Winthrop WA 352 F10
Winton Qld 499 M8, 451, **471**
Winton Vic. 224 C2, 235 L7
Winton North Vic. 224 C1
Winulta SA 294 I7
Winwill Qld 482 G8
Winya Qld 483 K3
Wiragulla NSW 108 B2
Wirha SA 293 H2, 295 Q10
Wirlinga NSW 123 Q13, 235 Q3, 236 C1
Wirrabara SA 295 K2, 297 J13
Wirrega SA 293 H6
Wirrega North SA 293 H5, 295 Q13
Wirrida SA 301 Q13
Wirrimah NSW 115 C1, 116 E9
Wirrinya NSW 116 C7
Wirrinya West NSW 116 C7
Wirrulla SA 303 Q10
Wisanger SA 294 H11
Wiseleigh Vic. 227 Q4, 236 G12
Wisemans Creek NSW 100 C6, 116 H7
Wisemans Ferry NSW 101 M3, 117 L6, 46, **89**
Wishart Qld 481 K5
Wishbone WA 364 H7
Wistow SA 288 E12, 289 I3, 290 I3
Witchcliffe WA 357 C10, 359 C8, 335
Withcott Qld 482 F8
Witheren Qld 483 M13
Withersfield Qld 492 H11
Witjira National Park SA 298 C1, 411 M13, **263**, 268
Witta Qld 483 L1, 486 A10, 491 P7
Wittenbra NSW 118 E10
Wittenoom WA 365 I4, 368 B4, 345
Wittitrin NSW 105 D4, 119 O11
Wivenhoe Tas. 544 G6
Wivenhoe Pocket Qld 483 J7
Woden ACT 135 E4, 136 E13, 137 C4, 138 G3
Wodonga Vic. 123 P13, 235 P4, 236 B2, 44, **200**, 201
Wokalup WA 357 H2, 364 C7
Woko National Park NSW 119 L13
Wokurna SA 295 J5
Wollar NSW 116 I2
Wollemi National Park NSW 100 I2, 117 J3, 75, 80
Wollert Vic. 213 K4, 226 D2, 234 G13
Wollombi NSW 108 A13, 117 L4, 53
Wollomombi NSW 119 M8
Wollongbar NSW 119 Q3
Wollongong NSW 110, 112 H6, 29, 53, **89**
Wollstonecraft NSW 95 L7
Wollun NSW 119 K10
Wolseley SA 230 A7, 293 I7
Wolumla NSW 113 F9, 115 G11, 237 Q7

Womalilla Qld 490 E6
Wombarra NSW 101 M12, 112 H4
Wombat NSW 115 C2, 116 D10
Wombelano Vic. 230 D11
Wombeyan Caves NSW 100 F13, 116 I9, 85
Womboota NSW 123 K13, 234 E3
Won Wron Vic. 227 L9
Wonboyn Lake NSW 113 F13, 115 G12, 237 Q9
Wondai Qld 491 N6, **471**, **473**
Wondalga NSW 115 B6, 116 D13
Wonga Qld 489 B2, 495 M5
Wonga Park Vic. 210 C5
Wongan Hills WA 366 D6
Wongarbon NSW 116 F2
Wongarra Vic. 217 H11
Wongawilli NSW 112 G7
Wonglepong Qld 483 M12
Wongulla SA 293 E1, 295 N8
Wonnerup WA 357 E7, 359 G2, 364 B8
Wonthaggi Vic. 226 G10, 153, **200**
Wonwondah East Vic. 230 G10
Wonwondah North Vic. 230 G10
Wonyip Vic. 227 J9
Wood Wood Vic. 122 G10, 233 M9
Woodanilling WA 364 G8
Woodbridge Tas. 538 G10, 543 L10
Woodburn NSW 119 Q4, 491 Q13, 61
Woodburne Vic. 212 D6, 219 B2
Woodbury Tas. 543 M4, 545 M13
Woodchester SA 288 F13, 293 C2, 295 L10
Woodenbong NSW 119 O1, 491 P11
Woodend Vic. 212 G2, 226 A1, 229 R2, 234 D12, 173, 180, **200**, **202**
Woodfield Vic. 235 K10
Woodford NSW 100 I7, 103 K8
Woodford Qld 483 L3, 491 P7
Woodforde SA 285 N5
Woodgate Qld 491 P3, 430, 454
Woodglen Vic. 227 O4, 236 E13
Woodhouselee NSW 115 F3, 116 H10
Woodlands Qld 482 H8
Woodlands WA 354 D11
Woodlawn Qld 482 C2
Woodleigh Vic. 213 N12
Woodleighton Qld 482 D3
Woodridge Qld 481 L8, 483 M9
Woods Point SA 293 E2, 295 N10
Woods Point Vic. 213 R4, 227 J2, 235 M13, 184
Woods Reef NSW 119 J8
Woods Well SA 293 E5, 295 N13
Woodsdale Tas. 543 N6, 530
Woodsedge Vic. 181
Woodside SA 288 E10, 289 I1, 293 C2, 295 L9, 247
Woodside Vic. 227 M9, 189
Woodside Beach Vic. 227 M9
Woodstock NSW 116 F7
Woodstock Qld 492 G1, 495 P13, 468
Woodstock Tas. 538 F9, 543 K10
Woodstock Vic. 213 K4, 226 D2, 234 G13
Woodstock Vic. 223 O2, 231 P10, 234 B9
Woodvale Vic. 231 Q9, 234 C8
Woodvale WA 354 D3
Woodville NSW 108 C6, 117 M4
Woodville SA 284 F3
Woodville West SA 284 E4
Woody Island WA 326
Woody Point Qld 463
Woohlpooer Vic. 228 G2, 230 G13
Wool Bay SA 294 I9

Wool Wool Vic. 212 A10, 217 E5, 229 M8
Woolamai Vic. 213 N13, 226 F9
Woolbrook NSW 119 K10
Woolgoolga NSW 119 P7, **89**
Wooli NSW 119 Q6
Woollahra NSW 95 O11, 99 Q1, 40
Woolloomooloo NSW 40
Woolloongabba Qld 476 H13, 478 G13, 480 H2, 417
Woolomin NSW 119 K11
Woolooga Qld 491 O5
Woolooware NSW 99 L11
Woolooowin Qld 478 G9
Woolshed Vic. 235 O5, 236 A3
Woolsthorpe Vic. 228 H8
Woolwich NSW 95 K8
Woomargama NSW 123 Q12, 235 R2
Woombye Qld 483 M1, 486 E9
Woomelang Vic. 122 F12, 231 J2, 233 J13
Woomera SA 296 F6, 250, 275, 279, **280**
Woongoolba Qld 483 O10
Woonona NSW 112 H5
Wooragee Vic. 235 O5, 236 B3
Wooragee North NSW 235 O4, 236 B2
Woorak Vic. 230 E6
Woorak West Vic. 230 E6
Wooramel Roadhouse WA 365 C10
Woorarra Vic. 227 J10
Wooreen Vic. 213 P12, 226 H8
Woori Yallock Vic. 213 N6, 216 D9, 226 F4
Woorim Qld 483 N5, 433
Woorinen Vic. 122 H11, 233 M10
Woorinen North Vic. 122 H10, 233 M10
Woornack Vic. 232 I10
Woorndoo Vic. 229 J6
Wooroonook Vic. 231 L6
Wooroonooran National Park Qld 489 G12, 495 N7, 425, 443, 446, **458**
Woosang Vic. 231 M7
Wootha Qld 483 L2, 486 B12
Wootong Vale Vic. 228 E4
Wootton NSW 117 O2
Worlds End SA 295 M5
Worongary Qld 483 N13, 485 C7
Woronora NSW 98 G10
Woronora Heights NSW 98 G10
Worsley WA 357 I4, 364 D8
Wowan Qld 493 N12, 426
Woy Woy NSW 104 F8, **89–90**
Wrattonbully SA 228 A1, 230 A12, 293 I9
Wrightley Vic. 224 C6, 235 L9
Wroxham Vic. 115 F12, 237 O10
Wubin WA 366 D5, 340
Wudinna SA 294 C3, 296 B13, **280**
Wujal Wujal Qld 495 M4
Wuk Wuk Vic. 227 P4, 236 E13
Wulagi NT 400 I5
Wulgulmerang Vic. 115 B11, 236 I8
Wulguru Qld 487 F13
Wundowie WA 356 F3, 364 E3
Wunghnu Vic. 123 M13, 234 I4, 187
Wunkar SA 295 P8
Wurruck Vic. 227 M6
Wurtulla Qld 486 I11
Wutul Qld 482 E3
Wy Yung Vic. 227 P4, 236 F13
Wyalkatchem WA 364 G1, 366 E7
Wyalong NSW 116 B8, 123 R6
Wyan NSW 119 O4, 491 P13
Wyandra Qld 490 B8
Wyanga NSW 116 D3
Wyangala Dam NSW 115 E1, 116 F8

Wybong NSW 117 K2
Wycarbah Qld 493 N11
Wycheproof Vic. 122 G13, 231 L5, **202**
Wychitella Vic. 231 N6
Wycliffe Well Roadhouse NT 409 K13, 411 K2
Wye River Vic. 217 I11, 183
Wyee NSW 101 Q1, 108 G13, 117 M5
Wyeebo Vic. 236 E3
Wyelangta Vic. 217 E11
Wyena Tas. 541 P5, 545 M7
Wyening WA 364 E1
Wylie Creek NSW 119 N2
Wymah NSW 123 Q13, 235 R3, 236 D1
Wymlet Vic. 232 F8
Wynarka SA 293 F2, 295 O10
Wynbring SA 303 N4
Wyndham NSW 113 D9, 115 F11, 237 P7
Wyndham WA 363 N1, 371 P4, 344, **347–8**
Wynn Vale SA 287 O8
Wynnum Qld 479 N9, 483 N7, 418
Wynnum West Qld 479 M10
Wynyard Tas. 544 F5, 514, **532–3**
Wyomi SA 293 F8
Wyong NSW 101 P2, 104 F1, 117 M6, **90**
Wyong Creek NSW 101 P2, 104 D2
Wyperfeld National Park Vic. 122 C11, 230 D2, 232 E12, 147, **176**, 178, 179, 191
Wyreema Qld 482 E8
Wyrra NSW 116 B8, 123 R5
Wyrrabalong National Park NSW 101 Q4, 104 H4, 83, 84
Wyuna Vic. 234 G5
Wyurta Downs NSW 121 P6

Yaamba Qld 493 N10
Yaapeet Vic. 122 D12, 230 F3
Yabba North Vic. 235 J5
Yabba South Vic. 235 J5
Yabba Valley Vic. 235 R5, 236 D3
Yabmana Vic. 294 F5
Yacka SA 295 K4
Yackandandah Vic. 235 P5, 236 B3, 186, 200, **202**
Yagoona NSW 94 D12, 98 G2
Yahl SA 228 A6, 293 H12
Yalangur Qld 482 E6
Yalata SA 302 I7
Yalata Roadhouse SA 302 I7, 333
Yalboroo Qld 493 J4
Yalbraith NSW 100 D13, 115 G2, 116 H9
Yalca Vic. 234 H3
Yalca North Vic. 234 H3
Yalgogrin North NSW 116 A8, 123 P6
Yalgogrin South NSW 116 A9, 123 P7
Yalgoo WA 366 D3, **348**
Yalgorup National Park WA 356 A11, 357 F1, 364 B6, 366 B9, 319, 342
Yalla Y Poora Vic. 222 E10
Yallakool NSW 123 J11
Yallambie Vic. 209 O4
Yallaroi NSW 118 I4, 491 K13
Yalleroi Qld 492 D12, 499 R12
Yallingup WA 357 B7, 359 C2, 364 A9, 366 B10, 316, 319, 335, **348**
Yallourn North Vic. 227 J7
Yallunda Flat SA 294 D7
Yaloak Vale Vic. 212 F5, 223 P13
Yalwal NSW 112 B12, 115 I4, 117 J11
Yamala Qld 493 J11
Yamba NSW 119 Q5, 72, **90**
Yamba Roadhouse SA 122 A7, 232 A4, 295 R7, 268
Yambacoona Tas. 542 A8
Yambuk Vic. 228 G9, 190
Yambuna Vic. 234 G4
Yamsion Qld 482 C3
Yan Yean Vic. 213 K4, 226 D2, 234 G13
Yanac Vic. 230 C5, 186
Yanac South Vic. 230 C6
Yanakie Vic. 227 J11
Yanchep WA 356 A1, 364 C2, 366 C7, **348**
Yanchep National Park WA 356 B1, 364 C2, 366 B7, 317, **322**, 346, 348
Yanco NSW 123 O8, 71, **90**
Yandaran Qld 491 O2
Yanderra NSW 101 J13, 112 D4, 115 I2, 117 J9
Yandilla Qld 482 A10
Yandina Qld 486 E6, **473**
Yando Vic. 122 I13, 231 O5, 234 A4
Yandoit Vic. 212 E1, 223 O7, 229 P1, 231 P12, 234 B11, 170
Yaninee SA 294 B2, 296 B12
Yanipy Vic. 230 C8
Yankalilla SA 289 D7, 293 B3, 295 K11, **280**
Yantabulla NSW 121 L3
Yantanabie SA 294 A1, 303 Q11
Yaouk NSW 114 H2, 135 B12, 138 E7
Yapeen Vic. 212 E1, 223 P6
Yaraka Qld 501 O2
Yarck Vic. 213 N1, 235 J10
Yarding WA 364 I3
Yargullen Qld 482 C7
Yarloop WA 356 C13, 357 H1, 364 C7, 328
Yaroomba Qld 486 H6
Yaroona SA 288 B12, 289 G3, 290 E4
Yarra NSW 115 F4, 116 H11
Yarra Bend Vic. 209 M8
Yarra Creek Tas. 542 B9
Yarra Glen Vic. 210 G1, 213 M5, 216 B6, 226 E3, 152, 177, 178, 197
Yarra Junction Vic. 213 N6, 216 E9, 226 G4
Yarra Ranges National Park Vic. 213 O4, 216 F6, 226 G2, 227 J3, 235 J13, **175**
Yarra Valley Vic. 216, 141, 152, 174, 177, 197
Yarrabah Qld 489 G8
Yarrabandai NSW 116 C5
Yarrabin NSW 116 G3
Yarraby Vic. 233 M9
Yarragee NSW 139 M8, 73
Yarragon Vic. 213 Q10, 226 I7, **202**
Yarralin NT 408 D3
Yarralumla ACT 134 B10, 136 F11, 137 D1, 129, 130
Yarram Vic. 227 L9, **203**
Yarramalong NSW 101 O2, 104 B1
Yarraman NSW 118 H12
Yarraman Qld 482 F2, 491 N7
Yarramony WA 364 E2
Yarrangobilly NSW 115 C6, 138 C5
Yarranlea Qld 482 B9
Yarrara Vic. 122 B8, 232 C5
Yarras NSW 105 B7, 119 N12
Yarraville Vic. 208 I9
Yarrawalla South Vic. 231 P6, 234 B4
Yarrawarrah NSW 98 G12
Yarrawonga Vic. 123 N13, 235 L3, 201, **203–4**
Yarrie Lake NSW 118 F8
Yarrock Vic. 230 B6
Yarroweyah Vic. 123 M13, 234 I3
Yarrowitch NSW 119 M11
Yarrowyck NSW 119 K8
Yarto Vic. 230 G1, 232 G12
Yarwun Qld 493 P12
Yass NSW 115 D4, 116 F11, **90**
Yatala Qld 483 N10
Yatala Vale SA 287 P7
Yatchaw Vic. 228 F5
Yatina SA 295 L2, 297 K12
Yatpool Vic. 122 D7, 232 G4
Yatteyatah NSW 115 I5, 117 J12, 139 P3
Yaugher Vic. 217 H9
Yea Vic. 213 M1, 234 I11, **204**
Yealering WA 364 H5, 366 E9, 346
Yearinan NSW 118 F11
Yearinga Vic. 230 B7
Yednia Qld 483 J1
Yeelanna SA 294 D6
Yeerip Vic. 235 L5
Yeerongpilly Qld 480 F4
Yelarbon Qld 119 J2, 491 L12
Yellangip Vic. 230 H5
Yellingbo Vic. 213 M6, 216 D10
Yellowdine WA 366 G7
Yelta Vic. 232 F3, 88
Yelta SA 294 I6
Yelverton WA 357 C8, 359 D4, 364 A9
Yenda NSW 123 O7
Yendon Vic. 212 D5, 223 N12, 229 P4
Yengo National Park NSW 101 L1, 117 K5, 80
Yennora NSW 94 B10
Yeo Yeo NSW 115 B3, 116 D10
Yeodene Vic. 212 B12, 217 G8, 229 N9
Yeoval NSW 116 E4
Yeppoon Qld 493 O10, 464, **473**
Yering Vic. 210 G3
Yerong Creek NSW 116 A13, 123 Q11
Yeronga Qld 480 G3
Yerranderie NSW 100 G11, 52, 68
Yerrinbool NSW 101 J13, 112 D5, 115 I2, 117 J9
Yetholme NSW 100 D4, 116 H6
Yetman NSW 119 J3, 491 L12
Yeungroon Vic. 231 M7
Yilliminning WA 364 G6
Yimbun Qld 482 I3
Yin Barun Vic. 224 A4
Yinkanie SA 295 P7
Yinnar Vic. 227 J8
Yirrkala NT 407 P5, 396
Yokine WA 354 G10
Yolla Tas. 544 F6
Yongala SA 295 L2, 297 K13
Yoogali NSW 123 N7
Yoongarillup WA 357 E8, 359 G4, 364 B9
York WA 356 I4, 364 F3, 366 D8, **348**
York Plains Tas. 543 M5
Yorke Peninsula SA 294 H8, 240, 249, **255**
Yorke Valley SA 294 I7
Yorketown SA 294 I9, **280**
Yorkeys Knob Qld 489 F7
Yornaning WA 364 F6
Yoting WA 364 H3
Youanmite Vic. 123 M13, 235 J4
Youarang Vic. 235 J4
Youndegin WA 364 G3
Young NSW 115 C2, 116 E9, **90**
Youngtown Tas. 541 O11
Yowah Qld 501 P10, 442
Yowaka National Park NSW 113 E11, 115 F11, 237 P8
Yowie Bay NSW 99 J11
Yowrie NSW 113 F3, 115 G9, 139 K12
Yuelamu NT 410 G5
Yuendumu NT 410 F5
Yulara NT 404 E10, 410 E11, 382, 386, **396**
Yuleba Qld 490 I7
Yulecart Vic. 228 F5
Yumali SA 293 F3, 295 O11
Yumba Qld 455
Yuna WA 366 B3
Yundi SA 290 E8, 278
Yundool Vic. 235 K5
Yungaburra Qld 489 D12, 425, **473**
Yungera Vic. 122 G9, 233 L7
Yunta SA 291 H13, 295 N1, 297 N11
Yuraygir National Park NSW 119 Q5, **59**, 64, 72, 89, 90
Yurgo SA 293 F2, 295 O10
Yuroke Vic. 213 J4, 226 C2, 234 F13
Yuulong Vic. 217 D11

Zanthus WA 367 L6
Zeehan Tas. 542 D1, 544 D11, 505, 514, 526, 528
Zeerust Vic. 234 H5
Zetland NSW 95 M12, 99 O2
Zillmere Qld 478 G6

Suggestion Form

This 15th edition of *Explore Australia* is updated from information supplied by consultants, tourist organisations and the general public. We would welcome suggestions from you. Please use the form below to supply us with any information you feel is relevant.

Suggestions for improvement

Text: ....
....
....

Maps: ....
....
....

Suggested amendment or addition

Text

Town Name	Amendment/Addition

Maps

Page no.	Grid	Amendment/Addition

Have you purchased a copy of *Explore Australia* before? ....

If so, what edition? ....

Optional

Name: ....

Address: ....

Please cut out and send to:
    Managing Editor
    Penguin Cartographic
    A division of Penguin Books Australia Ltd
    487 Maroondah Hwy
    Ringwood Vic. 3134

Accident Action

Those vital first moments

Treating an unconscious person

1. CLEAR AIRWAY
Lie victim on side and tilt head back.

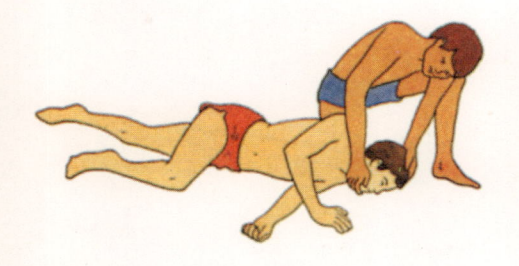

2. CLEAR MOUTH
Quickly clear mouth, using fingers if necessary. If breathing, leave on side.

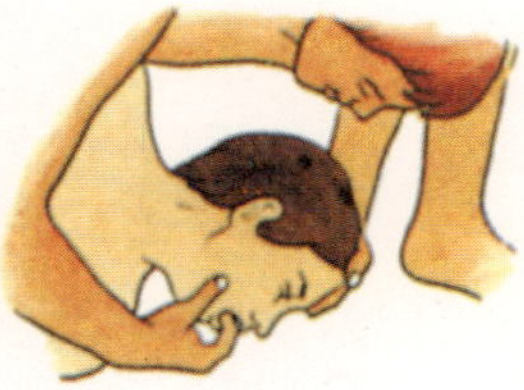

3. TILT HEAD
IF NOT BREATHING, place victim on back. Tilt head back. Support the jaw, keeping fingers away from neck.

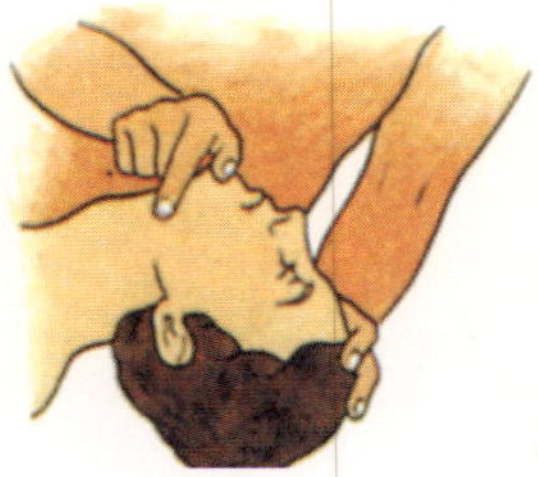

4. BLOW INTO MOUTH
Kneel beside victim's head. Place your widely open mouth over victim's slightly open mouth, sealing nostrils with your cheek. Blow until victim's chest rises.

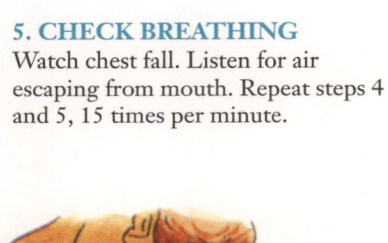

5. CHECK BREATHING
Watch chest fall. Listen for air escaping from mouth. Repeat steps 4 and 5, 15 times per minute.

6. RECOVERY POSITION
When breathing begins, place victim on side, head back, jaw supported, face pointing slightly towards ground.

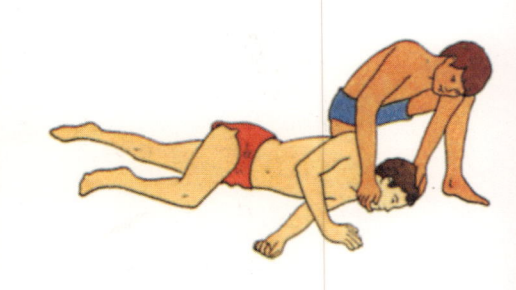

NOTE: For an injured child, cover mouth and nose with your mouth. Blow until chest rises (20 times per minute).

7. IF TRAPPED IN CAR
If victim is unconscious and trapped in the car, still tilt head back and support the jaw.

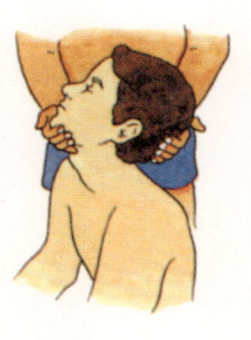

SEND SOMEONE FOR AN AMBULANCE.

DO NOT LEAVE AN UNCONSCIOUS PERSON.